South Africa

THE ROUGH GUIDE

There are more than one hundred Rough Guide titles
covering destinations from Amsterdam to Zimbabwe

Forthcoming titles include
Bangkok • Barbados • Edinburgh
Japan • Jordan • Syria

Rough Guide Reference Series
Classical Music • European Football • The Internet • Jazz • Opera
Rock Music • World Music

Rough Guide Phrasebooks
Czech • French • German • Greek • Hindi & Urdu • Indonesian • Italian
Mandarin Chinese • Mexican Spanish • Polish • Portuguese • Russian
Spanish • Thai • Turkish • Vietnamese

Rough Guides on the Internet
http://www.roughguides.com/
http://www.hotwired.com/rough

ROUGH GUIDE CREDITS

Text editor: Sarah Dallas
Series editor: Mark Ellingham
Editorial: Martin Dunford, Jonathan Buckley, Samantha Cook, Jo Mead, Kate Berens, Amanda Tomlin, Ann-Marie Shaw, Vivienne Heller, Paul Gray, Chris Schüler, Helena Smith, Julia Kelly, Caroline Osbourne, Judith Bamber, Kieran Falconer (UK); Andrew Rosenberg (US)
Online editors: Alan Spicer (UK); Geronimo Madrid (US)

Production: Susanne Hillen, Andy Hilliard, Judy Pang, Link Hall, Nicola Williamson, Helen Ostick
Cartography: Melissa Flack, David Callier, Maxine Burke
Finance: John Fisher, Celia Crowley, Catherine Gillespie
Marketing and Publicity: Richard Trillo, Simon Carloss, Niki Smith (UK); Jean-Marie Kelly, SoRelle Braun (US)
Administration: Tania Hummel, Alexander Mark Rogers

ACKNOWLEDGEMENTS

This book is dedicated to two babies born during the course of the writing: Lungelolakhe-Joseph and Gabriel McCrea-Pinchuck. A big thank you to Link for production, Melissa and Maxine for maps, Nikky Twyman for proofreading, and Martin Dunford for help and advice throughout the project.

Barbara and Tony would like to thank our families in South Africa, Silke Ziehl for a home and place to write in London, Nina Saunders for her invaluable contribution to Durban, Bronwyn Kaplan, Peta Lee, Rodney and Roz Harber, Roger Field, Anne and John Field, Ida Cooper, Wendy Torien, Steve Shapiro, Stanley Singer, Daphne Knight, Ben Maclennan, Jeanne Berger, Don Pinnock, Margy Ramsey, the Armstrongs, Anne Marais, Trevor Dearlove (National Parks), Jeff Gaisford (Natal Parks), Sodwana Dive Retreat, the very many unmentioned people within the tourist industry, as well as friends, who gave us time, accommodation, meals and information, whose inside knowledge has made a huge contribution to this book, and thanks most especially to David Bristow for infallible orientating and steering. And finally thanks to our editor Sarah Dallas for her cool head, hard work and limitless patience.

Greg would like to thank: my mother Elizabeth, wife Lindiwe and son Lungelo for their love and forbearance while I wrote; Rob Allingham for the music; Liz Legum for supplies; Mi Hlatshwayo for being such a good *umkongi*; Miriam Wheeldon, Robbie and Cathy, Bram Kruger, Shaun de Waal for literary efforts and Cathy Tyacke in Johannesburg; Ruan Hoffman in Pretoria; the Middletons, the Lesotho Tourist Board, Mick and Di Jones, Jonathan at Semonkong and Duncan Dragon in Lesotho; Lindbergh Lodge and the Van Barts in the Northwest; the staff of the Big Bend Inn in Swaziland; and finally Sarah Dallas for her patience and tact as editor.

The authors of the Rough Guide to South Africa

Barbara McCrea was born in Zimbabwe and went to university in South Africa, going on to teach African literature at the University Durban-Westville for two years before coming to London in 1983. Driven by homesickness, she first wrote *The Rough Guide to Zimbabwe and Botswana* with Tony Pinchuck, before tackling even lengthier travels for the South African guide. Besides writing and living between South Africa and London, she works as a movement education teacher.

Tony Pinchuck launched his travels hitching around the country when he was fifteen. While at university studying African politics he drew political cartoon strips, several of which which were banned by the apartheid government, after which he left for the UK. He has since lived in Britain, where he has earned a living as a designer, cartoonist, editor and writer and has published numerous articles on southern Africa as well as nine books, including *The Rough Guide to Zimbabwe and Botswana*, and *Mandela for Beginners*. Since the installation of democracy in South Africa, he has run journalism courses there for university students.

Greg Salter-Mthembu first went to South Africa in 1989 in search of gospel music to promote in the UK, and has been going back ever since, most recently to live, work less and get married. He now has a young Capetonian son and a burning ambition to start Cape Town's first Zairean music nightclub.

PUBLISHING INFORMATION

This first edition published 1997 by Rough Guides Ltd, 1 Mercer Street, London WC2H 9QJ
Distributed by the Penguin Group:
Penguin Books Ltd, 27 Wrights Lane, London W8 5TZ
Penguin Books USA Inc., 375 Hudson Street, New York 10014, USA
Penguin Books Australia Ltd, 487 Maroondah Highway, PO Box 257, Ringwood, Victoria 3134, Australia
Penguin Books Canada Ltd, 10 Alcorn Avenue, Toronto, Ontario, Canada M4V 1E4
Penguin Books (NZ) Ltd, 182–190 Wairau Road, Auckland 10, New Zealand
Typeset in Linotron Univers and Century Old Style to an original design by Andrew Oliver
Printed in England by Clays Ltd, St Ives PLC
Illustrations in Part One and Part Three by Edward Briant; illustrations on p.1 and p.645 by Henry Iles

No part of this book may be reproduced in any form without permission from the publisher except for the quotation of brief passages in reviews.
© Barbara McCrea, Tony Pinchuck and Greg Salter-Mthembu, 1997
720pp, includes index
A catalogue record for this book is available from the British Library.
ISBN 1-85828-238-1

The publishers and authors have done their best to ensure the accuracy and currency of all the information in *The Rough Guide to South Africa*, however, they can accept no responsibility for any loss, injury or inconvenience sustained by any traveller as a result of information or advice contained in the guide.

South Africa

THE ROUGH GUIDE

written and researched by

Barbara McCrea, Tony Pinchuck and Greg Salter-Mthembu

with additional accounts by

Donald Reid

THE ROUGH GUIDES

We set out to do something different when the first Rough Guide was published in 1982. Mark Ellingham, just out of university, was travelling in Greece. He brought along the popular guides of the day, but found they were all lacking in some way. They were either strong on ruins and museums but went on for pages without mentioning a beach or taverna. Or they were so conscious of the need to save money that they lost sight of Greece's cultural and historical significance. Also, none of the books told him anything about Greece's contemporary life – its politics, its culture, its people, and how they lived.

So with no job in prospect, Mark decided to write his own guidebook, one which aimed to provide practical information that was second to none, detailing the best beaches and the hottest clubs and restaurants, while also giving hard-hitting accounts of every sight, both famous and obscure, and providing up-to-the-minute information on contemporary culture. It was a guide that encouraged independent travellers to find the best of Greece, and was a great success, getting shortlisted for the Thomas Cook travel guide award,

and encouraging Mark, along with three friends, to expand the series.

The Rough Guide list grew rapidly and the letters flooded in, indicating a much broader readership than had been anticipated, but one which uniformly appreciated the Rough Guide mix of practical detail and humour, irreverence and enthusiasm. Things haven't changed. The same four friends who began the series are still the caretakers of the Rough Guide mission today: to provide the most reliable, up-to-date and entertaining information to independent-minded travellers of all ages, on all budgets.

We now publish 100 titles and have offices in London and New York. The travel guides are written and researched by a dedicated team of more than 100 authors, based in Britain, Europe, the USA and Australia. We have also created a unique series of phrasebooks to accompany the travel series, along with an acclaimed series of music guides, and a best-selling pocket guide to the Internet and World Wide Web. We also publish comprehensive travel information on our two websites:

http://www.hotwired.com/rough
and http://www.roughguides.com/

HELP US UPDATE

We've gone to a lot of effort to ensure that this first edition of *The Rough Guide to South Africa* is as complete and up-to-date as possible. South Africa is changing fast, however, and if you feel there are places we've underrated or overpraised, or find that we've missed something good or covered something which has now gone, then please write; suggestions, comments or corrections are much appreciated.

All letters are answered and we'll acknowledge you in the second edition. A free copy of that (or any other *Rough Guide* if you prefer) will be sent for the best letters.
Please mark letters: "South Africa Update" and send to:
Rough Guides, 1 Mercer Street, London WC2H 9QJ,
or Rough Guides, 375 Hudson St, 9th floor, New York, NY 10014.
Or send email to: mail@roughguides.co.uk

CONTENTS

Introduction xii

PART ONE — BASICS — 1

Getting there: from Britain and Ireland	3
from the USA and Canada	8
from Australia and New Zealand	11
Red tape and visas	13
Health	15
Travel insurance	19
Costs, money and banks	21
Maps, information and websites	22
Getting around	25
Accommodation	31
Parks, reserves and wilderness areas	36
Wildlife	40
Food and drink	41
Post, phones and email services	44
The media	46
Opening hours and holidays	47
Photography	48
Spectator sports	49
Activities and outdoor pursuits	50
Trouble and the police	52
Travellers with disabilities	54
Gay and lesbian travellers	56
Directory	57

PART TWO — THE GUIDE — 59

● CHAPTER 1: CAPE TOWN AND THE PENINSULA 61–121

Arrival and information	64
City transport	65
Accommodation	68
The City	78
The Waterfront	86
The Southern Suburbs	88
Constantia and its winelands	93
Table Mountain	94
The Atlantic Seaboard	97
The False Bay Seaboard	99
Simon's Town	102
Table Bay and the Northern Suburbs	106
Cape Flats and the African townships	107
Eating and drinking	108
Nightlife and entertainment	112
Activites	116
Shopping	118
Listings	119
Moving on from Cape Town	120
Travel details	121

● CHAPTER 2: THE WESTERN CAPE 122–218

The Winelands	123
Stellenbosch	128
The Stellenbosch wine estates	132
Paarl	136
Franschhoek	142
Breede River Valley and the Little Karoo	146
Worcester and Ceres	147
Tulbagh	148

Robertson and McGregor	150	The Garden Route	180
Montagu	152	Mossel Bay	182
Oudtshoorn and around	154	Knysna and around	190
Cango Caves	157	Plettenberg Bay and around	198
Calitzdorp and the Groenfontein Valley	158	Tsitsikamma National Park	203
De Rust	159	Storms River Mouth	206
Prince Albert and around	159	The West Coast	207
The N1 from Worcester to Beaufort West	160	Langebaan Lagoon	210
The Overberg Interior and the Whale Coast	164	Cederberg	215
Hermanus	171	Clanwilliam	217
De Hoop Nature Reserve	179	Travel details	218

• CHAPTER 3: THE NORTHERN CAPE 219–256

Kimberley	223	Augrabies Falls National Park	238
Arrival, information and orientation	225	Kalahari Gemsbok National Park	239
Accommodation	225	Kuruman and around	243
The City	227	Namaqualand	245
The Big Hole	227	Northern Cape Flower Routes	246
Eating, drinking and nightlife	230	Calvinia and around	250
Listings	231	Springbok and around	251
Around Kimberley	231	The West Coast	253
The Kalahari	234	Richtersveld National Park	255
Upington	234	Travel details	256

• CHAPTER 4: THE EASTERN CAPE 257–334

Port Elizabeth	261	Bisho	303
Addo Elephant Park	269	Fort Hare	303
Shamwari Game Reserve	270	Hogsback	305
Jeffrey's Bay	270	The Eastern Cape Drakensberg	309
Port Alfred	273	Rhodes	310
Grahamstown	277	The Wild Coast region	314
Inland to the Karoo fringes	284	Coffee Bay and around	323
Graaff-Reinet	288	Umtata and around	324
Nieu Bethesda	293	Port St Johns	328
East London and around	296	Travel details	333
King William's Town	301		

• CHAPTER 5: KWAZULU-NATAL 335–426

Durban	337	The Drakensberg	381
Arrival and information	340	The Zululand coast and game reserves	393
The City	346	Hluhluwe-Umfolozi Park	396
Nightlife and entertainment	357	Greater St Lucia Wetland Park	399
Outdoor activities	359	Mkuzi Game Reserve	403
Shopping	360	Phinda Private Game Reserve	406
Listings	362	Northern Maputaland	406
Around Durban	363	Ndumo Game Reserve	411
The South Coast	364	Itala Game Reserve	413
The Dolphin Coast	370	Central Zululand and the Battlefields	414
Pietermaritzburg	374	Travel details	425
The Midlands	380		

• CHAPTER 6: FREE STATE 427–446

Bloemfontein	429	Golden Gate Highlands National Park	440
Arrival and information	430	Clarens	441
Accommodation	431	Fouriesburg and around	443
The City	432	Rustler's Valley	443
Eating and drinking	434	Ficksburg	444
Nightlife and entertainment	435	Clocolan and around	444
Listings	435	Ladybrand	445
The Highlands Route	438	Travel details	446

• CHAPTER 7: GAUTENG 447–496

Johannesburg	449	Around Johannesburg	481
Arrival & information	452	Pretoria	482
City transport	453	Arrival and information	486
Accommodation	455	Accommodation	487
The City	459	The City	487
Soweto	469	Eating and drinking	492
Eating and drinking	472	Nightlife and entertainment	493
Entertainment, nightlife and culture	475	Listing	494
Shopping	478	Around Pretoria	495
Listings	479	Travel details	495

• CHAPTER 8: THE NORTHWEST PROVINCE 497–516

The Magaliesberg	501	Mafikeng and around	510
Rustenburg and around	501	Lichtenburg and around	512
Sun City	503	Potchefstroom	513
Pilanesberg Game Reserve	504	Klerksdorp	514
Groot Marico	506	Wolmaransstad	515
Zeerust	508	Bloemhof and Christiana	516
Mmabatho and around	508	Travel details	516

• CHAPTER 9: MPUMALANGA AND THE KRUGER NATIONAL PARK 517–554

The Escarpment	519	Phalaborwa	528
Sabie	520	The Lowveld and gateways to southern Kruger	529
Pilgrim's Rest	522	Nelspruit	530
Graskop	523	Barberton	532
Blyde River Canyon and Blydepoort Dam	524	Kruger National Park	538
Gateways to Central Kruger	526	Private Game Reserves	550
Hoedspruit	527	Travel details	554

• CHAPTER 10: NORTHERN PROVINCE 555–582

The Central Region	558	The far north	574
Pietersburg	562	Venda	578
Letaba	565	Travel details	582
Waterberg	569		

● CHAPTER 11: LESOTHO 583—620

Tips on travel in Lesotho	588	Katse and the Lesotho Highlands Water Project	610
Maseru and the Central Districts	590	The Southern Districts	612
Roma and Semonkong	599	Mafeteng, Mohale's Hoek and Moyeni	614
The road to Thaba Tseka	601	Mount Moorosi, Qacha's Nek and the	
The northern districts	603	Sehlabathebe National Park	617
Buthe-Buthe to the Sani Pass	607	Travel details	620

● CHAPTER 12: SWAZILAND 621—644

Tips on travel in Swaziland	624	Hawane Dam Nature Reserve	638
Mbabane and around	626	The Northeast	638
The eZulwini Valley and Lobamba	630	Mlawula Nature Reserve	639
Mlilwane Wildlife Sanctuary	632	Hlane Royal National Park	640
Manzini	634	The South	641
Piggs Peak and the northwest	636	Mkhaya Nature Reserve	643
Malolotja Nature Reserve	637	Travel details	644

PART THREE CONTEXTS 645

South Africa: the historical framework	647	Books	677
Literature	663	Music	683
South African writers	669	Language	690
Index	693		

LIST OF MAPS

South Africa	xii–xiii	Port Elizabeth Beachfront and		Bloemfontein	430
Main intercity bus routes	26	Suburbs	262	The Highland Route	438
Major parks and wilderness areas		Central Port Elizabeth	264	**Gauteng**	447
	36	Port Alfred	274	Greater Johannesburg	449
Chapter divisions	59	Grahamstown	277	Johannesburg accommodation	
Cape Town	62	Cradock	286		456–457
Cape Town Centre and Waterfront	69	Graaff-Reinet	289	Central Johannesburg	460
Southern suburbs, False Bay and		East London	297	Northern suburbs	466
Atlantic Seaboard	90	The wild coast	315	Pretoria	484–485
Western Cape	124–125	Umtata	325	**Northwest Province**	498–499
Stellenbosch	129	**KwaZulu-Natal**	336	The Mageliesberg	501
Stellenbosch Wine Route	133	Durban suburbs	338	Mmabatho and Mafikeng	509
Paarl	137	Durban City Centre and Beachfront		**Mpumalanga**	518
Franschhoek	142		348–349	Blyde River Canyon	525
Hermanus	171	The Holiday Coast	364	Nelspruit	531
The Garden Route and Little Karoo		Pietermartizburg	375	Kruger National Park	539
	180–181	The Drakensberg	382	**Northern Province**	556–557
Knysna	191	Zululand coast and Game Reserves		Pietersburg	563
Plettenberg Bay	199		394	Letaba	565
Northern Cape	220–221	Hluhluwe-Umfolozi Park.	397	**Lesotho**	584
Kimberley	224	Mkuzi Game Reserve	404	Maseru	592
Upington	235	The Zulu Heartland and the		**Swaziland**	622
Kalahari Gemsbok National Park	240	Battlefields	415	Mbabane	626
Eastern Cape	258–259	**Free State**	427	Manzini	635

MAP SYMBOLS

⊷N8⊷ National road	◉ Hotel	⊤ Public gardens	
⊨R27⊨ Regional road	▲ Campsite	⊞ Hospital	
⊨M5⊨ Metropolitan road	⌂ Rest camp	ⓘ Information centre	
—— Minor road	卅 Picnic site	⊠ Post office	
······ Untarred road	❀ Vineyard	◐ Swimming pool	
▬▬▬ Pedestrianized road	✕ Battlefield	⚑ Golf course	
▪▪▪▪▪▪ Road under construction	♦ Museum	★ Public transport stop	
━━━ Railway	◉ Cave	♦ Other point of interest	
- - - - Path	▪ Hide	■ Building	
▬ ▪ ▬ International border	⮃ Viewpoint	⊞ Church	
━ ·· ━ Province border	⑂ Waterfall	⁺+⁺ Cemetery	
- - - - Chapter division boundary	⩫ Marshland	National park/nature reserve	
⸸ Border post	▲ Mountain peak	Park	
✕ Airport	⌁⌁ Mountain range	Beach	

INTRODUCTION

South Africa is a large and massively diverse country. The size of France and Spain combined, it varies from the picturesque Garden Route towns of the Western Cape to the raw stretch of subtropical coast in northern KwaZulu-Natal. It's also one of the great cultural meeting points of the African continent, a fact obscured by years of enforced racial segregation, but now manifest in its big cities.

Above all this is an incredibly beautiful country. But it's also something of an enigma, and a visit presents some uniquely South African challenges; it has the best travel facilities on the African continent but also the most difficult surface to scratch. After so long as an international pariah, the "rainbow nation" is still struggling to find its identity.

Many visitors are pleasantly surprised by South Africa's **excellent infrastructure**, which draws favourable comparison with countries such as Australia or the United States. Good air links and bus networks, excellent roads and a growing number of first-class B&Bs make South Africa perfect touring country. For those on a budget, rapidly mushrooming **backpackers' hostels** and a couple of backpacker buses provide an efficient means of exploring. The picture isn't all rosy, however. Apartheid may be dead, but its heritage still shapes South Africa in a very physical way. The country was organized for the benefit of whites, so it's easy to get a very white-orientated experience of Africa. Nowhere is this more in evidence than in the layout of towns and cities, where African areas (often desperately poor) are usually tucked out of sight. As a visitor, you'll have to make an effort to meet members of the country's African majority on equal terms, and you'll need to take a special tour to visit the black townships – or even to know they exist.

South Africa's **population** doesn't simply reduce to black and white. The country's majority group are the **Africans** (76 percent of the population); **whites** make up 13 percent, followed by **coloureds** (8.5 percent) – descendants of white settlers, slaves and Africans, who speak English and Afrikaans and make up the majority in the Western Cape. **Indians** (2.5 percent), most of whom live in KwaZulu-Natal, came to South Africa around the turn of the century as indentured labourers.

Although a growing number of theme parks pander to a tourist appetite for ethnic **culture**, South Africa draws as much from global influences as it does from home-grown sources; you won't be able to tell a power-dressed Xhosa from a jeans-wearing Zulu in downtown Johannesburg. **Music** is one area where South Africans really hold their own, and there's nowhere better than Jo'burg to go clubbing. Up in the Drakensberg, the countless images painted thousands of years ago onto rock faces by **San** people (the now-extinct first South Africans) give a glimpse into the country's rich artistic heritage.

Crime isn't the indiscriminate phenomenon that press reports suggest, but it is an issue. Really, it's a question of perspective – taking care but not becoming paranoid. Patterns of crime aren't uniform and, statistically at least, the odds of becoming a victim are highest in downtown Johannesburg, where violent crime is a daily reality. Other cities aren't exempt, but present a reduced risk – similar to, say, some parts of the United States; many country areas are safe by any standards.

Where to go

While you could circuit the whole of South Africa in a matter of weeks, a more satisfying approach is to focus your attention on one section of the country. Every one of the nine provinces (plus Lesotho and Swaziland) holds at least a couple of compelling reasons to visit, although, depending on the time of year and your interests, you'd be wise to concentrate on either the **west** or the **east**.

The **west**, best visited in the warmer months (Nov–April), has the outstanding attraction of **Cape Town**, worth visiting for its matchless setting beneath Table Mountain, at the foot of the continent. Half a day's drive from here can deliver any other destination in the **Western Cape**, a province which owes its distinctive character to the fact that it has the longest-established colonial heritage in the country. You'll find gabled Cape Dutch architecture, historic towns and vineyard-draped mountains in the **Winelands**; forested coast along the **Garden Route**; and a dry interior punctuated by Afrikaner *dorps* in the **Little Karoo**.

If the west sounds a bit too pretty and you're after a more "African" experience, head for the **eastern** flank of the country, best visited in the cooler months (May–Oct). **Johannesburg** is likely to be your point of entry to this area, and its frenetic street life, soaring office blocks and lively mix of people make it quite unlike anywhere else in the country. Half a day away by car lie the Northern Province and Mpumalanga, which share the mighty **Kruger National Park**. Of South Africa's roughly two dozen major parks, the Kruger flashes like a beacon to first-time visitors homing in on game-viewing opportunities, and is unrivalled on the continent for its cross-section of mammal species.

Kruger combines brilliantly with KwaZulu-Natal to the south, and an excellent short cut is to drive through tiny, landlocked **Swaziland**, which has attractions all of its own; a unique Swazi culture and a number of well-managed game parks. Once in **KwaZulu-Natal**, you'll be spoilt for superb game and birdlife; **Hluhluwe-Umfolozi Park** is the best place in the world to see endangered rhinos and there are several other outstanding **small game reserves** nearby, such as Itala, Mkuzi and Ndumo. If it's hiking and nature you want, nothing rivals the soaring **Drakensberg** range. Meanwhile **Durban** is, after Cape Town, the only city in South Africa worth visiting in its own right; a busy, cultural melting pot with a bustling Indian district and lively beachfront. The long stretch of beaches north and south of Durban is the most developed in the country; but head north towards the Mozambique border and you'll be on the wildest stretch of **coast** in South Africa.

Long sandy **beaches**, developed only in pockets, are characteristic of much of the 2500km of shoreline that curves from the cool Atlantic along the Northern Cape round to the subtropical Indian Ocean that foams onto KwaZulu-Natal's shores. Along its length, the pumping waves are excellent for **surfing**, yet don't teem with a crush of boards; **Jeffrey's Bay** on the Eastern Cape coast is a favourite spot. Much of the Eastern Cape coast is equally appealing, whether you just want to stroll, sunbathe or take in backdrops of mountains and hulking sand dunes. **Scuba-diving**, especially in KwaZulu-Natal, opens up a world of coral reefs rich with colourful **fish**, and southeast of the Western Cape winelands, along the **Whale Coast**, is one of South Africa's unsung attractions – some of the best shore-based **whale-watching** in the world.

With time in hand you might want to leave the big cities, the coast and game parks, and drive through the sparse but exhilarating **interior**, with its open horizons, switchback mountain passes, rocks, scrubby vegetation and isolated *dorps*. The offerings of the **Northern Cape** and **Northwest Province**, while less obvious than Kruger, Cape Town and the Garden Route, can reveal surprises. Visit the western section of the Northern Cape in August or September, and you'll be treated to a riot of colourful **wildflowers**. From the staunchly Afrikaner heartland of **Free State**, you're well poised to visit the very undeveloped kingdom of **Lesotho**, set in the mountains between the Free State and KwaZulu-Natal. Lesotho has few vestiges of royalty left today, but it does offer plenty of spectacular highland scenery, best explored on a sturdy, sure-footed Lesotho pony.

Climate: when to go

South Africa is a predominantly sunny country, but when it does get cold you really feel it, because indoor heating is limited and everything is geared to the fine weather that's the norm. You'll need to pack with the weather in mind, especially if you're going in winter. Southern hemisphere seasons are the reverse of the north, with **midwinter**

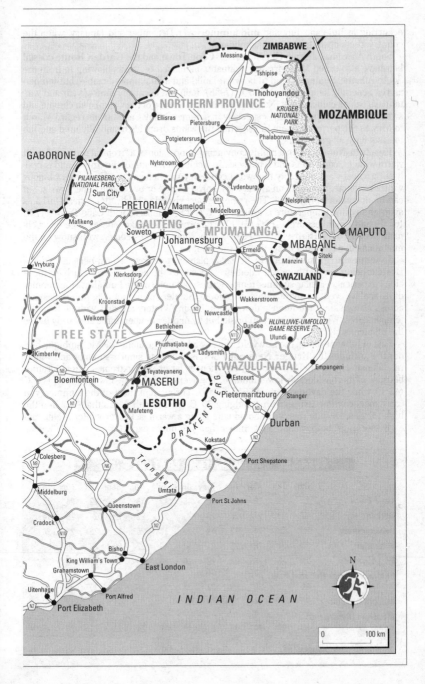

occurring in June and July and **midsummer** over December and January, when the country shuts down for its annual holiday.

South Africa has distinct climatic zones. **Cape Town** and the **Garden Route** coastal belt have a so-called Mediterranean climate, influenced by winds blowing in from the South Atlantic. Summers tend to be warm, mild and a little unpredictable, but temperatures generally keep below the 26°C (79°F). Rain can fall at any time of year and winter days can be cold and wet. Nagging winds are a feature of the Cape Town climate and sweep down for days at a time, especially in summer. Many Capetonians regard March to May as the perfect season; this is when the winds drop, it's beautifully mild and the tourists have all gone home.

KwaZulu-Natal puts on a highly convincing impression of a "tropical province", with warm winters, coral reefs and tepid seas. In fact it's well south of the tropics and is really subtropical – a technicality that won't concern you when you're enjoying its fabulous winter sunshine. Summers on average are only a degree or two above Cape Town's, but can be uncomfortably humid. The region is best visited in midwinter, when Durban's average daytime temperature is around 22°C (72°F) compared with Cape Town's 17°C (63°F) and Johannesburg's 16°C (61°F). The province's Drakensberg range has a climate similar to the Highveld (see below), only some degrees cooler, with snow on the mountains in winter and misty days in the summer.

Johannesburg and **Pretoria** lie on a plateau and have a near-perfect climate. Despite being several hundred kilometres closer to the equator than Durban, these cities experience similar summer temperatures, but none of the humidity. Hot summer days are relieved by pyrotechnic afternoon thunderstorms with lightning flashing across slatey skies, and intense downpours of rain. Winters are dry, with chilly night temperatures. Winter days start off brisk, but by midday temperatures are rarely below the mid-teens (15°C).

East of Johannesburg, the **Lowveld**, the low-lying wedge along the Mozambique border that includes the **Kruger National Park**, is subject to similar summer and winter rainfall patterns to the Highveld, but experiences far greater extremes of temperature because of its considerably lower altitude. The average night-time low for winter is 6°C (43°F) while the daytime high is 25°C (77°F). Throughout most of the summer, you can expect daytime temperatures nudging 30°C (86°F), with peaks that soar into the high thirties. Despite this, you should take along a warm jacket for winter nights and early mornings; both can get a lot chillier than you might expect.

AVERAGE MAXIMUM TEMPERATURES (°C)												
	Jan	Feb	Mar	Apr	May	June	July	Aug	Sept	Oct	Nov	Dec
Cape Town	27	27	26	23	20	19	17	18	19	22	24	26
Durban	27	28	27	26	24	23	22	22	23	24	25	26
Johannesburg	26	26	24	22	19	16	16	20	23	25	25	26
Kimberley	33	31	28	25	21	19	19	22	25	28	30	32
Port Elizabeth	25	26	25	23	22	20	20	20	20	21	22	24
Skukuza (Kruger National Park)												
	31	31	30	29	27	25	25	26	29	29	30	30
Maseru (Lesotho)	20	17	14	11	9	7	7	9	11	14	17	20
Mbabane (Swaziland)												
	25	25	24	23	21	19	19	21	23	24	24	25

°C = (°F - 32) multiplied by 5/9

PART ONE

THE
BASICS

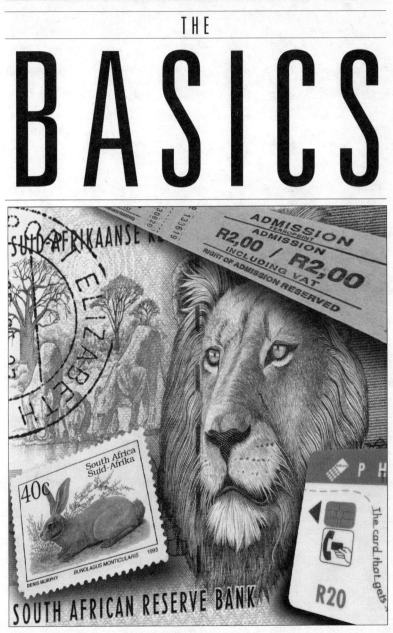

GETTING THERE FROM BRITAIN AND IRELAND

Most people travel to South Africa by air and it has never been cheaper or easier to get there, with an increase in the number of scheduled flights and plunging prices following the end of apartheid in the 1990s. From London there are direct flights to Johannesburg, Cape Town and Durban; the cheapest usually go via mainland Europe or Africa and involve changes of plane.

Fares depend on which **season** you're flying. To give a rough idea, the rock-bottom **basic season** is in April and May (the South African autumn); a rung up, the **low season** runs from June to November (winter and early spring); the more expensive **shoulder season** covers mid-January to the end of March; while by far the most expensive **high season** falls over the first half of January and most of December (midsummer). Expect some variation on these dates from one airline to the next.

Also worth considering is an **"open-jaw" ticket** which allows you to fly into one South African destination and out from another (say Johannesburg and Cape Town) or even to fly out from another African country. On some airlines these fares are no more expensive than a straightforward return ticket and they have the great advantage of avoiding tedious backtracking if you're touring.

Overland options (see p.6) include journeys via East Africa, either driving or travelling by rail or on economy buses. Organized trips that show you the sights run on a number of routes, some starting in Europe.

NONSTOP FLIGHTS FROM BRITAIN

South African Airways (*SAA*) and *British Airways* (*BA*) fly daily and *Virgin Atlantic* flies six times a week from Heathrow direct to **Johannesburg**, a journey taking eleven hours – the fastest available. Both *SAA* and *BA* operate direct flights to **Cape Town** (11hr 30min) four times a week and to **Durban** (14hr), via Johannesburg, three times a week. Basic/high season scheduled fares – APEX – go for £690/£1025 basic season/high season to Johannesburg; and £733/£1065 to Cape Town.

You can usually pick up fares for a lot less by booking through **discount agents** (see box on p.5), who will often be able to sell you the same scheduled seat cheaper or do you a deal on a direct **charter flight**, although you'll have to start planning this several weeks in advance during peak season. Look through the classified sections of the Sunday newspapers – the *Sunday Times* and *Observer* especially – and if you live in London, *Time Out* magazine and the *Evening Standard* newspaper for the latest cheap deals; you may be able to pick up a return flight to Johannesburg for around £400–500 direct and to Cape Town for around £500 direct. Keep an eye out also for "seat sales" from the airlines throughout the year, which sometimes bring fares in basic season down to £400 and below.

FLIGHTS VIA EUROPE

The growing popularity of South Africa means there's a choice of easy flights from London **via Europe**. Convenient transfers and discounted prices make these definitely worth considering, although you pay the price of longer journey times and lingering in transit lounges. London to Johannesburg tickets on a number of European carriers, including *Air France* via Paris, *Lufthansa* via Frankfurt, *KLM* via Amsterdam, *Olympic Airways* via Athens and *Sabena* via Brussels, sometimes come up for under £350 in low season. Some of these airlines continue on to Cape Town after stopping in Johannesburg.

FLIGHTS VIA AFRICA

Cheap flights from London are also often available **via other African countries**. One of the best carriers is *Air Namibia* which flies from

AIRLINES FLYING FROM THE UK TO SOUTH AFRICA

Air France, 10 Warwick St, 1st Floor, London W1R 5RA (☎0181/742 6600).

Air Namibia, Beaumont House, Lambton Rd, West Wimbledon, London SW20 0LW (☎0181/944 6181).

Air Zimbabwe, Colette House, 52–55 Piccadilly, London W1V 9AA (☎0171/491 0009).

Alitalia, 27–28 Piccadilly, London W1P 9PF (☎0171/602 7111).

Balkan Bulgarian Airlines, 322 Regent St, London W1R 5AB (☎0171/637 7637).

British Airways, 156 Regent St, London W1R 5TA, and branches throughout the UK (all enquiries ☎0345/222111).

Egyptair, 296 Regent St, London W1R 6PH (☎0171/734 2395).

Emirates Airlines, 95 Cromwell Rd, London SW7 4DL (☎0171/808 0808).

Ethiopian Airlines, 4th Floor, 166 Piccadilly, London W1V 9DE (☎0171/491 9119).

KLM Royal Dutch Airlines, Reservations (☎0990/750900); ticket office at Terminal 4, Heathrow.

Kenya Airways, 16 Conduit St, London W1 (☎0171/409 0277).

Lufthansa German Airlines, 10 Old Bond St, London W1X 4EN; Phoenix House, 78 St Vincent St, Glasgow G2 5UB (☎0345/737747).

Olympic Airways, 11 Conduit St, London W1R 0LP (☎0171/409 3400).

Sabena, 10 Putney Hill, London SW15 6AA (☎0345/581291).

South African Airways, St Georges House, 61 Conduit St, London W1R ONE (☎0171/312 5000).

Swissair, Swiss Centre, 10 Wardour St, London W1V 4BJ (☎0171/434 7300).

Virgin Atlantic Airways, *Virgin Megastore*, 14 Oxford St, London W1 (☎01293/747747).

London to Windhoek several times a week and frequently offers competitive fares on to Johannesburg or Cape Town (special prices can be as low as £370 return from London to Johannesburg). *Air Namibia* has good African regional connections and is also useful if you're exploring the subcontinent beyond South Africa. *Air Zimbabwe* flies from Gatwick to Harare with onward flights to Cape Town (once a week), Durban (once a week) and Johannesburg (twice a week). A number of other airlines, such as *Kenya Airways*, via Nairobi, *Egyptair* via Cairo, and *Emirates* via Dubai, offer connections to Johannesburg.

ROUND-THE-WORLD TICKETS

Round-the-world tickets provide an extremely economical way of travelling if you want to include South Africa in an extended tour taking in several continents. Routings almost always include Australia; but that aside, there's a wide choice of destinations. A popular combination is London–Johannesburg–Perth (own arrangements to Sydney)–Sydney–Los Angeles–London and costs under £650 in May and June, or around £950 in September and October. For the same price you can fly to Harare (or another African destination) and make your way overland to Johannesburg, from where you can fly out to Perth.

PACKAGES AND ORGANIZED TOURS

There are few traditional sea-and-sun **packages** to South Africa. After all, there's not much point flying for at least eleven hours just to cool out on a beach for a couple of weeks when you can do it far cheaper much closer to home. Package tours therefore tend to include some form of travelling around the country. The least imaginative of these are highly organized sightseeing **bus tours**, with punishing whistle-stop itineraries that promise more interaction with the other passengers than with local people. These through-the-window holidays can be booked at most of the large high-street travel agents, such as *Thomas Cook* or *Going Places*.

A more satisfactory alternative are **tailor-made packages** that prearrange all or part of your holiday, but leave you to travel on your own. Quite a number of well-informed tour operators and travel agents have an excellent knowledge of South Africa and specialize in such packages. If time is tighter than money, it's

FLIGHT AGENTS IN THE UK

Bridge the World, 47 Chalk Farm Rd, London NW1 8AN (☎0171/911 0900). *Specializes in round-the-world tickets, with good deals aimed at the backpacker market.*

Campus Travel, 52 Grosvenor Gdns, London SW1W 0AG (☎0171/730 8111); 541 Bristol Rd, Selly Oak, Birmingham B29 6AU (☎0121/414 1848); 61 Ditchling Rd, Brighton BN1 4SD (☎01273/570226); 39 Queen's Rd, Clifton, Bristol BS8 1QE (☎0117/929 2494); 5 Emmanuel St, Cambridge CB1 1NE (☎01223/324283); 53 Forest Rd, Edinburgh EH1 2QP (☎0131/668 3303); 166 Deansgate, Manchester M3 3FE (☎0161/833 2046); 105–106 St Aldates, Oxford OX1 1DD (☎01865/242067). *Student/youth travel specialists, with branches also in YHA shops and on university campuses all over Britain.*

Comet Travel, 21 Newman St, London W1P 4DD (☎0171/580 5000). *Agents for* Air Namibia *and* SAA.

Council Travel, 28a Poland St, London W1V 3DB (☎0171/437 7767). *Flights and student discounts.*

Flightbookers, 177–178 Tottenham Court Rd, London W1P 0LX (☎0171/757 2444). *Low fares on an extensive offering of scheduled flights. Very handy hours, open daily (Mon–Fri 9am–7pm, Sat 9am–5pm, Sun 10am–5pm).*

The London Flight Centre, 131 Earls Court Rd, London SW5 9RH (☎0171/244 6411); 47 Notting Hill Gate, London W11 3JS (☎0171/727 4290); Shop 33, The Broadway Centre, Hammersmith, London W6 9YE (☎0181/748 6777). *Long-established agent dealing in discount flights.*

North South Travel, Moulsham Mill Centre, Parkway, Chelmsford, Essex CM2 7PX (☎01245/492882). *Friendly, competitive agency offering discounted fares worldwide. Profits are used to support projects in the developing world, especially the promotion of sustainable tourism.*

Nouvelles Frontières, 2/3 Woodstock St, London W1R 1HE (☎0171/629 7772). *French-owned tour operator specializing in charter flights and packages that take in African destinations. Most charter flights go from or through Paris.*

Quest Worldwide, 10 Richmond Rd, Kingston, Surrey, KT2 5HL (Australia & worldwide ☎0181/547 3322). *Specialists in round-the-world and Australasian discount fares.*

STA Travel, 86 Old Brompton Rd, London SW7 3LH (☎0171/937 9921); 117 Euston Rd, London NW1 2SX (☎0171/361 6161); 38 Store St, London WC1E 7BZ (worldwide ☎0171/361 6262; Europe ☎0171/361 6161); 25 Queens Rd, Bristol BS8 1QE (☎0117/929 4399); 38 Sidney St, Cambridge CB2 3HX (☎01223/366966); 88 Vicar Lane, Leeds LS1 7JH (☎0113/244 9212); 75 Deansgate, Manchester M3 2BW (☎0161/834 0668); 36 George St, Oxford OX1 2OJ (☎01865/792800); and branches in Birmingham, Canterbury, Cardiff, Coventry, Durham, Glasgow, Loughborough, Nottingham, Warwick and Sheffield. *Worldwide specialists in low-cost flights and tours for students and under-26s, though other customers are welcome.*

Trailfinders, 42–50 Earls Court Rd, London W8 6FT (☎0171/938 3366); 194 Kensington High St, London W8 7RG (☎0171/938 3939); 58 Deansgate, Manchester M3 2FF (☎0161/839 6969); 254–284 Sauchiehall St, Glasgow G2 3EH (☎0141/353 2224); 22–24 Priory Queensway, Birmingham B4 6BS (☎0121/236 1234); 48 Corn St, Bristol BS1 1HQ (☎0117/929 9000). *One of the best-informed and most efficient agents for independent travellers. They produce a very useful quarterly magazine worth scrutinizing for round-the-world routes (for free copy, call ☎0171/938 3366). All branches open daily.*

Travel Bag, 52 Regent St, London W1R 6DX or 12 High St, Alton, Hants GU34 1BN (southern Africa ☎0171/287 5535). *Discount flights worldwide including southern Africa. Officially appointed* Qantas *agent.*

The Travel Bug, 125a Gloucester Rd, London SW7 4SF (☎0171/835 2000); 597 Cheetham Hill Rd, Manchester M8 5EJ (☎0161/721 4000). *Large range of discounted tickets. Official* South African Airways *agent.*

definitely worth drawing on their years of knowledge and expertise.

Fly-drive packages are also worth considering if you want to simply have your transport taken care of, but want the freedom to arrange the rest of your visit. Packages are available in conjunction with *BA, SAA* and *Virgin* – the three airlines that fly direct from Heathrow to South Africa. Prices for a one-week basic package for two people travelling together ranges from £700 to £1000 per person (depending on season). Car rental can be extended for around £200 a week.

TOUR OPERATORS IN THE UK

Abercrombie and Kent, Sloane Square House, Holbein Place, London SW1W 8NS (☎0171/730 9600). *Large upmarket operator with comprehensive and professional programmes in southern Africa, including South Africa, Lesotho and Swaziland.*

Africa Travel Centre, 21 Leigh St, London WC1H 9QX (☎0171/387 1211). *Experienced and knowledgeable Africa specialists with a wide range of affordable options, including days' travelling around the Cape Peninsula for £1500, and a ten-day city and safari tour at £1895.*

Art of Travel, 21 The Bakehouse, Bakery Place, 119 Altenberg Gardens, London SW11 (☎0171/738 2038). *Highly flexible specialist agent offering fully inclusive holidays to South Africa, including Swaziland, to suit a range of budgets, using tried and tested local operators.*

Discover the World, 29 Nork Way, Banstead, Surrey SM7 1PB (☎01737/218800). *Well-established safari holiday specialist. Tempting packages include seventeen-day train journey from Johannesburg to Cape Town, with safari excursions en route (£2000;) and ten-days' whale- and wildlife-watching in the Cape (£1458). They also organize more general itineraries and fly-drives.*

Grenadier Travel, 11–12 West Stockwell St, Colchester CO1 1HN (☎01206/549585). *Small but expert agent with genuine knowledge of South Africa and an affection for the region based on several years' residence. Highly personalized, upmarket trips with great attention to detail.*

Hayes & Jarvis, Hayes House, 152 King St, London W6 0QU (☎0181/748 5050). *Long-established operator, whose wide-ranging options stretch from budget self-catering and no-frills safaris to luxury tours. Exotic weddings organized.*

Jetsave, Sussex House, London Rd, East Grinstead, West Sussex RH19 1LD (☎01342/322525). *Agents for* South African Airways Holidays *which include fly-drive packages with the national carrier which from Heathrow to Johannesburg, Cape Town or Durban.*

Kuoni Worldwide, Kuoni House, Dorking, Surrey RH5 4AZ (Africa ☎01306/743000). *Flexible packages from this reputable long-haul operator, with good deals for families.*

Okavango Tours and Safaris, Gadd House, Arcadia Ave, London N3 2TJ (☎0181/343 3283). *Old hands with on-the-ground knowledge of the subcontinent, this company say they can meet most of your requirements for South Africa.*

Sunvil Discovery, Sunvil House, Upper Square, Old Isleworth, Middlesex TW7 7BJ (☎0181/232 9797). *Tailored holidays offered throughout southern Africa.*

Thomas Cook Holidays (☎01733/267171, fax 505784), 12 Coningsby Rd, Peterborough PE3 8XP and high streets across Britain. *Fly-drive packages with* South African *or* British Airways *from Heathrow to Johannesburg, Cape Town or Durban.*

Virgin Holidays (☎01293/617181, fax 536957), The Galleria, Ground Floor, Station Rd, Crawley, West Sussex RH10 1WW. *Fly-drive packages in conjunction with* Virgin Atlantic Airlines *flying from Heathrow to Johannesburg.*

Worldwide Journeys and Expeditions, 8 Comeragh Rd, London W14 9HP (☎0171/381 8638). *Outstanding tailor-made travel programmes by a company that will steer you to the smaller, better-value options. One popular itinerary is their eight-day "Highlights of South Africa", which includes game-viewing in Kruger, touring the Drakensberg, and the down to the Garden Route and Cape Town (from £2295).*

OVERLAND OPTIONS

Road conditions in Africa are inconsistent. Major tarred routes are often perfectly good, but in some countries, where maintenance tends to be poor, they can get badly potholed. Some roads – usually those leading off the main arteries – are seasonal and will be out of commission during heavy rains. African roads also have a reputation for erratic opening and closing of borders. It's wise to keep up with the news, as conflicts and coups occasionally erupt.

At the time of writing, unrest in Sudan and the Democratic Republic of the Congo cut a swath right across Africa, from the Red Sea to the Atlantic Ocean, making overland travel from north to south inadvisable for all but the holidays-in-hell brigade. Things may change, but for the moment driving through Eastern Africa provides the most feasible – and adventurous – route, starting in **Kenya** and heading through **Tanzania**, **Malawi**, **Zambia** and **Zimbabwe** eventually to touch the southern tip of the continent at **Cape Town**.

OVERLAND OPERATORS IN THE UK

Dragoman, 14 Camp Green, Debenham, Stowmarket, Suffolk IP14 6LA (☎01728/861133). *Extended overland journeys in purpose-built expedition vehicles through Africa. Shorter camping and hotel-based safaris also offered.*

Encounter Overland, 267 Old Brompton Rd, London SW5 9JA (☎0171/370 6845). *Wide range of overland trips in southern Africa as well as six-month treks from London or Nairobi to Cape Town.*

Exodus, 9 Weir Rd, London SW12 0LT (☎0181/675 5550). *Adventure-tour operators, set up over twenty years ago, running nine-week overland trips from Kenya to Cape Town and short tours in South Africa, including backed-up mountain biking in the Western Cape.*

Explore Worldwide, 1 Frederick St, Aldershot, Hampshire GU11 1LQ (☎01252/319448). *Overland*

trips inside southern Africa, with a popular trip starting in Cape Town and heading east along the Garden Route and through Swaziland to Johannesburg. They also offer trips that take in Namibia, Botswana and Zimbabwe.

Guerba Expeditions, Wessex House, Station Rd, Westbury, Wiltshire BA13 3JN (☎01373/826611). *Huge range of trans-African overland trips including Gibraltar or Nairobi to Cape Town and shorter pick-and-mix trips in southern Africa. Agents for Drifters, a South Africa-based overland company that operates trips inside the country.*

Kumuka Expeditions, 40 Earls Court Rd, London W8 6EJ (☎0171/937 8855). *Overland 22-day trips from Victoria Falls to Cape Town, and short tours around South Africa using local operators.*

Travelling in the immediate vicinity of South Africa is a different story, with excellent roads from Namibia, Botswana and Zimbabwe to South Africa.

ORGANIZED OVERLAND TRIPS

Several overland operators run **trans-Africa routes** starting in Britain, Europe or Nairobi and working their way down to Cape Town. Some companies have stopped traversing the full length of the continent, due to the impassibility of Sudan and the Congo, but others simply fly clients over the awkward sections. A 31-week trip from **Gibraltar to Cape Town** via West Africa costs in the region of £4500–5000 (land arrangements only). For a more modest eleven-

AIRLINES, AGENTS AND TOUR OPERATORS IN IRELAND

AIRLINES

Aer Lingus, Northern Ireland reservations (☎0645/737 747); Dublin reservations (☎01/844 4777). Branches at: 40 O'Connell St, Dublin (☎01/844 4777); 2 Academy St, Cork (☎021/327 155); and 36 O'Connell St, Limerick (☎061/474 239).

British Midland, Northern Ireland reservations (☎0345/554 554); Dublin reservations (☎01/283 8833).

Lufthansa, Dublin reservations (☎01/844 5544).

Olympic Airways, Franklin House, 142 Pembroke Rd, Ballsbridge, Dublin 4 (☎01/608 0090).

Virgin Atlantic, Club Travel Offices, 30 Lower Abbey St, Dublin 1 (☎01/873 3388).

AGENTS AND TOUR OPERATORS

Liffey Travel, 12 Upper O'Connell St, Dublin 1 (☎01/878 8322). *Package tour specialists.*

Thomas Cook, 11 Donegall Place, Belfast (☎01232/242341); 118 Grafton St, Dublin 2 (☎01/677 1721). *Package holiday and flight agent with occasional discount offers.*

Trailfinders, 4–5 Dawson St, Dublin 2 (☎01/677 7888). *Competitive fares out of all Irish airports, as well as deals on hotels, insurance, tours and car rental worldwide.*

USIT, branches at: Fountain Centre, College St, Belfast BT1 6ET (☎01232/324073); 10 Market Parade, Patrick St, Cork (☎021/270900); 33 Ferryquay St, Derry (☎01504/371888); Aston Quay, Dublin 2 (☎01/602 1600); Victoria Place, Eyre Square, Galway (☎091/565177); Central Buildings, O'Connell St, Limerick (☎061/415064); 36 Georges St, Waterford (☎051/872601). *Student and youth specialists for flights and trains.*

week trip from **Nairobi to Cape Town** via Harare, expect to pay in the region of £2000. An increasing number of operators are also offering overland trips within southern Africa, taking in **South Africa and its neighbours**. Other trips just take in the well-worn **South African routes** from Cape Town, down the Garden Route through to the Kruger National Park and on to Johannesburg.

FLIGHTS FROM IRELAND

There are no direct flights from Ireland to South Africa and prices tend to be higher than nonstop routings from Britain. With the frequency of connections from Belfast and, to an even greater extent, from Dublin to London and several cities on mainland Europe, you shouldn't have a problem arranging a convenient connection if you book well in advance.

From Belfast to Johannesburg *KLM* flies via Amsterdam and *Olympic Airways* via Athens, both with a four-hour delay between flights, while the *Lufthansa* connection with a *South African Airways* flight involves a significantly shorter delay. **From Dublin**, the choice of flights to Johannesburg is a lot wider and the interval between flights much shorter. Among the airlines flying this route are: *Aer Lingus* connecting with *SAA* in Frankfurt; *British Midland* connecting with *SAA* at Heathrow; and *Sabena* via Brussels. Apart from these, your travel agent should be able to arrange a routing to suit you.

When it comes to **packages**, you're best off contacting one of the British-based companies listed on p.6, or booking through one of the agents in the box p.7.

GETTING THERE FROM THE USA AND CANADA

From New York it's possible to fly direct to Johannesburg in just over sixteen hours. South African Airways (SAA) and American Airlines both operate daily, nonstop flights from New York to Johannesburg. SAA also operates five flights a week from Miami to Cape Town.

Most other flights stop off in Europe en route to South Africa; **British Airways** have several flights a week from New York via London, with a fast connection of roughly one hour to Johannesburg, Cape Town and Durban. **Delta** won't take you all the way, but they can, on most days of the week, connect you with a partner airline that flies into Johannesburg (usually *Swissair* in Zurich) with only a short stopover. Otherwise, you'll probably arrive in Europe in the morning and have to wait until late at night or early the following morning to complete your journey. **Virgin Atlantic** flies daily from New York to Johannesburg via London, and **KLM** flies from New York to Johannesburg via Amsterdam every day except Friday.

The **high season** for travel from North America to South Africa, when fares are generally most expensive, is June to August and mid-December to mid-January. The rest of the year is low season (there is no shoulder season).

FARES

The cheapest of the airlines' published fares is usually an **APEX** (Advance Purchase Excursion Fare) ticket which is likely to come with restrictions – booking in advance, minimum and maximum stay and penalties if you wish to change your schedule.

Typical lowest standard APEX **fares** to Johannesburg for low/high seasons are as follows: Chicago ($1619/$2169); Los Angeles ($1699/$2249); New York ($1198/$1899);

NORTH AMERICAN DISCOUNT AGENTS AND TOUR OPERATORS

DISCOUNT AGENTS

Air Brokers International, 323 Geary St, Suite 411, San Francisco, CA 94102 (☎1-800/883-3273 or 415/387-1383). *Consolidator and specialist in RTW tickets.*

Council Travel, 205 E42nd St, New York, NY 10017 (☎1-800/226-8624) *Student/budget travel agency.*

Now Voyager, 74 Varick St, Suite 307, New York, NY 10013 (☎212/431-1616) *Courier flight broker and consolidator.*

High Adventure Travel, 353 Sacramento St, Suite 600, San Francisco, CA 94111 (☎1-800/350-0612 or 415/912-5600; http://www.highadv.com). *Round-the-world and Circle Pacific tickets. The*

website features an interactive database that lets you build your own RTW itinerary.

STA Travel, 10 Downing St, New York, NY 10014 (☎1-800/777-0112 or 212/627-3111; http://www.sta-travel.com/), and other branches in the Los Angeles, San Francisco and Boston areas. *Worldwide discount travel firm specializing in student/youth fares; also student IDs, travel insurance, car rental, rail passes, etc.*

Travel Cuts, 243 College St, Toronto, ON M5T 1P7 (☎416/979-2406 or 800/667-2887 in Canada; ☎888/238-2887 in US). *Specialists in student travel, IDs and all other travel services.*

TOUR OPERATORS

Although phone numbers are given here, you're better off making tour reservations through your **local travel agent**. An agent will make all the phone calls, sort out the snafus and arrange flights, insurance and the like – all at no extra cost to you.

Abercrombie and Kent (☎1-800/323-7308) *Leading upscale operator with over thirty years of experience organizing African safaris. Package options include a nine-night "Highlights of South Africa" priced at $3800 and a twelve-night "Family Safari" for $5240 (adults) and $3995 (kids). Prices exclude flight from the US.*

Adventure Center (☎1-800/227-8747) *Wide variety of affordable packages, ranging from a five-day "Kruger Bushveld Safari" for around $395, to a thirteen-day "South African Panorama" priced at $3350.*

Africatours (☎1-800/235-3692) *Medium to pricey customized tours.*

Big Five Tours (☎212/481-1919). *Range of packages include sixteen-day "Grand Classic", with game-viewing, history and archeology, at $4595 (including round-trip flight from New York).*

Bushtracks (☎415/326-8689). *Upmarket, customized tours for travellers interested in wildlife photography; at around $400–$450 per day.*

Mountain Travel-Sobek (US: ☎1-800/227-2384; Canada: ☎1-800/282-8747). *Packages include sev-*

enteen-day "Wild South Africa" tour which includes hiking and game-viewing. Land cost is $3990.

Safaricentre (☎1-800/223-6046) *Wide choice of packages from budget to upmarket. On the cheaper end of the scale there's a five-day camping tour of the Bushveld at $425 per person; or an eighteen-day package that includes game-viewing, hiking, a visit to Swaziland and a day in the wine country for $1375 (land only).*

Saga Holidays (☎1-800/343-0273). *Group packages for the over-50s, including seventeen-night tour with game-viewing, at $4600 per person (flights included).*

Wilderness Travel (☎1-800/368-2794). *Options include an eighteen-day tour with game-viewing, hiking and cultural sightseeing for around $4000, which is limited to eight people.*

Worldwide Adventures/Quest Nature Tours (☎1-800/387-1483). *Packages include an eighteen-day mixed-accommodation hiking/trekking/game-viewing/cultural tour for $1750, and a more upscale fourteen-day-hotel-/lodge-accommodated game-viewing and bird-watching tour for $2295.*

Toronto (CDN$2587/$2839); Vancouver (CDN$2779/$3031). From New York to Durban, you can expect to pay around $2004/$2210. Fares from New York to Cape Town are roughly $1299/$2296, and from Miami to Cape Town around $1299/$1899.

SHOPPING FOR TICKETS

You can normally cut costs further, and maybe avoid some of the restrictions of the APEX ticket, by going through a specialist flight agent – either a **consolidator**, who buys up blocks of tickets from the airlines and sells them at a discount, or a **discount agent**, who in addition to dealing with discounted flights may also offer special student and youth fares and a range of other travel-related services such as travel insurance, rail passes, car rental, tours and the like. Some agents specialize in **charter flights**, which may be cheaper than anything available on a scheduled flight, but again departure dates are fixed and withdrawal penalties are high.

Low-/high-season **discount/student rates** can be found for New York to Johannesburg ($1046/$1292); New York to Cape Town or Durban ($1450/$1555); and Toronto to Johannesburg (CDN$1499/CDN$1899).

It's also worth looking out for limited **special offers** from the major carriers, which you'll find advertised from time to time in the newspapers, often giving little notice before the deadline for making reservations expires.

You might want to check if an airline hikes its fares on their US–South Africa route for **weekend travel**. For instance, *SAA* charges the same rates seven days a week, whereas *British Airways* fares are $25–30 more expensive (each direction) at weekends.

Also worth considering is an **"open-jaw" ticket**, which allows you to arrive in one city, travel overland, then depart from another. Flying from New York into Johannesburg and out of Cape Town in low/high seasons costs around $2035/$2240.

Finally, if you have time to make the most of it, a **round-the-world** (RTW) ticket might be your best option. Obviously, the price varies considerably, depending on your itinerary and whether you want to keep part of your trip open for overland travel. The ticket is usualy valid for one year, with departure and return to the US often the only fixed dates. At the budget end of the scale, a low-season New York–London–Johannesburg–Delhi/Bombay–Bangkok–Hong Kong RTW ticket could cost around $1775.

AIRLINES IN THE US AND CANADA

American Airlines, Manhattan Air Terminal, 100 E42nd St, New York (☎1-800/624-6262); 44 Gerrard St W Toronto, ON M5G 2K2 (same phone number).

British Airways, 530 5th Ave (between 44th and 45th), New York, NY 10036 (☎1-800/247-9297); 4120 Yonge St, North York, Toronto, ON M2P 2B8 (☎1-800/668-1059); http://www.british-airways.com/

Canadian Airlines, in Canada (☎1-800/665-1177); in US (☎1-800/426-7000); http://www.cdnair.ca/

Delta, 1 Penn Plaza, New York, NY 10119 (☎1-800/241-4141 or 404/765-5000); 2 Bloor St, Suite 502, Toronto (☎1-800/241-4141); http://www.delta-air.com/

KLM, 437 Madison Ave (between 49th & 50th), New York (☎1-800/374-7747); 777 Bay St, Toronto (☎1-800/361-5073); http://www.klm.nl/

South African Airways, 900 3rd Ave, New York, NY 10022 (☎1-800/722-9675); http://www.saa.co.za/saa/.

Swissair, in US (☎1-800/221-4750); in Canada (☎1-800/267-9477); http://www.swissair.com/

Virgin Atlantic Airways, 100 E42nd St (at Park Ave), New York, NY (☎1-800/862-8621); http://www.fly.virgin.com/atlantic/

GETTING THERE FROM AUSTRALIA & NEW ZEALAND

Southern Africa is an undeniably expensive destination for travellers from Australia and New Zealand. Fares are steep, and a ticket to Europe with a stopover in South Africa, or even a round-the-world (RTW) ticket, generally represents better value than a straightforward return.

There are flights from both the eastern states and Western Australia to Johannesburg and Cape Town, but New Zealanders have to fly via Sydney. *South African Airways* (*SAA*), *Qantas*, *Air New Zealand* and *British Airways* all fly to South Africa; some of the Asian (*Air Lanka*, *Malaysian*, *Singapore* and *Thai*) and Middle Eastern (*Gulf Air*) airlines tend to be less expensive, but their routings often entail more stopovers en route.

FARES

Whatever kind of ticket you're after, your first call should be to one of the **specialist travel agents** listed in the box overleaf, who can fill you in on all the latest **fares** and any special offers. If you're a student or under 26, you may be able to undercut some of the prices given here; *STA* is a good place to start. All the fares quoted are for travel during low or shoulder seasons; flying at peak times (primarily mid-May to 31 Aug & Dec to mid-Jan) can add substantially to these prices.

Johannesburg is the main South African gateway airport for flights from Australia, though there are also services to Cape Town, which tend to cost another A$100–200. When

the airlines have surplus capacity, special fares can be as low as A$1689. Otherwise, the best return fares you're likely to find are around A$1899 from the eastern states, A$1629 from Western Australia. From New Zealand, fares start at NZ$2220.

"**Open-jaw**" tickets enable you to fly into Johannesburg and out of Cape Town (or vice versa), which can save valuable time spent backtracking; fares start from A$2100/NZ$2449. If you plan to visit South Africa **en route to Europe**, you can expect to pay in the region of A$2299/NZ$2649.

ROUND-THE-WORLD TICKETS

Given these fares and routings, **round-the-world tickets** that take in **South Africa** are worth considering, especially if you have the time to make the most of a few stopovers. Ultimately, your choice of route will depend on where else you want to visit besides South Africa, but possible itineraries include: starting from either **Melbourne**, **Sydney or Brisbane,** flying to Johannesburg, then travelling overland to Cape Town, before flying to London, and taking in Amsterdam, New York and San Francisco on the way back home (from A$2439); or, starting from **Perth,** flying to Denpasar, Casablanca, Istanbul, Nairobi, then down to Cape Town and Johannesburg on the return leg to Perth (from A$2299).

From New Zealand, you could fly from Auckland to Sydney, Bangkok and London, returning via Johannesburg and Perth back to Auckland. Fares for this route start at NZ$2899.

PACKAGES AND ORGANIZED TOURS

Package holidays from Australia and New Zealand to South Africa tend to be either expensive or of the extended **overland** variety, although airlines are beginning to put together bargain fly-drive options as demand increases. At the luxury end of the market, tailor-made **safaris** will set you back around A$6499/NZ$7200 for a two-week trip. *Bench International's* "Safari and Cape Town Special" is a slightly more affordable option, combining six nights on Makutsi Safari Farm with four nights in Cape Town, visiting Cape Point and the

Winelands (from A$1890, excluding flights). **Fly-drive** deals can often be found for little more than the cost of a flight alone: *Qantas Holidays*, for example, offer return flights to Johannesburg, seven days' car rental and your first night's accommodation for A$2000–2499 (depending on season).

Adventure tours are worth considering if you want to cover a lot of ground or get to places that could be difficult to reach independently. *Contiki* offer a fully inclusive fourteen-day bus tour, with prices starting from A$4259, including return flights. Companies such as *Encounter Overland*, *Explore Worldwide* and *Peregrine* run extended camping trips taking in the Kruger National Park, Swaziland, the Drakensberg mountains and the Garden Route to Cape Town (20–28 days, A$1710–2090, air fares extra).

AIRLINES AND AGENTS IN AUSTRALIA AND NEW ZEALAND

AIRLINES

Air Lanka, 64 York St, Sydney (☎02/9321 9234); 6/44 Emily Place, Auckland (☎09/309 2425).

Air New Zealand, 5 Elizabeth St, Sydney (☎13 2476); 139 Queen St, Auckland (☎09/357 3000).

British Airways, 26/201 Kent St, Sydney (☎02/9258 3300); 154 Queen St, Auckland (☎09/356 8690).

Gulf Air, 64 York St, Sydney (☎02/9321 9199).

Malaysian Airlines, 16 Spring St, Sydney (☎13 2627); 12/12 Swanson St, Auckland (☎09/373 2741).

Qantas, 70 Hunter St, Sydney (☎13 1211); 154 Queen St, Auckland (☎09/357 8900 or 0800/808 767).

Singapore Airlines, 17 Bridge St, Sydney (☎13 1011); corner of Albert and Fanshawe Streets, Auckland (☎09/379 3209).

South African Airways, 5 Elizabeth St, Sydney (☎02/9223 4402).

Thai Airways, 75 Pitt St, Sydney (☎13 1960); 22 Fanshawe St, Auckland (☎09/377 3886).

TRAVEL AGENTS

Anywhere Travel, 345 Anzac Parade, Kingsford, Sydney (☎02/9663 0411).

Brisbane Discount Travel, 260 Queen St, Brisbane (☎07/3229 9211).

Budget Travel, 16 Fort St, Auckland, plus branches around the city (☎09/366 0061 or 0800/808 040).

Destinations Unlimited, 3 Milford Rd, Auckland (☎09/373 4033).

Flight Centres *Australia*: 82 Elizabeth St, Sydney, plus branches nationwide (☎13 1600); *New Zealand*: 205 Queen St, Auckland (☎09/309 6171), plus branches nationwide.

Northern Gateway, 22 Cavenagh St, Darwin (☎08/8941 1394).

STA Travel, *Australia*: 702 Harris St, Ultimo, Sydney; 256 Flinders St, Melbourne; other offices in state capitals and major universities (nearest branch ☎13 1776, fastfare telesales ☎1300/360 960); *New Zealand*: 10 High St, Auckland (☎09/309 0458, fastfare telesales ☎09/366 6673), plus branches in Wellington, Christchurch, Dunedin, Palmerston North, Hamilton and at major universities. Web site: www.statravelaus.com.au; email: traveller@statravelaus.com.au

Thomas Cook, *Australia*: 175 Pitt St, Sydney; 257 Collins St, Melbourne, plus branches in other state capitals (local branch ☎13 1771, *Thomas Cook Direct* telesales ☎1800/063 913); *New Zealand*: 96 Anzac Ave, Auckland (☎09/379 3920).

SPECIALIST AGENTS

These agents specialize in African travel arrangements, and can help with flights, accommodation and car rental, as well as fully inclusive tours.

Africa Adventures, 1/862 Hay St, Perth (☎08/9321 1259).

Africa Travel Centre, 456 Kent St, Sydney (☎02/9267 3048 & 1800/622 984); 21 Remuera Rd, Auckland (☎09/520 2000).

African Experts, 82 Elizabeth St, Sydney (☎02/9235 3522).

Lion Travel, 6/10 Lorne St, Auckland (☎09/373 5942).

TOUR OPERATORS IN AUSTRALIA AND NEW ZEALAND

Abercrombie and Kent, 90 Bridport St, Albert Park, Melbourne (☎03/9699 9766); 14/17 Victoria St, Auckland (☎09/358 4200). *Luxury tours of southern and eastern Africa.*

African Wildlife Safaris, 1/259 Coventry St, Melbourne (☎03/9696 2899). *Upmarket camping and lodge-based safaris to southern Africa.*

Bench International, 36 Clarence St, Sydney (☎02/9290 2877 or 1800/221 451); 21 Remuera Rd, Auckland (☎09/520 2000). *African tours, focusing on wildlife and safaris.*

Contiki Holidays for 18–35s, 35 Spring St, Bondi Junction, Sydney (☎02/9511 2200). *Frenetic tours for the young and adventurous.*

Encounter, Suite 15, 600 Lonsdale St, Melbourne (☎03/9670 1123 or 1800/654 152). *Overland tours – from ten days to 32 weeks.*

Explore Worldwide, book through *Adventure World*, 73 Walker St, North Sydney (☎02/9956 7766 or 1800/221 931), plus branches in Brisbane and Perth; 101 Great South Rd, Remuera, Auckland (☎09/524 5118). *Small-group tours and treks.*

Hartley's Safaris, 11/465 Kent St, Sydney (☎02/9264 5710). *Luxury, individually tailored safaris.*

Peregrine Adventures, 258 Lonsdale St, Melbourne (☎03/9663 8611), plus offices in Brisbane, Sydney, Adelaide and Perth. *Adventure tours and all-inclusive game safaris throughout Africa.*

Qantas Holidays, book through travel agents (see box opposite). *Fly-drive and flight-and-accommodation packages.*

RED TAPE AND VISAS

Citizens of the USA, Canada, Australia and New Zealand need only a valid passport to stay for up to three months in South Africa. EU nationals with a valid passport can stay for up to six months. All visitors need a valid return ticket; if you try to enter South Africa without one, you may be required to deposit the equivalent of your fare home with customs (the money will be refunded to you after you have left the country). Visitors must also be able to prove that they have sufficient funds to cover their stay.

Citizens of African and former Eastern Bloc countries do require a visa to enter South Africa, and this must be purchased before arrival, as visas are not issued at the border. If you come under this category and plan on travelling to Lesotho and Swaziland during your trip, you'll need a **multi-entry visa** to get back into South Africa. If you don't have one, it it will be issued free of charge on return, although this can be time-consuming.

For longer stays in South Africa, **visa extensions** may be granted in the Aliens Control Section at one of the main offices of the Department of Home Affairs, where you will be quizzed about your intentions and your funds. In Cape Town, the Department of Home Affairs office is at 56 Barrack St (☎021/462 4970); in Johannesburg, you'll find it at 77 Harrison St (☎011/836 3228).

Very few citizens need a **visa** to enter **Swaziland** – and those that do will be issued with one free of charge at the border. Visa requirements for **Lesotho** are in a state of flux; you'd be well advised to check the latest situation before you travel. At the time of writing citizens of the USA, Canada, Australia and New Zealand *do* need a visa, which is issued and paid for on arrival; EU nationals do not need visas. For visa extensions in Lesotho, contact the Department of Immigration and Passport Services, Kingsway, Maseru (☎31 7339).

CUSTOMS

At present the **duty free** allowance in South Africa is as follows: two litres of wine and one litre of spirits, 400 cigarettes and 50 cigars and 250g of tobacco per person.

South Africa, Lesotho and Swaziland are members of the Southern African Common Customs Union, which means that there is no internal customs control between those countries.

SOUTH AFRICAN DIPLOMATIC MISSIONS ABROAD

Australia Rhodes Place, Yarralumla, Canberra, ACT 2600 (☎02/6273 2424).

Botswana Plot 5131, Kopanyo House, Nelson Mandela Drive, Gaborone (☎304 800).

Canada 15 Sussex Drive, Ottawa (☎613/744 0330); Suite 2515, Exchange Tower, Toronto (☎416/364 0314).

France 59 Quai d'Orsay, Paris (☎01/4555 9237).

Germany Auf de Hostert 3, Bonn (☎228/82010).

Malawi Mpico Bldg, City Centre, Capital City, Lilongwe (☎78 3722)

Mozambique Avenue Eduardo Mondlane 41, Maputo (☎01/491614).

Namibia RSA House, corner of Jan Jonker and Nelson Mandela avenues, Windhoek (☎061/229 765).

New Zealand no representative.

UK South Africa House, Trafalgar Square, London WC2N 5DP (☎0171/930 4488).

USA 3051 Massachusetts Ave NW, Washington DC (☎202/232 4400); Suite 300, 50 North La Cienega Blvd, Beverly Hills, CA (☎213/ 657 9200).

Zimbabwe Temple Bar House, corner of Baker Ave and Angwa, Harare (☎04/753147).

KINGDOM OF LESOTHO DIPLOMATIC MISSIONS ABROAD

Canada 202 Clemow Ave, Ottawa (☎613/236-9449).

South Africa 6th Floor, Momentum Centre, 343 Pretorius St, Pretoria (☎012/322 6090).

UK 7 Chesham Place, Belgravia, London SW1 8HN (☎0171/235 5686).

USA 2511 Massachusetts Ave NW, Washington DC 20008 (☎202/979-5533).

KINGDOM OF SWAZILAND DIPLOMATIC MISSIONS ABROAD

Canada 130 Albert St, Ottawa, Ontario (☎613/567-1480).

South Africa Infotech Bldg, 1090 Arcadia St, Hatfield, Pretoria 0083 (☎012/342 5784).

UK 20 Buckingham Gate, London SW1A 6LB (☎0171/630 6611).

USA 3400 International Drive, Washington DC 20008 (☎202/362-6683).

HEALTH

You can put aside most of the health fears that may be justified in some parts of Africa; run-down hospitals and bizarre tropical diseases aren't typical of South Africa. As in the rest of Africa, however, HIV is rampant, but there's little chance of catching it other than through intravenous drug taking or unprotected sex.

There are generally high standards of hygiene and safe **drinking water** in all tourist areas. The only hazard you're likely to encounter, and the one the majority of visitors are most blasé about, is the **sun**, which can cause short- and long-term illness. In some parts of the country there is a risk of catching **malaria**, and you will need to take precautions. See p.18 for details.

INOCULATIONS

Although no specific **inoculations** are compulsory if you arrive from the West, it's wise to ensure that your **polio** and **tetanus** jabs are up to date. A **yellow fever** vaccination certificate is necessary if you've come from a country where the disease is endemic, such as Kenya or Tanzania or tropical South America.

In addition to these, the Hospital for Tropical Diseases in London recommends a course of shots against **typhoid** and a Havrix injection against **hepatitis A**, which is caught from contaminated food or water. This is a worst-case scenario, as you probably won't be travelling in areas where these illnesses pose a serious threat. The cholera vaccination is unpleasant, pretty ineffective and not recommended unless you are going to be working for a period in very deprived areas. In any case, despite their terrible reputation, typhoid fever and cholera are both eminently curable and few, if any, visitors to South Africa ever catch them. Hepatitis B vaccine is essential only for people involved in health work. The disease is spread by the transfer of blood products, usually dirty needles, so most travellers need not worry about it. If you decide to have an armful of jabs, start organizing them six weeks before departure.

If you're going to another African country first and need the yellow fever jab, remember that a yellow fever certificate only becomes valid ten days after you've had the shot.

STAYING HEALTHY

The surest way of staying healthy is to keep your resistance up by eating a **balanced regular diet** and by avoiding **stress** – sometimes more easily said than done. The following tips should help you to stay well on your travels and assist you over the illness if you do succumb.

WATER – AND STOMACH UPSETS

Stomach upsets from food are rare. Salad and ice – the danger items in many other Third World countries – are only found in hotels and restaurants. Both are perfectly safe. As anywhere, though, don't keep food for too long, be sure to wash fruit and vegetables as thoroughly as possible, and don't overindulge on fruit – no matter how tempting – when you first arrive.

If you do get a **stomach bug**, the best cure is lots of water and rest. Papayas, the flesh as well as the pips, are a good tonic to offset the runs. Otherwise, most chemists should have name-brand anti-diarrhoea remedies. These – Lomotil, Codeine phosphate, etc – shouldn't be overused.

Avoid jumping for **antibiotics** at the first sign of illness: keep them as a last resort – they don't work on viruses and annihilate your "gut flora" (most of which you want to keep), making you more susceptible next time round. Most upsets will resolve themselves by adopting a sensible fat-free diet for a couple of days, but if they do persist unabated (or are accompanied by other unusual symptoms) then see a doctor as soon as possible.

THE SUN

The **sun** is likely to be the worst hazard you'll encounter in southern Africa, particularly if you have a fair skin. The danger of overexposure to the sun is something white South Africans haven't yet caught onto; locals still regard their tans as more important than their health.

The sun in the southern hemisphere is far more intense and transmits far more ultraviolet than it does in the north (even in the sunshine states of the USA). It's wise to limit your exposure to this major cause of **skin cancer**. If on returning home you notice any changes to any mole on your body you should see your doctor, as melanomas can be

MEDICAL RESOURCES FOR TRAVELLERS

For a comprehensive and sobering account of the health problems which travellers encounter worldwide, consult the regularly updated *Traveller's Health*, edited by Dr Richard Dawood (OUP;Viking Penguin).

AUSTRALIA AND NEW ZEALAND

Travellers' Medical and Vaccination Centre, 7/428 George St, Sydney (☎02/9221 7133); 3/393 Little Bourke St, Melbourne (☎03/9602 5788); 6/29 Gilbert Place, Adelaide (☎08/8212 7522); 6/247 Adelaide St, Brisbane (☎07/3221 9066); 1 Mill St, Perth (☎08/9321 1977); http//:www.tmvc.com.au

Auckland Hospital, Park Rd, Grafton, Auckland (☎09/379 7440).

BRITAIN AND IRELAND

British Airways Travel Clinics, Flightbookers, 177 Tottenham Court Rd, London W1 7RA (Mon–Fri 9.30am–6pm, Sat 10am–2pm; ☎0171/439 9584), walk-in service, but appointments recommended. Appointment-only branches at 101 Cheapside, London EC2 (Mon–Fri 9–11.45am & 12.15–4.45pm; ☎0171/606 2977) and at the *BA* terminal in London's Victoria Station (8.15–11.30am & 12.30–3.40pm; ☎01276/685040). *BA* also operates around forty regional clinics throughout the country (call ☎0171/831 5333 for the one nearest to you); airport locations at Gatwick and Heathrow.

Healthline (☎0839/337733; 49p per minute; code for South Africa ☎73) and **Health-Fax** (☎0991/991992; £1.50 per minute; code for South Africa ☎235). *Up-to-the-minute recorded advice provided by the Hospital for Tropical Diseases on how to stay healthy abroad. Computer-operated system dishes out detailed health information about South Africa and all its neighbouring countries. Health-Fax sends the same information to a fax number you specify. This actually works out cheaper because you spend less time on the line being interrogated, you don't have to scribble madly to get the information down, and you end up with a written report you can peruse at leisure. You will need the codes in brackets above to access the appropriate information.*

Hospital for Tropical Diseases, St Pancras Hospital, 4 St Pancras Way, London NW1 0PE (☎0171/388 9600). *Travel clinic offering consultations, jabs and any other medical gear you might need such as mosquito nets or anti-malaria pills. Consultations cost £15, a fee which is* waived if you have jabs as well. Most jabs cost around £10.

MASTA (Medical Advisory Services for Travellers Abroad), Bureau of Hygiene and Tropical Diseases, Keppel St, London WC1E 7HT (☎0171/631 4408). *Commercial service providing detailed "health briefs" for all countries, and a Travellers' Healthline (☎0891/224100) providing written information tailored to your journey by return of post.*

Trailfinders Immunization Centre, 194 Kensington High St, London W8 7RG (Mon–Wed & Fri 9am–5pm, Thurs 9am–6pm, Sat 9.30am–3.30pm; ☎0171/938 3999). *Walk-in advice and inoculation service operated by the respected and knowledgeable travel agency.*

USA AND CANADA

Canadian Society for International Health, 170 Laurier Ave W, Suite 902, Ottawa, ON K1P 5V5 (☎613/230-2654). *Distributes a free pamphlet*, Health Information for Canadian Travellers, *containing an extensive list of travel health centres in Canada.*

Center for Disease Control, 1600 Clifton Rd, NE, Atlanta, GA 30333 (☎404/639-3311; http://www.cdc.gov/travel/travel.html) *publishes outbreak warnings, suggested inoculations, precautions and other background information for travellers. Their website is very useful.*

International Association for Medical Assistance to Travellers (IAMAT), 417 Center St, Lewiston, NY 14092 (☎716/754-4883), and 40 Regal Rd, Guelph, ON N1K 1B5 (☎519/836-0102). *Non-profit organization supported by donations, and providing a list of English-speaking doctors in South Africa, climate charts and leaflets on various diseases and inoculations.*

Travel Medicine, 351 Pleasant St, Suite 312, Northampton, MA 01060 (☎1-800/872-8633). *Sells first-aid kits, mosquito netting, water filters and other health-related travel products.*

Travelers Medical Center, 31 Washington Square, New York, NY 10011 (☎212/982-1600). *Consultation service on immunizations and treatment of diseases for people travelling to developing countries.*

removed if caught early, but malignant melanomas can prove fatal if ignored.

Short-term effects of **overexposure** to the sun include burning, nausea and headaches. This usually comes from overeager tanning and has the nasty side effect of leaving you looking like a lobster. The fairer your skin the slower you should take tanning. Start with short periods of exposure and **high protection suncreen** (at least SPF 15), and gradually increase your time in the sun and decrease the factor of your screen. Many people with fair skins, especially those who freckle easily, should take extra care, starting with a very high factor screen (SPF 25–30) and continue using at least SPF 15 for the rest of their stay. There's no shame in smearing sensitive areas of your face with total block cream, which contains zinc and has been made fashionable by cricketers and skiers.

A **broad-brimmed hat** and sunglasses are recommended, especially for children, who should ideally be kept well-covered at the seaside. Overexposure to the sun can cause sunburn to the surface of the eye, inflammation of the cornea and can result in serious short- and long-term damage. Good **sunglasses** can reduce ultraviolet light exposure to the eye by 50 percent. Look for a pair that absorbs at least 95 percent of UVR (which is invisible to the human eye) as well as UVB.

AIDS AND SEXUALLY TRANSMITTED DISEASES

Your biggest chance of catching **AIDS** in South Africa is through unprotected sex. AIDS and other venereal diseases are widespread in southern Africa in both men and women. The chance of catching the virus through sexual contact is very real. Follow the usual precautions regarding safer sex: abstain – or at the very least use a condom. There's no special risk from medical treatment in the country, but if you're travelling overland and you want to play it safe take your own needle and transfusion kit.

BILHARZIA

One ailment which you need to take seriously throughout sub-Saharan Africa is **bilharzia**, carried in most of South Africa's fresh waterways except in the mountains. Bilharzia (schistosomiasis) is spread by a tiny, waterborne parasite. These worm-like flukes leave their water-snail hosts and burrow into human skin to multiply in the bloodstream. They work their way to the walls of the intestine or bladder where they begin to lay eggs.

Avoid swimming in dams and rivers where possible. If you're canoeing or can't avoid the water, have a test when you return home. White water is no guarantee of safety; although the snails favour sheltered areas, the flukes can be swept downstream. The chances are you'll have avoided bilharzia even if you swam in the Orange River, but it's best to be sure.

Symptoms may be no more than a feeling of lassitude and ill health. Once infection is established, abdominal pain and blood in the urine and stools are common. Fortunately it's easily and effectively treated these days with praziquantel, although the drug can make you feel ill for a few days. No vaccine is available and none foreseen.

MEDICAL KIT

Most medicines and medical gear can be bought in pharmacies all over South Africa, so there's no need to lumber yourself with too heavy a **medical kit**. Only in deeply rural areas where few visitors ever go to are you likely to be caught short. If you need specialized drugs bring your own supply, but any first-aid items can be easily replaced. A very **basic kit** should include:

Antibiotics Potentially useful if you're heading off the beaten track. A broad-spectrum variety is best.

Antiseptic cream *Bacitracin* is a reliable brand. *Nelson's* natural calendular ointment is invaluable for stings, rashes, cuts, sores or cracked skin.

Bandages One wide and one narrow.

Eyedrops Wonderfully soothing if you're travelling on dusty roads.

Fine tweezers Useful for removing thorns or glass.

Insect repellent Essential in malarial areas (see p.18).

Lip salve/chapstick Invaluable for dry lips.

Paracetamol Safer than aspirin for pain and fever relief.

Sticking plasters

MALARIA

Malaria is endemic in tropical Africa: many Africans have it in their bloodstream and get occasional bouts of fever. Most of South Africa is free of the disease, but there is a risk in the **Kruger National Park**, **Northern Natal**, along the **Mozambique border** and in **Swaziland**. Protection against malaria is essential if you're planning on travelling to these areas.

Malaria is caused by a parasite carried in the saliva of the female anopheles mosquito. It has a variable incubation period of a few days to several weeks, so you can become ill long after being bitten. If you go down with it, you'll know: the fever, shivering and headaches are like severe flu and come in waves, usually beginning in the early evening. Malaria is not infectious but it can be dangerous and even fatal if not treated quickly.

PREVENTION

No antimalarial drug is totally effective – your only sure-fire protection is to **avoid getting bitten**. Malaria-carrying mosquitoes are active between dusk and dawn, so avoid being out at this time, or at least cover yourself well.

Sleep under a **mosquito net** when possible, making sure to tuck it under the mattress, and burn **mosquito coils** (which you can buy everywhere) for a peaceful, if noxious, night. Whenever the mosquitoes are particularly bad – and that's not often – cover your exposed parts with something strong. **Insect repellents** containing diethyltoluamide work well. Other locally produced repellents such as *Peaceful Sleep* are widely available.

Electric mosquito-destroyers which you fit with a pad every night are less pungent than mosquito coils, but you need electricity. Mosquito "buzzers" are useless.

Doctors can advise on which kind of **antimalarial tablets** to take – generally the latest anti-resistant creation – and you can buy most without a prescription at a pharmacy before you leave. It's important to keep a routine and cover the period before and after your trip with doses. The combination of chloroquine and proguanil is the prophylactic recommended for **South Africa** by the World Health Organization. For the low-lying areas of **Swaziland**, the WHO recommends mefloquine (Larium). However, there have been some controversies surrounding the side effects of Larium recently, and you should consult your doctor before deciding which drug to take.

It's important to keep taking the tablets even once you leave a malarial zone, as the parasites remain present in your bloodstream for some weeks after being bitten.

IF YOU FALL ILL

Malaria's warning signs include flu-like symptoms, fever, diarrhoea and joint pains. If you come down with any of these from one week after arriving in a malaria zone to three months after leaving, you should immediately see a doctor and have a blood test. Don't compare yourself with local people who may have considerable immunity. The priority, if you think you might be getting a fever, is treatment. Delay is potentially risky.

TEETH AND EYES

Dental care in South Africa is well up to British and North American standards and considerably cheaper. You'll find **dentists** in all the cities and most smaller towns. Dentists are listed after doctors at the beginning of each town in the telephone directory. You can buy cleaning kit for most types of **contact lenses** in the larger centres.

SNAKES, INSECTS AND OTHER UNDESIRABLES

South Africa features all sorts of potential bites, stings and rashes – which rarely, if ever, materialize.

Snakes are present, but hardly ever seen as they move out of the way quickly. Puff and Berg adders are the most dangerous because they lie in paths and don't move, but they're not commonly encountered by travellers. The best advice if you get bitten is to remember what the snake looked like and get yourself to a clinic or hospital. Most bites are not fatal and the worst thing is to panic: desperate measures with razor blades and tourniquets risk doing more harm than good.

Tick-bite fever is occasionally contacted from walking in the bush, particularly in long wet grass. The offending ticks can be minute and you may not spot them. Symptoms appear a week later – swollen glands and severe aching of the bones, backache and fever. Since it is a self-limiting disease, it will run its course in three or four days. Ticks you may find on yourself are not dangerous; just repulsive at first. Make sure you pull out the head as well as the body (it's not painful). A good way of removing small ones is to smear

Vaseline or grease over them, making them release their hold.

Scorpions and spiders abound, but are hardly ever seen unless you turn over logs and stones. If you're collecting wood for a campfire, knock or shake it before picking it up. Contrary to popular myth, scorpion stings and spider bites are painful but almost never fatal. Most are harmless and should be left alone. A simple precaution when camping is to shake out your shoes and clothes in the morning before you get dressed.

Rabies is present throughout southern Africa. Be wary of strange animals and go immediately to a clinic if bitten. Rabies can be treated effectively with a course of injections.

HOSPITALS AND DOCTORS

Public **hospitals** in South Africa are fairly well-equipped and attempt to maintain standards, but they are under huge pressures under which they are unfortunately deteriorating. Expect long waits and frequently indifferent treatment. Private hospitals or clinics, which conform more closely to British or North American standards, are usually a better option for travellers. You're likely to get more personal treatment and the costs are nowhere as prohibitive as in the US; besides which, if you're adequately insured these shouldn't pose a problem. Private hospitals are given in the town listings throughout the Guide.

TRAVEL INSURANCE

It's very important to take out a good travel insurance policy for a trip to South Africa. The policy can be quite comprehensive, anticipating anything from lost or stolen baggage and missed connections to charter companies going bankrupt; however, certain policies (notably in North America) only cover medical costs.

If you plan to participate in adventure activities, watersports or do some hiking, you'll probably have to pay an extra premium; check carefully that any insurance policy you are considering will cover you in case of an accident. Note also that very few insurers will arrange on-the-spot payments in the event of a major expense or loss; you will usually be reimbursed only after going home. In all cases of loss or theft of goods, you will have

to contact the local police to have a report made out so that your insurer can process the claim.

BRITAIN

Most British travel agents and tour operators will offer you insurance when you book your flight or holiday, and some will insist you take it. These policies are usually reasonable value, though as ever you should **check the small print**. If you feel the cover is inadequate, or you want to compare prices, travel agents, insurance brokers and banks should be able to help. Most companies offer at least two tiers, the more basic essentially covering medical expenses and limited loss of property, while the upper tier will include things like loss of money, delayed flights or baggage and will promise to pay out more on lost property and medical expenses. The cheapest basic cover for South Africa starts at around £30 for seventeen days, £50 for a month, and £85 for three months – but it's always worth shopping around. If you have a good "all risks" **home insurance policy** it may well cover your possessions against loss or theft even when overseas, and many **private medical schemes** also cover you when abroad – make sure you know the procedure and the helpline number.

As well as the companies listed in the box overleaf, *Campus Travel* and *STA* (see box on p.5 for addresses) offer competitive travel insurance schemes. *Columbus* also offers one of the best annual multi-trip policies, as well as long-term cover for periods up to a year.

USA AND CANADA

Before buying an insurance policy, North American travellers should **check that they're not already covered**. Canadian provincial health plans typically provide some overseas medical coverage, although they are unlikely to pick up the full tab in the event of a mishap. Holders of official **student/teacher/youth cards** are entitled to accident coverage and hospital in-patient benefits – the annual membership is far less than the cost of comparable insurance. **Students** may also find that their student health coverage extends during the vacations and for one term beyond the date of last enrolment. Bank and credit cards (particularly *American Express*) often provide certain levels of medical or other insurance, and travel insurance may also be included if you use a major credit or charge card to pay for your trip. **Home-owners' or renters'** insurance often covers theft or loss of documents, money and valuables while overseas.

After exhausting the possibilities above, you might want to contact a specialist **travel insurance** company; your travel agent can usually recommend one, or see the box below.

Travel insurance **policies** vary: some are comprehensive while others cover only certain risks (accidents, illnesses, delayed or lost luggage, cancelled flights, etc). In particular, ask whether the policy pays medical costs upfront or reimburses you later, and whether it provides for medical evacuation to your home country. For policies that include lost or stolen luggage, check exactly what is and isn't covered, and make sure the per-article limit will cover your most valuable possession. Most North American travel policies apply only to items lost, stolen or damaged while in the custody of an identifiable, responsible third party – hotel porter, airline, luggage consignment, etc. Even in these cases you will have to contact the local police within a certain time limit to have a complete report made out so that your insurer can process the claim.

The best **premiums** are usually to be had through student/youth travel agencies – *STA Travel*, for example, currently offer a comprehensive policy for fifteen days, valid for travel the world over, at $80–105 for one month.

AUSTRALIA AND NEW ZEALAND

Travel insurance is available from most **travel agents** (see p.12) or direct from **insurance companies** (see box) for periods ranging from a few days to a year or even longer. Most policies are similar in premium and coverage – but if you plan to indulge in **high-risk activities** such as mountaineering, bungee jumping or scuba diving, check the policy carefully to make sure you'll be covered. Two weeks' cover for a trip to southern Africa should cost roughly A$130/NZ$145, while you can expect to pay around A$190/NZ$210 for a stay of one month.

TRAVEL INSURANCE COMPANIES

Most travel agents will arrange travel insurance at no extra charge. The following insurance companies can be called directly.

AUSTRALIA AND NEW ZEALAND
Cover More, 9/32 Walker St, North Sydney (☎02/9202 8000 or 1800/251 881).

Ready Plan, 141 Walker St, Dandenong, Melbourne (☎03/9791 5077 or 1800/337 462); 10/63 Albert St, Auckland (☎09/379 3208).

BRITAIN
Columbus Travel Insurance, 17 Devonshire Square, London EC2M 4SQ (☎0171/375 0011).

Endsleigh Insurance, 97–107 Southampton Row, London WC1B 4AG (☎0171/436 4451).

Frizzell Insurance, Frizzell House, County Gates, Bournemouth, Dorset BH1 2NF (☎01202/292333).

USA AND CANADA
Access America (☎1-800/284-8300).

Carefree Travel Insurance (☎1-800/323-3149).

Desjardins Travel Insurance – Canada only (☎1-800/463-7830).

STA Travel (☎1-800/777-0112 or 212/627-3111); http://www.sta-travel.com

Travel Guard (☎1-800/826-1300); http://www.noelgroup.com.

Travel Insurance Services (☎1-800/937-1387).

COSTS, MONEY AND BANKS

Visitors coming from Europe, North America or Australasia will find South Africa cheap by comparison. Since the twenty percent fall in the rand in 1996, foreign visitors have found that their money goes a lot further here than at home. However, South Africa is more expensive than other African countries.

What you spend depends on the kind of trip you want to have. If If you're prepared to stay in backpackers' lodges, travel on public or backpacker transport and eat cheaply, you can get by on under **US$30/£20** a day – less if you're camping. If you plan on staying in B&Bs and guesthouses, and on eating out regularly, you should allow for anything between **US$30** and **US$60 (£20–40)** a day. In luxury hotels and game lodges, expect to pay upwards of **US$100/£60** per day. Extras such as car rental, scuba diving, horse-riding and safaris will obviously add to these figures substantially.

You'll almost always find a decent **place to stay** for under US$25/£15 a night, especially if there are two of you. Backpackers' lodges currently cost under US$7/£5 per person and most B&Bs charge less than US$25/£15 per head for a couple. A hotel costing US$50/£30 or over per head should have something special to justify the price, although, in Cape Town particularly, this cannot be guaranteed. Prices tend to be highest over the Christmas and Easter holidays, especially at the coast.

Food and **drink** are both good value, especially if you stick to local markets. Most **restaurants** cost US$5–10 (£3–7) for a reasonable three-course meal. Cape Town and the Winelands are

more expensive: an average meal will cost you around US$20/£13, and you can expect to fork out up to US$30/£19 per person at an upmarket restaurant. At restaurants used by working-class blacks, you can fill up on hearty stews for less than US$1/60p, but these places can feel rather intimidating to travellers new to the country, and are best visited with a local guide. Almost all imported goods, books and international phone calls are very expensive.

Despite the size of the country, **transport** is inexpensive, especially compared to Europe, Australia and the US. Even using luxury and tourist **bus** services will not set you back much, considering the distances that are usually involved. If you're travelling around on *Intercape* or *Translux* buses, it makes sense to buy one of their variety of passes (see "Getting around" on p.25), which will save you money. Internal **flights** can be pricey; pre-planning as far in advance as possible will help keep costs down. **Driving** may not be the cheapest way of getting around, given the cost of car rental, but in many parts of the country it's the only realistic option. For this reason, you might consider buying a used car for around US$4500/£2800. **Rental cars** usually cost US$35–50 (£22–32) a day. **Fuel**, though rising in price, is still very inexpensive; roughly US35c/25p (R2.50) a litre.

What you'll pay **on safari** will depend very much on whether you stay in government-run national parks, where accommodation in a rondavel can cost as little as US$6/£4 per night, or fully catered for on an upmarket private reserve, where prices can rocket up to as much as US$500/£320 a night.

Most **museums** and **art galleries** charge an entry fee – usually quite low. Because the rand is so unstable at the moment, we haven't included exact entry fees for museums and galleries, but have indicated whether or not you will need to pay something to get in.

MONEY AND THE EXCHANGE RATE

South Africa's currency is the **rand** (R), often called the "buck". Notes come in R10, 20, 50, 100 and 200 denominations and there are coins of R1, 2, 5, 10, 20 and 50 cents, as well as R1, 2 and 5. At the time of writing, the exchange rate was

R7.3 to the pound sterling, R4.5 to the US dollar and R5.8 to the Australian dollar.

All but the tiniest settlement has a **bank** where you can **change money** swiftly and easily. **Banking hours** are Monday to Friday 9am to 3.30pm, and Saturday 9am to 11am, with banks in smaller towns usually closing down for lunch. In major cities, some banks operate bureaus de change that stay open until 7pm.

Outside banking hours, some hotels will change money, although you can expect to pay a fairly hefty commission. You can also change money at branches of *American Express* and *Rennies Travel.*

TRAVELLERS CHEQUES, CASH AND CREDIT CARDS

Travellers cheques are the safest way to carry your funds into South Africa, as they can be replaced if lost or stolen. *American Express, Visa* and *Thomas Cook* are all widely recognized. However, they'll be useless if you're heading into

remote areas, where you'll need to carry **cash**, preferably in a very safe place, such as a leather pouch under your waistband.

Credit cards can carry come in very handy for hotel bookings and for paying for more mainstream and upmarket tourist facilities, and they are essential for car rental. *Visa* and *Mastercard* (*Access*) are the cards most widely accepted in major cities. *American Express* is not widely accepted. Like travellers' cheques, though, credit cards won't be accepted in small *dorps* and rural areas such as the Wild Coast and Northern Cape, where you'll need cash for most transactions.

Visa, Mastercard and most international ATM cards (check with your bank before departing) can be used to withdraw money at **automatic teller machines** (ATMs), found open 24 hours a day in the cities. When the ATM asks what type of account you have, press "cheque". Curiously, this works better with the ATMs at smaller banks like *Nedbank, Volksas* and *United Bank* than the larger ones such as *First National Bank* and *Standard Bank.*

MAPS, INFORMATION AND WEBSITES

South Africa is experiencing a boom in tourism, and you should have no difficulty finding maps, books and brochures before you leave. The South African Tourism Board (SATOUR) is well-organized: if there's an office near you, it's worth paying a visit to pick up their free map and browse through

their information on hotels and organized tours. Alternatively, you can surf through South Africa's growing internet presence for up-to-date travel details, and maps you can print out.

MAPS

Many regional place names in South Africa have changed recently, so if you buy a **map** before you leave make sure that it's bang up to date. *Bartholomew* produce an excellent map of **South Africa**, including Lesotho and Swaziland (1: 2,000,000), as part of their *World Travel Map* series. Also worth investing in are *MapStudio's Miniplan* maps of major cities such as Cape Town, Durban and Pretoria: these are a convenient size and have useful details, such as hotels, cinemas, post offices and hospitals. *MapStudio* also produce good regional maps, featuring scenic routes and street maps of major towns, and a fine Natal Drakensberg map which shows hiking trails, picnic spots, campsites and places of interest.

SPECIALIST BOOK AND MAP SUPPLIERS

AUSTRALIA AND NEW ZEALAND

Adelaide *The Map Shop*, 16a Peel St (☎08/8231 2033).

Auckland *Specialty Maps*, 58 Albert St (☎09/307 2217).

Melbourne *Bowyangs*, 372 Little Bourke St (☎03/9670 4383).

Sydney *Travel Bookshop*, 20 Bridge St (☎02/9241 3554).

Perth *Perth Map Centre*, 891 Hay St (☎08/9322 5733).

BRITAIN

Aberdeen *Aberdeen Map Shop*, 74 Skene St, AB10 1QE (☎01224/637999).

Glasgow *John Smith and Sons*, 57–61 St Vincent St, G2 5TB (☎0141/221 7472).

Inverness *James Thin Melven's Bookshop*, 29 Union St, IV1 1QA (☎01463/233500).

London *Daunt Books*, 83 Marylebone High St, W1M 3DE (☎0171/224 2295), and 193 Haverstock Hill, NW3 4QL (☎0171/794 4006); *National Map Centre*, 22–24 Caxton St, SW1 0QU (☎0171/222 2466); *Stanfords*, 12–14 Long Acre, WC2E 9LP (☎0171/836 1321 for enquiries and **mail order**), 52 Grosvenor Gdns, SW1W 0AG (☎0171/730 1314) and 156 Regent St, W1R 5TA (☎0171/434 4744); *The Travel Bookshop*, 13–15 Blenheim Crescent, W11 2EE (☎0171/229 5260).

CANADA

Montréal *Ulysses Travel Bookshop*, 4176 St-Denis (☎514/843-9447).

Toronto *Open Air Books and Maps*, 25 Toronto St, ON M5R 2C1 (☎416/363-0719).

Vancouver *World Wide Books and Maps*, 736 Granville St, BC V6Z 1E4 (☎604/687-3320).

USA

California *Book Passage*, 51 Tamal Vista Blvd, Corte Madera, CA 94925 (☎415/927-0960); *Map Link*, 30 S La Petera Lane, Unit #5, Santa Barbara, CA 93117 (☎805/692-6777); *Phileas Fogg's Books & Maps*, #87 Stanford Shopping Center, Palo Alto, CA 94304 (☎1-800/533-FOGG); *Rand McNally*, 595 Market St, San Francisco, CA 94105 (☎415/777-3131); *Sierra Club Bookstore*, 6014 College Ave, Oakland, CA 94618 (☎510/658-7470; mail order ☎415/977-5600).

Chicago *Rand McNally*, 444 N Michigan Ave, Chicago, IL 60611 (☎312/321-1751).

New York *The Complete Traveler Bookstore*, 199 Madison Ave, NY 10016 (☎212/685-9007); *Rand McNally*, 150 E 52nd St, New York, NY 10022 (☎212/758-7488); *Traveler's Bookstore*, 22 W 52nd St, New York, NY 10019 (☎212/664-0995).

Washington DC *The Map Store Inc.*, 1636 1st St, Washington DC 20006 (☎202/628-2608).

Mail order *Rand McNally* ☎1-800/333-0136 ext 2111.

South Africa's motoring organization, the Automobile Association (AA) offers a wide selection of maps, free to AA members, which you can pick up from their offices. Their *New South African Book of* *the Road* is an invaluable combination of good **road maps**, a large range of city and town maps alongside information about South African flora, fauna and architecture, and troubleshooting for your car.

SOUTH AFRICAN TOURIST OFFICES

Head office 442 Rigel Avenue South, Erasmusrand 0181, Private Bag X164, Pretoria 0001 (☎012/347 0600, fax 45 4889).

Australia 6/285 Clarence St, Sydney, NSW 2000 (☎02/9261 3424, fax 9261 3414).

Canada Suite 2, 4117 Lawrence Avenue East, Scarborough, Ontario M1E 2S2 (☎ & fax 416/283-0563).

UK 5–6 Alt Grove, Wimbledon SW19 4DZ (☎0181/944 8080, fax 944 6705).

USA 500 Fifth Ave, Suite 2040, New York, NY 10110 (☎212/730-2929, fax 764-1980); Suite 1524, 9841 Airport Blvd, Los Angeles, CA 90045 (☎310/641-8444, fax 641-5812).

Zimbabwe Mon Repos Building, Newlands Shopping Centre, Harare (☎4/70 7766, fax 78 6489).

INFORMATION IN SOUTH AFRICA

Nearly every town in South Africa, even down to the sleepiest *dorp*, has some sort of **tourist information office** – sometimes connected to the museum or post office – where you can pick up local maps, lists of B&Bs and travel advice. In larger cities such as Cape Town and Durban, you'll find several branches offering everything from hotel bookings to organized safari trips.

We've given precise **opening hours** of tourist information offices in most cases; they generally adhere to a standard schedule of 8.30am to noon and 2pm to 5pm, Monday to Friday, with many offices also open from 9am to noon on Saturdays.

In this fast-changing country, often the best way of finding out what's happening is by word of mouth, and for this **backpackers' hostels** are invaluable. If you're planning on seeing South Africa on a budget, rest assured that the useful notice boards, constant traveller traffic and largely helpful and friendly staff you'll encounter in the hostels will greatly smooth your travels.

SOUTH AFRICA ON THE INTERNET

ANC Homepage
http://www.anc.org.za
Dry but informative official website of the ANC, with daily news briefings, government documents, and links to other African websites.

Mail & Guardian
http://www.mg.co.za/mg
The *Mail & Guardian*'s homepage is a good first step into South Africa's internet scene. The site is a superb resource, with a huge variety of links to other sites all over the country, including numerous travel homepages. It includes a very useful homepage dedicated to surveying South Africa's online travel resources.

Nelson Mandela Biography
http://www.anc.org.za/people/mandela.html
Fine website packed with information on Mandela, with selected speeches and writing, excerpts and photos from Mandela's autobiography and numerous articles about the president.

National Parks
http://africa.com/-venture/ntpks/npbhome.htm
Comprehensive information on game parks and safaris in South Africa and Swaziland, including details of adventure holidays, trails, photographic safaris and more. Links to many different tour operators. Up-to-date price lists and online booking facilities.

Satour
http://africa.com/satour
Tourism Board site aimed at the travel industry as well as tourists. The "Travel Guide" section takes you through South Africa's nine regions, with city descriptions, travel tips and online booking facilities.

South African Airways
http://www.saa.co.za/saa/yesnet2.htm
Useful site for checking current flight schedules, prices and routes.

Train timetables
http://www.m.ac.za/departments/iwr/staff/daf/sartrain.html
Transnet's online schedules include route details, times and fares.

Vincent Williams
http://mickey.iafrica.com/-vincent/index.htm
Entertaining site chronicling the life of a man who lives in the coloured ghettos of Cape Town, and which gives an excellent taste of life in his part of town.

Virtual Africa
http://www.africa.com/docs/satravel.htm
Growing site with a striking travel and tourism page, providing links to the National Parks Board, Satour and others.

GETTING AROUND

Despite the large distances, travelling around most of South Africa is fairly straightforward, with a well-organized network of public transport, a good range of car rental companies, the best road system in Africa, and the continent's most comprehensive network of internal flights. The only weak point is public transport in urban areas, which is almost universally poor and often dangerous. Urban South Africans who can afford to do so tend to use private transport, and if you are planning to spend much time in any one town you'd be well advised to do the same. It's virtually impossible to get to the national parks by public transport; even if you do manage, you'll most likely need a car once you're there.

BUSES

South Africa's three established **intercity bus companies** are *Greyhound*, *Intercape* and *Translux*, who together reach nearly every town in the country. Travel on these buses (more common-

ly known as coaches) is safe, comfortable and good value. Fares vary according to distances covered. In general, you can expect to pay roughly R300 (US$65/£45) from Johannesburg to Cape Town, and the same amount from Cape Town to Durban.

If you're planning on making several long journeys, it's worth investing in a **pass**. By joining *Greyhound's* "Frequent Traveller Club" (fill in the form at one of their offices), each journey you make earns you points which can eventually buy you a free bus journey. *Greyhound* also operate the "Hound-about Travel Pass", which gives you seven days' unlimited travel over a thirty-day period for around R1050 (US$210/£130); fifteen days over a thirty-day period for R36 (US$410/£260); or thirty days over a sixty-day period for R300 (US$640/£400). If you make fifteen bus journeys with *Translux*, present your tickets at one of their offices and you'll get your next journey free. *Intercape* do not offer any passes.

The **Baz Bus** and the **Hopper Bus** operate an extremely useful hop-on/hop-off system aimed at backpackers and budget travellers. The *Baz Bus* route is the most extensive, running up and down the coast in both directions between Cape Town and Durban. From Durban, the *Baz* follows a loop through Zululand and Swaziland to Johannesburg and Pretoria, from where it heads down via the northern Drakensberg and Pietermaritzburg to Durban. Meanwhile, the *Hopper* runs between Cape Town and Cintsa in the Eastern Cape, though it will probably run as far as Durban by 1998. Both bus companies will pick you up from (and drop you off at) your backpacker accommodation and deposit you there, except in instances where the place is too remote – in which case the owner of the relevant backpackers' lodge will generally come to pick you up instead. The only

ENGLISH/AFRIKAANS STREET NAMES

Many towns have **bilingual street names** with English and Afrikaans alternatives sometimes appearing along the same road. This applies particularly in Afrikaans areas away from the large cities, where direct translations are sometimes used. Some common variations you may encounter are listed below:

Church	*Kerk*	First	*Eerste*	Kort	*Short*	Parsonage		Second	*Tweede*
Crescent	*Singel*	Fourth	*Vierde*	Main	*Hoof*		*Pastorie*	Third	*Derde*
Fifth	*Vyfde*	High	*Hoog*	Market	*Mark*	Road	*Pad*		

Bulawayo, Hwange & Victoria Falls △   △ Harare

MAIN INTERCITY BUS ROUTES

drawback with these buses, apart from occasionally erratic timing, is that the people you'll meet on them will almost exclusively be other backpackers, rather than local people.

As well as the major bus companies, there is a national network of more **inexpensive buses**, some of which are operated by *Translux's* sister company *Transcity* (sometimes called *Transtate*), and others operated by a host of small private companies. The buses are primarily aimed at black people, and it is difficult to get much information about them from travel agents and tourist information offices. *Translux* offers some information about the *Transcity* service, but to find out more – and to enquire about other private company services – you will need to enquire at the main bus station the day before you travel. Apart from saving money, travelling on these buses also enables you to meet South African black travellers, who are distinctly thin on the ground on the luxury coaches.

All bus journeys can be **booked** through *Computicket*, the national booking service that also offers cinema and concert seats, for no extra charge. This can be done by phone or in person at *Computicket's* offices.

MINIBUS TAXIS

Minibus taxis travel absolutely everywhere in South Africa, covering relatively short hops from town to town, commuter trips from township to town and back, and routes within larger towns and cities. However, the problems associated with them – unroadworthy vehicles, dangerous drivers and violent feuds between the different taxi associations who compete for custom – mean that, at least in busy urban areas, you should avoid using them. This is particularly true in cities, where minibus taxi ranks tend to be a magnet for petty criminals. The other problem with minibus taxis is that there is rarely much room to put luggage. However, despite all these drawbacks, don't rule out using this form of transport altogether. Without a car, minibus taxis will often be your only option for getting around in remote areas, where you're unlikely to encounter

INTERCITY BUS COMPANIES

Baz Bus National (☎021/439 2323); Durban–Johannesburg (☎031/23 6585).

Greyhound Johannesburg (☎011/830 1301); Pretoria (☎012/323 1154); Cape Town (☎021/418 4310); Durban (☎03/309 7830); Port Elizabeth (☎041/56 4879); Bloemfontein (☎051/430 2361).

Hopper Bus (☎041/51 2332).

Intercape Pretoria (☎012/654 4114); Cape Town (☎021/386 4400); Port Elizabeth (☎041/56 0055).

Translux Johannesburg (☎011/774 3333); Pretoria (☎012/315 2333); Cape Town (☎021/405 3333); Durban (☎031/361 8333); Port Elizabeth (☎041/507 3333); East London (☎0431/44 2333).

---

trouble. You should, however, be prepared for some long waits. **Fares** are very low. Try to have the exact change, and pass your fare to the row of passengers in front of you; eventually all the fares end up with the conductor, who dishes any change. There are no passes available for minibus taxis.

TRAINS

Travelling by **train** is just about the slowest way of getting around South Africa: the journey from Johannesburg to Cape Town, for example, takes 27 hours – compared to 19 hours by bus. Unless you've got a lot of time on your hands, you may be better off taking the bus, although rail travel does have the advantage of giving you a free night's accommodation.

First- and second-class travel is in compartments equipped with washbasins and with seats that convert into bunks at night. The principal distinction between the two is that second-class cabins accommodate up to six people, while first-class takes a maximum of four, has a shower in each carriage and tends to be quieter. Coupés which take two people in first or three people in second (although you pay for three if you want it to yourself) are ideal if you're travelling as a couple. Third-class travel isn't recommended. Seating in first and second classes is comfortable and so are the bunks, which offer the real possibility of getting a good night's sleep. If you don't have a sleeping bag, you can rent fresh cotton sheets and blankets for the night, which are brought around by a bedding attendant who'll make up your bed in the evening. It's best to buy your bedding voucher when you book your train ticket.

Spoornet run most of the intercity rail services. **Ticket prices** for first-class seats are comparable to the cost of a bus journey over the same distance, with second-class compartments costing considerably less. Train tickets must be booked in advance at railway stations or at *Spoornet* offices in the large cities.

A word of warning about **security** on trains. Don't leave your valuables unattended in your compartment, unless you have some way of locking it, and make sure you close the window before you go, as thieves work the stations, especially around Gauteng. This may mean you won't want to eat in the dining car, so it's worth bringing your own food and drink, although someone usually comes round selling tea or coffee once or twice during the journey.

South Africa offers a handful of **luxury trains** worth considering if you want to travel in plush surroundings, often through wonderful scenery, and don't mind paying through the nose for the privilege. The celebrated **Blue Train** runs from Pretoria to Cape Town, and from Pretoria to Victoria Falls. The full Pretoria–Cape Town fare is around R4500 (US$1000/£625) for the 29-hour journey. Passengers must be dressed in "smart casual" clothes during the day, and have to change into formal wear for the evening meal. You can reserve a seat on this popular train by booking through *Blue Train*'s offices in Johannesburg (☎011/773 7631); Pretoria (☎012/315 3038); Cape Town (☎021/405 2672) or Durban (☎031/361 7550). Another luxury rail option is offered by **Rovos Rail** (☎012 /323 6052 or 21 4020), running from Cape Town to Pretoria, Pretoria to Victoria Falls, and Cape Town to Knysna.

INTERNAL FLIGHTS

Flying between destinations in South Africa is an attractive option if time is short and, though not particularly cheap, it compares favourably with the money you'll spend covering long distances in a rented car, stopping over at places en route.

The three main airlines offering domestic flights are *South African Airways* (*SAA*), *British*

Airways/Comair and *Sun Air*. *Sun Air* and *British Airways/Comair* almost always work out cheaper than *SAA* and its subsidiary, *SA Airlink*, and the earlier you book the less you'll pay. Booking flights through travel agents is the best idea, as they will know of the cheapest available fares.

SAA has the most extensive flight network, serving the major hubs of Johannesburg, Cape Town and Durban, as well as Bloemfontein, East London, George, Kimberley, Margate, Mmabatho, Nelspruit, Phalaborwa, Pietermaritzburg, Pietersburg, Plettenberg Bay, Sun City, Ulundi, Umtata and Upington. As a rough guideline, you can expect to pay R360 and upwards from Johannesburg to Cape Town, and R400 and upwards from Cape Town to Durban.

British Airways/Comair serves Johannesburg, Cape Town and Durban, and also offers flights to Port Elizabeth, Richard's Bay, Skukuza in the Kruger National Park, and Manzini in Swaziland. *Sun Air* only flies between Johannesburg, Cape Town and Durban.

If you expect to fly a fair amount, there are a number of **passes** that can save money. *BA/Comair*, *Sun Air* and *SAA* all operate **frequent-flyer programmes**, for which you must first fill out forms available at travel agents. Neither *SAA* nor *Sun Air* award air miles for their cheapest fares, but *SAA* gives you half the usual amount. None of the airlines offer discounts for students or pensioners.

Travellers expecting to make more than four flights in and around South Africa will save considerably with the **African Explorer Pass**, available on *SAA* and *SA Express* internal and regional flights. To qualify for the pass, you need an international flight to South Africa on any airline, and must quote your ticket number to your travel agent or *SAA* or over the phone. The pass, valid for 45 days from the date of issue, gives up to sixty percent savings on between four and eight flights, and you will also save on VAT.

DRIVING

Given the excellent bus services, you won't need to **drive** to get between the major centres in South Africa, but it's the only way to make it to remote areas where public transport is sporadic. South Africa has a generally well-maintained network of highways and a high proportion of its secondary and tertiary roads are tarred and drivable at speed. The only real challenge you'll face is **other drivers**.

If your visit is a long one – six weeks or more – it's worth considering **buying a vehicle**, which you can then sell at the end of your trip. On shorter trips, **renting a vehicle**, though not cheap, will enable you to explore areas in depth and at your own pace.

Fuel is cheap, at around R2.50 a litre for standard leaded. The usual fuel in coastal areas is **97** and **93 octane** on the highveld, with many filling stations now offering **unleaded**, too.

Filling stations are frequent on the major routes of the country, and usually open 24 hours a day, so it's hard to run out of fuel. If you wander off these, though, stations are less frequent, so do fill up regularly if you're on a long journey. Stations are rarely self-service. Instead, poorly paid attendants will fill up your car, check oil, water and tyre pressure if you ask them to, and often clean your windscreen even if you don't. A tip is always appreciated, though not obligatory. The transition from lowveld to highveld affects the timing of a small proportion of engines, so it's a good idea to have a quick retuning if you notice a loss of power.

REGULATIONS AND DRIVING TIPS

Foreign **licences** are valid in South Africa for up to six months provided that they are printed in English and have the driver's photograph on them. If you don't have such a licence, you'll need to get an International Driving Permit before arriving in South Africa (available from national motoring

---

AIRLINES IN SOUTH AFRICA

British Airways/Comair Johannesburg (☎011/ 921 0222); East and Western Cape (toll free ☎0800 961 1196); Durban (toll free ☎0800 131 4155)

Eastern Airlines Johannesburg (☎011/390 1545); Umtata (☎0471/36 0127).

Nationwide Air Johannesburg (☎011/390 1660).

Sun Air Johannesburg (☎011/397 2244); Cape Town (☎021/ 934 0918); Durban (☎031/469 3444).

South African Airways Central reservations (☎0800/11 4799).

organizations). When driving, make sure you have your driving licence and your passport on you at all times.

You drive on the **left-hand side** (as in the UK); **speed limits** range from 60kph in built-up areas, 100kph on rural roads, and 120kph on highways and major arteries. You should note that traffic lights are called **robots** in South Africa.

You won't find many roundabouts in the country; instead, there are **four-way stops**, where the rule is that the person who got there first leaves first, and you are not expected to give way to the right.

South Africa has among the world's worst road accident statistics – the result of reckless driving, **drunken drivers** or defective, overloaded vehicles. Keep your distance from cars in front, as domino-style pile-ups are particularly common. Watch out also for overtaking traffic coming towards you; overtakers often assume that you will head for the hard shoulder to avoid an accident – it is legal to do this, but it's also dangerous, so be careful. If you do pull into the hard shoulder to let a car take over, the other driver will probably thank you by flashing its hazard lights. As in many parts of the world, if oncoming cars flash their headlights at you, it probably means that there is a speed trap up ahead.

Other potential **hazards** include animals on the road in rural areas. This can be especially dangerous at night, so drive slowly at that time. Finally, the large **distances** between major towns means that falling asleep at the wheel, especially when travelling through long stretches of flat landscape in the Karoo or the Free State, is a real danger. Plan your car journeys carefully to include plenty of breaks and stopovers. Driving in Johannesburg, you risk the danger of being **carjacked**; see p.52 for safety hints.

CAR RENTAL

Renting a car can be quite expensive, but it's recommended if you want to travel widely and don't fancy being governed by public transport timetables. Prebooking your car with a travel agent before flying out is the cheapest way of doing it, and will provide more favourable terms and conditions (such as unlimited mileage and lower insurance excesses).

The major car rental companies present in South Africa are *Alisa* (☎0800/02 1515), *Avis* (☎0800/021 111), *Budget* (☎0800/01 6622), *Europcar* (☎0800/01 1344), *Hertz* (☎021/386 1560), *Imperial* (☎0800/13 1000) and *Tempest* (☎0800/03 1666) – see box on p.30 for international phone numbers. As a rough guideline you can expect to **pay** upwards of R1000 (US$225/£150) including collision damage and theft waivers, as well as about 200 free kilometres. Unlimited distance will cost more but is usually worth it if you're doing a lot of driving over a short period. Most companies stipulate that drivers must be a **minimum age** of 21.

The advantage of renting through major companies is that you do not have to return the car to where you hired it from, but can deposit it in some other major centre instead; though rental companies will usually levy a charge for this. If you're planning on driving into Lesotho and Swaziland, check that the company allows it – some don't. Insurance often doesn't cover you if you drive off the tar, so check for this too. Local firms are almost always cheaper, but usually have restrictions on how far away from base you can go.

Camper vans can be a good idea for getting to remote places where accommodation is scarce. You should expect to pay around R600 (US$120/£85) per day for a vehicle that sleeps two, R650 (US$130/£95) for one with three berths and R750 (US$150/£110) for a van that accommodates five people. Some companies offer standby rates that knock fifteen to twenty percent off the price if you book at short notice (one week or less ahead). Vans come fully equipped with crockery and cutlery, but only the five-berth vans normally have a built-in toilet, although portaloos can usually be rented for very little extra. The downside of camper vans is that they struggle up hills and guzzle a lot of fuel (15 litres per 100km in the smaller vans, and 20 litres per 100km in the larger ones), which could partly offset any savings on accommodation.

One of the biggest **camper-van rental companies** is *Britz Africa*, which has branches in Johannesburg (☎011/396 1860, fax 396 1937), Cape Town (☎021/981 8947, fax 981 8946) and Durban (☎031/72 9326, fax 72 9329), and will pick you up from the airport and return you for about R70 (US$15/£10). *Rainbow Camper Hire* is another company with offices in Johannesburg (☎011/396 1445, fax 396 1757), Cape Town (☎021/948 0743, fax 949 7515) and Durban (☎031/72 9326, fax 72 9329). Along the Garden Route you can rent camper vans from *Knysna Camper Hire* (☎0445/22444, fax 82 5887) in Knysna.

INTERNATIONAL CAR RENTAL AGENCIES

UK
Avis ☎0990/900 500
Budget ☎0800/181 181
Europcar ☎0345/222 525
Hertz ☎0990/996 699

AUSTRALIA
Avis ☎1800/225 533
Budget ☎132 727
Hertz ☎133 039

NEW ZEALAND
Avis ☎09/526 2847
Budget ☎09/375 2222
Hertz ☎09/309 0989

NORTH AMERICA
Avis ☎1-800/331-1084; http://www.avis.com/
Budget ☎1-800/527-0700;
    http://www.budgetrentacar.com
Hertz ☎1-800/654 3001; http://www.hertz.com

BUYING A CAR

Surpisingly, **buying a used vehicle** in South Africa is more expensive than in most Western countries, and you will have to spend at least R20,000 (US$4500/£2800) to be sure of getting something reliable. However, you should be able to get your money back when you sell it, providing you haven't paid over the odds for the vehicle in the first place, although it can take a few weeks to get the price you deserve.

Buying from a **dealer** will generally up the price by ten to twenty percent, but should enable you to get a warranty for the vehicle – useful if it turns out to be unroadworthy. Bear in mind that the warranty is only worth having if you are able to return the car back to the dealer who issued it, which is likely to be tricky if you're travelling around the country.

Alternatively, you can buy a car through the **small ads** in the newspapers or in the growing number of free ads papers. If you do this, it helps to know something about the kind of vehicle you are buying, as no guarantee will be offered for its roadworthiness. If you don't trust your own mechanical abilities, enlist the services of the AA, who offer to check out cars for about R400 (US$90/£55). It's a good idea to go for a car that still has a few months of its road tax left, otherwise you will have to fork out for another year's worth of tax when you register the car in your name.

Beware of **rust**: cars from coastal regions, particularly those from Cape Town, are most likely to be on the rusty side. The least rusty vehicles are usually from the Northern Cape or somewhere equally dry.

When you buy a vehicle, make sure you get the registration document from the previous owner, as you'll need it when you come to register the vehicle in your name. You should also make sure you have a contact number for the previous owner, just in case the car turns out to have been stolen. After buying the car, you need to ensure that it's **roadworthy**. This involves taking it to the nearest testing station and paying for it to be put through a series of pretty basic tests. One possible problem that can arise is that the engine serial numbers do not all match up. If this happens, you'll have to take the vehicle to a police testing station where they run a series of computer checks to see if the car has been stolen.

Once you've got the roadworthy certificate, head for the nearest vehicle registration centre with your certificate, registration document, driving licence, passport and about R100 (US$20/£14): all this should be enough to procure you your own registration document for the vehicle.

Selling a vehicle is a lot more simple than buying one. All you need is the registration document to give to the new owner, a completed form for the transfer of ownership (which you can pick up from any vehicle registration centre), and a photocopy of the new owner's ID book or passport. Once you have handed over the keys and the new owner has driven away, you need to present the completed form and photocopy to a vehicle registration centre.

Most South Africans drive without any form of **insurance** but you would be foolish to do the same. Aim to buy a third-party insurance policy, preferably comprehensive, as soon as you take charge of a new vehicle. **Joining the AA** is a good idea, and you can join for a short period – say a couple of months. Their maps, travel advice and emergency services can be invaluable if you're driving around the country.

CYCLING

It's easy to see why **cycling** is popular in South Africa: you can get to stunning destinations on good roads unclogged by traffic, and many towns have decent cycle shops for spares and equipment. You'll need to be fit, though, as South Africa is a hilly place and many roads climb punishing gradients. The weather can make life difficult too: if it isn't raining, there is a good chance of it being very hot, so carry plenty of liquids. An increasing number of backpackers' hostels rent out mountain bikes for reasonable rates, making it easy to do plenty of cycling without having to transport your bike into the country. Cycling on the main roads is not recommended.

HITCHING

Generally speaking, **hitching** in most areas of South Africa is not a very good idea, particularly in large towns and cities. Even in rural areas it's risky and, while you might encounter wonderful hospitality and interesting companions, it's advisable not to hitch if you have any doubts at all.

If you must hitchhike, it's essential to take a number of precautions to maximize your safety. Avoid hitching alone, and being dropped off in isolated areas between *dorps*. Ask drivers where they are going before you say where you want to go, and keep your bags with you: having them locked in the boot makes a hasty escape more difficult. Check the notice boards in backpackers' lodges for people offering or looking to share lifts – that way, you can meet the driver in advance.

ACCOMMODATION

While you shouldn't expect the kind of bargains found in other Third World countries, accommodation in South Africa does offer good value for money. On average B&B prices are only slightly cheaper than they are in Britain, but rooms almost always come with private bath, and you'll often have the use of a garden or swimming pool. The recent growth in backpacker accommodation means that you should be able to find a hostel in most areas, and many will offer excellent facilities. Finally, at the camping and self-catering end of the scale, you'll be spoilt for choice: this is the preferred form of holiday accommodation of South African themselves, and the country is amply supplied with caravan parks, camping resorts and self-catering apartments and cottages.

Advance booking is vital if you're planning on staying in a national park or in popular areas such as Cape Town or the Garden Route, or if you're visiting during high season. South Africa's **peak season** is during the midsummer Christmas school holiday period (roughly Dec 4–Jan 21), which coincides with many foreign tourists piling in to catch their winter tan. The Easter school holiday (March 20–April 15) is a shorter and less intense period, when South African families migrate to the coast and inland resorts. At both Christmas and Easter, **prices** for budget and mid-priced accommodation (but not camping or backpacking) can as much as double, and most places get booked up months ahead.

There's a lull in the midwinter **low season** (June–Aug), during which time you should have no problem finding plenty of good-value places to stay, at least outside Cape Town and the Garden Route.

HOTELS

Generally speaking, South Africa's cheaper **hotels** are throwbacks to the 1950s and 1960s and can't keep up with the new profusion of guesthouses and B&Bs – many have degenerated into watering holes that earn most of their keep

ACCOMMODATION PRICE CODES

All the accommodation listed in the Guide has been categorized into one of seven price bands, as set out below. The rates quoted, unless otherwise stated, represent the most expensive per-person rate for a double or single room outside high season (Dec–Jan), except for category ①, which are per-person rates for a dorm bed in backpacker accommodation, or a campsite.

① **Up to R50 per person**. Dormitory accommodation and double rooms at backpackers' lodges with shared washing and cooking facilities fall into this category.

② **R50-100 per person**. At the bottom end of this range are upmarket backpackers' lodges (rare but burgeoning) with double rooms, and downmarket B&Bs, both with shared bathrooms. At the top end you'll get slightly run-down hotels, good self-catering accommodation on farms, at resorts and in towns, and good B&Bs offering rooms with bath in less touristy areas. The most basic national parks accommodation in rondavels with shared washing and cooking facilities also fall into the upper range of this category.

③ **R100–150 per person**. Basic mid-range hotels, good B&Bs and guesthouses, which should have a degree of style and will usually have a garden and swimming pool. Some en-suite self-catering national parks chalets are within the top half of this range.

④ **R150–200 per person**. Stylish B&Bs and guesthouses in popular areas, and exceptional places off the beaten track. This category also includes good mid-range hotels and the best en-suite national parks accommodation.

⑤ **R200–250 per person**. The starting range for luxury and style whether in a guesthouse, upmarket hotel or country lodge. Expect spacious en-suite rooms, and gardens with swimming pools (and even jacuzzis), first-class service and above-average food.

⑥ **R250–300 per person**. As above, but the location ought to be outstanding for this price, perhaps with sea or mountain views.

⑦ **Over R300 per person**. The sky's the limit here and, given the excellent standards you can expect for less money, we only recommend places in this category if they are truly out of the ordinary or if their huge reputation demands inclusion.

---

from their bar. Hotels are really only worth considering at the middle to the top end of the scale, and then only if you want plenty of facilities and luxurious accommodation and are prepared to pay through the nose for it. At some of the most expensive places you'll be paying for the social cachet of the name and may find equal facilities nearby far cheaper.

At the **bottom end** you can expect unremarkable en-suite rooms in the region of US$20/£15 per person. In smaller places off the tourist routes, you'll often have a choice of one or two hotels of this type, and these are rarely good value. There are exceptions of course: hotels with real charm in *dorps* where you'd least expect them, and we've included many of those in this guide.

At **mid-range** hotels you'll usually pay between $US25–50 (£15–30), and you can expect fairly decent standards, often in old and characterful buildings that have been refurbished. Many hotels in this middle category are comparable to guesthouses for the same price, but they offer a decent alternative if you prefer hotel anonymity and facilities such as room service, private telephone and TV. Many mid-priced hotels – especially those on main routes in the interior – get fully booked up during the week by travelling salesmen; but over the weekends, when they're often empty, you can often negotiate reasonable discounts. Along the coastal holiday strips such as the Garden Route and southern KwaZulu-Natal and all the major seaside towns in between, medium-priced hotels are ubiquitous and frequently offer rooms right on the beachfront.

South Africa's main hotel chains include *Holiday Inn*, *Protea*, *Southern Sun* and *Karos*, all of which offer reliable but rather soulless accommodation. At this **upmarket** end of the scale, prices can be high – anything from US$60/£40 to over US$150/£100 per person. If you're going to dig that deep in your pocket, you'd probably be better off at one of the many pleasant country hotels with beautiful gardens tucked away in scenic parts of the country, such as the Garden Route and the KwaZulu-Natal midlands. It's worth being warned about South Africa's idiosyncrasy over "smart casual" wear, which is demanded by many smarter hotels after 6pm. The directive applies mainly to men, and in practice means you'll need a pair of slacks, a decent shirt with a collar and closed shoes.

CARAVAN PARKS, RESORTS AND CAMPING

Caravanning was once the favourite way of enjoying a cheap family holiday in South Africa, and this accounts for the very large number of caravan parks dotted across the length and breadth of the country. Recently, however, their popularity has declined and with it the standard of many of the country's **municipal caravan parks and campsites**. Today, municipal campsites are generally pretty scruffy places, though you may find the odd pleasant one in rural areas, or near small *dorps*. Staying in a municipal campsite adjoining a city or large town will often be more grief than it's worth; not only will facilities generally be run-down, but theft is a big risk. In most municipal sites you can expect to pay roughly US$15/£10 per site.

All in all, you're best off heading for the better-organized **privately owned resorts**, where for roughly the same price you'll get greater comfort and a lot more facilities. Although private resorts sometimes give off a holiday-camp vibe, they usually have good washing and cooking facilities, self-catering chalets, shops selling basic goods, *braai* stands and swimming pools.

Virtually every **national park** in the country – and many provincial reserves – have campsites and in some of the really remote places, such as

parts of KwaZulu-Natal, camping may be your only option. At national parks you can rely on well-maintained washing facilities and there are often communal kitchen areas or at the very least a *braai* stand and running water as well as decent communal shower, toilet and washing facilities (known locally as "ablutions").

Camping rough is not recommended anywhere in the country, and with so many proper campsites, even in very remote areas, it's very unlikely you'll have to pitch a tent anywhere else.

BACKPACKERS' LODGES AND YOUTH HOSTELS

Backpackers' lodges are the fastest-growing type of accommodation in South Africa and their quality is improving all the time. Most offer basic hostel accommodation in a dormitory for under US$8/£5 per person, and many have a few double rooms which cost only a little more. The hostels usually have communal kitchens, an on-site restaurant or café, TV, internet facilities and bike rental.

South Africa's backpackers' lodges are invariably good meeting points, with large notice boards filled with advertisements for other hostels and backpacker facilities, and a constant stream of travellers passing through. Many hostels operate their own reasonably priced tours and excursions into the surrounding areas, and will be able to pick you up from railway stations or bus stops (especially *Baz* and *Hopper* bus stops) if you phone in advance. The only problem with staying in this kind of accommodation

---

YOUTH HOSTEL ASSOCIATIONS

South Africa, *Hostelling International South Africa*, 3rd Floor, St George's House, 73 St George's Mall, Cape Town 8001 (☎021/24 2511, fax 24 4119; email: hisa@gem.co.za).

England and Wales, *Youth Hostel Association* (*YHA*), Trevelyan House, 8 St Stephen's Hill, St Albans, Herts AL1 2DY (☎01727/855 215); London information office: 14 Southampton St, London WC2 7HY (☎0171/836 1036).

Northern Ireland, *Youth Hostel Association of Northern Ireland*, 22 Donegal Rd, Belfast BT12 5JN (☎01232/324 733).

Ireland, *An Oige*, 61 Mountjoy St, Dublin 7 (☎01/830 4555).

Scotland, *Scottish Youth Hostel Association*, 7 Glebe Crescent, Stirling FK8 2JA (☎01786/451 181).

Canada, *Canada Hostelling Association*, Room 400, 205 Catherine St, Ottawa, ON K2P (☎1-800/663-5777).

USA, *Hostelling International-American Youth Hostels* (*HI-AYH*), 733 15th St NW, Suite 840, PO Box 37613, Washington DC 20005 (☎202/783-6161; http://www.hostels.com).

Australia, *Australia Youth Hostels Association*, 422 Kent St, Sydney (☎02/9261 1111); 205 King St, Melbourne (☎03/9670 9611); 236 William St, Perth (☎08/9227 5122).

New Zealand, *Youth Hostels Association of New Zealand*, PO Box 436, Christchurch (☎03/379 9970).

YHA BOOKINGS

The following hostels in South Africa can be **booked** in advance through your local *Youth Hostel Association* office:

Cape Town: *Abe Bailey Youth Hostel, Albergo for Backpackers, Ashanti Lodge, Belvidere Accommodation Centre* and *Cloudbreak Backpackers.*

Durban: *Banana Backpackers, Durban Beach Youth Hostel* and *Tekweni Backpackers.*

Eastern and Western Cape: *Albergo for Backpackers* (Plettenberg Bay), *Backpackers' Oasis* (Oudtshoorn), *East London Backpackers* (East London), *George*

Backpackers (George), *Jeffreys Bay Backpackers* (Jeffreys Bay), *Knysna Backpackers* (Knysna), *Mossel Bay Backpackers* (Mossel Bay), *Port Elizabeth Backpackers* (Port Elizabeth), *Stumble Inn* (Stellenbosch) and *Zoete Inval Backpackers* (Hermanus).

Johannesburg: *Backpackers Ritz, Fairview Youth Hostel, Johannesburg Central Hostel* and *Kew Youth Hostel.*

Kimberley: *Gum Tree Lodge.*

is that you tend to meet the same people over and over again as you travel around.

Recently, an **upmarket** variant on backpackers' lodges has started to appear, aimed at thirty-somethings who want reasonably priced, casual accommodation, but are looking for something a little more stylish and sedate than the usual backpackers' lodge. At these places, you'll be able to get a very decent double room for around $US15/£10, and can still expect congenial communal areas. Although still uncommon at the time of writing, upmarket backpackers' lodges are bound to mushroom and we've listed them throughout this guide where appropriate.

South Africa's **youth hostel** scene is on the small side; around thirty backpackers' lodges around the country are affiliated to *Hostelling International South Africa* (*HISA*), part of the international *Youth Hostel Association* network. Located in most of the major tourist centres, some of these hostels can be prebooked via the International Booking Network (see box above), which enables you to book and pay for accommodation in advance through your local *YHA* office.

HISA has also put together a "Go-as-you-please" package available to *YHA* membership card holders. The package consists of prepaid dormitory accommodation vouchers, which are valid for up to a year and save you having to carry cash, and discounted travel passes for use on the *Translux* intercity bus network.

SELF-CATERING

Away from the resorts, **self-catering accommodation** in cottages, apartments and small complexes provides the cheapest option outside of staying in a backpackers' lodge. A self-catering holiday almost always clocks up at less than US$15/£10 per person per night for two people sharing. Apartments often sleep up to six people, and because rates are mostly quoted for entire units this can be an extremely economical option if you're travelling as a family or in a group. Even though you don't usually get breakfast (although this is sometimes offered for a small extra charge), you can save a lot of money by cooking for yourself, and you'll get a sense of freedom and privacy missing from the nicest guesthouse or B&B.

Apart from chalets at the ropiest of municipal caravan parks, standards of self-catering accommodation are usually quite high. Cottages or apartments generally come fully equipped with crockery and cutlery – and even microwaves and TVs in the more modern places. Linen and towels are often, but not always, provided – check before you book in.

One of the best things about self-catering is the wide choice of location you'll get. There are self-catering options on farms, near beaches, in forests and in wilderness areas, as well as in practically every town and city. We've listed many places throughout this guide – however, they are so widespread that it's always worth enquiring locally at tourist information bureaus.

B&BS, GUESTHOUSES AND FARMSTAYS

More and more South Africans are opening their homes to visitors, and in some places you'll be spoilt for choice. The most basic **B&B** consists of just one or two rooms inside a house, where you share washing facilities with the owners and pay around US$15/£10 per person. Far more common are the efficiently run B&Bs with en-suite rooms, often in garden cottages or annexes to the main house, and frequently with tea-making facilities and the use of a garden; for these you can expect to pay around US$25–40 (£15–25). In several places, Cape Town being the most notable, B&Bs are not allowed to display signs outside, but usually they will have signposts in their front garden, and often there will also be clear official signs pointing from the main street. It's worth asking to see your room first and get a feel for the place; South Africans are highly hospitable and at some B&Bs you run a real risk of being overwhelmed by attentive hosts and having little privacy.

The defining line between a B&B and a **guesthouse** can seem a little hazy. According to official definition, guesthouses are professionally run establishments without a public bar that rent out between four and fourteen rooms – they are dedicated lodgings rather than offshoots of someone's home. For practical purposes guesthouses fall somewhere between B&Bs and better hotels in facilities, atmosphere and cost. Prices start at around US$30/£20 per person and many offer a dinner, bed and breakfast rate.

Along many roads in the countryide you will see signs for *Bed en Ontbyd* (Afrikaans for "bed and breakfast") – this signals **farmstay** accommodation. As with urban B&Bs you will either be staying in rooms in the main homestead or in a cottage in its garden. On a farmstay you can usually expect a hearty Afrikaner breakfast and prices a little below urban B&Bs. Some farmstays offer hiking, horse-riding, and other activities and excursions – there are some real gems dotted about, which we've listed in this guide. tourist information bureaus will almost always have lists of farms in the area which rent out rooms or cottages.

NATIONAL PARKS ACCOMMODATION

Almost every **national park** in the country has a choice of several types of accommodation.

Classic pre-1970s accommodation is often arranged in circles facing inward without a view – a pity as national parks are invariably in beautiful settings. However, there will always be one or two that do have vistas and it's worth your while trying to secure a bed in one of these. Fortunately, recent fashion has been towards architect-designed rest camps with imaginative accommodation of a good standard, that makes the most of the site while emphasizing privacy (something the KwaZulu-Natal parks excel at).

Accommodation options include **campsites**, which cost about US$15/£10 per site; one-room **rondavels** with shared washing and cooking facilities for under US$15/£10 per person; and self-contained **chalets** with private bath or shower and cooking facilities, which come out at about US$30/£25. For groups of four to six people there are self-contained **cottages** with private bath and kitchen, where the price of the whole unit is around US$100/£65 for a four-sleeper, and US$130/£85 for a six-sleeper – this can work out fairly reasonably for a group.

In all national parks accommodation (apart from camping) you will get bedding, towels, a fridge and basic cooking utensils. The ultimate wildlife accommodation is in the **private game reserves**, most of which are around the Kruger National Park. Here you'll pay big bucks, but will get a far more intimate experience of the wild. At this level, accommodation is invariably luxurious and can be in large en-suite walk-in tents, small thatched rondavels or plush rooms with air conditioning in the larger and most expensive lodges. Prices start at US$150/£100 per person per night and can rise to several times that amount at the most fashionable spots. It's worth remembering that, high as these prices are, all your meals and game drives are included and you're essentially paying for an exclusive experience of the bush rather than for just a bed (see p.39 for more details).

PARKS, RESERVES AND WILDERNESS AREAS

No other African country has as rich a variety of parks, reserves and wilderness areas as South Africa. Literally hundreds of game reserves and state forests pepper the terrain, creating a bewildering but enticing choice. While there are dozens of unsung treasures among these, the big destinations amount to just over a dozen parks protecting the country's major game reserves and wilderness areas. With few exceptions these fall under the Natal Parks Board, which controls most of the public conservation areas in KwaZulu-Natal, and the National Parks Board, which covers the rest of the country.

It's important to realize that only some national parks are also game reserves; the chart opposite details what to expect from the major parks. **Wildlife** is what most people come for, and here again South Africa excels. But don't let the Big Five (buffalo, elephant, leopard, lion and rhino) blinker

you into missing out on the marvellous **wilderness areas** that take in dramatic landscapes and less-publicized animal life. There are parks protecting marine and coastal areas, wetlands, endangered species, forests, deserts and mountains, usually with the added attraction of animals, birds, insects, reptiles or marine mammals.

If you had to choose just one of the country's top three parks, **Kruger**, stretching up the east flank of Mpumalanga and Northern Province, would lead the pack for its sheer size (it's larger than Wales), its range of animals, its varied Lowveld habitats and unbeatable game-viewing opportunities. After Kruger, the **Tsitsikamma**, in the Western Cape, attracts large numbers of visitors for its ancient forests, cliff-faced oceans, the surging Storms River Mouth and the Otter Trail, South Africa's most popular **hike**. For epic mountain landscapes, nowhere in the country can touch the **Natal Drakensberg Park**, which takes in a

MAJOR PARKS AND WILDERNESS AREAS

MAJOR PARKS AND WILDERNESS AREAS

KEY	PARK	PRINCIPAL FOCUS	DESCRIPTION AND HIGHLIGHTS	DETAILS
WESTERN CAPE				
1	**Karoo NP**	Desert reserve	Arid mountainous landscape with ancient fossils, herbivores and wild flowers in spring.	p.163
2	**Tsitsikamma NP**	Marine and coastal	Cliff, tidal pools, deep gorges and evergreen forests. Snorkelling, scuba and forest trails.	p.203
3	**Wilderness NP**	Marine and coastal	Lakes, rivers, lagoons, forest, fynbos, beaches and the sea.	p.188
4	**West Coast NP**	Marine and coastal	Wetland wilderness with birding and watersports.	p.210
EASTERN CAPE				
5	**Addo Elephant NP**	Endangered species	Home to more than 200 elephants, Cape buffaloes and various antelopes.	p.269
6	**Mountain Zebra NP**	Endangered species	Dramatic hilly landscape in flat country with rare mountain zebras and other herbivores.	p.288
NORTHERN CAPE				
7	**Kalahari-Gemsbok NP**	Desert/game reserve	Remote desert with rust-red dunes, desert lions, shy leopards and thousands of antelopes.	p.239
8	**Augrabies Falls NP**	Desert reserve	Orange River plummets down a deep ravine. Rhinos, antelopes and prolific birdlife.	p.238
FREE STATE				
9	**Golden Gate NP**	Mountain enclave	Resort at the foot of rich sandstone formations in the heart of the Maluti Mountains. Trails.	p.440
NORTHWEST				
10	**Pilanesberg NP**	Game reserve	Mountain-encircled grassland trampled by the Big Five, accessible from Johannesburg.	p.504
NORTHERN PROVINCE/MPUMALANGA				
11	**Kruger NP**	Game reserve	The largest, best-stocked and most popular game reserve in the subcontinent.	p.537
KWAZULU-NATAL				
12	**Greater St Lucia**	Coastal wetland	Vast patchwork of wetlands, wilderness, coast and game reserves.	p.399
13	**Hluhluwe-Umfolozi GR**	Game reserve	KwaZulu-Natal's hillier, smaller answer to Kruger is among the top African spots for rhinos.	p.396
14	**Itala GR**	Game reserve	Lesser-known small gem of a game reserve in mountainous country.	p.413
15	**Mkuzi GR**	Game/bird reserve	Top birding venue, excellent for rhinos and other herbivores. Walks in wild fig forest.	p.403
16	**Natal Drakensberg Pk**	Mountain reserve	A series of parks covering the highest, most stirring and most dramatic peaks in SA.	p.381

PARK ENTRY FEES, RESERVATIONS AND ENQUIRIES

Entry fees into parks vary; some charge according to vehicle, others according to person. In general, the very most you'll be charged is R40 per person (and usually much less). Most of South Africa's major national parks have accommodation which can be **booked** in advance (and in high season, this should be several months in advance) through the National Parks Board, except for Pilanesberg, which should be booked through Pilanesberg National Park, and the KwaZulu Natal reserves, which should be booked through the Natal Parks Board.

National Parks Board, PO Box 787, Pretoria 0001; street address: 643 Leyds St, Muckleneuk, Pretoria (☎012/343 1991, fax 343 0905); PO Box 7400, Roggebaai 8012, Cape Town; street address: 44 Long St, City Centre, Cape Town (☎021/22 2810, fax 24 6211).

Natal Parks Board, PO Box 1750, Pietermaritzburg 3200 (☎0331/47 1981 enquiries only, 47 1891, fax 47 1980).

Pilanesberg National Park, PO Box 937, Lonehill 2062 (☎011/465 5423, fax 465 1228).

series of reserves on the KwaZulu-Natal border with Lesotho and offers gentle hikes along watercourses as well as ambitious mountaineering for serious climbers.

The unchallenged status of Kruger National Park as the place for packing in elephants, lions and casts of thousands of animals, tends to put the **KwaZulu-Natal parks** in the shade; quite undeservedly, as they have several points going for them. As well as offering the best places for seeing **rhino**, these parks feel less developed than Kruger, often provide superior (but no more expensive) accommodation and are just as accessible for self-driving. Another facility you'll find in the Natal parks are guided walks with an armed guard – something not available at Kruger. Both Kruger and Natal parks offer **night drives**, which is a popular way to catch sight of the elusive denizens that creep around after dark.

SAFARIS

If it's **wildlife** you've come to see, you'll find South Africa hard to beat. The country has the best-managed **national parks** in Africa, with well-organized rest camps, developed over four decades to provide cheap holidays for white South African families, and offering reasonably priced accommodation, campsites and good self-catering facilities.

Game-viewing isn't a cheap business, and mostly you get what you pay for. The **least expensive** way of experiencing a game park is as a group renting a car and **driving yourself** around a national park, taking advantage of the self-catering and camping facilities. Another budget alternative, worth considering if you're alone and have no transport, is staying outside Kruger and taking game drives with a safari company

into the park. There's a backpackers' lodge nearby, several hotels and B&Bs offering safari excursions. Two disadvantages of this are that you miss out on the experience of waking up in wild places and you end up spending considerably more hours on the road. But during South African school holidays, when Kruger is booked to capacity, you may have no other option.

In addition to the state-run parks there are expensive **private reserves**, frequently abutting onto them and sharing the same wildlife population. For your money you'll see the same animals, but under more exclusive conditions, staying at luxurious game lodges staffed by well-informed rangers who lead game-viewing outings in open-topped Land-Rovers. If you're new to the African bush and its wildlife, consider shelling out and spending at least two nights at one of the safari lodges on the private reserves abutting Kruger and then set out on your own. If money's no object, don't bother with self-driving at all.

A word of warning: be wary of any cheap deals on "safari farms" in the vicinity of Kruger. These are generally fine if you want to see animals in what are essentially huge zoos and make an acceptable overnight stop en route to Kruger, but are no substitute for a real wilderness experience – sooner or later you hit fences and gates on your game drive. Some of the better places in this category are given in the relevant chapters.

Spotting game takes skill and experience. It's easier than you'd think to mistake a rhino for a large boulder, or to miss the king of the beasts in the tall, lion-coloured grass – African game is after all designed with camouflage in mind. Don't expect the quantity of animals you get in wildlife documentaries, which edit months of filming into half an hour: what you see is always a matter of luck, patience and skill. The section of the Guide on Kruger National Park (see p.537) gives advice on how to go about spotting game and how to enjoy and understand what you do see – whether it's a brightly coloured lizard in a rest camp, head-butting giraffes at a waterhole or dust-kicking rhinos. For other **books** that can enhance your visit to a game reserve, see p.681.

Although the Kruger is the focus for most of South Africa's safari activity, particularly for venturing into the wilderness with skilled guides, the KwaZulu-Natal game reserves – foremost among them **Hluhluwe-Umfolozi**, **Mkuzi** and **Itala** – offer rewarding opportunities for self-drive touring. The same applies to the **Pilanesberg Game Reserve** in Northwest Province, while the remote **Kalahari-Gemsbok National Park** on the border of Botswana promises truly exciting wilderness driving. A number of extremely upmarket operations offer the whole game-lodge experience on private reserves, where your vehicle stays in the car park and you walk or are driven around by a guide. Among the most prestigious of these are **Phinda** in KwaZulu-Natal and **Tswalu** in the Northern Cape.

SELF-DRIVE SAFARIS

Self-driving involves the thrill of spotting game yourself, rather than relying on a game ranger, and gives you the freedom to stick around for as long as you like. For people with **children** self-driving is the principal way you can get into a game reserve, as most of the upmarket lodges don't admit children under 12. You also have the advantage of going at your own pace, and may choose to cover a route that takes in both the Mpumalanga reserves and those in KwaZulu-Natal, just a few hours away – an appealing combination of one large and some more intimate reserves, which will cover very different terrain.

As far as **accommodation** is concerned, camping works out at under US$6/£4 per person; basic chalets with shared washing facilities start at around US$9/£6; and en-suite accommodation ranges from US$23–38 (£15–25). En-suite accommodation is in serviced, thatched rondavels with linen provided. The cheaper units usually don't have their own kitchen, although everywhere you go will have a fridge, tea-making facilities and somewhere to *braai*. In several of the Natal parks rest camps you aren't allowed to use the kitchen, but must give your food to the camp chef and attendants who cook or prepare your meal for you, serve you and wash up, at no extra cost. **Advance booking** is essential to secure a place to stay in a national park – this is especially true during holiday season.

Most game reserve rest camps have a **shop** selling supplies for picnics or *braais*, as well as a **restaurant**.

If you plan to self-drive, consider investing in good animal and bird field **guides**; once in the park, you'll find them indispensible for identification and learning about what you see. The same applies to a decent pair of **binoculars**. Finally, whether you're cooking or not, it's worth taking a thermos for tea and a cool bag to keep water cold.

The one real disadvantage of self-driving is that you can end up jostling with other cars to get a view, especially when it comes to lion-watching. Also, you may not know what signs to look out for in order to spot game; and unless you travel in a minibus or 4WD vehicle you're unlikely to be high enough off the ground to be able to see across the *veld*.

PRIVATE RESERVES AND LODGES

If you choose well, the ultimate South African game experience has to be in a **private reserve** or **lodge**. The advantage of private reserves is that you spend time in a small group and relax while your game-viewing activities are organized, and because you rarely see other visitors you get a stronger sense of the wild than you ever could at one of the big Kruger rest camps. Most of all, you get the benefit of knowledgeable rangers, who can explain the terrain and small-scale wildlife as they drive you around looking for game.

Nowhere are the private reserves more developed than along the west flank of the **Kruger**, where you'll find the top-dollar prestigious lodges as well as some places offering more bang for fewer bucks.

Smaller private reserves accommodate between ten and sixteen guests, which gives you very close contact with your hosts and the opportunity to ask about flora and fauna around meal tables and at teatimes. Larger camps often cater to two or three times as many people, and resemble hotels in the bush, though you'll always have a game ranger and see the same quantity of game. Many safari lodges have their own waterholes, overlooked by the bar, from which you can watch animals drinking.

Accommodation is in luxurious safari tents with private bathrooms, or in a variety of chalets – some thatch and brick, some stylish luxury suites. A couple of places have "bush-showers" (a hoisted bucket of hot water with a shower nozzle attached) behind reed screens but open to the sky – one of the great thrills of the bush is taking a shower under the southern sky. Some chalets or tents have gaslights or lanterns in the absence of electricity. **Food** is usually good and plentiful, and vegetarians can be catered for.

A **typical day** at a private camp or lodge starts at dawn for tea or coffee followed by guided game-viewing on foot, or driving. After a mid-morning brunch/breakfast, there's the chance to spend time on a viewing platform or in a hide, qui-etly watching the passing scene. Late-afternoon game-viewing is a repeat of early morning but culminates with sundowners as the light fades, and often turns into a night drive with spotlights out looking for nocturnal creatures.

Prices, which include accommodation, meals and all game activities, do vary widely – at US$105–500 (£70–350) per person per day. In this instance, expensive doesn't necessarily mean better and you might find that the cheaper camps in the same areas are more to your taste, simply because of the plainer and wilder atmosphere that is more in keeping with the bush. The ultra-expensive camps offer more luxury and social cachet, but not necessarily better game-viewing.

WILDLIFE

South Africa has a century-long history of wildlife conservation and its budget is the biggest on the African continent. It's no surprise, therefore, that this country is rich in wildlife, and you'll see herds of animals here that elsewhere on the continent are heading for extinction. The Big Five (lion, elephant, buffalo, rhino and leopard) are all present, together with all the herbivores you could want: elephant, giraffe, zebra, hippo and many species of antelope (buck). South Africa also happens to be one of the best places in the world for shore sightings of marine mammals – whales and dolphins.

Hunters and development have meant that you'll need to make some effort to trawl out to the game reserves, to which most large mammals are now restricted. Photos and information for identification of the commonest larger mammals can be found in our colour wildlife section. For specific advice on safaris, and for a rundown on the game reserves, see the entries below.

LARGE MAMMMALS

Antelope are South Africa's most common species and if you spend any time at all game-viewing, the prolific impala are likely to become a very familiar sight. Other common herbivores that you're bound to come across include zebra, giraffe, hippo and buffalo. Wherever you find grazers and browsers, **predators** aren't far behind. The big cats are there (as well as smaller and lesser-known felines such as the caracal and black-footed cat), but are only found far from human habitation. Night brings out a different cast, and any operator taking game drives will have a spotlight to reveal hyenas, spring hares and – if you're lucky – porcupines, pangolins and leopards.

SMALLER CREATURES

Spiders and **scorpions** will do their best to get away from you, while the **butterflies** are all you could hope for. **Lizards** are common, often beautifully coloured and completely harmless, as are the prehistoric-looking chameleons, which are found absolutely everywhere, even in suburban gardens. Don't be disturbed if you see small gravity-defying reptiles running across the ceiling: they're insect-eating geckos (whose adhesive toes allow the acrobatics) and should be encouraged.

BIRDLIFE

South Africa is home to over seven hundred species of **birds** – a great attraction to ornithologists from all over. Water birds include the small jackass penguin, the sacred ibis, the Egyptian goose and the lesser flamingo. Larger species range from the huge, land-bound ostrich, to the graceful blue crane, while raptors include the

rather frightening-looking martial eagle and the metre-high secretary bird. Many of the country's birds are detailed in their relevant habitats throughout this book.

THE COAST

Far from being just a place to catch a tan, South Africa's beaches and **coastal areas** harbour a huge variety of life that includes crustaceans who leave their crisscrossing trails on the beaches, minute living universes in rock pools, otters, seals, birds and marine mammals, of which whales and dolphins are the real highlight. How and where to see them is outlined in the relevant chapters.

DON'T FEED BUNS TO THE ELEPHANTS

Wildlife in South Africa is now almost exclusively confined to the game reserves, which are in fenced-off enclaves that are meticulously managed – a fact that led one warden at the Kruger National Park to comment wryly that the place was little more than a very big farm.

Like all exaggerations this carries a germ of truth: most of the major game reserves are crisscrossed by tarred roads and have facilities that include filling stations and shops that sell fresh milk and daily newspapers – trappings of civilization that can lull you into seeing the animals as props in a theme park. Don't be fooled in all the game reserves – animals in all the game reserves are wild and potentially dangerous. So don't be tempted to **feed buns to elephants** or to step out of your car to get a better snap of a lion – idiotic as it may seem, both have been done by visitors who didn't live to relate the experience.

FOOD AND DRINK

South Africa doesn't really have a coherent indigenous cuisine, although attempts have been made to elevate Cape cuisine to this sta-

tus. Traditional African food tends to focus around stiff grain porridge (similar to Italian polenta) accompanied by meat or vegetable-based sauces. Among white South Africans, Afrikaners have evolved a style of cooking known as boerekos ("farmer's food") that tends to be cholesterol-rich and can be heavy-going if you're not used to it. People of British extraction favour the traditional English style of meat and overcooked vegetables.

With its thousands of kilometres of coast, South Africa is blessed with a vast array of seafoods, from oysters to numerous species of fish – and this is where you should focus your culinary attention. In all the major cities you'll find reasonably priced restaurants covering an ever-increasing range of international styles and eclectic local adaptations.

SOUTH AFRICAN FOOD

Although South Africa's indigenous offerings are few, you can still expect to eat well in this country. The variety of food available is huge and context is always important – you may not want to eat *boerewors* at a restaurant; but at a *braai* under the stars, accompanied by a few beers, it's almost obligatory.

CAPE CUISINE

Styles of cooking brought by Asian slaves have evolved into **Cape cuisine** (sometimes known as Cape Malay food – a misnomer given that few slaves came from Malaysia). Characterized by sweet aromatic curries, Cape cuisine is worth sampling at least once, especially in Cape Town where it developed and is associated with the Muslim community. Although it can be delicious, there isn't that much variety and few restaurants specialize in it. Despite this, most of the dishes considered as Cape cuisine have actually crept into the South African diet, many becoming part of the Afrikaner culinary vocabulary. For details of particular dishes see "Eating and drinking" in Chapter One, p.108.

OTHER ETHNIC AND REGIONAL INFLUENCES

Although there's nothing as distinct as regional cuisines in South Africa, you will find changes of emphasis and local specialities in different parts of the country. **Natal**, for instance, particularly around Durban and Pietermaritzburg, is especially good for Indian food. The South African contribution to this great multifaceted tradition is the humble **bunny chow**, a cheap takeaway consisting of a hollowed out half-loaf of white bread originally filled with curried beans, but nowadays with anything from curried chicken to sardines (see p.354).

Because of its proximity to Mozambique, **Portuguese food** made early inroads into South Africa, predominantly through the use of hot and spicy *peri-peri* seasoning, which goes extremely well with *braais*. The best-known example of this is delicious **peri-peri chicken**, which you will find all over. **Italian food** has also been around for a while, brought over with POWs from the North Africa campaign who were incarcerated here and stayed on after World War II. You'll find some excellent Italian restaurants in the cities, from small pizzerias to smarter restaurants going the whole hog.

Eastern European **Jewish food** came with turn-of-the-century refugees and you'll find bagels, chopped liver and chopped herring at delis and some supermarkets.

VEGETARIAN FOOD

While not quite a **vegetarian** paradise, South Africa is nevertheless vegetarian-savvy and you'll find at least one concession to meatless food on most menus. Even steakhouses will have something palatable on offer and generally offer the best salad bars around; especially at the Spur

---

THE BRAAI AND BOEREKOS

Braai (short for *braaivleis*), is an Afrikaans word literally translated as "meat grill" and is probably the only place you'll catch an unreconstructed white South African man cooking. A *braai* is basically a **barbecue**, but white South Africans have perfected the form, and at any national park, nature reserve or resort you'll never be far from a permanent *braai* stand.

Barbecuing is an intensely social activity and is usually done among family and friends accompanied by gallons of beer. You can *braai* anything, but a traditional barbecue meal consists of huge slabs of steak, lamb cutlets and **boerewors** ("farmer's sausage"), a deliciously spicy South African speciality. Potatoes and onions wrapped in aluminium foil and placed in the embers are a usual accompaniment. The real skill in *braai* comes in knowing when the coals are hot enough to cook the meat and in concocting the marinades and sauces. A variant on the *braai* is **potjiekos** ("pot food"), in which the food is cooked, preferably outdoor over an open fire, in a three-legged cast-iron cauldron.

In a similar vein, but cooked indoors is **boerekos** ("farmers' food"), a diet eaten mainly by Afrikaners. Much of it is similar to English food, but taken to cholesterol-rich extremes, with even the vegetables prepared with sugar and butter. Should you spend the night on an Afrikaans farm, you could well find yourself waking up to a breakfast of several eggs, steak, piles of bacon and *boerewors*. *Boerekos* comes into its own in its variety of over-the-top desserts, including *koeksisters* (plaited doughnuts saturated with syrup) and *melktert* (literally "milk tart"), a solid rich custard in a flan case.

chain, where you can fill up on greens for under US$3/£2. If you're self-catering in the larger cities, head for the delicious dips and breads at delis and *Woolworth's* and *Pick'n'Pay* supermarkets. South Africa's choice of vegetables and fruit is wide and inexpensive compared to Europe.

PLACES AND PRICES

Restaurants in South Africa offer outstanding value compared with Britain or North America. In every city you'll find places where you can eat a good main course for well under US$8/£5 and for US$13/£15 you can expect the very best. Restaurants with imaginative menus are found in all the larger centres. **Franschhoek**, a small *dorp* in the Winelands, has established itself as a culinary centre for the country, where you'll find some fine eateries in extremely close proximity. As a rule restaurants are licensed but Muslim establishments serving Cape cuisine don't allow alcohol at all.

An attractive phenomenon in the big cities, especially Cape Town, has been the rise of the continental-style **cafés** – easy-going, informal places where you can eat just as well as you would in a regular restaurant, but also drink coffee all night without the feeling that you're expected to order food. A reasonable meal in a café is unlikely to set you back more than US$6–8/£4–5. Café service tends to be slick and friendly, and opening hours long. Make sure you don't confuse this new type of café with the traditional South African café found in even the tiniest country town. The equivalent of a corner store elsewhere, they commonly sell a few magazines, soft drinks, sweets, crisps and an odd collection of tins and dry goods. Their only concession to ready-to-eat food is normally a meat pie heated in a microwave oven or a leg of chicken that spent a little too long incubating in the warmer.

If popularity is the yardstick, then South Africa's real national cuisine is to be found in its **franchise restaurants**, which you'll find in every town of any size. The usual international names like *KFC* and *Wimpy* are omnipresent, but these are no match for South Africa's own home-grown American-style steakhouses, such as **Spurs**, **Steers** and **Saddles**, projecting a wholesome Wild West image that has successfully been roping in South African families for decades. South Africa's great contribution to the world of fast food is the **Nando's Chickenland** chain, which grills excellent Portuguese-style chicken, served under a variety of spicy sauces. Expect to pay US$3–8/£2–5 for a filling main course at any of these places.

DRINKING

Although South Africa yearns to be a major wine-producing country, **beer** is indisputably the national drink. Beer is as much an emblem of South African manhood as the *braai* is for whites – and unlike the *braai* it cuts through all race and class divisions. Pubs and bars are not the centres of social activity they are in the US or the UK, although in the African townships **shebeens** or informal bars do occupy this position. Whites tend to do their drinking at home. In city centres, **bars** have traditionally been rough, men-only places, women being corralled into stiff lounges or ladies' bars attached to hotels. The **Irish/British-style pub** is beginning to make an appearance under the invasion of a series of franchised names, but has no deep roots in South African culture. Beer, wines and spirits can be bought at supermarkets and bottle stores (the equivalent of the British off-licence), which generally keep normal shopping hours, although some stay open as late as 6.30pm. Generally, don't expect to be able to buy liquor at night or on Sundays.

BEER

South Africans tend to be fiercely loyal to their brand of **beer**, though they all taste similar, given that virtually all beer in the country is produced by the huge *South African Breweries* monopoly. **Lager** is the predominant style, and to a British palate is likely to taste a bit thin and bland, though it can be wonderfully refreshing drunk ice-cold on a sweltering day. One or two microbreweries have sprung up, best known of which is *Mitchell's* in Knysna, which produces some distinctive ales. These can be found at some bottle stores and bars between Cape Town and Port Elizabeth. **Imported beers** are starting to make an appearance, but they're rather expensive by comparison with the local product.

WINES

South Africa's **wine industry** is rising out of years in the doldrums, casting aside a 350-year-old tradition of trying to make French wine, and is entering the world market as **Cape winemakers**. Exports are rising and, though South African wines haven't reached the general standards of Australian wine (yet), make no mistake: this country produces some excellent wines that can give the Aussies a good run for their money – and it's dead cheap.

Prices for quaffable bottles start at under US$3/£2. The country's most expensive wine – a Pinot Noir from the Hamilton Russell Estate – sells for less than US$26/£17 and is considered outrageously expensive by locals. This means that anyone with an adventurous streak can indulge in a bacchanalia of wine sampling without breaking the bank. Wine is available throughout the country, but the best way to sample it is by visiting **wineries**, some of which charge a small tasting fee to discourage freeloading.

The oldest and most rewarding wine-producing regions are the **Constantia estates** in Cape Town (see p.93) and the region known as the **Winelands** around the towns of Stellenbosch (see p.132), Paarl (see p.136) and Franschhoek (see p.142), which all have institutionalized wine routes. Other wine-producing areas include: the Klein Karoo (see p.147), Robertson (see p.150), the Swartland (see p.208), the Orange River (see p.236) and Walker Bay (see p.172).

SOFT DRINKS AND FRUIT JUICE

There are no surprises when it comes to **soft drinks**, with all the usual names available. What does stand out is the South African **fruit juice**. The range is broad and includes what must be one of the most extensive selections of unsweetened juices in the world under the *Liquifruit* and *Ceres* labels.

POST, PHONES AND EMAIL SERVICES

Most towns of any size have a **post office**, generally open Monday to Friday 8.30am to 4.30pm and Saturday 8am to noon (closing earlier in some places). The deceptively familiar feel of South African post offices can lull you into expecting an efficient British- or US-style service. In fact, post within the country is slow, erratic and unreliable, and money and valuables are frequently stolen en route. For important items, it makes sense to use one of the private courier services such as *Federal Express*, which are more expensive, but far more reliable.

Expect domestic delivery times from one city to another of about a week – longer if a rural town is involved at either end. **International airmail** deliveries are often quicker, especially if you're sending or receiving at Johannesburg, Cape Town or Durban – the cities with direct flights to London. By surface mail you can expect your letter or package to take anything up to six weeks to get from South Africa to London. **Stamps** are available only at post offices and are relatively inexpensive compared to Britain or North America. You'll find **poste restante** facilities at the main post office in most larger centres, and in many backpackers' hostels.

PHONES

South Africa's **telephone system**, operated by the state monopoly, *Telkom*, works well and public phone booths are easily found in every city and town, with increasing numbers being installed in rural areas – a tangible result of the new government's policy of taking services to the people. There are two types of *Telkom* phone: coin- or card-operated. **International calls** can be made from virtually any of them, and for this it helps to have a card, as you'll be lucky to stay on the line for more than a minute or two for R10. **Cards** are available at *Telkom* offices, post offices, and newsagents. They come in R10, 20, 50 and 100 denominations, and you can tell from the liquid crystal display on the phone how many units you have left. If you are going to be making a lot of calls, especially international ones, the R50 or 100 cards will be the most useful.

CHANGES TO PHONE NUMBERS

Phone numbers in various areas of the country are being changed as South Africa progessively upgrades and expands its network. Some of the numbers given in this book may go out of date during its lifetime. If you have a problem getting through, contact the free directory enquiry service on ☎1023.

The cheapest time to make international calls is Monday to Friday 8pm to 8am and during the weekends. **Reverse-charge calls** are made through a service called *International Booked Calls*, on ☎0900.

If you need to use the phone while staying at a **hotel**, be sure to ask what their rate is – the surcharge is often extortionate. In cities you'll find **private phone bureaus**, where you can make your call on a normal phone and pay afterwards, but, while it's more comfortable to sit down, these cost considerably more than a *Telkom* phone booth. Some of these bureaus will also send and receive **faxes** for you, which though expensive, may turn out cheaper than making a phone call. Many newsagents also offer fax services, which they advertise in their windows.

Mobile phones (known locally as cellular or cellphones) operate on the GSM digital system and are well-established in South Africa, with two competing networks covering all the main areas and the national roads connecting them. If you want to use your GSM phone in South Africa you will need to arrange a **roaming agreement** with your provider at home – but be warned this is likely to be an expensive way of keeping in touch. Mobile phone **rental** can be arranged at the airports in the main cities as well as through other providers in town. If you are phoning someone who is on a mobile phone, remember that calls are usually more expensive than the *Telkom* network, for you as well as the recipient.

EMAIL

The unreliability of mail and the expense of phones have provided the motivation for early adoption of **email** and the internet: both are remarkably well-established for this relatively poor country. Many hotels, safari lodges and tourism service providers have email addresses, and this is the cheapest way to make contact over distance. If you're planning on using a computer for email in South Africa, find out whether your service provider has any agreements with local companies. The international provider *Compuserve* has nodes all over the country (although connections in smaller places can be painfully slow), which allows you to use your own ID just as if you were at home through local nodes; this keeps call costs down to local rates. Every city has at least one **cybercafé** where you can surf the net, and an increasing number of **backpackers' hostels** have internet and email facilities.

DIRECTORY ENQUIRIES AND INTERNATIONAL CODES

Telkom operates an extremely useful (and free) **directory enquiry service** (☎1023). However, English is not the first language of many of the operators who answer the calls and, with standards of literacy quite a lot lower than in Europe or North America, be prepared to be patient and to help the operator with spelling. Also remember that the English accent people are accustomed to here may be very different to your own – so talk slowly and clearly.

INTERNATIONAL CALLS

To call southern Africa **from overseas**, dial the international access code (☎00 from the UK; ☎011 from the US and Canada; ☎0011 from Australia) followed by the country code. Remember to leave out any zeros in front of domestic area codes. The international codes are:

South Africa ☎27   Lesotho ☎266   Swaziland ☎268

To dial **out of South Africa**, the international access code is ☎09. To dial **out of Lesotho and Swaziland**, the code is ☎00. Remember to omit any zeros in front of the city, town or area code of the place you're phoning. Outgoing international codes from South Africa include:

Australia ☎09 61   Ireland ☎09 353   New Zealand 09 64   UK ☎09 44   USA and Canada ☎09 1

THE MEDIA

South Africa's press is rather parochial, with one or two notable exceptions. Unlike Britain, the country lacks a strong tradition of national papers and instead has many local papers of varying quality. Meanwhile, television is faced with having to transform itself from an apartheid mouthpiece into a democratic voice – no mean task. Radio is where South Africa is finding it easiest to meet the multicultural needs of a diverse and scattered audience, and deregulation of the airwaves has already brought to life scores of new stations.

NEWSPAPERS

Of the roughly twenty **daily newspapers**, most of which are published in English or Afrikaans, the only one that qualifies as a national is the weekly *Mail & Guardian*, which is available throughout the country, and benefits enormously from its close association with the London *Guardian* (from which it draws most of its international coverage). The *Mail & Guardian* is unquestionably the country's intellectual heavyweight, although its dense reporting can be a bit heavy-going. The *Sowetan*, targeted at a mainly black Jo'burg audience, is also widely available across the country and provides a less exclusively white perspective on South African issues.

Of the English dailies, the *Star* in Johannesburg is one of the best, while *Business Day* is South Africa's equivalent of the *Financial Times* or the *Wall Street Journal*. **Local papers** are useful for listings; in Cape Town you'll find the *Cape Times*, and the *Cape Argus*, sister paper to the *Star*, which identifies itself with issues local to the "mother city". Durban brings out the *Daily News* and the *Natal Mercury* in the morning and evening, while Port Elizabeth offers the *Eastern Province Herald* – a gossipy broadsheet which beats with the heart of a tabloid. Finally, East London has the *Daily Dispatch*, an Eastern Cape paper packed with local news.

The easiest places for **buying newspapers** are corner stores and newsagents, especially the *CNA* chain. These places also sell **international press**, such as *Time* and *Newsweek*, and the weekly editions of the London *Daily Mail*, the *Telegraph* and the *Express*.

TELEVISION

Every day twelve million South African adults tune into the SABC's three public **TV** channels, which churn out a mixed bag of domestic dramas, game shows, soaps and documentaries, filled out with lashings of familiar imports. **SABC 1, 2** and **3** share the unenviable task of trying to deliver an integrated service, while having to split their time between the eleven official languages. This massive mission would tax the resources of even a rich, industrialized country, but for a Third World one like South Africa it's a crippling project. In practice English turns out to be most widely used, with SABC 3 broadcasting almost exclusively in

---

BBC WORLD SERVICES AND VOA

The **BBC World Service** gives wider coverage than local South African stations, and broadcasts some excellent programmes in its **Africa Service**. There can be considerable variation in reception, so it's worth surfing the airwaves to find the sharpest frequency. As a rule of thumb, the lower ones (below 7000kHz) tend to provide better reception from late afternoon and throughout the evening, while the higher ones are usually better during the early morning till about midday.

Frequencies for the BBC's principal English-language broadcasts on short wave are as follows (given in kHz; times are local): 3255 (5–8am & 6pm–midnight); 6005 (5–6pm & 11pm–midnight); 6190 (5–10.15am & noon–midnight); 9600 (5–10am); 1183 (7.30am–9pm); 11940 (8–10.15am & noon–6pm); 15400 (9.30am–noon & 7–9.15pm); and 21660 (1–4.30pm & 5.30–7pm). The BBC also relays these broadcasts on medium wave 1197 (midnight–9.15am, 3–4.30pm & 5.30pm–midnight).

The **Voice of America**'s English-language broadcasts to Africa can be picked up on the following short-wave frequencies: 6035 (8–9am & 6.30pm–midnight); 6080 (5–9am), 7375 (7pm–midnight) and 7415 (7pm–midnight).

the language, while SABC 2 and SABC 3 spread themselves thinly across all the remaining ten languages with some English creeping in even here. A selection of sports, movies, news and specialist channels are available to subscribers to the **M-Net** satellite service.

RADIO

Given South Africa's low literacy rate and widespread poverty, it's little surprise that **radio** is its most popular medium, since receivers are cheap and broadcasts can penetrate into even the remotest rural area. The SABC operates a national radio station for each of the eleven official language groups. The English-language service, **SAfm** is of a generally high standard; its best offerings are the highly polished evening and morning news programmes. The SABC also runs 5FM Stereo, a national pop station broadcasting Top 40 tracks, while their Radio Metro is targeted at black urban listeners. These aside, there are scores of regional, commercial and community stations, broadcasting a range of material, which makes surfing the airwaves an enjoyably serendipitous experience, wherever you are in the country. See p.476 for new stations operating in the Gauteng area.

OPENING HOURS AND HOLIDAYS

The working day starts and finishes early in South Africa: shops and businesses generally open on weekdays at 8.30am and close at 4.30pm or 5pm. In small towns, many places close for an hour over lunch. Shops and businesses close around noon on Saturdays for the day, and most shops are closed on Sundays. However, in every neighbourhood, you'll find what South Africans call "cafés" – not places where you get coffee, but corner stores where you can buy milk, bread and essentials after hours.

It's always best to do business in the morning and get out early. **Banking hours** are generally 8.30am to 3.30pm Monday to Friday, Saturday 8am to 11am, but you'll find **bureaux de change** in the major cities open until at least 5pm and often later in big cities (see "Listings" for each city for late openings) and open at the international airports to meet flights. Post offices are generally open 8.30am to 4.30pm on weekdays, and Saturdays 8am to 11.30am. Government departments are open 8am to 4pm weekdays.

HOLIDAYS

School holidays in South Africa can disrupt your plans, especially if you want to camp, or stay in the national parks and the cheaper end of accommodation (self-catering, cheaper B&Bs, etc), all of which are likely to be booked solid during that period. If you do travel to South Africa over the school holidays, book your accommodation well in advance – especially for the national parks.

The longest and busiest holiday period is **Christmas**, which for schools stretches from around December 4 to January 21. Flights and train berths can be hard to get from December 16 to January 2, when many businesses and offices close for their annual break. You should book your flights – long-haul and domestic – as early as six months in advance for the Christmas period. The remaining school holidays cover roughly the following periods: Easter; March 20 to April 15; winter; June 20 to July 21; spring; and September 19 to October 7.

SOUTH AFRICAN PUBLIC HOLIDAYS
January 1 New Year's Day
March 21 Human Rights Day
Good Friday
Easter Sunday
Easter Monday
April 27 Freedom Day
May 1 Workers' Day
June 16 Youth Day
August 9 National Women's Day
September 24 Heritage Day
December 16 Day of Reconciliation
Christmas Day
December 26 Day of Goodwill

PHOTOGRAPHY

South Africa is outstandingly photogenic and you won't need to be a professional to get striking photographs. What kind of camera you take depends on how much weight you're prepared to carry around, how much of a tourist you want to look, and whether or not you plan to photograph animals.

Small, compact cameras are handy as you can keep them unobtrusively in your pocket and whip them out for a quick shot. But they're hopeless for wildlife – a nearby lion will end up a furry speck in savannah. Compacts are also potentially dangerous – tales abound of tourists with little cameras sneaking up too close for comfort to big game and ending up hurt.

If you take your photography seriously, you'll probably want a single-lens reflex camera (SLR) and two or three lenses – a heavy and cumbersome option. For decent wildlife photography you definitely need a **telephoto lens**. A 300mm lens is a good all-rounder: any bigger and you'll need a tripod. The smallest you could get away with for animals is 200mm, while 400mm is the best for birds. All long lenses need fast film, or you'll find you're restricted to the largest apertures, and hence the narrowest depth of focus. If you simply want good snaps from your SLR, think about one well-chosen zoom lens.

PROTECTION

The biggest problem can be **dust**, which tends to penetrate straight into a normal camera case or cloth bag. When travelling in dry, dusty regions, cameras need to be inside sealed plastic bags, or in some dustproof container, and taken out only for the business of taking pictures. You'll need to carry a blower-brush to blow dust off lenses.

Another problem is South Africa's **heat**. Never leave your camera or films lying in the sun. The film in a camera left exposed on a car seat, for instance, will be completely ruined. Keep rolls of film cool in the middle of your clothes or sleeping bag.

LIGHT READING

You really have to rely on a judicious combination of the camera's **light readings** and your own common sense. The contrast between light and shade can be huge, so expose for the subject and not the general scene. This can mean setting your camera to manual, approaching the subject to get a reading and then using that. With a zoom you can zoom in for a reading and then return. Some of the new multi-mode cameras will do much of this for you.

If you're photographing black people, especially in strong light, use more exposure than usual, otherwise they'll be underexposed; the light and your eyes (which are more sophisticated than any camera) can deceive you.

Early morning and late afternoon are the best times for photography. At midday, with the sun overhead, the light is flat and everything is lost in glare.

FILM

Film is readily available in South Africa. Don't let anyone tell you it's unnecessary to have fast film because the sun is so bright in Africa. Even if you opt for a compact with a fast lens (ie one that's very light-sensitive) you'll need at least some 400 ASA film if you want to take pictures at dawn and dusk and in heavy cloud or forest. With long lenses on an SLR, fast film is essential.

SUBJECTS AND PEOPLE

Photographing animals is a question of patience and resisting taking endless pictures of nothing happening. If you can't get close enough, don't waste your film. While taking photos, try keeping both eyes open and, in a vehicle, always turn off your engine.

You should always ask before taking photographs of **people** or, for example, of a dwelling decorated with colourful paintings. Some kind of interaction and exchange is customarily implied: people often ask for a copy of the photograph and you'll end up with several names and addresses and a list of promises.

SPECTATOR SPORTS

South Africa is a sports-fanatical nation, where devotion has been heightened by the re-entrance of the national teams into international competitions since the lifting of the sports boycott. The big spectator sports are soccer, rugby and cricket, with racing also a firm favourite and, since the 1996 Olympics, athletics too.

Soccer is the country's most popular game, with a primarily black and coloured following, and it is only now starting to attract the kind of serious money that could soon see South Africa as one of the world's top soccer nations. The professional season runs from August to May, with teams competing in the **Premier Soccer League** (PSL). A new knockout competition with big prize money called the Rothman's Cup was also announced in May 1997. Unlike rugby teams, soccer teams do not own their own grounds and are forced to rent them for specific fixtures. In most places, there is only one choice of ground so it does not make much difference to the fans, but in Gauteng, the heartland of South African soccer, all the big clubs have to use the same grounds, which has prevented the development of the kind of terrace fan culture you find elsewhere. Nonetheless, soccer crowds are generally witty and good-spirited, perhaps because alcohol is banned, though violence is now on the increase at Gauteng games. A remarkable feature of South African soccer games is the absence of police, as the clubs themselves provide the security. The two big club names in South African soccer are undoubtedly the **Kaiser Chiefs** and the **Orlando Pirates**. They are both Sowetan clubs, but have a nationwide following, and their derbies are the highlight of the PSL's fixture list. Games are played on weekday evenings (usually at 7.30pm or 8.30pm) and at 3pm on Saturdays, and cost about R15. The national squad, nicknamed **Bafana Bafana** ("our lads") hit African soccer by storm in 1996 when it won the African Cup of Nations, and seem likely to follow this up with an appearance at the next World Cup. They play typically South African soccer – imaginative and strong on spec-

tacular athletic feats that have the crowd cheering, but a tendency to run out of energy in the second half and thus risk throwing the game away. Even games they should win have that element of unpredictability that makes for great spectator sport.

Rugby is hugely popular with whites, especially Afrikaners, though the South African **Springboks'** victory in the 1995 World Cup greatly broadened the game's appeal. The competition attracted fanatical attention nationwide, particularly when President Nelson Mandela donned a springbok jersey (long associated exclusively with whites) when he presented the cup to the winning side. Although the national rugby administration has been slow to capitalize on this opportunity to turn the sport into a truly national game, the fact remains that South Africa is extraordinarily good at rugby, and that you are likely to witness high-quality, if brutal play when you watch either provincial or international games. The main provincial competition is the **Curry Cup**, with games played from March to October, almost always on Saturdays at around 3.30pm. Admission is between R20 and R40. International games are played throughout the year and are invariably popular, so you will need to get tickets well in advance.

Cricket is dominated by the one-day game, at which the country excels, with longer matches reserved almost exclusively for the international level. The provincial season runs from October to April, and the main competition is the **Standard Bank Cup**. Games are played throughout the week, and admission is around R25 for standing and R35 for a seat. There are now so many international games that attendances have started to fall, and cricket administrators may start cutting back. Nonetheless, you stand a good chance of being around for an international test or one-day series if you are in the country for a month or more. South African cricket teams have historically been almost solidly white, but a few coloureds are now playing. Attempts to promote the game in black townships have now begun, though it will be some time before they bear fruit.

ACTIVITIES AND OUTDOOR PURSUITS

South Africa's diverse landscape of mountains, forests, rugged coast and sandy beaches, as well as miles of veld and game-trampled national parks, make this supreme outdoor terrain, a fact that hasn't been missed by the South Africans themselves, who have been playing in the outdoors for decades. The result is a well-developed infrastructure for activities, an impressive national network of hiking trails and plenty of commercial operators selling adventure sports.

HIKING TRAILS

Over the past twenty years **hiking** has taken off in a big way in South Africa, and this country has the most comprehensive system of footpaths in Africa (inspired by the US Appalachian Hiking Trail).

Wherever you are – even in the middle of Johannesburg – you won't be far from some sort of trail. The best ones are in wilderness areas, where you'll find waymarked paths that vary from half-hour strolls to major hiking expeditions of two to seven days that take you right into the heart of some of the most beautiful parts of the country. Overnight hiking trails are normally well laid out, with painted footprints or other markers to indicate the route and campsites or huts along the way (but you need to carry all your own equipment). Numbers are limited on most, and many trails are so popular that they become booked up many months in advance, so it's worth arranging these beforehand – although you can often find a place by just turning up and hoping for a cancellation. If you want to do a fair amount of walking but don't want to launch out on a long expedition, consider basing yourself in one of the wilderness

areas such as the **Drakensberg**, where you can stay in chalets and set off on a series of day walks, returning each night.

Unique to Africa are **guided wilderness trails**, where you walk in game country (such as the Kruger National Park), accompanied by an armed guide. These walks should be regarded as a way to get a feel for the wild rather than actually see any wildlife, as you'll encounter far fewer animals on foot than from a vehicle. Specialist trails include mountain biking, canoeing, horseback trails and camel trails. A handful of trails have also been set up specifically for people with disabilities, mostly for the visually impaired or people confined to wheelchairs.

WATERSPORTS

Don't expect balmy Mediterranean seas in South Africa: of its 2500km of coastline, only the stretch along the Indian Ocean seaboard of KwaZulu-Natal can be considered tropical, and along the entire coast an energetic surf pounds the shore. In **Cape Town**, sea bathing is only comfortable between November and March. Generally, the further east you go from here the warmer the water becomes and the longer the bathing season. Sea temperatures that rarely drop below 18°C make the **KwaZulu-Natal** coast warm enough for a dip at any time of year. A word of warning: dangerous undertows and riptides are present along the coast and you should try to bathe where lifeguards are present. Failing that (and guards aren't that common away from main resorts out of season) you should follow local advice and always treat the ocean with respect.

The pumping surf is of course precisely what makes South Africa among the world's finest

---

TRAIL BOOKS

Numerous books exist covering hikes in specific regions of South Africa, but these two general guides are extremely useful.

Jaynee Levy *The Complete Guide to Walks & Trails in Southern Africa* (Struik). Levy was important in helping establish the system of trails, and this is the most comprehensive guide to the region as a whole, with all the basic information and contact addresses you'll need to trail anywhere in the subcontinent.

Willie and Sandra Olivier *Hiking Trails of Southern Africa* (Southern). Covers less ground than Levy, dealing with only the 44 most important trails, but writes them up with greater depth and gives excellent natural history commentary on each trail.

spots for **surfing**. The country's perfect wave at **Jeffrey's Bay** was immortalized on celluloid in the 1960s cult movie *Endless Summer*, but any surfer will tell you that there are equal, if not better, breaks all the way along the coast from the Namibian to the Mozambique border. Surfers can be a cliquey bunch, but the South African community has a reputation for being among the friendliest in the world and, provided you pay your dues, you should find yourself easily accepted. Some of the world's top shapers work here and you can pick up an excellent board at a fraction of European or American prices. If you can face the humiliation of being regarded by the pro-surfers as a "tea bag" or "doormat", boogie-boarding and body-surfing make easy alternatives to the real thing, require less skill or dedication and are great fun. **Windsurfing** (or sailboarding) is another popular sport you'll find at many resorts, where you'll be able to rent gear.

Scuba diving is a recreation that's growing in popularity and South Africa is one of the cheapest places in the world to get an internationally recognized open-water certificate that will allow you to dive anywhere in the world, with courses at all the coastal cities as well as a number of other resorts. The most rewarding diving is along the St Lucia Marine Reserve in northern KwaZulu-Natal coast, where 100,000 dives go under every year for its coral reefs and fluorescent fish. You won't find corals and bright colours along the Cape coast, but the huge number of sunken vessels makes wreck-diving popular and you can encounter the swaying rhythms of giant kelp forests.

KwaZulu-Natal is also good for **snorkelling** and there are some underwater trails elsewhere in the country, most notable of which is in the Tsitsikamma National Park.

Fishing is another well-developed South African activity and the coasts yield 250 species caught through rock, bay or surf angling. The confluence of the warm Indian and cooler Atlantic east of the Cape Peninsula, brings one of the highest concentrations of game fish in the world, including longfin, tunny and marlin. Inland you'll find plenty of rivers and dams stocked with freshwater fish, while trout fishing is extremely well-

established in Mpumalanga, the northern sections of the Eastern Cape and the KwaZulu-Natal Midlands.

If you want to find out how it feels to be bait, there are a couple of places along the southern Cape and Garden Route where you can go on **shark-cage dives** and come face to face with deadly great whites.

On inland waterways, South African holiday-makers are keen **speedboaters**, an activity that goes hand in hand with **waterskiing**. **Kayaking** and **canoeing** are also very popular and you can often rent craft at resorts or national parks that lie along rivers. For the more adventurous, there's **white-water rafting**, with some decent trips along the Tugela River in KwaZulu-Natal and on the Orange River.

OTHER ACTIVITIES

There are ample opportunities for aerial activities in South Africa. In the Winelands you can go **ballooning**; and **paragliding** offers a thrilling way to see Cape Town, by diving off Lion's Head and riding the thermals. More down-to-earth options include **mountaineering** and **rock climbing**, both of which have a huge following in South Africa. If you decide to go **skiing** at one or two resorts in the Eastern and Western Cape, you'll be able to go home with a quirky experience of Africa. And finally, if you can't choose between being airborne or earthbound, you can always bounce between the two by **bungee jumping** off the Gouritz River Bridge near Mossel Bay.

Horse-riding is a sport you'll find at virtually every resort, whether inland or along the coast, for two hours or two days. You can ride in the Drakensberg from the Natal parks, or go pony trekking for several days in Lesotho. Take your own hat, as not everyone provides them. **Bird-watching** is another activity you can do almost anywhere, either casually on your own, or as part of a guided trip with one of the several experts operating in South Africa. Among the very best bird-watching spots are Mkuzi and Ndumo game reserves in KwaZulu-Natal. **Golf** lovers will have a fabulous time in South Africa as courses are prolific and are frequently in stunningly beautiful locations.

TROUBLE AND THE POLICE

Despite horror stories of sky-high crime rates, most people visit South Africa without incident. This is not to minimize the problem – crime is probably the most serious difficulty facing the country and it is unacceptably high by any standards. However, once you realize that crime follows demographic patterns, the scale becomes less terrifying. The greatest proportion of violent crime takes place in the poorer areas – predominantly townships – and in Johannesburg, where the dangers are the worst in the country. Be careful, but don't be paranoid.

While levels of crime in major centres outside Gauteng, such as Port Elizabeth, Cape Town or Durban, are probably higher than (say) the metropolitan United States, many other areas such as the Garden Route are safer than most places in the world. Outside city centres and major tourist venues, **police presence** is almost non-existent, and the police have a rather poor image. It's best to rely on your own resources. This is exactly what many middle-class people now do, by subscribing to the services of armed, **private security firms** to protect their property. Protecting property and "security" are major national obsessions, and it's difficult to imagine what many South Africans would discuss at their dinner parties if the problem disappeared. The other obvious manifestation of this obsession is the huge number of alarms, bars, high walls and electronically controlled gates you'll find, not just in the suburbs, but even in less deprived areas of some townships.

SAFETY TIPS

In general

- Try not to look like a tourist.
- Dress down.
- Don't carry a camera or video openly visible in cities.
- Avoid wearing jewellery or expensive watches.
- Leave your expensive designer shades at home – they are sometimes pulled off people's faces.
- Remain calm and co-operative if you are robbed.

On foot

- Grasp bags firmly under your arm.
- Don't carry excessive sums of money on you (but have enough to satisfy a mugger).
- Don't put your wallet in your back trouser pocket.
- Always know where your valuables are.
- Don't leave valuables exposed (on a seat or the ground) while having a meal or drink.
- Develop an awareness of what people in the street around you are doing.
- Don't let anyone get too close to you – especially people in groups.
- In big cities, travel around in pairs or groups.

On the beach

- Take only the bare essentials to the beach.
- Don't leave valuables, especially cameras, unattended.
- Some people pin car keys to their swimming gear, or you can put them in a waterproof wallet or splash box and take them into the water with you.

On the road

- Lock all your car doors, especially in cities.
- Keep your rear windows sufficiently rolled up to keep out opportunistic hands.
- Never leave anything worth stealing in view when your car is unattended.

At cash machines

Automatic teller machines (ATMs) are favourite hunting grounds for sophisticated conmen who use cunning rather than force to steal money. Never underestimate their ability and don't get drawn into any interaction at an ATM, no matter how well-spoken, friendly or distressed the other person appears. You can avoid trouble by following the pointers below.

- Never help anyone who claims to be having problem with a cash machine – tell them to contact the bank.
- Never accept help from strangers if you have a problem at a cash machine.
- Don't allow people to crowd you while withdrawing money.
- If in doubt, go to another machine.
- Never allow anyone to see you punch in your personal identification number (PIN).
- If your card gets swallowed, report it without delay.

Guns, both licensed and illicit, are an everyday part of life, routinely and openly carried by police. In many high streets you'll spot firearm shops rubbing shoulders with places selling clothes or books; and you'll come across notices asking you to deposit your weapon before entering the premises.

If you fall victim to a **mugging**, you should take very seriously the usual advice not to resist and do as you're told. The chances of this happening can be greatly minimized by using common sense and following a few simple rules (see box). If you're staying in Johannesburg, it pays to be extra alert; for specific guidelines, see our box on p.452.

POLICE

For many black South Africans, the **South African Police** (SAP) still carry strong associations of collaboration with apartheid and a lot of public relations work has yet to be done to turn the police into a genuine people's law enforcement agency. Poorly paid, shot at (and frequently hit), underfunded, badly equipped, barely respected and demoralized, the police keep a low profile. If you ever get stopped, at a roadblock for example (one of the likeliest encounters), always be courteous. And remember that under South African law you are required to carry your driver's licence at all times. If you are robbed, don't expect too much crime-cracking enthusiasm (and don't expect to get back your property), but you will need to report the incident to the police, who should give you a case reference for insurance purposes.

DRUGS, DRINKING AND DRIVING

Dagga (cannabis in dried leaf form) is South Africa's most widely produced and widely used drug. The quality is generally good, but this doesn't alter the fact that it is illegal. Grown in hot regions like Natal (the source of Durban poison),

Swaziland (Swazi Gold) and as a cash crop in parts of the Transkei, it is fairly easily available, but you should take particular care when scoring as people have run into trouble dealing with unfamilar local conditions. Otherwise, if you're reasonably discreet you should encounter no problems. Rave culture is big in South Africa, and together with **ecstasy** is principally a white, middle-class thing.

Strangely, for a country that sometimes seems to be on one massive binge, South Africa has laws that prohibit **drinking** in public – not that anyone pays any attention to them. The **drink-drive laws** are also routinely and brazenly flouted, making the country's roads the one real danger you should be concerned about. Levels of alcohol consumption go some way to explaining why during the Christmas holidays over a thousand people die in an annual orgy of carnage on the roads. People routinely stock up their cars with booze for long journeys and even at filling stations you'll find places selling liquor.

WOMEN AND SEXUAL HARASSMENT

South Africa's extremely high incidence of **rape** doesn't as a rule affect tourists. In fact you're very unlikely to need to fend off the unwanted attentions of men. However, women should avoid travelling on their own, nor should they hitchhike or walk alone in deserted areas. This applies equally to cities, the countryside or anywhere after dark. Minibus taxis should be ruled out as a means of transport after dark, especially if you're not exactly sure of local geography. **Sexual harassment** is rare, but you should nevertheless walk assertively in crowded areas such as minibus taxi termini in big cities. At heart the majority of the country's males, regardless of race, hold on to fairly sexist attitudes. Sometimes your eagerness to be friendly may be taken as a sexual overture – always be sensitive to potential crossed wires and unintended signals.

TRAVELLERS WITH DISABILITIES

Facilities for disabled travellers in South Africa are not as sophisticated as you'd get in the First World, but overall they are sufficient to ensure you have a satisfactory visit.

By accident, rather than design, you'll find pretty good accessibility to many buildings, as South Africans tend to build low (single-storey bungalows are the norm), with the result that you'll have to deal with fewer stairs than you may be accustomed to. Because the car is king, you'll frequently find that you can drive to, and park right outside, your destination.

A growing number of popular tourist attractions are being designed to facilitate **disabled access**. For example, the Kirstenbosch Botanical Gardens in Cape Town have Braille and wheelchair trails, while trails aimed specifically at disabled travellers are on offer at Kamberg Nature Reserve in the Drakensberg and in the Karoo National Park. The longest trail so far is a six-kilometre walk with a tapping rail and guide ropes in the Palmiet Nature Reserve in Durban. Cape Town's Waterfront, one of the top national attractions, has specially designed parking bays as well as ramps and broad walkways around the development itself. Sun City in Northwest Province, as well as a growing number of national parks, is also disability-friendly.

PLANNING A HOLIDAY

There are **organized tours** and holidays specifically for people with disabilities – the contacts in the box below will be able to put you in touch with specialists for trips to South Africa. If you want to be more independent, it's important to become an authority on where you must be self-reliant and where you can expect help, especially regarding transport and accommodation. It is also vital to be honest – to know your limitations and make sure others know them. If you do not use a wheelchair all the time but your walking capabilities are limited, remember that you are likely to need to cover greater distances while travelling (often over rougher terrain and in hotter temperatures) than you are used to. If you do use a wheelchair, have it serviced before you go and take a repair kit with you.

Read your **travel insurance** small print carefully to make sure that people with a pre-existing medical condition are not excluded. *Tripscope* (see box below) can provide a current list of appropriate insurers. Use your travel agent to make your journey as straightforward as possible; airline or bus companies can cope better if they are expecting you, with a wheelchair provided at airports and staff primed to help. A **medical certificate** of your fitness to travel, provided by your doctor, is also extremely useful, and some airlines or insurance companies may insist on it. Make sure you have extra supplies of drugs – carried with you if you fly – and a prescription including the generic name in case of emergency. Carry spares of any clothing or equipment that might be hard to find; if there's an association representing

people with your disability, contact them early in the planning process.

TRANSPORT

All the major **airlines** flying to South Africa can provide assistance for disabled passengers, but you should give them notice of your needs when booking. As far as domestic air travel is concerned, *South African Airways* provides passenger aid units at all principal airports.

Car rental of automatics with hand controls can be arranged for no extra charge through *Avis* or *Budget* (see p.30) at all the major centres, but a month's prior notice is recommended. Many garages along the main routes, especially along the N1 between Johannesburg and Cape Town, have wheelchair-accessible **toilets**. A Special Parking Disc, which allows **parking** concessions

BEFORE YOU LEAVE: USEFUL ORGANIZATIONS

UK

Access Travel, 16 Haweswater Ave, Astley, Lancashire M29 7BL (☎01942/888844). *Tour operator that can arrange flights, transfer and accommodation. This is a small business: staff personally check out places before recommendation and can provide first-hand impressions on conditions in South Africa, guarantee accommodation standards and recommend suitable places to stay on game farms as well as other places of interest. ATOL bonded, established five years.*

Holiday Care Service, 2nd Floor, Imperial Building, Victoria Rd, Horley, Surrey RH6 7PZ (☎01293/774535). *Provides free lists of accessible accommodation abroad – European, American and long-haul destinations – plus a list of accessible attractions in the UK. Information on financial help for holidays available.*

RADAR (*Royal Association for Disability and Rehabilitation*), 12 City Forum, 250 City Rd, London EC1V 8AF (☎0171/250 3222; Minicom ☎0171/250 4119). *Produce an annual holiday guide for long-haul destinations including South Africa, but information tends to be rather basic (£5 inc. p&p).*

Tripscope, The Courtyard, Evelyn Rd, London W4 5JL (☎0181/994 9294). *Registered charity providing a national telephone information service offering useful advice for first-time disabled air travellers, and they can provide an up-to-date list*

of insurers offering appropriate policies for your needs.

NORTH AMERICA

Directions Unlimited, 720 N Bedford Rd, Bedford Hills, NY 10507 (☎914/241-1700). *Travel agency specializing in custom tours for people with disabilities.*

Mobility International USA, PO Box 10767, Eugene, OR 97440 (Voice and TDD ☎541/343-1284). *Information and referral services, access guides, tours and exchange programmes. Annual membership US$25 (includes quarterly newsletter).*

Society for the Advancement of Travel for the Handicapped (*SATH*), 347 5th Ave, Suite 610, New York, NY 10016 (☎212/447-7284; http://www.sittravel.com/). *Non-profit travel-industry referral service that passes queries onto its members as appropriate – allow plenty of time for a response.*

Travel Information Service (☎215/456-9600). *Telephone information and referral service.*

Twin Peaks Press, Box 129, Vancouver, WA 98666 (☎360/694-2462 or 1-800/637-2256). *Publisher of the Directory of Travel Agencies for the Disabled* (US$19.95), *listing more than 370 agencies worldwide; Travel for the Disabled* (US$19.95); *the Directory of Accessible Van Rentals* (US$9.95) *and Wheelchair Vagabond* (US$14.95), *loaded with personal tips.*

to people with severe mobility impairment, can be obtained for the Johannesburg area through the *Independent Living Centre* (see box, p.54) and for elsewhere in the country through the local traffic department. You should bring any appropriate disc or badge from your home country, which can be used to get a temporary disc.

ACCOMMODATION

South Africa has a growing number of **hotels** with facilities for disabled people. The *South African Tourism Board* publishes an accommodation guide, available from all their offices (see p.23), which includes up-to-date information about disability-friendly establishments. In the national parks, specially adapted huts are available in the Kruger and Karoo national parks. For further details of facilities in other parks, contact the National Parks Board and Natal Parks Board (see p.54 for addresses).

ACTIVITIES AND TOURS

Activities and tours are opening up for disabled travellers to South Africa, ranging from the relatively sedate to the more energetic. Organized tours offer the possibility for wheelchair-bound visitors to take part in safaris, sport and a vast range of adventure activities, including white-water rafting, horse-riding and parasailing. Tours can either be taken as self-drive trips or group packages.

GAY AND LESBIAN TRAVELLERS

South Africa has the world's first and only gay- and lesbian-friendly constitution, and Africa's most developed and diverse gay and lesbian scene. Not only is homosexuality legal between consenting adults of 18 or over, but the constitution outlaws any discrimination on the grounds of sexual orientation. This means that, for once, you have the law on your side.

Outside the big cities, however, South Africa is a pretty conservative place where open displays of public affection between gay and lesbian people are unlikely to go down well; many whites will find it unchristian, while blacks will think it un-African.

Outright is a bimonthly glossy **magazine** (☎011/648 5032) aimed at gay and lesbian readers (though with an emphasis on men), which features up-to-date information on the club scene, particularly in Johannesburg, advertisements for gay-owned or gay-friendly accommodation and shops, as well as plenty of feature articles. *Gay Pages* is another glossy, which comes out twice a year, and combines features with lots of advertisements. Also worth keeping an eye out for is the newspaper *Exit*, which covers much the same ground.

A useful contact is the **Gay and Lesbian Coalition** (☎021/448 0505), a powerful lobbying organization who also work to advance the interests of black gay and lesbian people. Staff here can let you know about new contact groups currently springing up all over the country.

CAPE TOWN

Cape Town is South Africa's – and indeed, the African continent's – gay capital. The country's only gay **travel agent**, *Gay esCape* (☎021/23 9001; e-mail: gayesc@cis.co.za; home page: http://www.icafe.co.za/gayes), is the quickest and surest way of finding out about the latest developments in the gay scene, both here and throughout South Africa – they can also tell you about *Stepping Out*, a new gay travel directory which hopes to establish itself as a Bible for gay travellers to South Africa.

Getting to know Cape Town's lively gay scene, with its clubs, cafés and restaurants, is made easy by consulting *Gay esCape*'s helpful little map to gay Cape Town. The city hosts an annual **drag ball**, a hugely popular event currently dubbed the "Twinkly Sea" after the underwater-themed party of 1995. Up until now the ball has been held in December, but the date may change to early January, so contact *Gay esCape* for the latest information. While in town, be sure to tune into Bush Radio's (89.5FM) gay programme, called **In the Pink**, every Thursday between 8.30pm and 9.30pm. To contact Cape Town's 24-hour **Gay Helpline**, phone ☎021/21 5420. Like much else in the city, Cape Town's gay scene is white-dominated, though gay clubs are starting to emerge in the surroundings townships too.

JOHANNESBURG AND PRETORIA

The gay scene is a lot more multiracial in **Johannesburg**, especially in the clubs. Useful contacts here include *Glow* (Gay and Lesbian Organization of the Witwatersrand, 3–9pm; ☎011/336 5081 or 648 5873) and the *Lesbian Forum* (☎011/336 5081). *Activate* (☎011/725 6710) is Gauteng's gay and lesbian information and support centre, while *Nkateko* (☎011/939 1190) is a new group working for black lesbian and gay empowerment. If you are near Johannesburg in September, make sure you are there for the **annual pride parade** through the streets of the city.

The **Pretoria** gay and lesbian scene has grown enormously over the past few years. *Glop* (Gay and Lesbian Organization of Pretoria, Tues–Fri 7–10pm; ☎012/46 9888) has put together a very handy map showing places to go, and is a useful contact once you're in the city.

AIDS INFORMATION AND COUNSELLING CENTRE BRANCHES	
Bloemfontein	☎051/405 8544
Cape Town	☎021/400 3400
Durban	☎031/300 3104
East London	☎0431/34 2382
Johannesburg	☎011/725 6710
Kimberley	☎0531/80 6212
Klerksdorp	☎0184/62 2151
Nelspruit	☎0131/159 2167
Pietermaritzburg	☎0331/42 7031
Pietersburg	☎0152/91 4962
Port Elizabeth	☎041/506 1415
Pretoria	☎012/313 7988

DIRECTORY

AIRPORT TAX An arrival tax of R60 is included in your international air fare, while R39 is added to the price of tickets for flights to other countries in southern Africa and R17 for domestic flights.

BARGAINING Haggling at markets and with street traders isn't a part of South African shopping culture. Most marketeers are trying to earn an honest living and are generally not trying to rip you off, so bargaining just isn't expected.

BEGGING The coexistence of poverty and wealth in close proximity, and the absence of a social security safety net, make begging a widespread and inevitable phenomenon in South Africa. What you do when confronted by someone asking for money (or even food) is a sticky matter of conscience, but giving to every beggar you encounter is simply not a workable possibility. Your choices are to not give at all, to give selectively, or to make a donation to one of the recognized charities that is trying to alleviate the worst consequences of deprivation – the way many middle-class South Africans salve their consciences. An extension of begging is people offering services you may not have asked for. Common examples are self-appointed car attendants who hang around parking places, direct you into your parking bay and offer to look after your vehicle while you're away – essentially an offer you can't refuse. Agree to pay when you return (around R3–5 should do the trick) provided they've done their job. Offers to clean your car are also very common (R10 is standard).

CONTRACEPTION Despite a serious AIDS problem, South Africa is remarkably coy about contraception and you shouldn't expect to find condoms anywhere other than in pharmacies. As far as the pill goes, this can also be bought through a pharmacy, but only with a doctor's prescription. The safest option is to bring your own supply.

ELECTRICITY Electricity runs on 220/230V, 50Hz AC and sockets take round-pinned plugs. Most hotel rooms have sockets that will take 110V electric razors, but for other appliances US visitors will need a transformer.

EMERGENCIES Police ☎10111, Ambulance ☎10177.

KIDS On the whole South Africa is more child-friendly than Britain and the country has developed a holiday infrastructure for self-driving local families. You'll find family rooms at many lower- to middle-range hotels and motels and the national parks often have rooms with bunks in them. However, you may hit problems if you try to go to any of the upmarket hotels or private game lodges, which frequently exclude children under 12.

LAUNDRIES Most towns have self-operated launderettes where for a reasonable sum you can also often have a serviced wash which can include ironing.

TAX Value-added tax (VAT) of fourteen percent is levied on most goods and services, though it's usually already included in any quoted price. Foreign visitors can claim back VAT on any goods over R250. To do this you must present the tax invoice and your passport at the airport just before you fly out.

TIME There is only one time zone, two hours ahead of GMT, throughout the region. If you're flying from anywhere in Europe you shouldn't experience any jet lag, as you'll be travelling virtually due south, which won't mess with your body clock.

TIPPING Ten to fifteen percent of the tab is the normal tip at restaurants and for taxis – but don't feel obliged if the service has been shoddy. Keep in mind that many of the people who'll be serving you will be black South Africans, who rely on tips to supplement a meagre wage on which they support huge extended families. When in doubt, err on the side of generosity, as gratuities are seldom unwelcome. Porters at hotels normally get about R3 per bag. There are no self-service garages in South Africa; someone will always be on hand to fill your vehicle and clean your windscreen, for which you should tip around R3–5. It is also usual at hotels to leave some money for the person who services your room. Many establishments, especially private game lodges, take (voluntary) communal tips when you check out – by far the fairest system, which ensures that all the low-profile staff behind the scenes get their share.

WEIGHTS AND MEASURES South Africa is fully metricated, and kilometres, grammes, kilogrammes, litres and degrees Celsius are the norm. Shoe sizes follow the British system.

METRIC CONVERSION TABLE

1 centimetre (cm) = 0.394in	1 inch (in) = 2.54cm	1 foot (ft) = 30.48cm
1 metre (m) = 100cm	1 metre = 39.37in	1 yard (yd) = 0.91m
1 kilometre (km) = 1000m	1 kilometre = 0.621 miles	1 mile = 1610m
1 hectare = 10,000 square metres	1 hectare = 2.471 acres	1 acre = 0.4 hectares
1 litre = 0.22 UK gal	1 UK gallon (gal) = 4.55 litres	
1 litre = 0.26 US gal	1 US gallon (gal) = 5.46 litres	
1 gramme (g) = 0.035oz	1 ounce (oz) = 28.57 g	
1 kilogramme (kg) = 1000g	1 kilogramme = 2.2lb	1 pound (lb) = 454g

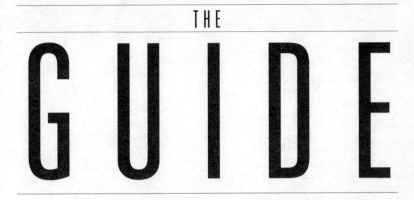

PART TWO

THE

GUIDE

CHAPTER ONE

CAPE TOWN AND THE PENINSULA

CAPE TOWN is southern Africa's most beautiful, most romantic and most-visited city. Indeed, few urban centres anywhere can match its setting along the **Cape Peninsula** spine, which slides like the mighty tail of the continent into the Atlantic Ocean. By far the most striking – and famous – of its sights is **Table Mountain**, frequently mantled by clouds, and rearing up from the middle of the city to provide a constantly changing vista to the suburbs below.

More than a scenic backdrop, Table Mountain is the solid core of Cape Town, dividing the city into distinct zones with public gardens, wilderness, forests, hiking routes, vineyards and desirable residential areas trailing down its lower slopes. Standing on the tabletop, you can look north for a giddy view of the **city centre**, its docks filled with matchbox ships. Looking west, beyond the mountainous Twelve Apostles, the drop is sheer and your eye will sweep across Africa's priciest real estate, clinging to the slopes along the chilly Atlantic seaboard. Turning south, beyond the leafy middle-class suburbs of Newlands and Constantia, lies the warmer but more distant **False Bay seaboard**, which curves around before fading off to **Cape Point**. Finally, relegated to the grim industrial east, are the coloured **townships** and black **ghettos**, spluttering in winter under the smoky pall of coal fires – your stark introduction to Cape Town when driving in.

To enjoy Cape Town you need to spend time **outdoors**, as Capetonians do, often choosing mountain bikes in preference to cars and turning **adventure activities** into an obsession. Sailboarders from around the world head for Table Bay for some of the world's best windsurfing, and the brave (or unhinged) jump off Lion's Head and paraglide down close to the Clifton beachfront. But the city offers sedate pleasures as well, along its hundreds of hiking trails and 150km of beaches, as well as in its marvellous botanical gardens and wine estates.

Cape Town's rich urban texture is immediately apparent in the **diverse architecture**: indigenous Cape Dutch architecture, rooted in the Netherlands, finds its apotheosis in the Constantia wine estates, which were themselves brought to new heights by French refugees in the seventeenth century; Muslim slaves, freed in the nineteenth century, added their minarets to the skyline; and the English who invaded, and freed these slaves, introduced their Georgian and Victorian building styles. In the tightly packed terraces of twentieth-century Bo-Kaap and the tenements of District Six, coloured descendants of slaves evolved a unique brand of jazz, which is still played in the Cape Flats and some city-centre clubs.

Sadly, when most travellers expound the unarguable delights of Cape Town, they are referring only to genteel Cape Town – the formerly whites-only areas. The harsh reality for most Capetonians is one of crowded **shantytowns**, sky-high murder rates, taxi wars, racketeering and gangland terror. In 1996 a further element was added when the Muslim fundamentalist group PAGAD (People Against Gangsterism and Drugs) took the law into their own hands, lynched a leading drugs baron and declared a jihad

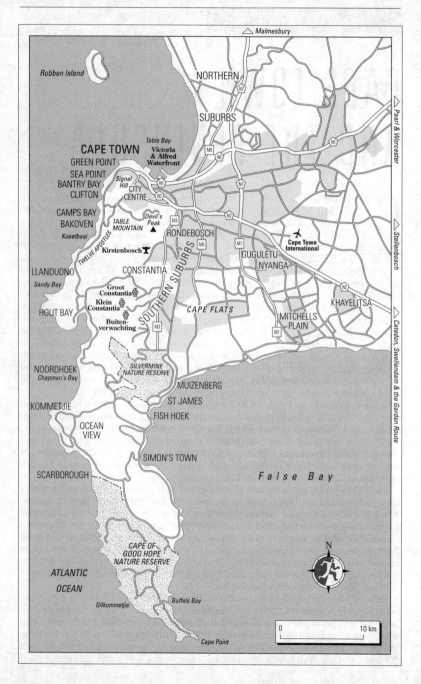

ACCOMMODATION PRICE CODES

All the accommodation listed in the Guide has been categorized into one of seven price bands, as set out below. The rates quoted, unless otherwise stated, represent the most expensive per-person rate for a double or single room outside high season (Dec–Jan), except for category ①, which are per-person rates for a dorm bed in backpacker accommodation, or a campsite. For more accommodation details, see p.31.

① R0–50	② R50–100	③ R100–150
④ R150–200	⑤ R200–250	⑥ R250–300
	⑦ Over R300	

against the gangs. While the gangs tend to restrict their activities to the Cape Flats townships, crime is nonetheless a problem in central Cape Town, but it's a risk you can minimize by taking a few simple precautions (see Basics, p.52).

Some history

San hunter-gatherers, South Africa's first human inhabitants, moved freely through the Cape Peninsula for tens of millennia before being edged into the interior some 2000 years ago by the arrival of sheep-herding **Khoikhoi** migrants from the north. Over the next 1600 years the Khoikhoi held sway over the Cape pastures. **Portuguese** mariners, in search of a stopoff point en route to East Africa and the East Indies, first rounded the Cape in the 1480s, and named it "Cabo de Boa Esperanza" ("Cape of Good Hope"), but their attempts at trading with the Khoikhoi were short-lived, and no Europeans seriously attempted to create a permanent stopping-off point until the **Dutch East India Company** (VOC) cruised into Table Bay in 1652 and set up shop.

The VOC, the world's largest corporation at the time, planned little more at the Cape than a halfway stop to provide fresh produce to their ships travelling between Europe and the East in search of spices, slaves and profit. Their small landing party, led by **Jan Van Riebeeck**, built a mud fort where the Grand Parade now stands and established **vegetable gardens**, which they hoped to work with Khoikhoi labour.

The Khoikhoi were understandably reluctant to exchange their perfectly satisfactory lives for the restrictions of formal employment, so van Riebeeck began to import **slaves** in 1658. The growth of the Dutch settlement alarmed the Khoikhoi, who declared war in 1659 to drive the Europeans out, but were defeated and had to cede the Peninsula to the colonists.

During the early eighteenth century, Western Cape Khoikhoi society disintegrated, **German** and **French** religious refugees swelled the European population, and slavery became the economic backbone of the colony, which was now a minor colonial village of canals and low, whitewashed, flat-roofed houses. By 1750, Cape Town had become a town of over 1000 buildings, with 2500 inhabitants.

In 1795, **Britain**, deeply concerned by Napoleonic expansionism, grabbed Cape Town to secure the strategic sea route to the East. This was not welcomed by the settlement's Calvinist Dutch burghers, but was better news for the substantially Muslim slave population, as Britain ordered the **abolition of slavery** and allowed **freedom of religion**. It wasn't long before South Africa's first mosque, built by freed slaves, shot up in Dorp Street in the Bo-Kaap.

By the turn of the nineteenth century, Cape Town had become one of the most cosmopolitan places anywhere and a sea port of major significance, growing under the influence of the British Empire. The Commercial Exchange went up in 1819, followed by department stores, banks and insurance company buildings. In the 1860s the docks were begun, Victoria Road from the city to Sea Point was built, and the suburban railway line to Wynberg was laid. Since slavery had been abolished, Victorian Cape Town had to be built with **convict labour** recruited from the ranks of Xhosa contract labourers and prisoners transported from the Eastern Cape. Racial segregation wasn't far behind, and an outbreak of bubonic plague in 1901 gave the town council an excuse to establish **Ndabeni**, Cape Town's first black location, near Maitland.

In 1910, Cape Town was drawn into the political centre of the newly federated South Africa (see p.653) when it became the **legislative capital** of the Union. Africans and coloureds, excluded from the cosy deal between Boers and Brits, had to find expression in the workplace, flexing their collective muscle on the docks in 1919, where they formed the mighty **Industrial and Commercial Union** which boasted 200,000 members in its heyday.

Increasing industrialization brought an influx of black workers, who were housed in the locations of **Gugulethu** and **Nyanga**, built in 1945. Three years later, the National Party came to power, promising a fearful white electorate that it would reverse the flow of Africans to the cities. In Cape Town it introduced a policy favouring coloureds for jobs, admitting only African men with work and forbidding the construction of family accommodation for Africans.

Langa township became a stronghold of the **Pan Africanist Congress** (PAC), which organized a peaceful anti-pass demonstration in Cape Town on April 8, 1960. Police fired on the crowd, killing three and wounding many more, and the government declared a state of emergency, and banned anti-apartheid opposition groups, including the PAC and ANC.

In 1966 the notorious **Group Areas Act** was used to uproot whole coloured communities from District Six and to move them to the desolate **Cape Flats**, where rampant gangsterism took vicious root and today remains one of Cape Town's most pressing problems. Compounding the injury, the National Party stripped away coloured representation on the town council in 1972.

Eleven years later, at a huge meeting on the Cape Flats, the extra-parliamentary opposition defied government repression and re-formed as the **United Democratic Front**, heralding a period of intensified struggle to topple apartheid. In 1986 one of the major pillars crumbled when the government was forced to scrap influx control; and blacks began pouring into Cape Town seeking work and erecting shantytowns, making Cape Town one of the fastest-growing cities in the world. On February 11, 1990, the city's history took a neat twist, when, just hours after being released from prison, **Nelson Mandela** made his first public speech from the balcony of City Hall to a jubilant crowd spilling across the Grand Parade, the very site of the first Dutch fort.

The **telephone code** for Cape Town is ☎021.

Arrival and information

One of the world's great moments of **arrival** is cruising into Table Bay on a luxury liner. For most, however, the approach is much less picturesque – indeed, it can be something of a shock. Whether you come in by air or road, there's small chance of avoiding the grey, industrial sprawl and the miles of squatter camps that line the N2 into town.

The airport

Cape Town International Airport (flight information ☎934 0407) is on the Cape Flats, 22km and half an hour's drive (longer during rush hour: 7–9am & 4–5.30pm) from the city centre. The *Intercape* **shuttle bus** (☎386 4414 at the airport or ☎419 8888 in Cape Town) between the airport and Cape Town station, in the centre of town, costs around R30 each way and operates until the last flight in the evening. *Intercape* has its desk at the domestic terminal; services run from both the international and domestic terminals. There's also the more expensive **airport express bus**, which will take you, by prior arrangement, to any destination in the peninsula. Metered **taxis** rank in reasonable numbers outside both terminals and cost about three times as much as the shuttle bus. Inside the terminals, you'll find the desks of the major **car rental** firms. There are no trains from the airport.

A **bureau de change** is open to co-incide with international arrivals, but exchange rates are more advantageous at banks in the city. The **Captour** desk (daily 7am–5pm) can provide information on accommodation.

Intercity buses and trains
Greyhound (☎418 4312), *Intercape* (☎386 4400) and *Translux* (☎405 3333) inter-city **buses** and mainline **trains** from other provinces all terminate in the centre of town around the interlinked central **Railway Station** and **Golden Acre** shopping complex, at the junction of Strand and Adderley streets. The complex can be a confusing muddle, but you'll find everything you need for your next move within a couple of blocks: tourist information, city buses, taxis and suburban trains.

Information
The most useful place to gather **information** is around the **railway station**, where all transport (trains, buses, airport shuttles and urban transport) terminates and information offices converge. On the Adderley Street side of the station, the **Tourism Gateway** is a complex housing various agencies, and is the base for many tour buses. Here you'll find the useful **Captour** office (Mon–Fri 8am–7pm, Sat 9am–5pm; ☎418 5202 or 418 5214), which operates a comprehensive accommodation booking service and can provide free city maps. Also here is **Satour** (Mon–Thurs 8am–4.30pm, Fri 8am–4pm, Sat 10am–12.30pm; ☎21 6274), helpful for general information about South Africa.

An alternative source of information, especially good for backpackers, is *One World Travellers Space*, 309 Long St (daily 10am–6pm; ☎ & fax 23 0777), in the centre. Although principally a commercial operation making bookings for tours, this is also a place where you'll get sympathetic advice on all backpacker-ish matters. Services include baggage storage, a travellers' notice board, and mail-holding facilities. You can also chill out in their armchairs, watch TV, have a coffee and listen to CDs from their extensive selection of African music.

If you're planning to explore beyond the confines of the city centre, you'll need to invest in a detailed **street atlas**, easily found at most bookshops, including the ubiquitous *CNA* chain. MapStudio's *A to Z Streetmap* is the cheapest and adequate for the centre and most of the suburbs, although it doesn't cover Simon's Town. Specialist guides are worth looking for if you have a particular interest you want to pursue. There are countless **guide books** on walks around Cape Town, hikes up Table Mountain, dive sites, fishing locations, surfing breaks and windsurfing spots. For the best-stocked shelves and nicest atmosphere, head for either of the two *Exclusive Books* stores in the Lower Mall, Cavendish Square, Claremont (☎64 3030), and Victoria Wharf, the Victoria and Alfred Waterfront (☎419 0905). Both are open seven days a week until 9pm (except Sun, when opening is more restricted). You'll also find some useful books on all aspects of South Africa at the second-hand bookshops down Longmarket Street.

City transport

Cape Town's city centre is compact enough to get around on foot. For further afield you'll need public transport, which is better here than anywhere else in South Africa. Around the central suburbs there's a reasonable **bus network** and a regular **train** service cuts

USEFUL BUS SERVICES

CITY BUS TERMINALS

Adderley Street, outside *OK Bazaars* supermarket: buses to Sea Point, Hout Bay and southern suburbs.

Golden Acre Bus Terminus, outside Golden Acre Shopping Centre in Adderley Street: buses to Table Mountain, Camps Bay and Table Bay.

Grand Parade, in Strand Street behind the railway station is the main bus station, where there's an information booth.

Tourism Gateway, outside *Captour* in Adderley Street: buses to Waterfront.

CITY TO:

Sea Point (direct): Golden Acre•Mouille Point•Main Road Sea Point. *Mon–Sat; 13+ per day.*

Camps Bay (circular via Table Mountain): Golden Acre•Adderley St•Wale St •Buitengracht St•Kloofnek Rd•Kloofnek• Camps Bay Drive•Victoria Rd•Main Rd Sea Point•Adderley St•Golden Acre. *Mon–Sun hourly.*

Table Mountain (circular): Golden Acre•Sea Point•Camps Bay•Kloofnek•City. *Mon–Fri half hourly; Sat & Sun hourly.*

Table Mountain: Adderley St•Wale St• Buitengracht St•New Church St•Kloof Nek Rd•Kloof Nek Terminus. *Mon–Sat hourly.*

Kirstenbosch: Adderley St•Hout Bay•World of Birds•Kirstenbosch. *Daily every 2hr.*

Hout Bay: Adderley St•Kirstenbosch•World of Birds•HoutBay. *Daily every 2hr.*

Waterfront: Tourism Gateway•Strand St•Buitengracht St•Waterfront. *Daily every 10min.*

WATERFRONT TO:

City: Waterfront•Tourism Gateway. *Daily every 10min.*

Camps Bay: Waterfront•Sea Point (Queen/ Beach Rds)•Camps Bay•Lower Cable Station•Waterfront. *Daily every 40min.*

Sea Point: Waterfront•Mouille Point•Green Point•Three Anchor Bay •Beach Road Sea

Point. *Mon–Fri every 20min, Sat & Sun every 15min.*

Sea Point via Camps Bay (circular): Waterfront•City (Adderley Street)•Lower Cable Station•Camps Bay•Beach Road Sea Point• Waterfront. *Daily every 40min.*

through the southern suburbs to Muizenberg and from there down the False Bay seaboard to Simon's Town. Transport along the Atlantic coast is poor, with the exception of the inner-city suburbs as far as Sea Point, which are served by frequent buses, and Hout Bay, which is directly linked to the city centre by bus. Cape Town **taxis** range from metered, minibus or Rikkis (small, open-sided, three-wheel vehicles). Taking public transport after dark isn't recommended. Make every effort to take metered taxis at night, and if you're forced to use public transport take sensible precautions, such as travelling in a group (especially women) and avoiding third-class carriages on trains.

If you're planning on staying for more than a few days, it's worth investing in a **Cape Town Card**, which entitles foreign visitors to unlimited travel on all *Golden Arrow* buses and Metro Rail trains in the Peninsula. The pass is available from the Cape Card Information Desk, on the top floor of the Tourism Gateway, 3 Adderley St, and costs R35 for a four-day card and R55 for a seven-day one.

Buses

Within the central area, **buses** are the most convenient way of getting around, especially those serving the Waterfront, Sea Point, Kloof Nek (for the Lower Cable Station) and Camps Bay. There is also a regular but infrequent service to Kirstenbosch, Hout

Bay and *World of Birds*. Don't attempt to catch a bus to the suburbs – take the train, unless you have a penchant for slow journeys in old rigs. All the principal terminals are around Adderley Street and Golden Acre (see box opposite). Tickets are sold on buses by the driver, and if you're planning on using them frequently, consider buying a **Ten-Ride Clip Card**, which will save you money. For timetables, enquire at the *Golden Arrow* booth at the Grand Parade **central bus terminal** or at *Captour*, in Adderley Street, or phone *Golden Arrow* (direct line ☎934 0540 or toll free ☎0801/21 2111).

Taxis, minibus taxis and Rikkis

The term **"taxi"** is no less ambiguous in Cape Town than elsewhere in South Africa: it's used to refer to conventional metered cars, jam-packed minibuses and their more upmarket cousins, Rikkis.

Metered taxis
Metered taxis, regulated by the Cape Town Municipality, don't cruise up and down looking for fares; you'll need to go to the taxi ranks around town, including the Waterfront, the train station and Greenmarket Square. Alternatively, you can phone to be picked up (see "Listings" at the end of the chapter for reliable taxi companies). Taxis must have the driver's name and identification clearly on display and the meter clearly visible. Fares work out at around R5 a kilometre. This is expensive compared to other forms of transport, but worth it at night, when metered taxis are the safest way of getting around.

Minibus taxis
Minibus taxis are cheap, frequent and bomb up and down the main routes at tearaway speeds. As well as the crazed driving, be prepared for the pickpockets who work the taxi ranks. Minibus taxis can be hailed from the street or boarded at the central taxi rank, adjacent to the railway station. Once you've boarded, pay the *guardjie* (assistant), who sits near the driver, and tell him when you want to get off. Fares should be under R2 for most trips. A word of warning: minibus taxi companies throughout South Africa are riven by factions, which from time to time declare war on each other. Ask at your accommodation for the current safety of this mode of transport.

Rikkis
Rikkis are more visitor-friendly versions of minibus taxis, carrying not more than nine passengers, and aimed principally at tourists. They cruise around the centre and can be hailed (if you're lucky enough to spot one), or you can phone for a lift. In Cape Town (7am–6pm; ☎23 4888 or 23 4892) they are restricted to the City Bowl, the Waterfront and the Atlantic seaboard as far as Camps Bay – they don't go into the suburbs. Fares are kept down by picking up and dropping off passengers along the way (between R5 and R15). Rikkis also operate mini-tours to destinations that include Cape Point and Stellenbosch, for which they charge R60–80 an hour for a whole vehicle.

Trains

Cape Town's **train** service (information ☎405 2991) is an efficient, if slightly tatty, urban line which runs through the **southern suburbs**, all the way from the city to Simon's Town. It reaches the False Bay coast at Muizenberg and continues south, sometimes spectacularly close to the ocean. Trains run overground, and there are no signposts on the streets, so you'll have to look at a map or ask around to find the stations. Tickets must be bought in advance at the station. You're best off on a reasonably priced first-class carriage; curiously, there's no second class, and third class is not recommended. A first-class single from Cape Town to Muizenberg works out at a little under R5.

Trains leave every ten minutes at peak times (Mon–Fri 5.30–8am & 3.30–6pm) for the southern suburbs as far as Retreat, and every twenty minutes as far as Fish Hoek. At other times there are one to two trains per hour, until the last one at 10.30pm. All the way to Simon's Town there are one or two trains every hour, the last one leaving at 9.30pm. Rikkis (☎786 2136) meet every Simon's Town train between 6.40am and 6.20pm. The other three lines run from Cape Town to Strand (through the Cape Flats) and to the outlying towns of Stellenbosch and Wellington. Because they run through the Flats, some sections of these are not as safe as the Simon's Town train.

Trains tend to run closely to the published timetable, which can be bought from newsagents or stations.

Driving in Cape Town

The usual precautions for defensive **driving** in South Africa apply, but Cape Town has a few peculiarities all of its own. The unwritten rule of the road on the Peninsula is that minibus taxis have the right of way. Don't mess with them: their vehicles are bigger than yours, they carry handguns and will also routinely run red lights (as will most Capetonians). Don't assume green means safe: pretend you're a pedestrian (look left, look right and left again), then cross if it's safe.

Cape Town's freeways appear to have been conceived by a manic fairground designer. Take care approaching them: the on-ramps frequently feed directly into the fast lane (and Capetonians furiously exceed the 100kph freeway speed limit). Signs on freeways make no concession to outsiders. There's often little warning of branches off to the suburbs, only the final destination of the highway being given. Your best bet is to plan your journey carefully and make sure you know exactly where you're going.

Car and bike rental

There are dozens of **car rental** companies in Cape Town. To find out who's currently operating and to get the best deal, either pick up one of the brochures at the *Captour* office (see "Arrival and information") or look in the *Yellow Pages* telephone directory. Among the cheapest are *Golden Oldies* (☎24 3951) and *Discount Drive Car Hire* (☎439 2078), which rent out older vehicles at up to half the price of the others. For one-way rental (to drive down the Garden Route and fly out of Port Elizabeth), you'll have to rely on one of the bigger companies, which are pricier, but have nationwide offices – such as *Imperial* (☎23 3300) – *Dolphin* (☎toll free 0800/01 1344), *Key* (☎386 2633), or *Avis*, 84 Strand St (☎24 1177).

For **motorbike rental**, *Le Cap Motorcycle Hire*, 3 Carisbrook St (☎23 0823), can provide all the necessary gear as well, while **bicycle**s are available from *Rent 'n' Ride*, Park Road, Mouille Point (☎434 1122), and *Mike Hopkins Cycles*, 133a Bree St (☎23 2527). *Fly bike*, on the corner of Somerset and Chiappini roads, on the outskirts of the city centre (☎21 1328) rents out 70cc and 100cc automatic **scooters** for R120–150 per day including a helmet.

Accommodation

Finding a **place to stay** in Cape Town isn't always easy, especially with the city's growing popularity, and there are few signs that this will change. December to January (the main annual school holidays) is peak season, when many South Africans head for the coast. If you're lucky enough to find anywhere at this time, expect to pay up to twice as much as at other times. The foreign tourist season, too, is progressively stretching and now extends throughout summer from October to March. The only way to guarantee the kind of place you want is to **book ahead**.

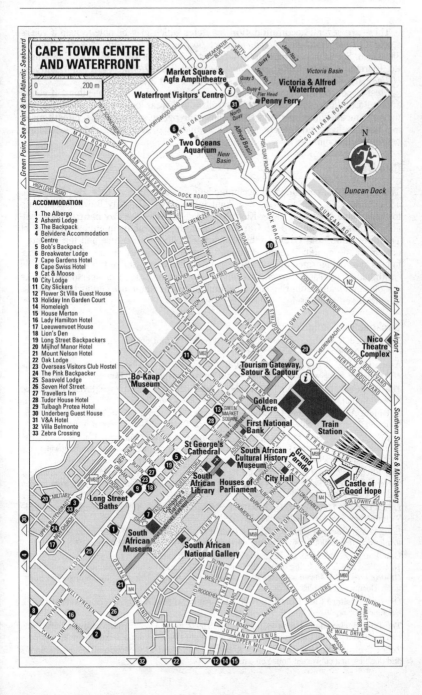

CAPE TOWN CENTRE AND WATERFRONT

0   200 m

Green Point, Sea Point and the Atlantic Seaboard

Market Square &
Agfa Amphitheatre

Waterfront Visitors' Centre

Victoria & Alfred
Waterfront

Penny Ferry

Two Oceans
Aquarium

Duncan Dock

ACCOMMODATION

1 The Albergo
2 Ashanti Lodge
3 The Backpack
4 Belvidere Accommodation
   Centre
5 Bob's Backpack
6 Breakwater Lodge
7 Cape Gardens Hotel
8 Cape Swiss Hotel
9 Cat & Moose
10 City Lodge
11 City Slickers
12 Flower St Villa Guest House
13 Holiday Inn Garden Court
14 Homeleigh
15 House Merton
16 Lady Hamilton Hotel
17 Leeuwenvoet House
18 Lion's Den
19 Long Street Backpackers
20 Mijlhof Manor Hotel
21 Mount Nelson Hotel
22 Oak Lodge
23 Overseas Visitors Club Hostel
24 The Pink Backpacker
25 Saasveld Lodge
26 Seven Hof Street
27 Travellers Inn
28 Tudor House Hotel
29 Tulbagh Protea Hotel
30 Underberg Guest House
31 V&A Hotel
32 Villa Belmonte
33 Zebra Crossing

Bo-Kaap
Museum

Nico
Theatre
Complex

Tourism Gateway,
Satour & Captour

Golden
Acre

First National
Bank

Train
Station

St George's
Cathedral

South African
Cultural History
Museum

Grand
Parade

South
African
Library

Houses of
Parliament

City Hall

Castle of
Good Hope

Long Street
Baths

South
African
Museum

South African
National Gallery

There are several **accommodation agencies** which may be able to help if you're stuck: *Captour Hotel and Accommodation Booking Centre,* 3 Adderley St (Mon–Fri 8am–5pm, Sat 8.30am–1pm, Sun 9am–1pm; ☎418 5214 or 418 5216); *B&B,* 17 Talana Rd, Claremont (☎683 3505); *The Home Accommodation Hotline* (☎75 7130); and *A–Z Holiday Accommodation,* 11 Elgin Rd, Milnerton (☎551 2785).

Most Cape Town accommodation is fairly decent, with a few exceptions. If you're after a B&B, don't expect to be able to stroll around areas looking for somewhere: you must phone ahead, as operators aren't allowed to put up signs. **Hotels, guesthouses** and **backpackers' hostels** are usually clearly indicated, but it's still advisable to phone before heading out.

City Bowl

The greatest concentration of accommodation is around the **City Bowl** and the adjacent seaside strip as far as Sea Point (see below). The City Bowl, creeping up towards Table Mountain, along Kloof Nek Road, includes the **city centre,** the down-at-heel and lively suburb of **Gardens,** and the desirable inner-city suburbs of **Tamboerskloof** and **Oranjezicht,** which are close to the centre and ten minutes' drive over the mountain to the stunning Camps Bay coast. A cluster of backpackers' lodges are concentrated on Long Street in the city centre, and at the lower end of its continuation up Kloof Street. Further up, the sweaty ranks of apartment blocks dissolve into leafier suburbs, and you'll find the pricier and more comfortable **B&Bs, guesthouses** and **hotels**.

Backpackers' lodges

The Albergo, 5 Beckham St, Gardens (☎22 1849, fax 23 0515). Doubles and dorms in this pleasant converted house along a side street, just off the main drag. ①.

Ashanti Lodge, 11 Hof St, Gardens (☎23 8721, fax 23 8790). Well-located lodge, just behind the *Mount Nelson Hotel,* with a nice garden, swimming pool and courtyard. Doubles and dorms. ①.

The Backpack, 74 New Church St, Tamboerskloof (☎23 4530, fax 23 0065). Stylishly decorated house, offering dorms and doubles, with a courtyard and a bar. ①.

Belvidere Accommodation Centre, Higgo Crescent, off Bellevue Rd (☎23 0615). Historic Cape house on the mountainside, convenient for the centre. Dorms and family rooms available. ①.

Cat & Moose, 305 Long St (☎23 5456, fax 23 8210). Most characterful of the Long St lodges, run by interesting and informed Capetonians. There are plans for a plunge pool and climbing wall in the courtyard garden. Doubles ②, dorms ①.

City Slickers, 25 Rose St (☎22 2357, fax 22 2355). Purpose-built, professionally run backpackers' lodge with small lockable double rooms mostly with bunks, 5min from Adderley St. Roof garden with views of Table Mountain. ①.

Lion's Den, 255 Long St (☎ & fax 23 9003). Dorms and doubles on offer at this friendly, respectable Victorian building converted into a lodge. ①.

Long Street Backpackers, 209 Long St (☎23 0615). The oldest Long St backpackers' lodge, in a former apartment block converted into dorms and doubles. Safe, clean and basic. ①.

Oak Lodge, 21 Breda St, Gardens (☎45 6182). More an event than a backpackers' lodge in this 1860s Victorian house being overhauled with dramatic dungeons and dragon murals, and a lively atmosphere. There's even a chance of working off your rent by helping with the ongoing renovations. Dorms and doubles available. ①.

Overseas Visitors Club Hostel, 230 Upper Long St (☎24 6800). Airy high ceilings and dorms with balconies. ①.

The Pink Backpacker, 116 New Church St (☎23 6992, fax 26 1350). Brightly coloured, run-of-the-mill lodge you wouldn't want to wake up to after a night's hard drinking. Dorms only. ①.

Zebra Crossing, 82 New Church St (☎ & fax 22 1265). Standard backpackers' lodge with dorms and doubles, in a converted house on a main road. ①.

Guesthouses and B&Bs

African Sun, 3 Florida Rd, Vredehoek (☎ & fax 461 1601). Secluded, fully equipped self-catering apartment close to the city centre, stylishly furnished with pared-back ethnic decor and own patio garden. Good value, at the bottom of its range. ③.

Ambleside Guesthouse, 11 Forest Rd, Oranjezicht (☎45 2503). Inexpensive, slightly stuffy rooms, some with bath, in a nice part of town. ③.

Flower Street Villa Guest House, 3 Flower St, Oranjezicht (☎45 7517). Spacious rooms in a former nursing home. Rates include breakfast. Triples and doubles (with or without bathroom) ③, quadruples ②.

Homeleigh, 14 Forest Rd, Oranjezicht (☎46 5417). Self-catering flat for four in a quiet street. ③.

House Merton, 12 Forest Rd, Oranjezicht (☎45 6417). Rooms with bath in a comfortable private house. ③.

Leeuwenvoet House, 93 New Church St, Tamboerskloof (☎24 1133, fax 24 0495). Tranquil guesthouse along a main drag with lots of oregon pine and wicker. All rooms have bath. ④.

Saasveld Lodge, 73 Kloof St, Tamboerskloof (☎24 6169, fax 24 5397). Clean but rather impersonal lodge on a noisy thoroughfare, with TV and phone in rooms. Bed-only rate ③.

7 Hof Street, 7 Hof St, Gardens (☎24 4984). Room in a private house in a nice part of town. ③.

Travellers Inn, 208 Long St (☎24 9272, fax 24 9278). Somewhere between a backpackers' lodge and a guesthouse in character, you won't be swinging many cats in their mean-sized rooms. Room-only rate ②.

Underberg Guest House, 6 Tamboerskloof Rd, Tamboerskloof (☎26 2262, fax 24 4059). Centrally located, fairly large guesthouse. ④.

Hotels

Breakwater Lodge, Portswood Rd, Waterfront (☎406 1911, fax 406 1436). Sparklingly clean hotel in the city's old prison building. Excellent value, 5min from the Waterfront. Rooms with bath ③, with shared showers ②. Rate excludes breakfast.

Cape Gardens Hotel, 88 Queen Victoria St, Gardens (☎23 1260, fax 23 2088). Functional hotel bang in the centre, opposite the Botanical Gardens. ④.

Cape Swiss Hotel, corner of Kloof and Camp streets (☎23 8190, fax 26 1975). Three-star comfort in this high-rise hotel on the corner of two main roads, in the middle of fashionable Tamboerskloof. Rate excludes breakfast. ⑤.

City Lodge, corner of Alfred and Dock roads, Waterfront (☎419 9450, fax 419 0460). Rather austere but perfectly adequate hotel in the Waterfront development. ⑤.

Holiday Inn Garden Court, 10 Greenmarket Square (☎23 2040, fax 23 3664). Just what you'd expect from the assembly-line chain, remarkable only for its central setting on the famous Greenmarket Square. Rate excludes breakfast. ⑤.

Lady Hamilton Hotel, Union St, Gardens (☎24 1460, fax 23 7788). Reasonably priced, smart hotel in the central Gardens area. Rate excludes breakfast. ④

Mijlhof Manor Hotel, 5 Military Rd, Tamboerskloof (☎26 1476, fax 22 2046). Fairly decent hotel in a nice area near town. Rate excludes breakfast. ⑤.

Mount Nelson Hotel, 76 Orange St, Gardens (☎23 1000, fax 24 7472). Cape Town's *grande dame*: a fine and famous establishment that takes itself very seriously and overcharges accordingly. Rate excludes breakfast. ⑦.

Tudor House Hotel, 153 Longmarket, Greenmarket Square (☎24 1335, fax 23 1198). Rooms with bath, balconies and cheapo furnishings, overlooking Greenmarket Square. ③.

Tulbagh Protea Hotel, Ryk Tulbagh Square (☎21 5140, fax 21 4648). Centrally situated member of a respectable South African chain, but in a somewhat grim location. ⑥.

V&A Hotel, Pierhead, Waterfront (☎419 6677, fax 419 8955). Squeaky-clean atmosphere, bang in the middle of the Waterfront development. ⑦.

Villa Belmonte, 33 Belmont Ave, Oranjezicht (☎462 1576, fax 462 1579). South Africa's smallest four-star hotel feels like a country lodge in the middle of the city. Wonderful views of the sea and Table Mountain. Rooms are themed and prices vary according to size. Book six months ahead for balcony rooms. ⑥–⑦.

Southern suburbs

The southern suburbs – the formerly whites-only areas closest to the mountain – are convenient for the Simon's Town train line, providing easy access to both the city centre and the False Bay seaboard. Closest to town, **Observatory**, with its narrow streets, tightly packed Victorian cottages and large student population, has a bohemian ambience, and some congenial bars and and restaurants, while the more southerly areas of **Rosebank**, **Claremont**, **Newlands** and **Rondebosch** become greener and more suburban the further from town you go. Poshest of all are the semi-rural areas close to the mountain and along the road to Hout Bay. Of these, **Constantia** is the oldest and most salubrious suburb in Cape Town, boasting functioning wine estates and country-style hotels. Although there is a limited bus service along Hout Bay Main Road, generally you'll need your own transport.

Budget self-catering and backpackers' lodges

Allandale Holiday Cottages, 72 Swaanswyk Rd, Tokai (☎75 3320, fax 72 9744). Sixteen self-catering brick cottages on the slopes of Constantiaberg, right next to Tokai Forest, with a pool and tennis courts. ③.

The Green Elephant, 57 Milton Rd, Observatory (☎ & fax 448 6359). Basic dorms and doubles in a large, vibey house just off Main Rd. The owner leads outdoor expeditions around Cape Town. ①.

The Lodge, 36 Milton Rd, Observatory (☎ & fax 448 6536). Clean, quiet and homely house with a pool; good value for a couple sharing. Dorms ①, doubles ②.

Guesthouses and B&Bs

Bed & Break Ltd, 17 Talana Rd, Claremont (☎683 3503). All rooms with bath in a quiet suburban street, 20min walk from the station and Cavendish Square shops. ②–③.

Gloucester House Bed & Breakfast, 54 Weltevreden Ave, Rondebosch (☎ & fax 689 3894). Conveniently close to Rondebosch station, and all rooms have a bath. ③.

Carmichael House, 11 Wolmunster Rd, Mowbray (☎689 8350, fax 689 8097). Turn-of-the-century house with nice big rooms and a pool, near *Baxter Theatre*. Rooms ③, suites ④.

Constantia Lodge, Duntaw Close, off Rhodes Drive, Constantia (☎794 2410, fax 794 2418). Luxurious and beautifully situated guesthouse, close to Cecilia Forest. ⑥.

Constantia Uitsig, Spaanschemat River Rd, Constantia (☎794 6500, fax 794 7605). Charming cottages on a wine estate. ⑦.

The Coach House, 20 Mortimer Rd, Wynberg (☎761 6493). Cottage in converted barn near shops and Wynberg station. ③.

Elephant Eye Lodge, 9 Sunwood Drive, Tokai (☎752 432). Friendly B&B in converted Cape farmhouse, minutes' walk from Tokai Forest and with its own large grounds. ③.

Feldenhausen Ave, 24 Feldenhausen Ave, Claremont (☎650 3402, fax 650 4041). Self-catering cottage sleeping two, close to Cavendish Square shops and Claremont train station. ③.

Groot Moddergat House, off Main Rd, Hout Bay (☎790 1110). Thoroughly pleasant establishment in a semi-rural setting. ④.

Houtkapperspoort, Hout Bay Rd (☎794 5216, fax 794 2907). A great rural feel at these 26 stone and brick self-catering cottages close to Constantia Nek, with paths leading onto the mountain. Highly recommended. ④.

Kenilworth Guest House, 38 Greenfield Rd, Kenilworth (☎761 6181, fax 761 6185). Victorian house, nicely furnished, with tranquil garden and rooms without bath. Very convenient for the station. ③.

Koornhoop Manor House, corner of Wrensch and Nuttal roads, Observatory (☎ & fax 448 0595). Immaculate rooms in this Victorian house with a quiet garden, close to the station. ③.

Little Ruo, 11 Willow Rd, Constantia (☎794 2247, fax 794 1981). Very pleasant and reasonably priced B&B and self-catering units set in huge grounds in landscaped garden with willows, a stream and a saltwater pool. Self-catering units ④, B&B ③.

Riverview Guest Lodge, Anson Rd, Observatory (☎47 9056, fax 47 5192). Large and reasonably priced guesthouse, handy for transport. Rate excludes breakfast. ③.

Rodenberg Guest House, 8 Myrtle Rd, Rondebosch (☎689 4852, fax 689 2065). Gracious Victorian home very close to the station. All rooms with bath. ③.

The Stables, Chantecler Rd, Constantia (☎794 3653). Converted farmhouse, with comfortable, English-style rooms with patios and verandahs. Fabulous breakfasts are served. ③.

Tadworth Cottage, 9 Uitsig Rd, Constantia (☎& fax 794 6083). Reasonably priced double rooms in desirable Constantia, but you'll need your own transport. ③.

Walloon Farm, Walloon Close, Constantia (☎794 4406, fax 794 1471). Guesthouse in an area more suburban than some Constantia places, but still very pleasant. ⑤.

Hotels

Baxter Suites, Lyle Rd, opposite Baxter Theatre, Rondebosch (☎689 7070, fax 789 7295). Serviced flats near station and shops. ③.

The Courtyard, Liesbeek Ave, Mowbray (☎448 3929, fax 448 5494). The height of luxury in an exceptionally beautiful eighteenth-century Cape Dutch homestead, next door to Valkenberg Mental Hospital. Breakfast is extra. ⑦.

Greenways Hotel, Torquay Ave, Claremont (☎761 1792, fax 791 0878). Small, private hotel in a historic Cape Dutch house. All rooms with bath. Prices depend on size of room and view. ⑥–⑦.

Vineyard Hotel, Colinton Rd, Newlands (☎683 3044, fax 683 3365). For total colonial elegance, this historic Cape Dutch house offers unequalled views and is one of Cape Town's best, at half the price of the *Mount Nelson*. ⑤–⑥.

Atlantic seaboard

Down the Atlantic seaboard the urban ribbon extends through the inner-city seaside suburbs of **Green Point** and **Sea Point**, historically Cape Town's hotel and high-rise land, now a dense conglomeration of every type of accommodation. At night, Green Point is a magnet for the city's prostitutes, and petty crime is rampant. Sea Point mixes tacky and gentrified and has many of Cape Town's best restaurants, as well as a leading gay cruising zone along the seaside promenade. Rikkis operate as far as Sea Point, and buses to the centre are frequent and take under ten minutes. Moving south along Victoria Drive, the luxury mountainside suburb of **Camps Bay** has soaring views over the Atlantic, while the nearby **Llandudno** has similar vistas but fewer places to stay. Further down the coast, **Hout Bay** is the main urban concentration along the lower half of the peninsula, with its own harbour, a pleasant waterfront development, and the only public transport beyond Camps Bay, with direct buses from the centre along the coast or across the mountain via the southern suburbs. South of Hout Bay is the semi-rural settlement of **Noordhoek**, which has the best walking beach along the coast and is close to the Cape of Good Hope Nature Reserve. The quiet but windy village of **Scarborough**, nestled around Smit's Bay, is the last settlement on the Atlantic coastline before Cape Point, and offers a couple of places to stay.

Green Point and Sea Point

Crammed with a wide range of hostels and hotels, **Green Point** and **Sea Point** are good places to head for if your budget is tight. Sea Point also boasts lively restaurants and trendy coffee shops along its bustling Main Road.

BACKPACKERS' LODGES

Bird's Eye View, 55 High Level Rd, Green Point (☎434 4143). Supremely hospitable and spacious accommodation in a large family home, still occupied by the two original women owners. Dorms sleeping four to six people, and a double room, are on offer. ①.

Bunkers, 15 Graham Rd, Sea Point (☎ & fax 434 7899). Unexceptional eight-bed dorms in a private house, with camping on the lawn. The owner also has reasonably priced rooms around Sea Point – a good bet if you're stuck. ①–②.

Bunkhouse for Backpackers, 23 Antrim Rd, Sea Point (☎ & fax 434 5695). One of the best-run lodges in the area: sociable and busy, with a swimming pool, pool table, and lockers in each room. ①.

Hip-Hop, 11 Vesperdene Rd, Green Point (☎439 2104, fax 439 8688). Camping, dorms and doubles at this pleasantly decorated and lively lodge. Can be noisy though, and it's not as clean as you might wish. ①.

St John's Waterfront Lodge, 4/6 Braemar Rd, Green Point (☎ & fax 439 1404). Expertly run by friendly and helpful staff, with two pools and a great garden. Highly recommended, despite the slightly unsavoury neighbourhood. Dorms and triples ①, doubles ②.

GUESTHOUSES AND B&BS

Ascot Manor, 369 Main Rd, Sea Point (☎439 3885). Small guesthouse close to the Waterfront and Clifton beach. ③.

El-Hann, 5 Scholtz Rd, Three Anchor Bay (☎434 0968). Repro furniture and rooms with bath in a quiet cul-de-sac. ④.

The Glen Guest House, 3 The Glen, Sea Point (☎439 2256). Seriously upmarket establishment with large airy rooms, all with bath. ⑦.

Kinneret Guest House, 11 Arthur's Rd, Sea Point (☎439 9237, fax 434 8998). Comfortable doubles amid outrageously camp interior decor. Love it or hate it, it's perfect for the promenade and beachfront. ④.

Leeuwenzee Guest House, 199 High Level Rd, Sea Point (☎439 9516, fax 439 9550). Small, clean rooms somewhat devoid of character, with a swimming pool. ③–④.

Olaf's Guest House, 24 Wisbeach Rd, Sea Point (☎439 8943, fax 439 5057). Clean, comfortable Victorian house, nicely decorated, and offering personal attention. ④.

Oliver Guest House, 8 Oliver Rd, Sea Point (☎439 9237, fax 434 8998). Sister to *Kinneret Guest House*, but more plainly furnished and better value. ③.

Stonehurst Guest House, 3 Frere Rd (☎434 9670, fax 439 8131). Airy Victorian residence with original fittings and Cape furniture. Self-catering with no meals provided, but there's a kitchen and guest lounge. All rooms have bath. ③.

Villa Rosa, 277 High Level Rd, Sea Point (☎434 2768). Friendly guesthouse decorated with simplicity and style. Some rooms have sea views, but the main drawback is the busy road. ③.

HOTELS

Carnaby Hotel, corner of Main and St Bede's roads, Three Anchor Bay (☎439 7410). Clean, good-value hotel with small rooms. Shared facilities ②, en suite ③.

Claridges Hotel, 47 Main Rd, Sea Point (☎434 1171). Formerly a student residence in one of the less savoury Sea Point localities, near a brothel. ④.

Karos Arthur's Seat Hotel, Arthur's Rd, Sea Point (☎434 1187). Excellent and convenient for the beach, but pricey. ⑧.

Lion's Head Lodge, 319 Main Rd, Sea Point (☎434 4163, fax 439 3818). No-nonsense, functional rooms that serve the purpose, but have no flair. Rate excludes breakfast. The lodge also offers fully equipped apartments. ③.

Palm Garden Protea Hotel, 75 Regent Rd, Sea Point (☎439 1171, fax 434 0741). In central Sea Point with a grand views of Lion's Head. ⑤.

Peninsula All-Suite Hotel, Beachfront, Sea Point (☎439 8888, fax 439 8886). Very good, upmarket apartments; a fine bet if you can afford it. ⑦.

Ritz Inn, Main Rd, Sea Point (☎439 6010, fax 434 0809). Enormous block, best known for its revolving restaurant on the 22nd floor with views of sea and mountain. With over 200 rooms, you'll never feel alone. ④.

Winchester Mansions Hotel, 221 Beach Rd, Sea Point (☎434 2351, fax 434 0215). Elegant and charming hotel right on the seafront. The pricier sea-facing rooms have the nicest views in Sea Point. ⑥–⑦.

Camps Bay

Bay Hotel, Victoria Rd (☎438 4444, fax 438 4455). Luxurious, glitzy hotel which occasionally hosts the mildly famous, on the fashionable beachfront strip. Mountain-facing rooms ⑥, sea-facing rooms ⑦.

Diamond House, 61 Hely Hutchinson Ave (☎438 1344, fax 438 1557). Comfortable rooms with bath in a house set against the hillside, set away from the beach. ⑥.

House Michelitsch, 41 Hely Hutchinson Ave (☎438 9148). Self-contained apartment with own balcony, halfway up the mountain. ③.

Leeukop, 25 Sedgemoor Rd (☎438 1361, fax 438 1675). Best B&B accommodation in Camps Bay, in two stylishly arty flats near the beach. ③–④.

Stan's Halt, The Glen (☎ & fax 438 9037). Cape Town's most tranquil backpackers' hostel is in a former nineteenth-century hunting lodge in the heart of woodlands, 15min walk to Clifton beach. The only snag is the 30min walk from the nearest public transport. Take the Kloof Nek bus from Adderley St (outside *OK Bazaar*) and get off at Kloof Nek; then walk down to the right towards Clifton, following the hostel signs. ①.

Views, 58 Hely Hutchinson Ave (☎ & fax 438 1622). En-suite rooms on the hillside. ④.

Llandudno

B4 Richmond, 5 Logies Rd (☎790 4108). Pleasant B&B, with a garden and swimming pool. ④.

Far Horizon Apartments, 17 Bosman Ave (☎ & fax 790 1734). Perfectly decent self-catering two-bedroom flats sleeping four, as close to the beach as you can get. Cheap if there are four of you. ④.

Llandudno Heights, 19 Llandudno Rd (☎ & fax 438 2305). Open-plan flats sleeping three, just off the main road, away from the beach, with a terrace garden. ③.

Hout Bay

Bayview Manor, 8 Flora Close (☎790 2061, fax 790 5096). Comfortable rooms with bath, set in isolation high on a hill. The drive up through less salubrious parts of the village might be a disincentive. ③.

Beach House, Royal Ave (☎ & fax 790 4228). Comfortable doubles in a modern guesthouse, close to the beach and near Mariner's Wharf. ③.

Chapman's Peak Hotel, Main Rd (☎790 1036). Restaurant with a few rooms with bath, some facing the sea. Not luxurious, but pleasant enough, and one of the best places in town for sunsets. Rate excludes breakfast. ⑤–⑥.

Dune Lodge, 8 Edward St (☎790 4228). Comfortable and modern, if slightly sterile rooms (with bath) across the road from Mariner's Wharf. ③.

Hout Bay Manor, Main Rd (☎790 5960, fax 790 4952). Elegant country-style hotel away from the sea. ⑤–⑥.

Noordhoek

Chapman's Peak Caravan Farm, Dassenheuvel (☎789 1225). 3km from the beach, so best with a car. Campsite and on-site caravans (bring your own linen). ①.

Imhoff Caravan Park, 1 Wireless Rd, Kommetjie (☎783 2871). 500m from the beach, this is the nicest campsite in the area. Two-bedroom self-catering chalets also available; camping ①, chalets ③–④.

Monkey Valley Beach, Mountain Rd, Chapman's Peak (☎789 1391, fax 789 1143). It's a 10min walk to the beach from these double-storey, thatched cottages on the slopes of Chapman's Peak. ⑤–⑥.

Scarborough

Scarborough Backpackers, 330 Main Rd (☎780 1154). On the left-hand side of the main road on the way to Cape Point, this small hostel run by a surfer offers dorms only, a tiny bar and kitchen, and some space to camp. ①.

Beach Break, 365 Rooibok St (☎ & fax 780 1517). Well-equipped, self-catering apartment with three rooms, a short walk from the sea, and off to the right of Main Road. ②.

False Bay

Down the eastern side of the peninsula, the still-bracing waters of the **False Bay coast** are warmer than the Atlantic, and the public transport is better than anywhere else. This is a good place to stay if you want to be by the sea and away from the centre. The suburban railway runs through the southern suburbs to hit the coast at **Muizenberg**, the oldest and most developed of Cape Town's seaside suburbs. To its south are a series of settlements, including **St James**, **Kalk Bay**, **Fish Hoek** and **Simon's Town**, which, as the third-oldest urban settlement in South Africa, has its own well-established identity.

Muizenberg and St James

Abe Bailey Youth Hostel, corner of Maynard and Westbury roads, Muizenberg (☎ & fax 788 2301). Dorms and doubles are on offer at this respectable outfit, a 5min walk from the beach. ①.

Alexander Mews Guest House, 10 Alexander Rd, Muizenberg (☎788 3541). Somewhat sombre and impersonal guesthouse in one of Muizenberg's less attractive streets. ③.

Greens Hotel, 90 Beach Rd, Muizenberg (☎788 1131, fax 788 7415). Basic hotel with clean rooms, worth considering only for its beachfront position. Bed-only rate; ③.

Shrimpton Manor, 19 Alexander Rd, Muizenberg (☎ & fax 788 1128). Lavishly furnished small hotel, a few blocks back from the seafront. ③–④.

Sonstraal Guest House, 6 Axminster Rd, Muizenberg (☎ & fax 788 1611). Kitsch decor and the most extravagantly generous breakfast in Cape Town. 5min from the beach. ④.

Spray, 105 Main Rd, St James (☎788 8018). One of the best and most reasonably priced B&Bs along the False Bay seaboard. The two bedrooms (with bath) are about 30m from the shore, with superb views across the bay. Book well in advance. ②.

Sunbird Lodge, 66 Clovelly Rd, Clovelly (☎782 2778). Tiny self-catering place which sleeps four, close to beach. ③.

Zandvlei Caravan Park, 1km from Muizenberg Beach (enquiries to: Director, Civic Amenities, PO Box 298, Cape Town 8000; ☎88 5215). Campsites and self-catering accommodation. ①.

Kalk Bay

Castle Hill, 37 Gatesville Rd, Kalk Bay (☎788 2554, fax 788 3843). Stylishly restored Edwardian guesthouse with large, high-ceilinged rooms, and fretwork balconies with unparalleled views of the sun rising across the bay. Magnificent. ④.

Chartfield Guest House, corner of Gatesville and Norman roads, Kalk Bay (☎788 3793, fax 788 8674). Comfortable and unpretentious accommodation halfway up the hill, offering rooms with baths. Ask for one of the semicircular rooms on the corner with 180° views, or the loft. ②–③.

Harbourside Backpackers, 136 Main Rd, Kalk Bay (☎788 2943, fax 788 6452). Popular hangout with beds on platforms offering views of the harbour. A party atmosphere prevails, but there are quieter doubles on the lower of its upstairs floors. Very cheap restaurant open to public. Dorms and doubles. ①.

Innesfail, 6 Dalebrook Rd, Kalk Bay (☎788 8928, fax 788 8929). Modest hotel with simple rooms off Kalk Bay Main Rd and a few minutes' walk across the railway line to the sea. ③.

Fish Hoek

Avenue Hotel, 7 First Ave, Fish Hoek (☎782 6026, fax 782 5693). Comfortable hotel within walking distance of beach, but without its own sea view. ③.

Beaufort B&B, 34 Main Rd, Fish Hoek (☎782 4037, fax 782 4227). Cheap and clean, with a boarding-house feel. Right on the main road, but plenty of rooms make it a good bet if you're stuck. ③.

Nautilus Lodge, Simon's Town Rd (☎ & fax 782 4168) Magnificent sea views from every suite in this self-catering establishment. Cheaper than its posher neighbour, *Tudor House*. ③.

Outspan Lodge, 16 Kommetjie Rd, Fish Hoek (☎782 1140). Principally a residential establishment, this lodge away from the beach rents cheap, adequate rooms with bath. ④.

Sunny Cove Manor, 72 Simon's Town Rd, Fish Hoek (☎782 2274, fax 782 6665). Outstanding sea views (except for the back room) in this cheerful B&B, 3min from Sunny Cove station. ④.

Tudor House by the Sea, 43 Simon's Town Rd, Fish Hoek (☎782 6238). Runner-up to the best B&B in South Africa in 1995. Luxury self-catering apartments on the water's edge have slightly stuffy decor, but incredible views. Book as far ahead as possible. ④.

The Wave Backpackers, 288 Main Rd, Clovelly (☎782 3659). Dorms and doubles and a very reasonable B&B rate, just across the road from the beach. Kitchen for self-catering, free airport pick-ups and a 5min walk along the beach to Fish Hoek station. ①.

Simon's Town

Ark Studio, 4 Grant Ave, Boulders (☎786 2526). Thoroughly comfortable and fully equipped apartments sleeping two, with sweeping views across the sea. Breakfast an optional extra. ③.

Blue Lantern Holiday Cabins, Main Rd, Froggy Pond, Simon's Town (☎786 2113). Small, fully equipped timber cabins of varying sizes, outside the centre of town. The flimsy walls could be a problem if your neighbours are partying. ②.

Bosky Dell on Boulders Beach, 5 Grant Ave, Boulders, Simon's Town (☎23 1818, fax 23 1827). Self-catering units so close to the beach that inquisitive penguins frequently pad into the garden. Comfortable rooms (some with views), and a private path to the beach. ④.

Boulders Beach Backpackers, 4 Boulders Place, Boulders Beach (☎786 1758, fax 786 1825). A sixteen-bed dorm and a double room, sharing the kitchen and lounge. Breakfast is available at *Boulders Beach Guest House* next door. ①.

Boulders Beach Guest House, Boulders Place, off Bellevue Rd, Simon's Town (☎786 1758). B&B on the parking lot rather than the beach, but 2min walk to the water, and with a sea view. ③–④.

British Hotel, 90 St George's St, Simon's Town (☎790 4930). Three-bedroom, self-catering apartments in a grand 1898 Victorian hotel. This is an experience rather than just somewhere to stay. Enquire at *Brad's Bakery* next door. Huge units with high ceilings and enormous balconies overlooking the street and the docks (④), and more modest doubles (with bath) ③.

Eick House, corner of Main Rd and Ixia Crescent, Murdock Valley, Simon's Town (☎ & fax 786 2187). Self-catering, six-bed apartment with modern decor, a good view and its own terrace, and a B&B unit (②–③).

Kijabe Lodge, 32 Disa Rd, Murdock Valley (☎786 2433). High on the hillside, a little away from the seafront, with amazing views. Reasonably priced with exceptionally hospitable owners. ②.

Lord Nelson Inn, 58 St George's St (☎786 1386, fax 786 1009). Comfortable little inn overlooking the harbour in the village centre. The best rooms have sea views. ③–④.

Oatlands Holiday Village, Froggy Pond (☎786 1410, fax 786 1162). Slightly cramped, fully equipped self-catering chalets of varying size. ③.

Seaforth Beach Bungalows, corner of Main and Seaforth roads (☎786 1463). Despite the name, they're not on the beach and there's no sea view, but the beach is a short walk away. Tiny, old-fashioned timber units. Flats sleeping six ①, cabins ②.

Table Bay and the northern suburbs

Around the N2 and north of the city are the **northern suburbs**, the most boring suburban expanse on the entire Cape Peninsula. With the notable exception of **Bloubergstrand**, which has some shred of its origins as a fishing village, and a couple of adjacent places along the edge of Table Bay, which are noted for the ultimate view of Table Mountain, there is every reason to pump hard on the accelerator if you're driving through. Public transport is limited to a handful of buses from the city centre transporting workers to and from the Koeberg nuclear reactor, north of Blouberg, at the beginning and end of the working day.

Blouberg Windsurf & Leisure, 28 Pikkewyn Rd, Bloubergstrand (☎56 1663). Budget self-catering accommodation, overlooking a lake. ②.

Blue Peter Hotel, Popham Rd, Bloubergstrand (☎56 1956, fax 56 1364). Popular, well-appointed and expensive hotel, right on the beach. ⑤.

Cape View, 50 Sir David Baird Drive, Bloubergstrand (☎ & fax 56 2127). Pick of the area, this well-run and friendly guesthouse offers comfortable rooms and is nicely located, minutes from good restaurants and the beach. ⑤.

Cotswold Guest House, 6 Cotswold Drive, Milnerton (☎551 3637). Away from the beach, but with luxurious accommodation and pleasant staff. ⑤–⑥.

Dolphin Beach Hotel, Marine Drive, Table Bay (☎557 8140, fax 557 8147). Modern hotel where you pay primarily for the view. Nice long walks on Milnerton Beach. ⑦.

Batavia Street, 8 Batavia St, Bloubergstrand (☎ & fax 56 1169). Self-catering apartment for up to four people, one street away from the sea without the views, but reasonably priced. ②.

55 Stadler Road, 55 Stadler Rd (☎56 1281). Unpretentious, fully equipped self-catering apartment right on the beach. A bargain. ②.

Ou Skip Caravan Park, Otto Du Plessis Drive, Melkbosstrand (☎553 2058). On-site caravans for rent, some distance from Cape Town. A good deal for families or small groups. ①–②.

Rockhaven Lodge, 3 Sir David Baird Drive, Bloubergstrand (☎56 2414, fax 56 1501). Pleasant guesthouse close to the beach and restaurants. ⑥.

Sunset Lodge, 41 Gull Rd, Bloubergstrand (☎ & fax 56 1818). Modern house on a hill, with views. ④.

The City

Between two mountainous flanks, reaching away from the docks, through the intense city centre and up the mountain is the **City Bowl** (made up of the Upper and Lower city centres and the Waterfront) where lively areas, like Long Street, the Bo-Kaap and Gardens rub shoulders with the serious new wealth of Tamboerskloof and Oranjezicht. Straggling south from the centre along the eastern slope of the mountain, the predominantly white **southern suburbs** become progressively more affluent as you move from arty Observatory through the comfortably middle-class districts of Rondebosch and Newlands, culminating with the Constantia wine estates. Along the coastal belt, the **Atlantic seaboard** is drier and sunnier, with the wealthiest areas like Clifton and Camps Bay clinging to the mountainside above the sea, white sands and rocky beaches. The **False Bay** coast is wetter, softer and greener, and the sea here usually several degrees warmer than the western peninsula, making Muizenberg, Fish Hoek and Simon's Town the most popular bathing beaches in Cape Town. Curling northeast around Table Bay, the **northern suburbs**, taking in Parow, Milnerton and Bloubergstrand are exceptionally dull suburbs, traditionally with an Afrikaans flavour. South of these, and extending seemingly endlessly along the N2 into the interior, the coloured **Cape Flats townships** jostle with the desolate, litter-strewn **African ghettos** of Nyanga, Langa and Gugulethu, which relentlessly overflow into kilometre after kilometre of tin and cardboard shantytowns.

The Upper City Centre

The **Upper City Centre**, the entire area from Strand Street to the southern foot of the mountain, is a collage of Georgian, Cape Dutch, Victorian and twentieth-century architecture, as well as the place where Europe, Asia and Africa meet in markets, alleyways and mosques. Among the substantial drawcards here are **Parliament**, the **Botanical Gardens** and many of Cape Town's major **museums**.

Strand Street marks the edge of Cape Town's original beachfront (though you'd never guess it today), and all urban development to its north stands on reclaimed land. To its south, heading towards Table Mountain, are the remains of the city's 350-year-old historic core, which has survived the ravages of modernization and apartheid-inspired urban clearance to emerge with enough charm to make it South Africa's most pleasing city centre.

Adderley Street, slicing through the Upper City from the railway station in the north to the Gardens in the south, is the obvious orientation axis. To its east, and close to each other just off Strand Street, are the **Castle of Good Hope**, the site of **District Six**, the **Grand Parade** and the **City Hall**. The district to the west of Adderley Street is the closest South Africa gets to a European quarter – a tight network of streets with cafés, buskers, bookstores, street stalls and antique shops congregating around the pedestrianized **St George's Mall** and **Greenmarket Square**. The **Bo-Kaap**, or Muslim district, three blocks further west across Buitengracht (which means the "Outer Canal", but is actually a street), exudes a piquant contrast to this, with its minarets, spice shops and cafés selling curried snacks.

South of Adderley Street, where it takes a sharp right into Wale Street, is the symbolic heart of Cape Town (and arguably South Africa), with **Parliament**, museums, archives and De Tuynhuys, the official residence of the President, arranged around the **Botanical Gardens**.

Adderley Street

Once *the* place to shop in Cape Town, **Adderley Street**, lined with centuries of handsome buildings, is still worth a stroll today, for what grand architecture remains. Its attractive streetscape has been seriously blemished by a series of large 1960s shopping centres, but just minutes away from crowded malls, among the streets and alleys around Greenmarket Square, you can still find some human scale and historic texture.

Adderley Street was formerly the "Heerengracht" ("Gentlemen's Canal") – a waterway which ran from the Botanical Gardens down to the sea. Low-walled channels, ditches, bridges and sluices which ran through Cape Town earned it the name "Little Amsterdam". During the nineteenth century, the canals were buried underground, and in 1850 Heerengracht was renamed Adderley Street (see box overleaf). There's little evidence of the canals today, except in name – one section of the street is still called Heerengracht and a parallel street to its west is called Buitengracht.

The destruction of old Cape Town continued well into the twentieth century, with the razing of many of the older buildings. One of the ugliest newcomers is the **Golden Acre** shopping complex, built in the 1970s, and today Cape Town's unavoidable hub. Dominating the north (harbour) end of Adderley Street, Golden Acre employs an unfriendly network of subways and walkways to draw together all the major arrival points into town. The *Metrorail* urban transit and mainline stations, the central bus terminals, the taxi ranks and tiered parking garages all congregate around this enormous, darkened shopping mall. Among the sidewalks and pedestrianized sections outside, you'll find a tightly packed **flea market**, where you can browse through curios, crafts and electronic goods (but watch your wallet).

A little further south lies a **flower market** run by members of the Bo-Kaap Muslim community. As you wander up, two grandiose banks stand on opposite sides of Adderley Street. The fussier of the two is the **Standard Bank**: fronted by Corinthian columns and covered with a tall dome, it seems like a temple to the partnership of empire and finance. The **First National Bank**, completed in 1913, was the last South African building designed by Sir Herbert Baker (see p.467). Inside the banking hall, a solid timber circular writing desk, with the original inkwells still in place, resembles an altar.

At the top corner of Adderley Street, just as it veers sharply west into Wale Street, you'll find the **South African Cultural History Museum** (Mon–Sat 9.30am–4.30pm; small entry fee). Originally the slave lodge of the Dutch East India Company, then the colony's main brothel, the building was turned over to another form of entertainment in 1810, when the Supreme Court moved in, and its proceedings were opened to the public. Uninspiring displays spread themselves thinly, and apparently randomly, over so many topics that your appetite is whetted but never satisfied. The upper floor brings together weapons, silver and toys, while the lower floor has tasters from a selection of

ADDERLEY STREET

Although the Dutch used Robben Island (see p.86) as a political prison, the South African mainland only narrowly escaped becoming a second Australia, where British felons and enemies of the state could be dumped. By the 1840s, "respectable Australians" were lobbying for a ban on the transportation of criminals to the Antipodes. The British authorities responded by trying to divert convicts to the Cape. In 1848, the *Neptune*, with a cargo of 282 prisoners, set sail for Cape Town, where the news of their departure was met with outrage. Five thousand citizens gathered on the Grand Parade to hear prominent liberals denounce the British government, and when the ship docked in September 1849 governor Sir Harry Smith forbade any criminal from landing. In London, politician Charles Adderley successfully addressed Parliament in support of the Cape colonists. In February 1850, the *Neptune* set off for Tasmania, and grateful Capetonians renamed the city's main thoroughfare **Adderley Street**.

cultures, including Japanese, Tibetan and Dutch, but has little on local indigenous culture. The most interesting of the downstairs rooms cover topics you aren't likely to see elsewhere, including a social history of Cape Town, displays of coins, paintings, clothes and furniture. The "Cape Kaleidoscope" exhibition in the entrance hall is worth taking in for its interesting crash course in the political and economic history of South Africa's first European settlement.

Castle of Good Hope

From the outside, South Africa's oldest building looks somewhat miserable, and its position on Darling Street, behind the railway station and city bus terminal, does nothing to dispel this. Nevertheless the **Castle of Good Hope** (daily except public holidays 9am–4pm) is well worth the modest entrance fee to experience the meticulous ten-year restoration which has returned the decor to the British Regency style introduced in 1798.

Completed in 1679, the Castle (as it's commonly known) replaced Van Riebeeck's earlier mud and timber fort, which stood on the site of the Grand Parade. For 150 years it was the symbolic heart of the Cape adminstration, and the centre of social and economic life. In the late nineteenth century, when the colony had expanded far beyond its walls, there were at least three attempts to demolish it, as it was regarded as a white elephant that was costly to maintain. Inside, there's a powerful atmosphere of calm and a strong sense of order in the Castle's pentagonal plan, based on Renaissance engineering principles. Ironically, there was nothing ordered about its construction over thirteen years, with work constantly coming to a standstill either because of labour shortages or insufficient materials. The original seaward entrance had to be moved to its present position, because the spring tide sometimes came crashing in – a remarkable thought given how far aground it is now.

There are three collections of varying interest inside: the uninspiring **Military Museum** has displays on the conflicts that dogged the early settlement; the **Secunde's House** has furnishings, paintings and *objets d'art* that filled the living space of the deputy governor; and the **William Fehr Collection**, one of the country's most important exhibits of decorative arts, includes paintings of the settlement, eighteenth- and nineteenth-century Dutch and Indonesian furniture, and seventeenth- and eighteenth-century Chinese and Japanese porcelain. **Free tours** (9am–3pm; Feb–Nov hourly; Dec & Jan every 30min) are useful for orientation and cover the main features. There is a very pleasant tea shop in the Castle courtyard. The Castle is also home to the Defence Force's Western Province Command and you may catch a glimpse of armed soldiers marching in and stepping through the elegant courtyard as Table Mountain peers over the west wall.

The Grand Parade and the City Hall

The **Grand Parade**, on the west of the Castle, is where the residents of District Six used to come to trade. On Wednesdays and Saturdays it still transforms itself into a **market**, where you can buy a whole array of bargains ranging from used clothes to spicy food. The Grand Parade appeared on TV screens throughout the world on February 11, 1990, when 100,000 people gathered to hear **Nelson Mandela** make his first speech, from the balcony of City Hall, after being released from prison. The **City Hall** is a slightly fussy Edwardian building dressed in Bath stone, that despite its drab surroundings looks impressive against Table Mountain.

District Six

South of the Castle, in the shadow of Devil's Peak, is a vacant lot shown on maps as the suburb of Zonnebloem. Before being torn out by apartheid two decades ago, it was **District Six**, an impoverished but lively community of 55,000 people, predominantly coloured Muslims. Once known as the soul of Cape Town, this inner-city slum harboured a rich cultural life in its narrow alleys and crowded tenements. Along the cobbled streets hawkers rubbed shoulders with prostitutes, gangsters, drunks and gamblers, while craftsmen plied their trade in small workshops. This was a rich place of the South African imagination, inspiring novels, poems, jazz and a blockbuster musical.

In 1966, apartheid ideologues declared District Six a **White Group Area** and the bulldozers moved in, taking fifteen years to drive its presence from the skyline. Today only the mosques and churches remain. But, in the wake of the demolition gangs, international and domestic outcry was so great that the area was never developed apart from a few luxury town houses on its fringes and the hefty Cape Technikon, a college which now occupies nearly a quarter of the former suburb.

On the northern boundary, at 25a Buitenkant St, is the **District Six Museum** (Mon–Sat 10am–4.30pm; donation). Formerly the Central Methodist Mission Church offered solidarity and ministry to the victims of forced removals, right up to the 1980s, and was a venue for anti-apartheid gatherings. Today, the church houses a collection of documentary photographs and a huge map laid out on the floor. It is a deeply moving place, hinting at the sense of collective loss experienced by an entire community. This living installation, intended as much for residents as tourists, invites visitors to jot down comments, memories or reflections (as powerfully evocative as the exhibit itself) on any part of the display. There are few places in Cape Town that speak more eloquently of the effect of apartheid on the day-to-day lives of men and women.

Long Street

Seedy but trendy **Long Street** lies at the heart of a lively central area, and is one of Cape Town's most fascinating thoroughfares. At the edge of the Bo-Kaap, its mosques attract Muslims from across the way, while the nightclubs and bars pull tourists, young locals and the old-timers who never stopped coming.

When it was first settled by Muslims, some three hundred years ago, Long Street marked Cape Town's boundary. By the 1960s, it had become a sleazy alley of drinking holes and whorehouses. Miraculously it's all still here, but with a whiff of gentrification. Georgian-style mosques still coexist with Victorian bottle stores, brothels live above old-fashioned locksmiths, pawnbrokers alongside purveyors of porn. There are gun shops next to delicatessens, and wonderful antique dealers rubbing shoulders with coffee shops. Also here are several excellent second-hand bookshops and more **backpackers' lodges** per metre than on any other street in Cape Town.

Long Street Baths (Mon–Fri 7am–10pm, Sat 7am–7pm, Sun 8am–7pm), at the top of the road, where it hits Buitensingel (meaning "Outer Crescent"), is a Cape Town institution. Established in 1906, the steam rooms, great for relaxing on a winter's day, are open on separate days to men (Mon, Thurs & Sat) and women (Tues, Wed & Fri).

A four-hour session (R45) gets you a private cubicle and towel, access to the dry or wet steam rooms, the plunge pool and a short massage. Swimming (R4) is communal.

Greenmarket Square and around

Turning east from Long Street into Shortmarket Street, you'll skim the edge of **Greenmarket Square**, worth at least a few minutes' exploration to soak up the distinctly European atmosphere, with cobbled streets, coffee shops and grand buildings. As its name implies, the square started as a vegetable market, then spent many ignominious years as a car park. Human life has returned and it's now a flea market, selling crafts, jewellery and hippie clobber. This is also one of the few places in Cape Town to buy from Zaireans, selling masks and malachite carvings.

St George's Mall, to the square's east, is a pedestrianized road starting at Thibault Square, near the railway station, and ending at Wale Street, across from St George's Cathedral. There are a number of coffee shops and snack bars inside, but not much else to draw you here, although it does make a more pleasant route from the station to the Gardens than neighbouring Adderley Street. Nearby, at Queen Victoria and Wale streets, **St George's Cathedral** is more interesting for its history than for its Herbert Baker Victorian Gothic design; on September 7, 1986, **Desmond Tutu** hammered on its doors symbolically demanding to be enthroned as South Africa's first black archbishop. Three years later, he heralded the last days of apartheid by leading 30,000 people from the Cathedral to the City Hall, where he coined his now famous slogan for the new order. "We are the rainbow people!" he told the crowd. "We are the new people of South Africa!"

Government Avenue and the Company's Gardens

A stroll down **Government Avenue**, the southwest extension of Adderley Street, makes for one of the most serene walks in central Cape Town. This oak-lined boulevard runs past the rear of Parliament through the Gardens, and its benches are frequently occupied by snoring *bergies* (tramps).

On the right as you enter the north end of the avenue looms the **South African Library** (Mon–Fri 9am–6pm, Sat 9am–1pm; free), one of the country's best collections of antique historical and natural history books, covering southern Africa. Built with revenue from a tax on wine, it opened in 1822 as one of the first free libraries in the world.

Stretching from here to the South African Museum, the **Company's Gardens** were the initial *raison d'être* for the Dutch settlement at the Cape. Established in 1652 to supply fresh greens to Dutch East India Company trading ships travelling between the Netherlands and the East, the Gardens were initially worked by imported slave labour. This proved too expensive, as the slaves had to be shipped in, fed and housed, so the Company phased out its own farming and granted land to free burghers, from whom it bought fresh produce (see p.649). At the end of the seventeenth century, the gardens were turned over to botanical horticulture for Cape Town's growing colonial elite. Ponds, lawns, landscaping and a crisscross web of oak-shaded walkways were introduced. Today, they are full of exotic plants, the result of long-standing European interest in Cape botany; Swedish scientists have been sailing out since the seventeeth century to classify and name specimens.

The gardens are a pleasant place to meander: Cecil Rhodes certainly thought so – it was during a stroll here that he plotted the invasion of Zimbabwe. Rhodes also introduced an army of small, furry colonizers to the gardens: the grey squirrels. There's a statue of Rhodes here, as well as an outdoor café.

Continuing along Government Avenue from the South African Library, past the rear of Parliament, you can peer through an iron gate to see the grand buildings and tended flowerbeds of **De Tuynhuys**, the official office (but not residence) of the president. One party of tourists in 1996 stood aghast as Nelson Mandela strolled across the lawns for a friendly chat – but don't hold your breath.

A little further along, the tree-lined walkway opens out into a formal gravel area with ponds and statues, around which are sited the National Gallery to the east, and the South African Museum and Planetarium to the west .

The South African National Gallery

At the south end of Government Avenue, the **South African National Gallery** (Mon 1–5pm, Tues–Sun 10am–5pm; free) is a must for anyone interested in the local art scene, and includes a small but excellent permanent collection of contemporary South African art. You'll also find a fine display of traditional works from the southeast of the continent, based around a small collection donated by the German government. The exhibits, which include beadwork, carvings and craft objects, were chosen for their aesthetic qualities and rarity, and represent the gallery's policy of focusing on neglected parts of South Africa's heritage. A room of minor works by various British artists includes Pre-Raphaelites, George Romney, Thomas Gainsborough and Joshua Reynolds. The gallery has a good café serving light lunches, snacks, coffees and cakes, as well as a gallery shop – excellent for one-off gifts and souvenirs with a genuinely local flavour.

The South African Museum and Planetarium

Despite having a collection that should command anyone's attention, the **South African Museum**, west of Government Avenue, at 25 Queen Victoria St (daily 10am–5pm; small entry fee), is a troubled and controversial place. Essentially a natural history museum, it also contains ethnographic exhibits, thus implying that tribal people are part of the animal world. The ethnographic galleries downstairs are nevertheless stunning and will make a great contribution (should they be moved to the Cultural History Museum, as has been mooted). They include life casts of San hunter-gatherers, now virtually extinct in South Africa, and superb dioramas depicting nineteenth-century San life. There are very good displays on the traditional arts and crafts of several African tribes, some exceptional examples of rock art (entire chunks of caves sitting in the display cases) and casts of stone birds found at Great Zimbabwe, across South Africa's border. Upstairs, the natural history galleries display stuffed mammals, dioramas of prehistoric Karoo reptiles and Table Mountain flora and fauna. The highlight is the four-storey whale well, in which a collection of beautiful whale skeletons hang like massive mobiles, accompanied by the eerie strains of their song.

The attached **Planetarium** (daily 10am–5pm; small entry fee; shows Tues–Fri 1pm, Sat noon, 1pm & 2.30pm, Sun 2pm & 3.30pm) is recommended for the chance to see the southern sky. There's also a changing programme of often interesting shows covering topics such as San sky myths. Leaflets at the museum provide a list of forthcoming attractions and you can buy a monthly chart of the current night sky, which is very handy, especially if you're staying in an area without streetlights and can actually see the stars.

Houses of Parliament

South Africa's **Houses of Parliament**, east of Government Avenue, on Parliament Street, are not one building but a complex of interlinking ones, with labyrinthine corridors connecting hundreds of offices, debating chambers and miscellaneous other rooms. Many of these rooms are relics of the 1980s reformist phase of apartheid when, in the interests of racial segregation, there were three distinct legislative complexes sited here to cater to different "races".

The original wing, completed in 1885, is an imposing Victorian Neoclassical building which first served as the legislative assembly of the Cape Colony. After the Boer republics and British colonies amalgamated in 1910, it became the Parliament of the Union of South Africa. This is the old Parliament where over seven decades of repressive legislation, including apartheid laws, were passed. It's also where **Hendrik Verwoerd**, the arch-theorist of apartheid met his bloody end, not at the hand of a political activist, but stabbed to death by a parliamentary messenger, who inexplicably went off the rails. Verwoerd's portrait, depicting him as a man of vision and *gravitas*, used to hang over the main entrance to the dining room. In 1996 it was removed, along with paintings of generations of white parliamentarians.

The new chamber was built in 1983 as part of the **tricameral parliament**, P.W. Botha's attempt to avert majority rule by trying to co-opt Indians and coloureds – but in their own separate debating chambers. The "tricameral" chamber, where the three non-African "races" on occasions met together, is now the **National Assembly**, where you can watch sessions of democratic South Africa's historic First Parliament, which will sit until the next election in 1999.

Day tickets to watch sessions are available from the Parliamentary Public Relations Section, Room 12 (ask for directions at the entrance desk), in the old Parliament building. Most interesting is **question time** (Wed 3pm onwards), when you can hear ministers being quizzed by MPs if Parliament is sitting. The ANC sits to the right of the speaker, so if you want to see them you should enter the gallery at the rear via the right entrance. The minority parties sit opposite. You're most unlikely to see the President, who is not a member of parliament and rarely attends sittings. When he does, for the opening of Parliament or for visits by foreign leaders, seats are invariably already snapped up.

Free one-hour **tours** of Parliament (Mon–Fri 11am & 2pm) take in the old and new debating chambers, the library and museum, and should be booked in advance through the Public Relations Section (☎403 2460 or 403 2461 or 403 2462).

The Bo-Kaap

Minutes from Parliament, on the slopes of Signal Hill, is the **Bo-Kaap**, one of Cape Town's oldest and most fascinating residential areas. Its streets are a facade of brightly coloured nineteenth-century Dutch and Georgian terraces which conceal a network of alleyways that are the arteries of its **Muslim community**. The Bo-Kaap harbours its own strong identity, made all the more unique by the destruction of District Six, with which it had much in common. A particular dialect of Afrikaans is spoken here, although it is steadily being eroded by English, which has a higher social status and lacks the associations with apartheid.

Bo-Kaap residents are descended from dissidents and slaves imported here by the Dutch in the sixteenth and seventeenth centuries. They became known collectively as "Cape Malays", a term you'll still hear, even though it's a complete misnomer: fewer than one percent of slaves actually came from Malaysia. Most originated from Africa, India, Madagascar and Sri Lanka.

The easiest way to get to the Bo-Kaap is by foot along Wale Street, which trails up from the south end of Adderley Street and across Buitengracht, to become the main drag of the Bo-Kaap. There's a deceptively quaint feel to the area; apart from Wale Street, this is not really a place to explore alone. A good place to head for is the **Bo-Kaap Museum**, 71 Wale St (Mon–Sat 9.30am–4.30pm; small entry fee), near the Buitengracht end. Consisting mainly of the house and possessions of a wealthy nineteenth-century Cape Muslim family, the museum also has exhibits exploring the local brand of Islam, which has its own unique traditions and nearly two dozen *kramats* (shrines) dotted about the peninsula. One block south of the museum, at Dorp Street, is the **Auwal**, South Africa's first official mosque, founded in 1795 by "Tuan Guru", a Muslim activist. Ten more mosques, whose minarets give spice to the quarter's skyline, now serve its 10,000 residents.

Modern, low-cost developments, looking down from the heights of Signal Hill onto the photogenic Bo-Kaap townscape, have helped alleviate the community's housing shortage, but have added nothing to the architectural charm of the protected historic core bounded by Dorp and Strand streets, and Buitengracht and Pentz streets. A small Muslim shantytown, tucked away next to the old quarry below the cemetery, brings the immediacy of South Africa's housing crisis right to the edge of the city centre.

The only way to get under the skin of the Bo-Kaap is on one of the several **tours** that takes in the museum and walks you around the district. The best (and cheapest) of these is the three-hour walk, costing R25, run by *Bo-Kaap Community Guided Tours* (bookings on ☎24 0014), which is based at the museum and operated by insiders whose knowledge goes beyond the standard tour-guide script.

The Lower City Centre

The **Lower City Centre** has for centuries been a marginal area between Cape Town and the sea. The area stretches north of Strand Street to the shore, taking in the still-functional **Duncan Dock** and Cape Town's biggest shopping and entertainment complex at the **Victoria and Alfred Waterfront**. In the mid-nineteenth century, the city's middle classes viewed the quarter with a mixture of alarm and excitement – a tension which remains today.

Lower Long Street divides the area just inland from the docklands into two. To the east is the Foreshore, an ugly post-World War II wasteland of grey corporate architecture, among which is the **Nico Theatre**, Cape Town's prestige arts complex. To the west, in sharp contrast, is the city's densely packed clubbing and pubbing locality.

Clubland: west of Lower Long Street

As long as the docks have existed, there's been life after dark west of Lower Long Street, particularly along **Waterkant Street**, and at the northern ends of **Bree** and **Loop streets**, where they intersect Waterkant. Frequented by sailors, dock-workers and prostitutes, Cape Town's red-light district used to be a hard-drinking, drugged-up, apartheid-free zone where some of the city's best jazz was played and raids by the police were a regular part of the scene. These days, with its high density of **nightclubs** and **pubs**, the area has become the best place in Cape Town to club-crawl and one of the few places where you're guaranteed action seven nights a week. See "Nightlife and entertainment" for club details.

The Foreshore

The **Foreshore**, an area of reclaimed land north of Strand Street, stretching to the docks, and east of Lower Long Street, is a ham-handed post-World War II development, which was intended to turn Cape Town's harbour into a heavily symbolic gateway to Africa, but instead turned out as a series of large concrete boxes surrounded by acres of windswept tarmac parking lots.

Heerengracht, a truncated two-lane carriageway running from Adderley Street to the harbour, and punctuated at either end by massive roundabouts, each solemnly guarded by statues of Jan Van Riebeeck and Bartholomeu Dias, was meant to be the ceremonial axis through this grand scheme, joining the city to the sea, but it never quite makes it to the water, coming to a disappointing standstill at the dock perimeter fence, before bearing east under the dismal shadow of the N1 and N2 flyovers.

The only building worth visiting here is the **Nico Theatre Complex**, Cape Town's major performance venue, in DF Malan Street just east of Heerengracht. Incorporating the large *Main Theatre*, it also houses the small *Arena Theatre* and an opera house. The complex is currently making attempts to throw off the burden of a long association with the apartheid establishment by branching out into Afrocentric productions (see "Nightlife and entertainment" for more details).

Duncan Dock

North of the Foreshore, **Duncan Dock** is Cape Town's working harbour and presents a forbidding industrial landscape of large ships and towering cranes cut off from the city by an enormous perimeter fence. It's a fabulous place to take moody photographs of gigantic hulks against Table Mountain, and has an excellent Taiwanese restaurant, but is not the kind of area you'd want to linger alone in.

Work started on the dock in 1938, swallowing the city beachfronts at Woodstock and Paarden Island to cater for the growing supertanker traffic that was outstripping the capacity of the Victoria and Alfred Docks (see below).

The Waterfront

The Victoria and Alfred Waterfront (known simply as the Waterfront), adjoining the west of Duncan Dock, is Cape Town's original Victorian harbour which, after two decades of stagnation, began redevelopment at the start of the 1990s as the city's central shopping area, its

ROBBEN ISLAND

Nelson Mandela is the most famous Robben Island prisoner, but certainly not the first. In the seventeenth century, the island was established as a place of banishment for those who offended the political order – first of the Dutch, later the British and most recently the Afrikaner Nationalists. The first political prisoner was the Strandloper leader **Autshumato**, who learnt English in the early seventeenth century and became an emissary of the British. After the Dutch settlement was established, he was jailed on the island in 1658 by Jan Van Riebeeck. Throughout the seventeenth century a succession of East Indies political prisoners were exiled here for opposing Dutch colonial rule. Many Muslim holy men from the Dutch East Indies found themselves here, going on to establish Islam at the Cape once they were freed.

During the nineteenth century, the **British** used Robben Island as a dumping ground for deserters, criminals and political prisoners, in much the same way as they used Australia. Captured **Xhosa leaders** who defied the Empire were taken by sea from the Eastern to the Western Cape to be imprisoned, many ending up on Robben Island. In 1846, the island's brief was extended to include a whole range of the **socially marginalized**. Criminals and political detainees were joined by vagrants, prostitutes, lunatics and the chronically ill. All were victim to a regime of brutality and maltreatment, even in hospital. In the 1890s, a leper colony existed alongside the social outcasts. Lunatics were removed in 1921 and the lepers in 1930. During World War II the **Defence Force** took over the island to set up defensive guns against a feared Axis invasion, which never came.

Robben Island's greatest era of notoriety began in 1961 when it was taken over by the **Prisons Department**. Prisoners arriving at the island prison were greeted by a slogan on the gate that read: "Welcome to Robben Island: We Serve with Pride." By 1963 when Nelson Mandela arrived, it had become a maximum security prison. All the warders, and none of the prisoners, were white. Common-law and political prisoners were housed together prior to 1971, when they were separated in an attempt to isolate the politicals further.

Conditions were harsh, especially as there is nothing between the island and the South Pole; icy winds routinely blow in from across the Atlantic. Prisoners were made to wear shorts and flimsy jerseys, and were routinely beaten, while many were forced to do hard labour. Nelson Mandela, like every other prisoner, slept on a thin mat on the floor until 1973, when he was given a bed because he was ill. Like the other prisoners, he was kept in solitary confinement in a cell measuring two metres square for sixteen hours a day. In the early 1960s, prisoners were only allowed to send and receive one letter every six months.

Remarkably, the prisoners found ways to of **protesting**, using hunger strikes and other means, and winning improved conditions over the years. The island also became a university behind bars, where people of different political views and generations met. It was not unknown for prisoners to give academic help to their warders. The last political prisoners were released from Robben Island in 1991 and the remaining common-law prisoners were transferred to the mainland in 1996. On January 1, 1997, control of Robben Island was transferred from the Department of Correctional Services to the Department of the Arts, Culture, Science and Technology, which has now established it as a a museum. The government is putting forward the island for UN World Heritage Site status.

most fashionable eating and drinking venue, and a safe place to dally for an hour or two. A cocktail of period buildings, neo-Victorian shopping malls, piers with waterside walkways, and a functioning harbour, as well as the magnificent backdrop of Table Mountain, complement the wide range of restaurants, outdoor cafés, pubs, clubs, cinemas, museums and outdoor entertainment. This is one of the most popular attractions in Cape Town.

The Waterfront has drawn fire, though, for presenting a sanitized, Anglo-Saxon version of its history, with little acknowledgement of the thousands of slaves, press-ganged sailors, impoverished fishermen and prostitutes who made the place work and created its real historical atmosphere. Controversy here is nothing new – arguments raged throughout the first half of the nineteenth century over the need for a proper dock. The Cape was often known as the "Cape of Storms" because of its vicious weather, which left dozens of wrecks littering Table Bay. Many makeshifts were attempted, including the construction of a lighthouse in 1823, and the start on a jetty at the bottom of Bree Street in 1832. The clamour for a harbour grew with the expansion of sea traffic arriving at the Cape in the 1850s, and reached its peak in 1860, when the Lloyds marine insurance company refused the risk of covering ships dropping anchor in Table Bay.

The British colonial government eventually agreed that a harbour was needed and, on a suitably stormy September day in 1860, at a huge ceremony, the teenage Prince Alfred tipped the first batch of stones into Table Bay to begin the **Breakwater**, the westernmost arm of the harbour, which was subsequently completed with convict labour. In 1869 the dock, consisting of two main basins, was completed and the sea was allowed in.

The **Victoria Basin**, and the smaller **Alfred Basin** to its west, now joined by the even more westerly **New Basin**, create the Waterfront's geography of piers and quays, with most of the activity concentrated around the north side. The **Waterfront Visitors' Centre**, set back from the northwest of the Victoria Basin on Dock Road (☎418 2369), can provide maps, bookings for tours and taxis, and an excellent booklet that guides you round 32 social history display boards dotted about the harbour. If you're simply sauntering, you'll get by without a map, as the Waterfront is replete with visitor-friendly signposts, and the constant presence of Table Mountain makes orientation simple.

Northeast of the visitor's centre, the action centres around **Market Square** and the **Agfa Amphitheatre**, where you can often catch free rock or jazz performances and sometimes hear the Cape Town Symphony Orchestra.

TOURS TO ROBBEN ISLAND

The only **tours** allowed onto Robben Island are ones run by the Department of Arts. Three ferries run every day (9.30am, 11.45am & 1.15pm) departing from the Embarkation Point on Jetty 1 at the Waterfront. Tickets on these heavily subscribed tours cannot be booked ahead and are only available in person from the Embarkation Office (daily 7.30am–5pm; ☎419 1300).

At the time of writing the tours (R80) were still in a fairly raw state, but there are hopes that they will improve greatly. Don't expect too much from the commentary that accompanies the tours, which lacks polish, but go rather to see this potent symbol of apartheid for yourself. The ferry trip takes about half an hour. The visit takes in Section B of the prison, where you'll see **Mandela's cell** as well as the horrifically crowded **dormitory cells** which accommodated sixty to seventy prisoners in cramped and freezing conditions. A bus ride around the island takes in the **leper graveyard**, the **leper church** designed by Sir Herbert Baker and the **lime quarry**, where Mandela and the other prisoners worked quarrying lime, ruining their eyes from the relentless glare. Perhaps one of the saddest and most poignant sites is **Robert Sobukwe's house**. Leader of the Pan Africanist Congress (see p.655), Sobukwe was kept here in solitary confinement and not allowed to speak to anyone, even his warder. Sobukwe was considered such a dangerous political figure that after his sentence expired the apartheid government drummed up the General Amendment Act, specifically to prolong his detention indefinitely.

Boat trips

A couple of minutes east of the Agfa Amphitheatre brings you to the dockside, and to Quays 4 and 5. **Boat trips** and **cruises** are on offer here, including trips to Robben Island (see box, p.86). Tickets for trips other than Robben Island are available from the outdoor vendors or the office in the Old Port Captain's Building on the adjacent Pierhead. The dowdy brick building at the end of Quay 5 was once the Department of Correctional Services' embarkation point for prisoners exiled to Robben Island.

From the Pierhead jetty you can catch the **penny ferry** rowing boat, or the motorized **water taxi service**, both of which will take you all over the Waterfront. One very pleasant short hop, costing R1, transports you from the Pierhead to **Carradines**, with its bar/restaurant, and a jetty where Cape fur seals come to sun themselves. The taxi returns by a slighly longer route, taking in the tip of Jetty No. 1. Look out for more seals lying atop the buffer tyres, which hang from the harbour wall.

Two Oceans Aquarium

Bear west from the Pierhead along the adjacent North Quay, past the swanky *Victoria and Alfred Hotel*, towards the northwest corner of New Basin, and you'll reach what is without question the highlight of the Waterfront – **Two Oceans Aquarium** (daily 10am–6.30pm). Dedicated to exhibiting the unique ecosystem of Africa's southern coast, this museum is great fun and alone justifies a visit to the Waterfront. Downstairs in the auditorium, scheduled videos cover South Africa's marine life and related topics (such as underwater photography); on the same floor, you'll find tanks containing a jaw-dropping array of bizarre sea creatures. You can even have a feel of them – if you are inclined – in the shallow "touch pool". Upstairs, the ambitious River Ecosystem, Kelp Forest and Open Ocean exhibits display complex interactions in a living and changing environment. The first of these has penguins flapping about rocks, and diving and swimming underwater, while sea birds fly about the rafters.

GETTING TO AND FROM THE WATERFRONT

The Waterfront is one of the easiest points to **reach** in Cape Town by **public transport**. Waterfront Buses (☎418 2369) leave from outside the Tourism Gateway in Adderley Street every ten minutes (daily 6.30am–11pm) and from Beach Road in Sea Point every twenty minutes, and terminate at Breakwater Boulevard. The *Golden Arrow Beachcomber* service (☎ toll free 0801/21 2111) runs two circular services (daily every 40min) from the Waterfront, both going via Sea Point, Camps Bay and Table Mountain; one of the services takes in the City as well. If you want to leave by **cab**, head for the taxi rank on Breakwater Boulevard. Arriving by **car**, you'll find yourself well catered for, with several car parks and garages.

The southern suburbs

The bulk of Cape Town's residential sprawl extends east into South Africa's interior away from Table Mountain and the city centre. It's here that the **southern suburbs**, the formerly whites-only residential areas, cut a swath from town, down the east side of Table Mountain, ending just before Muizenberg on the False Bay coast. All the main suburban attractions are concentrated in this area and, not surprisingly, the best shopping areas and cinemas.

From anywhere in the southern suburbs you can see Table Mountain rising above Cape Town. The area offers some quick escapes from the city heat into forests, gardens and vineyards, all hugging the eastern slopes of the mountain, and its extension, the

Constantiaberg. The suburbs themselves are pleasant enough places to stay, eat and shop, but sights are thin on the ground.

Woodstock, Salt River and Observatory

First and oldest of the suburbs as you take an easterly exit from town is **Woodstock**, unleafy and windblown, but redeemed by some nice Victorian buildings, originally occupied by working-class coloureds, and gradually yuppifying.

To its east, **Salt River** is a harsh, industrial, mainly coloured area, built initially for workers and artisans, while **Observatory**, abutting its southern end, is generally regarded as Cape Town's bohemian hub, a reputation fuelled by its proximity to the University of Cape Town in Rondebosch and its large student population. Many of the houses here are student digs, but the narrow Victorian streets are also home to young professionals, hippies and arty types. The refreshingly unrestored, peeling arcades on Observatory's Lower Main Road, and the streets off it, have some nice cafés and lively bars, as well as a wholefood shop, an African fabrics shop, one of Cape Town's few African restaurants and a couple of antiques emporiums. The huge *Groote Schuur Hospital* overlooking the freeway which sweeps through Observatory, was the site of the world's first heart transplant in 1967.

Mowbray and Rosebank

Heading along Station Road, away from the mountain and south of Observatory, is **Mowbray**, originally called "Drie Koppen" ("Three Heads"), after the heads of three slaves impaled there in 1724, but its name was sanitized in the 1840s. In the nineteenth century, this was the home of philologist Willem Bleek, who lived with a group of Khoisan convicts given up by the colonial authorities, so that he could study their languages and world-view. Bleek's pioneering work still forms the basis of much of what we know about traditional Khoisan life.

Rosebank, to Mowbray's south, has a substantial student community, some staying in the so-called "Tampax Towers", the unmistakable circular residential blocks on Main Road. Just beyond them is the brown-bricked **Baxter Theatre**, one of Cape Town's premier arts complexes (see "Theatre, performance and cinema").

Irma Stern Museum

Irma Stern is acknowledged as one of South Africa's pioneering artists of the twentieth century, more for the fact that she brought modern European ideas to the colonies than for any huge contribution she made to world art. The **UCT Irma Stern Museum** on Cecil Road, Rosebank (Tues–Sat 10am–5pm; small entry fee), was the artist's home for 38 years until her death in 1966. The museum is definitely worth visiting to see Stern's collection of Iberian, African, Oriental and ancient artefacts. The whole house, in fact, reflects the artist's fascination with **exoticism**, starting with her own Gauguinesque paintings of "native types", the fantastic carved doors she brought back from Zanzibar, and the very untypical garden that brings a touch of the tropics to Cape Town with its exuberant bamboo thickets and palm trees.

Born in a backwater town in South Africa in 1894 to German Jewish parents, Stern studied at Germany's Weimar Academy, against whose conservatism she reacted. She adopted **expressionist distortion** in her paintings, some of which were included in the Neue Sezession Exhibition in Berlin in 1918. Although her work was appreciated in Europe when she returned to South Africa after World War II, critics claimed that her style was simply a cover for technical incompetence. Stern went on several expeditions into Africa in the 1940s and 1950s, where she found the source for her intensely sensuous work that shocked contemporary South Africa, but has led historians to regard her as the towering figure of her generation.

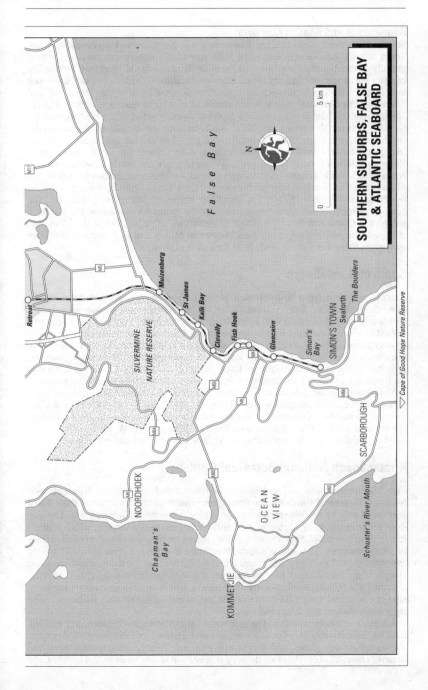

SOUTHERN SUBURBS, FALSE BAY & ATLANTIC SEABOARD

5 km

0

N

False Bay

Retreat

M17

M5

Muizenberg

St James

Kalk Bay

SILVERMINE NATURE RESERVE

Clovelly

Fish Hoek

Glencairn

M5

M6

M64

M4

Simon's Bay

SIMON'S TOWN

Seaforth

The Boulders

M4

NOORDHOEK

M6

Chapman's Bay

M65

OCEAN VIEW

KOMMETJIE

M65

SCARBOROUGH

Schuster's River Mouth

▷ Cape of Good Hope Nature Reserve

Rondebosch and Rhodes Memorial

South of Rosebank, neighbouring **Rondebosch** is home to the **University of Cape Town** (UCT), handsomely festooned with nineteenth-century creepers and sitting grandly on the mountainside, overlooking Main Road and the M3 highway. Next to the campus north towards the city is the **Rhodes Memorial**, built to resemble a Greek temple, and grandiosely conspicuous against the slopes of Devil's Peak. The monument celebrates Cecil Rhodes' energy with a sculpture of a horse rearing up wildly, and the empire-builder's bust is planted at the top of a towering set of stairs. His large estate, **Groote Schuur**, bordering on Main Road, became the official prime ministerial residence of the Cape, now South Africa's presidential seat occupied by Nelson Mandela. Mandela lives here when he is in Cape Town (his private home is in Houghton, Johannesburg). Even more eye-catching are the herds of wildebeest and zebra, nonchalantly grazing on the slopes around the Memorial, as cars fly past on the M3, and the **Tea Garden**, with terrific views of Cape Town. From here you can walk to the King's Blockhouse, formerly a signalling station to Muizenberg, and onto the contour path which follows the eastern side of the mountain, way above the southern suburbs to Constantia Nek (see "Table Mountain walks", p.96). Below the Memorial, alongside the M3, is the incongruous **Mostert's Mill**, a real mill built two centuries ago, when there were wheat fields here instead of highways.

South of Rondebosch

Continuing **south from Rondebosch** along the Van der Stel Freeway or along the more congested Main Road, you pass some of Cape Town's most prestigious suburbs. **Newlands**, almost merging with Rondebosch, is home to the city's famous rugby and cricket stadiums, while the well-heeled suburb of **Claremont** to its south is becoming an alternative focus to the city centre for shopping and entertainment, with two cinema complexes and several malls. A little further on, **Bishopscourt**, as its name suggests, is home to the Anglican bishop of Cape Town and it was in a mansion here that Archbishop Desmond Tutu lived even in the years when blacks weren't supposed to live in whites-only suburbs. Partly because of its prime siting – some plots have views of both Newlands Forest and the sea – this is one of the most prestigious areas in Cape Town and a number of consuls live here on huge properties behind the high walls that are about all you'll see passing the area. Further down the line, **Wynberg** is known for its Maynardville open-air theatre and quaint little row of shops and eateries.

Kirstenbosch National Botanical Gardens

Five kilometres south of Rondebosch, in Rhodes Avenue, are the **Kirstenbosch National Botanical Gardens**, the third most popular tourist attraction in Cape Town (exceeded only by the Waterfront and the cable-car trip up Table Mountain). The gardens are magnificent, glorying in lush shrubs and exuberant blooms, which trail off into fynbos, covering a huge expanse of the rugged eastern slopes and wooded ravines of Table Mountain. The setting is quite breathtaking – this is a great place to have tea and stroll around gazing up the mountain, or to wander onto the paths, which meander steeply to the top. If you're here in summer, one of the undoubted delights is to bring a picnic for a Sunday evening **open-air concert**, where you can lie back on the lawn, sip Cape wine and savour the mountain air and sunset light. There's a tea house, open daily for breakfast, and lunch and teas.

Kirstenbosch is the oldest and largest botanical garden in South Africa, and was created by Cecil Rhodes in 1895 (his camphor and fig trees are still here). Today, over 22,000 indigenous plants, and a research unit and library, attract researchers and botanists from all over. There's a nursery selling local plants, while characteristic Cape plants, found nowhere else in the world, are cultivated on the slopes. Little signboards and paved paths guide you through the highlights of the gardens, with trees and plants identified to enhance the rambling. The most interesting route is the one created for blind visitors, with labels in braille and an abundance of aromatic and textured plants.

The cultivated gardens blend seamlessly into the mountainside, as there are no fences cutting off the way to the top of Table Mountain. From here, you can make your way up the mountain: two popular paths, starting from the Contour Path above Kirstenbosch, are Nursery Ravine and Skeleton Gorge (see "Table Mountain Walks", p.97). Note that women should not walk alone in the isolated upper reaches of Kirstenbosch.

Getting to the gardens

There are two **bus routes** to Kirstenbosch; the Adderley Street to Hout Bay service, which operates five buses a day (2hr), and the service from Mowbray station (three buses a day), which is linked by trains to central Cape Town. There is no train service directly to the gardens. If you're **driving,** take the M5, and leave it at the Rhodes Avenue turnoff.

Constantia and its winelands

South of Kirstenbosch lie the elegant suburbs of **Constantia** and the Cape's oldest **winelands**. Luxuriating on the lower slopes of Table Mountain and the Constantiaberg, with tantalizing views of False Bay, the winelands are an easy drive from town, not more than ten minutes off the Van der Stel Freeway (the M3), which runs between the centre and Muizenberg.

The winelands started cultivated life in 1685 as the farm of **Simon van der Stel**, the governor charged with opening up the fledgling Dutch colony to the interior. Thrusting himself wholeheartedly into the task, he selected for his own use an enormous tract of the choicest land set against the Constantiaberg, the section of the peninsula just south of Table Mountain. He named the estate after his daughter Constancia, and this is now (with a minor change of spelling) the name of Cape Town's oldest and most prestigious residential area. Exuding the easy ambience of landed wealth, Constantia is a green and pleasant place, shaded by oak forests and punctuated with farm stalls, riding schools, designer Cape Dutch-style shopping centres and, of course, the vineyards.

Constantia grapes have been making wine since van der Stel's first ouput in 1705. After his death in 1712, the estate was divided up and sold off as the modern **Groot Constantia**, **Klein Constantia** and **Buitenverwachting**. In 1990, the nearby Steenberg Estate was bought up by a large Johannesburg mining conglomerate and is worth keeping an eye on for its future output. All **four estates** are open to the public and offer tastings; definitely worth devoting a few hours to if you aren't heading further afield to the Winelands proper.

There is no public **transport** to Constantia, but Groot Constantia features on most organized tours of Cape Town or the peninsula. To get to the estates **by car**, take the sign-posted Groot Constantia off-ramp from the M3 onto Ladies Mile Extension, and keep following the signs to Groot Constantia. Buitenverwachting and Klein Constantia are on Klein Constantia Road, just off Ladies Mile Extension, and are clearly signposted.

Groot Constantia

The largest estate and the one most geared to tourists is **Groot Constantia**, among Cape Town's four most-visited attractions. Its big pull is that it retains the rump of van der Stel's original estate, as well as the original buildings. There is a **museum** (daily 10am–5pm; entry fee), a gift shop, art gallery and two restaurants. **Cellar tours** start every hour on the hour (10am–4pm; entry fee) and there's **wine tasting** between 10am and 4.30pm.

Despite the commercialism, Groot Constantia is impressive, though its portrayal of life in a seventeenth-century colonial chateau makes scant reference to the slave labour that underpinned its operations. The **manor house**, a quintessential Cape Dutch building, was van der Stel's original home, modified at the end of the eighteenth century by the French architect Thibault. Walking straight through it, down the ceremonial axis, you'll come to the cellar, fronted with a carved pediment, depicting a riotous bacchanalia, which represents fertility.

Klein Constantia and Buitenverwachting

Smaller in scale than Groot Constantia, Klein Constantia and Buitenverwachting both offer free wine tasting in less regimented conditions than at the bigger estate, and although the buildings are far humbler the settings are equally beautiful. **Klein Constantia**, on Klein Constantia Road (wine tasting and sales Mon–Fri 9am–5pm, Sat 9am–1pm) has a friendly atmosphere and produces some fine wines. Something of a curiosity is its **Vin de Constance**, the recreation of an eighteenth-century Constantia wine which was a favourite of Napoleon, Frederick the Great and Bismarck. It's a delicious dessert wine, packaged in a replica of the original bottle, and makes an original souvenir. As well as wine, there's wildlife here: look out for the guinea fowls that roam the estate munching on the beetles that attack young vine leaves; in summer, migrant steppe buzzards prey on unsuspecting starlings, which eat the grapes.

Buitenverwachting, also on Klein Constantia Road (wine tasting and sales Mon–Fri 9am–5pm, Sat 9am–1pm), pioneered environmentally friendly viniculture in South Africa at the beginning of the 1990s. It carries its "holistic" approach right down to its workers, who enjoy some of the best living conditions of any South African farm. Unusual labour practices include the provision of two social workers, weekly visits by a doctor to the farm clinic, and worker involvement in the selection of new staff. Buitenverwachting's expensive **restaurant** (Tues–Fri noon–3pm & 7pm–midnight) is regularly voted one of South Africa's ten best. For a day out on the farm (they have cattle and horses, too), Buitenverwachting provides **picnic lunches** (Mon–Sat noon–2.30pm), which must be prebooked (☎794 1012 or 794 2122).

Table Mountain

The icon that for hundreds of years and from hundreds of kilometres announced Cape Town to seafarers, **Table Mountain**, flat-topped, with dramatic cliffs and eroded gorges, dominates the northern end of the peninsula. Its north face overlooks the city centre with **Lion's Head** and **Signal Hill** to the west and **Devil's Peak** to the east. The west face is made up of a series of gabled formations known as the **Twelve Apostles**. The southwest towers over Hout Bay and the east over the southern suburbs.

The mountain is a compelling feature in the middle of the city. It's a wilderness where you'll find wildlife and a substantial 1400 species of **flora**. Indigenous mammals include baboons, dassies (hyraxes) and porcupines, while the animals that resemble mountain goats are Himalayan tahrs, descended from specimens introduced by Cecil Rhodes onto his estate, and which escaped to flourish on the mountain.

Walks, climbs and cable cars

Reckoned the most-climbed massif in the world, **Table Mountain** has suffered under the constant pounding of hikers and wanton vandalism, though the damage isn't always

TABLE MOUNTAIN SAFETY

MAKE SURE YOU . . .
- Don't climb alone.
- Inform someone you're going up the mountain.
- Tell them your route, when you're leaving and when you expect to be back.
- Leave early enough to give yourself time to complete your route during daylight.
- Don't try to descend via an unknown route. If you get lost in poor weather, seek shelter and keep warm and wait for help.
- Avoid leaving any litter on the mountain.
- Avoid making fires. No cooking (even on portable stoves) is allowed.

WEAR . . .
- Good footwear. Boots or running shoes are recommended.
- A broad-rimmed hat.

TAKE . . .
- A backpack.
- A water bottle (filled with water, not beer). Allow two litres per person.
- Enough food: sandwiches, glucose sweets, nuts, raisins, juice.
- A warm jersey.
- A windbreaker.
- A raincoat
- Sunglasses.
- High-factor sunscreen.
- Money for the cable car.
- Plasters for blisters.
- A map (available from Cape Union Mart at the Waterfront, or Cavendish Square Shopping Cente in Claremont).

obvious – certainly not from the dizzying vista at the top. The harm done isn't all one way, either; every year the mountain strikes back, taking its toll of lives. One of the commonest causes of difficulties is people losing the track (often due to sudden mist falling) and ending up trapped. If you plan on tackling one of the hundreds of walks and climbs on its slopes, go properly prepared (see box above).

The cable car

The least challenging, but certainly not least interesting, way up the mountain, is via the **cable car**, which offers dizzying views across Table Bay and the Atlantic. The journey is a Cape Town must: don't go home without doing it.

To cope with half a million visitors jostling to ride the cable car to the top of the mountain, a state-of-the art Swiss system was installed in 1997. The floor of the fish-bowl-shaped car is designed to complete a 360-degree rotation on its way to the top, giving passengers a full panorama. Regular departures leave from the lower cableway station (daily May–Nov 8.30am–6pm, Dec–April 8am–10pm; ☎ 24 5148 or 21 4615) on Tafelberg Road. To get there, take the **Kloofnek bus** from the Adderley Street terminus to Kloofnek; from here you can catch the **cable shuttle** to the lower station.

Signal Hill and Lion's Head

From the roundabout at the top of Kloofnek a road leads all the way along **Signal Hill** to a car park and lookout with good views over Table Bay, the docks and the city. A cannon was formerly used for sending signals to ships at anchor in the bay, and the Noon

Gun, still fired from its slopes daily, sends a thunderous rumble through the Bo-Kaap below. Halfway along the road is a sacred Islamic *kramat*, or shrine, one of several dotted around the Peninsula which "protect" the city. You can also walk up **Lion's Head**, an unstrenuous and popular hike which seems to bring out half of Cape Town every full moon. But be prepared to use fixed chains to climb up a couple of short but steep rocky outcrops.

Climbs and walks

Climbing the mountain will give you a greater sense of achievement than being ferried up by the cable car, but proceed with extreme caution: it may look sunny and clear when you leave, but at the top you could find a very different story. The weather is subject to rapid changes, both in general and in small localized areas. The main hazards are sun, mist and violent winds. Unless you're going with a knowledgeable guide, attempt only the simplest routes (the ones outlined here).

PLATTEKLIP GORGE AND MACLEAR'S BEACON

The first recorded ascent to the summit of Table Mountain was by the Portuguese captain Antonio de Saldanha in 1503. He wisely chose **Platteklip Gorge**, the gap visible from the front table which, as it turns out, is the most accessible way up. A short and easy extension will get you to Maclear's Beacon which, at 1086m, is the highest point on the mountain. The Platteklip route has the added advantage of depositing you up at the Upper Cable Station, so you can hop on a car to get back down.

The route starts out at the **Lower Cable Station**. From here, walk along Tafelberg Road until you see a high embankment built from stone and maintained with wire netting. Just beyond and to the left of a small dam is a sign pointing to Platteklip Gorge. A steep fifteen-minute climb brings you onto the **upper contour path**. About 25m east, take the path indicated by a sign reading "Contour Path/Platteklip Gorge". The path zigzags from here onwards and is very clear. The gorge is the biggest cleavage on whole mountain, leading directly and safely to the top, but it's a very steep slog which will take **two to three hours** if you're reasonably fit. Once on top, turn right and ascend the last short section onto the **front table**, for a breathtaking view of the city. A sign points the way to the **Upper Cable Station** – a fifteen-minute walk along a concrete path thronging with visitors.

Maclear's Beacon is about 35 minutes from the top of the Platteklip Gorge on a path leading eastward. A waymarked path of white squares on little yellow footsteps guides you all the way. The path crosses the front table with Maclear's Beacon visible at all times. From the top you'll get views of False Bay and the Hottentots Holland Mountains to the east.

THE PIPE TRACK

One of the most rewarding and easiest walks along the mountainside takes the **Pipe Track**, a service road which follows water pipes from the mountain reservoirs to Kloof Nek. The track runs on the level for roughly 7km, on the west flank of Table Mountain, beneath the Twelve Apostles, following the mountain's contours and offering fantastic views of the Atlantic. The Pipe Track isn't a circular route, so you can turn back at any point. The whole walk can take up to three hours.

The route begins at some stone steps at **Kloof Nek** opposite the bus terminus, just to the west of Tafelberg Road turnoff (if you're driving, park on Tafelberg Road). Steps lead up alongside forestry staff houses before the road levels off under some pines. The path intersects several ascents up the mountain. The first, after about 45 minutes, is indicated by a sign to **Blinkwater Ravine** (closed to the public due to rockfalls). A further ten to fifteen minutes brings you to the **Kasteelspoort** ascent (signposted under gum trees) followed by **Woody Ravine** and the last, roughly 25 minutes after Kasteelspoort, at **Slangolie Ravine**, where the path ends. The rock bed on Slangolie is steep, unstable and to be avoided. Turn back when you see the first of the **Woodhead Tunnel** danger signs.

SKELETON GORGE AND NURSERY RAVINE
You can combine a visit to the gardens at Kirstenbosch with an ascent up Table Mountain via one route and a descent down another, ending at the Kirstenbosch National Botanical Gardens' restaurant for tea. Starting at the restaurant, follow the well-signposted **Skeleton Gorge** signs, which lead you onto the **Contour Path**. At the Contour Path, a plaque indicates that this is **Smuts' Track**, the route favoured by Jan Smuts, the Boer leader, statesman, philosopher, friend to the British and South African prime minister. The plaque marks the start of a broad-stepped climb up Skeleton Gorge, involving wooden steps, stone steps, wooden ladders and loose boulders. It requires reasonable fitness, but can take as little as an hour. Be prepared for steep ravines and difficult rock climbs and under no circumstances stray off the path. Skeleton can be an unpleasant way down, especally in the wet season when it gets slippery.

Nursery Ravine is recommended for the descent. At the top of Skeleton Gorge, walk a few metres to your right to a sign indicating **Kasteelspoort**. It's just 35 minutes from the top of Skeleton along this path to the head of Nursery Ravine. The descent returns you to the 310-metre Contour Path, which leads back to Kirstenbosch. This entire walk lasts about five hours.

The Atlantic seaboard

Table Mountain's steep drop into the ocean along much of the western peninsula forces the suburbs along the **Atlantic seaboard** into a ribbon of developments clinging dramatically to the slopes. The sea washing the west side of the peninsula is freezing; far colder than on the False Bay seaboard. Although not ideal for bathing, the Atlantic makes up for this with some of the most incredible coastal roads in the world, particularly beyond **Sea Point**.

Green Point and Sea Point

Inland from the Waterfront and stretching for about a kilometre to the west, **Green Point** is one of the closest suburbs to the city centre, with a growing supply of budget accommodation, but little else to recommend it. Green Point's Main Road is notorious as a major hangout for prostitutes and their pimps, who are conveniently close here to their gangland turf in the Bo-Kaap.

Continuing southwest along Main Road, Green Point merges with the more fashionable **Sea Point**, one of the long-established haunts of Cape Town's gourmands. Middle-class couples, pram-pushing mothers, street kids and drunks living together create a blend of respectability and seediness that dissipates as you move into the wealthier suburbs down the Atlantic seaboard.

Sea Point is Cape Town's most densely populated former white suburb, with high-rise hotels and apartments interspersed with Victorian bungalows, and is one of the best places to find accommodation. The rocky shoreline, a block down from Main Road, has the closest beaches to the city centre, although the sea is unsuitable for swimming. Halfway along the kilometre-long beach promenade, running alongside Beach Road, you'll catch views of **Graaff's Pool**, an institutionalized and exclusively male nudist spot, while at the westernmost end is the only place in the vicinity to swim, at the spanking-new Olympic-sized **saltwater pool**, alongside the crashing surf.

Clifton to Sandy Bay

Suburbia proper begins south of Sea Point at Bantry Bay. Fashionable **Clifton**, on the next cove, is sheltered by Lion's Head. The sea here is good for surfing and safe for swimming, but bone-chillingly cold. Sitting on the most expensive real estate in Africa, Clifton is studded with fabulous seaside apartments and four wonderful sandy **beaches**, reached via steep stairways. First Beach (they're all numbered) is colonized by pneumatic male ball-players, surfers and their female counterparts, so avoid it unless your tan is up to scratch. Second and Third beaches are split between the teenies and thirtysomethings; if in doubt, head for Fourth, which has become the family beach because it has the fewest steps. There are regular **buses** to Clifton from the city centre.

A little to the south, **Camps Bay** suburb climbs the slopes of Table Mountain and is scooped into a small amphitheatre, bounded by the Lion's Head and the Twelve Apostles sections of the Table Mountain range. This and the airborne views across the Atlantic make Camps Bay one of the most desirable places to live in Cape Town. The main drag, Victoria Road, skirts the coast and is packed with trendy restaurants, while the wide sandy beach, in refreshing contrast, shines because of its sheer ordinariness. Enjoyed by families of all shapes and colours, Camps Bay Beach positively throngs around the Christmas and Easter breaks. However, it's exposed to the southeasterly wind, and there's the usual Atlantic chill and an occasional dangerous backwash.

There's little development between Camps Bay and **Llandudno**, a wonderful cove, 20km from Cape Town along Victoria Road (not served by public transport). A steep and narrow road winds down past smart homes to the shore, where the sandy beach is punctuated at either end by granite boulders. This is a good sunbathing spot and a choice one for bring-your-own sundowners. The small car park frequently spills over into the suburban streets at peak periods.

Isolated **Sandy Bay**, Cape Town's main nudist beach, can only be reached via a twenty-minute walk from Llandudno. In the apartheid days, the South African police went to ingenious lengths to trap nudists, but nowadays the beach is relaxed, so feel free to come as undressed as feels comfortable. Among the dunes and fynbos there are no houses – in fact, no facilities whatsoever – so bring whatever supplies you may need. To get there, take the path from the south end of the Llandudno car park, through fynbos vegetation and across some rocks, to the beach. It's a fairly easy walk, but if you're barefoot watch out for broken glass.

Hout Bay

Although no longer the quaint fishing village it once was, **Hout Bay** still has a functioning fishing harbour and is the centre of the local crayfish industry. Leopards no longer stalk its *kranse* and *koppies*, but their former presence is recalled by a bronze statue looking down from Chapman's Peak Drive. Despite ugly modern development and a growing shantytown, the natural setting is quite awesome. Next to the harbour and car park, the little **Mariner's Wharf** waterfront development has the *Seafood Emporium* selling fresh fish and there's a restaurant upstairs. This is a good place to pick up fresh *snoek*, a Cape speciality.

The sea off the long slender **beach** is no good for swimming – too cold, too close to the harbour and too prone to fish scales floating in its surf – but the beach is perfect for walking. Away from the harbour, the village is just managing to hang onto its historic ambience, with the **Hout Bay Museum**, 4 St Andrews Rd (Tues–Sat 10am–12.30pm & 2–4.30pm), offering good exhibits on Strandloper culture and the local fishing industry. Nearby, **World of Birds**, Valley Road (daily 9am–5pm; R14), is one of the world's largest bird parks, with large walk-through aviaries. This is a great chance to see unusual species like African blue cranes and Australian cassowaries. You can easily get there **by bus** on the Hout Bay service, which pulls in on its way from Adderley Street. Alternatively, go down to the estuary near the harbour to see local birds in their natural environment for free; kingfishers and blacksmith plovers are among commonly sighted residents.

Hout Bay is at a convenient junction for the rest of the peninsula and has the highest concentration of places to stay south of Sea Point, including the upmarket, country-style *Bay Hotel*. From Cape Town it's 20km along either the coast or inland via Constantia. Several **buses** (see p.66) leave from Adderley Street every day along the latter route and you can also catch minibus taxis. Crossing the peninsula spine from Simon's Town it's 26km (on the Glencairn Expressway).

Chapman's Peak Drive to Scarborough

Continuing south along the coast, **Chapman's Peak Drive** is a thrilling journey along terrifyingly narrow hairpin bends. For 10km the road carves into the mountainside on the one side, dropping precipitously hundreds of metres to the ocean on the other. Unceasingly spectacular views take in the breadth of Hout Bay to the 331-metre high sentinel on a curved outcrop. Viewpoints are provided along the route, but take care in high winds as it can be dangerous, with occasional rockfalls, although this doesn't seem to bother the scores of cyclists who sweat their way round, making considerate driving a necessity.

Noordhoek, a low-key settlement at the end of the descent from Chapman's Peak Drive, consists of small holdings in a gentle valley with a long white untamed beach stretching 3km across Chapman's Bay to Kommetjie. The sands are fantastic for walking and horse-riding, but can resemble a sandblaster when the southeaster blows. Swimming is hazardous, though surfers relish the rough waters around the rocks to the north. For refreshment, the only place around here is the excellent *Red Herring*, set back from the sea, about ten minutes on foot from the car park, with fine views from its outdoor deck.

Although only a few kilometres south of Noordhoek along the beach, getting to **Kommetjie** by road involves a 15km haul inland up the peninsula spine south along Noordhoek Road, taking a west turn into Kommetjie Road, to descend again. The beach's small basin (*kommetjie*), which is always a few degrees above the surrounding sea temperature, is perfect for swimming. Just to its north, **Long Beach** is a favourite surfing spot, used by devotees even during the chilly winter months.

Almost ten kilometres south by road from Kommetjie, the developing village of **Scarborough** is the most far-flung suburb along the peninsula. A long wide beach edges temptingly to its south just beyond Schusters River Lagoon – resist its potentially treacherous sea and stick to the lagoon. A crayfish processing plant, based here, and the local *Camel Rock* restaurant, make this a good place to stop and eat.

The False Bay seaboard

In summer, the waters of **False Bay** are several degrees warmer than those on the Atlantic seaboard, which is why Cape Town's oldest and most popular seaside development is along this flank of the peninsula. A series of village-like suburbs, backing onto the mountains, each served by a Metro Rail Station, is dotted all the way south from **Muizenberg**, through **St James**, **Kalk Bay**, **Fish Hoek** and down to **Simon's Town**. Each has its own character with restaurants, shops and places to stay, while Simon's Town, one of South Africa's oldest settlements, is worth taking in as a day-trip and makes a useful base for visiting the **Cape of Good Hope Nature Reserve** and **Cape Point**.

Muizenberg

Once South Africa's most fashionable beachfront, today **Muizenberg** is overcrowded, overdeveloped and rather tacky. Brightly coloured bathing boxes are reminders of an

CAPE TOWN'S TOP WHALE SPOTS

Cape Town's **best whale-watching spots** are on the **False Bay** side of the peninsula, and you'll need binoculars to get a decent sighting. Along this side, look out for whale signboards, indicating good places to spend time looking for them.

Boyes Drive, running along the mountainside behind Muizenberg and Kalk Bay, provides an outstanding vantage point. To get there **by car**, head out on the M3 from town to Muizenberg, taking a sharp right into Boyes Drive, at Lakeside, from where the road begins to climb, descending finally to join Main Road between Kalk Bay and Fish Hoek. Alternatively, sticking close to the shore along Main Road, the stretch between **Fish Hoek** and **Simon's Town** is recommended, with a particularly nice spot above the rocks at the south end of Fish Hoek Beach, as you walk toward Glencairn. **Boulders Beach** at the southern end of Simon's Town has a whale signboard, and smooth rocky outcrops above the sea to sit on and gaze out over the sea. Even better vantage points are further down the coast between Simon's Town and **Smitswinkel Bay**, where the road goes higher along the mountainside.

Without a car, it's easy enough to go **by train** to Fish Hoek or Simon's Town and whale-spot from the beach walkway which goes along the coast, just below the railway line.

If you're on a **coach trip**, or **driving** around the peninsula, you could also look out to sea at **Chapman's Peak** towards Hout Bay and also between **Llandudno** and **Sea Point**, where the road curves along the ocean. This side of the peninsula is not as rewarding as the warmer False Bay side. Outside Cape Town, the best place of all is ninety minutes away, at **Hermanus** and the other towns dotted around Walker Bay (see p.172).

Information on exactly where whales have been sighted in the past 24 hours is available from the **Whale Watch Hotline** (☎ toll free 0800/22 8222).

elegant heyday, when it was visited by the likes of Agatha Christie, who enjoyed riding its waves while holidaying here in the 1920s: "Whenever we could steal time off," she wrote, "we got out our surf boards and went surfing."

Despite the tawdriness, Muizenberg's gently shelving, sandy **beach** is the most popular along the peninsula. It's safe for bathing, the water tends to be flat and warm, there's good surfing in its breakers, and it's also the closest beach to Cape Town by train. This is also the most developed of the peninsula's beaches, with a pavilion complex around the car park featuring tea shops, a waterslide and minigolf. Along the beachfront and Main Road you'll also find shops, cafés and restaurants catering to the seaside trade. Muizenberg is one of the most heavily policed beaches, particularly at peak times, and there is a secure left-luggage office near the changing rooms.

Getting there is best done by train: from the centre it's a 45-minute journey – the train's first seaside stop as it trundles through the southern suburbs on its way to Simon's Town. By car, take the M3 through the posh suburbs, or the slightly quicker M5 via the less salubrious Cape Flats to Muizenberg. During peak season, finding a place to leave your vehicle can be near impossible.

The Historical Mile

Striking out south from Muizenberg, Main Road and the railway line hug the shore all the way to Simon's Town. A short stretch, starting at Muizenberg station, is known as the **Historical Mile**, dotted with a run of notable buildings, and easily explored on foot. **Muizenberg station**, an Edwardian-style building completed in 1913, is now a national monument, while further towards Simon's Town the **Posthuys**, a ruggedly white-washed and thatched building dating from 1673, is a fine example of the Cape vernacular style. **Rhodes' Cottage** (daily except Mon 10am–5pm; free), was bought in 1899 by the millionaire politician who dreamt of a railway from the Cape to Cairo through

British territory. He died here in 1902 before his grander dwelling next door (closed to the public) could be completed. Rhodes' Cottage contains memorabilia which paint a distinctly rosy portrait of the man, with photographs, a model of the Big Hole in Kimberley (where Rhodes made his fortune at the diamond diggings), and a curious diorama of World's View in Zimbabwe's Matopos Hills, where he lies buried.

Most idiosyncratic of the buildings along the historic mile, and closest to St James, is the **Natale Labia Museum** (daily except Mon 10am–5pm; closed Aug), completed in 1930 as the residence of the Italian Consul. Built in eighteenth-century Venetian style, it sits incongruously amid the Main Road townscape. Inside, heavy lace obscures the magnificent view, but there's an excellent restaurant, which serves up breakfasts, light meals and teas in the ersatz-Baroque interior or on the Italianate patio.

St James

St James, 2km south of Muizenberg, and just one stop by train, is more upmarket than its northern neighbour, and its pleasing, villagey feel makes it a nice place to hop off the train for tea. Although sheltered from the southeaster, the rocky beaches here don't make for great sea swimming, but there's a tidal pool that is safe for toddlers and great for bathing at high tide, when enormous breakers crash over the sea wall.

Kalk Bay

Moving south from Muizenberg, **Kalk Bay**, one of the most southerly and smallest of Cape Town's suburbs, is a lively **working harbour**, with wooden fishing vessels, mountain views, and the villagey shopping precinct packed with trendy coffee shops, antique dealers and curiosity shops.

Apart from the larger Hout Bay, Kalk Bay is the only harbour settlement still worked by coloured fishermen. The settlement is arranged around the small docks, where you can watch the boats come in and buy fresh fish, which are flung onto the quayside and noisily auctioned off in a spirited display. Kalk Bay somehow managed to slip through the net of the Group Areas Act, making it one of the few places on the peninsula with an intact coloured community. To purchase direct from the fishermen, phone the harbour master to find out when the boats are due back (note that boats never venture out when the southeaster is blowing).

Perched on the harbour wall in the station building, pounded by waves, is the popular *Brass Bell* restaurant, one of Kalk Bay's biggest attractions (see "Eating and drinking"), one of the few restaurants along the peninsula where you can actually sit next to the sea. If you want to try your hand at **fishing**, *Harbourside Backpackers*, 136 Main Rd (☎788 2943) arranges trips, which leave at 4.30am.

Rising up behind the Kalk Bay settlement is **Silver Mine Nature Reserve**, which runs across the Peninsula's spine, almost stetching to the west side at Chapman's Peak. Part of the Table Mountain chain, it offers walks and drives with fabulous views of False Bay, the mountains, indigenous forest and montane fynbos, and is most easily reached via the Ou Kaapseweg ("Old Cape Road") through Tokai.

Fish Hoek

In contrast to its neighbour Kalk Bay, **Fish Hoek**, further south, is one of the dreariest suburbs along the entire False Bay coast. Right up till the 1990s, a now-repealed law banned the sale of alcohol here, boosting the town's image as a dull retirement home.

That said, Fish Hoek does boast one of the best family **beaches**. The best and safest swimming is at the southern end of the beach, where the surf is moderately warm, tame and much enjoyed by boogie boarders. Facilities include changing rooms, toilets, fresh water, and a surprisingly good restaurant right on the beach (see "Eating and drinking").

From behind the restaurant, **Jager's Walk**, a picturesque pathway, skirts the rocky shoreline above the sea as far as Sunny Cove. The walkway provides a good vantage point for seeing whales when they're in the vicinity.

By car you can strike west south of Fish Hoek across the peninsula's spine to the Atlantic coast. The scenic Ou Kaapseweg takes you to Noordhoek. Alternatively, you can branch off north to Chapman's Drive. The Cape Town to Simon's Town train stops at Kalk Bay station, just opposite the beach.

Simon's Town

South Africa's principal naval base, **Simon's Town** isn't the hard-drinking, raucous place you might expect or hope for. Just 40km from Cape Town, the country's third-oldest European settlement is exceptionally pretty, with a near-perfectly preserved streetscape, marred on the ocean side by the domineering **naval dockyard**. But this, and glimpses of naval squaddies training behind the high walls or strolling to the station in their crisp white uniforms, are what give the place its distinct character.

Roughly halfway down the coast to Cape Point, Simon's Town makes the perfect base for a mellow break along the peninsula, offering easy day-trips by train to Cape Town. Just a few kilometres to the south is the rock-strewn **Boulders Beach**, with its colony of nonchalant jackass penguins – reason in themselves to venture here.

Some history

Founded in 1687 as the winter anchorage of the Dutch East India Company, Simon's Town was modestly named by **Governor Simon van der Stel** after himself. Its most celebrated visitor was Lord Nelson, who convalesced here as a midshipman returning home from the East in 1776. Nineteen years later, the British sailed into Simon's Town and occupied it as a bridgehead for their invasion of Cape Town and the **first British occupation of the Cape**. After just seven years they left, only to return in 1806. Simon's Town remained a British base until 1957, when it was handed over to South Africa.

There are fleeting hints, such as the odd mosque, that the town's exclusively white appearance isn't the whole story. In fact, the first **Muslims** arrived from the East Indies in the early eighteenth century, imported as slaves to build the Dutch naval base. After the British banning of the slave trade in 1807, ships were compelled to disgorge their human cargo at Simon's Town, where one district became known as "Black Town". In 1967, when Simon's Town was declared a White Group Area, there were 1200 well-established coloured familes descended from these slaves. By 1973 the majority had been **forcibly removed**, because of the Group Areas Act (see "History", p.655), to the desolate township of Ocean View (ironically, one of the few places along the peninsula not to enjoy a sea vista). Their departure made a significant impact, and dwellings were destroyed or allowed to rot, depriving the town of significant historic buildings. In 1973, town clerk Charles Chevalier complained that "the loss of the non-white population has had a depressing effect on the commercial life of the town".

Arrival and information

Trains run from Cape Town roughly every hour during the day. The trip takes an hour, the last twenty minutes from Muizenberg skirting the coast right next to the shoreline. Trains are met at Simon's Town by Rikki taxis. A thoroughly pleasant outing is to take one of the restaurant trains pulling *Biggsy's Restaurant Carriage & Wine Bar*, which runs five return trips a day (Tues–Sun) and serves lunches, salads and highly recommended breakfasts. *Biggsy's* leaves from Platform 1 at Cape Town station, but space is limited, so you should book (☎683 6020).

By car, the quickest way to get here from Cape Town is via the M3 or M5 freeways to Muizenberg and then follow the coast road to Simon's Town. There are no buses to Simon's Town.

The Town

A short way south of the station, a signposted road to the left points to the museums. The **Simon's Town Museum** (Mon–Fri 9am–4pm, Sat 10am–1pm) on Court Road is in the Old Residency built in 1772 for the Governor of the Dutch East India Company. It also served as the slave quarters (the dungeons are in the basement) and town brothel. The motley collection includes maritime material and an inordinate amount on Able Seaman Just Nuisance, a much-celebrated seafaring Great Dane. At the **South African Naval Museum** next door, lively displays include the inside of a submarine, the bridge of a ship simulating rocking, and loads of official portraits of South African Navy big guns with double-barrelled names, from 1922 to the present.

Across the road, the *British Hotel* is a pompous piece of Victoriana, still renting out rooms, and festooned with a grossly outsized banner bearing the portrait of Queen Elizabeth II. For the best **bread**, **pastries**, **pies** and everything else you'll need for a picnic at Cape Point, pop into *Brad's Bakery* next door, which also acts as an excellent self-appointed **information bureau** and accommodation agency.

The Beaches

Nearest to the station, **Long Beach** offers no shade and is therefore little used. However, on windless days it can be pleasant for long walks, with views of the Hottentots Holland Mountains, and its tidal pool is safe for bathing. Access is by a number of gaps in a brick wall alongside the main road and about midway along the beach (opposite Hopkirk Way), by a flight of steps. There are changing rooms and toilets nearby, and fresh water.

One of the best beaches for swimming is at **Seaforth**, where clear, deep waters lap around rocks. It's calm, protected and safe, but not pretty (bounded on one side by the looming grey mass of the naval base). There's plenty of lawn shaded by palm trees though, and an excellent restaurant, the *Seaforth*.

Two kilometres from the station towards Cape Point takes you out of town and to **Boulders**, the most popular local beach, with a number of places to stay, but no shops. The area takes its name from the huge, rounded rocks that create a collection of little coves with sandy beaches and clear, natural sea pools. But the main reason people come here is for the jackass **penguins** in the **Boulders Coastal Park** (small entry fee when attendant is present), a small fenced reserve on Boulders Beach. Passing sailors used to prey on the quirky birds and their eggs, but the penguins are extremely laid-back, paying little attention to visitors. More recently they have fallen victim to vandals, but are now under the protective wing of a semi-official guard. Jackass penguins usually live on islands off the west side of the South African coast; the Boulders birds form one of only two mainland colonies in the world. This is also the only place where the endangered species are actually increasing in numbers, so it's a rare opportunity to get a close look at them.

Almost 5km to the south is the popular **Miller's Point** resort, which has a number of small sandy beaches and a tidal pool protected from the southeaster. There's a **campsite** at the caravan park, with great sea views. Along Main Road, the notable *Black Marlin* seafood restaurant attracts busloads of tourists, while the boulders around the point attract rock agama and black zonure lizards and dassies.

The last place before the you get to the Cape of Good Hope Nature Reserve is **Smitswinkelbaai**, a little cove with a small beach, which is safe for swimming but feels the full blast of the southeaster. It's not accessible by car, as local property owners fiercely guard their privacy. To get there, you must park next to the road and walk down a seemingly endless succession of stairs.

Cape of Good Hope Nature Reserve

Most people come to **Cape of Good Hope Nature Reserve** (daily: summer 7am–6pm; winter 7am–5pm; small entry fee) to see the southernmost tip of Africa and the place where the Indian and Atlantic oceans meet at **Cape Point**. In fact, it's the site of neither, but is nevertheless an awesomely dramatic spot, which should on no account be missed. The reserve sits atop massive sea cliffs with huge views, strong seas, and an even wilder wind, which whips off caps and sunglasses as visitors gaze southwards from the old lighthouse buttress. The continent's real tip is at **Cape Agulhas**, some 300km southeast of here, but Cape Point is a lot easier to get to than Agulhas and a lot more exciting.

There is no public transport to the reserve. To get there **by car**, take the M3 to Muizenberg, continuing on the M4 via Simon's Town to the reserve gates, where you'll be given a good map with the main driving and walking routes, as well as the tidal pools and other facilities.

From the car park, the famous viewpoint is a short, steep walk, crawling with tourists, up to the original lighthouse. A **funicular** runs the less energetic to the top, where there's a restaurant. There is also a restaurant at the car park, which has outdoor seating (but it's usually too windy to be pleasant) and huge picture windows taking in the drop to the sea below. Most people come to the Point as part of a round-trip, returning via Kommetjie and the especially scenic Chapman's Peak Drive.

FYNBOS

Early Dutch settlers were alarmed by the paucity of good timber on the Cape Peninsula's hillsides, which were covered by nondescript, scrubby bush they described as *fijn bosch* (literally "fine bush") and which is now known by its Afrikaans name **fynbos** (pronounced "fayn-bos"). They set about planting exotics, like the oaks that now shade central Cape Town, and over the ensuing centuries their descendants established pine forests on the sides of Table Mountain in an effort to create a landscape that fulfilled their European idea of the picturesque. It's only relatively recently that Capetonians have come to proudly claim fynbos as part of the peninsula's cultural heritage, and Table Mountain pines have been felled to be recycled as books and articles about fynbos. Fynbos is remarkable for its astonishing variety of plants, making up eighty percent of the vegetation of the **Cape Floral Kingdom**, the smallest and richest of the floral kingdoms; its 8500 species make it one of the world's biodiversity hot spots. Only the South American rainforests come anywhere near matching its incredible concentration of diversity.

The Cape Peninsula alone, measuring less than 500 square kilometres, has 2256 plant species (nearly twice as many as Britain, which is 5000 times bigger). While the other five floral kingdoms cover vast areas such as Australia or the northern hemisphere, the entire Cape kingdom stretches across a relatively narrow coastal crescent from Niewoudville in the west, through Cape Town and across to Grahamstown in the east.

The four basic types of fynbos are: **proteas** (South Africa's national flower you'll see sold in bouquets at the airport if nowhere else); **ericas**, amounting to 600 species of heather (against 26 in the rest of the world); **restios** or reeds; and geophytes, including ground orchids and the startling flaming red **disas**, which can be seen in flower on Table Mountain in late summer.

CAPE WILDLIFE

Along with indigenous plants and flowers, you may well spot some of the **animals** that harbour in the Cape of Good Hope Nature Reserve fynbos habitat. **Baboons** lope along the rocky shoreline and can be a menace. Keep your car windows up and watch out, as they're adept at slyly swiping picnics and it's not unknown for them to invade vehicles. There are also **bontebok**, **eland** and **red hartebeest**, as well as **Cape rhebok** and **grysbok** grazing on the heathery slopes. If you're very lucky you may even see some of the extremely rare **Cape mountain zebras**.

Ostriches stride through the low fynbos, and occasionally **jackass penguins** come ashore. A distinctive bird on the rocky shores is the **black oystercatcher** with a bright red beak, jabbing limpets off the rocks. You'll also see **Cape cormorants** in large flocks on the beach or rocks, often drying their outstretched wings. Running up and down the water's edge are **white-fronted plovers** and **sanderlings** which probe for food left by the receding waves. Finally, as on any other beach walk in the Cape, you'll see piles of shiny brown **ecklonia kelp** on the beach or floating in dark beds in the wave-swells.

Numerous **tours** spend a day stopping off at the peninsula highlights. *Day Trippers* (☎531 3274 or 461 4599) run fun tours for R120 (including a picnic lunch), and give you the option of cycling part of the way, along two of the most awesome stretches of the route. *Green Life Eco-Tours* do a full-day tour which combines a walk in the reserve with a visit to the penguins at Simon's Town, as well as going in the cable car up Table Mountain. *Captour* (☎468 5415 or 083/653 9744) operates a reliable Cape Point and Table Mountain day-trip every day.

Cape Point and around

Cape Point is the treacherous promontory of rocks, winds and swells that navigators since the Portuguese in the fifteenth century had to contend with when they "rounded the Cape" on their way to the East. Plenty of wrecks lie submerged off its coast, and at **Olifantsbos** on the west side you can walk to two wrecks: one a US ship sunk in 1942, and the other a South African coaster which ran aground in 1965. The **Old Lighthouse**, built in 1860, was too often dangerously shrouded in cloud, failing to keep ships off the rocks, so another was built lower down in 1914, not always successful in averting disasters but still the most powerful light beaming onto the sea from South Africa.

The sea and mountain scenery in the reserve are reason enough to travel the 66km from central Cape Town. Most visitors make a beeline for Cape Point, seeing the rest of the reserve through a vehicle window, but walking is the best way to appreciate indigenous **Cape flora**. At first glance the landscape appears rocky and bleak, with short, wind-cropped plants, but the vegetation is surprisingly rich – there are as many plant varieties in this small reserve as in the whole of Britain. Amazingly, many bright blooms in Britain and the US, such as geraniums, freesias, gladioli, daisies, lilies and irises, are hybrids grown from indigenous Cape plants.

Swimming and walking

There are several waymarked **walks** in the Cape of Good Hope Nature Reserve. If you're planning a big hike it's best to set out early, as shade is rare and the wind can be foul, especially during summer, often increasing in intensity as the day goes on. One of the most straightforward **hiking routes** is the signposted forty-minute trek from the car park at **Cape Point** to the more westerly **Cape of Good Hope**. For exploring the shoreline, a clear path runs down the Atlantic side from Hoek van Bobbejaan. A convenient place to join it is at **Gifkommetjie**, which is signposted off Cape Point Road. From the car park, several sandy tracks drop quite steeply down the slope across rocks, and through bushes and milkwood trees to the shore, along which you can walk in either direction. Alternatively, take a copy of the Government Printer's 1:50,000 map 3318 CD Cape Town for some more intrepid exploration. Take water on any walk in the reserve, as there are no reliable fresh sources.

You'll find the **beaches** along signposted sideroads branching out from Cape Point Road, the main route through the reserve, going from the entrance gate to the car park at Cape Point. The sea is too dangerous for swimming, but there are safe tidal pools at the adjacent **Buffels Bay** and **Bordjiesrif**, midway along the east shore. Both have *braai* stands, but more southerly Buffels Bay is the nicer, with big lawned areas and some sheltered spots to have a picnic.

Table Bay and the northern suburbs

The **northern suburbs**, middle-class and Afrikaner-dominated, curl around the edge of Table Bay, north from Duncan Dock, and east along the N2 freeway. Few tourists see more of this area than the strip along the coast from Milnerton to Blouberg, and with good reason: the main attraction here is the much-snapped view of Table Mountain across the bay, otherwise the northern suburbs are an unappetizing sprawl of starter homes and new developments (this is one of the few areas of Cape Town where there's room for expansion).

Nevertheless, the long sandy beaches are ideal for a sunset walk, when you can watch the glowing orb slip into the sea close to **Robben Island** (see p.86). The sea is cold, and often windy, but windsurfers and kite-fliers do well here. **Big Bay** (*Grootbaai*), close to the principal resort of **Bloubergstrand** (usually shortened to Blouberg), draws windsurfing enthusiasts from all over the world for annual competitions.

By car, take the N1 from the city centre and the Milnerton/Paarden Island off-ramp to get onto Marina Drive which follows the coast to Milnerton, Tableview, Blouberg, Melkbosstrand, Koeberg nuclear power station and right on up the west coast to the Namibia border.

Milnerton to Melkbosstrand

The beachfront strip at **Milnerton**, closest to central Cape Town, is a banal, neon-lit fast-food haven, offering little reason to stop off, unless you're one of the surfing devotees who brave the water for the break off the lighthouse, undeterred by the debris floating across from the docks.

To the west is **Table View**, noted for its easy access to the beach, beachside parking and its classic view of Table Mountain. Nearby **Bloubergstrand**, 25km from the city, is the only place to draw you out to Table Bay. Once a fishing village, this is a good place to walk and take in the views, and you can sample one of Blouberg's outdoor restaurants for meals or tea.

By the time you get to **Melkbosstrand** and find yourself driving through dry, low scrub, you will feel well and truly out of Cape Town. Melkbos, 30km from Cape Town, has a caravan park and one or two places to stay, but few people choose to, perhaps because the settlement is so close to Koeberg, the country's only **nuclear power station**, which generates electricity for the Western Cape. It is said that the sea around Melkbos is a few degrees warmer than elsewhere around here, heated by the water used to cool the reactor. The radioactive waste itself is deposited 600km to the north at Vaalputs.

The Cape Flats and the African townships

East of the northern and southern suburbs, among the industrial smokestacks and the windswept Cape Flats, reaching well beyond the airport, is Cape Town's largest residential block, taking in the **coloured districts**, **African townships** and shantytown **squatter camps**, which are only visited on packaged township tours.

The **Cape Flats** are exactly that: barren, windswept and flat. You can't miss them along the N2 as you drive into Cape Town from the airport. Exclusively inhabited by Africans and coloureds, in their own separate areas, they can be both shocking and heartening. If you manage to get inside and talk to people, you'll see unimaginable squalor and hear countless stories of personal courage and stoicism. The safest way inside is via a **tour** (see box below); venturing in on your own isn't a good idea as the apartheid ghettos are crime-ridden, and thanks to them Cape Town has earned an unenviable reputation as the "murder capital of the world".

Some history

The African townships were set up as dormitories to provide labour forces for white Cape Town, not as places to build a life, which is why they had no facilities and no real hub. The **men-only hostels**, another apartheid relic, are at the root of many of the area's social problems. During the 1950s, the government set out a blueprint to turn the tide of Africans flooding into Cape Town. No African was permitted to settle permanently in the Cape west of a line near the Fish River, the old frontier over 1000km from Cape Town; women were entirely banned from seeking work in Cape Town and men prohibited from bringing their wives to join them. By 1970 there were ten men for every woman in Langa.

In the end, apartheid failed to prevent the influx of work-seekers desperate to come to Cape Town. Where people couldn't find legal accommodation they set up the **squatter camps** of makeshift tin, cardboard and plastic sheeting. During the 1970s and 1980s, the government attempted to eradicate these by demolishing them and destroying anything left inside. But no sooner had the police left than the camps reappeared, and they are now a permanent feature of the Cape Flats. One of the best known of all South Africa's squatter camps is **Crossroads**, whose inhabitants suffered campaigns of harassment that included killings and continuous attempts to bulldoze it out of existence. Through sheer determination – and no little desperation – its residents hung on and eventually won the right to stay. Today, the government is making attempts to improve conditions in the shantytowns by bringing in running water and sanitation. The lack of facilities is starting to change, with families moving in and ad hoc traders beginning to fill the gaps.

CAPE FLATS TOURS

In the darkest days of apartheid, during the late 1980s, the African townships were no-go areas for outsiders – particularly whites or police. Although today that's over, and many people welcome visitors, your best chance of getting in and coming out safely is to join one of the **township tours**, which will give you a chance to meet local people. The popular *One City Tours* (☎387 5351) takes visitors on a three-hour journey around the African areas of Langa, Khayelitsha, Guguletu and Crossroads. Tours leave from Tourism Gateway in Adderley Street and are led by residents of the townships.

For a chance to see the upbeat side of Cape Flats nightlife, *Heart Stoppers* (☎761 0811 or 683 3990) operate tours of three nightspots in an evening: because there are few clubs in the African areas, these tend to concentrate on the coloured districts.

Langa and Mitchell's Plain

Langa is the oldest and most central township, lying just east of the white suburb of Pinelands and north of the N2. In this relentlessly grey and random place, without the tiniest patch of green relief, you'll find women selling sheep and goats' heads, alongside state-of-the-art public phone bureaus run by enterprising township businessmen from inside recycled cargo containers. Nuclear families live in smart suburban houses while, not far away, there are former men-only hostels where as many as three families share one room.

South of the African ghettos is **Mitchell's Plain**, a coloured area stretching down to the False Bay coast, which you'll skirt if you take the M5 to Muizenberg. More salubrious than any of the African townships, Mitchell's Plain reflects how under apartheid lighter skins meant better conditions, even if you weren't quite white. But for coloureds the forced removals were no less tragic, many being summarily forced to vacate family homes because their suburb had been declared a White Group Area. Many families were relocated here when District Six was razed, and their communities never fully recovered – one of the symptoms of dislocation are the violent gangs, which have become an everyday part of Mitchell's Plain youth culture.

Eating and drinking

Cape cuisine is engaged in a desperate bid to produce a unique South African culinary style. While there's nothing wrong with it, the style is never going to take the world by storm and you'd be hard-pushed to eat it more than once or twice during your stay. It's fortunate then that Cape Town scores with its large number of relaxed and convivial restaurants serving imaginative and healthy food of a high quality that doesn't cost an arm and a leg. The range of styles is broad – and widening all the time.

Cape cuisine, the only truly local food, is a spicy hybrid of the cooking styles brought to South Africa and adapted to local conditions by slaves principally from Asia and Madagascar. Mild and semi-sweet curries with a strong Indonesian influence predominate and includes: *bredie* (stew), of which *waterblommetjiebredie* (made using water hyacinths), is a speciality; *bobotie*, a spicy minced dish served under a savoury custard; and *sosaties*, a local version of kebab using mincemeat. Of the desserts, dates stuffed with almonds make a light and delicious end to a meal, while *malva* pudding is a wickedly rich combination of milk, sugar, cream and apricot jam. There are only one or two restaurants dedicated to this style of cooking, but dishes influenced by Cape cuisine are relatively common elsewhere. As far as **seafood** goes, Cape Town offers cold-water fishes such as kingklip and snoek, not found along the coast to the east. Apart from *smoorsnoek*, a delicious spicy speciality you'll find in restaurants serving Cape cuisine, on the whole snoek isn't widely available as a main course at restaurants. You will, however, find smoked snoek and snoek pâté as starters, and every fish-and-chip shop in town offers fried snoek as an option in season.

Given Cape cuisine's strong links with the local (teetotal) Muslim community, you'll rarely be able to enjoy Cape wines at restaurants serving Cape food, particularly in the Bo-Kaap. However, just about everywhere else in Cape Town, **wine** drinking (see also p.127 and p.44) is a matter of fierce local loyalty and most meals are accompanied by it. Apart from the Constantia estates, whose restaurants serve their own wines, you'll find much the same choice here as you would in any of the bigger centres, but in no other city in the country does it feel more right to be sampling Cape wines than here under the gaze of Table Mountain.

For **self-catering**, see "Self-catering: food and wine", on p.119.

Restaurants

The greatest concentration of **restaurants** is in the central district around the **City Bowl**, **Sea Point** and the **Waterfront**. For Cape cuisine, the best places are *Biesmillah* in the Bo-Kaap, or *Kaapse Tafel* in the city centre. As far as prices go, expect to pay under R25 for a main course at an inexpensive restaurant, up to R40 at a medium one, and upwards of that at an expensive one.

City Bowl and the Waterfront

Aldo's, Shop 153, Ground Floor, Victoria Basin, Waterfront (☎21 7876). Good but expensive traditional Italian food. Daily until 10.45pm.

Amigos Tapas, 162 Kloof St, Gardens. A trifle too self-conscious to be true *tapas*, but a tasty mixture of Greek meze combined with Italian and Spanish food. Medium-priced and lively, with some tables outside. Daily until midnight.

Anatoli, 24 Napier St, De Waterkant. Turkish restaurant in a turn-of-the-century warehouse that buzzes with atmosphere. Excellent meze include pickled octopus and stuffed mussels. The dolmades are exceptionally delicious, as are the pressed dates topped with a puff of cream. Tues–Sun until 11pm.

Biesmillah, corner of Wale and Pentz streets. One of the oldest and best-known restaurants for medium-priced, traditional Cape cuisine. No alcohol permitted. Daily noon–3pm & 6–11pm.

Buccaneer Steakhouse, 64 Orange St, Gardens. Good steaks and sauces in an atmosphere bordering on dowdy, making for a supremely relaxed and low-cost evening.

Floris Smit Huijs, 55 Church St (☎23 3414). The beautiful decor in this eighteenth-century town house is as big an attraction as the mid-priced, eclectic international cuisine. Daily until 10.30pm.

Greek Boyz, Kloof St, Tamboerskloof (☎24 2282). One of Cape Town's top four restaurants is a triumph of Greek cuisine. Exceptionally good value, the food is fresh and luscious. Try the ever-so-tender *calamari* in lemon sauce.

Jewel Tavern, near Yacht Club off Duncan Rd, Duncan Docks. This unpretentious Taiwanese sailors' eating house has been discovered by Cape Town's *bon viveurs*. Superb, mid-priced Chinese food, including stunning hot and sour soup and spring rolls made while you watch.

Kaapse Tafel, Montreux Building, 90 Queen Victoria St (☎23 1651). Twenty years in the business of traditional Cape cuisine hasn't diminished this restaurant's excellent reputation. Good for *bobotie* and medium-priced Cape seafood. Closed Sun.

Mama Africa, 178 Long St. Mid-priced food from around the continent in a relaxed atmosphere. The highight is a 12mbar in the form of a green mamba. Mon–Sat until midnight.

Mexican Kitchen, 13 Bloem St. Cheap, casual restaurant serving up good-value burritos, enchiladas, *calamari fajitas* and *nachos*. They also do deli-style takeaways. Mon–Sat until midnight.

Mussel Cracker, Shop 222, First Floor, Victoria Basin, Waterfront (☎419 4300). Eat your way through the fine (and pricey) seafood buffet at one of the few Waterfront restaurants of note.

Vasco da Gama Tavern, 3 Alfred St. Known locally as the "Portuguese embassy", this unpretentious restaurant with a blaring TV is a genuine working man's pub. Grilled tongue with bread, accompanied by wine mixed with Coke, are standard. It's also a great seafood restaurant at half the price and better than many of the upmarket joints.

Wangthai Restaurant, 31 Heerengracht St, off Adderley St. Solid, medium-priced Thai food with a good wider variety. Daily until late.

Yindees, 80 Kloof St, Gardens (☎22 1012). Undeniably the best Thai in Cape Town. Great, mid-priced food and brilliant spicy prawn soup served by dour waiters. Mon–Sat until late.

Southern suburbs

Africa Café, 213 Lower Main Rd, Observatory (☎47 9553). Sample inexpensive food from around the dark continent in a suitably *fauve* atmosphere. Mon–Sat until midnight.

Constantia Uitsig Restaurant, Spaanschemat River Rd, Constantia (☎794 4480). Very successful, rather pricey restaurant on a wine estate. Views across the Constantia Valley and good Provençale food have made this one of South Africa's top ten restaurants. Daily until late.

Fellini's Trattoria, 79 Durban Rd, Little Mowbray. Good imitation of an Italian restaurant, with medium-priced menu marred by poor service. Tues–Sun until 11pm.

Pancho's Mexican Kitchen, 127 Lower Main Rd, Observatory (☎47 4854). Highly popular and inexpensive cantina-style restaurant serving Mexican dishes. Overzealous frying has led to it being described as "Cape Town's other oil depot". Daily until late.

Parks, 114 Constantia Rd, Wynberg (☎797 8202). The most elegant and expensive eating in the southern suburbs outside the wine estates, in restored Victorian town house with original menu and personal, almost pedantic service and attention to detail.

Atlantic seaboard

Aris Souvlaki, 150 Main Rd, Sea Point. Reliable, inexpensive terrace restaurant for Greek *shwarma* and *souvlaki*. You can also get takeaways. Daily until 11pm.

Blues, 9 The Promenade, Victoria Rd, Camps Bay (☎438 2040). Spectacular views make this over-rated Californian-style restaurant one of the most popular in town. Brace yourself for poor service and ringing mobile phones. Daily until midnight.

Caponero, 142 Main Rd, Sea Point. Superb, thick-based pizzas with indulgently rich fillings and seafood toppings to remember. Daily until late.

Chicken Bar, 110 Main Rd, Sea Point. Touch nothing here apart from the chicken, which is very good and reasonably priced.

Little Bombay, 245 Main Rd, Sea Point. Excellent food at Cape Town's only vegetarian Indian restaurant. Their Thalis give you a cheap and tasty set meal. Unlicensed, so bring your own booze. Daily until late.

Mario's, 89 Main Rd, Green Point (☎439 6644). Italian food with attitude. If you can handle slow service, rude waiters and expensive wine, their pastas and casseroles are certainly worth it.

Nando's Chickenland, 128 Main Rd, Sea Point. South Africa's answer to *KFC*. Surprisingly good grilled Portuguese-style *peri-peri* poultry. Daily until 10pm.

Ons Huisie, Stadler Rd, Bloubergstrand (☎56 1553). Come to enjoy the romantic 1816 fisherman's cottage (now a national monument), rather than their fish. Closed Tues.

Pizzeria Napoletana, 178 Main Rd, Sea Point. A family business since 1956, the best Italian joint in Cape Town offers solid, good-value and tasty cuisine. Try the Veal Parmigiano, or their crayfish – the most generous you'll find on the Peninsula. Closed Mon.

Red Herring, Beach Rd/Pine St, Noordhoek (☎789 1783). Beautiful sea and mountain views at this relaxed, mid-priced, out-of-town restaurant. A good place for line fish. Daily until late.

The Round House, The Glen, Camps Bay (☎438 2320). *Nouvelle cuisine* at one of the snottiest, but not too expensive, restaurants in town, housed aptly in Lord Charles Somerset's hunting lodge. Daily until late.

San Marco, 92 Main Rd, Sea Point (☎439 2758). Stunning, mid-priced Italian seafood. The grilled *calamari* tossed in chilli and garlic is wonderful, and their antipasto trolley is especially good for vegetarians. They also serve wonderful *gelato*. Closed Tues.

Theo's Steaks, Beach Rd, Mouille Point (☎439 3494). Upmarket ambience right on the beachfront, offering superb mid-priced beef and seafood. Daily until 10pm.

Wooden Bridge, Golf Club, Woodbridge Island, Milnerton (☎52 2423). You'll enjoy a classic post-card view of Table Mountain across the bay at this mid-priced restaurant. Seafood is the speciality, but you'll find all sorts of continental cuisine here. Tues–Sat until 11.30pm.

Zorba, 229d Main Rd, Sea Point. Tasty, good-value Greek dishes, as well as generous tender steaks and delightful salads under a hopelessly kitsch (but delicious) thousand islands dressing. Mon–Sat until 11pm.

False Bay seaboard

Brass Bell, Kalk Bay station, Kalk Bay (☎788 5456). Arguably the best place in town to eat, with views of both Table and the Hottentots Holland mountains, although the mid-priced seafood meals don't quite match the magnificent setting. There's also a pub with live music some nights. Daily until late.

Fish Hoek Galley Seafood Restaurant, Beach Rd, Fish Hoek. Informal restaurant right on the beach. Their excellent-value seafood platter attracts busloads of Japanese tourists. Mon–Sat until 10pm.

Gaylords, 65 Main Rd, Muizenberg. The tacky interior belies an imaginative menu which adapts great Indian cooking and local ingredients to create something unique and inexpensive. Wed–Sat until 10pm.

Mia's Place, corner of Norman and Gatesville roads, Kalk Bay (☎788 3793). Fragrant, moderately priced Indian food in a stunning setting indoors surrounded by Oregon pine or outdoors on the stone patio with bay views. Excellent seafood curries and butter chicken, the perennial favourite.

Coffee and snacks

Recently Cape Town's centre has begun to enjoy a renaissance, and **continental-style cafés** are springing up in their numbers, offering easy-going places where you can eat a meal, or just linger over a drink or coffee. Service tends to be slick and friendly, and the cafés stay open late into the night.

Surprisingly for a warm and sunny city, Cape Town has few **outdoor snack bars** and even fewer seaside ones, which is a pity given the 150km of peninsula coastline. Fortunately the idea is beginning to catch on, and more and more places around town, especially the more relaxed cafés, are managing to create room for a few outdoor tables and chairs during the summer months. You'll always find somewhere with harbour views at the **Waterfront**. For **garden settings**, try the Company Gardens in town, the *Jonkerhuis* on the Groot Constantia Wine Estate or Kirstenbosch Botanical Gardens. For **Table Mountain vistas**, try *Aladdin* in Sea Point or Rhodes Memorial on its slopes, with panoramas across the city. For **seaside settings** there's the choice of *Mariner's Wharf Bistro* or *Suikerbossie* in Hout Bay, the *Red Herring* at Noordhoek, the *Brass Bell* at Kalk Bay station (see opposite) or *Wimpy* at Sea Point.

City Bowl and the Waterfront

Aladdin, Nedbank Centre, 15 Kloof Rd, Sea Point. Patio coffee shop with views of Table Mountain, serving up cheap Israeli-style *shwarma*, houmous and vegetarian alternatives. Daily until 11pm.

Café Bardeli, Long St Studios, off Kloof St. Excruciatingly stylish, the epitome of café society where the food is suitably chic but also very good. A film-set favourite, with Cape Town's highest quotient of supermodels per square metre.

Café Paradiso, 110 Kloof St. Good, medium-priced Greek and Mediterranean dishes, including a weigh-your-plate meze bar and outside terrace with views up to the mountain and down over the city and docks.

Col'Cacchio, Seef House, 42 Hans Strydom Ave, Foreshore. Offbeat pizza restaurant which often spills onto the pavement outside. Has over forty different and quite original pizza toppings, such as smoked salmon, sour cream and caviar.

Company Gardens, Slow service and standard sandwiches and teas in pleasant surroundings. A good bet if you're already in the centre of town.

Hartlief Gourmet, Shop 28, Gardens Centre, Mill St, Gardens. Essentially a takeaway, this meat-centred deli has an exceptional selection of foods. German specialities include sauerkraut fried with strips of bacon. Mon–Fri until 6pm, Sat until 1pm.

i-Cafe, 273 Long St. Plug into the info superhighway for R10 an hour. Frequented by university students, net junkies or people just looking for a good sandwich and a coffee.

Mr Pickwick's, 158 Long St. Hearty and cheap "tin-plate" meals, including a range of hot and cold "foot-long" sandwiches. Few have been known to finish them, never mind depart hungry. Open so late that no one really knows when, if ever, it closes.

Old Townhouse, corner of Church and Keerom streets, city centre. Teas and light lunches in the courtyard of a historic building, close to Greenmarket Square.

Plaizier, NBS Waldorf Building, 47 Burg St. Best coffee in town (but no outdoor seating), as well as light meals and wonderful cakes. Mon–Fri until 3.30pm, Sat until 2pm.

Yellow Pepper, 138 Long St. Good lunch spot near town centre, featuring big plate-glass windows to gawk at bustling Long St, and pasta bakes that will set you fair for a hard afternoon's sightseeing or shopping.

Sea Point and Green Point

Chariots Italian Coffee Bar, 107 Main Rd, Green Point. Stylish decor and great, inexpensive food make this a fashionable haunt for Cape Town's yuppies. Come for *foccaccia* with simple fillings and good coffee. Daily until 11.30pm.

Giovanni's Deliworld, Main Rd, Green Point. No outdoor seating, but this trendy Italian deli/coffee shop is good for a coffee, snack or takeaway.

Rieses Delicatessen, 367 Main Rd, Sea Point. Fine sandwiches served up at a local institution, with outdoor seating. Try their salt beef on rye. Daily until mid-evening.

Wimpy, Sea Point Carousel, Beach Rd. Run-down, ramshackle and seedy fast-food outlet with wonderful views.

Southern suburbs

Café Carte Blanche, 42a Trill Rd, Observatory. Former curio shop decorated with Eastern artefacts, where you can sip wine under a Persian carpet or quaff beer on a Mongolian bedspread. Small, unique and exotic.

Enrica Rocca, 19 Wolfe St,Wynberg. A real Italian – no red checked tablecloths and straw chianti bottles with candles – with a vast antipasto spread followed by a limited range of interesting pasta dishes.

Gardener's Cottage, Montebello Estate, Newlands. Set in a complex of old farm buildings under old pine trees, and serving hearty breakfasts and lunches as well as tea and coffee. Worthwhile if you want to browse through the neighbouring arts and crafts workshops.

Jonkershuis, Groot Constantia Wine Estate, Constantia. Enjoy an outdoor lunch or tea surrounded by vineyards and mountains.

Kirstenbosch Gardens, Rhodes Drive, Newlands. Good outdoor English breakfasts and Cape Town's most boring tea (a choice of apple pie or scones) in the lovely gardens at the foot of Table Mountain.

Rhodes Memorial Tea Garden, Rhodes Estate, Rondebosch. Set on the side of Devil's Peak, this is one of Cape Town's best tea gardens, offering views across the city to the sea. Good for snack lunches and teas. Closed Sun am & Mon.

Atlantic seaboard

Mariners Wharf Bistro, The Harbour, Hout Bay. Relaxed, well-run place with terrace seating overlooking the harbour. Good for seafood to eat in or take away.

Red Herring, corner of Beach Rd and Pine St, Noordhoek. Snacks and drinks on the upstairs deck, which offers marvellous sea and mountain views.

Suikerbossie, Victoria Drive, Hout Bay. A Cape Town outdoor institution with great views of Hout Bay, making it popular with tourists. This is a fine spot for afternoon tea.

False Bay seaboard

Café Matisse, 76 Main Rd, Kalk Bay. Popular, relaxed café serving pizzas and light meals. The work of local artists is exhibited on the walls, and the café often hosts musical evenings or poetry readings.

Nightlife and entertainment

If you've come to Cape Town looking for any especially African or cosmopolitan **entertainment** you're bound to be disappointed. Suburbanites thrive on the usual mid-Atlantic fare of mainstream movies, classical concerts and the odd play, while **clubbing** and **pubbing** tends to cut sharply down ethnic lines with distinct white and coloured venues. The African townships weren't intended by their apartheid planners to be places of pleasure, and never developed much of a club culture.

The fact that segregation still marks out Cape Town's nightlife from Johannesburg's or Durban's may come as a surprise in the legislative capital of the "Rainbow Nation", with supposedly the most liberal tradition in the country. However, this owes as much to geography as social attitudes, with Table Mountain, once again, defining the boundary. The City Bowl is also the **nightlife** centre of Cape Town, with pubs and clubs clustering in the heart of the city and along Kloof Street towards the suburbs.

To find out what's on, check out the *Review* section in the inside back pages of the weekly *Mail & Guardian*, which comes out every Friday and covers exhibitions, movies, music and performance in Jo'burg, Durban and Cape Town. Alternatively, look at the *Cape Weekend* supplement to the *Weekend Argus,* which hits the streets on Saturdays and offers similar coverage, with the bonus of quaintly provincial-sounding listings of local activities ranging from big events at the Planetarium to local cake sales.

Pubs, clubs and Cape jazz

The distinction between **clubs** and **pubs** is fuzzy in Cape Town – drinking and dancing often take place at the same venue. Activity is centred around the lower end of **Long and Loop streets**, the only place in the city where you can spend an entire evening strolling around and sampling the nightlife. To a lesser extent, the **Waterfront** also holds out the promise of an evening's meandering, with a handful of pubs, clubs and coffee bars, but in the more artificial, and safer, mall atmosphere. The only real indigenous flavour in town, **Cape jazz**, can be found in the coloured clubs on the Cape Flats, where you can also catch **jazzing**, hugely popular ballroom dancing to 1950s bossa nova and tango. Outside the Flats, local jazz can be found in town centre haunts, of which *Mannenberg's* is the best. The most famous exponent of Cape jazz music is **Abdullah Ibrahim** (aka Dollar Brand), but there are many other talented performers to look out for.

One of the best ways to get into the Cape Town jazz scene is on a **jazz tour** operated by *Heart Stoppers* (☎761 0811 or 683 3990). These excursions can accommodate your particular interests while taking in three or four clubs between 8.30pm and 2.30am.

White clubs in the city centre and inner-city suburbs frequently change names and policy (rather than venue). Cape Town youth is quite capable of getting down and partying, although the sounds and styles tend to be derivative of whatever was going on "overseas" some time ago. The best source of **information** is the peninsula-wide *Good Hope FM* (94–97MHz), which specializes in American-style soul and hip-hop and announces forthcoming gigs. There's also *Bush Radio* (88.9MHz), a community station which can only be picked up in the city centre and Cape Flats and broadcasts mainly to a coloured audience.

City Bowl

Angels, Somerset Rd/Napier St. A complex of gay clubs with a courtyard at the back. *Detour* is the place to hang out and get down.

Crow Bar Pub, 43 Waterkant St. One-time winner of the "Bar of the Year" award recreates a London pub.

Dock Road Cafe, Waterfront. Lively cabaret spot in the cocoon of the Waterfront that stages live jazz from time to time.

The Fireman's Arms, 25 Merchau St. Pub serving first-class steaks at a third of the price of the restaurants.

Green Dolphin Jazz Restaurant, Victoria and Alfred Arcade, Waterfront (☎21 7471). Smooth and sophisticated venue with live music every night. Phone to find out about forthcoming attractions.

Havana Bar, 45 Waterkant St. One of the clutch of trendy bars down Waterkant St, and a port of call for the "Tequila Girl", who wanders from one drinking hole to the next wearing a gun belt stocked with bottles of the liquid dynamite which she adminsters (along with lemon and salt). Young, wild and noisy.

Kimberley Hotel, 48 Roeland St. Frequented by white working-class men, this old pub is full of photographs and memorabilia of Edwardian Cape Town. The delightful upstairs verandah is a good place to survey the passing urban scene.

The Lounge, 194 Long St. Trendy late-night drinking hole in a gorgeous Victorian building. Popular with a twenty-something film-industry set with money to burn.

Mama Africa, 178 Long St. The food's not that African but the atmosphere is good and the decor stunning. Go upstairs just to gape at the 500-bottle *Coca Cola* chandelier and the green mamba snake bar.

Manhattan Cafe, 74 Waterkant St. Gay-friendly bar/restaurant serving up cheap eats, where you can sit on the verandah and check out the passing scene or join the throng standing outside with their drinks.

Mannenberg's Jazz Cafe, 2nd Floor, Dumbarton House, Adderley and Church Streets (☎23 8595). Live music seven nights a week, with jazz-funk and the greats of Cape township jazz. Near Parliament, it's also the place to see leading yuppie politicians relaxing after a long debate.

Mr Pickwicks, 158 Long St. Small, crowded speakeasy-style bar playing British rock, and frequented by an art and ad-agency crowd. Meals are served until 2am and the place closes several hours later. Take care when leaving late at night.

Perseverance Tavern, 83 Buitenkant St. The oldest pub in town, and mainly a drinking hole for city workers before they trek home to the suburbs. There's a roaring fire in winter and an outdoor patio for warmer weather.

The Shebeen, Bree St. Wire sculptures, and drinks served in tin mugs in a stylized parody of a township drinking dive.

Stag's Head, 71 Hope St. Seedy, cockroach-ridden establishment with huge windows looking onto the street. Raucous, rough and sometimes scary. It's bliss for pool players, with tables upstairs and down.

Southern suburbs

Don Pedro's, 113 Roodebloem Rd, Woodstock. Late-night arty hangout that feels like a corner café, with a motley collection of non-matching tables and chairs. Linger all evening over a beer or a coffee without feeling hassled. They also serve good pizzas and fish dishes.

Heidelberg Tavern, 92 Station Rd, Observatory. Based on a German bierkeller, this student hangout near the university has long wooden tables and an outdoor beer garden.

Peddars on the Bend, Spaanschemat River Rd, Constantia. Posh bar in the poshest suburb with a delightful outdoor area shaded by oaks.

The Planet, Station Rd, Observatory. A local institution and great venue for hanging out until late.

Atlantic seaboard

Ambassador Hotel, 34 Victoria Rd, Bantry Bay, Sea Point. Snotty bar attached to a smart hotel, with stunning cliff and sea views.

Chapman's Peak Hotel, Main Rd, Hout Bay. Beautiful for sunsets over the bay, accompanied by greasy and delicious *calamari*.

Dizzy Jazz Café, 41 The Drive, Camps Bay. Crowded and lively nightspot with a big verandah, draught beer and sea views. Live jazz on Fridays and Saturdays.

La Med, Glen Country Club, Victoria Road, Clifton. Overlooking the rocks at Clifton, this is a favourite place for hang-gliders from Lion's Head to drop in after landing in the field adjacent to the pub.

False Bay seaboard

The Light Fantastic, York Rd, Muizenberg. Good bar and cabaret.

Muizenberg Station, Main Rd, Muizenberg. Favoured haunt of local fishermen and great views upstairs at *La Mer* restaurant.

Cape Flats

Baker Street Jazz Club, Halt Rd/28th Ave. Large, live jazz club operating on Wednesdays, Fridays and Saturdays. This is one of the best places for jazz dancing.

Blue Note, Club Galaxy, Cine 400, College Rd, Rylands. One of Cape Town's oldest jazz venues, much favoured by serious musicians.

Club Montreal, York St, Sherwood Park. Nightclub and bar staging live performances on Saturday and Sunday nights. Great spot to see jazz dancing.

Goodfellas Jazz Club, 13 Halt Rd, Elsies River. Mainly jazz-fusion club, with special guests on Sunday nights.

Riff's Jazz Pub, 39 Wetton Rd, Wetton. Good for jazz funk and fusion every night of the week.

Classical music

Although you won't be coming to Cape Town specifically for its **classical music**, there are a handful of venues with decent programmes. However, the only real reason to go to a concert here is to enjoy the combination of music and wonderful outdoor setting. By far the venues are the Kirstenbosch National Botanical Gardens and the Josephine Mill during the summer concert season. Scan the *Cape Times* or the *Cape Argus* to find out what's on at the venues below.

The Baxter Theatre, Main Rd, Rondebosch (☎685 7880). Occasional opera performances and lunchtime concerts in an impressive auditorium.

Josephine Mill, Boundary Rd, Newlands (☎686 4939). The Nedbank Summer Concert Season delivers a varied menu of outdoor music along the Liesbeek River, including classical and choral performances on Sundays from November to February.

Kirstenbosch Botanical Gardens, Rhodes Drive, Newlands (☎762 1166). A stunning setting, whatever the music, at the foot of Table Mountain. The Appletiser Summer Sunset Concerts provide an eclectic programme to accompany your picnic.

Natale Labia Museum, 192 Main Rd, Muizenberg (☎788 4106). Chamber music on the fourth Sunday of every month, in this imitation Baroque former residence of the Italian consul.

Nico Theatre, DF Malan St, Foreshore (☎21 7839). Opera, musicals, lunchtime and Sunday afternoon concerts at the Western Cape's premier theatre complex.

Theatre, performance and cinema

Live performance is suffering in the new South Africa as resources are being directed towards essentials like restructuring education, and away from what is seen as elitist activity, such as **theatre**. While there are some fine playwrights in the country, exciting performances are few and far between. Your best bet of catching something good is by checking out what's on at the province's showpiece theatre, the *Nico*, or the more innovative *Baxter*. It's worth keeping an eye on the press, as there are occasional surprises.

Theatres

Baxter Theatre Complex, Main Rd, Rosebank (☎685 7880). Administered by the University of Cape Town, the *Baxter* houses three theatres. It has attempted to accommodate the changing face of South Africa by putting on visiting shows from Jo'burg, as well as classical and contemporary material.

Dock Road Café & Theatre, Waterfront (☎25 4334). Populist venue staging mainstream productions, including local musicals.

Herschel Theatre, 21 Herschel Rd, Claremont (☎64 4010). Primarily school groups and amateur productions.

Little Theatre, University of Cape Town, Orange St (☎24 2340). Showcase for innovative work from the University drama school.

Long Street Theatre, Waterkant St, off Long St at entrance to St John's Arcade (☎418 3496). Alternative arts, culture and experimental theatre venue with a resident band fusing rock and African rhythms.

Maynardville Open-Air Theatre, corner of Church and Wolfe streets, Wynberg (☎21 5470). Exclusively Shakespearean works performed in the park and under the stars during January and February.

Nico Theatre Complex, DF Malan St, Foreshore (☎21 5470). Opera house and two theatres, which is home to *CAPAB*, the Western Cape's theatre company. High-quality productions of classical and contemporary theatre, with belated attempts to explore indigenous forms.

Theatre on the Bay, Link St, Camps Bay (☎438 3301). Farces, reviews and lightweight comedies are the standard fare.

Cinema

South Africa's indigenous film industry is fledgling at best, and the local taste for **cinema** runs mainly to mainstream Hollywood. All the major cinemas advertise daily in the *Cape Times* and the *Cape Argus*. The two main movie companies, Ster-Kinekor and Nu Metro, have a number of multi-screen complexes in the city centre and the suburbs. Most convenient for visitors are the *Ster-Kinekor Golden Acre* (☎25 2720) on Adderley Street, bang in the centre; the *Nu-Metro V&A Waterfront* (☎419 9700); the *Ster-Kinekor Cavendish Square* (☎683 4063 or 683 4064) and *Nu-Metro Atrium* (☎683 1122), both in Main Road, Claremont; and the *Constantia Rosebank* (☎686 6649), Main Road, Rosebank.

For independent releases, check out the cinemas at the Claremont shopping complex. Cape Town has two art cinemas: the *Labia*, 68 Orange St (☎24 5927) and the *Baxter*, Main Rd, Rondebosch (☎689 1069). Neither advertises widely, so pop in for one of their programmes, or give them a call. Worth noting also is the *Imax Cinema* at the Waterfront, one of the world's largest screens, which shows visual spectacles and wonderful nature documentaries.

Outdoor activities

Capetonians take their **leisure** seriously and the city provides every opportunity for pitting yourself against all four elements, whether riding the winds on a sailboard, hangglider or even a kite; tackling the oceans with surfboard or scuba gear; coming down the mountain on a rope or bike; or simply letting everyone else get on with it while you soak in the sun, sink a few beers and watch the cricket.

Spectator sports

Cricket. This is keenly followed by many Capetonians, with international and local events taking place at Newlands Cricket Ground, 61 Campground Rd, Newlands (☎64 4146). If there's anything going on in town, it will almost certainly get high-profile coverage in the press.

Rugby. Exceeding even cricket as an obsession, rugby manages to bring South Africa's white community to a virtual standstill of TV-watching. Newlands Stadium, on Campground Road in Newlands, is one of the country's major venues for international and provincial contests.

Running. The Two Oceans Marathon, another of the Cape's big events, is in fact a 56km marathon and a half, and takes place every April.

Participation sports

Abseiling You can slide off Table Mountain with *Abseil Africa* (☎25 4332) for around R90 for a half-day trip.

Bird-watching The peninsula's varied habitats attract nearly four hundred different species of bird. Fertile ground for the activity is on Lion's Head, in Kirstenbosch Gardens and the Cape of Good Hope Nature Reserve, as well as at Kommetjie and Hout Bay. For a more institutionalized experience, there's *World of Birds*, Valley Rd, Hout Bay (☎790 2730), and you can find out about guided outings with knowledgeable guides through the *Cape Bird Club* (☎686 8795).

Golf The Milnerton course, Bridge Rd, Milnerton (☎52 1047), is tucked in between a lagoon and the Table Bay and boasts classic views of Table Mountain. Other popular local courses are at *Rondebosch Golf Club*, Klipfontein Rd, Rondebosch (☎689 4176), and *Royal Cape Golf Club*, 174 Ottery Rd, Wynberg (☎761 6551).

Gyms *Health and Racquet* clubs are upmarket but well-appointed gyms dotted around the peninsula. Contact their head office (☎794 2382) to find out where the nearest one is to you

Horse-riding *Horse Trail Safaris*, Indicator Lodge, Skaapskraal Rd, Ottery (☎73 4396), offers riding along the spectacular Noordhoek Beach, as does *Sleepy Hollow Horse Riding*, Sleepy Hollow Lane, Noordhoek (☎789 2341).

Kite-flying *The Kite Shop* (☎21 6231) can bring you face to face with another friend of the Cape southeaster – power kite flying. You can harness yourself up to big, powerful kites for some exhilarating adventures on buggies and skis.

Mountain-biking *Hopkins Tours and Rentals* (☎23 2527) will show you the rough and tough way down Table Mountain – R100 for a three-hour guided ride including the rent of fairly decent bikes. Also try *Rent'n'Ride*, 1 Park Rd, Mouille Point (☎434 1122), who offer good off-road biking in Silvermine Nature Reserve and Jonkershoek near Stellenbosch.

Paragliding *Parapente* (☎705 5801) offer a one-day introductory course for R250 or a tandem flight from Lion's Head in Cape Town for R350.

Road cycling The 105km *Argus Pick'n'Pay Cycle Tour*, the largest individually timed bike race in the world with over 25,000 participants, takes place in early March. Entries close in early January: contact *Western Province Pedal Power Association* (☎689 8420). Otherwise, cycling is popular all over the peninsula, and is a great way to take in the scenery.

Rock climbing You can learn how to rock-climb up Table Mountain's famous facade with the *Cape Town School of Mountaineering* (☎61 9679), who charge R600 for a four-day course.

Rollerblading Especially popular along the long, smooth promenade that runs from Mouille Point to Sea Point, rollerblading is a growing activity. You can rent blades from *Rent 'n' Ride*, 1 Park Rd, Mouille Point (☎434 1122).

Sailing Cape Town's largest seafaring event is the biennial *Cape to Rio Yacht Race* held in January in even years. If this is too long to wait, you might consider one of the more modest cruises, most of which leave from the Waterfront. From here you can pick up countless Robben Island cruises (but only the official one docks at the island, see p.86), sunset outings into Table Bay, and the romantic two-hour trip to Clifton and back that includes a bottle of bubbly.

Scuba diving Cape waters are cold but can be clear and are good for wrecks. Contact the *Atlantic Underwater Club*, Bay Rd, Mouille Point (☎439 0701 or 439 9322), for information about dives. Courses, equipment rental and dives can be arranged through *Orca Industries* (☎61 9673), *Blue Print Diving*, Shop 5, Quay 5, Waterfront (☎418 5806), *Ocean Divers International*, Protea Ritz, Main Rd, Sea Point (☎439 1803), and *Scuba Venture*, Avalon Building, 8 Mill St, Gardens (☎461 2709).

Surfing Top spots include Big Bay at Bloubergstrand, where competitions are held every summer, Llandudno, Muizenberg, Kalk Bay, and Long Beach at Kommetjie and Noordhoek. For further information, contact the *Western Province Surfing Association* (☎64 2972 or 788 8218).

Surf skiing/canoeing/kayaking Contact *Coastal Kayak Trails* (☎551 8739).

Swimming There are surf livesaver patrols on duty at Milnerton, Camps Bay, Llandudno, Muizenberg and Fish Hoek beaches. Snorkelling trips to swim with seals at Seal Island are arranged by *Hout Bay Two Ocean Divers* (☎438 9317).

Walking Contact Richard Behne (☎761 9900), a guide recognized by the *Mountain Club of South Africa* (☎45 3412). The best places for gentle strolls are Newlands Forest, up from Rhodes Memorial, and any beaches. For longer walks, head for anywhere on Table Mountain (see p.94), Tokai Forest, Silvermine Nature Reserve or Cape Point Nature Reserve.

Windsurfing In summer most Capetonians moan about the howling southeaster; if you've got a smile on your face you're probably into windsurfing. One of the best spots is 75min north of Cape Town, at Langebaan. Otherwise the place to go is Bloubergstrand. For further help, contact *Cape Windsurf Centre*, Langebaan (☎02287/21114).

Shopping

Cape Town's **Waterfront** is the country's most popular **shopping** venue, but beautiful as it is it lacks the grittier feel of the city centre. You can buy all the functional goods you'll need at the Waterfront and all the most upmarket shops are here too, but you should expect to pay above the odds for everything. For crafts, second-hand books, antiques and food you'll be better off looking to the city centre and the suburban shopping areas.

Arts, crafts, souvenirs and curios

Cape Town is not known for its indigenous **arts and crafts** in the way, say, Durban is, and much of the stuff you'll buy here is from elsewhere in Africa. Goods from Zimbabwe and Zambia are particularly well-represented. There are several places in the city centre and the Waterfront, but you'll often pick up the same arts and crafts for a lot less money at the **markets** scattered around town.

African Image, branches at corner of Church and Burg streets, city centre, and Shop 6228, Victoria Wharf, Waterfront. This is your best port of call for authentic African arts and crafts, from fabrics, antique sculpture to beadwork, but the goods are a little overrated and overpriced.

Cape Heritage Shop, corner of Church and Burg streets, city centre. Well-chosen selection of Cape craft items, including jewellery, fabrics and ceramics.

Cape Town Station, Forecourt, Adderley St, city centre. Thronging ranks of market traders selling radios, leather goods and African crafts. Mon–Fri 8am–5pm, Sat 8am–2pm.

Constantia Craft Market, Alphen Common, corner of Spaanschemat River and Ladies Mile roads, Constantia. Sizable outdoor flea market where you can pick up good local crafts and items from around the continent, ride a camel or a pony and have a cup of tea. First and last Saturday and first Sunday of the month.

Greenmarket Square, Burg St, city centre. Open-air market that's the best place in town for colourful handmade Cape Town beachwear from T-shirts to shorts and sandals, as well as a venue for antiques and knick-knacks. Mon–Fri 8am–5pm, Sat 8am–2pm.

Out of Africa, Shop 125, Victoria Wharf, Waterfront (☎418 5505). Expensive baskets, beads and African arts and antiques in the pleasant spending fields of the Waterfront.

The Red Shed Craft Workshop, Victoria Wharf, Waterfront. Craft market where craftworkers make and sell ceramics, textiles, candles and jewellery. Mon–Sat 9am–9pm, Sun 10am–9pm.

Rose Korber, 48 Sedgemoor Rd, Camps Bay (☎438 9152, fax 438 6262). This should be the first stop for the serious collector, with an exceptional selection of top contemporary art and craft from around the continent.

Waterfront Craft Market, Waterfront. High-quality handcrafted items. Daily 9.30am–6pm.

Books

Long Street is the best place for second-hand and remaindered books, with several highly browsable places.

Book Warehouse, Main Rd, Rondebosch (☎64 2230). Small shop expertly staffed, with a fine collection of books. Mon–Fri 9am–5pm, Sat 9am–1pm.

Clarke's Antiquarian, 211 Long St, city centre (☎23 5739). The best bookshop in Cape Town for South African books, with tightly packed shelves and brilliantly well-informed staff. Mon–Fri 8.45am–5pm, Sat 8.45am–1pm.

Exclusive Books. The friendliest bookshop chain for just browsing away an hour, well-stocked with books and magazines. Branches at: Lower Mall, Cavendish Square, Claremont (Mon–Thurs 8.30am–9pm, Fri & Sat 8.30am–10pm, Sun 10am–5.30pm; ☎64 3030); Victoria Wharf, V&A Waterfront (Mon–Fri 9am–10.30pm, Sat 9am–11pm, Sun 10am–9pm; ☎419 0905); Constantia Village Shopping Centre, Spaanschemat River Rd, Constantia (Mon–Fri 8.30am–9pm, Sat 9am–9pm, Sun 9am–5pm; ☎794 7800).

Self-catering: food and wine

It should come as no surprise that **self-catering** is the cheapest way to eat in Cape Town, and it can also be good fun. Apart from *braai*-ing, which takes place anywhere at any excuse, there are countless places on beaches, in the forests or up the mountain where you can enjoy a terrific picnic or you may just want to buy stuff to cook back at your accommodation.

Thanks to the city's cosmopolitan population there are some excellent (if pricey) **delicatessens**, several of which are strung along Main Road, Green Point and Sea Point. Among the many are *Giovanni's* in Green Point, for delicious Italian foods, while the *New York Bagel Deli* in Sea Point has the best bagels in town and a great selection of Eastern European Jewish fillings.

The easiest places to shop for food are at the large **supermarket chains**, and none is better than *Woolworth's*, South Africa's equivalent of the British *Marks & Spencer*. It's excellent for quality fast-cook meals, fresh produce and cold foods, such as olives, houmous and various Mediterranean dips. There are several branches around town, but the most convenient ones are in Adderley Street and at the Claremont shops. In a similar vein, *Pick 'n' Pay*, which has branches at the Waterfront, Main Road, Camps Bay and Claremont shops, does excellent-value ready grilled chickens for under R20. The larger branches of the better supermarkets also have fishmonger counters where you can buy **fresh fish**, but by far the most atmospheric way to acquire seafood is at either Kalk Bay or Hout Bay harbours (see p.73).

You'll also find delicious food and some unusual **fruit and vegetables** at the more sophisticated farm stalls, such as the *Old Cape Farm Stall* at the turnoff to Groot Constantia, on Constantia Nek Road. Check out also the fruit and veg sellers on sidewalks and street corners, whose produce is usually cheap and good.

For **wine**, the supermarkets tend to have decent selections at competitive prices, but for more interesting labels and well-informed staff, there are some first-rate specialist wine merchants in town. One of the best known is *Vaughan Johnson's*, on Dock Road, at the Waterfront, which has a huge range of labels from all over the country, arranged in alphabetical order. Another good selection is at *Picardy*, Shop 5, Seeff House, Hans Strydom Avenue, in the city centre.

Listings

Airlines *Air France* (☎21 4760); *Air Namibia* (☎21 6685); *Air New Zealand* (☎419 9382); *Air Portugal* (☎21 7224); *Air Zimbabwe* (*Compass Tours* ☎419 4370); *Alitalia* (☎21 6335); *British Airways* (☎ toll free 0800/01 1747); *British Airways/Comair* (☎934 8818); *KLM Royal Dutch Airlines* (☎21 1870 or 934 3495); *Lufthansa* (☎25 1490 or 934 8534); *Nationwide* (☎936 2050); *Olympic Airways* (☎23 0260); *Qantas* (☎419 9382); *SA Airlink* (☎ toll free 0800/11 4799); *Sabena* (☎21 7873); *South African Airways* (domestic ☎403 1111; international ☎936 2358); *Sun Air* (☎934 0918); *Swissair* (☎21 4938).

Banks Main branches are easy to find in the shopping areas of the city centre, the middle-class suburbs and at the Waterfront. Banking hours are Mon–Fri 8.30am–3.30pm, Sat 8–11am. Wherever you find banks, you'll also find automatic teller machines (ATMs).

Bureaux de change For foreign exchange transactions outside normal banking hours, try one of the following: *Rennies Travel*, St George's St (Mon–Fri 8.30am–5pm, Sat 9am–noon; ☎25 2370); *Trustbank*, Cape Town International Airport (open to accommodate international flights, ☎934 0223); *American Express*, Waterfront (Mon–Fri 9am–7pm, Sat & Sun 9am–5pm; ☎419 3917); *Rennies Foreign Exchange*, Waterfront (Mon–Fri 9am–7pm, Sat & Sun 10am–5pm; ☎418 3744).

Car parks These are dotted all over the place in this car-friendly city. There are pay and display car parks at street level all over the city centre, where hustlers will offer to look after your car and clean it for a tip, especially on the Grand Parade and Loop and Church streets. If you want to park in peace, head for one of the multi-storey parking garages. There's one attached to the Golden Acre complex and another at the north end of Lower Burg St.

Cell phone rental is available by the day, week or month from *Cellcity,* Kiosk 5, Victoria Wharf Centre, Waterfront (☎418 1306).

Credit and bank card theft ☎080 953 4300 or 418 5600.

Embassies and consulates *Australia,* 14th Floor, BP Centre, Thibault Square (☎419 5425); *Canada* Reserve Bank Building, Hout St (☎23 5240); *France,* 2 Dean St, Gardens (☎23 1575); *Germany,* 825 St Martini Gdns, Queen Victoria St (☎24 2410); *Israel,* Church Square House, Plein St (☎45 7207); *Netherlands,* 100 Strand St (☎21 5660); *Sweden,* 17th Floor, Southern Life Centre, 8 Riebeeck St (☎25 1687); *Switzerland,* 9th Floor, Waldorf Building, 80 St George's Mall (☎25 3670); *UK* Southern Life Centre, 8 Riebeeck St (☎25 3670); *USA,* 4th Floor, Broadway Centre, Heernegracht (☎21 4280).

Emergencies Ambulance ☎10177; Fire ☎535 1100 or 461 4141; Police (Flying Squad) ☎10111; Police (Tourist Assistance Unit) ☎418 2853; Rape Crisis ☎47 9762.

Gay contacts *Gay Escape,* 10th Floor, Guarantee House, 37 Burg St (☎23 9001), is a travel agency catering for both men and women, which organizes accommodation, activities and tours as well as providing information on clubs, pubs and parties. The *Gay, Lesbian and Bisexual Helpline* can be contacted on ☎21 5420.

Hospitals and doctors Doctors are listed in the telephone directory under "Medical". The largest hospital is *Groote Schuur,* Hospital Drive, Observatory (☎404 9111), just off the M3. *Somerset Hospital,* Beach Rd, Mouille Point (☎402 6911), nearer the centre, has outpatient and emergency departments and is convenient for the City Bowl and Atlantic seaboard.

Left luggage Cape Town railway station, Adderley St (Mon 7.30am–7pm, Tues–Thurs 7.30am–4pm, Fri 7.30am–6pm, Sat & Sun 6am–2.30pm; ☎405 2611).

Pharmacies with extended opening hours: *Hypermed Pharmacy,* York and Main roads, Green Point (Mon–Sat 8.30am–9pm, Sun 9am–9pm; ☎434 1414); *Sunset Pharmacy,* Sea Point Medical Centre, Kloof Rd, Sea Point (daily 8.30am–9pm; ☎434 3333); *Tamboerskloof Pharmacy,* 16 Kloof Nek Rd, Tamboerskloof (Mon–Fri 10am–8.30pm, Sat 10am–1pm & 6–9pm, Sun 10am–1pm & 6–8pm; ☎24 4450).

Police Head office: Caledon Square, Buitenkant St (☎461 7282); Tourist Assistance Unit, Tulbagh Square (☎418 2853).

Post office Main branch, Parliament St (Mon, Tues, Thurs & Fri 8am–4.30pm, Wed 8.30am–4.30pm, Sat 8am–noon; ☎461 5670) has a poste restante and enquiry desk.

Swimming *Long St Swimming Pool,* Long St (☎400 3302), is Cape Town's only heated indoor pool. *Newlands Swimming Pool,* Main and San Souci roads, Newlands (☎64 4197), is an Olympic-sized chlorinated pool. *Sea Point Swimming Pool,* Beach Rd, Sea Point (☎434 3341), is an enormous and wonderful sea-water pool.

Taxis There are a number of reliable companies, including *Unicab* (☎448 1720), *Marine Taxi Hire* (☎434 0434) and *Sea Point Taxis* (☎434 4444).

Telephones There are phone booths all over Cape Town taking phone cards and coins. For cash calls there are phones at the Main Post Office, Parliament St (Mon–Sat 8am–9.45pm, Sun and public holidays 9.30am–8.30pm).

Moving on from Cape Town

Cape Town's status as the undisputed tourism hub of South Africa has meant the development of an excellent network of connections to the rest of the country. **Flying** from Cape Town airport (☎934 0407) is the quickest and most expensive way of getting around, but useful if you need to cover large distances across the country. As far as overland travel goes, the intercity **express buses**, run by *Greyhound* (☎418 4312), *Intercape* (☎386 4400) and *Translux* (☎405 3333), offer a frequent, comprehensive and inexpensive service connecting Cape Town to major centres in the coastal provinces of **Northern**, **Western** and **Eastern Cape**, and **KwaZulu Natal**. There are also good bus connections to **Pretoria** and **Johannesburg**, which is the best place to head to if you want to reach the game-rich areas of Northern Province or Mpumalanga. Apart from the beautiful weekly journey by **train** between Cape Town and George, run by *Spoornet* (☎405 3871 or 405 3581), there is little to recommend the long train trips to Johannesburg and Durban, which cross some of South Africa's dreariest terrain. The cheapest way to get around is on one of the **backpacker buses**, which constantly run to and fro from Cape Town. The *Baz Bus* (☎439 2323) leaves Cape Town four times a week and runs along the coast as far as Port Elizabeth, with connections to Durban twice a week. The daily *Hopper Bus* (☎041/51 2332) goes to Mossel Bay, with connections to Port Elizabeth the next morning. From Port Elizabeth, the *Hopper* runs connections east along the coast to Cintsa via the inland town of Grahamstown.

travel details

Buses

To help you identify which **bus companies** go where, we've listed *Greyhound* (GH), *Intercape* (IC) and *Translux* (TL) where appropriate.

Cape Town to: Bloemfontein (4–5 daily;13hr; GH/IC/TL); Durban (3 daily; 20hr; GH/TL); East London (1–2 daily; 15hr 40min; GH/TL); George (5 daily; 6hr; GH/IC/TL); Graaff Reinet (1 daily except Mon & Wed; 9hr; TL); Grahamstown (1 daily; 12hr 25min; GH); Johannesburg (3 daily; 17hr; GH/IC/TL); Kimberley (1 daily except Wed; 11hr 45min; IC/TL); Knysna (5 daily; 6hr 50min; GH/IC/TL); Mossel Bay (5 daily; 5hr 15min; GH/IC/TL); Oudtshoorn (Tues, Thurs, Sat & Sun; 6hr 50min; TL); Pietermaritzburg (2 daily; 18hr 40min; GH/TL); Plettenberg Bay (5 daily; 7hr 30min; GH/IC/TL); Port Elizabeth (5 daily; 10hr; GH/IC/TL); Pretoria (3 daily; 18hr; GH/IC/TL); Stellenbosch (1–2 daily; 1hr; TL); Storms River (5 daily; 10hr 10min; GH/IC/TL); Umtata (1 daily; 18hr; GH); Upington (Mon, Wed, Fri & Sun; 10hr 30min; IC); Windhoek (Tues, Thurs, Fri & Sun; 16hr 30min; IC).

Trains

Two useful trains are the *Metro Rail* services connecting Cape Town with **Stellenbosch** and **Paarl**. Outside peak morning and evening hours, trains are irregular but run at approximately two-hour intervals. You should phone the station before leaving.

Cape Town to: Bloemfontein (every Mon; 23hr); Durban (every Mon; 36hr 25min); Johannesburg (1 daily; 24hr 55min); Kimberley (1 daily; 16hr 30min); Pietermaritzburg (every Mon; 34hr); Pretoria (1 daily; 26hr 20min).

Flights

Cape Town is a major **international point of entry** into South Africa, with flights from all around the world. It is also an important centre of the **domestic** network, and you can fly to virtually anywhere in the country from here. Services include:

Cape Town to: Bloemfontein (2–3 daily; 2hr 20min); Durban (8 daily; 2hr); East London (4 daily; 2hr); George (2 daily; 1hr); Johannesburg (hourly; 2hr); Kimberley (1 daily; 3hr); Port Elizabeth (5–6 daily; 1hr 30min); Upington (4 weekly; 1hr 45min); Walvis Bay (3 weekly; 2hr).

CHAPTER TWO

THE WESTERN CAPE

Most popular and arguably most beautiful of all South Africa's provinces, the **Western Cape** is also the least African area of the country. Visitors spend weeks here without exhausting its attractions, but frequently find themselves leaving slightly disappointed, never having quite got wind of an African beat. Of South Africa's nine provinces, only the Western Cape and the Northern Cape don't have an African majority; one person in five here is African, and the largest community, making up 55 percent of the population, are coloureds – people of mixed race descended from white settlers, indigenous Khoisan people and slaves from the East.

Although the Western Cape appears to conform more closely to the First World than any other part of the country, the impression is strictly superficial. Beneath the prosperous feel of the Winelands and the Garden Route lies a reality of Third World poverty in **squatter camps** on the outskirts well-to-do towns and on some **farms** where nineteenth-century labour practices prevail despite the end of apartheid.

Nevertheless, you can't fail to be moved by the sensuous physical beauty of the province's mountains, valleys and beaches. The **Winelands**, less than an hour from Cape Town, give full reign to the sybaritic pleasures of eating, drinking and visual feasting. Dutch colonial heritage reaches it peak in this region of gabled homesteads sitting among vineyards against a backdrop of slaty peaks.

To the northeast lies the **Breede River Valley**, a region usually bypassed along the N1 en route to Johannesburg, but featuring among its faceless fruit-farming towns some hideaways favoured by Capetonians as weekend retreats. Further east, the country opens into the timeless landscapes of the **Little Karoo**, the curtain-raiser to the semi-desert that drifts across one-third of South Africa's surface, and is nowhere more rewarding nor more easily accessed than here. Less visited than it deserves, the Little Karoo is skirted by the N1 to its north and the N2 to its south, and offers a succession of dramatic **passes** switchbacking across one mountain range after another.

Southeast of the Winelands, the **Overberg** is another region that remains hidden behind the mountains during a hasty journey east. The **Whale Coast**, an angry stretch of Indian Ocean to the south that has claimed hundreds of ships, is known for being the best area in the country for shore-based **whale-watching**, and there are a couple of pleasant coastal towns off the main routes along here.

The best-known name in the Western Cape is of course the **Garden Route**, a drive along the N2 that technically begins at **Mossel Bay**, where the freeway hits the coast, and continues for 185km to **Storms River**. In reality it is taken as part of a journey between Cape Town and Port Elizabeth, simply because these are the easiest places to catch flights and to pick up and drop off rental cars. The Garden Route proper can be driven in half a day, but to cover it so quickly would mean missing its essence, which can be found off the road in its coastal towns, lagoons, mountains and ancient forests, the highlight being the **Tsitsikamma National Park**, where the dark Storms River opens into the Indian Ocean. Partly because it lies along a single stretch of freeway, **public transport** along the Garden Route is better than anywhere in the country.

North of Cape Town, the less popular, remote and windswept **west coast** is usually explored during the wildflower months of August and September, when visitors converge on its centrepiece, the **West Coast National Park**. Its other major pull is the **Cederberg** mountain range, 200km north of Cape Town on the N7, a rocky wilderness with hikes and hidden rock art sites.

Apart from the annual explosion of wild flowers in the north, the Western Cape really scores on wilderness and flora, and is South Africa's **"fynbos" province"**. The plants you'll glimpse from afar all along the coast and up every mountainside look like a nondescript grey-green blur of vegetation, but on closer examination reveal a rich kingdom of delicate flowering plants that rival the Amazon Forest for biodiversity.

Several national parks and nature reserves make excellent places to explore fynbos, as do all the hikes mentioned in this chapter, but you shouldn't expect to see much African wildlife here. Most reserves have a few zebra or antelope, but the Big Five disappeared donkey's years ago – reflecting the fact that South Africa's longest colonized province was also the first to taste the devastatingly destructive power of firearms. By the same means, indigenous **Khoikhoi and San people** were virtually extinguished in the nineteenth century and **Africans** kept at arm's-length, some 1000km away on the "Eastern Frontier", which accounts for their relatively small numbers in the Western Cape.

THE WINELANDS

South Africa has over a dozen recognized wine routes extending to the Karoo and way into the Northern Cape, but the area known as **the Winelands** is restricted to the oldest wineries outside the Peninsula, which are within a sixty-kilometre radius of Cape Town. The district takes in the earliest European settlements at Stellenbosch, Paarl, Franschhoek and Somerset West, each with its own wine route. On the hillsides and in the valleys around these towns you'll find a flawless blending of traditional Cape Dutch **architecture** with landscape.

The Winelands are best covered in your own car, as half the pleasure is the drive through the countryside. Without private transport, your most sensible option is to head for **Stellenbosch**, which is served by regular trains from Cape Town. The most satisfying of the Wineland towns, it enjoys an easy elegance, beautiful streetscapes, a couple of decent museums and plenty of visitor facilities. If you're in a car, one of the region's scenic highlights is the drive along the R310 through the **Helshoogte Pass** between Stellenbosch and **Paarl**, which can also be reached on the *Metro Rail* link from Cape Town. The workaday farming town of the region, Paarl is credited as the

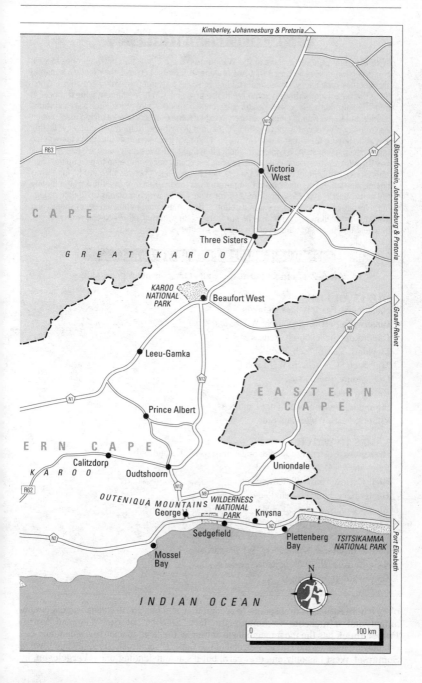

TACKLING THE WINEFIELDS

With over one hundred estates in the **Winelands**, the big question is which ones to visit. Our selection covers wineries that are of general interest because they feature beautiful architecture or scenery, or are entertaining in some way, not primarily because they produce the best wine (although some are in the first rank). When planning your trip bear in mind that although all the wineries offer tastings many offer a lot more, such as restaurants, picnics and horse-riding. Choose an area to explore and don't try to take on too many wineries in a day unless you want to return home in a dizzy haze. Remember that wine tasting and wine buying are supposed to be fun, so don't take it too seriously and don't take on too much. Even if you aren't a wine buff, you'll often find staff at tasting rooms are happy to talk you through a wine, which can be interesting, especially once you begin to pick up the characteristics of different wines. Most estates will charge a fee of between R2 and R8 for a wine-tasting session. If you plan on anything more than the briefest of tours, think about buying the authoritative *John Platter's South African Wine Guide*, which provides up-to-date ratings of the produce of every winery in the country. *Wine* magazine, published every month and available from all newsagents, has useful features on wineries, places to eat, wine reviews, information on latest bottlings and a diary of events.

ROUGH GUIDES FAVOURITE LABELS

An A–Z of old favourites, rising stars and plain good value

OLD FAVOURITES
Backsberg, Paarl. Whites and reds.
Blaauwklippen, Stellenbosch. Whites and reds.
Kanonkop, Stellenbosch. Reds.
Lievland, Stellenbosch. Reds.
Meerlust, Stellenbosch. Whites and reds.
Overgaauw, Paarl. Reds.
Rust en Vrede, Stellenbosch. Reds.
Simonsig, Stellenbosch. Whites and reds.
Villiera, Paarl. Whites and reds.

NAMES TO WATCH
Brampton, Rustenberg Estate, Stellenbosch. Whites and reds.
Fairview, Paarl. Whites and reds.
Glen Carlou, Paarl. Whites and reds.
Hartenberg, Stellenbosch. Reds.
Klawervlei, Stellenbosch. Reds.
Klein Constantia, Constantia. Whites and reds.
Morgenhof, Stellenbosch. Whites and reds.
Plaisir de Merle, Simonsberg. Whites and reds.
Saxenburg, Stellenbosch. Reds.
Veenwouden, Paarl. Reds.

place where Afrikaans first sprang to recognition, and has an Afrikaans language monument and a museum to honour the fact. Smallest of the Wineland towns, **Franschhoek** has the most magnificent setting at the head of a narrow valley, and has established itself as the culinary capital of the Cape. By contrast, the sprawling town of **Somerset West** has only one drawcard, but it's an outstanding one – **Vergelegen**, by

RISING STARS
Buitenverwachting, Constantia. Whites and reds.
Grangehurst, Stellenbosch. Reds.
Jordan, Stellenbosch. Whites.
Mulderbosch, Stellenbosch. White and *Faithful Hound* (red blend).
Stellenzicht, Stellenbosch. Whites and reds.
Thelema, Stellenbosch. Whites and reds.
Vergelegen, Somerset West. Whites and reds.

VALUE FOR MONEY
Backsberg, Paarl. Cabernet Sauvignon, Merlot, Shiraz, Pinotage.
Bergendal, Stellenbosch. Bergenblanc and Bergenrood.
Chateau Libertas, Stellenbosch. Red blend.
De Leuwen Jagt, Paarl. Cabernet Sauvignon-Merlot blend.
Fairview, Paarl. Range of whites and reds.
Fleur du Cap, Bergkleder winery, Stellenbosch. Merlot, Shiraz and noble late-harvest dessert wine.
Hartenberg, Stellenbosch. Cabernet-Shiraz blend.
Lievland, Stellenbosch. Lievlander red blend.
Nederburg, Paarl. Kap Sekt champagne-style bubbly.
Pongrácz, Bergkleder winery, Stellenbosch. Cap classique, champagne-style bubbly.
Villiera, Paarl. Huge range of whites, reds and Tradition (Carte Rouge), a champagne-style bubbly.
Vlottenburg, Stellenbosch. Cabernet Sauvignon, Merlot, Pinotage.

ROUGH GUIDE FAVOURITE ESTATES

- **Boschendal Estate**, Franschhoek (see p.144). Best-organized mass-tourist venue offering conducted tours, beautiful buildings, shops and a choice of restaurants.
- **Delaire**, Stellenbosch (see p.134). Best mountain view across the Helshoogte Pass.
- **Cabrière Estate**, Franschhoek (see p.144). Most eccentric uncorking using *sabrage* – slicing clean through the neck of a bubbly bottle with a sabre.
- **Fairview Estate**, Paarl (see p.141). Great family venue with a famous goat tower, peacocks, cheese and wine.
- **La Motte Estate**, Franschhoek (see p.144). Best tasting room, decorated with marble, glass and oak barrels.
- **Rhebokskloof Estate**, Paarl (see p.140). Trendiest restaurant, overlooking a swan lake.
- **Rustenberg Estate**, Stellenbosch (see p.134). Most bucolic setting, with a historic gabled milking shed.
- **Vergelegen**, Somerset West (see p.135). The estate that has it all: fabulous buildings, a small museum, beautiful gardens, good wines to taste and a choice of restaurants.

far the most stunning of all the Wineland estates, which can be tacked onto a tour of the Stellenbosch wine route.

Summer is the best time to visit, when days are longer, as are opening hours, the vines are in leaf and there's activity at the wineries. In winter the wine has been made, there are fewer cellar tours and there's not much going on.

Stellenbosch

Dappled avenues of three-century-old oaks are the defining feature of **STELLEN-BOSCH**, 46km east of Cape Town – a fact reflected in its Afrikaans nickname *Die Eikestad* ("the oak city"). Street frontages of the same vintage, sidewalk cafés, water furrows and a European town layout centred on the Braak, a large village green, add up to a well-rooted urban texture that invites casual exploration. The city is the undisputed heart of the Winelands, having more urban attractions than either Paarl or Franschhoek, while at the same time being at the hub of the largest and oldest of the Cape **wine routes**.

The city is also home to **Stellenbosch University**, Afrikanerdom's most prestigious educational institution, which does something to enliven the atmosphere. But even the heady promise of plentiful alcohol and thousands of students haven't changed the fact that at heart this is a conservative place, which was once the intellectual engine room of apartheid, and fostered the likes of Dr **HF Verwoerd**, the prime minister who dreamed up Grand Apartheid. Today, the white establishment still has roots firmly in the National Party, the Dutch Reformed Church and the Broederbond (an Afrikaner secret society strongly linked to the National Party).

Some history

One of the first actions of **Simon van der Stel** after arriving at the Cape in November 1679 to take over as Dutch East India Company commander was to explore the area along the Eerste River ("first river"), where he came upon an enchanting little valley. Less than a month later it appeared on maps as Stellenbosch ("Stel's bush"), the first of several places dotted around the Cape, including Simonsberg overlooking the town, which the governor was to name after himself or members of his family.

Charged by the Dutch East India Company directors in the Netherlands with opening up the Cape interior, van der Stel soon settled the first **free burghers** in Stellenbosch. Within eight years, sixty freehold grants had been made and the area was regarded as full. Within twenty-five years Stellenbosch was established as a prosperous, semi-feudal society dominated by landowners, and in 1702 the Danish traveller, Abraham Bogaert, admired how it had "grown with fine dwellings, and how great a treasure of wine and grain is grown here". Eight years on, some of those fine thatch-roofed houses were destroyed by **fire**, but were soon rebuilt, and by the end of the century there were over a thousand houses and some substantial burgher **estates** in and around Stellenbosch, many of which are still standing.

Arrival and information

Coming to Stellenbosch **by car** gives you the freedom to explore the surrounding wineries at your leisure. The drive from Cape Town takes under an hour along either the N1 or N2. *Metro Rail* **trains** commute between Cape Town (information ☎405 2991) and Stellenbosch station (☎808 1111) roughly every two hours during the day, and take about an hour. Infrequent (and expensive) **intercity buses** from Cape Town and Port Elizabeth pass through Stellenbosch, calling at the train station.

The busy **tourist information bureau**, 36 Market St (☎883 3584, fax 883 8017; email: eikestad@iafrica.com), can provide basic information on local attractions, and can supply you with the *Discover Stellenbosch on Foot* leaflet, which describes a walking tour covering a daunting 62 sites.

> The **telephone code** for Stellenbosch is ☎021.

STELLENBOSCH

ACCOMMODATION

1 Avenues Guesthouse
2 Blombosch Guesthouse
3 Bonne Esperance
4 Cluver Lodge
5 D'Ouwe Werf
6 Just Joey
7 The Lanzerac
8 Michaelhouse
9 Natte Vallei
10 Stellenbosch Hotel
11 Stumble Inn
12 Victoria House
13 Villa Jonde
14 Weidenhof Lodge

The centre of Stellenbosch is small enough to explore on foot, but if you need to get further afield, contact *Rikkis* (☎887 2203), who provide transport in **tuk-tuks** that roam around collecting and dropping off passengers. They also offer excursions to wineries for around R20 per person per farm. For **car rental**, try *Budget Rent-a-Car* (☎883 9103), which also offers **bike rental**. *Stellenbosch Motorcycles*, Latsky St (☎883 9805), have a couple of motorbikes for rent at R100 per day (with 100km thrown in free), plus a charge per kilometre.

Accommodation

Stellenbosch has no shortage of **places to stay** and covers the field from backpacker's lodges to total luxury. Apart from the handful of out-of-town farmstays and the luxurious *Lanzerac*, all the accommodation is within easy walking distance of the town centre.

Guesthouses and hotels

Avenues Guest House, 32 The Avenue (☎887 1843, fax 887 2733). Friendly B&B done out in airy yellowwood and pine, with a twist of Laura Ashley, across the road from the Eerste River. An easy walk to the centre and university campus, where guests can use the swimming pool and three-storey gym. ④.

Blombosch Guest House, 61 Plein St (☎883 3674). Central guesthouse with eight double rooms, some with balconies. ②.

Bonne Esperance, 17 Van Riebeeck St (☎887 0225, fax 887 8328). Colonial elegance in a terrific double-storey Victorian villa. Good service, a verandah overlooking a lovely front garden, and a courtyard and swimming pool at the rear all help to justify the price. ④.

D'Ouwe Werf, 30 Church St (☎887 1608 or 887 4608, fax 887 4626). South Africa's oldest country inn, in the middle of town, dates back to the end of the nineteenth century. There are TVs and phones in every room plus a swimmming pool. ⑦.

Just Joey, corner of Noorwal and Helderberg streets (☎887 1799, fax 887 2899). Peachy pink guesthouse with comfortable rooms glowing with rose-tinted frills and drapes. ④.

The Lanzerac, Jonkershoek Rd, 1km from town (☎887 1132, fax 887 2310). The last word in Winelands luxury, this hotel wallows in a visual orgy of whitewashed buildings surrounded by vineyards and mountains. ⑦.

Michaelhouse, 29 Van Riebeeck St (☎ & fax 886 6343). Modern cast-iron decor with just a hint of the ethnic, offers a relief from the town's ubiquitous soft colours and floral prints. The garden terrace with trellised vines makes the perfect venue for a summery breakfast. ③–④.

Natte Valleij, 44 Klapmuts Rd (☎875 5171, fax 875 5475). En-suite B&B rooms off a courtyard or in cottage in an old whitewashed homestead with large gardens in the heart of the Winelands. Breakfast is served on the verandah and there's a swimming pool. ③.

Stellenbosch Hotel, corner of Dorp and Andringa streets (☎887 3644, fax 887 3673). Smart town-centre hotel in a restored nineteenth-century house, now declared a National Monument. Brass beds, capacious sofas, starched linen and atmosphere. ⑤–⑦.

Victoria House, 21 Van Riebeeck St (☎ & fax 883 2099, mobile 082/576 3807). Good-value, self-catering rooms in a serviced and comfortably furnished house with all the facilities you're likely to need plus shared lounge, kitchen and bathrooms, near the centre. ②.

Villa Jonde, 27 Noorwal-Wes (☎ & fax 883 3568). Rambling Edwardian house eccentrically furnished and generally unpretentious. Surrounded by a huge jungle of a garden in which you can lose yourself, it offers reasonable value at the bottom end of its price range. ③.

Backpacker's lodges

Cluver Lodge, 12 Cluver St (☎887 2123, fax 887 2397). Fourteen budget double rooms in a house sharing five bathrooms and three kitchens. ②.

Stumble Inn, 12 Market St (☎ & fax 887 4049). The obvious choice for backpackers, with friendly, switched-on staff and a chilled atmosphere in a turn-of-the-century house with a verandah and garden just down the road from the tourist information bureau. Doubles, dorms and camping. ①.

Weidenhof Lodge, 24 Weidenhof St (☎886 4679, fax 887 2397). Clean, friendly and functional pur-pose-built backpacker's lodge that frequently hosts large groups and has a great roof terrace. The owner is happy to offer advice on alternative accommodation. ①.

The Town

Stellenbosch's attractions lie principally in its setting and streetscape; it's a lovely place to simply wander around. The tourist information bureau in the Rhenish complex, Market St, is a good place to start your explorations. Heading north up this road you'll soon reach a whitewashed block that was the **VOC Kruithuis** (the Dutch East India Company's powder magazine), which houses a small and unprepossessing collection of four British uniforms, assorted rifles, some intriguing, but unexplained, little laptop-sized cannons and some powder kegs. From here, a right turn south around the **Braak**, the large green that occupies the centre of town, will take you past the **Rhenish Church** in Bloem Street, which was built in 1823 as a school for slaves and coloured people.

The Village Museum

Head north up Ryneveld Street, and you'll encounter Stellenbosch's highlight, the extremely enjoyable **Village Museum**, 18 Ryneveld St (Mon–Sat 9.30am–5pm, Sun 2–5pm, ☎887 2902), which cuts a cross-section through the town's architectural and social heritage by means of a complex of four fortuitously adjacent historical dwellings from different periods. They're beautifully conserved and furnished in peri-od style, and you'll bump into the odd worker dressed in contemporary costume. Earliest of the houses is the homely **Shreuderhuis**, a vernacular cottage built in 1709, with a small courtyard garden filled with aromatic herbs, pomegranate bushes and vine-draped pergolas – bearing more resemblance to the early Cape settlement's European aesthetics than to modern South Africa. Across the garden, **Blettermanhuis**, built in 1789 for the last Dutch East India Company-appointed mag-istate of Stellenbosch, is an archetypal eighteenth-century Cape Dutch house, built on an H-plan with six gables. **Grosvenor House**, opposite, was altered to its current form in 1803, and reflects the growing influence of English taste after the 1795 British occupation of the Cape. The Neoclassical facade with fluted pilasters supporting a pedimented entrance borrows from high fashion, current then at the heart of the growing Empire. The more modest **OM Bergh House**, across the road, is a typical Victorian dwelling that was once similar to Blettermanhuis, but was "modernized" in the mid-nineteenth century on a rectangular plan with a simplified facade without gables.

Dorp Street and around

From the Village Museum, head back south into **Dorp Street**, Stellenbosch's best-preserved historic axis, well worth a slow stroll just to soak in the ambience of build-ings, gables, oaks and roadside water furrows. Heading west along it, you'll spot the **wine-tasting centre** on your left and next door the much-celebrated **Oom Samie se Winkel**, which amounts to little more than a jam-packed Victorian-style general deal-er selling touristy knick-knacks, antiques, comestibles and wines, but is worth pop-ping into if only to sample some fish biltong. On your right, look out for **Krige's Cottages**, an unusual terrace of historic town houses at nos. 37–51, between Aan-die-Wagen-Weg and Krige streets. The houses were built as Cape Dutch cottages in the first half of the nineteenth century, and later Victorian features were added, resulting in an interesting hybrid, with gables housing Victorian attic windows and decorative Victorian verandahs with filigree ironwork fronting the elegant simplicity of Cape Dutch facades.

A left turn into Strand Street brings you to **Libertas Parva**, a fine example of an H-plan Cape Dutch manor, and home to the **Rembrandt van Rijn Art Museum** (Mon–Fri 9am–12.45pm & 2–5pm, Sat 10am–1pm & 2–5pm). Don't let the name fool you into expecting Old Dutch Masters – the museum is funded by the Rembrandt tobacco multinational. The gallery has a small but stimulating collection of South African art, including a wonderful 360-degree panorama of Cape Town rendered in pen, ink and watercolour by Josephus Jones in 1808; *The Conservationists Ball*, an acerbic tryptich by William Kentridge, a leading light among the current generation of South African artists; and a number of Irma Stern paintings and drawings to pad it all out. Adjacent in the same courtyard, the Libertas Parva Cellar houses the **Stellenryck Wine Museum** (Mon–Fri 9am–12.45pm & 2–5pm, Sat 10am–1pm & 2–5pm), which has some moderately interesting ancient amphorae, winepresses, wineglasses and old bottles, but shouldn't keep you nosing around for too long, unless you're a real buff.

Eating and drinking

You'll be spoilt for choices of good **places to eat** in Stellenbosch, both in the centre and on some of the surrounding estates. In the evenings, the student presence ensures a relaxed and sometimes raucous drinking culture.

Restaurants, pubs and cafés

De Akker, 90 Dorp St. Good spot for pub lunches in a cool joint enjoyed by unshod students accompanied by torn jeans and dogs.

De Cameron, 50 Plein St (☎883 3331). One of the best restaurants in town, offering southern Italian food, including pasta, pizzas and gnocchi, as well as first-rate seafood.

Lanzerac, *Lanzerac Hotel*, Jonkershoek Rd (☎887 1132). Formal restaurant among the vineyards on the outskirts of town, with an internationally inspired à la carte menu that changes once a month.

D'Ouwe Werf, 30 Church St (☎887 1608). In a beautiful courtyard with vines, this restaurant offers traditional Cape cuisine, including Karoo lamb, bobotie and oxtail brewed in red wine sauce. Their Black Forest cake is an excellent accompaniment to tea.

Ralph's, 13 Andringa St (☎883 3532). Stellenbosch's top restaurant is run by a master chef and features a terrific international menu that includes ostrich steak. Food is served amid 1980s-style red white and black decor, and wicker chairs.

Rustic Café, Bird St. Cheap to moderately priced pizzas, *nachos*, salads and Thai curries.

San Francisco Coffee Roastery, Drostdy Craft Market, Alexander St. A dead cert for a fine cup of coffee, with a choice of blends, flavoured coffees, muffins and light snacks.

Stellenbosch Wine Tasting Centre, 90 Dorp St (☎883 3814). Hundreds of Cape wines to taste, buy and quaff.

Vinkel en Koljander, *Lanzerac Hotel*, Jonkershoek Rd. Outdoor teas and traditional country dishes (soups, casseroles and light meals) served against a wonderfully scenic backdrop of mountains and vineyards.

Volkskombuis, Aan-de-Wagenweg, off Dorp St (☎887 2121). On the banks of the Eerste River, serving up Cape cuisine and *boerekos* at acceptable prices.

The Stellenbosch wine estates

Stellenbosch was the first locality in the country to wake up to the marketing potential of a **wine route**, which it launched in 1971. The tactic has been hugely successful and now draws tens of thousands of visitors from all over the world to the wineries, making this the most toured area in the Winelands. Although the region only accounts for fif-

Paarl

Wellington

Cape Town

N1

Lievland

R304 Simonsig
R44

Bottelary Rd

Kromme Rhee Rd

Morgenhof

Rustenburg

Wedge
Farm

Thelema

Stellenbosch
Station

Leur Rd

R310

Delaire

Franschhoek

Jordan

Neethlingshof

Overgaauw

R310

Lanzerac
Hotel

Stellenbosch

Eerste River

N

R306

R300

R102

Blaauwklippen

Annandale Rd

R44

R310

Strand Rd

0   5 km

STELLENBOSCH WINE ROUTE

Somerset West

teen percent of the country that's under vine, its wine route is the most extensive in South Africa and offers some of the Cape's best reds and overall the greatest diversity of wines. The wineries are all along a series of roads that radiate out from Stellenbosch. The selection below covers three of these roads, with the wineries arranged from Stellenbosch outwards, making each series easy to cover in a single journey. All the wineries have wine-route signposts along the main road.

Along the R44

The Klapmuts road (**R44**) north out of Stellenbosch, towards the N1, will lead you, after 3.7km, to **Morgenhof** (Mon–Fri 9am–4.30pm, Sat 10am–3pm; also Sept– May Sun 10am–3pm; ☎021/889 5510, fax 889 5266; small tasting charge). A French-owned chateau-style complex overlooked by the vine-covered Simonsberg, Morgenhof has a light and airy tasting room with a bar. Delicious light lunches are served outside, topped off, when available, by ripe berries and ice cream on the summery lawns. Among the wines worth sampling here are the Merlot, Cabernet Sauvignon and Sauvignon Blanc. Drive a further 3.6km north along the Klapmuts Road, and you'll reach the turn-off on your left to **Simonsig** (Mon–Fri 8.30am–4.45pm, Sat 8.30am–4.30pm; cellar tours Mon–Fri 10am & 3pm, Sat 10am; ☎021/882 2044, fax 882 2545; small tasting charge). The winery, just over 2km down Kromme Rhee Road, has an outdoor tasting area under vine-covered pergolas, from where you get majestic views back to Stellenbosch of hazy grey mountains, slaty peaks and vineyards. Although there's no restaurant, you can eat your own picnic at tables in a courtyard area cooled by a fountain. Of their first-class wines, their cutting-edge Pinotage is worth a try, as is their Kaapse Vonkel sparkling wine.

Back on the main road, **Lievland** (tasting and sales Mon–Fri 9am–5pm, Sat 9am–1pm; ☎021/875 5226, fax 875 5213), 4.5km north of the Simonsig turn-off, is the last of the Stellenbosch wineries on this section of the R44 – after this they fall under Paarl. In a farm environment, Lievland is an informal place where, if you're keen, you can ask to speak to the winemaker, who is an expert on Shiraz. This, unsurprisingly, is one of the wines you should try in their Cape Dutch tasting room, which dates back to 1823.

Driving straight back through Stellenbosch, 3.9km from town along the Strand Road (R44 south) brings you to **Blaauwklippen** (Mon–Fri 9am–5pm, Sat 9am–1pm; ☎021/880 0133, fax 880 0136; tasting charge), at the foot of the Stellenboschberg. Although big enough to take tour buses, Blaauwklippen isn't overly commercialized. Apart from the usual Cape Dutch buildings, there are inexpensive carriage rides through the vineyards, a horse-carriage museum, and a little shop selling soft drinks and knick-knacks. A coachman's lunch is served (Mon–Sat) on the verandah. The most celebrated wine from the Blaauwklippen cellar is their Zinfandel, rated South Africa's best of its type, with successive vintages winning international acknowledgement. If you continue south along the R44, you'll eventually reach Somerset West, centre of the Helderberg wine route, the highlight of which is **Vergelegen** (see p.135).

Along the R310

One of the closest estates to central Stellenbosch is **Rustenberg** (tasting and sales 8.30am–4.30pm, Sat 9am–12.30pm; ☎021/887 3153, fax 887 8466), which isn't a member of the official Stellenbosch wine route, but is one of the most alluring wine farms. To get there, join the R310 from the R44 to Paarl, just north of town. After just under 2km along the R310 to Franschhoek, turn into Ida's Valley for a further 2km, which, after a drive through orchards, sheep pastures and treed avenues, brings you to the estate. An unassuming working farm, Rustenberg hangs onto a romantic pastoral atmosphere, with a complex of three-hundred-year-old buildings, including two National Monuments, and a gabled Cape Dutch milking shed. The first vines were planted here in 1692, but the viniculture looks to the future, with an Australian winemaker bringing in New World know-how to revamp the old labels. Despite the slave bell in the farmyard, their labour practices are among the best in the Cape, with model worker housing and participatory management. No meals are laid on, so you should bring your own picnic to savour under the oaks, along with one of their wines, of which the Rustenberg Gold, a Bordeaux blend of Cabernet Sauvignon, Merlot and Cabernet Franc, has been coming out tops for years. Also look out for highly drinkable reds and whites under the name Brampton – their second label.

For the Winelands' best views – though not the best wines – head for **Delaire** (tasting and sales Mon–Sat 10am–5pm; ☎021/885 1756, fax 885 1270; tasting charge), on the **Helshoogte Pass**, 6km from Stellenbosch along the R310 to Franschhoek. The drive up from the pass through the slopes of the vineyard-covered hillside brings you to the tasting room and restaurant with views through oaks across the Groot Drakenstein and Simonsig Mountains and down into craggy valleys. One of the great mysteries of Delaire is its unexciting wines, given that neighbouring Thelema consistently produces some of the Cape's most brilliant reds and whites. **Thelema** is sadly not worth visiting, as there's little chance you'll find any examples of their best output to taste. In fact, when the British queen visited South Africa in 1995, the winemaker was forced to raid his private cellar to provide bottles of their world-class Sauvignon Blanc for a state banquet.

Along the R306 southwest

Moddergat Road (the R310) heads southwest out of Stellenbosch along the train tracks, branching off 5.4km later onto Polkadraai Road (the **R306**). Half a kilometre later you'll come to the driveway that leads up to **Neethlingshof** (tasting and sales Mon–Fri 9am–5pm, Sat & Sun 10am–4pm; ☎021/883 8988, fax 883 8941; small tasting charge), which has a beautifully restored Cape Dutch manor dating back to 1814, and two good restaurants (*Palm Terrace* serves light meals). The first vines were planted here in 1692 and Neethlingshof produces some good wines, but hits the high notes with its Noble Late Harvest sweet dessert wines, which are stunners. A further 500m along the R306 takes you to another turn-off to the north, along which after a short distance you'll reach **Overgaauw** (tasting and sales Mon–Fri 9am–12.30pm & 2–5pm, Sat 10am–12.30pm; ☎021/881 3815, fax 881 3436), notable for having the only Victorian tasting room in the Winelands with an atmosphere that's elegant and understated. A pioneering estate which turns out reds and ports of excellent quality, Overgaauw was the first in the country to produce Merlots and is the only one to make Sylvaner, a well-priced, easy-drinking dry white. None of this has gone to its head and it's a thoroughly convivial place to sample the grape.

Further north along the same road, **Jordan Vineyards** (Mon–Fri 10am–4.30pm, Sat 9am–2.30pm; ☎021/881 3441, fax 881 3426) is part of the new wave of Cape wineries, with a high-tech cellar, modern tasting room and friendly service. The drive there is half the fun, taking you into a *kloof* bounded by vineyards that get a whiff of the seas from both False Bay and Table Bay, which has obviously done something for their outstanding Chardonnay and Sauvignon Blanc.

Somerset West and Vergelegen

The only compelling reason to trawl out to the unpromising town of **SOMERSET WEST**, 50km east of Cape Town along the N2, is for **Vergelegen**, Lourensford Rd (daily 9.30am–4pm; ☎847 1334, fax 847 1608; entry fee includes wine tasting and cellar tours), a winery that is fair set on the ascendant and an absolute architectural treasure. Officially part of the Helderberg wine route, Vergelegen can easily be included as an extension to a visit to Stellenbosch, just 14km to the north.

Vergelegen represents a notorious episode of corruption and the arbitrary abuse of power at the Cape in the early years of Dutch East India Company rule. Built by Willem Adriaan van der Stel, who became governor in 1699 after the retirement of his father Simon, it is difficult to overestimate the impact of the estate as a grand Renaissance complex in the middle of the wild backwater that was the Cape at the turn of the eighteenth century. Willem Adriaan had illegally got hold of the land and had used Dutch East India Company slaves to build Vergelegen as well as Company resources to farm vast tracts of land in the surrounding areas. At the same time he abused his power as governor to corner most of the significant markets at the Cape. When this was brought to the notice of the Dutch East India Company in the Netherlands, Willem Adriaan was sacked and Vegelegen was ordered to be destroyed to discourage future miscreant governors. It's believed that the destruction was never fully carried out and the current building is thought to stand on the foundations of the original.

Vergelégen was the only wine estate visited by the British queen during her 1995 state visit to South Africa. This was a good choice, as there's enough here to occupy an easy couple of hours. The **interpretive centre**, just across the courtyard from the shop at the building entrance, provides a useful history and background to the estate which you can absorb in about ten minutes. Next door, the **wine-tasting centre** (closed Sun) offers a professionally run sampling with a brief talk through each label. The **homestead**, which was restored in 1917 to its current state by Lady Florence

Phillips, wife of a Johannesburg mining magnate, can also be visited. Its pale facade with a classical triangular gable and pilaster-decorated doorways is reached along an axis through an octagonal garden that dances with butterflies in summer. Massive grounds planted with chestnuts and camphor trees and ponds around every corner make this one of the most serene places in the Cape and one where you might want to linger.

Practicalities

Vergelegen is best reached **by car**. Although there are regular *Metro Rail* trains between Cape Town and Somerset West, the estate is too far from town to make this a serious option, unless you're prepared to hitch. To reach Vergelegen from Cape Town, take the N2 east past the International Airport, and leave the freeway at exit 43, signposted to Somerset West. This will bring you onto the R44, which you should follow into town. Once in Main Street, you'll see the turn-off to Lourensford Road (if you hit the town centre you've missed the turn-off), which you should follow for just over 3km to Vergelegen, which will be on your right.

Given its proximity to far nicer Stellenbosch, there's no reason to stay overnight in Somerset West. For **eating and drinking**, Vergelegen offers two excellent choices: at the chintzy *Lady Phillips Tea Garden* (☎852 6666) you can take tea or eat country-cuisine lunches (booking essential) of pies, quiches and pastas with an international flavour, while the less formal *Rose Terrace* offers outdoor light lunches of sandwiches on home-baked bread, cheese platters and wine by the glass.

Paarl

Although **PAARL** is attractively ensconced in a fertile valley brimming with historical monuments, at heart it's a parochial *dorp*, lacking either the sophistication of Stellenbosch or the new-found trendiness of Franschhoek. It can claim some virtue, however, from being a prosperous farming centre that earns its keep from the agricultural light industries – grain silos, canneries and flour mills – on the north side of town, and the cornucopia of grapes, guavas, olives, oranges and maize grown on the surrounding farms. Despite its small-town feel, Paarl has the largest municipality in the Winelands, with its most elite areas on the vined slopes of **Paarl Mountain**, the granite, domed formation that looks down over the town. In stark contrast with the cliquey conservatism of the predominantly white centre, the coloured townships on its periphery bear racy American names such as **Chicago** and **New Orleans**.

Some history

In 1657, just five years after the establishment of the Dutch East India Company refreshment station on the Cape Peninsula, a party under **Abraham Gabbema** pitched up in the Berg River Valley to look for trading opportunities with the Khoikhoi, and search for the legendary gold of Monomotapa. They obviously had treasure on the brain, because on awaking after a rainy night to the sight of the silvery dome of granite that dominates the valley, they dubbed it *Peerlbergh* ("pearl mountain"), which in its modified form, **Paarl**, became the name of the town.

Thirty years later, commander of the Cape, Simon van der Stel, granted strips of the Khoikhoi lands on the slopes of Paarl Mountain to French Huguenot and Dutch settlers. By the time Paarl was officially granted town status in 1840, it was still an outpost at the edge of the Drakenstein Mountains, a position from which it gained much benefit as a flourishing last-stop wagon-making and provisioning centre. This status was enhanced when the first **train line** in the Cape connected it to the Peninsula in 1863. Following in the spirit of the first Dutch adventurers of 1657, thousands of treasure-seekers brought custom to Paarl as the gateway to the interior during the diamond rush of the 1870s and the gold fever of the 1880s.

In the twentieth century the town holds deep historical significance for the two competing political forces that forged modern South Africa. **Afrikanerdom** regards Paarl as the hallowed ground on which their language movement was born in 1875 (see p.138), while for the **ANC** (and the international community), Paarl will be remembered as the place from which Nelson Mandela made the final steps of his long walk to freedom, when he walked out of **Victor Verster Prison** in 1990.

Arrival and information

Metro Rail and *Spoornet* **trains** from Cape Town pull in at Huguenot Station in Lady Grey Street at the north end of town, near to the central shops. *Greyhound* and *Intercape* intercity **buses** stop at Paarl Station, at the south end of town, close to the Laborie winery.

Paarl's **tourist information bureau**, 216 Main St (☎872 3829, fax 872 9376), has a selection of good maps and can help with finding accommodation. You can arrange **car rental** through *Avante Car Hire*, 272 Main St (☎872 5869), or *Wine Route Rent-a-Car*,

The **telephone code** for Paarl is ☎021.

THE HISTORY OF AFRIKAANS

Afrikaans is South Africa's third mother tongue, spoken by fifteen percent of the population and outstripped only by Zulu and Xhosa. English, by contrast, is the mother tongue of only nine percent of South Africans, and ranks fifth in the league of the eleven official languages.

Signs of the emergence of a new southern African dialect appeared as early as 1685, when HA van Rheede, a Dutch East India Company official from the Netherlands, complained about a "distorted and incomprehensible" version of Dutch being spoken in the Drakenstein Valley around modern-day Paarl. By absorbing English, French, German, Malay and indigenous words and expressions, the language continued to diverge from mainstream Dutch, and by the nineteenth century was widely used in the Cape by both white and coloured speakers, but was regarded by the elite as an inferior creole, unsuitable for literary or official communication. Even the first attempts by dominee **Stephanus du Toit** and the *Genootskap van Regte Afrikaners* ("League of True Afrikaners") to have Afrikaans recognized as a separate language from Dutch, and their launching in 1875, of *Die Patriot*, the first white Afrikaans **newspaper**, made little impact outside Paarl.

Ironically, it was the British defeat of the Afrikaner republics in the second **Anglo-Boer War** at the turn of the twentieth century that provided the catalyst for a mass white Afrikaans movement. The scorched-earth policy of the British had driven many Boers from the lands and produced a demoralized and semi-literate Boer underclass. The official British policy of the anglicization of South Africa helped to unite the white Afrikaner proletariat and elite against the common English enemy. In 1905, **Gustav Preller**, a young journalist from a working-class Boer background set about reinventing Afrikaans as a "white man's language". He aimed to eradicate the stigma of its "coloured" ties by substituting Dutch words for those with non-European origins. Preller began publishing the first of a series of populist magazines written in Afrikaans and glorifying Boer history and culture. Through this **Second Language Movement**, whites took spiritual control over Afrikaans and the pressure grew for its recognition as an official language, which came in 1925.

When the National Party took power in 1948, its apartheid policy went hand in hand with promoting the interests of its Afrikaans-speaking supporters and a concerted programme of the **upliftment of poor whites** began. Afrikaners were installed throughout the civil service and filled most posts in the public utilities. Despite the fact that there were more coloured than white Afrikaans speakers, the language quickly became associated with the **apartheid** establishment. This had electrifying consequences in the 1970s, when the government attempted to enforce Afrikaans as the sole medium of instruction in African schools, leading directly to the **Soweto uprising** in 1976, which marked the beginning of the end for Afrikaner hegemony in South Africa. The repressive period throughout the 1970s and 1980s and the forced removals under the Group Areas Act led many coloured Afrikaans speakers to adopt English in preference to their mother tongue, which they felt was tainted by apartheid.

There are few signs that Afrikaans will die out. Under the new constitution, existing **language rights** can't be diminished, which effectively means that Afrikaans will continue to be almost as widely used as before. It is now as much with coloured as white people that the future of the *taal* (language) rests.

23 Nantes St (☎872 8513, fax 872 8354). If you need to get around town in a hurry, contact *Paarl Radio Taxis* (☎872 5671). *Village Cycles*, 6 Commercial St (☎872 8909), on the corner of Commercial and Nantes streets, offers **bike rental**.

Accommodation

Most **places to stay** in town are either along or just off Main Street, many in historic buildings. In the absence of any backpackers' lodges, the cheapest options are the two resorts with chalets just outside town. One of South Africa's most outstanding places to stay is *Roggeland Country House*, which is not far from central Paarl.

Berg River Resort, 5km south of town on the R45 (☎863 1650, fax 863 2583). Rambling, run-down family holiday resort on the banks of the Berg River, with camping (①) and chalets (②), swimming pool and restaurant. There's an old mini-golf, and canoeing on the river. Bring your own towels.

Berghof, Monte Christo Ave (☎871 1099, fax 872 6126). The 22 rooms in this large, modern guesthouse at the top of a hill, are done out in marble, glass and impersonal motel furniture. The swimming pool commands one of the best sites in Paarl, with soaring views across town to the Drakenstein Mountains. ③–⑤.

Boschenmeer, 1km south of the N1 along the R303 (☎863 1250, fax 863 3082). Two-bed timber chalets overlooking a dam in a resort that's far more modern than *Berg River*. The chalets are fully equipped, with microwave and TV. Discounts Mon–Thurs. ②.

De Waenhuis, Second St (☎872 6643, fax 872 7921). Very central, tiny but fully equipped self-catering cottage a couple of blocks down from the tourist information bureau with TV, swimming pool and private entrance. ②.

Grande Roche, Plantasie St (☎863 2727, fax 863 2220). Stuffy, seriously upmarket hotel in the centre of town, surrounded by vineyards up against Paarl Mountain, with service that is meticulous to a fault. ⑦.

Lemoenkloof, 396a Main St (☎872 3782, fax 872 7532). Comfortable and well-run guesthouse in a National Monument that has both 1820s Cape Dutch and Victorian features as well as TV and fridge in each room, and a swimming pool. ④.

Nantes Vue, 56 Mill St (☎872 7311, fax 872 6291). En-suite doubles decorated with artistic flair in a National Monument-turned-friendly guesthouse, where breakfast is served on the verandah overlooking a small garden. Good value, nudging the bottom of its price range. ③.

Queenslin, 2 Queen St (☎ & fax 863 1160). Two rooms with bath in a family home in a quiet part of town bounded on one side by vineyards and towered over by Paarl Rock. The rate excludes breakfast. ②.

Rodeberg Lodge, 74 Main St (☎863 3202, fax 863 3203). Plain period furnishing gives this huge, centrally located Victorian townhouse a cool, spacious atmosphere. Ask for a room at the back if traffic noise bothers you. ④.

Roggeland Country House, Roggeland Rd, Dal Jospehat Valley (☎868 2501, fax 868 2113). The accolades keep rolling in for this family-run inn which somehow manages to combine good service, outstanding food and informality. The homestead is an eighteenth-century masterpiece of Cape Dutch architecture, with bedrooms in outbuildings. Dinner, bed and breakfast rate. ⑦.

The Town and around

Unlike Stellenbosch, which is made for wandering, all you're likely to get from strolling around Paarl is a tired pair of legs for relatively little return. The most rewarding sightseeing in the centre can be had by driving down the two oak-lined kilometres of **Main Street**, which has the best-preserved historical frontage in town.

It's here you'll find the **Paarl Museum**, 303 Main St (Mon–Fri 10am–5pm, Sat 10am–noon; small entrance fee), in a handsome, thatched Cape Dutch building with one of the earliest surving gables (1787), in the "new style", characterized by triangular caps. The contents don't quite match up to the exterior, but include some reasonably enlightening panels on the architecture of the town, and several eccentric glass display cases of Victorian bric-a-brac. A token "Road to Reconciliation" exhibit takes on board the new South Africa, with displays of press cuttings covering Paarl during the apartheid years. Among these you'll find passing mention of the fact that Nelson Mandela spent some time here as a "guest" of the town – his last years in jail, in fact. Leaving the museum from the east, a turn left into Van der Lingen Street and then right into Pastorie Street will bring you to the **Afrikaans Taal Museum** (Mon–Fri 9am–1pm & 2–5pm; free), which chronicles a white Nationalist version of the development of the Afrikaans language (see box opposite). Located in the house of Gideon Malherbe

(1833–1921), one of the founders of the League of True Afrikaners, the museum's displays are in Afrikaans, and a leaflet available from the reception desk gives an English summary of exhibits. Some brief material gives an alternative history of Afrikaans, placing new emphasis on the role of slaves and coloured South Africans in its evolution.

The only other sight of any interest in Paarl itself is the grandiose **Taal Monument** (daily 9am–5pm; free), the controversial memorial to the Afrikaans language, which stands on the top of Paarl Mountain. To get there, drive south along Main Street past the head office of the *KWV*, and follow the signs to your right up the slope of the mountain. The monument is as important a place of pilgrimage for Afrikaners as the Voortrekker Monument in Pretoria, although when it was erected in 1973 critics joked that monuments were usually erected to the dead. Close up , it's not as intrusive as you might fear, although the best thing is the truly magnificent panorama across to the Peninsula and False Bay in one direction and the Winelands ranges in the other.

About 1km north of the N1 on the R303 (Mon–Fri 9am–5pm, Sat 9.30am–3.30pm; ☎872 3420), is **Clementina van der Walt Ceramic Studio**, one of the best craft shops in the Winelands, selling tableware from the studio of Clementina van der Walt, who has created a mock-ethnic style with mass appeal. The shop also stocks hand-selected items of cutlery, wonderful fabrics from South Africa and the rest of the continent, and wooden bowls – all well-priced, superior quality stuff, miles away from airport art.

Victor Verster Prison

Roughly 9km south of the N1 as it cuts through Paarl, along the R303, the southern extension of Jan van Riebeeck Street, stands **Victor Verster Prison**, Nelson Mandela's last place of incarceration. It was through the gates at Victor Verster (not Pollsmoor in Cape Town or Robben Island as many people believe) that Mandela walked to his freedom on February 11, 1990, and was here that the first images of him in 27 years were bounced around the world – under the Prisons Act not even old pictures of him could be published for his 27 years of incarceration. The jail looks rather like an upmarket boys' school fronted by rugby fields beneath hazy mountains, and there's something bizarre about seeing a prison sign nonchalantly slipped in among all the vineyard and wine route pointers. Since you can't go inside, the usual tourist thing is to have yourself snapped standing in front of the of the gates, though raising a clenched fist and shouting "Amandla!" is strictly optional.

The wineries

Retracing your route to town, and turning left into Langenhoven Street and left again into Main Street, will bring you to the entrance of **Laborie**, Taillefert St (Mon–Fri 9am–4.30pm, Sat 9am–1pm; ☎807 3095; tasting charge), one of the most impressive Paarl wineries, made all the more remarkable for being right in town. The beautiful manor is fronted by a rose garden, acres of close-cropped lawns, historic buildings and oak trees – all towered over by the Taal Monument. There's a truly wonderful tasting room balcony, jettying out over the vineyards trailing up Paarl Mountain. Try the Chardonnay, Sauvignon Blanc and the Pineau de Laborie, the world's first pot stilled eau de vie made entirely from Pinotage grapes – delicious and well-priced. They also produce a nice Cap Classique, a champagne-style sparkling wine.

Back towards the centre along the main drag, Jan Philips Drive, a dirt track, takes a detour along the hillside past **Paarl Mountain Nature Reserve**, emerging 11km later at the north end of town to rejoin Main Street. If you take a left turn from Jan Philips, after 1.7km you'll reach **Rhebokskloof** (Mon–Fri 9am–5pm, Sat & Sun 9am–4pm; ☎863 8386, fax 863 8906; tasting free), a highly photogenic wine estate, overlooking a shallow *kloof* that borders on a mountain nature reserve. The estate has a growing reputation for its restaurant (see "Eating and drinking"), which overlooks an artificial lake with swans. Although wine tasting is free, for a small charge you can book (24hr in advance) for a formal tasting that incudes a talk on wine, a video and a cellar tour. The Cabernet Sauvignon, Pinotage and Merlot are well worth sampling.

Back on the southern fringes of town, **Fairview** (Mon–Fri 8.30am–5pm, Sat 8.30am–1pm; ☎863 2450, fax 863 2591; tasting free) promises the most fun of all the Paarl estates, with much more than just wine tasting on offer. To get there, take the R101 (the southwest extension of Main Road) out of town, turning right at the sign and continuing for 2.3km down a minor road, to the estate entrance. Your arrival is marked by a spiral goat tower, the emblem of the estate, whose inhabitants are publicly milked every afternoon. A deli sells sausages and cold meats for picnics on the lawn, and you can also sample and buy the goat's, sheep's and cow's cheeses made on the estate. As far as wine tasting goes, Fairview is an innovative, family-run place offering interesting tastings, but it can get a bit hectic when the tour buses roll in, so try to phone ahead to find out when they're expected. The first-rate wines here include Shiraz-Merlot, Merlot and Chardonnay – all fabulous and all good value.

From here the **Backsberg Estate** (Mon–Fri 8.30am–5pm, Sat 8.30am–1pm; ☎875 5141, fax 875 5144; tasting charge), south of the R101 along the very minor WR1, can be reached easily by backtracking from Fairview, turning right into the R101, and continuing a short way before turning left. After passing the Simonsvlei winery, go a short way till you strike a T-junction at the WR1, where you should turn left and you will almost immediately get to the winery entrance. Outdoor seating with views of the rose garden and vineyard makes this busy estate a nice place to while away some time. Their wines are of a high standard and, when you can lay hands on them, the Cabernet Sauvignon, Merlot, Shiraz and Pinotage represent good value. For something unusual, sample the Malbec and, if you're into spirits, their international-award-winning brandy.

Eating and drinking

Paarl isn't a gourmet centre, but it does boast one of South Africa's most expensive **restaurants** (at the *Grande Roche*), as well as a couple of outstanding places in the surrounding countryside, where you can enjoy good food accompanied by great views of the vineyards and mountains.

Restaurants and cafés

Bizzi Lizzi, Van der Lingen Square. Pleasant coffee shop serving light meals and breakfasts.

Bosman's Restaurant, *Grande Roche Hotel*, Plantasie St (☎863 2727). One of the best and most expensive restaurants in the country (winning accolades year after year) offers superb European cuisine and outstanding service that can be a bit stifling.

I Campanelli, Breda St. Low-key Italian restaurant, popular with locals.

The Coffee Place, 191 Main St. Light, seasonal food served indoors or in the garden.

The Country Elephant, Simondium Rd (☎874 1355). Provençale-style cuisine served amid bright decor or on a terrace for alfresco summer meals with views of Klein Drakenstein. Choose from a local wine list, tasty starters, and meat, fish or poultry main courses.

Gabi's Coffee Shop, 57 Lady Grey St. Bistro/bar handy for light meals.

Laborie Restaurant & Wine House, Taillefert St (☎808 7429). Seasonal à la carte and traditional Cape set menu lunches every day and dinners. Tues–Sat.

Rhebokskloof Restaurant, Rhebokskloof Minor Rd (☎863 8606). Intimate Victorian eatery and a larger Cape Dutch restaurant offering set and à la carte menus with interesting combinations.

Roggeland Country House, Roggeland Rd, Dal Jospehat Valley (☎868 2501). Not primarily run as a restaurant, you can sometimes book in here for the imaginative set menu inspired by the regional produce of Paarl, using vegetables and herbs grown in its own gardens. Beautifully prepared dishes are accompanied by a selected wine, each of which you are talked through. Booking is essential.

Wagon Wheels Steakhouse, 57 Lady Grey St. Out-of-the-ordinary steakhouse with surprisingly tasty sauces, and seafood alternatives.

Franschhoek

It's only relatively recently that **FRANSCHHOEK**, 33km from Stellenbosch and 29km from Paarl, has emerged from being the dowdy *dorp* of the Winelands to become the culinary capital of the Western Cape. Its late Victorian architecture, lightly seasoned with bland modern bungalows, can't match the elegance of Stellenbosch, but the terrific setting, hemmed in on three sides by mountains, the vineyards down every other backstreet, and some vigorous myth-making, have created a place fashion-conscious urbanites from Cape Town will drive out to just for Sunday lunch. And, while Capetonians dine here, Jo'burg designers, investors and bankers are buying up the place, as are German industrialists, an Italian count who flies to his estate by helicopter, and President Bongo of Gabon.

Some history

Between 1688 and 1700 about two hundred **French Huguenots**, desperate to escape religious persecution in France, accepted a Dutch East India offer of passage to the Cape and the grant of lands. They made contact with the area's earliest settlers, groups of **Khoi herders**. Conflict between the French newcomers and the Khoi followed familiar lines, with the white settlers gradually dispossessing the herdsmen, and forcing them either further into the hinterland or into servitude on their farms. The establishment of white hegemony was swift and by 1713 the area was known as *de france hoek*, but because of explicit Company policy, French-speaking died out within a generation. However, many of the estates are still known by their original French names. The town itself occupies parts of the original farms of La Cotte and Cabrière and is relatively young, having been established around a church built in 1833.

Arrival, information and accommodation

There's no public transport to Franschhoek or in the town itself; the only way to get here is in your own car. The **tourist information bureau** (☎ & fax 876 3603) is in

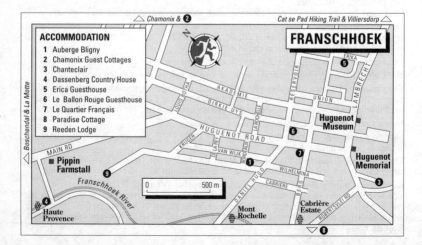

The **telephone code** for Franschhoek is ☎021.

Main Road, just north of the junction with Kruger Street, and can provide information about **places to stay** in the area. Franschhoek is small enough to explore on foot, though for more speed and greater range you can always rent a **mountain bike** from *Le Ballon Rouge*, 12 Reservoir Rd (☎876 2651). One- or two-hour **horseback tours** of Franschhoek's wineries for around R50 an hour can be arranged through *Mont Rochelle Equestrian Centre* (☎876 2635 or 083/300 4368). A four-cellar ride for roughly R100 takes in Cabrière, Haute Provence and Môreson, at each of which you taste one wine, and ends at Mont Rochelle, where you get to try their whole range.

Accommodation

Auberge Bligny, 28 Van Wijk St (☎876 3767, fax 876 3483). Centrally located Victorian house furnished in country style, with florals and checks and with a nice guest lounge. ③.

Le Ballon Rouge Guest House, 12 Reservoir Rd (☎876 2651). Small B&B offering rooms which lead onto a side street-facing verandah, in a Victorian town house with brass bedsteads and floral fabrics. ④.

Chamonix Guest Cottages, Uitkyk St (☎876 2498, fax 876 3237). Fully equipped self-catering cottages surrounded by vineyards on a wine farm. ②–③.

Chanteclair, signposted just west of the Huguenot Monument (☎876 3685). The best thing about this guesthouse, which stands on a massive property, is that you feel you're in the country, yet are only minutes from town. Unfussy rooms in English country style, and breakfast outside on the verandah looking out onto a lovely garden and orchard. ③–⑤.

Dassenberg Country House, off Main Rd (☎ & fax 876 2107). Beautiful and peaceful place with B&B rooms (③) and two self-catering cottages (②).

Erica Guest House, 4 Erika St (☎876 2425, fax 876 2825). Modern, centrally located suburban house with spotless accommodation. One the cheapest B&Bs in town, offering low-priced rooms with no views, and more expensive ones with small patios leading onto a lawn. ③.

Le Quartier Francais, corner of Berg and Wilhelmina streets (☎876 2151, fax 876 3105). The most luxurious place to stay in Franschhoek, with two suites (one with its own pool) and fifteen huge rooms decorated with sunny fabrics, thick duvets and fireplaces for winter, all arranged around herb and flower gardens and the swimming pool. Child-friendly, and pricey, but worth it for a special occasion. ⑦.

Paradise Cottage, Roberstsvlei Rd (☎876 2160). Among the cheapest rooms in the valley, in old, basic accommodation on a farm. ②.

Reeden Lodge, off Cabrière St (☎ & fax 876 3174). Lovely self-catering cottage on a farm on a river near Cabrière Estate, within walking distance of town. ②.

The Town and its wineries

Away from the wining and dining, Franschhoek's attractions are limited to hiking, horse-riding or cycling in the valley, or visiting the institutionalized Huguenot Monument and adjacent museum, which together occupy a prime position at the head of Huguenot Road, where it forms a T-junction with Lambrecht Street. The **Huguenot Monument** consists of three skinny, interlocking arches, which symbolize the Holy Trinity, emphasizing the importance of religion to the Huguenot settlers. The **Huguenot Museum** (Mon–Fri 9am–5pm, Sat 9am–1pm & 2–5pm, Sun 2–5pm; small entrance fee) gives comprehensive coverage of Huguenot history, culture and of their contribution to modern South Africa.

The best **hike** in the vicinity is the Cat se Pad ("cat's path"), which starts on your left just under a kilometre from the museum as you head out of town up the Franschhoek Pass. The walk leads into fynbos with proteas and gives instant access to the mountains that surround the valley. The first two-kilometre section gets you to the top of the pass and you can keep going for another 10km in the direction of Villiersdorp.

The wineries

Franschhoek's **wineries** are small enough and sufficiently close together to make it a breeze to visit two or three on foot, by mountain bike or even on horseback. Heading north through town from the Huguenot Monument, you'll find virtually all the wineries along branches that are signposted off Huguenot Road and its extension, Main Road.

Close to the Monument, **Cabrière Estate**, Berg Rd (Mon–Fri 11am–1pm & 2–4.30pm, Sat 11am–1pm; ☎876 2630), is reached through groves of fruit trees that lead up to the homestead and tasting room. The winery is notable for its Pinot Noirs and colourful wine-maker Achim von Arnim, whose presence guarantees an eventful visit; try to catch him when he slices off the upper neck of a bubbly bottle with a sabre, sending flying the neatly detached cork wrapped in the severed top ring of glass. Next door, **Mont Rochelle**, Daniel Hugo Road (May–Aug Tues–Sat 11am–4pm; Sept–April Sun 11am–1pm; ☎876 3000), has one of the most stunning settings in Franschhoek and an unusual cellar in a converted nineteenth-century fruit-packing shed, edged by eaves decorated with fretwork, stained-glass windows and chandeliers. Look out for the promising new wines under their premium Mont Rochelle label – the first South African wines to be bottled by an all-woman team.

Returning to Huguenot Road, keep heading north and turn right into Uitkyk Street to get to **Chamonix** (daily 9.30am–4pm; ☎876 2498), which holds its tastings in the cosy *Blacksmith's Cottage* (where you can also get a light meal). The estate's most consistent wines are their Cabernet Sauvignon and Chardonnay, but they also produce Chamonix schnapps from pear, peach, plum, apple and nectarine, and for teetotallers, Eau de Chamonix. There's a good restaurant here too (see "Eating and drinking").

A left turn just after the Pippin Farm Stall a little further along, where Huguenot merges with Main Street, will bring you to **Haute Provence** (daily 9am–4pm; ☎876 3195 or 876 2416), across the train tracks. This is one of the most casual and friendly estates, where you can sit in comfy armchairs in a tasting room with a traditional *riet-dak* (cane and mud ceiling), surrounded by paintings by well-known South African artists. The estate is best known for "Angels' Tears", a fruity blend of Chenin Blanc and Muscat d'Alexandrie grapes, whose name derives from the legend of a French village where angels came at night to taste the new vintage and wept for joy at its brilliance. Although the wine is highly drinkable, come for the genial ambience rather than to hear heavenly sighs. In contrast, **La Motte Estate** (Mon–Fri 9am–4.30pm, Sat 9am–noon; ☎876 3119), further along Main Road (here called the R45), presents a supremely cool front, with a superb designer tasting room that looks onto the cellar through a sheer wall of glass. This was the estate that put to rest once and for all the long-held notion that Franschhoek was a poor region for producing red wines. Among the wines, you'll find a good Shiraz and Cabernet Sauvignon and a stunning blend known as "Mille~nium", which sells out quickly.

If you have time for only one estate around here, **Boschendal** (Feb–Nov Mon–Fri 8.30am–4.30pm, Sat 10am–12.30pm; Dec & Jan Mon–Sat 8.30am–4.30pm, Sun 8.30am–12.30pm; ☎874 1031) is the obvious choice. Equidistant between Franschhoek and Stellenbosch at the junction of the R45 and R310, it is geared to absorbing busloads of tourists, who lap up its impressive Cape Dutch buildings, tree-lined avenues, choice of restaurants and cafés (see "Eating and drinking"), and of course its wines. Now owned by a massive Anglo-American corporation, Boschendal is one of the world's longest-established New World wine estates, dating back to 1685, when its lands were granted to Huguenot settler Jean Le Long. The Cape Dutch manor was built in 1812 by Paul de Villiers and his wife, whose initials appear on the front gable. Wine tasting takes place at the *Taphuis*, where you can sit indoors or sip under shady trees. Of its Reserve range, look out for the Merlot, and Shiraz; and from its extensive regular range, try the Sauvignon Blanc, Chardonnay and the Boschendal brut bubbly.

Eating and drinking

Eating and drinking is what Franschhoek is all about, so there's little point in making the effort to get here without sampling at least one or two of its excellent restaurants, some of which number among the Cape's best. **Restaurants** in town are concentrated down Huguenot Road, but there are a number of excellent alternatives in the more rustic environment of the surrounding wine estates. **Booking** is essential. Franschhoek's cuisine tends to be French-inspired, but not exclusively so, and salmon trout is a local speciality. For coffee or a sandwich, head for one of the many **cafés** in town, or book a picnic hamper at one of the wineries and eat alfresco within sipping distance of the vineyards.

Restaurants

Le Ballon Rouge, 12 Reservoir St (☎876 2071). The splash-out menu covers an eclectic range of Mediterranean flavours from Greek starters to their marvellous *focaccia* filled with smoked chicken breast, five-leaf salad and a sweet curry dressing.

Boschendal, junction of the R45 and R310 to Stellenbosch (☎847 1252). Legendary for its pricey but exhaustive daily buffet lunch which will set you up for rest of day. Eat as much as you can from the spread of soup, oysters, kalimari, roasts, casseroles salads, Cape specialities, cheeseboard and desserts.

Bread & Wine, Môreson Farm, Happy Valley Rd, off the R45 (☎876 3692). Mediterranean farmhouse lunches accompanied by the estate's own wines in a friendly venue beside a fountain in a courtyard surrounded by orchards and vineyards.

Chez Michel, Huguenot Rd (☎876 2671). Franschhoek's oldest eating place is a congenial bistro patronized by locals, in a Victorian house. The emphasis is continental and the mid-range menu incorporates steak, seafood and excellent home-made gateaux.

Haute Cabrière, Franschhoek Pass (☎876 3688). A bunker-like venue with an interesting mix-and-match menu planned around Cabrière wines, available by the glass or bottle. There are no starters or main courses but you can order half-portions from a choice that takes in salmon trout, lamb, ratatouille, wonderful desserts and home-made chocolates. There's a helipad on the roof should you wish to fly in.

La Maison de Chamonix, Uitkyk St (☎867 2393). French-based menu that includes oysters and smoked salmon trout inside or outdoors on an estate surrounded by views of the valley.

La Petite Ferme, Franschhoek Pass. Justifiably one of the most popular Franschhoek lunch and tea venues in a Victorian-style building with superb views across the valley. Country-fare meals include light salads, but their party piece is the deboned smoked salmon trout.

Polfyntjies Country Restaurant, Main Rd (☎876 3217). Gourmet versions of South African favourites such as boerewors, *bredie* and bobotie, as well as local salmon trout in several versions, cold soups and salads. All is served up in a 1860s farmhouse, with the wine list offering among the best drinking value in Franschhoek. Phone first to check they're open.

Le Quartier Francais, 16 Huguenot Rd (☎876 2151). Excellent choice for a no-holds-barred formal meal with a local flavour and an imaginative edge at the place that made Franschhoek synonymous with food. Choose from vegetarian noodles, snoek and lemongrass *soasaties* or grilled salmon trout cutlets with saffron potatoes, followed by delicious desserts.

Light meals, delis and picnics

Boschendal, junction of R45 and R310 to Stellenbosch(☎874 1252). *Le Café* does light, sit-down lunches, while *Le Pique Nique* offers deluxe picnic hampers daily under the shady pines. Booking for both is essential.

Brinjals Bistro, 18 Huguenot Rd. Teas and Mediterranean-style lunches using seasonal ingredients, served in a relaxed atmosphere.

Dominic's Restaurant & Tea Garden, 66 Huguenot St. Inexpensive, casual place with an alfresco eating area.

Frandeli, Co-op Building, Huguenot Rd. Licensed deli which serves delicious, filled *focaccias* and bagels accompanied by beer or wine to eat in or take away.

Gideon's Pancake House, 50 Huguenot Rd. Tasty savoury or sweet pancakes with a touch of Cape Muslim flavours.

Mont Rochelle, off Main Rd (☎876 3000). Picnic baskets are on offer every day at one of Franschhoek's most scenic wineries.

Pippin Farm Stall, Main Rd. Includes Franschhoek trout among its delicious foods, which you can use to make up your own budget picnic.

Ralf's Country Restaurant & Village Pub, 3 Main Rd. Relaxed and inexpensive joint with an outdoor eating area.

BREEDE RIVER VALLEY AND THE LITTLE KAROO

One of the most rewarding journeys in the Western Cape is an inland counterpart to the Garden Route – the **mountain route** from Cape Town to Port Elizabeth. Nowhere near as well known as the coastal journey, this trip will take you through some of the most dramatic passes and *poorts* (valley routes) in the country and crosses a fading frontier of *dorps* and drylands.

Beyond the Paarl and Stellenbosch winelands, a vast hinterland fans out away from Cape Town. Just outside Paarl, the Huguenot Tunnel punches through the Dutoitsberg mountain range to emerge in the fruit-growing and wine-making country of the **Breede River Valley**, where mountains give way to a jigsaw of valleys, each quite distinct in character. It's here, not in the more developed Winelands proper, that so many calendar shots are taken of isolated whitewashed homesteads dwarfed by vine-covered hills.

Although the Breede River Valley is part of a through route to the Eastern Cape via Oudtshoorn, its towns also make convenient excursions from Cape Town. **Worcester**, the large functional hub of the region, is only 110km from Cape Town, while to its north, **Tulbagh**, a more promising destination, with a perfectly restored provincial Cape Dutch street, is an easy 130km from the city. South from Worcester, the R60 shadows the groove cut by the Breede River and provides access to the rather dull little town of **Robertson**, centre of yet another wine route. Some 19km south lies **McGregor**, a small, laid-back town with a rural feel, and an excellent choice for a weekend stay. Nearby and a similar distance from the Cape Peninsula, the pleasant historic spa town of **Montagu** is towered over by precipitous red-streaked cliffs that attract serious mountaineers from all over the country.

Continuing east from Montagu, the R62 meanders into the Garden Route's backyard, the **Little Karoo** (or Klein Karoo), a vast and brittle khaki-coloured hinterland (the name is a Khoi word meaning "hard and dry"). The Little Karoo provides the easiest access to the semi-desert that seeps across one-third of South Africa's surface. Open treeless plains, sporadically vegetated with low, wiry scrub, and dotted with flat-topped hills, dissolve eventually into the **Great Karoo**, which extends into the southern Free State and well into the Eastern and Northern cape provinces. The Great Karoo is the harsh frontier which a succession of South Africans occupied by turns: San hunters, Khoi herders, Griqua (coloured) farmers and Afrikaner trekkers. Today Afrikaans is the dominant language, used by white and coloured speakers, the latter having absorbed what remained of the Khoi.

The unsung surprise along the way is **Calitzdorp**, a rustic little *dorp*, five to six hours' solid driving from Cape Town, down whose backstreets a few unassuming wine farms produce some of South Africa's best port. Around here you'll find neglected valleys where some of the old Karoo clings on tenuously in an almost feudal relationship between farmsteads and faded scatterings of coloured workers' cottages. By contrast, the well-trumpeted attractions of **Oudtshoorn**, half an hour further on, are the ostrich

PASSES AND POORTS OF THE LITTLE KAROO

The Little Karoo is hemmed in to the north by the Langeberg range and to the south the Outeniqua (the range that separates it from the Garden Route). In between lie a gauntlet of mountains and valleys that for centuries made this area virtually impassable for wheeled transport. In the nineteenth century, the British began to tackle the problem and dozens of **passes** were built through the Cape's mountains, 34 of which were engineered by the brilliant road-builder Andrew Geddes Bain and his son Thomas. In 1878 Anthony Trollope commented that the **Outeniqua Pass**, just north of George on the way to Oudtshoorn, equalled "some of the mountain roads through the Pyrenees", a description which just as easily applies today to any number of other Little Karoo passes. In fact, whatever the Little Karoo lacks in museums and art galleries is amply compensated for by the towering drama of these Victorian masterpieces.

In **Afrikaans** there are two words for pass: **pas**, meaning "a route over the mountains" and **poort**, meaning "a valley route", often following a river. Most passes are narrow, winding and steep, and frequently untarred, so they need to be driven slowly. In any case, you won't want to rush past such fantastic views, so it's worth bringing along food and drink to enjoy at the numerous picnic spots along the way. Below, we've listed a selection of some of the best of the passes and *poorts*:

- **Meiringspoort**, just north of De Rust. Tarred road through a gorge in the Swartberg, which keeps crossing a light-brown river, while huge slabs of folded and zigzagging rock rise up on either side. There's a picnic spot at each fording place and a waterfall at Ford 17 (they're all numbered). You can walk from here for 2–12km into the mountains (see p.159).
- **Swartberg Pass**, between Oudtshoorn and Prince ALFRED. Over-the-Swartberg counterpart of Meiringspoort, with 1:7 gradients (see p.159).
- **Cogmanskloof Pass**, between Ashton and Montagu. A five-kilometre route that is at its most dramatic as it blasts through a rock face into the Montagu valley (see p.153).
- **Gamkaskloof Pass** (aka *Die Hel* or "The Hell"), accessed from the summit of the Swartberg Pass. Arguably the most awesome of all the passes leading into a dramatic and now unoccupied valley. You have to return the same way, as there is no circular route (see p.160).
- **Prince Alfred's Pass**, between the N2 just east of Knysna and Avontuur on the R62.
- **Du Toit's Kloof Pass**, between Paarl and Worcester. The more exciting alternative to the Huguenot Toll Tunnel, with 1:9 gradients (see p.147).

farms and the massive **Cango Caves**, one of the country's biggest tourist draws. Less than 70km from the coast, with good transport connections, Oudtshoorn marks the convergence of the mountain and coastal roads and is usually treated as a leisurely day-trip away from the Garden Route.

Slicing up through the northernmost third of the Klein Karoo, on its way to Johannesburg, the N1 slips past **Matjiesfontein**, a wonderfully preserved Victorian railway town, and the mountainous **Karoo National Park**, both just off the main road and definitely worth breaking a trip for.

Worcester and Ceres

The fastest way to navigate the mountains from Paarl into the Breede River Valley is via the **Huguenot Toll Tunnel**, which burrows straight through to the other side, but misses the wonderful scenery of driving over the **Du Toit's Kloof Pass**. Much slower but far more interesting, the pass works its way through a series of wonderful mountain ranges with views onto distant farms and villages in the valleys.

WORCESTER, which is 31km from Paarl through the tunnel, is a relatively large town for this part of the world, and features some attractive historic frontage down Church Street, but not enough to demand much of your time. An agricultural centre with a number of factories, it's at the centre of a wine-making region, consisting mostly of co-operatives producing bulk plonk that makes up about one-fifth of national output. There really isn't much reason to dally here, apart from visiting the **Kleinplasie Living Open Air Museum** (Mon–Sat 9am–4.30pm, Sun 10.30am–4.30pm; small entry fee), which depicts the life on the Karoo frontier between 1690 and 1900. Made up of about two dozen reconstructed buildings, with staff in old-style workshops engaged in crafts and home industries, the museum is fairly absorbing. Keep a lookout in particular for the corbelled shepherd's hut, which represents a vernacular style unique to the Karoo, using domed stone roofs rather than beam and lintel construction – a response to the dearth of timber in the treeless expanse. There's a **restaurant** and **café** on site, and next door a wine shop sells a good selection of labels from the Worcester wineries. The museum is just outside the centre of town – to get there, turn right off High Street onto the Robertson road.

Taking the R43 north from Worcester for 49km brings you to **CERES**, another farming centre which, like several in the vicinity, is highly missable. Its most notable claim to fame is the factory that produces most of South Africa's delicious juices (same fruit, different labels: *Ceres, Liquifruit, Just Juice* and all the other fruity labels come from one plant on the outskirts of town).

Tulbagh

Altogether the most rewarding destination in the northern section of the Breede River Valley is **TULBAGH**, easily visited in a day from Cape Town, which lies 130km south. You could drive into town, down Van der Stel Street and out the other end, and assume from this unexceptional main street that Tulbagh was just another humdrum *dorp*. But one block west, on **Church Street**, is the most perfectly restored eighteenth- and nineteenth-century streetscape. Although only a fraction of what you see here is the original frontage (the town having been flattened in 1969 by an earthquake), this is no Disneyland, because even if the facades aren't original they're unquestionably authentic and undoubtedly beautiful.

Arrival, information and accommodation

There's no public transport to Tulbagh; the only way you'll make it here is by **car**, taking either the **R43** from Worcester or the **R301** from Paarl. One of the highlights of the drive is crossing the beautiful **Bain's Kloof Pass**, which connects these two routes.

The town's **tourist information bureau**, 4 Church St (Mon–Fri 9am–4.30pm, Sat 9am–4pm, Sun 11am–4pm; ☎ & fax 0236/30 1348), can give advice on activities and accommodation in the area. *Tulbagh Valley Trails*, 30 Church St (☎0236/30 1448), offer **mountain-bike rental** – an excellent way to get to wineries or other local attractions.

The cheapest **place to stay** is *Kliprivier Park Holiday Resort* (☎0236/30 0506), one of the nicest municipal caravan parks in the country, with campsites (①) and very basic chalets (②), some of which are on the edge of a dam and have excellent views of the mountains. Good-value B&B accommodation is available at *No 30 Church St* (☎ & fax 0236/30 1448; ②) in a double or triple room with a shower at the back of a friendly historic house, which has a courtyard under vines. Nearby, *De Oude Herberg*, 6 Church St (☎0236/30 0260; ④), is a well-positioned B&B offering comfortable rooms with French doors opening onto the verandah. Roughly 1.5km north of town, *Hunter's Retreat* (☎ & fax 0236/30 0582; ③–④) has plain and airy B&B rooms and spacious two-storey thatched cottages with lounges on a working farm, where you can see cattle, ostriches and sheep. Finally, the family-oriented *Wild Olive Farm* (☎0236/30 1160; ②), 2km down a dirt track on a turn-off 6km from Tulbagh towards Wolseley, offers a choice of five fully equipped self-catering cottages with mountain views. Guests are given milk and eggs and can buy meat for *braais*.

The Town

The best way to enjoy Tulbagh is to stroll up **Church Street** and take in the houses, gardens and the development in the style of gables that are an essential element of Cape Dutch architecture. After the 1969 earthquake, **restoration** of the buildings took place using salvaged materials from the ruins, and following photographic and hand-drawn records. At least six different styles can be distinguished just along this short road. At no. 23, **Paddagang** ("frog passage") was originally a *taphuis* ("wine house"), so it's fitting that it's now a restaurant with a wine house attached, which is recommended for its wonderful labels all featuring comical frogs rather than for the liquor itself. Although the gabled **Old Church**, built in 1743, is of some interest, you won't be missing much if you don't spend long over the collection of bric-a-brac inside which constitutes the **Oude Kerk Volksmuseum**, 2 Church St (Mon–Fri 8am–1pm & 2–5pm, Sat 10am–1pm & 2–4pm, Sun 11am–1pm & 2–4pm; small entry fee). The museum has three annexes (Mon–Fri 9am–1pm & 2–5pm) at nos. 4, 14 and 22, which won't keep you busy for too long either. No. 4 has photographs of old houses in Tulbagh before the earthquake and traces the histories of the families who lived in them.

Outside town, **De Oude Drostdy Museum** (Mon–Sat 10am–1pm & 2–5pm; Sun 2.30–5pm), 4km to the north on the extension of van der Stel Street, is an impressive Cape Dutch spectacle designed by the French architect Louis-Michel Thibault. Apart from some very nice pieces of furniture and a pleasantly relaxed atmosphere, the museum's main draw is the startling view of the mountains and farmlands that confronts you as you step out through the front doors.

Eating and drinking

Apart its historic streetscape, Tulbagh's biggest attraction is the *Paddagang Restaurant and Wine House*, 23 Church St (☎0236/30 0242). Established in 1821 as one of the first taverns in the Cape, it serves moderately priced traditional regional **cooking** and locally produced **wines** and has lovely gardens, where you can sit outside under vines. The restaurant is open for breakfast and lunch daily, but for supper only on Saturday. Traditional curries and country cuisine are on offer at *De Oude Herberg*, Church St, which opens daily for breakfast, lunch, tea and dinner and has terrace seating. *Pieter Potter* (☎0236/30 1626), despite an unpromising location in busy van der Stel Street, does reasonably priced steak, ribs and excellent fish lunches and dinners from Tuesday to Saturday until late, and lunch only on Sunday. Another pleasant surprise is *Restaurant Kerzenlicht* (☎0236/30 1614), at the *Hotel Tulbagh* in van der Stel Street, which is notable for its well-priced fish dishes.

Robertson and McGregor

ROBERTSON, 77km off the N2, is the largest town in the interesting stretch of the Breede River Valley that connects Worcester to Oudtshoorn. Its size, however, does nothing to mitigate the fact that Robertson is, unfortunately, a big yawn that dies completely over weekends. The only conceivable reason for popping into this fruit-picking town, is to visit the **Robertson Winery** (Mon–Fri 8am–12.30pm & 1.30–5pm; Sat, school holidays 9am–12.30pm) just off the R60, which breaks the general co-operative mould by producing some good-value and fairly quaffable Chardonnays and Colombards that are cheaper here than in the shops. In fact the Robertson Valley has its own **wine route**, which extends to McGregor and Bonnievale in the south (see box).

If you're not stocking up on liquor, press straight on to **MCGREGOR**, fifteen minutes to the south, at the end of a minor road signposted off the R60. Although it's been described as South Africa's best-preserved Victorian Karoo village, you certainly shouldn't expect anything like a quaint English hamlet – a description which might just about apply to Greyton just 14km away on the well-watered side of the mountains (see p.165). Still, McGregor is an attractive enough place, with whitewashed cottages glaring in the summer daylight amid the low rusty steel wool scrub, and a quiet, relaxed atmosphere that has attracted a small population of spiritual seekers and alternative types. In the shadow of the Dutch Reformed church down the high street, you'll find a **retreat centre** and a Waldorf school. The time to pull out your camera is in the late afternoon, when the sinking sun suffuses the landscape with deeply saturated colours.

McGregor gained some modest prosperity in the nineteenth century by becoming a centre of the whipstock industry, supplying wagoners and transport riders with long bamboo sticks for goading oxen. There aren't too many ox-drawn wagons today and, apart from farming, tourism (which is still quite limited) is beginning to develop. Residents are being urged to build in harmony with existing style and thus maintain the town's character.

Apart from its spare beauty – and it's worth taking a late-afternoon stroll down one of the dirt roads out of town – the main reason people come here is to walk the Boesmanskloof Traverse (see p.166), which crosses to Greyton on the other side of the mountain.

McGregor practicalities

Voortrekker Street is McGregor's main thoroughfare, where you'll find a small, clearly signposted **tourist information bureau** (Mon–Fri 10am–5pm, Sat 9am–12.30pm; ☎02353/856). The dirt roads around town are perfect for cycling and you can arrange **bike rental** through *Villagers Art and Coffee Shop*, also in the main road. All the central **accommodation** is in Voortrekker Street, or clearly indicated off it. Cheapest of the lot is the *McGregor* (☎02353/925, fax 620; ②), which has en-suite rooms and some rooms sharing bath, but can get noisy over weekends due to its public bar. For more flair, head for the friendly *McGregor B&B* (☎02353/656; ②), which has three attractive en-suite rooms and serves a substantial continental breakfast. For tranquil self-catering, *McGregor Country Cottages* (☎02353/816, fax 840; ②) offers a complex of eight workers' dwellings with traditional reed ceilings, surrounded by gardens, orchards and vegetable patches with a pool. The smartest place in town is the *Old Mill Lodge* (☎ & fax 02353/841; full board ④), a set of cottages surrounded by vineyards and gardens with

ROBERTSON VALLEY WINERIES: PICK OF THE BUNCH

The **Robertson Valley** is responsible for some ten per cent of South Africa's vineyards. Its soils have an ideal acidity level for growing grapes, but because it's hot and dry intense irrigation is necessary. Its best wines tend to be chenin blancs and colombards and it can conjure up some good Muscadels. We've picked out the best of its roughly two dozen wineries.

Along the road from Robertson to Bonnivale

● **Bon Courage**, not far southeast of Robertson, on the right-hand side (Mon–Fri 9am–5pm, Sat 9am–12.30pm; ☎02351/4178, fax 3581). Tasting room in a beautiful old homestead along the Breede River. Notable for its sweet whites, including Muscadel.

● **Van Loveren**, south of Bon Courage, on the right-hand side (Mon–Fri 8.30am–1pm & 2–5pm, Sat 9.30am–1pm; ☎0234/51505, fax 51336). Wine tasting in a lovely garden at a friendly estate that produces a quaffable Chardonnay and Pinot Gris.

● **De Wetshof**, slightly south of Van Loveren on the left (Mon–Fri 8.30am–4.30pm, Sat 9.30am–1pm; ☎0234/51857). Top-notch estate producing several excellent wines including Chardonnay, several variants on Rhine riesling and their great Finesse.

Along the R60 from Robertson to Worcester

● **Graham Beck**, north of Robertson (June–Sept Mon–Fri 10am–5pm; Sat 9am–5pm; ☎02351/61214, fax 5164). High-flying estate determined to make an international splash – and succeeding big-time with orders from the British supermarket giants, including *Tesco* and *Marks and Spencer*. Daringly modern tasting room where you can savour their outstanding Chardonnay and a first-class pioneering champagne-style Chardonnay bubbly.

● **Nuy**, turn-off 53km north of Robertson (Mon–Fri 8.30am–4.30pm, Sat 8.30am–12.30pm; ☎0231/70271). Not strictly on the Robertson Valley wine route, but one of South Africa's most successful wine-making co-operatives which can easily be taken in as part of it. As well as visiting the winery, you can buy, but not taste, their wines from a stall along the main road. Their lovely Colombard is excellent value and the romantically named Chants de Nuit is a pleasant curiosity that will hit the dust after 1999, because its ingredients include Ferdinand de Lesseps grapes, which have been declared "unclassifiable" by wine-making authorities.

---

a swimming pool. Outside town you'll find self-catering accommodation at *Dove Cottage* on Rhebokskraal Farm (☎02353/951, fax 739; ②), 2km from town (enquire at *Villagers Art and Coffee Shop*, Voortrekker St). A restored cottage on a beautiful fruit and grape farm, it's secluded and cosy, with views of mountains and the Karoo, and offers good walking opportunities. Some 8km from the centre, *Whipstock Farm* (☎ & fax 02353/733; full board ③), on the southerly continuation of Voortrekker Street, has restored cottages on an old citrus, almond and grape farm in the mountains. Whipstock is 5km from the McGregor side of the Boesmanskloof Traverse, and the owners will fetch or pick you up from the trail for free. There's horse-riding and swimming on offer, and bikes and canoes are available to rent. Another option for walkers are the basic huts rented out by Mr Oosthuizen (☎02353/735; ①) at the McGregor side of the Traverse, where only beds and water are provided and you must bring everything else, including sleeping bags.

Villagers is a good place for daytime **snacks** and **teas**, and has a verandah to watch the passing scene in Voortrekker Street. In the same street, the good-value *Lion House Tea Lounge & Dining Room* serves hearty bangers and mash, as well as curries. Light lunches are on offer at the *Old Mill Lodge*, where you can also splash out on a four-course set evening meal, but must book for this by lunchtime.

Montagu

Without a doubt **MONTAGU** is the ultimate Breede River Valley destination, and approaching from the south through Cogman's Kloof Gorge numbers among the most dramatic arrivals in the country. A short five-kilometre winding road blasts through a rock face into a tight valley dramatically opening out to Montagu, which is small enough to capture in one glance. Soaring mountains rise up in vast arches of twisted strata that display reds and ochres, and from September to October the gentler tints of peach and apricot blossoms flood the valley. Not only is Montagu very pleasing, with sufficient Victorian architecure to create an historic character, but there's enough to do here to more than justify an overnight stay.

The town was named in 1851 after **John Montagu**, the visionary British Secretary of the Cape, who realized that the colony would never develop without decent communications and was responsible for commissioning the first **mountain passes** that connected remote areas to Cape Town. The grateful farmers of Agter Cogman's Kloof ("behind Cogman's Kloof") leapt at the chance of a snappier name for their village and called it after him.

Arrival, information and accommodation

Intercity **bus services** to Montagu are sparse and inconvenient. *Translux* (☎021/405 3333) stops here three times a week on its journey between Cape Town and Port Elizabeth, arriving at *Avalon Hotel* in Bath Street either in the late evening or before sunrise. The cheaper and more convenient *Munniks* (☎021/637 1850) service picks up at the *Spur* steakhouse. Montagu's **tourist information bureau**, Bath St (Mon–Fri 8.45am–1pm, 2–4.45pm, Sat 9am–noon; ☎0234/41116 or 42471), is useful for picking up information about local attractions.

Accommodation

Even if you're visiting for the springs, it is far nicer to find somewhere to **stay** in town rather than at the spa, which amounts to little more than a large crowded resort, especially at weekends and school holidays. If you do get stuck, the tourist information bureau (see above) can help.

Avalon Springs Hotel (☎0234/41150, fax 41906). One of two options at Montagu Springs, this tacky pink hotel offers B&B rooms and cheaper self-catering flats. ④–⑤.

Cynthia's, 3 Krom St (☎0234/42760, fax 41326). Six self-catering cottages dotted around the west side of town, all in old houses, with gardens and *braai* areas, and near the starting point for hiking trails. ②.

John Montagu Victorian Guest House, 30 Joubert St (☎ & fax 0234/41331). En-suite rooms at this guesthouse two streets up from Bath St, with enough period furniture and knick-knacks to create an historic ambience without being oppressive. ③.

Kingna Lodge (☎0234/41066, fax 42405). Nelson Mandela's choice when he hit town in 1995, this large period house delivers a Victorian atmosphere with a vengeance. The emphasis is on excellent personal service and excellent food and there's a verandah for tea and a swimming pool and jacuzzi at the back. Dinner, bed and breakfast. ⑤.

Mimosa Lodge, Church St (☎0234/42351, fax 42418). Handsome Edwardian double-storey house just off Bath St, with an emphasis on food using local ingredients. Rooms are en suite – the best are upstairs, with a balcony. Dinner, bed and breakfast. ⑤.

Montagu Caravan Park (☎0234/42675), at the west end of Bath St, across the Keisie River. Slightly scruffy municipal park, offering campsites and cheap chalets which sleep four – but you'll need to bring your own bedding and towels. ①.

Montagu Rose Guest House, 19 Kohler St (☎0234/42681, fax 42780). Well-run guesthouse in a modern home with very personalized service and a hallway plastered with thankyou notes and cards. ③.

Montagu Springs (☎0234/41050, fax 42235). Stay in one of the resort's 120 chalets that sleep four and (a hot tip) are substantially cheaper from Sunday to Thursday and outside school holidays. ③–④.

Squirrel's Corner, corner of Bloem and Jouberts streets (☎0234/41081, fax 51610). One of the cheapest B&Bs in town, with three basic spotless rooms in a family house two blocks from the main road. They also have a cheaper three-bedroom self-catering cottage in Church St. ②.

The Town and around

Highly photogenic, Montagu is a place in which you can happily foot it around, taking in the interesting buildings or simply enjoying the setting, with its mountains, valleys and farms. There are also a couple of museums, neither of which is outstanding. The best thing about the **Montagu Museum**, 41 Long St (Mon–Fri 9am–1pm & 2.15–5pm, Sat & Sun 10.30am–12.30pm; small entry fee), housed in a pleasant old church, is its herbal project, which traces back traditional Khoisan knowledge about the medicinal properties of local plants. Work is being done in conjunction with the Pharmacology Department at the University of Cape Town and you can buy *Herbal Remedies: Montagu Museum*, which details some of the findings. The herbs themselves are also on sale, and some of them are grown in the gardens of the **Joubert House Museum** (Mon–Fri 9.30am–1pm & 2.15–5pm, Sat 10am–noon; small entry fee), one block west at 25 Long St. Built in 1853, this was one of the first houses standing in a vast plot which was originally a town farm, and has peach-pip floors fixed with beeswax, typical of the area.

Montagu's main draw is the **Montagu Springs Resort** (daily 8am–11pm; entry fee), about 3km northwest ot town, on the R318. Several open-air pools of different temper-

---

MONTAGU ACTIVITIES

To most people Montagu is best known for its hot springs, but serious **rock climbers** come for its cliff faces, which are regarded as among the country's most challenging. You can also explore the mountains on a couple of **trails** or more effortlessly still on a tractor ride onto one of the peaks that offer stunning panoramas. Montagu is also conveniently positioned for excursions along both the Robertson and Klein Karoo wine routes (see p.151).

Three **hikes** begin from the Old Mill at the north end of Tanner Street, from where you can also take a gentle meander at the foot of cliffs in a small park. **Maps** for the hikes are available from Montagu's tourist information bureau. Shortest of the hikes is the Lover's Walk, a 2.2km stroll through Bath Kloof (or Badkloof) that follows the Keisie River to the hot springs and is open between 7am and 6pm. A more substantial walk is the 12km Cogman's Kloof Hiking Trail, which can be completed in three to six hours. Only the first 2km are steep, after which it's an easy walk at a medium altitude, which gives nice views of Montagu, the ravines and mountains. Most ambitious is the 15.6km Bloupunt Hiking Trail, which gets you up to an altitude of over 1000m and can be completed in six to nine hours. The walk passes through terrain with ravines, mountain streams, craggy cliffs and rock formations and from the summit of Bloupunt you can see as far as McGregor and Robertson. Throughout the year, you will see dassies and klipspringers as well as a large variety of wild flowers because of the presence of perennial streams. The fynbos vegetation includes proteas, ericas, aloes, lilies, watsonias and wild orchids. Carry a waterbottle to fill up at a waterpoint about halfway up the mountain.

If you don't feel like walking up the Langeberg Mountains, you can still get to the top on a highly recommended three-hour **tractor ride** (Wed 10am, Sat 9.30am & 2pm; book at the tourist information bureau ☎0234/42471), from Protea Farm, which is 29km along the Koo/Touws River road (R318). Remember to take warm clothes as it can be brisk up there.

atures and a couple of jacuzzis are spectacularly situated at the foot of cliffs – an effect unfortunately not enhanced by the neon lights of a tawdry hotel complex and some fast-food joints. Avoid coming here at weekends if you can – when it becomes a mass of splashing bodies – but first thing in the morning or last thing at night, when the outside air is cooler, the steaming waters provide a wonderfully relaxing alcohol-free nightcap. The springs are popular with coloured and Indian families, who were previously barred under apartheid; this has driven some rednecks to establish a racially exclusive spring on a farm outside town, where only whites are allowed.

You can also reach the resort **on foot**, by following the Keisie River which flows along the north edge of town.

Eating and drinking

When it comes to **eating**, Montagu has several good places in town. *Something Special Coffee Shop*, Bath St (☎0234/42436), is a great daytime venue in a listed Cape Dutch building, serving sandwiches, milkshakes and coffee. The best place for **lunch**, the *Montagu Country Inn* (☎0234/614 3125), is also on Bath Street and does an especially good-value eat-as-much-as-you-can ploughman's platter. *Romano's Italian Restaurant*, Church St (closed Sun), does reasonably priced pasta and pizza dishes, while *Preston's* (☎0234/41633) in Bath Street is a small, intimate nightspot recommended for its sole and oxtail. The ultimate eating experience is the superb five-course meal, served with silver cutlery and candles, at *Kingna Lodge* (☎0234/41066), where you'll need to book by lunchtime and vegetarians can be catered for. For **self-catering** and snacks, *Montagu Dry Fruit Farmstall*, Bath St (Mon–Fri 7am–6pm, Sat 8am–2pm, Sun 7am–1pm), sells dried fruit, biltong, boerewors, bread, milk and cheese.

Oudtshoorn and around

The slogan promoting **OUDTSHOORN** as the "ostrich capital of the world" makes one think of a sad bunch of PR consultants with their heads in the sand. The town is indeed crammed with **ostrich farms**, several of which you can visit, and the local souvenir shops keep busy dreaming up 1001 tacky ways to recycle ostrich parts. But Oudtshoorn has two other big draws: it's the best base for visiting the nearby **Cango Caves**, and the town is known for its sunshine and pleasant climate. Only 63km of tar separate Oudtshoorn from Wilderness on the coast, yet the weather couldn't be more different, and this is especially good news in winter, when a cold downpour along the Garden Route can give the lie to the idea of "sunny South Africa".

Some 50km west of Oudtshoorn, **Calitzdorp** is a delightfully unassuming Victorian village that can be taken as a circular excursion incorporating the scenic **Groenfontein Valley**. Alternatively its wineries and one or two tea shops hold out the chance of a breather if you're travelling on the R62 mountain route through the Little Karoo. A town with similar origins to Calitzdorp, but 35km in the opposite direction, is **De Rust**, which has benefited greatly from lying on the national road connecting the N1 to the Garden Route, but is little more than a pleasant pit stop on a journey north.

Some history

Until the 1860s Oudtshoorn was just a small village named in honour of Geesje Ernestina Johanna van Oudtshoorn, wife of the first civil commissioner for George. By the 1860s, **ostriches**, which occur in the wild in Africa, were being raised under the ideal conditions of the Oudtshoorn Valley, where the warm climate and loamy soils enabled lucerne, the favourite diet of the flightless birds, to be grown. It was the quirky Victorian fashion for large feathers that turned the ostriches into a source of serious wealth. By the 1880s, hundreds of thousands of kilogrammes of feathers were being exported and birds were changing hands for up to £1000 a pair – an unimaginable sum in those days. On the back of this boom, sharp businessmen made their fortunes, ignorant farmers got ripped off and labourers drew the shortest straw of all. The latter were mostly coloured descendants of the Outeniqua and Attaqua Khoikhoi and trekboers, who received derisory wages supplemented by rations of food, wine, spirits and tobacco – a practice which still continues on some farms. In the early twentieth century, the most successful farmers and traders built themselves the "feather palaces", ostentatious sandstone Edwardian piles that have become the defining feature of Oudtshoorn.

Arrival and information

Few people other than business travellers arrive in Oudtshoorn by air and there are no shuttles into town from **SM Greeff airport** (☎0443/29 2088), 2km from the centre of town, off Park Street. This is inconvenient if you're travelling on the *Greyhound, Intercape* or *Translux* intercity **buses**, because they, too, stop at the airport. However, there is a payphone at the airport, which is handy if you have arranged for staff at a hotel or lodge to pick you up. Far more convenient are the backpackers' buses, which will drop you off anywhere in town. The *Greenline* commuter bus, which leaves Oudtshoorn for George at the crack of dawn and returns at the end of the day, stopping at the backpackers' lodge, is a cheap but not a wildly convenient alternative.

Oudtshoorn's **tourist information bureau** (Mon–Fri 8am–6pm, Sat 8.30am–1pm; ☎0443/29 2532), at the *Queens Hotel*, Baron van Reede St, is good for information about the caves, ostrich farms and local accommodation. *Backpackers Oasis* (see below) is another excellent source of information about what to do in the vicinity.

Accommodation

Oudtshoorn has a number of large **hotels** catering mainly to tour buses, plenty of good quality B&Bs and guesthouses, a centrally located campsite with chalets, and one of the country's best-run backpackers' lodges. While accommodation is plentiful, it's also in great demand, so you should book in advance. The tourist information bureau (see above) offers a free accommodation booking service for all budgets.

Adley House, 209 Jan van Riebeeck Rd (☎ & fax 0443/22 4533). Edwardian-styled sandstone home built during the ostrich boom with eight en-suite rooms (all with TV) a swimming pool and garden to relax in. ④.

Backpackers Oasis, 3 Church St, Oudtshoorn (☎0443/29 1163). Professionally run, friendly and helpful backpackers' lodge that can provide you with all sorts of information about the area, as well as organize cycling trips with excellent bikes. Every evening there's an ostrich *potjie* and a relaxed jamming session on African instruments around the fire. Dorms and doubles. ①.

Bedstop, 69 van der Riet St (☎0443/224746). Modest rooms with gardens where you can sit outside, and *braai*. The rate is slightly cheaper if you don't have breakfast. ②.

Bisibee, 171 Church St (☎0443/224784, fax 292 373). Recommended B&B a few blocks from the centre, with five good-value rooms in a colonial-style home with verandahs, a large garden, swimming pool and a *braai* area. ③.

De Oude Meul, signposted on the R328 to Cango Caves, 18km from Oudtshoorn (☎0443/22 7190). A row of pleasant rooms facing onto a small lake and hills in Schoemanspoort, on a nursery ostrich farm. B&B as well as self-catering available, and very good dinners are served. ③.

Kannaland Lodge, 126 St John St (☎0443/29 2685, fax 29 2686). Reliable if predictable modern hotel-style rooms conveniently located in the centre. You can buy meat packs and *braai* in the garden, and also use the kitchen. ③.

Kleinplaas Holiday Resort, 171 Baron van Reede St (☎0443/22 5811). Shady camping and fully equipped brick chalets conveniently close to town, with a swimming pool and laundrette. ①.

Oakdene Guest House, 99 Baron van Reede St (☎0443/22 4838, fax 29 2645). Bright and friend-ly house with verandahs and spacious, wooden-floored rooms, decorated with strong earthy colours, hand-woven rugs and bedspreads, and paintings by South African artists. ③.

Old Parsonage, 141 High St (☎29 1751). Bedrooms sharing bathrooms or en suite in a fabulous centrally located sandstone, double-storey Dutch Reformed Church parsonage that is still in use and has a very pleasant garden. ②

Oue Werf, signposted on the R328 to Cango Caves, 15km from Oudtshoorn (☎ & fax 0443/22 8712). Farmhouse B&B in old farmstead in Schoemanshoek Valley, with good walks, bird-watching and a swimming pool. A good option if you're visiting the caves and want to stay in the country. ③.

Rosenhof Country Lodge, 264 Baron van Reede St (☎0443/22 2232, fax 22 3021). The most ele-gant place to stay in Oudtshoorn, on the edge of town, with twelve white cottages arranged around a restored Victorian house set in a beautiful rose garden filled with herbs, manicured lawns, a foun-tain and swimming pool. The lodge has its own restaurant serving cordon bleu food, using local ingredients. ⑥.

Queens Hotel, Baron van Reede St (☎0443/22 2101, fax 22 2104). Nicest of the smart hotels in Oudtshoorn, with all the facilities and right in the centre, *Queens* has been stylishly renovated and offers cool relief in the summer, with marble floors, a fountain, swimming pool and the *Langenhoven Restaurant* with an upstairs terrace and ostrich on the menu. ④.

Villa Morne B&B, 216 Jan van Riebeeck Rd, 1km north of the centre (☎083/700 8534, fax 0443/29 2916). 1960s modernist-style house, with breakfast on the patio and use of a small swimming pool ③.

The Town and the ostrich farms

Oudtshoorn's town centre is a pretty straightforward place to negotiate, and has little more than a couple of museums worth checking out if you've time to kill. The town's main interest lies in its Victorian and Edwardian sandstone buildings, some of which are unusually grand and elegant for a Karoo *dorp*.

The **CP Nel Museum** (Mon–Sat 9am–5pm; entry fee), on the corner of Baron van Reede Street and Voortrekker Road, is a good place to start your explorations. A hand-some sandstone building, it was built in 1906 as a boys' school, but now houses an eccentric and fairly intriguing collection of items relating to ostriches. Nearby, **Le Roux Town House**, on the corner of Loop and High streets (Mon–Fri 9am–1pm & 2–5pm), is a perfectly preserved family town house, and the only way to get a glimpse of one of the much-vaunted feather palaces. The beautifully preserved furnishings were all imported from Europe between 1900 and 1920, and there is plenty to stroll around and admire here.

Many people come to Oudtshoorn to see, or even ride, **ostriches**. You don't actually have to visit one of the ostrich farms to view Africa's biggest bird, as you're bound to see flocks of them as you drive past farms in the vicinity or past truckloads of the birds on their way to the butcher (feathers are no longer fashionable and these days ostrich-es are raised for their low-cholesterol flesh). A number of show farms offer tours (45–90min) costing around R20 a person, which include a commentary, the chance to sit on an ostrich and the spectacle of jockeys racing the birds. Best of the bunch is *Cango Ostrich and Butterfly Farm* (☎0443/22 4623, fax 22 8241), on the main road between Oudtshoorn and the Cango Caves, which takes only one group of visitors at a time and offers more personal attention than most of the others.

Eating and drinking

Oudtshoorn has a choice of several **places to eat**, all strung out along Baron van Reede Street, and all catering to the tourist trade.

Bernard se Taphuis, Baron van Reede St (☎0443/22 3208). Opposite the tourist information bureau, this is a large, central restaurant with a pleasant outdoor terrace upstairs. A good place to sample ostrich, game dishes, steaks and Afrikaner specialities at a medium price.

Fijne Keuken Restaurant, Baron van Reede St. In a house converted into a cosy restaurant with tables in several rooms as well as on the verandah, this is the nicest spot in town for just a drink, or a reasonably priced meal with enormous salads, pasta and the obligatory ostrich dish.

Headlines, Baron van Reede St (☎0443/22 3434). Good-value coffee shop and restaurant on the corner of St John's St, serving up good sandwiches, ostrich kebabs and steakhouse-style food and fish. A good place to come for a quick lunch.

Santa Fe Spur, Baron van Reede St. Popular chain, between Olivier and St John's streets, and serving good-value steaks, burgers, salads and cheaper takeaways.

Cango Caves

The **Cango Caves** number among South Africa's top ten attractions, drawing a quarter of a million visitors each year to gasp at their fantastic, cavernous spaces, dripping rocks and rising columns of calcite. In the two centuries since they became known to the public, the caves have been seriously battered by human intervention, but they still represent a stunning landscape growing inside the Swartberg foothills. Don't go expecting a serene and contemplative experience, though: the only way of getting inside the caves is on a guided tour accompanied by a hammed-up commentary.

Cango is a Khoi word meaning "a wet place" – spot-on, given that the caves' awesome formations are the work of water constantly percolating through rock and dissolving limestone on the way. The solution drips from the roof of the cave and down the walls, depositing calcium carbonate which gradually builds up. Although the caves are many millions of years old, the calcite formations that you see today are geological youngsters, dating back a mere 100,000 years.

Some history

San hunter-gatherers sheltered in the entrance caves for millennia before white settlers arrived, but it's unlikely that they ever made it to the lightless underground chambers. **Jacobus van Zyl**, a Karoo farmer, was probably the first person to penetrate beneath the surface, when he slid down on a rope into the darkness in July 1780, armed only with a lamp.

Over the next couple of centuries the caves were visited and pillaged by growing numbers of callers, some of whom were photographed cheerfully carting off wagonloads of limestone columns. In the 1960s and 1970s the caves were made accessible to mass consumption when a restaurant and curio complex were built, the rock-strewn floor was evened out with concrete, ladders and walkways were installed and the caverns were turned into a kitsch extravaganza with coloured lights, piped music and an indecipherable commentary that drew hundreds of thousands of visitors every year. Even apartheid put the boot in: under the premiership of Dr Hendrik Verwoerd, the arch-ideologue of racial segregation, a separate "non-whites" entrance was hacked through one wall, resulting in a disastrous through-draft that began dehydrating the caves.

Fortunately the worst excesses have now ended. Concerts are no longer allowed inside the chambers and the coloured lights have been removed. But the debate over how best to use these geological formations continues. According to David Bristow, editor of the South African travel magazine, *Getaway*, "the battle lines have been drawn between those who believe the caves are a lot of attractive rocks that should be at the disposal of the local council for all manner of entertainment and mass tourism, and those who believe they are a fragile ecosystem and should be protected as possibly one of our finest ecotourism destinations".

Practicalities

Apart from reasonably priced trips organized by *Backpackers Oasis* (☎0443/29 1163) in Oudtshoorn, there is no public **transport** to the Cango Caves. To **drive** here from Oudtshoorn, head north along Baron van Reede Street, and continue on the R328 for 32km to the caves. The visitors' complex resembles a Swiss ski resort – a bizarre image amidst the hot dryness – and houses a mass-catering **restaurant** with nice views of the mountains and valley, and a souvenir shop. Below the complex you'll find shady picnic sites at the edge of a river that cuts its way into the mountains and along which there are hiking trails. The nearest **accommodation** is beautifully set on the river, at *Cango Mountain Resort* (☎0443/22 4506; ②), signposted 27km from Oudtshoorn and 3km from the main road en route to the caves. This is the best self-catering accommodation in the area, with especially nice timber chalets. A small shop on site sells basics.

Three **tours** leave every hour on the hour (daily 9am–4pm). The half-hour "Scenic Tour" (R10) takes in the two largest and most spectacular caves, but is too short to give you a decent idea of the whole system. Most people join the one-hour "Standard Tour" (R15), which gets you through the first six chambers. If you're an adrenaline junkie, the ninety-minute "Adventure Tour" (R20) is a must; this takes you into the deepest sections open to the public, where the openings become smaller and smaller. Squeezing through tight openings with names like "Lumbago Walk", "Devil's Chimney" and "The Letterbox" is not recommended for the overweight, faint-hearted or the claustrophobic, and you should wear oldish clothes and shoes with grip to negotiate the slippery floors.

Calitzdorp and the Groenfontein Valley

Just 50km west of Oudtshoorn, the tiny Karoo village of **CALITZDORP** hangs in a tor-por of midday stillness. After the bustle of the "ostrich capital", it comes as a welcome surprise, with its attractive, unpretentious Victorian streets and a handful of wineries. There's nothing much to do here, apart from have tea, taste some wine and wander through the streets.

The low-key **tourist information bureau** (☎04437/33312), near the New Byzantine-style Dutch Reformed church, has some first-class brochures about the village and its surrounds, as well as information about the wineries and accommodation. Some of South Africa's best ports are produced at the three modest wineries signpost-ed down sideroads, a few hundred metres from the centre. The most highly recom-mended is *Die Krans Estate* (Mon–Fri 8am–5pm, Sat 9am–4pm; ☎04437/33314, fax 33562; tasting free), where you can sample their wines and ports (one of which is reck-oned to be among the country's top three), and stretch your legs on a thirty-minute **vineyard walk** in lovely countryside. *Boplaas Estate* (Mon–Fri 8am–5pm, Sat 9am–1pm; ☎04437/33326, fax 33750; tasting charge) also produces some fine ports and is worth a quick look to see their massive reed-ceiling tasting room that feels like a can-tina that fell off the set of a spaghetti western. If you've time for one more winery, head for the *Calitzdorp Wine Cellar* (Mon–Fri 8am–1pm & 2–5pm, Sat 8am–noon; ☎04437/33301, fax 33110; tasting free), where the main attraction is the stunning view from the tasting room into the Gamka River Valley.

Places to stay include the cheap, airy B&B rooms with verandahs at *Die Dorpshuis* (☎04437/33453; ②), which is centrally located, opposite the church, and the comfort-able, country-style *Welgevonden Guest House* (☎ & fax 04437/33642; ③), St Helena Rd, 300m from the main road, on a small Chardonnay farm. *Die Dorpshuis* is also a good place to **eat**, serving reasonably priced sandwiches, teas, light meals and heavier tradi-tional Karoo food, such as stews.

Heading east out of town, you can return to Oudtshoorn on the tarred R62, but it would be a pity to miss out on the more circuitous scenic route that diverts just outside

Calitzdorp and drops into the Groenfontein Valley. The narrow dirt road twists through the Swartberg foothills, past numerous whitewashed Karoo cottages and farms, and eventually joins the R328 which goes to Oudtshoorn.

De Rust

Hemmed in by Cape fold mountains, **DE RUST**, 35km northeast of Oudtshoorn, is a drive-through town on the N12 that cuts between the Garden Route and the N1 that races to Johannesburg. This accounts for the fact that most of the buildings along the town's small main road all seem to be selling something: teas, crafts, and biltong or ostrich products galore. You'll need to reach for your phrase book (or consult our language glossary on p.691) in this very Afrikaans village, which has a safe, calm atmosphere with gardens that make a bright contrast with the surrounding stony, dry hills. De Rust is a nice enough place to stop to stretch your legs and have a drink, but there's little reason to spend the night here.

Greyhound and *Translux* intercity **buses** from Gauteng stop off on their way to Knysna at the *De Rust Hotel*, while *Intercape* buses pull in at the Shell Garage – both central locations. You can **camp** at *De Oude Stal*, Burger St (①), a caravan park that has grassy stands and peacocks and figs in the yard. For beds in town, the clean and cheap *Afsaal Gastehuis* (☎04439/2134; ②) has two dark, old-fashioned rooms facing onto the main road. A self-catering cottage in a quiet part of the village is bookable through the *Country Kitchen* ((☎04439/2306). There's an outstanding place to stay some 15km out of town, off the R341 to Uniondale: *Oulap Country House* (☎04439/2250, fax 2298; ④–⑤), a Karoo farm in the Swartberg Mountains, run by film producer and storyteller Jans Rautenbach and his wife. Rooms are furnished with antiques and South African paintings and, besides using the house as a base to explore Oudtshoorn and around, you can explore the grounds and use the swimming pool. A hearty dinner is included in the rate.

The nicest **eating** places in town are the two tea shops in the main road, both with gardens: *Herries*, marked by a purple elephant outside, has pleasant seating under shady trees, while *Country Kitchen* serves outdoor teas and sells home-baked produce. For fresh bread, rusks, cakes and indoor teas you could also try *Die Groen Bliktrommel*, on the same road.

Prince Albert and around

Isolation and poverty have left intact the traditional rural architecture of **PRINCE ALBERT**, an attractive little town 70km north of Oudtshoorn, across the loops and razorbacks of the Swartberg Pass. Although firmly in the thirstlands of the South African interior, occupying the cusp between the Little and Great Karoo, Prince Albert is all the more striking for being quenched by a perennial spring, whose water trickles down furrows along its streets – a gift that propagates fruit trees and gardens.

Supremely old-fashioned displays make window-shopping as much fun as in any country museum, but the essence of Prince Albert is in the fleeting impressions that give the flavour of a Karoo *dorp* like nowhere else: the silver steeple of the Dutch Reformed church puncturing a deep-blue sky, residents sauntering along or progressing slowly down the main street on squeaky bikes. Visitors mostly come to Prince Albert for the drive through its two southerly gateways – the **Swartberg Pass** and **Meiringspoort** – generally driving in one way, spending the night in town and driving out the other. The town is also an excellent base for some thrilling walks and drives in the mountains – the ultimate being a journey into **Die Hel** (see box overleaf).

GOING TO HELL

Prince Albert is one of the best places to launch off on a trip into **Die Hel** (aka "Hell", "The Hell" or "Gamkaskloof"). Die Hel is not on the way to anywhere and, although it doesn't look very far on the map, by **car** you'll need to allow for two and a half hours in either direction to make this spectacular but tortuous expedition into the valley. Although the journey is on a dirt road, you won't need a 4WD vehicle, but you should definitely not attempt the drive in the killing heat of December or January. On **foot**, this makes a thrilling trip of two or three days. Reasonably priced **guided hikes** are operated by the owners of the *Prince Albert of Saxe-Coburg Lodge* in Prince Albert (see "Practicalities"), but note that they will only take minimum parties of four people. **Accommodation** can be arranged through the Lodge in primitive self-catering huts (②). There's no electricity in the valley and you'll have to heat water using a wood-fired boiler. There are no shops or any other facilities in the valley, so you'll need to stock up on food and supplies before heading off.

Practicalities

The only way to get to Prince Albert is by **car**, but once here the place is easily and most rewardingly handled on foot. A number of moderately priced B&Bs, self-catering places and a good and relatively inexpensive hotel make finding **accommodation** here a breeze. *Onze Rus*, 47 Church St (☎04436/380; ②), has cool, thatched B&B rooms attached to a restored Cape Dutch house, while *Kuierhuis*, 51 Church St (☎04436/770; ②), offers simple rooms with twin beds in a Cape Dutch house with a beautiful cottage garden. If you're **hiking** in the area, head for the *Prince Albert of Saxe-Coburg Lodge*, 60 Church St (☎04436/366; ②), where the owners hike regularly in the Swartberg Mountains and organize trips to Die Hel. The B&B rooms are in their house, with the best ones opening onto the back garden and duck pond, and the owners also rent a house with yellowwood floors at 15 Church St (②), which can sleep up to six and is available only for one party at a time. The smartest place in town is the *Swartberg*, 77 Church St (☎04436/332, fax 383; ③–④), a hotel in a Victorian double-storey National Monument, smothered in magenta bougainvillea. Traditional Karoo dinners are served in an atmospheric dining room, and there's a swimming pool.

When it comes to **eating**, the *Swartberg* is open to non-residents and is the only place in town for three-course dinners, which are formal but very good. For something more casual, the *Pancake Place*, Church St, does very reasonably priced bobotie and is open all day until 8pm (Sun 5pm). A nice place for tea or lunch is the *Wild Olive*, one block south of the hotel in Church Street, in a bright, butterscotch building. If you want to pick up food for the road, there's nowhere better than *Sampie se Plaasstal*, where you'll find excellent dried fruit and rusks, as well as local olives which are among the best in South Africa.

The N1 from Worcester to Beaufort West

The **N1** is the main highway between Cape Town and Johannesburg, and with the majority of flights still arriving in Johannesburg it's common for visitors to arrive there and drive down to the coast. This account, however, assumes you'll be starting your journey in Cape Town and heading north. While this route isn't particularly inspiring, and won't take you through the diversity of the country, it does lead you into the **Karoo**, the huge semi-desert that fills the centre-west of South Africa. The various towns along the way have a couple of interesting historic buildings and some of the flavour of the isolated Karoo in their street scenes – definitely enough to fill an hour if you're looking for a break from the long journey. The most compelling places are undoubtedly the Victorian village of **Matjiesfontein** and the **Karoo National Park** at Beaufort West, both of which can be regarded as destinations in their own right.

Worcester to Beaufort West

Some 30km beyond **Worcester**, on the outer edge of the Western Cape mountains, is the **De Doorns Valley**, full of vineyards, small white cottages, farm stalls and strangely contorted mountains, closed in from both ends and often forgotten among the classic valleys of the Cape winelands. Staff at the local **tourist information bureau** (☎02322/2835) in *De Doorns Wynkelder* (a winery), just off the road about halfway down the valley, are enthusiastic and will help you out if you're keen to explore this tranquil and pleasantly rustic area. **Touwsrivier**, 46km on, is a small, flat town with a service station and not much else, though in the town's hotel you'll find two pillars used by astronomers in 1880 to measure the distance of the sun from the earth.

Matjiesfontein

Pressing on, one of the quirkier manifestations of Victorian colonialism lies 54km east of Touwsrivier at the historic village of **MATJIESFONTEIN** (pronounced "Mikey's-fontayn"). Little more than two dusty streets beside a train track, the village resembles a film set rather than a Karoo *dorp*: every building, including the grand railway station, is a classic period piece, with tin roofs, pastel walls, well-tended gardens and Victorian frills. At the eastern end of the main street is the centrepiece, the *Lord Milner*, a hotel decked out with turrets and balconies and fountains by the entrance. If you're passing by, make sure you stop at least for a look around, and at less than three hours' drive from Cape Town the village is worth considering as a two-day trip of its own.

The origins of this curious place lie in the enterprise of a young Scottish entrepreneur, Jimmy Logan, who came to Cape Town to work on the railways and obtained the concession to sell refreshments to passengers all the way along the line from Cape Town to Bulawayo. He built Matjiesfontein as a health resort – making much play on the clean Karoo air – and it became a gathering point for the wealthy and influential around the turn of the century.

Today the village is doing brisk trade as a treasured relic. You can still come here in the classical manner on the mainline train (although it's a leisurely rather than direct journey), and **stay** at the *Lord Milner* (☎023/551 3011, fax 551 3020; ③), either in one of the grand, antique-filled rooms in the hotel itself or in one of the annexes in the surrounding houses. Inside the hotel there are huge portraits on the wall, polished brass fittings and, perhaps taking the theme a touch too far, rather surly service from waitresses dressed in black and white, with doilies on their heads. For **eating and drinking**, the hotel has a dimly lit dining room and a wonderfully aged and creaking bar. Along the main street, you'll find a tea room, souvenir shop and post office, all in attractive Victorian houses.

Laingsburg and Leeu-Gamka

There's little incentive to stop at **LAINGSBURG**, a town only 27km further along the N1 which marks the start of the long, lonely spaces of the Karoo. A service station lies on the road as it pulls around the Buffels River, and there are a couple of nondescript hotels and a cosy **caravan park** just up behind the service station, with tiny rondavels (①). As you drive through town, look out for the sign on the central reservation showing the water level during the catastrophic flood here in 1981 – it's level (if not more) with the roof of your car. Just outside Laingsburg, beside the road, is an Anglo-Boer War blockhouse, still largely intact on the outside and one of the best examples of these you'll see. These were built by the British at frequent intervals along the railway line to protect their main supply route; in all they built some eight thousand blockhouses (at £16 each), prompting Boer General Christiaan de Wet to pass comment on the British "blockhead" system.

One of the longest empty stretches is along the next 124km until you reach **LEEU-GAMKA**, with a filling station and a tiny Anglo-Boer War cemetery which just about has room for the grave of Private Schultz, the tallest man in the British army. There must have been some feline hunting around here at some point, as both barrels of the name Leeu-Gamka mean "lion" – the first being Afrikaans and the second a Khoi word for the king of the beasts, who hasn't padded the Western Cape for decades.

Beaufort West

For over 100km on either side of **BEAUFORT WEST**, the scenery from the N1 is far away and hazy, so the appearance of the Nieuwveld Mountains, which rise up behind town, give the place a certain distinction. Beyond that, however, Beaufort West is not a pretty place, with the N1 traffic trundling through its centre (watch out for speed traps and remember to stop at traffic lights), and it devotes most of its attention to servicing road-weary travellers.

As befits a town which is the oldest municipality in South Africa, most of the old buildings you'll see have a very municipal stolidity to them. Principal among these is the town's **museum**, 87 Donkin St (Mon–Fri 9am–12.45pm & 1.45–4.45pm; entry fee), in the old town hall, which houses an exhibition honouring the glamorous life and achievements of Beaufort West's Professor Christiaan Barnard, who performed the world's first human heart transplant operation at *Groote Schuur Hospital* in Cape Town in 1967.

Practicalities

The intercity **buses** all pull into the *Oasis Hotel* in Donkin Street. The town's helpful **tourist information bureau**, 63 Donkin St (☎0201/51160), is one block along from the museum. Beaufort West has no shortage of **accommodation**, though much of it is for mass consumption and fairly characterless. There's a municipal **camping** and caravan park under some trees on the right as you come into the main part of town on Donkin Street, but as with other camping options along the N1 it's a bit scruffy and unappealing. If you want to camp, you're better off going to the Karoo National Park, which is just a few kilometres out of town (see opposite). Ideal for backpackers, *Donkin House*, 14 Donkin St (☎0201/4287; ①), is more of a simple guesthouse than a hostel, but has a swimming pool and some communal space to hang out in. Another budget option is the *Formule 1*, 144 Donkin St (☎0201/52421; ②), part of a fast-bed chain that delivers slick, ultra-modern rooms which resemble a ship cabin. Also part of a chain, the *Wagon Wheel Protea* (☎0201/2145 or central reservations toll-free ☎0800/11 9000; ②–③), off the N1 on the northern fringe of town, offers predictable motel cleanliness, with a few cheaper rooms. *Clyde House*, 25 Donkin St (☎0201/4083; ③), has quite lavish accommodation in a pink, double-storey house built in 1839, and dishes up good breakfast in the coffee shop downstairs. For more elegance, make straight for the *Matoppo Inn* (☎0201/51055, fax 51080; ④–⑤), on the corner of Bird and Meintjies streets, which has upmarket rooms in the town's old *drostdy*, or magistrate's house.

When it comes to **eating**, you could do worse than the breakfasts and lunches in the coffee shop next to the craft gallery at *Clyde House* on Donkin Street. For dinner, *Ye Olde Thatch* restaurant, 155 Donkin St, is a bit gloomy inside but the menu is decent enough. Across the road is *Mac Young's*, an upmarket, Scottish-themed restaurant nestled behind a Caltex service station. Popular with Afrikaners, anyone with a Scottish ancestor within five generations will find the cringe factor rather high. Opposite the *Formule 1* hotel is the formulaic but reliable *Saddles Steak House*.

Karoo National Park

Unassuming and undervalued, the **Karoo National Park** (daily 5am–10pm; entry fee) has been emerging in recent years as a reserve with much more to offer than first meets the eye. Although it doesn't immediately feel very Karoo-like (there are too many mountains), the themes of the semi-desert are undoubtedly here, and after a night gazing at the dazzling sky, or a hot day learning about the unexpectedly intricate flora of the region, you'll start to appreciate this park's special value. Many of the slightly graceless facilities are recognizable from national parks elsewhere in South Africa, but here you do get the sense that the management are working hard to help people enjoy the place.

Much of what you take from here is in the landscape and the serene atmosphere: despite the recent introduction of some **black rhino**, big game is limited, although there are some impressive raptors, including the **black eagle**. The designated drives you can take around a limited section of the 600-square-kilometre park aren't terribly exciting; however, a recent innovation is a wider-ranging 4WD trail in Parks Board vehicles, with the opportunity to overnight out in the *veld* in a remote mountain hut, at a cost of around R200 per person.

Near the main rest camp there is an environmental education centre, along with three **trails**: an eleven-kilometre day-walk; a short but informative tree trail; and a very imaginative fossil trail (designed to accommodate wheelchairs and incorporating Braille boards), which tells the fascinating 250-million-year-old geological history of the area and shows fossils of the unusual animals found here in the times when the Karoo was a vast inland sea.

Practicalities

The entrance gate to Karoo National Park is right on the N1, 2km south of Beaufort West. The reception and rest camp are a couple of kilometres into the park, hidden among the appealing flat-topped mountains in a way that makes you feel as though you are a million miles from the town and the highway. At reception is a shop and **restaurant** (Mon–Sat 8am–8.30pm, Sun 8am–7pm), and there is a swimming pool nearby. **Accommodation** is in various large chalets (③), strung out on either side of the main complex, with the campsite (①) hidden away over a rise. If you're intending to overnight in Beaufort West during a long trip, it's well worth considering coming out to the park instead of staying in town. For more information about the park, phone

☎0201/52828; for **bookings** contact the National Parks Board in Pretoria (☎012/343 1991) or in Cape Town (☎021/22 2810).

THE OVERBERG INTERIOR AND THE WHALE COAST

East of the Winelands lies a vaguely defined region known as the **Overberg** (Afrikaans for "over the mountain"). In the seventeenth century, when even Stellenbosch, Franschhoek and Paarl were remote outposts, to the Dutch settlers everywhere beyond them was a fuzzy hinterland that drifted off into the arid sands of the Karoo. These days it extends to an ill-defined point between Arniston and Mossel Bay on the coast and somewhere east of Swellendam in the interior.

Of the two main routes through the Overberg, the **N2** strikes out across the less interesting interior, a four- to five-hour stretch most people endure rather than enjoy to get to the Garden Route – but you can make it less of a chore with a couple of well-chosen stops along the way. North of the N2 is **Greyton**, a pleasant village used by Capetonians as a relaxing weekend retreat, and the starting point of the **Boesmanskloof Traverse** – a terrific one-day trail across the mountains into the Karoo. The Moravian mission station of **Genadendal**, five minutes down the road from Greyton, has a strange Afro-Germanic ambience that offers a couple of hours' pleasant strolling. Along the N2 itself the only places that justify a restorative stop are **Caledon**, for its Victorian thermal springs, and **Swellendam**, for its well-preserved streetscape as well as one of South Africa's best country museums.

The real draw of the area is the **Whale Coast**, close enough for an easy outing from Cape Town, yet surprisingly undeveloped. The exception is popular **Hermanus**, which owes its fame to its status as the whale-watching capital of South Africa. The whole of this southern Cape coast, in fact, is prime territory for land-based **whale-watching**. Also along this section of coast is **Cape Aghulas**, the southernmost place on the continent, which sadly fails to deliver the drama its location promises. Nearby (and far more worthwhile) is Arniston, one of the best-preserved fishing villages in the country, and a little to its east the **De Hoop Nature Reserve**, an exciting wilderness of bleached dunes, craggy coast and more whales.

Caledon

The first impression of **CALEDON** is the huge, cathedral-like grain silos that dwarf its church spires. A declining farming town some 111km east of Cape Town, Caledon built its former prosperity on its wheat, barley and malt trade, but today is slowly declining. The town's burghers are gambling on reversing their fortunes through a massive casino complex mooted to be built around the town's one natural asset – its **thermal springs**. For the moment the public can still wallow in the steaming mineral water at Caledon's terrific historic **Victorian bathhouse** (daily 8am–10pm; R10) in the grounds of the *Overberger Hotel*.

You can make this highly recommended rest-stop with only a minor detour from the N2: to get to the spa follow the Overberger sign, which if you're coming from Cape Town is a little way beyond the town-centre indicator. Use of the springs predates by centuries the Victorians, who built the wrought-iron structure in the nineteenth century. When the Dutch arrived here in the eighteenth century, Khoi people were already wallowing in steaming holes dug in the ground – a practice imitated by the settlers.

Apart from the spa, Caledon has a couple of other decent attractions. The **museum** (Mon–Fri 8am–1pm & 2–4.30pm, Sat 9am–1pm; ☎0281/21511; small entry fee), above the tourist information bureau at 16 Constitution St, consists of a collection of mainly domestic items displayed in the old Freemasons Meeting Hall and at a house faithfully restored to "Victorian Caledon style" (1837–1901), diagonally opposite. The most enjoyable way to see the collections is on a guided tour led by curator Mangia Galli, whose brilliantly well-informed commentary makes fascinating connections between seemingly trivial household items and the broader tapestry of history – you can also arrange agricultural tours through him.

Caledon's outdoor attraction is the **Wildflower Garden and Nature Reserve**, where you can wander through fynbos, aloes and succulents on a lovely long walk along a rocky, wooded *kloof* into the mountains, or head out on the ten-kilometre Meiring Trail, which goes deep into the nature reserve.

Practicalities

All three of intercity **buses** stop off at the *Alexandra Hotel* on Market Square in the centre of town. Caledon's **tourist information bureau**, 16 Constitution St (Mon–Fri 8am–1pm & 2–4.30pm, Sat 9am–1pm; ☎0281/21511), has literature about the area as well as details of places to stay. **Accommodation** is limited but reasonably priced. The cheapest beds in town are in a self-catering cottage with a verandah at the *Painted Lady*, 3 Donkin St (☎0281/41290 or evenings 22093; ②). Also good value are the rooms at the *Manor B&B*, 40 Mill St (☎083/212 1836 or evenings 0281/22862; ②), a late Victorian house with a garden, close to hot springs. Smartest of the lot is the *Overberger*, Narina Ave (☎0281/41271, fax 41270; ⑥), a conference venue on the edge of town with nice views of wheat fields, and gardens with a pool and spa facilities. Out of town you'll find *Oom Barrie se Huisie* (☎0281/41080 or 48903; ①), a cottage that sleeps six, clearly signposted off the R406 between Caledon and Greyton. Extremely rural, the building is set in rolling wheatlands, and has a double room and space for four in the attic. The house has no electricity or phone, although there is hot and cold running water and a fully equipped kitchen, and linen is available on request.

Eating comes down to snacks during the day at the *Venster* restaurant in the Wildflower Garden or at the swish *Overberger Hotel*, which is surprisingly good value for a light meal, and you'll get the benefit of views from the terrace. For self-catering, you can buy home-baked products, including fresh bread, every Friday at the *Museum Shop*, Donkin St, around the corner from the museum.

Greyton and the Boesmanskloof Traverse

The best things about **GREYTON**, a small holiday and retirement village 46km north of Caledon, based around a core of Georgian and Victorian buildings, are the unploughed Riviersonderend ("endless river") Mountains which set it off from the cultivated landscape typical of most of the Western Cape. There's no industry here and the only modern development is the fair quantity of repro Georgian houses along its streets. The calm, bucolic atmosphere created by the shady oaks hides a real tension in the town between the folk who want to retain the sleepy ambience and keep out economic activity and those who see a need to create jobs for the 500-strong coloured community who don't have the privilege of living here in golden retirement or on holiday.

Apart from estate agents selling the rural dream to city dwellers who come to set up businesses, so little money changes hands here that there isn't even a bank. The town's big attraction is the superb **Boesmanskloof Hiking Trail** (see box overleaf), which crosses the mountains to McGregor. Apart from that – and some shorter walks – there's very little to do but stroll down the streets and potter about in the handful of antique and tea shops.

Arrival and information

As there's no public transport to Greyton, the only way to get here is by **car**, the best route being just west of Caledon on the R406, which is tarred all the way. Don't attempt to tackle the untarred route from Riviersonderend, which will hammer your suspension. The **tourist information bureau** (Tues–Fri 10am–noon & 2.30–4.30pm; ☎028/254 9414, fax 254 9665) is in the public library along the main road as you come into town, and has information about places to stay. Greyton is ideal for cycling and you can arrange **mountain-bike rental** through *Shamrock Garden Services* (☎028/254 9559).

THE BOESMANSKLOOF TRAIL

One of the best reasons to come to Greyton is to walk the fourteen-kilometre **Boesmanskloof Traverse**, which takes you from the gentle, oaked streets of **Greyton** across the Riviersonderend mountain range to the glaring Karoo scrubland around the town of **McGregor**. The stark contrast over so short a distance is staggering, made all the more so by the fact that no direct roads connect the two towns; to drive from one to the other involves a circuitous two hours on the road.

The classic way to cover the Traverse is to walk from Greyton to **Die Galg** (14km from McGregor), where people commonly spend the night, returning the same way to Greyton the following day. The route rises and falls a fair bit so you'll have to contend with some uphill walking, but the whole way can be easily completed in a day if you're reasonably fit. If you don't want to go all the way you can still have a rewarding outing, venturing part of the way and returning to Greyton for the evening. A decent day's walk takes you to **Oak Falls**, 9km from Greyton, the highlight of the route. Composed of a series of cascades, its most impressive feature is a large dark pool, where you can rest and swim in the tannin-coloured water.

The walk takes you through over fifty species of wonderful montane fynbos and if you come at the right time of year you can find yourself walking through magnificent groves of flowering proteas. Mammals include small antelope, caracals, baboons and dassies, but you're not likely to see many of them, so go for the scenery, with the rugged Riviersonderend Mountains, *kloofs*, streams, waterfalls and pools.

Trail practicalities

You're free to walk the first 5km of the trail and back, but if you want to complete the whole thing from Greyton to Die Galg you will need a **permit**, which limits numbers to fifty people per day. Over weekends the trail gets extremely full and permits must be arranged in advance through the Manager, Vrolijkheid Nature Reserve, Private Bag X614, 6705 Robertson (☎02353/621 or 671). During the week you can buy a permit on the day of your hike from the Greyton Municipal Offices, DS Botha St (Mon–Fri 8am–1pm & 2–3.30pm; ☎028/254 9620). You'll get a **map** when you buy the permit, although you don't strictly need one as the Traverse is very clearly marked out. A booklet is available to accompany the interpretation trail, covering the McGregor half of the route. This is keyed to numbered points along the way and helps you to get more out of the walk by drawing your attention to what's around you. The walk isn't particularly strenuous but you should wear good shoes. It's also worth noting that this is a winter rainfall area, and can be wet at that time of year. Summers are hot and dry.

Accommodation on the McGregor side presents two possibilities: staying at the overnight hiking dorms (☎02353/735; ①), equipped with a fridge, cooker and beds (but no bedding) at Die Galg – the other end of trail; or *Whipstock Farm* (☎ & fax 02353/733; ③), 4km beyond Die Galg, from where the farm owners will collect you free of charge.

Accommodation

Many of Greyton's holiday homes are rented out by a central agency (contact Gerald Shrock on ☎028/254 9046) when not in use by owners. Winters can be cold in this mountainous country; it's worth getting a place with a fireplace if you're here at that time of the year. The large municipal **campsite** (☎028/254 9620; ①), 2.5km out of town and signposted off Main Road, is in a lovely setting on the banks of the Riviersonderend, with amenities limited to an ablution block with hot and cold water. For budget beds, you won't find cheaper than *Oak Tree Hikers Loft*, 25 Oak St (☎028/254 9820; ①), a modest holiday house just off the main road with basic rooms supplied with beds and mattresses aimed at hikers doing the Boesmanskloof Trail; the drawback is that it's rented out to groups (minimum seven). Cheapest of the **B&Bs** is *Bullocks*, Main Road (☎028/254 9948; ②), while *High Hopes B&B*, 76 Main Rd (☎028/254 9898; ③), is in a beautiful country-style home set in a magificent garden with a huge ornamental pond and delicious non-bacon and eggs breakfasts.

Of the **self-catering** options, *Webbers*, 1 Main St (☎028/254 9998; ②), is a two-bedroom apartment that sleeps four, attached to a house, with the use of a courtyard. *Little Mandalay*, Caledon Street (☎028/254 9818; ②), just off Main Road, is a 100-year-old fully equipped garden cottage that sleeps two and has a lovely pergola outside. *La Vue*, on the corner of West and Park streets (☎028/254 9658; ②), just outside the centre, has a fully equipped self-catering cottage that sleeps two and has *braai* facilities. Cheapest of the **guesthouses** is the *Guinea Fowl*, DS Botha St (☎028/254 9550; ③), while the *Post House*, Main Rd (☎028/254 9995, fax 254 9920; ④–⑤), has en-suite bedrooms furnished with Edwardian and country furniture and named after Beatrix Potter characters. The very comfortable *Greyton Lodge*, 46 Main Rd (☎028/254 9876, fax 254 9672; ③–④), is the smartest place in town, and should be your first choice if money is no object.

Eating and drinking

Greyton's best place for **eating** light meals and teas is on the sunny verandah of *Abbey Rose*, Main Rd, where you can get soups, crêpes, omelettes, salads, sandwiches and waffles. The unpretentious *Kennedy's Steak House* offers reasonably priced slabs of beef, burgers and fish, while the *Greyton Country Restaurant*, run by a charming French proprietor, has decent English food during the day throughout the week, and dinners on Tuesday, Friday and Saturday. Candle-lit four-course meals are on offer at the *Post House* and *Greyton Lodge*.

Genadendal

GENADENDAL, whose name means "valley of grace", was established in 1737 and is South Africa's oldest mission station, founded by Moravians (some of the ochre and earthy-pink architecture hints at Central-European influences). The village is essentially an excursion from Greyton, 6km to its west, as there's nowhere to stay in Genadendal itself.

Genadendal's focus is around **Church Square**, which is dominated by a very Germanic church building dating back to 1891. The old bell outside dates back to the eighteenth century, when it became the centre of a flaming row between the local farmers and the mission station. The scrap broke out when missionary Georg Schmidt annoyed the local white farmers by forming a small Christian congregation with impoverished Khoi – who were on the threshold of extinction – and giving refuge to maltreated labourers from local farms. What really got the farmers' goat was the fact that while they, white Christians, were illiterate, Schmidt was teaching blacks, whom they considered uncivilized, to read and write. The Dutch Reformed Church, under the control of the Dutch East India Company, waded in when Schmidt began baptizing converts, and prohibited the mission from ringing the bell which called the faithful to prayer.

At one stage during the eighteenth century, Genadendal was the largest settlement in southern Africa after Cape Town. Although it never became more than a village, Genadendal experienced a golden age in the nineteenth century, with a flourishing economy based on home industries. In 1838 it established the first teacher training college in the country, which the government closed in 1926, on the grounds that coloured people didn't need tertiary education and should be employed as workers on local farms – a policy which effectively ground the community into poverty. In 1995, in recognition of the mission's role, Nelson Mandela renamed his official residence in Cape Town "Genadendal".

Today the population of this principally coloured town numbers around four thousand people adhering to a variety of Christian sects – no longer just Moravianism. The **Mission Museum** (Mon–Thurs 9am–1pm & 2–5pm, Fri 9am–3.30pm, Sat 9am–noon; small entry fee), adjacent to Church Square, is moderately interesting and provides some clues as to why Moravians came here. You should allow up to two hours to explore the museum and wander through the town, down to the rural graveyard, spiked with tombstones dating back to the early nineteenth century. Genadendal offers few visitor facilities, but there is a **tea room**, just off Church Square, where you can get refreshments.

The Genadendal Trail

While you're here, you can venture a short way from the village into the surrounding countryside along the **Genadendal Trail**. The full 25-kilometre two-day circular trail requires a high level of fitness, particularly for the first 2km of the second day. But much of the rest is fairly easy-going and passes through montane fynbos inhabited by a variety of small antelope, caracals and the odd leopard. **Booking** and **permits** are essential and can be arranged through Vrolijkheid Nature Reserve, Private Bag X614, Robertson 6705 (☎02353/621 or 671). Overnight **accommodation** on *De Hoek Farm* at the halfway point can be arranged through the owner (☎02351/2176).

Swellendam

Although **SWELLENDAM**, 97km east of Caledon, is an unquestionably attractive historic town at the foot of the Langeberg and has one of the best country museums in South Africa, it doesn't make more than a congenial halfway stop along the N2 between Cape Town and the Garden Route. South Africa's third-oldest white settlement, Swellendam was established in 1745 by Baron Gustav van Imhoff, a visiting Dutch East India Company bigwig, who was deeply concerned about the "moral degeneration" of burghers who were trekking further and further from Cape Town and out of Company control. Of no less concern to the Baron was the loss of revenue from these vagabonds, who were neglecting to pay the Company for the right to hold land and were fiddling their annual tax returns. Following a brief hiccup in 1795, when burghers declared a "free republic" (quickly extinguished when Britain occupied the Cape), the town grew into a prosperous rural centre known for its wagon-making, and for being the last "civilized" port of call for trekboers heading out into the interior.

The income generated from this helped build Swellendam's gracious homes, many of which went up in smoke in the fire of 1865, which razed much of the town centre. In 1950, transport planners ripped out many of the oaks that had survived the blaze to widen the main road. Nevertheless, this dozy *dorp* survived with just enough charm to lure you off the national road.

The only building in the centre to survive these ravages is the **Cape Dutch Oefeninghuis**, 36 Voortrek St, which now houses the tourist information bureau. Built in 1838, it was first used as a place for religious activity, and then as a school for freed slaves, and has surreal-looking stopped clocks carved into either gable end, below which there's a real clock above the entrance. Diagonally opposite and slightly east at no. 11, the **Dutch Reformed church**, dating from 1910, incorporates Gothic windows, a Baroque spire, Renaissance portico elements and Cape Dutch gables into a wedding cake of a building that, against the odds, agreeably holds its own.

Arrival and information

The *Greyhound, Intercape* and *Translux* intercity **buses** travelling between Cape Town and Port Elizabeth all pull in at the *Swellengrebel Hotel*, 91 Voortrek St, in the centre of town. The *Baz* and *Hopper* backpacker buses will drop you off at any of the central accommodation. Swellendam has a very switched-on **tourist information bureau**, 36 Voortrek St (Mon–Fri 9am–1pm & 2–5pm, Sat 9am–12.30pm; ☎ & fax 0291/42770), which can provide frank and helpful advice about local attractions and will book accommodation.

You can easily cover the town centre on foot, but should you want to explore further afield or go on the seventeen-kilometre mountain-bike trail, which starts in Voortrek Street, you can arrange **bike rental** from *Reitzhof B&B*, 9 Moolman St (☎0291/43554).

Accommodation

Swellendam's budget **accommodation** starts with the *Swellendam Caravan Park*, Glen Barry Rd (☎0291/42705), which has functional campsites (①) and basic en-suite thatched cottages (②), which are dead cheap if you bring your own bedding and there are four of you sharing. In the same price bracket, but a lot more sociable, *Swellendam Backpackers*, 5 Lichtenstein St (☎0291/42648; ①), is a friendly place and, of the two hostels, is the more geared up for backpackers, with camping, dorms and doubles; staff can also arrange river rafting and canoeing trips. *Waenhuis Backpackers*, 5 Buitekant St (☎0291/42281), has only one dorm (①), but also offers reasonably priced B&B rooms (②) in an elegant house.

The nicest **B&Bs** in town are in historic Cape Dutch or Georgian houses. Pick of the bunch is the well-run *Pond Cottage*, 21 Buitekant St (☎0291/42036; ②), offering a cottage in a lovely garden with a double bed and fully equipped kitchen, and two rooms inside the house. Other options include *Moolmanshof*, 217 Voortrek St (☎0291/43258; ②), with comfortable country-style rooms inside a Cape Dutch homestead, and *Cypress Cottage*, 3 Voortrek St (☎0291/43296; ②), which has reasonable rooms in a small cottage behind the amazing main house (one of the oldest in town), and the same owners also have similarly priced rooms in the nicer *Tuishuis* next door. The *Old Mill*, 241–243 Voortrek St (☎0291/42790; ③), has two picturesque cottages and a small restaurant serving light meals during the day. If you're feeling sociable, *Roosje Van De Kaap*, Drostdy St (☎0291/43001; ③), owned by a pair of chatty yuppies, makes a convivial choice in a beautiful house, but some of the rooms are tiny. Just outside the centre of town are Swellendam's best and most expensive lodgings at *Klippe Rivier Homestead* (☎0291/43341; ⑦), off the western end of Voortrek Street, across the Klippe River, with opulent bedrooms in a magificent 1820 mansion.

Strand to Cape Hangklip

The main reason you'd take the coastal route that skirts the eastern shore of False Bay is to get to Hermanus, but scenically the drive has much to recommend it, especially once you get past the commuter settlements close to Cape Town. Leaving the N2 from Cape Town at Somerset West, the first coastal settlement you hit is **STRAND**, a massive industrial centre on the edge of Cape Town. Although it has a good beach, this isn't sufficient reason to stop off and the R44 quickly gets you to the ongoing commuter development of **Gordon's Bay**, your last chance for a decent sea swim for some distance. After here the mountains bear down on the sea and the road works its way around the folding mountainside with the sea crashing against the rocks. Rock-strewn and without a tree in sight, the barren landscape has a raw dramatic quality that takes you just inland of **Cape Hangklip**, the tip of False Bay, which earned its name from the fact that Hangklip frequently fooled Portuguese mariners into thinking they were rounding the Cape of Good Hope. A dirt road takes you down to **HANGKLIP** itself, where a succcession of dwellers have made their homes since humans left stone axes here over 20,000 years ago. In the nineteenth century, outlaws hung out in Hangklip's remote caves, but were flushed out in 1852, leaving the area to the baboons that now hole up here.

Betty's Bay and around

Cape Hangklip roughly marks the point at which the commuters become holidaymakers. Just around the corner, **BETTY'S BAY** was developed as a seaside retreat for Capetonians wanting to get away from the city. Prosaically named after Betty Youlden, daughter of the director of the first company to try to develop the area, this rather boring collection of holiday cottages hosts a colony of **jackass penguins**. The best time to see the birds is in the morning or evening between April and June. Jackass penguins mate for life and return to the same nest every year, but here are suffering from interference with their turf by perlemoen (a type of large shellfish) poachers. Residents urge you to tell local shopkeepers if you see poaching taking place.

Betty's Bay is not geared up to visitors, though you can **eat** at the Harold Porter Botanical Garden (see below).

Harold Porter National Botanical Garden

Creeping up the the mountains just above Betty's Bay, **Harold Porter National Botanical Garden** (daily 8am–6pm; small entry fee) is a wild sanctuary of coastal and montane fynbos that makes a good stop along the R44, if only to picnic or have tea at its outdoor **café**. Once here, you'll probably get lured at least some of the way up the *kloof* that runs through the reserve. The relatively compact botanical garden extends over two square kilometres from the mountains, through marshland down to coastal dunes. As you get higher up, you are treated to sea views in one direction and rugged mountains in the other.

Although wildlife in the form of small **antelope**, **baboons** and **leopards** are present, they are rarely sighted and you should look out instead for the birds and blooms. In January you can see brilliant red disas in all their glory, while the nerine lilies flower in March. Keep an eye open for colourful, nectar-loving sunbirds and scores of other **bird species** that occur here. Four **trails** of between one and three hours meander through the gardens, but you can just as easily take yourself off on an impromptu stroll, up and across the red-stained waters (caused by phenols and tannins leaching from the fynbos) running through Disa Kloof.

Kleinmond

Because of its isolation, **KLEINMOND**, roughly 12km northeast of Betty's Bay, was an outlaws' stronghold for some two hundred years. In the twentieth century, however, relatively easy access has turned the town into a holiday spot for Capetonians and for farmers from the surrounding areas. An impressive confluence of sea, dune, tidal estuary and mountain waterfalls combines with a ten-kilometre crescent **beach** that curves across the Bot River Mouth to Mudge Point, a promontory that completes the vista as you look east. Swimming is safest close to the *Beach House* hotel, but take care not to venture beyond where you see other bathers.

The cheapest **accommodation** is at the couple of caravan parks, signposted from the main road, where you can camp. Better of the two is the *Palmiet* (☎02823/4050; ①), which is quieter and closer to the safely swimmable river. The main caravan park, the

Kleinmond (☎02823/4050; ①), is unappealingly close to the main road which slices the village in half. For self-catering, *Our Kaia*, 12 5th Ave (☎021/686 8454 or 02823/4555; ②–③), has an apartment and a house, both with verandahs overlooking the beach. *Sandown Lodge B&B*, 7 Strand St (☎ & fax 02823/4586; ③), is a family home on the beachfront offering four rooms with private showers but no sea views, and two lounges that have fabulous views of Sandown Bay.

The most luxurious place is *Beach House*, Beach Rd (☎02823/3130, fax 4022; ⑦), a small hotel whose spacious rooms, with king-size beds, white wicker furniture and tastefully understated floral fabrics, look out over Sandown Bay, the lagoon and mountains and enjoy the sound of the endlessly pounding surf. If you're going to fork out to stay here, you may as well stay in one of the luxury sea-facing rooms. *Beach House* is also the best place for eating, with an expensive formal **restaurant**, which serves pleasant English-style food. For something cheaper, there are a couple of take-away places along the main road through town.

Hermanus, Walker Bay and around

On the edge of rocky cliffs and backed by mountains, **HERMANUS**, 112km east of Cape Town, sits at northernmost end of Walker Bay, an inlet whose protective curve attracts calving whales as it slides south to the promontory of Danger Point. The town trumpets itself as the **whale capital** of South Africa and, to prove it, has an official

HERMANUS

Walker Bay

ACCOMMODATION
1 Auberge Burgundy
2 Esplanade Holiday Apartments
3 Forty Five Marine Drive
4 Glenugie Pavilion Guesthouse
5 Hermanus Travellers Lodge
6 Kenjockity
7 Marine Hotel
8 Onrus Caravan Park
9 Whale Cottage Guesthouse
10 Windsor Hotel
11 Zoete Inval

Hermanus Accommodation Centre

Museum
Old Harbour

0   500 m

N

whale crier (apparently the world's only one) who struts around armed with a mobile phone and a dried kelp horn through which he yells the latest sightings. There is still the barest trace of a once-quiet cliff-edge fishing village around the historic harbour and in some understated seaside cottages, but for the most part Hermanus has gorged itself on its whale-generated income that has produced modern shopping malls, super-markets and craft shops.

Ignoring the hype, **Walker Bay** does provide some of the finest shore-based whale-watching in the world and, even if there are better spots nearby, Hermanus is the best setup anywhere in the country to exploit it. From about July, southern right whales start appearing in the warmer sheltered bays of the Western Cape (see p.200). Whales aside, Hermanus has good swimming and walking **beaches**, three excellent **wineries** you can visit and makes a good base for exploring the rest of the Overberg.

Southeast down Walker Bay, the unprepossessing town of **De Kelders** outshines its smarter neighbour as a whale-watching spot, but at nothing much else; and just inland of it, the wonderful and very upmarket **Grootbos Nature Reserve** is one of the best places in the country to learn about fynbos. Heading further down the bay, you hit the fishing town of **Gansbaai** (Afrikaans for "goose bay") which these days is far better known for its sharks than its waterfowl. Curving back to Hermanus, **Danger Point** is the promontory that marks Walker Bay's southern extent, and marks the spot where HMS *Birkenhead* literally went down in history.

An easy excursion from Hermanus takes you through attractive and relatively untrammelled farming country to **Bredasdorp**, a junction town on the R316 that gives you the choice of branching out to Africa's disappointing southern tip at **Cape Aghulas**; the well-preserved Moravian mission town of **Elim**; or the fishing village of **Arniston**, which is the least-developed and nicest town along the Whale Coast.

Arrival and information

Scant public transport passes through Hermanus, the exception being the infrequent *Chilwans* **bus** (☎021/904 0808), which comes from Cape Town on Friday and Saturday and stops opposite the *Marine Hotel*, before continuing on to Gansbaai. The *Hopper* and *Baz* backpacker buses offer the only regular transport that comes anywhere near here; both drop off at Bot River, 28km to the north on the N2. You can usually arrange for the backpackers' lodge to collect you, which won't normally involve a long wait, as the buses carry mobile phones and call ahead when their arrival is imminent. Most people come to Hermanus by **car**, which takes about ninety minutes from Cape Town. Travelling along the N2 and striking south onto the R43 at Bot River is the more direct of the two main routes, but the winding road which hugs the coast from Strand, leaving the N2 just before Sir Lowrie's Pass, is the more scenic.

There's a helpful **tourist information bureau** (Mon–Fri 9am–5pm, Sat 9am–3pm, Sun 9am–1pm; ☎0283/22629, fax 70 0305; email: infoburo@ilink.nis.za) in Main Road, with maps and useful brochures about the area as well. The bureau also operates a free accommodation-finding service.

Accommodation

You'll find very few places to rent along the shore in Hermanus, as they're all in pri-vate hands, but there are some **hotels** and **self-catering apartments**. The nearest and nicest **campsite** in the vicinity is in the quiet adjacent village of **Onrus**, where there are also a couple of B&Bs. If there are more than two of you, the best option may be to rent a whole house or apartment through *Hermanus Accommodation Centre*, which is on the corner of Church and Myrtle lanes (☎0283/70 0004; email: hermanus@iafrica.com).

Auberge Burgundy, 16 Harbour Rd (☎0283/70 1201, fax 70 1204). Newly erected imitation-Provençal country house in the town centre projecting a stylish Mediterranean feel, with imported French fabrics and a lavender garden. Breakfast is served across the road at the *Burgundy*, Hermanus's top restaurant, under the same ownership. ⑥.

Esplanade Holiday Apartments, Marine Drive (☎0283/23610). Close to the Windsor Hotel, these run-down but clean self-catering apartments offer variable facilities in an unbeatable position for sea views and whale-watching. ②.

Forty Five Marine Drive, 45 Marine Drive, Hermanus (☎0283/23727). Spanking new apartments which are more expensive than the *Marine Hotel* if there are two of you, but worth considering for their fabulous sea frontage if there are four sharing. ⑤.

Glenugie Pavilion Guest House, Roos St, Onrus (☎083/269 2666). Lovely 1920s house with lots of timber and stylish green and white exterior, in this small village next to Hermanus. ④.

Green Shutters, 3 Moffat St, Hermanus (☎ & fax 0283/23117). Fully equipped self-catering cottage sleeping four in a garden set well back from the seafront. ②.

Hermanus Travellers' Lodge, Tweefontein Farm, Hemel En Aarde Valley (☎0283/22829). Dorms and doubles at this slightly shabby backpackers' lodge, 5km from Hermanus in a secluded country setting. The owners will pick up from the *Hopper* or *Baz* bus stops at Bot River on the N2. You can also get lifts to town when they're going in. Dorms and doubles. ①.

Kenjockity, 15 Church St (☎ & fax 0283/21772). Centrally located and friendly B&B, where you can't see the sea but you can hear the whales at night in season. The best rooms have their own private sitting room and are en suite, while backpackers can sometimes be accommodated in smaller, cheaper rooms. ②–③.

Marine Hotel, Marine Drive (☎0283/70 1000, fax 70 0160). This grand, old-fashioned seafront hotel is Hermanus's best, and it's good value, as long as you don't mind the slightly formal atmosphere. It's worth booking early and paying extra for a sea-facing room. There's a jacuzzi, an indoor swimming pool and it's a short way down the cliff to the tidal pool. ④.

Onrus Caravan Park (☎0283/61210). In the adjacent village of Onrus, so away from the Hermanus hype, but close enough for the restaurants, shops and facilities. ①.

Pendle Place, 44 Luyt St (☎0283/22556). Quiet, self-contained B&B flatlet in the garden of a house belonging to Brenda Johnson – who wrote the Johannesburg *Star*'s cookery column for years and bakes great cakes. Rooms have electric kettle and fridge, but no cooking facilities. ②.

Whale Cottage Guest House, 20 Main Rd (☎0283/70 0929, fax 70 0912). Simple, pleasantly furnished guesthouse offering five rooms decorated with marine themes. The only drawback is it's away from the sea. ③–④.

Windsor Hotel, Marine Drive (☎0283/23727, fax 22181). The town's second hotel has the best location in town – right on the edge of the cliffs – but otherwise isn't a patch on the *Marine*. Booking is essential, and it's worth paying a little extra for a sea-facing room. ④.

Zoete Inval, 23 Main Rd (☎ & fax 0283/21242; email: zoetein@ilink.nis.za). Hermanus's most popular backpackers' lodge run by an enthusiastic couple with huge amounts of carefully prepared information for guests. Dorms (①) and doubles (②).

The Town and around

Main Road, the continuation of the R43, meanders through Hermanus, briefly becoming Seventh Street before again resuming its persona as the national road. **Market Square**, just above the old harbour and to the south of Main Street, is the closest thing to a centre, and here you'll find the heaviest concentration of restaurants, craft shops and flea markets – the principal forms of entertainment in town when the whales are taking time out.

Just below Market Square is the **Old Harbour Museum** (Mon–Sat 9am–1pm & 2–4pm), whose only real attraction is its live transmission of whale calls from a hydrophone anchored in the bay to its audio room (replaced by recordings out of season). Among the other uncompelling displays, you'll find lots of fishing tackle and some sharks' jaws. Outside the museum, a few colourful boats, used by local fishermen between 1855 and 1961, create a photogenic vignette in the tiny harbour.

An almost continuous five-kilometre cliff path through coastal fynbos hugs the rocky coastline from the old harbour to Grotto Beach in the eastern suburbs. For one short stretch the path heads away from the coast and follows Main Street before returning to the shore. East of the Old Harbour, just below the *Marine Hotel*, a beautiful **tidal pool** offers the only sea swimming around the town centre's craggy coast. For **beaches**, you have to head out east across the Mossel River to the suburbs, where you'll find a decent choice, starting with secluded **Langbaai**, closest to town, a cove beneath cliffs at the bottom of Sixth Avenue. **Voëlklip**, at the bottom of Eighth Avenue, has grassed terraces and is great for picnics if you prefer your sandwiches unseasoned with sand. Adjacent is **Kammabaai**, with the best surfing break around Hermanus, and 1km further east, **Grotto Beach** marks the start of a twelve-kilometre curve of dazzlingly white sand that stretches all the way to De Kelders.

Hemel-en-Aarde Valley: the Walker Bay wineries

On the eastern edge of Hermanus, **Rotary Way** is a fantastic ten-kilometre drive that follows the mountain spine through beautiful montane fynbos offering sweeping views of the town, the Hemel-en-Aarde Valley ("heaven and earth valley") and Walker Bay from Kleinmond to Danger Point. To get there from town, turn right just after the sports ground, and take a track straddled by a pair of white gateposts labelled "Rotary Way". The road is tarred for part of the way before becoming dirt, and eventually peters out altogether, which means you have to return the same way.

Some of South Africa's top wines come from the adjacent **Hemel-en-Aarde Valley**, about fifteen minutes by car west of Hermanus. Vineyards in the area date back to the early nineteenth century when the Klein Hemel-en-Aarde Vineyard was part of a Moravian mission station, but winemaking has been established here for little over a decade. Three small **wineries** are dotted along a few gravel kilometres of the R320 to Caledon, which branches off the main road to Cape Town 2km west of Hermanus, and are worth popping into, for their intimate tasting rooms and first-class wines, and to sample the stark scrubby mountains just inland.

Newest of the three wineries, *Whale Haven Winery* (tastings and sales Mon–Fri 9.30am–5pm, Sat 10.30am–1pm; ☎0283/21585; no tasting charge), a couple of hundred metres after the Caledon turn-off, released its first vintage in 1995 and its reputation has been growing since. Wines to look out for are the merlot, which is very highly rated and the baleine noire, a fruity merlot and shiraz blend that resembles beaujolais and is best drunk young.

The most established of the Walker Bay wineries, *Hamilton Russell* (tasting and sales Mon–Fri 9am–5pm, Sat 9am–1pm; ☎0283/23595, fax 21797; no tasting charge) produces South Africa's two priciest wines, a Chardonnay and a Pinot Noir, and is noted for its exceptionally good Chardonnays. If you're set on sampling a particular wine, be sure to phone ahead as some vintages sell out fast. *Hamilton Russell* also bottle a range of wines under the very collectable Southern Right label, which can't be bought at the estate, but is available at the town liquor stores, where they quickly sell out as souvenirs in the whale season. Adjacent to *Hamilton Russell*, towards Caledon, *Bouchard Finlayson* (Mon–Fri 9am–5pm, Sat 10.30am–12.30pm; ☎0283/23515) is another Walker Bay establishment with a formidable reputation, which consistently scores highly with its Pinot Noir, Chardonnays and Sauvignon Blanc.

Eating and drinking

Seafood is the obvious thing to eat in Hermanus, and you'll find plenty of good restaurants serving it. The town's farm stall and deli-style foodshops are very handy if you're **self-catering**. One of the best places to stock up on goodies is *Hemel-en-Aarde Food*, 2 Broad St, which sells cheeses, delicious breads, cakes and organic produce.

WHALE-WATCHING

The Southern Cape, including Cape Town, provides some of the easiest and best places in the world to **watch whales**. You don't need to rent a boat or take a pricey tour to get out to sea; if you come at the right time of year, whales are often visible from the shore, although a good pair of binoculars will come in useful for when they are far out.

All nine of the great whale species of the southern hemisphere pass by South Africa's shores, but the most commonly seen off Cape Town are **southern right whales** (their name comes from being the "right" one to kill because of their high oil and bone yields and the fact that, conveniently, they float when dead). Southern right whales are black and easily recognized from their pale, brownish **callosities** (rock gardens). These unappealing patches of raised, roughened skin on their snouts and heads have a distinct pattern on each animal, which helps scientists keep track of some of them. What gives away the presence of a whale is the blow or spout, a tall smoky plume which disperses after a few seconds and is actually the whale breathing out before it surfaces. If luck is on your side, you may see whales breaching – the movement when they thrust high out of the water and fall back with a great splash.

Female whales come inshore for calving in sheltered bays, and stay to nurse their young for up to three months. The period from August to October is the best time to see them, although they start appearing in June and some stay around until December. When the calves are big enough, the whales head off south again, to colder, stormy waters, where they feed on enormous quantities of plankton, making up for the nursing months when the females don't eat at all. Though you're most likely to see females and young, you may see **males** early in the season boisterously flopping about the females, though they neither help rear the calves or form lasting bonds with females.

The Overberg's hottest whale spots

Although Hermanus is best known and most geared up for whale-watching, it's also the most congested venue during the whale season and there are equally good – if not better – spots elsewhere along the Walker Bay coast.

In **Hermanus** itself the best vantage points are from the concreted cliff paths, which ring the rocky shore from New Harbour to Grotto Beach. There are interpretation boards at three of the popular vantage points (Gearing's Point, Die Gang and Bientang's Cave). At their worst, you'll find the paths two or three deep with people.

In fact aficionados claim that **De Kelders** (see p.176), some 39 km east of Hermanus, is even better, while **De Hoop Nature Reserve** (see p.179), east of Arniston, is reckoned by some to be the ultimate place along the entire southern African coast for whale-watching, with far greater numbers of southern rights breaching here than anywhere else.

Dial M for marine mammals

During the season, the **Whale Information Hotline** (☎083/212 1074) can tell you where the latest sightings have been.

Bientang's Cave, off Marine Drive (☎0283/23454). Next to the old harbour, this is the priciest restaurant in town, and is known for its seafood and fabulous location in a cave on the rocks just above the sea – where you can sit outside. Opening hours can be erratic, so phone before you set out.

The Burgundy, Marine Drive (☎0283/22800). Above the old harbour, and arguably Hermanus's top restaurant, serving fairly expensive French-style food in one of the town's oldest buildings. There's indoor and outdoor seating, from where you can watch whales or people. Closed Mon.

Charlie's Tapas, Market Square (☎0283/70 0110). Sit inside or outside for reliable, if unspectacular, medium-priced food.

Fisherman's Cottage, Lemms Corner (☎0283/23642). Excellent pub off Market Square, with verandah seating in an old cottage. Serves reasonably priced fish and chips. Closed Sun.

Green's Bistro, 310 Tenth St, Voëlklip Beach (☎0283/77 1048). Reasonably priced seafood and home cooking on the east side of town at another good restaurant. Closed Tues & Sun evenings.

Hermanus Fish Shoppe, Market Square. Cheap take-away fish and chips, seafood salads and fresh seafood to cook yourself.

Marine Hotel, Marine Drive. Excellent-value pub lunches of the fish-and-chips/sausage-and-mash variety.

Milkwood Restaurant, Atlantic Drive, Onrus (☎0283/61516). Nice outdoor venue especially recommended for medium-priced steaks, 5min drive west of Hermanus, on the estuary, shaded by milkwood trees.

Nautilus, Grotto Beach (☎0283/77 0090). Casual old eatery right on the beach, with moderately priced seafood and steaks.

Ouzeri and Trattoria, 60 St Peter's Lane (☎0283/70 0532). Fairly standard joint with slow service. The menu switches between Greek and Italian food and includes good-value pizzas and pasta.

Listings

Automobile Association Emergency rescue supernumber toll free ☎0800/01 0101.

Banks (Mon–Fri 9am–3.30pm, Sat 8.30–11am) are easy to find in the centre of the town. Wherever you find banks you'll find automatic teller machines (ATMs). Opening hours are Mon–Fri 9am–3.30pm, Sat 8.30–11am.

Emergencies Ambulance ☎10177; Fire ☎361 0000; Police (Flying Squad) ☎10111; Rape Crisis ☎23 2323.

Hospitals and doctors *Hermanus Private Hospital*, Hospital St, off Main Rd (☎0283/70 017), has a 24hr casualty service.

Pharmacy *Hermanus*, 145 Main Rd (☎0283/24039). Opening hours are Mon–Fri 8am–6.30pm, Sat 8am–1pm, Sun 10am–noon & 6.30–7.30pm.

Taxis Phone for a *Rikkis*(☎0283/76 3827) for the cheapest way to get to the beach – the price goes down the more of you there are. *Grab-a Cab* (☎0283/21388) does short trips in the Hermanus environs as well as trips to Cape Town airport and city centre. Although not cheap it's very popular, so book well in advance.

Telephones There are phone booths all over Hermanus's shopping centre, taking phone cards and coins. For directory enquiries, dial ☎1023.

Grootbos and De Kelders

East of Hermanus the R43 takes a detour inland around the Klein River Lagoon, past the riverside hamlet of **Stanford**, before reaching the private **Grootbos Nature Reserve** (☎02834/20381, fax 40552; ⑦; minimum stay two nights), a highlight of the area, and 33km from Hermanus. Rolling across undulating, fynbos-covered country, this luxury reserve has superb middle-distance views of the coast, and is promoted as a "fynbos lodge", where experts guide you through the Western Cape's unique and richly varied plant kingdom. Outings are available in 4WD vehicles, on foot or on horseback. **Accommodation** is in self-contained stone cottages with ethnic-chic furnishings, polished granite kitchen surfaces, imported fittings, temperature-controlled showers, multiple sundecks and views of the mountain from one side and the sea from the other. The rate includes a three-course dinner served in the main lodge, breakfast in your own cottage and a choice of activities, including guided horse-rides, walks or drives through the fynbos and conducted beach hikes.

The nearest coast is a couple of kilometres to the east at **DE KELDERS**, a haphazard and treeless hamlet that stares from bleak cliffs across Walker Bay to Hermanus. Despite surpassing fashionable Hermanus as a whale-watching venue, De Kelders has somehow escaped the hype, and this small aggregation of holiday homes remains a backwater devoid of facilities with only a couple of places renting out rooms. *De Kelders* (☎02834/40421, fax 40165; ②) is a typically unsophisticated country **hotel** which has seen little modernization since the 1960s, but has a great verandah for tea, with unbeatable views overlooking the bay, and does cheap pub lunches. The *Mooi Uitsig Guest*

House, 124 Cliff Rd (☎02834/4180; ④), has overpriced B&B rooms mitigated by a whale-watching deck with sublime views.

Continuing west past the guesthouse to the end of Cliff Road, you'll reach a car park from which you can clamber down to the **Klipgat strandloper caves**, which were excavated in the early 1990s and evidence of modern human habitation found from 80,000 years ago. It became unoccupied for a few thousand years and was again used by Khoisan people 20,000 years ago. Shells, middens, tools and bones were uncovered, and some of these are now displayed in the South African Museum in Cape Town (see p.75).

Gansbaai and Danger Point

From the Klipgat caves, the waymarked **Duiwelsgats Hiking Trail** goes east for 7km as far as Gansbaai and is a good way to explore this beautiful coastline. **GANSBAAI** itself is a workaday place, economically dependent on its fishing industry and the seafood canning factory at the harbour. This all serves to give the place a more gutsy feel than the surrounding holidaylands, but there's little reason to spend time here unless you want to engage in **great white shark safaris**, Gansbaai's other major industry, an appropriately competitive and cutthroat business, with a number of operators engaged in a blind feeding frenzy to attract punters. Boats go out from Gansbaai to Dyer Island, east of Danger Point, where great white sharks come to feed on the resident colony of seals. Sharks are baited and, while you do stand a chance of seeing one, sightings are certainly not guaranteed, especially over December and January, when there are plenty of seal pups to keep the sharks well-fed. Even if a shark does come it may not hang around long enough for all the people on the boat to get into the cage for a viewing (only two can fit in at a time). For more information, contact the Hermanus or Gansbaai tourist information bureaus.

There's little reason to stay in Gansbaai other than for the budget **accommodation** offered by *Great White Backpackers* (contact *Southcoast Seafaris* ☎02834/41380 or 082/553 0999, fax 02834/41381; ①), a pair of 1950s houses converted into plainly furnished lodges with small dorms and doubles.

Danger Point, the southernmost point of Walker Bay, is where British naval history was allegedly made. True to its name, the Point lured the ill-fated *Birkenhead* onto its hidden rocks on February 26, 1852 and, as was the custom, the captain of the troopship gave the order: "Every man for himself." Displaying true British pluck, the soldiers are said to have lined up in their ranks on deck where they stood stock-still, knowing that if one man broke ranks it would lead to a rush that might overwhelm the lifeboats carrying women and children to safety. The precedent of "women and chil-

---

DYER ISLAND AND SHARK ALLEY

How a black American came to be living on an island off South Africa is something of a mystery. But according to records **Samson Dyer** arrived here in 1806, and made a living collecting guano on the island that subsequently took his name. Dyer Island is home to substantial **jackass penguin** and **seal breeding colonies**, both of which are prized morsels among great white sharks. So shark-infested is the channel between the island and the mainland at some times of year that it is known as **"Shark Alley"**, and these waters are used extensively by operators of great white viewing trips. In 1996, a group of West African castaways washed up here having been put out to sea by the unscrupulous skipper of a Taiwanese merchant vessel whom they had paid to take them to the east, where they hoped to find work. One of them drowned in the process, but the rest (amazingly) survived five days at sea, including a stint down Shark Alley clinging to pieces of timber and barrels.

dren first", which became known as the **Birkenhead Drill**, was thus established, even though 445 lives were lost in the disaster.

Cape Aghulas and Elim

Along the east flank of the Danger Point promontory, the rocky and shallow coastline with heavy swells and strong currents makes this one of South Africa's most treacherous stretches of coast – one that has taken over 250 wrecks and around 2500 lives. Its rocky terrain also accounts for the lack of a coastal road from Gansbaai and Danger Point to **Cape Aghulas** – the southernmost tip of Africa. Apart from this one fact, there's nothing to recommend the place, which is approached through an ugly sprawl of houses. Flat, barren and windswept, it will leave you wishing that you took the left fork to Arniston. To get to Aghulas from Hermanus you have to go inland and take the R316 to Bredasdorp, where the road splits and you take the west branch for 43km to Aghulas or the east one for 24km to Arniston.

A far better reason to venture along the network of dirt roads that crisscrosses the Whale Coast interior is to visit **ELIM**, a Moravian mission station, 40km northwest of Aghulas, founded in 1824. The whole village is a National Monument of streets lined with thatched, whitewashed houses and fig trees. There's nothing twee about this extraordinarily undeveloped and untouristy place which doesn't have a bottle store or even a tea shop. Facilities amount to a couple of tiny stores where coloured kids play video games. With no museum to visit and no places to stay, this is a place to simply drive or stroll around.

Arniston

After the cool deep blues of the Atlantic to the west, the tepid azure of the Indian Ocean at **ARNISTON** is truly startling; and it's made all the more dazzling by its white dunes interspersed with rocky ledges. This is one of the best places to stay in the Overberg and is refreshingly unbuilt-up compared to Hermanus and places closer to Cape Town. The village is known to locals by its Afrikaans name, Waenhuiskrans ("wagon-house cliff"), after a huge cave 1.5km south of town, which trekboers reckoned was spacious enough for a wagon and span of oxen (the largest thing they could think of). The English name derives from a British Ship, the *Arniston*, which hit the rocks here in 1815.

Conversely, the shallow seas that are treacherous for vessels give Arniston the safest **swimming** waters along the Whale Coast. Apart from sea bathing, **Kassiesbaai**, a community of starkly beautiful limewashed cottages, now collectively declared a National Monument, is the principal attraction of this unspoilt hamlet. Its beautifully simple dwellings are invariably the ones that show up in coffee-table books whenever picturesque fishing villages are called for. But as the home to the coloured fishing families that have for generations made their living here, it sits a little uneasily as a living community that's a bit of a theme park for visitors, who stalk the streets with their cameras. You can't stay in the cottages; all the holiday accommodation is in the adjacent new section of town, which has managed miraculously to blend in with the spirit of the old village.

The only regular entertainment here is wandering down to the harbour at high tide to watch the fishing boats being shoved down the slipway by a tractor that ends up half submerged. Otherwise, swimming and a few beach walks offer breaks from the supreme languor. You can swim next to the slipway or at **Roman Beach**, the main swimming beach, which is next along, heading away from the harbour.

Heading north through Kassiesbaai, at low tide, you can walk 5km along an unspoilt beach unmarred by buildings until you reach an unassuming fence – resist the temptation to climb over this, as it marks the boundary of the local missile-testing range.

Taking the other direction for 1.5km along spectacular cliffs and the road, you'll reach the vast cave after which the town is named; this is a walk worth doing simply for the fynbos-covered dunes you'll cross on the way. From the car park it's a short signposted walk down to the dunes and the cave, which can only be reached at low tide. The rocks can be slippery and have sharp sections, so be sure to wear shoes with tough soles and a good grip.

Practicalities

As there's no public transport to Arniston, your only option is to **drive** here. **Accommodation** is limited to one hotel, some self-catering cottages and a handful of B&Bs, which get snapped up quickly during school holidays and over weekends. At the *Waenhuis Caravan Park* (☎02847/59620), along the main road into Arniston, you can either pitch your own tent (①) or stay in small, four-bed en-suite bungalows (①–②), which have no sea views, but are only a couple of minutes' walk to the beach. Cooking equipment is available at a small charge, but you'll need to bring your own bedding and towels. Alternatively, limewashed self-catering mock-Arniston houses can be rented from *Arniston Seaside Cottages* (☎02847/59772, fax 59125; out of season ②), well signposted from the national road, along the street behind the hotel. The cottages are fully equipped and are charged per person out of season – in season (Dec, Jan & Easter school holidays) you pay for the total number of beds in the unit. Just behind the hotel, *Southwinds*, Huxham St (☎ & fax 02847/59303; ③), has three double B&B suites looking onto a courtyard garden. The smartest place to stay is the *Arniston* (☎02847/59000, fax 59633; ⑤–⑦), a luxurious and well-run hotel in a central position along the seafront. Guests are offered extras, such as massage, and this is the only place in the village offering sea views from some rooms.

The village has three **restaurants**, all of which serve fresh fish caught locally. *Waenhuis*, Du Preez St (a continuation of the national road), is the least expensive, and is decorated to resemble a fishermen's tavern. The other two restaurants are at the hotel and have sea views. The informal and reasonably priced *Slipway* serves steaks, burgers and the like, while the hotel's main restaurant is far more formal and quite pricey. You can buy **fresh fish** from the fishermen at the slipway near the hotel.

De Hoop Nature Reserve

It's surprising that a reserve with as much going for it as **De Hoop** (daily 7am–6pm; small entry fee) has the humble status of a nature reserve, when it's quite probably the wilderness highlight of the Western Cape. Although the reserve makes a relatively easy day outing from Hermanus, you'll find it far more rewarding to come here for a night or more.

Breathtaking coastline is edged by bleached sand dunes that stand 90m high in places, and rocky formations that at one point open to the sea in a massive craggy arch. The flora and fauna is impressive too, encompassing 86 species of mammal, 260 different birds, 1500 varieties of plants, and it's reckoned to be the ultimate place in South Africa (surpassing even Hermanus and De Kelders) to see **southern right whales**. If you're here for a couple of days in season, chances are you'll see some whales. July to September is best for whale-watching, but you stand a very good chance of a sighting right through June to November. Inland, **zebra**, **bontebok** and other **antelope** congregate on a plain near the reserve accommodation. Apart from swimming and strolling along the length of white sandy beach, there are hiking and mountain-biking trails, but you'll need to bring your own bike as there's nowhere here to rent one.

Practicalities

De Hoop is along a signposted dirt road that spurs off the R319 as it heads out of Bredasdorp, 50km to its west. **Accommodation** is restricted to a campsite (①) and self-catering cottages (②) set on an estuary well back from the sea. The cottages are equipped with a cooker, fridge and electricity, but you'll need to bring your own bedding, kitchen utensils and food. **Booking** should be made through the Manager, De Hoop Nature Reserve, Private Bag X16, 7280 Bredasdorp (☎028/542 1126, fax 542 1679). Overnight visitors must report to the reserve office, about 4km into the reserve, by 4pm. Be sure to stock up on supplies before you come – the nearest shop is 15km away, in the hamlet of **Ouplaas**.

THE GARDEN ROUTE

The **Garden Route**, a slender stretch of coastal plain between Mossel Bay and Storms River Mouth, bears a legendary status as South Africa's paradise – reflected in local names such as **Garden of Eden** and **Wilderness**. A soft, green 198-kilometre forested swath, cut by rivers from the mountains to the north, which tumble down to its southern rocky shores and sandy beaches, it was heaven to the **Khoi** herders, who lived off its natural bounty and called it *Outeniqua* ("the man laden with honey").

This Eden was quickly destroyed in the eighteenth century with the arrival of Dutch **woodcutters**, who had exhausted the forests around Cape Town and set about doing the same in Outeniqua, and killing or dispersing the Khoi and San in the process. Birds

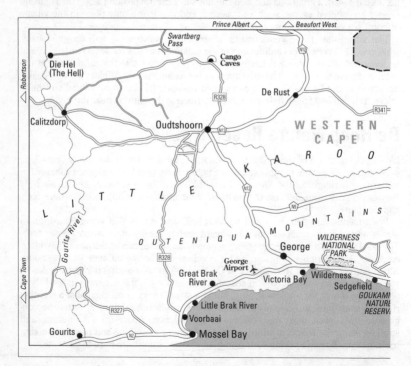

and animals suffered too from the encroachment of Europeans. The Swedish naturalist Johan Victorin, who came in the 1850s, shot and feasted on the species he had come to study, some of which, including the endangered narina trogon, he noted were "beautiful and good to eat".

Despite the dense appearance of the area, what you see today are only the remnants of one of Africa's great **forests**; much of the indigenous hardwoods have been replaced by exotic pine plantations and the only milk and honey you'll find now is in the many shops that service the Garden Route coastal resorts. **Conservation** may have halted the wholesale destruction of the indigenous woodlands, but a huge growth in tourism and the influx of urbanites seeking a quiet life in the relatively crime-free Garden Route towns threatens to rob the area of its remaining tranquillity.

Most visitors take the Garden Route as a **journey** between Cape Town and Port Elizabeth, dallying for a little more than day or two to do a bit of shopping or sightseeing. The rapid passage cut by the excellent N2 makes it all too easy to have a fast scenic drive – and end up disappointed because you don't see that much from the road. To make the journey worthwhile, you'll need to slow down, take some detours off the highway and explore a little to find secluded coves, walks in the forests or **mountain passes** in the Karoo.

The Garden Route coast is dominated by three inlets – Mossel Bay, the Knysna Lagoon and Plettenberg Bay – each with its own town. Oldest of these and closest to Cape Town is **Mossel Bay**, an industrial centre of some charm, that marks the official start of the Garden Route. **Knysna**, though younger, exudes a well-rooted urban character and is the nicest of the coastal towns, with one major drawback – unlike

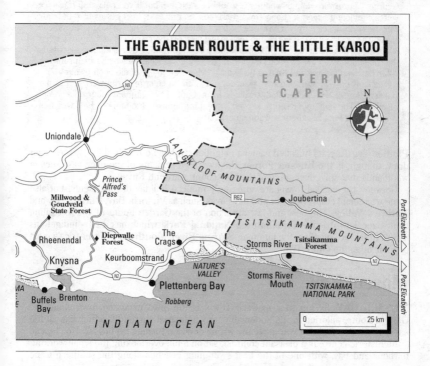

GARDEN ROUTE TRANSPORT

The coastal zone between Cape Town and Port Elizabeth, which takes in the **Garden Route**, is probably the best-served stretch of South Africa for **transport**. The excellent N2 makes **driving** along here an absolute breeze, and if you take it straight you'd have to try pretty hard to get lost.

Most user-friendly among the public transport options are the two **backpacker buses**, the nine-seater *Hopper Bus* (daily Cape Town–Mossel Bay and Mossel Bay–Port Elizabeth; ☎041/51 2332) and the larger *Baz Bus* (4 weekly Cape Town–Port Elizabeth; ☎021/439 2323). Both are recommended if you're exploring the Garden Route and want the freedom to get on and off at will. The *Hopper Bus* provides the only means, other than driving yourself, of getting down to Storms River Mouth, which is arguably the ultimate attraction of the whole route. Both buses offer a door-to-door service within the central districts of all the towns along the way, and both have the advantage over the large intercity lines that they will happily carry outdoor gear, such as surfboards or mountain bikes. Although the buses take standby passengers if there's space available, you should book ahead if you want to secure your seat.

The **intercity buses** *Intercape*, *Greyhound* and *Translux* are best for covering longer distances comfortably and cheaply. They stop off at Mossel Bay, George, Wilderness, Sedgefield, Knysna and Storms River (the village but not the Mouth, which is some distance away), but don't offer a door-to-door service and often don't go right into town, instead letting passengers off at filling stations on the highway.

The weekly Southern Cross **train** between Cape Town and Port Elizabeth used to be South Africa's great railway journey – before the tracks got washed away in 1997 near George. There were doubts whether it would be restored, but if you enjoy rail travel it's worth contacting *Spoornet* (Cape Town ☎021/405 3871 or 3581; Port Elizabeth ☎ 041/507 2400 or 2222) to see if the train is back on track. Reckoned to be one of the most dramatic stretches of railroad in the world, one section just west of George curves and climbs a steep 300m in just 26km. Another train, which is more of a day's outing than serious transport, is the *Outeniqua Choo Tjoe*, a goods train with passenger carriages attached, which runs the 30km between George and Knysna twice daily (Mon–Sat) in either direction (see p.187).

Finally, if time is tight you may want to go **by air** to George at the west end of the Garden Route, with scheduled services from Cape Town, Johannesburg and Port Elizabeth. The only other centre served by regular flights is Plettenberg Bay, which is connected to Port Elizabeth and Johannesburg.

Plettenberg Bay, its tinselled eastern neighbour, it has no beach of its own. A major draw, though, is the **Knysna Forest**, the awesome remants of the once vast ancient woodlands that still cover some of the hilly country around Knysna.

Between the coastal towns are some ugly modern holiday developments, but also some wonderful empty beaches and tiny coves, such as **Victoria Bay**, **Buffels Bay** and **Nature's Valley**. The best and last attraction of the Garden Route (if you're coming from Cape Town) is the **Tsitsikamma National Park**, which has it all – indigenous forest, dramatic coastline, the pumping **Storms River Mouth** and South Africa's most popular hike, the **Otter Trail**.

Mossel Bay

MOSSEL BAY, 397km west of Cape Town, is the most maligned town along the Garden Route, pilloried for its undeniably ugly industrial surrounds which can all too easily make you feel that you made the wrong decision turning off the N2. Don't panic – the historic centre is a pleasant contrast, set on a hill overlooking the small working harbour and bay, with one of the best swimming beaches along the southern Cape coast. The town takes on a strong Afrikaans flavour over Christmas when Karoo farmers with their families descend in droves to occupy its caravan parks and chalets. While Mossel Bay's modest attractions are unlikely to hold you for more than a night, it has some decent accommodation and a first-class restaurant, which make it a good place to stop to gather your breath before launching out into the thick of the Garden Route.

Some history

Mossel Bay bears poignant **historical significance** as the place where indigenous Khoi cattle herders discovered the existence of Europeans in a bloody encounter that set the tone for five hundred years of race relations on the subcontinent. A group of Portuguese mariners under captain **Bartholomeu Dias** set sail from Portugal in August 1487 and months later rounded the Cape of Good Hope in search of a sea route to the riches of India. In February 1488, they became the first Europeans to make landfall along the South African coast, when they pulled in for water to the safety of an inlet they called Aguado de São Bras ("Watering Place of St Blaize"), now Mossel Bay.

The Khoikhoi were organized into distinct groups, each under its own chief and each with territorial rights over pastures and water sources. The Portuguese, who were flouting local social conventions, saw it as "bad manners" when the Khoikhoi tried to drive them off the spring. In a mutual babble of incomprehension the Khoi began stoning the Portuguese, who retaliated with crossbow fire that left one of the herders dead.

Arrival and information

The N2 bypasses Mossel Bay and, of the **buses**, only the *Hopper* and *Baz* come right into town. *Baz* drops off at *Mossel Bay Backpackers* and *Santos Express*; the *Hopper* will take you to any accommodation in the town. The large **intercity buses** all stop at Shell Voorbaai Service Station, 7km from the centre, at the junction of the national highway and the road into town. The town itself is small enough to negotiate on foot, but should you need transport contact *Rendezvous Cape* (☎0444/91 3781 or 082/891 8454), which runs a **taxi** service.

The busy **tourist information bureau** (Mon–Fri 9am–5pm, Sat 9am–1pm; ☎0444/91 2202, fax 3077), bang in the centre, on the corner of Church and Market streets, has shelves of brochures about Mossel Bay and the rest of the Garden Route. The staff can provide a small but very adequate **map** of the town.

Accommodation

Mossel Bay has a broad range of **accommodation**, including a number of reasonable B&Bs which can be booked through the tourist information bureau (see above).

Allemans Dorpshuis, 94 Montagu St (☎0444/3621). Comfortable B&B in a nineteenth-century house with Victorian furnishings on a hill three blocks from the tourist bureau. ②.

De Bakke, George Rd (☎0444/91 2915). Rock-bottom cheap camping at the municipal site just back from the beach, with sea views and self-catering chalets. ①–②.

Huijs te Marquette, 1 Marsh St (☎ & fax 0444/91 3182). Pleasant, if rather fussily furnished B&B close to the Point, with no views but a lovely courtyard ideal for sundowners. ③.

Mossel Bay Backpackers, 1 Marsh St (☎ & fax 0444/91 3182). Cheapest dorms and doubles in town, in a small suburban house attached to a guesthouse conveniently located between the centre and the Point. ①.

Mossel Bay Guest House, 61 Bruns Rd (☎0444/91 2000, fax 4900). Comfortable rooms in a suburban home. ③.

Old Post Office Tree Guest House, Bartholomeu Dias Museum Complex, Market St (☎0444/91 3738, fax 91 3104). Opposite the tourist bureau and close to Santos Beach and the museums, in an old Cape Dutch manor house, this stylish guesthouse is by far the best place in town, with breakfast served at the *Gannet*, Mossel Bay's nicest restaurant. ④–⑤.

Point Caravan Park, Bland St (☎0444/3501). Along the rocky Point, this is not as nice for swimming, but it's close to the start of the St Blaize hiking trail. ③.

Santos Express (☎0444/91 1995). This stationary train on Santos Beach, just metres from the surf, has the best location in town, and offers train compartments with up to three sharing. ①.

Santos Protea Hotel, Santos Rd (☎0444/7103, fax 91 1945). Priciest option in town, in a great location overlooking the beach, but with a rate that doesn't include breakfast. ④.

The Town

It's fitting that Mossel Bay's main urban attraction is its **Bartholomeu Dias Museum Complex**, housed in a collection of historic buildings well integrated into the small town centre. The buildings are all within a couple of minutes' walk of each other and the tourist bureau, and are pleasantly diverting. The highlight is the **Maritime Museum** (Mon–Fri 9am–4.45pm, Sat & Sun 10am–4pm), a spiral gallery with displays on the history of Portuguese, Dutch and British seafaring, arranged around a full-size replica of Dias' original caravel (small boarding fee payable at reception). The ship was built in Portugal and sailed from Lisbon to Mossel Bay in 1987 to celebrate the 500th anniversary of Dias' historic journey. You can't fail to be awed by the idea of the original mariners setting out on the high seas into *terra incognita* on such a small vessel. More astonishingly, the crew were accommodated above deck with only a sailcloth for protection against the elements.

The one Mossel Bay attraction that most South Africans have heard of is the **Post Office Tree**, which grows just outside the Maritime Museum. Sixteenth-century mariners used to leave messages for passing ships in an old boot under a milkwood tree somewhere around here and the plaque claims that "this may well" be the same tree. You can post mail here in a large, boot-shaped letterbox and have it stamped with a special postmark.

Of the remaining exhibitions, the **Shell Museum and Aquarium** (Mon–Fri 9am–4.45pm, Sat 10am–1pm, Sun 2–5pm; entry by donation), next to the Post Office Tree, is the only one worth taking time to visit. This is your chance to see some of the beautiful shells found off the South African coast, as well as specimens from around the world. Displays of living shellfish, including cowries with their inhabitants still at home, are quite fascinating.

A short walk north down the hill from the Maritime Museum gets you to **Santos Beach**, the main town strand, and the only north-facing beach in South Africa – which gives it exceptionally long sunny afternoons. Adjacent to the small town harbour, the beach provides some of the finest swimming along the Garden Route, with uncharacteristically gentle surf, small waves and a perfect depth for practising your crawl.

East of the harbour, the coast bulges south towards the **Point**, which has a couple of franchised restaurants and a popular bar/restaurant (see "Eating and drinking") with a deck at the ocean's edge, from which you may see dolphins cruising past, as well as a surreal 500-metre rocky channel known as the **Aquarium**, which is extensively used as a natural tidal pool.

Dives, shark encounters and hikes

Given that the seals of **Seal Island**, about 10km northwest of Santos Beach, are a highly popular delicacy among **great white sharks**, you'd be forgiven for wondering why **scuba diving** remains so popular off Mossel Bay, but it does. In 1990, the unfortunate Monique Price became the first fully kitted scuba diver to fall victim to a great white attack just off the island, and divers are warned to avoid its immediate environs. There are, however, several rewarding diving and snorkelling spots around Mossel Bay, and full facilities, including certification courses and one-off dives, are available from *Mossel Bay Divers* (☎ & fax 0444/91 1441), at *Santos Protea Hotel*, Santos Rd. These aren't tropical seas, so don't expect clear warm waters, but you do stand a good chance of seeing octopus, squid and sea stars.

If you want to see sharks face to face, there are a couple of operators taking **shark cage dives**, much to the disquiet of many Mossel Bay burghers, who are unhappy about great whites being baited so close to swimming beaches and dive sites; they refer queries to Gansbaai (see p.177), a comfortable distance away, where at least five operators churn the water fighting it out for clients.

Cruises around Seal Island to see the jackass penguin and seal colonies can be taken on the *Romonza* (☎ & fax 0444/3101) or the *Orpa* (☎083/265 9732) – medium-sized yachts which launch from the yacht marina in the harbour. You can stay ashore and still see the coast on the **St Blaize Hiking Trail**, an easy-going fifteen-kilometre walk (roughly 4hr each way) along the southern shore of Mossel Bay. The route starts from Bat's Cave, just below the lighthouse at the Point, and heads west as far as Dana Bay, taking in magnificent coastal views of cliffs, rocks, bays and coves. A **map** is available from the tourist information bureau (see "Arrival and information").

Eating and drinking

As far as **eating** is concerned, you'll find all the usual franchised joints, including *Saddles*, which is at the Point and dishes up predictable steaks and burgers. For **light meals** in town, *Annie's Kitchen*, on Church Street, serves sandwiches and a cheap hot lunch, while *Café Baruch*, Liberty Centre, Bland St, is good for toasted sandwiches and salads and does decent coffee. For **takeaways**, *Snoekies*, Powrie St, is has the best fried fish and chips. Mossel Bay's lively **drinking** spot is *Tidals Waterfront Tavern & Pub*, which buzzes until the early hours on Fridays and Saturdays in a stunning seaside location overlooking cliffs and the open sea.

For more substantial **meals**, the *Gannet* on Market Street serves moderately priced seafood dishes with considerable flair, enjoyed all the better in the stylish garden with glimpses across the dusk-washed harbour.

George

There's little reason to visit **GEORGE**, 66km northeast of Mossel Bay, unless you're starting or finishing a trip on the *Outeniqua Choo Tjoe*. This large inland working town, a five-kilometre detour off the N2, hasn't even a beach to recommend it, and all that's left of the forests and quaint character that was turned on by Anthony Trollop, when he visited in 1877 and was moved to describe it as the "prettiest village on the face of the earth", are some historic buildings, of which the **St George Cathedral**, consecrated in 1850, is the most notable. Other than that, the **George Museum** (Mon–Fri 9am–4.30pm, Sat 9am–12.30pm; donation) is worth half an hour, if only to visit the **PW Botha collection**. Once your horror subsides at the blind adulation for one of the most ruthless proponents of apartheid, you can adjust your mind-set for a brief insight into the psychosis that gripped South Africa's white Nationalists for half a century. Botha (see box), the former parliamentary representative for George, was the last of South Africa's apartheid hardliners and the immediate predecessor of FW De Klerk, who negotiated the demise of minority rule.

Arrival and information

Arriving in George by **air**, you'll land at the small George Airport, 10km west of town on the N2. There's no public transport from here into town; most tourists flying in pick up a car from one of the three rental companies here and push off down the Garden

THE IMPERIAL PRESIDENCY OF PW BOTHA

Pieter Willem Botha is credited with setting up an autocratic "Imperial Presidency" in South Africa, but in retrospect he was actually the King Canute of apartheid, closing his eyes to the incoming tide of democracy and believing that by wagging his finger (his favoured gesture of intimidation) he could turn it back.

A National Party hack from the age of 20, Botha worked his way up through the ranks, getting elected an MP in 1948 when the first apartheid government took power. He became leader of the **National Party** in the **Cape Province** and was promoted through various cabinet posts until he became **Minister of Defence**, a position he used to edge out Prime Minister John Vorster in 1978. Botha immediately set about modernizing apartheid, modifying his own role from that of a British-style prime minister answerable to parliament and making himself an executive president who took vital decisions in the secrecy of a President's Council heavily weighted with army top brass.

Informed by the army that the battle to preserve the apartheid status quo was unwinnable purely by the use of force, Botha embarked on his **Total Strategy**, which involved reforms to peripheral aspects of apartheid and the fostering of a black middle class as a buffer against the ANC, while pumping vast sums of money into building an enormous military that crossed South Africa's borders to bully or crush **neighbouring countries** into submission. South African refugees in Botswana and Zimbabwe were bombed, Angola was invaded and arms were run to rebels in Mozambique and the country reduced to rubble – a policy which has returned to haunt South Africa with those same weapons now returning across the border and into the hands of criminals. Inside the country, security forces enjoyed a free hand to murder, maim and torture **opponents of apartheid** on a scale which only fully emerged in 1996 and 1997, under the investigations of the Truth and Reconciliation Commission.

Botha's intransigence led to his greatest blunder in 1985, when he responded to international calls for change by hinting that he would announce significant reforms at his party congress that would irreversibly jettison apartheid. This so-called **Rubicon speech** was a disaster, as Botha proved to have insufficient steel to swim against the current of white right-wing thinking. The speech ruled out significant concessions to black South Africans. The immediate result was a flight of capital from the country and intensified sanctions. Perhaps worst of all for the apartheid regime, the Chase Manhattan Bank refused to roll over its massive loan to South Africa, leaving the country an uncreditworthy pariah.

Botha blustered and wagged his finger at the opposition through the late 1980s, while his bloated military sucked the state coffers dry. Even National Party stalwarts realized that his policies were leading to ruin, and in 1989, when he suffered a stroke, the party was quick to replace him with FW de Klerk, who announced the reforms the world had expected from Botha's Rubicon speech.

Botha lives out his retirement near George, where, it is reported, he still harbours deep resentments against his National Party colleagues, whom he believes betrayed him. He has declined to apologize for any of the actions taken under his presidency to bolster apartheid.

Route. By train, scheduled *Spoornet* and *Outeniqua Choo Tjoe* services arrive at George Station (℡0441/73 8288), at the southeast end of Market and Hibernia streets. *Intercape*, *Translux* and *Greyhound* **intercity buses** pull in at St Mark's Square in a dubious part of town – if you're arriving here at night, arrange to be picked up. Of the **backpacker buses**, *Baz* drops off at the backpackers' hostel and the *Hopper* at any of the town accommodation. **Minibus taxis**, useful mainly for shuttles to and from Oudtshoorn, arrive in Cradock Street.

George's very helpful **tourist information bureau**, 124 York St (Mon–Fri 8am–4.30pm, Sat 9am–noon; ℡0441/863 9295), can provide town maps and help with accommodation bookings.

Accommodation

Places to stay are plentiful. *George Tourist Resort*, York St (☎0441/74 5205, fax 74 4255), offers camping (①) and chalets (②) set in pleasant gardens, with a swimming pool, a shop and laundry facilities. Camping is also possible at *George Backpackers' Hostel*, York St (☎0441/74 7807; ①), 1km from the town centre, with dorms and doubles in an annexe in the garden. Pick of the budget **B&Bs** is *Number 10 Caledon Street* (☎0441/73 4983; ③), a spotless guesthouse in a quiet street around the corner from the museum, featuring balconies with mountain views and a garden to relax in. One rung up, and nicer than the town's hotels, *Bramble Lodge* (☎0441/70 8541, fax 70 8542; ⑤; ask about winter discounts), is on a farm about 5km from the airport, and offers a free shuttle service. Guests stay in six luxurious rooms with views onto the Outeniqua Mountains and the farm's lake. *Bramble Lodge* is also renowned for its excellent **dinners**, available to non-residents. If you're set on staying in a hotel, head for the *George III*, King George Drive (☎0441/74 7659, fax 74 7664; ⑤), slightly out of the centre in a quiet setting, offering comfortable rooms, each with their own verandah.

Eating and drinking

For **meals** on a budget, the *Pancake Tearoom* in George Arcade serves cheap lunches, including boerewors roll, meat and veg or their speciality – filled pancakes. Traditional Afrikaner *boerekos* is served at the good-value *De Oude Werf*, 53 York St. The station restaurant does cheap pub lunches – handy if you're on the midday *Outeniqua Choo Tjoe*. The rather formal but mid-priced *Copper Pot* (☎0441/74 3191), in the Multi Centre on the corner of Market and Meade streets, is George's best restaurant, and specializes in seafood. For cheaper food, head next door to its sister bistro, the *Wine Barrel* (☎0441/73 4370).

Victoria Bay and Wilderness

Some 9km south of George and 3km off the N2 is **VICTORIA BAY**, a small sandy beach wedged into a cove between cliffs. One of the genuine gems of the Garden Route, it packs out to the brim during the December holidays with day-trippers, and despite its benign aspect of a grassy sunbathing area, safe swimming and a tidal pool, it rates as one of the top **surfing** spots in South Africa. Best of all, because of the cliffs there's only a single row of houses along the beachfront, with two of the most dreamily positioned guesthouses along the coast.

There's no public **transport** to Victoria Bay, although a lot of people hitch the few kilometres from the N2. The only place to buy **food** is from a small beachside kiosk selling light refreshments and unexciting snacks. **Accommodation** is in somewhat better supply – the cheapest option being *Victoria Bay Caravan Park*, on the left as you approach the beach (☎0441/74 4040 or 71 2161; ①), which has magnificently located campsites on the clifftop overlooking the beach. Budget rooms are available at *Sea Breeze Holiday Resort* (☎0441/71 2679, fax 71 2971; ②), along the main road into the settlement. Here you can rent a variety of large, modern double-storey holiday cabanas, sleeping from four to six people. The cabanas have no sea views, but it's an easy stroll to the beach. Just metres from the sea, *The Waves*, Victoria Bay Rd (☎ & fax 0441/71 1785; ⑤, ask about winter discounts), offers two front rooms in a high-ceilinged period house in an unbeatable location. A little further along the same road, *Land's End Guest House* (☎0441/71 3168, fax 75 0068; ④) has two wonderful self-catering studio apartments sleeping two with views out to sea from the bed, and also offers similarly priced B&B accommodation.

Wilderness and around

East of Victoria Bay, across the Kaaimans River, the beach at **WILDERNESS** is so close to the N2 that you can pull over for a quick dip and barely interrupt your journey. Unfortunately this is also the worst thing about the place, as it is sliced up by the national road, leaving the village and lakes stranded inland. Tradition has it that Wilderness village earned its name after a young man called Van den Berg bought the property in 1830 for £183 as a blind lot at a Cape Town auction. When he got engaged, his fiancée insisted that their first year of marriage should be spent out of town in the wilderness, so he romantically (or perhaps opportunistically) named his property Wilderness and built a hut on it.

If the hut's still there, you'll struggle to find it among the sprawl of retirement homes, holiday houses and 2500 beds for rent in the area. Take your life in your hands and cross the N2 to get to the **beach**, which is renowned for its long stretch of sand, backed by tall dunes, rudely blighted by holiday houses that compete to outdo each other. Once in the water, stay close to the shoreline: this part of the coast is notorious for its unpredictable currents.

The tiny **village centre**, on the north side of the N2, has a filling station, a few shops and an excellent **tourist information bureau** in Leila's Lane (Mon–Fri 8.30am–12.30pm & 2–5pm, Sat 9am–12.30pm; ☎0441/877 0045). One of the cheapest **places to stay** is *Fairy Knowe Backpackers* (☎082/880 9589, fax 0441/877 1403; ①), a characterful nineteenth-century coaching inn, beautifully set in woodlands near the Touws River, and offering small dorms and a double room. This is the only backpackers' lodge in the country with its **own train station**, a fact which absolutely begs that you arrive here on the *Outeniqua Choo Tjoe* (ask ahead to be let off here, as the stop is unscheduled). Meals are available on request and mountain bikes can be rented. Also well away from the sea, *Island Lake Holiday Resort* (☎ & fax 0441/877 1194; ①), Lakes Rd, 2km from the Hoekwil/Island Lake turn-off on the N2, has camping and self-catering bungalows (①) which sleep four on one of the quietest and prettiest spots on the lakes. Good swimming and more budget accommodation are to be had at *Trails and Holiday Resort* (☎04455/31914, fax 32006; ①) on Swartvlei Lake, with camping, furnished caravans (bring your own bedding and towels) and timber chalets (①). For greater comfort, head for *Fairy Knowe* (☎0441/877 1100, fax 877 0364), on Dumbleton Road (follow the signposts from the N2), an old-fashioned hotel away from the beach, with the best rooms facing onto the Touws River (④) and cheaper garden-facing rooms (③). The best views in Wilderness are from the *Mes-Amis Homestead*, Buxton Close (☎ & fax 0441/877 1928; ④), which has good double rooms, each with a terrace and sliding doors looking out to sea.

The best place to **eat** is in the village centre at *Tom's Tavern* (☎0441/877 0353), which serves up a range of steaks, pizzas, pasta and seafood of variable quality.

Wilderness National Park

Stretching east from Wilderness village is the **Wilderness National Park** (reception daily Feb–Nov 8am–1pm & 2–5pm; Dec & Jan 7am–8pm; ☎0441/877 1197, fax 877 0111; booking through National Parks Board ☎012/343 1991 or 021/22 2810, fax 012/343 0905 or 021/24 6211; entry fee), the least aptly named national park in South Africa, as it never feels very far from the rumbling N2. Although the park takes in beach frontage, it's the **forests** you should come for; the 16km of inland waterways and the variety of habitats that include coastal and montane fynbos, evergreen forests and wetlands which attract 250 species of **birds** and many more holidaymakers. There are several waymarked **trails** lasting from one to four hours, all well worth doing to get a feeling of the indigenous vegetation and escape the N2 and holiday homes – the reception issues trail maps. You can also rent **canoes** from reception and take to the water.

There are two **rest camps**, both on the west side of the park and clearly signposted off the N2. *Ebb and Flow*, right on the river, is cheap, old, away from the hustle and has two-person huts (②), some with communal ablutions. *Wilderness Restcamp* offers more modern accommodation in spacious log cabins on stilts (④) and cottages, both sleeping four, which makes poor value if there are only two of you. If, on the other hand, you pitch up without a booking you can get them at a per-person rate (②) which is very reasonable. Cheaper chalavans (②) sleeping up to six have shared ablution facilities. **Camping** (①) at both rest camps is far and away the best budget option. There is a **shop** selling milk, bread and basic groceries at reception.

Sedgefield and the Goukamma Reserve

The drive between Wilderness and Sedgefield gives glimpses on your left of dark-coloured lakes which eventually surge out to sea, 21km later, through a lagoon at **SEDGEFIELD**, a lacklustre holiday village with a safe swimming **beach** that makes a refreshing pit stop. Sedgefield's unpromising appearance of shops, restaurants and B&Bs lining the highway belies an undeveloped beachfront, cut through by a wide lagoon, a few kilometres off the road. The beach is especially beautiful because all the houses are set back behind the sand dunes.

Despite this forest of holiday homes, there is little **accommodation** for casual visitors away from the highway. The one exception is *Landfall Resort* (☎04455/6573), a low-key and old-fashioned place which allows camping (①) and rents out on-site caravans (①) with attached kitchens, toilets and showers. The resort also rents out more spacious two-bedroom cottages (②) which sleep six.

Sedgefield provides a good base from which to explore **Goukamma Nature and Marine Reserve** and the western extent of **Groenvlei**, a freshwater lake that falls within it. An unassuming sanctuary of around 220 square kilometres, Goukamma ranges west as far as the small seaside resort of Buffels Bay to absorb 14km of beach frontage, some of the highest vegetated dunes in the country and walking country covered with coastal fynbos and dense thickets of milkwood, yellowwood and candlewood trees.

The area has long been popular with anglers, who come to catch the six **fish** species that inhabit Groenvlei. Away from the water you stand a small chance of spotting one of the area's **mammals**, including bushbuck, grysbok, mongoose, vervet monkeys, caracals and otters. Because of the diversity of coastal and wetland habitats, this is also good avifauna territory, with over 220 different kinds of **birds** recorded, including fish eagles, Knysna louries, kingfishers, and very rare African black oystercatchers. Off the shore, southern right **whales** often make an appearance during their August to December breeding season and bottlenose and common **dolphins** can show up at any time of year.

Apart from angling and bird-watching, the Goukamma offers a number of self-guided **activities**, including safe **swimming** in Groenvlei or **canoeing** – you can rent craft at the *Lake Pleasant Holiday Resort* (see overleaf). There are several day-long hiking **trails** that enable you to explore different habitats – if you plan on hiking you should pick up the Cape Nature Conservation map from the *Lake Pleasant Hotel*. A beach walk, which takes around four hours one way, traverses the full 14km of crumbly cliffs and sands between the Platbank car park on the western side and the Rowwehoek one at the other. A slightly longer trek across the dunes also takes you from one end of the reserve to the other, but via an inland route. A shorter circular walk starts at the reserve office and goes through a milkwood forest.

Practicalities

Two roads off the N2 provide **access** to the Goukamma Reserve. At the westernmost side, a dirt road that runs down to Platbank beach takes you past the tiny settlement of **Lake**

Pleasant on the south bank of Groenvlei, which consists of little more than a hotel and holiday resort. On the eastern side, access is via the Buffels Bay road, along which the Goukamma office is reached about halfway. There are no public roads within the reserve.

Accommodation in the Goukamma Nature Reserve should be booked well in advance through the Manager, Goukamma Nature and Marine Reserve, PO Box 331, Knysna 6570 (☎ & fax 0445/83 0042). The choice is limited to a basic bushcamp on the southern shore of the lake, reached by a road past the hotel turn-off; and on the Buffels Bay side to a thatched rondavel overlooking the Goukamma River. At **Lake Pleasant**, on the western edge of the reserve, you have the choice of the *Lake Pleasant Hotel* (☎0445/31313, fax 32040; email: lake.pleasant@pixie.co.za; ③–④), which has country-style public spaces, a lovely garden and simple rooms which look onto thick reed-beds around the lake, disturbed by the constant rumble of the N2; or the cheaper anglers- and family-oriented *Lake Pleasant Holiday Resort* (☎ & fax 0445/31985; ①), which has shady campsites, self-catering chalets, a store selling basics and and an exceptionally well-stocked anglers' shop. The resort also rents out mountain bikes, rowing boats and canoes. For **light meals**, the *Swan Pub* at the *Lake Pleasant* serves reasonably priced pub lunches.

Another possibility is to stay at **Buffels Bay**, 10km down a turn-off that is 13km east of Sedgefield along the N2. This haphazard little development at the east of the reserve has a few places to stay, the cheapest being the *Buffels Bay Caravan Park* at the Point (☎0445/83 0045; ①), and one of the best being the spacious, fully equipped *Buffalo Bay Apartments*, 160 Walker Drive (☎0445/83 0218; ④), overlooking the bay.

Knysna and around

South Africa's 1990s tourist boom has rudely shaken **KNYSNA** (pronounced "Nizena") from its gentle backwoods drowse, which for decades made this the hippie and craftwork capital and quiet retirement village of the country. The town, 102km east of Mossel Bay, now stands as the undisputed hub of the Garden Route despite having no beaches of its own, a shortcoming it makes up for through its hilly setting around the **lagoon**, a broad body of water that fills and drains each day with the tides. The lagoon's narrow mouth is guarded by the **Heads**, a pair of steep rocky promontories, the western side being a private nature reserve and the eastern one an exclusive residential area soaring above the Indian Ocean from dramatic cliffs.

Knysna's distinctive atmosphere derives from its small historic core of Georgian and Victorian buildings, which gives it a character absent from most of the Garden Route holiday towns. Coffee shops, craft galleries, street traders and a modest nightlife add to the attractions, and you may find yourself tempted to stay longer than just one night. That the town has outgrown itself is evident from the cars and tour buses which, especially in December and January, clog Main Street, the constricted artery that merges with the N2 as it toddles into town.

Some history

At the beginning of the nineteenth century, the only white settlements outside Cape Town were a handful of villages that would have considered themselves lucky to have even one horse. Knysna, an undeveloped backwater hidden in the forest, was no exception. The name comes from a Khoi word which means "hard to reach", and this remained its defining character well into the twentieth century. One important figure was not deterred by the distance – **George Rex**, a colourful colonial administrator, who had placed himself beyond the pale of decent colonial society by taking on a coloured mistress. Shunned by his peers in Britain, he headed for Knysna at the turn of the nineteenth century in the hope of making a killing shipping out hardwood from the Knysna Lagoon.

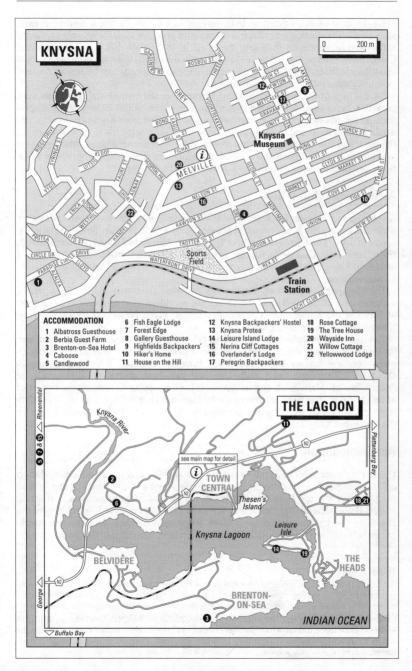

KNYSNA

0   200 m

BADOUX'S RD
BOSBOU ST
THESEN
HILL ST
NEWTON ST
METCALFE ST
GRAHAM ST
UNITY ST
GREY
VOORTREKKER
BOND ST
HILL ST
FICHAT
MELVILLE
Knysna Museum
SPRING ST
CHURCH ST
PITT ST
CLYDE ST
MARKET ST
COVE ST
TIDE ST
STRAND ST
NELSON ST
RAWSON ST
HEDGE ST
GORDON ST
UNION ST
NEW ST
RIDGE DRIVE
SYRINGA ST
VYGIE
UITSIG
KLOOF
FAURE ST
SHORT
AGNAR ST
ERICA
RIDGE
WESTHILL
HANDEL ST
PROTEA
LLOYD ST
CIRCLE DR
CIRCLE DRIVE
PARADISE
LLOYD
ALFALFA
TROTTER ST
WATERFRONT DRIVE
Sports Field
REX ST
Train Station
YACHT CLUB RD

ACCOMMODATION

1 Albatross Guesthouse	**6** Fish Eagle Lodge	**12** Knysna Backpackers' Hostel	**18** Rose Cottage
2 Berbia Guest Farm	**7** Forest Edge	**13** Knysna Protea	**19** The Tree House
3 Brenton-on-Sea Hotel	**8** Gallery Guesthouse	**14** Leisure Island Lodge	**20** Wayside Inn
4 Caboose	**9** Highfields Backpackers'	**15** Nerina Cliff Cottages	**21** Willow Cottage
5 Candlewood	**10** Hiker's Home	**16** Overlander's Lodge	**22** Yellowwood Lodge
	11 House on the Hill	**17** Peregrin Backpackers	

THE LAGOON

Rheenendal
Knysna River
5 7 & 15
see main map for detail
TOWN CENTRAL
Thesen's Island
Pletenberg Bay
BELVIDÈRE
George
Knysna Lagoon
Leisure Isle
THE HEADS
BRENTON-ON-SEA
INDIAN OCEAN
Buffalo Bay

By the time of Rex's death in 1839, Knysna had become a major **timber centre**, attracting white woodcutters who felled trees with primitive tools for miserly payments, and looked set eventually to destroy the forest. In 1872 Prince Alfred, on his visit to the Cape, contributed to this wanton destruction when he made a detour here to come and shoot an elephant. The forest only narrowly escaped devastation by far-sighted and effective conservation policies introduced in the 1880s.

By the turn of the twentieth century, Knysna was still remote and its forests were inhabited by isolated and inbred communities made up of the impoverished descendants of the woodcutters. As late as 1914, if you travelled from Knysna to George you would have to open and close 58 gates along the 75-kilometre track. Fifteen years on, the passes in the region proved too much for George Bernard Shaw, who did some impromptu off-road driving and crashed into a bush, forcing Mrs Shaw to spend a couple of weeks in bed at Knysna's *Royal Hotel* with a broken leg.

Arrival and information

Greyhound and *Translux* **intercity buses** drop passengers off at Bern's Service Station, while *Intercape* pulls in at Fernwood Service Station, both in Main Street, right in the centre of town. The **Outeniqua Choo Tjoe**, South Africa's last scheduled mixed steam **train**, runs from George to Knysna twice daily (Mon–Sat; ☎0445/21361), where it arrives at Knysna Station. The *Baz* and *Hopper* buses will pull into any of the town accommodation.

For **transport** around town, *Knysna Tuk-Tuk Mini Tours* (☎0445/82 5878) operates a shuttle service that will meet the *Choo Tjoe*, provide airport transfers from George, and trips to the Knysna Forest and Cango Caves. *Rikkis* (☎0445/82 650) taxis serve Knysna and the surrounding areas.

Knysna's **tourist information bureau** (Mon–Fri 8.30am–6pm, Sat 9am–3pm, Sun 9am–1pm; ☎0445/21610, fax 21646), on the corner of Main and Gray streets, provides maps and information about the town. Privately operated **information kiosks** (Mon–Fri 8.30am–5pm, Sat 8.30am–1pm, Sun 9am–1pm; ☎0445/82 5878) on Pledge Square, just off Main Road, and in Woodmill Lane Shopping Centre, on the corner of Main and Long streets, are also very useful sources of information and can take bookings for a whole range of activities, including ferry cruises on the lagoon and tickets for the *Outeniqua Choo Tjoe*.

Accommodation

Housed in the same office as the tourist information bureau is a busy **accommodation** office, whose staff are extremely knowledgeable about all the options in and around town and can arrange bookings. Knysna caters well for backpackers, but is short on budget B&Bs. The best places to stay are away from the main road, with views of the Heads or the lagoon. Out of town there are some excellent and very reasonably priced self-catering cottages right in the forest, where you can get well away from the town buzz.

Town centre
Albatross Guest House, corner of Albatross Rd and Paradise Circle (☎ & fax 0445/24498). En-suite cottage-style rooms leading onto a garden with a swimming pool, one block up from the lagoon and main road in a quiet wooded area. For scuba divers an added plus is the resident dive master. ③.

Caboose, corner of Gray and Trotter streets (☎0445/82 5850, fax 82 5224). Dead-cheap sleepers in spotless but cramped train-style compartments – part of a huge modern timber complex with pleasant public spaces, including a swimming pool and sun deck. Have no illusions, though – even though you have your own shower, you'll be using it directly over the toilet. ②.

Gallery Guest House, 10 Hill St (☎0445/22510). Gracious double-storey colonial house within easy walking distance of town, with arty decor and balcony views across the the the lagoon to the Heads. ③.

Highfields Backpackers' Guest House, 2 Graham St (☎0445/82 6266). Best of the backpackers' lodges, with stylish decor, a friendly atmosphere, swimming pool and sun deck. There's no bar, which makes this a good bet if you're after some peace and quiet. Reasonably priced excursions can be arranged to the Heads, the *Mitchell's Brewery* and Brenton. ①.

Hikers' Home, 17 Tide St (☎0445/24362). Clean and sociable backpackers' lodge that attracts travellers keen on mellowing out in the garden and partying, with TV, bar and mountain-bike rental. Dorms and doubles. ①.

Knysna Backpackers' Hostel, 42 Queen St (☎0445/22554). Claims to being the only backpackers' lodge with a bit of a lagoon view, and this is indeed its principal recommendation.

Knysna Protea Hotel, 51 Main St (☎0445/22127, fax 23568). Smart hotel offering luxury rooms and cheaper ones without air conditioning along the busy main street. ③–④.

Overlander's Lodge, 11 Nelson St (☎0445/82 5920). Popular backpackers' lodge which achieves a delicate balance between being organized and relaxed. Camping is available, and there are clean 24-bed dorms and double rooms inside the house, and an outside bar. ①.

Peregrin Backpackers, 37 Queen St (☎0445/23647). Although pretty standard, this lodge with camping, six-bed dorms as well as doubles, generates consistently positive feedback. ①.

Wayside Inn, Pledge Square (☎ & fax 0445/82 6011). Clean and smart place done out with white linen on black wrought-iron bedsteads and sisal matting. Right in the centre, it makes a pleasing night stop, but without public spaces is not somewhere to spend your holiday. Continental breakfast is served in your room on a wicker tray. ⑤.

Yellowwood Lodge, corner of Handel and Short streets (☎0445/82 5906, fax 24230). Clean, comfortable rooms in a light and airy, non-smoking, nineteenth-century guesthouse with period furniture, one street back from the main road. May–Sept discounts. ④–⑤.

Eastern suburbs

House on the Hill, 60 Milkwood Drive (☎0445/21326). Two B&B rooms in a friendly and cheap suburban house with good views and repro furniture, well away from the action. ②.

Leisure Isle Lodge, 87 Bayswater Drive, Leisure Isle (☎0445/23923). Knysna's top guesthouse, right on the edge of the lagoon at a good swimming spot, exudes a quiet and restful atmosphere. Heated outdoor pool, spacious rooms, under-carpet heating. Choice of back rooms or more expensive lagoon-facing units. ④–⑥.

Rose Cottage, 34 Wilson St (☎0445/22824; email: mmfs@pixie.co.sa). Small but immaculate en-suite room ideal for overnighting, and large, pleasant and good-value self-catering cottage good for two adults and a child, with patio, use of swimming pool and garden. ②.

The Tree House, 37 Cearn Drive, Leisure Isle (☎ & fax 0445/82 6326). Lovely self-catering cottage on the lagoon near an excellent swimming spot with two bedrooms, two bathrooms, TV, video and large sun deck screened by a huge tree. ③.

Willow Cottage, 34a Wilson St (☎0445/82 6095 or 23111). Highly recommended double-storey self-catering cottage overlooking a beautiful garden with clear views of the lagoon from the balcony. ②.

West of town

Berbia Guest Farm, Welbedacht Rd, off the N2 towards George (☎0445/82 5429). Four en-suite rooms, attractively furnished in warm colours, on a farm along a winding road 6km from Knysna. All rooms lead onto a swimming pool, from which you can see the lagoon and Heads in the distance. No self-catering facilities, apart from *braai* stands. ③.

Fish Eagle Lodge, off Welbedacht Rd (☎ & fax 0445/82 5431). Swiss-style self-catering chalets that come with breakfast, phones, TV and views of the lagoon. April–Aug discounts. ③–④.

The beaches and the forest

Brenton-on-Sea Hotel, Brenton beachfront (☎ & fax 0445/81 0081). The only seaside hotel in the area, overlooking the long curve of Brenton beach which swings round to Buffalo Bay. Pretty ordinary motel-style rooms make it a place to stay for the location rather than style. May–Nov discounts.

Self-catering chalets sleeping six are only worth considering if there are four or more of you. B&B rooms are also available. ⑤.

Candlewood and Nerina Cliffs Cottages, Rheenendal (☎0445/4624, fax 4611). Wonderful place for several nights' stay, 20min drive from Knysna in a choice of two cottages on a scenic citrus farm. *Candlewood* (③) sleeps six in an old-fashioned holiday chalet with a fabulous garden. Nearby *Nerina Cliffs Cottage* (②) is about as remote as you'll find on the Garden Route, along a rough farm road which brings you to a timber house perched on the edge of cliffs overlooking the real Knysna Forest, in a part wild enough to have the occasional leopard breezing through the area. A fantastic deck jettying out over the chasm is big enough to sleep out on in summer. There's no electricity and the fridge, heater, lights, hot water and cooker all run off gas. You can canoe and swim on the farm lake.

Forest Edge Cottages, Rheenendal (☎0445/4704, fax 4773). Ideal if you want to be close to the forest itself, these traditional tin-roofed cottages have verandahs built in the local vernacular style. The self-contained, fully equipped and serviced two-bedroom cottages sleep four. Forest walks and cycling trails start from the cottage and you can rent mountain bikes. ②.

The Town and around

Knysna wraps around the **lagoon**, with its oldest part – the town centre – on the northern side, while along the eastern shore the exclusive suburbs include **Leisure Isle**, which is connected to the shore by a narrow causeway, and the **Heads**, a network of winding roads curling their way up to the heights overlooking the craggy coast and a wild Indian Ocean.

Main Street is the hub of the city centre, and its principal attraction is the collection of craft and woodwork shops that line up along the road. The **Knysna Museum** (Mon–Fri 9.30am–1pm & 2–4.30pm, Sat 9.30am–1pm; small entry fee), on the corner of Queen and Main streets, contains a complex of minor exhibits that can comfortably occupy an undemanding half-hour; attractions here include South Africa's first **Angling Museum**, an extensive collection of antique nets and rods, which traces the changing technology of the activity. Look out for the preserved coelacanth, one of several specimens in the country of a fish that was long thought to have been extinct until one turned up in a fishing net in 1939 (see p.277).

A short way from the centre in the industrial area, **Mitchell's Brewery**, Arend Rd (☎0445/24685), off George Rex Drive via Vigilance and Sandpiper roads, offers thirty-minute tours (Mon–Fri 10.30am), where for next to nothing you get to sample their four kinds of beer, including Foresters Draught, a Pilsner-type lager, and Bosun's Bitter, an ale modelled on Yorkshire bitter. The brewery is too far to reach on foot; you're best off taking a Rikki if you don't have your own transport, or staying in town and sampling the beers at one of the pubs.

The main reason to make for **Leisure Isle** is for the excellent swimming it offers in the lagoon and the views out to sea through the gap between the Heads. The best bathing spots are along the southern shore of the island, particularly the western section along Bayswater Drive; but check a tide table, as the swimming is only good around high tide (and then only in summer).

Continuing south along George Rex Drive gets you to the web of roads that wind up through the small suburban areas of the Heads and Coney Glen to the top of the **eastern Head**, from which you get fantastic views out to sea.

The beaches

Don't come to Knysna for a beach holiday: the closest sands are 20km away, around the western edge of the lagoon at **Brenton-on-Sea**. On the shores of the beautifully sandy Buffels Bay, this is is a tiny settlement with an unexceptional hotel situated on a quite exceptional beach. A few kilometres inland is the quaint and very upmarket settlement of **Belvidere**, through which visitors are prohibited from driving (but you can walk around). Although **Buffels Bay** (see p.182), the next beach to the west, is along the same continuous stretch of sand as Brenton-on-Sea, there's no direct route there; you have to return to the N2 and proceed from there. In the opposite direction from Knysna things are little better, with the closest patch of sand lying to the east at **Noetzie**, a town known more for its eccentric holiday homes built to look like castles than for its seaside.

Eating, drinking and nightlife

Knysna has a livelier atmosphere than you might expect from a Garden Route town, buzzing at **night** to the strains of pretty good music at *Tin Roof Blues*. As far as **food** goes, oysters are an obvious choice, with the farm here, but you'll also find good restaurants catering to other palates and one or two excellent **coffee shops** if you need a caffeine shot on your way through town.

The Anchorage, Garden Route Shopping Centre, Main St (☎0445/22230). City-centre seafood and steak restaurant where you can be guaranteed fresh fish every day.

Coffee Connection, Main Rd. The best coffee in town, with a wide choice of blends – including flavoured beans – as well as snacks.

Crab Creek, Belvidere Rd (☎0445/87 1043). Worth coming to for the great views on the banks of the lagoon rather than for its average seafood menu.

Cranzgot's, Knysna Heads. Popular young meeting place in an outstanding setting right on the rocks beneath the Heads. The rather indifferent menu features a selection of coffees, snacks and pizzas.

Knysna Oyster Company, Long St Thesens Island (☎0445/22168; Mon–Thurs 8am–5pm, Fri 8am–4pm, Sat & Sun 9am–3pm). Tasting tavern at one of the world's largest oyster farms, where you can feast on mussels or cultivated oysters served with bread and a choice of sauces. Pickled hake, snoek and angel pâté are on offer, as well as take-away oysters by the dozen, which are best eaten sitting at the edge of the lagoon. Mouthwatering.

La Loerie, 57 Main St (☎0441/21616). Knysna's top restaurant is a consistently excellent and intimate place, where you can eat fresh lagoon oysters and some of the best fish along the Garden Route.

Macintosh's, Thesen's Building, Long St. Fantastic selection of fruit and vegetables, as well as Thai, Chinese and Indian herbs, displayed in baskets and laid out on hessian.

O Pescador, on the Brenton/Belvidere turn-off from the N2 (☎0445/387 1386). Out-of-town restaurant known for its Portuguese cuisine, of which the house speciality is Mozambique prawns. Open daily.

Pink Umbrella, 14 Kingsway, Leisure Island (☎0445/22409). Highly popular alfresco place done out in sugar-pink decor and renowned for sumptuous chocolate desserts. Serves exclusively seafood and vegetarian dishes, except on Saturday nights when they spit-roast a lamb. Booking is essential.

Sailor Sam, Millwood Place, Main St. Excellent take-away fish and chips as well as sole, kalimari and prawns. Daily 11am–9pm.

CRUISES

One of the obligatory excursions around Knysna is a **cruise** across the lagoon to the Heads. *Knysna Ferries* (☎0445/82 5520) runs six ninety-minute trips a day from the Tapas Jetty on Thesen's Island. Another option is offered by the larger double-decker *MV John Benn*, which has a bar on board, runs cruises to the Heads and provides the only means for reaching the private Featherbed Nature Reserve on the western side of the Heads. The entire trip takes four hours and includes a 4WD shuttle to the top of the western Head with the option of walking the 2km back downhill to enjoy spectacular views and see the local flora and fauna, including Knysna louries.

Booking is essential for ferry trips and can be done through the tourist information bureau or the information kiosks on Pledge Square or in Woodmill Shopping centre (see p.192).

Tin Roof Blues, corner of St George's and Main roads. Good live music performed by local and visiting bands from across the country.

Woodbury's Delicatessen, Woodmill Shopping Lane, off Long and Main streets. Fantastic place to stock up for a gourmet picnic, with the most delicious take-away sandwiches in town (generous fillings in crusty Portuguese rolls). You can eat your tuck at the tables outside in the paved mall.

Listings

Automobile Association Emergency rescue supernumber toll free ☎0800/01 0101.

Banks are easy to find down Main St. Wherever you find banks you'll find automatic teller machines (ATMs). Opening hours are Mon–Fri 9am–3.30pm and Sat 8.30–11am.

Emergencies Ambulance ☎10177; Fire ☎82 5066; Police ☎10111.

Hospitals and doctors The best first port of call for medical treatment is the *International Medical Centre* (for appointments ☎0445/82 6272, after hours ☎82 6366, mobile ☎083/610 0546), which is geared to travellers and operates an affordable drop-in service for emergencies and can arrange appointments for non-urgent problems. The centre incorporates a *British Airways Travel Clinic*, which offers travel health advice, vaccinations and current malaria prophylaxis.

Laundry *The Knysna Wash Tub*, 20 Gray St, is open Mon–Fri 7.30am–5.30pm, Sat 7.30am–1pm.

Pharmacy *Marine Pharmacy*, on the corner of Main and Grey streets, has extended opening hours (Mon–Fri 8am–9pm, Sat 8am–1pm & 5–9pm, Sun 9.30am–1pm and 5–9pm; ☎0445/82 5614).

Taxis *Rikkis* (☎0445/82 6540) covers Knysna and surrounds as far as Buffalo Bay to the west and Plettenberg Bay to the east.

Telephones There are phone booths all over Knysna's centre, taking phone cards and coins. For directory enquiries, dial ☎1023.

The Knysna forests

The best reason to come to Knysna is for its **forests**, although these are now only the shreds of a once magnificent woodland that was home to **Khoi** clans and harboured a thrilling variety of wildlife, including elephant herds. A marvellous wonderland of strange species and a seemingly boundless timber resource, they attracted European explorers and naturalists, and in their wake woodcutters, businessmen like George Rex and gold-diggers, all bent on making their fortunes here.

THE KNYSNA ELEPHANTS

Traffic signs warning motorists about elephants along the N2 between Knysna and Plettenberg Bay are rather optimistic: by 1995 there appeared to have been only one indigenous pachyderm left. Such is the mystique attached to the **Knysna elephants** that locals tend to be a little cagey about just how few they are. By 1860, the thousands that had formerly wandered the once vast forests were down to five hundred, and by 1920 (twelve years after they were protected by law), there were only twenty animals left. Loss of habitat and consequent malnutrition seem to have been the cause rather than full-scale hunting.

An attempt was made in 1995 to create a breeding herd by introducing three young cows from the Kruger National Park, who it was hoped would breed with the Forest's lone bull. The "bull" turned out to be a cow and fled in terror when confonted with the three teenagers. In the chase that followed, one young elephant died from pneumonia, brought on by stress. By 1997 the two surviving aliens had moved east and were causing destruction to farmland near Plettenberg Bay. The *National Parks Board*, working with local wildlife organizations, decided to relocate them to Shamwari Game Reserve, some 300km to the east near Port Elizabeth.

French explorer Francois Le Vaillant was one of the first **Europeans** to sample the delights of these forests. He travelled through in the eighteenth century with Khoi trackers, who shot and cooked an elephant; the explorer found the animal's feet so "delicious" that he wagered that "never can our modern epicures have such a dainty at their tables". Two hundred years later, all that's left of the Khoi people are some names of local places. The legendary Knysna elephants have hardly fared better, and are teetering on certain extinction.

Eleventh-hour **conservation** has ensured that some of the handsome hardwoods have survived to maturity in reserves of woodland that can still take your breath away. A number of walks have been laid out in several of the forests and this is unquestionably one of the best ways to experience the forests. The devastating success of the nineteenth-century timber industry means that all these reserves are some distance from Knysna itself and require transport to get to.

Goudveld State Forest

The beautiful **Goudveld State Forest** (daily 6am–6pm), just over 30km northwest of Knysna, is a mixture of plantation and indigenous woodland that takes its name from the gold boom (*goudveld* is Afrikaans for goldfields) that brought hundreds of prospectors to the mining town of **Millwood** in the 1880s. The six hundred small-time diggers who were here by 1886 scouring out the hillsides and panning Jubilee Creek for alluvial gold were rapidly followed by larger syndicates, and a flourishing little town quickly sprang up, with six hotels, three newspapers and a music hall. The singing and dancing was shortlived and bust followed boom in 1890 after most of the mining companies went to the wall. The ever-hopeful diggers took off for the newly discovered Johannesburg goldfields, and Millwood was left a deserted **ghost town**. Over the years its buildings were demolished or relocated, leaving an old store known as "Materolli" as the only original building standing. Today, the old town is completely overgrown, apart from signs indicating where the old streets stood. In **Jubilee Creek**, which provides a lovely shady walk along a burbling stream, the holes scraped or blasted out of the hillside are still clearly visible. Some of the old mine works have been restored and there are plans to restore the **old reduction works** around the co-co pan track which is still there after a century.

The forest itself is still lovely, featuring tall, indigenous trees, a delightful valley with a stream, and plenty of swimming holes and picnic sites. To **get there** from Knysna, follow the N2 west toward George, turning right onto the Rheenendal road just after the Knysna River, and continue for about 25km, following the Goudveld signposts.

GUIDED FOREST WALKS

One of the nicest ways to explore Goudveld State Forest is on a **guided walk** with **Judith Hopley**, who leads excellent walks that achieve the right balance of information and anecdote. Incredibly informative and helpful, Hopley gives a handle on the forest in terms of identifying the trees and understanding the ecology of the whole system. Apart from scientific information she also passes on forest lore that she has picked up from years spent talking to foresters and forest guards. She is also able to include a tour of a furniture factory that works with Knysna hardwoods.

Judith has written *On Foot in the Garden Route*, a useful catalogue of fifty relatively easy hikes in the area. To join one of the guided walks, turn up at the Rheenendal Post Office on Wednesdays or Thursday at 10am. **Getting there** from Knysna, take the N2 west toward George, turning right onto the Rheenendal road just after the Knysna River. For more **information**, call ☎0445/4788 (7–9am & 6–9pm).

Diepwalle Forest

The only elephants you can expect to see in the **Diepwalle Forest** (daily 6am–6pm; entry fee), just over 20km northeast of Knysna, are on the painted markers indicating the three main hikes through these woodlands, which are the last haunt of Knysna's almost extinct elephant population. However, if you're quiet and alert, you do stand a chance of seeing vervet monkeys, bushbuck and blue duiker.

Diepwalle (meaning "deep wall") is one of the highlights of the Knysna area and is renowned for its impressive density of huge trees, especially yellowwoods. Once the budget timber of South Africa, **yellowwood** was considered an inferior local substitute in place of imported pine, and found its way into the structure, floorboards, window frames and doors of thousands of often quite modest nineteenth-century houses in the Western and Eastern Cape. Now its deep golden grain is so sought-after that it commands premium prices at the annual auctions.

The **three main hiking routes** cover between 7km and 9km of terrain, and pass through flat to gently undulating country covered by indigenous forest and montane fynbos. If you're moderately fit, the hikes should take two to two-and-a-half hours. All trails begin at the Forest Station. **To get there** from Knysna, follow the N2 east towards Plettenberg Bay, after 7km turning left onto the R339, which you should take for about 16km in the direction of Avontuur and Uniondale. The Forest Station is 10.5km after the tar gives way to gravel.

The nine-kilometre **Arboretum Trail**, marked by black elephants, starts a short way back along the road you drove in on, and passes down to a stream edged with tree ferns. Across the stream you'll come to the much-photographed **Big Tree**, a six hundred-year-old Goliath. The easy-going nine-kilometre **Ashoekheuwel Trail**, marked by white elephants, crosses the Gouna River, where there's a large pool allegedly used by real pachyderms. Most difficult of the three hikes is the rewarding seven-kilometre **Velboeksdraai Trail**, marked by red elephants, which passes along the foothills of the Outeniquas. Take care here to stick to the elephant markers, as they overlap with a series of painted footprints marking the Outeniqua Trail, which you shouldn't take. Just before the Veldboeksdraai picnic site, there's another mighty yellowwood regarded by some as the most beautiful in the forest.

Plettenberg Bay and around

Over the Christmas holidays 40,000 residents from Johannesburg's wealthy northern suburbs decamp to **PLETTENBERG BAY** (usually called "Plett"), 33km east of Knysna, and the flashiest of the Garden Route's seaside towns. This is sufficient reason to give it a miss at Christmas, when prices double, accommodation becomes impossible to find and everything gets very crowded. Yet, during low season, sipping champagne and sucking oysters while watching the sunset from a bar can be wonderful – the ugly developments on the surrounding hills somehow don't seem so bad because the bay views really are stupendous. The deep-blue **Tsitsikamma Mountains** drop sharply to the inlet and its large estuary, providing the constant vista to the town and its suburbs. The bay generously curves over several kilometres of white sands, which are separated from the mountains by forest. The proximity of the wooded slopes breathing onto the sea makes this a green and temperate location that receives rainfall throughout the year.

Southern right **whales** make an appearance every winter and are a seriously underrated attraction. Less particular are the **dolphins** who can be seen hunting or riding the surf, often in substantial numbers, throughout the year. **Swimming** is safe, and though the waters are never tropically warm they reach a comfortable temperature between

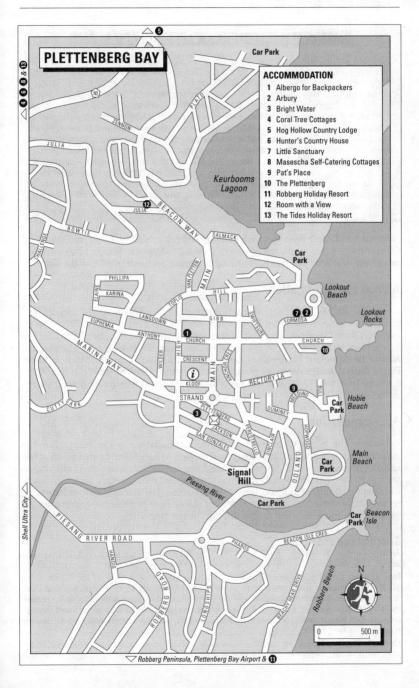

PLETTENBERG BAY

ACCOMMODATION

1. Albergo for Backpackers
2. Arbury
3. Bright Water
4. Coral Tree Cottages
5. Hog Hollow Country Lodge
6. Hunter's Country House
7. Little Sanctuary
8. Masescha Self-Catering Cottages
9. Pat's Place
10. The Plettenberg
11. Robberg Holiday Resort
12. Room with a View
13. The Tides Holiday Resort

WHALE-WATCHING AT PLETTENBERG BAY

Elevated ocean panoramas give Plettenberg Bay outstanding vantages for watching **southern right whales** during their breeding season between June and October. Phone the *Whale Hotline* (☎04457/33743) for information about their current where-abouts. An especially good watching point is the area between the wreck of the *Athene* at the southern end of Lookout Beach and the Keurbooms River. The Robberg Peninsula is also excellent, looming protectively over this whale nursery and giving a grandstand view of the bay. Other good town watching points are from Beachy Head Road at Robberg Beach; Signal Hill in San Gonzales Street past the post office and police station; the *Beacon Isle Hotel*; and the deck of the *Lookout* restaurant on Lookout Beach. Outside Plett, the Kranshoek viewpoint and hiking trail offers wonderful whale-watching points along the route. To get there, head for Knysna, taking the Harkerville turn-off, and continue for 7km. It's also possible to view the occasional pair (mother and calf) at Nature's Valley, 20km from Plett on the R102, and from Storms River Mouth. For more information about whales, see Hermanus on p.172.

November and April. River and rock **fishing** yield rewards all year long, and one of the Garden Route's best short **hikes** covers a circuit rounds the Robberg Peninsula – a great tongue of headland that licks around to contain the western edge of the bay.

Arrival and information

SA Airlink **flights** from Johannesburg arrive daily at Plettenberg Bay airport, and three times a week there are flights from Durban via Port Elizabeth. There is no transport from the airport into town. **Intercity buses** stop at the Shell Ultra City service station, just off the N2 in Marine Way, 2km from the town centre. The *Baz* and *Hopper* **backpacker buses** drop passengers off at their accommodation in town. Plett's **tourist information bureau**, Victoria Cottage, Kloof St (Mon–Fri 8am–5pm, Sat 8am–1pm; ☎04457/34065), has maps of the town and can help with finding accommodation.

Accommodation

Because of the hilly terrain, much of the **accommodation** in Plettenberg Bay has views of the sea and mountains, though you're likely to have to put up with views of holiday developments as well. Surprisingly perhaps, for such an unapologetically upmarket resort, Plett has a backpackers' lodge, camping and some cheaper accommodation, with additional self-catering available at **Keurbooms**, just across the river. Rates skyrocket at Christmas and Easter, and several places have two rates, depending on the quality of the room. July and August are the cheapest months.

Guesthouses and hotels

Arbury, Formosa St (☎04457/32193, fax 32189). Two B&B flatlets, each with a deck, bedroom and lounge, in an unbeatable location a 2min walk from Lookout Beach, and close to the centre. ④.

Hog Hollow Country Lodge, Askop Rd, The Crags, 16km east of Plett off the N2 (☎ & fax 04457/48879; email: hog.hollow@pixie.co.za; ④–⑤). Nine ethnically styled double rooms on a private nature reserve overlooking valleys and the Tsitsikamma Mountains, with walks on the property. This is a country rather than a beach place, though you could hike for a couple of hours through forest to Keurbooms Beach, or drive it in 15min. Friendly, with a congenial outdoor deck and top reputation for food. ④–⑤.

Hunter's Country House, off the N2, 10km west of Plett on the way to Knysna (☎04457/7818, fax 7878, email: hunters@pixie.co.za). Set in a woodland area, this award-winning hotel is the best

Garden Route stay, with an emphasis on country comfort rather than seaside glitz, at half the price of the much-vaunted *Plettenberg*. Accommodation is in thatched cottages set in well-established gardens, each with an open fireplace and private patio. ⑥–⑦.

Little Sanctuary, 14 Formosa St (☎04457/31344, fax 31603). Next door to the *Arbury*, as close to the beach as you can get, offering bedrooms with bath and private verandah overlooking the sea. ④.

Pat's Place, 4 Meeding St (☎04457/33180). One of the cheapest B&Bs in Plett, in an old timber and iron house 3min walk to Hobie Beach. Rooms don't have bath, but they're pleasantly decorated. In the front rooms you can lie in bed and look at the sea. ②–③.

The Plettenberg, Lookout Rocks (☎04457/32030, fax 32074). Plett's most luxurious hotel offers unbeatable views straight onto the ocean. ⑦.

Room with a View, 5 Julia Ave (☎04457/3186, fax 34208). Luxury home, back from the beach, but with good views, offering seriously upmarket B&B rooms with TV, video and a champagne breakfast served on your own private deck. ⑤.

Backpackers' lodges and self-catering

Albergo for Backpackers, 8 Church St (☎04457/34434). Unexceptional backpackers' lodge in the centre of the town, with dorms and a couple of doubles. Canoes, bikes, surf and boogie boards are available to rent, and staff offer rides out to Robberg Nature Reserve. ①.

Bright Water, 15 Jackson St (☎ & fax 04457/30467 or 48623). Three en-suite double rooms in this centrally located, homely suburban house where you can rent the whole place or just a room, and have use of the kitchen. The owner lives across the road. ②–③.

Coral Tree Cottages (☎04457/7822, fax 7869). Off the N2, 11km west of Plettenberg Bay. High-quality, well-furnished and spacious self-catering thatched cottages, although unfortunately the roar of the N2 is never absent. ③.

Masescha Self-Catering Cottages, 1km north off the N2, signposted 12km west from Plettenberg Bay (☎04457/7647, fax 7645). Three reasonably-priced self-catering whitewashed cottages plainly furnished on a farm. The outdoor sitting areas are surrounded by pleasant gardens and a forest, and there's a pool. Good for families or couples, it also has an indigenous plant nursery and natural history bookshop. Breakfast is available as an extra. ②.

Robberg Holiday Resort, Robberg Rd (☎ & fax 04457/32571). Close to Robberg Nature Reserve and Robberg Beach, this budget option is suitable only if you have your own transport. There's camping (①) and cheap self-catering bungalows without bathrooms (①) and also en-suite accommodation. (②).

The Tides Holiday Resort, 2km west of Plett off the N2 (☎ & fax 04457/32478). Reasonably-priced en-suite double rooms and slightly more expensive self-catering units, with breakfast offered as an extra charge. ②.

The Town and its beaches

Plett's town **centre**, at the top of the hill, consists of a conglomeration of supermarkets, swimwear shops, estate agents and restaurants aimed largely at the holiday trade. It's the **beaches** people come for – and there's a fair choice. Southeast of the town centre on a rocky promontory is **Beacon Isle**, dominated by a 1960s hotel, an eyesore blighting a fabulous location. Beacon Isle Beach, or **Main Beach**, right at the central shore of the bay, is where the fishing boats and seacats anchor a little out to sea. The small waves here make for calm swimming and this is an ideal family spot. To the east is **Lookout Rocks**, which draw surfers to the break off a needle of rocks known as the Point and the predictable surf of **Lookout Beach**, to its east, which is also one of the nicest stretches of sand for bathers, body-surfers or sun lizards. Lookout Beach has the added attraction of a marvellously located restaurant (see "Eating, drinking and nightlife"), from which you can often catch sight of the **dolphins** that often breeze into the bay. From here you can walk kilometres down the beach towards Keurbooms and the **Keurbooms Lagoon**.

Besides the obvious draw of walking around the protective arm of the Robberg Peninsula (see below), you can go **horse-riding** through the surrounding forest, fynbos and grassland at *Southern Comfort Farm* (☎04457/30306; booking essential), 6km

WALKING IN THE ROBBERG NATURE AND MARINE RESERVE

One of the Garden Route's nicest walks is the four-hour, nine-kilometre **circular route** around the spectacular rocky peninsula of **Robberg**, where you can completely escape Plett's ugly development and experience the coast in its wildest state, with its enormous horizons and lovely vegetation. Much of the walk takes you along high cliffs, from where you can often look down on seals surfacing near the rocks, dolphins arching through the water and, in winter, whales further out in the bay. If you don't have time for the full circular walk, there is a **shorter two-hour hike** and a **thirty-minute ramble**. A map indicating these is available at the reserve gate when you pay to get in (daily Feb–Nov 7am–5pm; Dec–Jan 7am–8pm; ☎04457/32125; small entry fee).

You'll need sturdy walking shoes as the terrain is rocky and steep in parts, and the walk involves some some serious rock-hopping on the west side. Don't forget to bring a hat and a bottle of water, as there's no drinking water for much of the walk and no tea rooms. There's no public transport to the reserve; if you aren't in a car, you can get a reasonably-priced **transfer** with the *Albergo for Backpackers* (see p.201). **To get there by car**, take Strand Street towards Beacon Island, turn right into Piesangs Valley Road, and 200m further on, turn left into Robberg Road. Follow the airport signs, continuing for 3.5km and then turn left toward *Robberg Holiday Resort*, where you'll find the gate to the reserve 500m beyond the resort.

from town. Two-hour rides cost from R70 per person, and staff can pick you up for a small fee from the Shell Garage, where all intercity buses drop off. Alternatively, *Equitrailing* (☎04457/30599, mobile 082/955 0373) runs similar full-day trails, full-moon rides and champagne breakfast trails through similar terrain. For **beach rides**, head out to *Keurbooms River Hotel* (☎04457/34065), where one-hour beach rides leave throughout the day.

Eating, drinking and nightlife

The *Cave*, Plett's young rave spot, is one of the liveliest **clubs** on the Garden Route, and for some travellers it's the principal draw of the town. You'll also find some pleasant beachside **pubs** with terrific views, and a handful of decent **restaurants** serving locally caught fresh fish.

The Boardwalk, Yellowwood Centre, corner of Main and Crescent streets. Cosy, eclectic restaurant serving up tasty seafood, steaks and baked potatoes.

The Cave, in the *Arches* hotel, Marine Drive, off the N2 (☎04457/32118). A young crowd raves it up here, especially at weekends and in the December holidays. Phone first to check dates and opening hours.

Cornuti Restaurant, Shop 1, Seaview Properties, Perestrella St. Good place to fill up on cheap pasta dishes and pizzas.

Fish Eagle Creek, on the Keurbooms Lagoon, just off the N2 between Plettenberg Bay and Keurbooms (☎04457/9445). Reasonably priced meals served at this pleasant pub with outdoor seating on the edge of the calm lagoon. Their fresh fish and chips are especially recommended.

Islander Eating Place, on the N2 between Plett and Knysna (☎04457/7776). Popular, high-quality restaurant for seafood, where you can eat as much as you like for a set price. Booking essential.

Kelly's Pub, Florina Place, Main St. Lively pub with pool tables and balconies for taking in the sea air.

The Lookout, Lookout Beach. Marvellous bay views at this casual restaurant-cum-pub right on the beach, where you can eat reasonably priced fresh fish, or more expensive crayfish, and, if you're lucky, watch whales and dolphins rollicking in the surf.

Moby Dick, Main Beach. Pleasant place for a drink, particularly out of season – in summer it draws a lively boogie-board crowd.

Old Nick Tea Garden, on the N2 between Plett and Keurbooms (☎04457/31395). Good place for outdoor tea, and more especially recommended as the best **craft shop** in the area, especially for woven goods.

Rusty Nail, Main St. Rough-and-ready fishermen's bar with windows looking out on the bay. Popular with locals rather than holidaymakers.

Keurboomstrand

Some 14km east of Plettenberg Bay, across the Keurbooms River, is the uncluttered resort of **KEURBOOMSTRAND**, which shares the same bay and has equally wonderful beaches, but is less safe for swimming. A calm and attractive place, Keurboomstrand has few facilities, and if you're intending to stay here you should stock up in Plettenberg Bay beforehand. The safest place for swimming is at **Arch Rock**, in front of the caravan park, though **Picnic Rock Beach** is also pretty good.

If you can tear yourself away from the beach, **canoeing** up the Keurbooms River gives an alternative perspective on the area, but you'll need a permit from *Nature Conservation* (☎04457/32125), who rent out fairly basic canoes for day- or overnight trips. The forest comes right down to the river edge, and as the gorge narrows and you go higher the journey gets better, because you leave behind the pleasure boats and water-skiers who are restricted to an area near the caravan park. Don't be put off by the river's Coca-Cola colour (which comes from harmless oxides in the water): it's quite fresh, and wonderful to swim in during the summer. If you're renting a boat, you can stop and picnic at any of the little beaches upriver. While you're here, keep an eye out for the pink-flowering Keurboom trees which give their name to the river and resort.

Places to stay include one of the country's best family-oriented campsites, *Keurbooms Avontura* (☎04457/9309), signposted off the N2, 6km east of Plett. Here you can choose from campsites on the shady banks of the river (①), self-catering cabins (②) or chalets (③). Canoes and motorboats are available to rent, and there's a swimming pool. Just a short walk to the sea, *Dune Park*, off Keurbooms Strand Road on the right (☎04457/9606), offers camping (①) and timber chalets (③) behind the sand dunes, but has no sea view. Finally, *Arch Rock Chalets and Caravan Park* (☎04457/9409) features a shady campsite and rather old chalets right on the seashore, but gets packed with families in the summer. The only place in Keurboomstrand for **eating and drinking** is the *Singing Kettle*, which has an unbeatable location right on the beach and makes a great whale- and dolphin-spotting venue.

Tsitsikamma National Park

The **Tsitsikamma National Park** (open daily; entry fee), roughly midway between Plettenberg Bay and Port Elizabeth, is the highlight of any Garden Route trip, and you'd be crazy to pass up its highlight, the **Storm's River Mouth**, which is the most dramatic estuary on this exhilarating stretch of coast. This is where South Africa's ultimate hike, the five-day **Otter Trail**, begins.

Starting from just beyond Keurboomstrand in the west, the national park extends into the Eastern Cape along a narrow 68-kilometre belt of coast, with dramatic foamy surges of rocky coast, deep river gorges and ancient hardwood forest teetering on the edge of tangled, green cliffs. Established in 1964, Tsitsikamma was South Africa's first marine reserve, stretching 5.5km out to sea, with an **underwater trail** open to snorkellers and licensed scuba divers.

Tsitsikamma has two sections: **De Vasselot** in the west and **Storms River** in the east. Both sections can only be reached down the park's own winding tarred road from the N2 (there's no way of getting from one to the other through the park itself). De Vasselot incorporates **Nature's Valley**, the only resort in the park, and the most low-key settlement on the Garden Route, with a fabulous sandy beach which stretches for 3km.

De Vasselot

The **De Vasselot** section, at the western end of Tsitsikamma, extends inland into a rugged and hilly interior incised with narrow valleys and traversed by a series of footpaths. **Walking** is the main activity here, and the area is covered with waymarked routes of varying lengths, including the highly popular Otter Trail (see box). **Nature's Valley** is a pleasingly old-fashioned settlement on the Groot River Lagoon with 20km of beach. Bypassed by the N2, the intercity buses, tour parties and most motorists, who can't be bothered to contend with the tortuous mountain passes to get down here, this is the right destination if you're after a quiet time along the Garden Route.

There are plenty of good **walks** at Nature's Valley, many starting from the De Vasselot campsite, where you can pick up maps and information about birds and trees. One of the loveliest places to head for is **Salt River Mouth**, 3km to the west of Nature's

---

MAJOR GARDEN ROUTE HIKES

If you're keen on walking and the outdoors, and want to schedule in at least one long walk somewhere in the country during your holiday, the Garden Route provides some fine possibilities. Indeed, walking is the only way to really experience the Garden Route's forests and coast and escape the clutter of holiday homes and roaring N2.

The **hikes** listed below are two to five days long. You'll need to carry all your food, a sleeping bag for use in the communal hiking huts (mattresses are provided), lightweight cooking utensils and stove, and waterproofs. You should also wear proper, worn-in hiking boots. For day-hikes and walks lasting only a couple of hours, a good bet is Judith Hopley's *On Foot in the Garden Route*, available from Knysna's tourist information bureau (see p.192) and several other outlets on the Garden Route.

OUTENIQUA HIKING TRAIL
Wilderness
Start: Beervlei (old Forest Station – eight overnight huts)
End: Harkerville Forestry Station
Distance: 108km
Duration: seven days (shorter versions possible)
Permit: Department of Forestry, Knysna (☎0445/23037 or Forestry Office ☎82 5466)
Features: Indigenous forest, including giant yellowwood trees, pine plantations and gold-mining remains at Millwood.

HARKERVILLE COAST HIKING TRAIL
Start and end: Harkerville Forestry Station, 12km west of Plettenberg Bay, signposted off the N2
Distance: 26.6km
Duration: two days
Permit: Department of Forestry, Kynsna (☎0445/23037 or Forestry Office ☎82 5466)
Features: Magnificent rocky coastline, indigenous forest and fynbos. Lots of rock scrambling and some exposed, narrow ledges above the sea. Don't attempt this hike if you're scared of heights or are unfit. Monkeys, baboons and fish eagles are common, and you may also spot dolphins or whales. Closer to the roads, this trail isn't as remote in feeling as the Otter Trail, but is a good second best.

Valley, where you can swim and picnic – though you'll need to ford the tannin-dark river at low tide. This walk starts and ends at the café at Nature's Valley. Also recommended is the circular six-kilometre **Kalanderkloof Trail**, which starts at the De Vasselot campsite, winds up to a lookout point, and descends via a narrow river gorge graced with a profusion of huge Outeniqua yellowwood trees and Cape wild bananas.

Practicalities

Public **transport** to Nature's Valley is limited to the *Hopper* and *Baz* **backpacker buses**, which deposit you at the De Vasselot rest camp or the village centre – little more than a restaurant and small shop which acts as an informal **information bureau** and can help with accommodation.

The cheapest **place to stay** is 1km north of Nature's Valley, at the De Vasselot rest camp, which has campsites (①) tucked into indigenous forest, and basic forest huts (①) with communal ablution facilities. **Bookings** must be made through the National Parks Board, PO Box 7400, Roggebaai, Cape Town 8012 (☎021/22 2810, fax 24 6211), or PO Box 787, Pretoria 0001 (☎012/343 1991, fax 343 0905). In Nature's Valley itself, most

OTTER TRAIL

Tsitsikamma National Park

Start: Storms River Mouth

End: Nature's Valley

Distance: 42km

Duration: five days

Permit: National Parks Board (☎012/343 1991, fax 24 6211, or ☎ 021/22 2810, fax 343 0905). Bookings are taken up to twelve months in advance. The maximum number of people on the trail is twelve. Cost: R200 per person.

Features: South Africa's first established hiking trail is a coastal walk crossing rivers, tidal pools and indigenous forest. You may see dolphins, whales and seals, and the spoor of the Cape clawless otter – although virtually impossible to spot, they're certainly around. Short daily stretches between log-hut nightstops gives plenty of time to walk slowly, and enjoy the vegetation and birds. Some parts of the hike are steep, so you need to be fit. The Bloukrans River has to be crossed by wading or swimming: go at low tide and waterproof your backpack.

TSITSIKAMMA TRAIL

Tsitsikamma

Start: Nature's Valley Caravan Park

End: Storm's River Bridge

Distance: 64km

Duration: five days, shorter versions possible

Permit: SAFCOL (☎042/391 0393)

Features: Not to be confused with Otter Trail, this is an inland walk through indigenous forest, long stretches of open fynbos and the Tsitsikamma mountain range. Five overnight huts accommodate thirty people. It's not a difficult hike, and you won't cover more than 17km in a day. However, after heavy rains the rivers can be hard to cross.

accommodation consists of holiday cottages, which means you can forget about finding anywhere to stay during the Christmas holidays, when their owners occupy them. The situation reverses for the rest of the year, and a number are rented out by *Bib's* (☎04457/6834), as B&Bs (③) and expensive but comfortable backpacker rooms (①–②).

If you're self-catering, stock up on supplies before you get here. The only place to buy a meal is at the *Valley Inn* **restaurant**, on the corner of Forest and St Michael streets, which serves seafood, steaks, burgers and toasted sandwiches and provides the only nightlife apart from gazing at the stars.

Storms River Mouth

In contrast to the languid lagoon and long soft sands of Nature's Valley, **Storms River Mouth**, 55km from Plettenberg Bay, presents the elemental face of the Garden Route, where the dark Storms River surges through a gorge to wrestle with the surf. **Storms River Mouth Restcamp** (☎042/541 1607), sited on tended lawns, is poised between a craggy shoreline of black rocks pounded by foamy white surf, and steeply raking forested cliffs, and is without a doubt the ultimate location along the southern Cape coast. Don't confuse this with Storms River Village just off the N2, which is nowhere near the sea, and has little to recommend it, apart from a variety of places to stay if you can't get in at the Mouth.

Walking is the main activity at the Mouth, and at the visitors' office at the rest camp you can get **maps** of short, waymarked trails that leave from here. The trails take in the coast, and there are steep walks up the forested cliffs where you can see 800-year-old yellowwood trees with views onto a wide stretch of ocean. Most rewarding is the **three-kilometre hike** west from the rest camp along the start of the Otter Trail to a fantastic waterfall pool at the base of fifty-metre-high falls where you can swim right on the edge of the shore. Less demanding is the kilometre-long **boardwalk stroll** from the restaurant to the suspension bridge to see the river mouth. On your way to the bridge, don't miss the dank *strandloper* ("beachcomber") **cave** – hunter-gatherers frequented this area between 5000 and 2000 years ago, living off seafood in wave-cut caves near the river mouth. A modest display shows an excavated midden, with clear layers of little bones and shells.

If you're desperate to walk the **Otter Trail** (see box, p.205) which begins at Storms River, and have been told that it is full, don't despair. As a single person or a couple, you stand a chance of getting in on the back of a last-minute cancellation, so it may be worth hanging out at the Mouth for a night or two. Since the trail is booked long in advance, there is often a chance that someone won't turn up.

Swimming at the Mouth is restricted to a safe and pristine little sandy bay below the restaurant which can be icy in summer if there are easterly winds and cold upwellings of deep water from the continental shelf, only 25 nautical miles off the coast.

Practicalities

Storms River Mouth lies 18km south of Storms River Bridge, the boundary between the Eastern and Western Cape provinces, where most people stop to gaze into the deep river gorge and fill up at the most beautifully located filling and service station in the country. Even if your time is limited and you can't spend the night at Storms River Mouth, it's still worth nipping down for a meal, a restorative walk or a swim in the summer. The only public **transport** to Storms River Mouth is on the *Hopper Bus*, which comes to the **rest camp**. A wide variety of **accommodation** is available here (book through the *National Parks Board* in Pretoria ☎012/343 1991 or 343 1999; or Cape Town ☎021/22 2810), all with sea views, including superb campsites (①) just metres from where the surf breaks on the rocks; incredibly good-value two-person forest cabins (①), which provide bedding but no catering facilities; comfortable one-bedroom self-catering log cabins including breakfast (④); and oceanette mini-apartments close to the sea, also including breakfast (④). All these options get heavily subscribed in season, but are discounted from May to August.

The only **eating** place is the rest-camp restaurant, which serves breakfasts and à la carte meals, which are less memorable than the stunning views.

Storms River Village

STORMS RIVER VILLAGE lies about a kilometre south of the national road, has a number of places to stay, a general dealer selling basics and some activities, but is little more than a functional stop. There's a fair range of **accommodation**, starting at the cheapest with *Storms River Village Backpackers*, Main Rd, run by *Storms River Adventures* (☎042/750 3637), which has its office next to the post office. The backpackers' lodge has packed dorms (①) with twelve bunks in each, a small double room (①), and the use of a kitchen. *Armagh B&B* (☎042/541 1512, fax 541 1510; ③), along the turn-off into the village, also offers decent accommodation. For something smarter, try the *Tzitzikama Forest Inn* (☎042/541 1711, fax 541 1669; ⑤), which also sees tour buses. A couple of kilometres east of town along the N2 is the *Tsitsikamma Lodge* (☎042/750 3802, fax 750 3702;), which has its eye firmly on the German market, featuring jacuzzis in every room and a nudist hiking trail. A **coffee shop** next to the backpackers' lodge sells snacks. *Storms River Adventures* offers some **activities**, best of which is "Blackwater Tubing" down the the Storms River canyon for a half-day-trip. This is a far milder version of whitewater rafting, through the Tsitsikamma National Park to the sea at the Mouth – though you'll need a wet suit, as the water is cold and the river canyon shady.

THE WEST COAST

The **west coast** of South Africa – remote, windswept and flushed by the cold Atlantic ocean demands a special appreciation. For many years the black sheep of Western Cape tourism (a fact borne out by the prominence of industries such as fishing, and the iron-ore terminal at Saldanha Bay) it has been set upon by developers who seem all too ready to spoil the bleached, salty emptiness which many people had just started to value. This is a region roughly cut by nature, with sandy soil and dunes harbouring a distinctive coastal **fynbos** vegetation, a coastline almost devoid of natural inlets or safe harbours, fierce southeasterly winds in summer, dank fogs in the winter, and the ever-miraculous **wild flowers** which appear out of the *veld* in spring.

The southern West Coast region has many links to Namaqualand to the north – not least in the flowers – although this 200km or so of coastline is by far the most densely populated part of the coast and the **Swartland** region immediately inland is unusually fertile. North of Swartland lies the impressive **Cederberg mountain range**, an area of distinctive beauty, and a striking feature on the N7 highway, the main West Coast

---

WEST COAST FLOWERS

During August and September you will find displays of **wild flowers** across the West Coast region, with significant displays starting as far south as the inland town of Darling, just 80km north of Cape Town off the main R27 coastal route. Other excellent displays are to be found in the West Coast National Park and the hazy coastal landscapes around Cape Columbine and Lambert's Bay, while inland Clanwilliam is the centre of some good routes. For up-to-date advice and guidance, contact *Flowerline* in Cape Town (☎021/418 3705) or the helpful local information centres in Darling, Saldanha and Clanwilliam. For further tips on flower-viewing, see p.246.

artery between Cape Town and Namibia. North from **Clanwilliam**, the attractive town at the northern end of the Cederberg, the N7 connects with Vanrhynsdorp, strictly within the Western Cape but for practical purposes linked to the flower routes of Namaqualand in the Northern Cape (see p.219).

Outside the flower months of August and September, the West Coast has a wide range of attractions, particularly during summer when the lure of the sea and the cooler coast is strong. The area is well known for its **seafood**, always fresh, plentiful and much cheaper than in Cape Town, and also for a wide range of activities, most popularly hiking and horse-riding along the coast or in the mountains, various types of watersports, whale-spotting and some excellent bird-watching.

Swartland

Early of a morning it's not uncommon to find a tangy fog smothering the coastal plain inland from Melkbosstrand on the northern edge of Table Bay, but if the visibility is good the N7 highway north from Cape Town leads quickly into the pleasing and fertile **Swartland** landscape. *Swartland* means "black land", but while the rolling countryside takes on some attractive hues at different times of year it is never really black. The accepted theory is that before the area was cultivated the predominant vegetation was a grey-coloured bush called *renosterbos* ("rhinoceros bush") which seen from the surrounding ranges of hills gave the area a complexion sufficiently dark to justify the name.

Bounded to the west by the less fertile coastal strandveld and to the east by the tall mountain range running from the Boland mountains by Wellington to the Cederberg, Swartland is known best as a wheat-growing area, although it also supports dairy farms, horse studs, tobacco crops and vineyards famous for earthy red wines.

The N7 skirts a series of towns on its way north, including the largest in the region, **Malmesbury**. If you're travelling south towards Cape Town, look out for some unusual views of Table Mountain, and for tortoises, which you should take care to avoid as they cross the road.

Darling and around

The small country town of **DARLING** lies caught between Swartland and the West Coast, and as a result is famous both for its rolling countryside and dairy products and its displays of wild flowers in spring. Easily reached from Cape Town by the coastal R27 route, Darling boasts some handsome old buildings and has developed recently as a **artists' colony**, with one of South Africa's best-loved comedians, Pieter Dirk-Uys, establishing his most famous character, Evita Bezuidenhout, as the hostess of a weekend cabaret show at the tiny old railway station in the centre of town (for details of shows, bookings and dinner reservations, phone ☎02241/3145). Local painters are displayed at the well-cared-for **Darling Museum** (daily 9am–1pm & 2–4pm; small entry fee) on the corner of Pastorie and Hill streets, and an "Art Walk" to the homes and studios of local artists, photographers and jewellers is organized on the first weekend of every month (details from the museum).

Just under 20km to the south of Darling at **Mamre**, near the "lost" – or at least oddly adrift – coloured commuter town of Atlantis, an old Moravian **mission station** stands on the northern edge of town. Still active, it includes a series of old thatched mission cottages, a huge church and a working water mill, and remains one of the finest examples in the Western Cape of these pragmatic but bold early nineteenth-century outposts. If you're interested in specialized **tours** of the missions of the Cape, contact Mercia Bruce in Cape Town (☎021/576 1296).

Practicalities

Darling's **tourist information office** is inside the museum (daily 9am–1pm & 2–4pm; ☎02241/3361) and can offer useful advice on local attractions. Although Darling is well within the scope of a day-trip from Cape Town, it's also a good spot for a short **stay**. *The Old Buffers*, 9 Station Rd (☎02241/3008; ②–③), is a pleasant B&B in an old town house, and more rooms are available at the comfortable *Den Houte*, 25 Long St (☎02241/3000; ②–③). As well as the old railway station (see above), good **places to eat** include *Zum Schatzi*, a German restaurant on Long Street (☎02441/3095; closed Mon) or, for snacks and lunches, *Café Mosaic* on Main Road.

Riebeek West

To the northeast of Malmesbury lies an impressive island of hills, **Kasteelberg** ("castle mountains"), on the far side of which lie two small settlements, **Riebeek Kasteel** and **RIEBEEK WEST**. Roughly 3km north of Riebeek West on the road towards Moorreesburg is a turning to a *PPC Cement* works. Within the site, rather incongruously set among rumbling conveyor belts and grey dirt heaps, is the whitewashed cottage where **Jan Smuts**, the great South African statesman and soldier, was born in 1870. There isn't a great deal to see other than a simple old house with wooden floors and some contemporary artefacts inside, but, if you can suspend for a while the fact that it has been all but gobbled up by an industrial site, there are some pleasant lawns and flowerbeds and a handful of outbuildings to wander around – one of which displays an interesting series of storyboards about the eventful life and times of the man (see box).

Accommodation in Riebeek West is available in a Victorian house, *Carollanns* (☎02246/245; ②–③), visible from the main road, while good **meals** and rooms can also be found in the revitalized *Royal Hotel*, 33 Main St (☎02244/378; ③), in neighbouring Riebeek Kasteel.

JAN SMUTS

The life of **Jan Christiaan Smuts**, one of South Africa's greatest figures, perhaps embodies more than any other this country's strained relationship with itself in the first half of the twentieth century. Born to an Afrikaner farming family, Smuts spoke English with the distinctive linguistic burr of Swartland and distinguished himself as a scholar at Stellenbosch and then Cambridge universities. During the Anglo-Boer War he waged a wide-ranging and ultimately undefeated guerrilla campaign as the leader of a Boer commando. However, he came to believe in a unified South Africa under a British flag, and was appointed commander-in-chief of imperial forces in East Africa during World War I, attending meetings of the British War Cabinet in the final phases of the war. Smuts was **prime minister** of South Africa between 1919 and 1924 and again between 1939 and 1948, when he led South Africa into World War II on the British side but, rather like his fellow leader and statesman Winston Churchill, he failed to hold together support at home and lost the postwar general election in 1948 to the hardline Afrikaner DF Malan, who, coincidentally, grew up on the farm Allesvoloren, a few kilometres from Smuts' birthplace.

Smuts spent much of his career in domestic politics trying to hold together disparate political and social moralities among English and moderate Afrikaans-speaking whites, and is remembered by South Africans as a wily, tainted politician rather than as a great humanitarian. Yet he was, like very few South Africans before or since, a man of global vision and influence who as a 76-year-old played an important role in drafting the United Nations charter in 1946. He also published a philosophical treatise and was known for his love of nature and the outdoors, in particular Table Mountain in Cape Town, one of the popular routes up which carries his name.

Groot Winterhoek

Situated within the often hazy, fortress-like line of mountains on the eastern fringe of Swartland is the 300-square-kilometre **Groot Winterhoek Wilderness Area**, an excellent place for lonely hiking and camping, with sparkling swimming pools, typical Cape mountain fauna such as klipspringer, rhebok and elusive felines, distinctive fynbos vegetation and – as the name suggests – rather formidable winter conditions. It is also an area well worth exploring if you're a mountain biker or paraglider.

As this is a wilderness area, you are free to walk and camp where you wish, although there are a number of suggested trails varying in length from a few hours to a few days, and you must carry a **permit**. For details and **bookings**, contact the Cape Nature Conservation Office in Porterville (Mon–Fri 7.30am–4pm; ☎02623/2900).

Langebaan Lagoon

To the west of rural Swartland and immediately north of Cape Town's fast-developing northern coastal suburbs of Bloubergstrand and Table View, the west coast of South Africa starts off fairly much as it continues for many hundred of kilometres north – isolated fishing settlements and sand-dune vegetation of bleak but alluring windswept beauty. Other than river mouths, the only sea inlet and protected deep-water harbour on the entire South African Atlantic seaboard is at **Saldanha Bay**, some 100km north of Cape Town, which is connected to *Langebaan Lagoon*, the attractive centrepiece to the small but precious **West Coast National Park**.

While the holiday town of **Langebaan**, just to the north of the park on the eastern shore of the lagoon, has managed to keep its focus relatively frivolous and beach-oriented, industrial development has muscled into the northern part of the bay. The structures include a 1.5-kilometre-long causeway, an iron-ore railway terminal and a fast-rising steel and concrete works, and come as an ugly intrusion after the delicate simplicity of the national park. They also mean that the town of **Saldanha**, which once positioned itself as a sturdy fishing port with historic naval and military ties, is now grim, sullied and eminently avoidable.

West Coast National Park

The **West Coast National Park** (daily; entry fee) is one of the best places to savour the simple, unspoilt charm of the West Coast. The park protects over 40 percent of South Africa's remaining pristine strandveld and 35 percent of the country's salt marshes, and incorporates both the majority of Langebaan Lagoon and a Y-shaped area of land immediately around and below it.

Much of the appeal of the park is in what you see and taste soon after driving into it: uplifting views over the still lagoon to an olive-coloured, rocky hillside; the sharp, saline air; the calling gulls and Atlantic mists burning up in the harsh sunlight. This isn't a game park – a few larger antelope are located in the Postberg section of the park, an area open only during the spring flower season – but there are huge numbers of **birds**, including some 70,000 migrating waders. A number of well-organized interpretive walking trails lead through the dunes to the long, smooth, wave-punished Atlantic coastline, offering plenty of opportunity to learn about the hardy fynbos vegetation which so defines the look and feel of the West Coast region.

On the southern tip of the lagoon is a large old farmhouse and steading called *Geelbeck*, where there is an information centre, tea room and accommodation (see "Practicalities"). There are also a number of bird hides nearby, and all the main **trails** (up to a total of 30km) set out from here. If you continue from *Geelbeck* up the peninsula on the western side of the lagoon you will come to **Churchhaven**, a tiny village where there are some simple private cottages and where you can swim in the still, relatively warm water of the lagoon. A little further on is the demarcated **Postberg area**, open only during flower season but worth visiting at that time to see **zebra**, **gemsbok** and **wildebeest** wandering around among fields of wild flowers. The tip of the peninsula overlooking the mouth of Saldanha Bay is owned by the National Defence Force and remains inaccessible. The reserve also includes a number of islands around the mouth of the bay which are home to gannets, penguins, seals and, on one, a colony of albino rabbits.

Practicalities

There are two **entrance gates** to the park: one on the R27, roughly 10km north of the turning to Yzerfontein, and the other south of the town of Langebaan. The park isn't huge; if you're driving you'll cover the extent of the roads in a couple of hours. You can see a good chunk if you enter at one gate and come out at the other – but it's worth taking the roads slowly to enjoy the views, and a visit to the **information centre** at *Geelbeck* will allow you to appreciate a bit more of what you're seeing. Overnight **accommodation** is available here, principally for those walking the two-day trail, but there's nothing to stop you simply booking in for the night. Facilities are simple three- to seven-bed self-catering cottages (①), set attractively near the edge of the lagoon. The **tea room** (10am–3.45pm) on the back patio of the main farmhouse serves snacks and light meals, and there are some nice picnic spots around the park. To **book** accommodation and trails call, ☎02287/22798 or 22144.

The **best time to visit** the park is in spring, when the sun is shining and the flowers are out, although this is, inevitably, also the busiest period. Like much of the West Coast, the national park is chilly and wet in winter, and hot and wind-blasted in summer.

Langebaan

Once the home to the largest whaling station in the southern hemisphere, and for a while Cape Town's long-haul passenger flight terminus (when seaplanes from Europe touched down on the lagoon during World War II), **LANGEBAAN** is in some respects the gateway to the West Coast National Park. However, the town appears to have given itself almost entirely to sun, fun, watersports and a motley collection of what only real estate agents (of whom there is no shortage) could dare to call desirable seafront holiday homes. In summer and at weekends the holiday crowds are large and neon swimsuits, ice creams and speedboats dominate. Outside summer, the town falls deathly quiet.

If you're into **windsurfing** and have been wondering how to harness the big south-easter winds of summer, Langebaan could be just your thing. The *Cape Windsurf Centre* (daily: summer 9am–7pm; winter 10am–6pm; ☎02287/21114), on the beach on the northern edge of town, rents out all levels of equipment, including the latest, top-line gear, and offers windsurfing lessons. Right off the beach the water is flat, the sailing winds – as the ragged flags above the centre testify – anywhere from fresh to fearsome, and unless you catch a fast-running tide out towards the Atlantic it's all reasonably safe. The centre also rents out mountain bikes and paddle skis. If you want to rent other watersports equipment such as *Hobie Cat* sailing dinghies, canoes, jet bikes or boats for fishing, try *Lagoon Sports* on the beach in the main part of town, beside *Pearly's* restaurant at the end of Bree Street.

Practicalities

Tourist information is available in the library (Mon–Fri 9.30am–4.30pm, Sat 9am–noon; ☎02287/22115) at the corner of Oostewal (the road in from the R27) and Bree streets, although the presence of a giant papier-mâché seagull outside is a good indication of what Langebaan thinks the tourists want. **Accommodation** is plentiful – it's what the town exists on. The municipal **campsite** is a couple of blocks from the beach on Suffrens

Street, and though it claims not to allow tents without permission you'll probably get away with it. *Die Losieshuis*, 29 Main Rd (☎02287/21744; ①–②), near the beach, is a large back-packer-type house with several double rooms. Halfway between Langebaan and Saldanha is *Olifantskop* (☎02287/22326; ②–④), a guesthouse with a restaurant, bar, pool and equestrian centre. On the bay beside this is a burgeoning Greek-village-style holiday development called *Club Mykonos* (☎02287/22101; ④–⑤), the place to go if you feel you're missing a Costa del Cape flavour in your holiday. Langebaan's most upmarket option is *The Farmhouse* (☎02287/22062; ④), a luxury guesthouse with a good restaurant, set on a hill among some new houses at the southern end of town.

As with accommodation, there's a wide selection of **places to eat** in town. *Die Strandloper* (☎02287/2240 or 083/227 7195; bookings essential), just beyond the *Cape Windsurf Centre* on the road to Saldanha, is a good example of the West Coast's open-air seafood restaurants (see box, p.215). On the main beach itself in town, *Pearly's* is a crowded eating, drinking and ogling spot in a prime location, while *La Taverna* (closed Mon), on the corner of Bree and Oostewal streets, serves better food and some mighty, diet-destroying cakes.

Saldanha

SALDANHA is known chiefly for its links to the military (a military academy is sited here) and for the controversial iron-ore loading terminal built here in the 1970s. The iron ore arrives from Sishen in the Northern Cape, 861km away along a purpose-built railway line. The scheme has never been the success it was hoped for, and the latest attempt to paper over the cracks is the erection beside the terminal of a steel plant. This comes with the added bonus of a concrete works, being built to use up the waste material from the steel plant, which will require a ten-kilometre-long conveyor belt to be constructed between it and the coast north of Saldanha. You get the sense that it's in for a penny, in for a pound, leaving the country's environmentalists – the precious ecosystems and bird habitats of the West Coast National Park are only a few kilometres away – with their heads buried in their hands.

The town, seated on the northwestern hook of the bay, thinks of itself as a holiday place, but as an observer it's hard to be convinced. If you do spend time here, though, it's worth taking advantage of the availability of good **fresh seafood** which arrives daily from the fishing fleet. Interspersed with numerous fish-and-chip shops and fast-food chains along the cliff-edge seafront, you'll find some decent **places to eat**, including the unassuming *Hoedjiesbay Hotel*, or the rather swanky *Meresteijn* (☎02281/43345) at the top of the hill. Just under 4km north of town, but quickly returning back into the West Coast feel, is *Oranjevlei* (☎02281/42261), which offers seafood pub lunches (Mon–Sat), **B&B** (③) and plenty of character in one of the oldest farms in the area. The **West Coast Publicity Association** is run from an old cottage called *Oorlogsvlei* on Van Riebeeck Street (Mon–Fri 8.30am–1pm & 2–5pm; ☎02281/42088). Staff here are helpful and frank, and will assist you with information about accommodation or flowers in the wider region.

Around Cape Columbine

The coastline north of Vredenburg is classical West Coast territory: isolated fishing settlements with small, whitewashed cottages and a salty haze hanging over the lazy, glinting ocean. However, despite the quaint image, most of the settlements possess alarmingly expanding holiday developments, offering (naturally) whitewashed cottages in classical West Coast style. Although you can still find the odd lonely coastline and some genuine character in the old villages and their coloured inhabitants, the area feels as though it has reached that sad moment of tilting over from "best-kept secret" to over-subscribed building site.

North of Saldanha is a large inland farming centre, **VREDENBURG**, an unremarkable town in a featureless setting. Nearby are two different **accommodation** options. The first, just past the main crossroads of the R45 from Vredenburg and the R27 from Cape Town, is *Windstone Backpackers* (☎02286/61645; ①), a friendly base for exploring the region, where you can also organize horse trails along the coast or up in the Cederberg; the second is *Jacobsbaai* (☎02281/83105; ④), an upmarket and comfortable guesthouse right on the coast off the R238 between Saldanha and Vredenburg.

The best of the area is to be found around the village of **PATERNOSTER** (whose name comes from the prayer mumbled by Portuguese sailors crawling ashore from a shipwreck in the adjacent bay), and the nature reserves **around Cape Columbine**, Tieties Bay and south of Cape St Martin. There are some excellent **coastal hiking trails** through these reserves, including two long day-trails (details from West Coast Publicity Association, see opposite) and, if you have a larger group, a two-day hike with two nights accommodation in a simple cottage near Tieties Bay (contact Fred Botha on ☎021/96 8327). There is also an attractive, isolated **campsite** at Tieties Bay (☎02285/718).

For some choice West Coast delicacies and hospitality, head for the farm stall and **coffee shop**, *Die Winkel op Paternoster* ("the shop in Paternoster"), by the "Stop" sign on the main road.

St Helena Bay

St Helena Bay was the point where **Vasco da Gama** set foot in what is now South Africa during his epic voyage around the Cape and through to India in 1497. He wasn't the first European to round the Cape of Good Hope, nor the first to land, but his voyage did open up the route to the Cape, which was to give the Cape its strategic importance for four centuries. **Three granite lumps** on the shore between the fishing villages of St Helena Bay and Stompneus Bay serve as a memorial to his landing, and a no-expenses-spared **Da Gama Museum** (daily 8.30am–4.30pm; free) has also been established within the largest of the new housing developments in the area at **Shelley Point**. The museum is more a rainy-day affair than a must-see, but does include some well-devised storyboards, a collection of model ships and some early navigation devices.

Throbbing away in the background, as you stand at the granite memorial contemplating three months in a leaky boat, is a **lobster factory**, where you can usually buy fresh or frozen specimens if you enquire at reception. It's illegal to buy the lobsters if they're offered to you on the street, although in season you can obtain a permit to catch them for personal consumption (contact the Department of Sea Fisheries, ☎02281/41710). Strangely enough, fishermen once thought the lobster that got entangled in their net a pest, and during the nineteenth century sold wagonloads of them to farmers to be ground up and used as fertilizer.

Velddrif

At the northern end of the R27 from Cape Town and 15km east of St Helena Bay is **VELDDRIF**, a fishing town situated at the point where the Great Berg River meets the sea. Each year the Berg River **canoe marathon**, which begins up near Ceres, ends here at a marina development called Port Owen. In the quieter backwaters near the Velddrif bridge, you can still see individual fishermen in small boats landing catches of mullet or horse mackerel which are then dried and salted to make *bokkoms*, called by some a delicacy, but essentially a staple form of cheap protein for fishermen and farm workers on the West Coast. To see the rickety wooden jetties where the boats tie up and the frames and sheds by the shore where *bokkoms* are strung up to dry, turn right at the roundabout just over the bridge coming into town on the R27, and after a kilometre or so take the first right-hand turn down to the riverside.

In town, straight on at the roundabout onto Church Street and then right up a dirt driveway is the **West Coast Gallery** (Mon–Sat 9am–5pm), one of the best of its type in the area. Run by a local artist and essentially a shop, it displays a wide selection of art and crafts, including some interesting driftwood collages. You can also have a cup of coffee here, and explore the reed maze or have a game of pétanque in the grounds. Look out for the selection of sea-salt products, including flavoured salts, seaweeds and bath salts, produced on a small pan by the coast nearby.

Further up the Berg River there is a wealth of **birdlife** in the marshes and various wetlands. While you're here, you can take a bird-watching river cruise (☎02288/31253) or even stay in a **houseboat** (☎ & fax 021/462 1902), and there are some pleasant **self-catering cottages** and walking trails on the historic farm of *Langrietvlei* (☎ & fax 02288/30856; ①), halfway between Velddrif and Hopefield.

Lambert's Bay

The only settlement of any note between Velddrif and Port Nolloth, almost at the Namibian border, is **LAMBERT'S BAY**, 75km north of Velddrif (by indirect dirt road) and 70km due west of Clanwilliam (by tarred road). This is an important **fishing port**, although by the sights and sounds of the harbour you soon become aware that even the fishermen have to stand aside for the impressive colony of **gannets** on Bird Island in the centre of the bay. You can walk out to the island on the causeway which encloses the fishing-boat harbour for a closer look at the tightly packed, petulant, ear-piercing mass of gannets, along with a few disapproving-looking penguins and cormorants.

Lambert's Bay itself is rather short on charm; the fish-processing plant sits on the edge of the harbour, right in the town centre, giving you the feeling you're in a seat behind a pillar at the theatre. Nevertheless, its isolation means that there is some deserted coastline and nature nearby. You can wander off to see it for yourself, but there are some fun **desert safari trips** run from a lopsided wooden shack by the fishing harbour (☎027/432 1715). On these trips you'll be taken on a twilight walkabout looking for such things as sidewinding adders, swimming geckos and flightless dung beetles, with an outdoor *potjie* feast set up at the end. The same bunch also organize 4WD trails and boat trips to see the birds and sea life. Also on the active theme, horse trails, bird-watching and canoeing are organized at **Verlorenvlei**, a wetland inland from Eland's Bay to the south of Lambert's Bay, by *K'Taaibos Adventure* (☎ & fax 0263/684), who also offer rustic B&B **accommodation** in a stone cottage or luxury tents (③).

Practicalities

Tourist information at Lambert's Bay is available from the Sandveld Museum in Kerk Street (Mon–Fri 9am–1pm & 2–5pm, Sat 9am–1pm; ☎027/432 2335). There are a couple of **caravan parks** at either end of town, and no shortage of self-catering apartments, but nothing much by way of charm or character. If you need a proper bed for the night, head for Voortrekker Street in the centre of town, where the neat *Marine Protea* (☎027/432 1126; ③) offers comfortable hotel rooms, and *Raston Guesthouse* (☎027/432 2431; ②) has good-quality B&B accommodation.

Eating is one of Lambert's Bay's specialities. Good options include *Bosduifklip* (☎027/432 2735), an open-air restaurant set inland among some big rock formations 6km out of town along the R364, while the original West Coast open-air restaurant, *Muisboskerm* (☎027/432 1017), scores on location – right on the edge of the ocean, 5km south of the town. For a more conventional seafood restaurant, try *Die Kreef Huis* (☎027/432 2235; closed Sun) at the entrance to the harbour on Strand Street, or the easy-going *Villa Romano* (☎027/432 22835), a pizza and pasta restaurant one block along from the *Protea* hotel.

Cederberg

A bold and jagged outcrop of the Western Cape fold escarpment, the **Cederberg mountain range** is one of the most magical wilderness areas in the Western Cape. Rising with a striking presence on the eastern side of the Olifants River Valley, around 200km north of Cape Town, these high sandstone mountains and long, dry valleys manage to combine accessibility with remote harshness, offering something for hikers, campers, naturalists, rock climbers and even astronomers. In a number of places the pink-hued sandstone (which can glow with heartbreaking beauty in the light of a low sun) has been weathered into grotesque, gargoyle-like shapes and a number of memorable natural features – including the huge **Wolfberg Arch** and a thirty-metre-high free-standing pillar which is shaped like, and known as, the **Maltese Cross**. Throughout the area there are numerous San rock-art sites, an active array of Cape mountain fauna, from baboon and small antelope to leopard, lynx and aardwolf, and some notable mountain-fynbos flora, including the gnarled and tenacious Clanwilliam cedar and the rare snow protea.

The Cederberg is easily reached from Cape Town by way of the N7: the towns of **Citrusdal** and **Clanwilliam** lie just off the highway near, respectively, the southern and northern tips of the mountain range. Both make attractive bases from which to explore the area, particularly during spring flower season, although you can find simple accommodation right in the mountains themselves. From Clanwilliam, set beside a man-made dam, there are worthwhile routes out to Lambert's Bay on the coast (see opposite) and over a spectacular mountain pass to the remote and unique mission at **Wuppertal**.

Exploring the Cederberg

The **Cederberg Wilderness Area**, 710 square kilometres in extent, is reached by a dirt road 28km north of Citrusdal which leads off the N7 to the forest station at Algeria. The permit system for the area allows a certain number of people to be in each of three separate parts of the wilderness area, but you do have to arrange permits in advance through the Cape Nature Conservation Office (☎027/482 2812) in Algeria. Because it's a wilderness area, you can hike or camp where you like within the areas you hold a permit for. There are many designated **trails**, including routes to the main rock features and the two main peaks, **Sneeuberg** and **Tafelberg**. Camping is available at a pretty riverside site at Algeria, and unsophisticated but adequate **self-catering chalets** are also available through Cape Nature Conservation or at the farms inside the reserve: *Sanddrif* (☎ & fax 027/482 2825; ①), *Kromrivier* (☎027/482 2807; ①–②) and *Krakadouw* (☎027/482 2507; ①–②). At Dwarsrivier, by Sanddrif, there is an amateur

observatory, which on summer weekend evenings occasionally features an outdoor slide show and some high-powered telescopes for a closer look at the dazzling heavens.

Weather conditions are often extreme in the Cederberg, with frost and snow during winter, and blistering heat in summer. There are a number of rivers, however, which you can safely head to for a swim. If something even wetter excites you, the best **white-water rafting trips** in the Western Cape take place on the Doring River in the northern Cederberg from mid-July to mid-September. Weekend trips with *River Rafters* (☎021/72 5094) include one night sleeping under an overhang, and cost in the region of R500 per person. At the other end of the accommodation scale is *Bushman's Kloof* (☎027/482 2627; ⑦), northeast of Clanwilliam, a luxury **lodge** with some interesting (though not big) game and a resident rock-art specialist.

Pakhuis Pass and Wuppertal Mission

Leaving Clanwilliam to the northeast, the R364 winds up through the northern Cederberg over the **Pakhuis Pass**, a drive worth taking for its lonely roadside scenery and inspiring views. A turn-off from the road after it drops into the Doring River Valley takes you to Wuppertal mission station, but if you keep straight on for another 100km or so it leads though some remote and beautiful landscapes, renowned for their spectacular wild flowers in spring, to **Soetwater**, on the R27 between Nieuwoudtville and Calvinia (see pp.249–250).

Set deep in the wonderfully named Tra-tra valley, the Moravian **mission station at Wuppertal** is one of the oldest in the Western Cape and remains one of the more poetic and untouched settlements in South Africa. A tiny collection of thatched cottages with a few cultivated fields around its fringes, the mission is famous for making *velskoene* (literally "hide shoes"), suede footwear commonly known as "vellies" and part of the South African national dress. You can see the shoes being made and, of course, buy some here. Two small **guesthouses** and some **campsites** provide simple accommodation (☎027/482 3051; ①).

Citrusdal

Heading north from Piketberg on the N7, a long, flat plain reaches out to the line of Olifantsrivierberg Mountains, which the highway crosses by way of the impressive **Piekenierskloof Pass**, forged in 1857 by the indomitable road engineer Thomas Bain. Coming down the northern side of the pass, the town of **CITRUSDAL** appears in the rolling countryside of the Olifants River Valley with the dramatic mountainscape of the Cederberg behind. Strange as it may seem now, early Dutch explorers saw huge herds of elephants here as they travelled north towards Namaqualand, so falling upon a suitable name for the river.

There are no roads from Citrusdal into the heart of the Cederberg Wilderness Area – you have to carry on up the N7 to the Algeria turn-off – although there are various routes leading into the foothills justifiably popular with mountain bikers. You can get a **map** outlining these at *Sandvelhuise*, the town's upbeat **information centre** (Mon–Fri 9am–4.30pm, Sat 9am–noon; ☎022/921 3210) in a small complex off Muller Street, just up from the wide main street, Voortrekker. Staff here can provide useful information about self-catering cottages and guesthouses in the area. The centre also has a **tea room**. If you decide to stay (and Citrsudal is a good place to pause for a break and make some plans), there's a pleasant **campsite** with a pool in town (☎022/921 3145; ①–②), on the left-hand side as you come in over the bridge from the N7, and the garishly coloured *Cederberg Lodge* (☎022/921 2221; ③) has **hotel**-type accommodation on Voortrekker Street. Light **meals** are on offer at *Uitspan*, at 66 Voortrekker, painted a distinctive yellow and purple.

Beyond Citrusdal is some attractive countryside and farmland, including, as the town's name suggests, plenty of citrus groves. One of the principal attractions of this area is *The Baths* (☎022/921 3609; ①–③), a laid-back mineral **spa resort** with campsites, chalets and self-catering rooms in a large old stone building set around a series of hot pools. To get to it, turn right off the road leading into Citrusdal from the N7 and drive 16km down a good tarred road past the airfield – incidentally, one of the best places in the Western Cape for parachuting. Given that other hot-spring resorts in the Western Cape tend to be either rather snooty and expensive or tacky and overcrowded, this place hits a nice balance: it will be crowded, certainly, during holidays, but it has retained its simplicity and elegance and is a good spot to relax, particularly if you've been hauling over mountain and rock for a few days.

Clanwilliam

Also on the N7 but at the northern end of the Cederberg, **CLANWILLIAM** is an attractive, assured town which carries off with some aplomb its various roles – as a base for the Cederberg Wilderness Area, majestic and ragged behind it; as a centre for spring flowers; as a holiday resort focused on the neighbouring dam; and as a service centre for the lower part of the fertile irrigation schemes of the Olifants River Valley to the north. Established in the last years of the eighteenth century, this is one of the older settlements north of Cape Town, and features a number of historic buildings around town, including an **information centre** and **museum** (Mon–Fri 8.30am–5pm, Sat 8.30am–12.30pm; ☎027/482 2024; small entry fee for museum), situated in the old jail at the far end of Main Street. There are some genuinely interesting attractions in town, including a good commercial **art gallery**, *Kunhuis*, on Main Street, a traditional leather shoemaking factory on Ou Kaapseweg, and the country's main **rooibos tea-processing factory** (tours Mon–Fri 10am–noon & 2–4pm) next door. Just to the south of town, a wild-flower reserve, **Ramskop**, is set on a hillside inside the entrance to the dam resort.

To add to its charms, Clanwilliam is well-supplied with **accommodation**. You can **camp** on the edge of the dam in the *Clanwilliam Dam Resort* (☎027/482 2133; ①–②), which also has a collection of plain chalets. The resort is the only public access point to the dam – one of the country's top water-skiing venues – which in summer and at weekends can seem to be monopolized by speedboat louts. There isn't any local rental if you want to join in the watersports, unless you're a resident at the *Olifants Dam Motel* (☎027/482 2185; ③) on the N7 side of the dam, which has boats available. Other places to stay include a famous South African institution, *Strassberger's Clanwilliam Hotel* (☎027/482 1101; ③–④), on the town's main street. Dignified and well run, the hotel has an open-air pool, renowned restaurant (*Reinhold's*), a tea room and separate chalets. Finally, *St du Barrys* (☎027/482 1537; ③–④), on the way out of town on the Pakehuis road, is a country guesthouse with an upmarket feel, antique-filled rooms and thatched roofs.

Reinhold's undoubtedly has the best reputation in town as a **place to eat**, but if you fancy something a bit more casual head for *Olifantshuis Pizzeria and Olde Worlde Pub*, on the corner as you turn into Main Road off Augsburg Drive.

ROOIBOS TEA

Few things in South Africa create such devotion, derision, hype and, among visitors, suspicious bemusement, as **rooibos** (literally, "red bush") **tea**. Still sown and harvested by hand on many farms, rooibos is a type of fynbos plant grown only in the mountainous regions around Clanwilliam and Nieuwoudtville. The tan-coloured tea which is brewed from its leaves has been a traditional South African drink ever since it was developed by Asian slaves two centuries ago, but it is only in the last twenty years that it has broken free from its health-food-shop earnestness and established mainstream credibility as a light, refreshing and healthy (caffeine-free) drink. In homes and tea rooms throughout South Africa you'll find rooibos firmly entrenched alongside regular tea and coffee. Drink it with milk and sugar, or just with a slice of lemon and a teaspoon of honey.

travel details

Most **public transport** in the Western Cape originates in Cape Town and the main services are outlined in our "Travel details" at the end of Chapter One.

Trains

The most useful **trains** in the Western Cape are the two *Metro Rail* services connecting Cape Town with Stellenbosch and Paarl. Outside peak morning and evening hours, trains are irregular, but run at approximately two-hour intervals. Phone the station to confirm times.

Intercity buses

In addition to the major points of departure listed below, the **intercity buses** stop at a number of intermediate points. Principal routes are Cape Town – Port Elizabeth along the N2 coastal route, with an inland alternative along the Little Karoo mountain route; Cape Town–Johannesburg/ Pretoria along the N1; and Knysna–Johannesburg/Pretoria via Mossel Bay and the N12.

Beaufort West to: Cape Town (3–4 daily; 6hr); George (2–3 daily; 4hr); Johannesburg (3–4 daily; 11hr); Knysna (2–3 daily; 5hr); Mossel Bay (2–3 daily; 3hr); Oudtshoorn (2–3 daily; 2hr 15min); Paarl Pretoria (3–4 daily; 12hr).

George to: Cape Town (3–4 daily; 6hr); Durban (1 daily; 18hr); Johannesburg (daily except Sat 2–3 daily; 15hr); Knysna (3–4 daily; 1hr); Mossel Bay (3–4 daily; 45min); Oudtshoorn (daily except Sat 2–3 daily; 1hr 30min); Plettenberg Bay (3–4 daily; 1hr 30min); Port Elizabeth (3–4 daily; 4hr 30min); Pretoria (daily except Sat 2–3 daily; 16hr).

Knysna to: Cape Town (3–4 daily; 7hr); Durban (1 daily; 17hr); George (3–4 daily; 1hr); Johannesburg (daily except Sat 2–3 daily; 16hr); Mossel Bay (3–4 daily; 1hr 15min); Oudtshoorn (daily except Sat 2–3 daily; 2hr); Plettenberg Bay (3–4 daily; 1hr 30min); Port Elizabeth (3–4 daily; 4hr 30min); Pretoria (daily except Sat 2–3 daily; 17hr).

Mossel Bay to: Cape Town (3–4 daily; 5hr 30min); Durban (1 daily; 18hr 30min); George (3–4 daily; 45min); Johannesburg (daily except Sat 2–3 daily; 14hr); Knysna (3–4 daily; 1hr 15min); Oudtshoorn (daily except Sat 2–3 daily; 1hr 15min); Plettenberg Bay (3–4 daily; 2hr 15min); Port Elizabeth (3–4 daily; 4hr 30min); Pretoria (daily except Sat 2–3 daily; 15hr).

Oudtshoorn to: George (daily except Sat 2–3 daily; 1hr 30min); Johannesburg (daily except Sat 2–3 daily; 13hr 30min); Knysna (daily except Sat 2–3 daily; 2hr); Mossel Bay (daily except Sat 2–3 daily; 45min); Pretoria (daily except Sat 2-3 daily; 14hr 30min).

Paarl to: Beaufort West (4–5 daily; 5hr); Durban (2 daily; 18hr); East London (5 weekly; 15hr); Johannesburg (3–4 daily; 14hr); Pretoria (3–4 daily; 15hr).

Plettenberg Bay to: Cape Town (3–4 daily; 7hr 30min); Durban (1 daily; 16hr); George (3–4 daily; 1hr 30min); Knysna (3–4 daily; 1hr 30min); Mossel Bay (3–4 daily; 2hr 15min); Port Elizabeth (3–4 daily; 2hr 30min).

Backpacker buses

Both the *Baz* (☎021/439 2323) and *Hopper* (☎041/55 4000) **backpacker buses** travel along the N2 between Cape Town and Port Elizabeth, with a detour to Oudtshoorn. You can be let off anywhere along the way. The *Baz* runs five times a week in a single journey, while the *Hopper* does the trip in two legs: Cape Town–Mossel Bay and Mossel Bay–Port Elizabeth (daily in both directions) with the night spent in Mossel Bay.

Flights

George to: Cape Town (1–3 daily; 1hr); East London (3 weekly; 2hr); Johannesburg (3–4 daily; 1hr 30min); Port Elizabeth (5 weekly; 1hr 40min).

Plettenberg Bay to: Durban (3 weekly; 2hr 45min); Johannesburg (4 daily; 2hr 15min); Port Elizabeth (3 weekly; 50min).

CHAPTER THREE

NORTHERN CAPE

The vast **Northern Cape**, largest and most disseminated of South Africa's provinces, is not an easy region to tackle as a visitor. From the lonely **Atlantic West Coast** to the provincial capital, **Kimberley**, hard against its eastern border with the Free State, it covers over one-third of the nation's landmass – an area dominated by heat, brown aridity, empty spaces and huge travelling distances. However, while these characteristics themselves possess a surreal attraction, it is for the miracles of the desert you will come – the improbable swaths of flowers, and wild animals roaming among the dunes.

The most significant of these suprises is the **Orange River**, a large watercourse which flows, often with parched land stretching for hundreds of kilometres on either side, from the Drakensburg Highlands of Lesotho to the Atlantic, where it marks South Africa's northern border with Namibia. The river separates the two sparsely populated semi-desert ecosystems which fill the interior of the Northern Cape – the **Kalahari** and **Great Karoo**. It was by the Orange that **diamonds** were first discovered in the 1860s, although it was in the alluvial deposits of the Vaal River and nearby dry diggings around Kimberley that the story of diamonds would be played out in its most compelling detail.

A no less hard-won economic contribution of the Orange is in the large **irrigation schemes** which have created a stretch of incongruous green along the course of the river, principally around the isolated northern centre of **Upington**. A small but important town, Upington acts as a major gateway to the magnificent **Kalahari-Gemsbok National Park**, undoubtedly one of the finest game-viewing parks in South Africa, and the smaller **Augrabies Falls National Park**, where the Orange plunges with muscular drama into a large granite gorge.

On the western side of the province, the presence of the Atlantic Ocean means that the land, while still harsh and dry, is subject to different influences. It is in this region, **Namaqualand**, that the brief rains of winter produce one of nature's truly glorious transformations, when in August and September the land is carpeted by a magnificent display of multicoloured **wild flowers**.

Despite these impressive natural attractions, the most commonly encountered part of the Northern Cape is its southeastern corner, where both of the two main routes between Johannesburg and Cape Town, the **N1** and the **N12**, pass before meeting just northeast of Beaufort West in the Great Karoo. The N12, no longer in time or distance than the N1, presents a good opportunity to spend a day or so in Kimberley. Neither route, however, offers particularly inspiring scenery or sights, and anyone hoping to see a cross-section of South Africa by driving between Johannesburg and Cape Town will find themselves hot, tired and rather disappointed. A less obvious, but more attractive option is to take the **N14** from Johannesburg through Upington, passing the atmospheric old mission station at **Kuruman**, and on to **Springbok** and the main west coast route (the N7) to Cape Town. This route is only 400km longer than the N1 or N12 and, while it doesn't offer respite from long, empty landscapes, the sights on the way are more unusual. This route also puts both the Kalahari-Gemsbok National Park and little-visited **Richtersveld National Park** within striking distance and, in August and September, allows you to experience the full geographic extent of the magnificent Namaqualand flowers, something usually seen only in restrictive forays from Cape Town.

ACCOMMODATION PRICE CODES

All the accommodation listed in the Guide has been categorized into one of seven price bands, as set out below. The rates quoted, unless otherwise stated, represent the most expensive per-person rate for a double or single room outside high season (Dec & Jan), except for category ①, which are per-person rates for a dorm bed in backpacker accommodation, or a campsite. For more accommodation details, see p.31.

① R0–50	② R50–100	③ R100–150
④ R150–200	⑤ R200–250	⑥ R250–300
	⑦ Over R300	

Some history

The history of the Northern Cape area is intimately linked to the **San**, whose heritage is most prominently seen in the countless examples of **rock art** to be found across the province, as well, to a lesser extent, in their ancient legends and place names. The movement of Africans from the north and east and Europeans moving in from the southwest drove the San from their hunting grounds and eventually to extinction, yet for both sets of newcomers the semi-desert of the Karoo and the Kalahari offered little more than hopelessness and heartbreaking horizons. What it did offer – wealth under the dusty ground – the Europeans showed no restraint in pursuing, beginning with an expedition into Namaqualand to mine for copper led by **Governor Simon van der Stel** soon after the Dutch first established their settlement in the Cape. The other Europeans who made an early impression on the province were **trekboers**, Dutch burghers freed from the employment of the Dutch East India Company in the Cape who wanted to find new lands to farm away from the authoritarian company rule, and **missionaries**, the boldest of the early explorers, who established a framework of settlement and communication which was to be used by all who came after.

Within a few years of the discovery of **diamonds** in the area, a settlement of unprecedented size had grown up around Kimberley, which soon had more trappings of civilization than most of the southern hemisphere, with such things as public libraries and tramways, as well as South Africa's first urban "location" for Africans and coloureds. The British authorities in the Cape were quick to annex the new diamond fields, something which didn't endear them to either the Orange Free State or the mainly coloured **Griqua** people (see box p.436), who both claimed this ill-defined region. It was no surprise, therefore, that at the outbreak of the **Anglo-Boer War** in 1899 rich and strategic Kimberley was one of the first towns besieged by the Boer armies, and many reminders of the war can still be seen in the area.

In the **twentieth century** the harsh land has relented little and the predominant themes of the province have hardly changed. Kimberley is still the largest town, farming is still tempered by the lack of water, wealth is still gathered greedily from the ground and travellers into the interior are regarded as rare and bold.

KIMBERLEY AND AROUND

The **N12** highway which runs from Johannesburg through **Kimberley**, and then down to meet the N1 link to Cape Town, is the main reason most visitors find themselves in this area. Although the term suggests a wonderland of romance and riches, Kimberley and its "Diamond Fields" surrounds are mostly dry and uninspiring, and the city will never again know the importance and glamour it had for two heady decades at the end of the last century.

A SHORT HISTORY OF THE DIAMOND FIELDS

Before 1866, the area now known as the **Diamond Fields** was unpromising farmland, marked by occasional *koppies* and inhabited by pioneer farmers and an independent people of mixed race origins, called the Griquas. The outlook changed, however, after a 15-year-old boy noticed a shiny white pebble on the banks of the Orange River near Hopetown, about 120km southwest of Kimberley. Just as word of that discovery was spreading, another Hopetown resident, Schalk van Niekerk, acquired from a Griqua shepherd a massive 83.5 carat diamond. It is common practice for significant diamonds to be given a name, and these two became known, respectively, as "Eureka" and "The Star of South Africa". The Star was described at the time by the British Colonial Secretary as the "rock on which the future success of South Africa will be built". He was not far off the mark. Certainly in the short term the discoveries provoked wild optimism as thousands of prospectors made the gruelling trek across the Karoo to begin sifting through the alluvial deposits along the banks of the Orange and Vaal rivers. By 1873 there were an estimated 50,000 people living in the area.

Although there were plenty of diamonds to be found in the rivers, prospectors also began scratching around in the dry land between them, encouraged by tales of diamonds being found in farmhouse bricks made from local earth. Two of the most promising "dry diggings" were on a farm owned by two brothers, **Johannes** and **Diederick de Beer**. In 1871 the brothers sold the farm, which they had bought a few years previously for £50, to prospectors for the sum of £6300. The two sites were subsequently to become the **Kimberley Mine**, or "Big Hole", and the **De Beers Mine**, situated on either side of the city centre of Kimberley. The Big Hole was the focus of the most frenetic mining activity of the early years, and the shantytown which grew up around it, called New Rush, was the origin of the present city. In those days it was a heady, rugged place to live, with little authority or structure, but with prizes rich enough to attract bold men with big ideas. Of these, two very different, if equally ambitious, men rose to prominence in the new settlement. **Barney Barnato**, a flamboyant Cockney, established his power base at the Kimberley Mine, while **Cecil John Rhodes**, a parson's son who had come out to join his brother in South Africa to improve his health, gradually took over control of the De Beers Mine. The power struggle between the two men was intense, and culminated in the formation in 1888 of the De Beers Consolidated Mines Limited, an agreement which involved the transfer of over £5 million, an astronomic sum in those days, from Rhodes to Barnato.

This consolidation laid the foundation for De Beers' monopoly of the diamond industry in South Africa, something which has remained intact ever since. The rise of the gold fields on the Witwatersrand soon swamped Kimberley's importance, and although three of the five large mines in the area still produce diamonds, and the alluvial claims along the Vaal are still worked, the firm hand of De Beers has stifled the enterprise which initially gave the area its character.

For those passing through, however, there is enough in the area to justify a day doing a bit of modern-day prospecting, especially if you are into the complex history of South Africa. The biggest draw is Kimberley itself, but trips to the area's **Anglo-Boer War battlefields** and the **alluvial diamond diggings** around the Vaal River are well worth the effort. It's important to realize that, despite being the provincial capital, Kimberley does not really act as a gateway to the Northern Cape, being far nearer to Bloemfontein and the Free State. The obvious route to the Kalahari and Namaqualand from Johannesburg is along the N14 through Upington, and from Cape Town up the N7 to Springbok.

Kimberley

Despite being a provincial capital and the centre of production of one of the most valuable materials known to man, **KIMBERLEY** is neither a large nor glamorous city. Status and sophistication have been draining from it ever since the days of the diamond rush,

KIMBERLEY

De Beers Mine

Train Station

Sister Henriette
Stockdale Statue

Rhodes
Statue

William Humphries
Art Gallery

Africana
Library

Kimberley Club

City Hall/
Market Square

Harry
Oppenheimer
House

Oppenheimer Memorial
Gardens & Diggers' Fountain

Library

City Civic
Complex

Tram
terminus

De Beers
Head
Office

The Big
Hole

Star of the West pub

Kimberley Tram Line

Kimberley Mine Museum

ACCOMMODATION

1 Caravan Park
2 Diamond Protea Lodge
3 Edgerton House
4 Gum Tree Lodge
5 Holiday Inn
6 Jacaranda Cottage
7 Open Mine Caravan Park
8 Penbury Lodge
9 Savoy
10 Swann's Rest Guest House

△ & Bloemfontein

Halfway House pub 3

Bultfontein & Du Toitspan Mines 6

Honoured Dead Memorial & Airport ▷

△ Cape Town N12

△ Shell Ultra City, Johannesburg N12

△ Upington N8 10

300 m

when it was the fastest-growing city in the southern hemisphere and **Cecil Rhodes** held in his grip not only the fabulously wealthy diamond industry, but the heart and mind of the British Empire. Even the all-controlling **De Beers Group** (sometimes called the "grandfather" of Kimberley for the number of people it directly and indirectly employs) is now itself controlled by the huge Anglo-American conglomerate in Johannesburg and the city lives in the chilly shadow of the day when the diamonds finally dry up.

Spend a few hours seeking out what historical buildings remain, and take the opportunity of an **underground tour** of a working diamond mine, not forgetting to peer into the depths of the **Big Hole**, a remarkable, hand-dug chasm which takes up almost as much land area as the central business district (CBD) of the city itself, and you'll taste some of the opulence and energy which made the city famous.

The **telephone code** for Kimberley is ☎0531.

Arrival, information and orientation

Kimberley's **airport** (domestic flights only) lies 7km south of the city centre (information ☎851 1241). All the city's **car rental** firms are located here: *Avis* (☎851 1082), *Budget* (☎851 1182) and *Imperial* (☎851 1131). Arriving by **train**, you'll find yourself within easy walking distance of the town centre, though be warned that the daily service from Cape Town pulls in here at 2am, while trains from Johannesburg arrive at 6pm and 9pm. The main **bus** services terminate at the Shell Ultra City service station on the Transvaal Road (N12), an inconvenient 6km north of the city centre. There is no transport from here, so your best option is to hitch a lift. If you're arriving by **car** for a fleeting visit, you'll find plenty of parking space outside the tourist information office.

Kimberley's helpful **tourist information office** is in the City Civic Complex on Bulfontein Road (Mon–Fri 8am–3pm, Sat 8.30–11.30am; ☎82 7298), and is well worth making use of.

The fact that the best-known sight, the Big Hole, is under the ground doesn't make **orientation** immediately easy. However, the tell-tale mounds of dead earth lying immediately to the west of the CBD are a good indication of its location. Another useful landmark is the stern-looking **Harry Oppenheimer House**, often just referred to as "HOH", one of the town's few skyscrapers, near the tourist information office.

City transport

Kimberley is poorly served by public transport; beyond the city centre, which is walkable, getting around without a car isn't easy. There is a **taxi** company in town, *AA Taxis* (☎861 4015), which do not have the best reputation for reliability. **Bikes** can be rented from *Alphabeta's* in the Sanlam Arcade, 19a Jones St (☎81 1059), and they are also available at low cost for residents at the *Gum Tree* backpackers' lodge. Unusually for South Africa, Kimberley has a restored **tram** service, but its only function is to transport visitors to the Big Hole. Trams depart regularly from Market Square in the centre.

Accommodation

Kimberley's **accommodation** is targeted at through-traffic and business travellers, but there are a handful of pleasant guesthouses in historic buildings, and because the city isn't regarded as a main centre prices are generally reasonable. While most hotels are within walking distance of the centre, some of the guesthouses, and both the campsites, are over 2km away, and the backpackers' lodge is too far to consider walking if you have

CECIL JOHN RHODES

When **Cecil John Rhodes** first arrived in the Kimberley Diamond Fields he was 18 years old, a sickly youth sent out to join his brother for the sake of his health. Soon making money buying up claims, he returned to Britain to attend Oxford University, where his illnesses returned and he was given six months to live. He came back out to South Africa, where he was able to improve both his health and his business standing, allowing him to return to Oxford and graduate in 1881, by which time he had already founded the **De Beers Mining Company** and been elected an **MP** in the Cape Parliament. Within a decade Rhodes controlled ninety percent of the world's diamond production and was champing at the bit to expand his mining interests north into Africa, with the British Empire in tow. With much cajoling, bullying, brinkmanship and no little obfuscation in his dealing with imperial governments and African chiefs alike, he brought the territories north of the Limpopo under the control of his South African Company. That land – now Zimbabwe and Zambia – became known as Rhodesia in 1895, the same year as a Rhodes-backed invasion of the Transvaal Republic, the Jameson Raid, failed humiliatingly. Rhodes was forced to resign as prime minister of the Cape Colony, a post he had assumed in 1890 at the age of 37, while the Boers and the British slid towards war. He spent the first part of the war in besieged Kimberley, trying to organize the defences and bickering very publicly with the British commander. A year after the end of the war, aged only 49 and unmarried, he died at Muizenberg near Cape Town and was buried at an outlook called World's End in the Matopos Hills near Bulawayo in Zimbabwe.

luggage to carry. If you get stuck, the tourist information office (see above) can provide an accommodation list.

Hotels and guesthouses

Diamond Protea Lodge, 124 Du Toitspan Rd (☎81 1281, fax 81 1284). Rather overshadowed by the *Holiday Inn* next door, the *Diamond* is a bit more intimate, but still aimed primarily at business travellers. ③.

Edgerton House, 5 Egerton Rd (☎81 1150, fax 81 1785). Elegant guesthouse in a National Monument in historic Belgravia suburb. Thirteen rooms, a pool and a tea room prove a bit of a squeeze. Serves an expensive dinner. ④–⑦.

Holiday Inn Garden Court, 120 Du Toitspan Rd (☎31751, fax 82 1814). Reliably good rooms in this large six-storey hotel with a pool and a *Spur* steakhouse. ③–④.

Jacaranda Cottage, 95 Main Rd (extension of Du Toitspan) (☎32357). Separate apartment at the back of a suburban house southeast of the city centre. A bit flowery and fussy, but still one of the better B&Bs in town. ③.

Kimberley Club, 70–72 Du Toitspan Rd (☎82 4224). Run along lines of a London club, though the rooms fail to match grandeur of the rest of the building. Women not allowed into main bar. ③.

Pembury Lodge, 11 Currey St (☎81 6956). Pleasant historic house in city centre. The rooms (all en-suite) are a bit creaky, but boast some fascinating period pieces – ask for the one with old-fashioned shower. Good food is served in the attached restaurant. ②.

Savoy Hotel, 19 De Beers Rd (☎82 6211, fax 82 7021). Not in the best part of town, and very plain from the outside, but inside the *Savoy* retains an old-fashioned charm. ③.

Swann's Rest Guest House, 41 Swann's Way (☎861 3406). Two good-value, simple double rooms with a kitchenette at the back of a suburban house, 2km from the centre. Beware the confusing map on back of their leaflet – the best way to get here is to follow R64 west out of town, turn left at Pickering and left again into Swann's Way. ②.

Campsites and budget lodging

Gum Tree Lodge, Bloemfontein Rd (☎82 8577). Kimberley's only backpackers' lodge is an inconvenient 5km out of town, but is pleasantly shady and has a swimming pool. There's also a restaurant next door. The office is open 7am–10pm. ①.

Kimberley Caravan Park, Hull Rd, next to De Beers Stadium (☎83 2582). Unappealing municipal campsite in an insalubrious part of town, with igloo-style cabins for rent. ①.

Open Mine Caravan Park, West Circular Rd (☎80 6322). Privately run campsite located among the old mine heaps just beside Big Hole. Lush, neat and relatively quiet, with a pool, although the shade from the young trees isn't generous. There are rumours that a casino complex is to be built on the site. The office is open 6am–8pm. ①.

The City

Many of Kimberley's main sights lie on or near **Du Toitspan Road**, which slices diagonally across the city centre and becomes one of the main arteries out of town to the southeast. The **Big Hole** lies just west of the centre, while the more open central business district (CBD) lies to the south of Lennox Road.

The Big Hole: Kimberley Mine Museum

Although the **Big Hole**, just west of the city centre, is neither the only nor even the biggest hole in Kimberley, it remains the principal attraction of the city, and is certainly worth a look. The only official way to see it is from inside the **Kimberley Mine Museum** (daily 8am–6pm; entry fee) on the western side of the hole. To get there, drive to West Circular Road or take a tram from the City Hall (hourly at quarter past the hour 9.15am–4.15pm). The museum is spread out along the edge of the Big Hole and there are two viewing platforms, from where you can peer down into nothingness and look for the poetry and poignancy which undoubtedly still lingers where mountains were moved in a belief in the power of wealth. Balanced on the lip of the crater on the far side is the now diminutive outline of the city, almost swallowed up by the size and silence of the hollow below it.

The rest of the museum comprises a large collection of **historic buildings**, many of them original from the days of Rhodes and Barnato, which were moved here from the city centre when development and demolition threatened. With old shops, churches, bars, banks and sundry other period institutions, including *Barney Barnato's Boxing Academy*, there is enough property to create a fairly complete settlement, and most of the fixtures, fittings and artefacts are genuine. You can walk down these old Kimberley

KIMBERLEY'S BIG HOLE

Where there is now a gaping 500-metre-wide cavity was once a small hill on a typically dry northern Cape farm belonging to the brothers Johannes Nicolaas and Diederick Arnoldus de Beer. In the early 1870s, with diamonds known to be in the area, there were various work parties scratching around hoping for a lucky find. One, known as the "Red Cap Party", led by Fleetwood Rawstorne, was working at the base of Colesberg *koppie* in July 1871. The story goes that they sent one of their cooks to the top of the hill as a punishment for being drunk, telling him with a laugh and a clip round the ear not to return until he had found a diamond. The unnamed servant duly came back with a peace offering, and within two years there were over 50,000 people in the area frantically turning Colesberg *koppie* inside out. By 1914, when De Beers closed the mine, some 22.6 million tonnes of earth had been removed, yielding over 14.5 million carats of diamonds. Incredibly, the hole was dug to a depth of 240m entirely by pick and shovel, and remains the largest man-made excavation in the world. In its heyday, when tens of thousands of miners swarmed over the mine to work their ten-square-metre claim, and a network of ropes and pipes crisscrossed the surface, each day saw lives lost and fortunes either discovered or squandered. Once the mining could go no further from the surface, a shaft was dug which allowed further excavations beneath it to a depth of over 800m.

streets, peer into shop windows and wander through a couple of the buildings, but for a "living museum" the atmosphere is somewhat soporific. One of the more engaging parts is an area where you can buy a bucket of alluvial river diggings and sift through it on old sorting tables, in the hope of finding one of the mock diamonds planted among the gravel, which you can then exchange for some emminently undesirable prizes, such as faded postcards of the museum or fluffy keyrings. Your chances of striking lucky are about one in five – much better odds than the original miners faced.

Market Square and around

At the heart of the city centre is **Market Square**, dominated by the white, Corinthian-styled **City Hall**. As well as being the hub of buying and selling during the early diamond days, the square was the scene of two occasions significant in South Africa's history: the public crushing of gold-bearing rock from the Witwatersrand which persuaded Rhodes, Barnato and others to further their investments in gold-mining, and the departure in 1890 of the Pioneer Column which effectively established "white" Rhodesia. Around the square, the sense of movement and commerce is perpetuated by a large taxi rank and an assortment of scruffy but colourful stalls and traders.

One block west of Market Square along the tramline, at 36 Stockdale St, is the head office of **De Beers**, a dignified but unremarkable old building rather swallowed up by the city around it. You can read the brass plates by the door, but the building is not open to the public.

The Kimberley Club and around

Not far southwest of Market Square, on Du Toitspan Road, is the two-storey **Kimberley Club**, founded in 1881 by the movers and shakers of the new settlement. The club was modelled on gentlemen's clubs in London, but its colourful, enterprising bunch of members ensured the place was more dynamic than stuffy. It was claimed that there were more millionaires to the square foot here than any other place in the world, and acceptance within the club is said to have been a significant carrot in Rhodes' wooing of Barnato in 1888 (that, and a cheque for £5 million). Although the present building is the third on the site, it was completed in 1896 and would still have been known by Rhodes, whose presence seems no less dominant today than it would have been at the turn of the century, with countless portraits, busts and other memorabilia of the man in all parts of the building. As well as leather armchairs in the smoking lounge and marble in the hallway, there are plenty of fine antiques and a few quirky pieces such as a weighing chair presented to the club by Lord Randolph Churchill, Winston Churchill's father. If you want to look around or go for a drink in the bar, you'll get a much less chilly reception if you phone ahead and pay due respect to the club's rules, which include no jeans and T-shirts and no women in the main bar. It's also possible to spend a night at the club (see "Accommodation").

Across the road is the small but engrossing **Africana Library** (Mon–Fri 8am–12.45pm & 1.30–4.30pm), which specializes in historical material relevant to Kimberley and the Northern Cape. Opened in 1887, it retains many original features and is worth peeping into – one of the librarians will show you around if you ask nicely. One block away, on Chapel Street, the **Alexander McGregor Memorial Museum** (Mon–Fri 9am–5pm, Sat 9am–1pm, Sun 2–5pm; entry fee) is one of seven McGregor museums spread around the Diamond Fields area and is the repository for the stones, bones and bygone fashions of the collection.

The CBD

At the junction of Du Toitspan and Lennox roads stands a statue of **Cecil Rhodes**. Unusually, here he is portrayed astride a horse, although the tributes around the plinth spare little of the swagger common to most Rhodes memorials. Across the road in the grounds of St Cyprian's Cathedral, and a little more humble in tone, stands what is reputed to be the only statue of a nun in the world, depicting **Sister Henriette Stockdale**, a pioneer of nursing in South Africa.

Moving south of Lennox into the CBD area, you'll come to the **Oppenheimer Memorial Gardens**, which contain a bust of mining magnate Sir Ernest Oppenheimer and the striking **Diggers Fountain**. The combination maintains a balance of respect which Kimberley, to its credit, perpetuates between those who got dirt beneath their fingernails and those who made the money. The fountain depicts five miners holding high a massive sieve, and looks particularly impressive when floodlit at or after dusk. The tall building lurking above the gardens is **Harry Oppenheimer House** (HOH), the offices of De Beers' Central Selling Organisation, on the upper floors of which all of the company's South African-mined diamonds are assessed for caratage, colour, clarity and shape. So that this can be done in the best natural light, the building faces south and has special windows to eliminate glare. Not surprisingly, it isn't open to the public.

On the opposite side of the gardens to HOH lies an unexpected gem: the **William Humphreys Art Gallery** (Mon–Sat 10am–1pm & 2–5pm, Sun 2–5pm; free entry Wed), one of the country's top art galleries. Although dominated by European Old Masters when it opened in 1952, the collection has been moving with the times long enough to have established an impressively well-balanced representation of South African art, and shows no reservations about including traditional and contemporary work. The gallery was one of first places in the world to display San rock paintings as works of art rather than museum pieces.

Just south of the CBD, in the middle of a roundabout where Dalham and Memorial roads meet, is the **Honoured Dead Memorial**, a striking monument to the victims of the Kimberley siege during the Anglo-Boer War. Beside the memorial is the gun used in the siege known as **"Long Cecil"** – built in the De Beers' workshops to respond to the Boer's Long Tom cannon.

Belgravia

About 1km southeast of the CBD, along Du Toitspan Road, lies **Belgravia**, the residential suburb where most of Kimberley's wealthy families lived. A stroll around these streets is a good way to get a feel for the more refined side of the diamond age. The focus of the area is at the junction of Du Toitspan and Egerton roads, where you'll find the historic **Halfway House** pub. The pub takes its name from the fact that it is situated halfway between the De Beers and Bultfontein mines, and gained fame as a drive-in (or, in those days, ride-in) pub frequented by the celebrities of the pioneer days. Sure enough, the sign swinging outside shows a badly drawn Cecil Rhodes atop his horse, holding a glass of beer – though presumably not just "The Half" the inscription hints at (Cecil not being one to do things in part measures). Happily, the pub has not fallen victim to tourist kitsch and is still a popular local drinking hole.

Next door is **Edgerton House** (Mon–Sat 10am–4pm), a National Monument built in 1901 which has been converted into an upmarket guesthouse with a tea room in the internal courtyard (see "Accommodation"). Across the road is the famous **McGregor Museum** (Mon–Sat 9am–5pm, Sun 2–5pm), housed in a grand building and named after an early mayor of Kimberley. Inside you'll find natural and cultural history collections, as well as memorabilia pertaining to the siege. You can visit a couple of restored houses nearby: **The Bungalow**, the mansion of mining magnate HP Rudd, and **Dunluce**, an elegant Edwardian home, both on Lodge Road. Arrangements must be made at the museum if you want to see inside either house, although you can walk past both, along with over thirty other historic homes and points of interest, on a self-guided **walking tour** of Belgravia, details of which can be obtained from the tourist information office (see p.225).

UNDERGROUND MINE TOURS

One of the best ways to spend a morning in Kimberley is to join an **underground tour** of two of De Beers' working diamond mines – **Bultfontein** and **Dutoitspan** – both on the outskirts of the city. The nice thing about the tours is that, instead of being whisked around a sanitized visitors' centre, you are taken right to the working heart of the mine, amid the noise of turbines and engines, the dust, the mud, the heat and the thick air. After an introductory video and safety talk, visitors are kitted out with overalls, hard hats, torches and emergency oxygen packs – exactly the same gear as the miners wear – and then taken down (in groups of about twelve) to a depth of 825m by the shaft lift. Once down, you'll be shown around caves where kimberlite is loosened by explosions, dragged out into trolleys, crushed and then taken to the surface for cleaning and sifting. The tour is not a good idea for the timid or claustrophobic, and De Beers won't allow anyone under the age of 16 to go underground. It is, however, a rare and fascinating opportunity to get right to the rock face where diamonds are being extracted, and see in its raw form one of the industries which still lies at the centre of the South African economy and psyche. In the event you spot a diamond while underground, De Beers will give you 20 percent of its value, more (they claim) than it could fetch on the black market. Don't hold out too much expectation, though; mostly all you'll see is grey clay dirt.

The tours (Mon & Wed–Fri 8am, Tues 9.30am) last three and a half hours and cost around R50. You have to book beforehand (☎82 9651). Also available are surface tours of the same mines (Mon–Fri 9am & 11am), lasting one and a half hours.

Adjacent to the McGregor Museum on Egerton Road is the **Duggan-Cronin Gallery** (Mon–Sat 9am–5pm, Sun 2–5pm), which despite its stuffy-sounding name includes a large collection of endearingly unsophisticated photographs taken by Alfred Duggan-Cronin, a night watchman for De Beers, portraying different aspects of the lifestyles of the indigenous people of South Africa.

Eating, drinking and nightlife

Kimberley's limited selection of **restaurants** is dominated by the ubiquitous steakhouses, and beyond the handful of historic **pubs**, which can be entertaining for their atmosphere and clientele, there is little in the way of **nightlife**. If you're looking for a snack or a cup of **coffee** during the day, head for *Kaldi's Coffee House* in the Pick 'n' Pay arcade off Chapel Street. Alternatively, the refined *Edgerton Tea Garden*, on the corner of Du Toitspan and Egerton roads in Belgravia, offers afternoon tea.

Restaurants and pubs

Halfway House Pub, corner of Du Toitspan and Egerton roads. Cecil Rhodes' old refreshment stop, and still a popular, unpretentious local. Pub lunches available, although *Umberto's* restaurant next door is perhaps better for a slap-up meal.

Keg & Falcon, corner of Du Toitspan and Memorial roads. Traditional English theme pub which promises more than it delivers, but is very popular with locals.

Mario's, 159 Du Toitspan Rd (☎81 1738). In a small house across the road and just along from *Holiday Inn*, this restaurant offers the best atmosphere in town. You can eat outside – although it fronts a main road. Friendly staff, and a big menu. Mon–Fri 11.30am–2pm & 6–10.30pm, Sat 6–10.30pm.

Old Diggers Restaurant, Bloemfontein Rd, next to *Gum Tree Lodge*. Large dining hall, serving up cheap, wholesome meals, principally for residents of the backpackers' lodge, at all hours of the day. Takeaway is available, and there's a bar.

Penbury Lodge, 11 Currey St, city centre. Swiss owner and chef Peter Egli masterminds a fairly specialized, meat-oriented menu, with delicious results. Pub lunches are also available. Closed Sun.

Safari Steakhouse, corner of Transvaal/Jones and Old Main roads, Market Square. Classic, popular steakhouse which has being pumping out the protein for thirty years. Big on game: to order, simply point to the set of horns mounted on the wall to indicate which species you want. Among the imaginative menu is an elephant-sized, 1.1kg steak.

Star of the West, corner of West and North Circular roads. Near the Big Hole, Kimberley's oldest pub still serves beer to diggers after the diamond markets on Saturdays. This is a good place to come after a hard day's holing – and the solid pub lunches are a better option than the Mine Museum's tea room.

Tiffany's, in the *Savoy Hotel*, 19 De Beers Rd. A meal at Kimberley's most formal restaurant doesn't come cheap – and the atmosphere can be a bit intimidating – but the food is good.

Umberto's, corner of Du Toitspan and Egerton roads. Next door to the *Halfway House Pub*, this regular Italian restaurant, with red-checked tablecloths, serves up decent pizza and pasta. The rest of the menu is slightly pricier. Closed Sun.

Listings

Airlines *South African Airways*, 30 Currey St (☎22431).

Banks with automatic teller machines (ATMs) are easy to find in the shopping areas of the city centre. Opening hours are Mon–Fri 8.30am–3.30pm, Sat 8–11am.

Bus information *Greyhound* (☎81 1062); *Intercape* (☎021/386 4400); *Translux* (☎012/315 2333).

Emergencies Ambulance ☎81 1954; Fire ☎82 4211; Police ☎10111.

Hospitals and doctors Doctors are listed in the telephone directory under "Medical". The two best hospitals for visitors are *Medi City*, 177 Du Toitspan Rd (☎88 1111), and *Curomed*, 144 Du Toitspan Rd (☎81 4370).

Pharmacy with extended opening hours: *Piet Muller Pharmacy*, 52 Market Square (☎81 1787), is open daily until 9pm.

Post office The main branch is in Market Square.

Swimming *Karen Muir Pool* in Queen's Park, off Regiment Way, is an open-air pool. Open Sept–April.

Taxis *AA Taxis* can be booked by calling ☎861 4015.

Telephones There are phone booths all over town taking phone cards and coins.

Train information Phone ☎88 2631.

Around Kimberley

The handful of interesting places around Kimberley include **Barkly West**, the town where some of the first diamond camps sprung up in the 1860s, and the little-known **Vaalbos National Park**. Both lie off the **R31** which runs northwest out of Kimberley in the direction of Kuruman. This is one of the roads in the region where you will see signs warning you not to exceed 60kph because of the danger of kudu leaping out of the bushes by the side of the road. Few drivers heed the signs, but the threat is a real one, particularly at night, as these large antelope have little judgement of the speed of a vehicle and will try to jump over the beam of headlights, often with fatal results – not just for the kudu. The mostly unremarkable landscape lying to the south of Kimberley along the N12 was the setting for one of the most dramatic campaigns of the Anglo-Boer War, and if such history appeals to you the scenery around **Magersfontein** can suddenly transform into an intricate and moving storybook.

Barkly West

Originally a convenient crossing point of the Vaal River known as Klipdrif, the small town of **BARKLY WEST**, 35km northwest of Kimberley, was the first important focus of the diamond rush, out of which rose the short-lived **Klipdrif Republic**, proclaimed by mili-

---

DIAMONDS ARE FOR EVER

Diamonds originate near the centre of the earth as particles of carbon in the earth's mantle which are subjected to such high pressure and temperature that they crystallize to form diamonds. Millions of years ago the molten rock, or magma, in the mantle burst through weak points in the earth's crust as volcanoes, and it is in the pipe of cooled magma – called **kimberlite**, after Kimberley – that diamonds are found. Finding kimberlite, however, isn't necessarily a licence to print money – in every one hundred tonnes there will be about twenty carats (4g) of diamonds. The word "carat" comes from the carob bean, which, when dried, was used as a measure of weight, now standardized as 0.2g. (Carat has a different meaning in the context of gold, where it is a measure of purity.) De Beers estimate that fifty million pieces of diamond jewellery are bought each year, which represents a lot of people saying, "Will you marry me?"

---

tant miners as British, Boer and Griqua authorities squabbled about who was to control the area. Later, political representation came in the form of Cecil Rhodes, who was the MP for the town up to and including his time as prime minister of the Cape Colony. Visibly poor, Barkly West is in a fairly sorry state today, although the alluvial beds along the river on the fringes of town are still being worked, and on Saturday mornings diggers come to sell their week's findings to licensed buyers at the **Diamond Market**. Some of the older diggers still prospect by hand, finding perhaps just five good stones in a year and always hopeful of one "big one". If you do want to investigate further – and it can't be denied that a rough romance still surrounds the whole business – snooping around on your own is unadvisable. The best way to explore is with Dirk Potgeiter of *Diamond Tours Unlimited* (☎82 9834 or 083/265 4795), who offers some fascinating insider **tours** of the alluvial diggings. He will take you to meet both the old hand-prospectors and the more modern operators. The full package (roughly R400 per person) also includes an underground tour with De Beers (see p.230) in the morning, lunch and a visit to Vaalbos National Park in the late afternoon. Shorter, customized tours can also be arranged.

Barkly West's visitor facilities are minimal; you're best off staying in nearby Kimberley or Vaalbos and visiting this town during the day.

Vaalbos National Park

Some 19km north of Barkly West is the low-key **Vaalbos National Park**, proclaimed in 1986 and only opened to the public in 1994. The 180-square-kilometre park makes a very pleasant half-day or even overnight outing, as long as you are not hellbent on seeing big game and dramatic scenery. Its principal focus is to protect an area where three significant and contrasting southern African vegetation types converge – Kalahari thornveld, Karoo and grasveld – although it is also now involved in the protection of the **black rhino**, and these, together with **white rhino**, **giraffe**, **buffalo** and a variety of **antelope**, are the larger animals you can expect to encounter.

To get to the park coming from Barkly West, turn left from the R31 and drive along a signposted dirt road for about 6km. The park entrance is to the left-hand side of the road, immediately across a causeway through the Vaal River. The park is open daily from 5am to 6.30pm. For general information, phone ☎053/561 0088.

There is only one road through the park, with two circular routes at the far end of this road, in the area where most game is found. If you want to **stay overnight**, you can do so at the pleasant *Mekala* rest camp, which consists of three compact self-catering chalets (①–②), each with six beds, set in the umbrella-thorn bushveld. **Bookings** must be made through the *National Parks Board* in Pretoria (☎012/343 1991) or Cape Town (☎021/22 2810). An upmarket alternative to the rest camp is the private *Sydney-on-Vaal Guest Lodge* (☎053/561 0081; ⑦), reached by a gate next to the park entrance. The lodge has been set up in the old hotel and converted main-street shops of the abandoned town of Sydney which was, in the days of the diamond rush, a thriving settlement of 20,000 people. It is now a ghost colonial village, and the only way to visit it is as a resident of the lodge.

Wonderwerk Cave

If you're driving further along the R31 towards Kuruman, you will pass the intriguing **Wonderwerk** ("miracle") **cave**, a major archeological site which has revealed some of the earliest evidence of the production of fire in the world. There is a small visitors' centre on the site, run by the McGregor Museum in Kimberley, and a **campsite** and self-catering **chalet** run by the local farmer (☎053/384 0680; ①–②). If there are archeologists working in the cave and you're interested enough in what's going on to ask a few questions, you're likely to hear some fascinating things. If there's no one around, you'll have to ask at the farm for the gate to be unlocked. A small admission fee is charged.

Magersfontein

Just over 30km south of Kimberley along the N12, the Anglo-Boer War battlesite at **Magersfontein** provides a poignant reflection on the area's blood-spattered past. This is where Boer forces put trench warfare into effect against British troops, with devastating results (see box, below). Signposts point the way to a rather scruffy **Visitors' Centre** (daily 8am–5pm; entry fee), with tea room, viewpoint and various monuments situated on the western end of the line of hills. Out on the battlefield itself, now open *veld* with springbok grazing and the occasional car throwing up a plume of dust along the dirt road, the

---

THE KIMBERLEY CAMPAIGN

At the outbreak of the **Anglo-Boer War** the Boer forces identified diamond-rich Kimberley as an important strategic base, and quickly besieged the city, trapping its residents, including Cecil Rhodes, inside. In response, the British deployed an army under **Lord Methuen** to relieve the city. The army was compelled, by its size and lack of knowledge of the terrain, to advance from the coast along the line of the railway so that a supply of troops, water, food and equipment could be ensured.

Methuen first encountered Boer forces at Belmont, just across the Orange River. This encounter was followed by further battles at Graspan and Modder River, from where the Boers made a tactical withdrawal to Magersfontein, a range of hills about 30km south of Kimberley. Here, rather than defending the top of the ridge of hills, as was their ususal tactic, the Boer generals, under the leadership of General Cronjé but the tactical direction of **Koos de la Rey**, decided to dig a line of **trenches** along the bottom of the *koppie*. In the early hours of December 11, 1899, the British, led by the Highland Regiment fresh from campaigns in North Africa and India, and considered to be the cream of the British army, advanced on Magersfontein, fully expecting the enemy to be lined along the ridge. Just before dawn, as they fanned out into attack formation, four thousand Boers in the trenches just a few hundred metres away opened fire. The use of trenches was, at that point, a forgotten tactic in modern warfare, and the element of surprise caused devastation in the ranks of Highlanders. Those not killed or wounded in the first volleys were then pinned down by snipers for the rest of the day, unable to move in the coverless *veld* and suffering appallingly under the hot sun. The next day the British withdrew back to Modder River, and the relief of Kimberley, inside which relations between Rhodes and the leader of the British garrison were becoming fraught, was delayed for two months. The defeat was one in a series of three the British suffered within what became known as "Black Week", news of which sent shock waves through the British public expecting their forces to overrun the "crude farmers" before Christmas.

lines of **trenches** can still be seen, along with other memorials, including a pair of granite crosses marking the graves of Scandinavian soldiers who fought on the Boer side.

One of the most enjoyable ways of finding out more about the history is to book a one-day **battlefield tour** with Steve Lunderstedt (☎86 1007 or 083/265 6436), a highly entertaining and well-informed military historian. The tours provide a vivid picture of the campaign, with trips to battle sites, fortifications and gun positions, and walks on the battlefields to get a sense of the terrain and look for old shells and other evidence of fighting.

If you want to **stay** in the area instead of heading back to Kimberley, a good option is *Langberg Guest Farm*, 21km south of Kimberley on the N12 (☎82 1001; ②), a very hospitable B&B set in several Cape Dutch horse stables on a historic farm at the western end of the Magersfontein battlefield. The food here is excellent and the rooms good value.

THE KALAHARI

The Northern Cape has no shortage of dry, endless expanses, but the most emotive by far is the **Kalahari**. The very name holds a resonance of sun-bleached, faraway spaces and the unknown vastness of the African interior, something at once harsh and magical. The name derives from the word *kgalagadi* ("place without water"), and is used in a general sense to describe the semi-desert which stretches north from the Orange River to the Okavango Delta in northern Botswana, west into Namibia and east until the bushveld begins to dominate in the catchment areas of the Vaal and Limpopo rivers.

The Kalahari here is characterized by surprisingly high, thinly vegetated red or orange sand dunes scored with dry river beds and large, shimmering saltpans. Like most deserts (although this is strictly semi-desert), daytime temperatures are searingly hot in summer and numbingly cold at night in winter. North from the Orange, South Africa's largest river which flows defiantly through the parched regions, the land is populated only by tough, hard-working farmers and communities largely (although not wholly) descended from the nomadic Khoi. For many land-users, there is an increasing realization that **ecotourism**, rather than a First World luxury, may be the only viable option on huge areas of land where both stock farming and hunting provide at best a marginal living.

Upington, the main town of the area, stands on the northern bank of the Orange, at the heart of an irrigated corridor of intensive wheat, cotton and, most prominently, grape farms. At the far end of the farming belt, about an hour east, the Orange picks up speed, and froths and tumbles into a huge granite gorge at **Augrabies Falls**, a powerful spectacle and the focus of a growing national park.

The undoubted highlight of this area is the **Kalahari-Gemsbok National Park**, tucked into a spear of South African territory thrusting up between Namibia and Botswana. A sanctuary rich in game, the park is well worth the long trek you'll have to make to get there. The options if you're coming to it directly from Johannesburg along the N14 highway are either to turn off at **Kuruman**, site of a famous nineteenth-century **mission station** established by Robert and Mary Moffat, along the R31 (a long, bleak dirt road which should only be tackled in a sturdy vehicle), or to travel on to Upington, the established gateway for the park, from where the road is tarred for half the way.

Upington

As an inevitable focus of trips heading to the Kalahari-Gemsbok and Augrabies national parks, as well those to and from Namaqualand, **UPINGTON** is a good place to stop to gather supplies, organize a park tour or onward accommodation, or simply draw breath. Situated on the banks of the Orange River, it can also be a mellow spot, although savage summer temperatures mean you probably won't want to linger for much longer than is necessary. The climate doesn't necessarily improve once you leave, but at least you're on your way to something interesting.

Arrival and information

Arriving by **car**, you'll quickly find yourself in or near the centre of town, where parking is easy, although it's always worth hunting for a bit of shade. *Translux* (☎054/28 2203) and *Intercape* (☎054/27091) **buses** will either take you to the *Protea* hotels right in the heart of town or to the railway station, a ten-minute walk away. Upington's **airport** (☎054/31 1364) is 7km northeast of town, on Diedericks Road. *Avis* **car rental** (☎054/25746) is based at the airport.

Central Upington is compact and easy to get around, with most of the activity on the three main streets running parallel to the river. You'll find the helpful **tourist information office** in the library building, halfway down Le Roux Street (Mon–Fri 8am–5.30pm, Sat 9am–noon; ☎054/27064). If you want to **book a tour** from Upington to either of the national parks, see the box on p.237.

4WD vehicles are available to rent from *Walker's Midas*, 53 Market St (☎054/25441), who offer good deals with unlimited mileage (they also rent out standard cars at decent rates).

Accommodation

There are enough **places to stay** in Upington for you to find something appropriate, although bear in mind that tourism here is still geared to South African holidaymakers,

UPINGTON

Orange River Wine △ Cellers Co-op   Kalahari Gemsbok National Park, Spitskop Nature Reserve, N10 Namibia △

ACCOMMODATION
1 Die Eiland
2 Le Must Guest Rooms
3 Lemon Tree Cottage
4 Protea Oasis
5 The Three Gables
6 Upington Protea
7 Yebo Budget B&B

Kalahari-Oranje Museum

Orange River

Kimberley, South African Dried Fruit Co-op

and the tastes of international travellers are not always catered for or even understood. The tourist information office (see above) can provide a list of guesthouses.

Die Eiland, on an island in the river immediately opposite the town centre (☎054/31 1553). Huge, popular, and well-run resort with pleasant campsite and self-catering chalets, the best of which are right by the river and sleep four. ①–②.

Lemon Tree Cottage, 14 Budler St (☎054/22255). Comfortable self-catering apartment at the east end of the town centre (near the post office), in the grounds of an attractive house with a sultry tropical garden backing onto the river. ③.

Le Must Guest Rooms, 12 Murray Ave (☎054/25015). Centrally located B&B in a double-storey Cape Dutch house on the riverbank. Choose from three tasteful doubles and three singles. ②.

The Three Gables, 34 Bult St (☎054/31 1220). Decent B&B in a suburban area near the police station. One room in a mini-apartment in the large garden and one with a living room under the main house. ②.

Upington Protea, 24 Schröeder St (☎054/25414). More characterful of the town's two *Protea* hotels, this has a few rooms looking out onto the river. A *Spur Steak Ranch* is downstairs. ③.

Yebo Budget B&B, 21 Morant St (☎082/574 4486). Although advertised as a backpackers' lodge, this is more a pleasantly unfussy house with double rooms, a pool and space for lounging around. Great value, and there's always a chance of some interesting people passing through. ①.

The town and around

Upington's main disappointment is that you can see very little of the Orange River once you're in the town centre. The best place to glimpse it is from the grounds of the **Kalahari-Oranje Museum**, at the southern end of Schröder Street. The museum itself (Mon–Fri 9am–12.15pm & 2–5pm; entry fee), based in the 1875 mission church which was the origin of the settlement here, tells a fairly predictable history. The grounds are pleasant enough, though – and you should look out for a quirky sculpture of a donkey. A couple of kilometres away at the other end of Schröder Street is an equally bizarre **statue of a camel**, which commemorates Upington's days as a frontier station, when the police – often mounted quite sensibly on camels – had to patrol large tracts of the wider Kalahari area, dealing variously with Griqua rebels, recalcitrant San bands and hostile German forces based in Namibian territory.

Thanks to irrigation schemes, Upington is surrounded by vineyards. Remarkably enough, ten percent of the country's grapes are grown in this stretch – mostly table grapes and dried fruit, but wine is also produced. **Vineyard tours** can be arranged through *Ben Ora* (☎054/491 1253), while factory tours and tastings are available at both the *Orange River Wine Cellars Co-op* in the industrial estate west of the town centre off Dakota Road, and the *South African Dried Fruit Co-op* on Louisvale Road, on the way out of town across the bridge.

Spitskop Nature Reserve

About 13km north of town along the R360, **Spitskop Nature Reserve** (dawn to dusk; ☎054/22336; entry fee) offers an accessible taste of the the semi-desert, although with its limited array of rather skittish antelope and other large game, the experience lacks the fullness you'll get when you venture further afield. The name "Spitskop" refers to a small rocky hill which offers some expansive and worthwhile views of the surrounding plains. At its base is a quiet **campsite** and simple **chalet**, which are worth considering if you want to avoid staying in town (both ①). There are hiking and mountain-bike trails throughout the reserve, and you can take game-viewing drives in your own car.

KALAHARI TOURS FROM UPINGTON

Upington is a good place to arrange a **tour** of the North Cape's national parks. Most operators will be able to customize tours to suit your requirements. For details and prices, which vary depending on how many people are on the tour, phone the companies directly.

• **Kalahari Tours and Travel** (☎082/493 5041). Budget tour of the Kalahari area; includes Augrabies Falls, canoeing on the Orange, the Roaring Sands, a game farm and return coach fares to Upington from Cape Town or Johannesburg. A three-day extension up to the Kalahari-Gemsbok park is extra.

• **Spitskop Tours and Safaris** (☎054/22336). The next level up. Includes Augrabies Falls, the Mier settlement, and two days in the Kalahari-Gemsbok park. Led by a local farmer/hunter who is knowledgeable about the animals and North Cape area.

• **Molopo Kalahari Safaris** (☎083/305 4227). A variety of tours offered by the acknowledged expert on 4WD in the area, including a three-day guided-drive tour of the Kalahari-Gemsbok park and a longer safari with 4WD into Botswana. More upmarket, but well-run and authoritative.

Eating and drinking

As the only large centre for hundreds of kilometres, Upington will seem like culinary heaven compared to the towns you'll pass through to get here. If ever conditions were right for you to appreciate a franchised **steakhouse**, this is it and, sure enough, they are lined up in anticipation in the town centre. Without doubt the best **restaurant** is *Le Must*, hidden behind some extravagant shrubbery at 11 Schröder St (☎054/24971), and serving up very imaginative South African and Provençal dishes.

For **coffee** or a snack, head for the *San Francisco* coffee shop, located in the mall bordered by Market and Hill streets, or, if your Afrikaans is feeling strong, *De Oude Kerkje Koffie Kôner* on the corner of River and Le Roux streets. Decent places to drown a **beer** include *Scotty's Bar* in the *Upington Protea*, 24 Schröeder St, and *O'Hagan's*, a few doors away.

On to the Augrabies Falls

From Upington, you're well-positioned to head to **Augrabies Falls National Park**, one of South Africa's most dramatic natural spectacles. The falls can easily be visited as a day-trip from Upington, although there is some decent accommodation both in the park itself and nearby. The route from Upington is west along the **N14**, following the Orange River and its rich fringe of vineyards, orchards and alfalfa fields. Along the road are two pleasant **campsites** situated on islands in the river: one at **Kanoneiland** and the other at **Die Punt**, 20km further south.

Some 39km southwest of Upington, the road passes through **KEIMOES**, where, if you have time, it's worth driving to the top of **Tierberg Reserve**, a small *koppie* at the eastern end of town which commands impressive views over the riverine farming strip and the harsh semi-desert beyond.

The town of **KAKAMAS**, 32km from Augrabies Falls, offers a few options if you're looking for somewhere to **stay** near the park. Along Voortrekker, the shady main street, is the *Waterwiel Protea* (☎054/431 0838; ③) and the friendly *Lapa-side* guesthouse (☎054/431 0150; ②). Slightly closer to the national park is *Ebenaeser Guesthouse* (☎054/431 1029; ②), set among the vineyards about halfway between Kakamas and the turning to Augrabies. To **camp**, follow the signpost to *Die Mas* (☎054/431 1150; ①), a secluded, privately owned camping and caravan site among the vineyards beside the river. The best **restaurant** in town is *Rodio*, in a modern mall behind the post office on Voortrekker.

Augrabies Falls National Park

Roaring out of the barren semi-desert just over 100km west of Upington, and sending great plumes of spray up above the brown horizon, is the most spectacular moment in the 2000-kilometre progress of the Orange River; the mighty waterfall still known by its Khoikhoi name, *Aukoerebis*, "the place of great noise".

At peak flow, the huge volume of water plunging through a narrow channel at the head of a deep granite gorge actually compares with the more docile periods at Victoria Falls and Niagara, although **Augrabies** lacks both the soul-wrenching grandeur of its larger rivals, and the prettiness of waterfalls which tumble from a greater height. However, it is free of rampant commercialization, and in its eerie desert setting, with the azure evening sky wide and smooth above, the falls provide a moving and absorbing experience.

The falls

To **view** the falls, walk across the smooth granite domes beside the main rest camp to the fence along the edge of the gorge. The sides of the canyon are shaped like a smooth parabola and there are many tales of curious visitors going too far in their quest to peer at the falls and sliding helplessly into the seething maelstrom below. Although there is the odd miraculous survival – most famously a Scandanavian who was stripped of all his clothes by the force of the water before he was plucked out – over twenty have died since the national park was proclaimed in 1966. There is now a large fence, but ever since the suspension bridge across the gorge washed away there is no one spot where you can get a clear view of the main event, and the temptation to edge closer and closer to the edge of the gorge for a better look is strong. By being forced to try different viewpoints, however, including a dramatic spot very close to the frothing water just as it is about to launch itself over the falls, you end up with a better impression of the river and gorge as a whole.

The atmosphere, always noisy and awesome, is at its best near **sunset**, as the softer sun shines straight into the west-facing gorge and the echoing roar disappears off into a suddenly empty, ceilingless light-blue sky. To see more of the gorge, walk the short distance from the rest camp to **Arrow Point** or, if you're prepared to let the modern world intervene, drive on the link roads round to **Ararat** or **Echo Corner**.

The rest of the park

The rest of the park covers an extensive 184 square kilometres on both sides of the river. The land is dry and harsh, with plants typical of arid areas such as *kokerboom* (quiver tree), camelthorn and Namaqua fig providing sparse ground cover. The landscape is not without interest, however, and there are various striking rock formations in the park, notably some **potholes** scoured out by the river when it ran a different course to its present one, and **Moon Rock**, a huge dome of smooth, flaking granite rising out of the flat plains. If you drive on the (untarred) roads which go into the park you'll probably spot some of the resident fauna, notably **eland**, **klipspringer** and other small antelope. You are as likely to see the smaller animals, including dassie, mongoose and lizards, on foot as you wander around the falls and the camp.

Practicalities

A visit to Augrabies is included on a number of tours running out of Upington (see box, p.237). If you're coming independently, you'll have difficulty getting here without your own car. It is possible to visit the park as a **day visitor**, a practical option if you're based in Upington or travelling on elsewhere, as in a couple of hours you can gather a good impression of the falls and gorge.

Augrabies is open daily (April–Sept 6.30am–10pm; Oct–March 6am–10pm). The **entrance gate** is 30km from the N14 along a good, tarred road; the park's **reception** (7am–7pm; ☎054/451 0050) is a little way inside. Facilities in the main camp include swimming pools, various levels of self-catering **chalets** and cottages (②–③), and a large **camping** and caravan area (①). To **book** accommodation, phone ☎012/343 1991. Alongside the reception area is a shop, a self-service snack bar and a smart **restaurant** with views looking out over rocks towards the gorge.

Various **adventure activities** are promoted by the park, but none really match the adrenalin surge of the falls themselves. What can be fun is the "Augrabies Rush", a half-day trip on small rafts down 8km of increasingly swift river immediately above the falls. The trip is run by *Walkers on the Wild Side* (☎054/451 0177).

The best time to visit Augrabies is from March to May, when the temperatures are slightly cooler and the river is at its maximum flow after summer rainfall up in the Lesotho catchment areas.

On to Gemsbok

The journey to **Kalahari-Gemsbok National Park** is, whichever way you travel, a long, hot and weary one. You'll see plenty of the classic **red dunes** of the Kalahari, and every so often a huge, crazily paved grey saltpan, but the vegetation has been largely denuded and there is no shortage of desolate images, such as broken windmills and the rusting frames of motor cars, drowning in the desert sand.

From Upington, the R360 is tarred for 150km, after which it becomes dirt, while the longer approach via the R31 is tarred only between Kuruman and Hotazel. Drive carefully when you're on dirt roads, and be extra alert at corners where deep sand can build up, and beware of dust clouds when you pass another vehicle. It's also a good idea to reduce the pressure in your tyres by about half a bar before setting off. If you're just visiting the park, there's no need to go to the extra expense of renting a 4WD; a normal, reasonably strong sedan car will do fine, but bear in mind that the higher the clearance the better – a car packed with four adults might struggle.

There are several **accommodation** options on the way, worth considering for a more homely experience before or after visiting the park. Remember, however, that the park's best game-viewing is to be had first thing in the morning, so stopping en route isn't really an option if you're on a tight schedule. *Rooipan*, off the R360 (☎054902/91 2411; ③), is a farmhouse offering full board, as well as a strategically placed tea room roughly halfway between Upington and the park, off the R360. At the turnoff, the *Yebo-Gogo* farmstall, a caravan brightly painted in the colours of the South African flag, is good for a drink or snack. Closer to the park, at **Andriesvale**, the *Molopo Lodge* (☎054/511 0008; ③) offers rondavels arranged around a very enticing pool. Andriesvale also has a **filling station** and a small shop. Some 7km east, along the R31 dirt road to Kuruman, is *Cromdale* (☎054902, ext 4; ②), which has a tea room and small overnight cottage. Another 30km on is *Loch Broom* (☎054902, ext 91 6620; ③), a friendly guesthouse on a typical Kalahari farm.

Kalahari-Gemsbok National Park

While it represents only a small section of the vast Kalahari desert, the **Kalahari-Gemsbok National Park** (referred to sometimes by locals as "Gemsbok Park", but never "Kalahari Park") is the second-largest national park in South Africa. Proclaimed in 1931 to protect the game-rich area from the incursions of hunters, the park covers

KALAHARI GEMSBOK
NATIONAL PARK

nearly ten thousand square kilometres wedged into an area bounded on its northern and eastern side by the dry Nossob river bed, on its western side by the Namibian border, and to the south by the dry Auob River and a strip of land running parallel to this. There are fences along the western and southern boundaries, but not along the Nossob, on the other side of which lie Botswana and that country's even larger Gemsbok National Park. A joint management committee ensures that the two parks are run as a single unit, allowing game to move freely along the ancient migration routes which are so necessary for survival in the desert.

The means of survival are very immediate criteria for most of the park's life forms, where any vegetation has to survive temperature extremes between 40° and 10°C, and a meagre rainfall of 200mm per annum. Life is not easy, and that it flourishes in such profusion and detail is the enduring wonder of the Kalahari.

Access and information

The two alternatives to making the long drive to Kalahari-Gemsbok are to go on a **package tour** (see p.237) or to **fly** by private charter plane to Twee Rivieren (contact *Walkers Fly-In Safaris*; ☎054/25441), from where you can pick up a car by prior arrangement with *Avis* in Upington (see p.235).

The only entrance to the park is at **Twee Rivieren**. Opening hours vary from month to month, but if you arrive any time between 7am and 6pm, you'll find the gates open. The park's airstrip is here, as is the **Visitors' Centre** (☎054/561 0021), with exhibitions and slide shows worth checking out. All the roads in the park are sand, but they're in good condition, and a normal sedan car will be perfectly adequate given that you're likely to be driving much slower than the 50kph speed limit to give yourself a chance to spot some game. **Fuel** is available at all three rest camps (see below).

The best time to visit the park is between **March** and **May**, when there is still some greenery left from the summer rain and the sun is not as intense as in summer.

Accommodation

It's important to try to **book your accommodation** (☎012/343 1991 or 021/22 2810) as far ahead as possible as the park is becoming increasingly popular and, especially during school holidays, it can be impossible to find space. For safety reasons you'll be given a **permit** when you arrive, and you have to sign in and out whenever you are leaving or arriving at a rest camp. The first (and most developed) of the three **rest camps** is right by the entrance and offers functional but pleasant self-catering chalets, with thatched roofs and nice patio areas. Also here is a sizable caravan and **camping** site, the park's only swimming pool, and a mediocre **restaurant** with inflexible opening hours (7.30–8.30am, noon–2pm & 6.30–8.30pm). A takeaway and a shop are nearby. The other two camps are at **Mata Mata**, 120km away at the end of the road which follows the course of the Auob River, and at **Nossob**, 160km along the Nossob River road. Both these camps are much more basic than Twee Rivieren, but they hold so much of the raw flavour of the desert that it really is worth making the effort to get to one or the other. Both have fully equipped family cottages, simple three-person huts and caravan and camping sites. If your time is limited, the shorter distance to Mata Mata makes more sense, but if you have longer Nossob is better both for atmosphere and game-viewing: as well as hearing the lions roaring at night, you'll probably have your best chance of seeing them in this area. Not far from the Nossob camp is a water hole which has a hide overlooking it and is lit up at night. The only chance of **camping** outside the rest camps is on the Botswana side. You can get there via Twee Rivieren, but arrangements are through the Department of Wildlife and National Parks in Maun, Botswana (☎09267/66 0376).

The park

Following the long slog to get to Twee Rivieren, be prepared to clock up even more mileage inside the park. The shortest circular game drive is over 100km long, not far short of the distance to Mata Mata rest camp. Although the network of roads through the park looks limited, it is in fact one of the most attractive things about Kalahari-Gemsbok. The main roads follow the **river beds**, and this is where the game – and their predators – are most likely to be. Water flows very rarely in the two rivers, but frequent **boreholes** have been drilled to provide water for the game. Larger **trees** such as camelthorn and *witgat* (shepherd's tree), offer a degree of shade and nutrition, and desert-adapted plants, including types of melon and cucumber, are a source of moisture for the animals. Both the outlying camps are located along the main roads which follow the river beds, so by making your way to them you're going through the best game-viewing areas.

Much of the park is dominated by **red sand dunes**, which, when seen from the air, lie strung out in long, wave-like bands across the ocean of desert. From your car, the perspective is a different one, as you are in the valley of the river bed. However, this doesn't prevent the path from offering one of the finest **game-viewing** experiences in South Africa – not only for the animals, but for the setting, with its broad landscapes, the crisp light of morning and the huge skies. **Photographers** especially prosper in the clear viewing and wonderful light, a fact you can confirm for yourself in the exhibition at the Visitors' Centre at Twee Rivieren camp or in any number of glossy coffee-table wildlife books.

The focus in Kalahari-Gemsbok is on game drives; there aren't many alternative activities on offer. During the main holiday season, short walks across the dunes are organized at Twee Rivieren as a way of seeing some of the smaller manifestations of life in the park, but you'll have to ask to find out whether these are available at other times.

Seeing the animals

The game-viewing highlights in Kalahari-Gemsbok are, inevitably, the predators, headed by the **Kalahari lion** and, enjoying rare status alongside the Big Five, **gemsbok**, the large, lolloping animal with classically straight, V-shaped horns. You won't find buffalo, elephant or rhino, but their presence is hardly missed. Of the remaining Big Five, the **leopard**, as elsewhere, is not uncommon, but manages to remain elusive. In the wide open spaces, with its light colours blending so well with the sandy environment, lion here have an image as noble and inspiring as anywhere in Africa. Although they are not considered a separate species, the Kalahari lions commonly have much darker manes than those found in the bushveld, and studies have shown their behavioural and eating patterns to be distinctively well-adapted to the semi-desert conditions here.

Beyond the Big Five, there is much to absorb you, both large and small, with various species of **antelope, hyena, jackal, bat-eared fox, cheetah,** and some extravagant **birdlife**, including raptors, bustards and ostrich.

The best time to take your game drives is as early as possible in the morning, when you're more likely to see game out in the open. The shortest drive you are likely to take will be four or five hours long, so an early start means less time outside as the desert sun approaches its zenith. The last couple of hours of light in the afternoon are also a good time for game (and for taking photographs), but it's a lot more relaxing to go out for a little foray from your base than to be en route for a new camp, destined to arrive just as it's getting dark. The middle section of the day, especially during summer, is a necessarily inactive time for both animals and humans, so don't plan too full a programme.

Kuruman and around

Lying on the border between the Northern Cape and Northwest Province, the historic settlement of **KURUMAN** is an important stop on the way to the Kalahari-Gemsbok Park if you're travelling from Gauteng. The settlement grew up around **The Eye**, a natural spring which, since time immemorial and through drought and flood, has consistently delivered twenty million litres a day of crystal-clear water. The Eye was the focal point for a rather unsettled Tswana clan called the **Batlhaping**, whose chief, Mothibi, first invited missionaries to live among his people in the early nineteenth century, a decision which led to the building of the famous **Mission Station** by Robert Moffat, and the establishment of Kuruman as the "Gateway to the Interior" of darkest Africa.

Kuruman's town centre is pretty scruffy, dominated by cut-price chain stores, faceless bulk-buying supermarkets and litter-strewn minibus taxi ranks. The only sight of interest is The Eye, just along from the information office, and even here there's not much to look at: a moss-covered slab of rock dribbling water and a lily-covered pond surrounded by a high green fence, which you'll be charged a nominal sum to get past.

Moffat Mission Station

Of far greater interest than Kuruman itself, lying on the outskirts of town, just over 4km from the N14 along the R31 to Hotazel, is the **Moffat Mission Station** (Mon–Fri 8am–6pm, Sun 3–6pm, closed Sat). This collection of old stone-and-red-clay buildings was, for many years in the mid-nineteenth century, the focal point of that vague concept, the South African "Interior". It was here that a large, often gruff, energetic Scot, **Robert Moffat**, and his demure but equally determined wife, **Mary**, established a mission station (see box) where they lived for fifty years. During this time they produced the first Tswana Bible, a remarkable feat of publishing, and saw their eldest daughter, also called Mary, married to missionary/explorer, **David Livingstone**.

THE MOFFATS AND THEIR MISSION

Robert and Mary Moffat, newly married and envoys of the London Missionary Society, arrived in the Kuruman area in 1820, initially at a place rather charmingly mistranslated by early explorers as "Lattakoo", about 14km from Kuruman. As a former market gardener, however, Moffat soon saw the advantages of irrigating the flow of The Eye of Kuruman, and began to build his mission on the closest land wide and flat enough to plough.

Moffat didn't clock up too many converts – by the time he had built his 800-seater church he had just nine – but the challenge of preaching and establishing a school inspired him not only to learn the local language, which he did by living for a period in a remote Tswana village, but also to attempt the daunting task of **translating the Bible** into Tswana, which he then published on an iron printing press, now on display in the old mission schoolroom.

The late nineteenth century was a time when the popular imagination of Victorian Britain about "Darkest Africa" was at its height and missionaries had the status of movie stars today. The Moffats may have lived for fifty years in a remote outpost of Africa, but they were treated as celebrities when they retired back to Britain in 1870, not least because of the continuing exploits of their son-in-law. The Mission at Kuruman, meanwhile, carried on until the passing of the Group Areas Act of 1950, which brought about the end of the school and the church as a functioning place of (multiracial) worship. The old Mission, neglected and forgotten, was revived in the 1980s as an interdenominational trust, and a retreat and conference centre has been built behind the old village, under the supervision of a permanent warden and volunteer staff.

The Mission is a pleasant place in which spend a few hours wandering around. Charmingly overgrown and shaded by tall acacia and camelthorn trees, the old village includes the Moffat homestead, with furniture and exhibits inside, the schoolroom housing the Tswana printing press, and the large rough-stone church, with rows of pews standing on an uneven clay floor, huge rafters holding up a thatched roof and shafts of sunlight angling in through the small windows and split wooden door. In front of the homestead is the furrow which carried water from The Eye, and beyond that, in Mary Moffat's garden, is the stump of the almond tree (it was taken out by lightning) under which David Livingstone proposed to his future wife. It wasn't the last tree Livingstone (who had been recruited as a missionary by Robert Moffat during a lecture tour in Britain) was to make famous during his forays into darkest Africa. It was under a tree in Ujiji on the shores of Lake Tanganyika that he famously encountered HM Stanley, and when he died a few years later, in Ilala in present-day Zambia, his servants cut out his heart and buried it under a tree there. Appropriately, when the rest of his body returned to Britain for a state funeral at Westminster Abbey, one of the pall-bearers was his father-in-law, Robert Moffat.

Practicalities

Ignore misleading street signs for the **tourist information office** (Mon–Fri 7.30am–1pm & 2–4.30pm; ☎05373/21095); the building you want is on Main Road (the N14), between the main junction with Voortrekker (the R31) and The Eye. The office is located in the old *drostdy* (magistrate's house), which also has a pleasant **tea room** inside.

The cheapest **room** in town is at the Moffat Mission (☎05373/21352; ①), in the conference centre just behind the old homestead. Bear in mind, however, that this a quiet retreat, not a lively hostel. For a bit more money, there's a basic but friendly B&B, *High Hopes* (☎05373/22763; ①–②), on Seolin Road, or you might try *Janke Guest House*, 16 Chapman St (☎05373/22792; ③), a large house obvious from the road as you head out towards the Mission. You can **camp** at *Kuruman Caravan Park* (☎05373/21479; ①–②), 500m from Main Road on the Kimberley road, although *Red Sands Country Lodge* (☎05373/23133; ①–②), a resort set among some hills 15km along the N14 towards Upington, is a much more pleasant option if you avoid noisy weekends and school holidays. *Red Sands* also has chalets and a restaurant.

The best of a very limited choice of **eating** places in Kuruman is *Over-de-Voor* restaurant, on Main Road, in a small white building with a green roof, across from The Eye.

On to Tswalu Private Desert Reserve

Some 60km north of Kuruman is a tiny settlement which vies with Pofadder as being the epitome of dead-end, deserted *dorps* in the Northern Cape: **Hotazel**. The town's name, coined by the first surveyors of the land, is its outstanding feature and, unless you're braving the long R31 to get to the Kalahari-Gemsbok park, you can get by with telling your friends: "*Sjue*, I was up in the Northern Cape, not far from that place called Hotazel. And boy, wasn't it just."

The one other reason you might be out on this road is to get to the upmarket **Tswalu Private Desert Reserve** (☎011/784 6832, fax 784 7667), an impeccably stylish and expensive game lodge tucked under the 1500-metre-high Korannaberg Mountains, not far from the tiny settlement of Sonstraal. Recently opened by the *Conservation Corporation* (the Terence Conran of eco-tourism), the lodge is the largest privately owned game reserve in South Africa. Its owner, an Englishman, has spent R50 million bringing nine thousand head of game to this desert setting, including **buffalo**, **lion** and, by special arrangement with the Namibian government, eight highly endangered **desert black rhino**. Part rich man's dream, part dedicated wildlife protection project, and part glamorous safari experience, Tswalu is designed to compete with the finest of the private game lodges of the Kruger Park and Natal. A package stay here will put you in your own luxurious thatched stone house, complete with wooden deck giving splendid views of the Kalahari. Sumptuous meals, a swimming pool and game drives are included in the **price** – roughly US$400 per person per night, with a low-season rate of US$260 per night.

NAMAQUALAND

"Namaqualand . . . tells the truth about the brevity of life, while offering flowers as symbols of hope and courage. We are able to believe that, like flowers buffeted, beaten and scarred by external forces, we can still attain moments of excellence and great beauty."

Freeman Patterson

Namaqualand is another of the regions in the Northern Cape with a name which conjures up a blend of desolation and magic. It is the land of the **Nama** people, Khoikhoi herders who were divided between the Little Nama, who lived south of the **Orange River**, and the Great Nama, who lived north of the river in what is now Namibia. Still sparsely populated, the region stretches south from the Orange to the empty **Knersvlakte** plains around Vanrhynsdorp, and from the **Atlantic coast** east to the edge of the winter rainfall area, somewhere beyond **Pofadder** in Bushmanland. Above all Namaqualand is synonymous with the incredible annual display of brightly coloured **wild flowers** which carpet the landscape in August and September, undoubtedly one of South Africa's most compelling spectacles. Outside the flower season – and it's worth noting that the "season" here is in August and September – swaths of orange, purple and white daisies are about the last thing you'd expect to emerge from the dry, empty landscape. Yet there is a tenacious beauty about the landscape, with mountain deserts, mineral-bearing granite hills, and drought-defiant succulents. An oft-quoted saying about the region, but one worth repeating, is that in Namaqualand you weep twice – once when you first arrive and once when you have to leave.

The area is reached by the **N7** highway which runs north from Cape Town. While flowers occur as far south as Darling (see p.208), the town of **Vanrhynsdorp** marks the start of the northern section of the flower area, with the region's capital, **Springbok**, well-placed right at its heart. From here roads lead north to the Orange River and Namibia, west to the coast at **Port Nolloth** and the remote but spectacular **Richtersveld National Park**, and east along the **N14** to Upington.

THE PRIVATE WORLD OF FLOWERS

The seeds of the multicoloured daisies, mesembryanthemums (*vygies*), aloes, gladioli and lilies, which make up the spectacular **flowers of Namaqualand**, lie dormant under the soil through the harshest droughts of summer, waiting for the rain that sometimes takes years to fall. Because different species – about four thousand species of plant are found in the area – react to different conditions, in any given place the flowers will come at different times each year, and any attempt to predict the venues of the best displays will always be fraught with uncertainty.

One of the keys is **winter rainfall**, unusual in semi-desert ecosystems, which is why the flowers appear only in August and September; and the other is **temperature**, which is why flowers rarely open before 10am and on cool or cloudy days the displays are muted. In simple terms, the flowers stay closed to protect their pollen from being blown away by the wind, which they assume is blowing if the temperature is below 16°C.

Northern Cape flower routes

Flower-viewing anywhere in Namaqualand demands that you spend a lot of time in your **car**, simply because the distances in this region are so great and because flowers can never be guaranteed and you may spend some time tracking them down. If you don't have a car your options are limited. Walking among the flowers is a highly recommended way of seeing them, but you have to get to them in the first place, and bus tours tend to be inflexible. **Cycling** is an option, although with accommodation at a premium in the flower season you'd need to organize your itinerary carefully, as it becomes a frustrating business when you're told that the best displays are 20km away.

The pre-eminence of the car means that the best way to approach the flower region is by thinking in terms of **routes**: either drives between two centres, or loops out from and returning to a specific town. Any route generally involves a combination of main roads to get to different areas and back roads to get into the countryside, where you can drive slowly or stop and get out to look at the flowers a bit more closely.

The flower areas of Namaqualand are most commonly approached from Cape Town and, while coming this far north involves a lot more time and effort than making one- or two-day trips out of Cape Town, the rewards are found in the variety of landscapes, and thus flowers, that you will encounter, the openness and breadth of the scenery and, perhaps above all, in realizing the vast geographical scope of this remarkable phenomenon.

FLOWER TACTICS

- A few days before you get to the flower areas, try and plan where the flowers are most likely to be. They follow the rainfall, so early in the season they will be out near the coast, moving steadily inland. Phone the tourist information offices in the area for guidance and for help organizing accommodation. Decide whether you'd rather stay on a farm or in one of the main centres, such as Calvinia or Springbok, from where you can follow a wider range of routes. You can also contact the central Flowerline in Cape Town (☎021/418 3705) for help and information.

- Day by day, plan your route before you head out. Speak to your hosts, who often have inside information about the best spots on a particular day, or talk to the tourist information offices or Flowerline. Be warned, however, that their information is more public and you do sometimes get "gold rush" situations, with everyone flocking to certain places.

- Remember that the flowers open up around 10am and close between 3pm and 4pm, which gives you plenty of time for a good breakfast and to get yourself where you want to be. Because the flowers orientate themselves to face the sun, it's best to drive westwards in the morning, eastwards in afternoon, and generally from south to north.

- Get out of your car! All the most dedicated flower-watchers have muddy patches on their knees.

- Although it goes without saying, don't pick the flowers. Take pictures or, if you're hopeless at that, buy a book such as *Garden of the Gods* by Freeman Patterson.

- Pack warm clothes, as it gets chilly at night.

- If it's rainy or dull, drive down to the coast, go for a walk in the mountains or improve your Voortrekker history in the museums in places such as Vanrhynsdorp, Calvinia or Springbok.

Vanrhynsdorp to Springbok

Although not strictly part of Namaqualand and still within the Western Cape, the town of **Vanrhynsdorp** is really the gateway to the Northern Cape flower routes. It marks the crossroads between the main road north, the N7, and the R27 which connects with **Calvinia** and ultimately Upington, on the northern fringe of the Great Karoo. The stretch of N7 between Vanrhynsdorp and **Springbok** eventually becomes attractive among the **Kamiesberg Mountains** between Garies and Springbok, although the 100km of **Knersvlakte** plains immediately north of Vanrhynsdorp can seem bleak and grey, particularly out of flower season.

Vanrhynsdorp and around

The main street in **VANRHYNSDORP** is Van Riebeeck, dominated by a tall church steeple at its far end. The town's **museum** is here (Mon–Fri 8am–1pm & 2–4.30pm), featuring a collection of old domestic and military pieces, neither compelling nor dreadfully dull and, as with many such places, there's always a bit of gentle fun to be had in looking out for poor English translations on the labels.

If you travel to the outskirts of town on Voortrekker Street, which runs parallel to and south of Van Riebeeck, you'll soon reach a **succulent nursery** (☎02727/91062) run by Buys Wiese, an expert in the succulents which grow in such profusion in the area. Of the 105 succulent species found in the world, 83 grow in this area, many of them endemic. You can buy plants at the nursery or, more practically for overseas visitors, obtain a permit for the three-kilometre-long **succulent trail**, situated 25km north of town off the N7 and a worthwhile diversion if you're travelling on that way. As well as displaying a fascinating range of succulents, the walk introduces you to the unusual **Knersvlakte**, the name given to the bleak plains covered in small white pebbles which lie to the north of Vanrhynsdorp. The word "Knersvlakte" means "plains of the gnashing teeth", and is taken to refer to the sound made by wagon wheels toiling across the fierce terrain, which you may notice bears a resemblance to the pebble-dash effect people pay large sums to have adorning their suburban driveway.

PRACTICALITIES

The first thing you come to after turning off the highway into town are two service stations, open 24 hours a day for **fuel** and **food**. The Shell garage is also the halt for intercity **buses** and **minibus taxis** departing for Cape Town, Springbok or Upington. There's a simple but friendly **tourist information office** (Mon–Fri 8am–1pm & 2–4.30pm; ☎02727/91552) in the museum, on the right as you approach the church.

If you're planning on **staying** more than one night, you're probably best off looking for somewhere on a farm or in the nearby mountains. The *Namaqualand Country Lodge*, Voortrekker St (☎02727/91633; ②), is the town's hotel, unexpectedly filled with African artefacts but a bit dark and plain. Best of the nearby guesthouses is *Van Rhyn's*, on Van Riebeeck Street (☎02727/91429; ②), which offers reasonable rooms in a converted stable. On the outskirts of town, the *Vanrhynsdorp Caravan Park*, Gifberg Rd (☎02727/91287; ①), is reasonably quiet out of season and has a cheap **campsite** and self-catering **chalets**. Some 29km out of town, on the slopes of a nearby mountain, *Gifberg Farm* (☎02727/91555; ①–②) has a guesthouse, some old cottages and a network of paths and trails. A good base for finding flowers is the friendly *Aties Farm Guesthouse* (☎02727/91534; ②), signposted 7km south of town and then a further 7km along a dirt road.

Garies and Kamieskroon

North from Vanrhynsdorp the N7 carries on across the Knersvlakte, towards some distant hills, before passing **GARIES**, the first town inside the boundary of the Northern Cape. A sleep *dorp* for much of the year, Garies comes to life during the flower season,

KAMIESKROON PHOTOGRAPHIC WORKSHOPS

If you're in Namaqualand for the flowers, it's likely you'll take a few photos, although capturing the immensity and spectacle of the landscapes on film is no easy task. One way of improving your chances is to book a place on one of the popular **Photography Workshops** at the Kamieskroon Hotel. Here you'll learn more about your camera, your eye, and the inspiring landscape and flora of Namaqualand, and hear the odd epiphany about the meaning of life. The residential courses last for a week, and involve lectures, tuition and field work under the instruction of the dynamic Colla Swart (whose family run the hotel), local photographer JJ van Heerden and the internationally renowned Canadian photographer **Freeman Patterson**, whose coffee-table book on the flowers of Namaqualand, *The Garden of the Gods*, is a classic portrait of the region. Although flowers are the principal focus, workshops are also held in the autumn (March & April), when field work takes place around the dunes on the Atlantic coast near Hondeklip Bay. The workshops are often booked out, so contact the hotel as far in advance as you can (☎027/672 1614, fax 672 1675).

when the **Town Hall** is used as a flower information centre and casual market. There are a couple of **hotels**, of which the *Garies* (☎027/652 1042; ②) is reasonable. Further along Main Street, a left- rather than a right-hand turn if you're coming in from the N7 leads to a pleasant caravan park (☎027/652 1014) with a bit of grass for **camping** and some nice views up the Green Valley.

About 50km north of Garies, the village of **KAMIESKROON** is set among the Kamiesberg Mountains, beneath the rocky peak – or *kroon* – from which it takes its name. There isn't much to the village other than a pretty setting, the crisp air of the mountains and, in flower season, a sense of the privilege of being at the heart of the garden of the gods. As you come off the highway the village is to the right, while to the left is the *Kamieskroon* (☎027/672 1614, fax 672 1675; ②), seemingly an inauspicious wayside **hotel**, but in fact one of the few vibrant, creative nodes of Namaqualand. The hotel has become famous for running photographic workshops during the flower season (see box above), and is the centre for a growing number of activities in the surrounding Kamiesberg. The hotel also has a **camping** area, which is a much better option than the caravan park in the village.

Deeper into the mountains, at places east of Kamieskroon such as **Lelifontein** and **Nourivier**, the land is owned and farmed as a community project by the local Nama people, and in places you will see families living in traditional *matjieshuis* (reed huts). These settlements, many of which are still based around a mission, are connected by dirt roads, and so make good flower-viewing routes. A place worth going to in flower season, even if you're just passing through on the highway, is the **Skilpad Wildflower Reserve** (in flower season 8am–5pm; entry fee), an area established by the World Wildlife Fund, 7km to the west of Kamieskroon. The displays here tend to be more reliable than elsewhere, and this is one place where you will see great swaths of orange colour.

Vanrhynsdorp to Calvinia

Heading **east from Vanrhynsdorp towards Calvinia** on the R27, you have a very clear impression of the sudden elevation of the land from the plains up to the Bokkeveld escarpment, which the road tackles by way of **Van Rhyn's Pass**, complete with a couple of neck-achingly tight hairpins near the top. There is an excellent viewpoint, signposted soon after you reach the plateau, which looks out over the plains. You'll notice (as the early settlers did, much to their relief, after hauling their ox wagons up the escarpment) that the vegetation on top of the plateau is suddenly more fertile.

Halfway between **Nieuwoudtville** and Calvinia, the R27 is joined by the **R364**, a dirt road which connects with **Clanwilliam** via the inspiring Botterkloof and Pakhuis passes. This is one of the more spectacular remote drives in the Western Cape area, particularly if there are flowers decorating the roadsides.

Nieuwoudtville

Ten kilometres on from the top of the pass, the R27 passes just to the north of attractive **NIEUWOUDTVILLE**, with its appealing collection of tin-roofed, honey-coloured sandstone buildings. On your left as you drive through on Voortrekker Road (the only tarred road), look out for a grand **church** set in a large plot of happily unkempt ground. An **information centre** (☎02762/81336) operates out of the house in the church grounds during flower season only and is a reliable source of local advice. The flower season in Nieuwoudtville is also notable for the highly recommended tours run by **Neil MacGregor**, one of the gurus of Namaqualand flowers, on his farm, Glenlyon (see box below). Year-round, local **information** is available from the **municipality office** (☎02726/81316), next to the telephones on the corner of Van Rieebeck and Voortrekker roads.

Places to stay include the simple *Nieuwoudtville Hotel* (☎02726/81046; ②) and three pleasant guesthouses run by the *Smitswinkel* restaurant (☎02726/81426; ②). Just over 1km outside town is a pleasant **campsite**; book a spot here through the municipality office (see above). For somewhere to **eat**, head for *Smitswinkel* on Neethling Street (open for lunch and afternoon tea year-round, and also dinner during the flower season), or the *braai* house attached to the village store on the corner of Voortrekker and Nassau roads.

Around Nieuwoudtville

Some 2km east of Nieuwoudtville on the R27 is the town's **wild flower reserve**, an area which, because it is at the edge of the escarpment and receives unusually high rainfall, boasts over three hundred different species. Seven kilometres north from town, towards the settlement of Loeriesfontein, is **Bokkeveld Nature Reserve** and its ninety-metre waterfall which, when the Doring River is flowing between April and October, tumbles down into an impressive gorge where large raptors can sometimes be seen soaring around the tall cliffs.

Worthwhile for those who have a bit of time in the area, and also worth considering out of flower season, is a hike or visit to **Oorlogskloof Nature Reserve**, perched on the edge of the escarpment south of Nieuwoudtville. The entrance to the reserve,

---

GLENLYON

The old Bedford bus is called – naturally – Flora, and she is one of the great characters of Nieuwoudtville. Behind the wheel is another, **Neil MacGregor**, a man whose love and knowledge of the botany of the land he has farmed all his life has won him admiration not just in Namaqualand, but around the world. The visitors' book at **Glenlyon**, Neil and Neva MacGregor's farm just outside town, includes such names as David Attenborough, who came with the BBC Wildlife team to film *The Private World of Plants*, and Sir Ghilleam Prance, director of Kew Gardens in London. Each flower season, during the months of August and September, Neil and Flora take tours around the farm, a 65-square-kilometre property where he breeds pure merino sheep and has been striving for three decades to prove that farming and the spectacular natural flora can flourish successfully alongside one another. The party piece at Glenlyon are orange bulbinellas, but Neil's enthusiasm and expertise soon have you down on your hands and knees examining all kinds of fascinating flowers. Tours lasts for two and a half hours and depart each day during the season at 2pm. For details, phone ☎02726/81200.

which has various hiking and mountain-bike trails and natural swimming pools, is through **Driefontein Farm**, about 20km south of Nieuwoudtville, but you must contact the conservator at the municipality office in town before visiting (Mon–Fri 8am–4.30pm; ☎02726/81159, after hours 81010).

Some of the farms around Nieuwoudtville offer **accommodation** in classic old thatched Karoo cottages, ranging from typically hearty farmhouse B&B to more basic self-catering rooms. *Kliprivier* (☎02726/81204; ①–②) and *Papkuilsfontein* (☎02726/81246; ②) are recommended.

Calvinia and around

Despite its stern name, bestowed by an early dominee, **CALVINIA** has quite an appealing prospect beneath the Hantam Mountains. The town acts as a service centre for a large area, but it isn't a place you'll want to spend a lot of time in, unless you are here for the flowers in the surrounding area. Outside flower season the **climate** can make the area fairly unwelcoming, with temperatures climbing towards 40°C during summer and dipping below freezing in winter, when snow is sometimes seen on the mountains.

The centre of Calvinia is dominated by the **Dutch Reformed church**, although it now has to vie for your attention with a cylindrical water storage tank dressed up as huge red **postbox**, just along on Hope Street. The idea behind this was to create a tourist attraction, and however crass the concept it does turn heads. Letters and postcards posted in the box will be stamped with a special postmark. Immediately opposite the postbox is a more serious attraction, **Hantam Huis** (Mon & Wed–Fri 9am–5pm, Sat 9am–1pm; open Tues & evenings during flower season), the oldest building in Calvinia, which has won various awards for its restoration. Inside it's principally a tea room (see "Practicalities") and gift shop.

The large **Calvinia Museum** (Mon–Fri 8am–1pm & 2–5pm, Sat 8am–noon; small entry fee) is housed in a 1920 Art Deco synagogue on Church Street, a link to the sizable Jewish community which once lived in town but has since melted away (one of its more famous sons is the Shakespearean actor Antony Sher, who was born in nearby Middlepost). Inside are some extensive displays of settler life, including old wooden flour mills, printing presses, huge forge bellows and no fewer than six pianos. There are also some bizarre exhibits, which include a black wedding dress and a display of *dagga* (marijuana) pipes. Predictably, a display cabinet displaying the memorabilia of the town's two rugby Springboks is as large as that showing San artefacts.

Practicalities

Despite its isolation, Calvinia is on a main cross-country route, and *Intercape* **buses** and **minibus taxis** travelling between Upington, Vanrhynsdorp and Cape Town stop at Trokkies Service Station at the western entrance to town. Tickets for the *Intercape* services are available in, of all places, the butcher's shop on Hope Street (☎0273/41 1073). You'll find the **tourist information office** (Mon–Fri 8am–1pm & 2–5pm, Sat 8am–noon; ☎0273/41 1712) in the museum, where staff give you details of the **flower routes** in the Hantam district.

The most characterful **accommodation** option is the collection of old town houses operated by *Hantam Huis* (☎0273/41 1606, fax 41 1777; ③) – all wooden floors, lace curtains and quirky antique furnishings. The houses are self-catering, but you can make arrangements with *Hantam Huis* for meals. Elsewhere, the *Commercial* on Water Street (☎0273/41 1020; ②) offers standard hotel rooms, and behind the bar is the engaging "tycoon of Calvinia", 76-year-old Cecil Traut, a man with a long, grey beard, a soft voice and a collection of over two thousand different ties which decorate every wall, nook and cranny of the bar. The **camping and caravan park** (☎0273/41 1011; ①) is on the corner of Station and Hofmeyr streets, on the way through town towards the Upington road. For food, *Hantam Huis* is the place to head, though it's closed in evenings outside flower season. The *Paladium* café on Stigling Street sells tasty **ice cream**. Remember that the word for ice cream in Afrikaans is *roomys*, which, when writ large on a shop front, can cause some confusion if you're crawling around town looking for accommodation.

Into the Great Karoo

Just beyond Calvinia the road splits, with the R27 going north through **Brandvlei** and **Kenhardt** towards Upington, while the R63 goes west through **Williston** and **Carnarvon** to Victoria West and the main N12 route between Cape Town and Johannesburg via Kimberley. Other than their sheer isolation, these Karoo settlements throw up the odd interesting feature, such as ancient fossil remains and corbelled houses; whitewashed, beehive-like constructions built because of the lack of timber available for roofs.

South of Calvinia there is a remote area of land shaded on the maps as the **Tankwa-Karoo National Park**. It has been gazetted to protect a sector of succulent Karoo habitat, but is still in recovery phase after overgrazing by sheep and is not open to the public.

THE GREAT KAROO

Strange though it may seem, the **Great Karoo**, the vast, dry, empty interior of South Africa was, some 250 million years ago, an equally vast inland lake. It was populated by tiny marine creatures and, around its fringes, dinosaur-like amphibians, some of which left their footprints in the mud which have been preserved as fossils, making the area a fascinating one for paleontologists. The contrast now could hardly be greater, with slow creaking windmills struggling to bring water to the surface and the baked, brown-red earth roamed only by small herds of antelope or tough merino sheep.

Farmers here talk about the terrain in terms of hectares per sheep rather than sheep per hectare. The summer heat is fierce, the winter biting cold, the rain elusive, and the soil all but barren. Yet the Karoo has a special place for many South Africans, who take an almost perverse joy in the crisp air, the colours of the scattered *koppies* at sunset, the vastness of the pale sky, the depth of the darkness at night and the jostling galaxies of stars.

Springbok and around

SPRINGBOK is the main commercial and administrative centre of Namaqualand, and an important staging post on the N7. It lies around 550km from Cape Town, just over 100km south of the border with Namibia, and marks the junction with the **N14** which runs right across the Northern Cape through Upington and ultimately on to Johannesburg. Springbok's great assets are its strategic position and reliable supply of good information, food and bed space.

The main action in town is centred on a mound of granite boulders called "Klipkoppie" ("rocky hill"), the site of a British fort blown up by General Jan Smuts' commando during the Anglo-Boer War. A short walk up Monument Street will bring you to the town's **museum** (Mon–Fri 8.30am–3.30pm) in an old synagogue, and a little way along from this at the back of town is the **Blue Mine**, the first commercial copper mine in South Africa, sunk in 1852.

Following the R355 past Springbok airport to the southwest of town for around 10km will take you to **Goegap Nature Reserve** (daily 8am–9pm), an important area described as "Namaqualand in miniature". The reserve incorporates the **Hester Malan Wild Flower Garden**, always a draw during the flower season. Two-day hiking trails, mountain bike trails, horse riding and 4WD routes are on offer; the Visitors' Centre (8am–4pm ;☎0251/21880) can provide details. **Accommodation** is available in a couple of large chalets (②).

Practicalities

Flights from Cape Town arrive at Springbok's **airport** (☎0251/22380), 5km out of town along the R355 road to Goegap Nature Reserve. *Intercape* **buses** drop off in front of the *Springbok Lodge*, while the **minibus taxi** rank is on Landros Street, behind the *First National Bank*. VIP minibuses (☎0251/22006) serve Port Nolloth, Upington and Kimberley. For **car rentals**, try *Jowell's* on Voortrekker Road (☎0251/23125), or *Richtersveld Challenge*, Jurie Kotze Rd (☎0251/21905), for 4WD. Springbok's very useful **tourist information centre** (Mon–Fri 7.30am–4.15pm, daily during flower season; ☎0251/22011) is in the little Anglican church beside the post office on Namakwa Street. Another valuable source of local wisdom (and good **food**) is the **Springbok Lodge & Restaurant** on the corner or Voortrekker and Keerom roads. This local institution, whose owner, Jopie Kotze, sits rather like a godfather behind a counter at the back of the restaurant, is a hub for travellers, information-swapping and local chitchat.

The cheapest and most original **accommodation** is at *Namastat* (☎0251/22435; ①–②), a small cluster of *matjieshuis* 2km south of Springbok on the road in from the N7. There are shared washing facilities and a bar. For **camping**, *Springbok Caravan Park* (☎0251/81584; ①) is 2km out of town along the R355 to Goegap, and has a swimming pool, but is near the noisy highway. Back in town, *Springbok Lodge* (☎0251/21321, fax 22718; ①–②) encompasses a variety of houses, mostly painted in white and yellow and including dorms, self-catering and large doubles with lounge, air conditioning and bath. Go to Jopie's desk at the back of the restaurant to make arrangements. The smartest hotel is the Art Deco *Masonic Hotel* on Van Riebeeck Street (☎0251/21505; ③).

North to the Namibian border

Only 8km north of Springbok on the N7 is the slightly scruffy little town of **OKIEP**, which took over from Springbok as the copper-mining centre of Namaqualand in the 1880s. Miners and engineers from the tin mines in Cornwall arrived to help establish the mines, and you can still visit both the easily identified **smokestack** and **Cornish beam pump** beside it; visits are arranged through the *Okiep Country Hotel* (☎0251/41000; ②–③), under the palm trees on the main street.

Some 40km further north, **Stienkopf** marks the junction of the N7 with the **R382** to Port Nolloth and the Richtersveld National Park. Then, for the next 50km the N7 crosses some fairly bleak Namaqualand plains, before beginning to descend through a band of rocky hills, burnt black and ochre in the heat, and into a haunting pass with the Scrabble-winning name of **Vwfmylpoort**. The road then breaks through into the green flood plain of the **Orange River**, which marks South Africa's northern border with Namibia. The gathering of buildings on the South African side of the river is called **Vioolsdrif**, but there isn't much here apart from a filling station, a dusty store and a high-fenced government building.

A turning here along a dirt road traces the south bank of the Orange, 20km along which is a **campsite** right on the edge of the river called *Peace of Paradise* (leave a message at ☎02521/8667; ①). It certainly lives up to its name, with some lush green grass to camp on, the meandering river to swim in and a bar serving ice-cold beer.

If you're going on into Namibia from Vioolsdrif you have to clear immigration and customs on either side of the bridge; the border is open 24 hours a day. The town on the Namibian side, **Noordoewer**, has a collection of service stations and *Camel Lodge* (☎09264/637 or 7171; ③), a hotel with a bar and restaurant which might be very welcome after the long, hot road.

Springbok to Upington

The **N14** from **Springbok to Upington** is long and, after leaving the mountains around Springbok, increasingly flat and empty. This is big telegraph-pole country: the more you can see stretching off to a shimmering horizon, the longer and straighter the road. The scarcity of trees means that a number of the poles have been adopted as hosts for huge brown **sociable weaver nests**, a distinctive feature of these arid northern regions.

Pella

Roughly 150km from Springbok is a turning to **PELLA**, an intriguing settlement established around a mission station. After the turning off the N14, take the right-hand fork after 3km and follow the dirt road for another 10km towards the range of mountains which are in fact following the course of the Orange River. Pella is a simple gathering of shacks, sandy roads and a few stone or brick buildings in the midst of which a striking yellow **cathedral** stands in an open, dusty white plot surrounded by stately date palm trees. The cathedral was built – remarkably – by a group of French missionaries in the 1880s who, lacking an experienced cathedral-builder in their group, used the *Encyclopédie des Arts et Métiers* for guidance. The surrounding attractive mission buildings are still home to a community of nuns, and the cathedral itself is in continual use. There are two small **museums** among the mission buildings; if they're not open, ask at the mission office.

On the corner where the road into Pella swings left to pass the mission you'll find the *Kultuur Koffie Kroeg*, a **coffee shop** run by a local woman and her daughters from a flimsy-looking reed house. With *kokkerboom* trunks for stools and coffee brewing on an open fire in the back yard, it's a triumph of local enterprise relished by the few visitors who make it this far. There is a **campsite** (☎0254/2101; ask for Mrs Gouws) at **Pella Drift**, a little way further along the road down to the banks of the Orange. Be warned, however, that the peace of the rocky hills and river is disturbed by the constant drone of the pumping station.

Pofadder

Back on the N14, and about 15km further on, the famously hot and remote town of **POFADDER** won't delay you for long, except perhaps to take a photo to prove you've been there. The name, much ridiculed by South Africans (it is Afrikaans for puff adder, a particularly nasty snake found around the country), in fact refers to a nineteenth-century bandit called Klaas Pofadder, who spent most of his time on an island in the Orange River near Upington but had a hideout here. There is a **hotel** in town, the *Pofadder* on Voortrekker St (☎02532/ask for 43; ②), and a triangle of grass at the caravan park a couple of blocks away if you want to pitch a **tent** (☎02532/ask for 36; ①).

The West Coast

North from St Helena Bay, the hook of land 100km north of Cape Town, the long, lonely **west coast** of South Africa has two simple components: the cold, grey Atlantic Ocean, and the dominant sandveld vegetation, hardy but infertile. There isn't much more to the region: between the mouth of the Olifants River at Papendorp, parallel to Vanrhynsdorp, and the Orange River over 400km to the north, there is just one tarred road connecting the N7 highway to the coast, which leads to the only settlement of any significance, **Port Nolloth**.

Access to much of the coast is restricted due to **diamond-mining**, which has in many cases involved disturbance on a huge scale to the sandveld and coastal dunes. The first diamonds were discovered in Namaqualand in 1925, which confirmed that diamonds could be carried the length of the Orange, washed out into the ocean, and then dispersed by currents and the processes of longshore drift. Although inital prospecting was carried out along the course of the Orange and in the coastal dunes, it is the diamonds lying offshore on the sea bed which are now the more eagerly chased, mostly by boats operating with huge underwater "vacuum cleaners" and scuba divers working in often dangerous conditions underneath the boats.

During the flower season, the rains fall first on the coastal areas, and you can often see displays beginning about 20km inland, making the few roads down to the coast from the N7 worthwhile options for day routes. The dirt road through the **Spektakel pass** between Springbok and Kleinzee is one of the most spectacular drives in Namaqualand, and the **Anenous pass** on the R382 between Steinkopf on the N7 and Port Nolloth is also impressive. Along this road, too, you will see wandering herds of goats belonging to the pastoral **Nama** people who live in the area, as well as the intriguing peaks and intimidating valleys of the Richtersveld, the mountain desert which occupies the area immediately south of the Orange River.

Port Nolloth

PORT NOLLOTH is an odd but delightful place, where in the hazy, windblown sunshine the horizons are never quite in focus and the heavy fogs of the mornings shroud the town in a quiet eeriness. Populated by an eclectic mix of races and professions, including fishermen, diamond boat-owners, fortune-seeking scuba divers, scuba-diver-seeking girls and a significant Portuguese community, Port Nolloth is a place with a whiff of mystery and excitement. Tales are thick about "IDB" (illegal diamond buying), and if you have an imaginative mind you'll find plenty to feed it on. Why, as locals will point out to wide-eyed visitors, are there four second-hand furniture shops and three second-hand car dealers in a town with only a few thousand people?

Attractions in town are limited, though a stroll to the harbour along the sand-strewn roads to the beach or the different parts of town always throws up a few memorable scenes. There is a small **museum** (Mon–Fri 8.30am–12.30pm) on the corner of the main road and Beach Road, with an adhoc collection of fishing castoffs. The best reason to go here is to chat to the curator and local guide, Issac, who claims to speak nine of South Africa's eleven languages and play Spanish rumba.

A **minibus** to and from Springbok is run by *VIP Taxis* (☎0255/8215). The best sources of local **information** are the musuem and, immediately next door, *Bedrock Lodge* (☎ & fax 0255/8865; ①–②), which also makes a wonderful **place to stay**, in a stylish old beach house with wooden floors and laid-back staff.

Despite the size of the town, the mix of people and professions keeps a generous range of **restaurants** in business. Best of the bunch is the cosy, relaxed *Crow's Nest*, in a garage-type building opposite the *Scotia Inn*. There's also a good **espresso bar**, *Maresol*, on the main road.

North of Port Nolloth

Diamond activity is also much in evidence if you drive **north from Port Nolloth** towards the closed diamond town, **Alexander Bay**, the most westerly point of South Africa, at the mouth of the Orange River. It is connected by a bridge to Oranjemund on the Namibian side, although this too is closed to all but Alexkor employees.

The main reason for anyone to be coming along this road is en route to the Richtersveld National Park, and for those looking for a base either side of their visit to the park there is a very pleasant **place to stay** at *Brandkaros*, 27km from Alexander Bay (☎0256/831 1856; ①–②), a farm with rondavels and a **campsite** 400m from the river.

CANOEING TRIPS TO THE ORANGE RIVER

One way to enjoy the majesty of mountain-desert landscape of the Richtersveld is to take a **canoe down the Orange River**. By the time it reaches northern Namaqualand the river is broad and easy-paced, so the few rapids you encounter tend to rouse you from slumber rather than quicken the pulse. Dramatic rock formations and varied birdlife are the highlights of the trip, but above all relaxation is the key. Trips from Noordoewer last four to six days, with camps set up by the riverbank en route. For more details, contact Felix Unite (pronounced "Unit") on ☎021/683 6433, or *River Rafters* on ☎021/72 5094, both based in Cape Town.

Richtersveld National Park

The area of northwestern Namaqualand known as the **Richtersveld** covers an area roughly bounded by the Orange River to the north, the N7 to the east, the R382 to Port Nolloth to the south and the Atlantic Ocean on its western side. The **Richtersveld National Park**, created in 1991, covers 1600 square kilometres of the most dramatic parts of the region, tucked into an omega-shaped loop in the Orange, land impressive as much for its fierce hostility as its rugged scenery. Names such as Hellskloof, Skeleton Gorge, Devil's Tooth and Gorgon's Head are indicative of the austerity of the inhospitable brown mountainscape, tempered only by a surprisingly broad range of hardy succulents, mighty rock formations, the magnificence of the light cast at dawn and dusk, and the glittering canopy of stars at night. There is little fauna in the park other than lizards and klipspringers, although along the Orange there is a surprisingly rich birdlife.

The rainfall in parts of the park is as low as 50mm per annum, making this the only true desert – and mountain desert at that – in South Africa. In summer the daytime heat can be unbearable, at night in winter the cold drops below freezing, and in spring a few flowers will sometimes make their miraculous appearance on the bare, burnt hillsides and sandy plains.

Practicalities

Facilities at Richtersveld are extremely limited – this is not the place for a casual visit. Normal (sedan) cars are not allowed inside the park; the only way to explore is in a **four-wheel-drive** (4WD) or a pick-up with a high enough clearance to handle the sandy river beds and rough mountain passes between the designated campsites. On arrival, visitors must report to the park headquarters, **Sendelingsdrift**, 94km from Alexander Bay. No driving is allowed at night, and the only fuel available is at the park headquarters. It is recommended that you travel in groups of two vehicles.

Accommodation is in three chalets at Sendelingsdrift (②). The designated campsites around the park have no shelter or facilities. Water is scarce, and only very limited stores are available at the park headquarters. It is possible to **hike** with a guide in the park between April and September along designated trails of one, two or three nights' duration.

The most popular time to visit is during the winter months, when the days are coolest. Avoid coming here in the summer, when temperatures have been recorded at over 50°C. For **bookings** contact the *National Parks Board* in Pretoria (☎012/343 1991) or Cape Town (☎021/22 2810), and for more information contact the park itself (☎0256/831 1506). There is an admission fee for entering the park.

Probably the most realistic way of seeing Richtersveld is as part of a guided **4WD tour**. The most experienced operation is *Richtersveld Challenge* (☎0251/21905, fax 81460), based in Springbok, while the *Richtersveld Experience* (☎ & fax 0255/8041), based in Port Nolloth, is aimed more at budget travellers. Both offer trips of varying lengths into the park and surrounding areas, and will be able to combine a trip with hiking or canoeing along a section of the Orange if requested. You can rent 4WD vehicles from either company, although prices don't drop much from the full guided tour, and you have to make sure you are fully equipped.

travel details

Trains

Kimberley to: Cape Town (1 daily; 16hr 55min); Durban (weekly; 19hr 45min); Johannesburg (1 daily; 9hr 25min).

Buses

Calvinia to: Cape Town (4 weekly; 5hr 45min); Upington (4 weekly; 4hr 45min).

Kimberley to: Cape Town (1 daily; 11hr 40min); Johannesburg (1 daily; 5hr 15min).

Kuruman to Johannesburg (4 weekly; 6hr); Upington (4 weekly; 3hr).

Springbok to: Cape Town (4 weekly; 6hr 30min).

Upington to: Calvinia (4 weekly; 4hr 45min); Cape Town (4 weekly; 10hr 30min); Johannesburg (4 weekly; 9hr).

Flights

Kimberley to: Cape Town (1 daily; 2hr 10min); Johannesburg (4 daily; 1hr 15min).

Springbok to: Cape Town (1 daily Mon–Fri; 1hr 20min).

Upington to: Cape Town (6 weekly; 1hr 50min); Johannesburg (6 weekly; 1hr 50min).

CHAPTER FOUR

THE EASTERN CAPE

The **Eastern Cape** stretches from just beyond the Storms River in the west to the Mtamvuna River in the east, its northern boundaries defined by the Orange River and the southern fringes of the Lesotho Drakensberg. The region is a lot poorer than its western neighbour, a fact seemingly reflected in its harsher, drier landscapes chewed at by sheep, ostriches and angora goats, with pineapple plantations covering the hills nearer the coast.

Although you won't find the swanky guesthouses and hotels that typify the Western Cape, the unsophisticated coastal resorts of the Eastern Cape can offer 1000km of barely developed coastline, with long, empty stretches of sand in the west erupting into the dramatic rock formations of the Wild Coast as you head east.

Just over the border with the Western Cape, **Port Elizabeth** was renowned during the 1950s as an ANC-led centre of **anti-apartheid resistance**, and many of South Africa's current political figures cut their political teeth in the nearby townships of New Brighton and Motherwell. Although it's not a place to pencil in for a long stay, Port Elizabeth has enough buzz to justify a day or two of your time. The city is also the transport hub of the Eastern Cape, with buses and flights radiating out along the coast and to all the major centres of the country.

The entire Eastern Cape coast offers excellent surfing breaks, but it's **Jeffrey's Bay**, 75km west of Port Elizabeth, that made international fame after being featured in the 1960s cult film *Endless Summer*. Two nearby game reserves, **Addo Elephant Park** and **Shamwari**, can't compete with the big game country of the Kruger National Park or KwaZulu-Natal, but they are the only major wildlife areas in the southern half of South Africa, and can be tacked onto the end of a drive along the Garden Route.

Moving further up the coast, **East London**, the area's second largest city, teeters on the edge of the former Ciskei *bantustan* and is the main base if you're heading into the Wild Coast. The coastal vegetation becomes progressively more tropical here, and beyond East London's unenticing urban limits the **Wild Coast** features the country's most deserted beaches – their isolation assured by rough dirt roads that lead off the N2 highway. This dramatically beautiful coast is a long way off becoming a South African riviera (most travellers bypass it altogether) but backpackers are beating a path to the two favoured resorts of **Coffee Bay** and **Port St Johns**, both served by buses.

ACCOMMODATION PRICE CODES

All the accommodation listed in the Guide has been categorized into one of seven price bands, as set out below. The rates quoted, unless otherwise stated, represent the most expensive per-person rate for a double or single room outside high season (Dec–Jan), except for category ①, which are per-person rates for a dorm bed in backpacker accommodation, or a campsite. For more accommodation details, see p.31.

① R0–50	② R50–100	③ R100–150
④ R150–200	⑤ R200–250	⑥ R250–300
	⑦ Over R300	

The Eastern Cape interior holds considerable interest in its sparse landscapes, prickly succulents and a handful of isolated but handsome settlements. Venturing further north to the edge of southeastern Lesotho, the **Eastern Cape Drakensberg** makes a remote and thrilling setting for mountain walks, taking in ancient San rock art and even skiing in winter. Unlike the KwaZulu-Natal Drakensberg, there are no resort hotels or national parks, and much of the area is only accessible on dirt roads, with trails established on private farms. The scenery is marvellous though, and the tiny Victorian hamlet of·**Rhodes** well worth the effort of getting to if you're after somewhere really unspoilt.

Some history

The stark contrasts between wealth and poverty that cut through the **Eastern Cape** were forged in the nineteenth century when the British drew the Cape colonial frontier along the Kei River, 1000km east of Cape Town, and fought over half a dozen campaigns to keep the **Xhosa** at bay on its east bank. In the 1820s the British shipped in thousands of settlers to bolster white numbers and reinforce the line. West of the Kei, you'll encounter fenced-off white farms, pretty historic towns and industrial development; while across the river, the scourges of imperialism and apartheid have left little but overgrazed communal lands dotted with traditional huts and skinny cattle.

Even for a country where everything is suffused with politics, the Eastern Cape's identity is excessively political. South Africa's black trade unions have deep roots in its soil, which also spawned many anti-apartheid African leaders, including ANC president **Nelson Mandela**, his heir apparent, **Thabo Mbeki**, and black consciousness leader **Steve Biko**, who died in 1977 at the hands of Port Elizabeth security police. The Transkei or **Wild Coast** region, wedged between the Kei and KwaZulu-Natal, was the testing ground for grand apartheid when it became the prototype in 1963 for the *bantustan* system of racial segregation. In 1976 the South African government gave it notional "independence", under the puppet leadership of the Matanzima brothers in the hope that several million Xhosa-speaking South Africans, who were surplus to industry's needs, could be dumped in the territory and thereby become foreigners in "white South Africa". When the Transkei was reincorporated into South Africa in 1994, it became part of the new Eastern Cape province, which is now struggling for economic survival under the weight of its apartheid-era legacy.

PORT ELIZABETH AND THE WESTERN REGION

A city of flyovers and sprawling townships, **Port Elizabeth** is the industrial hub of the Eastern Cape, where African shanty dwellers scrape a living on the dust-and-plastic fringes of well-tended middle-class suburbs. Port Elizabeth was the arrival point in 1820 for four thousand British settlers, whose immigration doubled the English-speaking population of South Africa. Today, their descendants risk the hellish national roads from Gauteng every Christmas, to speed down to the "Friendly City" and holiday along the institutionalized beachfront, with its tacky burger bars and performing dolphins. The best reason to wash up here is to launch out along, or finish, a tour of the **Garden Route**, Port Elizabeth being the largest city in the province and the prime transport nexus, with an airport, good road links to the rest of the country and car rental facilities. The port's industrial feel is mitigated by some good city beaches, and should you end up killing time here you'll find diversion in beautiful **coastal walks** a few kilometres from town and in the small **historical centre**. There are also a couple of excellent township tours which give you one of the best introductions to apartheid and the new

South Africa, and are a welcome contrast to the Garden Route's beach focus. With time in hand, **Addo Elephant Park** is a recommended day's excursion out of the city.

Considerably preferable to Port Elizabeth for a few days at the seaside are the handful of **resorts** to its east along the **East London coast road**, where the shoreline is a magnificent sweep of endless beaches and mountainous dunes. The inland route to East London deviates away from the coast to pass through **Grahamstown**, a handsome university town, worth at least a night (more if you're interested in English settler history and the frontier conflicts with the Xhosa). Nearby, pretty settler villages trace the spread of the **1820 Settlers** into the interior.

A couple of hundred kilometres north from Port Elizabeth, a vast semi-desert of flat-topped hills and treeless plains opens out to extend across a third of South Africa. Its name, the **Karoo**, means "hard and dry" in the tongue of the Khoikhoi pastoralists, who were exterminated by Dutch frontiersmen. The oldest and best known of these is the picture-postcard town of **Graaff-Reinet**, which is solidly on bus route tours. Just a few kilometres away is the awesome **Valley of Desolation**, and the village of **Nieu Betheseda**, best known for its eccentric Owl House. Nearly as pretty as Graaff-Reinet, though not as architecturally rich, the town of **Cradock**, to its east, has the added attractions of mineral baths and the rugged **Mountain Zebra National Park**. Some of the best places to stay in the *platteland*, or interior, are on a sheep farm or in a historically listed guesthouse.

Port Elizabeth

Approaching **PORT ELIZABETH** (commonly known as "PE") from the east, the stink from the smokestacks along the N2 is enough to warn you that this is one of South Africa's least appealing seaside cities. Any claims PE makes for its exciting urban culture are exaggerated, and much of the architectural beauty it might once have enjoyed has been ravaged by industrialization and thoughtless modernization. Having said that, one or two buildings stand out from a featureless **city-centre** streetscape and a couple of pretty rows of Victorian terraces still remain in the suburb of **Central**. And Port Elizabeth is a small, manageable city, agreeable enough for a day or two. Its substantial attraction is its outstanding **swimming beaches**, which stretch south away from the city centre, and are among the country's safest. If you want to learn to scuba dive, PE offers one of the least expensive PADI certified courses in the world.

The transport hub of the Eastern Cape, Port Elizabeth is well-served by flights, trains, buses and car rental companies, making it an ideal springboard for trips west along the **Garden Route**, east through the **Transkei**, or north into the **Eastern Cape hinterland**. There are also a number of rewarding day excursions from here to **Addo Elephant Park**, **Shamwari Game Reserve** and the **Groendal** and **Baviaanskloof Wilderness Areas**.

Arrival and information

Port Elizabeth Airport is conveniently situated on the edge of Walmer suburb, 4km from the city centre (arrivals and departures ☎51 2984). From here the **Supercab Shuttle** (☎52 3720) minibus will get you into town very reasonably, stopping at all the main hotels, and making unscheduled stops on request. A metered **taxi** from the airport will cost you twice as much. **By train**, you'll arrive at the centrally located station (☎507 2222, or 507 2111 after hours), from where you'll need to catch a bus or taxi to

The **telephone code** for Port Elizabeth is ☎041.

PORT ELIZABETH BEACHFRONT AND SUBURBS

ACCOMMODATION
1 Beach Hotel
2 Caboose Sleepers
3 Fernando's Guesthouse & Grill
4 First Avenue Lodge
5 Hotel Formule 1
6 The Humewood
7 King's Beach Backpacker Hostel
8 Margate Place

your accommodation. Both the *Baz Bus* (☎021/439 2323) and the *Hopper Bus* (☎51 2332) will drop you off at any central location. **By long-distance bus**, you can alight at Greenacres shopping mall in Newton Park suburb, or continue to the town terminals of each of the long-distance coach lines – far more convenient if you're going to stay in the suburb of Central. *Translux* (☎507 3333) ends its run at the train station; *Greyhound* (☎56 4879) nearby, in Fleming Street; and *InterCape* (☎56 0055) stops at 107 Main St. Of the **regional bus services**, *Minilux Luxury Minibuses* (☎55 8556) from East London, Port Alfred and Grahamstown stop at the railway station before terminating at the *Holiday Inn Garden Court,* on the beachfront, while the *Leopard Express* (☎0461/24589) from Grahamstown stops at the airport.

Information

The extremely helpful **Port Elizabeth Publicity Association** (Mon–Fri 8am–4.30pm, Sat & Sun 9am–3pm; ☎55 8884, fax 55 3564) has an office in the Donkin Lighthouse Building on the Donkin Reserve in Central. A recorded touch-tone visitor information service (☎56 1773) provides up-to-date details of transport, tours, accommodation, what's on and eating out. If you're spending any length of time in the city, *Braby's Map Book of Port Elizabeth* is invaluable. Frequently out of stock at the *CNA* chain of newsagents, it should be available from *Fogarty's Bookshop* at The Bridge shopping mall (see p.267). The *Automobile Association* (☎34 1313) also has a good selection of maps at their shop in the Greenacres shopping mall.

City transport and tours

If you are staying in the the inner-city suburb of Central, exploring the city **on foot** is a realistic possibility. The self-guided **Heritage Walk** (map available at the Publicity Association) takes you past interesting buildings, as well as nice cafés and pubs. However, for any serious exploration of PE, or for getting to and from the beachfront, **renting a car** is your best option, as the city's transit system leaves much to be desired (see "Listings" for reliable rental firms). **Buses** operated by *Algoa Bus Company*, the municipal service, are inexpensive, but infrequent, running from the Market Square Bus Depot to the suburbs, the beaches and Greenacres shopping mall. Timetable and route information is available on ☎41 4241 or toll free ☎0801/42 1444. PE's **minibus taxis**, as elsewhere in the country, are wracked with internal conflict and periodic internecine clashes around the main minibus taxi ranks. They do run from town to the beachfront on a regular basis, but are the least recommended way to travel. **Metered taxis** are reliable but more expensive. They don't have ranks so you'll need to phone for service, and if you're going to the bus or railway stations, or the airport, it's advisable to book ahead (see "Listings" for taxi firms).

Tours

Bus tours are a quick and easy way to see the city's highlights; *Friendly City Tours* (☎55 1801) operate four ninety-minute commentated tours every day, starting from the *Elizabeth Sun Hotel*. The best way to get an insight into **African** Port Elizabeth is to take a reasonably priced tour with *Gqebera Tours* (☎51257282, mobile 082/955 1039), which go into Walmer township, and arrange for you to have a meal with a Xhosa family. These tours are a safe and enjoyable way of meeting local people in the convivial environment of a *shebeen*. Finally, *Calabash Tours* (☎ & fax 55 6162, mobile 083/303 7553) operate the highly illuminating "Real City Tour", which focuses on Port Elizabeth's history and culture, and includes a display of traditional dancing and lunch in the townships. Tours run four days a week, and start at 10am and 4pm.

Accommodation

The obvious, if most expensive, **place to stay** is at the **beachfront**, where hotels styled in a curious 1930s fusion of Art Deco and colonial architecture remain an intact and delightful local idiosyncrasy. Cheaper but away from the sea, the well-preserved Victorian suburb of **Central** makes a pleasant alternative, with B&B accommodation and a few backpackers' lodges, and plenty of restaurants. There are a couple of excellent places in the less convenient, but greener, outlying suburbs of **Mill Park** and **Walmer**.

During the December and January peak holiday period, the beachfront becomes the focus for most of the city's action, while February and March are much quieter, yet still offer perfect beach weather. PE is subject to strong winds. When these sweep across town the beachfront becomes a sandblaster and you'd be better off booking into Central for the night: *Bed 'n' Breakfast Eastern Cape*, 22 Burford Crescent, Linkside (☎ & fax 33 3716) is a central booking agency for the area.

Beachfront

Beach Hotel, Marine Drive, Humewood (☎ & fax 53 2161). Comfortable 1930s-style hotel, across the road from popular Hobie Beach. There's a great patio bar overlooking the sea, offering snacks, cocktails and cold beer. Ask about the weekend specials. ③–④.

Caboose Sleepers, Brookes Hill Drive, Humewood (☎56 0088). Tiny, wood-panelled rooms which sleep up to three people. The cramped sleepers are made up for by a roomy, stylish lounge, sun deck and good self-catering facilities. ②.

First Avenue Lodge, 3 First Ave, Summerstrand (☎53 3037, fax 34 5905). Self-catering or B&B accommodation in this pleasant establishment with a pool. Airport transfers are available. ②.

Hotel Formule 1, corner of Beach Rd and Laroche Drive (☎55 6380). Budget rooms with bath in this clean but rather impersonal hotel. ②.

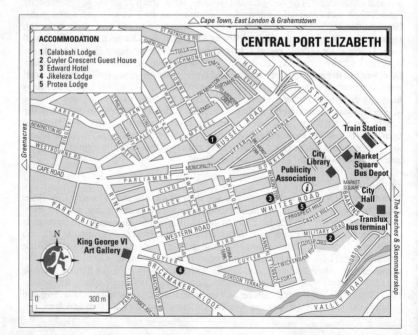

The Humewood, 33 Beach Rd, Humewood (☎ & fax 55 8961). Lovely rooms, a good bar, and a nice sun deck in a "family" hotel that has resisted modernization. ③.

King's Beach Backpacker Hostel, 41 Windermere Rd, Humewood (☎55 8113 or 32 2345). In a former family home, and attracting a lively mix of young travellers. Camping facilities, 24hr check-ins, safe baggage- and mail-holding, self-catering kitchens and weekly rates. ①.

Margate Place, 5 Margate St, Summerstrand (☎ & fax 53 3252). Fairly upmarket B&B, each self-contained cottage with its own kitchen, private patio and *braai*, plus use of the pool. ③.

Central

Calabash Lodge, 8 Dollery St (☎55 6162). Cool simplicity, with cotton sheets and a touch of the ethnic in a stylish, well-located house, offering rooms with or without bath. This beats the rest of the town's B&Bs hands down. Highly recommended. ②.

Cuyler Crescent Guest House, 19 Cuyler Crescent (☎55 3672, fax 55 6946). Among the city's top B&Bs, in the former home of the artist Alex Kiddie, one of PE's great eccentrics. Beautiful, art-adorned rooms, with a jacuzzi, hydro-, and aromatherapy treatments on offer. ③.

Edward Hotel, Belmont Terrace (☎56 2056, fax 56 4925). Edwardian landmark which has remained relatively intact, bang in the middle of historic Central. Great for a drink, tea, a ride in the vintage lift, or their speciality – breakfast. ④.

Jikeleza Lodge, 44 Cuyler St (☎ & fax 56 3721). Port Elizabeth's best backpackers' lodge, with no more than three beds per dorm, and two doubles. Friendly, and a good source of local info. ①.

Protea Lodge, 17 Prospect Hill (☎ & fax 55 1721). Nice old Victorian house in an interesting street, in the middle of Central, with friendly staff. 24hr check-ins, safe baggage- and mail-holding, self-catering kitchens and weekly rates. ②.

The suburbs

Fernandos Guest House & Grill, 102 Cape Rd, Mill Park (☎33 2823, fax 34 5228). Popular string of Victorian houses offering reasonable rates, self-catering facilities and full board. ②–③.

The City

Port Elizabeth's **city centre** is marred by the network of freeways perched on forests of concrete piles that cuts a swath across the south of town, blocking off the city from the harbour. The city's white population retreated to the suburbs some time ago, taking the big department stores with them, and leaving the centre to African traders, self-appointed parking attendants, and township shoppers.

City Hall and Central

The symbolic heart of town is the **City Hall**, standing in **Market Square**, a large empty space surrounded by some striking mid-Victorian buildings, adjacent to the railway and bus stations on the edge of the harbour. But the dejection of the quarter, under the grimy shadow of a flyover, conspires against it ever pumping any real life into the district. Nevertheless, the **City Library**, on the corner of Whites Road and Main Street, is a real attraction, especially the second floor, with its beautiful stained-glass dome and windows and magical little balconies of bookshelves – a Victorian cathedral to the spirits of knowledge.

In stark contrast, the old Sanlam Building at 44 Strand St, was the notorious secret police centre where Steve Biko (see p.302) was tortured. In 1997 the building was renamed the **Steve Biko Building**, to coincide with the twentieth anniversary of his death. Now a boarding house mostly for students, the building has a small sixth-floor library with books, cuttings and photographs of Biko on view (for a small entry fee), in the same room where Biko was interrogated.

Heading west up hilly **Donkin Street**, past its exceptionally well-preserved Victorian street frontage, you'll come upon a curious stone pyramid which commemorates the city's namesake, **Elizabeth Donkin**. Elizabeth was the young wife of the Cape's acting governor in 1820, Sir Rufane Donkin; she died of fever in India in 1818.

Moving east from here through **Central**, up Havelock Street then south into Rink Street, you'll reach St George's Park and the **King George VI Art Gallery**, 1 Park Drive (Mon–Fri 8.30am–5pm, Sat 9am–4.30pm, Sun 2–4.30pm; free) which has an interesting collection of contemporary local work, visiting exhibitions and a small but good gallery shop selling postcards and local arts and crafts. **St George's Park** itself is a huge circular green, dominated by the St George's Cricket Ground, and with a public swimming pool, a tiny but beautiful glasshouse and a couple of war memorials (one of them to horses which died under fire). North of Central's Russell Road boundary, you cross into **North End**, the city's industrial and administrative hub, where many fine old buildings were torn down to make way for the granite slabs of apartheid-era government offices. Worth a wander to get a feel of the city beyond the sanitized tourist haunts, North End is loud and lively, filled with African herbalists, Indian spice shops, gents' outfitters with impeccable window displays and snack bars selling mutton *rotis* and *bunny chow*.

The beachfront and around

PE's best hope of redemption is through its **beaches** which, due to the protection provided by Algoa Bay, are safe for swimming and clean enough to make beachcombing a pleasure. The beachfront strip starts about 2km south of the city centre at **King's Beach**, though a built-up curve of strand with a children's paddling pool is the best place to swim and sunbathe, and is uncomfortably crowded only at Christmas and on New Year's Day. Nearby, **Humewood Beach** retains much of its original architectural features and is likewise great for swimming, with a big, sandy beach. One of Humewood's highlights is the *Apple Express*, a beautifully restored steam train which runs on occasional Sundays from Humewood Station (leaving at 9.30am) to Thornhill Village, stopping on Van Staden's River Bridge, the highest narrow-gauge railway bridge in the world. After a leisurely lunch at the *Thornhill Hotel*, the train ambles back to Humewood, arriving at 4pm. Tickets can be booked through *Spoornet* (☎507 2333) or the Port Elizabeth Publicity Association (see p.263).

Across Humewood Road is a complex housing the **Port Elizabeth Museum** (daily 9am–5pm; small entry fee), which has a surprisingly good display on Xhosa people, and the **Oceanarium** (daily 9am–1pm & 2–5pm; dolphin shows 11am & 3pm; entrance fee), whose performing seals and dolphins attract hordes of excited children during the December holidays. The Oceanarium plays a major conservation role in the area, and the creatures currently performing were born in captivity – once they die the show will be over. There's also a **Snake Park** (same hours), if you fancy gawping at imprisoned reptiles. Next door, **Brookes Pavilion** offers a variety of restaurants with great views. Beyond that, to the south, **Hobie Beach** and **Summerstrand** are great for walking and sunbathing.

Marine Drive continues down the coast as far as **Schoenmakerskop**, along impressive coastline that alternates between rocky shores and sandy beaches. From Schoenmakerskop you can walk the eight-kilometre **Sacramento Trail**, a shoreline path which leads to the huge-duned **Sardinia Bay**, the wildest and most dramatic piece

---

DIVING

Although the Indian Ocean around Port Elizabeth isn't tropically clear and warm, **diving** here is good, especially for soft corals. For PADI dive courses recognized internationally, try *Pro Dive Scuba Instruction*, the Red Windmill, Beach Road, Summerstrand (☎583 5316).

of coast in the area. To get there by road, turn right at the Schoenmakerskop intersection and follow the road until it signals left to Sardinia Bay.

The suburbs

PE's **suburbs** offer little to draw you away from the beachfront, unless you're a shopaholic, in which case you should make a beeline for **Newton Park**, 5km west of the centre and home to **Greenacres** and **The Bridge**, vast shopping malls to which all the city-centre department stores have relocated en masse. So strong is their status as the consumerist heart of Port Elizabeth that bus companies use it as an alternative terminus for travellers wishing to avoid the city centre.

Tranquil and leafy, 2km southwest of the centre, near the airport, **Walmer** suburb sits complacently between two irreconcilable landscapes. To its left, on the city side, is **Settlers' Park Nature Reserve**, with entrances on Park Drive and Third Avenue, which follows the Baakens River Valley from Valley Road, south of Main Street, to Newton Park, and has 54 square kilometres of indigenous growth and impressive cliffs. To its right lies **Walmer Township**, a dilapidated jumble of houses and shacks, divided from the mansions of Walmer's millionaires by a single strip of wasteland. Despite some recent small improvements, conditions here are generally appalling. The area is home to many of the domestic workers serving the suburban surrounds, and it's not unusual to find township cattle grazing on the wide grassy pavements which line Walmer's wealthy streets. A recommended tour can take you into the area (see "City transport and tours", p.263).

Eating, drinking and nightlife

There's little that's outstanding about PE's **restaurants**, but at least you'll find places to suit most budgets, especially along the beachfront, and in Central, where there are more multiracial venues. Prices are much the same as the rest of the country, with fish an obvious choice. Apart from the hotel bars mentioned in the accommodation section, which are actually the best, there are a few other passable joints for a **drink**, and a couple of nightclubs.

Restaurants

Aviemore, 67 Parliament St (☎55 1125). Highly recommended (and expensive) restaurant in the centre, serving regional specialities, including springbok salad and seafood melange. Mon–Sat 6.30–10.30pm.

Casbah Roadhouse, Marine Drive. PE's nicest drive-in restaurant serves fine burgers and the best chips in town, at low prices. Daily until 1.30am.

Coachman Steakhouse, 10 Lawrence St (☎52 2511). Off Russell Rd in Central, you'll find a good, mid-priced meat menu, and New Orleans whorehouse decor, which is curiously not at odds with the cosily middle-class clientele. Daily 7–11pm.

De Kelder, Marine Drive, Summerstrand (☎53 2750). Best food in town in a wine-cellar ambience, with a pricey menu. Specialities include seafood, steak, poultry and veal dishes, cooked in a European continental style. Daily 12.30–2pm & 6.30–10pm.

Don Carlos, 153 Russell Rd (☎55 2828). Delightful, unassuming little Spanish restaurant, run by an elderly couple from Barcelona. You can bring your own wine without an outrageous corkage added to the bill. Their paella specials are cheap and delicious. Ring for opening times.

Le Med, 70 Parliament St (☎55 8711). Medium to expensive eating in a lively atmosphere. Choose from fish dishes and unusual specialities, such as *tagine*, a Middle Eastern stew cooked in an earthenware pot. Booking is essential.

Rome, corner of Campbell and Russell roads (☎56 2731). Mouthwatering pizza made in a wood-burning oven and served in a laid-back atmosphere, at decent prices.

Zorba's, 68 Parliament St. Varied, mid-priced menu includes tiger fish, stuffed squid and kebabs. There's a bar attached that stays open well after the restaurant has closed. Mon–Sat 6.30–10.30pm.

Bars

Keg & Fox, 31 Clyde St, Central. Great selection of local and imported beers and lagers. Generous glasses of wine, tasty cocktail snacks, and a very pleasant atmosphere.

Cadillac Jack's Rock 'n' Roll Diner, The Boardwalk, Marine Drive, Summerstrand. Incredibly popular summer spot which can get troublesome at night but boasts a great sea view, and a balcony for checking out near-naked, sun-bronzed bodies of both sexes.

Dockside Debbies, Bay Waterfront. Quaint old dockside building with harbour views – an excellent place for lunch, a sundowner or sushi. Downstairs is a gloriously ramshackle affair of ancient, mouldering piers and garishly painted chairs rescued from an ancient lifeboat. To get there, enter the harbour next to the central station and follow the signposts.

Nightlife

Local live **music** is limited, most talented performers having taken off to the brighter lights of Cape Town. You'll find no shortage of Neil Diamond clones, though, crooning away at the steakhouses and tapas bars. The occasional **concerts** that come to PE's Opera House, and the odd **cabaret** at other venues, are listed in the daily *Eastern Province Herald*. The *Centrestage Cabaret Theatre*, 12 Bird St, Central (☎55 1910), is an exciting new venue, with two stages, a bar and a restaurant.

The **cinema** situation is marginally better, with a good selection of current and art films showing at the *Kine Park Cinema*, 3 Rink St, Central (☎52 3311), and the usual Hollywood fare at the *Nu Metro*, 6th Ave, Walmer (☎51 5380), and at the *Ster Kinekor* (☎34 4551) in The Bridge shopping complex – check the *Herald* for programme details.

NIGHTCLUBS

Razzmatazz, 4th Floor, Central House, Grace St, Central (☎55 1851). PE's greatest jazz venue hosts some of Cape Town's best musicians, as well as sessions with young locals in a suitably dark and smoky haze. Cheap, friendly non-racial vibe, with Wednesday the best night.

Satchmo's Jazz Club, 12 Bird St, Central (☎55 1910). Weekly appearances by the top jazz names from Cape Town and Jo'burg at a cool club with a non-racial vibe.

Tiko's, Rose St, Central. Laid-back joint with African decor, where you'll often catch great jam sessions of original live music as well as some covers. Sells cheap, late-night munchies.

WU's, Belmont Terrace. Nice old building with mellow acid jazz vibe downstairs and louder house and jungle lifting the roof upstairs. Great non-aggressive pool venue where you can expect to see plenty of shiny happy youth in platforms and bell bottoms.

Listings

Airlines *SAA* ☎34 4444.

Airport Port Elizabeth Airport; arrivals and departures ☎51 2984.

Banks Main branches are easy to find in the shopping areas of the centre, and in *Greenacres* and *Newton Park* shopping malls. Banking hours are Mon–Fri 8.30am–3.30pm, Sat 8–11am. Wherever you find banks, you'll also find ATMs.

Car rental Companies based at the airport: *Alisa* (☎51 6550 or toll free 0800/21515); *Avis* (☎51 1306); *Budget* (☎51 4242/82); *Imperial* (☎51 4391); *Tempest* (☎51 1256). *Runabout Rentals* (☎35 1764 ext 3) rent out good second-hand cars and an Isuzu 4WD – perfect for driving around Addo Elephant Park.

Consulates *Germany*, 11 Uitenhage Rd, North End (☎57 22840); *UK*, Allied Building, 93 Main St (☎55 2423).

Doctors and dentists Listed in telephone directory under "Medical".

Emergencies Ambulance ☎10177; Fire ☎55 1555; Police ☎10111.

Hospitals *St George's* (private), Park Drive, Settlers Park (☎33 7921); *Provincial* (state), Gibson Rd, Central (☎392 3911).

Laundries *Automat*, 6a Parliament St, Central; *Rub & Tub*, Rink House, 70d Clyde St, Central. Open daily.

Pharmacy with extended opening hours: *Mount Road Medicine Depot*, 13 Lower Mount Rd (daily until 10.30pm; ☎54 3838).

Post offices Brookes Pavilion, Humewood, and Centrahill, Russell Rd, Central. Opening hours are Mon–Fri 9am–3.30pm, Sat 8.30–11am.

Taxis Good firms include *Amies* (☎57 3798), *Anchor* (☎54 4798 ext 2) and *Hurters Taxis* (☎55 7344).

Train information ☎041/507 2222, or 507 2111 after hours.

Travel agents *Pentravel*, The Bridge, Greenacres (☎33 3833); *ITC*, 50a Pickering St, Newton Park (☎35 2344).

Around Port Elizabeth

In a province not noted for its wildlife, Port Elizabeth holds the ace as the nearest centre to **Addo Elephant Park**, one of South Africa's most rewarding game reserves and the only one of substance in the Eastern Cape. Also within easy striking distance is the private **Shamwari Game Reserve**, a luxury game farm boasting the "Big Five" (elephant, lion, leopard, buffalo and rhino), although the lions are in pens. Southwest along the coast, **Jeffrey's Bay** attracts surfers the world over.

Addo Elephant Park

Addo Elephant Park (daily 7am–7pm; ☎0426/40 0556; entry fee), 50km northeast of Port Elizabeth, should be your first choice for a day's trip out of the city, and also makes for a rewarding and peaceful overnight stop. The Addo bush is thick, dry and prickly, making it difficult sometimes to spot any of the 200–300 elephants; when you do, though, it's often thrillingly close up. The best strategy is to ask at the park's reception where the elephants have last been seen, and also to head for the elevated viewing platform to scan the bush for large grey backs quietly moving about. Night drives with a National Parks driver can be booked at reception if you're spending the night in the park. Other animals to watch out for include **eland**, **kudu**, **buffalo** and **red hartebeest**.

A good break from waiting at waterholes or scouring the bush is to walk the six-kilometre circular **Spekboom Trail** which takes you through the indigenous spekboom *veld* which predominates in the park. The walking is in an area fenced off from the elephants, and gives you a real feel of the landscape.

Practicalities

To get to the Addo Park from Port Elizabeth, take the N2 in the direction of Grahamstown for about 11km before turning left onto the R335 which takes you through some dismal plastic-strewn shacklands to the prosperous citrus-farming village of Addo. The turn-off to the park is clearly signposted, 10km beyond the village. The network of roads within the park are not sealed, but they're in good condition. Without your own transport, you might consider taking a reasonably priced **tour** leaving everyday from Port Elizabeth with *Paradise Expeditions* (☎041/55 1977; ask for Graham Lind).

Maps of the park are available at Reception. **Accommodation** is in fully equipped, self-catering two- or four-bedroom cottages (bookings ☎021/22 2810; ②–③), overlooking a small dam where animals come to drink and birds congregate. **Camping** is also available (①) and there's a swimming pool and tennis courts. You'll find a decent **restaurant** (8am–9pm) next to Reception, dominated by the head of an enormous stuffed elephant, and a small groceries shop next door for drinks, snacks and basic catering. The park map indicates the locality of picnic and *braai* sites.

Shamwari Game Reserve

The private **Shamwari Game Reserve** (☎042/851 1196), 72km from PE, is the only place on the Eastern Cape where you can see the **Big Five** – even if the lions are kept in enclosures. The surroundings are marvellous, with dry hills and river-etched gorges stretching for miles. Safaris are aimed at the upmarket consumer, and if you're going to Natal or Mpumalanga you'd be better off spending your money in one of South Africa's great national game reserves. However, if you're only touring the Cape, or don't want to go into a malarial area, Shamwari will provide a satisfactory safari experience.

Day packages include lunch and a three- to four-hour game drive, and start at R250 per person. If you're **overnighting**, the accommodation, in a choice of Victorian and Edwardian homesteads, gives Shamwari a vastly different flavour to the traditional tented safari camp – although you'll still get to go on game drives in open land rovers. The lodges have been restored to their original nineteenth-century splendour and prices start at R1150 per person, including accommodation, full board and game drives. Unlike the national parks, Shamwari is not a place you can just drop into, and booking is essential.

Jeffrey's Bay

The only place of any interest along the 186-kilometre stretch of N2 from Port Elizabeth to Storms River is **JEFFREY'S BAY**, at least if you happen to be a surfer. Some 75km west of Port Elizabeth, off the N2, "J Bay", as it's known locally, is reputed to be one of the top three surfing spots in the world. Just thirty years ago, it consisted of nothing more than a few beachside shacks and a general store. Local residents, mostly conservative farmers, regarded the arriving surfers as lowlife, but were unable to ignore the commercial possibilities of their presence. Their contempt is visible in the town's design. Jeffreys is an irredeemably ugly dump, and the main street, **Da Gama Road**, running the length of the town, consists mainly of cheap brick buildings devoid of any civic sensibility. The town's rising fame corresponded with the boom in coastal development in the 1970s, and its hills are littered with huge, tasteless, executive vacation homes and the retirement dwellings of wealthy folk who rent them out during holiday season at astronomical prices.

For **surfing aficionados**, however, these are trifling details, given the possibility of the perfect wave. If you've come to surf, head for the break at **Super Tubes**, east of the main bathing beach, which produces an impressive and consistent swirling tube of white water that attracts surfers from all over the world throughout the year. Riding inside the vortex of a wave is considered the ultimate experience by surf buffs, but should only be attempted if you're an expert. Other key spots are at Kitchen Windows, Magna Tubes, the Point and Albatross. In a league of their own, **dolphins** regularly surf the waves here, and **whales** can sometimes be seen between June and October. For the less agile, Main Beach (in town), and Kabeljous-on-Sea (a few kilometres north) are the main **bathing areas**, with some wonderful seashells to be found between Main and Surfer's Point. Rock fishing is very popular, and the *Kouga Underwater Club*, (☎041/93 2259; ask for Jacques Marx) arranges scuba dives around the local reefs.

Practicalities

Getting to Jeffrey's Bay from Port Elizabeth without a car is straightforward. The *Hopper* bus (☎041/51 2332) calls in every morning at the J-Bay tourist office on its way to Plettenberg Bay and Knysna, from Port Elizabeth. The daily *Intercape* (PE/Cape Town service) stops at the *Savoy Protea Hotel* in Da Gama Road. Alternatively, you could take the *J-Bay Sunshine Express* (☎0423/93 2221, after hours 041/51 3790), a fifteen-seater minibus which doesn't follow a schedule, but can be booked at any time. It's convenient and reasonable if there's a group of you, since it can pick you up from the airport or anywhere else, and do a transfer at any time, but it's too expensive for just a couple.

The **tourist information office** (Mon–Fri 8am–5pm, Sat 9am–noon; ☎0423/93 2588) on the corner of Da Gama and Goedehoop roads, publishes a wide-ranging list of **places to stay**. Budget options are best booked in advance and include *Jeffrey's Bay Backpackers*, 12 Jeffreys St (☎0423/93 1379; ①), two blocks from Main Beach, with double-bed cabins, a bar, and bike and board hire. *Island Vibe*, 10 Dageradd St (☎0423/93 1625), is the other backpackers' lodge, offering camping in J Bay's best site, with 180-degree views. You'll find more comfortable cabins at *Beach Cabanas*, along Da Gama Road (☎0423/93 2323; ②). For a lot more luxury, head for *Diaz 15*, 15 Diaz Rd (☎0423/93 1779; ④), with two- and three-bedroom accommodation on Main Beach. Surfers who want to be near Super Tubes (the main surf beach), should try *Mount Joy Guest House*, 31 Mimosa St (☎0423/96 1932; ②), three minutes from the beach, and offering superb sea views. J-Bay has two municipal **campsites**, both on the beach with access to surfing breaks. The *Kabbeljous Caravan Park*, on the corner of Da Gama Road and Kabbeljous Street (☎0432/93 1111), is close to the town centre, while the *Jeffrey's Bay Caravan Park*, on the corner of Da Gama Road and Friesland Street (☎0432/93 1111), is less central.

For **eating**, Jeffrey's Bay has the usual collection of burger and steak bars, and lots of take-away places. *Le Grotto*, in Da Gama Road, is famous for its cheap, 1kg steaks. The ritziest restaurant in town is *Breakers* on Ferreira Street, which specializes in fish and game meats, and has a nice glassed-in patio. At the cheaper end, the *Sunflower*, 20 Da Gama Rd, offers breakfasts and some interesting pastas and salads, and also caters for vegetarians, while *Rendezvous*, at the corner of Da Gama and Goedehoop roads serves up pancakes, pasta and reasonably priced steaks and burgers.

SURFING ETIQUETTE

On the international surfer's map of the world, South Africa begins and ends at **Jeffrey's Bay**. Its legendary reputation was built on the 1960s cult movie *Endless Summer*, featuring surfer Bruce Brown trotting the globe in search of perpetual sunshine and the perfect wave (one of the breaks here is known as "Bruce's Beauties"). Although J Bay is by no means the best place to surf in South Africa – there are hundreds of good breaks up and down the coast between Cape Town and Durban – it is probably the place most single-mindedly devoted to the sport.

If you come here to surf, paddle-ski or boogie-board, you should take care to observe the fundamentals of **surfing etiquette**. On arriving at a new spot, always hang around the margins sussing out the scene, never intruding on someone else's patch and always remembering that you are a visitor. Surfers are highly territorial and there are clearly defined rules governing who takes precedence in the water. These often come down to proficiency. In the surfing pecking order, the rising stars are "grommets" or "surf rats", 16- or 17-year-olds who challenge the "old bullets" – twenty- or thirty-somethings whom they consider to be over the hill. Half-crazed rodeo riders of the swell, who take on large, seven-metre waves, are known as "hell men", while at the other end of the spectrum you'll find "doormats", "spongers" and "tea bags", who take to the sea on boogie- or knee-boards, and receive only marginally less contempt from surfers than paddle-skiers, who are termed "egg whippers" or "deckchairs". If you observe these conventions, the chances are you'll find South African surfers exceptionally friendly, ready to talk and happy to offer tips. And beginners will find it easy to find someone willing to get them started for a small fee.

Port Elizabeth to Port Alfred

One of South Africa's most undeveloped stretches of **coast**, with wide beaches and exhilarating surf, stretches east from **Port Elizabeth** for 150 sandy kilometres to **Port Alfred**. The sea temperature here is several degrees higher than around Cape Town (though not as warm as Natal, and never tropically clear), and the beaches are a walker's paradise, with shells, birds and rock pools to detain you. The only problem is the **wind**, which often affects the whole Eastern Cape coast – particularly in the afternoon, so set out as early as you can. The weather is most calm from April to July, and while it's not hot enough to tan you'll certainly be comfortable picnicking or walking along the beaches. April to July is also the optimum season for scuba diving, with the water at its clearest.

The beaches can be deserted out of season, apart from the occasional growl of **4WD vehicles** embossing their heavy tread into the sands. The question of vehicles on beaches bitterly divides South Africans, with fishermen and the expensive-toy brigade defending their freedom to drive on the sands, while ecologists and strollers complain of the disturbance they cause to coastal flora and fauna.

Thankfully, vehicles are banned on some parts of the coast, and you shouldn't encounter them on the **Alexandria Hiking Trail** – one of South Africa's best coastal walks over quite massive dunes. The twin resorts of **Bushman's River** and **Kenton-on-Sea**, each with a river dotted with boats, rocky coves and fabulous beaches for swimming and walking, are the most arresting spots along this coast. Most of the houses are holiday homes, unoccupied much of the year, belonging to white South Africans, but there is a fair bit of rentable **accommodation**, and the big plus of a regular bus service to Port Elizabeth or East London if you're without a car.

Alexandria State Forest and Diaz Cross

A fifty-kilometre tract of Eastern Cape beachfront is protected by the **Alexandria State Forest** and can be walked on the circular two-day **Alexandria Trail**, one of South Africa's finest **coastal hikes**, which winds through indigenous forest and across a deserty landscape of great hulking sand dunes, all the way to the ocean.

The 35-kilometre trail starts at the Alexandria Forestry Station, 8km from the R72. The signposted turn-off is on the right, just before you reach Alexandria, 86km from Port Elizabeth. There's an **overnight hut** (①) at the station, for use at the beginning or end of the trail, and another at Woody Cape, both with mattresses and drinking water, but no cooking facilities. There is no public transport to the starting point. The hike is quite tough-going, especially along the windy dunes. Tall posts with iron stays in the sand can get blown over, obscuring the route. But in fine weather the isolated beaches are magnificent. You'll need to **book** through *Alexandria Nature Reserve*, PO Box 50, Alexandria 6185 (☎046/653 0601). The **forest** itself, with yellowwood trees trailing lichen, is accessible on a seven-kilometre day-walk from the forestry station, with a nice picnic and *braai* place.

ALEXANDRIA, a pineapple- and chicory-growing centre, with a strip of shops and an imposing Dutch Reformed Church, is the closest town to the reserve. *Heritage Lodge* along the main street (☎046/653 0024; ③) is the only **place to stay**, if you want a more comfortable night at the beginning or end of the trail, but it's nothing special. From Alexandria, a good dirt road takes you 18km through the State Forest and farmland to the coast at **BOKNES**, a tiny resort, which is the start of an hour-long beach walk eastwards to the monument of **Diaz Cross**, commemorating the Portuguese adventurer and explorer, Bartholomeu Dias, who rounded the South African coast in 1487 in search a profitable new sea route between Europe and the East. The first

European to make recorded contact with the Khoikhoi, Dias was also the first to kill one of them. The cross, on a rocky promontory, marks the spot where he was forced by his crew to turn back to Cape Town, rather than face the journey eastwards.

Accommodation along this stretch of coast is in short supply. At **Cannon Rocks**, 2km west of Boknes, the *Cannon Rocks Holiday Resort* (☎046/654 0043), right on the beach, is the only place to stay; you can pitch a tent (①) or rent a luxury flat (⑤). Although there's a small shop, you're best off buying supplies from Alexandria, which is linked to Cannon Rocks by a tarred road.

Kenton-on-Sea and Bushman's River Mouth

Some 26km west of Alexandria, along a couple of river valleys, are the twin suburb-resorts of Kenton-on-Sea and Bushman's River Mouth, perfect for a few days' self-catering beach holiday. Totally unglamorous, they're a good choice if you want to be somewhere undemanding and beautiful. **KENTON-ON-SEA**, on a hill bounded by the Bushman's and Kariega rivers, has sandy beaches, sea-sculpted sandstone cliffs, rock pools and big shallow tidal pools to wallow in. You can rent **canoes** to go up the Bushman's River at the *Kenton Marina* (☎0464/81223), well signposted across the R67. **Swimming** in the rivers can be great, but avoid getting close to the entrance to the sea as strong riptides are frequent.

Intercape **buses** pull in at the shops next to the *Kenton Hotel* (☎0464/81333; ④), just off the main entrance to the resort as you leave the R67, perched on a hill with a couple of pine trees and views across the settlement to the sea. For **B&B**, book in advance through *Marlene Thompson* (☎0461/28001 or 28835), or *Tradewinds Agencies* (☎0464/81273; ④), which rents **self-catering** accommodation. Other practicalities include a couple of restaurants, mini-supermarkets, a bank with a cash machine, a post office and a filling station – all along the resort's main street.

BUSHMAN'S RIVER MOUTH is a similar resort, also with beaches and a river, but it's a lot smaller. You can **camp** at the well-kept caravan park, 2 Loerie Rd (follow the signs from the main turn-off), which is right in the centre (☎0464/81227) and a short walk to the river and sea. **Renting a cottage** is another option: enquire at one of the Kenton or Port Alfred agencies. In the tiny centre you'll find a large bottle store, a superette and a surprisingly good **restaurant**, the *Square Bistro*, which specializes in kudu steaks and seafood. Upstream along the Bushman's River and over the R67 is *Captain Jack's Floating Restaurant* (take the Riversbend turn-off from the R67 west of Bushman's), a shabby pontoon which doubles up as a pub, and serves hamburgers, chips and excellent calamari. The views of the steep cliffs, thick with euphorbia, amply compensate for any lack of flair.

Port Alfred

Of all the settlements between Port Elizabeth and East London, only **PORT ALFRED**, midway between the two, can make any claims to a town life outside the holiday season, when for a few weeks its small centre is transformed into a hectic bustle of cars and people. For the rest of the year, its large retired and (even larger), African population in the township are swelled every weekend by wetsuited surfers and partying university students from Grahamstown, less than an hour away.

Although it started life as a port for settler enterprises in the 1840s, Port Alfred was never quite suitable (the river kept silting up) and it quickly faded away into a resort. No large ships navigate the Kowie River, but plenty of **fishing boats** brave its turbulent mouth every day, watched by fascinated bystanders on the end of the pier. Nicknamed "Kowie" by locals, after the river, Port Alfred was named in honour of the second son

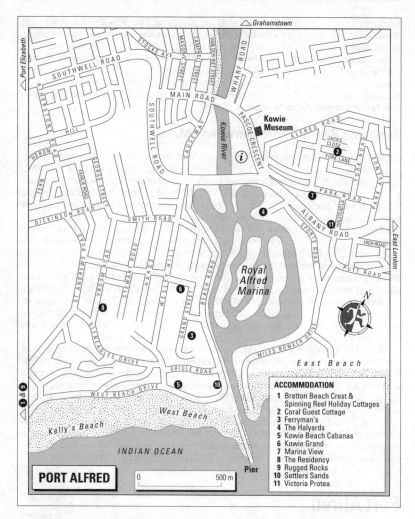

PORT ALFRED

0   500 m

ACCOMMODATION
1 Bretton Beach Crest &
   Spinning Reel Holiday Cottages
2 Coral Guest Cottage
3 Ferryman's
4 The Halyards
5 Kowie Beach Cabanas
6 Kowie Grand
7 Marina View
8 The Residency
9 Rugged Rocks
10 Settlers Sands
11 Victoria Protea

of Queen Victoria, although he never actually made it here. The prince, who visited the Cape in 1870, cancelled a trip to Port Alfred at the last minute, because the prospect of an elephant hunt seemed more appealing.

Arrival, information and orientation

Intercape **buses** travel in both directions between Port Elizabeth and East London pulling into the *Halyards Hotel*, off the main coastal road on the east side of the Kowie River (daily except Tues & Thurs). From here, it's about five minutes' walk to the **tourist information bureau**, Pascoe Crescent (Mon–Fri 8am–1pm & 2–4pm, Sat 8.30–11am; ☎0464/41235), off the main East London road, in the old Market building. From the market, cross the defunct railway line and river, and you'll be in Main Street, the town hub, lined with banks and shops. While you can manage without a car, renting a **bike** is a good idea; you'll find a selection at *Garro*, 41 Van der Riet St.

The **Kowie River** slices through Port Alfred, creating an **east** and **west bank**, with the town and most popular swimming beaches seated on the west, and the less-developed beaches stretching out along the east. The river is traversed by two bridges: a concrete bowstring-arch bridge that has become Port Alfred's symbol, and an older one, which leads straight into Main Street. Sadly, the natural lagoon was blasted away in the 1980s and replaced by a marina, floating with dozens of boats and artificial islands dotted with Toytown holiday homes. The *Halyards Hotel* and a pub constitute the town's less-than-lovely, caged-in waterfront.

Accommodation

Outside school holidays, you should have no problem finding a **place to stay**. The tourist information office (see above) publishes a useful list of accommodation, including B&Bs, and after hours there's a list posted up outside their office. The priciest and most-sought-after places are on **West Beach**. For cheaper options, head for the secluded cottages at Salt Vlei, 3km from West Beach – *Moore and Gardner*, 53 Campbell St (☎0464/42404), arrange lettings.

Hotels and guesthouses

Coral Guest Cottage, Jack's Close (☎0464/42849). B&B on one of the East Bank hills, with a 20min walk to East Beach. Comfortable rooms with bath in a restored corrugated-iron settler cottage. ②.

Ferryman's, Beach Rd (☎0464/41122). Nice, old-fashioned hotel, close to West Beach and overlooking the river. ②.

The Halyards, Royal Alfred Marina, Albany Rd (☎0464/42410). Smartest hotel in town, with stylish decor, but you could be anywhere in the world. ⑤.

Kowie Grand, Princes Ave (☎0464/41150). Right on top of West Bank, with fabulous views, but the rooms are a bit dingy and unappetizing. ③.

The Residency, 11 Vroom Rd (☎0464/24 5382). B&B in a beautifully restored Victorian house on the West Bank with a view of the sand dunes, but not the sea. ②.

Victoria Protea, towards East London on the national road just up the hill from the Marina (☎0464/41133). Comfortable, mid-range hotel. ④.

Camping and self-catering

Bretton Beach Crest & Spinning Reel Holiday Cottages, Freshwater Rd, Salt Vlei, 3km west of West Beach (☎0464/41606). Basic cottages set in dune bush, right on the seaside. The coast is rocky and poor for swimming, but great for shells. ②.

Kowie Beach Cabanas, West Beach (☎0464/42402). Luxury maisonettes (sleeping five) in the prime spot and consequently in the thick of holiday activity. ②.

Marina View, top of Park Rd, above the Marina (☎0464/24 4180). Self-catering flats with great views, and a 20min walk to the beach. ②.

Riverside Caravan Park, Mentone Rd (☎0464/42230). Nice park offering two-bedroomed chalets, but no camping. Peacefully set next to the river (but 3km from the beach). ①.

Rugged Rocks, Salt Vlei (☎0464/43112). Roughly 4km from town centre, at a rocky beach, with large discounts out of season. Bring your own bedding, and choose from ropy old cottages sleeping six (②), or new four-bed wooden chalets sleeping four (②).

Settlers Sands, West Beach (☎0464/41110). Close to the river mouth, these luxury timber chalets on stilts have terrific views. ②.

Medolino Carvan Park, Prince's Ave, Kowie West (☎0464/41651). Good camping facilities, self-catering chalets and a pool. ①.

The Town and its beaches

Port Alfred's attractions are firmly rooted in its **beaches** and the **Kowie River**. The town itself has little else to offer, apart from functional shopping in its one main street. Of passing interest is the tiny **Kowie Museum** (Mon–Sat 9.30am–12.30pm), opposite the tourist information office in Pascoe Crescent, featuring sepia photographs of Port Alfred before the marina and its mansions gobbled up the magnificent lagoon.

Beach life is focused on popular **West Beach**, where the river is sucked out to sea and the breakers pound in. From the café and stone pier, you'll get blasts of sea air watching surfers riding the breakers at the river mouth, and fishing boats making dramatic entries into the river from the open ocean. Fifteen minutes' walk along the beach takes you to **Kelly's Beach**, where you can swim safely in a gentle bay. **East Beach**, reached from the signposted road next to *Halyards Hotel*, is the best walking beach, with a backdrop of hilly dunes stretching as far as you can see into the distance. Port Alfred is home to the prestigious, registered **Kowie Dive School** (☎0464/42213), based at the *Halyards*. Boats go out to Fountain Rocks, and to a couple of nearby wrecks. Don't expect to see crystal waters and fluorescent fish (the Indian Ocean isn't tropical here), but you will come across colourful underwater denizens in the slightly murky water, as well as beautiful corals and sponges. For under R1000, you can qualify in a week for an internationally recognized diving certificate here.

Canoe trips, nature trails and riding

The two-day **Kowie Canoe Trail**, a 21-kilometre paddle up the Kowie River, is a much-sought-after trip and the only self-guided canoeing and hiking trail in South Africa (elsewhere you're accompanied by a nature conservation officer). Much of its charm is its colourful birdlife, and the landscape – hills of dense, dry bush which slope down to the river. Booking is essential (☎0464/42230) and, while weekends are almost always full, weekdays out of school holidays are easy to get, and cost under R50 per person. You **stay overnight** in a hut in the **Horseshoe Bend Nature Reserve**, where the river loops around in a brown, curving horseshoe. From here you can explore the forest on foot, and climb up the steep escarpment to get an impressive view over the horseshoe. The biggest difficulty on this trip is the tide – make sure you check the tide table in the local paper, and paddle with the flow, going up the river when the tide is coming in, and back to Port Alfred when the river is flowing out. If it's windy, stay close to the shore and ensure your gear is in waterproof bags.

If the trail is full, you can get a taste of the landscape **on foot** by driving to the reserve and taking the two-hour circular walk that trails down through thick bush to the Kowie River and along its banks. Look out for primeval **cycads**, some as much as a thousand years old, in the riverine woodland. It's not unusual to see tortoises, monkeys, bushbuck and duikers. By *bakkie* or 4WD, you can reach the reserve, 5km out of Port Alfred along the Bathurst Road. Turn left at the SANTA sign and follow the rough road down to the picnic sites, after getting a permit from the rangers. The other access point is 3km before you reach Bathurst, on a dirt road signposted "Waters Meeting", which takes you to the top of the escarpment for a postcard view of the horseshoe. If you're feeling energetic, you can walk down through the forest to the river to get a real feel of the landscape. Port Alfred has two **riding** establishments: *Glenhope Riding*, off the Bathurst Road (☎0464/25 0866), has nice horses, while the *Three Sisters Horse Trail*, signposted a few kilometres east of Port Alfred, off the East London road (☎0464/71 1269; booking essential), has access to one of the loveliest stretches of the coast, east of Port Alfred.

Eating

Port Alfred offers **fresh fish** galore, but the real surprise, and the biggest treat in town, is a private house serving authentic **Thai** food.

Butlers, 25 Van der Riet St. Next to the river, this is the town's swankiest restaurant, and is good for fish. Open lunch and supper.

Cockles & Mussels Tavern and Restaurant, 33 Van der Riet St. Big seafood platters served on tables on the lawn next to the river. This is also the only outdoor place for tea.

The Country Shoppe, 11 Princes Ave, along from the *Kowie Grand*. Teas and quiche-style lunches, served in a wood and iron settler house.

Dulce's, Campbell St, town centre. The only place in town for halfway decent coffee and sandwiches.

Fish and Chips, Bisquet Rd. Near the minibus taxi rank at the end of Main Rd where it joins the Port Elizabeth Rd. Serves up excellent freshly fried fish and chips.

Guidos on the Beach, Main Beach. Pizzas and pasta at a young place with atmosphere and beach views.

Ying Thai Restaurant, 6 York Rd (☎0464/41647). On the East Bank, and serving the best food in Port Alfred; outstanding, genuine Thai cuisine served in a front room of a private home. Booking essential. Fri and Sat eves only.

Grahamstown

Just over 50km inland from Port Alfred, but worlds apart in terms of ambience, **GRA-HAMSTOWN** projects an image of a cultured, historic town, quintessentially English, Protestant and refined. Dominated by its cathedral, university and public schools, this

ACCOMMODATION

1 Backpackers' Barn
2 Cathcart Arms Hotel
3 Caravan Park
4 Louisa Clayton
5 The Cock House
6 Gill Colette
7 Graham Protea Hotel
8 The Hermitage
9 Mrs Hendry
10 Historic Cottages
11 Settler's Inn

GRAHAMSTOWN

is a thoroughly pleasant place to wander through, with well-restored **Georgian** and **Victorian buildings** lining the streets, and pretty suburban gardens. Every July, the town hosts an **arts festival**, the largest of its kind in Africa.

As elsewhere in South Africa though, there's an alternative reality of conquest and dispossession. Climb up Gunfire Hill, where the fortress-like 1820 **Settlers National Monument** celebrates the achievement of South Africa's English-speaking immigrants, and you'll be able to see Makanaskop, the hill from which the **Xhosa** made their last stand against the British invaders. Strewn on its slopes and in its valleys are the desperately poor ghettos, where their descendants live in a town almost devoid of industry. Marking the gap are the Kowie Ditches (which you'll cross if you take the old East London Road out of town), a waterway which ran red with Xhosa blood in the 1819 battle of Grahamstown.

Despite all this, and the constant reminders of poverty, Grahamstown makes a good stopover, and the perfect base for excursions: a number of **historic villages** are within easy reach, some **game parks** are convenient for a day or weekend visit and, best of all, kilometres of **coast** are just 45 minutes' drive away. Cupped in a valley surrounded by hills, Grahamstown is compact; you'll only need a car or to take an organized tour for excursions out of town.

Some history

Grahamstown's sedate prettiness belies its beginnings as a **military outpost** in 1811. **Colonel Graham** made his name here (and gave it to the town), driving the Xhosa out of the Zuurveld, an area between the Bushman's and Fish rivers. The Fish River, 60km east of Grahamstown, marked the eastern boundary of **the frontier**, with Grahamstown as the capital. The ruthless expulsion of the Xhosa sparked off a series of nineteenth-century frontier wars.

A line of **forts** was built to defend the frontier, subsequently developing into the settlements, which now include Fort Beaufort, Fort Hare and Peddie, but these alone were not enough to hold the line, and the British decided to reinforce the frontier with a human barrier. With the promise of free land, they lured the dispossessed from a depressed Britain to occupy the lands west of the Fish River. In the migration mythology of English-speaking whites, these much-celebrated **1820 Settlers** came to take on a larger-than-life status as ancestors to whom many trace back their origins. However, far from the hoped-for paradise, the settlers, ill-equipped to deal with the rigours of their new life, found themselves in a nightmare; the plots given them were too small for cattle in the harsh Eastern Cape, and unsuitable for crops; drought, floods and disease were a constant problem, and the threat of Xhosa attack never far away.

Not surprisingly, many settlers abandoned their lands and headed to Grahamstown in the early 1820s. This brought prosperity and growth to the town, which enjoyed a boom in the 1840s, when it developed into the emporium of the frontier. Xhosa traders came to barter ivory and hides for beads, buttons and brass wire, while some colonists, who had persisted with farming in the surrounding district, traded **wool** from Spanish merino sheep which thrived in the Eastern Cape.

During the apartheid years, the Fish River marked the border of the **Ciskei**, one of the artificially created ethnic statelets in which many Africans were moved from "black spots", in white areas, to poverty-stricken resettlement villages. Even after the ANC victory in 1994 and the reintegration of the Ciskei into South Africa, the Fish continues to mark an unofficial border between prosperous farms on one side, and tin-roofed villages scattering the hills on the other.

Arrival and information

Grahamstown is on the N2, 127km from Port Elizabeth and is roughly an equidistant twelve hours by bus from Cape Town, Johannesburg and Durban. Both *Translux* and

Greyhound **buses** stop near the *Cathcart Arms Hotel* on Market Square, while the *Leopard Express* minibus, which connects Grahamstown daily with the nearest airport at Port Elizabeth, terminates in Hill Street, diagonally opposite the Cathedral. The *Hopper* bus (☎041/51 2322) operates a daily drop-off and pick-up service to any place in Grahamstown.

The **train station** is at the bottom of High Street, but sees only one train a day, a branch-line service connecting to the Johannesburg/Port Elizabeth line. With only one **taxi** company (☎082/652 0798) in town (and no buses), getting around is **on foot**. Fortunately Grahamstown is compact and the central accommodation and tourist information office are easily and safely reachable.

The very helpful **tourist office** (Mon–Thurs 8.30am–5pm, Fri 8.30am–4pm, Sat 9–11am; ☎0461/23241) is on High Street, next to the City Hall.

Accommodation

The only time you may have difficulty finding **a place to stay** is during the festival in July, when you'd be well-advised to book as early as March. Two agencies can arrange bookings: Marelene Thompson at *Fleur Petite Florist* (☎0461/28001, after hours 18835) and *Country Hospitality East Cape* (☎0461/28055) both cover places in town as well as farms in the surrounding area. There are only two budget central options: *Backpackers Barn* and the *Caravan Park*. For mid-range accommodation, the choicest B&Bs are in historic houses, and there's a good selection of hotels.

Hotels and B&Bs

Backpackers' Barn, 4 Trollope St (☎0461/29720). Cheapest beds in town, in a rambling old house on a hill above the train station. Clean dorms, a double room, a lounge and self-catering kitchen. Outings to the countryside and coast can be arranged. ①.

Caravan Park, on the right as you come into town from Port Elizabeth (☎0461/29112). Nicely located next to wooded hills, and an easy walk to town. Besides camping (①), there are rondavels with bunk beds and self-catering chalets which sleep five (bring your own linen). ②.

Cathcart Arms Hotel, 5 West St (☎0461/27111). Near the minibus taxi terminus, with comfortable rooms, country-style furniture, and a restaurant serving a fine seafood platter. ③.

Louisa Clayton, 1 Parker St (☎0461/23980). Two rooms with bath, 15min walk from the town centre; one inside the family house, the other in the garden. ③.

The Cock House, 10 Market St (☎0461/31 1287). Plush, pricey rooms in this beautiful house which last belonged to writer André Brink. ④.

Gill Colette, 6 Grey St (☎0461/22746, fax 31 1496). Two fully equipped, self-catering apartments opposite the Botanical Gardens, an easy walk to the centre. ②.

Graham Protea Hotel, 123 High St (☎0461/22324). Overpriced, but the most central of Grahamstown's hotels, a stone's throw from the University. ⑤.

The Hermitage, 14 Henry St (☎0461/31 1503). Best B&B in town, with bed and sitting room suites in a luxurious and stylish historic house. There are only two rooms, so book ahead. ③.

Mrs Hendry, 8 Bartholomew St & 1 Sheblon Lane, off Cross St (☎0461/29720). Settler cottage in the old part of town, with yellowwood stripped floors, and handy for the bus terminal. ③.

Historic Cottages, 1 Scott's Ave (☎0461/28936). The only B&B right in the centre, offering rooms with bath and basic self-catering facilities. ③.

Settler's Inn Hotel, off the N2, next to 1820 Settlers Monument (☎0461/27313). Just out of town with a motel feel, peaceful surroundings, a nice garden and pool. ③.

Farmstays

Craigdoone Farm, 10km from town on the Port Elizabeth Road, Howisonspoort (☎0461/28150). Fully equipped cottage in rugged, mountainous area, with breakfast provided. ②.

Table Farm, 15km from Grahamstown on the Cradock Road (☎0461/27854). Comfortable accommodation in large, en-suite bedrooms. ③.

The Town

Reminders of the **colonial past** are everywhere in central Grahamstown, not just in the architecture, but also the street names of Cape governors and soldiers: Cradock, Meyer, Somerset, Stockenstrom and Cuyler. The University itself, of course, is named after **Cecil John Rhodes**.

High Street

Virtually all the shops and banks you'll need are down **High Street**, Grahamstown's major shopping axis. Running from the station at its seedier east end, it continues past the Cathedral at the junction of Hill Street, terminating at the 150-year-old Drostdy Arch, the whitewashed entrance gate to the former courthouse, now of Rhodes University. The terraces of the nineteenth-century buildings lend a graceful air to High Street. You'll also see hawkers on the pavements selling small bags of fruit and vegetables, and may see young Xhosa men in new caps and jackets, with red clay on their faces, signifying that their initiation period is over. At the centre of the street is the **Cathedral of St Michael and St George**, opened in 1830 and, like many churches in the area, a refuge for women and children during the frontier wars. Inside, on the right as you come in, is a quietly ironic memorial tablet to Colonel John Graham, who commanded the frontier.

Rhodes University and the museums

Strung along Somerset Street, which runs at right angles to the top (west end) of High Street, is **Rhodes University** and a succession of modest museums – all are covered by a convenient multi-entry ticket, and can pleasantly take up a morning.

If you've time for only one, head for the **Natural Science Museum** (Mon–Fri 9.30am–1pm & 2–5pm, Sat & Sun 2–5pm), just south of the University entrance on the same side of the street. The display of Eastern Cape fauna and flora from 250 million years ago is excellent, with intriguing plant fossils and bones of dinosaurs, which once roamed these parts. Also worth a look is the **gallery of the curator** who worked for 48 years at the museum, which houses his personal collection of objects in beautiful old teak display cases.

Next door, the **History Museum** (Mon–Fri 9.30am–1pm & 2–5pm, Sat & Sun 2–5pm) houses a dusty collection of 1820 settler memorabilia, with nineteenth-century paintings and antique firearms, interesting mainly for their reminder of the intense conflicts that gave birth to modern South Africa. Upstairs, you'll find an exhibition on the role of clay in Xhosa social life (it's used to signify all major rites of passage).

Beyond Drostdy Arch, tucked behind some buildings at the corner of Somerset and Prince Alfred streets, is **ILAM**, the International Library of African Music (Mon–Fri 8am–5pm; ☎0461/31 8557). An absolute treasure trove of recordings of traditional African music from southern Africa, as well as Zaire, Rwanda, Uganda and Tanzania, the library also sells cassettes on request, and there's a collection of over 200 traditional instruments on view and for sale. If you want to be shown around, you'll need to phone beforehand.

On the same side of the road, the **JLB Smith Institute of Ichthyology** (Mon–Fri 8.30am–1pm & 2–5pm) is named after the Rhodes University scientist who shot to fame in 1939 after identifying the coelacanth, a "missing link" fish, caught off the East London coast, and thought to be extinct for fifty million years. In the foyer are two huge stuffed specimens, with fins which look like budding arms and legs. Far from being extinct, plenty of coelacanths have now been spotted by deep-sea divers; their preferred dwelling is in the pressurized, pitch-dark depths of the Indian Ocean around the Comoros Islands. There are no known colonies of them off the South African coast, they can't survive in aquaria, and it's still not known exactly how they reproduce.

Heading back down High Street and right onto Bathurst Street will bring you to the **Observatory Museum** (Mon–Fri 9.30am–1pm & 2–5pm), containing antique clutter in a restored building which was part-home, part-shop of a notable watchmaker and jeweller during the mid-1850s. The only reason to visit is to see the unusual rooftop Victorian camera obscura, which acts like a telescope, but projects the magnified images of the streets below, onto a wall.

The Provost, Monument and Botanical Gardens

One of Grahamstown's rewarding short walks starts at the **Provost** in Lucas Avenue, on the edge of the Botanical Gardens and University, and heads up through the gardens to the 1820 Settlers National Monument, on the hill above. Built as a prison last century, the whitewashed stone Provost is now a craft shop. Next to it you'll find some graves of British soldiers, killed by Xhosa wariors.

Strolling into the **Botanical Gardens** themselves, you'll hit the *Monkey Puzzle*, a pleasant outdoor place to have tea, lunch or a couple of drinks in the evening. Women should avoid wandering around the gardens alone, especially in the evenings, as there have been some muggings and rapes.

Looming on Gunfire Hill, the **1820 Settlers Monument**, built in 1974 to commemorate the British settlers, is an ugly fortress-like building, supposedly fashioned to look like a ship. The best reason to trudge up here is for the panoramic views, or to see something at the *Monument Theatre*.

Xhosa Grahamstown

Xhosa Grahamstown starts buzzing around **Market Square**, off Beaufort Street, where you'll see hawkers by the dozen and a busy minibus-taxi rank. In the late 1820s, the square was the trading venue for ivory, hides, wool and farm produce. If you're in the area, it's worth walking west of Market Square to see the restored **1820 settler cottages** in Cross and Bartholomew streets, some flat-roofed and double-storeyed, others with pitched tin roofs.

Beaufort Street, the main road for traffic passing through, leads up the hill towards the townships on the eastern side of town. At the top, the road cuts through a hill of white clay, where Xhosa people scratch out pigment for face markings. From this cutting, looking into the valley, well away from the squatters' shacks, you'll see some roughly made traditional huts, used during the seclusion period, when young men, **amakweta**, are inititated. All over the Eastern Cape, it's not unusual to see *amakweta* on the roadside wearing very little and smeared in white clay, which signifies that they've just been circumcised and initiated into manhood (Nelson Mandela went through the same ordeal, as a Xhosa speaker).

Beyond the cutting lies the treeless **Kings Flats** township where the **Umthathi Self-help Project** teaches men and women how to grow vegetables and raise chickens. Umathi's office in Grahamstown train station (☎0461/24450) can arrange for you to eat a meal with a local Xhosa family in a clean, bright township house. The money goes to the family and it's a great way to experience black South Africa authentically and in safety.

The best place to buy African crafts is at the **Power Station**, in the industrial area beyond the Monument, off the Port Elizabeth Road. It's signposted, and is a good half-hour's walk from town. If you don't want to go that far, look out for pavement sellers in High Street selling Power Station's characteristic pottery, brightly painted with animals, and wire goods.

Eating, drinking and entertainment

Eating prospects in Grahamstown are far from exciting, but at least one good pub, a decent coffee shop, and a couple of restaurants with pleasant settings go some way towards making up for the workaday fare. If you're making your own meals, the *Home Industries* shop on Hill Street is great for home-made pies, seasonal fruit and vegetables, and venison and ostrich eggs for gigantic omelettes (all their produce comes from local farms).

During the arts festival in July, the *Monument Theatre* is the primary venue for **shows**, but check *Grocott's Mail*, the local paper, to see if there's anything on at other times. **Nightlife** focuses on pubs. Grahamstown's two **cinemas**, the *Odeon* on Bathurst Street and *His Majesty's* in Hill Street, are old-fashioned, nostalgic fleapits.

Restaurants, tea shops and pubs

Calabash at *Graham Protea Hotel*, High St. Informal, low-cost dining in this bar and restaurant which serves especially good baked potatoes.

The Cock House, corner of Market and George streets (☎0461/31 1287). Grahamstown's smartest restaurant, offering *nouvelle cuisine* at a price.

Ella's, Hill St. A stone's throw from the south side of the cathedral, with the best coffee, cakes and atmosphere in town.

The Juice Bar, next to OK Arcade, High St. Relaxed daytime place with good fresh rolls, but not the freshly squeezed juice you might reasonably expect.

The Little Coffee Shop, OK Arcade, High St. Daytime café with decent espresso, passable sandwiches, but a rather gloomy interior.

Mad Hatters, 148 High St. Tea shop, wine bar and cybercafé, close to the University and serving generous pitta sandwiches. Popular with students and lecturers.

The Monkey Puzzle, Botanical Gardens. Pleasant outdoor restaurant and pub, popular with students, and the only place regularly serving up the regional speciality, kudu steak.

The Rat & Parrot, New St. Lively student bar and restaurant with decent food, notably those dishes cooked and served in individual pots, or *potjies* (the seafood *potjie* is outstanding).

Redwood Spur, High St, near the cathedral. Reliable American-style food,with big salads and late-night bottomless coffee, served with a smile by clean-cut young waiters.

The Terrace, just behind the Monument on the PE road. One of Grahamstown's few outdoor restaurants, and good for weekend breakfasts, pub lunches around the pool or sundowners. To get there, walk up through the Botanical Gardens to the Monument.

THE GRAHAMSTOWN FESTIVAL

Every July, Grahamstown bursts to overflowing, with visitors descending for the annual Standard Bank National Arts Festival – usually called the **Grahamstown Festival** or more simply "The Festival". The hub of the event is the 1820 Settlers Monument, which hosts not only big drama, dance and operatic productions in its theatres, but also art exhibitions and free early evening concerts. Grahamstown's festival proper began in 1974 when the Monument building was opened; today, it's the largest arts festival in Africa, and even has its own fringe festival. For eleven days, the town's population doubles to 100,000, with seemingly every home transformed into a B&B and the streets alive with colourful food stalls. Church halls, parks and sports fields become flea markets and several hundred shows are staged, spanning every conceivable type of performance.

The published festival programme is bulky, but absolutely essential, and it's worth planning your time carefully to avoid walking the very cold July streets, snooping around the markets and seeing nothing of the festival proper. The programme includes jazz, classical music, drama, dance, cabaret, opera, visual arts, crafts, films and a book fair. While work by African performers and artists is well-represented, and is perhaps the more interesting aspect of the festival for tourists, festival-goers and performers are still predominantly white. If you don't feel like taking in a show, the free art exhibitions at the museums, *Monument* and other smaller venues are always worth a look.

For more **information and bookings**, contact the *Grahamstown Foundation*, PO Box 304, Grahamstown 6140 (☎0461/27115, fax 24457).

Around Grahamstown

From Grahamstown, it's a short journey to the **coast**: Port Alfred and Kenton-on-Sea are both less than an hour by car (see p.273), and each has a historic settler village en route – **Bathurst** and **Salem** respectively. A bit further afield, you can meander down dirt roads, pausing at old settler churches and graves, and end up at the **Great Fish River**, which has a magnificent beach and wetland nature reserve (see p.294).

Grahamstown is also close to a couple of fine **wildlife reserves**, especially good for getting a look at the striking, dry bush particular to this area, and at some of the wildlife which, little over a century ago, roamed the land freely. *Backpackers Barn* (☎0461/29720) offer reasonably priced organized trips to the coast or inland, with a walking and outdoor emphasis.

Bathurst and around

Historically a significant centre, **BATHURST**, 45km south of Grahamstown, is today little more than a picturesque straggle of houses, gardens and curiosity shops. Nevertheless, for anyone with the remotest interest in the settler trail it's an intriguing place, the highlight being the **Toposcope**, a monument which indicates the locations of the original settlers' farms. The historic *Pig and Whistle Hotel* (☎0464/25 0673; ③), on the corner of the Grahamstown road as you drive into Bathurst, started life as a smithy in 1821, with an inn attached a few years later (if you decide to **stay**, ask for one of the old rooms upstairs). The water-powered **Bradshaw's Wool Mill** is a pleasant two-kilometre walk from the *Pig and Whistle,* and marks the spot where South Africa's wool industry started.

Across the road from the hotel, the *Bathurst Arms* serves meals, and has a few tables in the garden. You'll find inexpensive self-catering accommodation at *Hayhurst* (☎0464/25 0856; ②) on the Port Alfred Road, which has two converted railway buses, each with its own kitchen and bathroom, in a garden with a swimming pool. For B&B accommodation, *Cosy Corner* (☎0464/25 0955; ②) in Hill Street is good value, with a pool and *braai* facilities. Beyond Bathurst, 8km before you reach Port Alfred, and off the main road, is *Findon Guest Farm* (☎0464/42368; ②), the best B&B in the area – a beautiful, bright house with a pool.

Just outside Bathurst on the Port Alfred Road lies **Summerhill Farm**, designed with kids in mind: its pineapple farm and museum are housed in a monstrous yellow and green plastic pineapple, plonked in the middle of a field full of the genuine items. The area is a major farming district for the fruit and if you've always wondered how they're grown this is the place to find out; otherwise, just pop in to sample their freshly squeezed pineapple juice.

Salem and around

Grahamstown's closest nature reserve, **Thomas Baines**, is a hilly area 15km south of town on the road to Kenton-on-Sea. The main attraction here is **Settler's Dam**, good for picnics, *braais* and wandering around the vicinity of the dam. Walking elsewhere isn't permitted, as rhino and buffalo hang out in the thick, prickly bush. During late afternoons, you're very likely to see antelope grazing on open spaces.

SALEM, 20km southwest of Grahamstown, is a scrawny collection of settler homesteads dating back to 1822, surrounded by khaki scrub and arranged around a village green, dotted some Sundays with the bleached whites of local cricket teams. Salem's centrepiece is a little whitewashed **church**, which is now a national monument and worth a brief visit, though there's nowhere to get anything to eat or drink. Inside, a plaque commemorates Quaker **Richard Gush**, whose descendants still live in the hamlet. During the Sixth Frontier War, local settlers took refuge in a stone church, where they were confronted by Xhosa raiders. Fed up with the ceaseless conflict, Gush stepped out unarmed to confront the Xhosa about their grievances. On being told they were driven by hunger, he went inside and, to the irritation of his fellows, returned with armloads of food. The town was subsequently left in peace.

Moving on from Salem, 20km before you reach Kenton-on-Sea, is *Belton Hiking Trails* (☎0461/28395), with cheap dormitory **accommodation**, and self-catering facilities in a converted farmhouse. If the place is not booked out, you could get a room to yourself, though you'll need sleeping bags. There are several **hiking trails** on the farm, the longest taking you down to the Bushman's River. A further 6km on is the more upmarket *Kariega Park* (☎0461/31 1049; ③), a privately run and delightful game park, with balconied self-catering lodges set in the bush. Each lodge has three or four bedrooms. Besides walking through the reserve, you can also go swimming in the river or swimming pool.

The Great Fish River Reserve

Thirty four kilometres north of Grahamstown on the Fort Beaufort Road, lies the huge **Great Fish River Reserve** (☎0461/27909) – in fact an amalgamation of three separate reserves. Dry and prickly, its scrubby bush is thick with succulents, euphorbias and aloes, with a fair bit of **game** roaming around, including rhinos, giraffes, elephants and plenty of antelope. There are no big cats and, consequently, few tourists. Game is concentrated in the **Inyathi area**, and the best time to see the animals is in the late afternoon and early morning. Other parts of the park can be unrewarding if you're just out for the day.

If you want to make a weekend of it, there are the four **cabins** for rent at Bothas Post, which overlook the Kat River. Alternatively, *Bucklands Farm* (☎0461/22 8055; ②), hard by the reserve, has 17km of its own river frontage. There's a large modern prefab house in the farmyard for rent with single beds and bunks, which is equipped for self-catering, and reasonably priced.

Inland to the Karoo fringes

Travelling between Grahamstown and the towns of Cradock and Graaff-Reinet (the Eastern Cape's two most-visited Karoo towns), you'll be heading into **sheep farming country**, with the occasional *dorp* rising against the horizon, offering the chance to soak up the feel of an archetypal Eastern Cape one-horse outpost. The roads are quiet, and lined with rhythmically spaced telephone poles. Along the shimmering roadsides, people trudge long distances in the heat to unimaginable destinations in the middle of this vast emptiness. Dun-coloured sheep, angora goats and the odd springbok graze on brown stubble, and you'll often see groups of charcoal and grey ostriches in the *veld*, once farmed to satisfy an Edwardian feather fetish, and now reared to cater for a fashion for lean and healthy meat.

Adelaide, Bedford and Somerset East

The R63 west from Fort Beaufort (see p.307) brings you to **ADELAIDE**, a tiny Victorian market centre named after one of Queen Victoria's daughters. Arranged around a square, this drowsy place is dominated by the *Adelaide Century Lodge*

(☎046/684 1058; ②), which is no bad reason to **stay overnight**. Life centres around its bar, outside which you'll see local farmers' *bakkies*, loaded with patient sheep waiting for their owners to quench their thirst after a tough morning at the stock sales. Many of the hotel's original Victorian trimmings are still in place, including a dining room, which serves solid steak and fries **lunches**.

Twenty-two kilometres from Adelaide, in the foothills of the Kaga Mountains, is **BEDFORD**. Once the realm of Xhosa Chief Phato, it became one of the little "English" towns Cape governor Sir Harry Smith had promised to create. Now a drive-through place as you come off the road from Grahamstown, it nevertheless has a pleasant tea garden and craft shop and some nice settler buildings. In the mountainous backdrop you'll find a couple of **farmstays**, notably *Cavers*, PO Box 23, Bedford 5780 (☎046/685 0619; ②), a settler farm renowned for its mountain-spring-fed gardens, and which has a thatched two-bedroomed cottage with its own garden, and the use of a swimming pool and tennis courts.

Just under 60km east of Bedford lies **SOMERSET EAST**, a town which gets chewing during its biltong festival in June, and where Afrikaans matrons with tight perms, cardigans and plump brown arms stroll the main street. The historical part of the town merits a visit. Down Beaufort Street, on an axis with the white-spired Dutch Reformed Church is the **Somerset East Museum** (Mon–Fri 8am–1pm & 2–5pm), whose most interesting feature is the building itself, once the home of a Victorian pastor, and today with rose-petal jam for sale, attesting to a once isolated "civilized" life in this strange, dry land. Somerset's second attraction is the **Walter Battiss Art Gallery** (Mon–Fri 10am–1pm & 2–5pm), in a handsome two-storeyed house on the corner of Beaufort and Poulet streets. Inside you'll find a very uneven collection of drawings amd paintings by one of South Africa's best-known modern artists. It's worth a visit though; Batiss is noted for his sense of humour, which shines out even in this collection.

Cradock and around

CRADOCK, 240km north of Port Elizabeth, lies in the Karoo proper, the semi-desert heartland of South Africa, with knee-high bush, clear dry air and an enormous sense of space, reaching over horizons of slaty mountains. It makes a great stopover on the Port Elizabeth to Johannesburg run, not least because of the excellence of its accommodation in historical houses, and also for the **Mountain Zebra National Park**, which despite having no big cats is one of the country's top game parks.

On the surrounding sheep farms, you'll see the silvery **windmills** which have become an unofficial symbol of Cradock. Xhosa hawkers (often kids) stand along the main road around the city limits, selling intricately crafted wire model windmills, whose blades really do spin in the breeze. You're unlikely to see these anywhere else in South Africa apart from in Johannesburg galleries and on TV, where they first hit national stardom in a mobile phone advert.

Poverty, the motivation for this home industry, has overshadowed Cradock since the Frontier Wars of the last century and the subjugation of the Xhosa people that continued right up to the 1990s. Against this history of conquest, the town has provided fertile grounds for **resistance**: some members of the ANC were based in and around the town, and almost single-handedly kept the organization alive during the 1930s. In 1985, Cradock hit the headlines when anti-apartheid activist **Matthew Goniwe** (see box) and three of his colleagues were murdered.

Political controversy is also the theme at Cradock's biggest attraction, **Schreiner House**, 9 Cross St (Mon–Fri 8.45am–12.45pm & 2–4.30pm; small entrance fee). The house is dedicated to the life of the remarkable writer Olive Schreiner, best known for

CRADOCK

0   200 m

N

Mountain Zebra National Park & Bloemfontein

Great Fish River

DEARY AVE

MILNER STREET

ALBERT ST

ALBERTA STREET

HOSPITAL ST

NAESTED STREET

ALBERT ST

DUNDAS STREET

BEERENS STREET

STOCKENSTROOM STREET

ADDERLEY STREET

FRERE STREET

VICTORIA STREET

CAWOOD STREET

SPRIGG STREET

NAESTED STREET

❸

❷

DURBAN

Dutch Reformed Church

DURBAN

CHURCH STREET

Great Fish River Museum

ⓘ

VOORTREKKER STREET

MARKET STREET

CAWOOD STREET

SPRIGG STREET

Train Station

HARE ST

COMMISSIONER ST

BEERENS STREET

HIGH STREET

❺

❹

East London & Port Elizabeth

CROSS STREET

ACCOMMODATION
1 Cradock Spa
2 New Masonic Hotel
3 Sir John Cradock Guest House
4 Tuishuise
5 Victoria Manor

CROSS STREET

Shreiner House

▽ *Olive Schreiner's Grave*

her novel *The Story of an African Farm* (1883), the first work of imaginative power in South African literature. It was remarkable enough for a woman from the conservative backwoods of nineteenth-century Eastern Cape to write a novel (it was published under the pseudonym Ralph Iron), but even more amazing that she espoused ideas considered dangerously radical even a century later. While in London looking for a publisher, Schreiner mixed with the likes of Havelock Ellis and Eleanor Marx, returning to South Africa at the turn of the century to campaign for universal franchise for men and women irrespective of race. After a life of campaigning, Schreiner died in Cape Town in 1921 and is buried near Cradock on the Buffelskop peak, overlooking the Great Fish River Valley. Her **burial site** has become something of a place of pilgrimage and details of how to get there are available from the tourist information bureau (see opposite), along with a photocopied "OS Map". You'll need a car to get to the starting point, and you should allow a good half-day for the trip, which involves a very stiff climb.

Cradock's other highlights include the **Dutch Reformed Church** at the upper end of Church Street, based on London's St Martin's in the Field and completed in 1868, and a hot sulphur spring-fed **swimming pool**, Marlow Road (4.5km from town), which has indoor and open-air pools, and is a great place to relax after a long journey. The **Great Fish River Museum** behind the Town Hall (Tues–Fri 8am–1pm, Sat

8am–noon) is housed in an 1849 Dutch Reformed Church parsonage and depicts the early history of Eastern Cape pioneers.

Practicalities

Daily **trains** from Port Elizabeth to Johannesburg arrive at Cradock Station at the south end of Church Street at 7pm in the evening and far less conveniently at 4.30am going the other way. *Translux* **buses** pull in daily at *Struwig Motors* on Voortrekker Street, and link Cradock to Cape Town, East London, Port Elizabeth and Johannesburg.

Cradock is small and easily handled **on foot**, but you'll need transport to get to the sulphur spring pool or Zebra Park. There's an informal **taxi** service run by John Beukes (☎0481/71 1320). The very helpful and desperately overworked one-man **tourist information bureau** in Stockenstroom Street (☎0481/2383) can supply maps, accommodation lists and and information on farmstays.

Best bet for for budget **accommodation** are the B&B chalets at the pleasantly lawned *Cradock Spa* (☎0481/2709; ②), 4.5km out of town on the Marlowe Agricultural Road. For more comfort, head for the *Tuishuise* on Market Street (☎0481/71 1322; ③), where you can have an entire Victorian house, furnished with period decor, all to yourself. Other good options include the *Sir John Cradock Guest House*, Stockenstroom Street (☎0481/71 1443; ②), which has nicely furnished rooms with bath and a small garden. Of the two hotels, the old and characterful *Victoria Manor* (③), on Market Street, is the nicer, while the *New Masonic Hotel* in Stockenstroom Street (☎0481/3115; ③) offers standard bed and breakfast, and no funny handshakes. Out of town, the most accessible B&B farm is *Bergendal* (☎0481/4416 or 2239; ②), 12km south, off the main Port Elizabeth road.

Cradock's nicest **restaurant** is the *1814*, with a distinctive sloping red roof standing out on Main Road. Here you'll find tasty breakfasts, lunches and teas with an Afrikaans bias. If you're driving through in a hurry, there's a takeaway next door.

MATTHEW GONIWE AND THE SLAYING OF THE CRADOCK FOUR

Even by apartheid standards, 1985 was a dark year for South Africa. In July, the hawkish President PW Botha declared a state of emergency in response to a nationwide wave of popular resistance. By the end of the year, over five hundred people had been killed in police action. In this maelstrom of repression, **Matthew Goniwe** and three other Eastern Cape leaders from Cradock died in "mysterious" circumstances.

Goniwe, a prominent member and rural organizer for the United Democratic Front (UDF; a proxy organization for the then-banned ANC), left Vergenoeg township on the outskirts of Cradock early on June 27, 1985. Accompanied by **Fort Calata**, **Sparrow Mkhonto** and **Sicelo Mhlauli**, he was heading for a UDF meeting in Port Elizabeth. The four were never to return. On their way back home, they were ambushed, murdered and their bodies burnt and spread several kilometres apart. The nature of the murder indicated considerable planning and resources. A highly publicized inquest in 1989 could not find the necessary evidence to incriminate government forces. In May 1992 a chilling document leaked to the anti-apartheid *New Nation* newspaper revealed that a signal had been sent by Commandant du Plessis to General van Rensberg calling for Matthew Goniwe to be "permanently removed from society".

On the basis of the *New Nation* document, the inquest was reopened in 1993, and found that the assassins were members of the South African Defence Force. Dramatically, in 1997, during the **Truth and Reconciliation Commission** hearings, five members of the Port Elizabeth security police applied for amnesty to the Commission, confessing to the killings and explaining how they intercepted the car and murdered the Cradock Four. Whether it makes any difference to the families of the deceased or not, it's a relief that the truth has finally emerged.

Mountain Zebra National Park

When the **Mountain Zebra National Park** (daily: May–Sept 7.30am–6pm; Oct–April 7am–7pm) was created in 1937, there were only five Cape **mountain zebras** left on its 65 square kilometres. If that wasn't bad enough, four of them were males. At the time, environmental issues were far from being vote-winners; indeed, one cabinet minister referred to the threatened animals as "a lot of donkeys in football jerseys". Miraculously, conservationists managed to cobble together a breeding herd from the few survivors on surrounding farms, and the park now supports several hundred of them, while also translocating healthy numbers to different corners of South Africa.

Thrilling as it is to see members of a rare species, this is by no means the only attraction of the game reserve. **Hiking** is permitted, and is the best way to take in the exhilarating views across slaty layers of cropped mountains. There's an ambitious three-day hike, which must be booked through the *National Parks Board* (see "Practicalities"), with stops each night at a mountain hut. Be warned: it's a very hot hike in summer with little water about, and very cold in the winter. For those who just want to stroll, a number of **waymarked trails** lead the way through the valley and into the mountains.

If you're here for the animals your best bet is to travel by car. The park has a couple of good part-tar, part-gravel loop roads forming a rough figure of eight. Most rewarding is the 14.5-kilometre northernmost route, which circuits the Rooiplaat section where the plains game tend to congregate. Apart from zebra, keep an eye out for **springbok**, **blesbok** and **black wildebeest**.

Practicalities

Mountain Zebra National Park is 26km west of Cradock. To get there by **car**, head north out of Cradock on the N10, turning west after about 6km onto the Graaff Reinet Road. After a further 5km, turn left at the National Park sign onto a good gravel road, which reaches the park gate after a further 16km. Without your own transport, you could make an arrangement to be dropped off and collected from there by private taxi in Cradock (☎0481/71 1320).

The park has a good **campsite**, and twenty two-bedroomed self-catering lodges (②) offering outstanding mountain views. You'll need to **book** accommodation through the *National Parks Board*, PO Box 787, Pretoria (☎012/343 1991, fax 343 0905), or PO Box 7400, Rogge Bay 8012, Cape Town (☎021/22 2810, fax 246211). There's a twenty percent discount on accommodation and camping from June to September (excluding school holidays, when the park is always booked out).

A small shop at reception sells basics, souvenirs, alcohol and soft drinks, but if you're staying for a few days you should stock up in Cradock. There's also a restaurant, a post office, a filling station and a lovely swimming pool.

Graaff-Reinet

It's little wonder that the tour buses pull in to **GRAAFF-REINET** in their numbers; this is a beautiful town, and one of the few places in the Eastern Cape where you can wander freely day and night, taking in historical buildings and the odd museum, have a meal or a drink and stroll back to your accommodation. You don't even need a car to get to the town's sights.

Established in 1786, Graaff-Reinet is one of the oldest towns in South Africa, and much of its historical centre is intact. Exploring its charms takes at least a day and many people stop over en route from Johannesburg to the Garden Route. December is the busiest month, and you should definitely book well ahead if you want to stay over.

GRAAFF-REINET

N

ACCOMMODATION
1 Andries Stockenstroom
  Guest House
2 Camdeboo Cottages
3 Drostdy Hotel
4 Karoopark Holiday Cottages
5 Merwede Ruskamers
6 Urquart Caravan Park

0   200 m

Graaff-Reinet has a large population of Afrikaans-speaking coloured people, mostly living on the south side of town, some of slave origin, others the descendants of indigenous Khoi and San who were forced to work on frontier farms. The dry mountains surrounding the town are part of the **Karoo Nature Reserve**, whose main attraction is the **Valley of Desolation**, a B-movie name which disguises an impressive reality. The rocky canyon, echoing bird call and expansive skies of the valley shouldn't be missed.

Some history

By the late eighteenth century Dutch burghers had extended the Cape frontier northwards into the Sneeuwberg Mountains, traditionally the stomping ground of Khoi pastoralists and San hunter-gathers. Little more than brigands, the settlers had become accustomed to raiding Khoi cattle and attacking groups of San, killing the men and

ROBERT SOBUKWE AND THE AFRICANISTS

One of Graaff-Reinet's most brilliant and frequently forgotten sons is **Robert Managaliso Sobukwe**, founder of the Pan Africanist Congress (PAC). Born in 1923, Sobukwe won a scholarship to Healdtown, a boarding school near Fort Beaufort, going on to Fort Hare University (see p.303), where he joined the African National Congress Youth League. After graduating in 1947, he became a schoolteacher and then a lecturer at University of the Witwatersrand. A charismatic member of the Africanist wing of the ANC, who even the ultra-apartheid prime minister BJ Vorster acknowledged as "a man of magnetic personality", Sobukwe questioned the organization's strategy of co-operating with whites, and formed the breakaway PAC in 1959. The following year he launched the nationwide **anti-pass protests**, which ended in the Sharpeville massacre and his imprisonment on Robben Island for nine years. In 1969 he was released under a banning to Kimberley, where he died in 1978. Five thousand people attended his funeral in Graaff-Reinet. Unlike some of his current followers in the PAC, who have not always held back from anti-white rhetoric, Sobukwe was not a racist, maintaining rather that whites were capable, in time, of becoming genuine Africans.

abducting women and children to use as farm and domestic labourers. Friction escalated when the Khoi and San retaliated and, in 1786, the Cape authorities sent out a *landdrost* (magistrate) to establish **Graaff-Reinet**, from where he would administer the surrounding area and pacify the frontier.

Nine years later, *landdrost* Honoratus Maynier, following orders to stop vigilante rule by the white settlers and to curb the maltreatment of Khoi and San servants, was forced out of town at gunpoint by a group of burghers, bandying catch phrases from the recent French revolution. Declaring South Africa's **first Boer republic**, they complained that Maynier was "protecting the Hottentots and Kafirs against the Boers".

In 1800 Maynier was again put in charge of Graaff-Reinet and colonial control over the district was slowly consolidated, with vast tracts turned over to grazing sheep. The 1850s' **wool boom** brought prosperity to the town and established a pattern of farming and land ownership which continues today.

Arrival and information

Translux **buses** from Johannesburg and Port Elizabeth pull in daily at *Kudu Motors*, 84 Church St, a stone's throw south from the historical centre. However, for tickets and timetables you'll need to go to the *Translux* desk in the Old Library Museum on Church Street. This also houses the **tourist information bureau** (Mon–Fri 9am–12.30pm & 2–5pm, Sat 9am–noon; ☎0491/22479), where you can pick up maps and details on accommodation, including a list of more than a dozen people offering bed and breakfast in their homes.

Accommodation

Graaff-Reinet has plenty of decent **places to stay** in the centre, the nicest being in listed buildings. There's a well-maintained **campsite** on the edge of town, with good-value chalets, and a cheap rooming house closer to the centre. Staying in a private house can work out less expensive than a guesthouse, and many houses have pools, *braai* facilities and welcome kids, though you'll have less privacy. The tourist bureau can provide a list and map (see above). Like some other South African towns, private houses offering B&B are not allowed to put up notices, so it is pointless driving or walking around to find a B&B.

If the Karoo landscape grabs you, you might want to head for one of the **farmstays** around Nieu Bethesda and Graaff-Reinet, and witness some of the country's most dazzling night skies and spacious landscape.

In the centre

Andries Stockenstroom Guest House, 100 Cradock St (☎0491/24575). Handsome listed house a couple of streets behind the *Drostdy*, with air-conditioned rooms, and the best food in town. ③.

Camdeboo Cottages, 16 Parliament St (☎0491/23180). Bang in the historical centre, these fully equipped nineteenth-century cottages built around a courtyard are smallish but pleasant (with hot-water bottles in winter), and couldn't be better located. ②.

Drostdy Hotel, 30 Church St (☎0491/22161, fax 24582). Elegant Cape Dutch landmark in a prime location, with a candle-lit dining room, shady gardens and fountains. The rooms, in terraced artisan cottages behind the hotel, are comfortable but small. ④.

Karoopark Holiday Cottages, 81 Caledon St (☎0491/22557, fax 25730). Modern complex of two- and three-bedroomed self-catering cottages (③) and a B&B (③), set in a garden with a pool.

Merwede Ruskamers, 100 Caledon St (☎0491/23749). The cheapest rooms in town, offering doubles and mini-dorms, with breakfast thrown in. Perfectly clean but a trifle dingy, and there are no cooking facilities. ②.

Urquhart Caravan Park, on the outskirts of town, at the extension of Stockenstrom St, next to the Karoo Nature Reserve (☎0491/22136). Large, well-maintained park with campsites (①) and good-value rondavels, chalets and bungalows (②) next to the Sundays River. The bungalows are more roomy than the stuffy rondavels, and have linen. Bring your own *braai*.

Farmstays

Bloemhof Bed & Breakfast, 27km north of Graaff-Reinet on the N9, and 5km down a good gravel road (☎ & fax 0491/91 0959). Grand, turn-of-the-century homestead built on ostrich feather money, on a large sheep and game farm. ②.

Wellwood, off the N9, on the road to Nieu Bethesda, 31 km north of Graaff-Reinet (☎0491/91 0517). Self-catering four-bedroomed cottage on a farm famous for its private collection of Karoo reptiles, merino sheep stud and orange grove. Breakfast is extra and *braai* packs are available on request. The stunning fossil collection is not open to the public, but you can write for permission to see it (PO Box 204, Graaff-Reinet 6280). ②.

Wheatlands Country House, 50km south of town, and 8km off the R75 to Jansenville and Port Elizabeth (☎0491/91 0422). Five bedrooms in a 1912 manor house and working sheep farm, with large gardens. ②.

The Town

Graaff-Reinet's layout centres around the imposing 1886 **Dutch Reformed Church**, with its pointy steeple and cake-icing decoration. The town's main thoroughfare, **Church Street**, splits at either side of the church, heading northwest to the Valley of Desolation and northeast to Nieu Bethesda, Middelburg and eventually Johannesburg. On either side of Church Street, little roads fan out, lined with whitewashed Cape Dutch, Georgian and Victorian buildings – it's in these parts that you'll find the town's museums, restaurants and most attractive buildings.

Church Street itself bustles with antique shops and businesses with Karoo-inspired names, such as *Merino Pharmacy* and *Kudu Motors*. One block south of the church is the **Old Library Museum** (Mon–Fri 9am–12.30pm & 2–5pm, Sat 9am–noon), which doubles up as the tourist information bureau. The only attraction here is the collection of **fossil skulls** and skeletons of reptiles which populated the marshes, lakes and pools of prehistoric Karoo, some 230 million years ago. These Karoo dinosaurs were entombed in mud, and their bones became embedded in the present-day Karoo shale. The fossils were collected from the hills and sides of river channels in the surrounding area. There's an even better collection on Wellwood Farm (see "Farmstays", above), but you'll need to write for permission to see it.

Next door, in a restored 1821 mission church with Dutch gables, is the **Hester Rupert Art Museum** (Mon–Fri 10am–noon & 3–5pm, Sat & Sun 10am–noon), which features a representative selection of work by South African artists (primarily white) active in the mid-1960s. Much of it is dreary and derivative of European art, but a few pieces stand out. Look out in particular for Cecil Skotnes's woodcuts, the strong expressionistic work of Johannes Meintjies, and Irma Stern's very appealing paintings.

Opposite the Art Museum stands the graceful, whitewashed **Drostdy Hotel**, a historical building in its own right, as the former residence of the *landdrost*. Most of the hotel guests are housed behind the main building, in Stretch's Court, a cobbled lane of nineteenth-century cottages with brightly coloured shutters. It hasn't always been so twee: Drostdy's slaves used to dwell here and, after slavery ended in 1838, their descendants stayed on until they were kicked out under the 1950 Group Areas Act (when the area was zoned for whites only).

From the front steps of the Drostdy, you can look down Pastorie Street, lined with Cape Dutch buildings, to **Reinet House** (Mon–Fri 9am–12.30pm & 2–5pm, Sat 9am–noon, Sun 10am–noon), Graaff-Reinet's finest museum. Formerly a parsonage, it was built in 1812 in the traditional Cape Dutch H-plan, with six gables and a spiral stairway leading to the garden. Essentially a period house museum with wooden floors and airy rooms, it's filled with covetable furniture and intriguing household objects. Strangely enough, the museum is the only place allowed to distil an illicit home-brewed spirit called "Withond" (white dog), which has an exceptionally sharp bite. Little bottles of the clear liquor, labelled with a picture of a bull terrier, are sold at the front desk.

Eating

You'll find a fair number of centrally located **restaurants** and **tea shops** to cater for Graaff-Reinet's many visitors. The town's culinary highlight is unquestionably its French-Karoo restaurant, which attracts gourmands from across the country.

Almar Steakhouse & Coffee Shop, 30a Parsonage St. Steaks and hamburgers with a take-away section and an outdoor beer and coffee terrace. Daily 9am–10pm.

Andries Stockenstrom Dining Room, 100 Cradock St (☎0491/24575). Outstanding French-Karoo restaurant with imaginative game and mutton dishes and scrumptious desserts. Booking (weeks ahead in Dec) is essential as seating is limited. Not cheap, but you won't get better. Evenings only except Sun.

Die Kliphuis, 46 Bourke St. Open during the day only, this is a good place for tea and sandwiches or a light lunch, with the advantage of pavement tables. Closed Sun.

Drostdy Hotel, Church St. Unmatched garden setting for drinks or tea. Rather formal dinners in the grand dining room, offering a pricey English-style set menu, with the odd Afrikaans speciality thrown in. Their buffet lunches and breakfasts are better value.

Iets Anders, 3 Parsonage St (off Church St). Daytime café/bar serving reasonably priced Afrikaans specialities, such as like bobotie and rice, tomato *bredie* done in a three-legged pot, hearty breakfasts, sandwiches, hamburgers, home-made ginger beer and cakes including syrupy *koeksisters* and *melktert*.

Karoo Nature Reserve

The low-lying **Karoo Nature Reserve** (daily dawn to dusk; free) lies 5km north of the centre of Graaff-Reinet on the Murraysburg Road, and totally surrounds the town. Its indisputable highlight is the strikingly deep **Valley of Desolation**. By car, follow the narrow tarred road which starts at the reserve's entrance and ascends up the bush-flecked mountainside, passing a series of viewpoints, up to the cliffs overlooking the

Valley. Late afternoon is the best time to enjoy the scenery: this is when the tinted sun saturates the ochres and reds of the rock towers which soar from the valley floor. The views from the lip of the canyon, beyond the rocks and into the plains of Camdeboo, are truly thrilling, and even better when you tune into the echoing bird calls, especially when you see black eagles circling the dolomite towers, scanning the crevices for prey. There's a 45-minute looped **walk** along the canyon lip, well marked with a lizard emblem. For longer trails, and **staying overnight** in a hiker's hut, you'll need to book at the *Department of Nature Conservation* in Bourke Street (☎0491/24535), where you can also pick up detailed maps.

Nieu Bethesda

There's a mystique about the Karoo being at the unfathomable heart of South Africa, and if you want to get a sense of that dry, timeless centre **NIEU BETHESDA** is the place to do it. Winding into the mountains 50km north of Graaff-Reinet, much of its attraction lies in its spareness, set against expansive skies. The Karoo is drier and dustier than you may find palatable, however, especially in midsummer when it boils with harsh, bright light. There are no streetlamps, and on winter nights temperatures plummet to zero and the sky fills with icy stars.

Most people come to Nieu Bethesda to marvel or shudder at the **Owl House**, River Street (daily 9am–5pm; entry fee), once the home of Helen Martins, a reclusive artist who expressed her disturbing and fascinating inner world through her surroundings. Every corner of the house and garden has been transformed to meet her vision, and the walls inside the house glitter and prickle with crushed glass. At the back of the house, trapped by a stone wall and high chicken wire, are hundreds of glass and cement sculptures – camels, lambs, sphinxes and human figures. Owls with large eyes gaze from her tin-roofed verandah. Martins never exhibited or courted publicity, though since her death in 1976 many have visited the museum and pondered on her life in this Karoo backwater. South African playwright Athol Fugard, who loves the Karoo and has a house in Nieu Bethesda, used her life and creative toil to talk about himself in his celebrated play, *The Road to Mecca*.

Owl House aside, the whitewashed village has plenty of charm. It's a tranquil place, accessible on a good gravel road, with the sound of spring water flowing down furrows into the little windmilled allotments. An archetypal Karoo *dorp*, its minuscule white population of around two dozen has been split since the 1970s between hippie outsiders, attracted by the region's isolation, and conservative locals. Nearby, a few hundred coloureds somehow manage to eke out a living in this ungiving environment. Making the most of the creative forces and lack of distractions, the **Ibis Gallery** on the main road (☎04923/602) hosts first-rate exhibitions of contemporary South African art, some of it generated locally, and runs workshops in creative writing, printmaking, painting and drawing.

The **Compassberg Mountain**, one of the highest peaks in the Eastern Cape and part of the Sneeuberg range, dominates the Nieu Bethesda skyline, and can be climbed. Contact Peet van Heerden for details of Compassberg **trails** (☎04923/749), all operated from private farms.

Practicalities

Nieu Bethesda is 23km off the N9 between Graaff-Reinet and Middelburg. There's a **village shop** and butcher on the main road, but if you're self-catering you should stock up elsewhere, especially for fresh fruit and vegetables, which are scarce in the Karoo. There's a good selection of **places to stay**. The *Ibis Gallery* (see above) offers self-catering accommodation for short- or long-term stays, especially for artists, who can use studio space to work in the village. Best of the guesthouses is *Huis Nommer Een*, Murray Street (book through the *Village Inn*, ☎0491/667; ②), with three spacious rooms furnished in South African country-style, a farmy kitchen, and handsome verandah. Another option is *Stokkiesdraai Guest House*, Murray Street (☎0491/711; ②), which offers a two-bedroomed self-catering Karoo cottage. If you want to stay on a farmhouse, head for *Weltevreden Farm* (☎04923/740; ②), 13km north of the village, in the Sneeuberg Mountains, with two self-catering cottages, and walking and riding on offer. Alternatively, there's the friendly *Doornberg Farm* (☎ & fax 04923/749; ②), self-catering, and with a trampoline, pool, riding and hiking. Given how tiny Nieu Bethesda is, it's surprising to find any **restaurants** at all. Evening meals are restricted to the cosy *Stokkiesdraai Country Kitchen*, Martin Street (☎0491/711), which serves plain, home-cooked meals, but needs to be booked in advance – they also do roast lunches on Sundays. During the day you can get lunches and teas at the *Village Inn* (☎04923/667), along from the Owl House, in New Street. The owner is a fund of **information** about the area, and also takes bookings for some guesthouses.

EAST LONDON AND THE CENTRAL REGION

Some of the Eastern Cape's least-developed **coastline** lies between Port Alfred and East London, saved from the hands of developers because it fell into the neglected Xhosa *bantustan* of the Ciskei. **East London**, formerly a part of white South Africa, wedged uncomfortably between two *bantustans*, is the largest city in the central region of the province, with excellent city beaches for surfing and swimming and good transport links to Johannesburg and along the coast. Heading inland from here, **Fort Hare University** near Alice has educated political leaders across the subcontinent, including Nelson Mandela, and has the country's finest collection of contemporary black South African art. Sweeping up from Fort Hare's valley, the gentle, wooded **Amatola Mountains** yield up to the dramatic landscapes of the **Eastern Cape Drakensberg**, which offer hiking, horse-riding and even skiing opportunities. Before white settlers (or even the Xhosa), arrived, these towering formations were dominated by **San hunter-gatherers**, who decorated the rock faces with thousands of ritual **paintings**, many of which remain surprisingly vivid, depicting a cosmology in which the spiritual world melds into everyday reality.

The Coast: Fish River Mouth to East London

Heading 38km east of Port Alfred, along the R72, the **Great Fish River** was the boundary across which Britain drove the Xhosa in the Fourth Frontier War of 1811–12. It constitutes a major landmark, cutting through a steep-sided valley shrouded in prickly, thick bush. During the apartheid years, the river became the frontier of the notionally independent Ciskei *bantustan*, whose multi-million-rand border post on the east bank of the river stood unused until the 1990s, when it became a rather pleasant roadside tea room.

The **Great Fish River Wetland Reserve** is a preserved wetland area between the R72 and the river mouth, beautiful for the mauves, yellows and browns of the plants and the prolific birdlife. There's nowhere to stay, apart from **camping**, for which the best spots are in the coastal bush near the beach, where it's sheltered from the wind; but there are no facilities, bar crummy toilets and cold running water, and often no one supervising or collecting fees. **Without a car**, this is the only place you'll get to in the vicinity of the Fish – walk down the hill from the *Fish River Sun*, where the Port Alfred to East London bus makes a stop, four days a week.

Just across the Great Fish, conforming to the bizarre logic of apartheid, the luxurious *Fish River Sun Hotel* (☎0405/66 1102; ⑥) is where Eastern Cape whites could nip over the border to the South African-owned **hotel** to enjoy a spot of gambling, which was banned in "White South Africa". The *Sun* has arguably the best golf course in the country (open to non-residents) with stunning views of the river and beach. A few kilometres further east, the *Mpekweni Marine Resort* (☎0405/66 1026; ⑤–⑥) is very comfortable, but not as glitzy. Its position couldn't be better, though, with rooms close to the beautiful lagoon and beach, which the hotel has managed to purloin for its own private use.

Hamburg

One of the few resorts along the Pineapple Coast that feels like real Africa is **HAMBURG**, a low-key village on a good dirt road, 14km off the R72. The route passes through **Xhosa settlements** and shanties, where you'll see traditionally decorated thatch and mud huts. Look out for animals wandering perilously into your way and strolling around Hamburg itself, lending the town a truly rural feel. With plots currently being snapped up, this run-down backwater looks set for a slick rash of development. Hamburg is renowned for **fishing** and the muddy-bottomed Keiskamma River is excellent for catching prawns. The sea offers a good beach break for **surfers**.

Public **transport** is limited to the *Hopper Bus* (☎041/51 2332), which calls in daily, and the *Baz Bus* (☎021/439 2323), which travels along the coast and makes a detour into Hamburg off the main coastal road whenever someone requests a pick-up or drop-off. There are only two **places to stay**, both with terrific views over the wide, brown Keiskamma River and high olivey hills, but a three-kilometre walk to the beach. There's nothing at the beach except for a car park, broken-down toilets and kilometres of sand and sea. The *Hamburg Oyster Lodge,* Main Street (☎0405/88 1020), has closely packed bunks (①) and double rooms (①), and allows **camping**. You can get **meals** here, including fresh oysters. For more comfort, the nearby *Hamburg* (☎0405/88 1061; ③) has double rooms with bath and views onto gardens, an outside bar deck, a pool and a rate that includes dinner. **Fuel** is available at the hotel.

THE SHIPWRECK HIKING TRAIL

One of the most rewarding ways to explore this area of the coast is on foot. The **Shipwreck Hiking Trail** is an informal beach walk traversing the 64km between Great Fish River and Chalumna, along deserted beaches where you'll spot the odd shipwreck. The main hike takes three days and two nights (you can also do a shortened version). En route, the best **places to stay** are at **Kiwane**, which has basic chalets, **Hamburg**, with hotel and backpacker accommodation, and **Birha** and **Mpekweni**, which have camping only. There's no one supervising the trail and no need to book, as numbers are not restricted. The wildest section is the beach between Hamburg and Kiwane, though there'll undoubtedly be some fishermen and 4WDs churning up the sand. Kiwane has an especially lovely lagoon. Although primarily a beach walk, light running or walking shoes are recommended, as you may have to walk upriver to cross the Great Fish at Hamburg if there are no boats around, and clamber on rocks if you're collecting oysters and mussels to eat. Take the usual precautions against the sun and, if possible, walk at low tide when the sand is firm and easy to stride along. Alternatively, base yourself at Hamburg, right at the centre of the trail, and embark on day walks from here. For further information, contact the *Keiskamma Ecotourism Network* (☎ & fax 0433/22571).

East London and around

EAST LONDON, the second-largest city in the Eastern Cape, is the obvious jumping-off point for exploring the Transkei or the coast west to Port Elizabeth. It has good **connections** to the rest of the country by air, rail and coach, and you can enjoy some beach life here without a car. But without fine, warm weather, the city can be dreary. What does happen takes place along the beachfront, where there's a plethora of places to stay, eat and drink. **Nahoon Beach** is a great **surfing spot**, and the town has a dedicated and lively surfing scene. It's also gradually becoming a place for black holiday-makers – a post-apartheid phenomenon.

Away from the holiday strip, East London is dominated by an industrial centre served by **Mdantsane**, a huge African township, 20km from the city towards King William's Town. Apart from the active river port, there are several large factories, including *Mercedes Benz*, whose workers presented Nelson Mandela with a bright-red, top-of-the-range Mercedes as a coming-out-of-prison present.

Some history

East London began life as a permanent British settlement during the nineteenth-century **Frontier Wars**, when it was used as a beachhead to land military supplies needed to push back the Xhosa. British governor Sir Harry Smith, taken by its strategic possibilities as a port, optimistically called it **London** in 1848, after the capital of the Empire. Later it was changed to the Port of East London, not after London's East End, but because the port was on the east side of the Buffalo River. British connections are still obvious, though: East London's main thoroughfare is called Oxford Street and there's a Fleet Street and even a Belgravia suburb.

Before the British, and even the Xhosa, this was home to the **Khoikhoi** people, who called it "Place of the Buffalos". In the past the Buffalo River teemed with game, but they were gradually killed off with the arrival of British hunters.

Arrival, information and orientation

East London's small **airport** (☎46 0211), a few kilometres west of the centre on the R72, connects the city to all major centres. The **airport shuttle** (☎082/569 3599) meets all flights and drops off at the *Holiday Inn* on the beachfront. Coming in **by train** from Johannesburg, by *Translux* **bus** from Durban, or *Intercape* from Port Elizabeth, you'll pull in at East London's business and shopping centre. The *Greyhound* from Johannesburg takes you straight to the beachfront, dropping off at the *Kennaway Protea*. The *Hopper* bus comes in daily from Port Elizabeth and will drop you off anywhere central. From the train station, it's a thirty-minute walk to either of the backpackers' hostels at Eastern Beach, and a slightly shorter stroll to Orient Beach. Buses are scarce, but there are metered **taxis** outside the station.

Like most South African cities, East London is gridded, sprawling and, with uncongested roads and easy parking, far more orientated to **driving** than walking. **Public transport** connects the African townships to the centre, via speeding minibus taxis, and buses link the city's two hubs, the **city centre** and **beachfront**, primarily at the beginning and end of the working day.

Maps and a comprehensive list of B&Bs are available from the helpful **tourist information bureau**, 35 Argyle St, behind the City Hall (Mon–Fri 8.30am–4.30pm, Sat 8.30–11am; ☎26015).

The **telephone code** for East London is ☎0431.

Accommodation

To get the best out of East London, **stay** either at the beachfront, or up the hilly and wooded east coast, towards Gonubie. If you're on your way to Port Elizabeth, there are a couple of convenient places just beyond the airport. East London fills up over the Christmas period, when prices rise sharply. **Backpackers** have the choice between two good lodges at Eastern Beach, one of them spectacularly situated in a former life-guard's lookout. For longer-term accommodation, a couple of agencies can be helpful: try *Lauraine Kruger* (☎27457), or *Eastern Cape Holidaymakers* (☎43 7933), which also offers caravans, cottages and runs hiking trails.

Beachfront

East London's **beachfront** sports graceless blocks of holiday apartments and functional hotels, redeemed only by their fabulous views of the Indian Ocean. The really cheap hotels are mostly filled with long-term residents, and are often rough drinking hangouts – best avoided.

Backpackers, 128 Moore St, Quigney (☎23423). Bunks in a ramshackle old house behind the *Holiday Inn*, close to Eastern Beach and a 15min walk from town through back routes. Camping is allowed in the back garden, next to the washing line. ①.

Chapman House, 12 Ganteaume Crescent, Quigney (☎43 4134 or 4135). Two B&B flatlets very close to Orient Beach. ②.

Holiday Inn Garden Court, Beachfront (☎27260). Close to Eastern Beach and no surprises here. ⑤.

Hotel Majestic, Orient Rd, Beachfront (☎43 7477). Revamped 1920s hotel, just above Orient Beach, with more character than most on the beachfront. The best rooms look onto the sea. ②.

Kennaway Protea Hotel, Beachfront (☎25531). Comfortable rooms in a reliable hotel with exceptional views. ④.

King David Hotel, 27 Inverleith Terrace (☎23174). East London's smartest hotel, a few blocks up from the beachfront. ④.

Queens Hotel, 6 Currie St (☎23631). The only low-cost beachfront hotel worth considering, with ordinary rooms, and near the beach. ②.

Sugar Shack, Eastern Beach (☎2111). Brilliantly located, right on the beach, and with terrific views. Bright dorms and outdoor relaxation area. Expect a lively surfing and partying crowd. Free pick-up is available from town or the station. ①.

Windsor Cabanas, George Walker Parade, Quigney (☎43 3220). Luxury Spanish-style, self-catering pads near Orient Beach, with great views. Minimum of three nights' stay and not cheap. ⑤.

Windsor Courtyard, George Walker Parade, Quigney (☎43 3220). Part of the *Windsor Cabanas* complex, but offering a cheaper rate for B&B. ④.

Eastern suburbs and resorts

If the glitz of the main beachfront doesn't appeal, your best bet is to head for the mostly white suburbs of **Beacon Bay**, **Bonza Bay** or **Gonubie**, close to the river and sea. Besides a couple of old-fashioned hotels, these areas have a good selection of smart **B&Bs** in private houses. You'll need your own transport to get there, unless you arrange to be picked up beforehand or take a taxi. East London's **campsites** are out this way too, near the water.

Blue Lagoon Hotel, Blue Bend Place, Beacon Bay (☎47 4821). Very pleasant accommodation overlooking the river mouth and close to the beach. ③.

Bonza Bay Hotel, Kingfisher Ave, signposted off Old Transkei Rd (☎47 2401). Quiet old hotel which has seen better days, but is reasonably priced and has a lovely garden. A good bet if you want to spend your time on the beach. ②.

The Castle, 13 Acacia Drive, Beacon Bay (☎47 3866, mobile 082/492 0981). B&B with easy access to the Nahoon River nature trail and mouth. Pool, deck and *braai*. ③.

Dolphin Hotel, 85 Harewood Drive, Nahoon (☎35 1435). Plain 1950s suburban hotel: the prim style gives no hint of the lush vegetation and wonderful beach just a 15min walk away. ④.

Gonubie Hotel, 141 Main Rd (☎40 4010). Attractive hotel on the point at Gonubie, a short boardwalk from the beach. ⑤.

Gonubie Resort & Caravan Park, 19km east of town off the N2 (☎40 2021). Sheltered camping spots, near the beach. ①.

Nahoon Caravan Park, Beach Road, Nahoon (☎34 2129). At the Nahoon estuary, the secure camping area nestles among riverine trees with plenty of grassy sites. A short walk to the river and a bit further to the open beach. There's a small shop mostly open for ice creams and selling basics. You'll need your own transport or to take a taxi from the centre. ①.

Quintetta Guest Farm, Bonza Bay Rd, Beacon Bay (☎47 4729). Next to a golf course and pub, with horses and a pool, but 5km from the beach. ②.

West of the city

If you're flying into the airport and don't fancy sampling East London itself, there are a couple of pleasant overnight stops which are on this side of town.

Kidd's Beach Hotel, Kidd's Beach (☎04323/715). Some 35km west of East London, this exceedingly old-fashioned place has cheap doubles and is a 10min walk to the beach. The town itself has a 1950s ambience, great surfing and a crescent-shaped beach with a tea room. ②.

Lagoon Valley Holiday Resort & Caravan Park, Marine Drive (☎46 1080). Off the R72, on the banks of the Zaminyama River, with camping (①) and self-catering chalets (②). From here you can walk 1hr west along the beach to Cove Rock, best visited for all the sea birds which nest and gather on it, and the stupendous views you get by climbing onto it.

The City

East London's drab city centre is dominated by **Oxford Street**, the main shopping and banking precinct, parallel to Station Street and the train station. Although a major traffic thoroughfare, it is largely deserted at night, when you shouldn't wander around alone. White East Londoners have abandoned the centre altogether, preferring to shop in the sanitized suburban malls.

Apart from a couple of handsome buildings, East London's Victorian heart has progressively been demolished. From the station, built in 1877, you can walk a few blocks north up Cambridge Street to the city centre's principal landmark, the splendid terracotta and lacy-white **City Hall**, opened in 1899. Its tall, colourful clock tower in an otherwise dreary lot of modernish buildings is a useful orientation point. Also worth a look is the **Daily Dispatch Building**, at the corner of Caxton Street and Cambridge Road, with a surrounding colonial-style verandah. The newspaper, founded in 1879, made national headlines in the 1970s, when its then-editor, Donald Woods, earned the wrath of the apartheid government for being involved with black leader Steve Biko (see p.302), who contributed to the newspaper, under a pseudonym. Woods fled the country rather dramatically, after endless police harassment – a story told in the 1987 movie *Cry Freedom*.

One street north, Terminus Street leads to **Gately House** (Tues–Thurs 10am–1pm & 2–5pm, Sat & Sun 3–5pm), the Victorian home of the city's first mayor, John Gately. East of Terminus, across the railway line, is **Quigney**, an area of small colonial-style Victorian houses, some nicely restored with verandahs and corrugated-iron roofs, others run-down and cockroach-infested. Quigney slopes downhill to the **Esplanade** and **Orient Beach**, the safest place to swim and best accessed along Currie Street. The city's nicest **craft shop**, *Umzi Wethu Curio Shop*, 110 Moore St, is uphill from the *Holiday Inn*.

The dockland waterfront, **Latimer's Landing**, 4km from the centre, is the best place to eat fresh fish or simply while away a few hours. To get there, head west along Fleet Street towards the airport, and just before crossing the Buffalo Bridge head steeply down Pontoon Road to the working docks on the Buffalo River. Unlike the glitzy shopping centres of Cape Town or Johannesburg, this is a low-key and peaceful waterfront, with a characterful shipyard, and a couple of outdoor restaurants and pubs overlooking the river. **Boat trips** from here head either upriver or through the Buffalo harbour out to sea and along the beachfront shore. There's usually a boat moored at the Landing, but it's best to arrange something beforehand; *Yatch Miscky* (☎35 2232 or 43 9220) offers good-value runs, as do *The Albatross* (☎486036/43 3264) and *The Ferry* (☎0431/43 1187 or 43 1188).

A few kilometres north of the city centre, the **East London Museum**, Upper Oxford Street (Mon–Fri 9.30am–5pm, Sat 9.30am–noon, Sun 11am–4pm; entry fee) has a stunning collection of South Nguni beadwork, and contemporary wire sculpture, including an inventive wire car made by Mdantsane resident Phillip Ntliziywana. The museum's pride and joy, however, is its stuffed coelacanth, caught off the coast in the 1950s.

The beaches

East London's **Esplanade** loops from Orient Pier in a wide and beautiful sweep of rocks, beach and sand dunes to Eastern Beach, marred only by the motley assortment of holiday apartments, hotels and restaurants lining the beach. There's no public transport along here, but it's easy enough to walk from one side to the other. The beaches are half an hour's walk from the city centre, and buses are sporadic.

Tucked in next to the pier, with cranes poking their necks above it, **Orient Beach** is a wonderful place to swim, though it looks a bit grim and industrial. The waves are gentle and the water and sandy beach are clean. Red-hatted lifeguards lend a sense of security, and there are changing rooms, and a couple of small pools for kids. You pay a small fee to enter the beach area during the day, but it's free after 5pm.

From Orient Beach, the sea-walled Esplanade continues east, along sand and black rocks, to **Eastern Beach**, with its high, bush-capped sand dunes. Although far more attractive, Eastern Beach is not really safe for swimming, and muggings have been reported here recently. Don't leave your stuff unattended, and give the beach a wide berth at night. Heading northeast beyond Bats Cave, a distinctive chunk of rock jutting out to sea is popular **Nahoon Beach**, a long wash of sand, backed by dunes. This wonderful natural setting is superb for swimming and surfing, with some of the best waves in the world. However, Nahoon's image may be changing with the arrival of squatters who have established an area of makeshift homes with mountains of plastic bags in the tangled forest behind the dunes, edging onto the golf course and prestigious suburbs. Public transport is scant, but there are three **buses** a day from the Esplanade, or you can walk the 5km from the centre if you're feeling energetic. East of the Nahoon River, the coast curves into **Bonza Bay**, with kilometre of beach walks and a lazy lagoon at the mouth of the Quinera River. East London's best campsite, the *Nahoon*, is here (see "Accommodation"), nestling in the riverine trees.

Eating, drinking and nightlife

Although it's hardly a culinary capital, East London does have a couple of very decent places serving **fresh fish** in an outdoor setting: Latimer's Landing is the most congenial place to do this. **Drinking** spots abound, from beachfront sleaze at lowlife hotels to lively surfers' hangouts or swanky tipples overlooking the ocean. Some of the pubs double up as **live music** venues, as well as offering a bite to eat.

Beachfront

Jekyll & Hyde, Lock St Gaol, Fleet St, a couple of blocks up from Orient Beach. A favourite with the surf crowd, this bar often has live music.

Mignon's, Esplanade on the Orient Beach side of the *Aquarium*. Best Italian-style ice cream in town, with tea, coffee, cakes and savouries also on offer. Daytime only.

Monte Rio Spur, Beachfront, just above the Orient Beach car park. Good-value American-style burgers, steaks and salads.

Movenpick, upstairs at the paying entrance to Orient Beach. Excellent seafood at the beachfront's priciest restaurant, with dinner and dancing. Don't turn up in flip-flops.

O'Hagan's, Esplanade, midway along, next to the *Aquarium*. Spectacular setting on a terrace which juts out over the waves. Even when the weather is bad you can watch the surfers through the big windows. The food is unexciting, but the location more than makes up for it.

Platform One, New Papagello Centre, Esplanade. This pub jumps with drunken 19-year-olds.

Quarterdeck, Orient Beach, overlooking the paddling pool. One of the best beachside places for a quiet drink, with "catch of the day" fish served daily, at reasonable prices.

Saddles, King's Entertainment Centre, Esplanade. Choicest place in town for a steak. Informal atmosphere, big windows looking towards Eastern Beach. Popular with families and reasonably priced. They also do a vegetarian platter.

Central and Quigney

Casbah Restaurant, *King David Hotel*, Inverleith Terrace. Expensive but delicious food with a Middle Eastern touch, in East London's top hotel.

Country Rose Coffee Shop, Caxton House, Caxton St. The centre's nicest coffee shop, a stone's throw from the *Daily Dispatch* newspaper. Open sandwiches, gooey cakes, quiches, coffee and *rooibos*. Daytime only.

Dave's Kitchen, Pearce St. Centrally located, casual and friendly – good for pizzas and the like.

Latimer's Landing Waterfront

Hunter's Jetty. Pig out on meat, with great river views. Venison or lamb on a spit are really excellent, with hunks carved straight onto your plate.

Sportsman's Bar. Pub with a big satellite dish, liveliest when South African sports teams are battling it out internationally on the big screen. The sun deck overlooking the Buffalo River is great on a nice day.

Tug & Ferry. Less rowdy than its competition (see above), with drinks and meals inside or out on the quay.

Listings

Automobile Association ☎21271. Emergencies ☎0800/0101 01.

Banks Main branches are along Oxford Street with several 24hr ATMs at intersections with Union, Gladstone and Terminus streets.

Bus information ☎21251. *Hopper* bus ☎51 2332.

Car rental Good firms include *Dolphin* (☎46 2686) and *A/H* (☎43 9111).

Emergencies Ambulance ☎10177; Fire ☎0431/21212; Police (Flying Squad) ☎10111.

Garages *Stirling Motors*, 8 Old Transkei Rd, does repairs and is open 24hr. Closest to the beach is *Gavin White Motors*, 1 Currie St.

Hospitals *Frere Hospital* (state), Amalinda Drive (☎49 1111); *St Dominics* (private), 45 St Mark's Rd (☎43 4303).

Laundries *Wishing Well*, Currie St, or *Laundromat* (coin-operated washing machines and ironing) at the Edcott Centre, Oxford St.

Pharmacies which offer extended opening hours: *John Forbes*, 205a Oxford St (closes 10pm); *Hylton Boyd*, 211a Oxford St (closes 11pm).

Taxis *Springbok* ☎24400.

Train information ☎44 2020.

Travel agents *Rennies Travel*, Caxton House, Terminus St (☎21375); *Let's Travel*, Kennaway Building, Esplanade (☎43 2983).

The Amatola Mountains

Most visitors drive quickly through the scrubby, dry and poor area between East London and the **Amatola Mountains** proper, to reach the cool forests and holiday lands at the Hogsback. It's really worth deviating en route, though, to see the marvellous collection of African art at Fort Hare University, visit apartheid martyr Steve Biko's grave in King William's Town, and to take in bits of East Cape history, if you have the inclination.

King William's Town

More commonly known as "King", **KING WILLIAM'S TOWN**, 56km northeast of East London, started life as a military frontier and missionary outpost, and today has a large population drawn from the former Ciskei. If you're passing through, there's enough of historical interest here to satisfy at least half a day. To get a feel for **Xhosa history**, head for the **Kaffrarian Museum** (Mon–Fri 9am–12.45pm & 2–5pm) in Alexandra Road; the Xhosa Gallery has unusually good displays, including full accounts of the British tactics and campaigns which crushed the Xhosa. Traditional culture is well-represented, with contemporary exhibitions on current building styles. Don't miss Phillip Ntliziywana's imaginative bus and car sculptures made from wire and discarded bits and pieces.

Two blocks north of the museum, off Albert Road, is the nineteenth-century **Edward Street Cemetery**, notable for the story it tells of the conflicts in the area.

STEVE BIKO AND BLACK CONSCIOUSNESS

Steven Bantu Biko's brutal interrogation and death while in police custody triggered international outrage and turned opinion further against the apartheid regime. His death was followed by the banning of the Black Consciousness organizations, and helped lead to the imposition of a mandatory arms embargo against South Africa by the United Nations Security Council.

Born in 1946 in **King William's Town**, Biko's political ascent was a swift one, due in no small part to his eloquence, charisma and focused vision. While still a medical student at Natal University during the late 1960s, he was elected president of the exclusively black South African Students' Organisation (SASO) and started publishing articles in their journal, fiercely attacking white liberalism. In an atmosphere of repression – both ANC and PAC leaders were serving hefty sentences at the time – Biko's brand of **Black Consciousness** immediately caught on. He called for blacks to take destiny into their own hands, to unify and rid themselves of the "shackles that bind them to perpetual servitude". He became honorary president of the Black Peoples' Convention, an umbrella organization which attracted mainly young intellectuals and professionals. From 1973 onwards, Biko suffered banning, detention and other harassment at the hands of the state. In 1974, he defended himself in court, presenting his case so brilliantly that his profile in the international press soared.

Barred from straying out of King William's Town, Biko continued working and writing, frequently escaping out of his confinement. In 1976, black outrage burst into the open with the Soweto riots, when school pupils took to the streets to protest against the imposition of Afrikaans as the language of instruction in their schools. The police boot went in hard: hundreds were killed and imprisoned, and the search for "agitators" led to Biko's 101-day detention. In August the following year, he was stopped at a roadblock near Grahamstown (outside his restricted area), taken to Port Elizabeth, intensively interrogated and tortured. On September 12, 1977, he died from a brain haemorrhage, sustained at the hands of security police. No one was held accountable. Diplomats from thirteen Western countries joined the thousands of mourners at his funeral in King William's Town.

Besides a memorial to those killed in the innumerable frontier wars against the Xhosa, there is an open piece of ground on the far side of the cemetery which marks a mass grave. This is where hundreds of Xhosa were buried, their bodies emaciated as a result of the 1857 **Cattle Killing**, when many Xhosa people destroyed their cattle at the behest of the prophetess Nonquaquse – she promised that this would finally drive out the British (see p.319).

About fifteen minutes' walk north of the Kaffrarian, the **Missionary Museum** in Berkeley Street (Mon–Fri 9am–1pm & 2–5pm; small entry fee) is mainly of interest for the glimpse it gives into early educational institutions in the Eastern Cape, where South Africa's first professional blacks were schooled and, indeed, many of the new nation's current heavyweights, including Nelson Mandela himself.

King's only other attraction of note is **Steve Biko's grave**, a couple of kilometres out of town, tucked away at the end of a rutted dirt track that branches off the end of Cathcart Street. It's a moving place, and much humbler than you'd expect for such an important figure in black politics. The polished, charcoal-coloured tombstone sits quietly among a small patch of paupers' graves that make up Ginsburg Cemetery. To get there, take Cathcart Street south out of town (towards Grahamstown), turning left onto an unsignposted gravel road after the bridge (just before the turn-off to your right to Alice). Follow the road under the railway bridge and immediately take the right turn up an unpromising-looking road that leads to the cemetery. Biko is buried towards the back of the graveyard.

Practicalities

Alexandra Road is the town's main drag, where you'll find a 24-hour filling station and signs for King's **Information Bureau** (Mon–Fri 8.30am–5.30pm, Sat 8.30am–1pm; ☎0433/23369), which is in the public library opposite the Kaffrarian Museum, and can provide an accommodation list. The **minibus taxis** rank in Cathcart Street, with connections to East London, the rest of the Eastern Cape and further afield.

One of King's nicest **B&Bs** is *Bramble Hill*, 3 Upper Mount St (☎0433/23369; ③), with friendly owners who can fill you in on local history. Centrally located and in a Victorian house, it doubles up as a Montessori school. *Dreamers Guest House,* 29 Gordon St (☎0433/23012; ③), is also in a Victorian house, just off Alexandra Road, and has a pool, and real log fires in winter. Of the town's **hotels**, the *Grosvenor Lodge* (☎0433/21440; ④) in Taylor Street, near the Kaffrarian Museum, is the most salubrious; next best is the *Crown* in Wodehouse Street (☎0433/23025; ④). At the edge of town is King's little-used caravan park and **campsite**; ask at the Information Bureau whether it is currently OK to camp there.

For **eating and drinking**, *Archie's Pub & Pizzeria* in Taylor Street is popular, while *St Louis Spur*, in a prime spot at the corner of Alexandra Road and Cathcart Street, serves up the usual steaks and hamburgers. *Nando's* is a handy fast-food joint on Alexandra Road.

Bisho

Of little aesthetic interest in itself, **BISHO** is nevertheless is worth the six-kilometre detour from King, if only for its curiosity value and ostentatious architecture. Now the provincial capital of the Eastern Cape, the town is beset by dreary 1980s monumental town planning. The brainchild of Lennox Sebe, the apartheid *bantustan*'s first "president", the architecture of the previous capital achieves the improbable feat of combining dullness with grandiosity. Sebe is said to have been inspired by ancient buildings in Israel – quite possible given his strong links with the country, which provided arms and military training for his fiefdom.

As you approach Bisho, the **stadium** on the left is a grim reminder of apartheid atrocities. During the constitutional negotiations in 1991, Ciskei troops opened fire on a group of ANC supporters who were attempting to hold a rally at the sports ground. The protest centred around the continuing repression in the Ciskei, where the ANC was still outlawed. Twenty-eight were killed and two hundred injured. The outrage provoked by the massacre effectively spelt the end of the apartheid-backed Ciskei and was a milestone marking the demise of the old order.

The new order, embodied in the **Provincial Legislature** buildings, is a short hop from the town centre, but is grim and not worth the detour, despite its national importance. For a bit of light relief, you could nip over to the casino at the plush *Amatola Sun* (☎0433/91111; ⑦), the only **place to stay** in Bisho, and a few hundred metres from the Legislature. **Minibus taxis** from Cathcart Street in King William's Town ply the route between Bisho and King William's Town.

Fort Hare

Despite decades of deliberate neglect and relegation after 1959 to a "tribal" university under apartheid, **FORT HARE**, 64km west of King William's Town along the R63, is assured a place in South African history. Established in 1916 as a multiracial college by missionaries, it became the first institution in South Africa to deliver tertiary education to blacks. Many prominent African leaders, including Zimbabwe's president Robert Mugabe and Tanzania's Julius Nyerere came here for their tertiary education. But most famous, of course, is **Nelson Mandela**, making this an essential port of call if you're following Mandela's footprints. Sadly, though, the Wesley Residence from whose window the young Madiba reputedly used to climb to go ballroom dancing, has been pulled down. The spot it occupied is now the lawn just to your right as you enter through the main gate. **Freedom Square**, at the centre of the campus, is worth a visit to recall the many scenes of protest at the University – this is the spot where several members of the present government cut their teeth politically.

It's possible to visit **Beda Residence** where Robert Mugabe studied, though the dormitory where he stayed has been converted into single rooms. This is one of the pleasanter old residences; some of the others are pretty dilapidated owing to under-funding during the apartheid years. Virtually all students live on campus as Alice, the adjacent town, is too undeveloped to offer much in the way of digs.

If you have even the slightest interest in African art, take advantage of Fort Hare's **De Beers Art Gallery** (daily 8.30am–1pm & 2–4.15pm; free). From the outside, the cylindrical gallery resembles a high-security bank vault, which is perhaps appropriate. Once inside, you're faced with a veritable treasure trove of contemporary black south-ern **African art** – one of the most significant and least publicized collections anywhere. Pioneers of black painting, including Gerard Sekoto and Pemba, are represented, and you should look out for the lively oils of Dan Rakgoate. There are some stunning sculp-tures: Uneas Sithole's elongated *Is my friend the chameleon hiding?*; Percy Konqobe's *Ntsikana and his cow*; and Sydney Kumalo's *Robot man*. Also unmissable is the sequence of fifteen woodcuts by Lucky Sibiya called *Umabatha*, the Zulu adaptation of *Macbeth*. You'll have to make an appointment to see Fort Hare's **ethnographic collec-tion** – a major museum of traditional crafts and artefacts, with all sorts of rare and valu-able pieces, but as yet neither well-displayed in a permanent place nor publicized.

Practicalities

Ideally you'll have your own **transport** to reach Fort Hare, a couple of kilometres out-side the town of Alice, although from King William's Town there are **minibus taxis** to Alice, conveniently dropping off passengers at the University gates. A visit is best done as a day-trip from Grahamstown or East London, or as part of an excursion to the Hogsback. With the virtual lack of **accommodation** in Alice, you're better off staying either in Fort Beaufort or Hogsback – the choice of many of the University's lecturers.

Tours of the University and art gallery should be arranged beforehand through the University's public relations department (Mon–Fri 9am–5pm; ☎0404/22239). Getting into the University past the security personnel at the main gates can be tricky, espe-cially outside term time. Be polite and persistent: the art gallery, at least, is meant to be open for visits every day. If you haven't arranged a visit in advance, or you find the gallery closed, head for the public relations office at the entrance of the main adminis-tration buildings and ask someone to open up.

Alice

A handful of photogenically decaying colonial houses with peeling corrugated-iron roofs, and balconies smothered in creepers, constitute the main interest in **ALICE**. It's the closest town to the university, but can in no way be called a university town. The lengthy decay of the village reflects the second-class status accorded the university under Afrikaner Nationalist rule. There's one hopelessly tiny bookshop, a depressing reflection of local poverty and the high cost of books in South Africa, which puts them beyond the reach of the majority of the population – even the fifty percent who are lit-erate. Alice's two hotels are little more than run-down carousing joints. Of the two, the *Amatola* is favoured for drinking by university staff and students.

Just 1km east of the town centre is **Lovedale College**, older than Fort Hare, and no less significant in educating Africans. Built in 1842 as a Presbyterian mission station, it was soon

educating the country's first black professionals, and became an important publishing centre. The Xhosa language was first translated into written form here, and one of Lovedale's
students, J. Tengo Jabavu, was the founder of South Africa's first weekly African-language
paper, *Zabantsundu*. With the passing of the Bantu Education Act under the apartheid government, Lovedale was closed. Now that the college is in use again, you can drive in and
look at the Victorian buildings, but the actual site doesn't have any displays or information
– for that, visit the Missionary Museum in King William's Town (see p.302).

Hogsback

Made sweeter by the contrast with the hot valleys below, **HOGSBACK**, 32km north of
Alice (and 145km from East London), offers cool relief after hauling through prickly,
overgrazed country. For whites hankering after a British past, this village in the
Amatola Mountains represents a corner of England, a fantasy fed by mists, pine plantations and exotic trees such as oak, walnut and azaleas, and guaranteed snowfalls each
winter. In fact, the real attraction of the place is the **Afro-montane cloud forest**,
singing with bird calls and gauzy waterfalls, and populated by the odd troop of **samango monkeys**, which survive on the steep slopes above the pine plantations. Winding
your way up the mountains on the road from Alice, you'll have a good view of the forest, dense with yellowwood, stinkwood and Cape chestnut.

Hogsback is a great place to spend an unchallenging couple of days, with plenty of
walks, good air and many places to stay. The name "Hogsback", which applies to the area
as much as to the village, comes from the high rocky ridge (actually three peaks) resem-
bling a bushpig's spine, which runs above the settlement. Hogsback can be wet and cold,
even in summer, so bring a warm pullover, sturdy shoes and rain gear all year round.

The hamlet itself itself is strung out along 3km of gravel road, with lanes branching
out on either side to hotels and cottages. The closest thing to a **centre** is the small conglomeration of a general store, post office, filling station and some nearby craft shops.
Hogsback has its own **indigenous craft** you'll find nowhere else in the country: prepare to be pestered by Xhosa kids selling the characteristic unfired clay horses and
hogs with white markings. One of the best craft shops is the *Gallery*, on the main road,
selling with hand-dyed woolies, organic herbs and jams, and framed photographs capturing the landscape. *Storm Haven Crafts*, nearby, is smaller, but has some nice stuff,
and doubles up as Hogsback's Publicity Association (see "Practicalities").

Hogsback is prime **rambling** country with relatively easy trails (see box), with waymarked routes indicated by hogs painted onto trees. For a rewarding taste of indige-

---

THE AMATOLA TRAIL AND OTHERS

Ranked among South Africa's best forested mountain walks, the **Amatola Trail** is a tough
but fabulously beautiful five-night, 105km trail starting in the Pirie Forest, some 21km
north of King William's Town, and ending up at Hogsback. The main attraction of this
walk is the dense, high forest, and the numerous waterfalls, rivers and bathing pools.
There are also a number of shortened versions of the trail, but these can only be done
outside of school holidays, or at short notice if the huts are not filled. Best of the **short
trails** is the 36km **Zingcuka Loop** from Hogsback, which scales the Hogsback itself, and
has you walking along streams much of the way, past idyllic waterfalls and pools.

Right in the forest at the base of a cliff, the overnight hut has the luxury of a primitive
shower, and fire wood. To go on a trail, you'll need well-broken-in boots, waterproofs,
and warm clothes. You could get rained on between October and March. **Book** through
the *Keiskamma Ecotourism Network*, 9 Chamberlain St, King William's Town, 5600 (☎ &
fax 0433/22571).

nous forest, the Contour Path above the campsite makes an easy, one-hour walk. From this path, there is a route going steeply up **Tor Doone**, which overlooks the settlement, and is the easiest summit to climb. One of the most rewarding waterfall trails is the one-hour steep downhill walk to the spendid **Madonna and Child waterfall**. More demanding trails take you up to grassland plateaus and are best done as day-trips, with appropriate footwear and not alone. A number of short and long routes are detailed in inexpensive guidebooks available at the village shops.

Practicalities

It's worth spending a night or two in Hogsback, but you'll need a car, as no public transport serves the village. The *Little Red Bus* company in East London (☎082/569 3599) operates **day tours** to Hogsback, with lunch at the *Hogsback Inn*. On the main road, *Storm Haven Crafts* doubles up as the town's **Publicity Association** (☎045/962 1050), and can supply accommodation details.

Places to stay are plentiful, but the village tends to fill up during holidays and weekends, when you'll need to book ahead. Budget self-catering with private rooms (but no bedding) and communal kitchen and bath, is available at *The Amatola* on the main road (☎ & fax 045/962 1159; ①); they also have self-contained cottages with linen, which are slightly more expensive. Self-catering cottages abound; best of the bunch is *Petersfield* (☎ & fax 045/962 1159), a four-bedroom rondavel in a lovely garden with streams and an orchard, and the cottages at *The Edge* (☎ & fax 045/962 1159; ②). Both places are a couple of kilometres off the main road, and need to be booked in advance. For more luxury, head for *Hyde Park Chalets* (☎045/64269; ③) in Dinwiddie Lane. Of the hotels, *King's Lodge*, along the main road (☎045/962 1024; ③), is wood-panelled and bright and has the best food and bar, as well as two self-catering units (③). *Hogsback Inn* (☎045/962 1006; ⑤) offers old-fashioned country-inn ambience, with log fires, big gardens, and a rate which includes three meals. There's **camping** at *Forestry Caravan Park* (☎045/962 1055; ①), on the corner of the main road and Oak Avenue.

Hogsback has a general **shop** selling basic supplies. For **meals**, *Woodlands* on the main road is excellent, while *Little Timbers Tea Garden* (☎045/962 1082), 3km north of the village opposite St Patrick-on-the-Hill chapel, provides some of the most imaginative cakes in the Eastern Cape, but you must book. Good, reasonably priced teas and light lunches are served up in the coffee shop adjoining the *Gallery* shop.

Katberg

KATBERG, 13km on a gravel road off the R67 from Fort Beaufort to Queenstown, is a sort of poor relation of Hogsback, since it fell into the former Ciskei and never developed into a residential area. It's a beautiful thirty-kilometre drive from Hogsback to Katberg, though the roads are unsealed and get slippery after rain or snow. **To get there** from Hogsback, head north out of the village towards Seymour and Cathcart, ignore the turn to Cathcart and continue down Mitchell's Pass to Seymour. The turn-off to the Katberg and Hotel is just beyond Seymour.

Katberg is essentially a weekending spot with only one **place to stay**, the *Katberg Protea* (☎0404/31151 or 31152; ⑤), a mountain resort which offers a full-board rate, horse-riding, tennis and pleasant shady gardens. The hotel is certainly visitable for **tea** or a **meal** if you want to explore the rich indigenous **forest**, on a variety of one- to four-hour walking trails or horse-rides on the slopes below the dramatic escarpment cliffs.

Katberg Hiking Trails and the Mpofu Game Reserve

A challenging three-day, fifty-kilometre **hiking trail** traverses the Katberg and the **Mpofu Game Reserve**, with mountain huts to stay in on the way. Besides the possibility of seeing antelope, zebra, wildebeest, ostrich and birds of prey, you can also take in San rock paintings and swim in mountain pools. The Mpofu Reserve's entrance is off the R67, halfway between Fort Beaufort and Seymour. A shorter, forty-kilometre overnight trail starts and ends at the Katberg Forest Station, just above the *Katberg Hotel*. Both trails cost around R25 per person per night and must be booked through *Keiskamma Ecotourism Network*, 9 Chamberlain St, King William's Town 5600 (☎ & fax 0433/22571).

If you want to **stay** in the reserve before or after the trail, or do day-hikes instead, there are two, fully equipped self-catering lodges (②–③). Bookings should be made through the *Eastern Cape Tourism Board* (☎0401/95 2115).

Fort Beaufort

A farming town at the heart of a citrus and wool district, **FORT BEAUFORT**, 80km northwest of King William's Town, is nothing to get excited about. Founded as a link in the chain of forts built along the eastern frontier to "pacify the blacks", its moment in history came in 1845, when a Xhosa man called Tsili stole an axe from a shop here, precipitating the bloody **War of the Axe** – the Seventh Frontier War. The theft allowed the British to act on a growing and convenient belief among whites that Xhosa land would be put to better use in their own hands. In 1847, after literally bringing the Xhosa chiefs to their knees (forcing them at bayonet point to kiss his feet), Governor Harry Smith told the vanquished that their land would be divided into counties, towns and villages bearing English names. "You may no longer be naked and wicked barbarians," he informed them, "which you will ever be unless you labour and become industrious."

The axe shop is still here, as is the 1830 officer's mess, now the highly eccentric **Fort Beaufort Museum** which doubles up as a tourist office and resembles a bric-a-brac shop. Interesting items include a painting by the Victorian documentary oil colourist, Thomas Baines, and a proclamation by Sir Harry Smith inviting anyone with a gun to take a potluck shot at the Xhosa, with the incentive that they could keep any cattle they rustled. The other notable historical building is a **Martello Tower**, still intact and exactly the same as those built two hundred years ago along the British coastline to keep out the French. The underworked tourist office will direct you there and fill you in on local history.

Practicalities

For **accommodation**, head for Durban Street, where you'll find the unexceptional *Savoy* (☎04634/31146; ③), not far west of the museum on the other side of the road, with a couple of B&Bs nearby. A number of working merino and citrus estates in the district offer **farmstays**, one of the nicest being *Millbank*, an old settler homestead 24km out on the Queenstown Road (☎04634/32912; ②), where you can stroll through orange groves on the farm. The **tourist office** (☎04634/31555) in Fort Beaufort Museum can provide lists of others. The town's best **place to eat** is *Talita's* in Campbell Street. If you're just stopping at Fort Beaufort to fill up, the *Pondorosa Café*, next to the Total garage on the Queenstown Road, is friendly and serviceable.

East London to Aliwal North

Besides the mountainous scenery of the Amatolas, there's little to encourage a stop along the N6 highway from East London en route to Johannesburg until you reach the inviting **hot springs of Aliwal North**. The road traverses a region which was once home to **German settlers**. Between 1857 and 1859, over four thousand Germans arrived in the Eastern Cape, initially drawn from a German regiment fighting for the

British in the Crimea, and brought in by the Cape Governor to act as a buffer against the Xhosa. The once-cohesive German-speaking community has long been diluted, and the last settler farms were abandoned in the 1980s when the area came under the auspices of the Ciskei government.

Queenstown and around

There's no reason at all to pause in **QUEENSTOWN**, a sizable workaday shopping and administrative centre, 190km north of East London, serving a large and poor black rural community and white stock farmers. However, if you're here for the night on a cross-country journey, the **Lawrence de Lange** and **Longhill nature reserves** just out of town in the mountains are worth a visit. Entrance is free and there are rhino, zebra, wildebeest and a wide variety of antelope in the park, as well as picnic sites in the Longhill section of the reserve. From Cathcart Road, the main street, head out of town on Kingsway and Hangklip roads, and look out for signs to the reserve.

The best **place to stay** is in the middle-class suburbs above the railway line, where you'll find some excellent B&Bs. *Carthews Corner*, 1 Park Ave, Blue Rise (☎ & fax 0451/81881; ③) has garden cottages, a pool and *braai* facilities, and secure off-street parking – they can recommend other places if they're full. It's not advisable to camp in the run-down caravan park next to the busy East London road. Reliable **eating** comes down to the *Spur* in Cathcart Road.

The scenery around Queenstown is inviting and there are a couple of **game farms** worth a detour. *Carnarvon Estates*, PO Box 9, Sterkstroom 5425 (☎ & fax 045/856 0011), 50km north of Queenstown, is the most established. Here you'll see a variety of antelope in magnificent mountain scenery, with accommodation in a luxury farmhouse lodge (③–④) or a garden cottage (③).

Aliwal North

ALIWAL NORTH, 158km north of Queenstown, on the Orange River, borders Free State province and has a distinctly Afrikaans flavour. The town's name celebrates the smashing of the Sikhs at Aliwal in India in 1846 by the governor of the Cape Colony, Sir Harry Smith. (Aliwal South was the former name of Mossel Bay in the Western Cape.) More relevant to its Afrikaans character is the town's part in the **Second Anglo-Boer War**, when the Boers under General Olivier occupied the town and declared the Republic of Oliviersfontein in 1900. What remains of the short-lived republic is a sobering memorial to the Boers who died in concentration camps set up by the British. Historic interest aside, the main reason to come to Aliwal North is for its **curative mineral waters**, 3km from the centre, which merit a restorative stopoff.

The town is effectively divided into two: the central area dominated by the N6 traffic, and the area built up around the spa, which, although ugly, has the best places to stay, shop and eat. The **Spa** (7am–10pm; entry fee), signposted off the N6 and R58, centres around an Olympic-sized outdoor pool with palm trees and green lawns – perfect for swimming and relaxation. The indoor pools are much warmer, but not quite hot enough in winter. Admission also gives you access to the modest gym and tennis courts, but you'll need your own racquet and balls.

At the southern edge of town, signposted off the N6, is a symbolically heavy-handed **Boer War Concentration Camp Memorial**. On the site of two camp cemeteries, the memorial looks like a prison or crematorium from the outside. Inside, the walls are plastered with handmade grave stones of the 716 people who died (many of them Afrikaner children), from the terrible conditions in the tented camps set up by the British.

Arrival, information and accommodation

Translux **buses** between East London and Johannesburg pull in daily at the *CNA* newsagent in Somerset Street; bus tickets can be bought at *Dampier Motors* in the same street. The **tourist information office** at the northern entrance to town, near the Orange River bridge, can supply maps and lists of places to stay in the North Eastern Cape and over the river in the Eastern Free State mountains.

Most of the town's **accommodation** is clustered around the spa. There is a reasonable hotel in the centre, but this is only worth considering if you're not taking the waters.

Aliwal Spa, De Wet Drive (☎0551/2951, fax 3008). Municipally run outfit with a huge caravan park, camping and run-down bungalows. Also municipally run, but spanking new, are nice timber self-catering cottages set on a lake 8km beyond the campsite, known as *Islands*. When booking, ask specifically for these cottages – the best place to stay in Aliwal North. ②.

Balmoral Hotel, Somerset St (☎0551/2453). The only central hotel, on the main road through town with spacious en-suite rooms and a serviceable restaurant. Not the place to stay if the sound of big trucks bothers you. ③.

Buffelsbron Chalets, 35 Dan Pienaar Ave (☎0551/3129). Fully equipped and spotlessly clean self-catering brick chalets sleeping up to four people. ③.

Thatchers Spa Hotel, 14 Dan Pienaar Ave (☎0551/2772 or 4208). Over the road from the spa, offering the best-value hotel rooms in town with a fair bit of comfort, including electric blankets in winter and tea-making facilities in the en-suite rooms. ③.

Umtali Motel, Dan Pienaar Ave (☎0551/2400). At the end of the avenue, this is the smartest hotel, but it's a bit characterless and you'll need transport to get to the spa from here. ④.

Eating

If you're staying at the spa, you won't have to stray very far for something to eat; *Green Trees* is conveniently located right next to the pool, and serves up decent sandwiches, pancakes, burgers, omelettes and Cokes, from 8am to 8pm. Opposite the spa entrance, in Dan Pienaar Avenue, the smart *Pink Lady Steakhouse* offers reasonably priced fish and steak main courses. Back in the centre, the nicest place is *Kunsgallerie*, opposite the *Balmoral* in Somerset Street, which serves up good teas and light lunches, in a craft shop.

On to the Cape Drakensberg

Coming from Johannesburg, Aliwal North is where you branch off east to reach the **Cape Drakensberg**. A dramatic (goods-only) train line follows this mountainous route to Barkly East, with eight celebrated zigzagging reverses, much photographed by train buffs, and its highest station, called **Drizzly**. A **weekend train safari** now operates twice a month between East London and Barkly East; the train leaves East London on Friday evenings for the overnight trip to Aliwal North, heading off to Barkly East in the morning, and returning to Aliwal North that evening to spend the night on the train, before travelling back to East London on Sunday. The whole trip, including meals, costs from R1300 per person. Book through *Kei Leisure*, Latimer's Landing, PO Box 1410, East London 5200 (☎0431/43 3110, fax 43 3115).

The Eastern Cape Drakensberg

Although known misleadingly as South Africa's "little Switzerland" in tourist brochures, the **East Cape Drakensberg** are wonderful African mountains, horse-brown in winter and full of **San rock paintings**, sandstone **caves** and craggy sheep **farms**. One of the country's best-preserved and prettiest Victorian villages, **Rhodes** is the obvious goal in the region, and makes a good base for riding, walking, skiing and trout fishing. While it's very cold, dry and sunny in the winter, summer is idyllically green, with river pools to swim in. There are some appealing cottages for rent on farms, and a number of **hiking trails**, many of which offer the opportunity to see rock paintings and sleep in enormous caves. Since there is no national park in the Cape Drakensberg, activities are all done through private farms. For **bird-watchers**, the region is especially good for raptors (notably the rare lammergeier and Cape vulture), as well as orange-breasted rock jumpers and ground woodpeckers.

From Aliwal North to Rhodes Village

LADY GREY, 50km from Aliwal North and 5km off the R58, is the only place worth a stop en route to Rhodes, with one **hotel**, the *Mountain View Country Inn*, Botha Street (☎051/603 1103; ③), which has nice old-fashioned rooms with great views. The staff keep a list of **walks** to help you explore the surrounding peaks, and the owners can organize **fly-fishing**. Besides walking, the town's attractions amount to a visit to the tiny **museum** at the Dutch Reformed church, dominated by a Victorian horse-drawn hearse and more like a curiosity shop under dust covers than anything else. It is open by arrangement only, through the hotel. The first minister of the Dutch Reformed church was a Scot, **David Ross**, who used to preach both in Afrikaans and English. His anti-imperialist views got him imprisoned by the British during the Anglo-Boer War, after which he apparently never spoke his native tongue again.

Some 79km southeast of Lady Grey, **BARKLY EAST** serves a large surrounding farming community, and is the last place to get money and fill up your car if your destination is Rhodes. Don't expect much help from the **tourist information office**, which doubles up as the manual telephone exchange in the municipal offices. There is nothing at all to do in the town, so unless night is falling push on for another ninety minutes to Rhodes. The sixty-kilometre dirt road to Rhodes is tortuous and rough with sheer, unfenced drops – definitely not recommended in the dark or mist. The very comfortable *Elanli Guest House*, 33 Cole St (☎04542/185; ③), in a Victorian house on the signposted road to Elliot, provides the best **accommodation** in Barkly. There's also a little-used **campsite**, 100m off to the right as you hit town from Lady Grey.

Rhodes and around

Some 60km northeast of Barkly East, **RHODES** is almost too good to be true – a remote and beautiful village girdled by the Eastern Cape Drakensberg, the highest and most extensive mountain chain in the country, stretching east across Lesotho and up the west flank of KwaZulu-Natal into Mpumalanga.

Few people actually live here: like other villages in this region, Rhodes was progressively deserted as residents gravitated to the cities to make a living, leaving its Victorian tin-roofed architecture of gracious houses stuck in a very pleasing time warp. Today its *raison d'être* is as a low-key holiday place for people who appreciate its isolation, wood stoves and restored cottages. Although electricity reached the village a couple of years ago, very few establishments have it, and paraffin lamps and candles are the norm.

Given that Rhodes is not on the way to anywhere (on some maps it doesn't even appear), it is a place to go to for a few days, rather than an overnight stop. While nights are cool even in summer, in winter they are freezing, and there's no central heating, so pack warm clothes. The *Rhodes Hotel*, a general shop and a garage are at the heart of the village, which is not much more than a few crisscrossing gravel roads lined with pine trees. The trees were donated in the 1890s, so the story goes, after a group of scheming townsfolk hoped to extract a slush fund from **Cecil Rhodes**, by changing the

TIFFENDELL SKI RESORT

Tiffendell, South Africa's only **ski resort**, promotes itself as a little Switzerland, with Alpine ski lodges and European instructors on the slopes. However, it's essentially a venue for for fun-loving South Africans, most of whom are conspicuous consumers after a nonstop party (packages tend to include free booze from lunch to midnight). The resort is enormously successful, and for foreign visitors it provides, if nothing else, a quirky experience of Africa.

Skiing at Tiffendell is on **artificial snow** (despite regular winter falls, the real snow melts too quickly to provide a reliable piste). You can rent everything you need at the resort at an all-inclusive R215 per day. If you've never skied, this is a good place to take **lessons**, and at around R300 per day all-inclusive it's very reasonable. Three-day, fully inclusive packages, including on-site accommodation, work out at around R1200 per person. Day visitors need to book, as there is a maximum of 180 people on the slopes per day. The season runs from May 30 to August 31. **Book** through *Tiffendell*, 14 Fairway Ave, Linksfield North 2191 (☎011/640 5160, fax 485 2915).

The only on-site **accommodation** is at the lodge, which is usually full. Rooms are small and functional, with shared washing facilities. Many people stay at Rhodes village, one hour's 4WD across mountain passes, or on guest farms in the area. Of these, one of the nicest is *Burnbrae Mountain Hideaway*, PO Box 123, Barkly East 9786 (☎04542, ask for 7403; ④), 15km from Tiffendell, which also offers self-catering (③). On the farm there are rock paintings and caves you can hike to and, in the summer, trout fishing and riding. *Fetcani Glen*, PO Box 88, Barkly East (☎04542, ask for 7412) offers similar attractions with a rambling five-bedroomed farmhouse for hire and a beautiful river cutting through a sandstone gorge on the property.

The shortest route for **getting to Tiffendell** is via Rhodes, but the road is steep and needs 4WD at all times. The alternative starts 23km north of Barkly East, and if the road is wet or snowy needs a 4WD vehicle for the last 19km. If you don't have the right transport, both the *Rhodes Hotel* and Dave Walker do daily transfers to the resort from Rhodes (see below).

village's name in his honour. All they got from the astute entrepreneur was a sackful of seeds. While there is a post office and payphone, there are no banking facilities and no public transport in or out of the village.

Rhodes is busiest in the winter when **skiers** use it as a base for the Tiffendell slopes (see box), an hour's 4WD drive into the highest peaks of the Cape Drakensberg. December to May are the best months for swimming, trout fishing and hiking, all of which are easy to do using the village as a base. The rivers jump with rainbow and brown trout, stocked in the 1920s. This is one of the best places in the country to **fly-fish**, with all the solitude and glorious landscape you could hope for. Advice about where to fish can be given by the *Rhodes Hotel*; better still you can go out for a day or longer with Dave Walker of *Walkabout* (see "Accommodation"), who can organize permits which give you access to 150km of river, but you'll need all your own gear. Dave Walker also keeps excellent horses and operates **day-rides** from Rhodes, and two-day trails following old stock routes through the mountains, overnighting at a remote farmhouse.

Rock art sites

Rhodes is a good base for exploring millennia-old **San rock paintings**, the majority of which are on surrounding private farms which can be visited with the farmers' permission (some farms also take guests). The *National Monuments Council* (☎021/462 4502, fax 462 4509) in Cape Town has a comprehensive list, and Rhodes locals can point you to local farms such as *Buttermead* and *Hillbury*, which have their own paintings.

There are two sites accessible from Rhodes which you can drop in on. **Martin's Hoek**, 16km from the village, is worth a visit, not just for the well-preserved, photogenic paintings, but for the lovely, lonely valley you have to drive though to get there. The signposted turn-off to Martin's Hoek is 8km from Rhodes on the road to Barkly East. From the turn-off it's another 8km to the site, with parking and a couple of picnic tables. The paintings, which are fenced off, are on the cliff face opposite the parking area. It's a ten-minute uphill scramble, much easier than it first appears, with views out onto the rough and streaky sandstone peaks.

A second site, at **Denorben Farm**, 32km from Barkly East, offers the longest series of San paintings in the country. It's only 1km to the farm from the main road, and the long, painted panel is behind the house, at the bottom of the garden. A nominal entry fee is charged and there's a helpful information sheet on the images, many of which are confusing. Don't miss the impressive (unpainted) cave in the farm yard – it's common practice for farmers in the area to use overhangs as cosy sheep pens and sheds.

Rock art had an essentially religious purpose, usually recording experiences of trance states. Shamans' visions often included powerful animals like the eland, which you can see depicted at both Denorben and Martin's Hoek, and whose power shamans were able to access for healing. A dying eland is a metaphor for the shaman who enters a **trance** and takes on aspects of an animal. At Denorben there's a half-animal, half-human figure, an image of transformation during the trance state. Also at Denorben are painted figures dancing, clapping and singing, in the process of inducing trance. For more details on rock art, see p.384.

Accommodation

Gateshead Lodges, PO Box 15, Barkly East 5580 (☎04542, ask for Dave Walker on 9203). Several farmhouses and cottages on huge properties in marvellously remote and rugged territory, all within a large radius of Rhodes. Some cater specifically for fly-fishing, hiking, riding or bird-watching, while a few have caves and rock paintings on the property. All are clearly detailed in a pamphlet available from the above address. ②.

Ramseys, PO Box 1, Rhodes (☎04542/9240). *Ramseys* rent out a couple of cottages in the village, and a draughty former parsonage with single beds and bunks in large rooms. ②.

Rhodes Hotel, Main Rd (☎04542, ask for Rhodes 21). Decorative exterior and charming Victorian furnishings. Quiet horses are available for renting, there are tennis courts and the owner is a trout-fishing guide. Dinner, bed and breakfast. ④.

Rubicon Flats, PO Box 5, Rhodes (☎04542, ask for 9002). The best-value, and the warmest, place in town, this handsome old schoolhouse has been converted into self-catering rooms, each with an anthracite burner, and simple dorms. The owner, Mrs Reeders, also rents out self-catering cottages in the village. ②.

Walkabout, signposted off the main road (☎04542, ask for 9203). Relaxed house with a few guest rooms. Friendly owner, Dave Walker, knows a good deal about the area and can organize almost any activity, including fly-fishing and horse-riding. Dinner, bed and breakfast. ③.

Eating and drinking

For **eating**, your best choice is the *Walkabout*, which does home-cooked meals, and, if booked in advance, vegetarian food. Cheapest of all are the ready-cooked meals, such as curry and rice, from local farmer's wife Marian Henning (☎04542, ask for 9013), who'll deliver to your door. **Drinking** comes down to the *Rhodes* bar, one of the most atmospheric bars in the country. It's decorated with horns of Wydeman, the leader ox of the supply wagon from Barkly East, who dropped dead outside the hotel in 1896, and smoky relics of the days when this was a frontier town of gamblers, cattle rustlers and barroom shoot-outs, line the walls.

Naude's Nek and the route south

The most exhilarating drive out of Rhodes is along **Naude's Nek**, the highest mountain-pass road in the country, connecting Rhodes with **Maclear** to the south, in a series of snaking hairpin bends and huge views. If you're chiefly looking for scenery, it's not essential to do the whole route to Maclear. Many people go from Rhodes to the top of the pass and back as a half-day trip, the highlight of which is to make a call from the highest phone (with a crank handle) in the country, in a corrugated-iron booth in the middle of a sheep pen at the top of the pass.

While it's only 30km from Rhodes, the journey can take a couple of hours to the Nek because so many changing vistas en route demand stops. You don't need a 4WD, but if you feel precious about your car don't attempt this route, as the road is harsh. The surface deteriorates from the top of the pass to Maclear, with sharp stones and a hump down the centre of the road, which may scrape the bottom of your vehicle, and is definitely impassable after snow. If you're wanting to use this route into the Transkei and KwaZulu-Natal, check with the *Rhodes Hotel* as to the current states of the road (☎04542, ask for Rhodes 21).

If you're not aiming for the Transkei, you can loop west from Maclear, at the bottom of the escarpment, and take the tarred R56 towards **Dordrecht** and the N6. The string of small towns along the the R56 from Maclear to Dordrecht are unmemorable trading centres, with nowhere to stay. All along the route though, the high Drakensberg march along, providing a dramatic backdrop to the journey. **Sheep farming** is the mainstay of

---

NORTH EASTERN CAPE TRAILS AND HIKES

The **North Eastern Cape** is prime **walking** country, with expansive skies and long views across the mountains. There is no national park, so all walks have to be done (and booked) on private property, but are very reasonably priced for that. Three of the best trails are listed below.

* **Ben Macdhui Hiking Trail**. Three-day circular trail along a 51-kilometre route involving about eight hours' walking each day. Begins and ends at Rhodes village with highlights that include magnificent mountain scenery, wild flowers, waterfalls, the chance to see rare mountain birds (such as the bearded vulture) and climb Ben Macdhui, the highest mountain (3000m) in the Eastern Cape. Accommodation is in an old farmhouse and mountain hut, both equipped with beds, mattresses, drinking water, long-drop toilets, a gas stove, kettle, pans, basin and a coal stove for heating. Rhodes village makes a convenient place to stay at the start and finish of this hike. Book through Gideon van Zyl, PO Box 299, 5580 Barkly East (☎04542/7021 or 9212).
* **Woodcliffe Farm**. Variety of one- to four-day trails on a farm, 22km north of Maclear, on the Naude's Nek Road. Highlights include stunning Drakensberg scenery, rock art, dinosaur footprints on the Pot River and 185 bird species. Accommodation, in a self-catering cottage, can be used as a base for day-walks or at the start of a longer hike, while cave overhangs can be used on longer hikes. Maps are provided and planning advice is available for a route matching your fitness and time available. Book through Phyll Sephton, PO Box 65, Maclear 5480 (☎ & fax 045/323 1550).
* **Kranskop Hiking Trail**. One- to two-day hike on a farm, 33km north of Dordrecht, on the Barkly East Road. Highlights include some beautiful *kloofs*, sleeping overnight in a sandstone cave, and seeing some San rock art. Accommodation at the start or finish of the trail is in a comfortable rustic farm cottage sleeping twelve. Beds, mattresses, pillows, hot water, stove, fridge, lamps, candles and a coal stove are provided. Farm milk and meat are available. Book through Frans Slabbert, PO Box 85, Dordrecht 5435 (☎045/944 1014).

white farmers in the region, though rampant stock theft is putting many out of business. One farmer has employed armed San, ex-trackers from a defunct unit of the South African army, to patrol his farm.

The R56 gives access to a couple of **hiking trails** with farm cottages for rent in the southern part of the Cape Drakensberg, notably **Woodcliffe** near Maclear, and **Kranskop** near Dordrecht, both of which have caves and rock paintings (see box). If you're simply overnighting, or visiting rock-painting sites, *Peddlars*, PO Box 607, Elliot 5460 (☎045/313 2315; ④), at the bottom of Barkly Pass, is a good **place to stay**, with motel-style rooms on a farm, and a dinner, bed and breakfast rate.

THE WILD COAST REGION

The **Wild Coast region** is aptly named: this is one of South Africa's least tame areas – a vast stretch of undulating hills, lush forest and spectacular beaches skirting a section of the Indian Ocean notorious for its harrowing shipwrecks. The sense of wildness goes beyond the landscape, for this is the former **Transkei homeland**, a desperately poor region which during apartheid was disenfranchised and turned into a dumping ground for Africans who were either too old or too young for South African industry to make use of. Few whites live in the Wild Coast region; nearly everyone is **Xhosa**, and those in rural areas mostly live in traditional rondavels that dot the landscape for as far as the eye can see.

Despite the obvious hardship, it's refreshing – at least for visitors – to find that rural areas are still communally owned rather than parcelled up into private farms. Instead of the fenced-off spaces edged by squatter camps that you find in most of rural South Africa, here the land is unfenced and fully inhabited.

The **N2** highway runs through the middle of the Wild Coast region, passing through the old Transkei capital of **Umtata** and a host of unremarkable smaller towns along the way. Northwest of the N2, towards the Lesotho border and the Drakensberg mountains, you'll find beautiful hilly country and endless little villages, but the lack of accommodation and poor roads make travelling here difficult.

Far more accessible is the **coastal region**, which runs from just north of East London to the mouth of the **Mtamvuna River**. With its succession of great beaches, hidden reefs, patches of subtropical forest, rural Xhosa settlements and the attractive little towns of **Coffee Bay** and **Port St Johns**, which are both popular with backpackers, this region is one of the finest areas to visit in the Eastern Cape. In addition, there are five beautiful, state-run **nature reserves** along the coast; if you only have time to visit one or two, head for **Cwebe**, with its pretty waterfalls, lagoon, abundant birdlife and comfortable bungalow accommodation, or **Hluleka**, with its outstanding beaches and shoreline.

Wild Coast practicalities

Most roads in the Wild Coast region are **untarred** and, while generally passable in an ordinary car, they invariably take their mechanical toll. Always carry a tool kit, a spare tyre (preferably two), and take the roads slowly. Watch out for livestock on all Wild Coast roads, including the N2, and avoid driving in rainy weather and at night. **Public transport** throughout the region is poorly maintained and, except for the routes between Port St Johns and Coffee Bay, can be very time-consuming and occasionally dangerous. You're best off in your own vehicle, or relying on the *Baz Bus*, which covers a fair amount of territory in this region.

It is wise to book **accommodation** in advance: the East London-based *Wild Coast Holiday Reservations* (☎0431/43 6181; email: meross@iafrica.com) and the Umtata-

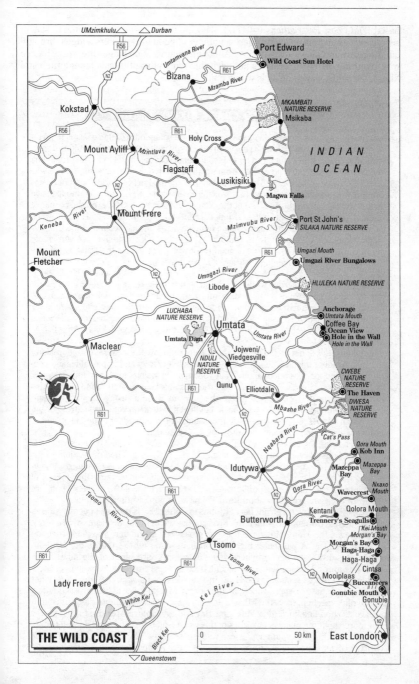

THE WILD COAST

0   50 km

based *Wild Coast Reservations* (☎0471/25344) are useful if you are planning to stay in several places on your journey. There a number of good backpackers' lodges throughout the coast, and plenty of campsites. Although security is no longer the worry it once was, **camping in rural areas** is not advisable – if you want to stay among the rural Xhosa, the safest way to do so is with a guide.

THE WILD COAST HIKING TRAIL

If you've got the time, an excellent way to take in the splendours of this coast is to go on the superb **Wild Coast Hiking Trail** (sometimes still called the Transkei Hiking Trail). This fourteen-day trail (which can be walked in small sections) runs from the Mtamvuna River to the Kei and must be walked from north to south only. It is divided into five sections: Mtamvuna to Msikaba; Msikaba to Port St. Johns; Port St. Johns to Coffee Bay; Coffee Bay to the Mbashe River; the Mbashe River to the Kei River. The inexpensive permits should be bought (in cash) at the Nature Conservation Office, on the corner of York and Victoria streets, in Umtata (Mon–Fri 8am–4.30pm; ☎0471/31 2711). The office can also furnish you with inexpensive and detailed maps of each section of the trail.

Accommodation is in basic huts, roughly 12km apart, which should give you ample time to reach them in a day. You will need to be well-prepared for the trails. Essentials to bring along include sleeping gear and a stove, water purifiers, a decent medical kit, old shoes for crossing rivers, and an air mattress or thick bin bags and an elastic band for floating your pack across while you do so. A tide table is vital – check the *Eastern Province Herald* newspaper for up-to-date information. Although you will often be able to dine in style on fresh fish caught by local fishermen, be sure to bring enough food for yourself just in case. Also useful is a good stock of small change, cigarettes and sweets to pay for the variety of services that will be offered to you along the way, from fish to ferry crossings.

The hiking trail is not well-marked. The idea is to follow the general direction along the coast, heading inland when the land becomes too craggy and impassable, and consulting the map for reference points. Plan your river crossings for thirty minutes after low tide, and avoid crossing at their estuaries, as sharks are often found there. Also avoid crossing near river mouths where there seems to be a strong outward current. Never swim with a rucksack on your back, but float it instead on your air mattress or bin bags. Watch where you are stepping in grassland, where puff adders often lurk, and in streams, where there are plenty of stingrays and stonefish.

The two northern sections of the trail are the least walked, but contain the most dramatic scenery, including several waterfalls that fall directly to the sea. The first section, which starts near the *Wild Coast Sun*, on the border with KwaZulu-Natal, is easy to get to, but reaching the second can be tricky, as if you drive to Msikaba you will have the problem of retrieving your car, while using public transport is nigh on impossible. These sections are notable for the wonderful **Mlambomkulu Falls** and striking **Cathedral Rock**.

The easily accessible trail from Port St Johns to Coffee Bay is the most popular stretch among hikers; crossing the Mngazana River in this section is made easier by the ferry. Further down, the Mdumbi River is tricky to cross walk inland until you judge that you can cross it easily. A particular highlight of this section on the trail is the **Hluleka Nature Reserve** (see p.324), where you stay on the third night of the hike. From Coffee Bay to the Mbashe River, the terrain becomes less rugged and more populated. One highlight of this section is the **Hole in the Wall** (see p.322), though you may not have too much time to appreciate it, as the nearby Mpako River is best crossed at low tide. The final section, from the Mbashe to the Kei, is little-walked, but passes through spectacular shoreline, including **Mazeppa Bay** and the **Qolora Mouth**.

For more about the many pecularities of this wonderful trail, you would do well to consult a specialist book on southern African wilderness hikes – the superb *Complete Guide to Walks and Trails in Southern Africa* by Jaynee Levy is the most authoritative.

To visit the region's **nature reserves** you'll need to book, and the best way to do this is by fax or in person at the Nature Conservation Office, on the corner of York and Victoria streets in Umtata (Mon–Fri 8am–4.30pm; ☎0471/31 2711, fax 31 2713). The office also takes bookings by post, but given the slowness of the the postal system this is only a realistic option if you're in South Africa for a month or more.

One highlight of many people's visits to the Wild Coast region, especially the Port St Johns area, is the ready availability of high-quality **cannabis** (*insango* in Xhosa). Be warned, though, that cannabis is as illegal here as anywhere else in South Africa and that the former Transkei police are trying to prove their worth to the national force with regular busts. Avoid the temptation to buy in large quantities, as it often turns out that the few tourists who have run into trouble in the region were trying to do just that.

The southern coast: East London to the Mbashe River

Once you get beyond the holiday resorts between East London and the Kei River, and cross what was once the border of Transkei, you'll find that the atmosphere changes completely. The rest of the southern Wild Coast is densely populated, with barely a hillside not liberally coated with brightly coloured rondavels facing east to the rising sun. Most of the region's resorts lie between East London and the Mbashe River, almost always at the end of difficult dirt roads that are mercifully not too far from the N2 highway. **Qolora Mouth**, where you can take fascinating trails that explore the tempestuous history of the region, is definitely worth a visit, while the **Cwebe Nature Reserve** stands out for its easy accessibility and the bonus of a comfortable hotel. There is only one backpackers' lodge in this stretch – in **Cintsa** – but it's a good one.

Cintsa, Haga-Haga and Morgan's Bay

By far the best of the smattering of resorts between East London and the Kei River are to be found at Cintsa and Morgan's Bay. To find **CINTSA**, take the Brakfontein exit (no. 26) off the N2, reverse down the highway back towards East London, take the next exit on your left, marked "East Coast Resorts" and follow the road for 16km until you see a sign pointing to Cintsa West and Cintsa Bay. Alternatively, you can take either the *Baz* (☎021/439 2323) or the *Hopper* (☎041/512332) **buses**, both of which will deliver you to the *Buccaneer's Retreat* (☎0431/383012; email: bucb-p@iafrica.com; ③). Primarily aimed at **backpackers**, with good dorms and excellent self-contained doubles, and set next to the beach amidst the dune forest (and with a swimming pool), the *Buccaneer's* offers a variety of sports and activities including surfing, dune-boarding, forest hiking and river cruises. The hostel is self-catering, but inexpensive communal meals are available. There are two **restaurants** in the village: *Crawfords*, which specializes in seafood, and *Cintsa Bay*, which serves up inexpensive, wholesome home-cooking. The local Xhosa community puts on **cultural displays** of traditional singing and dancing for hostel guests, for which the R20 (per person) charged goes towards a community centre.

The next resort north from Cintsa is **HAGA-HAGA**, dominated by the grim and box-like **hotel**, the *Haga-Haga* (☎04372/6302; ④). A short distance further along the coast, at **MORGAN'S BAY**, you'll find the *Morgan's Bay* (☎043/841 1062, fax 841 1130; ④), a full-board, family-oriented **hotel** with friendly management, good food and, of course, a statutory gorgeous beach right next to the hotel.

Kei Mouth

The Kei River marks the beginning of the Wild Coast proper, and **Kei Mouth** provides the tranquil setting for the first three of a succession of old-fashioned family hotels that span the coast's length. Only one hour's drive from East London and its weekend holi-daymakers, this area has become amongst the most manicured of the coast, and if you have the time you'll find it more rewarding to continue further north instead. To get to the Kei Mouth, turn off from the N2 at Mooiplaas, about 35km from East London. Ignore the turn-off to Haga-Haga and continue through pleasant grasslands for rough-ly 23km, until you reach the coast.

Accommodation includes the *Kei Mouth Beach* (☎043/841 1017; ④), a comfortable hotel close to the beach, offering rooms looking onto the sea, as well as deep-sea fish-ing and river cruises; the *Kei Sands* (☎043/841 1011; ④), a beachfront hotel with a nice sun-deck and swimming pool, offering both full-board and self-catering accommoda-tion; and the *Suncoast Cabanas* (☎043/841 1102; ④), nine thatched, self-catering cabanas arranged around a pleasant pool, a short stroll from the beach.

Butterworth

BUTTERWORTH, the oldest town in the Transkei, is located near the site of the Gcaleka chief Hintsa's Great Place, and was founded by Methodist missionaries in 1827. The town, known to Xhosa as *Gcuwa* (after the river running through it), derives its English name from the then-treasurer of the Wesleyan Mission Society, Reverend Butterworth, and was selected as the focal point of Transkeian industrial development in the 1970s, with its new industries drawing thousands of workers from the surround-ing countryside. Most of the industries have now closed, but the people are still living in sprawling townships and squatter camps around the town, where unemployment is worryingly high.

Whilst Butterworth itself is unattractive and a bit chaotic, with tatty department stores and supermarkets filled with shoppers, the nearby **Bawa Falls** on the Qolora River, which have a sheer drop of nearly 100m, are spectacular and well worth a visit. The poorly maintained dirt track which leads to them is just west of town past the Shell garage, but numerous twists and turns make the falls quite hard to find, so you will probably need to ask directions.

Practicalities

Butterworth is on the N2, just over 100km from East London, and if you are coming from there it is worth stopping off at the helpful **tourist information office** in the old border post on the Kei River, about halfway between the two towns, which has a good range of leaflets as well as reasonably priced Xhosa jewellery and fabrics.

The well-signposted road to Kentani and the Wild Coast is at the eastern end of Butterworth, past the Gcuwa bridge, and winds through the sprawling Zitulele Industrial Township, where the tar stops and gives way to an outrageously potholed dirt road that continues all the way to the coast. Butterworth's **bus** station is at the western end of town, next to the Shell garage, from where numerous buses and increasing num-bers of **minibus taxis** run to East London, Umtata and Kentani. Daily *Greyhound* and *Translux* buses both stop just off main road on Merriman Street, which is just before the Gcuwa bridge.

The N2 highway runs through Butterworth and is lined with **takeaways**, beer halls and filling stations. The only decent **accommodation** in town is the *Wayside Protea* (☎0474 4615; ③), which is reached by turning right down King Street off the main road, and taking the first right into Sauer Street, where you will see the hotel on your left. The rooms are not cheap, but they are comfortable, the hotel has safe underground parking, and a good **restaurant** serving lunchtime buffets and à la carte evening meals. The one drawback is that the hotel is right next to a busy taxi rank that swarms with people until late into the evening. The *German Restaurant* (☎0474 3852), just off the Kentani road at the eastern end of town, serves good-value steaks and German dishes.

Qolora Mouth

Heading east from Butterworth, and far more secluded than Kei Mouth, beautiful **Qolora Mouth** is best explored on one of the excellent **guided trails** run by two local residents: Trevor Wigley and Allan Burmeister. The trails include a popular three-hour walking and boating trip to the "gates" – the short, towering corridor of rock face through which the Qolora passes on its way to the sea. There's also a trail that explores the enormously varied shell life of the seashore and some of the coastline's many **ship-wrecks** – including the *Jacaranda*, a liner that went down in 1971 and whose rusting hull can still be clearly seen. If contacted in advance, Trevor can arrange a visit to a local *igqirha*, or traditional spiritual doctor, who enacts a typical consultation.

The spot on the Gxara River (which runs between the Qolora and the Kei), where the prophetess Nongqawuse had disastrous visions that induced the Xhosa to kill their cattle (see box below), is not far away, and Allan, who also works at the East London Museum, offers a ten-kilometre hike to the spot, providing lively historical commentary along the way. For the historically minded, there's a trail tracing the major **battle grounds** of the Final Frontier War between the Xhosa and the British in 1878. The Xhosa have not earned the same military reputation as the Zulu in

THE GREAT CATTLE KILLING

The 1850s were a low point for the Xhosa nation: most of their land had been seized by the British, drought was withering their crops, and cattle-sickness was decimating their precious herds. In 1856, a young woman called **Nongqawuse**, whose uncle Mhlakaza was a prophet, claimed to have seen and heard ancestral spirits in a pool on the Gxara River who told her that the Xhosa must **kill all their remaining cattle** and destroy their remaining crops. If they did this, claimed the spirits, new cattle and crops would arise, along with new people who would drive the whites into the sea.

As news of her prophecy spread, opinion was sharply divided amongst the Xhosa, with those whose herds had been badly affected by cattle-sickness most inclined to believe the young prophetess. A turning point came when the Gcaleka paramount chief Sarili visited Nongqawuse, became convinced she was telling the truth and ordered his subjects to start the killing. Thousands of cattle were killed but when the "new people" failed to material-ize on the expected day, the unbelievers who had not killed their herds were blamed. By February 1857, the next date for the appearance of the new people, over 200,000 cattle had been slaughtered and their corpses were festering everywhere. When the new people failed once more to materialize, it was too late for many Xhosa. By July there was wide-spread starvation, with 30,000 of an estimated population of 90,000 dying of hunger.

The British administration saw the famine as a perfect way to force the destitute Xhosa into working on white settlers' farms, and the Cape governor Sir George Grey closed down feeding stations established by missionaries to speed up the process. At the same time, he laid the blame for the disaster on Xhosa chiefs, and imprisoned many of them on Robben Island.

Not surprisingly, the 1856 cattle killing is often used by whites as evidence of the folly of black superstition. The Xhosa, however, have a different interpretation: "*Intombi kaMhlakaza yathetha ubuxoke*" goes the song – meaning "Mhlakaza's girl told lies".

European folklore, yet during this campaign they fought and held their own for a time against soldiers hardened in warfare in the African bush. This trail involves travelling in a 4WD vehicle and is thus more expensive than the others. All the trails can be **booked** through *Seagull's* or *Trennery's* (see below), or the East London Museum (☎0431/43 0686).

Practicalities

The easiest way to get to Qolora Mouth is to cross over the Kei Mouth on a small boat (which you can take your car on) that operates from 6am to 6pm in summer and from 7am to 5.30pm in winter. After disembarking, continue for another 10km on the dirt road to Gxara, where you should turn right and drive for a further 7km to the sea.

Qolora Mouth has two decent **resorts**: *Seagull's* (☎0474/3287; ④), near the rocky shoreline, and the more luxurious *Trennery's* (☎0474/4102; ⑤), slightly inland, with a great swimming pool. Both provide full-board accommodation, and are popular with South African families. The only budget option is *Allan's* (☎0431/43 0686, evenings 471299; ①), a ramshackle self-catering seaside cottage owned by tour guide Allan Burmeister.

Nxaxo Mouth

Nxaxo Mouth, just north of Qolora, is a tranquil location with fascinating mangrove swamps that teem with wildlife. It's an ideal place for hiking, shoreline fishing and general relaxation, as well as the more strenuous activities of canoeing, waterskiing and deep-sea fishing. All of this can be arranged through the only **accommodation** available, the *Wavecrest* (☎0474/3273; ④), a cluster of pleasant bungalows and family rooms that have recently been renovated, and a restaurant with a menu that's more imaginative than that of most along the Wild Coast.

To get there, return to Kentani and take the dirt road signposted to Nxaxo. This road is in poor condition, so take it slowly – and don't take it at all if it is raining hard and you do not have a four-wheel-drive vehicle.

Mazeppa Bay and Qora Mouth

Two of the best places for fishing and general relaxation on the Wild Coast lie further east from Nxaxo. To get to **MAZEPPA BAY**, take the signposted road from Kentani, and shortly after going through a spectacular narrow ridge – **Cat's Pass** – with great views of the surrounding countryside, take a signposted turn-off to the right and continue along a rough road to the coast. The *Mazeppa Bay* (☎0474/4771; ④) offers full-board **accommodation** in comfortable bungalows or family rooms in the hotel, and has the added attraction of its own island, which is connected to the mainland by a suspension bridge. Surfing is good near the bay, but Mazeppa is frequented by hammerhead sharks, so take care.

East of Mazeppa, **QORA MOUTH** has a good beach and a lagoon where you can swim, and is accessed by continuing past the Mazeppa Bay turn-off for around 30km along a potholed dirt road to the coast, passing through hilly lowland dotted with rondavels, river gorges and patches of subtropical forest. **Accommodation** is at the *Kob Inn* (☎0474/62 0246; ④), which features cosy, thatched bungalows, and a well-stocked bar with stunning views of the sea. Staff can arrange a boat and fishing tackle, and can also equip you for canoeing, waterskiing and boardsailing. There is a small ferry across the mouth that can transport you to some good hiking trails along the coast, grassland and nearby forest patches.

Idutywa and around

The small town of **IDUTYWA**, 35km north of Butterworth on the N2, is only a place to head for if you are short of fuel, or very hungry and tired. On the main road going through town you'll find passable *Max Frango's* and *Kentucky Fried Chicken* **takeaways** and the *Idutywa* (☎0474 271040; ③), a quiet **hotel** that is the only good place to stay on the main road between Butterworth and Umtata. Though the mattresses in the rooms are poor, the hotel is clean and its 1950s furniture lends the place a modest charm. The hotel's **restaurant**, the only one in town, serves a typical South African selection of steaks and grills.

SOME XHOSA TRADITIONS

The Wild Coast region is largely populated with **rural Xhosa**, who still practise traditions and customs that have faded in more urban areas. Many people, for example, still believe that the sea is inhabited by strange people who do not always welcome visitors, which explains the relative scarcity of the activities you would normally find thriving among seashore-dwelling people, such as fishing and diving.

Initiation for teenage boys and young men is still common. Young men usually leave their homes to stay in "circumcision lodges", dress in distinctive white paint and costumes and learn the customs of their clan. At the circumcision ceremony the young men are expected to make no sound while their foreskin is cut off (with no anaesthetic) with a single slice of a knife. After the ceremony, they wash off the paint and wrap themselves in new blankets, and all their possessions are thrown into a hut and set alight – they must turn away from this and not look back. There follows a feast to celebrate the beginning of manhood and the start of a year-long intermediary period during which they wear ochre-coloured clay on their faces. After this, they are counted as men. Boys who have gone through the experience of initiation together are supposed to remain bonded at a deep level for the rest of their lives.

Like other African peoples, although they believe in one God, *uThixo* or *uNhkulukhulu* (the great one), many Xhosa also believe that their **ancestors** play an active role in their lives. However, the ancestors' messages are often too obscure to be understood without the aid of specialists, or *amagqira*.

The Xhosa are patriarchal by tradition, with women's subordinate status symbolized by *lobola*, the dowry payment in cattle and cash that a prospective husband must make to her parents before he can marry her. If the woman is not a virgin, the man pays less. Married Xhosa women have the same right as men to smoke tobacco in **pipes**, and can often be seen doing so, with the pipes' long stems designed to prevent ash falling on babies suckling at their breasts. Pipes are shared between people, but each person must have their own stem, not just for matters of hygiene but also to prevent witchcraft: bits of the body make the most effective poisonous medicines against people, and that includes hair, skin and spittle.

The Xhosa did not wear cloth until it was introduced by Europeans, when it was quickly adopted. Today, what is now seen as traditional Xhosa cloth is almost always worn by women, mostly in the form of long skirts, beautifully embroidered with horizontal black stripes placed at varying intervals, which display themselves to subtle effect when the person wearing them is walking. Bags in matching colours with long shoulder straps are popular accessories, especially at weddings, when people put cash gifts inside them. The breasts of unmarried women were traditionally uncovered, while those of married women were usually covered with beads or matching cloth. These days, most women wear T-shirts. Almost all women, however, still cover their heads with scarves which are intricately tied to form two peaks above the forehead. The **traditional colours** of the Thembu and Bomvana clans are red or orange, while the colour of the Pondo and the Mpondomise clans is light blue. In practice, these traditions are not always observed, and married women from a number of clans often wear white instead.

A few kilometres east of town, a right-hand turn leads to **Colleywobbles**, the name given by British soldiers to a particularly tortuous and fascinating stretch of the Mbashe River about 10km down the dirt track. The river reaches the sea 50km further east, disgorging between the **Cwebe** and **Dwesa** nature reserves, but the best way for you to reach these two beautiful places is by continuing for another 60km or so along the N2 until **Jojweni** (sometimes still called Viedgesville), and turning right down the Coffee Bay road.

Dwesa Nature Reserve

North of Qora Mouth, the **Dwesa Nature Reserve** (daily 6am–6pm; small entry fee) is in the throes of a protracted dispute over land ownership, which has rendered its future uncertain. The reserve is still very much visitable and safe, but its facilities and trails have fallen into disrepair. This is a shame, because Dwesa *should* be one of the best places to stay on the coast, with rare animals like tree dassies and samango monkeys, pristine forest, grassland and coastline, and well-sited, self-catering wooden chalets and a campsite (①). To **stay** at Dwesa you need buy a permit in person or by fax from the Nature Conservation Office in Umtata (see p.326).

To get to the reserve, drive to Dwesa, take the Coffee Bay road off the N2 and then take the turn-off for Elliotdale. About 20km along the dirt road to the coast, turn right at a small signpost to Dwesa. The dirt road rapidly deteriorates, and should be taken slowly.

Cwebe Nature Reserve

North of the Mbashe River from Dwesa, the **Cwebe Nature Reserve** (daily 6am–6pm; small entry fee) makes up for its lack of big game by the fact that it is the only Eastern Cape reserve to provide full-board accommodation.

Three-quarters of the reserve is dense subtropical forest, brimming with flora and fauna. Stinkwood and samango monkeys, both of which have all but disappeared from most of southern Africa's east coast, are to be found here via a poorly maintained network of trails. Thankfully, the trail to the beautiful **Mbanyana Waterfall** is in good shape, and you should find it easily walkable from the *Haven* (see below) if the ground is dry. The remaining section of the reserve comprises rolling grassland and a long stretch of wonderful dune-filled shoreline lying in the shadow of the Mbashe lighthouse.

The *Haven* (☎0474/62 0247; ④) is privately owned, so you do not need to get a permit from Umtata before spending the night here, though you should book in advance with the hotel itself. The hotel's bungalows are dotted fairly close together on the fringes of a small golf course that is regularly grazed by **wildebeest**, and are a short walk through milkwoods to the sea.

The well-signposted road to Cwebe, though untarred, is in good shape and you should be able to drive it at regular speed. Take the Coffee Bay turn off the N2 at Jojweni and continue for another 20km to a tarred turn to the right with a small sign pointing to the *Haven*. You'll know you've gone too far if you go past a sign on the Coffee Bay road saying "Coffee Bay 54km". The road continues to small **Elliotdale**, the main administrative centre in the communal lands of the Bomvana people. Once through the town, turn off at a sign claiming the *Haven* to be 69km away onto a dirt road. In fact, it's much less than that and you should reach the reserve in less than an hour.

Hole in the Wall

The village of **HOLE IN THE WALL** has grown up on the shoreline near the large cliff that juts out of the sea a short distance from the Mpako River mouth, from which it gets its name. The cliff has a tunnel at its base through which huge waves pound during heavy seas, making a great crashing sound that has led the Xhosa to call it *esiKhaleni* ("the place of sound"). As well as good fishing and safe swimming, there are spectacular **hikes** all around, including a coastal walk to Coffee Bay.

A hotel and a backpackers' lodge make up the village's **accommodation** options. The *Hole in the Wall* (☎0475/44 2002; ③–④) is a collection of simple but comfortable cottages and rondavels, where you can either self-cater or eat at the hotel's restaurant. Perched up on the hill towards the actual Hole in the Wall is the nicely located *Hole in the Wall Backpackers' Lodge* (☎0475/44 2002; ①), which has wonderful views of the sea and surrounding area, reasonable accommodation and space for **camping**.

To get to Hole in the Wall by **minibus taxi** from Umtata, take a taxi to Mqanduli on the Coffee Bay road, and then one to Hole in the Wall. The *Baz* **bus** (☎021/439 2323) will deposit you at the Shell Ultra City just outside Umtata, from where the backpacker management will pick you up and take you to their hostel. By **car**, take the Coffee Bay road and turn right at the Hole in the Wall turn-off, from where it is another 15km along a potholed dirt road to Hole in the Wall.

Coffee Bay and around

The densely populated, gentle hills of **COFFEE BAY**, known to the Xhosa as *Tshontini* after a dense wood that grows there, mark the traditional boundary between the Bomvana and Pondo clans of the Xhosa nation. Despite the absence of nature reserves, the combination of easy access from an excellent tarred road all the way from the N2, nearby attractions like the famous Hole in the Wall (see above) and a laid-back, relaxed atmosphere, mean that Coffee Bay attracts more and more visitors every year. New backpackers' lodges have sprung up to accommodate the influx, but the village retains its feeling of idyllic obscurity. Neither the swimming nor fishing are particularly good, and though the surfing is supposed to be the best on the Wild Coast the main attractions here are the **coastal hikes** that take you through Xhosa villages through beautiful hilly countryside. The walk to Hole in the Wall is particularly outstanding: head south along the track from Coffee Bay, and turn left at a small sign just past the Telkom tower, from where it's another 5km along the coast.

You can watch **traditional dancing** on Mondays and Thursdays at Nomande Madlalisa's *Bayview Restaurant* (☎0475/44 2004) on the way out of Coffee Bay, and dine on inexpensive, sumptuous traditional Xhosa meals, which are mostly based around meat stews. For **crafts**, you'll find a tiny but inexpensive selection of Xhosa bead jewellery at the *Tsheze Community Development Centre* (Mon–Fri 8am–4pm), near the river.

Practicalities

There are plenty of **minibus taxis** running from Umtata to Coffee Bay. The **Baz Bus** will deposit you in Qunu, from where staff at the backpackers' lodge can pick you up. The drive by **car** is a fast and easy one along a good tarred road from the Jojweni junction with the N2, but the river leading to the village itself is frequently impassable, so you will probably have to park your car on the other side (where it should be quite safe), and wade across with your luggage.

Accommodation is at a traditional full-board hotel, the *Ocean View* (☎0475/44 2005; ④), a short distance from the rest of the village and a stone's throw from the sea, with the only **restaurant** for kilometres around. The scruffy but cheerful *Coffee Bay Backpackers* (☎0475/44 2005; ①) offers dorms, doubles, camping and a lively bar, but can only just cope with the number of visitors it attracts. Nearby, *Woodhouse Backpackers* (☎0475/44 2005; ①) is an attractive wooden complex with a good kitchen and a cosy bar, basic dorms and small doubles with mattresses but no beds. *White Clay*

Backpackers (☎0475/44 2005; ①) is a short walk from the village, in an isolated spot overlooking the sea, and offers comfortable dorms and one double. The municipal **campsite** (with cold water only) is superbly located in a patch of semi-forest by the sea, and has campsites and huts intended for those walking the Wild Coast Hiking Trail (see p.316).

Umtata River Mouth

The **Umtata River** disgorges a short distance from Coffee Bay into another soothing lagoon that is the site of a **hotel**, the *Anchorage* (☎0471/31 2887 or 34 0061), where you can either stay in old-fashioned but reasonably comfortable bungalow accommodation (③) or camp (①). A good way to see the surrounding area's gentle hills, coastal forest and shoreline is on **horseback**, which the hotel can arrange for you.

Getting to the river mouth **from Coffee Bay** involves negotiating the short but difficult coastal road and following signs to Umtata Mouth. First head back on the Umtata road from Coffee Bay for a short distance, and then take the Mdumbi turn on the right, just past the police station. **From Umtata**, you should follow the road to Port St Johns, turning right towards Ngqeleni, and right again at the turn-off to Umtata Mouth.

Hluleka Nature Reserve

One of the loveliest of the Wild Coast nature reserves, **Hluleka Nature Reserve** (daily 6am–6pm; small entry fee) consists of coastal forest whose coral trees flower scarlet in July and August, a strip of grassland and outstanding sandy beaches interspersed with rocky outcrops tattooed with extraordinary wind-shaped rock formations. Although Hluleka's trails are poorly maintained and frequently end up as dead ends, the reserve is sufficiently small that you can usually afford to get a little lost for a while. In the grassland strip you're likely to encounter wildebeest and maybe some of the zebra and blesbok that also roam the area.

Accommodation is in two sets of chalets (①), one on stilts overlooking the sea and the other further up the hill, in the forest. Both are spacious but poorly equipped and subject to electricity curfews, so bring candles. You'll also need all your own food, though you may be able to buy fish from local fishermen if you tell the reserve's staff, who will tip them off. **Permits** should be arranged via the Nature Conservation Office in Umtata (see p.326)

You can reach Hluleka along the difficult coastal road from Coffee Bay. After heading back on the Umtata road from Coffee Bay for a short distance, take the Mdumbi turn on the right, and continue for some 30km, when signs to Hluleka appear. Alternatively – and more easily – you can take the Hluleka turn on your right off the road from Umtata to Port St Johns (there is one before and one after Libode), and continue for another 70km to the coast.

Umtata and around

Straddling the Umtata River and the N2 highway, the fractious, shambolic town of **UMTATA** is the former capital of the Transkei and is the Wild Coast region's largest town. Unfortunately it's a pretty ugly place, its litter-strewn streets lined with nondescript 1970s office buildings and throbbing with pedestrians. However, the town is useful for stocking up and drawing breath for the next stage of your journey, and has the only office in the country that issues **permits** for the five nature reserves of the Wild Coast and the walking trails between them.

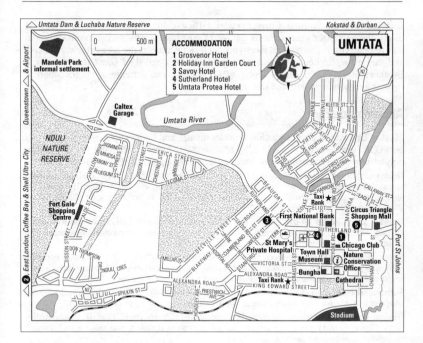

If you're travelling by car and heading on to the Wild Coast, Umtata is also your last chance to ensure that your vehicle is in good enough shape to cope with the generally poor state of Transkei's roads.

Some history

The Umtata River was traditionally the boundary between the Thembu and Pondo clans of the Xhosa nation, with the Thembu to the south and the Pondo to the north. Whites farmed by the river from the 1860s, and after Britain acquired Thembuland in 1875, Umtata was established as the site of one of its four magistracies. From 1976 until 1994, Umtata was the capital of the Transkei homeland and still has a parliament – now defunct – a smattering of showcase big buildings and a reputation for some of the most corrupt officialdom in South Africa.

Arrival and information

Umtata's small **Matanzima Airport** (☎0471/36 0023) lies 10km west of town on the Queenstown Road. There is no public transport from the airport, but you can rent a car from here (see "Listings"). *Greyhound* and *Translux* **buses** pull in at the Shell UltraCity, a few kilometres west of town, from where you can get a minibus taxi to the town centre. The *Baz Bus* stops at *Steers* at the Circus Triangle mall on the Port St Johns road for those heading on to the backpackers' lodge in Port St Johns, at Shell UltraCity for those going to Hole in the Wall, and further west at Qunu for those going to Coffee Bay. *Transtate* buses and most **minibus taxis** stop near the train station to the south of the CBD on Edward Street.

You'll find Umtata's **tourist office** (Mon–Fri 8am–4.30pm; ☎0471/31 2885) on the corner of York and Victoria streets, with useful maps and staff who know the area well.

Conveniently, the **Nature Conservation Office** (Mon–Fri 8am–4.30pm; ☎0471/31 2711), the only place you can book for Wild Coast hiking trails and accommodation in nature reserves, is downstairs. Here you can pick up maps of the areas you want to visit and buy a helpful booklet about the whole coastal strip. *Wild Coast Reservations*, 3 Beaufort St (Mon–Fri 8am–4.30pm; ☎0471/25344), can arrange accommodation at resorts and hotels throughout the region.

Accommodation

Most of Umtata's **accommodation** is pretty dismal, and budget options are few and far between. However, there is a handful of reasonable hotels in the centre of town. The only nearby place to **camp** is the Umtata Dam (see opposite), just northwest of town.

Grosvenor Hotel, corner of Sutherland and Madeira streets (☎0471/31 2118). B&B accommodation at this pleasant turn-of-the-century hotel in the heart of town, with safe parking. The rooms are old-fashioned and comfortable, and the hotel restaurant offers set menus on Tuesdays and Wednesdays. ③.

Holiday Inn Garden Court, N2 (☎0471/37 0181). Large modern building on the way out of Umtata, with a stylish pool, slot machines, a chic cocktail bar and a respectable restaurant. The rooms are unremarkable, though, and all the singles face the car park. ④.

Savoy Hotel, corner of Sutherland St and Savoy Terrace (☎0471/31 0791). Elegantly decaying hotel with good rooms and a restaurant with a steak-dominated set menu. There are three bars: a smart private one, a public bar with pool tables, and a Xhosa bar at the back. ③.

Sutherland Hotel, corner of Sutherland and Owen streets (☎0471/31 2281). Pretty shabby hotel, with rowdy public bars and no restaurant. But it's very cheap, and offers safe parking. ①.

Umtata Protea Hotel, corner of Sutherland and Madeira streets (☎0471/25654). Unimaginative hotel offering decent rooms, excellent service, good views of Umtata if your room is high enough up, reliable food and safe parking. ④.

The Town and around

Central Umtata comprises a small grid of busy streets bursting with pedestrians and lined with dull office buildings interspersed with the odd older architectural gem. One of these gems is the elegant **town hall** on Leeds Street, with a fine clock stuck at nearly 6pm which looks down onto a war memorial and pleasant gardens. One block south, opposite the tourist office, stands the town's small and neglected **museum** (Mon–Fri 8am–4.30pm; free), which has fairly informative displays of traditional Xhosa costume, local geology and an exhibit on the ANC that stops before the 1994 elections.

Continue further south to the corner of Owen and Alexandra streets for a peek at the distinctive, mustard-coloured old **parliament**, or *bungha*, built in 1927. The debating chambers are now closed, but the rest of the building is still being used as municipal offices and you can wander inside. One block east, on the corner of Alexandra and York streets, is an elegant sandstone Anglican **cathedral**, sadly permanently closed. A major taxi rank straggles along the opposite side of Alexandra Street, and behind it is the small **stadium** used by the Umtata Bucks soccer team. If you are in town for a few days and the weather is good, head for the pleasant open-air **swimming pool** (daily, 9am–12.30pm & 2–4.45pm; small entry fee) at the western end of Sutherland Street, near the junction with Stanford Street.

A little over 20km west of Umtata are the scattered dwellings of **Qunu**, which constitute the humble birthplace of **Nelson Mandela** (see box). Since Mandela was born here, the big changes in Qunu have been the N2 highway which now thunders through it, and a large and rather plain **presidential palace**, which you may photograph but not

NELSON MANDELA AND THE QUNU CONNECTION

Nelson Rolihlahla Mandela, surely the world's most popular statesman, was born near tiny **Qunu** in the even tinier village of Mvezo on July 18, 1918. His father was a member of the Xhosa royal house and a custodian of Xhosa history – he was also chief of Mvezo, until he crossed swords with the local white magistrate over a minor dispute concerning an ox. After his sacking, the family moved to a small *kraal* in Qunu, which Mandela remembers as consisting of several hundred poor households.

Mandela is often called **Madiba** – the name of his family's subclan of the Thembu clan. The name Nelson was given to him by a schoolteacher, and Rolihlahla means "pulling the branch of a tree" or, more colloquially, "troublemaker". Mandela has said that at home he was never allowed to ask any questions, but was expected to learn by observation. Later in life, he was shocked to visit the homes of whites and hear children firing questions at their parents and expecting replies.

Shortly after his father died, Mandela was summoned from Qunu to the royal palace at Mqhakeweni, where he sat in on disputes in court and learnt more about Xhosa culture. At 16 he was initiated – and burnt with shame for a long time afterwards at the cry he had let slip out when circumcised. He enrolled in Clarkebury, a college for the Thembu elite, then the Wesleyan college of Healdtown at Fort Beaufort, and finally the celebrated Fort Hare in Alice (see p.304), which has educated generations of African leaders.

Mandela was expelled from Fort Hare after clashing with the authorities and returned to Mqhakeweni. In 1941, faced with the prospect of an arranged marriage, he ran away to Johannesburg and there immersed himself in politics.

It was only in 1990 (at the age of 72) when, released from prison, Mandela was able to return to Qunu, visiting first the grave of his mother, who had died in his absence. He noted that the place seemed poorer than he remembered it, and that the children were now singing songs about AK47s and the armed struggle. However, he was relieved to find that none of the old spirit and warmth had left the community, and he arranged for a palace (or "country house" as he called it) to be built there. This palace has become the venue for Mandela's holidays and family reunions and has a floor plan identical to that of the house in Victor Verster prison where Mandela spent the last few years of his captivity. In his autobiography he writes: "The Victor Verster house was the first spacious and comfortable home I ever stayed in, and I liked it very much. I was familiar with its dimensions, so at Qunu I would not have to wander at night looking for the kitchen."

enter. **Tours** are available (called "Footsteps of the President") from *Kai Safaris*, based at East London Airport (☎0431/36 6494).

Nearby nature reserves

Though they can't compete with the wonderful subtropical forest reserves of the Wild Coast, the three small reserves close to Umtata are worth investigating if you're in town for a few days, or if you need a place to camp. **Umtata Dam** (daily 6am–7pm; small entry fee), a few kilometres northwest of town, is a tranquil spot, popular with anglers, and is the only place to **camp** near Umtata. To get there, take the Queenstown road and turn right after the Caltex garage past the Dela school. After this, turn left onto a dirt road at a sign pointing to the *Eastern Cape Appropriate Technology Unit*, drive past the growing informal settlement on your left, and take the first right turn after the bridge. There have been no reports of security problems here so far, but you'd be wise to check with staff at the gate before pitching your tent.

Turn left at the dam gates at a sign saying "boating and yachting" for the **Luchaba Nature Reserve** (daily 6am–7pm; small entry fee), and continue for another 2km. This somewhat drab grassland reserve flanks the dam and has blesbok, wildebeest and diverse birdlife, but no accommodation.

Roughly 3km south of Umtata, the **Nduli Nature Reserve** (daily 8am–6pm; small entry fee) is a pleasant patch of bushveld which is home to a variety of antelope, including blesbok and impala, as well as wildebeest, but has no accommodation. To get there, take the first turn right off the N2 out of Umtata after Sissons Street, onto an unmarked road; from here, it's a short distance to the gate.

Eating, drinking and nightlife

As well as the hotel restaurants, of which those at the *Protea* and *Holiday Inn* are the best (see "Accommodation"), there are several good **places to eat** in Umtata, and plenty of fast-food chains. In addition, you'll find street vendors on the corner of Sutherland and Sprigg streets near the *Protea*, selling tasty dishes like boerewors and *pap*. Umtata has a thriving **nightlife**, but exploring it without a local escort isn't recommended. The notable exception is the *Chicago*, on the corner of York and Leeds streets, opposite the Old Mutual building, which is open every night and plays a wide variety of sounds to a relatively mellow crowd.

Cafés and restaurants

Café de Didi, Fort Gale shopping complex, Sisson St. In Umtata's most upmarket suburb, north of the N2, and west of the CBD, this café offers a delicious selection of cakes.

China Restaurant, 22 Owen St (☎0471/24510). All sorts of interesting and reasonably priced Chinese dishes make this one of the best restaurants in town. Closed Sun.

La Piazza, Fort Gale shopping complex (☎0471/31 0795). Varied and tasty Italian-based menu, with a good range of salads and a friendly, family-oriented setting. Also does takeaways.

Nando's, 85 York Rd, opposite the town hall. South Africa's best fast-food chain, serving up the usual tasty menu. Closed Sun.

Prim's, corner of Leeds and Craister streets (☎0471/31 0995). Umtata's smartest and priciest restaurant serves high-quality dishes with a continental flavour in elegant surroundings. Closed Sun.

Listings

American Express The nearest office is in Port Elizabeth.

Automobile Association The nearest offices are in Durban and East London.

Banks *First National Bank*, corner of Sutherland and York streets; *Standard Bank*, corner of York and Leeds streets. Expect large queues. Where you find banks, you'll also find ATMs.

Car rental *Avis* (☎0471/360 066) is based at Matanzima Airport.

Emergencies Ambulance ☎22222; Police ☎10177 or ☎31 1333 (Flying Squad).

Garages *Fort Gale Motors* (☎0471/31 1683) on the Queenstown Rd has a reasonable reputation with locals, though the same level of service for those who are just passing through cannot be guaranteed.

Hospitals *St Mary's Private Hospital*, 30 Durham St (☎0471/31 2911).

Nature Conservation Office, corner of York and Victoria streets (☎0471/31 2711) is the only place to book for Wild Coast hiking trails and the national parks in this area.

Post office The main post office is on the corner of Sutherland and Durham streets.

Shopping The Circus Mall in the centre of town is the least hectic for shopping.

Travel agents *East West Travel*, 1 Toyi Properties, Victoria St (☎0471/22928), can arrange flight bookings, intercity bus travel and hotel accommodation in the region.

Port St Johns

The sixty-kilometre drive to **PORT ST JOHNS** from Umtata is one of the best journeys in the Wild Coast. After passing tiny **Libode**, with its small hotel and restaurant, you start the dramatic descent to the coast, passing by craggy ravines and epic vistas of forest and rondavel-spotted grassland. The road runs alongside the Mzimvubu River for the last few kilometres, giving you a perfect view of the Gates of St John, before reaching the town's square and taxi rank.

Port St Johns is a favoured destination for young backpackers, who are drawn by its stunning location at the mouth of the Mzimvubu River, dominated by Mount Thesiger on the west bank and Mount Sullivan on the east, and the copious quantities of strong cannabis which are grown around here. Even if the latter isn't your cup of tea, the town's famously laid-back atmosphere may tempt you to stay for longer than you intended. Port St Johns also has good fishing and swimming beaches, a wider choice of accommodation than anywhere else on the Wild Coast, and an excellent tarred road all the way into town.

Some history

The origins of Port St Johns' name is something of a mystery but may derive from the sixteenth-century Portuguese ship, *São João*, which was wrecked nearby, leaving around four hundred survivors to complete a 700-kilometre walk to Mozambique. Only eight survived and one of those was shipwrecked again near the Umtata river mouth two years later. He reportedly died of despair, unable to face the trek to Mozambique once more.

In 1878, in an effort to reduce gunrunning from the harbour, a representative of the Cape governor bought a fifteen-kilometre stretch of the river from the shore inland, and the land on the western side from the Pondo for R2000. While he was waiting for the money, an armed force arrived from Natal and annexed the eastern side of the river. A compromise was found by making Port St Johns a crown colony in its own right, though this was rescinded when the whole of Pondoland was annexed by Britain in 1895.

The area was then known for its **tobacco**, which was exported from Durban and East London. During the negotiations for the Act of Union (see p.653), the Transvaal demanded the cessation of the trade to allow its white tobacco growers to expand their business without competition. The Cape Colony obliged and in 1906 stopped exporting tobacco. Local farmers responded by switching to **cannabis** (*insango*), supplying the growing numbers of men from the area going to work on the Witwatersrand mines. Today, the cultivation and trade are as strong as ever, which may explain the presence of so many white South African hippies in the town.

Arrival and information

Port St Johns is easily reached by **minibus taxi** from Umtata: plenty run from the *Steer's* restaurant at the Circus Triangle mall on the Port St Johns road. This is also where the *Baz Bus* deposits backpackers going to Port St Johns.

If you're travelling from KwaZulu-Natal to Port St Johns by public transport, an alternative route is to go via the *Wild Coast Sun*, Bizana and Lusikisiki. This journey is most easily done by catching the local *Grimboys* bus from Durban, which runs daily directly to Port St Johns.

There is no information centre in town (though one is planned), but a number of lodges keep copies of a helpful hand-drawn map of the town by local resident Ben Dekker. Some lodge owners have also compiled their own information – the *Port St Johns Backpackers* offers the most comprehensive.

Accommodation

Port St Johns has the best selection of **accommodation** on the Wild Coast, with a healthy number of backpackers' lodges, old-fashioned hotels and nearby farm accommodation. For a memorable **township** experience, you can stay with the gregarious Ms

Constance Duna in the Port St Johns township (or "location", as they call it here) perched up on the hill between Port St Johns and Second Beach: you'll need to book with *Port St Johns Backpackers* (see below) and pay in advance.

Coastal Needles Hotel (☎0475/44 1031). Old-fashioned and musty rooms in a large, gently decaying hotel opposite the taxi rank in the centre of town. The restaurant serves inexpensive set meals. ②.

Ferry Point Backpackers (☎083/726 6332). Terrific assortment of dwellings perched dramatically on the eastern sea-facing cliffs of the Umzimvubu estuary, with dorms, doubles, family rooms and self-contained cottages. The emphasis, particularly at weekends, is on partying. If penniless and hard-working, you can earn your stay clearing alien vegetation. Turn off the Lusikisiki road after the Pondoland bridge, and crunch your way down 5km of terrible track. Alternatively, catch the ferry boat from Port St Johns before 6pm. ①.

Franco's (no phone). Rustic farm with huts for visitors northeast of town amidst lovely countryside, overlooking the Umtafufu estuary, with many Xhosa living nearby whom the owner knows well. A pleasant 4hr walk from Port St Johns and a very restful place to stay. Bring your own bedding and food, and a guide to show you the way – the two backpackers' lodges can arrange this. ①.

The Jetty (☎0475/44 1072). Tranquil lodge on the Umzimvubu's eastern bank, a short distance from the Pondoland bridge and Lusikisiki road, offering five en-suite rooms, an ample bar and choice fishing spots. You can rent boats for fishing trips or river cruises, and self-cater, although meals are available. ②–③.

Lily Lodge (☎0475/44 1229). Best known for its great seafood restaurant, this lodge has well-equipped and comfortable brick cottages set in a luxuriant subtropical garden, very close to Second Beach. To get there, take a signposted left turn off Second Beach Rd. ③.

The Lodge, Second Beach Rd (☎0475/44 1171). Charming and secluded B&B at the end of Second Beach Rd, with three tasteful rooms and the best wine and cooking in Port St Johns. Booking essential. ③.

Outspan Inn (☎0475/44 1057). B&B with wonderfully decorated en-suite rooms, some with high beds that give a sea view. The restaurant is one of the better places to eat in town. The *Inn* is behind the *Outspan* store, past the town hall on the road to First Beach. ③.

Port St Johns Backpackers. (no phone). Homely dorms and doubles at this mellow hostel staffed by friendly folk on the first turn to the right off the main road, after the post office. This is also the best place in Port St Johns to read up on surrounding attractions. Camping is permitted. ①.

Umngazi Bungalows (☎0475/44 1115). Set in the Umngazi River mouth just west of Port St Johns, this smart resort is arguably the best-designed and -equipped along the Wild Coast, though the rooms are small. The beach and pool are inviting and the buffet spread is particularly good. To get there, go back 10km on the Umtata road until the signpost, from which it's another 11km on a pot-holed dirt track. ④–⑤.

The Town and around

Although there is nothing much to see in town, Port St Johns is still a nice place to take a leisurely stroll, particularly during the early evening, when many residents are doing the same. The town's main attractions are its two beaches; **First Beach** is along the main road from the post office and offers good fishing, while **Second Beach**, 5km along a road off a right turn past the post office, is a fabulous swimming beach. Most people rarely go anywhere else, though the rocky coastline into the **Silaka Nature Reserve** (see opposite) and as far as the **Umngazi River Mouth** provides wonderful walks, as do the endless stretches of pristine beach east of the Mzimvubu River. The Mzimvubu is muddy in summer, disgorging topsoil washed down the Drakensberg from Lesotho, but clears up dramatically in winter, when it is clear and good for fishing.

Both the mountains of the **Gates of St John** merit a clamber to the top, from where you get a superb view of the lush surrounding landscape. The paths can be hard to find, though, and you'll be best off with a guide or at least a decent map. Two local residents, David and Steve, contactable through the backpackers' lodges (or on

☎083/305 2213), can take you further afield, deep into the Pondo heartland of **Mtambalala**, where you stay with locals and hike to the stunning **Magwa Falls** and beyond. They can also arrange visits to a nearby traditional healer.

For **crafts**, check out *Pondo People* on the east side of the Mzimvubu River across the Pondoland bridge; the speciality here is immaculate bead jewellery and clothing. *Jakotz*, next to *The Lodge* on Second Beach, sells African printed clothes, while *Bayou*, 5km up the Umtata road has a colourful selection of batik clothes, handmade furniture and herbal products.

Silaka Nature Reserve

Just south of town, the **Silaka Nature Reserve** (daily 6am–6pm; small entry fee) is a small reserve with a dramatic coastline, and comprises the idyllic **Third Beach**, dense tropical-forest areas – through which there are good trails – and a handful of animals, including zebra and wildebeest.

Accommodation is in spacious self-catering chalets (①) surrounded by grassland. Bookings can be made at the reserve itself, as well as in the Umtata Nature Conservation Office (see p.326). The reserve's hiking huts, intended for those walking the Wild Coast Hiking Trail (see p.316), are attractively located near Third Beach.

To get to the reserve, travel down the Second Beach road from Port St Johns and then up the treacherously steep dirt road to the reserve's office. If you are staying at *Port St Johns Backpackers*, the owner will drive you to the office himself, from where you'll have a very pleasant walk back along the coastline.

Eating and drinking

You'll have to search a bit for decent places to **eat and drink** in Port St Johns. If you're self-catering the picture is a lot brighter, with plenty of tempting local produce, including tropical fruits and fresh fish (sold on the beach), guaranteeing you won't go hungry.

Lily's Restaurant (☎0475/44 1229). On the way to Second Beach, this is the best restaurant in the area, serving up delicious and reasonably priced seafood. Enjoy the perfect view from the sun deck while you're eating. Closed Mon.

Outspann Inn. Near the town hall, this spacious restaurant has an interesting and inexpensive menu, but not much custom. Closed Sun.

Hippo's. On the main road, very near the Second Beach turn-off, *Hippo's* is popular with locals, and serves inexpensive traditional dishes such as samp and bean stews.

Coastal Needles. Cavernous hall in this faded central hotel, serving cheap meat dishes.

The Lodge (☎0475/44 1171). Tiny hotel restaurant at Second Beach serving good seafood and continental meals, with fine wines to wash it all down. Booking essential.

The northern Wild Coast and the KwaZulu-Natal enclave

For many visitors to the northern part of the Wild Coast, the main draw is the *Wild Coast Sun*, a hotel and casino on the border of KwaZulu-Natal. However, the stretch of coast from Port St Johns to the Mzamba River by the *Sun* is outstandingly beautiful, with three of only five waterfalls in the world that fall over 100m directly into the sea, as well as countless deserted beaches and cosy bays. The best way to see it is to walk (see p.332), though you can drive, with some difficulty, to the **Mkambati Nature Reserve**, which contains a good portion of this coast.

The **Lusikisiki** road from Port St Johns to the *Wild Coast Sun* via Bizana makes an interesting alternative to the N2 for getting from the Eastern Cape to KwaZulu-Natal.

The road through the Eastern Cape enclave in KwaZulu-Natal takes you into the rolling hills of **Ixopo**, made famous by Alan Paton's novel, *Cry the Beloved Country*.

Mkambati Nature Reserve

The largest of the Wild Coast reserves, **Mkambati** (daily 6am–6pm; small entry fee), covering eighty square kilometres, consists almost entirely of grassland, though it is flanked by the forested ravines of the Msikaba and Mtentu rivers, and a ravishing coastline of rocky promontories and deserted beaches. The park has plenty of **game**; you are likely to see eland, hartebeest, wildebeest and blesbok, as well as Cape vultures. The highlight, though, is the Mkambati River itself, which flows through the middle down a series of striking waterfalls, of which the **Horseshoe Falls** near the sea are the most spectacular.

Accommodation is either in the main lodge – available for a minimum of five people – which has double rooms with bath (②) or in self-catering cottages and rondavels (①). There's an unimpressive **restaurant** in the main lodge. Bookings must be made through the Nature Conservation Office in Umtata (see p.326).

To get to Mkambati from the N2, take the Flagstaff turn-off between Mount Ayliff and Kokstad, and just before Flagstaff, look out for signs to the *Holy Cross Hospital* and Mkambati. From there, a poor-quality dirt road, impassable in a standard car during rainy weather, takes you past the hospital to the reserve.

North to the Wild Coast Sun

The road from Port St Johns to the small, unremarkable town of **LUSIKISIKI** is untarred and hard to negotiate in wet weather for the first 16km, but tarred for the rest of the way to the *Wild Coast Sun*. Beyond Lusikisiki, the hills of Pondoland seem to stretch for miles, punctuated 50km later by the small village of **Flagstaff**. Roughly 30km further on, a junction leads back to the N2, and 20km beyond that through heavily populated hillsides is the busy town of **BIZANA**, 60km from the coast in an area where both **Oliver Tambo** and **Winnie Madikizela-Mandela** were born. The *Bizana Hotel* on the left side of the main road has a quiet **restaurant** serving good-value steaks and curries, but otherwise is not recommended as a place to stay.

Some 60km further along is the opulent *Wild Coast Sun* (☎039/305 9111; ⑦), in a well-chosen location by the Mzamba River mouth. Despite its tacky Pacific island-themed decor, some of the hotel complex is quite pleasant. Most people are here to gamble, but an impressive games arcade, ten-pin bowling, pony rides and minigolf are also on offer. **Accommodation** is in small, well-equipped rooms, with some suites looking onto the sea. You can **eat** tasty (if overpriced) fish steaks at the *Driftwood Terrace*, which has a fantastic sea view.

Opposite the complex is the **Mzamba Crafts Market**, arranged in a circle to resemble a traditional *kraal*. The central shop sells authentic crafts from all over southern Africa for reasonable prices, with local ones the cheapest, particularly the grasswork. Reject goods are on sale in the outlying huts for even better prices. **Taxis** and **buses** stop outside the market on their way to Bizana and **Port Edward** in KwaZulu-Natal.

Mount Ayliff and Mount Frere

The quickest and busiest way from the Eastern Cape to KwaZulu-Natal is on the N2, passing by the scraggy towns of Mount Frere and Mount Ayliff, before reaching **Kokstad** and the provincial boundary. From the road you'll see hillsides dotted with densely packed dwellings. Closer inspection reveals that the hillsides are not coping well with the strain, as there are massive dongas creating scar-like craters in many places where huge volumes of topsoil have simply been washed away. **MOUNT FRERE** is about 100km from Umtata, and is called *kwaBhaca* in Xhosa, meaning "the place of the Bhaca", for it was here that many of those who ran south from the Zulu king Shaka ended up, earning the name *amaBhaca*, "the people who hide". Today, Mount Frere is a fairly rough town and you'd be wise to pass swiftly through. The small trading-station town of **MOUNT AYLIFF**, 44km further on, though not ideal either, nonetheless offers the pleasantly decayed, colonial *Mount Ayliff* (☎047382 50; ①), with basic **hotel** rooms that look out onto a large, rambling garden, and an inexpensive restaurant.

The Eastern Cape enclave in KwaZulu-Natal

The **Eastern Cape enclave in KwaZulu-Natal** for many years sat uncomfortably with the crass ethnic categorizations of past regimes, and the legacy of this lives on today. The people living in the enclave, whose main town is uMzimkhulu, are a mixture of Zulu, Pondo, Bhaca and Griqua, economically tied in the main to Pietermaritzburg and Durban. The apartheid regime yoked them with the Transkei, ostensibly on the grounds that most were Pondo, and thus part of the Xhosa nation, but in fact to tap them as a cheap labour reserve. Controversially, the area was included in the Eastern Cape when the boundaries were redrawn, in part because many in the area support the ANC and did not want to be part of a province ruled by the Zulu nationalist Inkhata Freedom Party.

The enclave is reached by turning off the N2 onto the R56 at the Stafford's Post junction towards **Ixopo**. It's scenic and pleasant enough to drive through, though not a good place to travel around in, and desperately poor, despite its extensive cornfields. **uMzimkhulu** is a busy transport centre, with a large taxi rank by its Shell garage and plenty of fast-food outlets to feed hungry passengers, most of whom are going to and from **Pietermaritzburg** and **Durban**. After passing the remnants of a small border post just east of the town, you will find yourself back in KwaZulu-Natal, a short distance from Ixopo.

travel details

All major transport in the Eastern Cape begins or ends at Port Elizabeth or East London – the two hubs of the province. In addition to train, intercity bus and air services, there are backpacker buses and scheduled minibuses making additional connections to one or two smaller centres. Failing these, the option remains of cheap and frequent (though unscheduled and less comfortable or safe) minibus taxis.

Trains

Two mainline trains, the *Amatola* from East London and the *Algoa* from Port Elizabeth, serve the Eastern Cape, both making several stops along the way to Johannesburg.

East London to: Bloemfontein (daily; 13hr); Johannesburg (daily; 20hr); Queenstown (daily; 4hr 30min).

Port Elizabeth to: Bloemfontein (daily; 11hr 30min); Cradock (daily; 4hr 30min); Johannesburg (daily; 18hr).

Intercity buses

The main bus routes run from Port Elizabeth (up the N10) and East London (up the N6) to join the N1 via Bloemfontein to Johannesburg and Pretoria; and along the coast to Cape Town in the west and Durban in the east. An alternative route goes inland through the Little Karoo to Cape Town.

East London to: Alexandria (5 weekly; 3hr); Aliwal North (daily; 5hr); Bloemfontein (daily; 7hr 30min); Cape Town (1–2 daily; 14hr 30min); Durban (2 daily; 9hr); Fish River Sun (5 weekly; 2hr 30min); George (1–2 daily; 8hr 30min);

Grahamstown (2 daily; 2hr); Johannesburg (daily; 13hr); Kenton-on-Sea (5 weekly; 3hr); King William's Town (2–3 daily; 45min); Knysna (1–2 daily; 7hr 30min); Mossel Bay (1–2 daily; 9hr); Paarl (5 weekly; 14hr 30min); Plettenberg Bay (1–2 daily; 7hr); Port Alfred (3 daily; 2hr 30min); Port Elizabeth (3 daily; 4hr); Port Shepstone (2 daily; 8hr); Pretoria (daily; 14hr); Sedgefield (1–2 daily; 8hr); Storms River (1–2 daily; 6hr); Swellendam; Umtata (2 daily; 3hr 30min); Wilderness (1–2 daily; 8hr 30min).

Port Elizabeth to: Alexandria (5 weekly; 1hr); Bloemfontein (1–2 daily; 10hr); Cape Town (5–6 daily; 11hr); Durban (2 daily; 13hr 30min); East London (3 daily; 4hr); Fish River Sun (5 weekly; 2hr); George (5–6 daily; 4hr 30min); Graaff-Reinet (5 weekly; 3hr 30min); Grahamstown (2 daily; 1hr 30min); Jeffrey's Bay (2 daily; 45min); Johannesburg (1–2 daily; 16hr); Kenton-on-Sea (5 weekly; 1hr 30min); King William's Town; Knysna (5–6 daily; 3hr 30min); Mossel Bay (5–6 daily; 4hr 30min); Paarl (4 weekly; 10hr); Plettenberg Bay (5–6 daily; 3hr); Port Alfred (5 weekly; 1hr 45min); Port Shepstone (2 daily; 12hr); Pretoria (1–2 daily; 17hr); Sedgefield (5–6 daily; 3hr 30min); Stellenbosch (6 weekly; 10hr); Storms River (5–6 daily; 2hr); Umtata (2 daily; 7hr 30min); Wilderness (4 daily; 3hr 30min).

Umtata to: Cape Town (1–3 daily; 17hr 30min); Durban (3 daily; 5hr 50min); East London (1–2 daily; 3hr); Johannesburg (2 daily; 12hr 45min); Port Elizabeth (1 daily; 5hr 40min); Pretoria (1 daily; 13hr 45min).

Backpacker buses

The *Baz* (5 times a week) and *Hopper* (daily) **backpacker buses** both ply the coastal route between Port Elizabeth and Cape Town. Neither goes straight through: the *Hopper* overnights in Mossel Bay and the *Baz* in Knysna. The Port Elizabeth-based *Hopper* (indicated as H where appropriate below) goes to East London as far as Cintsa via Grahamstown daily, while the *Baz* (indicated as B) goes all the way through to Durban four times a week.

Port Elizabeth to: Durban (4 weekly; 15hr 30min/B only); East London (1–2 daily; 2hr 30min); George (daily; 7hr 45min); Grahamstown (daily; 2hr 15min/H only); Jeffrey's Bay (1–2 daily; 1hr 45min); Knysna (1–2 daily; 6hr 30min); Mossel Bay (daily; 10hr 15min); Nature's Valley (1–2 daily; 4hr 30min); Oudtshoorn (daily; 9hr); Plettenberg Bay (1–2 daily; 5hr 30min); Port Alfred (4 weekly; 2hr 15min/B only); Port Shepstone (4 weekly; 14hr/B only); Storms River Mouth (daily; 3hr 30min/H only); Wilderness (daily; 7hr 15min); Umtata (4 weekly; 8hr 30min/B only).

Flights

East London to: Cape Town (4 daily; 2hr); Durban (3 daily; 1hr); George (6 weekly; 2hr); Johannesburg (4 daily; 1hr 20min); Port Elizabeth (1–3 daily; 45min).

Port Elizabeth to: Bloemfontein (4 weekly; 1hr 20min); Cape Town (4–8 daily; 1hr 15min); Durban (6–8 daily; 1hr 10min); East London (2–4 daily; 45min); George (6 weekly; 50min); Johannesburg (8–14 daily; 1hr 30min); Plettenberg Bay (3 weekly; 50min).

Umtata to: Durban (1 daily Mon–Fri; 1hr); Johannesburg (1–3 daily; 1hr 30min); Port Elizabeth (1 daily Mon, Thurs & Fri; 1hr 20min).

CHAPTER FIVE

KWAZULU-NATAL

KwaZulu-Natal, South Africa's most African province, harbours everything the continent is known for – beaches, wildlife, mountains and accessible ethnic culture – a combination no other province can match. It's also the country's most turbulent region, wracked by political violence that has riven its Zulu majority in a low-key but deadly war of attrition and vendetta. although still present, this long-term struggle between ANC supporters and followers of the **Inkatha Freedom Party** (which controls the provincial government) has died down since the 1994 election, and you certainly won't hear mention of it in official tourist literature.

For white South Africans, KwaZulu-Natal is well known for its subtropical **coastline**, which offers a temperate climate even in the winter, when the Cape can be showered by an icy downpour. This is where you'll find Africa's most intensely developed beaches, in a 250-kilometre ribbon of holiday homes that stretches along the shore from the Eastern Cape border in the south to the Tugela River in the north.

At the ribbon's centre lies **Durban**, the industrial hub of the province and the country's principal harbour. Apart from Cape Town, Durban is the only major city in South Africa that warrants a visit in its own right. British in origin, it carries a heady mixture of cultural flavours derived from its Zulu, Indian and white communities. You'll find palm trees fanning Victorian buildings, African squatters living precariously on truncated flyovers, high-rise offices towering over temples and curry houses, overdeveloped beachfronts, and everywhere an irrepressible fecundity.

Paradoxically, while the coasts on either side of Durban – the so-called **North and South coasts** – are South Africa's busiest and least enticing, north of the Tugela River are some of the most remote and pristine shores in the country. Here, **Maputaland**, a patchwork of wetlands, freshwater lakes, wilderness and Zulu villages, meets the sea at a virtually seamless stretch of sand that begins at the St Lucia Estuary and slips across the Mozambique border at **Kosi Bay**. Apart from southern **Lake St Lucia**, which is fairly developed in a low-key fashion, Maputaland is one of the most isolated regions in the country, traversed only by dirt roads. The reward at the end of one such track is **Rocktail Bay**, a dreamscape of tropical vegetation, tepid water and soft sands stretching as far as you can see in either direction. South Africa's best snorkelling and scuba diving lies just south of here, along the coral reefs off **Sodwana Bay**.

KwaZulu-Natal's marine life is matched on land by its **game reserves**, some of which are second only to the Kruger National Park and easily surpass it as the best place in the continent to see both black and white rhinos (though Kruger is better if you're bent on seeing lions and elephants). Concentrated in the north, just west of Maputaland, the reserves tend to be compact and beautiful places with some of the most stylish game-lodge accommodation in the country. Most famous and largest of the reserves is the **Hluhluwe-Umfolozi Park**, trampled by a respectable cross-section of wildlife that includes all of the Big Five. The low-key **Mkuzi** and **Ndumo** game reserves are two of South Africa's best destinations for bird-watching, while near the northern provincial border, most surprising of them all is the little-known **Itala Game Reserve**, a mountainous delight which year after year wins awards for its top-class accommodation.

The interior, north of the Tugela River, marks the **KwaZulu-Natal Battlefields**. This heartland of the nineteenth-century Zulu kingdom saw gruesome battles between

Boers and Zulus, British and Zulus and finally Boers and British. Today the area can be explored through battlefield tours – a memorable way of taking in some of South Africa's most turbulent history.

Since the nineteenth century, when KwaZulu-Natal was one of the most missionary-trammelled regions in the world, the **Zulus** have captured the popular imagination of the West and remain one of the province's major pulls for tourists, despite the fact that you're as likely to encounter a Zulu person dressed in jeans in Jo'burg as someone in traditional garb in KwaZulu-Natal. You'll find constant reminders of the old Zulu kingdom and its founder Shaka, including an excellent reconstruction of the beehive-hutted capital at **Ondini** and the more touristy **Shakaland**, near Eshowe.

The area south of the Tugela, designated in the mid-nineteenth century as "white man's country" and consolidated a century later under apartheid, represents the most English area of South Africa and is the least compelling section of the province. That's not to say the **Midlands** is unpleasant or lacking in beauty, but its rolling green sugar estates, polo clubs and rather contrived arts and crafts routes pale by comparison with the drama of the rest of the province.

From the Midlands, South Africa's highest peaks sweep west into the soaring **Drakensberg** range, known to the Zulus as the "Barrier of Spears". Protected by a chain of Natal Parks Board reserves, you'll find rest camps from where you can launch out on walks into the mountains or head out for ambitious hikes in the High Berg. With relatively little effort you can reap the huge reward of crystal rivers tumbling into marbled rock pools, peaks and rock faces enriched by ancient San paintings. Most elemental of all KwaZulu-Natal, the Berg sees dramatic thunderstorms in summer, with lightning flashing across huge charcoal skies.

KwaZulu-Natal experiences considerable variations in **climate**, from the occasional heavy winter snowstorms of the Drakensberg to the mellow, sunny days, pleasant sea temperatures and good surfing a couple of hundred kilometres away along the coast. This makes the region a popular winter getaway, but in midsummer (Jan, Feb & Dec) the low-lying areas, including Durban, the coastal belt and the game reserves, can experience an uncomfortably high humidity, relieved only by crashing thunderstorms.

DURBAN

Up to the 1970s, **DURBAN** was white South Africa's quintessential seaside playground – a status fostered by its tropical colours, oversized vegetation and an itinerant population of surfers, hedonists and holidaying Jo'burg families. The collapse in the 1980s of apartheid population-influx controls saw a growing stream of Africans flood in from rural KwaZulu-Natal – and even from as far afield as Zaire – to stake their claims in the

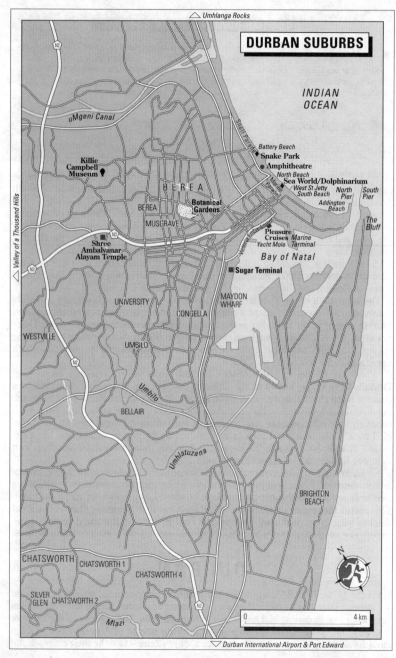

△ *Umhlanga Rocks*

DURBAN SUBURBS

*INDIAN
OCEAN*

uMgeni Canal

Battery Beach
Snake Park
● **Amphitheatre**
North Beach
Sea World/Dolphinarium
West St Jetty
South Beach
*North
Pier*
*South
Pier*
*Addington
Beach*

**Killie
Campbell
Museum**

B E R E A

BEREA

**Botanical
Gardens**

MUSGRAVE

*The
Bluff*

**Pleasure
Cruises**
Yacht Mole
*Marine
Terminal*

**Shree
Ambalvanar
Alayam Temple**

Bay of Natal

■ **Sugar Terminal**

UNIVERSITY

CONGELLA

MAYDON
WHARF

WESTVILLE

UMBILO

Umbilo

BELLAIR

Umhlatuzana

BRIGHTON
BEACH

CHATSWORTH
CHATSWORTH 1
CHATSWORTH 4

SILVER
GLEN
CHATSWORTH 2

Mlazi

0   4 km

N

◁ *Valley of a Thousand Hills*

▽ *Durban International Airport & Port Edward*

city centre with shantytowns and cardboard hovels that reveal the reality of one of the most unmistakably African conurbations in the country.

South Africa's third-largest city is a thriving industrial centre and the largest port in Africa, kept afloat by its **harbour**, which creates a photogenic place for meandering or eating and drinking at the dockside. Durban's second-largest population group, **Indians**, arrived here in the nineteenth century to work on the province's sugar plantations, and their mosques, bazaars and temples festooned with wildly coloured deities stand juxtaposed to the Victorian buildings that mark out the colonial centre.

The city's main interest lies not in its seaside, but its gritty urbanity, a seemingly endless struggle to reconcile competing **Indian**, **African** and **English cultures** and to keep the rampant vegetation at bay. There's enough here to keep you busy for a few days, looking at mosques, exploring the Indian area around Grey Street, or passing by the Dalton Road Zulu Market. However, most people come to Durban because it provides a logical springboard for the KwaZulu-Natal game parks, the Drakensberg and the Battlefields. Durban is well connected to the rest of South Africa by air and through intercity buses and trains, and some international flights touch down here.

Some history

Less than two hundred years ago, Durban was known to Europeans as **Port Natal**, a lagoon thick with mangroves, eyed by white adventurers who saw business opportunities in its ivory and hides. In 1824, a British party led by **Francis Farewell** persuaded the Zulu king, **Shaka**, to give them some land, which they planted with the Union Jack. Not long after the British went on to rename the settlement **Durban** after Sir Benjamin D'Urban, governor of the Cape Colony, whose support, they believed, might not come amiss later.

Britain's tenuous colonial toehold looked threatened in 1837 when **Boers** trundled over the Drakensberg in their ox wagons and declared their "Republic of Natalia" nearby. The threat was compounded the following year when a large force of now-hostile Zulus descended on the settlement and razed it, forcing the British residents to take refuge at sea in the *Comet*. Taking advantage of British absence, a group of Boers annexed Durban, later laying siege to a British detachment. This provided the cue for a much-celebrated piece of Victorian melodrama – familiar to every English-speaking school child in South Africa – when teenager **Dick King** heroically rode the 1000km from Durban to Grahamstown in ten days to alert the garrison there, which promptly dispatched a rescue detachment to relieve Durban.

While two-hundred-year-old Cape Town was on its way to becoming a cosmopolitan centre in the 1840s, Durban had a population of barely over one thousand, living basic existences in a near wilderness roamed by lions, leopards and hyenas. Things changed after Britain formally annexed the **Colony of Natal** in 1843; within ten years large-scale immigration of settlers from the mother country had begun. Over the next couple of decades all the niceties of English life – horse-racing, postal deliveries, two-storey houses and newspapers – started to make their appearance.

The promise of the industrial age, heralded in 1852 with the arrival of the first steamship, the *Sir Robert Peel* in Durban, actually pointed to the settlement's Achilles heel: the sand bar across the harbour mouth which prevented large vessels from entering. Work to clear it went on throughout the 1850s and beyond, while in 1860 the first railway tracks in town were laid and over three hundred indentured **Indian labourers** arrived to work in the KwaZulu-Natal cane fields, planting the seeds for South Africa's lucrative **sugar industry** and the city's now substantial Indian community.

The British **conquest of the Zulus** in 1879 and the imposition of taxes on them paved the way for their enforced entry into South Africa's growing cash economy and saw many heading north in the 1890s to work on the Gauteng goldfields, while others were drawn south to enter Durban's expanding economy. In 1895 the completion of the railway connecting Johannesburg and Durban accelerated the process of migrant labour, which still carries hundreds of thousands of Zulu workers to Johannesburg every year. This link to South Africa's industrial heartland, and the opening of Durban's harbour mouth to large ships in 1904, ensured the city's eventual pre-eminence as South Africa's principal harbour.

In 1922, in the face of growing Indian and African populations, Durban's strongly English city council introduced **legislation** to restrict the sale of land in the city to whites, predating Afrikaner-led apartheid by 26 years. During the boom years of World War II, **Africans** flooded into the city in yet greater numbers, leading to calls, which were ignored, for their recognition as permanent residents.

As **apartheid** began being strictly enforced in the 1950s, Durban saw a decade of ANC-led **protests**, starting with the country-wide Defiance Campaign in 1952 (see p.655) and reaching a peak in 1959 when *shebeen* queens (African women operating speakeasy bars) took to the streets and attacked municipal beer halls in protest at police harassment. The ANC was quick to seize this localized momentum and dovetailed it into nationwide marches and protests that led to nearly three years of turmoil, culminating in the apartheid government clampdown of 1961, when the authorities swamped the streets with troops, declared a state of emergency and banned the ANC. Left with no peaceful option, the ANC formed its armed wing, Umkhonto we Sizwe, with plans for a nationwide **bombing campaign** which by accident was initiated one day earlier than planned with an explosion in Durban on December 15, 1961. In the comprehensive swoop that followed, the government put most of the ANC's activists behind bars, effectively paving the way for a decade of unopposed apartheid.

Durban scored another first in 1973, when workers in the city initiated a wildcat strike, despite a total ban on black industrial action, heralding the rebirth of South Africa's **trade unions**, reawakening anti-apartheid activity and sparking the final phase of the country's road to democracy.

By the 1980s Durban had become the busiest port in Africa. By the 1990s, it was said to be the fastest-expanding city in the southern hemisphere, with thousands of people throwing up rude shacks in any open space or living rough in unimaginable numbers in the city centre.

Arrival and information

As a major industrial city and gateway to the country's densest ribbon of holiday beaches along the North and South coasts, Durban is served by international and domestic flights, intercity buses, backpacker buses, trains, and the ubiquitous informal minibus taxis.

The airport

Durban International Airport (international flight arrivals and departures ☎42 6111), 14km south of the centre on the Southern Freeway, receives flights from Europe, neighbouring countries and all the main centres inside South Africa. **Bus services** leave every hour (6am–9pm; ☎42 6111) from outside the domestic terminal to the *SAA* building on Aliwal Street in the city centre. For a small extra charge the bus will take you on request to any of the city-centre or beachfront hotels. More expensive is the *Super Shuttle* (☎469 0309 or 203 5407), which must be booked 24 hours ahead, and will pick up from either terminal and take you to anywhere in Durban. The shuttle is a better option than the rather unsalubrious **taxis** which rank outside the terminal exits. A **bank** at the international terminal keeps normal banking hours, and also opens whenever there are international arrivals.

The **telephone code** for Durban is ☎031.

Durban Station

Both the *Trans-Natal* service from Johannesburg and the interminable *Trans-Oranje* from Cape Town roll into the grim **New Durban Station** (☎361 7652), off NMR Avenue, just north of the main commercial centre. From here you can catch one of the *Mynah* buses (see "City transport"), which leave every fifteen minutes from outside the station, for the ten-minute ride into the city centre, pulling in at the Pine Street bus terminus, just east of Tourist Junction (see "information") in the same street. A more expensive and convenient option is to take one of the metered **taxis** that rank inside the station complex.

Intercity buses

The three main country-wide **bus operators**, *Greyhound* (☎309 7830), *Intercape* (☎021/386 4400) and *Translux* (☎361 8333) all end their runs at the **Motorcoach Terminal** attached to the train station complex. The *Margate Mini Coach* (☎03931/21406) from the South Coast pulls in both here and outside domestic departures at Durban airport. A number of smaller companies operating limited routes within the province use other arrival points: the *Cheetah Coach* (☎0331/42 2673) from Pietermaritzburg lets passengers off at the airport and outside the Local History Museum on Aliwal Street; the *Umhlanga Express* (☎561 2860) from Umhlanga Rocks drops off at a number of points in Durban, the most central of which is opposite Tourist Junction (see "Information"); the *Interport* service (☎0351/91791) leaving Richards Bay and travelling down the North Coast, winds up at the Pine Street bus terminal; and the *Baz* bus (☎021/439 2323), which travels in from Port Elizabeth on Tuesdays and Fridays, makes stops at all the Durban backpackers' lodges.

Long-distance minibus taxis

Long-distance **minibus taxis** from Gauteng arrive opposite the Umgeni Road entrance to the train station, while those from the South Coast and Transkei terminate at Berea Road in the Warwick Triangle area at the west of the city centre – both of these are very busy points where you should take care of your baggage. From both places, the city centre and beachfront accommodation is a fairly brisk walk away. If you're planning on staying in the Berea, you should catch a *Mynah* bus to Smith Street and the main bus depot, from where you'll be able to get another *Mynah* bus connection.

Information

The obvious first port of call for information is the central **Tourist Junction**, Old Station Building, 160 Pine St (Mon–Fri 8am–5pm, Sat & Sun 9am–2pm; ☎304 4934, fax 304 3868; email: funinsun@iafrica.com), which houses the city's tourist bureau, operating as *Durban Unlimited*, the Natal Parks Board booking office, accommodation agencies and a couple of travel agencies which book intercity coaches and tours.

Durban Unlimited can provide brochures and free maps of the city centre, but if you're planning on staying a while it's worth investing in one of the several street **map books** covering the city and suburbs in detail. *MapStudio* produces a whole range of maps from mid-priced fold-out plans of the city to pricier maps which include the surrounding areas. The best selection is at *Adams Bookshop*, 341 West St (☎304 8571) in the centre, or at *Exclusive Books*, Lower Level, Pavilion Shopping Centre, (☎265 0454), in the suburbs. You can also pick up maps at any branch of the *CNA* chain.

City transport

While **buses** cover the centre, beachfront and the Berea, you'll find it more difficult to get public transport to the suburbs. If you're **driving**, you'll find Durban fairly east to negotiate, though traffic on the freeways can be fast and aggressive.

Buses

Durban's most useful urban transport is offered by the cheap and regular **Mynah** (☎309 4126) and **Aqualine** (☎309 5942) **buses**, which cover the central districts, including the city centre, the beachfront and the Berea. If you want to get out to the more far-flung suburbs, *Durban Transport Municipal Buses* (phone number same as for *Mynah*), are quite functional though less salubrious and not as frequent. For quick and easy reference to times and routes, pop into the main bus depot, on the corner of Pine and Commercial streets, adjacent to the Workshop shopping mall, which is the starting point for local bus services.

Tuk tuks and mozziecabs

Cheaper than taxis, but more expensive than buses, **tuk tuks** are Asian-style three-wheel motorized rickshaws, while **mozziecabs** are Suzuki jeeps fashioned to resemble the original tuk tuks. Both will take you anywhere in central Durban, making them a convenient alternative to buses. The vehicles can take up to six people and work out cheaper the more of you there are in a group. Tuk tuks rank 24 hours a day at the *Beach Hotel*, opposite the Aquarium on Marine Parade, while mozziecabs (☎368 1114) must be contacted in advance for a pick-up.

Minibus taxis

Minibus taxis can be hailed down along any busy road – although they bear no obvious identification, you can usually recognize them by the frighteningly loud music blaring from their sound systems. To get to town or the beachfront from the Berea (or any

---

USEFUL BUS ROUTES FROM THE CITY CENTRE

- **To North/South Beach** (daily every 10min; 6.30am–11pm): *Mynah* buses leave from St Andrews Street on the north side of Albert Park, which stretches down to the Victoria Embankment at the western edge of the city centre (an inner-city strip of high-rise apartments best avoided at night, especially if you're carrying tourist trappings such as cameras). From here they turn north into Russell Street, before running all the way east to Marine Parade, where they either strike north as far as Battery Beach, or south as far as Addington Beach. Boards on the front of the bus indicate whether they are bound for North or South Beach. On their return trip buses head through the city centre along Smith instead of West Street.

- **To Berea – "Musgrave–Mitchell Park Circle"** (Mon–Fri every 10min; Sat slightly less frequent, Sun hourly; 6.30am–7pm). *Mynah* buses leave from the Pine Street bus depot and head east down Smith Street to the Berea, taking in Florida Road (restaurant strip) and Musgrave Road (Musgrave Centre), before returning to the city centre via Berea Road.

- **To Natal Society of Arts Gallery** (Mon–Fri every 30min; Sat less frequent, Sun 3 per day; 7am–5.30pm): *Aqualine* buses (route 86/87) leave from the Pine Street bus depot to Glenmore via Bulwer Road for the NSA Gallery.

DURBAN FERRIES

Apart from the journey from the north side of the harbour to the south, which saves a circuitous trek by road, scheduled **ferries** don't constitute a comprehensive form of transport in Durban. However, they can be an enjoyable way of seeing the harbour and spending a pleasant hour or so. *Durban Ferries* operates functional cruises (daily almost every hour 5am–11pm; ☎361 8727), taking fishermen, dock workers and sex workers across the harbour, departing opposite the Bat Centre jetty on the north side, at the bottom of Aliwal Street. From here the ferry sails around the harbour, taking in Pier 1 Container Depot and the Bluff before returning; the entire trip (including stops) takes two hours. One of the best ferries to catch is the 5pm departure, which gives you a chance to walk around the Bluff (known sometimes to the ferrymen as "West") and take in the sunset. The whole circuit is inexpensive and you can hop on and off along the way.

Another good service is the *Ferry Fun Rides* hopper ferry, operated by *Bay Services* (daily every 30min; 11am–7pm; ☎301 1953) that runs mini-rides along the northern harbour, serving the restaurants and pubs, starting at *Café Fish* ferry jetty on the Esplanade. As far as fun rides go, the *Sarie Marais* (☎305 4022) runs reasonably priced daily cruises at 11am around the harbour, and deep-sea outings at 11.30am and 2.30pm from the Gardiner Street jetty.

other suburb), stand along the sidewalk and signal assertively with an index finger. Once in the city centre, minibuses follow West Street to the beachfront, but turn south into Marine Parade as far as Addington Beach; you need to tell the driver where you want to get off.

Car and bike rental

The easiest way to explore Durban is in your own **car**. The city's freeways are well signposted, and careful map reading makes getting around pretty straightforward. You'll need to plan ahead, though, as Durban drivers are fast and there's no time to dither at lane changes and junctions. **Cycling** is fine along the beachfront, but hazardous on any major road. There are several **car rental** companies in Durban. To find out who's currently operating and where to get the best deal, either pick up one of the brochures at Tourist Junction or look in the *Yellow Pages* telephone directory. We've recommended some larger companies in "Listings" (p.362).

DURBAN TOURS

One of the safest and easiest ways to get under the skin of ethnic Durban is on a **guided tour**, which can get you into African and Indian areas or out-of-the-way places.

Tourist Junction, Old Station Building, 160 Pine St (☎304 4934, fax 304 3868). Staff here can arrange a number of excellent outings, including walking tours of the Grey Street area, "Oriental Durban" and the city centre and historical tours.

Tekweni Eco Tours, 169 Ninth Ave, PO Box 47773, Greyville (☎303 1199, fax 303 4369). Tours to Cato Manor township, east of the city centre, as well as day-trips to the Valley of a Thousand Hills and longer trips to the KwaZulu-Natal game parks.

Hamba Kahle Tours (☎707 1509). Options include a three-hour tour of Durban's townships, including Phoenix, where Gandhi lived, and a longer tour which takes in township *shebeens* and includes some partying.

Strelitzia Tours, 23 Serpentine Drive, Westville (☎86 1904). Daily minibus trips around the major sights, the centre and the Berea, as well as trips further afield, to the game parks and the Battlefields.

Accommodation

Durban's **accommodation** is concentrated along the **beachfront**, where sleek towers of chain hotels with sea views and swimming pools offer comfortable but pricey places to stay. Far more affordable are the scores of self-catering **apartments** (some with sea views, others a block or two back), which can be exceptional value for several people sharing. Staying at the beachfront ensures you're close to the action and only a few minutes from the central business district, and the area is well served with buses and taxis. Accommodation tends to be scarce during school holidays, and much more expensive in the peak holiday month of December.

The **city centre** is an obviously convenient location to stay, but it's not great at night, when the streets are deserted and potentially menacing. Taking private taxis or tuk tuks to your doorstep is recommended if you're returning to your hotel after dark. An alternative to the city centre and beachfront is the cool and leafy **Berea** residential area, ten minutes west of the centre and with excellent restaurants and cafés. You'll find the best backpackers' lodge here, as well as a couple of other budget guesthouses, and B&Bs where you can smell the frangipani and tropical scents on balmy nights.

Beachfront

The Balmoral, 125 Marine Parade (☎368 5940, fax 368 5955). Dark timbers and historical photographs of Durban when the wetlands were king create a serious, colonial atmosphere. The verandah is magnificent for sipping drinks on balmy summer nights while watching the buzz along the Marine Parade and the ocean beyond. ⑤.

The Beach Hotel, 107 Marine Parade (☎37 5511, fax 37 4222). Bland but spacious rooms with great views. The major drawcard is the lively sea-side verandah that buzzes with punters from the hotel's pubs and restaurants, which open onto the space. ④.

The Blue Waters Hotel, 175 Snell Parade (☎32 4272, fax 37 5817). Delightful 1950s Durban extravaganza opposite Battery Beach, with mangroves on the pavement and plush furnishing inside. The leisure lounge has great views onto the oceanfront. ④.

The Edward, Marine Parade (☎37 3681, fax 32 1692). Draping crystal chandeliers, dense colonial-style ambience and sea-view balconies make this Art Deco mansion the *grande dame* of the beachfront. The ladies' bar downstairs leads out onto a cool verandah. ⑥.

Golden Sands Holiday Apartments, 95 Snell Parade (☎368 2995, fax 37 1825). Functional self-catering apartments entirely saved by the (more expensive) rooms with magnificent sea views. Conveniently opposite North Beach and the Amphitheatre, the rooms are good value if there are three of you, and downright cheap for four or five sharing. ③.

Holiday Inn Crowne Plaza, 63 Snell Parade (☎37 1321, fax 32 5527). Spacious public rooms and an aquarium in the foyer make this 21-storey beachfront hotel a cool, calm retreat from the busy North Beach and Amphitheatre. ⑥.

Holiday Inn Garden Court–Marine Parade, 167 Marine Parade (☎37 3341, fax 32 9885). Crisp mirage with a cool through-breeze and tropical vegetation offering respite against the summer heat. While all the rooms face the sea, those on the top floors are best, and the vista from the thirtieth-floor swimming pool is fabulous. A back entrance across from Victoria Park provides handy access to the city centre. ⑤.

Holiday Inn Garden Court–North Beach, 83/91 Snell Parade (☎32 7361, fax 37 4058). Light and leafy hotel with all the trimmings and large rooms with separate sitting areas. Good beach access and 5min from the city centre by foot. ⑤.

Impala Holiday Flats, 40 Gillespie St (☎332 3232). Large family apartments and bachelor units sleeping two to six people, one block back from South Beach, close to the Wheel Shopping Centre and *Aldo's* and the *Villa D'Este* restaurants. ②.

Palace Protea Hotel, 211 Marine Parade (☎32 8351, fax 32 8307). Modern Art Deco landmark on Durban's Golden Mile, offering self-catering apartments opposite the Durban Fun Fair, and good access into the city centre along East St. ③.

San Marina Holiday Flats, 85 Hospital Rd (☎37 3842 or 37 0826). With fair-sized open-plan units, these self-catering apartments, an easy walk to Addington Beach, are a little pricey if there are just two of you, but can sleep up to five at a budget rate per person. ②–③.

Seaboard Protea Hotel & Holiday Flats, corner of West and Point roads (☎37 3601, fax 37 2600). Three-star hotel rooms and self-catering holiday apartments sleeping up to four, equidistant between the beach and town, in a tall block offering east-facing sea views. ③–④.

Silversands, 16 Erskine Terrace, South Beach (☎32 7931). Along the far end of Addington Beach, near the *Addington Hospital*, these spacious apartments sleeping two to six people (and cheaper for more sharing) are clean and comfortable. ③.

Treasured Holidays, Mangrove Beach Centre, 91 Somtseu Rd, North Beach (☎368 1192, fax 368 3411). Self-catering, fully equipped apartments that are clean and tastefully decorated in a combination of postmodern and wholesome family decor, diagonally opposite the Amphitheatre. Two to six sleepers work out cheaper per head in the larger units. ③.

City centre

Backpackers Club International, 154 Point Rd (☎32 0511). Conveniently located just 200m from the harbour and 350m from the nearest beach, with pool tables, a bar, bike rental and kitchen facilities. Meals are available and there's free collection from the airport or central Durban. ①.

Banana Backpackers, 61 Pine St, 1st Floor, Ambassador House (☎368 4062). Stuffy dorms and doubles in an old Durban building with a congenial courtyard. In the heart of the city, very close to Tourist Junction and the bus terminal. ①.

City Lodge Durban, corner of Brickhill and Old Fort roads (☎32 1447, fax 32 1483). Comfortable rooms in this smart hotel at the edge of the city, catering mainly to business travellers. ④.

Hotel Formule 1, corner of NMR Ave and Jeff Taylor St (☎301 1551). No frills at this clean, budget hotel right next to the train station, with a flat room rate making it only slightly pricier than a backpackers' hostel if there are two or three of you. ①–②.

Le Plaza Hotel, 9 Broad St (☎ & fax 301 2591). Reasonable rooms at the south end of the city, near the harbour and with an in-house restaurant. ④.

The Royal Hotel, 267 Smith St (☎304 0331, fax 307 6884). Durban's finest hotel, and a local institution in the city centre. It's used mainly by business visitors, but is worth considering if you can afford five-star splendour and fancy the liveried service. The legendary *Ulundi* Indian restaurant is also here. ⑦.

The Berea

Hotel California, 170 Florida Rd, Morningside (☎ & fax 303 1146). Genteel architecture and multiple eateries in an establishment above *Lams Restaurant* and *Bonkers* club, in the heart of the Florida Road nightlife strip. Avoid Wednesday nights if loud music is not your scene, as this is the night *Bonkers* sizzles. ③.

The Elephant House, 745 Ridge Rd (☎28 9580). B&B in Durban's oldest house, built in 1850 as a hunting lodge, in the tranquil part of the Ridge where the vegetation has won the day. The owners have a good collection of African literature. ③.

Florida Lodge, 258 Florida Lodge, Morningside (☎23 9436). Well-situated and extremely cheap guesthouse along lively Florida Rd, with direct bus routes into town. Parking space and TV lounge. Room-only rate. ①.

Napier House, 31 Napier Rd (☎207 6779). Clean, crisp rooms with the ambience of a country estate and an expansive view over the city. ④.

Nutall Gardens, 12 Nutall Gardens, Morningside (☎23 9045). Dignified opulence at a B&B in a quiet part of Durban, with rich colours, generous bedding and original South African artworks. ④.

Tekweni Backpackers, 9th Ave, Morningside (☎303 1433, fax 303 4369). Dorms and doubles at this favourite Durban backpacker spot in a converted old house well-situated just off Florida Rd. The atmosphere is chilled-out, and the bar serves drinks on a shady, cool verandah. Guests have the use of the kitchen, pool room, swimming pool and leisure lounge. ①.

The City

Durban's **city centre**, confined by the Bay of Natal to its south and the beaches of the Indian Ocean to its east, grew around the arrival point of the first white settlers. The remains of the historical heart, some monumental Victorian and Edwardian buildings, including the City Hall, are concentrated around **Francis Farewell Square**, five minutes by foot north of the bay. The central business area's flat grid, studded with high-rise buildings, is full of traffic and one-way street systems, and with no views of the ocean gives scarcely a hint you're in a seaside city.

On the western side of the city centre, around Grey and Victoria streets, is Durban's most fascinating area, the **Indian district.** This is where you'll find a pulsing warren of bazaars, alleyways, the Juma mosque and Victoria Street market, as well as Zulu traders selling *umuthi* (traditional herbal medicines). Although the laws which enforced the divide between the white-dominated business centre and the Indian district have gone, each area still bears a distinct feel. Further west and deeper downtown, the **Warwick Triangle**, situated in the hub of taxi ranks and bus depots, seethes with ceaseless activity. The poorest of the poor spend the nights on their market stalls here under plastic and cardboard, and *shebeens* do a brisk trade in this great African interchange of one of the world's most rapidly urbanizing cities.

Durban's **beachfront**, or "Golden Mile", on the eastern edge of the centre, is the magnet that pulls thousands upon thousands of white Jo'burgers down to "Durbs" every year. Although the beachfront's reputation for growing crime has sent many of the middle-class families scurrying out to safer beaches up the North and South coasts, you'll still find one of the city's greatest, and best-used, concentrations of restaurants and a surfeit of tacky family entertainment here.

South of the centre, skirting the north of the bay, **Victoria Embankment**, historically one of Durban's most desirable residential areas, is witnessing a decline as former residents attempt to escape its city-rim apartment blocks. The Embankment provides access to the northern side of the **harbour**, which despite its handful of trendy pubs and restaurants, offers a compelling industrial marinescape that is the real economic hub of the city. Protruding south from the southern corner of the city centre and the beachfront to enclose the northern half of the harbour, the **Point** is a seedy red-light peninsula which nevertheless has a couple of decent pubs and the best view of the city across the water.

Rising above the flat city centre and harbour is the **Berea**, a desirable residential district on a cooler ridge, which despite its proximity to the centre has luxuriant gardens alive with the sounds of birds, and fashionable restaurants, cinemas and shopping malls. Further afield lie the **western suburbs**, including Pinetown, Westville, Kloof, Gillitts and Hillcrest, while further still are the apartheid **ghettos** of KwaMashu, Inanda, Clermont to the northwest and Umlazi to the southwest – dormitory towns for blacks who commute vast distances to work every day. **Cato Manor**, the closest township to the city, provides an easily accessible vignette of South Africa's growing urban contradictions.

The centre

Francis Farewell Square, a sultry palm-fringed garden overlooked by some fine old buildings, stands at the heart of colonial Durban. Hemmed in by the centre's two main thoroughfares, West Street to its north and Smith Street to its south, it was here that the British adventurists, Francis Farewell and Henry Fynn, set up Durban's first white encampment to trade ivory with the Zulus. Today, down-and-outs enjoy its lawns, dotted with statues of city fathers, while the yellows and blues of the **Cenotaph**, a marvellous Art Deco monument to the fallen of World War I, creates an eye-catching focus for the square. The granite obelisk is decorated with ceramics depicting angels delivering the soul of a dead soldier. Regarded initially by Durban's prim citizens as improperly vibrant, it clearly also offended an anti-apartheid activist, who bombed it in 1984. Today the monument is intact. North of Farewell Square are the pathetic remnants of the **Natal Great Railway Station**, 160 Pine St, built in 1894 and recycled a century later as shops and the Tourist Junction information centre.

City Hall and around

On the south side of the Francis Farewell Square, the imposing neo-Baroque **City Hall**, erected in 1910, is the monumental centrepiece of the city-centre area and now houses the **Natural Science Museum** (Mon–Sat 8.30am–5pm, Sun 11am–5pm; free) on its ground floor. Along with an array of stuffed animals (useful if you want to bone up on your mammals before heading north to the game reserves), is the "KwaNunu" section, featuring oversized insects, such as cockroaches – all a little too close to home for anyone living in Durban, where such creatures, known as "Durban prawns", are an ongoing menace and a constant topic for urban legends.

A far better reason to cross the City Hall's threshold is to visit the **Durban Art Gallery** (same times; free) upstairs, which has a fine collection that includes Art Nouveau glassware by Lalique, bronzes by Rodin and Victorian paintings, but is most notable for its pioneering vision in the 1970s in becoming the first gallery in the country to collect **black South African art**. This approach has since expanded into the recognition of indigenous craft as an art form of equal status with painting or sculpture, which is why the gallery has an outstanding collection of *hlabisa* baskets, a refined form indigenous to KwaZulu-Natal. In no way to be confused with cheap souvenirs bought at roadside stalls, *hlabisa* represents a traditional craft, revived in the province around two decades ago, and now highly sought after by galleries and collectors worldwide. Although this is traditionally a woman's activity, one of the most highly regarded proponents of *hlabisa* is a man, **Reuben Ndwandwe**, whose work is particularly worth looking out for.

West of the City Hall, the **African Art Centre**, Guildhall Arcade, 35 Gardiner St (Mon–Thurs 8.30am–5pm, Fri 7.30am–4pm, Sat 9am–1pm, Sun 8am–12.30pm; free), is the heart of Durban's artistic life, where many rural artists sell their work. Primarily a gallery and shop, the centre is also involved in work to move rural craftsmen away from the production of curios and towards artistic expression. Tito Zungu, who draws pen-and-ink aeroplanes and boats; Bheki Myeni, who sculpts wooden insects; and Mzwakhe Mbatha, originally an airline cook, who now carves wooden aircraft, are a few artists who have gained recognition through this centre.

East of the City Hall, on the corner of Smith Street, the **Local History Museum** (Mon–Sat 8.30am–5pm, Sun 11am–5pm; free), with its entrance in Aliwal Street, occupies the Old Courthouse. Durban's first two-storey building was erected in 1866 in the Natal Verandah style, characterized by wide eaves to throw off heavy subtropical downpours. The atmosphere is somewhat austere, but, if you want to see a reconstruction of Henry Francis Fynn's daub and wattle hut, Durban's first European structure, then this is the place to come. A display of miniature models of historical figures including the Zulu kings from Shaka to Mpande resembles an arrested game of Battlefields. The temporary displays can be interesting: at the time of writing one featured the *amalisho*, or rickshaw pullers, who have provided the alternative transport in Durban since 1892.

North of the Local History Museum, along Aliwal Street, is **The Workshop**, a mall which sounds more interesting than it proves to be, although it does provide parking and every type of shop you're likely to need, conveniently close to Tourist Junction. On its north side, **Central Park**, with a lovely mosaic water fountain as its focus, offers a large green space. The **Exhibition Centre** in nearby Walnut Road is the venue for a busy Sunday flea market, where you can pick up trinkets, authentic didgeridoos and (a hot tip if you need footwear) handmade leather shoes and hiking boots from the

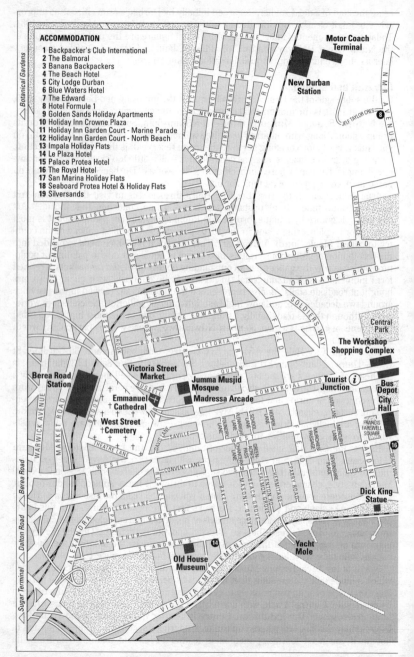

ACCOMMODATION
1 Backpacker's Club International
2 The Balmoral
3 Banana Backpackers
4 The Beach Hotel
5 City Lodge Durban
6 Blue Waters Hotel
7 The Edward
8 Hotel Formule 1
9 Golden Sands Holiday Apartments
10 Holiday Inn Crowne Plaza
11 Holiday Inn Garden Court - Marine Parade
12 Holiday Inn Garden Court - North Beach
13 Impala Holiday Flats
14 Le Plaza Hotel
15 Palace Protea Hotel
16 The Royal Hotel
17 San Marina Holiday Flats
18 Seaboard Protea Hotel & Holiday Flats
19 Silversands

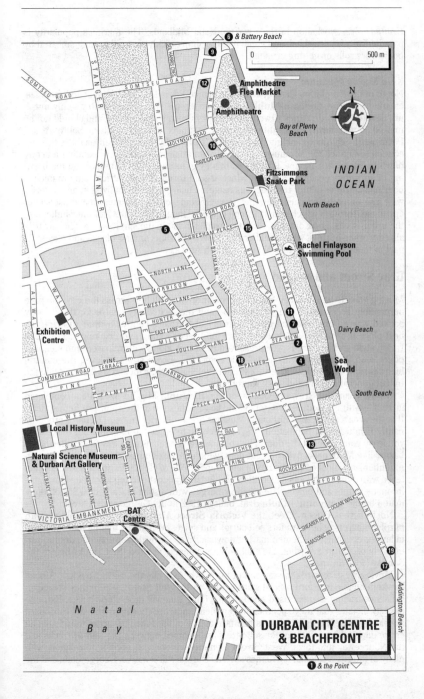

DURBAN CITY CENTRE & BEACHFRONT

Ground Cover workshop in the KwaZulu-Natal Midlands. The market's popularity is paradoxically its drawback and you'll need to shop quickly to avoid getting smeared by boerewors rolls or getting crushed.

Kwa Muhle Museum

North of the Exhibition Centre, at 130 Ordnance Rd, is Durban's newest and most fascinating museum, the **Kwa Muhle** (daily 8am–5pm). This is the country's only museum devoted to South Africa's twentieth-century urban social history, and should not be missed if you have the slightest interest in understanding modern South Africa. Permanent exhibitions include one on the "Durban System", which enabled the city council to finance the administration of African affairs without ever spending a penny of white ratepayers' money. It achieved this by granting itself a monopoly on the brewing of sorghum (grain beer) beer, which it sold through vast, African-only municipal beer halls. The resulting revenue was used to ensure that blacks lived in an "orderly" way. The exhibit also illustrates the "Pass System", one of the most hated aspects of apartheid, through which constant tabs could be kept on Africans and their influx into the urban areas. Look out, too, for photographs of life in the single-sex, artificially tribalized worker hostels, which deliberately sowed divisions among blacks and played its part in much of the current violence in South Africa.

Grey Street and around

Moving west to where **Grey Street** draws a north–south line across the city, the pace perceptibly accelerates, and you leave behind the formal city centre for the densely packed warren of shops and living quarters of Durban's central **Indian district**, the best place in town to sample local spicy food (see "Eating and drinking"). Post-1910 Union style architecture is well-preserved here and, along with minarets and steeples, punctuates the skyline with an eclectic roofscape. Down at street level, the cultural blend is rich, with African sidewalk vendors selling herbs, fruit and trinkets outside the Indian general dealers and spice merchants.

On the corner of Grey and Queen streets, the **Juma Musjid Mosque** – completed in 1927 – with gilt-domed minarets is the largest mosque in the southern hemisphere. It is the area's focal point, although Muslims are a minority among Durban's predominantly Hindu Indian population. You're welcome to enter the mosque, but make sure you leave your shoes at the door. The colonnaded verandahs give way to the alley of the bazaar-like **Madressa Arcade** next door, which provides tantalizing glimpses through mountains of coloured plastic bowls and draped bolts of cloth into general dealers cluttered with aluminium pots and kettles, and Indian traders peddling kerosene lamps, tailor-made outfits and beads. The arcade emerges with a start in Cathedral Street, dominated by the **Emmanuel Cathedral**, built in 1902 in the Gothic revival style.

North across Queen Street, the **Victoria Street Market** is a bright building with purple minarets, where traders sell curios and spices with labels that include "mother-in-law exterminator". The fish market downstairs can provide some hectic drama, particularly on Saturdays when the stall holders compete to shed their stocks before the Sunday close-down.

Moving west, towards the fag-end of town (where it hits the railway tracks), African hawkers unable to afford official stalls gather on **Russell Street**, where they scrape an existence trading *umuthi*, used goods or anything that will raise a few bucks. Extreme poverty dictates that they spend nights on their market pitches in plastic and cardboard hovels, because the daily minibus taxi fare to any of the township areas would cost an entire day's takings. West of Russell Street and jammed between the railway tracks and the N3 freeway into town, **West Street Cemetery** is zoned according to religion, with many of the city's colonial big names such as Durban's first mayor, George Cato, and the

Victorian documentary painter, Thomas Baines, buried here. In the Muslim section some tombstones are inscribed "hagee" or "hafez", the former indicating someone who has been to Mecca and the latter an individual who managed to memorize the entire Koran.

If the crowds feel too intimidating, you can always explore this area on one of the reasonably priced daily **walking tours** of the area from Tourist Junction (see box, p.343).

Warwick Triangle

In an Africanized *Bladerunner* setting west of Grey Street, concrete freeways run overhead chaotic roadways and minibus taxi ranks; here you'll find Durban's real urban heart of hawkers, shacks and *shebeens*. You'll need to be bold to explore the **Warwick Triangle**, which lies between Berea Road, Brooke Street and Cannongate – it's wise go in a group, leave your camera behind and wear nothing snatchable.

The gateway to the triangle is across Brooke Street, which until 1988 was known as "Slaughterhouse Road" (because butchers slaughtered livestock here) and through the Berea station concourse across the Market Road footbridge to the market area between Market Road and Warwick Avenue. The station concourse, which services African townships, pumps with reggae and the music of popular South African musicians such as Lucky Dube, while hawkers sell baseball caps, patent leather shoes and tortoise shells. As you move across the footbridge, take a look at the truncated flyover alongside the station, going nowhere, but now the site for shacks. On a buttress at the end of the flyover, an eight-metre mural of the African goddess Nomkhubulwana stretches out her arms in a gesture of greeting and protection.

Durban's major fruit, vegetable and flower **market** is between Warwick Avenue and Market Road, operating in the early morning only, with selling extending well beyond its walls in a dense mass of vendors. Shopping is frenetic; take your own basket and load up with the cheapest produce in town, from aubergines and jackfruit to beetlenut leaf for red-stained lips and a two-minute rush.

Victoria Embankment and the harbour vicinity

The **Victoria Embankment**, or the Esplanade, running along the harbour edge, south of the city, is Durban's palm-lined city avenue connecting Point Road in the east to Maydon Wharf Road, which leads to the container terminal piers and the dry dock off Bay Road in the west. During the city's early development in the nineteenth century, the Embankment was the prime residential area and it's here, one block north at the east end of the road, that the **Old House Museum**, 31 St Andrews St (Mon–Sat 8.30am–5pm, Sun 8.30–11.50am; small entry fee), is sited. Once the home of Sir John Robinson, who became Natal's first prime minister in 1893, the renovated settler house serves as a reminder of Durban's colonial heritage.

About 500m west along the Embankment you'll hit the entrance to the **Yacht Mole**, a slender breakwater jutting into the bay and home to the Point and Royal Natal Yacht clubs. A walk along here to look at the amazing variety of craft provides a photogenic view of Durban from across the water and a breather from the city traffic. A little further west along the dockside, a statue of **Dick King** re-enacts his heroic ride to save Durban (see p.339), and if you keep in the same direction along the Embankment you'll reach the **Bat Centre**, a focal point for arts in the city. This industrial-chic venue right on the dockside offers a concert hall, practical visual art workshops and yoga classes, while the *Blue Chip Café* provides a magnificent lookout for watching the passing harbour scene.

Back on the Esplanade, towards the Stanger Street intersection, enter the Harbour at Port Entrance no. 3 and follow the signs to the **Ocean Terminal Building**, which harks back to the romantic days of sea travel and is one of Durban's architectural masterpieces. Formerly the harbour reception building, this is now the headquarters for *Portnet*, the public utility that maintains South Africa's harbours. Although you can't enter the building, the view from outside it at night, looking back onto the city, is spectacular.

Striking south from from the city centre and Winder Street, the eastern extension of Victoria Embankment, **Point Road**, known in its heyday in the early 1900s as Africa's most exciting thoroughfare and Durban's hottest red-light district, cuts down the **Point**, the northernmost of the two arms that enclose the Bay of Natal to contain Durban's harbour. At the city end of the road are cheap and tawdry hotels which rent out rooms by the hour, late-night takeaways, loud drunks and scantily clad women lingering by the roadside.

Along the section between Camperdown and Browns roads, a row of derelict **warehouses** built between 1890 and 1900 provides the setting for occasional raves. **King's Battery Development** to the southwest, in the old gun battery building along the North Pier, has been refurbished as an eating and drinking venue (see "Eating and drinking" and "Nightlife and entertainment"). Situated at the mouth of the harbour with views of the South Pier and the Bluff across the water, the setting is gloriously surreal as ships are guided through the narrow harbour mouth by pilot tugs.

Maydon Wharf wraps around the harbour edge to the west in a photogenic complex of functional industrial architecture, most notable of which are the three dramatic sugar silos at the **Sugar Terminal**, 57 Maydon Wharf Rd, which are dedicated to storing Durban's white gold (one of the city's biggest revenue-earners) and whose design has been patented and used internationally. To find out about daily guided tours of the terminal, phone ☎303 0331.

Inland from the Sugar Terminal, across the Southern Freeway, the Dalton Road area clings closer to the city centre than any other African residential area. Craftsmen toil in the dingy hive of activity that constitutes **Dalton Road Market**, turning out traditional Zulu costume and regalia including *amabheshu* (leather aprons), shields, *izimboko* (staffs), dancing sticks and beadwork. Every Saturday night, the *Dalton Road Men's Hostel* comes alive with *isicatamiya* concerts (see box, p.686), which start around midnight and continue into the small hours. The concerts are competitions in which groups sing in unaccompanied harmony. This genuine Durban experience, not aimed at tourists, is well worth catching, but it's advisable to come to this ropy part of town at night (doors open around 11.30pm) only if you feel confident or are accompanied by a knowledgeable local.

The beachfront

Durban's **beachfront**, a high-energy holiday strip just east of the city centre, is South Africa's most developed seaside, and one to avoid unless you enjoy unabashed kitsch and garish amusement parks. This six-kilometre stretch from the Umgeni River in the north to the Point in the south was traditionally called the **Golden Mile**, but is fast becoming known as "Mugger's Mile", which is why so many middle-class Gauteng fam-

BEACHFRONT SAFETY

Durban's **beaches** are notorious hunting grounds for sharks – not of the piscean variety. **Muggings** are common, though frequently avoidable if you take precautions. Despite repeated warnings, tourists continue to venture onto beaches wearing expensive watches and jewellery and carrying large wads of cash – highly attractive bait. On the beachfront you should stay in a group, and at night never go out alone, no matter how enticing the seafront seems on a balmy evening. Street children are an occupational hazard in most South African cities and they positively thrive on the rich pickings of Durban's beachfront. No matter how small they look, make no mistake – many are skilful pickpockets and accomplished bag-snatchers.

ilies are breaking the habit of generations and deserting the beachfront for the safer (white middle-class) sands north and south of Durban.

Addington Beach, the southernmost swimming strand and a favourite spot for apprentice sufers, with a smaller swell, draws Durban families to its wide expanse of sand and lawns for sunbathing. Just north lies **South Beach**, the busiest beach in South Africa, which packs tight at peak times, and nets visitors with the start of the beachfront tourist tack: a refreshment and shopping complex and the dubious attraction of *Sea World Durban* (daily 9am–9pm; dolphin shows 10am, 11.30am, 1pm, 2.30pm & 4pm; shark feeding Tues, Thurs & Sun 12.30pm; R22), with its tropical aquaria, tanks of sharks, and performing dolphins, seals and penguins.

Further along Marine Parade, you'll find paddling pools, fountains, stepping stones, bridges, an aerial cableway and amusement rides. The only redeeming feature along here is the saltwater **Rachel Finlayson Baths** (☎37 2721), which offer sheltered swimming and sunbathing. Next is **Dairy Beach**, so called because of the milking factory that once stood here. Dairy Beach is now known as one of the best surfing beaches and is home to the Oceans Entertainment Centre, whose bars and restaurants are popular with the surfer-groupie crowd.

Dairy Beach adjoins **North Beach** and the adjacent **Bay of Plenty**, both of which make up the venue for the international Gunston 500 surfing contest held every July. North Beach is Durban's prime angling, bathing and surfing beach, made even more popular by the presence of hip bars and restaurants. Between Snell Parade and the pedestrian walkway at the Bay of Plenty is the **Amphitheatre**, the venue for Sunday flea markets, where local hawkers are joined by travelling merchants from Zimbabwe, Malawi and as far afield as Kenya, who trundle down the continent to sell their wares, trading for two weeks, before returning to restock. Any surplus goods are sold at cost to the Zulu traders who line the whole Marine Parade. The rickshaws also gather here with their ornate carriages and elaborately decorated Zulu pullers decked out in beads and streamers. Just north of the Bay of Plenty, on the corner of Snell Parade and Old Fort Road, is the **Fitzsimmons Snake Park** (daily 9am–5pm; R10), which offers the chance to gawp at reptiles in cramped glass boxes. Continuing north, the beachfront hype steadily diminishes with the less frenetic **Battery Beach**, with its good swimming and fewer crowds.

The Berea

West of the city centre, high on a ridge that cuts north–south, the **Berea** is Durban's oldest and most desirable residential district, where mansions and apartment blocks enjoy airy views to the harbour and the sea. Its palmy avenues provide an alternative focus for accommodation, eating and entertainment, away from the torrid atmosphere of the city centre and beachfront.

Undulating **Ridge Road** cuts a six-kilometre axis through the Berea from the Umgeni River in the north to the University of Natal. South of the N3, which passes through the Berea to the city, and east of Ridge Road, the **Natal Society of Arts (NSA)** (Tues–Fri 10am–6pm, Sat & Sun 10am–4pm; free), adjacent to Bulwer Park, provides a breezy venue for taking in fortnightly exhibitions of work by local artists and for relaxing in a great coffee shop. Designed for the local climate, the 1990s building is a spacious mass of interlinked volumes, divided by a timber screen that forms a verandah. The gallery shop has a good collection of original art pieces and cheaper, jazzy creations.

In **Upper Berea**, north of Berea Road, the **Botanical Gardens**, on the corner of Edith Benson and St Thomas roads, offers a pleasantly shady break from the surrounding urban torpor, with cool paths, excellent picnic spots (especially alongside the duck pond), a lovely tea house and a magnificent orchid collection. Established in 1849, the gardens are famous for their cycad collection, which includes *Encephalartos woodii*, one of the rarest specimens in the world. A notice board outside the entrance advertises forthcoming functions, including Natal Philharmonic Orchestra **concerts**, which are regularly held here.

Heading north for several blocks up Musgrave Road and west into Marriot Road, on the corner of Essenwood Road you'll find another magnificent garden at the **Killie Campbell Museum** (Tues & Thurs by appointment only; ☎207 3432; free). This is Durban's premier museum, and holds one of the finest private collections of Africana in the country. Housed in Muckleneuk, the Cape Dutch-revival former homestead of sugar baron Sir Marshal Campbell, it now falls under the University of Natal. Fine examples of KwaZulu-Natal's ethnic heritage are exhibited here, with a superb collection of Zulu crafts that includes tools, weapons, beadwork and pottery.

North of the Musgrave Shopping Centre, Musgrave Road briefly becomes Woodley Road before colliding with **Florida Road**, Durban's most fashionable place to eat, and characterized by many splendidly restored Edwardian villas, the majority of which are now offices. Most notable are **Atherton**, 295 Florida Rd, and **Cottam Grove**, 303 & 309 Florida Rd, both of which have been declared National Monuments.

Cato Manor

A short drive west of the city centre takes you through **Cato Manor**, a graphic slice through the Durban's twentieth-century history, where you can see the juxtaposition of African squatter camps, Hindu temples and entropic vegetation mingling in the heart of the city's middle-class suburbs. A large area in a valley below the Berea, Cato Manor was named after Durban's first mayor, **George Cato**, who arrived here in 1839. During the first half of this century, the district was home to much of Durban's Indian community, who built temples on its hills. They were later joined by Africans, who were forced into crowded slums because of the shortage of housing. In 1949, a petty incident flared up into Durban's worst **riot**, when thousands of Africans attacked Indian stores and houses, leaving 142 people dead.

Because Cato Manor was bang in the middle of white suburbs, the apartheid government began enforcing the Group Areas Act in the 1960s, and moved Africans north to KwaMashu and Indians south to Chatsworth, leaving a derelict wasteland guarded only by the handful of Hindu temples left standing. The vacuum was filled again in the late 1980s, when Africans pouring into Durban set up the closely packed tin shacks that line Bellair Road, which winds its way through Cato Manor's valley.

Along this interesting and safe drive it's well worth stopping to visit the **Shree Ambalvanar Alayam Second River Hindu Temple**, a National Monument in Bellair Road, which has no number but is on your right (just before the Edwin Swales freeway), if you're coming from town. The building is a 1947 reconstruction of the first Hindu temple in Africa, built in 1875 on the banks of the Umbilo River and subsequently destroyed by floods. The facade is adorned with a pantheon of wonderfully garish Hindu deities and the beautifully carved entrance doors are the originals salvaged from the flood. Around Easter every year the temple hosts a **firewalking festival** in which unshod devotees walk across red-hot coals to emerge unscathed. Visitors are welcome to join the melèe of thousands of worshippers who come every year to honour the goddess Draudpadi. To get to Bellair Road, leave the city centre on the M13, take the Brickfield Road exit, turning left into the M10; this becomes Bellair Road.

Eating and drinking

Eating out is a favourite pastime in Durban, whether you're a suburbanite relishing the seafood of a swanky restaurant or an African worker shelling out a few rand for a filling Indian take away. Although you'll find all types of cooking here, **Indian** food is what

Durban excels at – hardly surprising for a city with one of the largest Indian populations outside Asia. Perhaps less obviously, Durban also has some fine **Portuguese** restaurants, serving food which is often imported from Mozambique, with highly spiced *peri-peri* dishes, of which chicken is the most common variety and prawns the tastiest. And of course, in this port city **seafood** is excellent and found on the menu at most restaurants.

For a city that prides itself on its dedication to hedonism, Durban turns in disappointingly early, **closing time** for most restaurants being around 10.30pm. A notable exception is *Legends* in the Musgrave Shopping Centre, which is open past midnight. The best areas for restaurants are the city centre, along the beachfront and the Berea district. Prices are generally very reasonable, though you'll pay more for seafood. For Indian food, the best selection is in the Grey Street area; for fish, there's no better venue than the industrial marine landscape of the harbour. It's a good idea to **phone** before you set out, as opening hours tend to change frequently.

Durban's big contribution to the national fast-food scene is *bunny chow*, a cheap and filling scooped-out half-loaf of bread traditionally stuffed with curried beans, but now available with an array of mutton, vegetable, beef or even tinned fish curries. In a similar vein are curries wrapped in *roti* (a traditional Indian pancake). Down at the African markets and around the taxi ranks, you'll find *shisanyama* outlets, where you can buy a hunk of meat cooked on an open fire.

If you're **self-catering**, you can buy groceries at any of the supermarket chains which you'll find in shopping malls. **Tropical fruit** such as mangoes, papayas, bananas, litchis, pineapples, guavas and granadillas are available in season from supermarkets and street traders and at the Indian market off Warwick Avenue. In summer, try masala pineapple – cubes of the skewered fruit sprinkled with red-hot spices.

Beachfront

Aldo's, 15 Gillespie St (☎37 0900). One of Durban's oldest Italian restaurants, in the mid-price range, one street back from the beachfront, with a lively atmosphere. Their *panzarotti* (little spinach and ricotta-filled pockets) is recommended. Closed Sun.

The Chartroom Smorgasbord, *Edward Hotel*, 149 Marine Parade (☎37 3681). Delicious breakfasts on the terrace and very good smorgasbord lunches at one of the beachfront's hotels, where you'll find a magnificent and reasonably priced spread of seafoods, including crayfish oysters and kalamari. Open daily.

Coimbra, 130 Gillespie St (☎368 4614). Choose your own lobster in this first-class but mid-priced Portuguese restaurant frequented by businessmen, and in a seedy part of town. Closed Mon.

Villa D'Este, 29 Gillespie St (☎37 0264). One of the oldest and best places in town for seafood, clinging onto an old-fashioned Italian charm, with an expensive menu. Closed Mon.

City centre

Aangans, 86 Queen St. Wildly exotic but totally authentic and phenomenally cheap Indian cuisine, which you're encouraged to eat with your hands. Specials include the marvellous *malai kofta* (cottage cheese and potato dumplings filled with mixed fruit and cream in a cashew nut gravy), and their outstanding Butter Chicken. Closes 8.30pm.

Manjras, 56 Cathedral Rd. Highly affordable Indian cooking from the self-proclaimed "breyani kings", in a great location adjacent to the Juma Mosque near Grey Street, one of the most exciting parts of the city.

O Pescador, 52 Albany Grove (☎304 4138). As the name hints, seafood is the speciality at this moderately priced Portuguese restaurant, serving outstanding crab, with nutcracker, bib and the works. Their starters are recommended, as are their mussels in onion and tomato sauce. Closed all day Mon & Sat lunch.

Patel's Vegetarian House, Rama House, Grey St. One of the few places where Indians go to buy sweetmeats and also among the original homes of *bunny chow*.

Roma Revolving Restaurant, John Ross House (☎37 6707). Dine in orbit on the 32nd Floor, high above the city, with panoramic views. Decent but unexceptional moderately priced menu. Closed Sun.

Victoria Embankment and the Harbour

Café Fish, Yacht Mole, Victoria Embankment (☎301 3102). Beautiful and moderately priced restaurant looking out onto harbour, where eating the catch of the day is *de rigueur*.

Charlie Crofts Wharfside Diner, 18 Boatsman Rd, Maydon Wharf (☎307 2935). Right by a slipway in the industrial section of the harbour, their spicy kalamari grill is first-class.

The Famous Fish Co, North Pier, End of Point Rd (☎368 1060). Perfectly positioned at the port entrance, this seafood restaurant is recommended for the wonderful views of ships navigating the harbour mouth.

The Berea

Baan Thai, 138 Florida Rd, Morningside (☎303 4270). Unfailingly excellent Thai food including outstanding Ton Yum soup and steamed mussels, which are topped only by their honeyed duck at surprisingly moderate prices.

Blue Zoo Café, 6 Nimmo Rd (☎303 3568). Varied and unusual menu featuring delicious Cajun chicken, steaks, fish and salads with mango and chilli dressings. Beautifully located in Mitchell Park Gardens, with moderate prices. Tea Gardens open daily 8.30am–4.30pm. Closed Mon & Sun.

Chok Dee, Avondale Centre, Morningside (☎303 2198). Good, inexpensive Thai food in a red room decorated with Thai artefacts. Try their superb chicken mint salad. Closed Sun.

El Turko, 413 Windemere Rd, Morningside (☎23 7893). Cosy restaurant with pavement seating and a recommended *meze* platter with fiery olives and moderate prices. "Turkish Tigers" (vodka, condensed milk, cream and cinnamon) are worth trying to fire you up. Closed all day Sun & Sat lunch.

Gulzar, 69 Stamford Hill Rd, Morningside (☎309 6379). Durban's classiest Indian restaurant dishes up magnificent curries and tandooris amid Moorish decor and tasteful Oriental carpets. Closed Mon.

Indian Delights, 374 Brickfield Rd, Overport. Strictly vegetarian menu offering *puri-patha*, made of leaves, spread with a batter and spice, cut and fried and served with *roti*. Choose a sweetmeat to sample from the carnival of colours.

Queens Tavern, Stamford Hill Rd (☎309 4017). Indian cuisine adapted to bar culture in the old British Middle East Sporting & Dining Club building. A Durban landmark and a popular drinking hole with journalists from nearby Newspaper House. Try their basket of starters under umbrellas in the courtyard. Open until late; closed Sun.

Scoozi's Pizzeria, Silvervause Centre, Silverton Rd. Hip, mid-priced Italian joint with stylish menu featuring caviar avocado and sour-cream pizzas. Daily from lunchtime.

Two Moon Junction, 45 Windermere Rd, Morningside (☎303 3078). Reasonably priced Mediterranean cuisine, including vermicelli, salmon, brilliant strawberry and gooseberry salads and *millefleur* filo pastry dessert served in a techno-industrial aesthetic of steel bar-tops covered in fake Friesland cowhide set against a Corinthian column. Closed Sun.

Upstairs, 2a Avondale Centre, Morningside (☎23 9134). Dim sum starter with mouthwatering arrangement of sweet and hot sauces, spring rolls and assorted appetizers make this moderately priced Chinese cuisine worth travelling for. Order 24hr ahead for their exotic duck dish, consisting of smoked duck and skin served separately as a starter and reappearing as part of the stir-fry main meal. Closed Mon.

Coffee and snack shops

Café Geneve, 1st Floor, 384 Smith St. Specialist coffee shop serving light meals and excellent coffee, and providing a cool refuge from Durban's humidity. 6.30am–5pm. Closed Sun.

Clancey's on the Berea, Price Waterhouse, Silverton Rd. Durban's top deli serves up a generous café au lait that requires both hands. A fine after-movie venue and popular with the city's jewel-bedecked nouveau riche for Saturday breakfasts of croissants and jams. 7am until late. Closed Sun.

Java Java Cyber Café, 13 Marriot Rd, Berea (☎309 1575; email: javajava@sprintlink.co.za). Durban's relaxed vegetarian cybercafé in a converted old-style house is an alcohol-free zone, where the only mind-altering substances are their shelves of Marxist books and net-surfing. Cucumber Smoothie (grated cucumber served with yoghurt) is the house speciality. Tues–Thurs noon–1am, Fri 9am–2am, Sat 9am–3am.

Loafers Bakery & Coffee Shop, 514 Windermere Rd. Light and airy venue popular with Durbanites for Sunday morning breakfast. Budget but first-class full English breakfast. Daily 7am–4pm.

Press Club Coffee Shop, 26 Salisbury Centre. This is one of the few cafés in the city centre, and has menus on newsprint and a stylized, period feel. Full of city professionals, its daytime menu includes buttered buns, salmon and chives on rye, and good coffee. Daytime only; closed Sun.

Roxy, Marriot Rd. Excellent range of coffees, including flavoured beans, served by transvestite waitrons at this night-only venue. Closed Sun.

Take aways

Charlie Croft's Wharfside Diner, 18 Boatsman Rd, Maydon Wharf. Noted for its dockside setting and deli where you can pick and mix your own meal and pay by the weight.

Johnny's Takeaway, 179 Sparks Rd, Overport. From traditional beans *bunny chow* to chicken or fiery kebabs, this place just below the Berea isn't recommended for women alone late at night. Try their chip and cheese *roti* if you dare. Open all hours.

Sunrise Chip N' Ranch, 89 Sparks Rd, Overport. Fastest and tastiest *bunny chows* in town, 24hr a day at rock-bottom prices.

Victory Lounge, corner of Grey and Victoria streets. Hot and spicy *bunny chow* in the Indian quarter of the city centre.

Nightlife and entertainment

Durban is the grunge capital of South Africa and you'll find plenty of live **indie music** on offer, much of it derivative of European or North American trends. More interesting, but less accessible, are some of the **Zulu forms** such as *isicathamiya* and *maskanda*. On the **jazz** scene, the city's most indigenous offering is a spicy combination of American mixed with township jazz, Zulu forms and classical Indian music. Look out for performances by Gathering Forces II, featuring Darius Brubeck (son of Dave) and the classically trained Indian musician Deepak Ram.

The best place to hear **classical concerts** by the Natal Philharmonic Orchestra – more for the tropical ambience than the quality of performance – is at a sundowner concert held in the Botanical Gardens or the Village Green, a large open space along NMR Avenue. Check for listings and adverts in the press or on the notice board in the Gardens.

Durban has a fairly well-established and lively **gay scene**, with a handful of excellent nightclubs where heteros are also welcome.

For details of **what's on**, the *Mercury* is the better of Durban's two English-language dailies, while the Thursday edition of the *Daily News* has a comprehensive section on forthcoming events. *Natal on Saturday* gives an update on the latest drinking spots as well as where to go and what to do, while the Johannesburg-based weekly *Mail & Guardian* covers Durban nightlife in its What's On section towards the back of the paper.

Bars

123 Action Bar, Berea Rd. Seedy, grungy spot, with an authentic pool-bar feel and a large screen excellent for whiling way a Saturday afternoon watching sport.

Banana Joe's, Berea Rd. Speciality is cheap "shooters" (short, sharp schnapps) and noncompetitive pool where you won't feel out of place if you aren't Alex Higgins.

Riptide's Action Bar, South Beach Walk, below Sand Pebbles. A fitting place to come and watch the sun rise while trying to deal with Saturday-night post-clubbing tinnitus.

Sir Benjamin's Landing, Old Gun Emplacement. Most intriguing bar in town, in the middle of vessel maintanance works, off Maydon Wharf, reachable by ferry. You must climb some stairs to get to the top, and the atmosphere is homely, although the bar is frequented by heavy dockside types. Only beer is served, but you can take your own meat and get it *braai*-ed.

Thirsty's, King's Battery. Go for the view alone in this heavy hetero hunting ground, reachable by ferry.

Victoria Bar, Point Rd. Seedy but highly popular Portuguese venue good for boozing and watching sport on TV. *Catembe* (Coke and wine) is a house speciality, as is the excellent prawn curry.

Clubs

Anno Domini, Hermitage Lane, Small Craft Harbour, off Victoria Embankment, this is Durban's come-down bar, where ambient chill-out music plays for those still bumping and grinding at dawn. Open every night except Sat; opens Sun at 6am.

Club Zoom, West St. In the city centre, with its mirror balls, Durban's predominantly coloured bar has all the trimmimgs of a retro club. Come for the karaoke competitions and to see regulars The H Brothers do a first-class Stevie Wonder impression.

Retros, *Riviera Hotel*, Esplanade. Stomping ground for twenty-somethings whose cultural icons include Quentin Tarantino and Captain Strange. Dance floor, pool bar, chill-out room and balcony. Open Wed, Fri (1960s–1970s sounds) & Sat.

Stringfellas, corner of Point Rd and West St. In the city centre, this is the mother of all Indian clubs, attracting huge crowds to its two discos, two bars and comfy seating areas. Every second Sunday night features bhangra, the latest Eastern rave culture taking Durban by storm.

330, 330 Point Rd. Durban's definitive techno-rave club. Dress code is high fashion, accessories are body piercing, spring water and tiger balm ointment. Sat only.

Gay spots

Cheers, 66 Pine City Centre, Hill St, Pinetown. Open on the first Sunday of every month as an intimate lesbian venue, with pool tables and a dance floor throbbing to Euro-eclectic sounds.

The Club, 301 Umbilo Rd. South of the city centre, this lesbian club has the "longest bar in the world", a pool table and a dance floor with dim lighting that creates a personal ambience.

Garth's, Avonmore Centre, Berea. One of Durban's late-night spots is a cosy place for cakes, coffee and, the proprietor willing, piano recitals. With eccentric crockery, embellished plate hangings and comfy chairs, this place feels a bit like home.

Gossips, 423 West St, corner of Masonic Grove. In the city centre, and serving the legal eagles from the court during the day, by night *Gossips* welcomes a gay crowd to its great restaurant with understated decor.

Grumpies, Point Rd. A labyrinthine web of rooms, stairs and corridors, at this predominantly gay male hangout, which has bars and dance floors, and is convivial if you take your own company along.

Pandora's Box, Hunter St, Berea. Romantic decor meet 1990s minimalism, with a lime-green ice-cube bar, comfortable sofas for lounge lizards and a sprung dance floor for head-bangers.

Jazz

Centre for Jazz and Popular Music, University of Natal, South Ridge Rd (☎260 1111). "Jazz Happy Hour" every Wednesday at 5.30pm.

Bat Centre, Small Craft Harbour, entrance opposite Hermitage Lane, off Victoria Embankment. Probably the best jazz venue in Durban, with a free sundowner jazz concert on the deck every Friday from 5.30pm. On Friday and Saturday nights top local and international jazz musicians play in Bat Hall.

Funky's at the Bat Centre, Small Craft Harbour. Restaurant where you can hear good music. Many prominent Durban rock bands also appear here, including Urban Creep, Springbok Nude Girls, Breathe and jazz maestro Sipho Gumede.

The Rainbow, 23 Stanfield Lane, Pinetown. From Afro-fusion to jazz, occasional Sunday lunchtimes. Check press for programme details.

Tekweni Junction, corner of Umgeni Rd and Kolling St (☎309 1282). Predominantly African venue where it's best to go with someone who knows the town. Simple bar-restaurant with table soccer, pool and gambling machines. Famed for excellent curries and pap and samp. Fri & Sat from 9pm.

Theatre and cinema

There are two major **theatres** in town; the *Playhouse Drama Theatre*, 231 Smith St (☎36 9955), a mock-Tudor building which tends to host middle-of-the-road productions, but also sees performances by the resident progressive Playhouse Dance Company; and the *Elizabeth Sneddon Theatre*, University of Natal, on South Ridge Road (☎260 1111), a modern venue for university and visiting productions, which also hosts Monday lunchtime concerts, including Zulu traditional *maskanda* and piano recitals.

As far as movies go, the best and most convenient **cinemas** are the multiscreen complexes at the Musgrave Centre on Musgrave Road and the Workshop Mall in the city centre, both of which show all the mainstream releases. There are no art-house cinemas in Durban, but the Musgrave occasionally screens film-festival releases. For both cinema and live performances, check the press for details.

Outdoor activities

Durban's generous climate and beachside location foster a wide variety of **outdoor activities**. Not surprisingly for a city with such a British heritage, **cricket** and **horse-racing** are high on the agenda of spectator sports; the Kingsmead Cricket Ground, 2 Kingsmead Close (☎32 9703), is the principal cricket venue for local and international matches and is home to the **KwaZulu-Natal** provincial cricket team. You'll also have plenty of opportunity to watch **rugby** in season at King's Park Stadium, Walter Gilbert Rd, Stamford Hill (☎23 6368), which is the home to the local Sharks. **Horse-racing** is popular: the main season runs from May to August. and centres around the course at Greyville, Avondale Rd (☎309 4545). The Rothmans "July at Greyville" is South Africa's premier horse-racing event, drawing bets from across the length and breadth of the country and wildly exhibitionist fashions in the spectator boxes.

Surfing

Far more than a pastime, **surfing** in Durban amounts to an entire way of life. Night surfing competitions draw enormous crowds, as does the annual **Gunston 500**, the world's longest-running professional surfing competition, held at Durban every year in July. During this month, the city goes surf mad, with a large expo displaying the latest in surfing equipment and accessories.

The current favourite spot for surfers is **North Beach**, while good places to pick up surfing gear is the *Safari Surf Shop*, 28 Somtseu Rd (☎37 2176), where Spider Murphy, South Africa's top board-shaper will custom-make your board. This is a good opportunity to buy a world-class board far more cheaply than anything you'll find in Europe or North America. *Island Style Surf Shop,* 9 Pickering St, Marine Parade (☎328158), is a good bet for accessories. For rented boards, contact *Surf Zone*, 38 West St (☎36 8459), or their beach branch at the Ocean Action Centre (☎368 5818).

Diving and swimming

Diving is an obvious and pleasurable activity in KwaZulu-Natal's subtropical waters, but is somewhat limited immediately around Durban. The best diving spots around town are Vetches Pier, at the southern tip of Durban's beachfront, and Blood Reef at the tip of the Bluff. Further along the coast, Aliwal Shoal along the South Coast (see p.364) and Sodwana up the North Coast (p.370) are renowed for superb diving.

Scuba trips to these areas can be arranged from the *Trident Dive Shop & School*, 18 Boatmans Rd, Maydon Wharf (☎305 3081), which also operates diving courses, and sells, rents and services diving gear. *Underwater World*, 251 Point Rd (☎32 5820), is an equally reputable operator.

Durban's largest **swimming pool** is the heated *King's Park Olympic Swimming Pool* (☎23 0404) on NMR Avenue, between Argyle and Battery Beach roads in Stamford Hill. Convenient for the Berea are *Sutton Park Baths*, Stamford Hill Rd (☎303 1823), while the seawater *Rachel Finlayson Baths*, Lower Marine Parade (☎37 2721), are handy if you're staying near the beachfront.

Bird-watching and hiking

Bird-watching, a major activity in the green fringes of the city, is being encouraged by the Durban Metropolitan Open Space System (DMOSS), a project linking all the city parks via narrow green corridors. For organized bird-watching outings and courses, contact the *Wildlife Society of South Africa*, 100 Brand Rd, Glenwood (☎21 3126). Promising bird-watching areas include the Manor Gardens area; the Botanic Gardens, Botanic Gardens Road; the Berea; Burman Bush to the north of the city; Pigeon Valley, below the University of Natal; the Umgeni River Mouth; Virginia Bush, on the road to Umhlanga Rocks and the Havana Forest in Umhlanga, where the spotted thrush and green coucal have been spotted.

You can arrange to go **hiking** in the relatively close **Drakensberg** through one of the several hiking clubs that organize expeditions to Injasuti, Cathedral Peak and the Southern Berg. These can be contacted through the *Wildlife Society of South Africa* (see above), which organizes a variety of bush outings. Non-members are welcome. For kitting up, head for the *Quarter Master Store*, The Workshop, 99 Aliwal St (☎305 3087), and *Bushwackers*, 110 Pavilion Shopping Centre, Spine Rd, Westville (☎265 0102).

Fishing and canoeing

Fishing is done for fun and money in Durban and you can jostle with the locals on North Pier, or catch a ride on the ferry to the Bluff. A favorite local harbour spot is in front of Sir Benjamin's Landing, to which only the fishermen have access at low tide. Should your mood turn before the tide, you'll find it a wet journey to the shore. To take on the big fish, like barracuda, sailfish and sharks, contact *Deep Sea Cruising & Fishing*, 18 Grunter Gully, Bayhead (☎466 4300), which has a booking office on the corner of West Street and Marine Parade. For flies, tackle and all the gear you may need apart from Old Brown Sherry (South Africa's favourite mood-lifter during the slow bites), contact *Kings Sport*, 53 Hunter St (☎32 8251).

Canoeing, in all its forms, whether white-water, kayaking, solo or two-person, is popular in Durban, and the sailing and canoeing clubs are based on the banks of the Umgeni River. The **Dusi Marathon**, a major annual event, ends at the Umgeni River Mouth; for more information contact *Eric's Canoe Shop*, 320 North Coast Rd (☎579 4130).

Shopping

As one of South Africa's major cities, Durban has a fine supply of **shops**, making it a good centre to pick up general supplies and local books and records. But it's for **crafts and curios** that it scores particularly highly, being the largest city in KwaZulu-Natal, home turf to the Zulus, who produce a dazzling range of handmade goods (see box). The best places to browse for crafts are in the downtown markets, the weekend flea markets and the specialist shops around the city.

Fifteen minutes by car from central Durban along the N3 to Pietermaritzburg, you'll find the **Pavilion**, the largest retail complex on the east coast. KwaZulu-Natal's favourite promenading venue and Durban's shopping honeypot, the Pavilion is visited by over a million people a month and outstrips even the beachfront in popularity. If you're suffering from consumerist withdrawal, the Pavilion is a must, with everything

ZULU CRAFTS AND CURIOS

Durban's huge range of galleries, craft shops and markets make it one of the best centres in the country to pick up **Zulu crafts**. Traditional works include a range of functional items, such as woven beer strainers, grass brooms and basketry that can be extremely beautiful when well-crafted. Other traditional items are beadwork, pottery and Zulu regalia, of which *assegais* (spears), shields, leather kilts and drums are a few examples. However, drastic social changes in South Africa over the last century have affected the Zulus along with every other South African – black and white. The availability of cheap plastic crockery and enamelware has significantly eroded the time-consuming production of traditional ceramics and woven containers for domestic use. Instead, these personal household items are now frequently churned out en masse for sale to curio hunters who are indifferent to the authenticity or quality of what they are buying.

Fortunately the news isn't all bad and, although urbanization has stifled the production of much traditional craft, it has thrown up creative adaptations making use of new materials, or old materials used in new ways. Among these are beautifully decorated black and white **sandals** made from recycled rubber tyres, wildly colourful **baskets** woven from telephone wire and *sjamboks* (whips) decorated with bright insulation tape. On the more frivolous side are a whole genre of affordable curios that break away from the stereotypes of tribal woodcarvings and masks, and marry industrial materials with rural life or rural materials with industrial life. Attractive tin boxes made from flattened oil cans, chickens constructed from sheet plastic, and aircraft and little 4WD vehicles carved from wood are some of the results.

If you're serious about buying something really good, there is an entire movement of **master craftspeople** drawing on traditional forms to produce objects of the highest quality, many of which are sought after by art collectors. Among these many excellent craftworkers are woodcarver Vuminkosi Zulu; scrap-metal car sculptor Nkosinathi Gumede and potter Nesta Nala – track them down through the *Natal Society of Arts* shop in Berea.

from groceries to cinemas, banking facilities and restaurants, as well as plenty of safe parking and reliable security.

Books and music

Adams & Co, 341 West St (☎304 8571). In the city centre, this is Durban's oldest book store, and has an excellent selection of books on the history of Durban and KwaZulu-Natal.

Exclusive Books, Lower Level, Pavilion Shopping Centre (☎265 0454). Durban's flashiest general book store, where browsers are welcome to pore over titillating coffee-table books.

Ikes Bookshop, Boulevard Level, Overport City, corner of Sydenham and Ridge roads. Tiny second-hand bookshop with an interesting range of items covering KwaZulu-Natal's history and the fauna and flora of the area.

Look and Listen, Lower Level, Pavilion Shopping Centre (☎265 0826). Durban's best-stocked music shop, with a comprehensive range of indigenous music from the whole continent, including local favourites such as Ladysmith Black Mambazo and Hugh Masekela.

Crafts and curios

African Art Centre, 8 Guildhall Arcade, 35 Gardiner St (☎304 7915). Gallery and shop tucked away in the city and well worth a visit for its traditional and modern Zulu and Xhosa beadwork, beaded dolls, wire sculptures, woodcuts and tapestries.

The Bat Shop, The Bat Centre, Harbourside, off Victoria Embankment (☎32 9951). Contemporary works with an excellent collection by African artists, in a bright and colourful venue with masterful wireworks and robust ceramics.

Deco Jazz, 515 Currie Rd, Berea. Eco-friendly animal-skin-inspired prints on rich cotton fabrics and a range of functional accessories direct from the studio. Leopard, zebra and giraffe motifs add up to a cacophony of colours, stripes, dots and spots.

NSA Shop, Bulwer Rd, Berea. In a gallery building, this menagerie of hand-crafted goods includes a wonderful selection of functional art, including pewter cutlery, etchings and paintings.

Tourist Junction Shop, 160 Pine St (☎304 4934). Quality African artefacts, from Zulu basketwork to tribal masks and weaving.

Workshop, corner of Commercial and Aliwal streets. In part of the old station building, this is the city centre's largest shopping mall, and is a handy place to shop for gifts, souvenirs and curios.

Listings

Airlines *British Airways/Comair* (☎304 4741); *South African Airways* (☎450 2017); *SA Airlink* (☎0800/11 4799).

Automobile Association 352 Smith St (☎306 2851). Emergency rescue toll-free supernumber ☎0800/01 0101.

Banks Plenty of banks and ATMs are dotted throughout the shopping areas of the city centre, Berea and along the beachfront. Opening hours are Mon–Fri 9am–3.30pm, Sat 8.30–11am.

Bureau de change *First National Bank*, 32 West St, Marine Parade (☎031/37 9464; Mon–Fri 3.30–7pm, Sat 11am–6pm, Sun 10am–3pm), has extended hours for changing foreign currency.

Bicycle rental *Cycle-Logic*, 34 Cato St (☎031/32 2955).

Car parks are dotted all over the city; the most convenient ones in the centre are at Pine Arcade, at the west end of Pine St, and in the Workshop mall, on the corner of Commercial Rd and Aliwal St.

Car rental Among the larger companies with national networks are *Alisa* (☎toll free 0800/02 1515), *Avis* (☎toll free 0800/02 1111), *Budget* (☎toll free 0800/01 6622), *Europcar* (☎toll free 0800/01 1344), *Imperial* (☎toll free 0800/13 1000), *Key* (☎toll free 0800/32 5111), and *Tempest* (☎toll free 0800/03 1666). Smaller, more localized rental outfits include *Berea* (☎toll free 0800/33 3811), *Economy* (☎434 8304), *Rent & Drive* (☎32 2803), and *Windermere* (☎23 0339). For minibus rental, try *Berea* (☎0800/33 3811). Camper-van rental is available from *Britz Africa* (☎031/72 9326) and the considerably cheaper *Bobo Campers* (☎44 8633).

Embassies and consulates *Germany,* 4th Floor, Deloitte Touche House, 2 Devonshire Place, off Smith St (☎305 5677); *Netherlands,* 106 ABSA Building, corner of West and Field streets (☎304 1770); *UK*, 19th Floor, Marine Building, 22 Gardiner St (☎305 2929); *USA*, Durban Bay House, 333 Smith St (☎304 4737).

Emergencies Ambulance ☎10177; Fire ☎361 0000; Police (Flying Squad) ☎10111; Rape Crisis ☎23 2323.

Gay contacts Durban's gay chat group can be contacted on ☎81 3298.

Hospitals and doctors Doctors are listed in the telephone directory under "Medical practitioners". The main state hospital is the central *Addington*, Erskine Terrace, South Beach (☎32 2111), which offers a cheap 24hr emergency ward, but the level of care cannot be guaranteed. A preferable alternative is *Entabeni Private Hospital*, 148 South Ridge Rd, Berea (☎81 1344), which has a casualty unit and can also treat minor conditions, but where you will have to pay a deposit on admission and settle up before leaving town.

Laundries, *Musgrave Laundromat*, 2nd Level, Musgrave Centre (☎21 1936), and *Econ-O-Wash*, Ground Floor, Berea Centre, Berea Rd (☎21 0834) are both convenient for the Berea.

Left luggage Durban Station has inexpensive left-luggage facilities on the first floor (daily 6am–6pm).

Pharmacies offering extended opening hours: *Medicine Chest*, 155 Berea Rd, Berea (daily 8am–midnight; ☎305 6151); *Daynite Pharmacy*, corner of West St and Point Rd (daily 7.30am–10.30pm; ☎368 3666), which does free deliveries; *Mediquick Pharmacy*, 98 Overport Drive, outside Overport City Shopping Centre, Berea (8am–10pm; ☎29 3456), which delivers anywhere in town for a nominal charge.

Post office Main branch, corner of Gardiner and West streets, has a poste restante and enquiry desk. Opening hours are Mon–Fri 8.30am–4.30pm, Sat 8.30–11.30am.

Taxis Reliable firms include *Eagle* (☎368 1706), *Zippy* (☎202 7067) and *Swift* (☎32 5569).

Telephones There are phone booths all over Durban taking phone cards and coins. For directory enquiries, phone ☎1023.

AROUND DURBAN

The **North** or **South coasts** around Durban make an obvious and easy day/weekend trip out of the city if you want quieter beaches. The coast around Durban, with its easy access to Johannesburg, warmest waters in the country and decidedly tropical feel, has primarily been developed for white South African families on holiday. It's not at all unpleasant, or even remotely congested like the Mediterranean – there are kilometres of sandy beaches backed by wild banana trees, and the chance to spot dolphins, especially along the North Coast – but in a country with so many spectacular landscapes and wild places to visit, its blandness pales by comparison.

The South Coast draws diving enthusiasts to **Aliwal Shoal**, one of the country's top dive spots near Umkomaas, and is also notable for two nature reserves in the south: Oribi Gorge, inland from Port Shepstone, where you can overnight or visit by steam train; and Umtamvuna, inland from Port Edward, best visited to do day-walks along the Umtamvuna River.

Unless you're travelling to or from the Eastern Cape, the North Coast is preferable to the South Coast – it's a lot less built-up and tacky. **Umhlanga Rocks**, an upmarket resort less than half an hour's drive from Durban on the N2, offers beach walks, as well as great places to have a drink or meal, and gaze at the sea, and indeed is an alternative to staying in Durban itself. Further up the coast are a string of resorts which get more low-key the further north you go, all with sandy beaches and large tidal rock pools to swim in. Inland is sugar cane country, with a couple of upmarket guesthouses living up to the colonial-style grandeur of the early sugar barons. The old road north, the **R102**, which takes an inland route, is far more interesting than the coastal road, giving access to visiting Indian temples at **Tongaat**, the grave of one of the ANC's best-loved leaders, Albert Luthuli, at **Groutville**, and the Shaka memorial and museum, as well as the bustling Indian and African markets at **Stanger**.

Heading 80km northwest from Durban is **Pietermaritzburg**, the provincial capital, with an excellent art gallery and some interesting red-brick Victorian architecture combining with a vibrant mix of Zulu and Indian culture. Sampling Pietermaritzburg can be combined with the all-time favourite day-trip out of Durban – the **Valley of a Thousand Hills** – visitable by driving along the Old Main Road (R103) towards Pietermaritzburg. The outing to heady viewpoints of the folded hills amounts to taking in some great scenery and stopping for snacks or pub lunches along the way, or doing a bit of Zulu craft shopping.

Beyond Pietermaritzburg, and definitely more of a weekend stay than a day-trip, are the Natal **Midlands**, with appealing Drakensberg foothill scenery, trout fishing, numerous craft shops, and a number of hotels, guesthouses and cottages catering especially for the weekend trade. Although it's very pretty, the area is probably best experienced from the windows of your vehicle, as you head towards the real reward of the province, the stunningly beautiful **Drakensberg Mountains**.

Valley of a Thousand Hills

The evocatively named **Valley of a Thousand Hills**, 45km from Durban, makes for a picturesque drive along the edge of densely folded hills where Zulu people still live in traditional homesteads, and which visitors rarely venture into. The spectacular landscape goes some way to soothing any misgivings you might have about ethnographic "game-viewing", but it's only worth a special effort if you're not exploring the KwaZulu-Natal interior, where scenes like this occur in abundance. The trip to the valley and back can be easily done in half a day, and there are sufficient attractions laid on along the route to extend it to a full day's outing.

To reach the valley **by car**, head inland from Durban along the N3, following the Pinetown Road signs. At the Hillcrest/Old Main Road turn-off, turn right over the freeway onto the Old Main Road (R103) and continue along here to follow the scenic valley route. On the outskirts of Durban's suburbs, turn off at *Heidi's Farmstall* for the *Chantecler*, Clement Stott Rd (☎031/75 2613; ④–⑤), a quiet, English-style **hotel**, which has a pool and offers bar meals in the pub, an à la carte menu in the **restaurant** and teas and snacks in the garden.

Back on the R103 past the *Fainting Goat Centre*, which has some shops and a restaurant, you'll soon reach **Phezulu**, an African curio shop and a focal point of the drive. Here you'll find a reconstruction of a pre-colonial Zulu village, where you can watch touristy, but nonetheless spirited displays of **Zulu dancing** (daily 10am, 11.30am, 1.30pm & 3.30pm), set against the dramatic horizon of the valley. Part of *Phezulu's* untamed Africa setup is the **Assagay Safari Park** (daily 9am–4.30pm), 800m along the road, which brings you close to deadly serpents – though they're tucked away in cramped little glass boxes – and other penned animals. Give it a miss if you're heading onto the real game reserves, just a few hours away.

Follow the road for another 5km to the small settlement of **DRUMMOND** and the old-fashioned tin-roofed *Valley View* (☎0325/34560; ③), a **hotel** recommended for tea and scones or a pub **lunch**, as well as its Sunday carvery accompanied by breathtaking views. The hotel is distinguishable by its bright-green roof and the *Drum & Bell* pub sign. Also in Drummond, sharing the same heady vistas, the *Ravenscroft Dining Room & Coffee Shop* (Tues–Fri 11am–9pm, Sat 9.30am–9pm, Sun 9.30am–4pm; ☎0325/34598), dishes up excellent home-cooked cuisine.

Without your own transport, you can join one of the daily **tours** of the Valley offered by *Tekweni Eco Tours* (☎031/303 1433) or *DTBM Coach Tours* (☎031/368 2848).

The South Coast

The **South Coast**, the 160-kilometre seaboard from Durban to Port Edward on the Eastern Cape border, feels like a ribbon of seaside suburbs; thousands of families from the interior have jostled to build holiday homes along what is the closest stretch of sand to Johannesburg. But with truly exceptional beaches in northern Zululand and not far away in the Eastern Cape, it's difficult to justify coming to the South Coast unless you're travelling through KwaZulu-Natal and want to stay at the beach outside Durban. This

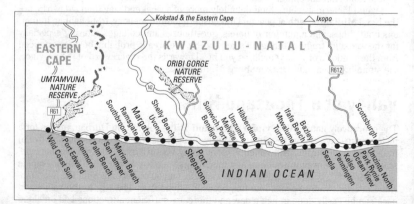

SOUTH COAST TRANSPORT

Driving by car, head for the **N2**, which zooms south from Durban as far as Port Shepstone, before heading inland to Kokstad. From Port Shepstone to Southbroom, the South Coast Toll Road is even faster and less traffic-clogged. By **air**, daily direct flights (90min) from Johannesburg on *SA Airlink* (central reservations, ☎toll free 0800/11 4799) go to Margate Airport (☎03931/73267).

If you're travelling to the South Coast by **intercity bus**, you've got two choices. *Malundi Bus Lines* (☎039682/3363) operates on Thursdays and Sundays from Pretoria, Johannesburg, Pietermaritzburg, Amanzimtoti, Scottburgh, Hibberdene, Port Shepstone, Shelly Beach and Margate. The bus doesn't drop off before or pick up passengers after Amanzimtoti. *Margate Mini Coach*, Gird Mowat Building, Marine Drive, Margate (☎03931/21406), has a daily service from Durban Station (*Translux* terminal) via Durban (*Royal Hotel*), Durban Airport (domestic arrivals), Amanzimtoti (prebooked only), Hibberdene (prebooked only), Hibberdene (Super Tube), Port Shepstone (*LSC Motors*) and Margate (post office). The *Baz* backpacker bus (☎021/439 2323 or 031/23 6585; email: bazbus@icon.co.za) runs from Port Elizabeth to Durban and back several times a week, pulling in at major South Coast resorts, although you can ask to be put off at intermediate destinations.

A steam **train**, the *Banana Express*, Princess Elizabeth Drive, Port Shepstone (☎0391/82 4821), chugs from Port Shepstone along a scenic narrow-gauge railway four times a week. A ninety-minute journey along the coastline and inland through banana groves and sugar-cane plantations to the hamlet of Izotsha costs R24, while the return trip (6hr 30min) to Paddock Station includes a 550-metre climb through green hills dotted with traditional Zulu villages.

may be especially tempting in the winter months when it's much warmer and sunnier along this stretch than anywhere else in the country.

South Coast beaches are sandy and backed by luxuriant wild banana trees wedged between the holiday developments. Many shelve steeply into the powerful surf – so you need to restrict swimming to where it's indicated as safe. Away from the sea, the land is very hilly and green, dotted with sugar cane fields, banana plantations and palm and pecan nut trees. Gardens are bright with exuberant flowering trees and shrubs, and in some places alive with monkeys.

Transport from Durban and Johannesburg to the South Coast is good (see box, p.356) and there are plenty of caravan parks next to the beaches, a couple of back-packers' lodges and a good number of mid-priced places to stay. **Margate**, 133km from Durban, is the transport and holiday hub of the area, with plenty of resorts lying to the east and west of it. **Port Shepstone**, 117km south of Durban, is the grim industrial and administrative centre along the coast, while **Oribi Gorge Nature Reserve**, just 21km inland from Port Shepstone, has lovely forest hikes and good-value accommodation.

Amanzimtoti, Warner Beach and Umkomaas

Some 27km south of Durban (and just minutes from Durban Airport), **AMANZIM-TOTI** is the largest town along the upper South Coast, yet feels more like a beachside suburb than a place in its own right. Outside weekends and school holidays – when its high-rise holiday developments are full to bursting point – it's worth coming here for a day's swimming and lounging on Nyoni Rocks beach.

If you're looking for somewhere to **stay**, however, **WARNER BEACH**, 3km to the south, is the place to head for. Far less developed than Amanzimtoti, Warner Beach offers some excellent surfing spots – as well as good swimming – and has the added attraction of a large tidal pool which is safe for small children. Overlooking the beach, *Angle Rock Backpackers*, 5 Ellcock Rd (☎031/96 2996; ①), is unquestionably a cut above the average **hostel**, with a swimming pool, four dorms and two doubles – all en suite with marble bathtubs. The atmosphere is supremely relaxed, and you may end up stay-ing longer than you planned. The lodge offers free use of surfboards and canoes. Warner Beach has a handful of decent pubs and **restaurants**: *Ouma's*, 117 Kingsway, is recommended for its South African flavours that revolve around *boerekos*. It opens at 10am for breakfast and serves up hearty meals until 10pm.

Roughly 16km further down the coast, **UMKOMAAS**, a faded town of buildings with corrugated-iron roofs, exudes an atmosphere that is more relaxed still. Perched on a headland with outstanding views across the sea, this is essentially a retirement village with beaches which are periodically discoloured by effluent washing down the Mkomazi River from the Saiccor cellulose mill, just upriver. For **diving** enthusiasts, Umkomaas is the perfect jumping-off point for **Aliwal Shoal**, a scattered reef quite close to the shore and one of southern Africa's top dive sites. On the beachfront, the *Whaler Dive Centre*, Roland Norris Drive (☎0323/31562, fax 31564; ①–②), offers a wide range of diving activities with self-catering **accommodation**. Their Open Water diving course leads to an internationally recognized certificate and costs around R1000 (excluding accommodation). The best time to dive is between May and September, when visibility is at its best. Some of the rewards for experienced divers include sight-ings of whale sharks, ragged-tooth sharks, potato bass, manta rays and eels, as well as shoals of tropical fish, corals and anemones.

Scottburgh to Port Shepstone

A further 9km south brings you to **SCOTTBURGH**, the oldest town along the South Coast and one of the most appealing because of its sheltered and lawn-covered beach fringes. The *Cutty Sark Protea* (☎0323/21230; ④) on the beachfront offers reasonable hotel **accommodation**, while self-catering and camping are available at the nearby *Scottburgh Caravan Park* (☎0323/20291, fax 22148; ①–②).

One of the few **backpackers' lodges** on the South Coast is *Club Tropicana*, PO Box 359, Annerley 4230 (☎039/681 3547; ①), some 51km south of Scottburgh. Signposted off the N2, it's 12km beyond **Hibberdene** on a farm a couple of kilometres inland from attractive **Banana Beach**. Unlike the Durban backpackers' lodges, there's no party scene here, but the lodge does offer access to rural Zulu areas where you can meet people on more equal terms, rather than in the artificial environment of a theme-park Zulu village set up for tourists. The owners have good contacts with diviners and people practising traditional medicine in Zulu villages, and are also involved in small-scale farming projects in areas devastated by apartheid and the fighting between Inkatha and the ANC. Accommodation is in basic dorms and doubles, cheap evening meals are on offer, and there are facilities for self-catering. There's no pressure to take part in any of the more socially minded activities; you can simply hang out and spend your days on Banana Beach. The *Baz* **bus** delivers them right to the doorstep, while the *Margate Mini Coach* takes passengers from Durban and drops them off a short walk away.

One unremarkable resort after another follows the shoreline from Hibberdene to gritty, sprawling **PORT SHEPSTONE**, a dismal place where you won't want to linger for long, although there are a couple of reasonable beaches just south of the town centre. Port Shepstone serves as a convenient gateway to the nearby Oribi Gorge Nature Reserve (see below), which is a lovely place to stop over if you're heading to Durban from the Eastern Cape. The town is also the place to hop on one of the *Banana Express* steam train journeys (see box, p.365), and take in some gorgeous coastal and inland scenery: one journey chugs inland to Oribi Gorge – very handy if this is on your itinerary.

Oribi Gorge Nature Reserve

Heading 21km inland from Port Shepstone, **Oribi Gorge Nature Reserve** (8am–4.30pm; small entry fee) is the South Coast's most compelling attraction: a compact and highly scenic area of cliffs rising from vast chasms and jungly forest traversed by the fast-flowing Umzimkulu and Umzimkulwana rivers.

A circular scenic drive descends from the rest camp into the Umzimkulu Valley, where a picnic site sits on the riverbank. Here the road winds upward again through thick forest before leaving the park and skirting north past the *Oribi Gorge Hotel* turn-off and then back to the reserve. There are numerous other idyllic picnic spots on the riverbanks (don't swim here as bilharzia parasites are present in the water) and way-marked **hikes** ranging from thirty-minute to day-long excursions leading to dizzying look-out points or through the forest (the reserve office can provide hiking maps). A recommended one-hour **walk** starts from the Umzimkulu car park and picnic site, crosses the river and heads immediately up some steps into the forest. You can hear the river through the dense vegetation, but you'll only see it when it opens out quite dramatically to reveal **Samango Falls** and a perfect little rock-bounded sandy beach.

Wildlife in the reserve includes bushbuck, common reedbuck, blue and grey duiker, but not oribi, which have left for the succulent shoots of the surrounding sugar cane plantations. You're more likely to hear than to see the shy samango monkeys, hiding in the high canopy of the forest, and although leopards are present it's probable that they'll see you before you catch sight of them.

Practicalities

Travelling **by car** to Durban from the Eastern Cape along the N2, you'll find the reserve just a few hundred metres off the main road. You can also get here by **steam train** from Port Shepstone on the *Banana Express* (see box, p.365), which offers packages (including a *braai* lunch) to Plains Station and road transfers to the reserve.

The nicest **accommodation** is in the Natal Parks Board huts (②) in the rest camp at the head of the Umzimkulwana Gorge, peering into the chasm of Oribi Gorge itself. There's a swimming pool here, and all crockery, cutlery and bedding is provided. A camp chef is available to cook meals if you bring your own ingredients. **Booking** ahead through the Natal Parks Board, PO Box 1750, Pietermaritzburg 3200 (☎0331/47 1981, fax 47 1980), is recommended. Alternatively, you can stay in the old-fashioned, colonial-style *Oribi Gorge* (☎039/687 0253; ③), a **hotel** some 16km from the rest camp, off the

Oribi Flats road, which offers good-value rooms, meals to suit most budgets and a pleasant outdoor tea area patrolled by a persistent pony with a sweet tooth.

The Hibiscus Coast

The 44km of coast from Port Shepstone to Port Edward has been dubbed the **Hibiscus Coast** possibly because of its luscious, bright gardens, luxury suburbs, beachside developments and attractive caravan parks. Although the whole area is built-up, the Hibiscus Coast gets nicer the further south you go.

Uvongo

Some 12km south of Port Shepstone, **UVONGO** is where the Vungu River narrows into a gorge and crashes down a **waterfall** before opening out onto a broad sandy beach. The waterfall is definitely the town's biggest attraction; elsewhere, tatty cliff-top developments have destroyed much of the natural vegetation. To see the falls, take the path from the bottom of the cliffs to the rear of the beach and follow the steps in the corner away from the river, following it through some undergrowth until you reach the viewpoint on a ledge. Uvongo's pleasant beach is the site of a daily market where Zulu women sell fruit, crafts and good-quality basketwork.

One of the most comfortable **places to stay** is *Glyndale Guest Lodge*, just east of the beach (☎03931/50918; ③), with a good full-board rate outside school holidays and nice gardens, a swimming pool and an excellent sea view. Nearby, the *Uvongo Beach Lodge*, Pioneer Rd (☎03931/50013, fax 51748; ②), is a bit old-fashioned and gloomy, but it's very cheap and is only a ten-minute stroll from the beach. If you're after a cottage for a weekend or short break, contact the *Holiday Cottage Accommodation Bureau*, PO Box 151, Uvongo 4270 (☎03931/50423).

The best place to **eat** is the *Pavilion*, a restaurant right on the beach with a curving glazed frontage looking out to sea.

Margate

The brash, built-up holiday town of **MARGATE**, 12km south of Uvongo, is the South Coast's undisputed tourism hub. Connected by daily direct *SAA* **flights** with Johannesburg and by **buses** with Gauteng and Durban (see box, p.365), Margate is as far as you'll get down the South Coast using public transport and has become a last bastion for white holiday-makers retreating from the beaches closer to Durban. A cacophony of high-rise apartments, fast-food outlets, and ice-cream parlours, Margate doesn't offer much in the way of undiscovered coves or hidden beaches, but its big plus point is that out of peak season you'll find a wide choice of good-value places to stay.

It's worth making use of Margate's **tourist information bureau** on the beachfront (Mon–Fri 8.30am–4pm, Sat 9–11am; ☎03931/22322), which can provide details of accommodation and general information about the whole South Coast area. Without a car, you'll find getting around the town easy enough using **tuk tuks**, which must be booked in advance (☎083/272 9593).

Margate's cheapest **place to stay** is the *De Wet Caravan Park*, St Andrews Ave, along the beachfront (☎03931/21022; ②), with fully equipped two-berth caravans and grassy campsites. A little more expensive but closer to the centre is *Skipper's*, Lagoon Rd (☎03931/51223, fax 51231; ②), an old-fashioned, but clean and well-maintained boarding house popular with backpackers and South African families, and overlooking the beach amusement park. Also excellent value is the more comfortable *Suntide*, Duke Rd (☎03931/74010; ②–③), a hotel with modern self-catering apartments in a quiet stretch right on the beach. The only drawback is that most doubles face onto the car park; you're best off paying a little extra and, even if there's only two of you, taking a larger, sea-facing four-bedder. The very comfortable *Margate*, Marine Drive (☎03931/21410, fax 73318; ③), is near the centre of town and right on the beach.

Southbroom, Palm Beach and Port Edward

Some 11km beyond Margate, **SOUTHBROOM** is known disparagingly as "Houghton-by-Sea" after Johannesburg's wealthiest suburb, which allegedly relocates here en masse in December. The town is predominantly a sumptuous development of large holiday houses set in expansive gardens that, out of season, can feel quite deserted. Huge dunes covered by lush vegetation sweep down to the sea and there are good long walks along the shore. The best place for swimming is **Marina Beach**, 3km south of Southbroom Beach. Southbroom is home to the area's most upmarket **hotel**, the tranquil *Country Lodge*, Main South Coast Rd (☎03931/78380, fax 78557; ④–⑤), a romantically secluded place surrounded by forest, away from the beachfront buzz.

Heading closer to Port Edward, which marks the border with the Eastern Cape, you'll soon get to one of the quietest spots along the South Coast: **PALM BEACH**, a rocky beach bordered with banana palms with a tidal pool for swimming. **Accommodation** in the *Greenhart Holiday Resort*, Palm Beach (☎03930/92285), is in mobile homes sleeping four (②) and a campsite (①). There is an on-site shop selling basics, and a very cheap restaurant serving kalamari, burgers and chips.

The main attraction of **PORT EDWARD**, 9km further on, is its proximity to the Umtamvuna Nature Reserve (see below). Nevertheless, it's a fairly relaxed and pleasant resort, with some nice sandy beaches. There are some some good **places to stay** near the beach. *Windwood Lodge*, Owen Ellis Drive (☎03930/32169; ②), is a smart, family-oriented guesthouse some 500m from the seafront. If you can handle the institutionalized flavour and characterless bungalows, the *Rusoord Holiday Resort*, Owen Ellis Drive (☎03930/32333, fax 32296; ②), has a perfect setting along the seafront and is close to the swimming beach, with cheap caravans, camping, rondavels and chalets ideal for families.

Moving west from Port Edward, the only **public transport** are the minibus taxis which form a lively rank on the R61 just outside town, collecting passengers for the Eastern Cape, many heading across the old Transkei border to gamble at the *Wild Coast Sun* casino (see p.332).

Umtamvuna Nature Reserve

The best nature walks in the whole of KwaZulu-Natal are to be found at the **Umtamvuna Nature Reserve** (April–Aug 7am–5pm, Sept–March 6am–6pm; small entry fee), some 8km north of Port Edward. Extending 19km upriver, along the tropical Umtamvuna River and the forested cliffs rising above it, the reserve is well known for its spring flowers, and the sunbirds and sugar birds feeding on the nectar. Also here is a famous colony of rare Cape vultures, though to see where they nest you'll have to be prepared for a whole day's walk. Waymarked paths are dotted throughout the reserve.

Umtamvuna is off the road to Izingolweni, signposted near Port Edward. There is no accommodation – if you want to **stay** overnight, head for one of the pleasant options nearby. *Umtamvuna River Lodge*, Old Pont Rd (☎03930/32313; ③), offering good B&B, is set amidst tranquil forested surroundings with abundant birdlife. The advantage of *Old Pont Holiday Resort*, Old Pont Rd, Banners Rest (☎03930/32211, fax 32033), is that it is right on the banks of the river, adjacent to the nature reserve, and is a good spot for fishing, with canoes for rent if you want a paddle. Caravans (③) and camping (①) are available, and there's a café and a useful shop selling basics.

Halfway between these two places is the excellent *Old Ferry* **restaurant** (☎03930/32410), which serves fine breakfasts, lunches, dinners and teas. You can sit upstairs on a thatched, open-air deck with fantastic views of the Umtamvuna River and enjoy tasty salads and reasonably priced main courses, including oxtail stew and vegetarian dishes.

North of Durban: the Dolphin Coast

The **Dolphin Coast** is the appealing name given to the eighty-kilometre stretch along the coast north of Durban, from Umhlanga Rocks to the mouth of the Tugela River. This narrow continental shelf combines with warm, shallow waters to create ideal conditions for attracting bottle-nosed dolphins all year round to feed. Though the chances of sighting a catecean are fairly high, you'd be unwise to base a visit solely around the possibility.

Less tacky and developed than the South Coast, the North Coast attracts an upmarket breed of holidaymaker, especially to the main resorts of **Ballito** and **Salt Rock**. If an easy beachside holiday close to Durban is what you're after, **Umhlanga Rocks**, less than half an hour's drive from the centre of the city, and served by public transport, is the best choice. The beaches here are long, steep and sandy, backed by banana palms, with warm strong surf, and shark nets to protect swimmers.

Rolling in from the coast are hills of **sugar cane** plantations, the main industry of the area (it was sugar barons who established the first holiday retreats along the coastline). Driving along the roads here you'll be competing with long transport trucks, which litter the tarmac with dry stalks and strands of cane.

The Dolphin Coast is still pretty well dominated by whites; the inland towns of **Verulam**, **Tongaat** and **Stanger** have substantial Zulu and Indian populations, but their lack of facilities for travellers makes it hard to spend much time in them.

Umhlanga Rocks

UMHLANGA ROCKS, 20km from the centre of Durban, is a substantial settlement with a permanent population of around 50,000, which merges with the suburb of Durban North, and makes a good day out from the city if you're after a beach walk, swim and a meal, or even an alternative place to stay. The town's main attraction is as a swish resort offering hotel-based holidays in its seven large (and numerous smaller) establishments. Apart from the pleasant, sandy **beach** dominated by a red-and-white lighthouse, the town's main focus is the shopping area along Chartwell Drive, where you'll find a collection of smart, well-stocked malls.

A couple of kilometres north of Umhlanga's centre, the **Natal Sharks Board**, Umhlanga Rocks Drive (☎031/561 1001; small entry fee), shows an intriguing, if slightly mawkish, multiscreen audiovisual (Mon–Thurs noon, 1pm, 3pm, also Mon, Tues & Thurs 2pm), which disabuses any notions of sharks as the hooligans of the oceans and plugs the work of the Board in maintaining Natal's shark nets. You can also see a dissection of one of the sharks that has recently fallen foul of the nets (Tues–Thurs 9am, Wed 11am & 2pm; entry fee). Although these nets protect swimmers all along the coast, they are controversial: endangered turtles and dolphins also die in them and by killing sharks the natural balance of the inshore ecosystem is affected. The Sharks Board is now investigating an electronic shark barrier which might improve the situation while still ensuring safe swimming. Without your own car, the best way of getting to the Sharks Board is by one of the tuk tuks which rank outside the Umhlanga Publicity Association (see below).

Practicalities

The **Umhlanga Publicity Association**, Chartwell Drive (Mon–Fri 8.30am–1pm & 2–4.30pm; ☎031/561 4257), is a useful source for maps and information about attrac-

THE WILDLIFE
OF EAST AND
SOUTHERN AFRICA

A ROUGH GUIDE

This field guide provides a quick reference to help you identify the larger mammals likely to be encountered in East and Southern Africa. It includes most species that are found throughout these regions, as well as a limited number whose range is more restricted. Straightforward photos show easily identified markings and features. The notes give you clear pointers about the kinds of **habitat** in which you are most likely to see each mammal; its daily rhythm (usually either **nocturnal or diurnal**); the kind of **social groups** it usually forms; and general **tips about sighting** it on safari, its rarity and its relations with humans.

◤ HABITAT ◤ DIURNAL/NOCTURNAL ◤ SOCIAL LIFE ☑ SIGHTING TIPS

Photographs © Bruce Coleman Picture Library. Text © Rough Guides, 1996.

Baboon *Papio cynocephalus*

◪ open country with trees and cliffs; adaptable, but always near water

◪ diurnal

◪ troops led by a dominant male

☑ common; several subspecies, including Yellow and Olive in East Africa and Chacma in Southern Africa; easily becomes used to humans, frequently a nuisance and occasionally dangerous

Eastern Black and White Colobus
Colobus guereza

◪ rainforest and well-watered savannah; almost entirely arboreal

◪ diurnal

◪ small troops

☑ troops maintain a limited home territory, so easily located, but can be hard to see at a great height; not found in Southern Africa

Patas Monkey *Erythrocebus patas*

◪ savannah and forest margins; tolerates some aridity; terrestrial except for sleeping and lookouts

◪ diurnal

◪ small troops

☑ widespread but infrequently seen; can run at high speed and stand on hind feet supported by tail; not found in Southern Africa

Vervet Monkey *Cercopithecus aethiops*

◪ most habitats except rainforest and arid lands; arboreal and terrestrial

◪ diurnal

◪ troops

☑ widespread and common; occasionally a nuisance where used to humans

PRIMATES

White-throated or Sykes'
Monkey/Samango
Cercopithecus mitis/albogularis
■ forests; arboreal and occasionally
terrestrial
■ diurnal
■ families or small troops
✓ widespread; shyer and less easily
habituated to humans than the Vervet

Aardvark *Orycteropus afer*
■ open or wooded termite country; softer
soil preferred
■ nocturnal
■ solitary
✓ rarely seen animal, the size of a small pig;
old burrows are common and often used
by warthogs

Spring Hare *Pedetes capensis*
■ savannah; softer soil areas preferred
■ nocturnal
■ burrows, usually with a pair and their
young; often linked into a network,
almost like a colony
✓ fairly widespread rabbit-sized rodent;
impressive and unmistakable kangaroo-
like leaper

Crested Porcupine
Hystrix africae-australis
■ adaptable to a wide range of habitats
■ nocturnal and sometimes active at dusk
■ family groups
✓ large rodent (up to 90cm in length),
rarely seen, but common away from
croplands, where it's hunted as a pest

Bat-eared Fox *Otocyon megalotis*
◪ open country
◪ mainly nocturnal; diurnal activity increases in cooler months
◪ monogamous pairs
☑ distribution coincides with termites, their favoured diet; they spend many hours foraging using sensitive hearing to pinpoint their underground prey

Black-backed Jackal *Canis mesomelas*
◪ broad range from moist mountain regions to desert, but drier areas preferred
◪ normally nocturnal, but diurnal in the safety of game reserves
◪ mostly monogamous pairs; sometimes family groups
☑ common; a bold scavenger, the size of a small dog, that steals even from lions; black saddle distinguishes it from the shyer Side-striped Jackal

Hunting Dog or Wild Dog
Lycaon pictus
◪ open savannah in the vicinity of grazing herds
◪ diurnal
◪ nomadic packs
☑ extremely rare and rarely seen, but widely noted when in the area; the size of a large dog, with distinctively rounded ears

Honey Badger or Ratel
Mellivora capensis
◪ very broad range of habitats
◪ mainly nocturnal
◪ usually solitary, but also found in pairs
☑ widespread, omnivorous, badger-sized animal; nowhere common; extremely aggressive

DOG RELATIVES – HONEY BADGER

African Civet *Civettictis civetta*

⊠ prefers woodland and dense vegetation

⊠ mainly nocturnal

⊠ solitary

☑ omnivorous, medium-dog-sized, short-legged prowler; not to be confused with the smaller genet

Common Genet *Genetta genetta*

⊠ light bush country, even arid areas; partly arboreal

⊠ nocturnal, but becomes active at dusk

⊠ solitary

☑ quite common, slender, cat-sized omnivore, often seen at game lodges, where it easily becomes habituated to humans

Banded Mongoose *Mungos mungo*

⊠ thick bush and dry forest

⊠ diurnal

⊠ lives in burrow colonies of up to thirty animals

☑ widespread and quite common, the size of a small cat; often seen in a group, hurriedly foraging through the undergrowth

Spotted Hyena *Crocuta crocuta*

⊠ tolerates a wide variety of habitat, with the exception of dense forest

⊠ nocturnal but also active at dusk; also diurnal in many parks

⊠ highly social, usually living in extended family groups

☑ the size of a large dog with a distinctive loping gait, quite common in parks; carnivorous scavenger and cooperative hunter; dangerous

WEASEL RELATIVES – SPOTTED HYENA

Caracal *Caracal caracal*

■ open bush and plains; occasionally arboreal

■ mostly nocturnal

■ solitary

✔ lynx-like wild cat; rather uncommon and rarely seen

Cheetah *Acionyx jubatus*

■ savannah, in the vicinity of plains grazers

■ diurnal

■ solitary or temporary nuclear family groups

✔ widespread but low population; much slighter build than the leopard, and distinguished from it by a small head, square snout and dark "tear mark" running from eye to jowl

Leopard *Panthera pardus*

■ highly adaptable; frequently arboreal

■ nocturnal; also cooler daylight hours

■ solitary

✔ the size of a very large dog; not uncommon, but shy and infrequently seen; rests in thick undergrowth or up trees; very dangerous

Lion *Panthera leo*

■ all habitats except desert and thick forest

■ nocturnal and diurnal

■ prides of three to forty; more usually six to twelve

✔ commonly seen resting in shade; dangerous

Serval *Felis serval*

⊠ reed beds or tall grassland near water

⊠ normally nocturnal but more diurnal than most cats

⊠ usually solitary

☑ some resemblance to, but far smaller than, the cheetah; most likely to be seen on roadsides or water margins at dawn or dusk

Rock Hyrax or Dassie *Procavia capensis*

⊠ rocky areas, from mountains to isolated outcrops

⊠ diurnal

⊠ colonies consisting of a territorial male with as many as thirty related females

☑ rabbit-sized; very common; often seen sunning themselves in the early morning on rocks

African Elephant *Loxodonta africana*

⊠ wide range of habitats, wherever there are trees and water

⊠ nocturnal and diurnal; sleeps as little as four hours a day

⊠ almost human in its complexity; cows and offspring in herds headed by a matriarch; bulls solitary or in bachelor herds

☑ look out for fresh dung (football-sized) and recently damaged trees; frequently seen at waterholes from late afternoon

CATS · HYRAX · ELEPHANT

Black Rhinoceros *Diceros bicornis*

◪ usually thick bush, altitudes up to 3500m

◪ active day and night, resting between periods of activity

◪ solitary

☑ extremely rare and in critical danger of extinction; largely confined to parks where most individuals are known to rangers; distinctive hooked lip for browsing; small head usually held high; bad eyesight; very dangerous

White Rhinoceros *Ceratotherium simum*

◪ savannah

◪ active day and night, resting between periods of activity

◪ mother/s and calves, or small, same-sex herds of immature animals; old males solitary

☑ rare, restricted to parks; distinctive wide mouth (hence "white" from Afrikaans *wijd*) for grazing; large head usually lowered; docile

Burchell's Zebra *Equus burchelli*

◪ savannah, with or without trees, up to 4500m

◪ active day and night, resting intermittently

◪ harems of several mares and foals led by a dominant stallion are usually grouped together, in herds of up to several thousand

☑ widespread and common inside and outside the parks; regional subspecies include *granti* (Grant's, East Africa) and *chapmani* (Chapman's, Southern Africa, right)

Grevy's Zebra *Equus grevyi*

◪ arid regions

◪ largely diurnal

◪ mares with foals and stallions generally keep to separate troops; stallions sometimes solitary and territorial

☑ easily distinguished from smaller Burchell's Zebra by narrow stripes and very large ears; rare and localized but easily seen; not found in Southern Africa

RHINOCEROSES · ZEBRAS

Warthog *Phacochoerus aethiopicus*
◨ savannah, up to an altitude of over 2000m
◨ diurnal
◨ family groups, usually of a female and her litter
☑ common; boars are distinguishable from sows by their prominent face "warts"

Hippopotamus *Hippopotamus amphibius*
◨ slow-flowing rivers, dams and lakes
◨ principally nocturnal, leaving the water to graze
◨ bulls are solitary, but other animals live in family groups headed by a matriarch
☑ usually seen by day in water, with top of head and ears breaking the surface; frequently aggressive and very dangerous when threatened or when retreat to water is blocked

Giraffe *Giraffa camelopardalis*
◨ wooded savannah and thorn country
◨ diurnal
◨ loose, non-territorial, leaderless herds
☑ common; many subspecies, of which Maasai (*G. c. tippelskirchi*, right), Reticulated (*G. c. reticulata*, bottom l.) and Rothschild's (*G. c. rothschildi*, bottom r.) are East African; markings of Southern African subspecies are intermediate between *tippelskirchi* and *rothschildi*

WARTHOG – HIPPOPOTAMUS – GIRAFFE

African or Cape Buffalo *Syncerus caffer*

▨ wide range of habitats, always near water, up to altitudes of 4000m

▨ nocturnal and diurnal, but inactive during the heat of the day

▨ gregarious, with cows and calves in huge herds; young bulls often form small bachelor herds; old bulls are usually solitary

✔ very common; scent much more acute than other senses; very dangerous, old bulls especially so

Hartebeest *Alcelaphus buselaphus*

▨ wide range of grassy habitats

▨ diurnal

▨ females and calves in small, wandering herds; territorial males solitary

✔ hard to confuse with any other antelope except the topi/tsessebe; many varieties, distinguishable by horn shape, including Coke's, Lichtenstein's, Jackson's (right), and Red or Cape; common, but much displaced by cattle grazing

Blue or White-bearded Wildebeest *Connochaetes taurinus*

▨ grasslands

▨ diurnal, occasionally also nocturnal

▨ intensely gregarious; wide variety of associations within mega-herds which may number over 100,000 animals

✔ unmistakable, nomadic grazer; long tail, mane and beard

Topi or Tsessebe *Damaliscus lunatus*

▨ grasslands, showing a marked preference for moist savannah, near water

▨ diurnal

▨ females and young form herds with an old male

✔ widespread, very fast runners; male often stands sentry on an abandoned termite hill, actually marking the territory against rivals, rather than defending against predators

Gerenuk *Litocranius walleri*
- ⊞ arid thorn country and semi-desert
- ◪ diurnal
- ◪ solitary or in small, territorial harems
- ☑ not uncommon; unmistakable giraffe-like neck; often browses standing upright on hind legs; the female is hornless; not found in Southern Africa

Grant's Gazelle *Gazella granti*
- ⊞ wide grassy plains with good visibility, sometimes far from water
- ◪ diurnal
- ◪ small, territorial harems
- ☑ larger than the similar Thomson's Gazelle, distinguished from it by the white rump patch which extends onto the back; the female has smaller horns than the male; not found in Southern Africa

Springbok *Antidorcas marsupalis*
- ⊞ arid plains
- ◪ seasonally variable, but usually cooler times of day
- ◪ highly gregarious, sometimes in thousands; various herding combinations of males, females and young
- ☑ medium-sized, delicately built gazelle; dark line through eye to mouth and lyre-shaped horns in both sexes; found only in Botswana, Namibia and South Africa

Thomson's Gazelle *Gazella thomsoni*
- ⊞ flat, short-grass savannah, near water
- ◪ diurnal
- ◪ gregarious, in a wide variety of social structures, often massing in the hundreds with other grazing species
- ☑ smaller than the similar Grant's Gazelle, distinguished from it by the black band on flank; the female has tiny horns; not found in Southern Africa

GAZELLES

Impala *Aepyceros melampus*
- ◧ open savannah near light woodland cover
- ◧ diurnal
- ◧ large herds of females overlap with several male territories; males highly territorial during the rut when they separate out breeding harems of up to twenty females
- ☑ common, medium-sized, no close relatives; distinctive high leaps when fleeing; the only antelope with a black tuft above the hooves; males have long, lyre-shaped horns

Red Lechwe *Kobus leche*
- ◧ floodplains and areas close to swampland
- ◧ nocturnal and diurnal
- ◧ herds of up to thirty females move through temporary ram territories; occasionally thousand-strong gatherings
- ☑ semi-aquatic antelope with distinctive angular rump; rams have large forward-pointing horns; not found in East Africa

Common Reedbuck *Redunca arundinum*
- ◧ reedbeds and tall grass near water
- ◧ nocturnal and diurnal
- ◧ monogamous pairs or family groups in territory defended by the male
- ☑ medium-sized antelope, with a plant diet unpalatable to other herbivores; only males have horns

Common or Defassa Waterbuck
Kobus ellipsiprymnus
- ◧ open woodland and savannah, near water
- ◧ nocturnal and diurnal
- ◧ territorial herds of females and young, led by dominant male, or territorial males visited by wandering female herds
- ☑ common, rather tame, large antelope; plant diet unpalatable to other herbivores; shaggy coat; only males have horns

Kirk's Dikdik *Rhincotragus kirki*

🅧 scrub and thornbush, often far from water

🅧 nocturnal and diurnal, with several sleeping periods

🅧 pairs for life, often accompanied by current and previous young

☑ tiny, hare-sized antelope, named after its alarm cry; only males have horns; not found in Southern Africa except Namibia

Common Duiker *Sylvicapra grimmia*

🅧 adaptable; prefers scrub and bush

🅧 nocturnal and diurnal

🅧 most commonly solitary; sometimes in pairs; occasionally monogamous

☑ widespread and common small antelope with a rounded back; seen close to cover; rams have short straight horns

Sitatunga *Tragelaphus spekei*

🅧 swamps

🅧 nocturnal and sometimes diurnal

🅧 territorial and mostly solitary or in pairs

☑ very localized and not likely to be mistaken for anything else; usually seen half submerged; females have no horns

Nyala *Tragelaphus angasi*

🅧 dense woodland near water

🅧 primarily nocturnal with some diurnal activity

🅧 flexible and non-territorial; the basic unit is a female and two offspring

☑ in size midway between the Kudu and Bushbuck, and easily mistaken for the latter; orange legs distinguish it; only males have horns; not found in East Africa

DWARF ANTELOPES - BUSHBUCK ANTELOPES

Bushbuck *Tragelaphus scriptus*

■ thick bush and woodland close to water

■ principally nocturnal, but also active during the day when cool

■ solitary, but casually sociable; sometimes grazes in small groups

✔ medium-sized antelope with white stripes and spots; often seen in thickets, or heard crashing through them; not to be confused with the far larger Nyala; the male has shortish straight horns

Eland *Taurotragus oryx*

■ highly adaptable; semi-desert to mountains, but prefers scrubby plains

■ nocturnal and diurnal

■ non-territorial herds of up to sixty with temporary gatherings of as many as a thousand

✔ common but shy; the largest and most powerful African antelope; both sexes have straight horns with a slight spiral

Greater Kudu *Tragelaphus strepsiceros*

■ semi-arid, hilly or undulating bush country; tolerant of drought

■ diurnal when secure; otherwise nocturnal

■ territorial; males usually solitary; females in small troops with young

✔ impressively big antelope (up to 1.5m at shoulder) with very long, spiral horns in the male; very localized; shy of humans and not often seen

Lesser Kudu *Tragelaphus imberbis*

■ semi-arid, hilly or undulating bush country; tolerant of drought

■ diurnal when secure; otherwise nocturnal

■ territorial; males usually solitary; females in small troops with young

✔ smaller than the Greater Kudu; only the male has horns; extremely shy and usually seen only as it disappears; not found in Southern Africa

Gemsbok *Oryx gazella gazella*

◨ open grasslands; also waterless wastelands; tolerant of prolonged drought

◨ nocturnal and diurnal

◨ highly hierarchical mixed herds of up to fifteen, led by a dominant bull

✔ large antelope with unmistakable horns in both sexes; subspecies *gazella* is one of several similar forms, sometimes considered separate species; not found in East Africa

Fringe-eared Oryx *Oryx gazella callotis*

◨ open grasslands; also waterless wastelands; tolerant of prolonged drought

◨ nocturnal and diurnal

◨ highly hierarchical mixed herds of up to fifteen, led by a dominant bull

✔ the *callotis* subspecies is one of two found in Kenya, the other, found in the northeast, being *Oryx g. beisa* (the Beisa Oryx); not found in Southern Africa

Roan Antelope *Hippotragus equinus*

◨ tall grassland near water

◨ nocturnal and diurnal; peak afternoon feeding

◨ small herds led by a dominant bull; herds of immature males; sometimes pairs in season

✔ large antelope, distinguished from the Sable by lighter, greyish colour, shorter horns (both sexes) and narrow, tufted ears

Sable Antelope *Hippotragus niger*

◨ open woodland with medium to tall grassland near water

◨ nocturnal and diurnal

◨ territorial; bulls divide into sub-territories, through which cows and young roam; herds of immature males; sometimes pairs in season

✔ large antelope; upper body dark brown to black; mask-like markings on the face; both sexes have huge curved horns

ORYXES · ROAN ANTELOPE · SABLE ANTELOPE

Grysbok *Raphicerus melanotis*

☒ thicket adjacent to open grassland

☒ nocturnal

☒ rams territorial; loose pairings

☑ small, rarely seen antelope; two
subspecies, Cape (*R. m. melanotis*, South
Africa, right) and Sharpe's (*R. m. sharpei*,
East Africa); distinguished from more
slender Steenbok by light underparts;
rams have short horns

Oribi *Ourebia ourebi*

☒ open grassland

☒ diurnal

☒ territorial harems consisting of male and
one to four females

☑ localized small antelope, but not hard to
see where common; only males have
horns; the Oribi is distinguished from the
smaller Grysbok and Steenbok by a black
tail and dark skin patch below the eye

Steenbok *Raphicerus campestris*

☒ dry savannah

☒ nocturnal and diurnal

☒ solitary or (less often) in pairs

☑ widespread small antelope, particularly in
Southern Africa, but shy; only males have
horns

Klipspringer *Oreotragus oreotragus*

☒ rocky country; cliffs and kopjes

☒ diurnal

☒ territorial ram with mate or small family
group; often restricted to small long-term
territories

☑ small antelope; horns normally only on
male; extremely agile on rocky terrain;
unusually high hooves, giving the
impression of walking on tiptoe

tions up the coast. Outside, you'll find the **tuk-tuk** rank and the ticket kiosk and **bus** stop for the *Umhlanga Express* (☎031/561 2860), which runs five times every weekday to the Tourist Junction in central Durban.

The *Beverly Hills Sun*, Lighthouse Rd (☎031/561 2211, fax 561 3711; ⑦), is without doubt the most sumptuous **place to stay**, while on the opposite side of the road the *Oyster Box* (☎031/561 2233, fax 561 4072; ③–⑥), the oldest hotel on the Dolphin Coast, oozes a more established elegance for less than half the price. The *Box* is also a great place for **tea or drinks**; you can sit on the outside terrace and gaze at the ocean. The town's best-value **B&B** is *Honey Pot Cottage*, 11 Hilken Drive, north of the M4 (☎031/561 3795, fax 561 2088; ③), which has en-suite units, set in gardens with a swimming pool.

Among the surfeit of cheap fast-food outlets, you'll find a handful of good **restaurants**, including *Cottonfields*, 2 Lagoon Drive, a popular local bistro and bar whose menu features *potjiekos*, traditional Afrikaner fare, served in a small three-legged cast-iron pots. If you can afford to splash out, look no further than *Razzmatazz*, at the *Umhlanga Sands Hotel*, Lagoon Drive. The restaurant has a great outdoor deck, and a prodigious reputation for its eclectic cuisine, which ranges from springbok fillets to Indonesian-style langoustines, and reputedly the best wine list in the province.

Umdloti, La Mercy and Tongaat

North of Umhlanga, the blur of development unexpectedly opens out into sugar cane hills and subtropical coastal vegetation. Plans for a big new international airport at La Mercy will certainly change this rural ambience, so get here while you can. **UMD-LOTI**, just 6km north of Umhlanga, has a safe swimming beach, as well as a fabulous natural rock pool, great for swimming or snorkelling on the calm inside of the shallow reef. A couple of kilometres further along at **LA MERCY** is a recommended **restaurant**; the long-established *Sea Bell*, a slightly tatty curry house under a dingy hotel, which is noted for its piquant prawns (there's also a vegetarian alternative) and marvellous sea views, from where you can occasionally sight dolphins.

Tongaat Beach, 12km further up the coast, is monopolized by the slighly old-fashioned *Westbrook Beach* (☎ & fax 0322/42021; ③), a **hotel** worth visiting for its **restaurant** with outdoor seating, casual atmosphere and superb wild oysters. The hotel also has its own wide beach and a swimming pool. A popular spot with **surfers** is the break at Westbrook Beach, just south of the parking area.

TONGAAT itself is a couple of kilometres inland from here across the N2 highway, a barrier between the coastal resorts and the gritty workings of Natal's sugar industry. Arriving in town you'll be confronted by a massive **sugar mill** pumping pungent white smoke from its towering chimneys, and people walking down the road chewing stalks of sugar cane. The town, fronted by neglected imitation-Cape Dutch cottages, has long associations with South Africa's Indian community and boasts a handful of garish temples. The most distinguished of these is the small but awesome **Shri Jugganath Puri Temple**, off the main road, on the corner of Catherine and Plane streets. A whitewashed, phallic building tipped by deities on each corner, and surrounded by mango trees, the temple is dedicated to Vishnu and is a National Monument, built at the turn of the century by the Sanskrit scholar Pandit Shrikishan Maharaj who came to Natal in 1895. To get to the temple, take the R102 towards Durban, turn right into Ganie Street at the first traffic lights after the police station, then left into Plane Street and left again into Catherine Street.

Ballito and Shaka's Rock

There's nothing very African about **BALLITO**, a Mediterranean-style resort 43km up the coast from Durban, with a splurge of time-shares, high-rise holiday apartments and shopping malls by the sea. Nevertheless, it's a pleasant enough place, with a beach offering safe swimming and full-time lifeguards, and a couple of natural rock pools for bathing – one at Ballito itself, and the other at the far northern end of Ballito beach, near the Santorini development.

The excellent **Dolphin Coast Publicity Association** (☎0322/61997, fax 62434), just behind the BP service station as you enter town, has an up-to-date list of B&Bs and can supply information about the surrounding area. The cheapest **place to stay** is the *Dolphin Coast Backpackers*, La Ballito Flats (☎0322/61644), which has a self-contained apartment sleeping six, near the beach. *Dolphin Holiday Resort*, a well-shaded campsite and collection of self-catering cottages on the corner of Compensation Beach Road and Hillary Drive (☎0322/62187; ②), has no sea view but is a five-minute walk from the beach. For more comfort, head for *Holland Farm Guest House*, Farm No. X7, Ensembi Rd (☎0322/91 8663, fax 91 8831; ④), which has country-style rooms and patios leading to a garden on a genuine anthurium flower farm. Equally comfortable is *Shorten's Country House*, Compensation Beach Rd (☎0322/71140, fax 71144; ⑥), a historic colonial homestead surrounded by wonderful gardens. Ballito's best **restaurant** is *Mariner's*, Ballito Shopping Centre, Compensation Beach Rd, which serves pricey but outstanding seafood.

Some 49km north of Durban, the rather tame coastal resort of **SHAKA'S ROCK** feels at odds with the name of Shaka, whose warrior reputation reverberated across southern Africa in the nineteenth century. More or less a continuation of Ballito, Shaka's Rock is dominated by the *Salt Rock*, Basil Hulett Drive (☎0322/5025, fax 5071; ③–④), a **hotel** built and still run by the Huletts, one of the region's biggest sugar families. The beach here is good for swimming, and there's a bell on a sea-facing deck outside the hotel which guests use to ring the alert when dolphins are spotted. Adjoining the hotel is its **caravan park** (②), situated on grassy terraces. Two tidal pools, great for swimming, are built into the rocks below the hotel; this is where Zulu women are reputed to have collected salt in King Shaka's day. An even better tidal rock pool is at Thompson's Bay, built on an elevated rocky platform with changing rooms and big enough for anyone wanting to swim serious lengths. To get to Thompson's Bay, simply walk back along the beach, towards Ballito.

Stanger and Groutville

You'll get far more of a sense of Shaka's legendary status as founder of the Zulu state by heading inland along the R102 to **STANGER**, which has a special place in the cosmology of Zulu nationalists. Roughly 70km north of Durban, Stanger is the site of the Zulu king's last *kraal* and the place where he was treacherously stabbed to death in 1828 by his half-brother Dingane who succeeded him. Shaka used his exceptional military talents to build up the Zulu state into the greatest power in southeast Africa by the mid-1820s – creating disquiet even among the British with their mighty army. The warrior is said to have been buried upright in a grain pit, and is commemorated by a small park and memorial in Couper Street, bang in the centre of town. Near the memorial is a rock with a groove worn into it – supposedly where Shaka sharpened his spears. These days, the park is the venue for a semi-religious pilgrimage by modern-day **Zulu warriors** from all over the country – members of the fiercely Zulu nationalist Inkatha Freedom Party (IFP), which controls the province. Every year, on September 24, they gather here to be addressed by their leader, **Chief Mangosuthu Buthelezi**, a mercurial figure who started his political life as an ANC member, but later fell out with the organization and is now playing the Zulu nationalist card in his bid for provincial autonomy.

At the rear of the garden, the **Dukuza Interpretative Centre** (Mon–Fri 8am–4pm, Sat & Sun 9am–4pm; free) has a small display on Shaka and a very good fifteen-minute audiovisual display. Nearby, the lively **Stanger Market** in Market Road, off King George Road, is where Zulu and Indian traders sell fresh spices, herbs, fruit and vegetables, not for the benefit of tourists (you're unlikely to meet any here) but simply for local consumption.

Some 8km south of Stanger on the R102, just across a rusty bridge over the Mvoti River, tiny **GROUTVILLE** is remarkable mainly for the grave of **Albert Luthuli**, one of South Africa's greatest nationalist leaders. A teacher and chief of the Zulus in Groutville, Luthuli became President General of the ANC in 1952. He espoused a non-violent struggle against apartheid and was awarded the Nobel Peace prize in 1960, which at home earned him a succession of banning orders restricting him to the Stanger area. In 1967 he died in mysterious circumstances in Stanger, apparently knocked down by a train. The chief is buried next to a whitewashed, nineteenth-century corrugated-iron mission church. Luthuli's life is recounted in his moving autobiography, *Let My People Go*.

Blythedale and Zinkwazi

The closest stretch of sand to Stanger is at **BLYTHEDALE**, some 8km away, where a ban on high-rise construction has preserved the deserted appearance of its endless **beach** and kept buildings screened behind the curtain of thick coastal vegetation. Swimming here is possible; shark nets are up between December and April and lifeguards are on duty in season. As with many spots along the KwaZulu-Natal coast, you're likely to see local fishermen trying their luck for shad, garrick, kingfish and barracuda. There's **camping** at *La Mouette Caravan Park*, 1 Umvoti Drive (☎0324/22547; ①), just back from the beach, and cottages to rent at *Mini Villas* across the road (☎0324/21277; ②–③). Slightly smarter cottages in a nicer setting are rented out by Mr Palsa (☎0324/21496; ②–③).

The northernmost and least-developed beach resort along the Dolphin Coast is **ZINKWAZI**, 13km beyond Blythedale, with mobile-home chalets (②–③) and campsites (①) set in lovely riverine gardens on the Zinkwazi River Estuary (☎0324/3344). Boat trips along the river are recommended for bird-watching enthusiasts.

Harold Johnson Nature Reserve

Abutting the Tugela River is the **Harold Johnson Nature Reserve** (☎0324/61574; entry fee), signposted 24km north of Stanger off the N2. With its well-preserved coastal bush, steep cliffs and gullies, this is a fine place to come for a day's visit or an overnight camp. At the main picnic site and parking area, you'll find a cultural **museum** housed in huts and featuring displays of Zulu beadwork and aspects of Zulu society. You can follow the two-kilometre "Remedies and Rituals" **trail** which starts from the picnic site and takes you through plants whose medicinal uses you can read about. Alternatively, pick up the "Thukela Trail" booklet and follow a walk which highlights various historical sites in the reserve, most of them connected to the Anglo-Zulu War of 1879 and Ultimatum Tree. This wild fig tree, all but demolished in a cyclone in 1987, was where the British issued their ultimatum to King Chetshwayo in 1878, part of which required the Zulus to demobilize their standing army. The British used his non-compliance as an excuse to attack the Zulus and crush their independence. The remains of Fort Pearson, from which the British launched out to invade Zululand, are also on the trail.

It's possible to simply turn up and camp at the reserve, but there are no shops or facilities, so be sure to stock up in Stanger beforehand.

Pietermaritzburg

Although **PIETERMARITZBURG** (often called "Maritzburg") sells itself as the best-preserved Victorian city in South Africa, with strong British connections, not that much of its colonial heritage remains, and it is actually a very South African city. **Zulus** make up the largest community, with people of **Indian** descent coming second, and those of **British** extraction a minority – albeit a high-profile one. This multiculturalism, together with a substantial student population, add up to a fairly lively city that's also safe and small enough to explore on foot.

Only 80km inland from Durban along the fast N3 freeway, Pietermaritzburg is an easy day's outing from the coastal city, and one you can do taking in the Valley of a Thousand Hills (see p.363) along the way. Maritzburg is also well-positioned for an overnight stop on your way to the Drakensberg (see p.381) or the Battlefields in the Ladysmith (see p.419) vicinity.

Some history

Pietermaritzburg's **Afrikaner** origins are reflected in its name; after slaughtering three thousand Zulus at the Battle of Blood River, the Voortrekkers established the fledgling **Republic of Natalia** in 1839, naming their capital in honour of the Boer leaders Piet Retief and Gerrit Maritz. The republic's independence was short-lived, and four years later **Britain** annexed it and spent the rest of the century transforming Pietermaritzburg into an English town stamped with all the grandeur and pomposity of empire. Even as the Afrikaners trekked north to escape the irksome British, English settlers were arriving from the south to swell the city's population, and during the closing decade of the nineteenth century Maritzburg was the most important centre in the colony of Natal with a population of nearly 10,000 (more than Durban at that time).

Indians arrived at the turn of this century, mostly as indentured labourers but also as traders. Among their number was a young, little-known lawyer called **Mohandas Gandhi**, who was to become a thorn in the side of the British in India. He later traced the embryo of his devastatingly successful tactic of passive resistance to an incident in 1893, when he was booted out of a first-class train compartment at Pietermaritzburg Station because he wasn't white.

Pietermaritzburg is the provincial capital of KwaZulu-Natal, but its exact status is ambiguous, as Ulundi in the former KwaZulu *bantustan* is currently tussling to be recognized as the political centre of the province.

Arrival and information

Daily flights from Johannesburg, used mainly by business travellers, arrive at the city's **Oribi airport** (✆61542), south of the town centre. The only means of getting from here to town is by taxi. It's far easier to fly into **Durban airport** (see p.340), which is connected twice daily to Pietermaritzburg by the *Cheetah* **shuttle bus** (✆42 2673). The journey takes about 75 minutes and the bus drops off outside the *Imperial Hotel*, 224 Loop St. The *Cheetah* also picks up passengers in the centre of Durban outside the local history museum in Aliwal Street. *Greyhound, Intercape* and *Translux* **intercity buses** pull in at the bus terminal on the north side of the information bureau, on the corner of Longmarket Street and Commercial Road. From here you can walk to the most central of the city hotels or take a taxi, which is also your best option to get to the suburban B&Bs.

The **telephone code** for Pietermaritzburg is ✆0331.

ACCOMMODATION
1 African Dreamzz
2 Ascot Inn
3 City Royal Hotel
4 Crossways Country Inn
5 Debbie's B&B
6 Duvet & Crumpets
7 Imperial Hotel
8 M'sunduzi Lodge
9 Rehoboth Cottages
10 Sunduzi Backpacker Lodge
11 Tudor Inn

PIETERMARITZBURG

If you're staying at either of the two backpackers' lodges, you can arrange for staff to pick you up. The *Baz* **backpacker bus** drops off at any of the central accommodation.

Arriving **by train**, you'll find yourself at the station (☎958 2006) at the unsavoury southwest end of Longmarket Street, one of the main city thoroughfares. The station's down-at-heel environs make it advisable to arrange beforehand to be collected, particularly at night.

The **tourist information bureau**, Publicity House, on the corner of Longmarket Street and Commercial Road (Mon–Fri 8.30am–4.30pm, Sat 8.30am–12.30pm; ☎45 1348, fax 94 3535), has a good selection of books and accommodation leaflets and also sells tickets for *Translux* and *Greyhound* buses. If you're planning on staying any length of time and will be travelling into the suburbs, a fold-out **map** of the whole city will come in handy. The best place to find one of these is at *Shuter & Shooter*, 230 Church St, which also stocks travel guides, natural history field guides and books covering Natal history.

The hectic minibus **taxi rank** is outside the tourist information bureau, and stretches from the bus terminus right down the block (destinations are posted outside the taxis). **Metered taxis** should be booked in advance (see "Listings", p.380), and in this compact city are unlikely to break the bank.

Accommodation

Pietermaritzburg has the whole gamut of **accommodation**, ranging from two good backpackers' lodges – conveniently located for the station and the central nightspots – to self-catering places and cheap B&Bs around the university on the south side of town, and more comfortable B&Bs in the lush northern suburbs – ideal if you're in a car. You'll also find a handful of good-value hotels in the city centre.

African Dreamzz, 30 Taunton Rd, Wembley (☎94 5141, fax 45 5937). One mini-suite in a family home on a large property 2km from the centre. Guests have use of the garden on a stream as well as the tennis court and swimming pool. ②.

Ascot Inn, 210 Woodhouse Rd, Scottsville (☎ & fax 67958). Complex of comfortable mock-colonial cottages set on large lawned property, next to Scottsville race course and the N3. Swimming pool. ②.

Brevisbrook, 28 Waverleydale Rd, Boughton (☎0331/44 1402, fax 45 3293). Three en-suite rooms with private entrances and use of a swimming pool and *braai* area in a large garden. Breakfast can be served on the patio. ③.

City Royal Hotel, 301 Burger St, City centre (☎94 7072, fax 94 7080). Pietermaritzburg's only four-star hotel is in a 1930s building that has been fully modernized and caters mainly to business travellers. Ask about their substantial discounts, offered over weekends and during school holidays. ④.

Crossways Country Inn, Old Howick Rd, Hilton (☎43 3267). Roughly 9km north of Pietermaritzburg, and a fine choice if you want to be out of town. Modelled on an English country pub, with nice old furniture, this is also a good place to stop off for teas and lunches. ③.

Debbie's, 17 Mills Circle, Hayfields (☎61719). Cheap B&B near the university, with a very friendly host. Accommodation is in two modest rooms, each with its own little garden, and is especially good value if you're sharing. Free lifts are offered to and from the bus station. ①– ②.

Duvet and Crumpets, 1 Freelands Place, Wembley (☎ & fax 94 4133). Self-catering or B&B in a simple but pleasantly furnished mini-apartment in a 1930s family home. ②.

Imperial Hotel, 224 Loop St, City centre (☎42 6551, fax 42 9796). Popular with business travellers, this grand red-brick hotel is looking a bit past its prime with a huge entrance foyer, large rooms and heavy staircases. ④.

M'sunduzi Lodge, 82 Henderson Rd, Athlone (☎ & fax 94 4388). A cut above the other B&Bs, this offers very comfortable, well-furnished mini-apartments with views across the city, attached to a sociable private house. Use of bar, jacuzzi and swimming pool – where huge breakfasts are served. ④.

Rehoboth, 276 Murray Rd, Hayfields (☎96 2312, fax 96 4008). Bright and cheerful mock-Victorian self-catering cottages set in large gardens 6km south of the centre. ②.

Sunduzi Backpacker Lodge, 140 Berg St (☎94 0072). Party atmosphere at this centrally located lodge close to all the town nightspots. Choose from the family house where bedrooms have been turned into dorms, or camping in the garden. Cheap meals (vegetarians catered for) are available, as are free pick-ups from the train or bus station. Friendly staff can help you arrange trips around the country. ①.

Tudor Inn, 18 Theatre Lane (☎42 1778, fax 45 1030). Immaculate and comfortable rooms at this lit-tle inn right in the characterful central Lanes area, run by a Portuguese proprietor who has creat-ed a European ambience. Each room has a small lounge area, phone and TV. ③.

The City

Most places of interest in Pietermaritzburg are within easy walking distance of the cen-tre's heart, which is crossed by the junction of **Commercial Road** and **Longmarket Street**, slicing across it from the train station in the southwest. The inevitable old apartheid divisions are marked out by roads and railways, with the African majority crammed into townships south of the station, as they used to be excluded from the city centre. By contrast, Indians were allowed to bring their business into the city fringes, but only as far as Boshoff Street, northeast of Commercial Road. Around here, and in the nearby Asian suburbs of Woodlands, Mountain Rise and Willowton, you'll find the greatest concentration of shops selling cheap spicy snacks like *rotis* and *bunny chows*, as well as the city centre's mosques and Hindu temples. On the hills, northwest of the centre, the predominantly white and affluent suburbs of Wembley, Athlone and Montrose look down from their heights at the sweaty buzz in the valley below, while south of the centre, **Natal University**, in Scottsville, is the magnet that attracts large numbers of students to set up digs in the suburban houses.

City Hall, Tatham Art Gallery and around

The **City Hall**, on the corner of Commercial Road and Church Street, once made inter-national fame when it was recognized by Ripley's *Believe it or Not* as the "largest work-laden brick building south of the equator". It's definitely worth a look as a great exam-ple of late Victorian red-brick civic architecture, self-assuredly holding the prime spot in town, with wonderful detailing and an impressive fifteen-metre clock tower.

Across Commercial Road, the **Tatham Art Gallery** (Tues–Fri 10am–6pm; free), another fine brick edifice, is the undoubted highlight of Pietermaritzburg's formal attractions and houses one of the country's best collections of international and local art. Completed in 1871 as the Supreme Court of the Colony of Natal, the building formed the central complex of the capital's defences when an invasion was feared dur-ing the Zulu War of 1879. In 1990 the building became home to the Tatham collection and the Zulus finally made it inside, with artworks by black South Africans exhibited alongside those by Pablo Picasso, Graham Sutherland, Edgar Degas, David Hockney and Henri Matisse.

Adjacent to the Tatham, firmly rooted on the corner of Longmarket and Commercial streets, the **Old Natal Parliament Building** represents a typical piece of imperial architecture. Started in 1889 for Queen Victoria's Jubilee, it borrows the grand lan-guage of columns and pediments from the Roman Empire. Standing amid the formal front gardens is a statue of the unamused "Queen Empress" wielding a distinctly Freudian combination of a sceptre and orb. From here, heading down **Longmarket Street** as far as Chapel Street, you'll pass a series of attractive period buildings, most notable of which are: the **post office**, a solid dressed stone pile built in 1903; the three-storey **Reid's Building**, a little further along and considered a daringly tall skyscraper in its day; and the **First National Bank**, even further along, which dates from 1903 and had its facade chosen from an Edwardian catalogue and shipped out from the mother country. Between this section of Longmarket and Church streets is the tightly gridded warren of alleyways known as the **Lanes**, a mostly pedestrianized quarter of lawyers' offices, takeaways, shops and an inordinate number of hairdressers. The area, which was the financial hub of Natal from 1888 to 1931, and housed four separate stock exchanges, is enjoyable to explore during the day, but is a notorious stamping ground of pickpockets, so stay alert and don't come here after dark. Any of the Lanes will bring you through to Church Street, which is worth wandering along back up to Commercial Road to take in some more period buildings.

On the corner of Chapel Street, **St Peter's Church**, completed in 1857, was the base for Bishop John Colenso after he was kicked out of the Church of England for his liberal theological ideas and his role in championing the Zulu cause against the British. As you head up Church Street, back toward the City Hall, you can't miss the **Gandhi Statue**, unveiled on June 6, 1993, on the centenary of his being thrown out of a first-class train carriage at Pietermaritzburg station because he wasn't white. Adjacent to Gandhi, the **Supreme Court Gardens** on the corner of Commercial Road and Church Street, are filled with monuments to Britons who died fighting against the Zulus, the Boers and other European powers in two world wars.

The museums

On the corner of Longmarket and Boshoff streets, the **Voortrekker Museum** (Mon–Fri 9am–4pm, Sat 8am–noon; free), centres on the original Church of the Vow, built in 1838 by Boers in honour of their victory over the Zulus three years earlier at the Battle of Blood River. The church was their part of a bargain allegedly struck with God (see p.422). The museum connects with the Voortrekker roots of Pietermaritzburg and is worth a fleeting visit to gain a little insight into life on trek. The most interesting items are the home-made children's toys and beautifully embroidered *kappies* (hats) which the women used to shield themselves from the sun. Across the lovely courtyard garden is the reconstructed house of **Andries Pretorius**, leader of the Voortrekkers at Blood River and the force behind the establishment of the Boer Republic of Natal. The thatched house, originally built in 1846, is appealing for its sheer simplicity, which stands in contrast to fussy Victorian fashion.

Less inspiring is the **Natal Museum**, 237 Loop St (Mon–Sat 9am–4.30pm, Sun 10am–5pm; small entry fee), one block east of the Old Natal Parliament, with an uncompelling collection of stuffed animals, dioramas, a small dinosaur display and a reconstruction of a late Victorian Maritzburg street. The best reason to visit is for the display of African sculpture, crafts and masks from across the continent, the highlight of which is a golden stool taken by British invaders as booty from the Asante people of Ghana.

ALAN PATON

Writer, teacher and politician **Alan Paton**, best known for his first novel *Cry, the Beloved Country*, was born in Pietermaritzburg in 1903. His visionary book, which focused international attention on the plight of black South Africans, was published in 1948 – the same year the National Party assumed power and began to put apartheid in place. Despite selling millions of copies worldwide, Paton's book coincided with a rising tide of repression inside the country and he entered politics to become a founder-member of the non-racial and fiercely anti-apartheid Liberal Party. He was president of the party from 1960 until 1968, when it was forced to disband by repressive legislation forbidding multiracial political organizations. Paton died in Durban in 1988, having published a number of works, including two biographies and his own autobiography. The following year the Alan Paton Centre (☎95 5622) was established at the University of Natal's archives building at 165 King Edward Ave. The Centre includes Paton's recreated study, personal memorabilia and documents.

Continuing down Loop Street for about 1km, you'll reach Pine Street, on the corner of which is the **Macrorie House Museum** (Tues–Thurs 9am–1pm, Sun 11am–4pm; small entry fee), a beautiful two-storey Victorian house with intricate wrought-iron detailing. The house, which contains furniture and relics of early British settlers, was built in 1862 and became the home of Bishop Macrorie from 1869 to 1891, after he arrived to take over from Bishop Colenso. Striking northwest up Pine Street brings you to the classically Victorian **Railway Station** at the end of Church Street. Although a little neglected in this now seedy part of town, the station remains notable for its alternating courses of red-brick and stone facings and for its fine wrought-iron lacework dripping from the forecourt eaves. As you enter the concourse, a small plaque on your left, just before the platform, records (yet again) that this was where Gandhi was thrown off a train for trying to occupy a first-class compartment reserved for whites.

Eating, drinking and nightlife

Pietermaritzburg has a fairly good choice of **restaurants**, as well as a handful of decent **nightclubs** and pubs, particularly along Commercial Road. Nightlife in the town centre is mostly white-dominated and you'll have to head to *Jezebel's* for a broader mix of people and sounds.

The two **cinema** complexes – the *Nu Metro*, in the Cascades Centre, McCarthy Drive, in the northern suburbs, and *Ster-Kinekor*, 50 Durban Rd, in Scottsville – show mainstream releases. The university's *Hexagon* and *Churchill* **theatres** host occasional productions – check the *Natal Witness* newspaper for details.

Restaurants and cafés

Café du Midi, 262 Boom St. In an old house with an outdoor garden serving moderately priced Mediterranean-style food. Good for outdoor coffee during the day.

Els Amicos, 380 Longmarket St (☎45 6524). Maritzburg's oldest restaurant in a colonial house is a popular place with a pleasant atmosphere, good prices and a varied menu.

Kara Nichha's, 470 Church St. Excellent, very cheap Indian takeaways, including filled *rotis* and Indian sweets.

Plaka Taverna, 117 Longmarket St (☎94 7727). Mid-priced Greek restaurant where you bring your own alcohol and can linger until the small hours.

Restaurant da Vinci, 117 Commercial Rd (☎45 6632). Rowdy American-Italian place with cheap pasta dishes and live music on Sunday evenings.

Spur, 50 Durban Rd, Scottsville. Popular chain for steaks, salads and unbeatably priced salad-box takeaways.

Tatham Art Gallery Coffee Shop, Commercial Rd. Best place in town for coffee and light lunches in the old Supreme Court, right in the centre, opposite the tourist information bureau.

Tropicana, 418 Longmarket St. Popular with Indian families, and serving up cheap curries and an extensive menu of burger and steak grills with chips.

Turtle Bay, 7 Wembley Terrace, Wembley, just off the N3 circle (☎94 5390). Excellent but pricey seafood restaurant in the northern suburbs.

Upper Crust, Longmarket St, opposite the taxi rank. Good for a range of bread, and imported foods such as olive oil and Swiss chocolate, with home-baked pastries and pies.

Bars and nightclubs

Buzz Bar, 204 Longmarket St. Lively nightspot with an emphasis on white South African music.

Cafe 21, 50 Durban Rd, Scottsville. Live bands occasionally play at this day and evening café near the university, and worth checking out if you're staying in the area.

Crowded House, 124 Balhambra Way. Pleasant indoor and outdoor bar which attracts a late-twenties crowd.

Jezebel's, 220 Commercial Rd. The city centre's only club that steers away from a predominantly white ambience. *Jezebel's* has a black American vibe, with discos on Thurs and Fri nights and live bands on Sat.

Keg and Elephant, 80 Commercial Rd. Cheap pub meals popular with a mix of students – black middle class and townsfolk.

Locker Room, 91 Commercial Rd. Young white dancing venue, with a sports bar and plenty of serious drinking.

McGinty's Irish Pub, 50 Durban Rd, Scottsville. Fairly smart pub with occasional live Irish music.

Listings

Banks are easy to find in the shopping areas of the city centre, as well as in all the suburban malls. Opening hours are Mon–Fri 8.30am–3.30pm, Sat 8–11am. Wherever you find banks you'll find automatic teller machines (ATMs).

Credit and bank card theft ☎toll free 0800 953 4300 or 418 5600.

Emergencies Ambulance ☎1 10177; Fire ☎42 1311; Police (Flying Squad) ☎1 0111; Rape Crisis ☎45 6279.

Hospitals and doctors Doctors are listed in the telephone directory under "Medical". For any medical emergencies, contact *Mediclinic*, Payn St (☎42 7023 or 42 7024).

Laundry *The Wash Tub*, Shop 2, Park Lane Centre, Commercial Rd (☎45 7458), is open daily 24 hrs.

Pharmacy offering extended opening hours is *PMB Medicine Depot*, 33 Commercial Rd (☎42 4581; Mon–Fri 6am–9.30pm, Sat 3–9.30pm, Sun 9am–1pm & 3–9.30pm).

Taxis *Junior Taxi Service*, 391 Berg St (☎94 5454), and *Wilken Taxis*, 90 Sanctuary Rd (☎42 3333), are two established firms.

Telephones There are public phones all over Pietermaritzburg taking phone cards and coins.

The Midlands

For most travellers, the verdant farmland that makes up the **Midlands** is picture-postcard terrain, whizzed through on the two-hour journey from Durban or Pietermaritzburg to the Drakensberg Mountains. There's really not much reason to dally here, unless you've time to kill, money to spend and fancy taking in the region's quaint, English-style county inns, tea shops and craft shops. From 1842 to 1897 battalion after battalion of British troops marched through the Midlands during a succession of wars to pacify first the Zulus and later the Boers. The region plays up its **British** connections, with trout fishing clubs, polo clubs (over eighty percent of the country's clubs are based here), posh boarding schools and old-fashioned country hotels. The cosy image is deceptive: security fences erected around most farms indicate deep levels of black resentment, with theft common and murder of white landowners not unusual.

Public relations consultants in the Midlands have been working overtime and have dreamt up the "**Midlands Meander**", a route that takes in a number of dispersed craftspeople, hotels and other minor attractions along a series of very attractive back routes. The scenery and little stopoffs are more appealing than any of the Midlands towns, which you can comfortably bypass in the certainty that you're not missing much. A number of upmarket country hotels offer plush accommodation, and there are B&Bs and self-catering cottages for cheaper stays. A free **map** outlining the attractions on this trip is available from most information bureaus throughout the vicinity.

The Midlands has an interesting historical footnote. Heading north out of Pietermaritzburg on the N3 through the Midlands, you're roughly tracing **Nelson Mandela's last journey** as a free man before being arrested in 1962 and imprisoned for 27 years. **Howick**, 18km north of Pietermaritzburg, is recorded as the place where his historic detention began. The actual spot is on the R103, 2km north of a sideroad heading to the Tweedie junction. On the run from the police, Mandela had been continuing his political activities, often travelling in disguise – a practice that earned him the nickname of the "Black Pimpernel". On this occasion he was masquerading as the chauffeur of a white friend, when their car was stopped on the old Howick road, apparently because of a tip-off. A memorial unveiled by Mandela himself in 1996 marks the unassuming spot, along farmland between a railway line and the road.

Midlands practicalities

For self-catering **accommodation** in the Midlands, contact *Underberg Hideaways*, 27 Ashby Rd, Pietermaritzburg 3201 (☎0331/44 3505, fax 44 2133), an agency renting out cottages (mostly costing less than R150 per person) on farms throughout the region. For more formal lodgings, **NOTTINGHAM ROAD**, 25km north of Howick along the R103, makes a good orientation point, with a couple of excellent country **hotels**. In the town centre, the *Nottingham Road*, 26 Nottingham Rd (☎0333/36151, fax 36167; ③), reputedly has the oldest pub in the province, dating back to 1854. The hotel has retained the character of a coaching inn and features hand-coloured portraits of British officers from the Zulu Wars. Just south of town, *Rawdon's*, Old Main Rd (☎ & fax 0333/36044; ⑤–⑥), is a gracious, thatched, English-style country estate looking onto its own trout lake with welcoming log fires for cool misty days and airy verandahs for the hot summer. Although this is a pricey place to stay, it's also highly tranquil, and has an atmospheric **pub** with an on-site brewery and a pleasant **tea room** – both of which are open to passers-by. For something more remote, head 22km west of Nottingham Road on the Loteni road, and turn off after 17km onto the D544. This will take you to rustic *Bramleigh Manor* (☎0333/36903), a large, thatched guesthouse(③) facing onto its own yellowwood and blackwood forests with fantastic trout fishing and two splendidly isolated self-catering cottages (③).

For **eating and drinking**, *Rawdon's* (see above) is excellent, as is the *Rose & Pig* (☎0333/37369), a pleasant pub with indoor and outdoor seating in the tiny hamlet of **ROSETTA**, 6km north of Nottingham Road on the R103. Another good choice is *Café Le Fort* (☎0333/36354; booking essential; daily except Mon & Tues) at **FORT NOTTINGHAM**, 13km from Nottingham Road on an unclassified road that heads southwest out of the village. The café here has a shady garden where you can tuck into very tasty Mediterranean-style food and afternoon teas.

THE DRAKENSBERG

The **Drakensberg**, South Africa's premier mountain wilderness, hugs the border with Lesotho for some 240km north to south, and is mostly a vast national park. The highest range in southern Africa, the "Dragon mountains" (or, in Zulu, the "barrier of spears") reach their highest peaks along the border with Lesotho. The mountain range is actually an escarpment separating a high interior plateau from the coastal lowlands of Natal, and is the source of many streams and rivers which flow out to the sea. Although this is a continuation of the same escarpment that divides the Mpumalanga highveld from the game rich lowveld of Kruger, and continues into the northeastern Cape, when people talk of the Drakensberg they invariably mean the range in KwaZulu-Natal.

For elating scenery – massive spires, rock buttresses, wide grasslands, glorious waterfalls, rivers, pools and fern-carpeted forests – the Drakensberg is unrivalled. This is a **hikers'** paradise, all the better for being wild, unpopulated and imbued with an intensity which is effortlessly spiritual. The Drakensberg is also one of the richest **San rock art** areas in the world. Over six hundred sites featuring more than 22,000 individual paintings by the original inhabitants of these mountains have been

THE DRAKENSBERG

recorded. You won't see anything like this number, as they are hidden all over the mountains, but there are three easily accessible caves at **Giant's Castle**, **Injusuti** and **Kamberg**.

There are no towns close to the mountains; instead the park is hemmed in by rural African areas – former "homeland" territory, unsignposted and unnamed on many maps, but interesting places to drive through and take in a slice of traditional **Zulu life**, complete with beehive-shaped huts.

In terms of **weather**, summers are warm but wet, with some cracking thunderstorms and misty days which block out the views. Winters tend to be dry, sunny and chilly, and you can expect freezing nights and, on the high peaks, occasional snow. Probably the best times for hiking are the transitional periods – spring or autumn.

Getting to the Drakensberg

There is no connecting road system through the Drakensberg, so it is not possible to drive from one end to the other. Besides **Sani Pass** in the south, which takes you into Lesotho on a hairpin dirt road requiring a four-wheel-drive vehicle, roads to the mountains branch off westwards from the N3, between Pietermaritzburg and **Ladysmith**, and come to a halt at various Natal Parks Board camps. There is no public transport to any of the Natal Parks camps.

The most practical way of visiting the Drakensberg is to base yourself in the northern, central or southern section of the mountains, staying either in the self-catering and camping options provided by Natal Parks or in one of several hotels which offer full-board rates. Without your own car, you'll have to go for the hotel option, and nearly all hotels in this area offer transfers from the *Greyhound* or *Translux* terminals in **Escourt** or Ladysmith. The highest concentration of hotels and resorts is in the **Central Berg** area, midway between Johannesburg and Durban.

The nearest commercial centres lie on or just off the arterial N3, and are useful for stocking up on supplies, filling up your car or arranging transport into the mountains. Largest and least appealing of these towns is **Estcourt**, 88km north of Pietermaritzburg. **Winterton**, 43km north, along the R74, which deviates westwards off the N3, and **Bergville**, another 23km further along, are two small villages with shops, filling stations and banks. If you get stuck around here, Winterton's *Bridge Hotel* (☎036/488 1554; ③), on the main road, offers half-price rates for backpackers, but don't be fooled into thinking that this is a cheap way of enjoying the Berg – the mountains are a good 50km away. *Ntabeni Backpackers*, 5km north of Winterton (☎036/488 1773; ①), is served by the *Baz Bus* and has dorms and a double. Staff here also offer trips into the Berg, but since the mountains are 50km away this is no cheap way to do it either, and it's worth examining alternatives closer to the mountains.

For **backpackers**, Sani Pass in the Southern Berg is easy to get to via a service from Durban and Pietermaritzburg, as well as on the *Hopper Bus* (☎041/51 2332) three days a week, from either the Wild Coast, or from Durban and Pietermaritzburg. *Baz Bus* (☎021/439 2323 or 031/23 6585) will get you from Johannesburg via the Northern Drakensberg (Winterton) to Pietermaritzburg and Durban.

Hiking in the Drakensberg

Whether you choose to take your time on easy walks or embark on a challenging three- or four-day trip into the mountains, **hiking** in the Natal Drakensberg is one of South Africa's top wilderness experiences. The marvel of setting out on foot in these mountains is that you're unlikely to encounter vehicles, settlements, or even many other people, and the scenery is nothing short of sublime.

THE SAN AND THEIR ROCK PAINTINGS

Southern Africa's earliest inhabitants and the most direct descendants of the late Stone Age, the **San** or "Bushmen" lived in the caves and shelters of the Drakensberg for thousands of years before the arrival first of the Nguni people and then white farmers. There is still some disagreement over what to call these early hunter-gatherers. Many liberal writers use the word "Bushmen" in a strictly non-pejorative sense – though the word was originally deeply insulting. Several historians and anthropologists have plumped for "San", but, as the term refers to a language group and not a culture, this isn't strictly accurate either. Since there is no agreed term, you'll find both words used in this book.

The San hunted and gathered on the subcontinent for a considerable period – paintings in Namibia date back 25,000 years. In the last two thousand years, the southward migration of Bantu-speaking farmers forced change on the San, but there is evidence that the two groups were able to live side by side. It was when white settlers began to annex lands for hunting and farming that tension built up. As the San started to take cattle from farmers, whites began to regard these people as vermin, and felt free to hunt them in genocidal campaigns in the Cape, and later in other areas, including the Drakensberg, until the San were literally wiped off the South African map.

San **artists** were also **shamans**, and painted trance-induced images, mostly depicting their **spiritual beliefs**. Interpreting their paintings of hunting, dancing and animals as realistic narratives of everyday life in the Drakensberg is thus quite pointless: to get the most out of the works, you'll have to dig a little deeper. J. Lewis-Williams makes the point that when we see a lamb in a stained-glass window in an old church we don't think of it as depicting a food source in past centuries, but know that it symbolizes Christ as the lamb of God. To interpret San art, a similar approach is required.

It's easy and rewarding to pick out some of the most significant elements in San paintings. The **medicine or trance dance** – journeying into the spiritual world in order to harness healing power – was the Bushmen's most important religious ritual and is depicted in much of their art. Look out for the postures which the shamans adopted during the dance, including arms outstretched behind them, bending forward, kneeling, or pointing fingers. Dots along the spine often relate to the sensation of energy boiling upwards, while lines on faces or coming out of the nose usually depict nosebleeds – a common side effect of the trance state. Other feelings experienced in trance, such as elongation, attenuation or the sensation of flight, are expressed by feathers or streamers.

To enter the spirit world, shamans often tapped into the power of certain **animals**. You'll see the spiral-horned **eland** depicted in every cave – not because these antelope were prolific in the Berg, but because they were considered to have more power than any other animal. Sometimes the elands are painted in layers to increase the store of potency. In any of the caves open to the public, you'll see fascinating figures in the process of transforming into their power animal. Besides antelope, other animals associated with trance are honeybees, felines, snakes and sometimes elephants and rhinos.

It's difficult to **date** the paintings in the Drakensberg with accuracy, but the oldest are likely to be at least eight hundred years old (although Bushmen lived in the area for thousands of years before that) and the most recent are believed to have been painted after the arrival of white people towards the end of the nineteenth century. The depictions of horses, cattle and white settlers, particularly in the Southern Berg, mark the end of the traditional way of life for the Drakensberg Bushmen, and it is possible that the settlers were painted by shamans as a supernatural technique to try to ward off people who destroyed them with all-too-real bullets.

Paintings weather and fade, many have been vandalized, and well-meaning people dabbing water on them to make them clearer, or touching them, has also caused them to disappear – so never be tempted!

The Drakensberg is divided into the High Berg and Little Berg. In the **High Berg,** you're in the land of spires and great rock buttresses, where the only places to sleep are in caves or, in some areas, mountaineers' huts. You'll need to be totally self-sufficient and obey wilderness rules, taking a trowel and loo paper with you and not fouling natural water with anything – which means carrying water away from the streams to wash in. Both huts and caves must be booked with whichever Natal Parks Board office you launch out from, and you'll also need to write down your route details in the mountain register. Slogging up the passes to the top of the mountains requires a high degree of fitness, some hiking experience and a companion or guide who knows the terrain.

If you're not bothered about reaching high peaks, the **Little Berg,** lower down, with its gentler summits, rivers, rock paintings, valleys and forests, is no less remote or beautiful. The Little Berg is also safer, and easy enough to explore if you're averagely fit. If you don't want to carry a backpack and sleep in caves or huts, it's quite feasible to base yourself at one of the Natal Park camps and set out on day-hikes, of which there are endless choices. It's also possible to do a two-day walk from one of the camps, spending one night in a cave (bookable from the office at the main camp). Two highly recommended bases for walking are **Injusuti** in the Giant's Castle Game Reserve (see p.388), or **Tendele** in the Royal Natal National Park (see p.392). If you want the added luxury of spending your nights in a hotel, you could do no better than basing yourself in the **Cathedral Peak** area at the *Cathedral Peak Hotel* (see p.391).

Each of the Natal Parks Board offices sells **books** on Drakensberg walks, as well as *Slingsby* **maps** (1:150,000), though some of the paths indicated have now disappeared. One of the best guides is David Bristow's *Drakensberg Walks*, published by Struik and available from the Natal Parks Board shops and many book stores. The book outlines 120 walks which vary in length from an hour to several days, and it's small enough to carry around with you.

At any time of year the **weather** can change rapidly, so always take sufficient clothing and food with you – including a hat; the sun is fierce and bright, even in winter. And it goes without saying that you should use tried and tested, well-worn hiking boots.

The Southern Berg

Although for the most part the **Southern Berg,** the closest mountains to Durban and Pietermaritzburg, lacks the drama and varied landscape found further north, its outstanding highlight is the hair-raising **Sani Pass,** a precipitous series of hairpins that twist to the top of the escarpment up to the highest point in southern Africa reachable on wheels. The Southern Berg, with its extensive grasslands, is also the terrain of the highly recommended **Giant's Cup Hiking Trail** (see box p.386), the only organized trail in the Drakensberg and an exhilarating introduction to the mountains.

Although Sani Pass is the Southern Berg's most popular destination, there are other holidaying areas to the south and north, also accessed from the R617. **Bushman's Nek** and **Garden Castle** in the extreme south are primarily mountain hotel resorts (though there is also a Natal Parks Board campsite at Garden Castle), while further north the Natal Parks Board offer campsites and cottages at **Cobham, Loteni** and **Kamberg,** and plenty of opportunity for trout fishing.

For anyone without their own transport, the Southern Berg is the most accessible part of the mountains, with connections to and from Durban and Pietermaritzburg and accommodation in backpackers' lodges and resort-style hotels.

Underberg and Himeville

The main access into this part of the Drakensberg is along the **R617**, which strikes out west off the N3 north of Pietermaritzburg (take the Bulwer/Merrivale off-ramp).

GIANT'S CUP HIKING TRAIL

The sixty-kilometre, five-day **Giant's Cup Hiking Trail** is the only laid-out trail in the Drakensberg and makes an excellent introduction to the mountains. The trail goes from Sani Pass in the north to Bushman's Nek in the south, through the foothills of the Southern Drakensberg, winding past eroded sandstone formations, overhangs with San paintings, grassy plains and beautiful valleys with river pools to swim in. No day's hike is more than 14km long and, although there are some steep sections, this is not a difficult trail – you need to be fit to enjoy it, but not an athlete. The trail is restricted to thirty people per day and tends to get booked out during holiday periods. **Booking** should be made through the Natal Parks Board (☎0331/47 1981, fax 47 1980), who provide a map and a trail booklet. The trail costs R30 per person per night.

The **mountain huts** at the four overnight stops have running water, toilets, tables and benches, and bunks with mattresses. It's essential to bring with you a camping stove, food and a sleeping bag. The trail can be shortened by missing the first day and starting out at Pholea Hut, an old farmhouse, where you'll spend the night, then terminating one day earlier at Swiman Hut, close to the Parks Board office at Garden Castle. You can also lengthen the trail by spending a extra night at Bushmen's Nek Hut, in an area with numerous caves and rock art sites.

Giant's Cup Trail is linear, so you'll need to arrange transport at the end of the hike to get back to where you parked. This can be arranged through *Himeville Toyota Service Station* (☎033/702 1121) or *Giant's Cup Motors* (☎033/702 1615), both of which can also pick you up or deposit you at Himeville if you don't have a car.

UNDERBERG on the R617, is the main gateway, with a good supermarket for stocking up and some emergency services should you run into difficulties in the mountains. There's also a **pharmacy**, *Sani Pharmacy* (☎033/701 1034, after hours 701 1955) and a private **hospital**, the *Riverview* (☎033/701 1516) for 24-hour emergencies and the *Automobile Association* offers a 24-hour breakdown service (☎033/702 1033).

HIMEVILLE, 9km north of Underberg, and the last village you'll find before heading up Sani Pass, also has a supermarket as well as the decent *Himeville Arms* (☎033/702 1305; ③), a country **inn** at the centre of the village, which makes a good stopoff before the final haul to the mountains.

Sani Pass

Sani Pass, the only road from KwaZulu-Natal into neighbouring Lesotho, connects South Africa to the tiny highland outpost of **Mokhotlong** in Lesotho (see p.608), once known as the "loneliest settlement in Africa" and still no great metropolis. But it's the pass itself, which zigzags into the clouds, that draws increasing numbers into the High Berg. Sani Pass is the only place in the KwaZulu-Natal Drakensberg range where you actually can drive up the mountains – though you'll need a 4WD vehicle to negotiate the road and a passport to cross the Lesotho border (open 8am–4pm). If you don't have your own transport, consider booking a trip with one of the handful of operators running journeys to the "roof of Africa", such as *Sani Pass Carriers* (see below).

Access and information

For all its isolation, Sani Pass is fairly straightforward to get to. By public transport, *White Mountain* **minibus taxis** (☎033/702 0612) offer safe and reliable connections between Pietermaritzburg and Underberg twice a day via Loteni. The the only snag with this is that you'll have to hitch the last 10km from Underberg to the start of the pass – though you may be able to arrange for hostel staff to pick you up. More direct transport is available on *Sani Pass Carriers* (☎ & fax 033/701 1017, after hours ☎701 1030), based in Underberg, who operate **bus** services from Pietermaritzburg (Mon–Fri; R60) and central Durban (Wed & Fri; R80) to any hotel or hostel in the Sani Pass area. This company can also get you up the pass in a Land Rover and organizes trips into Lesotho, as well as horse-riding trails and walking trips exploring rock art.

If you're touring around the country, you could do no better than take the *Hopper Bus* (☎041/51 2332, fax 041/51 2581), which travels to Underberg three times a week from Durban via Pietermaritzburg, and along the inland route to Underberg from the Wild Coast and Umtata.

Kwezintaba Tours (☎033/702 1228, fax 701 1300), also based in Underberg, operate reasonably priced weekly backpacking trips from Port St Johns in the Transkei; you'll need to phone for details, as the service operates according to demand.

Accommodation

You'll find most **accommodation** at the foot of the mountains, just before the pass hairpins its way up to the top. Closest to the start of the pass is *Wild West Sani Pass Youth Hostel*, Sani Pass Rd (☎033/702 0340; ①), offering self-catering accommodation with one dorm (eight beds) and doubles in rooms or rondavels, with shared toilets and washing facilities. The hostel is also very near to the start of Giant's Cup Hiking Trail (see box), and you can safely leave your car here before setting out on the trek. A little further down the road, cheap meals and more dorms and doubles are on offer at *Sani Lodge Backpackers Hostel*, Sani Pass Rd (☎ & fax 033/702 0330; ①), which has the advantage of being close to the *Sani Pass Hotel*, whose facilities you can use for a small fee. The hostel has pleasant verandahs and lawns and is convenient for walking to waterfalls and rock paintings. Nearby, and far more comfortable, the *Sani Pass Hotel* (☎033/702 1320, fax 702 0220; ⑤–⑥) has a full-board rate and plenty of extras – including sauna rooms and horse-riding and tennis facilities. If you're after a serious hiking vibe rather than a backpacking atmosphere, head for *Sani Top Chalets* (☎033/701 1466; ①), at the top of Sani Pass, just inside Lesotho, and offering basic, self-catering accommodation. For weekends or longer **farmstays**, contact *Underberg Hideaways* (☎0331/44 3505, fax 44 2133), who co-ordinate privately rented cottages and farmstays in this area.

South of Sani Pass: Cobham State Forest, Bushman's Nek and Garden Castle

The main reason to venture south of Sani Pass is if you're looking for a comfortable hotel break and have your own transport. If you're **hiking** through this area, though, the Natal Parks Board **camp** and overnight caves (☎0331/47 1981, fax 47 1980; ①) at **Cobham State Forest** (daily: April–Sept 6am–6pm;Oct–March 5am–7pm; small entry fee), 13km from Himeville, will come in very handy. This little-explored, rugged area features forested gorges, rock pools and waterfalls.

Deep in the mountains at **BUSHMAN'S NEK**, the *Bushman's Nek Timeshare Resort* (☎031/52 3217, fax 52 7717; ④; off-season reductions), 26km on an unsealed road off the R617, is the most laid-back **hotel** in the area. A little to the north, and a lot smarter, is *Drakensberg Gardens Golf & Leisure Resort* (☎031/37 4222; ④), in **GARDEN CAS-TLE**, 32km on an unsealed road off the R617. One of the oldest resorts in the district, with upmarket clientele from Durban and Gauteng, it has three restaurants and pubs, and some self-catering units (②).

North of Sani Pass: Loteni and Kamberg

Well off the beaten track and seldom explored by foreign visitors, the two Natal Parks camps at **Loteni** and **Kamberg** (daily: April–Sept, 6am–6pm;Oct–March 5am–7pm;

small entry fee) are worth venturing into for their isolated wilderness, good trout-fishing opportunities and, at Kamberg, some exquisite San rock paintings. **Accommodation** at both camps should be booked through the Natal Parks Board (☎0331/47 1981, fax 47 1980).

Nestling in a valley in the foothills of the Berg, **Loteni** is an attractive area with waterfalls and grasslands, reached either via Nottingham Road (76km) to its northwest, or from Himeville in the opposite direction. The Loteni River flowing through the reserve is stocked with brown trout and makes an excellent base for mountaineering through the peaks – some of the highest in the subcontinent – roughly 10km away. The small hutted camp has twelve cheap self-catering chalets (②) and a small campsite (①). There's a camp shop which sells basics, and you bring your own food and do your own cooking. Reservations for the campsite must be made through the camp manager (☎033722/1540).

The best reason to visit **Kamberg**, 42km west of Rosetta, is for the rock art at one of the three caves in the Drakensberg open to the public. At **Shelter Cave** (also known as "Game Pass Cave"), images of stylized figures in trance states and large, polychrome eland dance across the wall. The paintings can only be visited with a guard. You can arrange this beforehand, or join one of the guided tours which depart on Sundays from the rest camp at 8.30am – the walk there and back takes around four hours following a contour path through grasslands.

Kamberg's five-hut **rest camp** consists of three-bed units with communal ablutions and cooking by camp staff. As the nearest supplies are at Rosetta, you'll need to bring all your own food and drink. Walks from here are undemanding and very scenic, and there's a four-kilometre **wheelchair trail**.

The Central Drakensberg

The **Central Drakensberg** incorporates four distinct areas, all clearly signposted from the N3 and the R615. **Giant's Castle**, the site of a beautiful game reserve, is where you'll find an attractive horse-riding retreat, the popular Lammergeyer bird hide and access to important San rock paintings. More San art is at **Injasuti** to the north, principally a hiking destination and definitely the place to head for if you're after utter wilderness. Far more accessible and tourist-trammelled is **Champagne Valley**, with a healthy number of full-board hotels with ample sporting facilities, while to the north, and out on a limb, the hotel at **Cathedral Peak** is the best place to base yourself for some serious walking.

Giant's Castle Game Reserve

Giant's Castle Game Reserve (daily: April–Sept 6am–6pm; Oct–March 5am–7pm; small entry fee) was created to protect the dwindling numbers of **eland** which occurred in great numbers in the Drakensberg before the arrival of colonialists. The reserve is also home to antelope of the montane zone: oribi, grey rhebok, mountain reedbuck and bushbuck. Despite its four dozen mammal species and around 160 bird species, this is not a traditional game park – the way to see the wildlife here is by walking or hiking through the terrain, and not driving around in a car. There are no roads inside the reserve apart from access routes which terminate at the three main Natal Parks Board camps – **Giant's Castle**, **Hillside** and **Injasuti**. The reserve is bordered to the west by three of the four highest peaks in South Africa: Mafadi (the highest at 3410m); Popple Peak (3325m) and the bulky ramparts of Giant's Castle itself (3314 m).

One of the big attractions at Giant's Head is the thrilling **Lammergeyer Hide** (May–Sept Sat & Sun only), where you can see the rare lammergeyer, Cape vulture, black eagle, jackal buzzard and lanner falcon. These birds of prey are attracted here by the carcasses of animals put out by rangers during the winter months. The lammergeyer, a giant, black and golden bird with massive wings and a diamond-shaped tail, was thought to be extinct in southern Africa until only two decades ago. Today the bird is found only in mountainous areas such as the Himalayan foothills, and in South Africa only in the Drakensberg and Maluti mountains. According to David Bristow, the lammergeyer, a scavenger, is an evolutionary link between eagles and vultures. In order to visit the hide (from R30 per person), you'll have to **book** in advance through Giant's Castle Game Reserve, PO Box X7055, Escourt 3310 (☎0363/24718).

Giant's Castle has one of the three major **rock art sites** open to the public in the Drakensberg, with more than five hundred paintings at **Main Caves**, about a half-hour's easy walk up the Bushman's River Valley. There's a small entry fee and every hour between 9am to 3pm a game guard plays a recording of an interpretation of the paintings and shows you around a small on-site museum. Sadly, at the time of writing, the commentary was still based on now-discredited ideas about the nature of rock art and of Bushman society and failed to take into account the considerable amount of scientific research that has been done over the last thirty years. The slim booklet by Lewis-Williams, *Rock Paintings of the Natal Drakensberg*, published by the University of Natal Press, is one of the most up-to-date introductions to the subject.

If Natal Parks accommodation is full, you'll have to head for the one **hotel** which gives access to the reserve: *White Mountain Lodge*, Giant's Castle Hutted Camp Rd (☎0363/24437 or 24644, fax 24437; ②–③), 34 km on tar from Escourt. The hotel offers full-board accommodation and self-catering cottages, and is in the foothills and close to Zulu villages and farmlands – a short drive to the reserve or the horse-riding retreat at Hillside.

Giant's Castle

The most comfortable of the reserve's rest camps, Giant's Castle Hutted Camp (bookings through the Natal Parks Board, ☎0331/47 1981, fax 47 1980) has self-contained **bungalows** (③) with wonderful picture windows looking out to the peaks. There is no restaurant: you'll have to bring your own food and camp staff will prepare meals, as well as servicing the accommodation units. The **camp shop** sells frozen meat for *braai*-ing, some tinned food and beers, but you should preferably stock up before setting out here. The reserve's only **filling station** is here, at the main entrance.

There are **fabulous hiking** trails from the camp, with some of the best-located and -equipped hiking **huts** (①) in the Berg at Meander Hut, Giant's Hut and Bannerman's Hut. The only drawback is that there is no campsite at Giant's Castle Hutted Camp, so if you plan to overnight in the mountains you'll need to book your first or last night in one of the self-contained bungalows.

Hillside

Some 32km from the main Giant's Castle camp and 47km from Escourt, **Hillside** camp is the horse-riding centre of Giant's Castle. The two- and three-day **horse-riding trails** are hugely popular and should be **booked** a good while in advance (☎0331/47 1981, fax 0331/47 1980). The guided trails (R200, excluding food) take you into the mountains, where you'll spend nights in caves or huts. It is also possible to stay at Hillside and set out on half- or full-day rides, at around R30 per hour.

Accommodation at Hillside is in campsites (①), and one self-catering hut (②) which sleeps eight people and has no electricity, but is perfectly comfortable. Some groceries are available at the camp, but you should bring most supplies with you. Accommodation should be booked in advance with the Officer-in-Charge Hillside, PO Box 288, Escourt 3310 (daily 9am–noon; ☎0363/24435).

Injasuti

Some 50km from both Winterton and Escourt, and accessible from the R615, **Injasuti** is a hikers' dream: a place to drive to and then hike out into the mountains (there are ten different day-hikes varying from 1hr to 7hr), swimming in the rivers or looking at rock art. Injasuti tends to attract people who want to enjoy the mountains rather than home comforts, but even if you don't hike there are beautiful rivers right by the camp suitable for children to paddle in during the summer.

From the indicated turning off the R615, 30km of dirt road leads to the camp, passing through **Zulu villages** with traditional beehive huts and blocked by groups of Nguni cattle.

If you have even a passing interest in **rock art**, don't miss the paintings at **Battle Cave**, so named because of a series of rock paintings that apparently depict an armed conflict between two groups of Bushmen. There are estimated to be over 750 individual figures, people and animals beautifully painted in this extensive cave. The paintings are fenced off and can be visited only in the company of a Parks guide, who sets out most days at 8.30am on the three- to four-hour walk. Once at the cave, the guard will play a recorded commentary which explains the paintings. Lewis-Williams has argued that, contrary to popular belief, the battle scene is unlikely to depict a territorial conflict between two groups of Bushmen, because there is no evidence that such conflicts ever took place in a society which was very loosely organized and unterritorial. Instead, he claims, the paintings are about the San spiritual experience and shamanic trance, the battles taking place in the spiritual realm where marauding evil shamans shoot arrows of "sickness", while good shamans attempt, in their trance experience, to fight them off.

The only **accommodation** in this section of the mountains is in a Natal Parks Board camp, which has no-frills cottages (②) and a campsite (①). There's no restaurant and only a very basic little shop (which also sells beer), so you'll need to bring all your own supplies. Most people come here for the express purpose of taking to the hills and camping in one of the designated **caves**, which must be booked at reception and have absolutely no facilities.

Champagne Castle and Champagne Valley

Champagne Castle, the second-highest peak in South Africa, provides the most popular view in the Drakensberg, with scores of resorts in the valley cashing in on the soaring backdrop. The name, so the story goes, derives from an incident in 1861, when Major Grantham made the first recorded ascent of the peak, towing his batman, who inadvertently dropped the bottle of bubbly and christened the mountainside.

These days, Champagne tends to be enjoyed from the confines of the hotels down in the valley by cityslickers who refuse to follow in the major's footsteps, preferring to enjoy their tipple in comfortable surroundings. This overcivilized area, which lies outside Natal Parks reserve, is best avoided if you want to hike from your doorstep – you'll have to drive through the valley to the nearest Natal Parks Board camp at Monk's Cowl at the end of the road (camping only), from where plenty of hikes set off into the mountains. On the plus side, **Champagne Valley** is an easy 32-kilometre drive on tarred road (R600) all the way from Winterton, and has facilities absent in other parts of the Drakensberg, such as a supermarket, liquor store, greengrocers, laundry and a couple of restaurants, all indicated along the R600.

The **Ardmore Ceramic Art Studio** (daily 9am–4.30pm; ☎036/468 1314), 5km off the R600, is one of the highlights of the valley. The studio was started in the 1980s by fine arts graduate Fée Halsted-Berning with trainee Bonnie Ntshlintshali, a young Zulu girl suffering from polio. By 1990 they had collected a clutch of awards for their distinctive ceramic works, and the studio now has around forty people creating beautiful sculpture and crockery with wildly colourful and often impossibly irrational motifs that have included rhinos dressed as preachers, administering the sacrament to a congregation of wild animals. The works don't come cheap, but they make pretty unique objects to take home with you. The turn-off to the studio is clearly indicated, between the *Nest Hotel* and the *Drakensberg Sun*.

Accommodation

You shouldn't have any problem finding a **place to stay** in Champagne Valley: numerous hotels, family resorts and B&Bs are signposted off the R600. Perhaps the nicest **hotel** – though not the smartest – is the steadfastly old-fashioned *Champagne Castle* (☎036/468 1063, fax 468 1306; ⑤), which is as close to the mountains as you'll get by car, and just a few kilometres from the Natal Parks Board camp at Monk's Cowl. The hotel, which still insists on collar and tie for dinner, has comfortable en-suite chalets set in lovely gardens with a swimming pool and a rate which includes three (rather stodgy) meals a day.

For B&B accommodation, *Inkosana Lodge and Trekking* (☎036/468 1202; ③), 25km from Winterton on the R600, offers unpretentious, ethnic-style rooms, with beautiful gardens and a bit of a retreat-centre feel. Self-catering is available, and the lodge can provide transfers from Winterton and up to the Berg trailheads. *Ardmore Guest Farm* (☎036/468 1314, fax 468 1242; ③), also signposted off the R600, is a thoroughly hospitable B&B on a farm, attached to the highly recommended **Ardmore Ceramic Studio** (see opposite), and offering en-suite rondavels. Guests eat meals together from marvellous hand-crafted crockery made on the farm. Ardmore also operates **horse trails** in the Drakensberg foothills for experienced and novice riders, lasting from two hours to three days.

There are no Parks Board chalets, only a **campsite** (☎0364/68 1103; ①) at **Monk's Cowl**, at the end of the road through the valley, which serves as the trailhead for numerous hikes. The grassy campsite has toilets and showers, but the few kilometres of dirt road beyond *Champagne Castle Hotel* can be sodden in summer and rutted at other times, so drive with care.

Cathedral Peak

North of Monk's Cowl and the Champagne Valley resorts is the Mlambonja River Valley and **Cathedral Peak Hotel** (☎ & fax 036/488 1888; ④–⑤), the closest hotel in the Drakensberg to the mountains themselves, and within the Natal Parks' protected area. There are no other hotels in the vicinity, so the views are perfect. The *Cathedral Peak* is well signposted, 44km from either Winterton or Bergville, mostly on a dirt roads through Zulu villages, with the last 15km of road tarred.

Hiking trails start right from the hotel, which provides maps and books. One of the most popular day-walks is to the beautiful Rainbow Gorge. This eleven-kilometre round trip takes four to five hours, and follows the Ndumeni River with pools, rapids, falls, lichens, mosses and ferns to detain you. The hike can be wet, so wear proper walking boots. The hotel also operates guided trips up **Cathedral Peak** itself, a freestanding peak sticking out of the five-kilometre-long basalt Cathedral Ridge. You should expect the ten-kilometre round trip to take nine hours, which includes plenty of time at the top to revel in the views. It's a very steep climb, and the final section beyond Orange Peel Gap should only be tackled by experienced climbers – you'll probably be quite satisfied to stop at this point. The peak looks nothing like a cathedral (its Zulu name, *Mponjwane*, means "the horn on a heifer's head").

The only other place to stay is the small Natal Parks **campsite** (☎0364/88 1880; ①), opposite the Mike's Pass guardhouse, about 4km before the hotel. The guardhouse is the place to buy a permit to drive up **Mike's Pass**, a ten-kilometre twisting forestry road which takes you to a car park from where, on a clear day, you'll get outstanding views of the entire region. There's a scale model on top to help identify the peaks. An ordinary car will make the journey when the weather is dry and the road is hard, but you'll need a 4WD when it's wet.

The Northern Berg

The dramatically beautiful **Northern Berg** consists mainly of the **Royal Natal National Park,** with a few resorts scattered around the fringes and Zulu villages pressing around the borders. The Tugela River and its bouldered gorge offer some of the most awe-inspiring scenery in the area, while the Amphitheatre, the main geographical feature, is a striking, five-kilometre rock wall over which the Tugela plunges. With a complete cross-section of accommodation, the Northern Berg is a very desirable area to visit. The best place to get a real feeling of these pristine mountains and valleys is at **Tendele Camp**, the main Natal Parks camp, with chalets but oddly enough no camping.

Royal Natal National Park

The **Royal Natal National Park** (daily 24hr; small entry fee), 46km west of Bergville, is famed for its views of the **Amphitheatre**, a crescent-shaped rock edge of the escarpment which virtually encloses the park, and probably appears on more posters and postcards and in more books than any other single feature of the Drakensberg. Almost everyone does the **Tugela Gorge walk**, a fabulous six-hour round trip from Tendele, which gives close-up views of the Amphitheatre and the **Tugela Falls** leaping over the 500-metre-high rock wall.

The park itself is at the northern end of the high Drakensberg, tucked in between Lesotho to the west and Free State province to the north, and is the closest section of the Berg to Johannesburg. The three defining peaks are the Sentinel (3165m), the Eastern Buttress (3048) and the Mont Aux Sources (3282m), which is also where five rivers rise – hence its name, given by French missionaries in 1878. The park was established in 1916 but only earned its royal sobriquet in 1947 when the British family paid a visit.

Access and information

The only way to get into the Royal Natal is with your own transport along tarred roads all the way. Coming from Durban along the N3, take the Winterton/Berg Resorts turn-off and follow the clear signposts through the village of Bergville to the park entrance, some 46km away. Although there are plenty of **Zulu** settlements en route, **Bergville** is the nearest place to stock up on supplies. There is a basic provision store at the *Royal Natal National Park Hotel*, where you can buy bread, milk, meat, sugar and tinned food. The **visitors' centre** adjacent to the hotel sells books, maps, a good selection of hiking boots, and frozen and smoked trout.

Several of the resorts offer transfers from Bergville or the N3 if you book ahead and notify them, but they tend to be expensive.

Accommodation

Natal Parks Board **accommodation** consists of two campsites and the Tendele hutted camp. Also in the park, and creating a centre of sorts, is the *Royal Natal National Park Hotel*. Outside the park, just before you reach the entry gate, from Bergville, a well-signposted dirt road heading north is the location for the handful of resort-style hotels in the area.

Cavern (☎036/438 6270, fax 438 6334). The most tucked-away of the resorts, the *Cavern* is family-run, has an old-fashioned feel and adequate rooms, and is very much a South African weekend get-away with a swimming pool, horse-riding, Saturday night dances, a TV room and a rate which includes all meals. Transfers from the Durban/Johannesburg buses are available for R220 per return trip and must be booked beforehand. ⑤.

Hlalanathi Berg Resort (☎036/438 6308, fax 438 6852). Some 2km from the *Royal Natal*, this is a family resort offering camping, self-catering thatched chalets, trampolines, swimming pool, TV room as well as a sit-down and take-away restaurant serving cheap burgers, sandwiches and more substantial meals. During school holidays they insist on a five-night minimum stay. ①–②.

Mahai Campsite (☎036/438 6303, fax 438 6310). Adjacent to the hotel, this huge campsite set along the river caters for up to four hundred campers, and attracts hordes of South Africans with their tents and caravans over school holidays and weekends. From here you can strike straight into the mountains for some of the best walks in the Berg. ①.

Mont-Aux-Sources Hotel (☎ & fax 036/438 6230). Roughly 4km from the park, this smart but impersonal hotel has views of the Amphitheatre behind scrawny villages and cattle-chewed hillsides. ⑥.

Royal Natal National Park Hotel (☎036/438 6200, fax 438 6101). Old-fashioned place with decent enough rooms and pleasant gardens, though its dinner, bed and breakfast rate is not cheap. It's certainly well-situated for hiking, though the views from the hotel itself are disappointing – you'd hardly realize you're so close to the famous vistas. The hotel has a smart-casual dress rule (no jeans, T-shirts or open shoes) after 6pm. ⑤.

Rugged Glen Campsite, signposted 4km from Mahai (☎036/438 6303, fax 438 6310). A smaller and quieter campsite, but the views and walks aren't as good as from Mahai. The *Mont-Aux-Sources Hotel* is an easy walk away – handy if you want a substantial meal. ①.

Tendele Hutted Camp (☎0331/47 1981, fax 47 1980). At the end of the road, right in the mountains, this is one of the most-sought-after places to stay in South Africa, with splendid views of the Amphitheatre and excellent walks right from your front door. Accommodation is in comfortable en-suite units, the cheapest of which have fridges, kettles, toasters and eating utensils, but no kitchens, although chefs are on hand to cook your food for you. You'll need to bring all you need, as there is no shop or restaurant. You can walk or drive the couple of kilometres to the the hotel for a meal or basic provisions. ③–④.

THE ZULULAND COAST
AND GAME RESERVES

In startling contrast to the intensely developed 250-kilometre ribbon of the Holiday Coast, which runs north and south of Durban, the seaboard to the north of the Dolphin Coast drifts off into some of the wildest and most breathtaking sea frontage in South Africa – an imprecisely defined area known as **Maputaland**. Roughly speaking, Maputaland is the funnel-shaped slab wedged into the corner formed by Swaziland and Mozambique in the north, and confined to its east and west between the N2 and the coast.

If you've travelled along the Garden Route and wondered where stereotypical Africa was, the answer is right here in its tight patchwork of wilderness and **ancestral African lands**. The figures speak for themselves: Maputaland has more *nyangas* and *sangomas* (traditional healers and diviners) per head than anywhere else in the coun-

---

BOOKING ACCOMMODATION IN PARKS AND WILDERNESS AREAS

Maputaland incorporates the region of South Africa most densely packed with **game parks**, designated **wetlands** and **wilderness areas**. All the public resorts described in this section, with the exception of Tembe Elephant Park and Ndumo Game Reserve in the extreme north, fall under the **Natal Parks Board**, and **hutted accommodation** should be booked through Natal Parks Board Reservations, PO Box 1750, Pietermaritzburg 3200 (☎0331/47 1981, fax 47 1980). **Camping**, however, must be booked locally through the individual parks, whose addresses are given in each account.

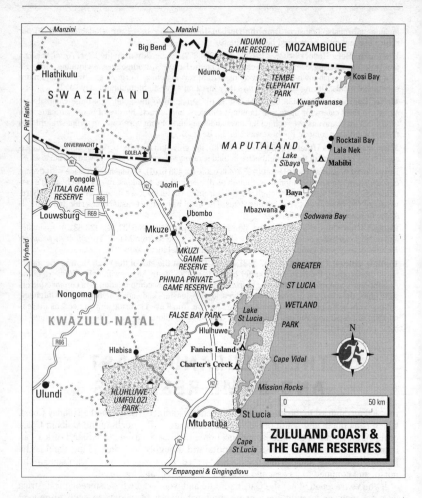

ZULULAND COAST &
THE GAME RESERVES

try. With one healer for every 550 people – compared with one Western doctor to 18,000 people – **traditional life** is hanging on in this forgotten corner of sub-Saharan Africa's most industrialized country.

It's only since the 1960s that **navigable tracks** have twisted their way through Maputaland's grasslands and tangled forests, and even today there's no tarred road leading all the way from the N2 to its 200km of virtually uninterrupted beachfront, most of which is still only accessible with a 4WD vehicle.

Driving for less than three hours on the N2 north from Durban gets you into the **big game country** of Hluhluwe-Umfolozi, which rivals even the Kruger National Park in beauty and a sense of the wild. Drive the same distance, but turn right instead of left at the Mtubatuba junction, and you'll hit the southernmost extent of South Africa's most satisfyingly "tropical" **coast**, protected all the way up to Mozambique by wetland reserve and marine sanctuaries. The coast gets remoter and more exhilarating the further north you head, with South Africa's best upmarket beachside stay at **Rocktail**

Bay, near Mozambique, where fewer than two dozen fortunate castaway guests have kilometres of rolling dunes and coastal forest to themselves.

So far the only major development blighting the area is the large modern industrial port of **Richards Bay**, 185km north of Durban, nudging the southern edge of Maputaland. But, with the possibility of a continuous strip of resorts all the way from Durban to the Mozambique border, there are real fears for the whole of this fragile ecosystem. Large mining interests have their eye on tearing at the titanium-rich dunes of the St Lucia Wetland, and there's talk of constructing a massive harbour at the remote mouth of the Kosi River in the far north.

Conservationists are hoping that the nomination of the area as South Africa's first **World Heritage Site** will stave off environmentally destructive developments, but conservation and poverty sit uncomfortably here; for **indigenous people** struggling to sustain a livelihood, the sight of visitors in their air-conditioned vehicles raising dust in their backyard leaves a bitter taste. In the past, African farmers were banned from planting crops in the wetlands, traditional fishermen were arrested for casting their nets on waters they believed to be theirs, and cattle herders had their livestock confiscated if they wandered into certain areas. It's not surprising that for some local people eco-tourism equals dispossession. This tension is one reason why **theft** is very high in the area. No matter how deserted a place looks, don't be lulled into leaving cameras or other valuables where they can be easily snatched.

Some locals, however, have responded more positively to the influx of visitors and Zululand is one of the best areas to buy **crafts**. Even on remote roads, you'll come across stalls with beautiful carvings, often suspended like windchimes from their roofs or from trees. Objects include platters, sticks or, in a more contemporary vein, little four-wheel-drive vehicles. More positive still is the growth of eco-tourism projects in the vicinity that involve partnership with the community. An example of this is **Phinda Private Game Reserve**, a seriously upmarket park near Mkuzi, that has brought tangible benefits to the local community and suggests a way in which business, communities and the environment can gain mutual benefit from tourism.

Richards Bay to Mtubabtuba

There's no conceivable reason for spending time in either **Empanegeni**, 173km north of Durban, or **RICHARDS BAY**, 12km east, on the coast. Two modern industrial sprawls that are the only centres of any size in the vicinity, they are completely at odds with the remote and pristine coast to the north and should be given short shrift, even if you happen to be making **transport** connections here. Given that you can avoid these towns on the *Baz* **backpacker bus**, which links up with transport to points along the Maputaland coast and to Hluhluwe-Umfolozi Park, you only need come here if you're **flying** into Richards Bay and plan on renting a car to make a quick getaway. *British Airways/Comair* (☎0351/41361) flies daily from Johannesburg, as does *SA Express* (☎0351/41040), which also flies twice a week from Durban and touches down at **Richards Bay airport** (☎0351/4161), 6km north of the town centre. **Car rental**, including 4WD, can be arranged from the airport through *Avis* (☎0351/98 6555, fax 43344), *Budget* (☎0351/98 7011, fax 45655) and *Imperial* (☎toll free 0800/118898). **Intercity buses** all arrive at the *Richards Hotel*, Hibberd Drive (☎0351/31301), with *Interport* (☎0351/91791) and *Greyhound* (☎031/309 7830) between them running three daily services from Durban; while *Greyhound* comes down daily and *Translux* (☎011/774 3333) three times a week from Johannesburg/Pretoria. If you're stuck here for the night, the **Richards Bay Publicity Association** (Mon–Fri 8am–4pm, Sat & Sun 8am–noon; ☎0351/97 4330), at the Small Craft Harbour, off John Ross Parkway, can help you find accommodation.

> The northern KwaZulu-Natal coastal region is **malarial.** For details on necessary precautions, see p.18.

Some 26km north of Richards Bay, the tiny village of **KWAMBONAMBI** lies on the *Baz* **backpacker bus** route, and is notable for being home to the *Amazulu Lodge Backpackers*, 5 Killarney Place (☎035/580 1009; email: amazulu@cdrive.co.za), an upmarket house offering camping (①), dorms (①) and double rooms (①), some with air conditioning. The hostel also has a swimming pool, sauna and a jacuzzi, but the biggest pull of the place is the fact that the staff offer day safaris to the Hluhluwe-Umfolozi Game Reserve and boat safaris on the St Lucia Estuary, as well diving trips to Sodwana Bay – a package that makes this one of the best options for exploring South Africa's northeast on a budget.

Another 38km further north, the crossroads of the R618 with the N2 offers the enticing choice of heading west for Hluhluwe-Umfolozi Game Reserve or west to the St Lucia Estuary – both an easy twenty minutes away.

Hluhluwe-Umfolozi Park

Hluhluwe-Umfolozi (daily: April–Sept 6am–6pm; Oct–March 5am–7pm; R25 per vehicle, R6 per person) is KwaZulu-Natal's most outstanding game reserve, and rated by some above even the Kruger. While it certainly can't match Kruger's sheer scale (Hluhluwe is a twentieth of the size) or its teeming game populations, its relatively compact 960 square kilometres have a wilder ambience. This has something to do with the fact that, apart from **Hilltop**, an elegant hotel-style rest camp in the northern half of the park, none of Hluhluwe's other rest camps is fenced off, and wild animals are free to wander through. The vegetation, with subtropical jungly forest in places and Tarzanish monkey ropes dripping over the rivers, adds to the sense of adventure.

Until recently the park was two distinct entities – hence its tongue-twisting double-barrel name – and the two sections have retained their separate characters, reinforced by the fact that a public road slices between them. The southern or **Umfolozi section** takes its name from a corruption of *mfulawozi*, a Zulu word that refers to the fibrous bushes that grow along its rivers. The topography here is characterized by wide, deep valleys incised by the Black and White Mfolozi rivers, with altitudes varying between 60 and 650 metres. Luxuriant riverine vegetation gives way in drier areas to a variety of woodland, savannah, thickets and grassy plains.

The notable feature of the northern **Hluhluwe section** is its river of the same name, so called because of the dangling monkey ropes that hang from the canopy of the riparian forest. A slender, slithering waterway, punctuated by elongated pools, the Hluhluwe rises in the mountains north of the park and passes along sandbanks, rock beds and steep cliffs in the game reserve before seeping away into the St Lucia wetlands to the east. The higher ground is covered by *veld* and dense thicket, while the well-watered ridges support the softer cover of ferns, lichens, mosses and orchid.

Some history

The sense of pristine wilderness you get at Hluhluwe-Umfolozi is entirely illusory – the result of careful **management** since the 1950s. Despite being the oldest proclaimed national park in Africa (it was created in 1895), Hluhluwe-Umfolozi's future as a game refuge has hung by a thread on several occasions in the last two hundred years. In the nineteenth century the park lay at the very centre of the **Zulu kingdom** and Umfolozi was the private hunting preserve of the Zulu king, Shaka. During Shaka's reign between 1818 and 1828 the area saw the most sustained campaign of hunting in Zulu history, but this was nothing compared to the destruction caused by white men in the twentieth century, when the park was twice de-proclaimed under pressure from neighbouring farmers whose cattle were being infected by **nagana**, a disease transmitted by tsetse flies from wild to domestic stock. Between 1929 and 1950 a crusade of game **extermination** was launched to wipe out the disease and saw 100,000 head of game from 16 species fall to the gun. Rhinos, alone, were spared.

It was only in 1952, when the park was handed over to the newly formed **Natal Parks Board**, that the slow process of resuscitation to the threadbare game reserve began. This was done with considerable flair and has been topped by the brilliant success of re-establishing its white rhino population from twenty animals at the turn of the century to nearly two thousand today. In 1994 the **white rhino** became the first species to be removed from the World Conservation Union's endangered list. Their survival is down mostly to efforts by conservationists in the Hluhluwe-Umfolozi Park, which has become the world's breeding bank for these animals.

Access and information

There is no public **transport** into Hluhluwe-Umfolozi. The only way of getting here without your own car is on one of the **tours**, such as those operated by *Amazulu Lodge Backpackers* (see p.407), 50km to the south in Kwambonambi. Access to the park is via one of three **gates**, two from the east along one of the two tarred roads that lead straight off the N2 into the park and the other from Ulundi in the west. The R618, which is 23km north of Kwambonambi, reaches **Mambeni Gate** after 27km, providing access to the southern section of the park. Some 46km beyond the R618 an unclassified, but signposted and tarred road takes you via **Memorial Gate** into the northernmost section of the park. A third gate, **Cengeni**, is accessible along a thirty-kilometre dirt road from Ulundi to the west. You cannot enter the park from the public road connecting Hlabisa and Mtubatuba, which slices through its centre.

Accommodation and eating

Accommodation is available at three public rest camps. The rest camps in the (southern) **Umfolozi section** are at **Masinda**, near the Mambeni Gate, which has just six four-bedded units, communal ablution facilities and a kitchen where camp chefs cook food from ingredients that you provide, and at **Mpila** in the centre of the section. Mpila commands excellent views of the surrounding wilderness and has twelve one-roomed huts with four beds each, communal ablutions and, like Masinda, cooks on hand to prepare your food. Mpila also has two self-contained three-bedroom cottages for seven people, with a cook on hand. Six self-catering chalets accommodate five people each. **Meal preparation times** from the central kitchen at both camps are daily 6.30 to 9am, noon–1.30pm and 4–7.30pm. There are no fences around the Umfolozi camps, which means you should take particular care when walking around, particularly at night.

The northern **Hluhluwe section** of the park has just one public rest camp, **Hilltop**, which is one of the best you'll find at any game reserve in the country. Set high on the edge of a slope, with sweeping views across the park's hills and valleys, the camp has modern, comfortable and varied accommodation, with twenty budget **rondavels** (②) that share communal ablutions and kitchen facilities. There are also 27 en-suite **two-bed chalets** (④) with bar fridges and tea- and coffee-making facilities, some with kitchenettes, as well as twenty **four-bed chalets** (④). **Bookings** for accommodation and wilderness trails should be made through Natal Parks Board Reservations (see p.393).

Hilltop also has a very pleasant **restaurant**, the *Mpunyane*, and the *Uzavolo Bar Lounge*, both attached to the central block. Hilltop is surrounded by an electric fence, which keeps out most animals. You may, however, come across nyala and other herbivores grazing around the chalets – they are both potentially dangerous and should be treated with respect.

Game-viewing and activities

Despite its compact size, Hluhluwe-Umfolozi is home to 84 mammal species and close on 350 varieties of bird. The Big Five are all here and it's no exaggeration to say that this is the best place in the world to see **rhinos** – both black and white. **Lions** had become extinct in Umfolozi until 1958, when a black-maned male made an appearance, apparently having traversed 400km from Mozambique. Females were later introduced and today there are around seventy of the big cats in the reserve, although they're not easy to see.

Other **predators** present are cheetah, leopard, spotted hyena and wild dog. **Herbivores** include blue wildebeest, buffalo, giraffe, hippo, impala, kudu, nyala and zebra. When it comes to **birds**, there are over a dozen species of **eagle**, as well as other

raptors including hawks, goshawks and honey buzzards. Other larger birds include ground hornbills, vultures, owls and herons, and there are hundreds of other beautiful species to look out for. **Reptiles** number in the sixties, including crocodiles and several types of venomous snake, none of which you're likely to see. Along the Hluhluwe River, keep an eye open for the harmless monitor lizards, which resemble miniture dragons.

Where Hluhluwe-Umfolozi really scores over the Kruger is in the variety of activities on offer. Apart from **self-driving** around the park, there are also **self-guided walks** near several of the rest camps, **guided trails** in the company of an armed game guard, and guided **night drives**. South Africa's first wilderness trail started in Umfolozi and the reserve has remained one of the best places in South Africa for taking a walk on the wild side. Four-night **wilderness trails**, on which gear is carried by pack donkeys, leave from the base camp – you sleep under canvas for the next two nights, returning on the fourth to base. These all-inclusive trails, which must be booked through the Natal Parks Board (see box, p.393) run from March to November and cost around R800 per person.

The Greater St Lucia Wetland Park

Five distinct ecosystems make up the **Greater St Lucia Wetland Park**, a 2750-square-kilometre patchwork of separate pieces locking together the St Lucia Reserve, St Lucia Park, False Bay Park, the St Lucia Marine Reserve, the Sodwana Bay National Park, the Cape Vidal State Forest, Mkuzi Game Reserve and other interlinking areas. Planned developments will make this the third-largest protected area in the country – it's already one of the most fascinating. The Wetland Park's origins as several separate reserves is readily apparent in the fact that few internal roads link one area to another and each section is reached by a separate road that spurs off the N2.

The most striking feature of the park is the 360-square-kilometre **Lake St Lucia**, South Africa's largest inland body of water, formed 25,000 years ago when the oceans receded. The lake is flanked by mountainous **dunes** covered by forest and grassland, whose peaks soar to an astonishing 200m above the beach to form a slender rampart against the Indian Ocean. Aside from the lake and dune ecosystems, the reserve protects a **marine zone** of warm tropical seas, coral reefs and endless sandy beaches; the **papyrus and reed wetland** of the Mkuze Swamps, on the north of the lake; and on the western shore dry **savannah and thornveld**. Any one of these would justify conservation but their confluence around the lake makes this a world-class wilderness.

St Lucia

It's a little strange to find a town inside a wilderness reserve and there's nothing contemplative about **ST LUCIA**, which lies at the mouth of the **St Lucia Estuary** in the extreme south of the park. Reached after 32km at the end of the R618 east, the town becomes so hectic in midsummer that it could put you off northern KwaZulu-Natal altogether. Fortunately it's singularly atypical of the area. Everything in St Lucia centres around **angling**: you can't miss the plethora of tackle and bait shops, seafood restaurants and four-wheel-drive vehicles buzzing up and down the main street bristling with fishing rods. A spin-off is that, out of season, when the hordes of anglers have left, there's plenty of accommodation across a broad range of budgets.

The town takes its name from the estuary, whose mouth was reached by Portuguese explorers in 1576, and which they named Santa Lucia. During the second half of the eighteenth century, landlocked Boers made attempts to claim the mouth as a port but were pipped at the post by the British who sent the HMS *Goshawk* in 1884 to annex the whole area, which then developed as a fishing resort. In the 1920s the town got its first hotel and in the 1950s St Lucia was connected to the mainland by a bridge.

St Lucia's best feature is the **estuary**, hidden behind the buildings along the main drag, and easy to miss if you drive quickly through. The main reason to fetch up here, however, is to get to **Cape Vidal** (see opposite), the real prize of the area, inside the St Lucia Wetlands National Park, where strictly limited accommodation may necessitate basing yourself in St Lucia town.

The Town

If you end up spending any time in St Lucia, one of the best things you can do is go on a two-hour **guided lake cruise** on the Natal Parks Board's *Santa Lucia*. From the deck you stand a good chance of seeing crocodiles and one of the eight hundred hippos that spend their days wallowing and snorting in Lake St Lucia, as well as pelicans, fish eagles, kingfishers and storks. Cruises leave daily at 8.30am, 10.30am and 2.30pm from the launch site next to the bridge on the west side of the estuary. **Bookings** are essential in peak season and can be made though the Natal Parks Board Office (☎035/590 1340, fax 590 1343), at the south end of Pelican Road.

Fishing and cruising aside, the **St Lucia Crocodile Centre** (daily 7am–5pm; crocodile feeding Sat 3pm; small entry fee), at the park gate at the north of town on the road to Cape Vidal, is worth an hour of your time if you have any interest in natural history. Rest assured that this isn't another of those exploitative wildlife freak-shows found throughout South Africa, but a serious educative spin-off of the Natal Parks Board's crocodile conservation campaign. Up until the end of the 1960s, crocodiles were regarded as pests, and this led to a hunting free-for-all that saw them facing extinction in the area. Just in time, it was realized that the reptiles have an important role in the ecoological cycle and the Parks Board began a successful **breeding programme**, returning the crocs to the wild to bolster numbers. The Crocodile Centre aims to rehabilitate the reputation of these maligned creatures, with informative displays and an astonishing cross-section of species (although only the Nile crocodile occurs in South Africa in the wild) lounging around enclosed pools. There's also a very good **bookshop** at the Centre, with items on natural history and cheap but informative booklets about the local coastal and wetland ecology.

Practicalities

The St Lucia Publicity Association, on the corner of Mackenzie Street and Katonkel Road (Mon–Fri 8am–5pm, Sat 8am–noon; ☎035/590 1075) isn't that hot on information about the town, but operates a very useful accommodation-finding service. For **information** about the Wetlands National Park your best bet is the Natal Parks Board office (daily 8am–4.30pm; ☎035/590 1340) at the south end of Pelican Road.

Out of season, cheap **accommodation** isn't hard to find and *Robbie's Place*, 25 Pelican St (☎ & fax 035/590 1328; ①), has clean basic self-catering double rooms at backpacker prices in a family house. *Jo a Lize*, Mackenzie St (☎035/590 1085, fax 590 1363), has self-contained, self-catering flats (②) and tiny but clean en-suite B&B units (③), while in the same street, the *Boma Hotel* (☎031 561 5179, fax 561 4144; ②), has spacious luxury self-catering cabanas, some of which have balconies with wonderful views of the estuary. The most comfortable and best B&B in town is *Kingfisher Lodge*, Mackenzie St (☎035/590 1015; ③).

For **eating**, the best place is the *Quarterdeck*, on the corner of Mackenzie Street and Albacore Drive, which serves good, reasonably priced seafood, including on occasion specialities like marlin, and does a bottomless plate of prawns for R50 every Sunday. If you want to enter the spirit of the place and catch your own fish, head for the *St Lucia Fishing Den*, next door, which sells rods, tackle and (should you fail to hook anything) fresh fish, as well as all the spices and condiments you'll need for a fish *braai*.

Cape Vidal

Another popular fishing spot, **CAPE VIDAL** (daily: April–Sept 6am–6pm; Oct–March 5am–7pm; small entry fee) has the real edge over St Lucia in that it's more difficult to reach and numbers are limited to just one hundred day-visitors' vehicles, while accommodation for overnight stays is limited to Natal Parks Board facilities. The only way of getting there is via St Lucia, from where you take a rough dirt road for 32km, navigating along a narrow bridge of land between the lake on the west and the Indian Ocean on the east. This one- to two-hour journey passes through pine plantations, open grassland and wetland areas.

Even if you aren't a keen ski-boat fisherman or surf-angler, there's enough stunning wilderness at Cape Vidal to get lost in or to keep you chilling out for several days. The sea is literally over the dunes, minutes from the Parks Board accommodation. An offshore reef shelters the coast from the high seas, making it safe for **swimming**, and if you're keen on **snorkelling** an underwater extravaganza of hard and soft corals and colourful fish awaits. Burly anglers who use the rocks for casting their lines into the wide ocean may look at you in disbelief if you go looking into the tiny water worlds of the **rock pools**, but you'll be rewarded with sightings of seaweeds, snails, crabs, sea cucumbers, anemones, urchins and small fish.

Large mammals and fish move just offshore in open seas beyond the reef. Cape Vidal is an excellent place for shore sightings of **humpback whales**, which breed off Mozambique, not far to the north in winter. In October they move south, drifting on the warm Agulhas current with their calves. If you're lucky you may see these and other whales from the vantage of the dunes, but without binoculars they'll just look like specks on the horizon. A **whale-watching tower**, reached through the dune forest south of the rest camp, provides an even higher viewpoint and has information boards about all the marine mammals that pass this way. Eighteen-metre plankton-feeding whale sharks, the largest and gentlest of the sharks, have been sighted off this coast in schools of up to seventy at a time and manta rays and dolphins, too, are common in these waters.

Practicalities

If you're planning to stay overnight, and this is highly recommended, prebook your **accommodation** before trawling out. There are only eighteen five-bed chalets and twelve eight-bed Swiss-style log cabins, all of which are en suite and fully equipped – all you need to bring is your own food and drink. Cabins are serviced and cleaned every morning by camp staff. There's a campsite with space for fifty tents in the dune forest near the beach, reservations for cabins and chalets should be made through Natal Parks Board Reservations (see box p.393). On **arrival** at Cape Vidal you should report to the Natal Parks Board Office (daily, 8am–12.30pm & 2–4.30pm).

Reservation for campsites is vital during school holidays and over long weekends and can be made in writing up to one year in advance through the Officer-in-Charge, Cape Vidal, Private Bag X01, St Lucia Estuary 3936 (☎035/590 1404, fax 590 1300). Although petrol and firewood can be bought at Cape Vidal, for all other **supplies** the nearest place to stock up is St Lucia.

The Western Shore

The **Western Shore** of Lake St Lucia marks the old seashore, harking back for aeons to a time when the ocean level was 2m higher than it is today. Decayed matter from marine animals has created a rich soil that once supported an extensive array of animal life, and although the Big Five were shot out ages ago there are still **birds** and over a hundred species of **butterfly** flitting about. Among the **herbivores** are suni, Africa's smallest antelope, as well as nyala and red duiker. With no dangerous predators apart from **crocodiles** (take care along the shore), the inland bushveld and woodlands are safe for walking without a guide.

The main activities along the Western Shore, which is accessible only in your own vehicle, are **fishing** and **bird-watching**. Most camps also have **waymarked trails** that make a thoroughly enjoyable way, if you're moderately energetic, to explore the lakeside vegetation and bir s. You should also keep an eye open for game, especially the water-loving reedbuck at take refuge in the swamps.

Charter's Creek

Primarily an anglers' retreat, **CHARTER'S CREEK** (April–Sept 6am–8pm; Oct–March 5am–8pm; small entry fee), which lies at the southern end of the lake, is also excellent for **bird-watching** and has two half-day **trails**. The major attraction here is the camp, situated on a cliff edge with views across the lake. From here you can look out for waterfowl and flamingos – even pelicans make an appearance – while permanent residents include hippos and crocodiles. The seven-kilometre **Isikhova Trail** and the five-kilometre **Umkhumbe Trail** both leave from the camp and shouldn't take more than two to three hours to complete. The trails take in typical Western Shore coastal forest and provide the opportunity to spot small **game**, including the tiny red duiker, with its short, backward-pointing horns. Other species occasionally encountered include mongooses, bushbuck, jackals, bushbabies and, commonest of all, vervet monkeys.

To get there, turn off the N2, some 20km north of Mtubatuba and follow the signs all the way to Charter's Creek via Nyalazi river halt. **Accommodation** is in a choice of a seven-bedded cottage (⑤), and huts (②) – ten four-bedded, fourteen three-bedded and one two-bedded – all of which are fully equipped. Servicing and cooking is done by camp staff, but you must provide your own food. Although you can't swim in the lake, there's a swimming pool at the camp for cooling off in. **Bookings** for accommodation should be made through the Natal Parks Board (see box, p.393).

Fanies Island

Not an island at all but part of the Western Shore, approximately 20km north of Charter's Creek as the crow flies, **FANIES ISLAND** (April–Sept 6am–8pm; Oct–March 5am–8pm; small entry fee) looks out onto reeded islands between networks of waterlogged paths worn away by hippos. The views are magnificent across the reed beds to the grasslands, forests and misty hill-like dunes of Cape Vidal on the coast. The large croc population here makes bathing or paddling inadvisable. Like all the Western Shore camps, Fanies Island is much favoured by anglers, but this is one of the most secluded.

The five-kilometre **Umkhiwane Trail** can be completed in two hours and goes through forest, open grassveld and swamp forest, and is highly recommended for bird-watching. Hippos, vervet monkeys, bushbuck, warthog, reed buck and waterbuck are among the common mammals you stand a good chance of seeing.

To get there follow the instructions for Charter's Creek, but at the junction follow the sign indicating a left turn for Fanies Island. The route is well signposted. **Accommodation** is available in a seven-bedded cottage (③–⑤, depending on numbers), twelve fully-equipped two-bedded rondavels (②) with their own fridges, but sharing an ablution block and a kitchen, where your food is prepared by camp chefs. There are twenty shady **campsites** for which **reservations** should be made through the Camp Manager, Fanies Island, PO Box 1259, Mtubabtuba 3935 (☎035/550 1631). All other accommodation should be booked through the Natal Parks Board (see box, p.393). **Fuel** is available at the camp, as are a limited range of basic foods, but you'll be far better off buying food in Hluhluwe or Mtubabtuba before you come.

False Bay Park

Situated about 20km north of Fanies Island, **FALSE BAY PARK** (April–Sept 6am–8pm, Oct–March 5am–8pm; small entry fee) perches on the west shore of a small, lozenge-shaped waterway connected to Lake St Lucia by a narrow steep-sided channel known colourfully as "Hell's Gates". Excellent for bird-watching, it's a quiet place, which doesn't see many tourists or even anglers despite offering opportunities to fish for both freshwater and marine species, as well as Cape salmon. The park gives an excellent, low-key experience of the lake, which you can get onto with **launch tours**. If you want to get out into the bush, the eight-kilometre **Dugandlovu Trail** and the ten-kilometre circular **Mpophomeni Trail**, will easily keep you busy for a couple of days. Both are clearly waymarked, pass through a variety of terrain and promise the possibility of seeing birds and a decent variety of antelope and other small mammals such as jackals, mongooses, servals, genets, warthogs and vervet monkeys.

To drive there, turn off the N2 to Hluhluwe village, 49km north of the Mtubatuba turn-off and continue east for 4km. Continue through town to a T-junction at the end of the road and follow the signposts for 15km to the False Bay gate. There's a **campsite** (①) at Lister's Point about midway down the west shore of False Bay, which has communal ablutions, but you must supply everything else. About 8km to the south, **Dugandlovu Rustic Camp** has four basic, four-bedded-huts (①) with cold showers, toilets, gas cookers and paraffin lamps. You must bring all your own gear, including linen and sleeping bags. **Bookings** for both camps must be made through the Officer-in-Charge, False Bay Park, PO Box 222, Hluhluwe 3960 (☎035/562 0425).

Mkuzi Game Reserve

Mkuzi Game Reserve (April–Sept 6am–6pm, Oct–March 5am–7pm; R25 per vehicle, R6 per person) is a major component of the Greater St Lucia Wetland Reserve, connected to the coastal plain by a slender corridor through which the Mkuze River flows before emptying itself in Lake St Lucia. Reached across the Lebombo mountains, 28km from Mkuze village on the N2, the reserve has no lions, but a rich cross-section of mammals covering 78 species inhabits its confines. It's for its varied and highly beautiful countryside and the avifauna that the reserve really rates – this is among the top spots for bird-watching in the country, with an impressive 430 species on record.

Defined to the west by the Lebombo mountains, Mkuzi marks the final haul of the coastal plain that stretches down the east of the continent from Kenya. The landscape varies from wetlands consisting of seasonal flood plains floating with waterlilies, reed beds and swamps, to savannah covered with grass. Elsewhere you'll come across stands of acacias (thorn trees) and in the south across the Mkuzi River you can wander through the cathedral-like fig forest that echoes to the shriek of trumpeter hornbills.

Access and information

There's no public **transport** into Mkuzi, and if you don't have your own vehicle you'll need to latch onto one of the **tours** that start in Mkuze village. The *Ghost Mountain Inn* (☎035/573 1025; ③–④) in the village, signposted off the N2, can provide information about bird-watching trips offered by *Ukubuka Bird Safaris* (☎035/573 1080) or straightforward half- or full-day game drives with *Maputaland Tours* (☎ & fax 035/573 1025) for which you should expect to pay R100–150 if there are two of you. If you're **self-driving**, the easiest way to get there is to leave the N2 at Mkuzi and follow the signs along a good dirt road for 28km to **Emshopi Gate**. An alternative route which leaves the N2 further south, 35km north of Hluhluwe village, involves a lot more driving on dirt and doesn't knock off that much distance. For navigating your way around the park, the reception office provides a clear map that shows all routes and distances.

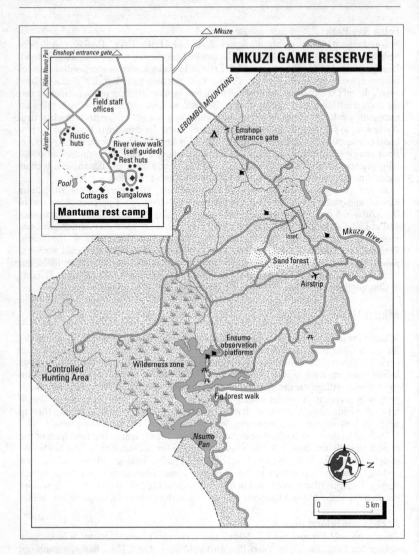

Accommodation

A **campsite** (①) is situated right at the entrance gate, while **Mantuma**, the main public rest camp, 9km into the park in the northern section, has a range of **accommodation**. Cheapest are the three-bedded rest huts (②) with shared ablution facilities and a kitchen, where a cook prepares your food for you. The most enticing units are the large traditional walk-in en-suite safari tents (②), each with its own roofed, but open-sided kitchen across the way. Nearby are three- and five-bedded en-suite bungalows (③–④) and a couple of seven-bedded cottages (④–⑤). All units are fully equipped and you need to bring just your own food and drink. **Reservations** for the campsite should be made through the Camp Superintendent, Mkuzi Game Reserve, PO BOX X550, Mkuze 3965 (☎035/673 1001). All other accommodation must be booked through Natal Parks Board Reservations (see box, p.393). Should the park be full, head for the *Ghost Mountain Inn* (☎035/573 1025; ③–④) in Mkuzi Village, which is also a pleasant place to have a **drink** or **meal**.

There's a **fuel pump** at the entrance gate where you can fill up your car, and a **shop** which sells basic supplies and books at the camp reception, but you really should plan to stock up in Mkuze village before heading out here.

Game-viewing and activities

Of the predators, **cheetah** and **leopard** are present but rarely glimpsed; you stand a better chance of seeing fox-like black-backed **jackals**. The obvious draw-card of Mkuzi, however, are its black and white **rhinos**. The **impala** antelope will also be hard to miss, and you should catch sight of the large, spiral-horned **eland** and **kudu**. **Baboons** and **vervet monkeys** are generally found rustling around in the trees and making a nuisance of themselves on the ground, while at night you could be treated to the eerie call of the thick-tailed **bushbaby** from the canopy.

Some 84km of road traverse Mkuze, but one of the best ways to see game is to stay put and wait for the animals to come to you. With exactly this in mind, several **hides**, clearly marked on the map given out at reception, have been erected at artificial water-holes and on the edge of pans. All animals have to drink at some time, particularly in the drier months when naturally occurring water is scarcer, so you're bound to have a relaxed and interesting time at a hide if you chill out with a pair of binoculars and a good field guide.

The two hides at **Nsumo Pan**, in the southern section of the park, apart from over-looking a very beautiful natural waterway, are superbly placed for observing waterfowl. The picnic site at Nsumo is one of the few places in the game reserve where you may leave your car and it makes a great place to stop and eat. Between July and September, if conditions are right, you can catch up to five hundred **birds** on the water at one time. Flocks of pelicans and flamingos make their appearance, as do kingfishers, fish eagles, waders, ducks, geese and countless other species.

From Nsumo you can embark on the three-kilometre self-guided **Mkuzi Fig Forest Trail** – another highlight of the reserve. Follow the signs from the car park to the Mkuze River, which can be crossed using a suspension bridge if the flow is too fast to allow rock-hopping. **Sycamore fig** forest is one of the rarest types of woodland in South Africa, and the stands of massive trees give the forest a gentle green glow. Look out for the flashing red flight feathers of fruit-eating **birds** like the purple-crested lourie or green pigeons and listen for the tap-tap of golden-tailed woodpeckers on the trees. **Monkeys** and **baboons**, which pass through from time to time pose no threat, except to steal your food, but you should keep alert to the possibility of encountering black rhinos or **hippos**, both of which are potentially dangerous and should be given a wide berth.

If you wish to explore other parts of Mkuzi on foot, you can go out on two-hour **conducted walks** with an armed guide. Many of the older guides speak very little English and their main function is to protect you. Current Parks Board policy, however, is to employ younger guides who speak English well and have a knowledge of the environment, so check out the situation when you book your walk at the rest-camp reception. More ambitious **three-day bushveld trails** are also available from March to November. On these, you'll be based at the trails camp in a remote part of the park, from which daily walks are accompanied by a well-informed trails ranger and a game guard. The trails cost around R800 per person, which includes all meals and accommodation, but you must bring your own snacks and drinks. For booking and further information, contact Natal Parks Board Reservations (see box, p.393).

Also not to be missed, and indicated on the map you'll get at the entrance gate, is a small **Crafts Centre**, where you can buy some great, inexpensive Zulu crafts made by people in the area.

Phinda Private Game Reserve

Although it's not one of the great South African game-viewing destinations, **Phinda Private Game Reserve**, on a private ranch, is certainly a contender for the most stylish. An irregular dribble of fenced-off land at the southern end of Mkuzi, the reserve offers a good chance of seeing **lion**, **cheetah** and both varieties of **rhino** on your game drives, but you can't help feeling it's all a bit too well-managed. At the moment the property is too small to sustain a self-regulating wildlife ecology, but if, as is hoped, it becomes integrated with surrounding parks (as has happened around the Kruger National Park) this could change dramatically.

Phinda is interesting, however, as an **eco-tourism** experiment based on the philosophy that to conserve wildlife in Africa it is necessary to bring tangible benefits to local communities. Not only has degraded farmland been returned to wilderness (*phinda* means "return" in Zulu), but more people are now employed providing services to tourists than when it was ranchland.

Whatever Phinda may lack as a wildlife destination is made up for abundantly in the sheer panache with which it provides fine-tuned luxury and hospitality to its upmarket clientele. **Accommodation** is at three lodges, with the Mountain Lodge providing vistas of the Lebombo range and the nearby St Lucia coastal plain; the Rock Lodge embracing a more intimate experience, with just six stone and glass chalets suspended off a cliff face; and the Forest Lodge offering stunning Afro-Japanese-style stilted timber houses, each tucked away discreetly among bush and trees. The **food**, described as "eclectic pan-African", is excellent. All game drives or walks are accompanied by well-informed expert guides, who are as good as any you'll find in South Africa.

Prices range from R1350 per person inclusive of all meals and game activities. **Bookings** should be made through *Conservation Corporation Africa*, Private Bag X27, Benmore 2010 (☎011/784 7077, fax 784 7667; email: reservations@conscorp.co.za), or through one of the specialist travel agents listed in "Basics". Unlike public parks, Phinda's wilderness is only open to its resident guests and you'll be given detailed instructions on **how to get there** when you make your booking.

Northern Maputaland

Northern Maputaland, roughly the region north of Mkuzi Game Reserve, is the remotest region of South Africa, mostly accessible only along dirt roads that work their tortuous way to the coast. For much of this area, a 4WD vehicle is essential and it's best to travel in two vehicles as there's nowhere to get repairs done and facilities are poor.

Some 11km north of **Mkuze** village, the longest tarred road in Maputaland snakes north and then east for 133km, before stopping abruptly at the busy, run-down settlement of **Kwangwanase** (Manguzi on some maps), 24km short of the coast. As it turns toward the sea, the road brushes past a short track that leads up to **Ndumo Game Reserve** and 8km later the entrance gate to **Tembe Elephant Park**, both hanging down from the Mozambique border. From Kwangwanase, 26km beyond Tembe, a road heads for Kosi Bay and the Mozambique border.

To its south, roads branch off this tarred spine, leading to **Mbazwana**, a tiny settlement that gains some status from being poised between **Sodwana Bay** to the south and **Lake Sibaya** to the north. Mbazwana can be reached by striking south off the tar at

Jozini, a small, dog-eared town that will seem like a thriving metropolis next to anything you're going to encounter beyond.

Sodwana Bay

A tiny scoop in the Zululand Coast, **SODWANA BAY** (daily; small entry fee) 19km south of Mbazwana along an unexpected interlude of tar, is the only breach in an almost flawless length of strand that extends from St Lucia for 170km to Kosi Bay. It's the fortuitous convergence of the bay, which makes it easy to launch boats, with the world's southernmost coral reefs that makes Sodwana the most popular base in the country for **scuba diving** and the most popular Natal Parks Board resort. Because the continental shelf comes extremely close to shore with near-vertical drops less than 1km away, it offers very deep waters, much loved by anglers, who gather here to launch out for some of South Africa's best **game fishing**.

When there's no one around, Sodwana Bay is paradise: a truly magnificent place with tepid waters, terrific sandy beaches, forest hikes, relaxed diving or snorkelling and plenty of cheap and basic accommodation. Over weekends and during school holidays, however, the picture changes, with fashion-conscious Jo'burgers tearing down to show off their designer wet suits while thick-set anglers from Gauteng, Free State and Mpumalanga kick up some sand with their heavy tread, drink themselves into a stupor and turn the beach into a massive 4WD car park. A gentler presence from mid-November to February are the leatherback **turtles**, which make their way onto Sodwana's beaches to reproduce, as they've been doing for the last 60,000 years (see box, p.410).

Access and accommodation

There is no public **transport** to Sodwana, although *Coral Divers* (see "Diving" overleaf) meets the *Baz Bus*, when it pulls into the village of Hluhluwe on its four-times-a-week run from Durban. Alternatively you can make arrangements through Kwambonambi-based *Amazulu Lodge Backpackers* (☎035/580 1009), which organizes diving trips. Hitching is possible, but even if you do succeed in thumbing a lift there the place is so spread out that getting around on foot is a major hassle. The park takes in the bay itself, while the desultory collection of shops and an upmarket lodge that pass for the **town** are 8km to the west, back along the Mbazwana Road.

Most **accommodation** is inside the park and tends to be pretty basic, apart from ten five-bedded (④) and ten eight-bedded (⑤) fully equipped **log cabins** provided by Natal Parks Board. Although the cabins are pricey for just two people, because there's a minimum charge they work out quite reasonably if there are three or more of you. There are also a staggering 446 **campsites** (①), which are levied at a minimum fee of R100 per site during public and school holidays as well as Friday and Saturday nights. The seasonal population explosion allegedly gives Sodwana the largest campsite in the southern hemisphere. **Bookings** for chalets should be made through the Natal Parks Board, (see box, p.393) while for campsites you should book through The Officer-in-Charge, Sodwana Bay National Park, PO BOX 310, Mbazwana 3974 (☎035/571 0051, fax 571 0115).

Apart from these, you can rent very basic **timber huts** (②) or bell tents on timber decks from the dive operators, when they aren't taken by scuba clients. These are offered by *Coral Divers* and *Sodwana Dive Retreats* (see "Diving" overleaf for details). The only **hotel** accommodation is at the expensive *Sodwana Bay Lodge & Hotel Resort* (☎035/571 0117, fax 571 0055; ⑤), which has comfortable en-suite reed chalets with thatched roofs and decks, but is 8km from the bay.

Diving

Unless you're a keen angler, the principal reason to come to Sodwana is for the **diving** off its coral reefs. More commonly found further north, coral reefs and bright tropical fish thrive here in the warm waters carried down the coast by the Agulhas Current. Both soft and hard **corals** robe the rocks with their convolutions and delicate formations and their range of textures, shades and colours. The waters are clear, silt-free and perfect for spotting some of the 1200 varieties of **fish** that inhabit the waters off northern KwaZulu-Natal, making it second only to the Great Barrier Reef in its richness.

The reefs are reached on dive boats, which weave a path through the surf. Closest to the bay, most commonly visited and consequently most stressed, is **Two Mile Reef**, which is 2km long, 900m wide, plumbs depths of betwen 9m and 34m and still offers eminently satisfying dives. Among the others is **Five Mile Reef**, which is further north and is known for its miniature staghorn corals, while beyond that **Seven Mile Reef** is inhabited by large anemone communities and offers protection to turtles and rays, which may be found resting here.

Of the operators with **concessions** for diving at Sodwana, only *Sodwana Dive Retreats* (☎031/307 4902 or 307 4903, fax 571 0042), based at *Sodwana Bay Lodge & Hotel Resort*, offers tuition leading to an internationally recognized **certificate**. If you want to learn to scuba dive in South Africa, this is unquestionably the best place to do it. They also do **dive packages** for people with open-water certificates, starting at R650 per person for three dives and two nights, hotel-style accommodation over a weekend on a dinner, bed and breakfast basis. A self-catering budget version staying in tents or very basic timber cabins (bring your own towels and sleeping bag) is also available. A slightly nicer self-catering budget alternative in more salubrious huts is offered by *Coral Divers*, PO Box 1840, Pietermaritzburg 3200 (☎0331/45 3076, fax 42 0144), which does packages starting at R450 for three nights and five dives over a weekend. Both companies offer discounted rates during the week.

Snorkelling, turtle tours and the Mngobolezeni Trail

If you don't want to go the whole hog with diving, you can still enjoy excellent **snorkelling** at Jesser Point, a tiny promontory at the southern end of the bay. Just off here is **Quarter Mile Reef**, which attracts a wide variety of fish, including moray eels and rays. Low tide is the best time to venture out – a sign on the beach indicates daily tide times. You can buy competitively priced snorkels and masks from the **dive shop** at *Sodwana Bay Lodge & Hotel Resort* (see "Access and accommodation") and they may be prepared to rent these as well as wet suits during off-peak periods.

During the December and January summer months when loggerhead and leatherback turtles (see box, p.410) come to nest and lay their eggs on the beach, Natal Parks Board operate well-informed guided **turtle tours**. Bookings for these must be made at the park reception, near the entrance gate.

The starting point for the five-kilometre circular **Mngobolezeni Trail** is just across from reception and winds its way through a variety of habitats, including woodland, to the coastal lake that gives the hike its name. Arrows and signs indicate the way – but take care not to get sidelined down one of the many game tracks that crisscross it. The walk takes around three hours and there's no drinkable water along the way, so you should take refreshment. **Crocodiles** live in the lake, as do hippos, who leave the water to feed, usually at dusk. If you encounter a hippo on land, treat it with the utmost respect: hippos are responsible for more human deaths than any other African mammal. Avoid getting between a hippo and its line of retreat, which will generally be the most direct route to the safety of the water. If you do disturb one, find a tree to hide behind or, even better, to climb!

Apart from hippos, you may be lucky enough to see some of the other animals that inhabit the dune forest and its surrounds, among them bushbuck, duiker (red and common), reedbuck and Tonga squirrels. An informative booklet, *Mngobolezeni Trail*, interprets points of interest along the way, and is available from reception.

Lake Sibaya and Baya Camp

On a windless day, **Lake Sibaya**, 10km due north of Sodwana, appears glassy, azure and flat. The waters are so transparent that when the Parks Board do a hippo count they just fly over and count the dark blobs that are clearly visible from the air. South Africa's largest natural freshwater lake covers 77 square kilometres, fringed by white sandy beaches that disappear into densely entwined forest. From the margins, timid crocodiles cut the lake surface, exchanging the warmth of the sun for the safety of the water. This is not an unpopulated wilderness: the lake fringes are dotted with traditional African lands and villages.

The only **accommodation** on the lake is at **Baya Camp**, on its western shore, 16km north of Mbazwana along a dirt track that traverses thick sand in places. Although you won't need a four-wheel-drive vehicle to get here, because of the thick sand you will need one to explore the forest areas around the lake.

Three four-bedded and four two-bedded chalets (②), connected by boardwalks, are each equipped with a handbasin with cold running water. The lounge, dining, kitchen and ablution facilities (with hot water if there's been enough sun to power the solar panels) are all shared. **Meals**, using your own food, are prepared by camp staff. **Reservations** can be made up to six months in advance through the Central Reservations Office, Department of Nature Conservation, Private Bag X9024, Pietermaritzburg 3200 (☎0331/94 6696, fax 42 1948). Don't just turn up expecting to find a vacant chalet, because if they're full you'll end up driving to the nearest hotel in Mkuze, some 111km away. There are no **facilities** apart from those already mentioned: the nearest shops and fuel are in Mbazwana, but you'd be better off stocking up at a larger centre, such as Mkuze or Jozini.

Boredom is a potential hazard in staying at Lake Sibaya, so consider coming here only if you're in a contemplative frame of mind as there's little to do apart from watch the hippos and crocs on the lake, survey the birdlife or embark on an exceptionally easy-going three-kilometre **circular walk** that starts from the viewing platform behind the camp. Nearby are two hides, and **bird-watching** can be rewarding with close on three hundred species present. Needless to say, with crocs and hippos lolling about, swimming in the lake would not be wise.

Mabibi

On the west side of Sibaya, **MABIBI** is probably the most remote and idyllic campsite in South Africa, made all the more appealing by the difficulty of getting there. Situated in luxuriant subtropical forest, about 20km from Sodwana up the coast towards Mozambique, the ten **campsites** (①) perch on a plateau at the top of monumental dunes that slide sharply down to the sea. The camp is protected from the winds by the dune forest and a boardwalk leads down the duneside to the **sea** – a walk that takes about ten minutes. This is truly one of the most undisturbed sections of coast in KwaZulu-Natal, and outside school holidays you stand a fair chance of having a perfect tropical beach all to yourself. You won't get the frenetic activity of outboard motors and four-wheel-drive vehicles found at Sodwana and other spots to the south, because they're banned within the Maputaland Coastal Forest Reserve, which Mabibi falls under.

The sea here is excellent for **surf angling** and the **snorkelling** matches that at Sodwana, with a rich tropical marine life thriving on the coral reefs offshore. A number of mammals live in the forest, but most of them – bushbabies, large-spotted genets and porcupines – only come out after dark, while others like suni and samango monkeys tend to be shy. Vervet monkeys, on the other hand, are fairly bold and you're bound to encounter a troop breezing through if you stay for more than a day.

The best **access** to the camp is along the tarred Kwangwanase (also called Manguzi) road from the N2, some 11km north of Mkuze. At the Manzengwenya intersection, turn right and follow the Mabibi signboards. Because this final 45km from the junction is along gravel and thick sand tracks, a 4WD vehicle or at least one with high clearance, such as a *bakkie* (pick-up truck), is essential. The closest **shops and fuel** are at Mbazwana, 60km to the south. The campsites can be **booked** up to six months in advance through the Central Reservations Office, Department of Nature Conservation, Private Bag X9024, Pietermaritzburg 3200 (☎0331/94 6696, fax 42 1948).

Rocktail Bay

South Africa's most sublime beachstay lies about 40km north of Mabibi along the coast at **ROCKTAIL BAY**, an even less accessible stretch of sand and sea that is restricted to guests who are prepared to shell out for the undeniable privilege of staying at the upmarket *Rocktail Bay Lodge*. Few parts of the South African coastline are as unspoilt at the beaches around here, and although there's no big game to pull in the punters, the bird-watching is excellent and you could see a number of rare and sought-after species, among them the green twinspot, green coucal, grey waxbill, purple-crested and Livingstone's louries as well as the Natal robin and emerald cuckoo. A rare and prized species to spot is the palmnut vulture.

Supreme idleness is one of the big attractions of the place, but if you're feeling perky you can go **snorkelling** in the bay at low tide (fins and snorkels are available to

---

MAPUTALAND'S TURTLES

The whole of the Maputaland coast is excellent for spotting **loggerhead** and **leatherback turtles** when they come ashore every year between October and February to breed, but Rocktail Bay is probably the best spot of all. Turtles coming from as far afield as Malindi in Kenya (3500km to the north) and Cape Agulhas (2000km west along the South African coastline) converge on the beaches of Maputaland to lay their eggs. Sea turtles have survived virtually unchanged for almost a hundred million years and it's reckoned that loggerheads have been using Maputaland's beaches to lay their eggs for 60,000 years.

When the female turtle's eggs are ripe she heads for the beach to lay her eggs. It is believed that the turtles are lured onto the beach by a hormone that oozes from the beach, a scent which she follows. The scent is believed to have been programmed into their subconscious while they were in their eggs. The myopic turtle, whose eyes are adapted to underwater vision, pulls herself along the beach in the dark until she encounters an obstruction such as a bank or a log, where she begins digging a pit using her front flippers until she has scooped out a nest big enough to hold her own volume. She then digs a flask-shaped hole about 50cm deep and lays her eggs into this, a process which takes about ten minutes.

The female turtle fills the hole and covers it with sand using her front flippers, disguising the place where the eggs are stored, and returns to the sea. After about two months the eggs hatch, and when the temperature drops below 28°C the entire clutch of hatched turtles will simultaneously race down the beach to the ocean. Only one in five hundred will survive to return. Once in the ocean, the hatchlings swim out to sea where they are either carried away by the Agulhas current into the Atlantic or along the Indian Ocean coast.

As the turtles are easily disturbed, only park officials are allowed on the beaches at night, escorting groups of visitors to watch the turtles.

guests), walk in the coastal forest, join an excursion to Black Rock or Lake Sibaya and go onto the beach to watch turtles during the summer egg-laying season. **Surf fishing** for shad, springer, kingfish, bonefish, stumpnose, barracuda and blacktail is another possibility.

Accommodation is in ten reed and thatched chalets with private toilets and showers raised on stilts into the forest canopy, each with its own wooden deck. This is the ideal place to get away: there's no phone, limited solar electricity (about 3hr per day), and the last few kilometres are so heavy-going that you leave your vehicle at the Coastal Forest Reserve office and have to be ferried in by four-wheel-drive.

Prices inclusive of all meals and activities come to US$190 and can be booked through *Wilderness Safaris*, PO Box 651171, Benmore 2010 (☎011/884 1458, fax 883 6255; email: wildrsa@iafrica.com).

Ndumo Game Reserve

Scenically one of the most beautiful of the KwaZulu-Natal reserves, **Ndumo** (daily dawn to dusk; R12 per vehicle, R5 per person) peers across the flood plain into Mozambique to the north and up to the Lebombo Mountains in the south. Its northern extent hugs up to the **Usutu River** which rises in Swaziland and defines South Africa's border with Mozambique. The turn-off to the reserve is 56km along the tar north of Jozini, with the final 15km along a rough gravel track.

No great volume of animals trammel the reserve, but the beauty, solitude and prolific birdlife here make this a good place to head for if you're not simply into the game of ticking off your list of **mammals** to see. That's not to underplay the 62 mammal species (including jackal, wildebeest, giraffe, hippo, hyena, zebra and both species of rhino) that occur here, but may be more difficult to see than elsewhere. For birdwatchers, though, Ndumo is in the big league, ranking among the country's birdwatching top spots. Of the staggering 420 different varieties that have been recorded here, among the **"target" bird species** for enthusiasts are the African broadbill, pinkthroated twinspot, gorgeous bushshrike, cuckoo hawk, southern banded snake eagle and the palmnut vulture.

As in other public game reserves, you can **self-drive** around some areas, one of the highlights being the trip to **Redcliffs**, where there's a picnic site with a towering vantage point that offers soaring views across the Usutu River into both Swaziland and Mozambique. KwaZulu-Natal Nature Conservation does open-topped 4WD outings in the mornings and evenings to the lovely **Inyamiti and Banzi pans**, which are inhabited by hippos and crocodiles and receive visits from an array of waterfowl. Guided **walking trails** are also available.

The small **public rest camp** is sited on a hill and has several old, but well-maintained, three-bedded **huts** (②), each with a fridge and handbasin with cold water. Ablutions are shared and camp chefs prepare your food for you. Meals are taken communally in the thatched dining room. A shop near the entrance gate sells basic supplies, but you'd be better off stocking up en route in Mkuze village. Accommodation **bookings** should be made through Central Reservations Office, Department of Nature Conservation, PO BOX X9024, Pietermaritzburg 3200 (☎0331/94 6696, fax 42 1948).

The private **Ndumo Wilderness Lodge** consists of a series of luxury en-suite safari tents on decks overlooking a beautiful pan in an area of the reserve closed to the general public. The units are connected by boardwalks on stilts above the flood level of the pan. The lounge area is an open-sided deck that jetties out towards the water and offers fabulous views of its crocodile-infested waters and the perfect vantage from which to watch water birds with a pair of binoculars. The lodge also lays on **game drives** and informative **guided walks** that help to give a more rewarding experience of the wild. Prices inclusive of all meals and game activities come to US$190 per person per day.

Bookings can be made through *Wilderness Safaris*, PO Box 651171, Benmore 2010 (☎011/884 1458, fax 883 6255; email: wildrsa@iafrica.com).

Tembe Elephant Park

Tembe was established in 1983 to protect **elephants** that had traditionally migrated seasonally between South Africa and Mozambique, but were falling victim to poaching and the war going on across the KwaZulu-Natal border.

Although the tarred road comes right up to the entrance gate of **Tembe**, 76km north of Jozini, once you cross its threshold you're into very undeveloped country that can only be accessed by a four-wheel-drive vehicle. Since only one party per day is permitted to visit the park, you're better off forgetting about coming here – it's far easier to see elephants in other places in South Africa, such as the Kruger Park (see p.537).

Kosi Bay

The northernmost place along the KwaZulu-Natal coast, **Kosi Bay** is at the centre of an enthralling area of waterways fringed by forest. Despite the name, this is not a bay at all, but a system of four lakes connected by narrow reed channels which eventually empty into the sea at Kosi Mouth. You will only be able to get to the mouth itself if you have a four-wheel-drive vehicle and are extremely intrepid.

One of the most striking images of Kosi Bay is of mazes of reed fences in the estuary and other parts of the lake system. These are **fish kraals** or traps built by local Tonga people, a practice that has been going on for hundreds of years. Custom has made the method of harvesting sustainable, because trap numbers are strictly controlled; they are passed down from father to son and designed to only capture four per-cent of the fish that pass through.

Staying at Kosi Bay, you're likely to feel yourself frustratingly aground and won't so much as glimpse the coast unless you sign up for the four-day **Amanzimnyama Trail**, which is one of the few ways for the general public to see South Africa's northernmost section of the Indian Ocean. The circular hike begins at the base camp on the west shore of Nhlange and passes through beautiful coastal forest, along the beach, through cycad and giant raffia palm groves. In summer there's the chance of seeing turtles on the beach. Beds, pots, cookers, ablution facilities and limited water are available at night stops along the route, but there's no electricity or refrigeration and you must bring your own eating utensils, food, bedding, torches and snorkelling gear. Mosquito repellent is recommended and this is one of the few parts of the country where it's advisable to use water purification tablets. **Bookings** for the trail, which costs R160 per person, should be made through KwaZulu Bureau of Natural Resources (see below).

A highly recommended alternative way to explore the area is on a **tour** guided by members of the **local community**, who can show you the lakes and the fish traps. Trips start just outside the rest camp from the reserve **office** (☎035/592 02036), where you can gather more information.

The KwaZulu Bureau of Natural Resources, 367 Loop St, Pietermaritzburg 3201 (☎0331/94 6698, fax 42 1984), rents out **accommodation** at its rest camp on the west shore of **Nhlage**, the largest of the lakes, in a two-bedded (②), five-bedded (②–⑤ – depending on numbers) and six-bedded lodge (③–⑥). There's a small **campsite** (①) nearby. Private accommodation is available nearby at *Kosi Bay Lodge* (☎ & fax 592 0037), 500m from the lake, in basic two-, four- or six-bedded reed chalets. There's a bar with a viewing deck and a restaurant serving run-of-the-mill fare.

Itala Game Reserve

West of Maputaland and close to the Swaziland border, the small **Itala Game Reserve** (daily: April–Sept 6am–6pm; Oct–March 5am–7pm; R20 per vehicle, R5 per person) is little-known, despite being one of the country's scenically most spectacular places to watch wildlife. The reserve's relative youth (it was only proclaimed in 1972) may be why it is frequently bypassed by visitors who rush for the big names such as Kruger and Hluhluwe-Umfolozi. This could soon change, especially as Itala's main camp, **Ntshondwe**, wins awards year after year as the best game-reserve rest camp in South Africa. Itala is notably mountainous and the terrain extremely varied; contained within a protective basin are numerous cliffs and rock faces.

If you're obsessed with seeing the Big Five, Itala is not the place to visit, as the king of the beasts is notably absent here, even though the rest of the other four make periodic appearances. Come instead for the most relaxed, uncrowded and beautifully set game-viewing you'll get in southern Africa. Like the rest of the KwaZulu-Natal game reserves, Itala is excellent for white **rhinos** and there is ample sufficiency of **plains game**, including zebras and giraffes. Of the **predators**, you could if you're very lucky bump into brown hyenas, cheetahs and leopards. But the best idea is to throw away your mammal check list and take a slow drive around the mountains into the valleys and along the watercourses. Because there are no lions, the game is relaxed, and on a quiet weekday watching **animal behaviour** can be pretty fascinating. Slow down, keep your eyes open, and you may recognize a rhino male defending his territory or two young giraffes testing their strength with neck wrestling. One of the most rewarding **drives** is along Ngubhu Loop, with a detour to Ngubhu picnic site.

There are some **self-guided trails** into the wooded mountainside above Ntshondwe, which give the chance to stretch your legs if you've spent a morning driving around. **Day and night drives** in open vehicles can be booked through Ntshodwe reception at a cost of R40 per person.

Practicalities

There's no public **transport** into the park, or even near to it, so self-driving is your only option. The main rest camp, **Ntshondwe**, 7km beyond the entrance gate, is ingeniously camouflaged against a high plateau with views at the foot of huge cliffs. There are no lawns or gardens; each chalet is surrounded by indigenous bush through which paved walkways weave their way around granite rocks and trees to the main reception area, which has a small shop, a restaurant, and bar with a deck overlooking a waterhole.

Accommodation at Ntshondwe is in two-bedroom chalets, either non-self-catering (③), in which case you eat in the restaurant or self-catering units (③), with two bedrooms, a fully equipped kitchen, lounge areas and verandahs. If you want an extremely pared-down bush experience, you won't beat the marvellous Doornkraal **campsite** (①), shaded by thorn trees and ilala palms, on the banks of the Mbizo River. Expect no frills here – it's cold showers in reed enclosures under the stars and cooking over wood fires, the only concession to civilization being a flushing toilet. **Bookings** for chalets should be made through the Natal Parks Board (see box, p.393) and, for camping, through the Officer-in-Charge, PO Box 42, Louwsburg 3150 (☎0388/75239, fax 75303).

If you're happy to shell out to eat in Ntshondwe's à la carte **restaurant**, which serves a surprisingly varied range of foods from escargot (not giant land snails fortunately) to steaks, don't bother with self-catering. Otherwise you will certainly need to stock up before you come, as the camp shop is poorly stocked with fresh foods and specializes in frozen meats and beers, which is great only if you plan to live on *braais* alone. Louwsburg's very small general dealer is a little better, but you'd be wise to pick up supplies at Vryheid,

Pongola, Mkuze or one of the larger villages en route. A cosy **bar** serves drinks, which taste even better outside on the deck, overlooking the waterhole and across the valleys.

CENTRAL ZULULAND AND THE BATTLEFIELDS

Central Zululand – the Zulu heartland – radiates out from the unlovely modern town of **Ulundi**, some 30km west of the Hluhluwe-Umfolozi Park. At the height of its influence in the 1820s and 1830s, under King Shaka, the core of the Zulu state lay between the the **Black Mfolozi River** in the north and in the south the **Tugela**, which discharges into the Indian Ocean, roughly 100km north of Durban.

Despite being a beautiful area of dry thornveld, large hills and big views, Central Zululand tends to be visited as a series of routes taking in museums and battlefield sites. The Zulu heartland, where you'll find **museums** relating to local history and culture, is concentrated just to the west of the Hluhluwe-Umfolozi Park, King Shaka's personal hunting preserve. The heartland can be taken as a side-trip from a visit to Hluhluwe-Umfolozi or Itala Game Reserve, which lies about 150km north of Ulundi.

Contained in a relatively small area to the west of the heartland are series of **battle sites** from wars fought in the nineteenth century, first between Zulus and Boers, then Zulus and the British and finally between the Boers and Brits. If it sounds boring, it needn't be, particularly if you're interested in history and in modern South African politics. But you'll be wasting your time if you attempt this area on you own: all you'll see is empty *veld* with a few memorials. Far better is to join a tour with one of the several excellent guides who make it their business to bring it all alive (see box, p.419).

The Zulu Heartland

Don't expect to see "tribal" people who conform to the Zulu myth outside **theme parks** such as Shakaland. Traditional dress and the **traditional lifestyle** are largely a nineteenth-century phenomenon, deliberately smashed by the British at the turn of the century, when they imposed a poll tax that had to be paid in cash – thus ending Zulu self-sufficiency, generating urbanization and forcing the Africans into the modern industrial economy, where they were needed as workers.

You will find beautiful crafts, at which Zulu society excels, the best examples being in museums such as the little-known but outstanding **Vukani Collection** in Eshowe. Also worth checking out is the reconstructed royal enclosure of Chetswayo, the last king of the independent Zulu, at **Ondini**, near Ulundi.

Some history

The truth behind the Zulus is difficult to isolate from the mythology, which was fed by both the Zulus themselves as well as white settlers. Accounts of the Zulu kingdom in the 1820s rely heavily on the diaries of the two adventurers **Henry Fynn** and **Nathaniel Isaacs**, who portrayed King Shaka as a mercurial and bloodthirsty tyrant who killed his subjects willy-nilly for a bit of fun. Despite their attempts to cover up their profligate regard for the truth, a letter from Isaacs to Fynn was uncovered in the 1940s. In it he encourages his friend, who was en route to London to publish his memoirs, to depict the Zulu kings as "bloodthirsty as you can, and describe frivolous crimes people lose their lives for. It all tends to swell up the work and make it interesting."

A current debate splits historians down the middle about the real extent of the **Zulu empire** during the nineteenth century. Some now question the conventional wisdom that

Shaka was the "African Napoleon", a military genius who transformed the politics of nine-teenth-century South Africa. What we do know is that in the 1820s Shaka consolidated a state, that was one of the most powerful political forces in the subcontinent and that internal dissent to his rule culminated in his assassination by his half-brother **Dingane** in 1828.

In the 1830s, pressure from whites exacerbated internal tensions in the Zulu state and reached a climax when a relatively small party of Boers obliterated Dingane's army at **Blood River**, leading to a split in the Zulu state, with one half following **King Mpande**. Collapse threatened when Mpande's sons Mbuyazi and Chetshwayo led opposing forces in a pitched battle for the succession. **Chetshwayo** emerged victorious and successfully set about rebuilding the state, but too late. Britain had already determined that its own interest would best be served by a confederated South Africa under its own control and a powerful Zulu state wasn't going to be allowed to stand in the way. On the banks of the Tugela River, the high commissioner, Sir Bartle Frere, delivered a Hobson's choice of an **ultimatum** that Chetshwayo should dismantle his polity or face invasion.

In January 1879, the British army crossed the Tugela and after a humiliating defeat of a massive British veteran force at Isandlwana the tide turned against the Zulus. By the end of July Zulu independence had been snuffed and Chetshwayo was being held prisoner in the Castle in Cape Town.

Gingindlovu

At **GINGINDLOVU** (shortened to "Ging" by local whites) the Zulus attacked a British relief column on April 2, 1879, as it was marching on Eshowe to relieve a siege. In one of the decisive battles of the Anglo-Zulu War, the colonial invaders delivered a crushing defeat to the Zulus that destroyed their morale, with the loss of only thirteen British lives. The following day the advancing British column continued on and successfully raised the Eshowe siege. There's nothing much to see in Gingindlovu, which is 50km north of Stanger along the R102, but it makes as good a base as any to explore the Zulu heartland and the Battlefields, and has the advantage of being a mere 15km from the coast.

The *Baz* **backpacker bus** pulls in and can drop you off at either of the two excellent **places to stay**, the cheaper being the eccentric and thoroughly entertaining *Inyezane Backpackers* (☎083/255 7345; email: inyezane@dbn.lia.net; ①) on a sugar farm just outside town. Accommodation consists of a series of eclectically decorated rondavels. The hostel is well known for its **mud baths**, and you can also learn to make your own curios out of elephant dung, or play traditional musical instruments. Also on a sugar estate, but at the opposite extreme of old-fashioned elegance, in a grand homestead that resembles something out of *Gone with the Wind*, is *Mine Own Country House* (☎0353/30 1262, fax 30 1025; ④–⑤), 4km north of Gingindlovu on the R102, with en-suite rooms, well-tended gardens, a swimming pool and tennis courts.

Eshowe

Visitors generally give a **ESHOWE** a miss on their way to the more obvious drama of the old Zulu capital at Ondini and the Battlefields, but the place deserves more than a passing glance as it offers a gentle introduction to the **Zulu heartland**. Apart from its attractively organic setting, interlacing with the Dhlinza Forest, this town, 22km inland from Gingindlovu, houses one of the finest historical and contemporary collections of Zulu crafts, has a half-decent museum and offers exceptional tours that take you under the skin of a modern KwaZulu-Natal country town. As befits a forested town in the heart of Zululand, its name has an onomatopoeic Zulu derivation evoked by the sound of the wind blowing through the trees.

Graham Chennels, former mayor and current proprietor of the *George Hotel* in Main Street, leads enthusiastic **tours** of Eshowe, taking in the white, coloured and African areas as well as the rural surrounds. This is one of the best and easiest ways of under-standing exactly how segregation worked under apartheid, and one of the most opti-mistic views of South Africa's future you're likely to find.

The Vukani Collection and Zululand Historical museums

One very good reason for coming to Eshowe is for the little-advertised **Vukani Collection Museum**, Osborn St (☎0354/75274, curator 74902; Tues & Thurs 9am–1pm, other times by request), which happens to be the largest and among the best collections of traditional **Zulu arts and crafts** in the world, containing over 3000 pieces. If you have any interest in local material culture this is an essential port of call. Better still, arrange a guided **tour** by the highly knowledgeable curator, who can put the items into a cultural and social context. On view you'll see a huge range of **baskets**, something Zulu culture excels at (and examples of which are held in many major inter-national art collections), each made for a specific purpose. There are also carvings, clothing, beadwork, tapestries and some outstanding ceramics, including works by **Nesta Nala**, one of the leading contemporary proponents of the form. After seeing the bench-mark examples here, you'll have a good idea about the quality of basketry and crafts you'll see for sale as you work your way around Zululand.

Also worth a visit is the **Zululand Historical Museum** (daily 9am–4pm; entry by donation), housed within the limewashed crenellations of **Fort Nongqayi**. The collec-tion is eccentric and informative by turns, but never dull. Among the displays is furni-ture belonging to **John Dunn**, the only white man to become a Zulu chief and to take 49 wives, so becoming the progenitor of Eshowe's coloured community, many of whom still carry his last name. You can also see Zulu household artefacts, the replica of a sil-ver beer mug given by Queen Victoria in London to Chetshwayo, the last king of the free Zulus in 1882 and displays on Zulu history. One of these covers the Bambatha Rebellion, in which Fort Nongqayi saw action, putting down the last armed resistance by Africans till the formation of the ANC's armed wing in the 1960s.

The large grounds around the museum are a great place to have a picnic. A twenty-minute trail leads to the **Mpushini Falls** and there's a one-hour self-guided walk through the majestic **Dhlinza Forest**, which has some hides where you can look out for forest birds.

Practicalities

The *Translux* **intercity bus** stops in front of the City Hall on its three-times-a-week haul between Pretoria/Johannesburg and Richards Bay, and the *Baz* **backpacker bus** also passes through town on its Durban–Johannesburg route.

The cheapest **accommodation** in town is at *Zululand Backpackers*, 38 Main St (☎0354/74919 or 42894, fax 41434, cell 082/492 6918; ①), which has camping, small dorms and doubles in a beautifully cared-for hostel. Outside, there's a big fig tree under which you can have meals and chill out. Mountain bikes are available to rent and there's a large swimming pool. Next door, the *George* (☎0354/74919; ②) offers good-value hotel accommodation at the bottom of its price range, with comfortable en-suite rooms with TVs. *Forest Lodge*, 128 Main St (☎0354/74079, fax 41908; ②), has fully equipped, self-catering units close to the forest and the falls, while *Amble Inn*, 116 Main St (☎0354/41300; ②), has eleven rooms and its own **restaurant**, which serves English-style meals. The *Curry Queen*, 25 Osborn Rd, serves tasty and spicy Indian-style food.

Shakaland and Simunye

North of Eshowe the winding R66 leaves behind the softer vistas of the Dhlinza Forest, the citrus groves and green seas of cane plantations and looks across huge views of the valleys that figure in the creation mythology of the Zulu nation. In no time you're into thornveld (acacias, rocky kopjes and aloes) and **theme park** country. Most accessible of these "Zulu-village hotels" is **Shakaland**, Norman Hurst Farm, Nkwalini (☎035/460 0912, fax 460 0824), 14km north of Eshowe off the R68, which just about manages to remain on the acceptable side of exploiting ethnic culture, but isn't quite as "authentic" as its publicity materials claim.

Built in 1984 as the set for the wildly romanticized TV series *Shaka Zulu*, Shakaland's management was taken over in 1988 by the *Protea* hotel chain. What the brochures don't tell you is that the village is a reconstruction of a nineteenth-century Zulu *kraal* (homestead) and is quite unrepresentative of how people live today. However, Shakaland does offer the chance to sample Zulu food in a spectacular dining area. **Tours** for day visitors (daily 11am & 12.30pm; R55, or R85 including lunch) begin with an audiovisual about the origin of the Zulus, followed by a guided walk around the huts, an explanation of traditional social organization, and concluding with some energetic dancing. **Accommodation** is available in luxury traditional beehive huts (⑥) with untraditional luxuries such as electricity and en-suite bathrooms.

In a different league, **Simunye** (☎03546/912, fax 824; ⑦), along the D256, off the R34, and 6km from Melmoth, offers a far more authentic experience of Zulu culture, introducing guests to contemporary ways of life as well as traditional customs. Visitors are conveyed to the camp by horse or on an ox-wagon and while there you'll get to see dancing, visit a working *kraal* and meet local people. **Accommodation** is either in stone and thatched huts at the main camp, which overlooks the Mfule River, or at a *kraal* in a beehive hut – either way there's no electricity.

Ulundi and Ondini

Some 83km north of Eshowe on the R66, **ULUNDI** is the former capital of the KwaZulu *bantustan* and lies at the centre of the **Makhosini Valley** ("valley of the kings"), which holds a semi-religious status among Zulu nationalists as the birthplace of the Zulu state and the area where several of its founding fathers lived and are now buried. Now that KwaZulu has been reintegrated with Natal, this rather unattractive modern town is tussling with Pietermaritzburg for pre-eminence in the province, but for the moment the two are joint capitals – a fact that brings joy to no one except the airlines that have to ferry legislators from one centre to the other. There's nothing in Ulundi itself that is worth stopping for, apart from its historical connections.

The **Battle of Ulundi Memorial**, just outside town on the untarred road to the Cengeni Gate of the Hluhluwe-Umfolozi Park, is the poignant spot that marks the final defeat of the Zulus. An understated small stone structure with a silver dome houses a series of plaques listing all the regiments on both sides involved in the last stand of the Zulus on July 4, 1879. The rectangular park around the memorial marks the site of the hollow infantry square adopted by the British and supported to devastating effect by seven- and nine-pounder guns.

By far the most interesting sight around here is the **Ondini Historical Reserve** (Mon–Fri 8am–4pm, Sat & Sun 9am–4pm; small entry fee), a few kilometres further along the road, which houses the reconstruction of the royal residence of **King Chetshwayo**, a site museum and a cultural museum. In 1872 Chetshwayo succeeded to the Zulu throne and set about rebuilding the Zulu state, which had been fracturing since the 1850s. His success at achieving this proved to be his undoing, because the British didn't want a strong united Zulu kingdom standing between them and their aim of a confederated South Africa under the Union Jack. After the decisive Battle of Ulundi, the royal residence at Ondini was razed to the ground and Chetshwayo was captured. Still puzzled by Britain's actions, Chetshwayo wrote to the British governor in 1881 from his exile at the Castle in Cape Town: "I have done you no wrong, therefore you must have some other object in view in invading my land." The *isigodlo*, or **royal enclo-**

sure, has been partially reconstructed with traditional Zulu beehive huts, which you can wander round, while the site museum has a model showing the full original arrangement. Among the items in the **Cultural Museum** is a major bead collection.

A **picnic site** has been provided in the extensive grounds of the reserve and there's **camping** (①) and accommodation in the traditional *umuzi* or homestead in a group of beehive **huts** (①–②) inside a stockade with beds and communal kitchens, with ablution facilities outside. **Bookings** for these should be made through the Clerk of the KwaZulu Monuments Council, PO BOX 523, Ulundi 3838 (☎0358/79 1223 or 79 1854).

The Battlefields

Most of the major KwaZulu-Natal Battlefields lie in the northwestern corner of the province, where first the Boers came out of the mountains from the northeast into Zulu territory and inflicted a severe defeat on the Zulu at **Blood River** in 1838, 13km southeast of the tiny town of Utrecht. Some four decades later the British spoiled for war and marched north to fight a series of battles against the Zulus, the most notable being at **Isandlwana and Rorke's Drift**, southeast of Dundee.

Twenty years on Britain again provoked war, this time against the **Boers** of the South African Republic and the Orange Free State to the north and west. The Second

---

GOING INTO BATTLE

There's little point in wandering around the Battlefields without a guide; all you'll see are stretches of *veld* and the odd memorial. Going along with a qualified **guide** will infinitely enhance your experience. Guides specialize in different battle sites, usually those closest to their base. You should expect to pay in the region of R100 and over for a day-trip.

Battlefield and Zulu Heartland Guides

Fred Duke (☎0381/80 7835). Specializes in the Zulu Battlefields in the Vryheid area, namely the sites at Hlobane, Kambula, Ulundi and Blood River as well as the Route Prince Imperial.

Maureen Richards (☎ & fax 0361/31 1233). Former curator of the Ladysmith Siege Museum and expert on the Anglo-Boer Battlefields, Spioenkop and Colenso, offers entertaining and highly informative tours.

David Rattray, PO BOX 3016 Rorke's Drift (☎03425/843, fax 0341/23319). Consummate storyteller, who infuses his accounts of Rorke's Drift and Isandlwana with emotion more than anyone else. This could easily be the best live performance you attend in South Africa.

John Turner, PO Box 10, Babanango (☎0358/35 0062). Highly qualified as a natural scientist, with a degree in animal behaviour, Dr Turner is able to combine tours of Hluhluwe-Umfolozi game reserve and ecological topics including birding and basic tree identification with Zulu historical sites and the Anglo-Zulu battlefield.

Foy Vermaak, PO Box 1358, Dundee 3000 (☎ & fax 03425/925). Based close to Isandlwana and Rorke's Drift sites, which he specializes in.

Do-it-Yourself

If you can't afford a guide, the next best thing is to buy an **audiotape**, which you can listen to in your car. These are available from reception at the Talana Museum (see p.421). Contact David Rattray direct to get hold of a copy of his excellent set of tapes covering Rorke's Drift and Isandlwana. The most authoritative book about the Anglo-Boer War is the highly entertaining *Boer War* by Thomas Pakenham.

Anglo-Boer War (also known as the South African War) was fought over control of the Gauteng goldfields. British troops were landed at Durban, in the British colony of Natal, and boldly marched north. Britain, accustomed to fighting enemies without firearms, believed the campaign would be quick, cheap and over by Christmas. But in the early stages of the war the huge but lumbering British machine proved no match for the mobile Boers who fought a guerrilla campaign that checked the advance of the redcoats in northern KwaZulu-Natal.

At **Ladysmith** the British endured months of an embarrassing siege, while nearby at **Spioenkop** bungling British leadership snatched defeat from the jaws of victory. Although the Empire successfully struck back, it took three years for it to defeat two of the smallest states in the world after committing half a million troops to the field in an operation that was the costliest campaign since the Napoleonic Wars nearly a century earlier.

Isandlwana and Rorke's Drift

On January 22, 1879 the British suffered one of the most humiliating defeats in their colonial history when virtually their entire force of 1700 men at **Isandlwana** was obliterated by a "bunch of savages armed just with sticks". That same evening, honour was restored when a motley group of British veterans and sick successfully defended the field hospital at **Rorke's Drift**, just across the Buffalo River from the site of the earlier disaster, against the same advancing Zulu force, a sequence of events heavily romanticized in the 1960s film *Zulu*, which made the reputation of an ever-grateful **Michael Caine** and led him to comment: "thank God for the Zulus."

If you're only planning to take in one battlefield site, then Isandlwana should be that one, and once you're making the effort you really should take in Rorke's Drift as well to complete the day's events. Isandlwana is just over 130km northwest of **Eshowe**, but the closest town of any size is **Dundee** about 70km to its west. Both Isandlwana and Rorke's Drift are eerily beautiful places, which you can visit and walk around on your own, but far more rewarding is to join a **tour** with one of the excellent battlefield guides, who can really paint a word picture of the battle against the mute landscape (see box p.419).

For somewhere to stay in the vicinity, you could do worse than the blink-and-you've-missed-it village of **BABANANGO**, 92km northwest of Eshowe, which consists of a shop or two and the *Babanango Hotel*, 16 Justice St (☎0358/350029; ④), a small atmospheric country hotel, that's renowned for its tiny *Stan's Pub*, which crams in piles of calling cards, girlie pics, Zulu War memorabilia, police helmets and a very friendly Great Dane. Babanango's rate includes dinner, bed and breakfast. A quieter alternative is *Babanango Valley Lodge* (☎0358/35 0062, fax 35 0160; ⑥), situated on a Natural Heritage Site, signposted 4km west of Babanango on the R68, deep in one of the most beautiful valleys anywhere, where you can be taken on walks to expore the veld, rocks and river. Accommodation is in pleasant en-suite rooms set in the garden, you get dinner and breakfast, and there's a swimming pool. The owner, Dr John Turner, is a registered guide with expertise in ecology as well as the cultural history of the Zulus and the Battlefields (see box, p.419).

A couple of other good alternatives exist, where you can stay in beautiful countryside at establishments run by battlefield guides. Near the minuscule settlement of **HELPMEKAAR**, along the R33 south of the Rorke's Drift battlefield and 30km south of Dundee, *Penny Farthing* (☎ & fax 03425/925; ③), is an historic pioneer farm still furnished with a lot of original objects and generations of hunting trophies, set in an area of big open grasslands, hills with walks and hiking trails on the farm. Host Foy Vermaak is a Battlefields guide (see box, p.419) who enjoys fireside chats on the subject and has a personal collection of memorabilia.

The ultimate Battlefields stay is at *Fugitives' Drift Lodge* (☎03425/843, fax 0341/23319; full-board rate ⑦), 9km north of **RORKE'S DRIFT**, where you're hosted by David Rattray who has made the Isandlwana and Rorke's Drift Battlefields his metier (see box, p.419). Located on a huge game farm, the lodge overlooks the drift where British survivors of Isandlwana fled across the Buffalo River. Rooms are in individual cottages that open onto lawns and gardens, and guests eat together in a cental dining room. If you're not staying at the lodge you can still join the tours (provided there is space), which are the most colourful and dramatic on offer.

Isandlwana

Dominated by an eerie hill, the **Isandlwana battlefield**, off the R68 between Nqutu and Babanango (daily 8am–5pm; small entry fee), remains unspoilt and unchanged apart from some small homesteads and the graves of those who fell. A small interpretation centre houses artefacts and mementos.

The monumental bungling and the scale of the Zulu victory over the British sent shock waves back to London. Following the British ultimatum to the Zulus, three colonial columns were sent to invade Zululand. King Chetshwayo responded by sending a force against each of these. On January 21, 1879, Zulu troops encamped 6km from Isandlwana Hill, where one of the British columns had set up camp. Unaware of the Zulus over the brow, the British commander took a large detachment to support another British force, leaving the men at Isandlwana undefended and unfortified.

Meanwhile, a British scouting party rode to the brow of a hill and were stunned to find the valley filled with 20,000 Zulu soldiers sitting in utter silence. Because of a superstition surrounding the phase of the moon, the Zulus were waiting for a more propitious moment to attack. On being discovered, they rose up and converged on the British encampment using the classic Zulu "horns of the bull" formation to outflank the unprotected British who they completely overran. Few of the 1200 British forces survived.

The British press at the time demonized the Zulus for disembowelling the dead, which must have made a pretty ghastly sight in the aftermath of the battle. In fact the practice had a religious significance for the Zulus, who believed that it released the spirit of the dead.

Rorke's Drift

Rorke's Drift is the most rewarding battlefield to visit on your own on account of its excellent **field museum** and interpretation centre (daily 8am–5pm; free) at the site. Although geographically close to Isandlwana, certainly near enough for a Zulu war party to run to, there are currently no direct linking roads and getting from one to the other involves a fairly long trip back to the R68, off which both sites can be reached.

Despite Chetshwayo's express orders to his men not to attack Rorke's Drift, a number of hot-headed young men were so fired up by their victory at Isandlwana and eager to "wash their spears" that they pushed on and attacked the hospital. For twelve hours spanning January 22 and 23, 1879, one hundred British soldiers repulsed repeated attacks by four thousand Zulus, thus saving tattered British honour and earning eleven Victoria Crosses – the largest number ever awarded in one battle.

While you're here, it's also worth taking in the **Rorke's Drift ELC Craft Centre** (Mon–Fri 8am–4.30pm, Sat 10am–3pm) at the site, which is known for its hand-printed fabrics and tapestries depicting rural scenes.

Dundee and the Talana Museum

Some 32km west of the Rorke's Drift turn-off, along the R68, **DUNDEE** is a one-trick coal-mining town you can safely miss because its single draw-card, the **Talana**

Museum (Mon–Fri 8am–4pm, Sat 10am–4pm, Sun noon–4pm; small entry fee) is 2km outside town on the Vryheid Road. The museum itself is excellent, consisting of nine historic buildings which are still standing from the time of the Battle of Talana Hill – the first engagement of the Anglo-Boer War in 1899, and a landmark for the British army, which wore khaki for the first time.

The museum is scattered around the grounds in a series of whitewashed buildings under shady blue gums, the most interesting of which is **Talana House**, which gives information about northern KwaZulu-Natal conflicts including Anglo-Zulu, Zulu-Boer and Anglo-Boer wars. Displays included weapons and uniforms, but most evocative are the photographs which really personalize the wars. Even if you're not really interested in military history, you're bound to find some fascinating detail, such as the POW camps Boers were exiled to in far-flung parts of the Empire including St Helena and the Far East. Often-neglected aspects of the Anglo-Boer War, including the roles of Africans and Indians, also get some coverage. In a photograph of Indian stretcher-bearers, you may be able to spot the youthful Mohandas Gandhi, who carried wounded British soldiers off the Spioenkop and Colenso Battlefields. The museum also has the lovely *Miners Rest Tea Shop*, which makes a far preferable stop for a **drink** and a **snack** than anywhere in town.

Blood River and Vryheid

You can't fail to be amazed by the monument at the **Blood River Battlefield** (daily 8am–5pm; small entry fee), 48km from Dundee on the way to Vryheid off the R33, which of all the Afrikaner quasi-religious shrines across the country definitely takes the cake. A replica laager of 64 life-size bronze wagons, stand on the site where on December 16, 1838 the Boers defeated a Zulu army. During the apartheid years, this date was celebrated by Afrikaners as the **Day of the Vow**, a public holiday honouring a supposed covenant made by the Boers with God himself that if he granted them victory, they would hold the day sacred. Afrikaners still visit the monument on this day, but under the new government the public holiday has been recycled as the Day of Reconciliation.

Back on the R33, it's 56km east to **VRYHEID** (meaning "freedom" in Afrikaans), one-time capital of the Nieuwe Republiek ("New Republic"), which for many whites, who refuse to fly the new South African flag, still represents some kind of Boer stronghold. Unless you're **stopping for the night** at the highly recommended, French-run *Villa Prince Imperial*, 201 Deputation St (☎0381/80 2610; ④), clearly signposted from the main street, there's little reason to delay leaving.

Ladysmith and around

LADYSMITH, 61km south of Dundee on the N11, owes what modest fame it has to one of the worst sieges in British military history nearly a century ago, and more recently to **Ladysmith Black Mambazo**, the local vocal group that helped Paul Simon revive a flagging career in the mid-1980s. Now one of South Africa's best-known black groups, Mambazo are rarely at home, so the only reason to hang out here is to explore the Anglo-Boer War in the town's museum, monuments and the surrounding Battlefields. Some 40km south of Ladysmith, near Chievely, is the spot where an armoured train carrying Winston Churchill was blown up by Boers. He developed

The **telephone code** for Ladysmith is ☎0361.

quite a respect for the Boers as a result of this encounter, and when he returned to England he reported to his colleagues that that the Boers were a more formidable opponent than they had imagined.

Some history

"[Ladysmith] is famous to the uttermost ends of the earth: centre of the world's attention, the scene of famous deeds", wrote a gung ho young journalist named Winston Churchill, who was covering the Anglo-Boer War for the *London Morning Post*. Lasting a 118 stinking days of filthy drinking water, powerlessness and the indignity of having 12,000 British troops pinned down by undisciplined farmers, who took regular pot shots at the town, the siege began on November 2, 1899. It was one of three sieges (the others being at Kimberley and Mafikeng) that kicked off the early stages of the war and shocked a British establishment that had fully expected to smartly sort out the Boers and have the troops home by Christmas.

Arrival and information

Of the **intercity buses** *Greyhound* (☎24181) pulls into Ted's Service Station on its Johannesburg–Durban route and *Translux* (☎27 1111) breaks its Bloemfontein–Durban run at the **train station** (☎27273). Daily trains arrive from Johannesburg and Durban, but arrival and departure times make taking the train an unrealistic option unless you're pressed. The **tourist information bureau**, Town Hall, Murchison St (Mon–Fri 8am–4pm, Sat 8am–noon; ☎22992), has a good selection of literature on the Battlefields. It's pretty easy to walk around Ladysmith's small centre, which is fortunate as there's no public transport.

Accommodation

There are plenty of **places to stay** in Ladysmith, some of them plugging right into the battlefield scene with proprietors offering themselves as "battlefield hosts" who you can come back to in the evening and discuss the day's experiences.

Blockhouse B&B, 5km from town on Windsor Dam Rd, off the R103 to Harrismith (☎32 4091). Eccentric farmhouse with its own blockhouse museum, probably the best private collection of Boer and Zulu war memorabilia, where you can linger for hours. Friendly hosts are battlefield enthusiasts who will share thoughts about the Boer War. Dinner, bed and breakfast rate, ③.

Bullers Rest Lodge, 61 Cove Crescent (☎26154). Smart thatched establishment on a ridge overlooking town. ③.

Mambasa Hutted Camp, off the R600 between Ladysmith and Winterton, adjoining Spioenkop Nature Reserve (☎488 1003, fax 488 1116). Cheapest accommodation in the Ladysmith Battlefields area in traditional Zulu beehive huts on the banks of the Tugela River. Furnished only with beds and mattresses, paraffin lamps, and with open fires for cooking meals, it also has a deepfreeze, hot and cold running water and flush toilets in a communal ablution block. Canoes and rubber tubes are available for use on the river. ①.

Royal Hotel, 140 Murchison St (☎ & fax 22176 or 2177 or 2178). In the heart of town, the original historic hotel that harboured the town's most privileged during the siege and was regularly shelled by the Boers is now a three-star establishment catering mainly to travelling reps. It's constantly full during the week, which makes booking essential at any time of year.

The Town

Along **Murchison Street**, the main artery running through Ladysmith, you'll find banks, the post office and shops as well as the the main tourist attractions. Of these the **Ladysmith Siege Museum** (Mon–Fri 8am–4pm, Sat 9am–1pm; small entry fee), next to the Town Hall, on the corner of Queen and Murchison streets, stands out as an essential starting point for any tour of the Anglo-Boer Battlefields. This compelling little museum tells the story of the war in a series of text and photographs, conveying the appalling conditions during the siege as well as key points in a war that helped shape twentieth-century South Africa, paving the way for its unification. The museum is also a good source of books about the war, written from both the British and Boer points of view.

Diagonally opposite, also in Murchison Street, stands the **Royal Hotel**, where the more privileged of the besieged passed their time, including Leander Starr Jameson and Frank Rhodes (brother of the more famous Cecil), who routinely lunched there. Both had been involved in 1895 in an attempt to overthrow the Boer government, which was why, some believed, the Boers regularly shelled the hotel around lunchtime.

Down Queen Street from the *Royal*, in Forbes Street, a **statue of Gandhi** stands self-possessed in front of the unprepossessing Vishnu Temple. Although the statue depicts Gandhi in his persona as the saintly Mahatma, his associations with Ladysmith go back before he had earned that title, to the Boer War, when he enrolled in the British army as a stretcher-bearer and trained members of Ladysmith's Indian community to do likewise. Gandhi, still at an early stage of his political learning curve, believed that by showing the British that Indians were loyal subjects they would grant independence to India.

Around the **Forbes and Lyell streets** areas, near the temple, Ladysmith presents an altogether more African face, thronging with people around the taxi ranks and informal market stalls set up on empty plots dotted between run-down Indian shopping malls, where people jive to the rhythm of backstreet music bars and mothers stroll with babies strapped to their backs.

The Muslim side of Ladysmith is represented by the **Soofie Mosque**, across the Klip River in Mosque Road, in the Indian suburb of Rose Park, said (most notably by the Publicity Association) to be the most beautiful mosque in the southern hemisphere.

Eating and drinking

The siege is over and horse is off the menu, but the *Royal Hotel*, with its three **restaurants**, is still the best place to eat in town. Less formal is the *Guinea Fowl Steakhouse*, Alfred St (☎28163), noted for its spare ribs, while *Savanna's Fast Foods*, Oval Shopping Centre, Murchison St, does the best Indian takeaways in town, serving cheap filled *rotis* and *breyanis* until 7pm. *Wimpy*, 7 Murchison St, is the only place to eat in a hurry and it stays open until 8pm.

Spioenkop

Spioenkop battlefield lies 35km west of Ladysmith and is set in the Spioenkop Nature Reserve (April–Sept 6am–6pm, Oct–March 6am–7pm). Bloodiest of all the Boer War battles, Spioenkop took more British lives than any other and taught the British command that wars fought by means of set-piece battles were no longer viable. After this, the guerrilla-style tactics of modern warfare were increasingly adopted.

Some 1700 British troops took the hill under cover of a mist without firing a shot, but were able to dig only shallow trenches because the surface was so hard. When the mist lifted they discovered that they had misjudged the crest of the hill. But their real failure was one of flawed command and desperately poor intelligence. Had the British reconnoitred properly they might have discovered that they were facing a motley collection of fewer than 500 Boers with only seven pieces of artillery and they could have called in their 1600 reserves to relieve them.

Despite holding lower ground, the Boers were able to keep the British, eight men per metre, pinned down for an entire sweltering midsummer day, while the Boers pounded them and shot at any helmet that peered over the trenches. Around six hundred British troops perished and were buried where they fell on the so-called "acre of massacre".

Meanwhile the Boers, who were aware of the 1600 British reinforcements at the base of the hill, had gradually been drifting off, and by the end of the day, unbeknownst to the British, there were only 350 Boers left. In the evening the British withdrew, leaving the hill to the enemy.

travel details

As the economic centre of KwaZulu–Natal, Durban is also its transport hub, with the majority of links into the province beginning or ending here. For travellers the most useful mode of transport could be the backpacker buses which provide access to interesting destinations not on other regular routes.

Buses

The main bus lines serving the principal routes from Durban to Johannesburg or Cape Town are *Translux* and *Greyhound* (☎031/361 7774), with supplementary services being offered twice daily by *Interport* up the north coast to Richards Bay (☎0351/91791) and one to two times daily down the South Coast as far as Margate by *Margate Mini Coach* (☎039/377 6406).

Durban to: Ballito (6 weekly; 35min); Bloemfontein (2–3 daily; 10–12hr); Cape Town (3 daily; 20hr); East London (2 daily; 9hr); Empangeni (2–3 daily; 2–3hr); Gingindlovu (2 daily; 1hr 30min); Grahamstown (2 daily; 12hr); Harrismith (1 daily; 4hr 30min); Johannesburg (7 daily; 11hr 30min); Kimberley (3 weekly; 11hr 30min); Knysna (1 daily; 15hr); Ladysmith (1 daily; 3hr 30min); Margate (1–2 daily; 2hr); Melmoth (6 weekly; 4hr); Pietermaritzburg (9 daily; 2hr 15min); Plettenberg Bay (1 daily; 14hr 30min); Port Elizabeth (2 daily; 13hr 30min); Port Shepstone (3–4 daily; 1hr 30min); Pretoria (7 daily; 9hr); Richards Bay (2–3 daily; 2hr 30min); Sedgefield (1 daily; 15hr); Stanger (6 weekly; 1hr); Umhlanga Rocks (6 weekly; 15min); Umtata (2 daily; 6hr); Upington (3 weekly; 16hr); Vryheid (6 weekly; 6hr).

Margate to: Durban (1–2 daily; 2hr); Johannesburg (2 weekly; 8hr 30min); Pretoria (2 weekly; 10hr).

Pietermaritzburg to: Bloemfontein (2–3 daily; 8hr 30min); Cape Town (2 daily; 19hr); Durban (9 daily; 2hr 15min); Johannesburg (6–7 daily; 7hr);

Kimberley (3 weekly; 10hr); Ladysmith (1 daily; 2hr); Pretoria (6–7 daily; 8hr).

Richards Bay to: Durban (2–3 daily; 2hr 30min); Gingindlovu (2 daily; 1hr 15min); Johannesburg (6 weekly; 9hr 30min); Pretoria (6 weekly; 10hr).

Backpacker buses

Among the most useful buses for travellers are the *Baz* and *Hopper* buses, which follow routes specifically designed to take in places of interest. The *Hopper* bus (☎041/51 2332) leaves Durban every Friday, Sunday and Tuesday for East London, travelling via Pietermaritzburg, Underberg (for the Southern Drakensberg), Kokstad, Umtata (with links available to the Wild Coast destinations of Port St Johns, Coffee Bay and Hole-in-the-Wall), and Cintsa. The *Baz* bus (☎031/23 6585) also goes to East London but along the South Coast towns of Warner Beach and Port Shepstone, after which it heads inland to Kokstad and then follows the same route as the *Hopper*. The *Baz* also goes from Durban to Johannesburg via the North Coast four times a week, passing through Ballito, Gingindlovu, Eshowe, Kwambonambi, Hluhluwe village, Mkuze and then onto Johannesburg and Pretoria via Swaziland. At the time of writing the bus went from Johannesburg to Durban via the Northern Drakensberg and Pietermaritzburg , but there were plans to run the Durban–Swaziland–Johannesburg loop in both directions from the beginning of 1998.

Trains

Durban to: Johannesburg (1 daily; 15hr); Pietermaritzburg (1 daily; 2hr 10min).

Flights

Durban to: Bloemfontein (11 weekly; 1hr 20min); Cape Town (11–14 daily; 2hr 15min); George (3 weekly; 3hr); Johannesburg (21 daily; 1hr 10min);

Pietermaritzburg (5 weekly; 25min); Plettenberg Bay (3 weekly; 2hr 50min); Port Elizabeth (7 daily; 1hr 20min); Richards Bay (16 weekly; 1hr 30min); Ulundi (16 weekly; 40min).

Margate to: Johannesburg (1 daily; 1hr 30min).

Pietermaritzburg to: Durban (5 weekly; 25min); Johannesburg (2–7 daily; 2hr 15min); Ulundi (10 weekly; 1hr 30min).

Richards Bay to: Durban (2 weekly; 40min); Johannesburg (2–4 daily; 1hr 20min).

CHAPTER SIX

FREE STATE

Free State lies at the centre of South Africa and is the traditional heartland of conservative **Afrikanerdom**, whose dourness seems to have oozed out into the sparsely populated, largely undemonstrative landscape. Most South Africans regard the Free State as the country's drive-through province, to be endured in an uninterrupted stupor of boredom on the N1 from Johannesburg to the Cape. And apart from a functional stop in the provincial capital, **Bloemfontein**, there's little reason to interrupt your journey, particularly in the gold-mining, industrialized north.

There's some relief to be had in the rest of the province though, in the flat farmlands rolling with miles of bright-yellow sunflowers, mauve and pink-petalled cosmos, maize and wheat fields glowing under immense blue skies. This is an area which Nelson Mandela described as gladdening his heart "no matter what my mood. When I am here I feel that nothing can shut me in, that my thoughts can roam as far as the horizons." However, especially if you're pressed for time, only the **Eastern Highlands**, the highly scenic flank which sweeps up to the Lesotho Drakensberg, is worth making the effort to see. Even as a transit route, it's a hundred times more rewarding than the N1, and is recommended if you're heading from Johannesburg to Port Elizabeth. Many travellers prefer it as a longer, but quieter route between Natal and the Garden Route, and it's also useful for avoiding the potholes and errant cattle of the N2 through the Transkei. The eastern Free State is also the **gateway to Lesotho**, with border posts close to each of the small towns on the South African side. You may well end up spending a night in one of them – no hard task since they're very pretty, all surrounded by mountains and cherry farms, and offer decent B&Bs.

The highlight of the Eastern Highlands is the **Golden Gate National Park**, designated a national park not for wildlife, but because of the beauty of the Maluti Mountains and its stripey red sandstone outcrops. From Golden Gate you can drive to the Sentinel car park via **Phuthadijhaba**, and hike up to the highest plateaus of the **Drakensberg**, an easier way than starting from a much lower altitude in the Royal Natal National Park. En route to Phuthadijhaba is the worthwhile **Basotho Cultural Village**. Since Golden Gate is an easy three- to four-hour drive from Johannesburg, it's very accessible, and from here you could do a round trip of the Highlands, taking in Lesotho as well. A fully tarred road runs inside Lesotho's border, mirroring the Highlands route, though quite different in the slices of rural Lesotho life you'll see. Just west of Golden Gate is **Clarens**, by far the nicest of the string of towns running south along the Lesotho border, with a distinctly arty feel, and some of the country's best riding at Bokpoort Farm. For young travellers, party-goers and ageing hippies the real focus of the region is **Rustler's Valley**, south of Clarens, where you can ride, hike in the hills or simply hang out on a truly magnificent farm.

Some history

Intriguing though it sounds, the name "Free State" is little more than a reminder that you're in redneck country. For nearly 150 years, the only people who were free in the Free State were its **white settlers**, who in 1854 were granted independence from Britain in a territory between the Orange and Vaal rivers, where they created a Boer Republic called the **Orange Free State**. The "Orange" part of the name came from the Orange River, which in its turn was named in 1777 by Colonel Robert Gordon, commander of the British garrison at the Cape, after the royal Dutch House of Orange.

The system of government in the republic, inspired by the US Constitution, was highly democratic – if you were a white male. Women didn't vote and Africans had no rights at all, and were even forbidden from owning land. Two expansionist military campaigns were launched in 1858 and 1865 to drive out independent **Basotho** people from fertile lands along the Caledon River, which had been their home since the sixteenth century. Many Basotho under paramount chief **Moshoeshoe** retreated to strongholds in the Drakensberg (see p.583). The thousands who remained were reduced to squatters, sharecroppers and labourers who faced poor wages on the 15,000 thinly distributed white farms.

Even by apartheid standards, the Orange Free State was bad news, being the only province to ban anyone of Asian descent from remaining within its borders for longer than 24 hours. Africans fared little better and in 1970, under the grand apartheid scheme, a tiny barren enclave wedged between Lesotho, KwaZulu-Natal and the Free State became **QwaQwa**, a "homeland" for southern Sotho people. As a result of forced clearances from white-designated areas, its population swelled from 24,000 to nearly half a million in the two decades after 1970, creating one of the worst rural slums in the country. Many men were forced to seek work as migrant labourers in the Gauteng gold mines. Another tiny area around Thaba Nchu, 63km east of Bloemfontein, was part of Bophutatswana, the Tswana *bantustan*, which became nominally independent from South Africa in 1977, but was never more than a series of disconnected fragments scattered all over the country, the capital at Mmabatho, in another shard of land in Northwest Province.

ACCOMMODATION PRICE CODES

All the accommodation listed in the Guide has been categorized into one of seven price bands, as set out below. The rates quoted, unless otherwise stated, represent the most expensive per-person rate for a double or single room outside high season (Dec & Jan), except for category ①, which are per-person rates for a dorm bed in backpacker accommodation, or a campsite. For more accommodation details, see p.31.

① R0–50	② R50–100	③ R100–150
④ R150–200	⑤ R200–250	⑥ R250–300
	⑦ Over R300	

The *bantustans* have since been reincorporated into South Africa, and after an ANC landslide in Free State province in the 1994 elections, the "Orange" part of the name, with its Dutch Calvinist associations, was dropped. In the provincial elections, the ANC took 77 percent of the vote, and the National Party took 13 percent. The Afrikaner separatist Freedom Front polled only 6 percent, far less well than expected in one of the three provinces considered its strongholds – signalling that the province may now begin to shake loose from its hitherto conservative image.

BLOEMFONTEIN

BLOEMFONTEIN isn't a place anyone actually visits, but because it lies at the crossroads of South Africa many travellers end up here to break a journey across the country. You're unlikely to be wracked by regret if you give the city a miss, but once here you'll find enough diversion for an afternoon – maybe even a day – in its surprisingly fine **Oliewenhuis Art Gallery**, set in beautiful gardens, and in the unmistakably provincial **President Brand Street**, lined with its mixed bag of handsome, sandstone public buildings.

As an overnight stop, the city fulfils its functional role admirably, providing an apparently disproportionate quantity of accommodation at reasonable prices – a result of its importance as the only centre of any size in a thinly spread province. People home in from all over the Free State for hospital treatment, for the university (highly regarded

---

GAUTENG TO BLOEMFONTEIN: SOME ROUTE TIPS

The great plus of taking the **N1** from Johannesburg to Bloemfontein is that it's the fastest way of covering the distance – and there's a lot to be said for getting the journey over with as quickly as possible. This no scenic route, however, especially the Gauteng section and the northern Free State, which is full of ugly industrial towns. Tollbooths are strategically positioned at intervals along the N1, but the charge hardly makes it worth taking free detours. **Kroonstad**, 207km south of Johannesburg, is the biggest town along the N1 before you get to Bloemfontein. The Kroon Park, a large, popular resort beside a river, with a swimming pool offers a pit stop if you want to cool off or get something to eat.

The alternative route from just south of the provincial border to Kroonstad goes via **Parys**, first along the R59 and turning onto the R721 at Vredefort, 13km south of Parys. But while Parys is quite green and pleasant, you're very likely to get stuck behind slow traffic, whereas the N1 at this point is still straight, smooth and wide.

The further south you go, the flatter the Free State becomes, and there's an exceptionally long, dull stretch between **Ventersburg** and Bloemfontein – with no services, a one-lane road and not a lot going for it.

Freshford House Museum
City Hall
Appeal Court
National Afrikaans
Literary Museum
The Old
Presidency
First Raadsaal
National Museum
Fourth
Raadsaal
Hertzog
Square
Intercity
bus stop
Bloemfontein
Station

ACCOMMODATION

1 City Lodge
2 Halevy House
3 Hobbit House
4 Holiday Inn Garden Court
5 Outspan Lodge
6 Rambling Rose
7 Stanville Inn
8 Taffy's Backpackers
9 Tredenham Guest House

BLOEMFONTEIN

0   500 m

Waverley, Oliewenhuis Art Gallery, 8 & 9

National Women's Monument & War Memorial

for its medical school) and its several boarding schools. It's also the seat of the provincial parliament and the judicial capital of the country – a sop tossed out to draw it into the Union when South Africa federated in 1910.

Bloemfontein's urban origins go back to 1846 when **Major Henry Warden** was dispatched to establish a fort and residency here to enforce British control over the unruly Boers, Griquas and Basotho, who were in a constant state of conflict. Knocking their heads together proved fruitless and he was withdrawn in frustration eight years later and the territory left to the Boers, who set up the capital of their republic here, using a schoolhouse built by Warden in 1849 as the **First Raadsaal** (parliament).

Arrival and information

Translux (☎408 3242), *Intercape* (☎33 3876) and *Greyhound* (☎430 2361) **buses** pull in at the central bus terminal in the new tourist complex at the east end of Park Avenue, opposite the swimming pool. Few travellers fly into **Bloemfontein Airport** (☎33 2901),

The **telephone code** for Bloemfontein is ☎051.

10km east of town on the N8, although there are scheduled flights between here and the major cities. There are no shuttle buses from the airport into town, so your only choice is to phone for a fairly expensive **taxi**, or **rent a car** from one of the big three rental companies, which have a presence here (see "Listings" for taxi and rental company phone numbers). By **train**, you'll arrive at Bloemfontein Station in Harvey Road at the east end of Maitland Street and by minibus taxi, you'll be dropped off at the rank in Hanger Street, one block west of the station. The area around the station and the minibus taxi rank is regarded by some residents as the dodgiest in the city centre, but there have been few actual incidents. Stay alert, and avoid the area at night if you can. Fortunately **metered taxis** usually rank outside the station; alternatively, you can phone for one (again, see "Listings" for numbers).

It's apparent that Bloemfontein isn't much of a tourist centre from the haphazard **tourist information bureau** (Mon–Fri 8am–4.15pm, Sat 8am–noon; ☎405 8490, fax 47 3859) in the City Hall, on the corner of President Brand and Charles streets, where you'll find **maps** of the city and may be able to gather some local information. There were plans to house a 24-hour tourist information desk and a coffee shop at the new tourist complex in Park Avenue at the time of writing.

Accommodation

Bloemfontein bears the distinction of having *Hobbit House*, which has been voted South Africa's best guesthouse. Also here is some of the cheapest overnight **accommodation** in South Africa, mainly concentrated around the hospitals, in Universitas suburb to the west of the city centre, and around Oranjesig to its south. However, you're best off heading for the nicer and more central suburbs of **Westdene** and **Waverley**, both north of the centre and easily reached on foot.

City Lodge, corner of Zastron St and Parfitt Ave, Westdene (☎447 9888, fax 447 5669). Unremarkable but good value, just outside the centre. Serves excellent breakfasts, and is handy for shops, restaurants and cinemas. ③.

De Oude Kraal, 35km south of Bloemfontein on the N1 off the Riversford exit (☎05215/636 or 733, fax 635). Restored original farmhouse famous for the Afrikaner opulence of its meals, with fireplaces in each en-suite room. Dinner, bed and breakfast rate. ④–⑤.

Halevy House, Markgraaff St (☎448 0271, fax 430 8749). City institittion in a turn-of-the-century hotel. The beautiful facade hides a down-at-heel reality that's quite acceptable, given the price. ②.

Hobbit House, 19 President Steyn Ave, Westdene (☎ & fax 447 0663). Winner in 1996 of two separate awards as South Africa's best guesthouse, this luxurious establishment is full of beautiful and comfortable antique furniture, with teddy bears tucked into every bed under hand-made quilts. With only five rooms, you'll need to book well in advance. Excellent three-course dinners are available. ④.

Holiday Inn Garden Court Bloemfontein, corner of Zastron and Melville streets, Westdene (☎447 0310, fax 430 5678). Best of the posh hotels, with large rooms, a nice swimming pool, and weekend discounts. ④.

Outspan Lodge, 32 Union Ave, Waverley (☎430 3483, fax 447 5531). Self-catering apartments on the R700, backing onto the Naval Hill Nature Reserve. Phones, TVs and kitchens with basic utensils. Outstanding value. ②.

Rambling Rose, 77 President Reitz St, Westdene (☎447 1634). Bright, comfortable garden rooms attached to a suburban house with a swimming pool. ③.

Stanville Inn, 85 Zastron St (☎47 7471). Tiny, well-maintained rooms in a five-storey apartment block, providing excellent value on a busy main road. ②.

Taffy's Backpackers, 18 Louis Botha St, Waverley (☎31 4533 or 405 5248; ask for Vilna). Salubrious suburban house in a pleasant street, 15min walk from the centre, with a big, well-equipped kitchen and a large garden. Ring for a free pick-up from the train or bus station. Small dorms, doubles and camping in the garden. ①.

Tredenham Guest House, off Eeufees Rd, just north of town (☎33 1285 or 33 1231). Colonial English farmhouse built in 1925, now Afrikaner-owned and furnished in period style. Good meals and relaxing atmosphere in a rural area, despite its proximity to town centre. The more expensive inside rooms are by far the best. ③–⑤.

The City

For a city with a countrywide reputation as the "biggest *dorp* in South Africa", Bloemfontein turns out to be quite agreeable, with a slightly unreal character due to the way so many of its late nineteenth- and early twentieth-century **public buildings** pay a pick 'n' mix homage to Mediterranean, British, Renaissance and classical influences. An almost nonexistent public transport system poses few obstacles to getting around; the central area can easily be crossed on foot in ten minutes.

City Hall and around

For the most rewarding stroll in the centre, head down **President Brand Street**, starting at the north end on the corner of Charles Street, where you'll see the **City Hall**, a monumental structure designed in the "new tradition style" by Gordon Leith, a former employee of Sir Herbert Baker, and built in 1934. On the opposite side of President Brand Street, **Hertzog Square** honours the dubious achievements of Boer general, high court judge and Afrikaner nationalist **J.B.M. Hertzog**, who founded the National Party in 1914, went on to become prime minister of the Union of South Africa in 1924 and was responsible for harsh segregationist legislation, including the stripping of voting rights from Africans in the Cape in 1936. Across the square at 36 Aliwal St, the **National Museum** (Mon–Sat 8am–5pm, Sun 1–6pm; small entry fee) is worth sticking your nose into for the rather good dinosaur fossil collection, the living beehive and an outstanding reconstruction of a turn-of-the-century Bloemfontein street. There's a general dealer, pharmacy, doctor's consulting rooms and a family scene which captures in frozen diorama a father telling off his son under a stern portrait of President Steyn, who looks on approvingly. The museum's tea room is a good place to take a break.

Returning to President Brand Street, south of the City Hall you'll come to the highest court in the country, the Roman-style **Appeal Court of South Africa**, built in 1929. Staring at it from across the road is the **Fourth Raadsaal**, regarded as the "architectural jewel" of the province. An imposing sandstone and red-brick building, typical of Free State construction of the period, the Raadsaal was the last parliament building of the independent Orange Free State republic (it's now the provincial legislature), and was built in 1890 in a style that manages to get away brilliantly with merging Greek, Roman and Renaissance elements.

National Afrikaans Literary Museum

One block south of the Appeal Court is the **National Afrikaans Literary Museum** (Mon–Fri 8am–noon & 1–3.45pm, Sat 9am–noon; free), in the Old Government Building, on the corner of President Brand and Maitland streets. Inside, an endless stream of offices have been reconstructed as the studies of the luminaries of Afrikaans writing, with name plates on the doors which make you feel rude for not knocking before going in. Look out for the display on **Eugene Marais**, the remarkable polymath who was active around the turn of the century and wrote a couple of trail-blazing natural histories on termites and baboons. Lawyer, poet of stature and journalist, he contributed articles to the *Observer* and *Times* in London and to the Reuter news agency. Also represented are the "Sestigers" (generation of the 1960s), including novelist **Andre Brink**, who was loudly critical of apartheid, especially after the 1970s, and poet **Breyten Breytenbach**, who went into exile in Paris in 1961. Breytenbach returned to South Africa under cover in 1975 to gain support for Okhela, a largely white section of the ANC, and was captured by the South African authorities and imprisoned for seven years, leading to the publication after his release of *The True Confessions of an Albino Terrorist*. Towards the end of the museum, a couple of rooms are devoted to displays of Afrikaans as a language of oppression, where coloured South Africans make their eleventh-hour appearance. One of the leading lights of coloured Afrikaans (which has its own distinct character) is the poet **Adam Small**, who in one display describes the predicament of being a member of an oppressed community, while at the same time being a speaker of Afrikaans, the language regarded during the uprisings of the 1970s as the language of the enemy. "I grew up with Afrikaans. Afrikaans is part of my culture," he is quoted as saying, "and when people said to you that Afrikaans was the language of the oppressor it pained you, because it was also the language you got from your parents, it was your mother tongue and it was beautiful and full of humanity."

The Supreme Court, Old Presidency and First Raadsaal

Carrying on south down President Brand Street to the corner of Selborne Street, opposite the Fire Station, the **Supreme Court**, completed in 1906, stands on the site of the home of the Fischers, a prominent Orange Free State Afrikaner family, whose heir, lawyer Bram Fischer, betrayed his Afrikaner tribal roots and defended Nelson Mandela during the 1963 Rivonia Trial (see p.656). After Mandela was found guilty and handed a life sentence, it was revealed that all the time Fischer had secretly been the leader of the proscribed Communist Party, and he too was jailed for life, later being released to die at home of cancer. You can visit the court by prior appointment (☎47 2631).

The **Old Presidency** (Tues–Fri 10am–noon & 1–4pm, Sat & Sun 2–5pm; free), on the opposite corner, was built on the site of the home of Major Henry Warden, the founder of Bloemfontein. Built in 1861 in "Scottish baronial style" as the official seat of the head of the republic, the Presidency is surprisingly plain, due as much to the impecunious condition of the state coffers as to the severe Calvinism that characterized the Boer republics. While you can go inside, you aren't going to get much of an idea of how the president lived because virtually none of the original furnishings remain. Turning east after the Old Presidency into St George's Street, you'll come to the **First Raadsaal** (Mon–Fri 10.15am–3pm, Sat & Sun 2–5pm), the oldest-surviving building in Bloemfontein. Built in 1849 by Major Warden as a school, the building was later used as a Dutch Reformed Church and venue for public meetings. At independence in 1854 it became first a meeting chamber for Free State Volksraad ("people's council") and subsequently reverted to a schoolhouse and church.

National Women's Monument and War Museum

Just over 2km south of the centre, along Monument Street, across the train tracks in an ugly industrial part of town, the solemn sandstone needle pointing skywards marks the **National Women's Monument and War Museum** (Mon–Fri 9am–4.30pm, Sat 9am–5pm, Sun 2–5pm; small entry fee), a memorial to the 26,370 Afrikaner women and children who died in British concentration camps during the second Anglo-Boer War. It's impossible to overestimate the depth of the scar left on the Afrikaner psyche by the concentration camps – probably the single most divisive issue between English and Afrikaans-speaking white South Africans, with reverberations even today. At the foot of the monument lies buried **Emily Hobhouse**, a British woman who energetically campaigned on behalf of the Boer internees. The interest of the adjacent museum lies principally in its status as a record of apartheid propaganda. The suffering it depicts isn't exactly untrue, just a little heavy-handed in its unrelenting dioramas of dignified Boers suffering at the hands of faceless British bastards. Two cursory panels on concentration camps for Africans (never widely publicized in South Africa in the old days), tacked on at the end, are a post-apartheid afterthought that at least provides a partial record of the more than 14,000 black South Africans who died incarcerated. Some visual relief to death and suffering is offered by a room near the entrance of the museum, lined with brilliant ceramic-tile tableaux, depicting scenes from the Anglo-Boer War. The tiles were discovered and brought here in 1969 after being uncovered when wallpaper was stripped off the walls of the Transvalia Theatre in Rotterdam, the Netherlands – an indication of how the war rallied the popular imagination in Europe on the side of the Boers.

Oliewenhuis Art Gallery and Freshford House Museum

The real highlight of Bloemfontein's museums is undoubtedly the **Oliewenhuis Art Gallery** on Harry Smith Street (Mon–Fri 8am–5pm, Sat 10am–5pm, Sun 1–5pm; free), about five minutes north of the centre by car. The collection is housed in a beautifully light neo-Cape Dutch manor set in large, attractive gardens that dissolve into wild bush traversed by short walking trails. The lightness of it all seeps into the gallery interior and creates an airy ambience for browsing through a surprisingly good range of **South African sculpture** and **painting**. Particularly satisfying is the landscape collection, which includes the strong, flashing strokes of a Van Gogh-esque interpretation of one of the city churches by **Bertha Everard**, and a **Thomas Baines** documentary painting of Bloemfontein as a tiny settlement in 1850. If you don't want to take in the culture, you can always have tea at the café under the trees on the lawn by a fountain – the most harmonious location in town.

Also to the north of the city centre, but not quite as far, **Freshford House Museum**, 31 Kellner St (Mon–Fri 10am–1pm, Sat & Sun 2–5pm; small entrance fee), makes a lightweight but enjoyable visit, especially if you're interested in **interiors**, as it has been refurbished impeccably in Victorian and Edwardian style. One highlight is a room authentically – and daringly – decorated in lime green, with three distinct William Morris wallpapers: one pattern up to the dado rail; another from there to the picture rail; and the third above that.

Eating and drinking

While Bloemfontein is no culinary capital and there are no regional specialities to sample, you can certainly have a good and inexpensive **meal** out, mostly in the city centre or the nearby suburbs of Westdene and Waverley, which are close to most of the accommodation. You'll also find the usual steakhouse chains scattered around the centre and in the shopping malls. For gluttonous **breakfasts**, the *City Lodge* and *Holiday Inn Garden Court* hotels (see "Accommodation") are always good bets.

JRR TOLKIEN

Bloemfontein's biggest surprise is that it's the birthplace of **John Ronald Revel Tolkien**, author of *Lord of the Rings* and *The Hobbit*, a fact which the city seems curiously reluctant to publicize. You're bound to come across wild claims that Tolkien's experience of the South African landscape inspired him to create the world of Bilbo Baggins. In fact, nothing could be further from the fantastical realm of mountains, forests and supernatural beings of *The Hobbit* than the flatness of the Free State and the down-to-earth Calvinism of its farming community. Some accounts claim that he was inspired by the Natal Drakensberg, while others say it was the Amatola Mountains around Hogsback. Both areas do have an otherworldly magic – the only problem is that Tolkien departed South Africa for good when he was 3 years old, never having set foot outside Bloemfontein.

Tolkien's father, Arthur, left his native Birmingham, where he worked for Lloyds Bank, for the better prospects of the colonies. He eventually rose to manager of the Bank of Africa in Bloemfontein, where JRR was born in 1892, in a house that stood on the corner of West Burger and Maitland streets, a couple of blocks east of President Brand Street. When Arthur Tolkien died in 1895, his wife returned to England with her two infant sons, and their house was later torn down to make way for a *Bradlow's* showroom, part of a cheap, nationwide furniture chain.

Restaurants and cafés

Barba's Café, Mimosa Mall, Kellner St (☎448 4406). Good Greek food, a diverse cocktail menu and the best coffee in town at this venue near the university, which draws the young and trendy to linger amid the starkly fashionable decor.

Beef Baron, 22 Second Ave (☎447 4290). True to its name, this is the place to come for beef, where your mug-shot could join those of other carnivores who downed 1.5kg steaks and survived. The wine cellar is excellent.

Café Oliewenhuis, Harry Smith St, signposted off the R700. Tables in the formal gardens at the back of the gallery, leading onto a nature reserve, make this Bloemfontein's nicest place for a relaxing outdoor tea or lunch, though the food itself is nothing to write home about.

District Six, 24 West Burger St (☎430 4440). Very affordable and freshly prepared Cape cuisine matching anything you'll find in Cape Town, including curries and *masala snoek*. Ring ahead to make sure they're open.

Le Petit Carousel, 38 First Ave (☎448 0251). Good place for vegetarians, with fresh vegetables, salads and tasty pâtés.

Oude Kraal, 35km south of town on the N1 (☎05215/636). Sunday lunch buffet blowout of rich, fattening Afrikaner-style food in lovely surroundings. Booking as far ahead as possible is mandatory to join the feast.

Revolving Restaurant, CR Swart Building, Elizabeth St (☎447 5315) Bloemfontein's most formal restaurant offers rotating city views and good meat and fish dishes. Thursday night is fish night, with plenty of seafood choices.

Roma Coffee Bar, 24 West Burger St (under *District Six* restaurant). Daytime only venue for good filter coffee and their legendary two-tone chocolate cake baked by a schoolgirl who won't divulge the recipe.

Sonneblom, 49 Second Ave. Eclectic coffee shop open evenings serving coffees with liqueur and basic meals.

Nightlife and entertainment

Finding out what's going on in Bloemfontein can be a problem for visitors, as there's no English-language newspaper. *Taffy's Backpackers* (see "Accommodation") is always a good source of information on up-to-the-minute drinking spots, but generally speaking **nightlife** is a pretty tame affair. Among the handful of bars in the centre worth checking out, *Barba's Café* (see "Eating and drinking") is a lively place for a drink, while *Déjà Vu*, a bar/nightclub favoured by bikers and punky types, at 158 Voortrekker St, is a good place for dancing.

The most interesting of Bloemfontein's handful of **theatres** is the *Observatory*, on the crest of Naval Hill, just north of the centre, because it's situated inside a real observatory in the city's nature reserve, which supports a few giraffe and some antelope. The most presitigious theatre is the *Sand du Plessis*, on the corner of Markgraaff and St Andrew streets. The recent removal of a prominent statue of HF Verwoerd, the arch-theorist and practitioner of apartheid, from in front of the theatre, ruffled local right-wing feathers. Bloemfontein has several **cinemas**, mostly in suburban shopping malls; the Mimosa Mall in Westdene has seven cinemas, and Noordstad in Eeufees Road (R700) has four, all showing standard, mainstream movies.

Listings

Airlines *South African Airways*, St Andrew's St (☎447 3811).

Automobile Association Sanlam Plaza, 17 Maitland St (☎447 6191). Emergency rescue super-number toll free ☎0800/01 0101.

Banks are easy to find in the the city centre and the shopping malls. Wherever you find banks you'll find automatic teller machines (ATMs). Opening hours are Mon–Fri 9am–3.30pm, Sat 8.30–11am.

Car rental *Avis* (☎33 2331), *Budget* (☎33 1178), *Imperial* (☎33 3511) all represented at the airport.

Emergencies Ambulance ☎10177; Fire ☎10178; Police (Flying Squad) ☎10111; Rape Crisis ☎447 6678.

Hospitals and doctors Doctors are listed in the telephone directory under "*Mediese Praktisyns*/Medical Practitioners". The main state hospital is *Universitas*, which offers a free 24hr emergency ward, but you may wait hours and the level of care is variable. Far better, if you can afford it or have travel insurance, is one of the private hospitals. These are *Hydromed*, Kellner St (☎404 6666), and *Rosepark*, Fichmed Centre, Gustav Crescent (☎22 6761).

Pharmacies with extended opening hours: *Medirex Pharmacy*, Southern Life Building, Maitland St (☎447 5822), is open Mon–Sat 8am–10.30pm, Sun 9am–10.30pm.

Post office Main branch, corner of East Burger and Maitland streets (Mon, Tues, Thurs & Fri 8am–4.30pm, Wed 8.30am–4.30pm, Sat 8am–noon).

Taxis Reliable firms include *Bloem Taxis* (☎33 3776); *President Taxis* (☎522 3399); *Rosestad* (☎451 1022).

Telephones There are phone booths all over Bloemfontein taking phone cards and coins. For local directory enquiries, phone ☎1023.

Train information Train station ☎408 2946; *Spoornet* ☎408 2941.

THE GRIQUAS

In the early nineteenth century, roving bands of cattle-herders and raiders with a reputation for horsemanship and fierce independence appeared on the eastern edge of the Cape Colony around the Orange River. They called themselves, with some pride, "Bastaards", being mixed descendants of European, Khoikhoi, Asian and African people. The missionaries who persuaded them to establish settlements at places such as Griquatown, Campbell and Philippolis also took exception to their name, which was changed to **Griqua**. Though Griqualand West was still theoretically independent, clashes with the Boers and squabbles over land ownership when diamonds were found in their territory saw them turning to the British for protection, faith which was all too hastily swallowed up by the gorging Cape Colony.

In 1861 three thousand Griquas from Philippolis under their leader Adam Kok III trekked across the Drakensberg to southern Natal to found **Griqualand East**, a pocket of land on the far side of the Drakensberg, south of Natal. That settlement failed, and slowly the Griquas dispersed and became subsumed into the wider coloured community, although there are still odd pockets of their descendants living in various places around the Northern, Western and Eastern Cape provinces.

South from Bloemfontein

Two major routes splay out and head south from Bloemfontein, the **N6** to the Eastern Cape via Aliwal North (see p.308) and the **N1** to the Western Cape via Colesberg (see p.437). Nothing much happens along either route apart from a couple of quirky small towns. Along the N6, **SMITHFIELD**, a tiny Free State *dorp*, 145km from Bloemfontein, has one of South Africa's top ten **restaurants** attached to the outstanding **guesthouse**, *Adam's Cottage* (☎05562 ext 21; ③), in a listed building. The guesthouse has three bedrooms (with bath), furnished with luxuries such as down duvets, mohair blankets and crisp white linen. The morning kicks off with hearty Russian breakfasts consisting of homemade *blinis*, soft scrambled eggs, caviar and chunky tomato sauce.

PHILIPPOLIS, 168km south of Bloemfontein along a slight detour off the N1 between Trompsburg and Colesberg, is the place where **Sir Laurens Van der Post** (see opposite) grew up. The road is quiet and typical of the upper Karoo, with a bit of distant scenery and the scattered signs of a scattered population. There isn't much to the town, although it was one of the first settlements north of the Orange River, established in the 1830s and named in honour of **Dr John Philip**, the British cleric who set up a mission station here. Way ahead of his time, Philip actively campaigned for the full integration of former slaves, Africans and coloured people into the white economic and social system, which he believed was the only way of ensuring peace, justice and stability.

Among the attractive old buildings that line the few streets is a small, white, flat-roofed house just before the post office on Voortrekker Street, the main thoroughfare running through the village, which has a plaque indicating that it was (according to tradition) the house of **Adam Kok III**, leader of the Griqua, people of Khoi and mixed descent who set up several statelets in the Northern Cape and vicinity in the nineteenth century (see box opposite).

There is an **information desk** and **accommodation** at *Die Waenhuis* guesthouse and tea room on Kok Street, which runs parallel to Voortrekker (☎773 0157; ②). The other guesthouse in town, the **Van der Post Guest House** (☎773 0324; ③) on Colin Fraser Street, is the old house of the Van der Post family. The guesthouse only accepts one party at a time, which allows for some privacy, and there is a small archive about the writer and his family inside, although you can only have access to the house if you are a guest. Laurens, the thirteenth of fifteen children, was born on a farm outside town in 1906 and moved here when he was still very young. In *The Lost World of the Kalahari* he says: "I was born near the Great River, in the heart of what for thousands of years had been great Bushman [San] country." Great River was a direct translation of "Gariep", the name the Khoi had used before the arrival of white settlers.

At the end of Voortrekker Street is the large **Dutch Reformed Church**, built on the site of the original Griqua mission station. Another good reason to take the Philippolis diversion is the chance to take a good look at the mighty **Orange River** – it's easier to stop and contemplate the river on a quiet country road than flashing over it at 120km per hour as you do on the highway.

Some 50km south of Philippolis on the N1 is **COLESBERG**, just over the Free State border in the Northern Cape (see p.219), but an excellent overnight stop if you want to push on beyond Bloemfontein, and want somewhere roughly halfway to Cape Town. Colesberg is a dry Karoo *dorp* at the centre of an area of sheep farms and horse-breeding studs, with ample accommodation.

LAURENS VAN DER POST

Growing up in Philippolis, **Laurens Van der Post**, the famous explorer, writer, soldier and philosopher, learnt of the stories and legends of the "Bushman", or San people who had once lived in the area but had been forced by the advance of African and European settlers into the northern deserts. "What drew me so strongly to the Bushman was that he appeared to belong to my native land as no other human being has ever belonged," he says, as he became entranced by the self-sufficient yet intensely spiritual and aesthetic way they lived. It prompted him to take a famous journey in search of the last remnants of the San, one he recorded in a book and film called *The Lost World of the Kalahari*. This narrative, along with a sequel called *The Heart of the Hunter*, were one of the first to prick the Western conscience with the idea that such a primitive "tribe" had anything to teach it. Van der Post was a Japanese prisoner of war during World War II – the book he wrote about his experiences, *The Seed and the Sower*, was made into the film *Merry Christmas, Mr Lawrence*. He lived in both London and South Africa, and died in 1996, aged 90.

THE HIGHLANDS ROUTE

Hugging the Lesotho border for 280 tarred kilometres from **Phuthadijhaba** (Witsieshoek) in the north to Wepener, beyond Ladybrand in the south, the **Highlands Route** offers one of South Africa's most scenic drives, taking you through colourfully streaked rock formations, cherry orchards and sandstone farming towns. Wedged into a corner between Lesotho and northern KwaZulu-Natal, Phuthadijhaba is the gateway to the Sentinel, the easiest route onto the **Drakensberg Escarpment**, the roof of southern Africa. Not far to the west is the highlight of the region, **Golden Gate Highlands National Park**, encompassing wide open mountain country. The park is an easy three- to four-hour drive from Johannesburg, which means you could use it as a first- or last-night stop if you're arriving or leaving from Johannesburg and don't want to spend the night in the city. Nearby, **Basotho Cultural Village** is worth visiting to gain some insight into Basotho traditions. The closest town to the Golden Gate is **Clarens**, a centre for arts and crafts and the most attractive of all the villages along the route.

Basotho Cultural Village

The **Basotho Cultural Village** (Mon–Fri 9am–4pm, Sat & Sun 9am–5pm; ☎ & fax 058/721 0300; email: basotho@dorea.co.za; entry fee), 20km east of Golden Gate National Park, is in the QwaQwa National Park which abuts Golden Gate, and caters to sanitized curiosity about traditional people's lives – in this case the **Basotho** people, who have lived in the vicinity for centuries and have a close affinity to people living just across the border in Lesotho. The main display at the village is a **courtyard of Basotho huts** from the sixteenth century to the present day, with people outside in traditional dress, playing different roles. Visitors are taken to meet the chief, hear musicians play, see a traditional healer throwing the bones and get the chance to sample traditional beer. Although the whole setup is contrived, the half-hour tour can be good fun.

The beautiful vernacular architecture of the huts, from organic, circular, sixteenth-century constructions to square ones with tin roofs and bright interior decor influenced by Boer scissorwork, is well worth seeing. Also interesting is the *litema*, or external decoration on houses, put on by women and still visible in rural Lesotho and Free State. The decoration varies from repeat patterns scratched into the mud-coloured plasterwork to vivid, modern motifs. While you're here, you can book to go on the intriguing two-hour **Matlakeng Herbal Trail**, guided by a traditional healer who gives an informed introduction to *veld* herbs. The tour also takes in a well-preserved **rock painting**. **Riding** on Basotho ponies is possible, but must also be booked beforehand.

There's a limited amount of very reasonably priced **accommodation** available in a couple of thatched, stone huts (②) with external toilets and washing facilities. A two-plate electric cooker and kettle are provided, along with basic utensils, and linen, blankets and towels. Views from the shuttered windows across the QwaQwa National Park are awesome, and this is a great place to stay, with an endless choice of casual walks. Don't expect to be looked after though, and be warned that the village is largely deserted at night, when the workers head back to contemporary urban Sotho life in Phuthadijhaba. A **curio shop** sells some quality local crafts (look out for raffia mats and baskets and the conical straw hats unique to this area and Lesotho), and the open-air **restaurant** serves teas and traditional food.

Phuthadijhaba and around

The only reason you're likely to drive through **PHUTHADIJHABA** (still sometimes called Witsieshoek), roughly 2km off the R712 and east of Golden Gate, is to reach the Witsieshoek Mountain Resort and the Sentinel car park, the easiest hiking access onto the High Drakensberg escarpment. Phuthadijhaba itself is rather bleak and functional, home to light industry and brick matchbox houses. In contrast to the emptiness of the landscape around Golden Gate, in Phuthadijhaba you'll see minibus taxis zipping around, and people and animals walking on the roadsides past shacks, their tin roofs

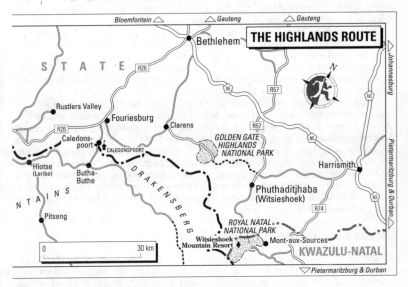

HIKING UP THE DRAKENSBERG ESCARPMENT

South Africa's most spectacular mountain views are from the **Drakensberg Escarpment** and the top of the **Amphitheatre**. Both of these require a high level of fitness if approached from KwaZulu-Natal (see p.335), but can be achieved relatively easily via the Free State from the Sentinel car park to a chain ladder, which gets you to the bottom of the final short onslaught on **Mont aux Sources**, the highest peak on the Escarpment (3278m). The ladder is reached after a tough ten-hour climb from the *Mahai* campsite in the Royal Natal National Park, or a 2.5-hour walk from the Sentinel car park (8km from Witsieshoek Mountain Resort) in the Free State. Set out early so you have the whole day for the excursion onto the Escarpment. A three-kilometre walk from the car park brings you to the foot of the thirty-metre high chain ladder, from whose top you can climb to the summit of Mont aux Sources. The downside of this short cut is that you'll find litter and other environmental degradation around the ladder, although no more than one hundred people are allowed up per day. Don't be lulled by your apparently easy conquest: it's always the Berg's prerogative to have the last word. Always tackle the magic ladder with enough food, water, clothes and a tent in which to sit out violent storms.

If the mountain bug has bitten, you can engage on some serious **hikes**, including a two-week trek along the Escarpment plateau to Sani Pass in the southern Drakensberg, or a five-day, 62-kilometre Escarpment traverse, sleeping in caves, from the Sentinel car park to Cathedral Peak in the Natal Drakensberg Park, roughly 40km southwest, taking in the most dramatic parts of the Berg. For any of these hikes, you'll need a map and the excellent *Drakensberg Walks* by David Bristow (see "Books", p.68), available in most bookshops. If you're starting a big hike at the Sentinel car park, you'll find accommodation in a mountain hut there, where 24-hour security protects vehicles. The hut has no hot water or electricity, so you may be better off at the more comfortable *Witsieshoek Mountain Inn* (see below). To book for the car park hut and one of the hundred places a day allocated to climb the chain ladder, phone ☎058/713 4191.

weighted down against the wind with stones. Phuthadijhaba was the artificially created capital of the former **QwaQwa** *bantustan*, and references to that miserable episode are still to be found in road signs and around town.

Signposted from here, the road to Witsieshoek culminates, about 15km from the town, in a fork, one branch of which ends at **Witsieshoek Mountain Inn** and the other at the **Sentinel car park**. The road is tarred until the final few kilometres. On maps it looks as if the Royal Natal National Park and Witsieshoek are adjoining, which they are, via footpaths up and down mountains, whereas by road the journey is about 100km, into KwaZulu-Natal and around the high peaks.

Witsieshoek Mountain Inn (☎058/713 6361 or 713 6362, fax 713 5274) represents one of the great lost opportunities of South African architecture, with the most spectacular setting of any mountain resort in the country but possibly the worst planning. **Accommodation** has been placed just below the brow of a plateau, thus denying guests one of the best views in the entire Drakensberg. Still, you can always walk out into the mountains to take in the views, and the functionality of the rooms is made up for by friendly service. The best rooms (④), with rates that include dinner, bed and breakfast, are the more expensive ones with views onto the Sentinel. There is a hikers' hostel (①) which sleeps twelve and has electricity and hot water – but you must bring your own sleeping bag.

Golden Gate Highlands National Park

Roughly 300km northeast of Bloemfontein on the R712, **Golden Gate Highlands National Park** (open daily; no entry fee) is Free State's only national park and was proclaimed for its outstanding beauty, rather than its wildlife. Although **eland, zebra,**

mountain reedbuck and **black wildebeest** roam the hillsides, the real attraction here is the unfettered space, eroded sandstone bastions and seamless blue skies. These rocks, grassy plateaus and incised valleys belong to the Drakensberg range, characterized here by spectacular yellow and red cliffs and overhangs. Sandwiches of purples, reds and ochres stripe the massive rocks, where you'll usually find butter-coloured segments at the top, because the softer, terracotta sandstone tends to erode more quickly.

A number of roughly hour-long **rambles** from the campsite into the sandstone ravines start from a direction board near the footbridge at the *Glen Reenen* campsite. There aren't many medium-length hikes in the park, the only exception being a half-day walk up **Wodehouse Kop**, which offers great views and is more physically challenging than any of the short rambles. The most strenuous hike is the two-day circular "Rhebok Trail", which involves some challenging hiking up and down the highest and lowest points of the park. Because the trail is so demanding you'll need to stay the previous night at *Glen Reenen*, where the trail begins, to make an early start (see "Practicalities", below). The Rhebok mountain hut on the trail provides basic accommodation for hikers. Bookings for the trail and hut must be made through the *National Parks Board*. **Horse-riding** is on offer, and can be booked through either rest camp, while **swimming** in the summer is possible in a natural waterfall pool close to *Glen Reenen* campsite.

Practicalities

Golden Gate is almost equidistant and easily reached from either Bloemfontein or Johannesburg, which is 320km to its north, on good, tarred roads all the way. There are no entry gates to the park. **Accommodation** is at two rest camps, close to one another and both right on the R712, a fact, which combined with the ease of access, deprives them of any sense of being wilderness retreats, though both have lush settings amidst the sandstone bastions. Cheaper of the two is *Glen Reenen*, with a **campsite** (①), which at peak holiday times becomes little more than a car park jammed with Afrikaner families and their caravans, and closely packed en-suite rondavels with kitchenettes (②). *Brandwag*, the more upmarket camp about a kilometre to the west, is a blot on the fabulous landscape, but offers well-equipped self-catering chalets (③) and comfortable hotel rooms (④) with bath, phones and TV. **Bookings** should be made through the *National Parks Board*, 44 Long St, Cape Town (☎021/22 2810, fax 24 6211), or 643 Leyds St, Muckleneuk, Pretoria (☎012/343 1991, fax 343 0905).

Fuel is available at *Glen Reenen*, which also has a provisions store selling basics, as well as frozen *braai* packs, firewood and alcohol. Your only choice for eating out here is at the restaurant at *Brandwag*. Alternatively, you could drive into nearby Clarens.

Clarens

Some 20km west of Golden Gate Highlands National Park lies the tree-fringed village of **CLARENS**, the most appealing of the settlements along the Highlands Route. Founded in 1912, Clarens is especially remarkable for its dressed stone architecture, which glows under the sandstone massif of the **Rooiberge** ("red mountains") and the **Malutis** to the southeast. The best time to see the village is in spring, amid the blossoming fruit trees, or in autumn, when the poplar leaves turn golden russet. Throughout the year though, Clarens's relaxed air makes it a rare phenomenon in the Free State – a *dorp* you'd actually want to explore, or sip a sidewalk lager and simply hang out in.

By a slightly tortuous set of associations, Clarens was named after the Swiss town where **Paul Kruger**, president of the South African Republic, ended his days. Kruger led a campaign in the Free State in 1865 against the Basotho under paramount chief Moshoeshoe and defeated them. Fate was fickle, and at the turn of the century, when Kruger found himself on the losing side against the British in the second Anglo-Boer War, he fled to Switzerland to live out his days in Clarens, where he died in 1904.

FARMSTAYS AND HORSE-RIDING AROUND CLARENS

Horse-riding is big along the Eastern Highlands and a couple of **farms** near Clarens provide outstanding riding opportunities onto the Drakensberg Escarpment, from where you can gaze across into Lesotho and at southern Africa's highest peaks.

One of the most interesting farms is friendly **Bokpoort**(☎ & fax 058/256 1181; ①–②), situated in brilliant hiking country, but more notable for its exceptional horse-riding. The B&B accommodation in self-catering farmhouse outbuildings is pretty basic, and there are three hikers' dorms, as well as a couple of doubles in small huts, and space for camping, with a pleasant communal cooking and eating place. For those on a B&B rate, a farmhouse brunch is served in a converted shearing shed. Bokpoort's big draw is the truly memorable Western-style riding in deep, comfortable cowboy saddles on sure-footed horses which help you feel very secure cantering on the hillsides. Short rides from the farmhouse take in San rock paintings, swimmable river-pools, and the chance of seeing eland, zebra and springbok on the adjoining game farm. Better still, owners Christo and Sunette lead reasonably priced two- or three-day riding trails (R600–700 including meals) into the mountains adjoining Lesotho. You carry your own bedroll and water-bottle on your horse and sleep on your saddle blanket in a hut in the mountains so remote that it can only be reached by helicopter or horse. A packhorse brings the food, and you ride about six hours a day, walking and cantering under the formidable supervision of Christo. Be sure to book well in advance for the longer trails, which are very popular and usually run over weekends.

Riding is also available at **Schaaplaats Cottage & Ashgar Connemara Stud** (☎ & fax 058/256 1176; ①–②), 6km south of Clarens off the R711 to Fouriesburg. This turn-of-the-century farm has a sandstone thatched cottage that sleeps five and an extremely cheap but basic shepherd's hut above the homestead. From here you can visit Boer War graves, San rock paintings and go horse-riding. There's also a chance to brush up your equestrian skills, as the owner is a qualified riding teacher.

Despite the Boer connection, Clarens has shed its redneck ties to become an **arts and crafts centre**, with a number of studios and shops peppering the streets. If you arrive around lunchtime on a weekend there's a chance you'll catch some local live music at one of the streetside cafés on **President Square**, the effective town centre in the middle of Main Street.

Any among the several **galleries** along Main Street and around President Square is worth a visit if you're after gifts or souvenirs; look out for the local Basotho tapestries, baskets and traditional hats. A real treat is the *Di Mezza & De Jager Trading Store*, which you can reach from the main road to Bethlehem, taking the Maluti Lodge turn-off. This is one of the few places in South Africa outside a museum where you're likely to catch an old-time general dealer that has barely changed in half a century. The shop is stocked to the brim with shelves of provisions, lamps, bicycle parts, sweets and colourful blankets, which are traditionally worn like cloaks by Basotho people in the district. The **blankets** make outstanding souvenirs if you're after something authentic.

Practicalities

When people in Clarens refer to "town", they mean Bethlehem, the largest centre of any size in the vicinity, some 30km to the north. Clarens itself has few facilities, no bank or large supermarket, but there's plenty of **accommodation**, both in the village (all signposted off Main Street and all easily walkable) and on surrounding farms. The cheapest place to stay is the *Clarens Inn*, Van Reenen St (☎058/256 1119), run by a musician and artist, with the choice between a functional dorm with a communal kitchen (①), or a self-catering unit sleeping six in two bedrooms (②). *Cottage Pie*, 89 Malherbe St (☎058/256 1214; ②), a B&B with self-catering garden chalets, is the town's premier guesthouse, offering breakfast on the patio and views onto a stream and the dramatic orange-and-black-striped cliffs that surround the village. *Christine's*, on Villiers Street (☎058/256 1077; ②), has a secluded cottage (self-catering) in a shady garden, as well as a B&B room in the main house. More conventional motel-style accommodation with phones and TVs in each room is available at the *Country Lodge* (☎ & fax 058/256 1354; ②–③), a resort on the edge of town, signposted just off the R712 to Bethlehem. In a similar vein, but smarter and more modern, the *Maluti Mountain Lodge* next door (☎058/256 1422; ④) is the most expensive place to stay in town, and offers pleasant rondavels in the garden.

Of the half-dozen or so **eating and drinking** places in Clarens, the *Country Living Gallery & Street Cafe Restaurant* on Main Street, is the busiest, owing to its reasonably priced pizzas, snacks, steaks and salads, and the 107 varieties of local and imported beers on offer. For a full-blown meal, head next door to the *Guinea-Feather*, Clarens's top restaurant, where you can sit outdoors and enjoy a mid-priced menu that includes oxtail in red wine sauce, trout, curries, pizzas and game. Breakfasts and teas are also available here from 8am onwards.

Fouriesburg and around

The funny little town of **FOURIESBURG**, 36km from Clarens on the R711, was given its name because of the high density of people called "Fourie" who were farming in the district. The hamlet hit the big time briefly in 1900, when it was proclaimed capital of the Orange Free State after Bloemfontein fell to the British in the Anglo-Boer War. Nothing much seems to have happened since, and one hundred years later they still haven't got round to rescinding the proclamation. Overshadowed by the **Maluti Mountains** and the **Witteberge** ("white mountains"), Fouriesburg serves as a decent overnight stop, with some good accommodation.

The nicest **place to stay** is the *Fouriesburg*, 17 Reitz St (☎058/223 0207, fax 223 0257; ②), a small, wonderfully antiquated hotel with a green, low-slung corrugated iron roof and comfortable rooms leading off the street-facing verandah. The owners let you rummage through the wine cellar to pick a bottle for dinner. Just under 2km out of town, the **Meiringskloof Nature Reserve** (☎058/223 0067), signposted from the centre, offers one of the free places worth **camping** (①) along the Highlands Route, and also a few stone self-catering chalets (②). Set in a sandstone *kloof* with plenty of trees, a swimming pool and a small grocery shop, the reserve (best avoided during holidays, when it gets packed) is the starting point for a number of short **hikes**, and the five-day **Brandwater trail** (phone for details). More upmarket is *Wyndford Holiday Farm* (☎058/223 0274, fax 223 0664; ④–⑤), just before the Caledonspoort border post, 9km from Fouriesburg. Popular with South African families, this is a fairly staid place proclaiming "old-fashioned Christian values", and offers thatched rondavels (with bath) in pleasant gardens at a rate that includes all meals and teas.

Rustler's Valley

In contrast to the conservatism of Fouriesburg, **Rustler's Valley** (☎ & fax 051/92 3939; email: wemad@cis.co.za), 27km to its south and well signposted off the R26, has set itself up as the New Age epicentre of South Africa. Located in a beautiful valley in the foothills of the Maluti Mountains, it brings together a mixture of rave culture, Gaia philosophy, and plain old-fashioned hippiedom. In this alternative getaway you need to be ready to submit to the wound-down atmosphere, in which everything is slow and haphazard, including the service. This, and the poor road, make it an unsatisfactory overnight stop, but if you can stay for a few days you're likely to have a highly sociable time. Scheduled events take place about once a month (calendar available from the above email address), and there's horse-riding, hikes, swimming in the dam, and bass and trout fishing. The biggest crowd-puller is the **Easter Festival**, which draws in hordes of young South Africans to listen to music, get down and chill out. By European or North American standards, the festivals are nothing special, but the setting certainly is, and for South Africans it's one of the country's major *jorls* (parties). **Accommodation** ranges from camping (①), backpacker dorms (①) and teepees (②), to thatched rondavels with bath (③) set among peach trees and decorated with bright goblins and fairies. A kitchen is available for backpackers only; everyone else must rely on the bar and **restaurant**, which serves good vegetarian food but isn't cheap. **Getting there** without your own transport entails finding your way to Ficksburg (see below), from where staff at Rustler's can pick you up. When you phone to book your accommodation, ask for the best way to get to Ficksburg from where you are. If you're driving, take care over the last section of dirt road, which in parts is pretty apalling.

Next door to Rustler's, in the same beautiful valley, and well signposted, is *Franshoek Polo Lodge* (☎ & fax 05192/3938, mobile 082/659 1966; ④). It's a more staid, but quite relaxed guest farm, ideal for horse-riding (you can even have polo lessons on the polo field). **Accommodation** is in pleasantly furnished rooms in a country-cottage style, without the frilly bits. Rates include a communal three-course farm dinner around a single table. While you're here, you might want to explore the eight- or fourteen-kilometre **hiking trails** on the farm, which take in a couple of spectacular sandstone overhangs that were used by San hunter-gatherers and later by Boer families hiding out during the Anglo-Boer War.

Ficksburg

FICKSBURG, 48km south of Fouriesburg, is the closest town to Rustler's Valley and the centre of South Africa's cherry and asparagus farming. The town's sandstone architecture gives it a pleasant ambience and this is a good place to make a stop halfway down the Highlands Route. An annual **Cherry Festival** in the third week of November is the highlight of Fickburg's calendar and features a marathon, floats, stalls, a "cherry queen" competition and a popular beer festival.

The cheapest way to stay here is by **camping** at *Thom Park* (☎05192/2122), a caravan park bang in the centre of town, on the corner of Bloem and McCabe streets. Nearby, the popular *Bella Rosa*, 21 Bloem St (☎05192/2623; ③), is a Victorian sandstone house with four nicely furnished **rooms** with bath. Dinner is available but must be booked, and tea is served on the very pleasant verandah. An alternative is *Green Acorn*, 7 Fontein St (☎05192/2746; ③), which has decent rooms with bath. As a last resort, you'll find rooms at the *Hoogland*, Market Square (☎05192/2214; ③), which also has a glassed-in coffee terrace upstairs and a pizzeria around the corner – the only public place serving **food** at night.

Clocolan and around

A tiny farming town dominated by its enormous grain silos, **CLOCOLAN**, 33km south of Ficksburg, has little to offer travellers aside from a visit to the **Lethoteng Weavers**, in a house on the main road. The weavers are south Sotho women who use angora rabbit and wool to produce lively tapestries based on traditional geometric motifs and imaginative illustrations of everyday life. To get to the main point of interest around here, you need to head some 9km out of town to **Tripolatania Farm** (☎05191/2475), the site of the **Tandjiesberg rock paintings**, some of the best examples of San art in the Free State. Panel after panel of rock paintings are overpainted with animal, human and supernatural motifs, which are interpreted in an excellent monograph available from the Bloemfontein Museum (see p.433) and sometimes from the farmer, from whom you have to collect keys and pay a small fee to get to the paintings.

If you're simply passing through, Clocolan's best overnight **accommodation** is at *Makoadi B&B* (☎943 0273; ③) on Makoadi Farm, signposted 1km from town, where three spacious rooms (with bath) off a verandah are furnished with antique farm items, ball and claw baths, and have original mud and dung floors. The owner sells beautiful home-spun angora jumpers. For longer stays, two outstanding farm cottages are to be found some way out of town. The first, *Evening Star Cottage* (☎051/932 3212; ③), 13km from Clocolan on the R703, is a romantically secluded self-catering thatched cottage tucked into a rocky outcrop, with French doors opening onto a balcony with views of farmlands and mountains. Lamps, candles and a mosquito net set the tone, and cooking is done on a fire outside in a beautiful rocky sitting area. The only drawback is that the toilet and bathroom are down the outside stairs, rather than en suite. The farm has a recommended **hiking trail** and serves tea in a converted monastery with an overgrown garden, where the owner sells her pottery. Another recommended getaway is the rustic *De Hoek* (bookings through *Jacana Country Retreats*, ☎012/346 3550 or 346 3551; ②), a four-bedroom house on a sandstone ridge with brass beds (bring your own bedding), dung floors, rough white walls, paraffin lamps (no electricity) and cooking on a coal stove. Two circular one-day **hiking trails** are available exclusively for *De Hoek* guests.

Ladybrand

LADYBRAND, just over 40km south of Clocolan, and on the main route into Lesotho, is one of the only towns in the Free State which is expanding, with a huge turnover of foreign currency in the local bank. This is due not to tourism, but to the Highlands Water Scheme across the nearby border in Lesotho (see p.583). The town gets its name from the mother of Johannes Brand, who was elected President of the Orange Free State four times after 1864. If you've got time to kill, it's worth popping to the **Catherina Brand Museum** in Church Street (Mon–Fri 10am–noon & 2–4pm; free) to see the small archeological exhibition, which displays fossils and stone tools found in the area, as well as reproductions of some of the rock paintings on Tripolitania Farm (see opposite). Other exhibits include a record of the Free State's oldest operating newspapers, and some historical background on Ladybrand.

Many of the foreign engineers and technicians working on the Highlands Water project in Lesotho choose to stay in Ladybrand rather than Maseru, so **accommodation** is in high demand, and doesn't come cheap. The only budget option is *Leliehoek Resort* (☎05191/40654), 2km south of the town hall, a rather run-down park with camping (①) and self-catering chalets (②). As to B&Bs, nothing along the Highlands Route can touch *Cranberry Cottage*, 37 Beeton St (☎05191/2290, fax 41168; ③), which offers comfortable country-style rooms and excellent dinners, with vegetarians well catered for. Under the same ownership, and a touch less expensive, are the equally imaginative self-catering units at the *Railway Station*, quirkily located in the refurbished ticket office, stationmaster's office and waiting rooms on the Ladybrand Station platform, which no longer serves passengers, but occasionally sees goods trains trundle by. The owners act as an unofficial tourist information centre and are able to give guests **information** on mountain-bike trails and horse-riding in town.

When it comes to **eating**, Ladybrand shapes up well for a *dorp*, offering pasta, pizza and good Irish coffee from a genuine Italian chef at *Imperio Romano*, in Church Street. In the absence of franchised steakhouses, the *Country Lodge Hotel* on Joubert Street serves as a popular family-style restaurant, where the coffee and peppermint crisp tart is recommended. For light meals, teas and coffees, *Zabi's Coffee Shop*, also on Church Street, is a good daytime venue for milkshakes, toasted sandwiches and coffee, while *Cranberry Cottage*, 37 Beeton St, serves up light lunches and teas in a quiet garden – the most relaxing spot in town.

travel details

Trains

Bloemfontein to: Cape Town (Fri; 20hr 45min); Durban (Tues; 16hr); East London (daily; 14hr 15min); Johannesburg (daily except Sat; 13hr); Port Elizabeth (daily; 12hr 15min); Pretoria (daily except Sat; 15hr 45min).

Buses

Bloemfontein to: Cape Town (4 daily; 11hr); Durban (2–3 daily; 9hr); East London (daily; 7hr 10min); Graaff Reinet (5 weekly; 7hr); Grahamstown (daily; 7hr 30min); Johannesburg (4–5 daily; 6hr); Knysna (5 weekly; 11hr); Mossel Bay (5 weekly; 9hr 30min); Oudtshoorn (5 weekly; 8hr); Pietermaritzburg (2–3; 8hr); Port Elizabeth (1–2 daily; 9hr); Pretoria (4–5 daily; 7hr).

Flights

Bloemfontein to: Cape Town (3 daily; 2hr 20min); Durban (2–3 daily; 1hr 15min); Johannesburg (9 daily Mon–Fri, 3 daily Sat & Sun; 1hr 10min); Port Elizabeth (1–2 daily; 2hr 20min).

GAUTENG

Gauteng means "Place of Gold" in Sotho, and no wonder: South Africa's smallest region comprises only 1.5 percent of its landmass, yet contributes over 40 percent of the GDP. Founded in 1994, this relatively new province is home to eight million people, and encompasses a section of the Magaliesberg mountains to the east, the gold-rich Witwatersrand to the south and west, on which are situated Johannesburg and Pretoria, and a host of grim satellite industrial towns.

Although lacking the spectacular attractions of the Cape Province or Mpumalanga, Gauteng has a subtle character all of its own. Startling outcrops of rock known as *koppies*, with intriguing and often lucrative geology, are set in open grassy plains of deep-red earth, and the usually mild climate is broken occasionally by spectacular lightning and massive summer storms, which can unleash torrents of water over the Transvaal plains within seconds. The area is also prone to drought, and the water supply is a constant and worsening problem. Yet the light, particularly at dawn and dusk, is a photographer's dream, rendering serene and compelling even the starkest of industrial landscapes.

The beating heart of Gauteng is **Johannesburg**, whose origins lie in the exploitation of **gold**. In keeping with its tough mining origins, this is a hectic, sometimes dangerous city, home to extreme contrasts of wealth and poverty. Most visitors leave as quickly as they can, but if you do stick around, you'll soon start to absorb its distinctive pleasures; this highly cosmopolitan city is home to some of the liveliest townships, and most vibrant cultural life in South Africa. Some 50km north lies dignified **Pretoria**, the country's administrative capital and historically an Afrikaner stronghold, but today increasingly international. Pretoria is near enough to the airport to offer an alternative to Johannesburg, if you're looking for somewhere more peaceful to stay.

The section of the **Magaliesberg Mountains** which creeps into Gauteng is a magnet for Johannesburgers desperate to escape the city's pollution and stress. Although the hills can be crowded, there's ample opportunity for nature trailing and hiking. Southeast of Johannesburg lies the little-known **Suikerbosrand Nature Reserve**, a pleasant surprise for those in search of game viewing, with zebra, cheetah and red hartebeest among its varied inhabitants. Gauteng also has some of the most ancient archeological sites in the world, and trips to the **Melville Koppies**, with the remains of Iron Age communties, and the astonishing **Sterkfontein Caves**, where the remains of pre-human primates have been found, are easily made from Johannesburg.

The wealth of the region may lie in gold, but since 1945 the **manufacturing industry** has far surpassed the profits of mines. This was a natural consequence of mining, as both the mines and their workers and families needed a wide range of goods. Mining profits enabled the necessary investment, and today there is more manufacturing in Gauteng than anywhere else in Africa. The mining industry is meanwhile in trouble: rising fixed costs and the fall in the value of gold mean that more and more mines are sliding into unprofitability. This has led to redundancies – the industry's workforce has shrunk from 700,000 to 330,000 in fifteen years, exacerbating Gauteng's unemployment problems.

Until 1994, much of the province, especially Pretoria, was renowned for white support for the restoration of apartheid, as proposed by the Conservative Party. But the elections of that year, and the local elections of 1995, have seen a turnaround; the **ANC** won both convincingly and will control the province for some years to come.

JOHANNESBURG

Fast-paced, frenetic **JOHANNESBURG** has had a reputation for immorality, greed and violence ever since its first plot auction in December 1886. Today, with a new political division ensuring that formerly white areas are administratively yoked with the black townships, the city is also struggling to cope with a dramatic change in racial composition.

Nowhere is the new tension more in evidence than in the previously all-white central business district, where an influx of poor blacks, and a soaring crime rate, has prompted the mass exodus of shops and restaurants to the northern suburbs. There will be a

GREATER JOHANNESBURG

continuous ribbon of development between Johannesburg and Pretoria, originally 54km apart, by the early part of the next century. Meanwhile, the black middle class is moving from township to suburb, while tens of thousands of immigrants from elsewhere in Africa are flooding into inner-city suburbs like Hillbrow and townships like Alexandra. Despite the changes, few township dwellers consider themselves true Johannesburgers, and the city's communities continue to be culturally segregated; as an outsider, it's hard to make inroads.

Johannesburg's contrasts are some of the most extreme in the world; poverty-stricken and overcrowded Alexandra is surrounded by some of the richest suburbs in South Africa, and downtown hundreds of homeless struggle to survive around the Stock Exchange. The contrast between suburb and township is mirrored nationwide, but is more extreme here because of the intense wealth of many of the suburbs, and the sheer size of the townships and their satellite squatter camps. Yet the city as a whole continues to suck in people and skills from all over the country, making it the financial, commercial and cultural powerhouse of South Africa.

A unifying strand through many lives, rich and poor, is the urgent desire to get ahead. Johannesburg is a profoundly entrepreneurial place, from its street hawkers to its boardroom executives. But it's not all about making money. In the evening, the city's renowned nightlife swings into action: Johannesburgers tend to party as hard as they work. The signals for the future are mixed, with everyday events confirming both bright optimism and deep cynicism. But it is this tension that gives the city its edge, making it amongst the most stimulating and provocative places in Africa.

Some history

Johannesburg dates back to 1886, when Australian prospector **George Harrison** found the main Witwatersrand gold-bearing reef. Almost immediately this quiet area of the Transvaal was swamped with diggers from near and far, and a tented city sprung up around the site. The Pretoria authorities were forced to proclaim a township nearby: they chose a useless triangle of land called the Randjeslaagte, which had been left unclaimed by local farmers. Johan Rissik, the surveyor, called it Johannesburg, either after himself, the chief of mining, Christiaan Johannes Joubert, or **Paul Johannes Kruger**.

Mining magnates such as Cecil Rhodes and Barney Barnato possessed the capital necessary to exploit what was the world's richest gold reef, and their **Chamber of Mines**, founded in 1889, attempted to bring some order to the digging frenzy, with common policies on recruitment, wages and working conditions. In 1893, due partly to pressure from white workers, and with the approval of the ZAR government, the chamber introduced the **colour bar**, which excluded black workers from all but manual labour.

By 1895, Johannesburg's population had soared to over 100,000, many of whom were not remotely Boer and had no interest in the ZAR's independence. Kruger and the burghers saw in these *uitlanders* (foreigners) a possible danger to their political supremacy, and denied them the vote, despite the income they generated for the state's coffers. Legislation was also passed to control the influx of blacks to Johannesburg, and Indians were forcibly moved out of the city into a western location. Before long, large shantytowns filled with blacks and Indians were springing up on the outskirts of Johannesburg.

In 1900 Johannesburg fell to the British, who had been attempting to annex the gold-rich area for some time. High Commissioner Sir Alfred Milner imported whiz kids from Oxford and Cambridge as his "kindergarten" to modernize the city. They lived in Parktown, and commissioned their houses from the celebrated English architect, **Sir Herbert Baker** (see p.467). At the same time, more black townships were established: **Sophiatown** was set up in 1903 in an area previously used for dumping sewage, and **Alexandra** was established two years later. Bubonic plague erupted on the northern fringes of the city in 1904, providing justification for the authorities to burn several Indian and African locations, including **Newtown**, just west of the centre.

Meanwhile, white mine workers were becoming unionized, and outbreaks of fighting over pay and working hours were a frequent occurrence. Their poorly paid black counterparts were also mobilizing; their main grievance was the ruling that skilled jobs were the preserve of white workers. Resentments came to a head in the **Rand Revolt** of 1922, after the Chamber of Mines, anxious to cut costs, decided to allow blacks into the skilled jobs previously held only by whites. White workers were furious: street battles broke out and lasted for four days. Government troops were called in to restore order and over 200 men were killed. Alarmed at the scale of white discontent, Prime Minister Jan Smuts ruled that the colour bar be maintained. Throughout the 1920s, the government passed laws restricting the movement of blacks.

During the 1930s, the township of **Orlando** became established southwest of the city, with accommodation for 80,000 blacks; this was the nucleus around which **Soweto** evolved. By 1945, 400,000 blacks were living in and around Johannesburg – an increase of 100 percent in a decade. In August 1946, 70,000 African Mineworkers Union members went on strike over working conditions. The government sent police in, and twelve miners were killed and over 1000 injured. Informal settlers on municipal land attempted a rent boycott that year, proclaiming "Asinamali!" ("We have no money!"). They were ignored, and non-rent payers were evicted. During the 1950s, *kwela*, a black urban culture unique to Johannesburg, began to emerge in the townships, and the new *marabi* jazz was played in illegal drinking houses called *shebeens*.

Forced removals, particularly from Sophiatown, began in 1955. Thousands of people were dumped far from the city centre, in the new township of Meadowlands, next to Orlando. Sophiatown was crassly renamed "Triomf" (triumph). The **ANC** found its mass base during this period, proclaiming the **Freedom Charter** in Kliptown, Soweto, that year. The 1950s was also the era of *Drum Magazine*, which revealed a sophisticated black Johannesburg culture, and introduced a host of talented journalists, like Can Temba and Casey "Kid" Motsisi, to the city and the world. *Mbaqanga* music emerged, with its heavy basslines and sensuous melodies capturing the bittersweet essence of life in the old townships.

The formation in 1972 of the **Black Consciousness Movement** (BCM) rekindled political activism, particularly among students in Soweto. On June 16, 1976, student riots erupted in the township, and the unrest spread nationwide (see p.657). The youth's war against the State escalated in the 1980s, resulting in regular **"states of emergency"**, during which the armed forces had permission to do anything they liked to contain revolt. Towards the end of the decade, the government relaxed "petty" apartheid, turning a blind eye to the growth of "grey" areas like Hillbrow – white suburbs where blacks were moving in.

The three years after **Nelson Mandela**'s release in 1990 saw widespread political violence on the Rand right up until the day before elections. However, as elsewhere in South Africa, the election on April 27, 1994 went off peacefully. The ANC won comfortably in Johannesburg, and confirmed their position in the local elections of 1995.

Since then, the city has moved into a new era. Ellis Park and the FNB stadium were centres of action in 1995 and 1996, when first the national **rugby team**, and then the national **soccer** team, won the World Cup and African Cup respectively. Johannesburg celebrated in style, displaying Latino levels of sporting fervour. The world learnt the tune of *Shosholoza*, a Zulu migrants' song transformed into a national sporting anthem.

The **telephone code** for Johannesburg is ☎011.

Arrival and information

Johannesburg's large **International Airport** (until recently known as *Jan Smuts*), lies 20km east of the city (international flight arrivals and departures ☎975 9963). The *Impala* **bus service** (half-hourly from the airport Mon–Fri & Sun 5.30am–10pm, Sat 5.30am–7pm) will take you to the Rotunda terminal, on the corner of Rissik and Wolmarans streets, in central Braamfontein for around R25. If your destination is the northern suburbs, you'll find it easier to take the **Sandton Shuttle** from the airport; tickets can be booked from the company's desk (☎884 3957), near the international arrivals exit. Taking a **taxi** from the airport is convenient and safe, but be sure to take

---

SAFETY AND CRIME IN JOHANNESBURG

With its extremes of poverty and wealth and its brash, get-ahead culture, it's perhaps hardly surprising that Johannesburg can be a dangerous place. As in all major cities, taking sensible precautions is likely to see you through safely, although the presence of illegal firearms makes taking extra care especially important.

If you're wandering around on foot, the crime you are most at risk from is **mugging**, and some areas carry a much higher risk than others. Be particularly alert when exploring the central business district (CBD), Braamfontein and Newtown; Joubert Park, Hillbrow and Berea are marginally safer, and Yeoville and Observatory safer still, but you still need to be wary in all these neighbourhoods. You are very unlikely to be mugged in Melville, Parktown or Rosebank. In high-risk areas, do your best not to look like a tourist. Study maps beforehand (not on street corners), try not to ask directions from passers-by and don't walk around with luggage. Try to look into the crowds coming your way, to see if there are any groups of young men (the main offenders) moving as a block. If you're carrying valuables, leave a portion of them easily available, so that any mugger is likely to be quickly satisfied and not investigate you further. Never resist muggers; running like hell can work, but some have guns, which you won't know about until too late.

You are unlikely to be mugged on **public transport**, but, as always, it's wise to stay alert, especially around busy spots such as the Rotunda and Eloff Street. Waiting for buses in the northern suburbs is generally safe.

Don't expect too much from the **police**. Keeping tourists safe is a priority in Durban and Cape Town, but in Johannesburg the battle has been lost and the police have other things on their agenda. Police on the street are rare, but if you do spot one, feel free to ask for an escort. The police station outside the *Carlton Hotel* in the CBD has officers who should be available to help. In an emergency, dial ☎10111.

If you're driving around, you're at risk of **car-jacking**, although staying in a hotel minimizes this risk (car-jackers tend to trail victims on their way home). Always keep all car doors locked and windows up – never wait in an unlocked car while a friend goes into a shop. The times when you are leaving or returning to your car are the most dangerous, so keep a good lookout, seek out secure and preferably guarded parking, and don't dawdle. Stopping at traffic lights, particularly at night, can also make you vulnerable – yet driving through them is riskier because of cars coming the other way. At traffic lights, keep a good distance between you and the car in front, make sure your windows are shut and doors locked, check your mirrors often, and keep your foot hovering over the accelerator. Repeat to yourself the mantra "Most people are never car-jacked."

Finally, don't let paranoia ruin your stay in the city. Remember that most Jo'burgers have no intention of doing you any harm at all. The best thing is to do as they do: juggle your fear and your bravado, without letting one swamp the other.

a metered Johannesburg airport taxi, make sure the driver knows where you're going before you set off, and be prepared to pay at least R80 for most destinations.

Greyhound (☎328 4040), *Intercape* (☎328 4571) and *Translux* (☎315 2333) **buses** and intercity **trains** (☎773 2944) arrive at the Rotunda (entrance on Wolmarans Street). From here, you're best off – and safest – taking a taxi to your final destination. Hillbrow, Yeoville, Observatory, Troyeville and Melville are all close by. Buses and minibuses run from the station to virtually everywhere, but waiting for them, especially surrounded by luggage, can be risky.

Information

The **Johannesburg Publicity Association** has an office in the international arrivals hall of the airport (Mon–Thurs 8am–4.30pm, Fri 8am–4pm, Sat & Sun 8am–1pm; ☎970 1220), from where you can arrange car rental and hotel bookings (but for expensive hotels only). There's a second branch in the Rotunda building on the corner of Rissik and Wolmarans streets (Mon–Fri 8am–4.30pm; ☎337 6650), while their head office is in the North State Building, on the corner of Kruis and Market streets (Mon–Fri 8am–4.30pm; ☎336 4961). At any of these outlets you can pick up the useful *Gateway* magazine and *Johannesburg Alive*, a free monthly **listings** guide to cultural and sporting events. The weekly national *Mail & Guardian*, and the two Johannesburg papers, the *Star* and the *Sowetan*, also publish listings, but they can be sketchy.

The *Gateway* has a **map** in its centre pages, but to get around the less central suburbs you'll need a detailed street guide. The hefty *Witwatersrand Street Guide* is the best and is available from *CNA* newsagents.

City transport

Johannesburg's **public transport system** leaves much to be desired: it's slow, unreliable, and after commuting hours practically nonexistent. **Cars** are the order of the day, especially for those living in the suburbs. If you're not driving, though, don't despair: with patience and a bit of stamina, it is possible to negotiate your way around the city using the buses, and some areas are easily explored **on foot.** You're highly unlikely to want to use the city's **train** system, which has a poor reputation and very limited services.

Cars and private taxis

By far the best way to explore Johannesburg is in your own **car**. Although road signs are can be poor, and local drivers pushy, the grid system at least removes some of the eccentricities that plague other big-city road networks. Familiarity with a few key roads and careful map reading makes getting around relatively straightforward. The **M1** connects the centre to the northern suburbs, flying over Newtown, through Braamfontein and Parktown, and heading into Houghton and Sandton, eventually turning into the N1 for Pretoria. Heading south, the M1 is one of the best routes to Soweto. The next artery west of the M1, also useful for heading north, is **Oxford Road**, which starts off in Parktown, and becomes Rivonia Road once it enters Sandton. West again is **Jan Smuts Avenue**, which passes through Rosebank and Dunkeld, before hitting Sandton.

The city is relatively well served for **car rental** (see "Listings" for telephone numbers). Local companies are the best bet: most offer good prices and old cars which are less likely to be stolen. For longer stays, **buying a car** is a practical option; the weekly *Junk Mail* has a large selection of private sales – expect to pay upwards of R20,000 for a decent vehicle. You can resell through *Junk Mail*, too, if you have a contact telephone number.

For short journeys around the city, use **private taxis**, which must always be telephoned in advance (see "Listings" for reliable firms). In the centre you'll find taxi ranks outside the *Carlton*, the *Sandton Sun* and *Sandton Towers* hotels. A journey to the CBD from the northern suburbs will cost at least R100.

Buses

Johannesburg's **buses** (many of which are double-deckers), offer the safest and cheapest public transport during weekdays. Most bus routes start and end at the main terminus (☎838 2125) in Vanderbijl Square, off Eloff Street, in the city centre; this is also where you can pick up timetables and route maps.

Buses only run between the suburbs and the centre, so are useless for getting from one suburb to another, unless they both lie on the same route to town. In a close reflection of their commuter role, most buses stop by 6.30pm, though a very few keep going until 9.30pm. Weekend services are poor, with very few routes in action and waits of at least one hour between buses.

SEVEN HANDY BUS ROUTES

These bus services are reduced on Saturdays and, apart from the 118, do not operate at all on Sundays.

Number	Route	Frequency
5	Eloff St; Park Station; Hillbrow; Parktown; Oxford Rd; Saxonwold; Houghton; Rosebank; Melrose; Ilovo	every 10–15min
10	Diagonal St; Eloff St; Hillbrow; Berea;	every 10–15min in morning
	Yeoville; Observatory; Orange Grove	every 35min–1hr in afternoon
22	Diagonal St; Nugget St; Eloff St; Yeoville; Bellevue East; Bruma	every 35min–1hr
31	Oriental Plaza; Newtown; Eloff St; Commissioner St; Judith's Paarl; Bez Valley	every 45min–1hr
67	Eloff St; Harrison St; Braamfontein; Richmond; Auckland Park; Melville	every 30–40min
75	Bree St; Braamfontein; Parktown; Jan Smuts Ave; Zoo Lake; Saxonwold, Parktown North	every 10–25min
118	Eloff St; Hillbrow; Berea; Yeoville	every 30min, Sat & Sun only

---

Minibus taxis

Even cheaper than buses, **minibus taxis** cover a far wider area, and can be picked up at ranks, or hailed mid-route by either raising your forefinger (if you're heading into town), pointing downwards (if you want to go uptown) or pointing towards yourself (if you want Park Station). The drawbacks, however, are worth bearing in mind; cramped cars, hair-raising driving, frequent accidents and petty criminals working the major taxi ranks have combined to deter most white Jo'burgers from using this mode of transport. If you do want to try one out, you'd be wise to wait at a smaller taxi rank, or wave one down en route – but never with bulky baggage.

CITY TOURS

One good way of taking in Johannesburg's main attractions, especially if you're here on a short stay, is to take one of the many **tours of the city** on offer. You'll find an abundance of travel agents here, and the market is competitive enough for agents to have to offer reasonable deals. For tours of Soweto, see box on p.470.

Chamber of Mines, 5 Hollard St, Marshall Town (☎838 8211). Tours of all the major mining houses, including *Anglo-American* and *Anglo-Vaal*. The day starts at 7.30am and is mainly taken up with a descent into the mine itself, sometimes kilometres beneath the ground, where you'll witness blasting and hacking first-hand. You'll hear fulsome technical explanations, and will go on a quick whip round the mine compounds, which are still largely ethnically segregated. The day finishes with a large meal in the mine clubhouse – worlds apart from the miners' canteen. R150.

Dumela Africa, PO Box 91217, Auckland Park, Johannesburg 2006 (☎837 9928). Minibus tours of Johannesburg, Gold Reef City, nearby parks, Sun City and Pretoria. Half-day excursions cost R110–150, and full days R285–330.

Neil Harrop's Original Balloon Safaris, PO Box 67, Randburg 2125 (☎705 3201, fax 705 3203). Expensive but wonderful waft over the Magaliesberg Mountains in a balloon early in the morning. You can't rely on the wind, of course, so you may end up not going on the day you've booked. R870 includes champagne breakfast.

Parktown Tours, Parktown & Westcliff Heritage Trust, Northwards, Rockridge Rd, Parktown (☎482 3349). Informative tour of the Parktown mansions, with guides decked out in head-turning nineteenth-century regalia. R50.

Springbok Atlas Tours, Leffin House, Eloff St, Johannesburg (☎493 0827). One of South Africa's major tour operators, offering bus tours of Johannesburg, Soweto, Gold Reef City and nearby parks.

Accommodation

Johannesburg has **accommodation** to suit every budget, and finding a room is usually not a problem. Where you decide to stay will depend less on availability than on the length of your visit and how concerned you are about safety. Some of the city's smartest hotels are in the **CBD** and **Braamfontein** and remain the preferred destination of business executives on fleeting visits. The high crime rate, however, makes these areas less useful for those interested in exploring, and both are easily accessible from elsewhere by day.

The safest – but also the blandest – areas to stay are undoubtedly the **northern suburbs**, which are also handy for public transport; **Rosebank** is the most convenient for access to downtown, and its streets are quite pleasant. Further to the west, off Barry Hertzog Drive, **Melville**, with its friendly cafés, is the most characterful of these suburbs, while **Parktown** is worth considering for its great location on a ridge overlooking the city and its fine colonial mansions.

East of the CBD, **Yeoville** has the best range of **budget accommodation**, and attracts lively crowds of backpackers. Nearby **Observatory** is quieter, with larger houses, and is a good place to be based if you like action, but not all the time. Riskier, but certainly exhilarating, the inner-city suburbs of **Hillbrow**, **Joubert Park** and **Berea** are the most Africanized places you'll find in Johannesburg. But they're not for the nervous.

Tourist infrastructure in the **townships** is minimal: the only hotel is in Soweto, the *Soweto International*, 8651, Zone 6, Diepkloof, Soweto (☎938 1637), poorly situated near a hospital and busy taxi rank. Staying with locals is the most rewarding way of experiencing the township, and this is best arranged through an experienced tour operator (see box, p.470).

Note that many hotels and hostels will send people to pick you up from the airport if you ring them, and some even tout for business in the arrivals lounge.

JOHANNESBURG ACCOMMODATION

ACCOMMODATION

1 Ah Hah Guesthouse
2 Backpackers' Underground
3 Bruma Lake Lodge
4 The Carlton
5 The Cottages
6 The Devonshire
7 Explorers' Club
8 Fairview Youth Hostel
9 Fountain Head Guesthouse
10 Holiday Inn Garden Court
11 Joel House

12 Johannesburg Central Youth Hostel
13 Karos Johannesburger
14 Kozy Korner
15 Parktown Place
16 The Pink House
17 Protea Gardens
18 The Ridge
19 Rockey St. Backpackers'
20 Sunnyside Park Holiday Inn
21 Traveller & Backpackers Retreat
22 Twin Steeples

CBD and Braamfontein

Carlton Hotel, Main St (☎331 8911, fax 331 3555). Part of the CBD's landmark Carlton Centre, very plush and a favourite with business travellers. Most city tours start from here. ⑧.

Devonshire Hotel, corner of Melle and Jorissen streets (☎339 5611 or 339 5612, fax 403 2495). The best views in Braamfontein from rooms at this smart executives' hotel, equipped with several bars and restaurants. ⑥.

Holiday Inn Garden Court, 84 Small St (☎336 7011, fax 336 0515). Near the Supreme Court – an unsafe part of town – this is a modern *Holiday Inn* with no surprises. ⑦.

Joubert Park, Hillbrow and Berea

Joel House, 61 Joel Rd, Berea (☎642 4426 or 642 4427, fax 642 5221). Stylish and popular guesthouse with a small garden, few rooms and Edwardian decor. A true haven of tranquillity. ③.

Johannesburg Central Youth Hostel, 4 Fife Ave, Berea (☎643 1213). Cheap dorms, camping and a garden (but no pool). ①–②.

Karos Johannesburger, 60 Twist St, Joubert Park (☎725 3753, fax 725 6309). Pleasant if rather characterless hotel, considerably more upmarket than its surroundings. ④.

Protea Gardens, 35 O'Reilly Rd, Berea (☎643 6610, fax 484 2622). The area's smartest hotel – all rooms with bath and TV – but on a Hillbrow street noted for its blatant drug dealing. ③.

The Ridge, 8 Abel Rd, Berea (☎643 4911). Pleasant hotel with two bars, a nightclub and restaurant, a patio, and pool tables. Choose a room away from the nightclub for a good night's sleep. ②.

Yeoville and Observatory

Backpackers' Underground, 20 Harley St, Yeoville (☎648 6132, fax 811 2760). Central Yeoville dorms and double rooms, with a pool and no curfew. Well-priced, friendly and safe. ①–②.

The Cottages, 30 Gill St, Observatory (☎648 4279, fax 487 2404). Superb cottages perched on the Observatory ridge, with a countrified atmosphere and organized hikes from the plot to the top of the *koppie*. Evening meals are available on request. ⑥.

Explorers' Club, 9 Innes St, Observatory (☎648 7138, fax 648 4673). Dorms and doubles in what is probably the best hostel in the area, with a fine verandah, pool, garden and a useful travel library, all 15min walk from Rockey St's bars and clubs. ①–②.

Fountain Head Guest House, 52 Urania St, Observatory (☎487 3564, fax 648 8009). Comfortable rooms in a stunning, Italian-style villa on Observatory ridge, with immaculate gardens and fountains, and great views. ⑤.

Pink House, 73 Becker St, Yeoville (☎ & fax 487 1991). Friendly hostel with dorms and doubles, right in the heart of Yeoville – near enough to stumble home to after a night out. There's a useful noticeboard, and good travel advice is available. ①–②.

Rockey Street Backpackers, 34 Regent St, Yeoville (☎648 8786, fax 648 8433). Two friendly adjacent houses close to Rockey St, with dorms and doubles, cooking facilities, a bar and a tiny swimming pool. Popular with non-English speakers. ①–②.

Eastern suburbs

Ah Ha Guest House, 17a Talisman Ave, Bedford View (☎616 3702, fax 615 3012). Silly name, but comfortable rooms and a decent swimming pool at this pleasant guesthouse. ④.

Bruma Lake Lodge, 41 Hans Pirow St, Bruma (☎615 1092, fax 615 6229). Near the airport and major shopping complexes, with dorms and doubles, a relaxed owner, a swimming pool and a small bar. ①–②.

Fairview Youth Hostel, 4 College St, Fairview (☎618 2048, fax 614 2823). Well-located hostel facing onto Commissioner St, and on a major bus route. There's a bar and kitchen, plus a pool and games room. ①–②.

Kozy Korner, 10 Milner Crescent, Kensington (☎615 5159, fax 455 4044). B&B with cosy beds in five plain rooms. Perfect for bus trips to the Eastgate shopping centre, or into town. ④.

Traveller & Backpackers' Retreat, 55 1st St, Bez Valley (☎614 2555, fax 614 2497). Quiet hostel with dorms and doubles. Well-established with continental European backpackers. ①–②.

Twin Steeples, 100 Ascot Rd, Judith's Paarl (☎614 8978, fax 614 7529). Wonderful old listed building, now converted into a B&B, and the most stylish accommodation in the area. ③.

Northern suburbs

Backpackers' Ritz, 6 North Rd (off Jan Smuts Ave), Dunkeld West (☎327 0229, fax 327 0233). Large two-house complex with pool, a tennis court and a good bar, popular with overlanders. Camping is allowed on the grounds. ①–②.

Don Apartments (☎442 7495, fax 442 8040). Choose from blocks of self-catering apartments in Rosebank and Sandton; all are tastefully furnished and well-equipped. ⑤–⑧.

Highgate Guest House, Side Rd, off East Rd, Morningside (☎ & fax 783 9585). In a rather lifeless cul-de-sac, offering slightly overpriced rooms in the house, and good-value self-catering cottages. ⑥–⑧.

Kew Youth Hostel, 5 Johannesburg Rd, Kew (☎ & fax 887 9072). The city's only black-owned hostel offers mostly dorms, and has few facilities apart from a swimming pool. Visitors are not allowed after 10pm. ①–②.

Melville House, 59 6th Ave, Melville (☎726 3503). Nicely located B&B with a great little garden and pleasantly decorated rooms. Easy access to central Melville. ④.

Michelangelo, Sandton Square (☎282 7000, fax 282 7171). Outrageously opulent, with prices to match, joined to the city's most upmarket shopping mall. ⑦.

Parktown Place, 12 Seymour Ave, Parktown (☎726 2521). Grand old building with only four bedrooms, a pool, wonderful grounds, and a self-catering cottage at the back (find it on "Johannesburg accommodation" map, p.456). ③.

Romney Cottage, 75 8th Ave, Parktown North (☎ & fax 442 7548). Excellent thatched B&B with cosy rooms and a pretty garden, just off Jan Smuts Ave. ⑤.

Rosebank Hotel, corner of Tyrwhitt and Sturdee avenues, Rosebank (☎447 2700, fax 447 3276). Smart modern hotel in handy location near Rosebank's many shops and restaurants. Aimed at business travellers, there's a pool, three restaurants (one with live music) and two bars. ⑦.

Sandton Sun & Sandton Towers, corner of Alice and Fifth streets, and corner of Maude and Fifth streets, Sandton (☎780 5000, fax 780 5002). Two luxury hotels standing opposite each other, and offering plush rooms, restaurants and a wide range of facilities. ⑧.

Sunnyside Park Holiday Inn, 2 York Rd, Parktown (☎643 7226, fax 642 0019). Elegant, if somewhat anonymous hotel in one of Parktown's finest buildings, formerly a governor's residence (find it on "Johannesburg accommodation", p.456). ⑦.

Sans Souci Hotel, 10 Guild Rd, Parktown West (☎726 3623, fax 480 5983). Wonderful old building on the Parktown ridge, with well-stocked bars, a swimming pool and a soothing garden. The rooms are in a 1960s extension, but are pleasant enough. Good-value buffet and restaurant lunches. ③.

Zoo Lodge, 2 Ashwold Rd, corner of Jan Smuts and Saxonwold avenues, Forest Town (☎486 0011, fax 838 7322). Dorms, singles and doubles, with a pool table and bar (but no pool). Forest Town is the suburb just north of Parktown, and is handy for Rosebank's shops. ①–②.

The City

Johannesburg is large, sprawling and poorly planned, with few conventional sights and a bewildering number of districts. The **central business district (CBD)** is where you'll find the city's most ostentatious buildings, serving mining, finance or the State, and a burgeoning multiracial street life, with office workers rubbing shoulders with hawkers, shoppers and gangsters. Across the train lines to the north lies **Braamfontein**, home to the highly rated University of Witwatersrand and, further north still, opulent **Parktown**, the original home of Johannesburg's richest residents. The seemingly endless **northern suburbs** that stretch from here to Pretoria throw up a few pleasant surprises, notably leafy **Melville**, with its lively parks and cafés, and **Rosebank**, the city's nicest place to shop. East of the centre, the buzzing inner-city districts of **Joubert Park**, **Berea** and **Hillbrow** are packed with migrants from all over the continent, while nearby **Yeoville** and **Observatory** exude a trendy ambience, with their lively ethnic mix and abundance of elegantly decaying houses. Further east still,

CENTRAL JOHANNESBURG

400 m

△ Oriental Plaza

the suburbs such as **Bezuidenhout (Bez) Valley** were, during apartheid, predominantly Portuguese, and today offer some great restaurants and bars. Southwest of the city centre lies another world: the vast **townships** of Soweto, Thokoza and Khatlehong, previously no-go zones for travellers, but today safe to explore with a reliable guide.

The CBD, Newtown and Braamfontein

With its towering office blocks and frenetic street life, it's easy to see why downtown Johannesburg has been dubbed "Africa's Manhattan". Unlike Manhattan, however, the **central business district** offers little beyond impressive office buildings to detain you, and the fact that it's one of Johannesburg's most crime-ridden areas means you can't afford to blank out as you stare up at the soaring skyscrapers. That said, the CBD is refreshingly multiracial; the sustained capital flight over the past few years has seen upmarket restaurants and shops replaced by a plethora of street traders, lending the area a bustling and genuinely African feel.

The **Carlton Centre**, which stands roughly halfway down Commissioner Street, is a good place to start explorations. The main attraction of this fifty-storey building is its top-floor **Observatory** (daily 9am–11.30pm; entry fee), which offers the most breathtaking views of Johannesburg you'll get. Five blocks west of here, on the corner of Loveday Street, the grandiose **Rand Club** is worth a quick look (though you can't go inside); this is where mining magnates come to dine and unwind. Completed in 1904, the building is actually the fourth one to occupy the site, as each successive club was replaced to reflect the owners' growing wealth. Four blocks south, going down Simmonds Street, on the corner of Frederick Street, lies the **Standard Bank Centre**, which houses an excellent gallery with changing exhibitions (Mon–Fri 8am–4.30pm, Sat 9am–1pm; free).

Moving west from Simmonds and Main streets leads to the forbidding **Magistrates Court** on West Street. The court holds bitter memories for many because of its role during apartheid, and is struggling to restore credibility. **Diagonal Street**, one of the most fascinating in the CBD, is two blocks north. A jumble of street traders and shops, some dating to the 1890 and selling traditional medicines (*umuthi*), Sotho blankets and inexpensive household items, give the street a very African buzz. Amid the noise and bustle stands the **Johannesburg Stock Exchange**, where you'll need to book to go on a tour of the trading floor and watch the dealers in action (Mon & Fri 11am, Tues–Thurs 11am & 4pm; ☎337 2200). Nearby, on the corner of Pritchard Street, the **Joomal Mosque**, built in 1918, is an elegant reminder of this district's past as a focal point for the Asian community.

Heading back east along Market Street, you soon reach the solemn **Public Library**, on the corner of Sauer Street (Mon–Sat 9am–5pm; free), and the recently revamped **Gauteng Legislature**, formerly the City Hall, on the corner of Harrison Street. The **First National Bank Museum** (Mon–Fri 9am–4pm; free) sits opposite. The museum itself is dull, but the exterior facade, built in 1902, is worth a pause. The main **Post Office** is one block east on the corner of Rissik Street. When this was completed in 1897, it was the tallest building in the city, and is still impressive, despite being dwarfed by later additions to the skyline. Whilst basically neo-Baroque in style, it has quirky Dutch touches, primarily in its gabling. The fourth floor and clock tower are later additions, timed to coincide with the accession of British king, Edward VII, in 1902.

Two of the last survivors of the CBD's department stores are reached by continuing east until you hit the busy bus ranks of Eloff Street, and then heading north for two blocks until Pritchard Street. Here you will find *Cuthberts*, which opened as a shoe shop in 1904, and *Markham's*, built in 1886. Completing the tour, the **Rand Supreme Court**, two blocks further east on Pritchard Street, was once another hated symbol of oppression, but has been making a new and better name for itself since 1994, with landmark rulings on the new constitution.

Newtown

Just west of the city centre, **Newtown**'s main draw is its **Cultural Precinct**, a cluster of buildings lying under the M1 highway, designed to inject some life into the area, and to some extent succeeding. At its heart, the large and excellent **Museum Africa**, 121 Bree St (Tues–Sun 9am–5pm; nominal entry fee), has three permanent exhibitions and numerous temporary displays. Most successful is "Johannesburg Transformations", a major exhibit with recreations of shacks and tenements (weird to find them in a musuem if you have just come from one), along with well-selected soundtracks from musical giants of the past, like *kwela* maestro Spokes Mashiane, and a plausible text. The overall effect is impressive and this is probably the best opportunity you'll have to get a sense of the city's history. Less successful is the **Bensusan Museum of Photography**, which grandly aspires to be a "newseum of the present and future" but adds up to little more than a selection of cameras, holograms and CD-ROMS – though camera buffs may find it rewarding. The **Museum of South African Rock Art** has few original paintings, as most of them are still on rocks scattered around South Africa, but there are some convincing replicas – which are as close as you'll get to the real thing without a hike up country. A useful text gives background on the artists and their work.

Next door, the **Market Theatre** was a fruit market until its conversion in 1976. There's an interesting mall outside, with a coffee shop, bookshop, two major music venues (see p.475) and the **Rembrandt van Rijn Gallery** (Tues–Sat 10am–5pm; free), Johannesburg's foremost non-commercial art gallery, with adventurous displays of fresh artistic talent. The cultural centre continues south of Jeppe Street, with a live music venue (*Megamusic*), a dance rehearsal and performing space called the **Dance Factory**, and the **Electric Workshop**, which is used for the annual Arts Alive Festival (see, "Entertainment, nightlife and culture", p.475). The city's best **flea market** takes place every Saturday outside the theatre (see "Shopping", p.478).

Moving south, over President and Main streets, you'll come to the infamous **John Vorster Square**, site of the Johannesburg police headquarters, where anti-apartheid activists were detained and tortured, and some fell to their deaths having "jumped" from the tenth floor. After this, it's a pleasant relief to find the remains of the old Indian neighbourhood just further west, where Jeppe Street turns into Minnaar Street. A busy commercial street ends up at the **Oriental Plaza**, an Indian-owned shopping complex, selling everything from suitcases and bric-a-brac to fabrics and spices. This is just about all that remains of Newtown's once-thriving Indian community, most of whom were forcibly removed in 1904 to make way for whites.

Braamfontein

The only time you're likely to visit **Braamfontein**, which starts at the main train station, and extends north as far as Empire Road, is for its transport facilities at the Rotunda and Park Station. The only other attractions marginally worth a visit are the **Civic Theatre** in Rissik Street, which hosts some of Johannesburg's best theatrical, musical and dance productions (see p.477), and the **University of the Witwatersrand**, otherwise known as "Wits", which lies in Braamfontein's northwest corner, on the corner of Jorissen Street and Jan Smuts Avenue. The university has played an important role in the country's history, educating many future leaders, and acting as a site of major intellectual and political struggles. Contained within its grounds, in Senate House, is the **Gertrude Posel Gallery** (Tues–Fri 10am–4pm; free), which has an extensive and interesting collection of traditional African art.

The inner-city suburbs: Joubert Park, Hillbrow and Berea

Johannesburg's **inner-city suburbs** are multicultural, and crime-ridden. These were the "grey areas" of Johannesburg, where apartheid first started to break down in the

1980s. The police turned a blind eye as large numbers of blacks started moving into these previously all-white areas from the townships. Today, most whites have left, and migrants from all over the continent, but especially Nigeria and the Congo Republic, have flooded in. The noise and street life can be intimidating at first, but these districts offer a fantastic insight into Johannesburg's changing racial composition. All three suburbs have their moments of architectural excellence, though their hectic street life may leave you disinclined to savour them at leisure.

Joubert Park

Joubert Park meets the CBD at Bree Street and extends as far as Smit Street, with the only inner-city green space, the park itself, its natural centre. Named after General Piet Joubert (who lost the South African Republic general election to Paul Kruger in 1893), the park, with pleasant fountains and a conservatory, is always filled with people, but most white South Africans avoid it for fear of mugging.

In the south of the park stands the **Johannesburg Art Gallery** (daily except Monday 10am–7pm; free), an elegant, predominantly nineteenth-century building that is among the most progressive galleries in the country. To get there, enter the park through the entrance on Klein Street. The regular exhibits inside include vast wooden sculptures by the visionary Venda artist Jackson Hlungwani that tower up to the gallery's ceilings. Elsewhere, the gallery shows a very South African mixture of African artworks and artefacts from the ceremonial to the purely decorative, and a range of European paintings, including some minor Dutch Masters. The special exhibitions are usually good, too; consult the *Mail & Guardian* newspaper for details.

At the park's southwest corner, on the corner of De Villiers and Wanderers streets stands the grand **St Mary's Cathedral**, built in 1926 and designed by Sir Herbert Baker (see box, p.467), but now largely deserted by its white patrons. Another Baker work stands northwest of Joubert Park, up Hospital Hill; the gracious **Medical Research Institute** was the architect's parting gesture before leaving for England. Look out for the bronze sculpture on the dome of the tower – a globe supported by three serpents. In the Institute's grounds, the **Adler Museum of the History of Medicine** (Mon–Fri 9am–4pm; free), includes recreations of an *umuthi* shop and an early twentieth-century pharmacist, along with a somewhat disturbing recreation of an early dentist's surgery. The main part of the museum has a bizarre selection of medical gadgets, including the world's first iron lung.

Hillbrow and Berea

Smit Street, which runs north of Joubert Park, marks the boundary with infamous and densely populated **Hillbrow**, dominated by multistorey apartment buildings, all crammed with people.

Hillbrow is best savoured by heading to its heart, the busy **Kotze** and **Pretoria streets**, which run parallel to each other, three blocks north of Smit Street. These thoroughfares, with their markets, clubs and bars, teem with activity and the nonstop action can be intimidating. A good idea is to stop in one of the several bars with balconies looking onto the street, and watch the day unfold in your own time.

Traditionally, Hillbrow attracts the city's new immigrants. Immediately after the war, the typical immigrant was English, Italian or East European. These days, Africans from all over the continent are arriving in their numbers, lending the area a uniquely pan-African atmosphere, with music from Lagos to Kinshasa pumping from the bars and clubs. Along the many side streets, the scene is distinctly seedier, with drug pushers hanging outside gaudy strip joints.

Keep an eye out for Hillbrow's most famous apartment building, the **Ponti** or "le petit Kinshasa", the round tower visible from miles around that is home to many of the suburb's Congolese immigrants. Also worth a look is the lovely mock-Tudor

Windybrow Theatre, tucked away on the corner of Nugget and Pietersen streets. The theatre was built in the 1920s, and performances are still held there regularly (see p.478).

Berea is mostly residential, dominated by tower blocks crammed with people. Its streets are increasingly monopolized by dealers and prostitutes, and most people who can afford to move away are doing so.

The eastern suburbs

Amongst the oldest of the city's suburbs, and home for years to Johannesburg's Jewish and Portuguese communities, as well as its bohemian whites, the eastern suburbs of **Yeoville** and **Observatory** have changed dramatically in recent years. Thousands of blacks, rich enough to avoid Hillbrow but too poor for the northern suburbs have arrived here from the townships, and lend the area a vibrant, frenetic street life. Should the fast pace start to grate, you can always head for the pleasant open space at **Bezuidenhout Park**.

Yeoville and Observatory

Lying east across the Harrow Road from Berea, and due north of Troyeville, **Yeoville** is Johannesburg's most vibrant and multiracial area. It's also a fairly relaxed and safe place to explore; the many restaurants and bars that line popular **Rockey Street** are filled with hip twenty-somethings, and the street life, though bustling, is not aggressive.

Yeoville used to be predominantly Jewish, but now its spacious houses and 1950s apartment blocks are filled with a wider mix of people, ranging from young artists – black and white – to yuppies who like the area's bohemian ambience. A visit here will definitely take you along the stretch of road which starts out from Berea as **Raleigh Street** and becomes **Rockey Street**, where you might want to stop in one of the many bars or cafés. The street markets, clothes shops and second-hand book stores along here offer ample opportunity for browsing and bargain-hunting; there's even a trendy mall, the **Piccadilly Centre**, on Scotch Corner, with a colourful selection of shops, cafés and a good nightclub (see "Entertainment, nightlife and culture" p.475). Rockey Street is fine to walk at night. Hundreds do, and at weekends the street has the closest Johannesburg gets to a carnival atmosphere. Trouble, when it surfaces, is usually connected to the drug dealers who frequent the parallel streets. Don't try to purchase anything from them and they should leave you alone.

Just before Rockey Street becomes Raleigh Street, you'll find a decent **park** at Yeoville Square, with a pleasant – and safe – public swimming pool next to the police station. At the bottom end of Yeoville on Harley Street stands an onion-shaped water tower, known simply as the **Yeoville Tower.** Built by Germans in 1914, it has miraculously escaped demolition during the city's many architectural purges, and remains one of the most bizarre and photogenic monuments you'll come across in Johannesburg.

At the other end of Rockey Street lies **Observatory**, whose leafy, residential streets are still dominated by affluent whites. There's not a lot to see here, but a pleasant walk can be had if you start at the end of Rockey Street, where Observatory Avenue starts, and wander east to Bezuidenhout Park.

Bezuidenhout Park and Bruma Lake

Further east again from Observatory are two of Johannesburg's best open spaces. **Bezuidenhout Park**, along Observatory Street, is popular with locals, especially at weekends, when large numbers park cars inside, turn up their hi-fis and drink the day away. The original homestead of the Bezuidenhouts, who owned the farm, is in the park, but is not open to the public.

Just east, across Queen Street, lies **Bruma Lake**, a shopping development around an artificial lake which, although relatively new, already appears decayed. The main attraction here is the vast, bustling **flea market** on Ernest Oppenheimer Drive (Tues–Fri 9.30am–6pm, Sat 8.30am–6pm, Sun 9am–6pm), one of the best places in Johannesburg to find curios, as long as you don't mind the pseudo-traditional dance troupes entertaining you as you browse. Just east again, off the R24, towards the airport, the ugly **Eastgate Shopping Centre** is reputedly the largest mall in Africa, and is much favoured by visitors from all over southern Africa.

The northern suburbs

Safe, prosperous and packed with shops and restaurants, the **northern suburbs** seem a world apart from the CBD and its surrounds. The name is actually a catch-all term for the seemingly endless urban sprawl that runs over 30km from Parktown almost as far as Pretoria. With the notable exception of Alexandra, this is a moneyed area, where plush shopping malls and well-tended parks are often the only communal meeting points. Despite the often numbing sheen of affluence, however, interesting pockets do exist and, as most of the suburbs are close to major arterial roads, they are easily explored by car.

Parktown

Parktown, the first elite residential area in Johannesburg, lies northwest of Hillbrow, over Empire Road. The first people to settle here were Sir Lionel Philips, president of the Chamber of Mines, and his wife Lady Florence. In 1892, seeking a residence that looked onto the Magaliesberg rather than the mine dumps, they had a house built on what was then the Braamfontein farm. The rest of the farm was planted with eucalyptus trees and became known as the Sachsenwald Forest, some which was given over to the Johannesburg Zoo a few years later. The remaining land was cut down in 1925 to make way for more residential developments.

Parktown's main attraction lies in its distinctive **architecture**, given shape by Sir Herbert Baker (see box overleaf), whose arrival in 1902 heralded a style particular to this district, which today is evident in the opulent mansions lining the streets. You can take in the grounds and interiors of Parktown's highlights via a **walking or bus tour** with the Parktown & Westcliff Heritage Trust (Mon–Fri 9am–1pm; ☎482 3349). Their guides, decked out in full Edwardian costume, are extremely knowledgeable and will lead you through the lavish grounds and mansions, some of which are quite inspired. You can walk the routes covered by the tours unguided, but without any access to the houses (the *Trust* publish a walking tour guide which you can pick up quite cheaply).

For your own tour, a good place to start is **Ridge Road**, just north of the Randjeslaagte beacon, which marks the northern point of old Johannesburg. To get there, turn north off Louis Botha at Boundary Road, which is a small road that is easily missed, and take the second left. The best of the houses on this street are **The View** at no. 18, built in 1897, with carved wooden verandahs and an elegant, red-brick exterior. Next door, **Hazeldene Hall** was built in 1902 and features cast-iron verandahs imported from Glasgow. Turning north into **York Road** will take you past **Sunnyside Hotel**, a massive complex which Lord Alfred Milner used as his governor's residence from 1900. The road curves to the left into Jubilee Road, with several palaces on its northern side; the neo-Queen-Anne-style **Emoyeni**, at no.15, built in 1905, is especially striking. At the corner of Jubilee Road and Victoria Avenue stands **Dolobran**, a weird and impressive house, also built in 1905, and with a perfect verandah, wonderful red-brick chimneys, red Marseilles roof tiles, and hallucinatory stained glass.

Crossing over the busy N1 onto **Rock Ridge Road**, you'll reach the **Northwards Mansion**, home of the Parktown Trust, and built by Sir Herbert Baker in 1904. Baker's

NORTHERN SUBURBS

ACCOMMODATION

1 Backpackers' Ritz
2 Highgate Guest House
3 Kew Youth Hostel
4 The Michelangelo
5 Romney Cottage
6 The Rosebank Cottage
7 Sandton Sun & Sandton Towers
8 Zoo Lodge

SIR HERBERT BAKER

South Africa's most famous architect, **Sir Herbert Baker**, was born in Kent, England, in 1862. The young Baker's training included apprenticing to his architect uncle in London at the age of 17, and attending classes at the Royal Academy and Architectural Association, where he took care to make the contacts he would use so skilfully in later life. By the time he left for the Cape in 1892, Baker was already a convert to the new so-called **Free Style**, which advocated an often bizarre, but roughly historical eclecticism. The young architect's favourite influences, which would crop up again and again in his work, were Renaissance Italian and medieval Kentish.

Once in the Cape, Baker met up with **Cecil Rhodes**, and this connection, assiduously cultivated, established him as a major architectural player. The second Anglo-Boer War began in 1899 and Rhodes, assuming eventual British victory, sent Baker off to study the classical architecture of Italy and Greece, hoping that he would return able to undertake the mission of creating a British imperial architecture in South Africa. Baker returned to South Africa deeply influenced by what he had seen. He was summoned by **Lord Alfred Milner**, the administrator of the defeated Transvaal, to fulfil Rhodes' hopes, and took up the challenge with enthusiasm. Baker began with the homes of the so-called "kindergarten": the young men, mostly Oxford- and Cambridge-educated, whom Milner had imported to bring British-style "good governance" to the defeated territory. The result was the **Parktown mansions**, the opulent houses which line the roads of Johannesburg's wealthiest suburb. In adherence to the architectural creeds he had learnt in England, Baker trained local craftsmen and used local materials for these mansions. He also pioneered the use of local *koppie* stone, lending a dramatic aspect even to unadventurous designs.

Baker's major public commissions were the **St George's Cathedral** in Cape Town, the **South African Institute for Medical Research** in Johannesburg, and the sober, assertive **Union Buildings** in Pretoria, which more than any other building express the British imperial dream – obsessed with classical precedent, and in a location chosen because of its similarity to the site of the Acropolis in Athens.

Baker left South Africa in 1913 to design the Secretariat in New Delhi, India. He returned to England on its completion, where he worked on South Africa House in Trafalgar Square, London, and was knighted in 1923. He died in 1946, and is buried in Westminster Abbey.

own residence is further along the road at no. 5, with a weighty wooden door at its entrance and a Roman-style atrium on the second floor. Rock Ridge leads to Eton Road and more Baker works: the attractive **St George's Church** and its rectory, which mix Kentish and Italian features and were built in local rock.

Zoo Lake, Houghton and Rosebank

Roughly 2km north of Parktown, off Jan Smuts Avenue, **Johannesburg Zoo** (daily 8.30am–5.30pm; admission fee), is home to over three thousand species, including polar bears. Despite recent attempts at revitalization, a sad air pervades, making this a good place for a melancholic wander, but not much else. Next door, and of greater interest, is the **National Museum of Military History** (daily 9am–4.30pm; small entry fee), where amongst the tanks, guns and uniforms you'll find a small gesture to the new government in the form of a display on **Umkhonto we Sizwe (MK)**, the armed wing of the ANC, although the other liberation armies are conspicuous by their absence. The display focuses on the wing's commander, Joe Modise, now Minister of Defence. Opposite the zoo, on the west side of Jan Smuts Avenue, is the artificial but pleasant **Zoo Lake**. The park here is a popular walking spot and hosts an all-day music event every September during the "Arts Alive" festival.

Moving east towards the lower end of **Houghton**, there's another green oasis in the **Houghton Wilds**. Far from wild, this is in fact a landscaped park covering rugged *koppie* outcrops either side of Houghton Drive (also known as the M31), just south of the junction with the M1. The park is excellent for strolling (but definitely not for women alone). You can follow a good trail northwards from the Wilds that runs along the Sandspruit stream to the **James and Ethel Gray Park**. Named after a city councillor and his historian wife, this contains the **Polish Memorial**, which is dedicated to the victims of Stalin's Katyn massacre of 1940 in Poland. There is a restful bird sanctuary, too, though it is not immune to the traffic roar. You can continue the trail from here into Sandton and beyond. Houghton is one of Johannesburg's wealthiest and greenest suburbs, and is where Nelson Mandela lives. Interestingly, it was the only constituency in the country to return an anti-apartheid MP, Helen Suzman, between 1961 and 1974.

Just north of Houghton, and west of Oxford Road, **Rosebank** is Johannesburg's best place to shop. The suburb brims with upmarket restaurants, shops and commercial galleries. Every Sunday, the **Rooftop Market** in the main mall at 50 Bath Ave offers a good selection of stalls and performance artists. The **Everard Read Gallery**, on the corner of Bath and Bolton roads (Mon–Sat 10am–7pm), has beautiful arts and crafts too, but is expensive. The **Jeffrey Sharpe Rare Books and Maps** shop, on the upper level of the mall on Cradock Avenue (Mon–Fri 9am–5pm, Sat 9am–1pm), sells fascinating Africana.

Melville

By far the most appealing of the northern suburbs, **Melville** lies west of Parktown and is best reached by car from the Kingsway Road (the western extension of Empire Road). The suburb's villagey atmosphere has proved highly attractive to the stressed ranks of Johannesburg's upwardly mobile, who are steadily buying up the property here. The main streets, especially 7th Street, are worth lingering in for their inviting coffee shops, restaurants, second-hand bookshops and quirky antique dealers.

The **Melville Koppies Nature Reserve**, just north of the suburb, contain archeological remains of both stone and Iron Age settlements, including smelters, which can be viewed on the third Sunday of every month, between September and May (☎782 7064). Plans are afoot to develop this valuable site and increase access. The reserve is part of the large Jan Van Riebeeck Park, that runs north and west for several kilometres, and also contains the **Johannesburg Botanic Gardens** in its northeast corner. Bonsai and herbal gardens, and a 24-acre rose garden (allegedly the largest in the world), plus plenty of open space, makes this a good place for walks and picnics.

Sandton and Randburg

Some 10km up the Oxford Road, **Sandton** is the archetypal northern suburb. It is outrageously rich, with plush shopping centres and endless rows of lavish houses protected by sophisticated security systems. A stroll through the vast **Village Walk Shopping Centre**, on the corner of Rivonia Road and Market Street, is perhaps the best way to appreciate the wealth of this suburb. Keep an eye out for the popular, TV-dominated *Sports Café*, which turns raucous and occasionally violent during big rugby games.

Further west, fast-developing **Randburg** is known primarily for its **Waterfront** on Republic Road. Themed restaurants, bars, amusement arcades and shops have been built around an artificial lake, along with cinemas and a flea market. Unusually for Johannesburg, some of the development is aimed at children; otherwise it's unexceptional.

Alexandra

The contrast between **Alexandra** (just east of the M1) and the suburbs that surround it could hardly be greater. This intensely crowded, desperately poor black township somehow avoided the forced removals of former governments. Despite the simple grid design its map suggests, the township is actually a bewildering maze of smashed-up streets, filled to bursting point with people.

Alexandra's overcrowding has worsened since the mass influx of Mozambican informal dwellers (squatters) in the late 1980s. The squatters' shacks, known to Alexandrans as *Maputo*, are perched precariously on the banks of the Jukskei River, which runs through the township, and get swept away in heavy rains. Politically militant since the **bus boycotts** of the 1940s, when mass action here prevented bus companies from raising their fares, Alexandra has long been an ANC stronghold, and paid dearly for it until the collapse of apartheid. Political violence is now a thing of the past, but the deprivation and crime remain; this is not a place to visit without a local guide. The inaccessibility is frustrating, as Alexandra has the best nightlife in the northern suburbs and good street markets. If you can't visit in person, tuning into its entertaining community radio station will at least give you a feel of this lively, though poverty-stricken suburb (see p.476).

The south

The suburbs immediately **south of the city centre** were traditionally the preserve of the white working class, but since the repeal of the Group Areas Act in 1990 blacks have started moving in, and, unusually in contemporary South Africa, many are wealthier than the original residents. Aside from **Gold Reef City** and **Soweto**, the only attraction of this area is the sizable **Klipriviersberg** nature reserve, just south of the N12, in Winchester Hills. Few Johannesburgers know about this undeveloped, unspoilt parkland, which provides wonderful views of the city to the north. To get there, take the N1 heading south, turn left into Columbine Avenue (M68), and then right a kilometre or two further, at Ormonde Street.

Gold Reef City

Gold Reef City (daily except Mon 9am–5pm; R40), 15km south of the city centre, is where old Johannesburg meets Disneyland; a large, gaudy entertainment complex built around the old no. 14 shaft of the Crown Mines. If you can take the overall tackiness and piped ragtime music, there are some points of interest at what is essentially a theme park, notably the **old gold mine** itself, which you can descend 200m into and get at least an inkling of how it is to work underground. Keep an eye out, too, for the tribal dancing that happens five times a day, as the dancers are excellent, even if their routines are a travesty of the real thing.

The museums dotted around the complex are generally disappointing, with the possible exceptions of those dedicated to early Johannesburg, such as Olthaver and Nourse House. Otherwise, the most enjoyable thing to do in Gold Reef City is check out the **rides** (all included in the entrance ticket): easily the best are "The Golden Loop" and "Thunder Mountain". In the unlikely event that you want to stay the night, the *Gold Reef City Hotel* (☎496 1626; ⑦) offers Victorian-themed decor, complete with a saloon, mock-oil lamps, and four-poster beds in the bedrooms. The restaurant serves a decent though pricey buffet.

To get to Gold Reef City, take the M1 heading south, and turn off at the Xavier Street off-ramp. Otherwise, join one of the many tours that go there, who advertise in nearly every hotel lobby.

Soweto

South Africa's most famous township, **Soweto** (short for "South West Townships") is home to its most extreme contrasts. The area has produced more Nobel Peace Prize winners than anywhere else in the world, yet suffers the highest rates of murder and

VISITING SOWETO

The best – and safest – way to **visit Soweto** is with a tour operator. By far the oldest, biggest and slickest operation is *Jimmy's Face to Face Tours*, Budget House, 130 Main St, Johannesburg (☎331 6109, fax 331 6209). Jimmy pioneered tours into the township, and his operation has grown steadily over the years. *Imbizo Tours* (☎ & fax 838 2667) run by the irrepressible Mandy Mankazana, provides stiff competition. Mandy is a mine of information and contacts, and her three-hour day tours and four-hour night tours of Soweto are excellent. Tours can also be customized, and *Imbizo* also organize evening *shebeen*-crawls. These can last up to five hours, depending on your stamina. Indicate what kind of company you would like to keep, from politicians to sports fanatics, and Mandy will select an appropriate *shebeen*.

Abantu Tours (☎648 7066, fax 648 2186) are another good company who offer jazz tours around clubs and stays with local people. For more politically orientated visits, contact *Tebu Travel Tours*, at the Tourist Rendezvous, on the corner of Prinsloo and Vermeulen streets, Pretoria (☎012/326 2875, fax 012/326 2821). The staff are well-briefed on the social and political realities of Soweto, and their tours can take you to hospitals and community centres, and elsewhere if you have a special interest, as well as the usual tourist highlights. *Tebu* can arrange private **accommodation** in Soweto and several other townships.

If you're **travelling to Soweto alone**, you can get there from town by a number of routes. Minibus taxis depart from the Carlton Centre on Commissioner Street all the time, but only travel this way if you're with a local, or being met at the taxi stop in Soweto. A number of roads lead to Soweto from the N1/M1, which runs from north to south through Johannesburg, and the N12, which runs east to west south of the city centre. There is also the Soweto Highway, or M70, which is what the minibus taxis use. This is most easily reached by travelling south down Simmonds Street in town, and then following signs to the M70.

rape; it is the richest township in South Africa, but has some of the most desperate poverty; it is the most political township, yet has the most nihilistic youth.

Soweto is huge, stretching as far as the eye can see, and divided into many neighbourhoods. On first sight it appears as an endless jumble of houses and shacks, overshadowed by palls of smoke. Once inside, parts of it have a villagey feel, especially if you are exploring by foot and, unlike anywhere else in Johannesburg, in Soweto people will often stop to greet you or to chat, regardless of your colour. As a visitor, though, you'll definitely need a guide, and not just for security reasons; the lack of obvious landmarks amidst the mile upon mile of bungalows can be highly confusing.

Unless you have a reliable connection in Soweto, the best way of seeing the township is via one of the many specialist **tours** now operating (see box above). For a reasonable sum, these will take you around the sites for between three and five hours, and some can arrange private accommodation.

Most of Soweto's tourist highlights are famous for purely historical reasons and are physically unimpressive. **Freedom Square** in Dube, for example, where the ANC's Freedom Charter was proclaimed to thousands in 1955, is now a scrawny wasteland near a taxi rank (though there are plans to upgrade it). Rather more striking are the **mansions** of the township's rich and famous, such as the Mandelas, Archbishop Desmond Tutu, and chat-show queen Felicia Mabuza-Suttle. They aren't open to the public, and their walls are high, affording a limited view. Winnie Mandela, however, has been known to have an open house at Christmas. Incidentally, in 1997, plagued by debts, she began bottling and selling soil from the Mandela garden to tourists.

The remains of the **Credo Mutwa Village** are in Dobsonville, northwest Soweto. You will need a guide to make sense of the weird statues and carvings, which Mutwa used to symbolize the mysteries of African religions. The village was attacked by students in 1976 for allegedly promoting tribalism, and has since been abandoned. Its huts and carvings are burnt and blackened, lending the village an eerie atmosphere.

The Johannesburg City Council has worked out a four-hour **hiking trail** that takes you into parts of the township not covered by the tours. Though rarely beautiful, and taking you through much litter and pollution, the trail is a fascinating experience, and enables you to meet many Sowetans, who generally express surprise, interest and hospitality. White non-residents have walked it, and no mishaps have been reported. Just stay alert, look confident and have a good map handy. The trail follows the Umhlangini tributary of the River Klip, starting at the Ipelegeng Anglican Centre (☎982 7612). This is at the junction of the Moroka and Phake roads, that separate Dube from Jabavu. From here, the journey follows the river west, through Jabavu, and then Zondi. At the railway line, the tour detours away from the river, north to Zondi Hill, and then snakes down to join the Motsamai stream, as it runs

THE SOWETO UPRISING OF 1976

The **student uprising** that began in Soweto in June 1976 was a defining moment in South African history. The revolt was sparked off by a government ruling that **Afrikaans** should be used on an equal basis with English in black secondary schools. Whilst this was feasible in some rural areas, it was quite impossible in the townships, where neither pupils nor teachers knew the language.

On June 16, student delegates from every Soweto school launched their long-planned mass protest march through the township and rally at the Orlando football stadium. Incredibly, details of the plan were kept secret from the omnipresent *impimpis* (informers). Soon after the march started, however, the police attacked, throwing tear gas and then firing. The crowd panicked, and demonstrators started throwing stones at the police. The police fired again. Out of this bedlam came the famous photograph of Hector Peterson, bleeding at the mouth, being carried by a friend, while a young girl looks on in anguished horror.

The police retreated to Orlando East, and students rushed to collect the injured and dead, erect barricades, and destroy everything they could belonging to the municipal authority, including beer halls. The attacks heightened the antagonism between the youth and many older people who thought that class boycotts were irresponsible given the students' already dismal employment prospects. Students responded angrily, accusing their elders of inactivity in the face of oppression, which they attributed in part to drunkenness. In a society that has traditionally regarded respect of the old by the young as sacrosanct, this was an historic departure and its effects still reverberate throughout South Africa's townships.

In the days following June 16, all Soweto schools were closed indefinitely, thousands of police were stationed throughout the township, and police brutality continued unabated. In the face of worldwide condemnation, the government insisted that there was no real problem, ascribing the violence to communist agitation. As evidence, it cited the clenched-fist salutes of the students, though this was really an indication of their support for the Black Consciousness Movement, founded by Steve Biko (see p.302). Meanwhile, rebellion spread to other townships, particularly in Cape Town. In Soweto, schools did not reopen until 1978, by which time many students had abandoned any hope of formal education. Some had left the country to join the military wings of the ANC and PAC. Others stayed at home, forming "street committees" to politicize and police the communities. Others drifted into unemployment.

Now the armed struggle is over, the problems that face the students of 1976 are manifold. As their parents warned, their lack of qualifications count against them in the job market, even if June 16 is now a national holiday, during which they are praised for their role in the struggle. The street committees have dissolved, but the guns remain. This generation needs better prospects if these weapons are ever to be silenced.

down through Zola and Naledi. The trail ends some way from where it starts, leaving you with little option but to retrace your steps to get back. Details of the hike may be found in "Johannesburg Trails", a leaflet only available from the Civic Centre in Braamfontein.

Also not included on the tourist itineraries, but vital to an understanding of Soweto, are its countless thousands of **churches**. Alongside all the major denominations, there are a host of smaller ones, mostly centred around a charismatic pastor. Church services in Soweto, as in all townships, are friendly affairs, with liberal doses of fantastic music and, depending on the denomination, religious ecstasy too. They are the most reliable places to make friends in Soweto you can trust. Be prepared to give at least a small testimony (a brief rundown of your spiritual life to date). Services last several hours, but no one will think it a crime if you leave before the end.

Eating and drinking

Despite the multiracial nature of Johannesburg, cultural interaction was obstructed for so long that a cuisine unique to the city has never emerged. However, you will have no problem finding almost every variety of food – and French, Italian and Portuguese **restaurants** are particularly popular. Service almost everywhere is famously poor, but complaining can help. For eating on the run, keep an eye out for *African Hut*, a take-away chain with exotic African delicacies such as tripe and ox hoof, and *Nando's*, a great Portuguese takeaway with outlets all over the city.

Not surprisingly for a city with such tough mining origins, **drinking** has always played a major part in Johannesburg's social life, often to the exclusion of all else. In most cases, bars are still male-dominated and for regulars only, but things are changing, especially in mixed areas like Yeoville. You'll find plenty of bars in Hillbrow, Berea and Troyeville, while in the northern suburbs you'll need to look for them in shopping centres.

CBD and Braamfontein

Countless takeaways and fast-food outlets serve the thousands of office workers in the **CBD** and **Braamfontein**, but there are also a few good restaurants and bars worth searching out. **Chinatown** in the CBD is a reliable stand-by if you get stuck, and most of the CBD's hotels have decent, if unimaginative restaurants attached.

Gramadoelas at the Market Theatre, Wolhuter St, Newtown (☎838 6960). Pleasant and popular spot specializing in Cape and African dishes, but not cheap. Closed Sun.

Hotel School Restaurant, 231 Smit St, Braamfontein (☎406 2954). Highly motivated chefs and waiters make up for any deficiencies in the end results, which are inexpensive, interesting and usually tasty. Closed Sat, Sun & during Technikon recesses.

Three Ships, *Carlton Hotel*, Main St, CBD (☎331 8911 ext 250). French-based cuisine, and there's always a special. A seven-course splurge is surprisingly reasonable. Closed lunch Sat, all day Sun & Mon.

Tong Lok, 7 Commissioner St, CBD. One of the best restaurants in Chinatown, and inexpensive too. Try *custard kok, beef congee* and other specialities. Closed Sun.

Yeng Chen Noodle Den, corner of Commissioner and Alexander streets, CBD. Small, inexpensive restaurant in Chinatown which is ideal for lunches if you're in the area.

Northern suburbs

The **northern suburbs** have Johannesburg's highest density of pleasant cafés and restaurants, many of them tucked away in shopping malls. You'll find places to suit most budgets, and everything from Italian to sushi, with an especially good selection of French restaurants.

Bodega, Standard Bank Building, corner of Tyrwhitt and Cradock avenues, Rosebank (☎447 3210). Reasonable, fairly priced Mediterranean food at this swish restaurant where diners come to see and be seen. Closed Sun.

The Bohemian, 5 Park Rd, Richmond. Just north of Empire Rd, near Melville. Unpretentious pool saloon serving up cheap, good Portuguese food. No cards.

The Carnivore, Muldersdrift Estate (☎957 2099). On the DF Malan extension, past Randburg and Honeydew. Join white South Africans as they guzzle crocodile, giraffe, ostrich and buffalo, along with more humdrum fleshy fare. As much as you can eat for a reasonable set price.

Catz Pyjamas, 7 Main Rd, Melville. Nothing impressive about the food or prices, but it's open 24hr a day, and draws an attractive crowd.

The Codfather, The Pavilion, Rivonia Rd, Morningside. Just north of Sandton, this take-away fish shop prepares your choice of fish on the spot, and the results are delicious. Open daily.

Cranks, The Mall, Cradock St, Rosebank (☎880 3442). Excellent, good-value Thai and Indonesian cooking. Some of the sauces are for sale and well worth buying.

Daruma, Park Gallery, Corlett Drive, Melrose North (☎447 2260). Popular and pricey Japanese restaurant serving wonderfully fresh food (especially the sushi) in elegant, authentic surroundings. Closed Mon & lunch Sun.

Hard Times Café, corner of 6th Ave and 5th streets, Melville. Nice quiet café, with a good pinball machine.

Isle de France, Cramerview Centre, 277 Main Rd, Bryanston (☎706 2837). In the far northern suburbs, just south of the N1 ring road. Expect expensive, excellent French provincial cooking in pleasant, spacious surroundings. Closed Sat lunch.

Koala Blu, 9 7th St, Melville (☎482 2477). Fashionable restaurant serving fine Thai food in a relaxed setting. The chicken with cashew nuts is outstanding.

Linger Longer, 58 Wierda Rd West, Wierda Valley West, Sandton (☎884 0465). Very classy French cuisine from an award-winning chef. Closed Sun & lunch Sat.

Maasai Boma, Shop 4, Rosebank Blvd, 189 Oxford Rd (☎788 5981). Good Kenyan restaurant, with live music on Fridays. Open daily.

Ohsho, Upper Level, Rosebank Mall, Rosebank (☎442 9109). Exquisitely prepared (and expensive) Japanese food in stylish and comfortable surroundings.

Osteria Tre Nanni, 9 Grafton Ave, Parktown North (☎327 0095). Near Zoo Lake, this is one of Jo'burg's best Italian restaurants, with a wide range of authentic food from northern Italy, and a comfortable ambience. Great home-made *grappa* liqueurs round off the evening. Book ahead.

Radium Beer Hall, 282 Louis Botha Ave, Orange Grove (☎728 3866). More famous as a pub and club, but the varied menu offers a steady stream of inexpensive specials, and is particularly good for fish. Closed Sun.

The Ritz, 17 3rd Ave, Parktown North (☎880 2470). The Franco-Italian dishes are quite expensive, but tastily creative. Closed lunch Sat, all day Sun.

Le Samovar, Hutton Court, Jan Smuts Ave, Hyde Park (☎788 3651). Just north of Rosebank, this very chic eating spot is ideal for breakfast, lunch and vodka. Closed Sun pm.

Sam's Café, 11 7th St, Melville (☎726 8142). Mostly Mediterranean dishes that are reliably tasty and very good value (particularly the specials). Closed lunch Sat, all day Sun.

San Francisco Coffee Shop, corner of 3rd Ave and 7th St, Melville. Good internet café, with small record shop attached, and reliably good coffee.

Shamiyana, 71 Corlett Drive, Bramley (☎786 8810). Reliable Indian cuisine with a good mix of inexpensive mild and hot dishes.

Willoughby & Co, Hyde Park Corner, Hyde Park (☎447 5187). A wide selection of fresh fish cooked with considerable panache, for moderate prices. Closed Mon dinner, all day Sun.

Zoo Lake, Zoo Lake, Parkview (☎646 2991). Smart though over-hyped restaurant in a splendid location. The game dishes and flambés are good, the wine list superb, and the final bill substantial. Closed dinner Sun, all day Mon.

Eastern suburbs

The **eastern suburbs** are where you'll find Johannesburg's best-value restaurants and most of its hippest bars. **Yeoville** and **Troyeville** are the areas to head for; Yeoville for its wide range of international cuisine and lively bars, and Troyeville for its very decent Portuguese restaurants, and somewhat more staid bars.

Arena Restaurant, corner of Derby and Bertrams streets, Bertrams. Neon-lit, popular black restaurant and bar. There's little choice, but the food is inexpensive and reliable, and the beer plentiful. No credit cards.

Bob's Bar, 76 Op de Bergen St, Troyeville. Late-night, well-decorated haunt of Troyeville's white alternative set. Screens B-movies at weekends. Closed Tues.

Gerhard's Bar, 128 Sivewright Ave, New Doornfontein. The walls of this old bar are covered in wonderful original photographs of Johannesburg, perfectly complementing its white, older clientele.

Gillooly's, Gillooly's Farm, Boeing Rd, Bedfordview (☎453 8066). The moderately priced food is nothing special, but the setting certainly is: an old Cape Dutch-style farmhouse, set in a pleasant open space.

Hearts 'n' Bones, 414 Commissioner St, on the corner of Grace, Fairview. Well-stocked bar, with a perfect balcony view of Johannesburg. Full of *boikies* (white, beery, cheery types), especially at weekends.

Iyavaya, 42 Hunter St, Yeoville (☎648 3500). Great atmosphere, a range of good-value African dishes and beverages, and a mixed clientele.

Milky Way Internet Café, 206 Times Square Building, on the corner of Raleigh and Fortesque streets, Yeoville (☎487 3608). On the second floor of the building, this feels more like an office than a café, but you can get food sent up from the *Time Square Café* below. Suitably ambient music, while you email away. Open daily until 8.30pm.

Mira D'Aires, Bertrams Spar Centre, Bezuidenhout St, Lorentzville. Good, inexpensive Portuguese restaurant in an unpromising venue. All the usual dishes, cooked with a genuine touch. Open daily.

The Portal, 430 Commissioner St, Troyeville. Perfect view of Johannesburg from this hip white-dominated bar, that heaves at weekends. Open daily until very late.

Rooftop Bar, 26 Rockey St, Yeoville. Above *Tandoor's*. Reliably grooved music, a pool table, pinball and mixed clientele, on a roof. Open daily.

Slowcoach, 65 Raleigh St, Yeoville. Calm 1940s station carriage, and a good antidote to the street. Open until midnight. Closed Mon.

Solar da Velha, corner of Princess and Beelaerts streets, Troyeville. Well-loved by the Portuguese community, particularly at lunchtime, for its inexpensive traditional dishes. Open daily.

Tre Gatti, 28a Bezuidenhout St, Troyeville. Portuguese-owned, but also serving inexpensive, good-quality Italian food, to eat in or take away. Closed Mon.

Two Plus One, 65 Op de Bergen St, Fairview. Brightly lit Portuguese canteen in a superb building, with a local clientele and good prices. Reliable dishes, particularly the chicken, and a good cabbage soup for starters, which is on the house.

Time Square Café, Time Square, Raleigh St, Yeoville. Tolerable Yugoslav and Israeli cuisine, in a café which stays open until 3am.

Southern and western suburbs

Decent restaurants are thin on the ground in the **southern suburbs**. What you'll find instead, especially in **Soweto**, are some great **bars**, ranging from the most basic to the fantastically opulent. The **western suburbs**, meanwhile, are home to a handful of classic Portuguese and Indian restaurants.

Blue Fountain, Mapetla, Soweto. Run by the notorious Godfrey Moloi, with a fountain in the middle, mirrors, rows of spirits, ice-cold beers, and a young, chic crowd.

Delhi Palace, 41 Central Rd, Fordsburg (☎838 6740). Near the Oriental Plaza and Newtown, this is one of the few good Indian restaurants in town, serving excellent tandooris and northern Indian dishes. No alcohol. Closed Mon.

555, Moletsani, Soweto. Informal, young people's *shebeen*, with a mix of soul and *kwaito* playing on the sound system. Attracts rival posses but remains calm nonetheless.

Pappies Tavern, Dlamini II, Soweto. Excellent *shebeen*, with a relaxed, soul-oriented music policy, and a good-humoured crowd.

Parreirinha & La Rochelle Beerhall, 9 6th St, La Rochelle. South of the CBD, serving up classic, moderately priced Portuguese cooking, in a down-to-earth, authentic setting. To get there, follow Van Wieligh St out of the CBD all the way down to La Rochelle.

Wandi's, Dube, Soweto. Classic *shebeen*, deservedly visited by every tour operator, yet still used by locals, for its good food.

Entertainment, nightlife and culture

Johannesburg has always had the best **entertainment** and **nightlife** in South Africa: the city draws top performers from all over the world, and its audiences are the most sophisticated around. Finding out **what's on** requires a bit of persistence, as there's no decent listings magazine. The *Mail & Guardian* publishes a sketchy weekly guide in print, while the Johannesburg Publicity Association's *Johannesburg Alive* can be helpful. For more alternative goings-on, a new magazine called *Get the Funk Out* aspires to cover the city's music scene. You'll find FM radio stations the best guide (see p.476). Tickets for most events can be booked from *Computicket* (☎445 8000).

Live music: jazz, blues and rock

Although Johannesburg dominates the South African **music scene**, the city's lack of venues means there isn't always good music on, even at weekends. Large concerts tend to happen at the Standard Bank Arena in Ellis Park or the FNB Stadium on the way to Soweto. Medium-sized acts generally play in the Newtown Cultural Precinct, especially at the *Megamusic Warehouse*. Newtown is also the place to find **jazz**, while **kwaito** bands pull enthusiastic crowds in Hillbrow and Yeoville. Music from the rest of Africa is filtering through slowly, with **Congolese bands** gigging regularly. In Soweto, live music is scarce due to a venue shortage, but there are hundreds of excellent clubs and all-night street parties.

CBD, Newtown and Braamfontein

Heart of Africa Brewpub, Market Theatre/Newtown Cultural precinct, corner of Bree and Wolhuter streets (☎838 6734). Has a solid reputation for reliable jazz and good beer.

Kippies, Market Theatre/Newtown Cultural Precinct, corner of Bree and Wolhuter streets (☎834 4714). *Kippies* has played host to South Africa's finest jazz acts for years, and continues to do so – not bad for a former municipal toilet. It's tiny, so bands are best seen during the week.

Megamusic Warehouse, Market Theatre/Newtown Cultural Precinct, corner of Bree and Wolhuter streets (☎834 2761). With good acoustics, but lousy ventilation, this venue attracts some excellent and varied acts, such as Mahlathini and Busi Mhlongo.

Wings Beat Bar, 8 Ameshof St, Braamfontein (☎339 4492). Showcases local rock and pop talent, with mixed results but very occasional gems.

Yeoville and Hillbrow

Jahnito's Live House, 43 Rockey St, Yeoville (☎648 9288). At the east end of Rockey St, just before the road turns residential. Small, but squeezes in two stages, one with live Central African sounds, the other playing soul, r&b and rap. Good early evening place to be.

Tandoor, 26 Rockey St, Yeoville (☎487 1569). Yeoville's main live-music venue is pretty good, if a bit seamy. The eclectic music selection veers towards the townships and the Congo.

La Frontière, Pretoria St, Hillbrow (☎642 4938). Next to *Thomas Cook*, and allegedly run by the criminal syndicates, this club features Central African sounds every weekend, and top township bands every Wed. The wide-ranging clientele is as much of a draw as the entertainment, and there's safe parking.

Northern suburbs

Bassline, 7 7th St, Melville (☎482 6915). Small, wine bar-style venue that has the most innovative selection of jazz and African bands in the city, and is reasonably priced.

Illovo Blues Room, Thrupp's Centre, Illovo (☎884 2593). A couple of kilometres north of Rosebank, this is deep in the heart of the northern suburbs, with an occasionally interesting selection of rock, blues and indie bands.

Morgan's Cat, Randburg Waterfront, Randburg (☎886 4408). Rock and pop bands play for free to suburban teenagers in a rather synthetic environment.

Roxy's Rhythm Bar, *Melville Hotel*, 20 Main Rd, Melville (☎726 6019). Veteran establishment hosting local indie bands.

206, 206 Louis Botha Ave, Orange Grove (☎728 5333). Friendly space featuring local and international blues and jazz bands.

Clubs

Johannesburg is the country's most desegregated city, a fact which has improved nightlife greatly. Add to that the stylish fashion sense of many Johannesburg *jollers* ("Good-timers"), and their celebrated love of a party, and you have the main ingredients for a memorable night out. **Hillbrow** and **Yeoville** are the heart of clubland, where you'll find an eclectic mix of disco, soul, hip-hop, *mbaqanga*, *kwaito* and Zairean *soukous*. In the predominantly white **northern suburbs**, rock and indie sounds are what you'll hear.

All-night **raves** take place every weekend in ever more unusual venues. Entrance is expensive, but the sessions go on all night. They are almost exclusively white. Tickets

---

LOCAL RADIO

In 1995, the **airwaves of Johannesburg** and the nation were transformed by the granting of over eighty new licences countrywide. Gauteng received over thirty of them, most of which operate from Greater Johannesburg. All but one are on FM. Reception is often poor, and presentation amateur, but the best stations have an energy and vitality lacking in their more established competitors. They all have community obligations, which are discharged more dutifully by some than by others, but most rely on DJs to attract their audience. The following is a selection of the early frontrunners, and tested favourites.

ALX FM, 89.1FM. Broadcasts out of the Alexandra township and can be picked up in most northern suburbs and some eastern ones. It focuses on township issues, but avoids excessive worthiness, and plays a fine selection of soul, r&b, reggae, *kwaito* and gospel, making it one of the most musically reliable stations around.

Hope FM, 102.2FM. Slick mix of very up-to-date US and South African sounds, with English-speaking DJs, and American evangelism at various points in the evening.

New Panhellenic Voice, 823MW. Broadcasts in vernacular only to Johannesburg's sizable Greek population. Wonderful Greek music is the compensation for those who don't speak the language.

Radio Clube Portuguese, 99.2FM. Broadcasts in Portuguese only, and plays great Portuguese, Spanish and Latin American sounds.

Radio 702, 702MW. Well-established local radio station famed for its lively discussion programmes and excellent presenters. Also good for local news.

Soweto Community Radio, 105.8FM. Features lots of community information and discussion, mostly in African languages and Sowetan slang. There's plenty of excellent South African gospel on Sundays; otherwise, the staples are American soul, *kwaito* and *mbaqanga*. Can only be picked up in Soweto and adjoining suburbs.

Voice of Soweto, 87.6FM. Soweto's finest DJs spin some great sounds. As they say in Jamaica, "a dem have the tunes, sah!", and so they do. Can only be picked up in Soweto and adjoining suburbs.

and information are available from the *Bizarre Centre*, on the corner of Rockey and Raymond streets in Yeoville (☎648 7808).

CBD, Braamfontein, and Newtown

Caesar's Palace, 61 Jorissen St, Braamfontein. Terribly tacky, but somehow perennially fashionable, the *Palace* aspires to Vegas, and plays rock and soul.

Carfax, 39 Pim St, Newtown. Hip venue offering performance art, jazz bands and house sounds.

Club Maputo, corner of Jeppe and Troye streets, CBD. In a crime-ridden part of town, but the club is usually safe, bar the odd fight over the entrance fee. Music policy is one of the best in Jo'burg, with Zairean *soukous, kwaito* and soul.

Doors, 161 Marshall St, CBD. Popular, cavernous club playing hard rock, Goth, and a smattering of ska and reggae, very loudly.

Razzmatazz, corner of Claim and Smit streets, CBD. Fashionable venue filled with beautiful people that stays open late, but lacks the music to keep you there.

Yeoville and Hillbrow

Base, corner of Twist and Kotze streets, Hillbrow. A heavy sound system and an excellent chill-out balcony overlooking the busy street. At weekends, this club pulls a well-dressed, cosmopolitan crowd, and plays soul and *kwaito*. Single women can get pestered.

Champs Elysées, Rockey St, Yeoville. Gay bar with bland decor, house music and outrageous clientele.

Da Flava, Rockey St, Yeoville. Popular venue playing fresh hip-hop, bubblegum and *kwaito* to a well-dressed party crowd.

Piccadilly Café, corner of Rockey and Cavendish streets, Yeoville. Soul, hip-hop, *kwaito*, and occasionally reggae at this garishly decorated venue that draws a hip young black crowd.

Northern suburbs

Krypton, Constantia Centre, Tyrwhitt Ave, Rosebank. Fashionable gay and bi club, but open to all, playing imported house, from garage to trance.

Pearl Harbour, 183 Oxford Rd, Rosebank. Very popular uptown spot, particularly on ladies' nights, when male strippers strut their stuff.

Radium Beer Hall, 282 Louis Botha Ave, Orange Grove. Mixed clientele and a mostly reliable selection of grooves, from rock to soul, and into *mbaqanga* and *kwaito*.

Classical music, film, theatre and dance

The Civic Theatre in Braamfontein is Johannesburg's premier venue for **theatre** and **opera** productions, but there are several other good venues, and the city is blessed with some innovative companies, including the Johannesburg Youth Theatre. South Africa's **National Symphony Orchestra** (☎714 4501) plays regularly at Linder Auditorium in Parktown. Johannesburg **dance** is going through a revival: key players are the Moving into Dance Academy, which is rearing new generations of South African choreographers, and the Dance Factory in the Newtown Cultural Precinct, with several dance companies revolving around it.

Alhambra, Siemert Rd, Doornfontein (☎402 7726). Three theatres in this attractive complex hosting large musicals and shows, from stand-up comedy to drama.

Johannesburg Civic Theatre, Loveday St, Braamfontein (☎403 3408). A good mix of mainstream shows and more adventurous productions at this impressive, four-stage venue.

Market Theatre, Newtown Cultural Precinct, Newtown (☎832 1641). Site of some of Johannesburg's finest performances, and celebrated for its innovative community theatre, and the odd costly epic.

Theatre on the Square, Mutual Square, Oxford Rd, Rosebank (☎442 5752). One of the very few theatres in the northern suburbs, though only open sporadically.

JOHANNESBURG FESTIVALS

Johannesburg is host to regular **festivals** in nearly every artistic field, and these are the most accessible and convenient way of sampling different aspects of the city's cultural life.

Arts Alive Festival, various venues (☎838 4563). The city's major festival for the performing arts takes place over two weeks, mainly in the Newtown Cultural Precinct, but also in some townships. Live music dominates, but dance, cabaret and theatre are also well-represented. "Jazz on the Lake", on Zoo Lake, is a mainstay of the festival, and always features major South African artists in front of big crowds. Every September.

Johannesburg Biennale, various venues (☎838 6407). This event grows continually; the last one involved core exhibitions of fine arts in fifteen venues, and dozens more informal ones, some in community arts centres. Visiting collections from overseas artists sometimes steal the local limelight, but the real revelation is the wealth of South African talent on display. Every October in years ending with an odd number.

FNB Vita Dance Umbrella, Wits Theatre, Braamfontein. The major national platform for South African choreography. Every February and March.

The Windybrow Theatre, Windybrow Theatre, Hillbrow (☎011 720 7009). Annual festival showcasing work generated by the theatre's community programme, which is often brilliant. Every March.

Windybrow Theatre, corner of Nugget and Pietersen streets, Hillbrow (☎720 7009). Staging mainly community theatre, throughout the year. The theatre's finest moment is its arts festival every March.

Film

The multi-screen *Nu-Metro* and *Ster-Kinekor* **cinemas** control the movie market and can be found all over the city, especially in shopping malls. Independent and foreign films can be found at the following:

Mall of Rosebank, corner of Bath and Baker streets, Rosebank (☎880 2866). Presents itself as the *grande dame* of the avant-garde, and screens a hip selection to a discerning audience.

Northcliff, corner of Weltevreden and Arbor streets, Blackheath (☎782 6818). Off DF Malan, just before the N1 highway, showing a good selection of art-house movies.

Sandton Select, Sandton City, corner of Rivonia and Sandton streets, Sandton (☎783 4430). Pleasant cinema with good programme, and surrounded by over twenty other screens showing mainstream movies.

Seven Arts, corner of Grant and William streets, Norwood (☎483 1680). Johannesburg's only independent cinema, run by award-winning cinematographer Italo Bernicchi. A haven for the weird, experimental, old or obscure (sometimes all four at once).

Village Walk Nu-Metro, Village Walk Mall, Rivonia Rd, Sandton (☎883 9558). One arts screen squeezed between the action movies, in a rather nondescript uptown mall.

Shopping

With its vast availability of goods, Johannesburg is a magnet for consumers from all over the subcontinent, who zoom down the highways to stock up before heading back the same day. For visitors, the city is the best place in South Africa to find **arts and crafts**, with excellent flea markets and galleries offering a plethora of goods, some of a very high quality. As the queen of **mall culture**, Johannesburg is also home to over twenty major malls (daily 8am–6pm), most of which are depressingly anonymous. A handful, however (listed below), are so plush and enormous that they merit a visit in their own right.

Malls

Hyde Park Mall, Jan Smuts Ave, Hyde Park. Trendy, upmarket mall awash with swanky cafés and *haute couture* outlets. A highlight here is a branch of the excellent *Exclusive Books* chain.

Randburg Waterfront, on Republic Rd, Randburg. Shopping complex built around an artificial lake, with restaurants, a flea market and a cinema alongside the clothes shops and chain stores.

Rosebank Mall, corner of Baker and Cradock streets, Rosebank. One of the city's nicest malls, with exclusive boutiques, crafts shops and – unusually – outdoor cafés, restaurants and walkways.

Sandton City Shopping Centre, corner of Sandton Drive and Rivonia Rd, Sandton. This enormous mall is worth a visit for its sheer size and mind-boggling abundance of shops, cinemas and attractions, including some good bookshops and African art galleries

Craft shops and markets

Art Africa, 66a Tyrone Ave, Parkview (☎486 2502). Good selection of innovative and more familiar items, with many ingeniously created out of recycled material.

Diagonal Street, CBD. This is the best place in South Africa to buy Sotho blankets, and is also good for *umuthi* medicine, and herbal cures particular to this part of the world.

Jacana, Rosebank Mall, 50 Bath Ave, Rosebank (☎880 5554). Stylish range of high-priced crafts.

M2 Highway, CBD. Informal market stretching for large tracts underneath this major artery, a few blocks south of Anderson St. Most stalls specialize in *umuthi*, but there are plenty of local crafts as well.

Mai Mai Bazaar, Albert St, underneath the M1, CBD. Once a migrants' hostel, now a great daily market selling Zulu crafts, medicines, food and clothes mainly to the local Zulu community.

Market Africa, Newtown. The city's liveliest flea market, next to the Market Theatre. Rifle through colourful blankets from Mali, Congolese masks and statues, and more. Sat 9am–4pm.

Rosebank Rooftop Market, Rosebank Mall, 50 Bath Ave, Rosebank. Reliable and entertaining place where you can browse through an impressive array of cottage-industry crafts and clothes. Sun 9am–5pm.

Zebra Crossing, 20a Rockey St, Yeoville. Good range of African crafts, but can be pricey. Mon–Sat 9am–5pm.

Music shops

Johannesburg is a good place to pick up a wide range of **African music**; the CBD (especially) has dozens of small shops selling cassettes of South African and American sounds. The *Musica* chain of shops are the most prevalent, and concentrate on soul and rock import CDs, with small selections of local music.

Bizarre Centre, corner of Rockey and Raymond streets, Yeoville. Best rave shop in Johannesburg.

Cadence Tropical, Time Square, Yeoville (☎648 7957). Without question South Africa's finest stockist of Central and West African music, and *the* place to find out about clubs currently playing these sounds. Closes at 10pm.

Kohinoor, 54 Market St, CBD. Excellent vinyl selection, as well as a wide range of tapes and CDs. The focus is on jazz, but you'll find all manner of South African styles here, ranging from gospel to *maskanda* and *mbaqanga*.

Record and Tape Centre, 39 Pretoria St, Hillbrow. Wide selection of international and South African music, with a fair amount on vinyl on offer. This is a good place to buy *kwaito*.

Rhythm Records, 28 Van Der Merwe St, Hillbrow. Broad range of rave and dance 12" imports.

Listings

Airlines *Air Afrique*, Sanlam Arena, 10 Cradock Ave, Rosebank (☎880 8537); *Air Botswana*, 301 Administration Building, Johannesburg International Airport (☎975 3614); *Air France*, Oxford Manor, Oxford Rd, Illovo (☎880 8040); *Air Malawi*, Surrey House, 35 Rissik St, Marshalltown (☎331 7627); *Air Namibia*, Dunkeld Place, 12 North Rd, Dunkeld West (☎442 4461); *Air Portugal*, Sanlam Centre, Jeppe St (☎337 3832); *Air Zimbabwe*, Carlton Centre, Commissioner St (☎331 1541);

Alitalia, Oxford Manor, Oxford Rd, Illovo (☎880 9254); *American Airlines*, Dunkeld Crescent (West), Albury Rd, Hyde Park (☎880 6370); *Balkan Airways*, Norwich Life Towers, 13 Fredman Drive, Sandton (☎883 0957); *British Airways*, 158 Jan Smuts Ave, Rosebank (☎441 8600); *Canadian Airlines*, Everite House, De Korte St, Braamfontein (☎339 4865); *Comair*, Rand Airport (☎827 9311); *Gulf Air*, Liberty Life Gardens, Marcia St, Bruma (☎616 7680); *Lesotho Airways*, International Departures, Johannesburg International Airport (☎970 1046); *Lufthansa*, 22 Girton Rd, Parktown (☎484 4722); *Olympic Airways*, JHI House, Cradock Ave, Rosebank (☎880 1614); *Qantas*, Village Walk, Maud St, Sandton (☎884 5300); *Royal Swazi Air*, Finance House, Oppenheimer Drive, Bruma (☎616 7323); *SA Airlink* (☎973 2941) *South African Airways*, Wolmarans St, Braamfontein (☎333 6504); *Sun Air*, Johannesburg International Airport (☎397 2233); *Virgin Atlantic*, Holiday House, H. Verwoed Drive, Randburg (☎886 6261).

American Express Foreign exchange bureau: Admirals Court, Tyrwhitt Ave, Rosebank (Mon–Fri 8.30am–4pm, Sat 9am–noon; ☎880 8382); cards: Nedbank Card division, Centurion House, 35 Melle St, Braamfontein (☎358 4000; after hours 358 5000).

Banks are everywhere, of virtually every international and domestic variety. Banking hours are Mon–Fri 9am–3.30pm, Sat 8.30–11.00am. Foreign exchange is available 24hr at Johannesburg International Airport.

Bookshops *Exclusive* is the best chain, and is well-represented in the northern suburbs. Branches include 30 Hyde Park Corner, Jan Smuts Ave (☎788 0998); Sandton City, Sandton (☎883 1010); and Village Walk, Maude St, Sandton (☎884 7614). For a good second-hand selection try *Yeoville Books*, 27a Rockey St, Yeoville (☎648 2002), or *Huxley's*, 31 Tyrwhitt Ave, Rosebank (☎447 4292), and *Jeffrey Sharpe Rare Books and Maps*, Cradock Ave Mall (☎788 0791), which specializes in Africana. The *Bookdealers* mini-chain specializes in second-hand books and remainders, and is staffed with enthusiasts. Find them at 12 7th St, Melville (☎726 4054) and at 29 Mutual Square, Rosebank (☎442 4089).

Bus companies (intercity) *Greyhound* ☎333 2130; *Intercape* ☎011 333 5231; *Translux* ☎011 774 3313.

Car rental National companies include *Protea* (☎402 6328), *Key* (☎392 2616), *Dolphin* (☎394 6605, or toll free 0800/01 1344), *Imperial* (☎337 2300 or toll free 0800/13 1000) and *Budget* (☎392 3929 or toll free 0800 016 662). For cheaper deals try *Apex* (☎402 5150), *Cheap Car Hire* (☎648 7300), *Afro Auto Rent* (☎792 8240) or *Dorset* (☎614 1177).

Cricket *Wanderers Club*, 21 North St, Illovo, near James and Ethel Gray Park (☎788 5010). Site of international test matches and the perfect place for fans to idle away an afternoon during the cricket season. To get there, head for Corlett Drive, which you can reach either from the M1 or Oxford Road – the cricket ground lies just off here.

Embassies all embassies and consulates are in Pretoria (see p.494).

Emergencies Ambulance ☎999; Police ☎10111; AA Breakdowns ☎0800/01 0101.

Hospitals *Johannesburg Hospital*, Parktown (☎488 4911), *JG Strijdom*, Auckland Park (☎489 1011), *Hillbrow*, Hospital Rd, Hillbrow (☎720 1121), and *Baragwanath*, Zone 6, Diepkloof, Soweto (☎933 1100) are all government-run, and have 24hr casualty departments. The city's top private hospital is *Morningside Clinic*, off Rivonia Rd (☎783 8901), in Morningside, near Sandton. *Millpark Hospital*, Guild St, Parktown (☎480 5600), is another private option.

Pharmacies can be found in every mall and suburban high street.

Post office The oldest and grandest is on the corner of Market and Rissik, in the CBD. Opening hours are Mon–Fri 8am–4.30pm, Sat 8am–noon.

Rugby Ellis Park, just off Bertrams Road in Ellis Park (☎42 8644), is a South African rugby shrine, particularly since the triumph of the national team in the 1995 World Cup. It's also the home ground of the formidable Transvaal team. Ellis Park comes into its own during major fixtures, where the atmosphere is electric. A number of buses run there.

Soccer Johannesburg dominates the South Africa's soccer scene, with the nation's two biggest teams, the Kaiser Chiefs and Orlando Pirates, based in Soweto. The *FNB Stadium*, off the Soweto Highway, on the NASREC road, is the premier venue; tickets are cheap, and there is safe parking. *Orlando Stadium*, in Orlando, Soweto, also hosts major games, though it's more run-down and less safe than the *FNB*.

Swimming Public pools include the superb, outdoor, Olympic-sized Ellis Park pool (Sept–March Mon–Fri 6.30am–9pm, Sat & Sun 6.30am–6pm), and decent pools in Bezuidenhout Park (Sept–March Mon–Fri 9am–5.50pm, Sat & Sun 9am–6pm), on Rockey St in Yeoville (Sept–March Mon–Sat 7.30am–6pm, Sun 8.30am–6pm), and in most middle-class suburbs.

Taxis *Maxi Taxis*, based in Yeoville (☎648 1212), use a rank in Cavendish St. *Rose Radio* (☎725 1111 or 725 3333) and *Good Hope* (☎725 6431) in Hillbrow control most of the market, even in the northern suburbs. There are usually taxis waiting outside the *Carlton*, the *Sandton Sun* and the *Sandton Towers*. If in Randburg, try *Randburg Taxis* (☎792 0189).

Around Johannesburg

Johannesburgers wanting to get away from it all tend to head for the **Magaliesberg Mountain** range, which stretches from Pretoria in the east to Rustenberg in the west. Much of the area is private farmland, but there are numerous resorts and hotels to cater for the weekend crowds.

The **Suikerbosrand Nature Reserve**, 40km south of Johannesburg, is the biggest and best nature reserve in Gauteng, offering interesting archeology and good hikes. Even more impressive, archeologically, are the world-renowned **Sterkfontein Caves**, where 3,000,000-year-old hominid bones were found recently, and the overcommercialized **Kromdraai Caves**, both of which are near the West Rand town of Krugersdorp, near Johannesburg.

Immediately east and west of the city, grim industrial towns such as Boksburg and Springs offer little to entice. The one exception is **Benoni**, in the east, where an excellent mining museum, the **Benoni Museum**, on the corner of Elston Avenue and Rothsay Street (Mon–Fri 9am–4.30pm; free), features intriguing exhibits on mining strikes in the late nineteenth and early twentieth century.

Suikerbosrand Nature Reserve

Though hardly in the same league as the epic parks of Kruger and the like, the **Suikerbosrand Nature Reserve** (Mon–Fri 7.15am–4pm, Sat & Sun 7am–5pm; ☎011/904 3930; entry fee), south of Johannesburg, is attractive nonetheless, and easy to get to from the city. The beautiful Suikerbosrand mountain range dominates the reserve, but you'll find gentle grassland plains too, with antelope, zebra and wildebeest, and even the odd cheetah and leopard.

The **visitors' centre**, at the entrance to the reserve, can supply maps and guidebooks. Next door, the **Diepkloof Farm Museum** is worth a visit, as careful renovation has ensured that the farm buildings look pretty much as they did when they were first built in 1850. The farm was worked by one Gabriel Marais, who participated in the Great Trek, but was burnt by British soldiers in the Anglo-Boer War, and remained neglected until the 1970s, when it was renovated. Most of the exhibits are aimed at Afrikaner children, and try to enthuse them about their fast-disappearing rural culture. However, other brief displays dwell on the sixteenth- to nineteenth-century settlements of Sotho and Tswana people, which were extensive, and have been excavated nearby.

You can **explore the reserve** on foot or by car, following a network of trails. Several hiking trails include overnight accommodation in camps (book at the visitors' centre). Alternatively, you can book out the very basic meditation hut, 18km from the visitors' centre. There's no electricity, but it's definitely quiet and undisturbed.

To get to the reserve and farm, take the N3 south of Johannesburg, and turn right onto the R550. The turn to the reserve is a few kilometres along the road, on your left.

Sterkfontein, Kromdraai and the Rhino Nature Reserve

Just over 40km west of Johannesburg lie the **Sterkfontein Caves** (daily except Mon 9am–4pm; ☎0152/956 6342; entry fee), Gauteng's oldest archeological site. Millions of years old, the caves are believed to have been inhabited by pre-human primates who lived here up to 3.5 million years ago. They first came to European attention in 1896, when an Italian lime prospector, Martinaglia, stumbled upon them. Martinaglia was only interested in the bat droppings, and promptly stripped them of it, thus destroying the caves' dolomite formation. Between 1936 and 1951, archeologist Dr Robert Broom excavated the caves and in 1947 found the skull of a female hominid that was over two million years old. Archeologists have nicknamed it "Mrs Ples". In 1995, another archeologist, Ronald Clark, found "Little Foot", the bones of a 3,000,000 year-old walking hominid, with big toes that functioned like our thumbs do today.

Fossilized wood samples and animal remains suggest that the area was once a tropical forest inhabited by lots of "Little Feet", as well as giant monkeys, long-legged hunting hyenas and sabre-toothed cats. One million years later, in a much drier climate, tool-making hominids had arrived on the scene, along with ostriches, horses and pigs. It seems likely that the caves were still being lived in when Mr Martinaglia came upon them.

Informed **guided tours** every half-hour take you around the main features. **To get to the caves**, travel west out of Johannesburg on the R47, until the R563 junction – about 40km. Turn right, and just over 2km further along is a sign on the right to the caves.

Equally old, but more commercially developed, the **Kromdraai Caves** (daily except Mon 9am–4pm; ☎957 0106), a few kilometres away, are billed as "wonder" caves. Expect carefully placed lighting inside, which often appeals to children, but far less substantial tours. These caves were mined for lime in the 1890s, which killed their dolomite production too. To get there, take the DF Malan Drive out of Johannesburg, and turn left at the Kromdraai junction, some 2km after crossing the R28.

You can also visit the Kromdraai Caves via the **Rhino Nature Reserve** (☎957 0039), which is a very short drive away. The reserve has ten white rhino, and plenty of wildebeest, hartebeest and giraffe, as well as all manner of antelope. It is pleasant, but not likely to hold you for more than an hour or two, though you can stay in a self-catering chalet if you pre-book. The reserve's restaurant serves hearty (if unimaginative) meat dishes.

Magaliesburg Village and around

Named after Mohali Mohale, a chief of the Po clan of the Ndebele people, **Magaliesburg Village** is a functional, though not wildly attractive village, serving its purpose well – that is, providing stressed city-dwellers with accommodation and facilities amid the fresh mountain air. If you plan on a jaunt up here, be sure to book **accommodation** ahead, especially at weekends. The nicest (and priciest) place to stay by far is *Mount Grace*, Rustenburg Rd (☎0142/77 1350, fax 011/880 3282; ⑦–⑧), magnificently located on a hilltop, and offering immaculate and stylish rooms. The restaurants here are superb, and there are outside concerts during the summer. If that's full, you could try the *Magaliesburg Country Hotel*, Rustenburg Rd (☎ & fax 0142/77 1109; ⑥), in the heart of the village, which is comfortable and has a good restaurant. For bed and breakfast, *Out of Africa* (☎ & fax 0142/77 1126; ⑥–⑦) offers luxury cottages by the river, tastefully decked out with antique furniture and original art. More cottages are on offer at *Valley Lodges*, Jenning St (☎0142/77 1301, fax 77 1306; ⑥–⑧).

The village lies on the R24, west of Krugersdorp. For a day-trip from Johannesburg, you can travel here by **steam train**: the *Magalies Valley Steamer* (☎011/773 9238) runs most weekends, and the fares for the three-hour return journey are quite reasonable, with lunch at the *Magaliesburg Country Hotel* included in the price.

PRETORIA

Gauteng's two major cities are just 50km apart, but could hardly be more different. **PRETORIA**, or *ePitoli* as it is known in the townships, has throughout much of its history been the epitome of staid traditionalism, with its graceful government buildings, wide avenues of purple flowering jacarandas, and staunchly Boer farming origins. Yet, although South Africa's administrative capital is seen by many South Africans as a bastion of **Afrikanerdom**, with its notorious supreme court and massive prison, things are changing. Ever since the nation's reacceptance into the international arena, Pretoria has become increasingly cosmopolitan, with a substantial diplomatic community living in Hatfield, east of the city centre. Furthermore, most Pretorians are not Afrikaner, but Sotho and Ndebele, a fact reflected in the ANC's substantial victories in the first democratic local elections of 1995. The city's Afrikaner community is hardly monolithic, either: as well as the stereotypical khaki-shorted rednecks, there are thousands of students, an active art scene and a thriving Afrikaans gay and lesbian community.

Pretoria is near enough to Johannesburg's airport to provide a practical alternative base for exploring Gauteng. The main attractions are that it's safer and less spread out than Johannesburg, and there is at least a sprinkling of things worth seeing. As well as the **Union Buildings** and **Church Square**, **Melrose House** is interesting and the **Police and Correctional Services museums** are compellingly bizarre. The city is unquestionably more boring than Johannesburg, but due to the risks associated with Johannesburg's excitements this is a price you might be willing to pay.

Some history

Unlike Johannesburg, Pretoria developed at a leisurely pace from its humble origins as a **Boer farming community** on the fertile land around the Apies River. When the city was founded in 1855 by **Marthinus Wessel Pretorius**, who named it after his father, Andries Pretorius, it was intended to be a unifying hub around which the new South African Republic (ZAR) would prosper. Embodying the Afrikaner conviction that the land they took was God-given, Pretoria's first building was a church. The town was then laid out in a grid of streets wide enough for teams of oxen brought in by farmers to turn corners.

In 1860 the city was proclaimed the capital of the new ZAR, the result of tireless efforts by Stephanus Schoeman to unite the squabbling statelets of the Transvaal. From this base, the settlers continued their campaigns against local African peoples, bringing thousands into service, particularly on farms. Infighting also continued amongst the settlers, and violent skirmishes between faction leaders were common. These leaders bought most of the best land, resulting in the dispossession and embitterment of many white trekkers, and the large-scale massacre of the wild animals of the region, particularly its elephants.

The British annexed Pretoria in 1877, and investment followed in their wake. Although it prospered and grew, farmer **Paul Kruger**, who was determined not to be subjugated by the British again, mobilized *commandos* of Afrikaner farmers to remove them. This resulted in the first Anglo-Boer War (1877–81). After defeat at Majuba on the Natal border, the colonial government abandoned the war and ceded **independence** in 1884.

Paul Kruger became ZAR president, and ruled until 1903. However, his mission to keep the ZAR Boer was confounded by geology. The discovery of **gold** in the Witwatersrand precipitated an unstoppable flood of foreigners. Kruger's policy of taxing the newcomers, while retaining the Boer monopoly on political power, worked for a while. Most of the elegant buildings of Church Square were built with mining revenues, while the *Raadsaal* (parliament) remained firmly in Boer hands. At the same time, the ZAR's military arsenal grew, largely thanks to imported German weapons.

ZAR independence ended with the second Anglo-Boer War (1899–02), but despite the brutality of the conflict Pretoria remained unscathed. With the creation of the **Union of South Africa** in 1910, the city became the administrative capital of the entire country. In 1913 Sir Herbert Baker built the epic Union Buildings to house the

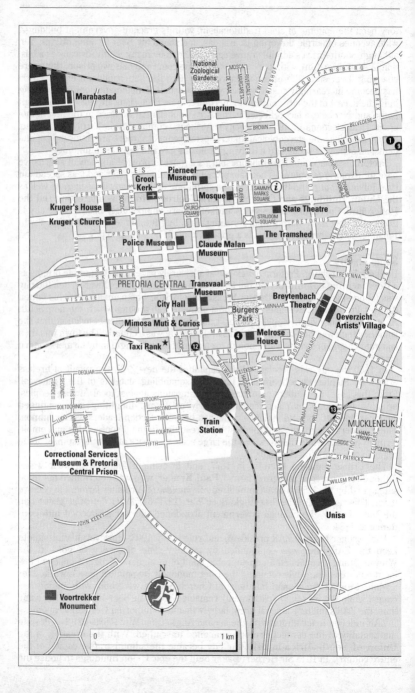

National Zoological Gardens

Marabastad

Aquarium

Pierneef Museum

Groot Kerk

Mosque

Kruger's House

Kruger's Church

State Theatre

Police Museum

Claude Malan Museum

The Tramshed

PRETORIA CENTRAL

Transvaal Museum

City Hall

Burgers Park

Breytenbach Theatre

Oeverzicht Artists' Village

Mimosa Muti & Curios

Melrose House

Taxi Rank

Train Station

Correctional Services Museum & Pretoria Central Prison

MUCKLENEUK

Unisa

Voortrekker Monument

N

0   1 km

PRETORIA

Union Buildings

TOM JENKINS

GOVERNMENT

GOVERNMENT

FAURE

BLACKWOOD

PINE

EAST CLYFFE

EAST

GEORGE

MERTON

THOMAS

PERCH

EASTWOOD

LISDOGAN

BALMORAL

HARCOURT

DUMBARTON

S.WASHINGTON BLVD

THE
WENLOCK

COLROYN

ROTHSAY

KERK

KERK

PRETORIUS

PRETORIUS

ARCADIA

SCHOEMAN

SCHOEMAN

HATFIELD

Pretoria Art Museum

ARCADIA

PARK

BURNETT

PROSPECT

Loftus
Versveld
Stadium

Pretoria
University

TROYE

CELLIERS

ESSELEN

FOURIE

WATER

SPUY

SUNNYSIDE

PARK

LAND

LINDSCHOTEN

VALLEY

MYRTLE

MARK

BRECHER

VILLA

BOND

KRKNES

UNIVERSITY

LYNNWOOD

BROOKS

ANDERSON

MURRAY

COLLEGE

BROOKLYN

MACKENZIE

MARAIS

MARAIS

CHARLES

CAMERON

WILLIAM

LEYDS

DWARS

REL

JORISSEN

REITZ

NEVILLE

TRUMP

RISSIK

WALKER

BEREA

BOURKE

RIDGE

LOVEDALE

MIDDLEBURG

DOUGLAS

SMITH

ORMOND

KRUIN

LUKAS

DEVENISH

ARNOLD

SIBELIUS

LEYDS

NICOLSON

KONGNGN

WITH

MACKIE

BOSHOFF

DR LATEGAN

TOTIUS

GEORGE STORRAR

GEORGE STORRAR

MENNING

VAN WOUW

BRONKHORST

FRANS DERDER

EPROS

ACCOMMODATION

1 Arcadia
2 Batiss Guesthouse
3 Hotel 224
4 Kia Ora Backpackers
5 La Maison
6 Malvern Guesthouse
7 Mazuri Backpackers
8 Mutsago Guesthouse
9 Orange Court Lodge
10 Pretoria Backpackers
11 Ronde Geluk
12 Victoria
13 Word of Mouth Backpackers

Anton Von Wouw Museum

civil service, and some ministries, including the office of the president, are still there today.

In 1928, the government laid the foundations of Pretoria's industry by establishing the **Iron and Steel Industrial Corporation** (Iscor), which rapidly generated a whole series of related and service industries. These, together with the civil service, ensured white Pretoria's quiet, insular prosperity. Meanwhile, increasing landlessness amongst blacks drove many of them into the city's burgeoning **townships**. Marabastad and Atteridgeville are the oldest, and Mamelodi is the biggest and poorest.

After the introduction of apartheid by the National Party in 1948 (see p.654), Pretoria acquired a hated reputation amongst the country's black population. Its **supreme court** and **central prison** were notorious: the source of the laws and regulations that made their lives a nightmare. As the poet **Mzwahke Mbuli** expressed it, in exasperation:

Central Prison – in Pretoria
Pass laws – in Pretoria
Pretoria – why you?

Mandela's inauguration at the Union Buildings in 1994 was the symbolic new beginning for Pretoria's political redemption. The change won't happen over night, but there are signs that things are moving in the right direction, not least in its confident and plausible bid to wrest the nation's parliament from Cape Town.

> The telephone code for Pretoria is ☎012.

Arrival and information

The nearest airport to Pretoria is **Johannesburg International Airport** (see p.452) some 50km away. From here, the only way to reach Pretoria is via one of the hourly *Impala* **buses**, which terminate at the city's Tourist Rendezvous Centre, downtown (see below). The journey takes about an hour. If you're arriving by **train** or intercity bus, you'll alight at the train station on the corner of Shelding and Paul Kruger streets, to the southwest of the city centre.

Pretoria's main point of **information** is the helpful **Tourist Rendezvous Centre** on the corner of Vermeulen and Prinsloo streets (daily 8am–5pm; ☎308 8937), where you should try to pick up *Be My Guest*, a free monthly publication handy for restaurant listings. **Satour** also has its offices in the centre, and can provide information and booking facilities for the whole country (☎323 1432).

City transport

Pretoria's city centre is easily explored on foot, but public transport is useful if you are heading slightly further afield. For journeys to the suburbs, you'll need the municipal **bus** services (information ☎313 0839), which start in **Church Square** and spread outwards. You buy the tickets – which are never more than a few rand – when you get on. Bus timetables are available from Church Square, the buses themselves and from pharmacies.

The best place to catch **minibus taxis** is from the corner of Jacob Maré and Bosman streets, just north of the railway station, though you can hail them from anywhere. As in Johannesburg, you can't hail metered **taxis**, but you'll usually find one at the Tourist Rendezvous (see "Arrival and information", above). Alternatively, cabs can be booked ahead by phone – we've listed some reliable firms in "Listings".

Only consider **car rental** if you are planning trips beyond Pretoria. *Rent-a-jalopy* (☎73 3006) is the cheapest, but it is in Queenswood, some way northeast of the town centre, which is hard to get to. It is easier but more expensive to go for the companies in the town centre (see "Listings", p.494).

Accommodation

Pretoria has plenty of soulless modern hotel complexes that range from the moderately to the expensively priced; the Tourist Rendezvous can provide you with detailed and updated lists. Nicer by far is to stay at one of the few **hotels** and **guesthouses** with genuine character, some of which are listed below. Bear in mind that apart from **Sunnyside** or **Arcadia**, everywhere apart from the townships dies at night. To stay with families in the townships, contact **Tebu Travel Tours** in the Tourist Rendezvous (☎326 2875), who can arrange it for you.

Arcadia Hotel, 515 Proes St (☎326 9311, fax 326 1067). Centrally located but somewhat over-priced, especially as there's no pool. Rooms are are comfortable and the restaurant reliable. ⑦.

Batiss Guesthouse, 3 Fook Island, 92 20th St, Menlo Park (☎ & fax 46 7318). Very comfortable B&B accommodation in the original home of eccentric artist Walter Batiss. Expect brightly painted floors, unusual decorations and a distinctly Greek feel. ⑥.

Hotel 224, corner of Leyds and Schoeman streets (☎44 5281, fax 44 3063). Single and double rooms in this fairly characterful mid-range hotel near the Union Buildings, with a restaurant and bar attached, and safe parking. ④.

Kia Ora Backpackers, 257 Jacob Maré St (☎322 4803, fax 322 4816). Excellent doubles and average dorms in this well-positioned spot next door to Melrose House, with a bar featuring live music. ①–②.

La Maison, 235 Hilda St, Hatfield (☎43 4341, fax 342 1531). Very pleasant guesthouse with immaculately tasteful rooms, lovely gardens and an outstanding restaurant. ⑥–⑦.

Malvern Guesthouse, 575 Schoeman St (☎341 7212). Small B&B handy for Arcadia's restaurants, and popular with students. Rooms are clean, with shared bath, but no TV. ③.

Mazuri Backpackers, 503 Reitz St, Sunnyside (☎ & fax 343 7782). Dorms and doubles at this small, laid-back hostel, with a communal kitchen, email facilities and a friendly owner. ①.

Mutsago Guesthouse, 327 Festival St, Hatfield (☎43 7193, fax 43 7635). Good B&B with pretty rooms and a nice swimming pool, near the university and a large shopping centre. ④–⑤.

Orange Court Lodge, corner of Vermeulen and Hamilton streets, Arcadia (☎326 6346, fax 326 2492). Self-catering suites in one of the oldest buildings in Pretoria. It's pleasant and secluded, despite being off a main road. Breakfast is available, and there's safe parking. ④.

Pretoria Backpackers, 34 Bourke St, Sunnyside (☎343 9754). Well-located for nightlife, and the owner knows the city well. The house is small though, and with so many backpackers about a pool would improve things. Offers daily shuttle to Johannesburg International Airport. ①–②.

Ronde Geluk, 570 Pretorius St, Arcadia (☎344 4850, fax 341 9221). Wonderful thatched cottages hidden away in central Pretoria, each self-contained and beautifully decorated. Breakfast is included in the price. ④.

Victoria Hotel, corner of Scheiding and Paul Kruger streets (☎323 6052). Historic building opposite the railway stataion offering plush accommodation, often filled with upmarket travellers taking luxury trains to Cape Town. ⑧.

Word of Mouth, 145 Berea St, corner of Mears and Muckleneuk (☎341 9661). Popular if cramped dorms and doubles in this two-house backpackers' establishment with a lively atmosphere. Free pick-up from Johannesburg International Airport and Pretoria's railway station is available. ①–②.

The City

Pretoria's city centre is compact grid of wide, busy streets, and is easily explored on foot. Its central hub is **Church Square**, with historic buildings and museums close by. To the north lie the vast Zoological Gardens, well worth a visit, while over in the east the Arcadia district is the site of the city's famous **Union Buildings**. Head south on any of the diagonal streets to explore **Sunnyside**, home to the city's friendliest street culture. Further east, **Hatfield**, close to Pretoria University, is filled with student bars, and is also the home of Pretoria's diplomats, who live in the swankiest houses in town. You need to travel 15km east out of town to find the sprawling township of **Mamelodi**; Pretoria's other major township, **Atteridgeville**, is equally far out of town to the west, off the N4, or R104, on the way to the Hartbeesport Dam and Sun City.

Church Square and the city centre

Attractive, pedestrianized **Church Square** is Pretoria's central point, and a good place to start exploring the city. It was here that Boer farmers *outspanned* their oxen when they came into town for the quarterly *Nagmaal* (Holy Communion) of the Dutch Reformed Church, turning the square temporarily into a campsite. Today this spot continues to be a meeting point for Pretorians, many of whom you'll see lounging in the sun or sipping coffee at *Café Riche*.

Nearly every important white meeting, protest or takeover the city has known happened in Church Square; the ZAR *Vierkleur* ("four colours") flag was lowered here in 1877 to make way for the Union Jack, only to rise again in 1881, after the British eviction from the republic; the British flag flew again in 1900 but was lowered for the last time in 1910; Paul Kruger was proclaimed head of state in the square four times, and 30,000 crammed it in 1904 for his memorial. Such historical resonances are viewed differently by Pretoria's black community, and the square's central **statue of Paul Kruger** – the work of Afrikaner sculptor Anton Van Wouw – is for many an unwanted relic of a dismal past. Van Wouw had to work fast: Kruger hated posing and the sculptor had little time with him. Nevertheless he still managed to produce this frighteningly miserable representation, set above four rugged Voortrekker archetypes.

Look out first for the old **Raadsaal** (parliament) on the southwest corner of the square, built in neo-Renaissance style in 1891, and still exuding the bourgeois respectability yearned for by the parliamentarians of the ZAR. Next door, the **Netherlands Bank Building**, built on the fortunes of the Rand, is one of the square's most impressive buildings. The grandiose **Palace of Justice**, on the northwest side of the square, was started in 1897, and used, half-completed, as a hospital for British troops during the second Anglo-Boer War. After its completion in 1902, the building was home to the Transvaal Supreme Court for many years. The new court is an ugly box which you will find sitting squatly in a street behind the Palace. It's worth going round to the back, as recent demolition has revealed the Palace's original rear facade and a fine balcony.

Sammy Marks Square and around

Moving east from Church Square, along Church Street, will take you towards Sammy Marks Square. Just before you get there, a left turn into Queen Street reveals the unexpected site of a bright white **mosque** sitting askew of its surroundings so as to face Mecca. Pretoria's Muslims, who reportedly got on well with Kruger, acquired the site in 1896, and the current building was constructed in 1927 by Cape artisans. The mosque is now hemmed in by ugly tower blocks, but is somehow all the more indomitable for that.

Garish **Sammy Marks Square** is named after the founder of South African Breweries (SAB), who was a patron of the city. Apart from the chain stores, the only thing worth checking out here is the excellent **library** (Mon–Fri 8am–5.50pm, Sat 8am–12.50pm; ☎313 8956) geared to adult education, with every available space decked out in Pretoria's trademark purple.

Cross Church Street for a brief taste of ghastly **Strijdom Square**, dominated by a vast and horrific bust of the man himself, encased in a modernistic arch. Prime minister from 1954 to 1958, Strijdom strongly supported apartheid and was a firm believer in "white supremacy". Some say it's high time the statue was replaced by a memorial to the victims of the random shooting at minibus taxis here by a right-wing delinquent namesake, Barend Strijdom, in 1993.

Heading back towards the south of Church Square, **Claude Malan Museum**, 48 Polleys Arcade, Pretorius St (Mon–Fri 8am–5pm, Sat 8am–1pm), has an excellent selection of antiques, and a shop which is well worth a browse. Nearby, at 458 Paul Kruger St, **Mimosa Muti & Curios** is more of a curio than a *umuthi* (medicine) shop these days, but is a welcome blast of African culture in a part of town that's still short of it. Cross Paul Kruger Street and turn right into Volkstem Street for the unmissably kitsch **Police Museum** (Mon–Fri 8am–3.30pm, Sat 8.30am–12.30am; free). Amid the tacky recreations of South African murders that made tabloid headlines, and scores of weapons old and new, are the latest exhibits, added since 1994, and by far the most interesting. You'll find recreations of the 1961 Sharpeville shootings, the murder of Black Consciousness leader Steve Biko in 1977, the 1992 Bisho massacre, and the assassination of the ANC military leader Chris Hani in 1993. Each of these except the last were perpetrated or orchestrated by the police, and the exhibits are there to signal self-reflection and commitment to change.

Paul Kruger's House and around

To find **Paul Kruger's House** (Mon–Sat 8.30am–4pm, Sun & public holidays 11am–4pm; R5), head west along Church Street, crossing Bosman and Schubart streets. On the way, you'll pass the striking former residence of the hated Department of Bantu Affairs, studded with white stone reliefs. The building now houses the police murder and robbery unit.

Kruger's House was built in 1884 by the English-speaking Charles Clark, described by Kruger as one of his "tame Englishmen", who mixed his cement with milk instead of water. Inside, the museum is rather dull, though you may find some of Kruger's effects interesting, like his large collection of spittoons. The *stoep* (verandah) is the most famous feature of the house, for here the old president would sit and chat to any white who chose to join him. Out at the back is Kruger's private railway coach, built in 1898, which he used during the second Anglo-Boer War.

Opposite is a characteristically grim Reformed church known as **Kruger's Church**. You'll find the **Groot Kerk** ("**Great Church**"), on the corner of Vermeulen and Bosman streets, more impressive. There's no need to go inside, but have a look at its strikingly ornate tower, one of the finest in the country.

North of Church Square

North of Church Square, a wander up Paul Kruger Street and a right turn into Vermeulen Street will take you to the **Pierneef Museum**, 231 Vermeulen St (Mon–Fri 8.30am–4pm; free). Jacob Hendrik Pierneef is often billed as the father of South African landscape art, and certainly his highly stylized representations, mostly painted in the 1920s, have been much imitated. His paintings are controversial for their expression of Afrikaner aspirations to own the landscapes they portray, but they are distinctive and evocative for all that. Head upstairs to view the permanent exhibition of Art Nouveau artist Wim Muller, whose talents were largely lost on the Transvaal when he lived there in the 1920s, but which have since received recognition. Further down the corridor is a tea room with an inviting selection of cakes. Further **north of here**, busy Proes and Struben streets are filled with cut-price stores, black shoppers and minibus taxis heading for the townships. Watch out for the gangs who work these streets, as a number of tourists have been mugged here.

Continue north across Bloed and Boom streets for the **National Zoological Gardens** (daily: May–Aug 8am–5.30pm; Sept–April 8am–6pm; entry fee), which is spacious and surprisingly good, housing rare species of antelope, a white rhinoceros, and a wide selection of South American as well as African animals. Night tours are a good idea, as you'll see some of the zoo's freakiest creatures at their most active. Next door, the **Pretoria Aquarium** (daily 8am–5pm; R7, children R5) is less impressive, but nonetheless has plenty of beasts, some very weird and highly poisonous. Hawkers sell curios outside, but you're better off heading a few blocks west for the bustling market at **Marabastad**, the city's first "non-white" area. While you're here, don't miss the intricately decorated Hindu **Mariammen Temple**, which is right next to the market.

South of Schoeman Street

The best thing about Pretoria **south of Schoeman Street** is restful **Burgers Park**, between Andries and Van der Walt streets. Named after ineffective ZAR president Thomas Burgers (who ruled between 1873 and 1877), the park has a good botanic garden, a quirkily designed curator's house and a pavilion at its centre, which was once the preserve of brass bands and all-white tea parties, but today is multiracial and a good place to relax.

Opposite the park's southern border, **Melrose House**, 275 Jacob Maré St (Tues, Wed, Fri & Sat 10am–5pm, Sun 10am–6pm; entry fee), is an overdecorated Victorian house with a wonderful conservatory, interesting exhibitions, and a very good African arts and crafts shop. The house was built in 1884 for local businessman George Heys, who made his money running mailcoach services. Lord Kitchener used the house during the second Anglo-Boer War, and the treaty of Vereeniging which ended hostilities was signed inside. Outside, a sumptuous tea garden serves up cakes and scones.

Head west of Burger Park along Minnaar Street, and then turn right into Paul Kruger Street for the **Transvaal Museum** (Mon–Sat 9am–5pm, Sun 11am–5pm; entry fee), Pretoria's oldest museum, and dedicated to natural history. Among the huge number of stuffed animals, models of dinosaurs and displays aimed with kids in mind are wonderful fossil remains, some over one million years old. In the Austin Roberts Bird Hall, you'll find an informative exhibit on South Africa's many species of birds. For the dedicated, a permanent geological exhibition has as many rock samples as you could possibly wish for.

Opposite the museum is the **City Hall**, with its eclectic mix of neo-Greek and Roman architecture, and two rather good statues of Andries and Marthinus Pretorius immediately outside. Go south one block to Jacob Maré Street to find the main minibus taxi rank, and continue south one block for the **Railway Station**, designed by Sir Herbert Baker. The **Victoria Hotel** opposite is an elegant building erected in 1896, when it was the railway workers' bar. Today, it is one of the smartest hotels in town (see "Accommodation", p.487).

Arcadia and the Union Buildings

Head east along Vermeulen or Church streets, and you'll soon reach the **Arcadia** district, where Pretoria's **Union Buildings**, the headquarters of the South African government, perch majestically on the main hill. Designed by Herbert Baker in 1910, allegedly to symbolize the union of Briton and Boer, the lashings of colonnades and lavish amphitheatre seem instead to glorify British imperial self-confidence. Nelson Mandela has an office inside, and the Buildings were famously the site of his inauguration in 1994. This was perhaps the first time their imperialist symbols were transformed, not least by the African praise-singers who delivered their odes from the amphitheatre, proclaiming Mandela as the latest in a long line of African heroes from Shaka to Hintsa, and beyond. You can walk around the buildings and their gardens, but can only go inside if you're on official business.

South of the Union Buildings, the **Pretoria Art Museum**, on the corner of Schoeman and Wessels streets (Tues & Thurs–Sat 10am–5pm, Wed 10am–8pm, Sun 10am–6pm; entry fee), houses an excellent selection of South African art and Dutch Masters, as well as some black artists, including Ephraim Ngatane. There is a small gallery just beyond the main entrance which is worth popping into for its contemporary exhibitions and small café.

Sunnyside and Hatfield

Southeast of the city centre, desegregated **Sunnyside** is one of the few areas of Pretoria that feels vaguely African, and its lively street life, distinctive old houses and multitude of cafés makes it a good place to wander. Don't miss the **Oeverzicht Artists' Village**, on the corner of Kotze and Gerard Moerdyk streets, a collection of attractive old cottages with interesting crafts shops and restaurants. Nearby, at 137 Gerard Moerdyk St, the **Breytenbach Theatre** is said to be haunted by the ghosts of those who died there when it was a hospital for Germans, and hosts mainly student productions. You'll find the tiny *Teaterhuise* around the back of the street. **Esselen Street** is Sunnyside's busiest thoroughfare, brimming with restaurants, bars and street hawkers. Nearby, the **Loftus Versveld Stadium** plays hosts to major rugby games.

It's worth continuing east to **Hatfield**, where **Pretoria University** houses a fantastic art collection, viewable by appointment only (☎420 3100). The collection includes seventeenth- and eighteenth-century furniture, Dutch Masters and beautiful ceramics from Europe and China. Some of the Chinese ceramics date back to the Han dynasty (206BC–221AD). The only art you can see without an appointment are the minimalist and metallic sculptures of Eduardo Villa in the Old University Library, which aren't really worth the effort. Otherwise, a stroll to Park, Burnett and Hilda streets will lead you to a plethora of studenty cafés, bars and restaurants.

To visit the elegant house and museum of acclaimed Afrikaner sculptor **Anton Van Wouw**, 26 Clark St (Tues–Fri 10am–4pm, Sat 10am–noon; free), you'll need to head southeast of the university to the wealthy suburb of **Brooklyn**. Van Wouw was responsible for most of the brooding effigies of Afrikaner public figures from the 1890s to 1930s that are scattered around the country, including the Kruger statue in Pretoria's Church Square (see p.487). His most famous work is the Voortrekker Monument, further south of the city (see below). The museum, designed by the celebrated architect Norman Eaton in 1938, houses a collection of his smaller pieces. Van Wouw's figures tend to be placed in rural settings, but here you'll find two striking, non-rural pieces, one of a mine worker and another showing an accused man, standing in the dock. Keep an eye out too for *The Guitar Player*, a feisty-looking woman strumming away with a trace of a smile on her face.

South to the Voortrekker Monument

Travelling south towards Johannesburg on Preller Road, you can't miss enormous **UNISA**, South Africa's largest university. Over 300,000 students are enrolled here – though most of them are on correspondence courses. Inside, on the fifth floor, there's a very good **art gallery** which hosts some of Pretoria's most innovative exhibitions, as well as a permanent collection exhibiting young South African talent of all races. You should telephone in advance to make sure the curator is here (daily 9am–5pm; ☎429 3111; free).

On the outskirts of Pretoria, west of UNISA, the chilling **Correctional Services Museum** (Tues–Fri 9am–3pm, Sun 10am–3pm; free), at Pretoria Central Prison, is well worth a visit. Make for Potgieter Street, which runs vertically three blocks west of Church Square, and stay on it while it becomes the R101 to Johannesburg. You'll see the notorious prison, where many famous political prisoners were held (and many executed), on your right. Be prepared to walk past depressed-looking visiting relatives on your way in. Inside the museum you can see artworks made by prisoners, including a life-sized statue of a destitute man crawling towards an expressionless prison warder, who has his arms outstretched, ready to correct him. There are also exhibits of knives concealed in Bibles and shoes, files in cakes and so forth. Most alarming by far are the group photos of various forbidding-looking prison warders through the ages, which seem a strange sort of propaganda for the prison service.

Continue out on the R101 and follow the signs to view the famous **Voortrekker Monument** (Mon–Sat 9am–4.45pm, Sun 11am–4.45pm; entry fee). This striking, austere block of granite was built in 1940 to commemorate Boer victory over the Zulu nation at Blood River on December 16, 1838, and its symbolism is crushingly heavy-handed. The monument is enclosed by reliefs of ox wagons, with a large statue of a woman standing outside, shaking her fist at imaginary oppressors. Inside, a series of moving reliefs depict scenes from the Great Trek. Outside, hidden by some trees, are two pint-sized replicas of the huts of Zulu kings Dingane and Cetshwayo. Incidentally, the first ever Afrikaans pornographic magazine, *Loslyf*, created a sensation in 1995 when it used the monument as the backdrop to a centrefold spread, causing outrage among those Afrikaners who still make a pilgrimage here every December 16.

Eating and drinking

Pretoria has plenty of good **restaurants**, but prices, especially in the centre, tend to be high. If you're on a budget, head for the suburbs of Sunnyside and Hatfield, where the choice is wider. The city's top restaurants are mostly in Arcadia and the outer suburbs. **Cafés** are numerous and varied; you'll find particularly attractive ones in Hatfield. Pretoria is a drinking town and has a host of **bars** to meet demand. Forget the bland ones that fill the city centre, and head for those in Sunnyside or Hatfield. Segregation has started to break down, but most bars are predominantly white. The bulk of the black community's drinking is still done in the townships, where *shebeens* abound.

Restaurants

Bacini's, 216 Esselen St, Sunnyside (☎341 0689). Popular and inexpensive Italian restaurant, with reasonably tasty dishes.

Brasserie de Paris, 525 Duncan St, Hatfield (☎342 5057). Faithful reproduction of the classic Parisian café, with pleasant terrace, spacious interior, moderate prices and a great menu. Closed Sun & lunchtime Sat.

Chagall's, 924 Park St, Hatfield (☎341 7511). Chic, expensive restaurant, with excellent food, wines to match, and a lovely setting a few kilometres out of town. Closed Sun & lunchtime Sat.

Die Werf, Plot 66, Olympus Rd, Pretoria East. A hearty selection of South African dishes is served up at this popular, good-value restaurant.

Fillings 4 Pancakes, 317 Esselen St, Sunnyside (☎343 1683). Pretoria's most right-on restaurant is explicitly gay-friendly, decked out in African fabrics, with funky music and simple, inexpensive, good food. There's an internet café attached.

Gerard Moerdyk, 752 Park St, Arcadia (☎344 4856). Beautifully cooked South African cuisine served at a price amidst lavish surroundings. Choose from ostrich, springbok pie and other intriguing dishes. Closed Sun & lunchtime Sat.

Hillside Tavern, Rynial Building, 320 The Hillside, Lynnwood (☎47 5119). Moderately priced restaurant, celebrated locally for its steaks.

Hong Kong, Shop 29, Brooklyn Mall, New Muckleneuk. Reliable, mid-priced Chinese food in inauspicious surroundings.

Machic-Chic, corner of Uitspan and Rossouw streets, Willows (☎807 0578). East of centre, off the N4, this is the finest Portuguese restaurant in Pretoria and is moderately priced, with a pleasant outdoor section.

La Madeleine, 258 Esselen St, Sunnyside (☎44 6076). Expensive, truly delicious dishes ranging from Provençale to quasi-Japanese. Booking essential.

Magic Samovar, 115 Gerard Moerdyk St, Sunnyside (☎341 9500). Large helpings of good-value Russian food, with occasional, traditional ensembles playing folk music to spice up proceedings.

La Perla, 211 Skinner St (☎322 2759). In the city centre, and serving classic, moderate-to-expensive European fish dishes like *bouillabaisse*, and line fish *grenobloise*.

Santorini, 57 Esselen St, Sunnyside. Very decent, inexpensive Greek restaurant on Sunnyside's busiest street.

Sirocco, 109 Gerard Moerdyk St, Sunnyside (☎341 3785). Restored Sunnyside house, providing an excellent setting for consistently good, moderately priced Mediterranean cuisine.

Bars and cafés

Café Riche, 2 Church Square West, city centre. One of the finest buildings in Pretoria provides the perfect setting for a hearty selection of cakes and teas: the ideal place to start your explorations of the city.

Café Tabac, The Yard, Duncan St, Hatfield. Quirky blend of antique shop and exquisite tea garden, with a neat vegetable patch and wagon wheel out the front.

Ed's Diner, Hatfield Galleries, Burnett St, Hatfield. 1950s nostalgia identical to other *Ed's Diners* around the world, that heaves with students in the evening when the in-house disco cranks up.

The Grapevine, 204 Sunnyside Galleries, Esselen St, Sunnyside. About the best bar on the street, with generally mellow and cheerful regulars.

Keg and Hound, 107 Arcadia St, Hatfield. Bearable themed British pub with a good selection of beers.

Odyssey, corner of Burnett and Festival streets, Hatfield. Internet café with passable coffee.

Star City Disco, corner of Bosman and Jacob Maré streets, near the bus station. Major black hang-out, especially at weekends, when good music and beer flow freely. Use a cab to get there and back.

Tings and Times, Hatfield Galleries, Burnett St, Hatfield. Popular student bar buzzing with talk of essay crises, money worries and jaunts up country.

Nightlife and entertainment

Pretoria lacks the rich **arts and music** scene of Johannesburg, and on weekends locals tend to head for the bright lights 50km south. However, if you're here on a brief visit, you should find enough to satisfy, especially if you make for **Sunnyside**, where Esselen Street and the surrounding area have the city's highest concentration of **nightclubs** and **music venues**. This is also where you'll find a thriving number of gay clubs, which work hard to keep Pretoria's gay community in the city over the weekend. Things are very different in Mamelodi and Atteridgeville, where plenty of small clubs play South African and soul sounds.

Theatre and cinema

Pretoria's main venue for **theatre**, **opera** and **classical concerts** is the *State Theatre* on Church Street (☎322 1665), which also has a good workshop. Nearby in Church Square, the *Basement Theatre* below *Café Riche* (☎328 3173) is an elegant, compact venue with a good record of adventurous productions. For a lively range of student productions, head for the *Breytenbach*, in Gerard Moerdyk Street, Sunnyside (☎44 4834). *Die Teaterhuise*, off Gerard Moerdyk Street in Sunnyside, is a tiny venue still establishing itself, but promising great things.

Pretoria's **cinemas** carry the typical selection of Hollywood fare, and the city is amongst the first to receive new releases. For the big releases, the *Nu-Metro* in Sammy Marks Square (☎326 6614) is reliable, and you'll find branches of *Ster-Kinekor* on Beatrix Street in Arcadia (☎341 7568) and on Jeppe Street in Sunnyside (☎44 4069). Back in the centre, on the corner of Schoeman and Van der Walt streets, *The Tramshed* (☎320 4300) screens a decent selection of non-mainstream films. *The Pretoria News* is a reliable source of theatre and cinema **listings**, while the national *Mail & Guardian* is good for coverage on the visual arts and theatre and the major musical events.

Live music and clubs

Bacaroos, Village Centre, 47 Esselen St, Sunnyside. Best on Friday nights, when its techno raves heave with hundreds of happy, sweaty white people.

Band Factory, corner of Meintjies and Esselen streets, Sunnyside. Gay rave club, open nightly.

Bootleggers, Glenwood Centre, Glenwood Rd, Lynnwood Glen (☎47 2025). Live music venue with frequently dodgy acts, so phone first.

Café Galleria, 60 Esselen St, Sunnyside. Live music bar with dismally grey interior but a nice performing space. Bands range from the iffy to the inspirational.

Crossroads Blues Bar, *The Tramshed* (upper level), corner of Schoeman and Van der Walt streets (☎322 3263). Hip, downtown venue, in the same complex as the cinema, hosting rock and blues bands.

Downtown, behind *Belgrave Hotel*, corner of Loop and Andries streets, near the railway station. Popular downtown gay rave club.

Steamers, by the railway station, city centre (north). Appropriately named gay bar, so dress for the occasion.

Tequila Sunrise Café, Village Centre, Esselen St, Sunnyside. Nice little venue featuring young bands. Musical proficiency isn't a high point here, but there's usually a good vibe.

Listings

Airlines All airline offices are in Johannesburg (see p.480).

American Express 4 Brooklyn Mall, 338 Bronkhorst St, New Muckleneuk (travel section: Mon–Fri 8.30am–5pm; foreign exchange: Mon–Fri 9am–4.30pm; ☎346 3580, after hours 345 4730).

Banks You'll find most banks and ATMs in the city centre around Church Square and along Church St.

Bookshops *Exclusive Books*, Sunnypark Centre, Esselen St, Sunnyside (☎44 1118) is the best.

Bus information Pretoria's bus terminal and information centre is on Church Square (☎313 0839). *Intercape* (☎328 4571), *Greyhound* (☎328 4040) and *Translux* (☎315 2333) have their terminal and office at the train station. *North Link Transport* (☎323 0379), which runs buses to Pietersburg and the north, departs from Bosman St, between Church and Pretorius streets.

Camping/hiking *Trappers Trading*, 79 Sanlam Centre, 252 Andries St (☎320 0247), is the best place in town to buy outdoor and camping gear.

Car rental *Avis*, 70 Schoeman St (☎325 1490); *Budget*, 456 Church St East, Arcadia (☎323 3658); *Dolphin*, Orange Court Lodge, Vermeulen St (☎326 3715); *Imperial*, corner of Pretorius and Potgieter streets (☎323 3259); *Rent-a-jalopy*, 1212 Bottrill St, Queenswood (☎73 3006); *Tempest*, 186 Struben St (☎324 5007).

Embassies and consulates *Australia*, 292 Orient St, Arcadia (☎342 3740); *Canada*, 1103 Arcadia St, Hatfield (☎342 6923); *France*, 807 George Ave, Arcadia (☎43 5564); *Germany*, 180 Blackwood St, Arcadia (☎344 3854); *Ireland*, Tulbagh Park, 1234 Church St, Colbyn (☎342 5062); *Lesotho*, 343 Pretorius St, Momentum Centre, 6th floor, West Tower (☎322 6090); *Malawi*, Delta Building, 471 Monica Rd, Lynnwood (☎47 7827); *Mozambique*, 199 Beckett St, Arcadia (☎343 7840); *Namibia*, suite 2, Eikendal, Tulbagh Park, 1234 Church St, Colbyn (☎342 3520); *Swaziland*, Infotech Building, 1090 Arcadia St, Arcadia (☎324 5782); *UK*, 255 Hill St, Arcadia (☎43 3121); *USA*, 877 Pretorius St, Arcadia (☎343 1048); *Zambia*, 353 Sanlam Building, Festival St, Hatfield (☎342 1541); *Zimbabwe*, 798 Merton St, Arcadia (☎342 5152).

Emergencies Ambulance ☎644 4515; Police ☎10111 or 326 2222; AA Breakdowns ☎0800/01 0101.

Flea markets Hatfield Flea Market, Hatfield Plaza, every Sun, is Pretoria's best flea market, with crafts, bric-a-brac and lively banter.

Hospitals For emergency hospital treatment, telephone or go straight to one of the hospitals with 24hr casualty services: *HF Verwoerd*, Doctor Savage Rd (☎329 1111), *Pretoria West*, Trans Oranje Rd (☎386 5111), or the private *Starcare Muelmed*, 577 Pretorius St, Arcadia (☎44 2362).

Laundries *De Luxe Drycleaners*, 479 Pretorius St, city centre (☎44 2251).

Pharmacies are to be found in every shopping mall. Good ones include *Berea*, 8 Rissik St, Sunnyside (☎44 7109), *Duncan Street*, 531 Duncan St, Hatfield (☎43 5055), *Station*, 509 Paul Kruger St (☎323 1238).

Police ☎10111 for emergencies. The central police station is on the corner of Pretorius and Bosman streets (☎326 2222).

Post offices The main post office is in Church Square. Other branches are at Nedbank Plaza, Beatrix St, Arcadia; 1127 Burnett St, Hatfield; and Jeppe St, Sunnyside. Opening hours are Mon–Fri 8am–4.30pm, Sat 8am–noon.

Taxis Reliable firms include *City Bug* (☎663 6316) *City Taxis* (☎21 5742) or *Rixi Mini Cabs* (☎325 8072).

Train information Pretoria Station (☎315 2757) is on Railway Street. For the half-hourly service to Johannesburg, phone ☎315 2268. For information on *Spoornet Special Steam Trains*, phone ☎315 2548. The luxurious *Blue Train* runs to Cape Town on Tues, Thurs and Sat, via Johannesburg (☎315 2111), while the even more sumptuous *Rovos Rail Trains* (☎323 6052) travels to Cape Town and Victoria Falls.

Around Pretoria

Doornkloof Farm in Irene, just south of Pretoria, makes a good day-trip from either Pretoria or Johannesburg. For many years this was the home of Prime Minister **Jan Smuts**, and the museum here (Mon–Fri 9.30am–4.30pm, Sat & Sun 9.30am–5pm; entry fee), while tending towards the hagiographic, does shed some light on one of South Africa's most enigmatic politicians. The massive library heralds Smuts's intellectual range and numerous mementos confirm his internationalism. Other displays focus on his military role as one of the most successful commanders of the Afrikaner forces during the Anglo-Boer Wars. To get to the museum, travel south from Pretoria on the M18 or R21 for about 20km, and take the turn-off to Irene.

The **Rietvlei Nature Reserve** is on the other side of the R21 from Irene. Though unspectacular and only open on Sundays and public holidays, it does at least offer Burchell's zebra, rhino and antelope, and plenty of birdlife around the dam (Sun & public holidays 9am–5pm; R10). The **Wonderboom Nature Reserve**, just north of Pretoria on the Voortrekker Road, surrounds a huge thousand year old fig tree, the *wonderboom* (wonder tree), which has mutated in all kinds of directions, and is quite a sight. The reserve also has a few trails to wander through, though there isn't much else to see.

Finally, the **Roodeplaat Dam Nature Reserve,** northeast of Pretoria, off the N1 and R513 also surrounds a dam, and provides **camping facilities** (☎012/ 808 0361). The reserve gets crowded at weekends and public holidays, but at other times you should find it quiet and restful.

travel details

Trains

Johannesburg to: Bloemfontein (1 daily; 13hr 20min); Cape Town (1 daily; 29hr 30min); Durban (1 daily; 13hr 30min); East London (1 daily; 19hr 45min); Kimberley (1 daily; 8hr 15min); Nelspruit (1 daily; 9hr 45min); Port Elizabeth (1 daily; 20 hr).

Pretoria to: Bloemfontein (1 daily; 14hr 50min); Cape Town (1 daily; 28hr); Johannesburg (32 daily; 1hr 30min); Kimberley (1 daily; 10hr 35min); Nelspruit (1 daily; 8hr 20min).

Buses

Johannesburg to: Bloemfontein (3–4 daily; 5–6hr); Cape Town (3–5 daily; 16–18hr); Durban (6 daily; 8–11hr); East London (1 daily; 11hr 30min); Kimberley (3–4 daily; 6–8hr); King William's Town (2 daily; 12hr 15min); Klerksdorp (3–5 daily; 2–4hr); Knysna (2–3 daily; 14–16hr); Kuruman (1 Tues, Thurs, Fri & Sun; 8hr 15min); Ladysmith (1 daily; 6hr 30min); Louis Trichardt (1 Tues, Thurs, Fri & Sun; 4hr 15min); Mossel Bay (1–2 daily; 14hr 30min); Nelspruit (1 daily; 5hr); Newcastle (1 daily; 4hr 45min); Oudtshoorn (1–2 daily; 13hr); Pietermaritzburg (7 daily; 6–8hr); Pietersburg (1–2 daily, except Sat; 3hr 45min); Plettenberg Bay (1 Tues & Fri; 15hr 30min); Port Elizabeth (2–4 daily; 13–15hr); Potchefstroom (1–3 daily; 1hr 30min); Pretoria (over 70 daily; 1hr); Queenstown (2 daily; 10hr); Rustenburg (1 daily; 2hr); Umtata (1 Mon, Wed, Fri & Sun; 12hr 45min).

Pretoria to: Aliwal North (2 daily; 9hr); Beaufort West (3–5 daily; 12–13hr); Bloemfontein (3–4 daily; 6–7hr); Cape Town (3–5 daily; 17hr); Durban (6 daily; 9hr); East London (1 daily; 12hr 30min); Ermelo (1 daily; 4hr 20min); George (1–2 daily; 16hr); Graaff Reinet (2 Mon–Sat; 11hr 45min); Harrismith (1 daily; 4hr 45min); Johannesburg (over 70 daily; 1hr); Kimberley (3–4 daily; 7hr); King William's Town (2 daily; 13hr 25min); Klerksdorp (3–5 daily; 3hr–4hr 30min); Knysna (2–3 daily; 16hr); Kuruman (1 Tues, Thurs, Fri & Sun; 9hr 15min); Ladysmith (1 daily; 7hr 30min); Louis Trichardt (1 Tues, Thurs, Fri & Sun; 5hr 15min); Mossel Bay (1–2 daily; 15hr 35min);

Nelspruit (1 daily; 4hr); Newcastle (1 daily; 4hr 45min); Oudtshoorn (1–2 daily; 14hr); Pietermaritzburg (7 daily; 7hr 15min); Pietersburg (1–2 daily, except Sat; 3hr); Plettenberg Bay (1 Tues & Fri; 16hr 30min); Port Elizabeth (2–4 daily; 16hr); Potchefstroom (1–3 daily; 2hr 30min); Queenstown (2 daily; 10–11hr); Umtata (1 Mon, Wed, Fri & Sun; 13hr 45min).

Flights

Johannesburg is a major **international point of entry** into South Africa, with flights from all around the world. The city is also an important centre of the **domestic** network, and you can fly to virtually anywhere in the country from here. Services include:

Johannesburg to: Bloemfontein (6 daily; 1hr 10min); Cape Town (20–26 daily; 2hr); Durban (17–22 daily; 1hr); East London (3 daily; 1hr 25min); Manzini (1 daily except Thurs & Sun; 1hr); Mmabatho (1 Mon–Fri; 1hr); Port Elizabeth (6–9 daily; 1hr 40min).

CHAPTER EIGHT

NORTHWEST PROVINCE

South Africa's **Northwest Province** is one of the country's most-visited but least-understood regions – renowned, among tourists at least, for the famously vulgar **Sun City** resort and **Pilanesberg Game Reserve**, but not much else. Few people venture beyond these attractions to explore this area in greater depth; consequently, it can be curiously rewarding to do so. There's a myriad of little *dorps* scattered throughout the region where few whites are fluent in English, and most blacks speak only Tswana. Outside the main cities, the old-fashioned hospitality you'll encounter, along with the stillness and tranquillity in the endless stretches of grassland and fields of *mielies*, are a refreshing change after hectic Johannesburg.

Northwest Province extends west from Gauteng to the Botswana border and the Kalahari desert. Along the province's eastern flank loom the **Magaliesberg Mountains**, one hundred times older than the Himalayas and these days dotted with holiday resorts for nature-starved Jo'burgers. If you're driving from Johannesburg to Cape Town and can afford a bit of meandering, try taking the **N12** through Northwest via Kimberley (in the Northern Cape); the road follows the Vaal River for hundreds of miles, and once you're past uninspiring **Potchefstroom** and **Klerksdorp**, a detour to the riverbanks provides a lovely breather, particularly to **Bloemhof** for its quiet nature reserve which teems with birdlife. The province also has a healthy number of **safari lodges**, where, depending on your budget, you can view game from a luxurious verandah, or camp in the bushveld under the stars.

The N4 from Gauteng will lead you to **Rustenberg** and its windswept **Nature Reserve**, where you can hike high enough to gaze down onto the shimmering plains beneath. **Groot Marico**, further west, is a friendly *dorp* with powerful home-brews and laid-back people to share them with. Nearby, the **Madikwe Game Reserve** is set to become one of South Africa's finest wildlife spots.

Relentless sun alleviated only by torrential rain makes summer in Northwest something of an endurance test: aim to come here in spring or autumn. Camping is especially rewarding in this part of South Africa; pitching a tent in the stillness of the *veld* allows you to savour the sense of timelessness before you head off once more.

Some history

San hunter-gatherers were Northwest's first inhabitants: they were displaced some one thousand years ago by Iron Age peoples from the north, who pitched their first settlements on low ground near watercourses. By the sixteenth century, these settlements had developed into stone-walled towns on hilltops; the largest, Karechuenya (near Madikwe), was estimated by a Scottish observer in 1820 to have at least 20,000 inhabitants – more than Cape Town had at that time. By the nineteenth century, the dominance of the Rolong, Taung, Tlhaping and Tlokwa clans was established. European observers classified them all as **Tswana**, but it's unclear whether these people regarded themselves as very different from people further east classified "Sotho".

The outbreak of intense **inter-clan violence** in the early 1800s was due to displacements caused by white settler expansion, and the new availability of firearms. Victory went to those who made alliance with the new arrivals, whether **Griqua** from the Northern Cape, or **Afrikaners** from further south. The Tlhaping were soon driven out,

eventually finding their way to Zambia. Mzilikazi's Ndebele ruled the region in the 1820s and 1830s, but they too were forced out, this time to modern Zimbabwe. The victories of the remaining clans was short-lived: their Griqua and Afrikaner allies soon evicted them from their land and forced them into service.

Potchefstroom and **Klerksdorp** were the first towns established here by the Afrikaners, and more followed, each forming the nucleus for a quarrelsome mini-state. In 1860 these mini-states amalgamated to form the **South African Republic** (ZAR), with Pretoria as its capital. The first Anglo-Boer War raged from 1877 until British defeat in 1881, with most of the province unaffected. In 1885, the British successfully fought the Afrikaners of the Goshen republic near Mmabatho and established the protectorate of north and south Bechuanaland – the north later became Botswana, while the south was annexed to the Cape Colony by Cecil Rhodes in 1895. British intervention meant that some land remaining in Tswana hands stayed that way, but by then the clans had lost almost everything. When **gold** was discovered on the Witwaters and and around Klerksdorp, Tswana men left in droves to work in the mines.

Of far greater impact was the **second Anglo-Boer War** (1899–1902). As well as the celebrated **siege of Mafikeng**, where British and Tswana forces held out for 217 days against Afrikaner troops (see p.511), there were protracted and nasty skirmishes up and down the Vaal River. Both Afrikaner and Tswana had their lands torched, and many were thrown into concentration camps by the dreaded Lord Kitchener.

The Union Treaty of 1910 left the province as the western part of the Transvaal, firmly in Afrikaner hands. Its smaller *dorps* soon became bywords for rural racism, epitomized in the 1980s by the fascistic AWB led by **Eugene Terreblanche**, whose power base was here. The migration of so many Tswana men and the lack of industrial development impeded the growth of a black working class in the province, which is why Northwest played a relatively minor role in the national struggle against apartheid.

The **Bophuthatswana** *bantustan* – or "Bop" – was created in 1977 out of the old "native reserves", the poor-quality land into which Tswana had been forced. Far from being a long-awaited "homeland" for blacks, Bop proved to be a confusing amalgamation of enclaves, ruled by the corrupt **Lucas Mangope**, who grew rich on the revenues from **Sol Kerzner**'s casinos in Sun City and the discovery of platinum. Bophuthatswana's short life came to an end with the elections of 1994, but its legacy lives on in the form of its notoriously corrupt civil servants, who are being retained until at least 1999. Since Bop's capital, **Mmabatho**, is also the capital of Northwest, these people have found the transition an easy one, and whilst there have not yet been scandals on a par with the Eastern Cape (which absorbed two *bantustans*), it is an ironic outcome, particularly for those who risked their lives fighting the Mangope regime.

The Magaliesberg

Northwest's finest asset is the **Magaliesberg mountain range**, which gets its name from the Tswana chief **Mogale** of the Kwena clan. Kwena people lived here from the seventeenth century until 1825, when most of them were forced out by the Ndebele chief Mzilikazi. Afrikaner farmers completed the removals, and today the dispossession of the Kwena in the Magaliesberg is complete.

The Magaliesberg are easily accessible from Johannesburg and Pretoria, with the result that great chunks have been fenced off and turned into time shares or resorts. Nevertheless, there are oases of unspoilt nature, notably the outstanding **Pilanesberg Game Reserve**, the lesser-known **Rustenburg Nature Reserve** and the **Mountain Sanctuary Park**, all preserved in something like their previous natural state and well-stocked with wildlife. The towns dotted throughout the mountains are fairly dull, though you're likely to want to stop at **Rustenburg** for its useful tourist information. If you're in the mood for some mind-boggling architecture and touristic opulence, **Sun City** provides the perfect gateway to Pilanesberg.

Rustenburg and around

Some 120km northwest of Johannesburg, the mining town of **RUSTENBURG** has the dubious distinction of being the birthplace of **Paul Kruger**, the ZAR's most famous president. However, the town's main appeal lies in its proximity to the **nature reserve**, and for the many pleasant country resorts which lie in the surrounding hills.

Arrival and information

Daily *Greyhound* **buses** from Johannesburg stop in Van Staden Street. You'll find Rustenburg's useful **tourist information office** (Mon–Fri 8am–1pm & 1.30–4.30pm; ☎0142/94 3194) on the corner of Plein and Burger streets.

THE MAGALIESBERG

ACCOMMODATION
1 Amble Inn
2 Anana Hotel
3 Cashane Hotel
4 Kloof Holiday Resort
5 Montana
6 Transvaal Hotel
7 Utopia

Accommodation

Rustenburg has a handful of **hotels** in town, but you'll get the most out of this area by staying in one of the many **country resorts** nearby (and listed below). Many of these do not have street addresses; we've indicated them on our map, and you should phone before you set out. Avoid the B&Bs advertised in the tourist office – they tend to be in the dull suburbs.

Amble Inn (☎0142/75 0608). Self-catering chalets southeast of town, in a pretty mountainside setting which, despite the owners' enormous dogs, is very restful. To get there, follow the Pretoria road, turning right at the sign for Rex and left at the Kromriver turn-off. Continue for about 10km. ②.

Ananda Hotel (☎0142/97 1742). Cosy accommodation in a fantastic spot west of town, with a wide range of sports facilities, a swimming pool and a decent restaurant. To get there, head out on the Malan Road, and at the T-junction out of town turn left and follow the signs. Caravans ①, rooms ③.

The Cashane, corner of Steen and Van Staden streets (☎0142/28541). One of the two hotels in the centre of town, and offering comfortable rooms with TV. There's a reasonable restaurant attached, but no pool. ③.

Kloof Holiday Resort (☎0142/97 1351). Uninspiring housing estate layout is made up for by the magnificent hill which towers above and which is within hiking distance. Avoid school holidays if you can, as the resort gets packed. The F chalets are the nicest and cheapest. To get there, follow the same directions as for the *Ananda* (above). Caravans ②, chalets ③.

Montana (☎0142/75 0113). Eight self-contained cottages on a long, thin, hikeable strip of the Magaliesberg. Cottages 6 and 7 have the best views. To get there, follow the Pretoria road, turning right at the sign for Rex and left at the Kromriver turn-off. Continue for about 20km. ③.

Transvaal, 33 Prinsloo St (☎0142/29351). Pleasant enough hotel in town, but with a loud disco downstairs that throbs with music all night on Fri and Sat. ③.

Utopia (☎0142/75 0352). Franchise operation renting out privately owned A-frame chalets next to Mountain Sanctuary Park. Self-catering, but with a restaurant and bar. This is not a place for hiking, but for taking in peaceful views from your chalet. To get there, follow the directions for *Montana* (see above). ②.

The town and around

There's not much to see in Rustenburg itself, apart from a compelling **Dutch Reformed Church** on Burger Street, and a mediocre **museum** (Mon–Fri 8.30am–4.30pm, Sat 9am–1pm, Sun 3–5pm; free), which contains a battered old ZAR flag.

Some 4km southwest of town, **Rustenburg Nature Reserve** (Mon–Fri 7.30am–4pm, Sat & Sun 10am–1pm; ☎0142/31050; entry fee) spans a spectacular portion of the Magaliesberg, and offers sweeping views and great hikes over terrain spotted with rock formations created by millennia of erosion. You'll find dry *veld* too, and streams coursing through the valleys that have generated a lush botany all of their own. Scattered around the reserve are aloes indigenous to the Magaliesberg, and the discreet *frithiapulchra*, a succulent with only its leaf tips exposed, flowering between November and March. Rustenburg is home to a host of **antelopes** – klipspringer, mountain reedbuck, sable and impala – and also **zebras**, and the many hilly crags are perfect for predatory birds – keep a lookout for the rare **black eagle** and **Cape vulture**, as well as parrots and paradise flycatchers.

The reserve can be explored on a day- or overnight hike. For **day-hikes**, head south out of town on Wolmarans Street and, some way down, take the left turn into Boekenhout Street, which leads to the reserve gate. From here, the road winds dramatically up to the mountaintop, where you'll find the **visitors' centre**, with useful maps and information on hikes and trails, as well as **camping** and *braai* facilities. The three-hour "Peglerae" interpretive trail takes in most of the reserve's best features, and the Parks Board puts out a good booklet to go with it.

To hike **overnight** at weekends you must book in advance, but during the week overnight huts are often available at short notice. Make for the **northern gate** by heading south out of Rustenburg on Smit Street, turning right some way down on Wildevy

Street, and then following the road to the gate. The overnight huts have firewood and cooking utensils, but you must bring all the food you need. The hikes last two days and two nights, with a leisurely nine-kilometre walk on the first day and a slightly more strenuous twelve-kilometre one on the second.

Smaller than Rustenburg Nature Reserve, but a gem nonetheless, **Mountain Sanctuary Park** (March–Aug 8am–5.30pm; Sept–Feb 8am–6.30pm; ☎0142/75 0114; entry fee), about 50km east of Rustenburg, has been allowed to return to a wilderness state, and is dotted with bilharzia-free streams safe for swimming in, and spectacular *kloofs* and gullies. You'll find klipspringer, rhebok and duiker wandering freely, and thousands of birds flying overhead. Chalets (②) and caravans (①) are available for **overnight stays**, but bring your own bedding. There's an extraordinary **swimming pool** by the caravans, which gives you the impression when bathing that you're on the edge of a precipice as you look out into the valley below. The simplest way to **get to the park** is to take the N4 as far as the Marikana turn-off, and then turn right (instead of left to Marikana). Once on this road, take the second dirt-track turning on your left and continue for about 3km.

Boekenhoutfontein Farm (daily except Mon 10am–5pm; small entry fee), home of Paul Kruger, lies some 20km north of the town – a short way from the R565 on the way to Sun City. Built in 1875, this is a plain house with flamboyant Victorian wallpaper. The main exhibits are the Kruger family Bible and grim-faced portraits of his clan.

Eating and drinking

Eating possibilities in Rustenburg are limited to a snack or grill; for anything more substantial, you should head for the **restaurants** some 6km out of town on the R30 (signposted as the Johannesburg road). Along here, *Karl's Bauernstube* (closed all day Mon, Sat lunch & Sun eve) serves up delicious German food and beers and is reasonably priced, while *Rustenburg's Bistro & Brewery* next door offers a surprising but appetizing choice between mid-priced Indonesian cooking or hearty steaks, washed down with delicious home-brewed **Dutch beer**.

Sun City

The famous casino-resort **SUN CITY** has fallen on hard times now that **gambling** is legal in South Africa. When entrepreneur Sol Kerzner built the vast complex some twenty years ago, however, the area was part of the Bophuthatswana *bantustan*, and was one of the few places in the country to throw dice legally. Thousands visited from "across the border" to sample Kerzner's blend of gambling, topless shows and over-the-top hotels. During apartheid, the resort played host to a series of high-profile rock concerts, with artists such as Elton John taking the stage despite the cultural boycott in operation at the time. These days, although the crowds have diminished, Sun City's bizarre and unique attractions haven't faded, and if you're in the area it's well worth popping in for a gawp, especially if you're travelling to Pilanesberg Game Reserve.

Arrival and information

You can **fly** to Sun City's small airport (roughly 7km away), from Johannesburg on *SA Airlink* (☎011/394 2430). Sun City **buses** drive from Johannesburg (book through *Computicket*; ☎011/331 9991) and Pretoria (book through Tourist Rendezvous; ☎012/313 7980) daily. If you're **driving** from Johannesburg, it's easier to take the R24 towards Rustenburg until you meet the N4, and then take the next right turn, the R565, which goes through Boshoek to Sun City. From Pretoria, follow the N4 past the Brits turn-off, and turn right onto the R556; from here it's roughly 70km to the resort.

Entrance to Sun City is a hefty R10. Arriving by car, you should drive right into the complex and head for the parking places nearest the Entertainment Centre. If you've arrived by plane or bus, use the free **monorail** that runs from the entrance all the way to the **information centre** (☎01465/71544). This is a good starting point for an exploration of Sun City (which, though it looks huge, is easily explored on foot), and can provide plenty of maps, leaflets and details of special offers. You can also book **game drives** into the Pilanesberg Game Reserve at the Safari Desk here (☎01465/21561).

Accommodation

The Cabanas (☎01465/21000). Practical for families, this cluster of self-catering holiday chalets offer the most inexpensive accommodation in Sun City. Moderately priced restaurants, an adventure playground and good indoor pool complete the picture. ④.

Cascades Hotel (☎01465/21000). After the *Palace*, this is the resort's most comfortable place to stay. Next door to the Entertainment Centre, it's a stylish high-rise, with "designer-tropical" decor, a mini rainforest and aviary, and outside lifts offering splendid views of Sun City and the surrounding hills. The inviting pool and bar are for residents only. ⑦.

Lost City Palace (☎01465/73121). Fantastically opulent hotel based on the theme of an African palace, with stunning carvings and sculptures, jungle murals and ultra-plush rooms. A stay here is bank-breakingly expensive but pretty unforgettable, and there are two outstanding restaurants. Room prices range from $400 to $4000 a night, and are payable for in foreign exchange only. ⑧.

Sun City Hotel (☎01465/21000). Near the resort entrance, and housing the main casino and nightclub. If you can handle the tackiness and sound of slot machines, this hotel is worth considering for the well-furnished rooms and three decent restaurants. ⑥.

The resort

The resort's showpiece is the **Lost City**, separated from the rest of Sun City by an entrance fee (R40) and the vibrating "Bridge of Time". On entering, you'll be met by **Valley of the Waves**, a gigantic pool area designed to look like a beach, complete with palm trees and waves. By far the best thing about Sun City, the Valley has two fabulous waterslides called "Viper" and "Mamba" that send you spinning down a dark tunnel on an inflated tyre at a truly terrifying speed.

Looking onto the water is the staggeringly opulent hotel, the *Lost City Palace* (see above). Despite the laughable mythology about it really being a lost city, the Palace really is rather splendid: a soaring edifice covered in elaborate woodcarvings and glowing mosaics, with beautiful, palatial interiors. You can pop in for a drink if you're not staying.

The **Entertainment Centre** is the focal point of the rest of Sun City. Here you'll find rows of bleeping slots faithfully fed tokens by their determined flock, and banks of arcade games. The centre's **cinema** has the best movie selection in Northwest, and the **concert hall** hosts regular beauty contests, music and sports events, which have improved since the lifting of the cultural and sports boycotts in the 1990s.

Watersports from windsailing to powerboating are offered on "Waterworld", a large, artificial lake near the *Cabanas* hotel, and you'll find tennis courts, a fitness centre and a golf course at the *Gary Player Country Club*.

Pilanesberg Game Reserve

Home to a huge variety of southern African animal life, the **Pilanesberg Game Reserve** (April–Aug 5.30am–7pm; Sept–March 5pm–8pm; entry fee) is Northwest's biggest tourist draw. Don't let the crowds put you off though: this huge, well-managed park offers game-viewing thrills aplenty, with a good chance of seeing all of the **Big Five**, along with **hippo**, **giraffe** and **cheetah**, as well as a vast range of **birdlife**. If you've only limited time in South Africa, and are based in Johannesburg, this is definitely the place to come to see some game.

Pilanesberg is the site of an earthquake that erupted some 1300 million years ago in what is now Lake Mankwe. Before the eruption, the magma's pressure cracked the earth's surface into unusual concentric circles. After the eruption, the earth's crust collapsed into the resulting underground vacuum, which squeezed the remaining magma into the cracks. The magma solidified, and now constitutes the park's many beautiful hills, which are in some ways Pilanesberg's finest feature, though often ignored by visitors more interested in scouring their slopes for wildlife. These hills were home to **Tswana** people until the 1970s, when "Operation Genesis" saw huge numbers of animals shipped from all over the country to create an impressive wildlife reserve.

You'll need at least a day to do Pilanesberg justice. If you're in your own car, aim to travel at under 20km per hour if you want to catch sight of the animals. A **map** available at the information centre (see below) explains the various habitats, enabling you to plan your journey around what you most want to see. Bear in mind, however, that other drivers have this map too, and areas recommended for popular animals tend to become congested. The most-sought-after big animals are lion, elephant, white and black rhino, hippo, giraffe, buffalo, cheetah and leopard. Most antelope species are here too, along with hundreds of bird species and snakes. At night, some fantastic creatures emerge, including the civet, porcupine and caracal, though their dislike of the large vehicles with spotlights used for night rides mean you will be lucky to catch a glimpse of them.

Practicalities

The main entrance to Pilanesberg is the **Manyane Gate**, on the eastern edge of the reserve. Driving **from Rustenburg**, you'll need to follow the R510 to Thabazimbi, and take a left turn near Mogwase. **From Sun City**, which is nestled in the southern border of the reserve, the nearest entrance is the **Bakubung Gate** west of the resort on the R565.

The park's **Reception** at the Manyane Gate (Mon–Thurs 7.30am–4.30pm, Fri 7.30am–8pm, Sat 7.30am–4.30pm, Sun 7.30am–3.30pm; closed daily 1–2pm; ☎01465/56135) can provide useful maps and leaflets. In the centre of the park, the **Pilanesberg information centre** (same hours) features displays and maps, and has a gift shop.

Pilanesberg is easily explored in your own car, but make sure you've got the official map and guidebook, keen eyes and plenty of time. The various picnic spots and hides dotted around are ideal for breaking the drive. Alternatively, you can book **game drives** (2.5hr) at the park's Reception, or at Sun City (see p.505); a good way to see the Big Five. *Pilanesberg Safaris* also operate **hiking trips**, which give you a genuine feel for the bush, and the chance to stand close to large and potentially dangerous animals, fortunately in the company of an armed warden. For a hefty R900 per person, you can waft above the park on a four-hour **balloon safari**, which includes food and drink.

LODGINGS

Pilanesberg's eight **lodgings** are, with the exception of *Tshukudu*, somewhat characterless and, with the exception of *Manyane*, fairly expensive. Most visitors stay at Sun City and explore the park on organized safaris. *Manyane* is the only place in the reserve where you can **camp** with your own tent. **Bookings** for everywhere except *Kwa Maritane* and *Tshukudu* must be made through Pilanesberg National Park, PO Box 937, Lonehill 2062 (☎011/465 5423, fax 465 1228).

Bakgatla Complex, near the Bakgatla Gate in the north. Well-situated, self-catering chalets that sleep five, set among weird-looking hillocks. ③.

Bakubung Lodge (☎01465/21861). On the southern edge of the park, just west of Sun City. The highlight at this large, modern lodge is the hippo pool just a stone's throw from the restaurant. Rooms are pleasant if bland, and guided walks and game drives are on offer. ⑦.

Kololo Camp. Nestled in the park's beautiful western hill ranges, and offering four tents sleeping twelve, which in high season must be booked as a single unit. The camp has wonderful views. ③.

Kwa Maritane Lodge (☎01465/21820). In the southeast corner of the park, near Pilanesberg Airport, this upmarket resort feels somehow detached from its fabulous surroundings. Full-board, plenty of facilities, and game drives. ⑦.

Mankwe Camp, by Mankwe Lake, in the centre of the park. Good-value bungalows and safari tents in a lovely setting, which is breathtaking at dawn and dusk. ②.

Manyane Complex & Caravan Park, just by the Manyane Gate. The low cost and convenience compensate for the distinctly un-bushlike atmosphere of this *Parks Board*-run camp. There's a bar and restaurant, pool, gym and mini-golf. Chalets with kitchen (②) or camping stands (①).

Metswedi Camp, in the northern hills of the park. Luxurious, fully catered safari camp with outstanding views. (⑦).

Tshukudu Lodge (☎01465/21861). Gaze out at big game from your verandah in an outstandingly beautiful setting in the southwest of the park. Picturesque thatched huts offer luxury accommodation (sunken baths, roaring log fires), and the high price includes all meals and game drives. ⑦.

The Central Region

Thanks to its scrawny and desolate dryness, Northwest Province's **Central Region** feels especially remote. **Mmabatho**, once the capital of Bophuthatswana and now capital of Northwest, forces reluctant bureaucratic pilgrimages on people from all over the province but remains profoundly uncosmopolitan. The city's monthly *What's On* magazine invariably reveals "not much", and the same is true, only more so, of **Zeerust**, **Groot Marico** and **Lichtenburg**. The region's appeal lies elsewhere, in the brooding plains and lush river valleys of Marico and the rarely visited game reserves, including **Botsalano** near the Botswana border. Then there are the remains of the rich but depressing history of the region, centring on the relentless dispossession of the Tswana, but also including the famed **siege of Mafikeng** during the second Anglo-Boer War, and the incredible **Lichtenburg diamond rush** of 1926. Finally, there are the people: local Tswana and Afrikaners are both short on English but long on hospitality, at least to visitors.

Groot Marico

GROOT MARICO, resting contentedly by the banks of the Marico River, just south of the N4 and 90km west of Rustenburg, gained fame through Herman Charles Bosman's short stories based on his time as a teacher here. The town's handful of attractions include the **Art Factory** (Mon–Sat 9am–5pm) on the main street, where you can pick up local Tswana cultural artefacts. Also worth a visit are the remains of **Tshwenyane** and **Karechuenya**, two Tswana towns built in the sixteenth and seventeenth centuries. They lie 36km northwest of town, on the Orion Farm (☎01428/23350), which is reached by taking the signposted turn-off from the Zeerust–Gaborone section of the N4, about 16km from Zeerust. If there are just one or two of you, enlist the help of Marico's information centre (see below). There's a display on these archeological findings at the Mafikeng Museum (see p.511).

Although prone to stultifying heat, particularly in summer, the hills of the Marico district are good for hiking, and when it all gets too much you can make for the river for cool relief. The water of the **Marico Oog**, a spring some 20km south of town, is particularly clear and refreshing: festooned with water lilies and surrounded by beautiful dolomitic rocks, it makes a tranquil place for a picnic.

The *Citylink* **bus** from Johannesburg to Mmabatho stops at the train station (20min from the village) on request, but you'll find it easiest to reach Groot Marico by **car**, following the reasonably good N4 highway. The town's helpful **information centre** (☎014252, ask for 85), which claims to be open 24 hours, is along the main

MAMPOER

Mampoer is the Afrikaans word for the fearsomely strong distilled alcohol so beloved by Marico locals for many years. Any fruit can be used to make *mampoer*, but **peach** is the most traditional: until 1878, much of Northwest's farmland grew peach trees solely devoted to this purpose. Things changed with the ZAR government's distilling tax, and new licensing system in 1894, and thousands of *mampoer* stills were destroyed. A few, however, escaped detection. One farmer, we are told, cleaned out his entire drainage system but made no attempt to conceal his fifteen barrels of *mampoer*. The inspectors found the barrels, split them open and poured the entire contents down the drain. Meanwhile, the canny farmer had his family stationed in the field where the pipe ended up with every container the household possessed, and managed to recover fourteen of the fifteen barrels.

To make *mampoer*, distillers put the fruit in a copper still and allow it to ferment until the juice is settled, at which point they light a fire under the still. A copper pipe leads from the top of the still to a drum filled with cold running water, which it coils inside. As the juice heats up, steam gathers at the top of the still and comes down the pipe, condensing when it reaches the coil in the drum. This liquid is distilled once more, this time over a low, slow fire. In the old days the alcohol content was measured by throwing a chunk of lard into a sample. If it floated halfway, the *mampoer* was perfect.

The drink is celebrated in Herman Charles Bosman's short story, **Willem Prinsloo's Peach Brandy**, set in the 1920s:

". . . we arrived at Willem Prinsloo's house. There were so many ox-waggons drawn up on the veld that the place looked like a laager [circle of wagons]. *Prinsloo met us at the door.*

'Go right through, kerels,' he said. 'The dancing is in the voorhuis [barn]. *The peach brandy is in the kitchen.'*

Although the voorhuis was big, it was so crowded as to make it almost impossible to dance. But it was not as crowded as the kitchen. Nor was the music in the voorhuis – which was provided by a number of men with guitars and concertinas – as loud as the music in the kitchen, where there was no band, but each man sang for himself.

We knew from these signs that the party was a success.

When I had been in the kitchen for about half an hour I decided to go into the voorhuis. It seemed a long way, now, from the kitchen to the voorhuis, and I had to lean against the wall several times to think. I passed a number of men who were also leaning against the wall like that, thinking. One man even found that he could think best by sitting on the floor with his head in his arms.

You could see that Willem Prinsloo made a pretty good peach brandy."

If you want to sample *mampoer*, head for Pieter Roets's **Vergenoeg Farm** (open most days, closed evenings) a few kilometres south of Marico along the untarred main road. Also on offer – and even more lethal – is *Doringdrood*, eighty percent proof and in a bottle wrapped in barbed wire to give you fair warning.

street from the *Bosveld Hotel* (look out for a small signpost). The *Bosveld* is Groot Marico's only **accommodation** option (☎014252, ask for 45; ②), and has good rooms, a restaurant and a bar where white locals, inspired by beer, brandy and their own good humour, have been known to dance traditional Afrikaans two-steps. For more relaxed accommodation, a **farmstay** can be booked through the information centre. The nicest **camping** spots around here are on the *Sallileni Farm*, 3km south of town, by the river (☎014252, ask for 114), and near the **Marico Dam** (☎014252, ask for Gronum Loots, 1303), north of town, where hot water and electricity are available. At weekends the dam is a magnet for local *braais*, fishing, drinking and watersports.

Zeerust and around

The large and unprepossessing regional centre of **ZEERUST**, 40km west of Groot Marico on the N4, is essentially a supplies town, and only worth stopping at on the way to Gaborone or one of the surrounding game reserves. There's an annual **mampoer festival** (check with tourist information centre for dates); otherwise, shops aside, there's precious little to see. Just outside town, the **Abjasterkop** is a striking, pointed hill which rewards a quick scramble or a more serious hike. You can park at the *Abjasterkop Hotel*, 2km east on the N4, and ask the manager for directions.

To find the luxurious private **Madikwe Game Reserve** (☎014778/89 1892; ⑦), head north of Zeerust on the N4 to the Botswana border. The third-largest reserve in South Africa, Madikwe is amply stocked with the Big Five (transported from Kruger Park) and hundreds of other species. Fabulous chalets look out onto the Marico River, and game drives are included in the very high price. Also near Zeerust is the **Klein Marico Resort** (☎01428/22038; chalet ②, camping ①; entry fee), which occupies a beautiful position high above the town. There are enough **antelope** to justify the entrance fee, and you'll find a restaurant serving moderately-priced meat dishes. The ugly brick chalets mercifully do not intrude on Klein Marico's soothing midweek tranquillity. To get there, head back to Groot Marico on the N4, turn off at the Total Garage and continue for 4km.

City Link (☎011/333 4412) and *Greyhound* (☎011/830 1301) **buses** arrive in Zeerust daily from Johannesburg. Decent **places to stay** include the *Transvaal*, 36 Kerk St (☎01428/22003; ②), which has a pleasant patio looking out onto the street, basic rooms and a solidly Afrikaner bar downstairs, and the *Erinbroch*, 5 President St (☎01428/21067; ③), a solid B&B. Some 2km east of town, on the N4, the *Abjaterskop* (☎01428/22008; hotel room ③, rondavel and camping ①) is in a magnificent hilly setting, ideal for hiking, and is the best **place to eat** in the area, with a restaurant with an à la carte menu, and a good bar.

Mmabatho and around

The capital of the former homeland of Bophuthatswana, **MMABATHO** is on the road to precious little. Unless you are travelling to Gaborone and don't mind the detour, you're unlikely to bother to come here. If you do, though, you'll be struck by the expensive-looking concrete buildings, which include a sports stadium and a massive shopping mall – all commissioned as city showpieces by the Bop dictator **Lucas Mangope**, largely from the revenues of Sun City. A visit to this area also gives you the chance to see the rarely visted Botsalano Game Reserve.

Mmabatho was created out of nothing in 1977 as the capital of the new "independent homeland" of Bophuthatswana. The city prospered fast, both from the discovery of platinum and the revenue from Sol Kerzner's gambling resort. One of the more positive legacies of those days is the impressive **Mmabana Cultural Centre**, on the outskirts of Mmabatho, at the southern end of the Mangope Highway. The centre offers a wide range of social and educational services, mostly to Tswana children, and can be visited by prior arrangement (☎0140/24100).

Just over 30km from town lies the **Botsalano Game Reserve** (daily 7.30am–4pm; camping ①, safari tent ③; ☎0140/86 2433; reservations ☎011/465 5423; entry fee), whose name means "friendship" in Tswana. **White rhino**, **giraffe** and other plains game roam the wooded grasslands, and the **birdlife** is fairly impressive, with around 140 different species. As well as being an inexpensive place to **camp**, you also stand a good chance of having Botsalano to yourself. To get there, take the road to the Ramatlabama border post (R503) for 20km; just before the border, take the Dinakana turn-off, and continue for about 7km to a crossroads. From here, take the turn marked

ZEERUST AND MMABATHO

MMABATHO & MAFIKENG

△ ① *Rooigrond & Sehuba Protea*

◁ *Manyane Game Reserve, Zeerust*

▷ *Airport, Lotlamoreng Dam & Vryburg*

△ *Botsalano Game Reserve, Botswana*

ACCOMMODATION
1 Hope Fountain Guest Farm
2 Mmabatho Sun
3 Molopo Sun
4 Montshiwa Guesthouse
5 Royal Palm Guesthouse
6 The Surrey
7 Windsor Lodge

Cooke's Lake Campsite

First National Bank

St John's Church

Mafikeng Museum

St Joseph's Convent

Victoria Hospital

Train Station

Taxi Rank

Mafikeng Cemetery

MAFIKENG

MONTSHIWA TOWN

Mmabana Cultural Centre

Megacity Shopping Mall

1 km

"Dinakana", and travel another 7km up a dirt track. The gate here should be open. If it isn't, drive another 12km to the management gate and enter from there.

Practicalities

SA Airlink (☎011/394 2430) operate two flights a day from Johannesburg to **Mmabatho International Airport**, roughly 17km from the town centre. From here, you'll have to rent a car to get downtown as there are no buses. *City Link* **buses** (☎011/333 4412) from the Johannesburg Rotunda terminate at the central Megacity Mall. Hordes of **minibus taxis** ply the tedious 5km between Mmabatho and Mafikeng. To reach Mmabatho **by car**, take the R49 from Zeerust and Vryburg, or the R503 from Lichtenburg. Mmabatho is only 25km from the Ramatlabama border post with Botswana, some 122km from Gaborone.

The **Northwest tourist information office** (Mon–Fri 8am–4.30pm; ☎0140/84 3040) is in the Electricity Centre, on the corner of the Mangope Highway and Dr Mogkobo Road. Barely signposted, the office is worth hunting out for its useful selection of literature on the province and Mmabatho itself.

Mmabatho has several decent **places to stay**: the centrally located *Molopo Sun* (☎0140/24 1849; ③), on University Road, offers comfortable rooms and a restaurant and pool. The rooms of the grander *Mmabatho Sun*, on Voortrekker Road (which connects Mmabatho to Mafikeng), are surprisingly poky for a casino-dominated hotel, but its three restaurants, two bars, two swimming pools, sauna and spa go some way towards compensating (☎0140/89 1111; ⑤). Finally, the *Montshiwa Guest House* (☎0140/21816; ①), in Montshiwa suburb, is one of the few Tswana-owned guesthouses in Northwest, and offers simple, good-value accommodation. The only decent **places to eat** in Mmabatho are at the restaurants of the *Molopo* and *Mmabatho Sun* hotels; for a wider choice, you're best off heading for Mafikeng (see below).

Mafikeng and around

Separated from Mmabatho by only 5km of poverty-stricken shacks, but considerably livelier than its neighbour, **MAFIKENG** is most famous for the Boer **siege** which occurred here in 1900, when Robert Baden-Powell defended the British garrison from six thousand Afrikaners (see box opposite). Today, the city's bustling centre and quiet colonial suburbs bear no trace of past dramas, and the main attraction is the excellent museum.

Arrival, information and accommodation

Daily *City Link* **buses** (☎011/333 4412) from Johannesburg stop in Mafikeng on their way to Mmabatho. **Minibus taxis** making the short hop from Mmabatho stop at the railway station, and at the corner of Warren and Shippard streets.

The best budget **accommodation** option is the central but rather run-down *Surrey*, 32 Shippard St (☎0140/81 0420; ①–②), with rooms that look onto the street, and a reasonable restaurant. Quieter and more comfortable, the nearby *Royal Palm Guest House*, 79 Sheppard St (☎0140/81 2218; ②), offers good-value B&B accommodation. The *Windsor Hotel Lodge*, 39 Tillard St (☎0140/81 1150; ③), is one of Mafikeng's best places to stay, but the rooms vary considerably, so ask to see yours before checking in. If you've got a car, it's worth staying a little way southeast of Mafikeng, in tiny **Rooigrond**. Here, the delightful *Hope Fountain Guest Farm* (☎01448/781; ②) offers cosy chalets in semi-rural surroundings, with breakfast included in the price. To get there, turn off the R503 at the Sehuba Protea sign, and follow the signs. The only **campsite** near town is *Cooke's Lake Camping Ground*, south of Mafikeng off the R503, with basic facilities but a noisy roadside location.

THE SIEGE OF MAFIKENG

Mafikeng was **besieged** within three days of the start of the second Anglo-Boer War (1899–1902) by generals Snyman and Cronje. **Colonel Robert Baden-Powell** (founder of the Boy Scouts) had the task of defending the town. This he did for 217 days, from October 16, 1899 until May 17, 1900, when relief arrived from Rhodesia and from the south. In the process, Baden-Powell became a British household name and hero, exemplifying imperial ability and courage under fire.

Mafikeng was strategically irrelevant to the war, and Baden-Powell's real achievement was to distract the six thousand Afrikaners besieging the town from fighting elsewhere. He relied heavily on the Barolong people for defence, labour and reconnaissance, but failed to record this either in his dispatches to London or in his memoirs. The Barolong received far fewer rations than the British and over one thousand subsequently died of starvation, yet none received any of the £29,000 raised in Britain for the rehabilitation of Mafikeng. To add insult to injury, not one Barolong was decorated for bravery, in contrast to the plentiful medals dished out to the British regiments, and none of the promises Baden-Powell made about land grants to them were ever kept.

The town and museum

Mafikeng's smattering of historic buildings make for a pleasant stroll. Starting from Victoria Street, four blocks north of Main Street, look out for the **Victoria Hospital**, which was pounded during the siege of 1900, and the elegant **St Joseph's Convent**. Three blocks south, on Martin Street, stands the splendid **St John's Anglican Church**, designed by Sir Herbert Baker and built in 1902. Nearby is the town's main attraction, the **Mafikeng Museum** (Mon–Fri 8am–4pm, Sat 10am–12.30pm; free), which has some intriguing exhibits on the San, with some of the range of poisons and weapons they hunt with, and photos of hand signals San make to each other when hunting in their customary silence. Tswana exhibits include a life-size recreation of a traditional hut, complete with stylish trademark enclosed porch, and samples of pottery and beadwork. An extensive display of herbs and medicines throws up some interesting specimens, including the sweet violet with five times the Vitamin C content of oranges, and a relative of the potato called the "mandrake", with awesomely hallucinogenic powers. The **Mafikeng Siege** is given a room of its own, filled with classic British imperial memorabilia, including a tattered flag, ration book, diaries and a wonderful collection of photos. Extensive quotations from Peter Warwick's *Black People and the SA War 1899–1902* intersperse the exhibits, offering a subversive account of the events. The Tswana writer and activist Sol Plaatje lived in Mafikeng for many years, and wrote a diary of the siege (see box above), and he receives a full, informative display. Keep an eye out too for the fascinating exhibit on Mafikeng and the railways, which provides evidence of the connection between their spread from Cape Town and Rhodes' mission to colonize Africa.

The only other sight in Mafikeng worth a visit is the **Cemetery** on Carrington Street, in the town's northwestern corner, next to the sleepy railway sidings. Dusty and unkempt, it counts amongst its headstones white iron crosses marking the graves of British soldiers. Some were casualties from the siege, and others are from the many other battles waged by the British against the Afrikaners and Tswana. Until the 1980s this was a whites-only cemetery, and still commemorates only the Europeans who died during the siege.

The game reserves

The **Manyane Game Reserve** (☎0140/81 6020; entry fee) lies 10km east of Mafikeng on the Zeerust Road (R49). Run by the Northwest Parks Board, it's well stocked with primarily herbivorous plains game, including **rhino** and **buffalo**, but the landscape is a bit flat and drab. You will can **stay** in pleasant chalets (④). Nearby, the **Wondergat** is a deep, water-filled cave whose bottom has only recently been reached. If you swim you might feel the warm stream 20m below the surface, which makes the water sparkle. On a good day, particularly in summer, this area makes a fine picnic spot. To reach the Wondergat, take the first right turn after Manyane, travel 4km and then take a left turn down a dirt track. Travel a further 8km and turn right.

The **Lotlamoreng Dam Resort** (daily 7am–noon; small entry fee) has two cold pools, *braai* stands, a tuck shop and bar that's popular with locals at weekends, but is quiet during the week. The resort's highlight is the remains of the Credo Mutwa Cultural Village inside its grounds, featuring *kraals* built in the traditional styles of South Africa's ethnic groups, and bizarre religious statues. The village was badly damaged in 1994 by members of the ANC youth wing for allegedly perpetuating tribal divisions, and today only goats roam the ruins. To find Lotlamoreng, travel 5km west of Mafikeng on the Vryburg road and turn right at the signs.

Lichtenburg and around

The deeply conservative *dorp* of **LICHTENBURG** lies some 65km southeast of Mmabatho on the R503, close to the N14 highway which connects the Northern Cape to Gauteng. Lichtenburg's name means "place of light"; when the town was proclaimed in 1873, it was hoped that the new settlement would bring some light to this forsaken spot. Progress was deadly slow until 1926, when a Tswana labourer on the Elandsputte farm of Jan Voorendyk discovered a **diamond**. News spread fast, and by 1927 the Lichtenburg diamond diggings were 36km long and 1.6km wide. Incredibly, a shantytown of 150,000 people had sprung up by then, sporting over 200 diamond-buying offices. The quantity of diamonds discovered here threatened the diamond market, but De Beers bought nearly every one to maintain its monopoly and the diamonds' worth.

The shantytown was famed for its **dust**, which was alleged to waft from Lichtenburger mouths as they spoke. By 1935, the rush had petered out, but a few prospectors continued working the diggings right up until 1993. Today only one company still works the diggings; you can watch its men in action by following the R505 north of Lichtenburg towards Zeerust, and turning left just before the Bakerville turn-off.

DIGGING FOR DIAMONDS

"Once you have found your first diamond, you will never give up looking." *Digger proverb*

According to digger mythology, all that anyone needs to find diamonds are a claim, a pick, a shovel, a wheelbarrow, and the luck of the gods. In practice, however, extra equipment comes in pretty handy. First off, you'll need a *dummy*, which is a swinging sieve in a frame that gets rid of larger stones. After this, you'll need a *washing machine*, which mixes the gravel left by the dummy with muddy water, its rotating arms and teeth holding the mixture in suspension. The diamonds and heavier gravel sink to the bottom, and the lighter gravel, called *tailings*, floats to the top and is poured out. Another sieve separates the tailings from the water, which is reused. After the washing machine, the remaining gravel is poured into a *sluice* and then a *washing tub*, which removes the last of the water, and grades the gravel into three sizes. These are then pored over with a knife, in the hope that this time there will be a diamond. In 1926, at the time of the Lichtenburg diggings, all this equipment cost around £600, which effectively meant you needed a diamond to pay for it . . .

In De La Rey Square, the **Lichtenburg Museum** (Tues–Fri 10am–noon & 1–5pm, Sat 10am–1pm; free) is worth a visit for its display on **General Koos De La Rey**, who tried and failed to capture Lichtenburg from the British in 1900. De La Rey was one of the Boer "bitter enders", who only stopped fighting in 1902 with the greatest of reluctance, and is credited with the invention of trench warfare (see p.233).

Accommodation is limited, the only hotel being the rather grim *Elgro* (✆01441/23051; ③), on the corner of Republiek and Melville streets. Far more comfortable is the *Melville*, 20 Melville St (✆01441/23514; ②), a B&B run by renowned South African illustrator and artist Carol Fourie. For **eating and drinking**, you could try the *Spur* steakhouse next door to the *Elgro*, or *O'Hagan's* pub on Melville Street. Marginally better than both is the *Taverne*, 145 Melville St, where you can tuck into a reasonably priced steak and dessert.

Nearby nature reserves

The **Lichtenburg Nature Reserve** (Mon–Fri 7am–4pm, Sat & Sun 8am–5.30pm; ✆01441/22818; entry fee; camping ①) has an unusual selection of wildlife, including an excellent vulture restaurant in its small forest. The vultures usually feed in the afternoon, but enquire at the gate for precise times if you enjoy the sight of birds devouring raw flesh. Less gory are the hundreds of birds you can watch from the hide by the lake. **To get to the reserve**, take the R505 north of the town to Ottoshoop and Zeerust, turning left 2km later at the easily missed signpost, and go under the railway bridge. The reserve is another 2km further on.

About 100km southwest of Lichtenburg on the N14 near Delareyville, you'll find the **Barberspan Nature Reserve** (✆053/948 1842; daily), a large, natural wetland that sits in striking contrast to the fields of *mielies*, and is home to tens of thousands of birds, including flamingos, herons, storks and ibis.

Along the Vaal River

The mighty **Vaal** (or Lekwa) was the historic boundary between the Orange Free State and the South African Republic (ZAR). Still the provincial boundary, separating Northwest from the Free State, today the Vaal runs alongside the N12 highway between Johannesburg and Kimberley. The landscape here is dominated by flat maize fields, but being close to the river is a bonus, providing you with opportunities for timely sorties from the beaten track.

Potchefstroom

One of the largest and oldest towns of Northwest, **POTCHEFSTROOM** is a classic Afrikaner settlement, with main streets wide enough to turn a wagon in, a large square and plenty of churches. Founded by Voortrekker leader **Andries Potgieter** on the banks of the Mooi River in 1837, "Potchefstroom" means "stream of chief Potgieter". Once the capital of the ZAR, today "Potch" is best known for its university, which has seen violent clashes between black and Afrikaner students since blacks were admitted in the 1990s.

A good place to start your explorations is with a stroll down Kerk Street, where the abandoned *Rendezvous Café* makes a pleasant Victorian landmark. Parallel Greyling Street is the site of the old *landrost* and post office; Potchefstroom played a major role in the ZAR's postal services, and black runners were employed here to deliver mail as far away as what is now Mpumalanga province, hundreds of kilometres away. The **Potchefstroom Museum** on Gouws Street (Mon–Fri 9am–5pm; free), houses one of the few remaining Voortrekker wagons used at the Battle of Blood River in 1838, when Voortrekkers defeated the Zulus.

You'll need a car to reach the town's other attractions. To get to **Pretorius House** (Mon–Fri 10am–1pm & 2–4pm, Sat 9am–1pm, Sun 2.30–5pm; small entry fee), the former home of Marthinus Pretorius, the ZAR's first president, head up Kerk Street until it turns into Van der Hoff Road, and continue a short distance – the house is on the right as you head north. It's a beautiful old house with whitewashed walls, green doors and a thatched roof, and is typical of nineteenth-century Afrikaner dwellings. Inside, you'll find dour photos and ornate wallpaper, minimal furnishings and a family Bible. On the opposite side of the street stands the **Totius Museum** (Mon–Fri 10am–1pm & 2–4pm, Sat 9am–1pm, Sun 2.30–5pm; free), recreated to be as it was when the poet lived here a century ago. Totius was a key figure in the Dutch Reformed Church and Afrikaans language movement: as well as establishing the church's theological college in Potchefstroom, he was one of the first poets to publish in Afrikaans, and translated the Bible into Afrikaans between 1923 and 1933. The most striking part of the museum is the poet's tome-filled study, but look out too for paintings by the celebrated and controversial Jacob Pierneef (see p.489), which were especially dedicated to Totius.

Practicalities.

Potchefstroom is well served by public transport; daily *Translux*, *Greyhound* and *Intercape* **buses** stop on Potgieter Street near the tourist information centre, on their route between Cape Town and Johannesburg via Kimberley. **Trains** from Cape Town and Johannesburg terminate at the train station west of the city centre (train information ☎0148/299 3205).

There's a helpful **tourist office** in the old library, on the corner of Kerk and Potgieter streets (Mon–Fri 7.45am–1pm & 1.45–4.30pm; ☎0148/293 1611), where you can pick up maps and leaflets about the town. The only budget **place to stay** is the charmless but functional *Lake Recreation Resort* (☎0148/299 5470; ①), north of the town centre on Tom Street, where you can rent a self-catering bungalow or **camp** amid good facilities. More central options include the mediocre *King's*, 23 Potgieter St (☎0148/297 5505; ②), and the Elgro, 60 Wolmarans St (☎0148/297 5411; ③).

Eating and drinking possibilities are limited to the steakhouses and pizza places on Potgieter and Kerk streets. For a coffee or light snack, head for *Expressivo* on Kerk Street.

Klerksdorp and around

Nondescript **KLERKSDORP**, 25km down the N12 from Potchefstroom, is a busy agricultural and mining centre near some of the world's largest gold mines. The only significant attraction here is the **Klerksdorp Museum** at the corner of Margaretha Prinsloo and Lombard streets (Mon–Fri 10am–1pm & 2–4.30pm, Sat 9.30am–noon, Sun 2–5pm; free). Hardly surprising for a former prison, this is a fairly creepy place, with displays of flogging equipment, solitary confinement and the like, very effective in evoking the once-grim conditions. The courtyard has been converted into a standard Afrikaner museum, complete with wagon and candle-making displays .

Some 11km northwest of Klerksdorp, the **Faan Meintjes Nature Reserve** (daily 10am–3pm; ☎018/462 7805; R12; caravan stands ①, chalets ②), has few carnivores of note, but plenty of **white rhino**, **giraffe** and **antelope** wandering its bushveld terrain. To reach the reserve, head north on Van Riebeeck (R30), which is also called Church Street, south of the N12, and turn right at the signpost a few kilometres later, along Brady Lane. There are **San rock paintings** nearby on the Bosworth farm, which you can visit by appointment through the owner of the *North Hills Country House* (see below).

AFRIKANER MUSEUMS

The former Transvaal and Orange Free State are filled with museums dedicated to the preservation and propagation of **Afrikaner mythology**. Typically, exhibits will include mementos from the Great Trek (wagons are particularly prized); displays of farm-life domesticity such as butter-churning and candle-making; children's toys (generally toy wagons made from bones); photos of Afrikaner generals from the Anglo-Boer Wars, with accompanying text about the "War of Liberation"; tattered Afrikaner flags, rifles and bullet belts; details of Afrikaner casualties of concentration camps and, finally, a plaque to tell you where the town's 1938 Voortrekker centenary monument is.

Many museums have recently had their grants cut, and widening the focus to include African culture is their only chance of renewing their financial lifeline.

Practicalities

Daily *Translux*, *Greyhound* and *Intercape* **buses** stop on Church Street on their way between Cape Town and Johannesburg via Kimberley. The **railway station** is just off Margaretha Prinsloo Street, a few blocks east of the city centre, with daily arrivals from Cape Town and Johannesburg (train information ☎018/406 2022).

Klerkdorp's **best place to stay** is unquestionably the *Fountain Villa Guest Lodge*, 21 Hendrik Potgieter Rd (☎018/464 1394; ③), a superb house in the old town sporting elegant turrets and wooden lattice work, and featuring an outstanding **restaurant** and an aromatherapy centre. Further out, on the road to the Faan Meintjes reserve, the *North Hills Country House* (☎018/468 6416; ④) provides comfortable rooms, excellent German cooking (with good dishes for vegetarians), and doubles up as an Arabian stud farm.

The road to Kimberley

Once past Klerksdorp, the N12 passes through vast stretches of maize-growing country. There are no big towns until **Kimberley** in the Northern Cape, and you'll find yourself passing through a succession of sleepy *dorps*. A string of small nature reserves on the banks of the Vaal and the excellent *Lindbergh Safari Lodge* provide good opportunities to break up your journey.

Wolmaransstad and around

WOLMARANSSTAD, 90km southwest of Klerksdorp on the N12, consists of little more than two or three streets with a handful of shops. There's a scraggy **campsite** off the R504 on the way to Leeudoringstad, but the nicest attraction in these parts is the *Lindbergh Safari Lodge* (☎01811/22041; ④–⑤), where you can get a tantalizing glimpse of how the Northwest *veld* looked before maize took over, when it was thronging with birds and wildlife. Set in a small nature reserve, the beautiful thatched lodge looks out onto a watering hole popular with wildlife, enabling indolent game-viewing from an armchair. The rooms are luxurious, and there's a simple bush camp if you'd rather self-cater. The main attraction of the lodge is that the absence of predators makes it safe to wander on foot, and get close up to the giraffe, antelope and other plains game. To reach *Lindbergh*, turn right onto a dirt road, off the N12 some 20km south of Wolmaransstad, and follow the signs to Rietpan, and then to Leeufontain. The lodge is about 15km from the main road in all, but the roads are bad and signposting poor, so aim to travel during the day.

Further down the road, the *Buisfontein Safari Lodge* (☎01811/6704; ③) is actually a collection of thatched chalets with a good restaurant attached. For a taste of the Vaal River, continue past Leeudoringstad and head east a few kilometres, avoiding the R504, to Bothaville for the *Wolwespruit Nature Reserve* (☎01813/2026; ①), which has a good **campsite**.

Bloemhof and Christiana

Heading further down the N12, tiny **BLOEMHOF** is an agricultural town that also serves as a stopover for buses on the long haul between Johannesburg and Cape Town. Laid out by one James Barkly on his farm in 1866, the town was named after a garden of flowers cultivated by his daughter. *Greyhound* **buses** arrive and leave from the Trek Garage on Prince Street; *Intercape* from outside the *Volkskas Bank* on the main street; and *Translux* buses from outside the post office. The only decent **place to stay** is the *Bloemhof* (☎01802/31211; ②), on the main street, offering rooms with TV and bath, and an adjoining windowless restaurant serving standard meaty fare. Ignore signs to a B&B on a side street, as it's situated right next to a particularly smelly factory.

Even smaller than Bloemhof, **CHRISTIANA** is just over 50km further south, its few shops straggled out along the main road. **Accommodation** is limited to the tolerable *Christiana* (☎0534/2326; ②), on the main street, which has a **restaurant** serving grills, and two bars: one decorated and for whites; the other windowless, shed-like, and for blacks. There's a decent **campsite** on the banks of the Vaal, with showers, *braai* facilities, and incredibly noisy birds. Across the river in the Free State, on the road to Hertzogville, are stunning **San rock carvings** said to be over 7000 years old. Sadly interspersed with pathetic graffiti, some carvings depict wildlife, whilst others are abstracts. You can find the carvings on the *Stowlands-on-Vaal Farm* (☎0534/3054), where the owner is planning to erect rondavels.

travel details

Trains

Bloemhof to: Cape Town (1 daily; 19hr); Johannesburg (1 daily; 5hr); Klerksdorp (1 daily; 2hr); Potchefstroom (1 daily; 3hr).

Klerksdorp to: Cape Town (1 daily; 23hr); Johannesburg (1 daily; 3hr 30min); Potchefstroom (1 daily; 50min).

Potchefstroom to: Cape Town (1 daily; 24hr); Johannesburg (1 daily; 2hr 20min); Klerksdorp (1 daily; 50min).

Klerksdorp to: Cape Town (1–2 daily; 15hr); Johannesburg (3–4 daily; 2hr); Kimberley (2–3 daily; 4hr); Potchefstroom (3–4 daily; 45min).

Mmabatho to: Johannesburg (1 daily; 3hr); Rustenburg (1 daily; 1hr).

Potchefstroom to: Cape Town (1–3 daily except Tues; 16hr); Johannesburg (3–4 daily; 2hr); Kimberley (2–3 daily; 4hr 15min); Klerksdorp (3–4 daily; 45min) .

Rustenburg to: Johannesburg (2 daily; 2hr); Mmabatho (1 daily; 1hr).

Sun City to: Johannesburg (2–3 daily; 2hr); Pretoria (1 daily; 2hr).

Zeerust to: Johannesburg (1 daily; 3hr 15min).

Buses

Bloemhof to: Cape Town (1 Mon, Wed & Fri–Sun; 13hr 45min); Johannesburg (2–3 daily; 3–4hr); Kimberley (2–3 daily; 2hr); Klerksdorp (2–3 daily; 2hr); Potchefstroom (2–3 daily; 2hr).

Christiana to: Cape Town (1 Tues & Sun; 12hr 15min); Kimberley (1–2 daily; 1hr 30min); Klerksdorp (1–2 daily; 2hr); Johannesburg (1–2 daily; 5hr); Potchefstroom (1–2 daily; 3hr).

Flights

Mmabatho to: Johannesburg (2 daily; 1hr).

Sun City to: Johannesburg (1–3 daily; 35min).

CHAPTER NINE

MPUMALANGA AND THE KRUGER NATIONAL PARK

Mpumalanga, "the land of the rising sun" to its Siswati- and Zulu-speaking residents, extends east from Gauteng to Mozambique and Swaziland. To many visitors the province is synonymous with the **Kruger National Park**, the real draw of South Africa's east flank, and one of Africa's best game parks. Kruger occupies most of Mpumalanga's eastern flank as well as that of Northern Province, and covers over 20,000 square kilometres – an area the size of Wales or Massachusetts. Unashamedly populist, Kruger is the easiest African game park to drive around in on your own, staying at one of its many well-run rest camps. Joined to its west, a number of **private reserves** offer the chance to escape the Kruger crush – at a price – with well-informed rangers conducting safaris in open vehicles.

Apart from the irresistible magnet of big-game country, Mpumalanga also has some spectacular scenery in the mountainous area known as the **Escarpment**, a couple of hours' drive west of Kruger and easily tacked onto a visit to the park. With the exception of **Pilgrim's Rest**, none of the Escarpment towns merits exploration, but they make good night stops to and from Kruger, and there are some famously stunning views as you drive around, where the bottom drops out of the mountains and hits the Lowveld. The most famous viewpoints – **God's Window**, **Bourke's Luck Potholes** and **Three Rondavels** – are along the lip of the Escarpment, which can be driven as a 156-kilometre looped day-trip from Sabie. The views of **Blyde River Canyon** are most famous of all and, while you can't drive into the canyon, there are some fabulous hiking opportunities in this area.

Jammed between the mountains and Kruger are the former African **bantustans**, created under apartheid: Lebowa for Sotho speakers and Gazankulu for Shangaan- and Tsonga-speaking people. The poverty of these artificial statelets was exacerbated in the 1980s when hundreds of thousands of Mozambicans fled into Gazankulu to escape the civil war in Mozambique. Even today, Mozambicans attempt to cross illegally into South Africa, braving lions, National Parks officials and anti-poaching units in Kruger in a quest to reach the "golden city" of Johannesburg.

ACCOMMODATION PRICE CODES

All the accommodation listed in the Guide has been categorized into one of seven price bands, as set out below. The rates quoted, unless otherwise stated, represent the most expensive per-person rate for a double or single room outside high season (Dec & Jan), except for category ①, which are per-person rates for a dorm bed in backpacker accommodation, or a campsite. For more accommodation details, see p.31.

① R0–50	② R50–100	③ R100–150
④ R150–200	⑤ R200–250	⑥ R250–300
	⑦ Over R300	

For overseas visitors, the **route** is usually the other way round, starting from Johannesburg and heading through the unappetizing industrial corridor traversed by the N4 as it races to **Nelspruit**, the modern capital of Mpumalanga, which is served by buses to Johannesburg, an airport and car rental facilities. From here the N4 continues to the **Mozambique** border. This route gives you access to the southernmost part of Kruger; from Nelspruit it's 62km to Malelane Gate and 51km to Numbi Gate. Nelspruit also connects with the road south through **Barberton** to Swaziland.

Descending the Escarpment on one of four mountain passes takes you into the tropical-fruit-growing and bushveld country of the Lowveld, with impressive views back towards the towering massif of the Escarpment. A number of places close to the **Blydepoort Dam** at the foot of the Blyde River Canyon can be taken in as bushveld breaks on the way to or from Kruger. In the same vicinity, around the tiny centre of **Hoedspruit**, roughly 90km via an eastwardly-arching route from the Escarpment, a number of small **game farms** offer cut-price game experiences that are good for an overnight stop but shouldn't be confused with the real thing. This you'll find nearby at the far pricier game lodges in the Manyeleti and Timbabavati private game reserves as well in Kruger itself.

THE ESCARPMENT

Four hours' drive east of Johannesburg International Airport takes you to one of the city's favoured mountain retreats: the waving grasslands and luxury guesthouses of the Mpumalanga Drakensberg, generally known as the **Escarpment**. This region mostly sees travellers purely on account of its proximity to the Kruger National Park, but it holds some of the most dramatic views in the country and its unfailing attraction is that they can be enjoyed with so little effort. Unlike the KwaZulu-Natal Drakensberg, this section of the range is one you can tour in your own car, stopping at one of the tourist towns for lunch and retiring to comfortable lodgings at the end of the day.

The little forestry towns of **Sabie** and **Graskop** have ample accommodation for all budgets and are convenient bases for exploring the area, but only **Pilgrim's Rest**, a reconstructed mining settlement from turn-of-the-century gold-rush days, merits a visit for itself. The overriding pull of the Escarpment is the **Blyde River Canyon**, whose dizzying views into one of the world's great gorges appear in every other South African tourist brochure. Most commonly gazed into from a number of viewpoints along the Escarpment lip, it can also be seen from the **Blyderivierspoort Nature Reserve** at its foot. The five-day **Blyderivierspoort Hiking Trail**, one of South Africa's best walks, starts at **God's Window** on the lip and takes in all the major viewpoints, while giving access to the flora and (if you're quiet and lucky) fauna of the reserve, which includes zebra, hippo, kudu and the entire range of South African primates – baboons, vervet and samango monkeys and bushbabies.

Dullstroom, Lydenburg and Long Tom Pass

Some 209km east of Johannesburg the R540 branches off the N4 at nondescript **Belfast**, to head into the hills, where the typical highveld countryside is covered by grasslands which wave tall green in summer, turning russet in winter.

Unless your passion is fly-fishing, chances are you'll find the tiny crossroads settlement of **DULLSTROOM**, 35km north of Belfast on the R540, just about as exciting as its name suggests. However, Dullstroom can be a useful place to stop over for a night on your way to Kruger National Park. The cheapest **accommodation** option is to camp at the dam or take one of the B&B rooms rented out at 503 Voortrekker St (☎01325/40053; ②), a home where you'll be treated like a family guest. More anonymous are the pleasantly cool rooms in the *Victorian Dullstroom Inn*, Teding van Berkhout St (☎01325/40071, fax 40278; ③). Of the upmarket country lodges that cater to fly-fishing enthusiasts, the most luxurious is *Walkerson's Country Manor* (☎01325/40246, fax 40260; ⑤), 20km north of Dullstroom on the R540. This is a small, sixteen-room hotel on a nature reserve, that provides exclusive fishing for its guests in its ten dams and 2km of river frontage. One notch down, with a rate which also includes dinner, the *Critchley Hackle Lodge*, Teding van Berghout St (☎01325/40145, fax 40262; ④), is a country-style hotel with stone and brick cottages, each with their own fireplace. Less pricey still, *The Poacher*, 66 Hugenoten St (☎ & fax 01325/40108; ③), is a small lodge with four rooms and has dam and river frontage and a tackle shop. Dullstroom's outstanding **restaurant**, *Tonteldoos*, in the main street, draws out gourmands from Jo'burg just for lunch and wins awards every year. The deli at the front of the restaurant stocks smoked trout and other delicacies.

Some 58km north of Dullstroom, functional **LYDENBURG** is the site of one of South Africa's major archeological discoveries, replicas of which are on display at the

Lydenburg Museum (Mon–Fri 9am–noon & 2–4.15pm, Sat & Sun 10am–4pm; small entry fee) in the Gustav Klingbiel Nature Reserve, 3km out of town along the R37 to Sabie. The **Lydenburg Heads**, seven ceramic masks which date back to the fifth century, are some of the first figurative sculptures in southern Africa, and they are rather beautiful, probably ceremonial and definitely unique – nothing like them has been found anywhere else. As well as replicas of these heads (the originals are in the South African Museum in Cape Town), there are excellent displays of human activity in the vicinity over the past million years or so.

Striking east from Lydenburg, the R37 twists its way up **Long Tom Pass**, which takes its name from the Scheider siege guns used here by the Boers during the 1899–1902 Second Anglo-Boer War against the British. Known as "Long Tom" because of their elongated necks, the artillery pieces were able to throw a 43kg shell a distance of 10km. You can still see the holes blasted by retreating Boers into the series of switchbacks cutting up the pass, known as "the Staircase".

Sabie, Pilgrim's Rest and Graskop

Only three towns occupy the heights of the Escarpment and of these **Sabie** is the largest, its personality split between serving the surrounding agroforestry industry, while trying to please the tourists that make it their base. Of the other two, **Pilgrim's Rest** unashamedly plays to the tour buses, pushing hard with its restored gold-rush buildings and themed museums, while the relatively uninteresting timber centre of **Graskop** is desperately working at its potential in an attempt to lay its hands on those elusive tourist bucks.

Sabie and around

SABIE (pronounced "sah-bee") is the centre of Mpumalanga's agroforestry industry, and with 450 square kilometres under active cultivation is dubiously proud of lying at the heart of South Africa's largest artificial forests. The extensive pine plantations look painfully monotonous next to the rich, jungly variety of the remaining pockets of indigenous woodland. Before the foresters arrived, Sabie made its name as a gold centre, with a lucky strike in 1895 at the Klein Sabie Falls. Mining stopped halfway through this century, and today the gold prospectors have been replaced by escapees from hectic Johannesburg, who make a living here running restaurants, B&Bs or craft shops. Sabie's compact size, slow pace, mildly arty ambience and gentle climate make it a congenial base – as long as you have your own transport – for exploring the Escarpment.

Arrival and information

There's no public **transport** to Sabie; the only way to get here is in your own car. The town lies on the R37, beyond Long Tom Pass. You'll find at least three privately run **tourist information bureaux** in Main Road, all touting information on accommodation and activities. None of them are impartial, and all are of limited use, so take your pick. In terms of shops, virtually everything you're likely to need is along Main Road or just off it.

Accommodation

You'll find a good supply of reasonably priced **accommodation** in Sabie, though prices can rise dramatically during South African school holidays. Avoid the rock-bottom B&Bs if you can: most of them offer no privacy.

Artist's Cafe, Hendriksdal, 15km south of Sabie along the R37 (☎013/764 2309). Colonial Africa in the beautifully converted station buildings of Hendriksdal siding, which still has goods trains trundling along its tracks. The stationmaster's house has been converted into a first-class restaurant. ④.

Castle Rock, 2km from centre on the Old Lydenburg Rd (☎013/764 1242). Ageing municipal caravan park with the cheapest campsites in town, pleasantly sited along a river, but beginning to suffer from neglect. ①.

Hillwatering Country House, Marula St, off Main St (☎013/764 1421, fax 764 1550). English country decor, antiques and a fabulous breakfast make this Sabie's ultimate overnight experience. The owner is a chef of note, so it's worth ordering dinner here to top it all off. ③.

Jock of the Bushveld, off Main Rd (☎013/764 2178, fax 764 3215). Well-maintained but unexceptional caravan park in the centre with backpackers' dorms and basic self-catering, en-suite chalet rooms. ①–②.

The Kranz, third turning left off the R537, at the airport sign (☎013/764 1330). Good-value accommodation in a comfortable house with en-suite rooms and a self-contained cottage. ③.

Merry Pebbles Holiday Resort, 2km from centre on the Old Lydenburg Rd (☎013/764 2266, fax 764 1629). Rated the third-best caravan park in the country and the pick of the Sabie self-catering establishments with camping and self-catering, en-suite chalets. ①–②.

Misty Mountain Lodge, 24km southwest of Sabie on Long Tom Pass (☎013/764 3377, fax 1482). Old-fashioned but pleasant self-catering units, some with splendid views across pine plantations into the valleys, and well-placed for walks into indigenous forest. ②–③.

Ute's Haus, Second St (☎013/764 2598). Good-value B&B and cheaper sister establishment to *Villa Ticino* around the corner, to which guests must walk in the morning for breakfast. ②.

Villa Ticino, corner of Louis Trichardt and 2nd streets (☎013/764 2598). Extremely hospitable Swiss-owned B&B with a terrace looking onto the hills. ③.

Winckler Guest House, 11 Potgieter St (☎013/764 2741). One en-suite room in this homely B&B, furnished in an Afrikaner old-world style, rented out by an owner who knows the area well. ③.

The Town and around

Sabie is segmented by **Main Street** (the continuation of the Long Tom Pass from Lydenburg), which meanders into the town centre where it hits **Main Road** at right angles. At the junction of the two, the compact **St Peter's**, an English-style country church designed in 1912 by Sir Herbert Baker, hides in a dense, verdant garden dominated by a gigantic jacaranda tree, which confetties the lawn with mauve petals in early summer.

A large number of **waterfalls** drop down the slopes just outside town. Travel only 7km from town, down the Old Lydenburg Road (which ends in a dead end), and you can take in three of the most impressive: **Bridal Veil**, **Horseshoe** and, appropriately left until last, **Lone Creek Falls** at the end of the road. Loveliest and easiest to reach of the three, Lone Creek is conveniently accessed down a paved, circular path which crosses a river and works its way back to the car park. More thrilling still are the 70-metre-high **Mac Mac Falls**, which are reached about 13km from Sabie along the Graskop road. Shimmering with dewy rainbows, the falls tumble into an inviting pool which is unfortunately fenced off. Although their name sounds like the sound of water splashing onto rock, the falls were actually named after the many people of Scottish descent who died looking for gold in the area and whose names appear on dozens of tombstones in the vicinity.

On the way to Lone Creek, *Sabie Horse Trails* (☎013/764 1011 ext 205; after hours ☎764 3324) operates **horse-riding** outings lasting from one hour to two days, depending on your level of experience. Along the same stretch of road you can stop off for a day's **trout fishing** at *Horseshoe Trout Farm* (☎013/764 2892), where you can also make a fire and barbecue your catch.

Eating and drinking

Sabie has a couple of very memorable **restaurants**, some relaxed places for light meals or drinks and one or two places you'd probably rather forget.

Artists' Café, Hendriksdal, 15km south of Sabie along the R37 (☎013/764 2309). The owners of this restaurant in converted station buildings cook up a real storm. Their Italian-style dishes are especially recommended. Prices are high, but the art-gallery setting and great atmosphere guarantee a memorable lunch or dinner. Booking essential.

Café Mocha, Main St. Daytime venue dishing up traditional South African food like *bobotie*, Cape curries, malva pudding and an extraordinary wine list which features wines from the smaller Cape estates.

Loggerhead Restaurant, corner of Main and Old Lydenburg roads. Pick of the bunch and reasonably priced, the *Loggerhead* is known for its trout dishes and imaginative menu, which includes items such as pork fillets stuffed with spinach and cheese, biltong salad, deep-fried ice cream cooked in filo pastry and a good Cape wine list.

Petena Pancakes, Main St. Cheap but unremarkable creperie with outdoor seating serving pancakes with savoury mince or fish as well as sweet fillings.

Zeederburg Coach House, Ford St. Restaurant and coffee house-cum-pub in an old colonial house with a verandah which attracts a laid-back crowd.

Pilgrim's Rest

Nestled in a valley 35km north of Sabie, **PILGRIM'S REST**, an almost too-perfectly restored gold-mining town, is an irresistible port of call for the scores of tour buses that meander through the Escarpment's passes every day. A collection of red-roofed corrugated-iron buildings, including a period bank, a filling station with pre-1920 fuel pumps and the wonderful Royal Hotel brimming with Victoriana, the place is undeniably photogenic, but you can't help feeling there's not much behind the romanticized gold-rush image, a suspicion that is confirmed when the village nods off after 5pm once the day-trippers have been spirited away.

Some history

Pilgrim's Rest owes its origins to South Africa's first **gold rush**, which predates the uncovering of the great Gauteng seams. In 1873 Alex "Wheelbarrow" Patterson discovered gold in the creek and tried but failed to keep his discovery secret. By the end of the year, Patterson had been joined by 1500 diggers hectically working 4000 claims. Far from the pristine little village of today, the **Pilgrim's Rest diggings** were the site of gruelling labour and unhygienic conditions. Many diggers arrived malnourished, suffering from dysentery and malaria after punishing treks through the Lowveld. Those who survived could expect drab lives in tents or, if they struck lucky, more permanent daub and wattle huts. The diggings were bought up by the Transvaal Gold Mining Estates (TGME) in 1896. In 1972 the TGME closed down its Beta Mine and Pilgrim's Rest was handed over to the provincial administration. In the 1980s the whole settlement was declared an historic monument. Hidden behind the hill to the southwest of town, away from tourist eyes, mining continues, with functional buildings, cyanide-filled slimes dams and great red scars hacked into the hillside in pursuit of the precious metal, having bulldozed away indigenous forest that got in the way.

Orientation, information and accommodation

Pilgrim's Rest stretches along its one main road and is divided into Uptown and Downtown. **Uptown**, to the east, centres around the *Royal Hotel* and the **tourist information centre** (daily 9am–12.45pm & 1.15–4.30pm; ☎013/768 1211), which can provide details on accommodation and the surrounding area. Uptown has the greatest concentration of shops and restaurants and consequently draws the bulk of tourists. **Downtown**, or Lower Town, just 1km to the west, has a more down-to-earth atmosphere – though many visitors slip in and out of Pilgrim's without realizing that this area even exists.

Alhough Pilgrim's Rest is by far the prettiest of the Escarpment towns, it has very little **accommodation**. In Lower Town, the self-catering *District Six Miners' Cottages* (☎013/768 1211; ②) offer authentic two-bedroomed 1920s workers' houses with verandahs overlooking the town and mountains; these are among the best places to stay on the Escarpment, and are very reasonably priced. Be sure to book ahead, as there is no on-site office if you simply turn up. The *Pilgrim's Rest Caravan Park* (☎013/768 1367), also in Lower Town, has a grassy campsite (②) with a river running through it, as well as fully equipped tents (②). The *Royal*, Main St, Upper Town (☎013/768 1100; ⑥), is a hotel which dates back to the gold-rush days and brims with luxurious Victoriana.

The Town

Apart from souvenir hunting and lingering in the cafés and tea shops, the main activity in Pilgrim's is visiting its handful of **museums**. Tickets for all the museums must be bought at the tourist information office before heading out (see opposite). You can whip through the three modest town "museums" in a matter of minutes, as they amount to little more than rooms reconstructed as they were in the gold-rush days. More interesting are the museums out of the centre. To get a really authentic impression of the gold-mining days, head for the open-air **Diggings Site Museum** on the edge of town on the Graskop Road (daily tours 10am, 11am, noon, 2pm & 3pm), where you can see demonstrations of alluvial gold-panning and get a bit of a garbled guided tour around the bleak diggers' huts, remnants of workings and machinery from the early mining days. The **Reduction Works** (open for guided tours only: Mon–Sat 10.30am & 2pm, Sun 10.30am), signposted from Lower Town, demonstrates how gold was processed . By contrast, if you want to see how those at the top lived, visit **Alanglade**, just west of the Downtown area (open for guided tours only: Mon–Sat 10.30am & 2pm; tickets at tourist centre in town), the reconstructed home of the former general manager of the mine. The house has a wonderful collection of early twentieth-century British fashion and decorative arts and shows a sheltered way of life far removed from either Africa or mining.

Eating and drinking

Pilgrim's Rest has plenty of restaurants and tea shops to provide for the daily influx from visitors using Graskop or Sabie as their base. Of the **places to eat**, only the *Digger's Den*, a lively, canteen-style place attached to the *Royal*, is open all day and every evening. For lunches the choice is wider: *Chaitow's*, a small café opposite the hotel, serves pricey but tasty pastas and pizzas, as well as smoked trout fillets and pâté. For something more exciting, head for *Edwin Wood's Wine Cellar*, below their wine shop on Main Street, which serves the best Cape wines with cheese platters and, their speciality, smoked wildebeest. In the Downtown area, *Scott's Café* serves light meals and has a pleasant **bar**.

Graskop

Some 15km east of Pilgrim's Rest, **GRASKOP** owes its place on the tourist map to *Harrie's Pancake Shop*, which serves much-imitated but rarely rivalled crêpes, and attracts all the tour buses doing the Escarpment viewpoints. The town itself is exceedingly ordinary, with timber trucks rumbling heavily through, and nothing at all to see in the centre. Its location, however, as the closest town to the Blyde River Canyon, which lies to the north, goes some way towards compensating, and the growing number of artists, together with a sizable gay community, are helping to shift Graskop's lumberjack image.

Practicalities

Given its size, Graskop has an surprisingly large crop of self-catering **places to stay**, starting with the budget *Municipal Tourist Park*, on the corner of Louis Trichardt Avenue and Hugenote Street (☎013/767 1126; ②), which has slightly dour chalets and rondavels. In a similar vein, the *Graskop Log Cabin Village*, Oorwinning St (☎013/767 1974, fax 767 1975; ②), is right in the centre of town and has a swimming pool but no views, unlike the *Panorama Rest Camp* (☎013/767 1091; ②), just outside town on the road to Hazyview, which has campsites and a variety of units sleeping two to eight people and gardens looking out over the Escarpment. Across the road, *Kloofsig Chalets* (☎013/767 1489; ④) make up for their slightly less spectacular siting with more modern and luxurious units. The only conventional **hotel** in town is the delightful *Graskop*, on the corner of High Street and Louis Trichardt Avenue(☎ & fax 013/767 1244; ③), which from the outside looks like a bog-standard travelling-salesmen's joint, but hides an attractive interior of African baskets, fabrics and sculptures and airy rooms decorated with flair. The hotel has a pool and offers weekend packages with health, fitness and hiking activities.

For **eating**, you won't get better than the legendary *Harrie's*, Louis Trichardt St, which has a nice outdoor terrace, serves sweet or savoury pancakes, and has an inside dining room with a roaring log fire in winter. *The Lonely Tree*, on the corner of Louis Trichardt and Kerk streets, works hard to compete, with pancakes, chocolate cake, filter coffee and good service, while *Eastern Delights*, a small groceries shop next to the Total garage in Main Street, does cheap Indian takeaways, including vegetarian options. For more substantial meals, head for the superb hotel restaurant at the *Graskop*.

Blyde River Canyon and Blydepoort Dam

There are few places in South Africa where you enjoy more dramatic scenery while barely leaving your car than the **Blyde River Canyon**, which drops sharply away from the Escarpment into the Lowveld, and is weathered out of strata of red rock and colossal formations. Protecting it, the **Blyde River Canyon Nature Reserve** (also known as Blyderivierspoort Nature Reserve) stretches from a narrow tail that tickles Graskop in the south and broadens itself into a great amphitheatre partially flooded by the **Blydepoort Dam** about 60km to the north. The views of the canyon are wonderful from both above and below, but the nicest way to take in the vistas is on an easy half-day's drive along the canyon lip.

Canyon viewpoints

Some 3km north of Graskop, the road branches and the easterly R534 takes a fifteen-kilometre loop past a series of intoxicating viewpoints with surprisingly banal names. The road winds through pine plantations until it comes to the turn-off to the **Pinnacle**, a gigantic quartzite column topped with trees, that thrusts out of a ferny gorge. After another 4km the road reaches **God's Window**, one of the most famous and consequently most developed of the viewpoints, with toilets and specially constructed stalls for curio sellers. The sheer drop, with views onto the Lowveld, makes God's Window well worth the effort to get to. The looping road returns to rejoin the R532, which from here heads north for 28km beyond the turn-off to reach **Bourke's Luck Potholes** – strange, smoothly scooped formations carved into the rocks at the confluence of the Treur and Blyde rivers by water-driven pebbles. The best view of all lies 14km beyond, at the **Three Rondavels**. The name describes only one small feature of this cinemascope vista: three cylinders in the shape of ships with the meandering Blyde River twisting its way hundreds of metres below. No photograph does justice to the sheer enormity of the view, punctuated by one series of cliffs after another buttressing into the valley.

The only place in the nature reserve where you can **stay** is *Aventura Blydepoort* (☎013/769 8005, fax 769 8059; email: aventura@iafrica.com), 5km north of the turn-off to the Three Rondavels lookout. The resort has comfortable, self-contained and fully equipped cottages, a swimming pool, supermarket, bottle store and filling station, but a bit of an institutionalized, family-oriented atmosphere.

Three Rondavels to Blydepoort Dam

The ninety-kilometre drive from the Three Rondavels viewpoint to the base of the canyon affords spectacular views of the Escarpment cliffs rising out of the Lowveld and

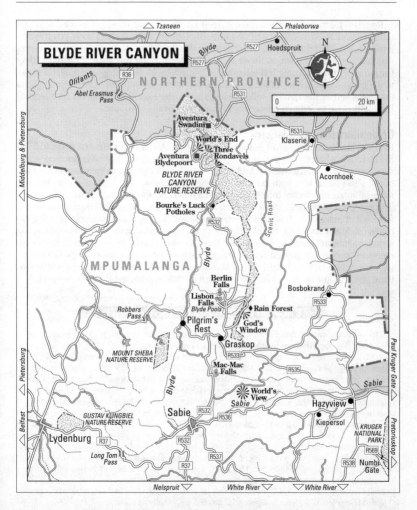

is easily incorporated into your itinerary if you're heading for Kruger. The drive winds west to join with the R36 and heads north to begin its descent through the Abel Erasmus Pass and then the JG Strijdom Tunnel, which plunges through the mountain, with the wide Lowveld plains opening out on the other side. The road takes a wide arching trajectory to circumnavigate the canyon.

Along the R527, near its junction with the R36, the **Monsoon Gallery** (☎ & fax 015/795 5114), 29km west of Hoedspruit, makes a good place to pause on your journey. This highly recommended African arts and crafts shop has an absorbing selection of authentic material, including ironwork and woodcarving from Zimbabwe, superb tapestries from the Karosswerkers factory near Tzaneen, Venda pots and jewellery. Linked to the gallery is an outstanding place to **eat** – *Mad Dogz Café* (daily for breakfasts, lunches and teas; Fri & Sat evenings for dinner). You'll also find a farm stall, an information bureau and very comfortable **B&B** accommodation at the *Blue Cottages* (☎015/795 5114; ③).

Roughly 15km further east, the untarred Driehoek road hives off to the south past the *Aventura Swadini* resort and on to the Blydepoort Dam. Alternatively you can continue on the R531 for a further 12km and take the tarred turn-off to the southwest, which leads straight down to the dam. At a dead end along this road, the **Blyde River Canyon Visitors' Centre** has interesting displays on local ecology and a useful model of the canyon that helps you get orientated. The best reason to come here though is for the vistas across the flooded valley below and for the excellent prospects for spending the night close to indigenous bushveld at the foot of the mountains.

Blydepoort accommodation

Reached along the same road as the visitors' centre, *Aventura Swadini* (✆ & fax 015/795 5141), has 78 **chalets** (③) that sleep up to five and a **campsite** (①) with stunning scenic surrounds, but a similar mass institutional feel to its sister resort on the mountain. A number of short trails start from here and you can take cruises on the Blydepoort Dam. Far more intimate, and highly recommended for a quiet and spectacular retreat, is the nearby *Trackers* (✆015/795 5033), which has an assortment of accommodation on a marvellous farm full of indigenous bushveld vegetation (as well as zebra and antelope) abutting the canyon's cliffs. Camping (①), self-catering chalets (②) and dinner, bed and breakfast (③) arrangements are available. A trained botanist, who lives on the farm, runs informative and extremely good-value **guided walks** through the indigenous vegetation. To get to *Trackers*, turn south into Driehoek road (as for the *Aventura* resort) and continue for a little over 6km, finally following the "D Rushworth" sign on your right to get to the homestead.

BLYDERIVIERSPOORT HIKING TRAIL

The only way to get directly into the canyon from the Escarpment is by walking there, and the five-day **Blyderivierspoort Hiking Trail** is a great way of doing this. Although the 65-kilometre route requires a fair degree of fitness, the gradients aren't generally too taxing and the walk could be undertaken by a hardy novice. The hike starts at God's Window, 5km north of Graskop, and works its way north, finally ending up at the Blydepoort Dam in the valley, 38km from Hoedspruit. There's a diversity of plant and animal life along the way and, even though the nature reserve's hippos, crocodiles, zebras, baboons and monkeys aren't that easy to spot, this is certainly your best shot.

Accommodation is provided along the way in four fully equipped huts that can sleep up to thirty people (the maximum allowed on the trail), with flush toilets, cold showers and firewood. You must carry all your own food. For somewhere to stay near the start or end of the trail, see our Graskop and Blyde River Canyon accounts. As the start and finish of the trail are 150km apart by road, you'll need to have access to two vehicles or make arrangements to get back to your starting point. Take note, too, that although the trail starts in malaria-free terrain, you will be ending up in the Lowveld, where this mosquito-transmitted disease is a potential hazard, especially in summer.

Reservations can be made up to six months in advance through the Officer-in-Charge, Blyderivierspoort Nature Reserve, Private Bag X431, Graskop 1270 (✆013/768 1216).

GATEWAYS TO CENTRAL KRUGER

Northeast of the Escarpment, you'll pass by little towns en route to the central section of Kruger National Park and the Manyeleti and Timbabvati private game reserves. If you're coming down the Escarpment along the R36/R527 from the Blyde River viewpoints, after about 75km you'll encounter a fork in the road. The more northerly road leads to **Hoedspruit** and **Klaserie**, both of which lie in the heart of bushveld **game farm** country where budget game-viewing is offered. Be warned that these are no substitute for the big game country of Kruger and its adjacent private reserves. Much further north and generally accessed from Pietersburg on the N1, **Phalaborwa** is unavoidable if you're heading into central Kruger through Phalaborwa Gate.

Hoedspruit

Lurking in the undulating Lowveld, 23km east of where the R531 splits off the R527, with the hazy blue mountains of the Escarpment still visible on the distant horizon, is the small service centre of **HOEDSPRUIT**. The town lies at the heart of a concentration of **private game reserves** and lodges. There aren't any sights here; the only reason you'll be passing through is on your way to Kruger or to stay in one of the game lodges, which, invariably, you will have booked long before you reach the area.

Generally what's on offer around Hoedspruit is a more affordable taste of the bush. As the price drops, however, so do a few other things, most importantly the quality of the game you're likely to see. What you do still get is a degree of pampered living, privacy and the opportunity of guided game-viewing, all of which can intensify your experience of the bush immeasurably when you get to Kruger.

Practicalities

Daily scheduled **flights** from Johannesburg on *British Airways/ComAir* arrive at Eastgate Airport (☎015/793 3681), some 14km south of Hoedspruit. For **car rental**, *Budget* (☎015/793 3681) have an office at the airport. For transfers to game lodges from here, contact *Eastgate Lodge Transfers* (☎015/793 3678). Hoedspruit itself is little more than a collection of gun shops, liquor stores, service stations and the odd grocery shop. The **Central Lowveld Tourism Association**, on the main street (☎015/793 2418), will be able to give you details about the different game lodges; they also have a separate kiosk on the western side of town along the R527, which offers more limited information.

Around Hoedspruit

As this is an area where animals are taken very seriously, it's not surprising to find the **Moholoholo Wildlife Rehabilitation Centre** (tours 9.30am & 3pm; bookings essential; ☎015/795 5236; entry fee), about 3km from the tarred turn-off to the Blydepoort Dam, on the R531 between the R40 and R527. Ex-ranger Brian Jones has embarked on an individual crusade to rescue and rehabilitate injured and abandoned animals, notably raptors, but also lion, leopard and countless others. The centre is part of a wider reserve and both night drives and early morning walks are offered. You can also make an easy tour of the rehabilitation cages and pens. Game-lodge-style self-catering (③) and fully catered **accommodation** (⑦) are both available.

Along similar lines, although larger in scale, is the **Hoedspruit Research and Breeding Centre for Endangered Species** (Mon–Sat 8.30am–4pm, also Sun during school holidays; ☎015/793 1633; entry fee), more commonly called the **Cheetah Project**, 20km south of Hoedspruit on the R40. Here a minibus will take you around a large number of pens and cages containing beautiful, silky-furred king cheetah, wild dog, blue crane and other endangered species bred for purposes of protection, restocking and research. While the centre gives you an opportunity to see some of these animals at close quarters, it does feel like a bit of a zoo and it can be tough work convincing yourself that it's all done in the name of science.

A new project in the area is the Shangaan cultural village, called **Nyani** (☎015/793 3816), 4km along the Guernsey Road which turns off the R40, 22km south of Hoedspruit. This is a fairly genuine effort developed by a local Shangaan man, who asked his grandparents' generation what the villages were like when they were children. He is currently reconstructing a Swazi village where backpackers will be able to stay .

Hoedspruit game farms

None of the following **game farms** have direct access to Big Five game-viewing, but they're worth considering as relatively inexpensive and comfortable places to stay deep in the bush on your way to or from Kruger. A number of farms also offer specialist activities.

Eyrie Birding Lodge, 36km from Hoedspruit on R531 (☎015/795 5775). Rather downhome accommodation in a fantastic, elevated position on the slopes of the Escarpment. Run by Dr Peter Milstein, one of South Africa's most knowledgeable experts on birds, and chosen by him as one of the finest bird-watching spots in the country. Full board. ⑤.

Kwa-Mbili, Thornybush Game Reserve, 30km east of Hoedspruit (☎015/793 2773). Intimate, unpretentious lodge with vibrant African decor, bush cuisine and plenty of game in the vicinity. A maximum of ten guests are housed in chalets or luxury tents. Activities on offer include game-viewing on foot and by mountain bike. Full board. ⑦.

Marc's Camp, just over 6km along Guernsey Rd (☎01528/32811). Fun and wacky place to stay, with accommodation up a stepladder in creaking tree houses above the Kaserie River. The rooms don't have electricity and bathrooms are shared. Game drives on a neighbouring estate are on offer but they don't take in the Big Five. Full board. ⑤.

Otter's Den, on R531 not far from junction with R521 (☎015/795 5250). Small and relaxing camp on a bush-covered island in the Blyde River recommended for fishing and bird-watching. There's a river-fed rock swimming pool and self-catering or full-board rate available. ④–⑤.

Tlhakan Chuni Camps & Trails, 10km north of Hoedspruit on R40 (☎015/793 2418). Basic but atmospheric reed-walled self-catering or full-board camp set on the riverbank by the confluence of the Blyde and Olifants rivers. The emphasis is on bird-watching and bushwalking. ②–⑤.

Tshukudu, 4km north of Hoedspruit on R40 (☎015/793 2078). Family-run farm good for kids, but not the place to come if you like your animals wild and hungry – here you might be accompanied on your early-morning game walk by cuddly, hand-reared lion cubs or a kindly elephant. Full board. ⑤.

Phalaborwa

The most northerly access to the central section of Kruger is at **PHALABORWA**, 74km north of Hoedspruit. The name means "better than the south", a cheeky sobriquet coined as the town developed on the back of its extensive mineral wealth. During the 1960s the borders of the park near Phalaborwa suddenly developed a kink, and large copper deposits were found, miraculously, just outside the protected national park area.

The only reason you'll be in Phalaborwa is on your way in or out of Kruger, and there's little to divert you on your way through unless you need a bed for the night. However, keen golfers shouldn't miss the chance of a round in the company of big game at the signposted **Hans Merensky Country Club** (☎01524/5931), where it's not unusual to see giraffes and elephants sauntering across the fairways. If you find yourself kicking your heels in the late afternoon you can whet your appetite before heading into the park with a short **microlight flight** over the park (contact ☎01524/5269 or tourist information), or a sundowner **boat trip** with *Jumbo River Safaris* (☎01524/86168).

You may see dust-encrusted vehicles driving around town which have long aerials with small flags attached to the top of them – this is so that they don't get squished by big trucks manoeuvring around the mines. Also unusual is the refugee camp on the outskirts of town which has sprung up because illegal immigrants from Mozambique, only 60km away on the other side of Kruger National Park, use Phalaborwa as a navigation aid, guiding themselves by the smoke of the chimneys by day, and the lights by night.

Arrival and information

Regular *SA Airlink* (☎01524/85823) flights arrive from Johannesburg at Hendrick van Eck **airport** (☎01524/85823), very close to Kruger's Phalaborwa Gate, off President Steyn Street. The closest rest camp from here is Letaba, 50km into the park. All Phalaborwa's car rental firms are represented at the airport: *Avis* (☎01524/5169),

Budget (☎01524/85404) and *Imperial* (☎01524/2376). *Phalaborwa Safaris* (☎01524/3197) offer transfers from the airport to game farms and lodges.

The town's **tourist information bureau** (☎01524/85860) is beside the main road (Hendrick van Eck) just before the gate into Kruger.

Phalaborwa has a good selection of **shops**, including the well-stocked *Link* pharmacy, open until 8pm, in the mall off Palm Street.

Accommodation

Phalaborwa has plenty of **places to stay**, but prices can be steep. *Elephant Walk*, 30 Anna Scheepers St (☎01524/4758; ①), is a small and friendly backpackers' lodge with camping facilities and budget tours into Kruger on offer. Equally relaxed, though a tad more upmarket, is *Sefapane Lodge*, Copper St (☎01524/87041, fax 87042; ③–④), a collection of neat beehive huts which achieves the feeling of a comfortable rest camp, with a restaurant, a nice pool and a poolside bar. *Steyn's Cottage*, 67 Bosvlier St (☎01524/2836; ③), is a fairly classy Victorian-style guesthouse, with a swimming pool, a tea garden and a restaurant, while the *Impala Protea Inn*, on the corner of Essenhout and Wildevy streets (☎01524/5681; ④), is pretty characterful as *Proteas* go, and has a pool and a pleasant pub. If you get stuck, head for the tourist bureau (see "Arrival and information"), which can supply a list of budget B&Bs.

Eating and drinking

For a relatively small town, Phalaborwa has a good selection of **places to eat**. The restaurant at *Sefapane Lodge* is pretty decent, and its sunken **bar** beside the swimming pool is the most convivial in town. There are two independent restaurants on Rooibos Street. *Monroe's* (Mon–Sat noon–10pm) serves inexpensive pizza, pasta and burgers, while the classier, though still moderately priced *Tiffany's* (☎01524/89 2021; Mon–Sat 7–10pm) has a wide-ranging menu. You'll find the usual steaks on offer at the *Campico Spur*. The best place for coffee is *Steyn's Cottage*, just across Hendrick van Eck Street from the main part of town.

THE LOWVELD AND GATEWAYS TO SOUTHERN KRUGER

Lying between the Mpumalanga section of the Drakensberg and the Mozambique coastal plain, the **Lowveld** is a region of savannah that stretches north as a narrow strip, opens out into Northern and Northwest provinces and engulfs most of Zimbabawe, Zambia and Central Africa. Closely associated at the turn of the century with fortune-seekers, hunters, gold-diggers and adventurers, these days the Lowveld's claim to fame is its proximity to the Kruger National Park and the adjacent private reserves. Although several of the towns wrapping around the game park fringes are pleasant enough, most people are here to get into big game country.

Largest of the Lowveld towns (and the capital of Mpumalanga), **Nelspruit** lies along the N4, five hours' drive from Johannesburg and accessible by air and bus (with direct flights from Durban as well). Heading north, the R40 passes through **White River**, **Hazyview** and **Klaserie**, a series of small towns, all of which are gateways into the Kruger and are well supplied with accommodation. Travel 32km south of Nelspruit and you'll reach **Barberton**, an attractive settlement in the hills with strong mining connections, which provides a useful launching pad for Swaziland, while **Komatipoort**, 97km east of Nelspruit, is a real subtropical frontier town, touching the Mozambique border and perfectly poised for getting into southeastern Kruger or for onward travel to KwaZulu-Natal through Swaziland.

The Lowveld area is **malarial**. For details on necessary precautions, see p.18.

Nelspruit

Mpumalanga's provincial capital, **NELSPRUIT**, 358km east of Johannesburg on the N4, is a traditionally conservative Afrikaner town fast transforming itself into one of South Africa's most relaxed and racially integrated cities. The town's importance lies in its status as the business capital of the province, but it is also a gateway into the southern pàrt of Kruger Park, and has the province's best **transport connections** with Johannesburg and Durban.

Arrival and information

Daily flights from Durban, Johannesburg and Maputo on *Metavia Airlines* (☎013/741 3142) and *SA Airlink* (☎013/752 5257) arrive at **Nelspruit International Airport** (☎013/741 4996), 12km southwest of town. This grandly named landing strip is served by the **car rental** offices of *Avis* (☎013/741 1087) and *Budget* (☎013/741 3871) – pretty handy as there's no transport into town. Camper van and 4WD vehicles are available to rent from *Mashona* (☎013/741 4447), also at the airport. Greyhound **intercity buses** from Johannesburg drop off and pick up outside *Lowveld Promotions* (☎013/752 5134), at the Joshua Doore Centre, on the corner of Paul Kruger and Louis Trichardt streets. Daily *Spoornet* **trains** between Johannesburg and Komatipoort (continuing on to Maputo three times a week) stop at **Nelspruit Station** off Andrew Street at the north end of the town centre, but the 3.20am arrival time from Johannesburg makes it practical to travel by train in a westerly direction only, getting off from Maputo or on for Johannesburg.

There's an excellent **tourist information bureau**, shop 5, Promenade Centre (Mon–Fri 8am–5pm, Sat & Sun 9am–4pm; ☎013/755 1988 or 755 1989, fax 755 1350), next to the *Promenade Hotel* in Louis Trichardt Street, which can provide maps and information about the town, and acts as Nelspruit's official AA agency. Staff can also arrange bookings for Kruger rest camps. Around Louis Trichardt, the main street, you'll find everything you need, from travel agents for arranging tours, to massive supermarkets for stocking up for a trip into Kruger.

Accommodation

Nelspruit's **accommodation** tends to be geared to business travellers and rooms are on the pricey side. If you're on a tight budget, head for the better-value options away from the centre or to the *Hotel Formule 1*, which offers the cheapest beds in town.

Hotel Bundu, 11km from Nelspruit off the R40 to White River (☎ & fax 013/758 1221 or 758 1222). Popular, good-value accommodation in an old-fashioned country hotel, decorated with animal hides and hunting trophies. Swimming pool, horse-riding and hiking trails to caves with rock paintings. Camping ①, Huts ②.

Bushveld Chalets, Kaapschehoop Rd, 6km from Nelspruit (☎013/741 3219 or 741 5058). Small, self-catering en-suite chalets near the airport. ③.

Hotel Formule 1, corner of N4 and Kaapschehoop Rd (☎013/741 4490).The only budget beds in the centre are in no-frills, en-suite boxes, which make for a functional night stop. Continental breakfast is available for small extra charge. ②.

Jörn's Guest House, 62 Hunter St (☎ & fax 013/752 3855). Recommended B&B run by a former hotelier in a private house with a nice garden offering Lowveld views and a swimming pool. ⑤.

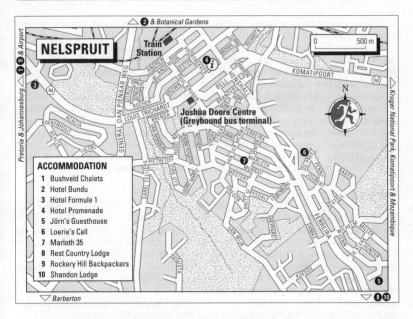

The Loerie's Call, 2 Du Preez St (☎ & fax 013/752 4844). Modern house with pool offering en-suite rooms with private verandahs looking onto the Crocodile River Valley. ⑥.

Marloth 35, 35 Marloth St (☎013/752 4529). Cheapest of Nelspruit's B&Bs, featuring simple furnishings in cool, ceramic-tiled rooms with breakfast served outdoors under sun umbrellas. Swimming pool and *braai* facilities. ③.

Hotel Promenade, Louis Trichardt St (☎013/753 3000). Nelspruit's smartest hotel is primarily aimed at business people but has the advantage of being bang in the centre of town. ⑥.

The Rest Country Lodge, Uitkyk Rd, 10km from Nelspruit (☎ & fax 013/744 9991 or 744 9992). Each luxury suite in this modern, purpose-built lodge has its own balcony with beautiful views over the Lowveld. Swimming pool, sun deck and verandah. ⑥.

Rockery Hill Backpackers, Kaapschehoop Rd (☎ & fax 013/741 5011). Some17km from Nelspruit, beyond the airport. Choose from camping, dorms, double cabins or an en-suite cottage on a farm with a communal kitchen and campfire cooking but no electricity. The owners come into town frequently and can usually arrange transfers. ①–②.

Shandon Lodge, 1 Saturn St (☎ & fax 013/744 9934). Rooms with private entrances arranged around a swimming pool in well-established and large suburban home run by friendly hosts who provide good food. ⑤.

The Town and around

Nelspruit grew in the 1890s as a base for transport riders, farmers and prospectors, but there is little evidence today of these historic origins. Most of the old buildings have been ripped out and replaced by shopping malls and freeways, and the town has a bustling and mildly prosperous feel, mostly due to the fact that it is a major commercial centre, not only for the Lowveld, but also for shoppers from Swaziland and Mozambique.

The town centre, roughly six streets crisscrossed by another six, could hardly be easier to get around. The N4 from Johannesburg to Komatipoort sweeps through town, briefly pausing to become **Louis Trichardt**, Nelspruit's main street, before reassuming its identity as the national highway.

Apart from the shops and supermarkets, Nelspruit's only real attraction lies just outside of town: the **Lowveld National Botanical Garden** (daily, May–Sept 8am–5.15pm; Oct–April 8am–6pm; small entry fee). Some 5km north of Nelspruit off the R40 and set on the banks of the Crocodile River, the gardens comes a close second to Cape Town's Kirstenbosch Gardens. Natural waterfalls and walks through humid rainforest make a very pleasant break from the boiling midday light. If you've been to Kruger, you'll have a chance to look at some of the same **trees** here, helpfully identified with labels. The plants are grouped according to habitat, and the garden specializes in **cycads** from around the world. There is also a grove of baobabs from South Africa and other African countries. A useful brochure sold at the entrance gate has a map showing the highlights of the garden and the paths through it.

Eating and drinking

Most of Nelspruit's **restaurants** are buried in shopping malls, where you'll find all the usual steakhouses and fast-food chains. *Spur*, in the Sanlam Centre on Louis Trichardt, is good for its salad selections and burgers, and you'll find spicey Portuguese-style chicken takeaways at *Nando's* in Brown Street off Louis Trichardt. *Café Mozart*, Promenade Centre, Louis Trichardt Street, does quiches, coffee and tea, and there are two steakhouses – *Steers* and *Mike's Kitchen* – in the same mall. For a more expensive and imaginative meal, head for *Costa Do Sol*, in Nel City, on the corner of Kruger and Louis Trichardt streets, which serves good Portuguese and Italian dishes. **Drinking** is done mostly at the restaurants or at the *Hotel Promenade* in the centre.

Listings

Airport information ☎082/893 5743.

Banks All the major banks and ATMs are in and around Louis Trichardt Street. Opening hours are Mon–Fri 8.30am–3.30pm, Sat 8.30–11am.

Emergencies Ambulance ☎013/10177; Fire ☎013/753 3331; Police ☎10111.

Hospitals *Nelmed Clinic* (☎013/755 2672) is open 24 hours a day and is suitable for non-emergency treatments. For more urgent consultations contact *Nelspruit Private Hospital* (☎013/744 7150).

Laundrette *The Laundrette* (open daily), is at the Youth Centre along the N4, next to Joshua Doore on the corner of Paul Kruger and Louis Trichardt streets.

Post office The main post office, in Voortrekker St, is open 8.30am–4pm.

Taxis *City Bug* (☎013/755 3792 or 755 3793) runs tuk-tuk shuttle services around the centre and to the suburbs.

Mozambique Embassy, Use the ME, Brown St (013/752 7396), for visa applications for Mozambique.

Barberton

Provided you have your own transport, **BARBERTON** makes a more relaxed staging post than Nelspruit for journeys between the south of the Kruger National Park and Swaziland. The town lies 36km south of Nelspruit and has a colonial backwater charm, a handful of historical sights, tropical vegetation and an attractive setting in a basin surrounded by mountains.

Barberton began its urban existence after Auguste Robert ("French Bob") discovered **gold** in 1883 on a nearby farm. Despite his attempts to keep the news to himself, other diggers realized something was up when French Bob began building a canal to his claims. The following year, **Graham Barber** discovered another incredibly rich gold reef and got his name hitched to the town at a riotous christening using a bottle of gin. An influx of shopkeepers, hoteliers, barmen and prostitutes, followed by ministers of religion whiffing the ripe scent of sin, soon joined the diggers in the rude tent, tin, thatch and mud frontier town, with nearly every second building functioning as a boozing joint. During the fabulous **boom** of the 1880s the mines slipped out of the grasp of the small-time prospectors and came under the control of the large corporates that still own them today.

Arrival and information

No scheduled public **transport** comes into Barberton: the closest transport hub is Nelspruit, from where you'll need to find a minibus taxi for Barberton. The excellent **tourist information bureau**, Crown St (Mon–Fri 8am–1pm & 2–4.30pm, Sat 8.30am–noon; ☎013/712 2121), can find you accommodation in the area, or point you to local walks, as well as supply you with reams of brochures and maps covering the whole province.

Accommodation

Because it's a bit off the main trail, Barberton is short on **places to stay**, but the prospects get better as you head a little out of town.

Digger's Retreat Hotel, Kaapmuiden Rd, 14km out of Barberton (☎013/719 9681). No-frills family hotel with rondavels, a swimming pool and a pub which fills up with workers from Consort Mine across the road. Good place from which to take gold-panning trips. ②–③.

Dixie Farm Cottage, Kaapmuiden Rd, 10km out of Barberton (☎013/719 9625). Three-bedroom cottage on a tobacco and cattle farm, with a big lawn and garden available on a B&B or self-catering basis, and dinners provided if you book ahead. ①–②.

Fountain Baths Guest House, 48 Pilgrim St (☎013/712 2707). Pleasant rooms and self-catering mini-apartments with a garden edging onto the hills and a swimming pool. ②.

Jock of the Bushveld Huts, Nelspruit Rd, 4km from town (☎013/712 4002). Reasonably priced thatched self-catering chalets on a litchi and mango farm, with horse-riding, swimming and microlight flights on offer. ②.

Kiaat Cottage, 6km from Barberton on the Agnes Mine road (☎013/712 4067). Self-catering cottage tastefully furnished and with magnificent views of the De Kaap Valley. ②.

The Phoenix, 20 Pilgrim St (☎013/712 4211). Barberton's only hotel has a long corridor of standard en-suite rooms where the noise of television seeps through doors. ④.

Weston Cottage, 17km out of Barberton towards Badplaas (☎013/712 3920). Cottage which sleeps four on a big cattle farm, done out in frilly florals and with self-catering and B&B rates. ②–③.

The Town

There are seven working **mines** around Barberton, and each has its own club and entertainment scene, which means you won't find miners packing out public bars as in the wild days of old. Neither do the mines run tours; since they are all fully operational, there's no time to humour a few visitors. However, there is one small-time prospector and hotelier outside Barberton (see box, p.534) who will give you a go at gold-panning, swilling water and sand in a big dish to watch for the telltale thread of gold appearing in the dark sand.

You can explore the mining history of the town at the **Barberton Museum**, 36 Pilgrim St (Mon–Fri 9am–4pm, Sat & Sun 9am–1pm & 2–4pm; small entry fee), three blocks east of the tourist information bureau. In a well-designed, modern building, the museum has good displays on the gold-rush era and, if phoned in advance, staff can do a gold-panning display for groups.

GOLD-PANNING AND HIKING AT BARBERTON

Unlike at Pilgrim's Rest, where you'll have to be content with merely watching how panning was done, at Barberton you can try it yourself. From *Digger's Retreat Hotel* (☎013/719 9681, fax 719 9684), 14km north of Barberton on the R38 to Kaapmuiden, proprietor Victor Nielson takes **gold-panning excursions** to the Noordkaap River, where you scoop up your own gravel to sift. He can extend the tour to **Eureka City**, an 1880s mining settlement which died forty years later. Eureka hasn't been reconstructed the way Pilgrim's Rest has and you'll only see walls and foundations, but you drive through a real mine to get there.

To get a sense of what the old mines were like, the two-kilometre circular **Fortuna Mine Hiking Trail**, just south of town, takes you through a disused tunnel built to transport gold-bearing ore to the Fortuna Mine. The actual tunnel is 600m long and you'll need to take a torch. The trail, which starts at the car park off Crown Street to the south of town, goes through an attractive area of identified indigenous trees before entering the tunnel, and once you're through you get good views of Barberton and the De Kaap Valley.

While you're here, pick up the map showing the location of the **Victorian houses** that fall under the musuem's supervision and make a good excuse to wander some of the streets and enjoy the flamboyant gardens. Built for a wealthy middle-class family and restored to its 1904 grandeur, **Belhaven House**, 18 Lee Rd, is a five-minute walk north from the museum and has an intriguing frontage, but is not always open. Further up Lee Road, **Fernlea House** (Mon–Fri 9am–12.30pm & 1.30–4pm) is a wood and iron structure, while **Stopforth House**, 18 Bowness St, to the east, is the most interesting of the three, and a guard can take you through the house at 10am, 11am, noon, 2pm and 3pm. The original wood and iron house and outbuildings were built by James Stopforth, a local baker and general dealer.

Eating and drinking

Barberton's best place to **eat** is the *Co-Co Pan* in Crown Street, which dishes up straightforward hamburgers, steaks and omelettes, and is cheap and friendly. Your best shot at meeting locals is to head downstairs to the lively **pub** below the restaurant. Next to the tourist information bureau on Crown Street is the pleasant *Victorian Tea Garden*, with a white gazebo straight out of a London park, and good tea and light snacks served outdoors.

Onwards to Swaziland

The closest and most beautiful route into Swaziland from Barberton is through the border crossing at Bulembu (open 8am–4pm), but the road is poor and should be avoided unless you're in a four-wheel-drive vehicle, or a fairly tough car in the dry season. A more practical option is to enter Swaziland via the Ngwenya/Oshoek (7am–10pm) or Jeppe's Reef/Matsamo (open 8am–4pm) border posts. There is no organized transport to Swaziland from either Nelspruit or Barberton.

The R40 from Nelspruit to Klaserie

The **R40** heads north from Nelspruit along the western border of the Kruger National Park, passing through prosperous tropical-fruit-growing farmlands and former black "homeland" areas where you'll find roadside fruit stalls and see people trudging along the roadsides pushing goods in wheelbarrows or carrying plastic water containers on their heads. Guesthouses, many of them fairly upmarket, pop up all along the way to Hazyview until you reach the densely populated former *bantustan* areas around **Bosbokrand**. Roadside lodgings reappear once you reach Klaserie, and many of them are on game farms – poor cousins to the pricier lodges right inside the game reserves to the east.

Hazyview

HAZYVIEW, 43km north of Nelspruit, is little more than a sprawl of shops buzzing with minibus taxis and small market stalls selling fruit and goods to the surrounding African community. The village's only interest lies in the fact that, just 19km from Numbi Gate, it's perfectly positioned for access to the game-rich southern section of Kruger National Park. This is one of the best bases for visitors who aren't spending the night in the park itself and would prefer to come home after a hard day's game-viewing to hotel comforts.

Practicalities

No public **transport** comes into Hazyview, but if you're staying at the local backpackers' lodge you can arrange transport with them from Nelspruit for a fee.

The village has a wide range of **accommodation**. At the bottom end of the scale, the *Kruger Park Backpackers*, Main Rd (☎ & fax 013/737 7224; ①), is pleasantly located under shady bushveld trees and offers campsites, dorms, rondavels and, nicest of all, Zulu beehive huts. There's a swimming pool and you can arrange day-trips into Kruger from here. Staying at the old-fashioned but comfortable *Numbi*, Main Rd (☎013/737 7301, fax 737 7525), won't break the bank either if you camp (①) or stay in their bungalows (③) – the place also has conventional hotel rooms (④). *Tembi*, along the R40, just north of the Sabie River (☎013/737 7729, fax 737 7036; ③) has reasonably priced en-suite B&B rooms. For somewhere out of the ordinary, make for *Thulamela*, 1km down White River Road, off the R40 (☎ & fax 013/737 7171, mobile 082/454 8278), which is run by a trained dietician who serves healthy breakfasts and puts you up in en-suite timber cottages, each with its own deck, jacuzzi and bushveld views. More luxurious accommodation is offered at *Hippo Hollow Country Estate* (☎013/737 7752, fax 737 7673; ④), along the R40 just south of town, with thatched cottages on the banks of the Sabie River featuring a communal eating, reception and bar area. Trips into Kruger with *Welcome Tours* leave from here every morning. Hazyview's most upmarket country lodge is the *Rissington Inn*, just south of town (☎013/737 7700, fax 737 7112; ④–⑤), which has a handful of plush rooms set in the gardens of a large homestead with a swimming pool and excellent food. To get there from Hazyview, take the R40 south and turn right at Kiaat Park, after the Haze Nissan garage on the left-hand side of the road.

All the hotels have **restaurants** open to the public, but if you fancy something a bit different head for *De Kraal* (Mon–Fri 8am–noon & 2–4pm, Sat 9–10am; ☎013/737 7853), a so-called "field kitchen" which recreates outdoor eating from "pioneer days", where you can blow out on barbecued warthog, wagon wheels (a beef delicacy) and freshly baked bread under the light of paraffin lamps hanging from the trees. To get there from Kruger, turn left just after the Total garage on the corner of the R40 and the Numbi Gate road.

On to Klaserie

The only reason you're likely to find yourself heading along the R40 from Hazyview is to gain access to the private game reserves – **Sabi Sand**, **Manyeleti** or **Timbavati** – that join up with the western flank of Kruger (covered on p.550). These reserves can also be reached via the more scenic routes along the Escarpment, but the Lowveld route isn't without its interest, if only as an antidote to the sanitized worlds of Kruger and the mountain resorts.

After Hazyview the R40 passes through irrigated farmlands and low hills dotted with bushveld trees. As you approach **Bosbokrand**, 28km to its north, the corridor between the Escarpment and big game country changes, with the sudden appearance of shanty-towns, busy roads, overgrazed lands and dense settlements interspersed with the odd papaya and banana tree. Also known by its English name "Bushbuck Ridge" (a direct translation from the Afrikaans), the town's name comes from the hilly finger that extends east from the Escarpment. Any bushbuck that might once have wandered here have long since been displaced by the cattle and goats that have chewed away the surrounding vegetation and now spill out into the roads.

Despite the fact that maps indicate little or no habitation, the busy and sometimes hazardous road passes through the former *bantustan* of **Lebowa**, where the people live crammed at a density six times greater than the provincial average. **Klaserie**, 42km north of Bosbokrand, lies in the middle of game farms and sits poised on the border between Mpumalanga and Northern Province. Head east here for **Orpen Gate**, 45km away, which gives access to the rewarding central section of Kruger National Park.

East to Komatipoort

Heading east from Nelspruit, the N4 roughly shadows the progress of the **Crocodile River**, which traces the southern boundary of Kruger National Park on its journey to the Indian Ocean through Mozambique. For 58km to the tiny settlement of **Malelane**, the road travels within view of the Crocodile's riverine forest, passing by lush, sub-tropical farmlands and the grey Dali-esque formations of granite *koppies*. Some 4km further on, the road turns off to Kruger's **Malelane Gate**, which is the most convenient entry point for Berg-en-Dal rest camp (see p.543). A signpost 12km east of Malelane indicates *Buhala Country House* (☎013/790 4372, fax 790 4306; ⑥), a fabulous **guest-house** on a mango, sugar cane and papaya farm, set high on the banks of the Crocodile, with views across the slow water into Kruger. Trips into Kruger can be arranged from here for around R200 per person.

Komatipoort

Of all the towns along the Kruger fringes, **KOMATIPOORT**, 87km east of Nelspruit, owes its frontier character least to tourism and far more to the fact that it stands at the cusp between one of Africa's richest countries and one of the world's poorest. The exotic flavour of this small, rambling town comes from its dusty streets dotted with small-time market traders selling tiny piles of tomatoes and onions, the vivid green of the surrounding cane plantations and the colourful wraps of Mozambican women. Despite a slightly seedy edge and the unshakable whiff of wheeling and dealing in sweaty hotel bars, it's a safe and friendly place, where you can enjoy a hint of what lies in Mozambique, just across the Crocodile River.

Komatipoort's **Ressano Garcia** border post is the bottleneck through which hundreds of dispossessed **Mozambicans** attempt to squeeze their way each day to get to the gold-paved streets of Johannesburg. Some who get turned back will chance their lives attempting to steal in through the wilds of Kruger, while the luckier ones who already have jobs on the mines pass through, drinking their earnings on the thrice-weekly train that takes them home to Maputo and returns this way with a fresh cargo of labour. Unless you're flying, this is your only South African gateway into Mozambique. A favoured holiday playground for white South Africans and Rhodesians up until the 1970s, when it gained majority rule, Mozambique was brought to its knees by a devastating, apartheid-sponsored war that brought tourism to an end for nearly two decades. Peace has thankfully returned and travellers are again beginning to explore and are returning with positive tales to tell.

Practicalities

Public transport to Komatipoort is limited to the daily train from Johannesburg, which arrives at **Komatipoort Station**, Nichol St, and **minibus taxis** from Nelspruit. If you're planning on heading into Mozambique, contact *Mozambique Tours* (☎013/790 8000 or 790 8222; ask for Carl Parsons), which can advise on visas and travel.

Places to stay include *Jackalberry Guest House*, 16 Gilfillan St (☎013/790 8111; ②), which has self-catering rooms in an unexceptional modern suburban house. Roughly 2km out of town, *Komati Holiday Resort* (②) also has self-catering accommodation in en-suite timber cabins set among indigenous thorn and fever trees. To get there, take the N4 towards Nelspruit for about 200m out of town and turn right at the Shell garage, following the signs to the resort. The only smart place to stay is the motel-style *Border Country Inn* (☎013/790 7328; ③), 3km out of town just before the border – a convenient stop if you want to make an early start into Mozambique in the morning.

Komatipoort's big surprise is that it has a couple of excellent **eating** places. *Hakunamatata*, 80 Rissik St (☎013/790 7283), is an informal place on the way to Crocodile Bridge that doubles up as a curio shop, and serves up plates of Maputo prawns for under R30. But the real humdinger is *Tambarina* (☎013/790 7057) in the same street, a Mozambican-style restaurant that captures the taste and feel of the former Portuguese colony, with vibrantly tropical decor and a courtyard shaded by mango trees.

KRUGER NATIONAL PARK AND THE PRIVATE RESERVES

Kruger National Park is arguably the emblem of South African tourism; the place that delivers best what most visitors to Africa want – wildlife. The park's success lies in making self-drive safaris relatively inexpensive, straightforward and safe, designed in the first place for self-catering South African families. But if you're looking for a sublime **wilderness experience**, forget about finding it here. The closest South Africa comes to fulfilling "Out of Africa" fantasies is in the **private game reserves** that rub up to the western flank of Kruger. These reserves are not just about good food and luxury accommodation; there is a real qualitative difference between scooting around on your own along tarred roads in a regular car and going off road in an open vehicle with a ranger who knows the bush inside out. Because there are no fences between these reserves and Kruger, they enjoy the identical animals, but the limited numbers of visitors makes for the exclusivity that you pay big bucks for.

However you choose to explore Kruger, be sure to relax and not to get too obsessed with seeing the Big Five. Remember that wildlife doesn't imitate TV documentaries and you're most unlikely to see lion-kills (you may not see a lion at all), or huge herds of wildebeest migrating across dusty savanna. There is always an element of luck involved in what you see, and this is exactly what makes game-spotting so addictive. To get the most out of your trip, a few **game-spotting tips** are outlined in the box overleaf which can make a big difference to your Kruger trip.

The emphasis in Kruger is on driving, and walking possibilities are limited, though many of the private reserves will offer escorted morning game walks. However, there are several three-night **wilderness trails** in different parts of the park, led by armed rangers – a fabulous way of getting in touch with the wilderness, but one you'll have to book for months in advance.

Kruger National Park is **malarial**. For details on necessary precautions, see p.18.

Animals, birds, reptiles and insects

Among the nearly 150 species of **mammals** which you may see in the park are cheetah, leopard, lion, spotted hyena, wild dog, black rhino, blue wildebeest, buffalo, Burchell's zebra, bushbuck, eland, elephant, giraffe, hippo, impala, kudu, mountain reedbuck, nyala, oribi, reedbuck, roan antelope, sable antelope, tsessebe, warthog, waterbuck and white rhino. The staggering 507 **bird species** include raptors, heftybeaked hornbills, ostriches and countless colourful specimens.

Keep your eyes open and you'll also see a variety of **reptiles**, **amphibians** and **insects** – most rewardingly in the grounds of the rest camps themselves. Although the camps are fenced off from big game, there's always something to see up the trees, in the bushes or even inside your rondavel. If you spot a miniature ET-like reptile crawling upside down on the ceiling, don't be tempted to kill it; it's an insect-eating gecko and is doing you a good turn. If, however, you have a horror of insects or frogs, stay away from Kruger in the rainy season (Nov–March), when they're more in evidence.

When to visit

Kruger is rewarding at any time of the year, though each season has certain advantages and drawbacks. If you don't like the heat, avoid high **summer** (Dec–Feb), when on a bad day temperatures can nudge 47°C – though they're generally in the mid- to high thirties. Throughout the summer (Nov–March) the heat can be tempered by short thunder showers. At this time of the year, everything becomes greener, softer and prettier, and from early November you're likely to spot cute young animals.

There's little rain from April to August, the cooler **winter** months, and the vegetation withers over this period, making it easier to spot game. Although daytime temperatures rise to the mid-twenties, the nights and early mornings can be freezing, especially in June and July, when you'll definitely need warm clothes. Rondavels in the rest camps are not heated.

Kruger National Park

A narrow strip of land hugging the Mozambique border, **Kruger National Park** stretches through the Northern Province into Mpumalanga, an astonishing 414-kilometre drive from Pafuri Gate in the north to Malelane Gate in the south, all of it along an arterial tarred road, with many well-kept gravel roads looping off the tar to provide routes for game drives.

Kruger is designed for self-driving and self-catering; if you don't have time in shop in Johannesburg or one of the nearby centres, you can hop in a car knowing you'll find supplies once you arrive, including milk, bread and even the daily newspapers at virtually every one of the thirteen rest camps (though not much in the way of fruit or vegetables). The park's popularity means that not only are you likely to share animal sightings with other motorists, but that **bookings** are at a premium, particularly during South African school holidays, and that at any time of year you may have to stay in whichever camp has accommodation, rather than in your first choice.

Some history

It's highly questionable whether Kruger National Park can be considered "a pristine wilderness", given that people have been living in or around it for thousands of years.

San hunter-gatherers have left their mark in the form of paintings and engravings at 150 sites that have so far been discovered and there's evidence of farming cultures at many places in the park. Around 1000 to 1300 AD centrally organized states were building stone palaces and engaging in **trade** that brought Chinese porcelain, jewellery and cloth into the area.

But it was the arrival of white **fortune seekers** in the second half of the nineteenth century that made the greatest impact on the region. The twentieth century has had an ambivalent attitude to the hunters, criminals and poachers (like the notorious ivory hunter Cecil Barnard), who made their livelihoods here, decimating game populations. Barnard's exploits are admiringly recounted in the *Ivory Trail* by TV Bulpin, while

KRUGER ESSENTIALS

ENTRY GATE ADMISSION FEES

To enter Kruger, you pay a fee per person plus a charge for the vehicle.

Adult	R10
Child (2–15)	R5
Vehicle	R20
Minibus	R25

OPENING HOURS

Gates

Every rest camp is fenced off and has an entrance gate which is closed and opened at the times indicated below. You are expected to return to your rest camp or leave the park prior to gate closing times. Except where specified, all times refer to both entrance and camp gates.

Jan	5am–6.30pm (camp); 5.30am–6.30pm (entry)
Feb	5.30am–6.30pm
March	5.30am–6pm
April	6am–5pm
May–Aug	6.30am–5.30pm
Sept	6am–6pm
Oct	5.30am–6pm
Nov & Dec	4.30am–6.30pm (camp); 5.30am–6.30pm (entry)

Reception at rest camps
8am–5.30pm

Shops
8am–half an hour after gate closing

Restaurants

Breakfast	7–9am
Lunch	noon–2pm
Supper	6–9pm

DRIVING

- Speed limits are: 50kph on tar, 40kph on untarred roads and 10kph in rest camps. Speed traps operate in some parts of the park.
- Approved roads only should be used. Don't drive on unmarked roads and never drive off-road.
- Never leave your car (it's illegal and dangerous), except at designated sites.

every other episode of the still-popular yarn, *Jock of the Bushveld*, set in the area, includes accounts of hunting. In the twentieth century African farmers were kicked off their traditional lands to create the park.

Paul Kruger, former president of the South African Republic is usually credited with having the foresight to set aside land for wildlife conservation. Kruger figures as a shrewd, larger-than-life figure in Afrikaner history and it was **James Stevenson-Hamilton**, the first warden of the national park, who cunningly put forward Kruger's name in order to soften up Afrikaner opposition to the creation of the park. In reality Stevenson-Hamilton knew that Kruger was no conservationist and was actually an inveterate hunter. Kruger "never in his life thought of animals except as biltong", Stevenson-Hamilton wrote in a private letter.

Orientation

Kruger can be divided roughly into three sections, each with a distinct character and terrain. If you have limited time, it's best to choose just one or two areas to explore; but if you're staying for five days or more, consider driving its length slowly, savouring the changes in landscape along the way. The southern, central and northern sections are sometimes referred to as "the circus", "the zoo" and "the wilderness" – sobriquets that carry more than a germ of truth.

The **southern section** has the greatest concentration of game, attracts the highest number of visitors and is the most easily accessible part of the park if you're coming from Johannesburg, which is 478km away on the N4 national highway. The park headquarters (Skukuza) are here, with an airport, car rental facilities, a filling station, a car repair workshop, a car wash, bank, post office and doctor, as well as enough rondavels to accommodate one thousand people. The **central section** also offers good game-viewing, as well as two of the most attractive camps in the park at **Olifants** and **Letaba**. The further north you go, the thinner both animal populations and visitors become, but it's the **northern section** that really conveys a sense of wilderness, reaching its zenith at the marvellously old-fashioned **Punda Maria** camp, which dates back to the 1930s.

Access

Without your own car, you've got two options for getting to Kruger: you can take one of the many **tours** on offer – some involving day-trips from points just outside the park, others involving camping inside the park – or you can fly into the **airport** and rent a car. However, flights to airports servicing Kruger, and car rental, are expensive, and there are no special deals.

By road

There are eight **entrance gates** along the western and southern borders of Kruger; where you enter will depend on where you're coming from and which camp you're heading to. **From Johannesburg**, the quickest way to get to Kruger is along the N4, which brushes along its southern boundary en route to Mozambique and quickly gets you close to the **southern gates** of Malelane, 411km away, and Crocodile Bridge, another 57km further on. These are also the closest if you're coming **from KwaZulu-Natal**, either via Barberton or Swaziland. If you've been exploring the **Blyde River Canyon** area, access is off the R538/R40 betweenWhite River and Klaserie to the **western gates** (Pretoriuskop, Paul Kruger, Orpen and Phalaborwa) leading into the southern and central sections of the park. The easiest way to get to the two **northern gates** on the west side is off the N1 from Johannesburg to Messina on the northern border, taking the R524 east at Louis Trichardt for Punda Maria Gate, or the R525, 58km further north, to Pafuri Gate.

Remember if you're trying to get from one part of the park to another that although it's far more fun driving inside, the speed limit (50kph on tar, 40kph on dirt) makes it a slow journey – and you're bound to make loads of stops to watch animals.

By air

British Airways/Comair (☎011/921 0222) flies out three times a day from **Johannesburg** to **Skukuza**, Kruger's headquarters. *SA Airlink* (☎toll free 0800/11 4799) flies three times every weekday (and less frequently over weekends) from Johannesburg to the town of **Phalaborwa** (see p.528), which lies just outside Phalaborwa Gate, and six times every weekday (less often over weekends) to **Nelspruit**, which is 45 minutes' drive from either Numbi or Malelane gates. *SA Airlink* also fly **from Durban** to Nelspruit four times a week. Both airlines offer fly-drive packages.

Car rental

For **car rental**, Johannesburg or Pretoria are obvious centres to make your arrangements, but closer to the Kruger you can sort out a vehicle at **Nelspruit International Airport**, 56km from Numbi Gate, through *Avis* (☎013/741 1087), *Budget* (☎013/741 3871) or *Imperial* (☎013/741 2834). **Phalaborwa Airport** also has branches of *Avis* (☎01524/5169), *Budget* (☎01524/85404) and *Imperial* (☎01524/2376), while at **Skukuza Airport** inside Kruger you'll only find *Avis* (☎013/735 5651).

Tours

One of the least expensive **tours** into Kruger is with *Bundu Bus Tours and Safaris* (☎011/693 1808, fax 693 4157, mobile 082/567 7041), which departs **from Johannesburg** and includes a trip through the Mpumalanga panoramic route to Kruger. All meals are included and accommodation for the first night is in chalets at Moholoholo Wildlife Rehabilitation Centre in Hoedspruit and the next two nights camping in in large dome tents in the southern or central camps of Kruger. The tours cost from R700 per person.

If you're short of time or just don't feel like driving from Johannesburg, the **fly-in safaris** operated by *British Airways/Comair* (☎011/921 0222) offer a choice of one-night safaris staying in public rest camps and more comprehensive tours that also take in the Escarpment. Prices range from R2000 to R4000.

From **Hazyview**, *Welcome Tours*, Hippo Hollow Country Estate (☎013/737 7945), operate half-day and full-day tours into the park (R190 and R260 per person, not including meals and refreshments), starting less than 20km from Numbi Gate. Daily departures are at 5–6am (depending on the time of year).

Accommodation: rest camps and bushveld camps

At most of Kruger's thirteen main **rest camps** the sounds of the African night tend to get drowned out by air conditioning and the merriment of *braaivleis* and beer. It's not all bad news, though; at least you'll have all the facilities you could ever want on hand. Nearly all camps have electricity, public telephones, petrol stations, shops, restaurants, laundrettes and snack bars. Some also have swimming pools and most offer night drives for viewing nocturnal animals on large trucks equipped with spotlights. Despite the suburban atmosphere, the rest camps can be quite pleasant, with walks around the

ACCOMMODATION BOOKINGS

Kruger's rest camps and bushveld camps are adminstered by the National Parks Board. If you're planning on staying at the park over the school holidays or weekends you should **book** your **accommodation** well ahead. Booking in writing opens thirteen months in advance. Closer to the date, you'll usually find somewhere, especially at off-peak times, if you're not too particular about where you stay in the park. Applications should be made to: National Parks Board, PO Box 787, Pretoria 0001 (☎012/343 1991, fax 343 0905), or PO Box 7400, Rogge Bay, Cape Town 8012 (☎021/22 2810, fax 24 6211).

edges, labelled trees to help you identify what you see on drives, and plenty of birds and smaller creatures around the camps themselves.

Kruger camps have a variety of accommodation. At most of them you'll find **thatched rondavels**, each with an outdoor eating area and facing communally towards each other rather than out towards the views. The best rondavels are on the camp perimeters or directly facing onto rivers. Nine of the rest camps have a **campsite** (with shared kitchen and washing facilities), which provide the park's cheapest accommodation (R40 for two people). Sites for **caravans** and **camper vans** are available wherever there's camping, cost up to R70 for two people and often have a power point. Some camps have **furnished tents** and **huts**, in configurations usually sleeping two to four people. Most of these have fridges and air conditioning, some come with basic crockery and cutlery, and all share communal kitchens and ablutions at prices ranging from R80 to R130 for two people. **En-suite chalets**, **rondavels** and **huts** come in several variations, ranging from those with just showers, toilets and fridges to ones fully equipped with kitchens. Prices range from **R190** to **R330** per couple, and often reflect how modern the camp is rather than the accommodation facilities.

For a more rustic (and pricier) experience, you'll need to head out to one of the handful of smaller **bushveld camps**, which dispense with all the niceties of shops and restaurants and get down to basics. These camps are more exclusive, being out of bounds to anyone not booked in to stay.

Southern Kruger rest camps

The so-called "circus" is the busiest section of the Kruger, with its hub at **Skukuza**, the biggest of all the Kruger camps and **Lower Sabie**, one of the most popular. Apart from containing some of the best places for seeing large quantities of game southern Kruger is also easily accessed from Johannesburg along the N4. At peak times of year this area can buzz with vehicles jostling to get up close to big cat sightings, which always appear to evoke poor human behaviour.

BERG-EN-DAL

In the southwest corner of the park, **Berg-en-Dal** is one of the newest camps, built in the 1980s and with modern chalets that break with the Kruger tradition of thatched rondavels. Set attractively among *koppies* in a shallow grassy basin (its Afrikaans name means "hill and dale"), 12km northwest of **Malelane Gate**, the camp overlooks the Matjulu stream and dam, both of which can be reached by means of a walkway running along the perimeter fence. The modern, fully equipped chalets with terraces are widely spaced to provide privacy and are landscaped among indigenous bushveld vegetation. Facilities include a beautifully positioned swimming pool, a shop selling a good range of food, a licensed restaurant, snack bar, filling station and laundrette.

CROCODILE BRIDGE

East of Berg-en-Dal, **Crocodile Bridge** is the least scintillating of Kruger's rest camps, and its position at the very southern edge of the park overlooking farmland does nothing to enhance your bush experience. Located at the **Crocodile Bridge Gate** on the north bank of the Crocodile River, the camp is reached via Komatipoort, 12km to its south on the Mozambique border. The main reason to spend the night here is if you're arriving late and don't have time to press on into the park. Facilities are limited to a laundrette and filling station, and a shop selling the most basic of supplies. Accommodation is in en-suite huts that sleep two to three people and have cooking facilities. If you're pushing north to Lower Sabie, it's worth taking the drive slowly, as this area, dotted with knobthorn and marula trees, is known for its herbivores, which include giraffe, kudu, steenbok, wildebeest, zebra, buffalo and waterbuck as well as ostrich, warthog and the magnificent black sable antelope. You should also keep your eyes peeled for predators such as lion, cheetah, hyena and jackal.

LOWER SABIE

Some 35km north of Crocodile Bridge, **Lower Sabie** occupies game-rich country that places it among the top three rest camps in the Kruger for mammal-spotting. The surrounding open savanna and the camp's position on the banks of the Sabie River attract animals coming to drink and graze, and the terrain around here is rated among the most beautiful in the southern Kruger. Within kilometres of the entrance gate to the camp, a number of waterholes and dams populated with crocodiles and hippos make good spots to park at and watch for game coming to quench their thirst. In the thorn thicket country hard by the west of the camp, you'll find promising terrain for catching sight of elephants moving between the trees as well as white rhino grazing on the sweet grasses, which also bring herds of buffalo and their wake, lions. Accommodation is in huts with shared ablutions as well as more expensive en-suite units with kitchens, some with river views. There's a restaurant, a cafeteria, a shop, a filling station and a laundrette.

PRETORIUSKOP

Due west of Lower Sabie, but not directly connected to it, **Pretoriuskop** is reached via **Numbi Gate**, 9km to its west. Set in an area of sourveld, characterized by granite outcrops, tall grass and sickle bush favoured by mountain reedbuck, sable and white rhino, the camp is in an area stalked by lions, wild dogs and side-striped jackals. However, given the dense bush you'll be more likely to spot larger species such as kudus and giraffes poking their necks over the bushes. Accommodation consists of en-suite cottages and rondavels in addition to cheaper units with shared ablution and cooking facilities. The camp has a restaurant, a snack bar, a shop, a laundrette, a swimming pool and a filling station. Night drives are on offer.

SKUKUZA

Kruger's largest rest camp, **Skukuza** lies at the centre of the best game-viewing area in the park. Its position can be a double-edged sword, because where you get large amounts of game, hordes of humans aren't far behind. Skukuza accommodates over one thousand people and resembles a small town. A sprawling collection of rondavels, it sits on the edge of the Sabie River, which is overlooked by a wide paved walkway furnished with park benches, from which you can watch crocodiles float by on the brown water looking like driftwood.

Skukuza is the hub of Kruger and has an airport you can fly into and a car rental agency. You can get repairs done here to your vehicle in the rest camp's garage and there's also a post office, a bank, a filling station, two restaurants, a cafeteria and a library at the central reception area. The closest entry point is through **Paul Kruger Gate**, 12km to the west, which in turn is 42km east of Hazyview. Accommodation is in a range of thatched, en-suite units, or more cheaply in some furnished East African-style tents in the caravan park, with shared ablutions and kitchens. Night drives and day drives in open vehicles can be arranged at the main complex, and cost around R60 and R100 per person respectively.

Central Kruger rest camps

Game-viewing can be extremely good in the "zoo", with the area between Skukuza and Satara reckoned to be one of the global hot spots for lions. At **Olifants** you'll find the Kruger's most dramatically located camp, with fantastic views into a river gorge, while **Satara** is the second-largest and one of the most popular – its placement is ideal for making sorties into fertile wildlife country.

ORPEN AND MAROELA

Like Crocodile Bridge, **Orpen** is located right by an entrance gate, 45km east of Klaserie, and is recommended mainly if you're arriving late and don't have time to make it further into the park before the camp gates close. Orpen is far preferable to its southern counterpart though, because although it's on the western periphery of Kruger, the substantial Timbavati Private Game Reserve lies to its west, so you're already well into the wilderness once you get here. Facilities are pretty basic, with a filling station and a reception that doubles up as a rudimentary shop. None of the accommodation is en suite and cooking is done in communal kitchens. The camp is small, peaceful and shaded by beautiful trees. If you want to camp you'll need to go to the small **Maroela** satellite camping area that overlooks the Timbavati River. It is situated approximately 4km from Orpen and has electricity. You must report to Orpen reception to check in before going to the campsite.

TAMBOTI

Not far from Orpen Gate into the park, **Tamboti** is reached by turning left 2km after Orpen and continuing for 1km. More basic than most, the camp consists exclusively of furnished walk-in tents with communal cooking and ablution facilities – you'll need to bring all your own implements. There are fridges and electric lights in the tents. All the tents have river views, but numbers 21 and 22 are particularly recommended both for their prime position on a bend in the river and the coolness of their shade.

SATARA

Due east of Orpen Gate, 46km straight along the tar, **Satara** ranks second only to Skukuza in size and the excellence of the game-viewing in its surrounding grassy plains. Set in the middle of flat grasslands, the camp commands no great views, but is preferable to Skukuza because it avoids the feeling of suburban boxes on top of each other. Accommodation is in cottages which are arranged around lawned areas shaded by large trees, which provides some relief from the midday sun. Facilities include a restaurant, cafeteria, shop, filling station, laundrette and vehicle repair workshop. About halfway along the tarred road between Satara and Skukuza, which is 92km to its south, the vicinity around Tshokwane picnic site reputedly has the highest concentration of lions in the world and is hence also a popular stamping ground for motorists.

The area around Satara itself is usually rewarding for sighting grazers, such as buffalo, wildebeest, zebra, kudu, impala and elephant.

OLIFANTS

Because of its terrific setting on cliffs overlooking the braided Olifants River, **Olifants**, 52km north of Satara, is reckoned by many to be the best rest camp in Kruger. It's quite possible to spend hours sitting on the benches on the covered look-out terrace, gazing into the valley whose airspace is crisscrossed by Bateleur eagles and yellow billed kites cruising the thermals, while the rushing of the water below creates a hypnotic rhythm. The camp has a charmingly old-fashioned feel. Accommodation is in thatched, en-suite rondavels, with numbers 1 to 24 possessing superb views overlooking the valley; it's worth booking well in advance to get one these sought-after chalets. The river marks the division between rugged, rocky *veld* with ghostly fever trees growing along the riverbanks to the south and to the north mopane woodland which attracts the large antelope such as eland, roan, sable and tsessebe. Also around here is promising country for spotting elephant, giraffe, lion, hyena and cheetah, and you should look out for the tiny klipspringer, a pretty antelope that inhabits rocky terrain which it nimbly negotiates by boulder-hopping. A highlight of the area are some of the dirt roads which loop along the Olifants River. Among the facilities you'll find at the camp are a restaurant, a snack bar, a shop and a laundrette.

LETABA

Set in mopane shrubland, **Letaba** is 34km north of Olifants, beautifully set on an oxbow curve along the Letaba River, a view which, sadly, very few of the rondavels enjoy. The restaurant does have great vistas of the floodplain, and you can spend a day just watching herds of buffalo mooching around, elephants drifting past and hosts of other plains game. The camp is old and quite large, a fact mitigated by large acacias and mopanes as well as ilala palms. Letaba is in the midst of good elephant country and has an interesting museum with exhibits on the life cycle of the large mammals as well as displays on the bull elephants with inordinately large tusks, who have trampled the area. Accommodation is in either en-suite rondavels or ones with shared ablution and cooking facilities as well as large furnished tents. All the usual restaurant, shopping and laundrette facilities are here, as well as a vehicle repair workshop.

Northern Kruger rest camps

You won't find edge-to-edge game in the northern "wilderness", but crossing the Tropic of Capricorn after **Mopani** camp gives a symbolic boost to the idea that you're entering hot savanna country. The north is the least visited of Kruger's regions and creates the most convincing impression of African wilderness, especially once you hit **Punda Maria** camp, which feels like a real old-time outpost in the bush.

MOPANI

Some 42km north of Letaba, **Mopani** is one of the newer camps in Kruger and overlooks the Pioneer Dam. A sprawling place in the middle of monotonous mopane shrub, its swimming pool provides cool relief after a long drive. Similarly, the dam, one of the few water sources in the vicinity, attracts animals to drink and provides an outstanding lookout for a variety of wildlife including elephant, buffalo and antelope. The modern en-suite accommodation, built of rough-hewn stone and thatch, is quite spread out and designed more for driving than walking. The restaurant is above the usual Kruger average and the bar has a good view across to the dam. Other facilities

GAME-VIEWING TIPS

- **Binoculars are a must** for scanning the horizon when you're out viewing. Don't try consciously to spot animals – many are well disguised. Instead, watch for any movement or something that strikes you as a bit out of place.

- **Look out for other stopped cars**, which are often a good indicator of a game-sighting.

- **Plan your game drive carefully** and invest in a detailed map of Kruger (available at virtually every rest camp). Use the map to choose a route which includes rivers or pans where you can stop and enjoy the scenery and birdlife while you wait for game to come down to drink, especially in the late afternoon.

- **Driving really slowly** pays off, particularly if you stop often. Switch off your engine when you stop, open your window and use your senses. Being in the bush isn't just about seeing animals: there are also the smells and sounds of the wilds, which complete the picture and provide useful clues. Twigs breaking or the alarm calls of animals can hint at something afoot.

- **Don't embark on overambitious drives** from your rest camp. You'll see as much game sitting quietly in your car as you would frantically driving around all day.

- **Take food and drink** with you. You don't want to have to break off that terrific lion-sighting because you're starving and can't miss lunch. Carry plenty of water to avoid dehydration or heatstroke. If you have your own teabags and milk you can make tea at the designated picnic sites, where there is always boiling water available, tables and chairs to enjoy your picnic in the wild, and *braai* places powered with gas.

- **Tuning into animal behaviour** can greatly enrich your experience and provides constant interest even on days when big cats stubbornly refuse to put in an appearance. Even commonplace species such as impala become fascinating when you understand what they're doing and why. Although the widely available *Safari Companion* by Richard Estes sounds like a manual on how to treat your porters, in fact it's an accessible and engrossing guide to the behaviour of African mammals (see "Books", p.682).

- **The best times of day** for game-viewing are when it's cooler during the early morning and late afternoon. Set out as soon as the camp gates open in the morning and go out again as the temperature starts dropping in the afternoon. Take a siesta during the midday heat, just as the animals do, when they head for deep shade where you're less likely to see them.

- **Take an interest in geology, trees and birds** and you need never be bored because "there's nothing going on". The excellent *Make the Most of Kruger*, available at most rest camps, is well worth investing in for the basic interpretation it provides of the park ecology and for filling in those empty moments.

include a shop, a laundrette and filling station, and you can go on organized night drives.

SHINGWEDZI

A fairly large camp featuring square, brick chalets and a few older, colonial-style white-wash and thatch bungalows, **Shingwedzi**, 63km north of Mopani, is sited in extensive grounds shaded by large mopane trees and palms. The dining room has a terrace, frequented by starlings and cheeky hornbills jostling to pounce on your food. From the terrace you get a long view down across the usually dry Shingwedzi River. Look out for the weavers' nests with their long, tube-like entrances hanging from the eaves outside reception and the cafeteria. Facilities include a restaurant, a cafeteria, a shop, a filling station and a swimming pool. Night drives are on offer.

PUNDA MARIA AND PAFURI

Kruger's northernmost camp, **Punda Maria**, 71km beyond Shingwedzi, is also the park's wildest and least visited. There's less concentration of game up here, but to aficionados, this is the real Kruger: a relaxed, tropical outpost near the Zimbabwe border, well away from the bustle of motorists. This isn't to say you won't see wildlife here (the Big Five all breeze through from time to time), it's simply that in its woodlands and dense mopane scrubland you have to work that much harder at game-spotting. The real rewards of Punda are in its landscapes and stunningly varied vegetation types, with a remarkable nine biomes all converging here, which also makes it paradise for bird-watchers. Some of the accommodation is in the original 1930s huts that ought to be declared National Monuments but are in danger of being pulled down for modernization. All units are en-suite and have fridges, while some have kitchens and the rest make use of communal cooking areas. The camp has a very simple restaurant, a small shop and a filling station. **Pafuri** picnic site, 46km north of Punda, should on no account be missed, as it's here that you'll experience the true richness of northern Kruger. The site is a large area under the shade of massive thorn trees, leadwoods and jackalberry trees on the banks of the Luvuvhu River and is the ultimate place for lunch. An interpretation board gives a fascinating account of human history in the area. There are *braai* facilities, a constantly boiling kettle to make your own tea and ice-cold canned drinks can be bought from the attendant.

Bushveld camps

Bushveld camps are far smaller, more remote and a whole lot more basic than the main rest camps. You won't find any shops or restaurants at these camps, but they are all within reasonable reach of larger rest camps – just in case you can't survive without a Coke. The appeal of the bushveld camps is that they get you away from day-to-day trivialities – and the tourist pack – and into the wilderness. The downside is that, with the exception of **Balule**, they all have **cottages** accommodating a minimum of four people, which means that you're going to pay at least R150 per person and a lot more if you're staying in one of the larger units that go for about R600–800 for up to four. Because of their exclusivity, the camps get booked up quickly, so stake your claim as early as possible. Most offer game drives during the day and at night.

BALULE

On the southern bank of the Olifants River, **Balule** is roughly 11km south of Olifants rest camp and 87km from Phalaborwa Gate. The only voltage you'll find at this very basic satellite to Olifants is in the electric fence that keeps out lions. The compact camp has two sections, one consisting of six spartan rondavels and another of fifteen camping and caravan sites. Each section has its own communal ablution and cooking facilities. Balule takes its bushveld identity seriously and luxuries are kept to a minimum – as is the price: this is the only bushveld camp where two can stay for under R100. There are iron washstands with enamel bowls, no windows and you can forget about air conditioning. You'll have to bring your own crockery, cutlery and utensils. You need to report to Olifants at least half an hour before the gates close.

BATELEUR

About 40km southwest of Shingwedzi rest camp, **Bateleur** is well off the beaten track, in the remote northern section of the park on the banks of the frequently dry Mashokwe stream. The camp has a timber viewing-deck, excellently placed for vistas of game coming to drink at a seasonally full waterhole. The nearby Silver Fish and Rooibosrand dams also attract game as well as birdlife in prodigious quantities. Seven family cottages can accommodate up to 34 people. Each has its own kitchenette and fridge, with electricity provided by solar panels.

BYAMITI
Byamiti is on the banks of the Mbyamiti River, about 41km northeast of the Malelane Gate and 26km west of Crocodile Bridge Gate. Its proximity to Crocodile Bridge Gate is one of the main advantages of this very southerly camp. Another plus point is that the terrain attracts large numbers of game including lion, elephant and rhinos. Fifteen family cottages, all with fully equipped kitchens, can accommodate a maximum of seventy visitors.

JAKKALSBESSIE
On the bank of the Sabie River, some 7km north of Skukuza rest camp, near the airfield, **Jakkalsbessie** is one of the less remote bush camps and is periodically treated to the

---

WILDERNESS TRAILS

Wilderness trails in Kruger won't bring you closer to game than driving would: the experience is really about getting closer to the vegetation and smaller creatures. Under the guidance of an experienced ranger, the two-day trails pass through areas of notable beauty that have a diverse plant and animal life. Groups (limited to eight people) spend three nights in four rustic, two-bed huts, served by reed-walled showers and flush toilets. Simple meals are provided. Trails cost in the region of R1000 per person fully inclusive.

The trails are closed over the Christmas school holidays and are heavily subscribed for the rest of the year. **Booking** in writing opens thirteen months in advance and is recommended if you have your heart set on a particular trail. Book through the National Parks Board, PO Box 787, Pretoria 0001 (☎012/343 1991, fax 343 0905), or PO Box 7400, Rogge Bay, Cape Town 8012 (☎021/22 2810, fax 24 6211).

- **Bushman Trail** covers the southwestern section of the park, near Berg-en-Dal rest camp. The trail camp is in a secluded valley, characterized by granite hills. San paintings in many of the hill shelters are an added feature of the trail.

- **Metsimetsi Trail** operates near Tshokane, with the camp at the foot of the mountain and overlooking a small waterhole. Black rhino and large predators move through the undulating savanna and rocky gorges and ravines.

- **Napi Trail** sets out from a camp between Skukuza and Pretoriuskop into woodland bushveld. Undulating terrain and granite hills suit the area's resident population of white rhino, while black rhino, elephant, lion and buffalo are also often seen. Birdlife is prolific.

- **Nyalaland Trail** is based in the remote northern section of the park along the Madzaringwe Stream north of Punda Maria. The area is known for its fever-tree and baobab forests, prolific birdlife and spectacular views.

- **Olifants Trail** has its camp on the southern bank of the Olifants River, from which it offers a magnificent view of the river. Riverine bush and gorges characterize the terrain, and lion, buffalo and elephant are often seen.

- **Sweni Trail** camp overlooks the Sweni stream in the wilderness area near Nwanetsi and provides a view of marula and knobthorn savanna. A resident pride of lions pads about here and is frequently seen.

- **Wolhuter Trail** walks in the vicinity of Berg-en-Dal and Pretoriuskop camp in the southern section of the park, where rhinos are relatively common, as is a wide variety of other game.

sound of aircraft taking off or landing at the Skukuza landing strip. Although it may be too close to the "city lights" of Skukuza for some, the camp is beautifully positioned on the Sabie River and has easy access to some of the richest game country in Kruger. Eight thatched cottages with fully equipped kitchens can accommodate a maximum of 32 people.

SHIMUWINI

On the upper reaches of the Shimuwini Dam, which is filled by the Letaba River, **Shimuwini** lies about 50km from the Phalaborwa Gate on the Mooiplaas Road. In mopane and bushwillow country, with sycamore figs along the banks of the river, this camp is not known for its game but is a perennial favourite among bird-watchers. It's an excellent place for spotting riverine bird species, including fish eagles. Up to 71 people can be accommodated in the fifteen family cottages which come equipped with kitchens and with verandahs.

SIRHENI

Sirheni is on the bank of Sirheni Dam, roughly 54km south of Punda Maria rest camp. Its siting on the edge of a dam makes Sirheni a fine spot for bird-watching, with some game also passing through the area. Its big pull, however, is its remote bushveld atmosphere in an area that sees few visitors. The fifteen one- or two-bedroom cottages, all equipped with kitchens, can accommodate eighty visitors.

TALAMATI

Lying on the banks of the usually dry Nwaswitsontso stream, about 31km south of Orpen Gate, **Talamiti** is in the varied terrain of mixed bushwillow woodland which attracts giraffe, kudu, wildebeest, zebra and predators like lion, hyena and jackal, as well as rhino and sable. The camp has the capacity for eighty people in its ten six-bed and five four-bed cottages.

The private game reserves

Outside Kruger's western boundaries, big game country continues and here you'll find the many exclusive and expensive **private game reserves** clustering on huge tracts of amalgamated land. The three major private reserves are **Sabi Sand** to the south and **Timbavati** and **Manyeleti**, adjoining the central section of the national park. All the reserves have a number of camps on them. They are unfenced; animals from Kruger can roam into private reserve territory. Private reserves are not places you drive yourself around in: if you do arrive by car you'll leave it at the gate and not see it again until you leave. What you pay for at these camps, besides all-inclusive luxury, is a well-informed game ranger who will take you out on game drives in open-topped vehicles, show you the animals and birds, and talk about their behaviour and the ecology of the area. You'll get the benefit of the ranger's sharp eyes and experience, which makes the game-spotting extremely rewarding. The other advantage is that you'll share the experience with very few others, and have your fantasies of wild Africa more fully satisfied than by staying in the park itself.

Which private camp you choose depends largely on what type of safari you're after: a more rustic experience with no electricity and the sounds of lions roaring at night, or a highly luxurious hotel in the bush where food is as important as your bush experience. All the camps follow the same basic formula of full board, and dawn and dusk game drives conducted by a ranger assisted by a tracker in open vehicles. Afternoon outings usually turn into night drives following sundowners in the bush, and you'll usually be able to fit in a walk as well if you wish.

The camps

Private camps aren't places you can casually pop into. You'll need to **book ahead** either directly through the contact addresses given below or through a specialist travel agent (such as those listed in "Basics"). There are scheduled flights from Johannesburg to Phalaborwa, Hoedspruit, Nelspruit and Skukuza, or from Durban to Nelspruit. Camps generally pick up guests from the airport. By car it will take five to six hours from Johannesburg. You will be given detailed instructions on how to get to your camp when you book.

Prices quoted are per person sharing a double unit and include all meals and activities, apart from the self-catering establishments, which don't include food. At the rock bottom, the cheapest camps for under R500 are extremely rustic places with the most basic of facilities (such as bucket showers), and are usually self-catering. What they do give you is exclusive access to the best of South Africa's big game country. For the real safari experience, staying in more comfortable en-suite units where you're fed and pampered you should expect to pay just under R1000. It should be stressed, though, that places for under R1000 are rare and therefore need to be booked well ahead. The really snazzy places, which are by far the majority, weigh in from R1000 to R2000 per person per night. On the whole, the huge price gulf between the bottom and top ends reflects the incidental extras, such as level of luxury and cuisine – and often simply reputation. All are en suite and have proper beds and a swimming pool unless specified.

Honeyguide

Manyeleti Game Reserve PO Box 786064, Sandton; 2146 (☎011/880 3912, fax 447 4326; email: hguide@global.co.za).

One of the best-value private reserves accommodates guests in large East African-style tents with beds. Each has a deck which overlooks a dry river bed fringed with riverine forest. Honeyguide puts out two vehicles which are in radio contact with each other and with neighbouring Khoka Moya, which multiplies your chances of a game-sighting. Honeyguide has access to 100 square kilometres of the Manyeleti which it shares with Khoka Moya, and there are seldom more than three vehicles out at a time. Surprising touches for a budget camp include fine, custom-made linen and tea brought to your tent in the morning. The food is good, the service excellent, the staff friendly, the game drives first class and the camp highly recommended. From R670. They also have the more basic Outpost Camp, which costs R360 per person.

Khoka Moya

Manyeleti Game Reserve; PO Box 15013, Sinoville 0129 (☎012/543 2134, fax 543 2135).

An easy-going, tasteful game lodge taking sixteen guests and verging on the luxurious, but still affordable for its type. Accommodation is in comfortable huts connected by board-walks set in semi-woodland savanna. From R650 per person all-in. They also run the Skybeds, a very basic reed camp deep in the bush beside a waterhole. Bucket shower with water heated on a fire. From R375 per person all-in (subject to a minimum of four people).

Leadwood Lodge

Sabi Sand Game Reserve; Exeter Game Lodges, 99 Belladonna Ave, West Acres ext 20, Nelspruit 1200; PO Box 2060, Nelspruit 1200 (☎013/741 3180, fax 741 3183; email: exeter@cis.co.za).

Operated by *Exeter Safaris*, one of the few self-catering outfits is also one of the cheapest private camps, and as a result is frequently booked out months ahead.

Accommodation is in five thatched, two-bed cottages dotted along the banks of the Sand River under jackalberry, leadwood and tamboti trees. The comfortably furnished air-conditioned units come with all cooking utensils; just bring your own food and drink. Full-time camp staff service the cottages, help with cooking and tend fires in the public area. Two daily game drives and a walk are included in the price, but you run the risk of these turning into a bit of a scrum as Leadwood shares traversing rights with Exeter's Main Lodge as well as two neighbouring outfits, all of which are liable to descend on the same game-sighting. Costs start at R410, including game drives but no meals. For a minimum of eight and maximum of ten people they also have Hunters' Lodge, another self-catering outfit which costs R385 per person. Book well ahead as their excellent value makes them highly popular.

Londolozi

Sabi Sand Game Reserve; Private Bag X27, Benmore 2010 (☎011/784 7077, fax 784 7667).

Leopards are almost synonymous with Londolozi and there are few places you'll stand a better chance of seeing these notoriously elusive stalkers in the wild. If you're prepared to fork out large sums to see cats, there's no better place to do it than at one of Londolozi's three camps, each of which carry the imaginative stamp of Conservation Corporation Africa, whose hallmark is unapologetic indulgence with a green conscience. Biggest and least exceptional of the three is Main Camp (US$450), which accommodates twenty in comfortable chalets. The best thing about it is the wonderful outdoor dining room surrounded by woodland and jettying out over the Sand River basin. But once you're spending this kind of money you may as well go the extra couple of hundred to stay in the more intimate surroundings of the two smaller camps. Bush Camp accommodates sixteen people and has a beautiful swimming pool from whose deck you can lounge and look onto the river with rates starting from US$500, while most exclusive is Tree Camp, built into a riverbank amid indigenous woodland at US$550 per person.

Ngala

Timbavati Game Reserve; Private Bag X27, Benmore 2010 (☎011/784 7077, fax 784 7667).

Despite being a member of "Small Luxury Hotels of the World", Ngala is actually rather large for a private game lodge, accommodating up to 42 people. Expect every indulgence you'd get at a top-quality hotel. Everything at Ngala conspires to feed "old Africa" fantasies, from thatched buildings crammed with stylish furniture and decorated with fine artefacts, right down to the silver and Villeroy and Boch crockery. Formal dinners (starched tablecloths and crystal wineglasses) by lamplight under the stars in the tree-canopied courtyard top off the day. Cottages US$400 and safari suite US$700.

Nottens Bush Camp

Sabi Sand Reserve; PO Box 622, Hazyview 1242 (☎013/735 5105, fax 735 5970).

Just over a decade old and still resisting the temptation to expand, this family-run outfit is one of the most popular small camps, but the fact that each evening is a hosted dinner party may not suit everyone. Accommodation for a maximum of ten is in double-bedded chalets lit by oil lamps, with tin roofs. The lack of electricity is an explicit part of the camp philosophy of bringing guests into contact with the bush and for the same reason game drives take place in one vehicle without the use of radio contact, which means that although the game here is excellent you stand a less than even chance of seeing the Big Five. To get closer to the wild, you can spend a night or two in their bush *boma* (open-topped enclosure). Evening meals are eaten around a large table, while breakfast and tea are served on a massive deck that acts as a viewing platform for the open plain that stretches out in front of the camp. From R950 per person.

Sabi Sabi

Sabi Sand Game Reserve; PO Box 52665, Saxonwold 2132 (☎011/483 3939, fax 483 3799).

Sabi Sabi is the largest outfit in the Sabi Sand Reserve and puts out more vehicles than any other, all in radio contact, so although your experience may be shared you stand an excellent chance of seeing game. Selati Lodge (R1950) is the most exclusive, consisting of seven pretty standard stone and thatch cottages without electricity and lit by oil lamps. Considerably larger, Bush and River lodges (R1850) have a hotel atmosphere and a big reception area. Bush Lodge has 22 chalets and 5 luxury suites in bushveld overlooking a waterhole, and River Lodge has 21 chalets and 2 luxury suites on the banks of the Sabi River. A cheaper and potentially more exciting option is the Ranger Training Experience (R750 per night), which caters to groups of four to seven participants, who spend minimum of three nights in Nkombe tented camp deep in the bush. The food is good, the beds comfortable and bush showers and toilets are provided. The course includes instruction by trained staff in flora and fauna, spoor identification and tracking skills, orienteering, bush survival techniques, ecology and habitat management, astronomy of the southern skies and four-wheel-drive handling, and promises to send you back to the metropolis with a better understanding of the bush than you'd get simply on game drives.

Tanda Tula

Timbavati Game Reserve; PO Box 32, Constantia 7848 (☎021/794 6500, fax 794 7605; email: cuisine@iafrica.com).

One of the longest-established and friendliest Mpumalanga bush camps has accommodation in twelve en-suite, East African-style walk-in tents, each with its own private deck overlooking the riparian forest of the usally dry Nhlaralumi River. The thatched dining room and bar also overlook the dry river bed, to which the guests sometimes decamp for silver-service dining under the stars. A small waterhole and hide, on site, offer game-viewing opportunities without leaving the camp and there's a much-needed swimming pool for cooling off in the sweltering summer. R1380 per person.

Umlani

Timbavati Game Reserve; PO Box 26350, Arcadia 0007 (☎012/329 3765, fax 329 6441; email: umlani@cis.co.za).

One of the cheapest bush camps gets down to basics with eight reed-walled huts overlooking the dry Nhlaralumi River. Each has an attached open-topped bush shower, heated by a wood boiler (there's no electricity) and the languid atmosphere is reinforced by several hammocks hanging lazily from trees with a plunge pool to dunk in when the midday heat becomes too much. Unusually for South Africa, the camp isn't fenced off, the emphasis being very much on a bush experience, with flimsy blinds over the windows. While it's not recommended if you freak out easily, there's barely another camp that will bring you closer to the feeling of being in the wild. Guests are encouraged to join guided morning walks to track game, and for an extra frisson you can spend the night alone, away from the camp in the stilted tree house overlooking a waterhole – highly recommended for full moon. An exceptional game experience, although the food isn't that great. R900 per person.

travel details

Mpumalanga is primarily a self-drive province and, apart from flights serving Skukuza and small service towns close to the private game reserves, scheduled transport amounts to a daily train service between Johannesburg and Nelspruit and, most practical of the lot, a daily *Greyhound* intercity bus between the two cities. If you want to get to anywhere else in the province you'll need to use Nelspruit as a springboard and take minibus taxis.

Trains

Nelspruit to Johannesburg (1 daily; 10hr); Maputo (3 weekly; 7hr); Pretoria (1 daily; 8hr).

Buses

Nelspruit to Johannesburg (daily; 5hr); Pretoria (daily; 4hr).

Flights

Nelspruit to Durban (1–2 daily; 1hr 30min); Johannesburg (3–6 daily; 1hr 50min); Maputo (daily; 1hr 35min).

Hoedspruit to Johannesburg (1 daily; 1hr).

Phalaborwa to Johannesburg (1–3 daily; 1hr).

Skukuza to Johannesburg (3 daily; 1hr 5min).

CHAPTER TEN

NORTHERN PROVINCE

T he **Northern Province** is South Africa's no-man's-land: a hot, thornbush-covered area caught between the dynamic heartland of Gauteng and, to the north, the Limpopo River, which acts as South Africa's border with Zimbabwe and, further west, Botswana. Towards the eastern side of the province is the game-rich lowveld, dominated by the seventy-kilometre-wide strip of Kruger National Park abutting the Mozambique border (covered in the previous chapter, p.537).

Running through the centre of this no-man's-land is the **N1** highway, often called here the "**Great North Road**". This is South Africa's umbilical cord to the rest of Africa, and the importance of the N1, and the weight of traffic which uses it, overshadow the rest of the province; indeed it's invariably the only part of the province most travellers see, with those travelling north eager to get to Zimbabwe, and those heading south impatient to reach Johannesburg.

The principal draws of the Northern Province lie in its three distinctive **mountain escarpments**, where the region's sense of wilderness is at its stongest. The most significant of these is the first rise of the **Drakensberg** escarpment, on its long and often spectacular sweep through South Africa. This north–south escarpment marks the descent from the highveld to the lowveld, but there is a lot to see in the mountains themselves, especially in the haunting, forested slopes of the **Letaba** area immediately to the east of **Pietersburg**, the provincial capital. This is a region of lakes, waterfalls, some excellent walking and comfortable country guesthouses.

On the otherwise unremarkable western side of the N1 lies the more sedate **Waterberg** massif, long a domain of cattle farming and hunting, which is fast becoming an important centre for conservation. In the north, lying parallel to the Limpopo and bisected by the N1, are the subtropical **Soutpansberg Mountains**, and the intriguing and still very independently minded **Venda** region, a former homeland, to the east. North of the Soutpansberg are wide plains dominated by surreal baobab trees, much in evidence along the N1 as it leads to the only (very busy) border post between South Africa and Zimbabwe, at Beitbridge.

Some history

It was across the Limpopo and into what is now the Northern Province that the first black Africans arrived in South Africa, sometime before 300AD. The various move-

---

ACCOMMODATION PRICE CODES

All the accommodation listed in the Guide has been categorized into one of seven price bands, as set out below. The rates quoted, unless otherwise stated, represent the most expensive per-person rate for a double or single room outside high season (Dec & Jan), except for category ①, which are per-person rates for a dorm bed in backpacker accommodation, or a campsite. For more accommodation details, see p.31.

① R0–50	② R50–100	③ R100–150
④ R150–200	⑤ R200–250	⑥ R250–300
	⑦ Over R300	

MALARIA IN THE NORTHERN PROVINCE

Parts of the Northern Province are malarial; you will need to take prophylactics, and exercise caution against mosquitoes if you are travelling in the lowveld, including Kruger National Park, or north of the Soutpansberg Mountains. The Waterberg and Letaba areas are not at present affected. However, the situation may change, and it's a good idea to double-check before you go. For reliable local advice contact the British Airways Travel Clinics in Cape Town (☎021/419 3172) or Johannesburg (☎011/807 3132).

---

ments and migrations, and of course trading, ensured a fluidity in the people who established themselves here, and the historical and cultural ties to the north are, as you might expect, stronger in this region than in other parts of South Africa. Traditional arts and crafts such as **pottery** and **woodcarving** are still an important part of life; legendary figures such as the **Rain Queen** retain great potency, and even **witchcraft** is still encountered in many places.

The arrival of the **Voortrekker** ox-wagons in the early nineteenth century brought profound changes to the orientation of the region. Their route roughly followed what is now the N1, founding such towns as Warmbaths, Nylstroom and Pietersburg. Led by men such as Louis Trichardt, Hermanus and Piet Potgieter, Andries Pretorius and Paul Kruger, the Voortrekkers who ventured this far north were determined people, and their conflicts with the local peoples were notoriously bitter. At **Makapan's Cave** near Potgietersrus, thousands of Ndebele were starved to death by an avenging Boer commando, while further to the north Venda forces forced the Voortrekkers to abandon the settlement they had established at **Schoemansdal** in the Soutpansberg.

In the twentieth century, the **apartheid years** saw some large chunks of the province hived off as homeland areas, with Venda becoming nationally independent and Lebowa and Gazankulu self-governing. Now reformed as one, the contrasts between the old homelands and the white farming areas are manifest throughout the province. Indeed, in the 1994 elections the Northern Province returned the highest-percentage vote in the country for both the ANC and the right-wing Afrikaner Freedom Front.

THE CENTRAL REGION

The core of the Northern Province, at least in terms of density of settlement and land use, lies along the N1 **from Warmbaths to Pietersburg**. The dominance of farming here, however, means there is little by way of sights or diversions until you cross into the mountains to the east of the highway, particularly along the R71 from Pietersburg into the otherworldly Letaba area.

The Great North Road

In between Pretoria and Beitbridge, the N1 highway or **Great North Road** links a series of towns established by the Voortrekker settlers. Most of these are little more than service centres for the surrounding farmland, and as such few have any real attraction beyond what they offer on a practical level – somewhere to sleep, eat or pass through on the way to somewhere else. Although all have significant black populations, the prevailing flavour of the towns is strongly Afrikaner, with little in the landscape to lighten the sometimes uncomfortable tone this sets.

The southernmost of the towns, **Warmbaths** and **Nylstroom** make a valiant attempt to rise above their mundane roots by catering for weekend and holiday tourists from

Gauteng with a glut of unexciting family-oriented resorts; **Potgietersrus** and the larger provincial capital, **Pietersburg**, are dominated by the highway. North of Pietersburg, there is a 100-kilometre stretch to Louis Trichardt and the Soutpansberg Mountains, an area covered separately (on p.574).

For all its grand title, the highway is rather a disappointment, although by South African standards it is fast and easy, if often busy. There is one toll just before Nylstroom, and sections of the road are being upgraded: the next phase of improvements are due to be made to the south of Pietersburg, where the highway will eventually bypass both Potgietersrus and Naboomspruit.

Warmbaths (Warmbad)

The Great North Road passes into the Northern Province approximately 40km north of Pretoria, with flat and undistinguished landscape predominating all the way up to the town of **WARMBATHS**, which lies a few kilometres to the west of the highway. Other than as a pitstop on the N1 or as the gateway to Thabazimbi and the southern Waterberg (see p.572), Warmbaths isn't of all that much interest, and for most people it is too close to Pretoria and too far from their ultimate destination to be much use as a base for exploring.

There is one point of interest in town: the **hot mineral spring**, from which the town takes its name, which has been engulfed by the sprawling *Adventura Warmbaths* watersports and leisure resort. This offers such things as waterslides and a water-skiing lake, and can attract up to 10,000 people during the holiday periods. You can see the source of the spring, which every hour pumps out 20,000 litres of water at 50°C, beside the entrance gate to the resort on Voortrekker Road. In the area surrounding the town, and in particular between it and Nylstroom, 30km to the north, there are any number of smaller holiday resorts – out of season dismal and deserted; at weekends and during school holidays, almost unbearably busy and noisy.

Practicalities

The **layout** of Warmbaths is quite confusing, but the town isn't large, and the key to orienting yourself is to find Voortrekker Road, on which is both the entrance to the *Adventura* resort and, opposite, the **tourist information office** (☎014/736 3694), beside the library. It isn't the most organized office, and there is no good map of the town available, but you should be able to get some help with accommodation if you need it. Remember to be specific about what you want, especially if your idea of a pleasant place to stay doesn't involve waterslides, caravans and copious *braai* facilities.

Accommodation in town is generally quite pricey, and high-season rates (including weekends) will often be more than double low-season rates. The cheapest option is holiday flats: you'll find a number of these along Moffat Street, parallel to Voortrekker, or ask at the tourist information office. The large, mustard-coloured *Elephant Springs Hotel* at 31 Sutter Rd (☎ & fax 014/736 2101; ③–④) is very central, quite hip and has a friendly bar and restaurant, while on the outskirts of town is an extravagantly grand B&B, *Chateau Annique*, off Swanepoel Street, (☎ & fax 014/736 2847; rooms ④–⑤, flats ③). The *Adventura Warmbaths* resort itself, on Voortrekker Road (☎014/736 2200, central reservations ☎012/346 2277; ③–④), has various chalets and hotel accommodation.

As a town by a main highway Warmbaths has a wide selection of **eating places**: your best bet is to head for the *Lion and Elephant* pub in the *Elephant Springs Hotel*, where you can get good, cheap pub grub or a fuller restaurant meal. It has a deck if you want to have a drink outside, and the toilets have been creatively decorated with the pages of the Afrikaans farmers' weekly *Die Landbouweekblad*. There's also the *Spur* and *Panarotti's Pizza and Pasta* – part of the *Adventura* resort but open to non-residents – and a new *O'Hagan's Irish Pub and Grill* at the junction between the R101 and the link road from the N1. There are also various fast-food takeaways around the centre of town.

Nylstroom

The most entertaining thing about **NYLSTROOM**, 27km north of Warmbaths on the R101, is the story behind its name. The legend goes that the first Voortrekkers discovered a reed-lined river, consulted their Bibles (the only reference books they carried) and decided that they had been travelling north for so long that they must surely be at the source of the Nile. The presence of a pyramid-shaped hill, Kranskop, the large mountain you can see clearly from the N1, only confirmed their theory.

The Little Nyl river (as it was dubbed) runs through the centre of the modern town, parallel to the bold main street, **Potgieter**. Along here, establishments like *Ammo Africa* and *Trappers Trading Co*, as well as an endless parade of orange dust-covered *bakkies*, proclaim the town's white farming roots. One of the more profitable local crops is table grapes, grown on large vineyards in the well-irrigated surrounding area.

Sights are few. In town there is a memorial **gateway** at the primary school (*Laerskool*) on Van Riebeeck Street which commemorates the women and children who died in a concentration camp sited there during the Anglo-Boer War. There's also, less predictably, a **mosque**, not far from the bridge over the river – testimony to the presence of an unexpectedly large Indian community.

Practicalities

If you want to avoid the toll (R8) on the N1, which is collected just before the R33 turn-off to Nylstroom, join the R101 at Warmbaths. If you don't want to stop in Nylstroom it's probably not worth coming off the N1 as the road is good and the toll charge isn't too hefty.

In Nylstroom, the **accommodation** options are the *Eurosun* campsite (☎014/717 1328; ①), beside the stadium on the northern side of the river, or a rather sugary but civilized guesthouse, *Pink Gables*, at 3 De Beer St, by the hospital on the Warmbaths road (☎014/717 5076; ②–③). There is a more upmarket country lodge, *Shangri-la* (☎014/717 5381, fax 717 3188; ⑤–⑦), at a turn-off 3km down the Eersbewoond road, a turning from the R33 between Nylstroom and the N1. It's pricey but comfortable; the surroundings are lush and it's filled with an eclectic mix of African memorabilia and interesting antique furniture.

There are **places to eat** in town along Potgieter and Voortrekker, most notably a plain restaurant at 100 Potgieter St called *Sparrow's*, and a slightly more lively place by the main crossroads on Potgieter which goes by the name of *Mampoer Boer Pub and Grill*. There is also a classier dining room at *Shangri-la Country Lodge*, though you must phone first for a booking (☎014/717 5381).

Just outside Nylstroom, the *Thaba Kgatla* guest lodge (☎ & fax 014/717 3959; ⑥–⑦) is a "village" of Tswana huts built among the ruins of an 800-year-old Iron Age site. The huts here have been designed to mix comfort with authenticity, but one unusual touch is that the owners of the lodge are making an attempt to breed the indigenous Western Sanga cattle and Pedi sheep, which the original inhabitants would have kept, not for meat but as a display of wealth.

Naboomspruit and Nylsvlei Nature Reserve

To the west of the N1, midway between Nylstroom and **NABOOMSPRUIT**, another resort-encircled highway town situated at the foot of the Swaershoek Mountains, is **Nylsvlei** – a 310-square kilometres nature reserve enclosing one of the most important wetland areas in South Africa. When the Nyl River is in flood, the *vlei* can spread out to as much as 7km in width, attracting over 150 species of bird, including a number of the country's rarest indigenous water birds. As well as picnic sites and bird- and game-viewing routes there is also a simple camping site.

ARCHEOLOGICAL SITES IN THE NORTHERN PROVINCE

Across the Northern Province, excavations at a number of important **archeological sites** have helped piece together a picture of the different people who have inhabited the land for thousands of years. Some of the most interesting sites are at places where iron was smelted, as the development from what was essentially a Stone Age culture to an Iron Age culture, with its associated improvement in tools for cultivation and war, was a vital part of the migration of black tribes into South Africa around 1500 years ago. Although the iron itself seldom survives the processes of erosion, the presence of slag and other wastes normally provide the strongest clues. Some of the most revealing excavations have taken place at **Thulamela**, inside Kruger National Park not far from the Punda Maria gate, **Bakone Malapa** cultural village outside Pietersburg, and **Masorini**, also in the Kruger park, not far from Phalaborwa.

The single most important site in the Northern Province is at **Mapungubwe**, the "Hill of the Jackals" situated by the confluence of the Limpopo and Shashi rivers where South Africa, Zimbabwe and Botswana meet. The site was only discovered in the 1930s, when a local farmer climbed the dome-shaped granite hill and found remains of stone walls, iron tools, graves, pottery and jewellery, including a tiny rhinoceros and a bowl, both made out of gold. It is now thought that the civilization which was centred at Mapungubwe later moved to the much more famous Great Zimbabwe.

Potgietersrus

A further 50km north of Naboomspruit on the N1 is **POTGIETERSRUS**, named after the Voortrekker hero Piet Potgieter, who died during a famous siege at Makapan's Cave in the hills which close in on the town to the north. The N1 runs right through the centre of town, although the new highway currently being built will bypass the town altogether.

The town recently attracted worldwide publicity when white locals tried to prevent black children entering what had been all-white schools during the apartheid years. The dogged racism the issue highlighted caused uneasiness in South Africa, and earned the town the unenviable title of racist capital of South Africa. Certainly there's little doubt that the old thinking still dies hard in the town and its agricultural hinterland – something you'll still pick up from such things as "Club Members Only" signs over bars and the attitude of locals you'll encounter in shops or restaurants. On the other hand, blacks crowd the main streets with stalls and, despite the continual crawl of traffic, give the place a bustling, lively feel.

MAKAPAN'S CAVE (MAKAPANSGAT)

In 1854, bent on revenge after a party of Voortrekkers had been ambushed, a Boer commando cornered the clan of Ndebele chief Makapan in the hills to the north of Potgietersrus. Led by Piet Potgieter, the nephew of Voortrekker leader Hermanus Potgieter who had been skinned alive not long before by kinsmen of Makapan, the Boers besieged the chief and an estimated three thousand of his followers inside the network of caves which ran through the hills. With little food and almost no water, the imprisoned Ndebele became increasingly desperate, and eventually seven hundred besieged men rushed out towards a nearby stream, only to be mown down by the patient Boers. When the siege was finally broken after four weeks, hundreds of rotting bodies were found inside. The Boers lost only two men, one of them Potgieter, whose body was "heroically" retrieved by a young Paul Kruger. A rather one-sided account of the siege is available at the museum in Potgietersrus.

One place worth stopping at is the **Arend Dieperink Museum** (Mon–Fri 8am–4.30pm), located in an old schoolhouse set back from Voortrekker Road (the N1), behind the tourist information office. It has a substantial collection of ploughs, tractors, wagons and farm implements outside; inside is more interesting, with well-labelled displays on the significant archeological discoveries made at Makapan's cave, 19km north of Potgietersrus, including that of three-million-year-old fossils of *Australopithecus africanus*, a predecessor of *Homo sapiens*. Access to the cave itself is only by arrangement with the museum.

Practicalities

The **train station** is four blocks to the east of Voortrekker Road; and the twice-weekly Translux **bus** stops at the *Wimpy* beside the Engen petrol station on Voortrekker. The well-organized **tourist information office** (☎0154/2244) is on Voortrekker Road as you come into the main part of town from the south, between Kruger and Van Riebeeck streets.

Most of the **accommodation** in Potgietersrus is in the form of travellers' overnight rooms, and as a result rates drop at weekends. There is a municipal caravan park (①) just off the N1 on the northern side of town, behind a parked steam locomotive. Given the lack of grass and unappealing views, however, you might prefer to head for *Tibani Lodge* (☎0154/491 5609; ①–③), 11km along the road to Percy Fyfe Nature Reserve, a formulaic holiday resort but somewhere to pitch a tent or sleep in a rondavel among the hills away from the highway. Another interesting spot just past here, *Thabaphaswa Hiking and Mountain Bike Trails* (☎0154/491 4882; ①) is a worthwhile place to explore if you have a couple of days to spare. The accommodation is unusual and rudimentary, but the trails are set in some impressive mountain scenery. Back in town the cheapest place to stay is the block of apartment rooms at *Lonely Oak Lodge*, on Van Riebeeck and Hodge (☎0154/491 4560; ②). On the northern edge of town there are a couple of travellers' hotels: *Oasis* (☎0154/4124; ③) and the ageing but respectable *Protea Park* (☎0154/3101, fax 6842; ④), which has a pool and a decent restaurant. On the southern side of the Nyl River 10km south of Potgietersrus on the N1 is a homely B&B, *Jaagbaan* (☎0154/7833; ②–③), while 32km north of Potgietersrus on the N1 is the *Ranch Hotel* (☎0152/293 7180; ④–⑥), a well-run, pleasant but pricey modern holiday hotel, though situated rather too close to the highway.

Since all the N1 traffic still plies its way through town, there are various obvious franchise **restaurants** and takeaways along or close to Voortrekker Road. The best is *Mike's Kitchen*, in the Spar Plaza off Retief Street, while *Brambles* in the *Protea Park* hotel is smart but not too expensive.

Pietersburg

Lying almost dead central in the province of which it is the capital, **PIETERSBURG** is also the largest city on the Great North Road between Pretoria and the border. It's mostly an administrative and industrial centre, and much of its energy derives from the large volume of traffic moving through the city on the N1. But it does have a couple of quirky attractions, including an excellent museum, and if you're heading towards the Letaba area, the lowveld and central Kruger National Park, Pietersburg is also the point to connect with the R71 to Tzaneen and Phalaborwa.

Arrival and information

The town has recently developed its air-force base into a public **airport**, called Gateway, located on the N1 5km north of the city. This is serviced by both domestic flights (*SA Airlink* ☎0152/293 2671) and occasional international connections from neighbouring countries. All the city's **car rental firms** are located here: *Avis* (☎0152/293 2699),

Budget (☎0152/293 2690) and *Imperial* (☎0152/293 1479). **Taxis** are also available on ☎0152/297 4493.

Daily **trains** running to and from Messina and Zimbabwe stop at the train station on the northern edge of the city centre, just off the R521 (an extension of Market Street). All the intercity **buses** pass through the centre of town: *Translux* stop at the *Big Bite* on Grobler Street, *Greyhound* at the Shell Ultra City and the *Zimmie Bus* at *SA Tours and Bookings* at 89a Schoeman St.

Pietersburg may not be well-endowed with attractions, but it doesn't want for tourist information services. The main **tourist information office** (☎0152/295 2011) is on the ground floor of the municipal buildings on the northern side of Civic Square – the best way to get to it is off Landros Mare Street; there are also more limited desks in the old information kiosk on the corner of Landros Mare and Vorster streets and at the nearby Irish House Museum on Market and Vorster, as well as a helpful budget travellers' tourist agent, *SA Tours and Bookings*, at 89a Schoeman St (☎0152/297 0816; email: satours@cis.co.za).

Accommodation
The municipal caravan park is situated at Union Park immediately beside the entrance to the city's large nature reserve; get to it by following Dorp Street south out of the city. While the proximity of the nature reserve doesn't really rub off, you can camp here and it has some inexpensive rondavels (①). Otherwise the options are as follows:

Aorangi, 7a Dorp St (☎0152/291 3919). Small and homely B&B in the centre of town. ③.

Arnotha's Lodge, 42 Hans van Rensburg St (☎0152/291 3393). Centrally located and long-established self-catering accommodation. ②.

Holiday Inn, on the corner of Vorster and Bok streets, (☎0152/291 2030, fax 291 3150). A couple of blocks from Civic Square, with an outdoor pool and a *Panarotti's* pasta and pizza restaurant attached. ④.

Ngwako, 7km along the R71 towards Tzaneen (☎ & fax 0152/293 6094). A more luxurious and comfortable guesthouse outside town noted especially for its excellent and innovative food. ④.

Kiesmet Guest House (☎0152/293 8207). A row of plain but decent units situated directly off the N1 near the SAB plant north of town. ③.

Plumtree Lodge, 138 Marshall St (☎0152/295 6153). Not far from the centre, a neat and comfortable lodge with a pool, a big garden and good rates over the weekend. ③–⑤.

The Town and around

Pietersburg has a busy, compact CBD set out on a grid pattern, with layers of industry and suburbia tightly packed around it. It may not be the most inspiring spot, but much of the Northern Province's drive and enterprise emanates from its capital. At its heart, the **Civic Centre**, a park area bounded on two sides by Landros Mare and Vorster streets, has an incongruous but entertaining array of sculptures, statues and monuments, and a white church housing the small but absorbing **Hugh Exton Photographic Museum** (Mon–Sat 9am–3.30pm, Sun 3–5pm; free), which displays the early years of Pietersburg through the work of a local commercial photographer, who quite evidently had a knack for taking excellent portraits. Opposite the park on the other side of Vorster is the old shop frontage of the **Irish House Museum** (Mon–Fri 8am–4pm, Sat 9am–noon, Sun 3–5pm; free), the town's neat and thoughtfully laid-out history and natural history museum.

For those inspired by the sculptures of the Civic Centre there is a small **art museum** above the library on Schoeman and Jorissen streets, together with an annexe of outdoor, industrial-type modern sculptures in a park on the left as you leave town on the N1 heading north.

However, the one sight in Pietersburg really worth putting aside time to see is the **Bakone Malapa Museum** (daily 8.30am–12.30pm & 1.30–3.30pm; except Mon pm; entry fee), 9km southeast of town on the R37. This is an open-air museum displaying the traditional way of life of the local Bakone people, a grouping within the Northern Sotho. A village of huts has been built in the traditional style, and fourteen people live permanently on site, working on crafts such as pottery and leatherworking through the day. One of them also acts as a guide, and will explain the different activities going on, as well as the architecture, history and legends of the site. It is a simple but genuine project, and one which succeeds in conveying some of the old way of life where many flashier examples have fallen short.

Eating and drinking

True to its functional role, Pietersburg has no shortage of standard chain **restaurants and takeaways**. For takeaways through the day try *Catz*, a German delicatessen in the Rentmeester arcade off Hans van Rensburg Street, and for a coffee and light lunches *Sarmi's* in the Nedbank arcade on Landros Mare Street. For dinner, there are an inordinate number of pizza restaurants in town, though the best such place is an Italian restaurant,*Villa Italia*, a small local chain at 55 Hans van Rensburg St. You'll also get good, inexpensive food at *Mike's Kitchen*, pleasantly situated on the southern side of the Civic Centre park area, off Church Street. Above this is a popular bar with regular live music, the *Ale and Thistle*. For a more upmarket and quite groovy restaurant, try *Café Pescatore*, on Hans van Rensburg St opposite Library Gardens (☎0152/291 1282), although the most refined, interesting (and expensive) option is at the out-of-town *Ngwako Guest House* (☎ & fax 0152/293 6094); bear in mind you'll have to book.

Letaba

The **Letaba** is a forested, lush, mountainous area east of Pietersburg which contrasts very sharply with the hot lowveld immediately east and the wide, flat bushveld to its west. It marks the first dramatic rise of the Drakensberg escarpment as it begins its sweep south through Mpumalanga, and in many ways is a less well-known alternative to the lush but crowded highlands of that province. The forestation begins around the mountain village of **Haenertsburg** and follows two very scenic parallel valleys to the largest centre in the area, **Tzaneen**. The colourful valleys are filled with still lakes surrounded by dark pine forests, sparkling rivers, misty peaks and, towards Tzaneen, intense subtropical crops such as tea, macadamia nuts and avocados. There are some very comfortable and beautifully located guesthouses, farmstalls and tea rooms, hiking trails and trout fishing, making the Letaba a highly soothing alternative to some of South Africa's more challenging environments.

Haenertsburg and around

The mellow village of **HAENERTSBURG** lies 60km from Pietersburg, high on a hillside looking down on the R71 as it winds down into the beginning of the thickly wooded Magoebaskloof valleys. Haenertsburg is an old gold-rush village, with wonderful views over the area they call the "Land of the Silver Mist", and one **main street**, along

EASTER GATHERINGS

On the 60km between Pietersburg and Haenertsburg there are two two huge, incongruous institutions, the **University of North** at **Turfloop**, and **Zion City Moria** at **Boyne**, identified by a huge Star of David on the hill above it. Each Easter, an incredible three million people gather here for the annual gathering of the Zion Christian Church, an independent, Africanized Christian Church. The symbols of followers of the church, a silver star or badge pinned onto the chest, and sometimes a grey peaked cap, are worn right across the northern areas of South Africa, and a certain amount of mystery and suspicion surrounds the movement. However, there isn't really anything to see other than during the Easter gathering, which is the one time you want to stay well clear, as three million people can cause some mighty traffic jams.

which you'll find a small pub, a friendly tea room, *The Elms*, which also has a gift shop and is the place to buy trout and ask about trout fishing, and a funky craft and coffee shop, *Greenwoods Trading Post* (☎0152/276 4472) – which sells some authentic and original African artefacts and jewellery, serves tasty lunches and acts as an enthusiastic local information bureau. They'll tell you about good picnic spots and short walks in the area, including a tough one up to the **Iron Crown**, the peak above the village.

Georges Valley Road and the Magoebaskloof Valleys

Just after Haenertsburg there is a turning to the right off the R71 which offers an alternative route to Tzaneen along the Georges Valley Road. There is, in fact, little to choose between the two options, and if you are spending any time in the area it's worth trying both.

The things to look out for along the Georges Valley Road are a **memorial to John Buchan**, the author who was captivated by the area when he came here not long after the Anglo-Boer War – "A place enchanted and consecrated," he described it – and the peaceful, almost Arthurian **Ebeneezer Dam**, a good spot for swimming and picnicking.

Staying on the R71 you come to the **Magoebaskloof Valleys**, named after the rogue chief Makgoba, who eventually had his head chopped off by an Impi serving under Abel Erasmus in 1895. About 4km beyond Haenertsburg there is a turning to the **Cheerio Gardens**, where a Cherry Blossom Festival is held each year at the end of September. If you miss the festival it still isn't hard to imagine the lush subtropical landscape bursting into extravagant colour; the **Letaba Tourism Assocation** (☎0152/276 4307) can give you details of various private show gardens in the area. Along this same turning, there is another wonderful little piece of backwoods life, at the tiny **Wegraakbos Dairy** (☎0152/276 1811), where cheese is made in traditional style over an open fire in a huge copper cauldron. A visit is thoroughly recommended: tours are at 9am, but you can visit the dairy throughout the day, and taste the cheese and walk around the farm and nearby woods.

As the R71 crosses over the Magoebaskloof pass it twists and turns impressively, with dark forests and long views alternating on either side. A sideroad leads into the **Woodbush State Forest**, where there is a network of roads (not all of them passable), two multi-day hiking trails and the famous **Debengeni Falls**, an attractive series of waterfalls, slithers and natural pools. There are some *braai* sites by the river (a small admission fee is charged), and you can swim in various places if you're careful, but the smooth, slippery rock is very dangerous and a sign indicates that a few folk who have tried the DIY waterslide haven't lived to recommend it.

Between the turn-off to Debengeni and Tzaneen the valley becomes broader, with huge stands of citrus, avocado and banana trees, as well as the rich green texture of tea bushes, covering the rolling hillsides. On the **Sapekoe Middlekop** tea estate not far from the junction of the R71 and R36, a winding road leads up to the **Pekoe View tea garden** (daily 10am–5pm) – the location of some of the best views in the whole valley. A shop sells packets of local tea and coffee, and there are also factory tours (daily except Sun & Mon 11am). Another interesting local product worth looking out for both here and in other local shops are *Avodeau* skin-care products, made in Tzaneen from avocado oil.

Accommodation

One of the main themes in the area around Haenertsburg and Magoebaskloof – and indeed around Tzaneen as well – is escape, and to that end there are a lot of attractive **places to stay**. Both *Greenwoods Trading Post* (☎0152/276 4472) in Haenertsburg or the Letaba Tourism Association will be able to help you find somewhere suitable.

At Den Eden farm off the R71 is a genuine *Log Cabin* (☎0152/276 4242; ②–③), set under some tall pine trees; off the same road, just before Haenertsburg, are *The Chalets* (☎0152/276 4264; ③), various Swiss-style self-catering chalets in a scenic setting. *BaliWillWill Farm* (☎0152/276 2212; ③), 1500m into the hills from Haenertsburg past the police station, offers B&B rooms in the farmhouse or in a simple self-catering flat.

Moving up a notch, the *Magoebaskloof Hotel*, on the R71 (☎0152/276 4276; ④–⑤), has probably the most spectacular view in the area from its front deck, but the rest, including a pub with an old red postbox outside, is fairly uninspired. Top of the range, and one of the finer country lodges in South Africa, is *Glenshiel*, 2km from Haenertsburg on the R71 (☎ & fax 0152/276 4335; ⑦), full of roaring fires, deep sofas, antiques and fine food.

Tzaneen and around

The dams and soaring gum forests surrounding **TZANEEN** are graceful and attractive. However, the town itself is fairly scruffy, well-endowed with shops and a useful transport hub, but worth avoiding as a place to stay. The one thing to see here is the **Tzaneen Museum** (Mon–Fri 9am–5pm, Sat 9am–1pm), situated in a tiny, four-roomed building in the grounds of the library at the top of Agatha Street. You'll need time: the dedicated curator and his assistants don't label any items, preferring to walk around with you and talk about the small but valuable collection, which includes sacred drums and other items associated with the Rain Queen. It's almost impossible to have a quick, casual visit, but it's essential to spare the time if you want to scratch a bit more deeply into the history and traditions of the region.

Practicalities

The **tourist information office** in town consists of an assortment of leaflets available in the library on Agatha Street; for more informed general information about the area contact Letaba Tourism in Haenertsburg (see above). A couple of locals run **minibus tours** to local attractions, including Modjadji, the Magoebaskloof Valleys and Kruger National Park. Contact *Letaba Active Tours* (☎ & fax 0152/307 3538) or Yvonne Clarke (☎0152/307 2000). The local bike shop, *G Sports* beside the cinema in the Oasis Mall off Voortrekker Street, should be able to tell you about good local **mountain-bike routes** (☎0152/307 2471).

There is a **daily minibus** which links Tzaneen with Pietersburg and Johannesburg operated by *North Link Tours* (☎0152/307 2950).

The **accommodation options** in town aren't inspiring, especially in comparison to what is available in the surrounding countryside, and it's a better idea to take the road leading out of town unto the Wolkberg Mountains to Agatha, which has some high-class country lodges and spectacular views out over the valleys and peaks of the escarpment (see overleaf for details).

If you're not inclined to do this, or don't have the time (or money), there's a caravan park on Old Gravelotte Road, *Fairview* (☎0152/307 2679; ①–②), which has some inexpensive chalets; *Arbor Park* on Soetdoring and Geelhout (☎0152/307 1831; ③) has plain overnight rooms in a small suburban business centre; and the *Karos Tzaneen Hotel*, in the centre of town at 1 Danie Joubert St (☎0152/307 3140; ④), is a large, shiny hotel gradually losing its lustre.

As for **food**, Tzaneen has a smattering of familiar takeaways and a few chain restaurants. There's the *Emerald Creek Spur* at 16 Morgan St, a *KFC* down Lannie St, where you'll also find *Nando's Chickenland* and – probably the best in town – the *Villa Italia*. Near the museum at 30 Agatha St there is a pleasant coffee shop, *Gazebo Gardens*, set in an old Victorian garden.

Agatha

AGATHA, the wife of an early mining commissioner, gave her name to a high plateau overlooking Tzaneen, now covered in forest but a cool and attractive place, especially if you can rise to a night at one of the top-class guesthouses set along the edge of the ridge. The best value of these is *Kings Warden Estate*, 12km from Tzaneen up Agatha Road (☎0152/307 3262; ②–④), a family-owned avocado farm with superbly lush gardens and four simple rooms, as well as a rustic self-catering stone cottage elsewhere on the farm. Turning left at the top of the hill, Old Coach Road leads to *The Coach House* (☎0152/307 3641, fax 307 1466; ⑤–⑦), a very classy, well-run establishment which is consistently quoted as one of the best small hotels in South Africa. The views from the breakfast balcony and pool area are breathtaking. In the opposite direction from the top of Agatha Road, *Sherwood's Country House* (☎0152/307 5512, fax 307 4216; ④) is a more intimate but slightly less-well-bred rival.

Finally, further down towards Tzaneen, the bizarre *Wayside Lodge Farm* (☎0152/307 4315; ②–③), is announced by huge giraffe and elephant statues outside. With a Buddhist garden, castles with beer-bottle-studded turrets and animal cages interspersed with some apartment-style accommodation, this is the eccentric alternative, though it's not quite as weird as it would like to be.

Modjadji Nature Reserve

The area around the rather downbeat village of **MODJADJI**, north of Tzaneen off the R36, is the home of the famous **Rain Queen**, the hereditary female monarch of a section of the Venda people whom legend maintains has the power to make rain, a useful talent in these often parched northern areas. Suitably, her home village is up in the mists on a mountain where a special form of ancient cycad, or tree fern, flourishes. The **Modjadji Nature Reserve** protects these plants in an area set on the very top of the hill, and incorporates some fine views (often obscured by the wispy mist) and various short but pleasant walking trails. There are a few facilities, such as a souvenir shop and information centre, which explains a bit more about the unique plants found here and, of course, the famous monarch.

Around 20km away from the turning to Modjadji lies the **Sunland Nursery**, which has a massive baobab tree with a pub inside where the owner will serve you a draught beer and relate a few of the strange stories that attach to his odd location. He'll put his case for this being the largest baobab in the world, a claim also made for a few others around the Northern Province. Still, it's fun to visit, especially if you've got time for a few convivial drinks, though you have to pay to get in (R10). A few kilometres further down the same road is **Hopefontein** (☎015/305 3607), a 50-square kilometre nature reserve where you can stay in one of two tree houses. You must phone beforehand to make arrangements.

Letsitele and around

LETSITELE is a small town 30km east of Tzaneen whose main function is as a waypoint to a few points of interest in the area of lowveld abutting the escarpment. To the south are the large nature and wilderness areas of **Legalameetse** and **Wolkberg**, places to explore if you have a few days and a penchant for empty, green landscapes. Near Letsitele itself is one of the most interesting handicraft projects in the province, **Karosswerkers**, who produce intricate and striking embroidered ethnic place mats, cushion covers and wall hangings. You can arrange to see the workshops, which employ over 150 local people, by phoning ☎015/345 1765, and you'll find their work on sale at the excellent Monsoon Gallery on the R527 west of Hoedspruit (see p.527).

North from Letsitele a road leads to the **Hans Merensky Nature Reserve**, the location of an *Aventura* resort, *Die Eiland* (☎0152/38759; ②–④), on the Letaba River, as well as the **Tsonga Kraal Open-Air Museum**, one of the first of its kind but now overtaken by other similar projects in the province. Between the reserve and Letsitele there's an ambitious new luxury game lodge, *Ndzalama* (☎0152/307 3065; prices from R190 pp self-catering to R600 pp all-inclusive), set on an 8000-hectare protected reserve, with rhino, elephant and various rare antelope. One outstanding feature of the reserve is the architecture of the lodge, bush camp and reconstructed Shangaan village, which have been beautifully designed to blend with the surrounding natural environment.

WATERBERG

And even now, . . . with the great gold-city belching its smoke almost within sight – even now, with invading civilization marching across the hills in seven-league boots, Waterberg still holds its charm.   Eugène Marais

Rising out of the plains to the west and north of the Great North Road, the **Waterberg** is one of the least-known and most intriguing of South Africa's significant mountain massifs. Once a place of lakes and swamps – hence its name – the elevated plateau can often seem a place as dry and sparse of water as its surrounding northern bushveld; yet it harbours a diversity of vegetation and topography which supports cattle-ranching, little-trumpeted hunting concessions and, increasingly, some of the country's foremost conservation projects.

These have developed over recent years to the extent that some ten percent of the Waterberg is now under formal conservation management. Indeed, the Waterberg is

---

EUGÈNE MARAIS (1872–1936)

A journalist who left South Africa to study law and medicine (simultaneously), in London during the 1890s, **Eugène Marais** was one of the most gifted yet troubled South Africans of his time. In the early 1900s he emerged as one of the first writers to make a literary mark in the "new" Afrikaans language, writing poetry and short stories. However, he also suffered from depression and ill health, and he retreated from his career as a lawyer to the remote Waterberg Mountains. His intense involvement with the natural world around him there led to the publication of two pioneering studies of animal behaviour: *The Soul of the Ape*, which was the result of some three-and-a-half years living in close proximity to a troop of baboons, and *The Soul of the White Ant*, a study of termites which argues that a termite nest is a single functioning composite similar to the human body. Still racked by ill health and increasingly addicted to morphine, he committed suicide in 1936.

---

being mooted as an undiscovered alternative to the lowveld areas around Kruger National Park. However, while it has impressive credentials as a vast area of true wilderness, and is certainly less commercialized, the game is less rich than around Kruger and the infrastructure still undeveloped. Rhino have been reintroduced, and elephant are found in a couple of reserves, but otherwise the highlights are large antelope, giraffe, hippo and the presence of leopard. It remains, also, an isolated region, detached from other main areas of interest and with scant transport links.

The largest single area is the new, but still mostly inaccessible, **Marakele National Park**, situated in the more mountainous southern section of the massif, but complemented by a patchwork of very dedicated private reserves around the central town of **Vaalwater**.

Northern Waterberg

The **northern section of the Waterberg**, centred on the small town of **Vaalwater**, is the beating heart of the region's conservation-centred approach to land use and tourism. The area can boast an embarrassing richness of conservation-centred reserves and game farms offering absorbing bush experiences on most levels, from luxury lodges to inexpensive self-catering cottages and wilderness campsites.

The scenery in this part of the Waterberg is subtle rather than dramatic, but you do pick up the rich intensity of the bush and the thrill of being close to it. The area also offers some exciting adventure activities, including bush hiking trails and some of the finest wilderness horse-riding in South Africa. The local **tourist information office**, run from a farm in the area, is very enthusiastic, organized and genuinely helpful. Contact Clare Beith on ☎014/7552 ext 4021.

Vaalwater

The town of **VAALWATER** is a small farming centre, and for the visitor offers little more than an orientation point on the R33, which connects Nylstroom, just off the N1, with Ellisras, and marks the junction with the tarred road to Melkrivier and Marken – along which the main conservation areas of the northeastern Waterberg are located.

If you need **accommodation** in town, the best B&B here is *Zeederberg Cottage* (☎014/755 3862; ②), situated by a service station on the northern side of town at the junction with the new road to Ellisras. Otherwise, there's *Bosveld Chalets and Caravan Park* (☎014/755 3696; ①–②), at 165 Davidson St, a small campsite off a suburban side street with some adequate if unexciting chalets. Also with rooms, and a small restaurant and lively locals' bar, is the *Vaalwater Hotel* (☎014/755 3686; ②), located on the right-hand side as you come into town from Nylstroom. It has recently upgraded itself to the "*International Hunter's Hotel*", which says quite a lot about what you can expect. If you are looking for **somewhere to eat**, there's a calmer atmosphere and reasonable range of meals at the *Waterhole Steakhouse* (☎014/755 3775), located in a new complex set amongst the gathering of shops by the Melkrivier turn-off.

If you're interested in finding out about **touring the Waterberg**, *Brown's Safari Services* (☎ & fax 014/755 3862), located in town by *Zeederberg Cottage*, can help with specialized or tailor-made tours and provide other advice about the area.

Around Vaalwater: game reserves and farms

Most of the lodges in the Waterberg are relatively remote and quite small, so it is advisable to prebook somewhere to stay, at least for your first couple of nights if you want to be sure of a room. Many of the reserves include various activities, usually game drives or walks, in their daily programme, so it's worthwhile arriving at a time when you can take full advantage of these. Game walks are an integral part of the Waterberg experience, and as such definitely worth experiencing. All the luxury lodges will offer these in the company of a guide, while the less expensive accommodation can normally recommend good hiking trails on their property or nearby.

Once in the area, you're likely to hear about – and be encouraged to seek out – some of the interesting and worthwhile projects going on in the area. For this reason, you may not want to book everything beforehand, although you should at least keep in mind the fact that any lodge where catering is included will need at least a day's notice.

Generally you will find that "luxury" here is not as high as in more developed parts of the country. On the other hand, most of the lodges recommended have a down-to-earth charm and friendliness which more than make up for any lack of pampering.

Full-board game lodges and reserves

The Waterberg owes much of its credibility and profile to the conservation ideals of *Lapalala Wilderness Area* (☎011/453 7645, fax 453 7649), a 350-square-kilometre reserve masterminded by Clive Walker, a highly regarded South African conservationist and artist, which provides sanctuary for a wide variety of endangered and rare animals (see box, p.572). The options here are to stay in the intimate and relaxed Rhino Camp (⑥), a tented bush camp situated right by the Lapalala River, or in one of the luxury rondavels at the main *Lapalala Lodge* (⑦). Full board and game drives are part of the package at both of these; also available are some basic but remote self-catering bush camps (②), some of which have a wonderfully atmospheric setting. Bush walks are always available, as are some topnotch horse trails, run by *Equus Horse Safaris* (☎011/788 3923).

There's a smaller, less-mainstream luxury lodge in the *Mokolo River Nature Reserve* (☎014755/2 ext Bulgerivier 1511, fax 083/264 9872; ⑦), set above a gorge in the Mokolo River and run with a determined conviction about the primacy of animals and the bush. Both elephants and rhino are found here, along with some very engaging, unpretentious hospitality.

Other lodges in this range worth considering include: *Tsotswane Lodge* (☎014755/3737; ⑦), a comfortable converted farmhouse in an isolated and atmospheric location; *Kgama Ranch* (☎0147552 ext 3013), a large farm with knowledgeable hosts and accommodation in reed houses; *Waterberg Game Reserve* (☎014755/2 ext 5912; ③–⑥), which has some rustic tree houses among its accommodation; and *Kudu Canyon* (☎011/608 2149; ③–④), with lively game drives and boat trips on an adjoining dam.

LAPALALA WILDERNESS AREA

The **Lapalala Wilderness Area** was established in 1981 by Clive Walker and businessman Dale Parker, and has since grown sevenfold in size and developed into one of the foremost conservation projects in South Africa. It makes few bones about putting tourism well down its list of priorities: it was the first private game reserve in the country to obtain the highly endangered black rhino, when five were acquired from Natal Parks Board for R2.2 million. It also promotes education through the Lapalala Wilderness School, established in 1985 and each year introducing some 3000 children from all over Africa to the principles and practice of conservation during week-long courses in the heart of the wilderness area. Lapalala is also the mainstay of the growing Waterberg Conservancy, a close-knit association of conservation-centred landowners which now embraces some 1200 square kilometres of the northeastern Waterberg.

Self-catering facilities

It's easy to overlook lower-priced accommodation when it comes to seeking out game in South Africa, often because you can't guarantee the quality game-viewing you get in the larger reserves. You can, however, experience the location more vividly by doing things cheaper, and this is especially so in a place like the Waterberg where the sense of the bush is as much part of the experience as the game itself. In Waterberg, there are a number of inexpensive **self-catering chalets or cottages** which often make arrangements with larger farms or reserves nearby for game walks or drives. Among these are *Shepherd's Tree Lodge* (☎014755/3652; ②), with accommodation in an old farmhouse and camping available; *Cattlelands* (☎0147552 ext 4021; ②), which offers accommodation in a large old farmhouse or small thatched cottage, with camping also available; *Mount Leisure* (☎014721/927; ③), situated between Nylstroom and Vaalwater, whose chalets have an impressive mountainside location; and *Podica* (☎0147552 ext 2905; ③) – a series of rondavels set on the banks of the Palala River.

Activity-based game farms

Some **game farms** promote activities along with straight game-watching. *Berglust* (☎014/763 2888 or 082/567 5142), for example, offer mountain-bike safaris, although they tend to do only group bookings; horse-riding safaris – not yet a common feature of big game areas in South Africa, mostly because of the problems inherent with taking horses into Big Five territory – are offered by the very professional *Equus Horse Safaris*, based in the *Lapalala Wilderness Area* (see p.571). *Horizon Horse Trails* (☎014755/3737 or 0147552 ext 2423), based at *Triple B Ranch*, offer similar safaris, of one to three days in length, on a slightly more down-to-earth, less luxurious basis, and including extra activities like joining a day's cattle-mustering on horseback – the ranch is a huge cattle stud farm. Also available are chuck wagon trails, hiking trails and comfortable, full-board accommodation in *Triple B's* historic old farmhouse (⑦).

Incidentally, if you're visiting the *Triple B* ranch, don't forget to visit the tiny stone **church** at Twenty-Four Rivers designed by the famous architect Sir Herbert Baker. He was commissioned by two maiden aunts who expected that he would do it for free, since it was a place of worship. Their assumption was, unsurprisingly, not shared by Baker.

Southern Waterberg

The **southern parts of the Waterberg** can boast more dramatic scenery than the land to the north, although it has many fewer game lodges and is dominated by the burgeoning **Marakele National Park**, which, though one of the bright new stars among South African game reserves, is still raw and undeveloped for visitors.

The main road into the area from Vaalwater is the R510, although there is also good access from the east via Warmbaths and from the south along the R511 and R510, both of which connect with the N4 highway west of Pretoria.

Thabazimbi and around

Southern Waterberg is centred around the town of **THABAZIMBI**, a place which lists mining and hunting as its core activities. Its name means "mountain of iron" and, while the town has a striking setting among some high peaks, it doesn't take too long to work out that large parts of the mountains have been dug up by the mines, well-sifted and then put back in place. Some locals have been heard to complain that they can feel the south wind blowing through town these days, something it never did before they rearranged the mountains.

There's not much point in hanging around, but if you need **accommodation** in town the *Hotel Kransberg* (☎014773/71586; ②–③) on Deena Street (off Eland Street) has rooms, while *Bonanza* (☎014773/71831; ①–②), signposted off the road towards Marakele National Park on the edge of town, is an unsophisticated resort with campsites and chalets. **Places to eat** include the windowless *Rhino Restaurant* at the hotel, which offers meat galore, and the *Pizza Cabin* in the Carpe Diem Centre, off 13th (Dertiende) Street.

Around Thabazimbi

Just under 7km south of Thabazimbi is the **Ben Alberts Nature Reserve**, which has a shady camping area, though the reserve isn't much to get excited by: as an adjunct to the mine, it is meant to act as a fig leaf to the towering man-made slag heap immediately behind. A further 15km south of town on the Rustenburg Road (R510) is the **Rhino Bushveld Eco-Park** (☎014773/71483; ③–⑥), a private reserve set in typical

---

HUNTING: A ROUGH GUIDE

To some it is barbaric blood lust, and to others it lies at the heart of conservation. The emotive issue of **hunting** is one you will encounter and hear vigorously debated in the Waterberg, as you will in many rural areas of South Africa where it is regarded as an essential part of life in the bush. It is also a multi-million-rand industry and, although you don't necessarily read about them in the guidebooks, there are many more hunting reserves in South Africa than there are eco-friendly game reserves.

In hunting reserves, the land is stocked with game specifically for the purpose of hunting, whereas in conservation-oriented game reserves the guiding principle is that tourists will pay simply to see the animals in their natural environment. However, wherever man has established artificial fences around a piece of land (which is just about everywhere), the idea of a completely natural environment is inevitably compromised, and intervention is necessary to maintain a realistic balance and diversity of nature within that area. Such intervention – "management" is a common euphemism – takes place even in the most conservation-oriented reserves. What is more at issue is the extent to which this process is commercialized. Some game reserves, knowing that they need to cull a certain number of animals, will allow paying clients to hunt for that quota, providing a valuable source of income for the reserve and its conservation ideals. However, inevitably this leads to grey areas. How many animals need to be culled, for instance, when there is money at stake? Whatever your beliefs, it is undoubtedly true that animals, many of them endangered species, are dying in large numbers in reserves all over South Africa, many of them needlessly, and many of them for profit.

bushveld which is attempting to push eco-tourism hand in hand with "wildlife management" (ie hunting). The butchery by the entrance isn't a particularly encouraging sign;
within the reserve, however, there are some reasonable bush camps (self-catering or
full board) and bush hiking trails with simple mountain huts.

Marakele National Park

In the mountains to the northeast of Thabazimbi, **Marakele National Park** is one of
South Africa's newest national parks, already an impressive 600 square kilometres, but
still growing as more land around it is bought up. At its core are the Kransberg, a striking assortment of odd-shaped peaks, plateaus and cliffs. The diversity of land and altitude means that a variety of interesting plants, including ferns, orchids, and even some
proteas and cycads, are found here, while the species of animals here have already
achieved an impressive breadth, with rhino, tsessebe, roan and sable antelope, red hartebeest and 800 breeding pairs of the endangered Cape vulture. A recent addition were
45 elephant, translocated from Kruger National Park, and there is an expectation that
lions will be introduced once the park gets a little larger.

The potential for the park is great, and it is destined to become a valuable and magnetic part of the efforts being made in conservation in the Waterberg as a whole. At present, however, access is limited: the only way of visiting the park is to book into a tented camp situated on the banks of the Matlabas River, which you will need a 4WD vehicle to get to. Bookings for this can be made through the National Parks Board on
☎012/343 1991 or ☎021/22 2810.

THE FAR NORTH

The **northernmost part of the Northern Province** is a hot, green, undeveloped
rural region with as much in common with Zimbabwe as it has with South Africa. The
essential geographical features of the area are the **Limpopo River**, the border between
South Africa and Zimbabwe (and, further west, Botswana), and the alluring
Soutpansberg Mountain range, aligned east–west just to the north of the area's main
town, **Louis Trichardt**. Both landmarks lie in the path of the N1 highway, still the main
route through the area, which crosses into Zimbabwe at **Beitbridge**.

As a first impression of South Africa for visitors arriving from Zimbabwe, the far
north cannot compete with the lure of attractions further south. Yet it is an area where
the lack of sophistication and isolated history of the people and culture make absorbing contrasts to other parts of the country. Perhaps the most significant manifestation
of the distinctness of the area is the **Venda** region, formerly an "independent" homeland under the apartheid regime. While economically impoverished, it (and its people)
remains rich in tradition, art and legend. East of the Venda lands is the northern tip of
Kruger National Park, a less-visited but intriguing part of the park (covered on
p.548); there are two entry gates to the park here, at **Punda Maria** and **Pafuri**.

The Soutpansberg area

The **Soutpansberg Mountains** have an unusual claim to distinction, named as they
are after a set of saltpans – one of the flatter natural features known to man. The name
came about after Voortrekker pioneers, under the leadership of Louis Trichardt, established their first settlement by the pans on the northern side of the mountain range.
While the settlement soon relocated to Schoemansdal, on the southern side, the
moniker stuck.

An impressive range of hills, particularly from the south, the Soutpansberg attract sufficient rainfall to create a subtropical climate, and lush farms along the southern slopes produce a range of exotic crops such as avocados, mangoes, bananas and macadamia nuts. In other parts the rocky *kloofs* and green hillsides offer some remote and unspoilt mountain retreats, shaded by up to 250 different species of tree and the home of monkey, small antelope, foraging warthog and some noble raptors.

The N1 highway bisects the range, passing through the main town of the north, **Louis Trichardt**, situated in the southern shadow of the mountains, then climbing over a low pass and descending through a pair of tunnels on the northern side. Once over the escarpment the highway runs north across mostly empty baobab plains to **Messina** and the **Limpopo**.

Louis Trichardt

With the N1 sliding through town, it doesn't take much to miss **LOUIS TRICHARDT**, basically a practical place to stop at the junction of the road leading into Venda and to the Punda Maria gate of Kruger National Park. With little on offer further north at Messina, however, this is the last town with a reasonable selection of shops and services before you reach the border; and, similarly, the first you hit if you're coming south. A centre for the surrounding mountain and bushveld farms, it has hung onto its traditional role as a white bastion in the hostile north, and you'll find its population overwhelmingly Afrikaans-speaking.

Practicalities

There is a well-organized and convenient **tourist information office** (Mon–Fri 8am–5pm, Sat 8am–3pm; ☎015/516 0040) situated beside *Safari Motors*, just off the highway at the most northerly of the three sets of traffic lights on the N1 as you come past town. The **train station** is at the southern end of Kruger Street; the **minibus taxi rank** for links into Venda and up to Beitbridge is near the corner of Trichardt and Kruger streets. *Translux* buses stop at the information office and *Northlink* buses use the *Bergwater Hotel*.

The best **accommodation** in the area is out of town itself, mainly in the foothills of the Soutpansberg (see p.576), but there are a few inexpensive places you can stay in town. The **municipal caravan park** is on Grobbelaar Street near the centre of town – it offers a bit of gloomy shade and grass for camping, but it is unattended and isn't really ly an attractive option. In town, the *Bergwater*, 5 Rissik Street, (☎015/516 0262; ②–③), has some decent-sized and relatively modern rooms upstairs with view over a small lake. Off Rissik Street, the *Carousel Lodge*, on Klein Street (☎015/516 4482; ①–②), is for the moment an unglamorous alternative, but has adequate and inexpensive self-catering rooms and dormitory planned. It also offers horseback and mountain-bike trails into Soutpansberg.

Outside town, the *Ben Lavin Nature Reserve*, signposted 8km south of town on the N1 (☎015/516 4534; ①–②), is a small reserve with a collection of larger antelope and giraffe, which makes a pleasant alternative stopover in the Louis Trichardt area. It has access to walking and mountain-bike trails (bikes can be hired) and a relaxed, neat rest camp with self-catering cottages and space to pitch a tent. The *Plaas Guesthouse*, 21km east of town along the R524 (☎015/516 4717; ③), is a very hospitable, friendly B&B on an avocado farm on the lush slopes of the Soutpansberg, with great breakfasts. There's also *Uitvlugt Cottage*, Roodewalpad, 6km northeast of town (☎015/516 4468; ②), a simple and rather jumbled self-catering flatlet, but in a pleasant farmlands setting.

There are various familiar take-away **food outlets** around the grid-set town centre. For a sit-down meal, the *Shenandoah Spur* steakhouse is on Kroeg Street and Magistrate Avenue, while *Vivo's*, a rather intimidating maroon-fronted bar and weekend nightclub on Trichardt Street, has an unexpectedly decent pub-type menu. There is also a pricier restaurant at the *Bergwater Hotel*.

Schoemansdal

A settlement established by the first Voortrekkers to reach the Soutpansberg, **SCHOE-MANSDAL**, off the R522 towards Vivo (Mon–Sat 9am–4pm), was abandoned around thirty years later, after it failed to stem attacks by Venda warriors. It was never again occupied. When control of the area was regained by the Zuid-Africaanische Republiek in 1898, a new settlement was established at Louis Trichardt, some 12km to the east, leaving Schoemansdal the only established Voortrekker settlement in the country not to become a modern town. Perhaps not surprisingly, the site of the historic village has been turned into an **outdoor museum of pioneering history**, with a number of old dwellings and buildings recreated and various aspects of settler life and domestic crafts on display. From the top of a wooden viewing platform you can make out the lines of grass where the streets of the settlement once were, as well as the archeological diggings which have been made on the site. It certainly paints a humble picture of pioneer Voortrekker life, and one that is not so readily evident in the collections of artefacts on display in dusty town houses. Having said that, the Schoemansdal museum is obviously dying a slow death of neglect, and has really become a place to absorb those interested in history rather than the wider audience it has the potential to attract.

Elim and around

Southeast of Louis Trichardt along the R578 lie some areas that used to form part of the self-governing homeland of Gazankulu (a Tsonga area, and they boast the leftover scruffiness and vibrant roadside action typical of such rural areas – most notably at **ELIM**, a cluster of stalls, minibuses and hoardings on the site of a long-established Swiss mission hospital. A short way from here, along the road to Levubu, is the modest but relaxing *Shiluvari Lakeside Lodge* (☎015/556 3406; ③), with lawns running down to the edge of Albasini Dam and views over the water to the Soutpansberg.

Continuing on the R578 from Elim crossroads, towards the town of Giyani, there are a series of rural arts and crafts workshops. This isn't strictly in Venda (see p.578), but the traditions and skills in arts and crafts are not dissimilar, and most of the workshops and small factories have simple, rural roots, making the trip to see them quite an adventure but definitely one well worth making. About 4km along this road, at the brow of a hill (directly opposite the road into *Tsonga Textiles*), the **Akanani development agency** is a small community centre with offices and workshops covering a range of practical subjects. This isn't a craft place, but they do have simple bunk rooms available (☎015/556 3133, ask for Nomsa) and will point you in the right direction for an interesting sunrise/sunset walk through the villages to nearby **Rivola Hill** (see box, p.581).

The Soutpansberg Mountains

Lush, rounded mountains rising to a height of over 1700m and cut by some dramatic outcrops of pinky-orange rock, the **Soutpansberg** seem to form a final barrier of colourful relief before the long hot plains either side of the Limpopo. Travelling north on the N1, you begin to climb immediately after leaving Louis Trichardt, up what becomes a narrow, winding road not easily negotiated by the heavy trucks which ply the Great North Road. Along this stretch you will pass a number of **hotels** which have used the lush surroundings to create a mountain-resort-type atmosphere. None are out-

> ### ELEPHANT TALK: AFRICA'S SHITTIEST SOUVENIRS
>
> One piece of modern Africana you shouldn't miss as you climb into the mountains from Louis Trichardt is along a rough farm road which turns off the N1 just past *Clouds End Hotel*. Lynne and Bruce Murray's **Elephant Talk** is an unusual home industry – the production of elephant-dung paper and products. They mix elephant-dung (personally gathered from the Tuli Block in Botswana) with recycled paper pulp to produce writing paper, cards and notelets. You can look in to see the paper being made by hand using traditional methods, and of course buy up some of their range of guaranteed fragrance-free and biodegradable paper souvenirs. Certainly it's a unique source of presents for those back home.

standing, and it is probably better to regard them as alternatives to a stopover in Louis Trichardt than attractions in their own right. The first two are on the southern side of the mountain range. The *Mountain View* (☎015/517 7031; ③), 9km north of town, is a little more pleasant, if slightly larger, than the *Clouds End* (☎015/517 7021; ③), 3km north of town. Also, just after the *Mountain View*, there is a turning (marked "Bluegumspoort") that provides a scenic drive along the face of the mountain range through stands of impressive eucalyptus. Once over the low pass, on the much less dramatic northern slopes, you'll find the well-run *Ingwe Ranch Motel* (☎015/517 7078; ③), which has a variety of rondavels and rooms, a coffee bar and one of the better restaurants in the area.

Mountain retreats

Beyond the well-worn route of the N1, you can get deeper into the more remote and wilder parts of the mountains if you have a couple of days to spare. Situated in the **Sand River gorge**, through which the rail line makes its pass through the mountains, *George's Place* (☎01554/641; ②–④) is a very rustic wood cabin overlooking one of the largest remaining wild fig forests in the country. Tucked away in the backwoods, it can accommodate five people and has no electricity. Both catered and self-catering is available. The spectacular dirt road leading to it from Waterpoort on the northern side of the Soutpansberg, however, requires both nerves and suspension of toughened steel.

Also in the Sand River gorge, but approached from the southern side (29km west of Louis Trichardt) is the equally escapist *Medike* (☎015/516 0481; ②), with accommodation in restored thatched stone cottages. For details of other retreats, contact the tourist information office in Louis Trichardt.

North to the border

Once over the Soutpansberg, the N1 runs across some hot, mostly featureless plains of dense bush and baobab trees for some 60km before reaching the town of **Messina**, the last settlement before the Zimbabwe border at the Limpopo River. There isn't anything much else in the region, although the famous Iron Age site at Mapungubwe, the "Hill of the Jackals", is located around 80km west of Messina, close to the confluence of the Shashe and Limpopo rivers. While there are plans to create a national park here, there are as yet no facilities.

Messina

Floating rather oddly 18km south of the border, **MESSINA** is above all a mining town, although it does mop up a fair bit of the traffic passing through on the N1. The border at Beitbridge is not open 24 hours a day, so there's always call for accommodation and food, which Messina does offer, but without flourish.

The one thing of note around Messina is the **Baobab Tree Reserve** which encircles the town. Baobab trees, the legend says, God planted upside down, with their roots in the air. You don't find the trees in great stands but rather dotted around the bushveld, each one with a plate nailed onto it displaying its protected status. Many are over a thousand years old, and the largest have been hollowed out inside and used as houses, bars, shops and even toilets. There are quite a number of fine examples by the roadside on the N1, although many of these are covered in graffiti. The entrance to the reserve, which doesn't have any facilities, is a couple of kilometres south of town.

Practicalities

The town's caravan and camping park, which has some grass and shade and is reasonably well-run, is on the left not long after you come into town from the south. Otherwise **accommodation** is a choice between *Günter's Country House*, 25 Irwin St (the R525 to Tshipise) (☎01553/41019 or 40484; ③), a civilized, pleasant B&B with a pool; the *Ilala Lodge* (☎01553/3220; ②), situated in the baobab reserve 8km northwest of town, with secluded stone chalets with pool; or, the least expensive option, the *Limpopo River Lodge*, on the N1 in the centre of town (☎01553/40204; ②) – a plain travellers' hotel with a certain creaking character and a restaurant attached.

When the time comes to **eat**, there are various takeaways, including a *Nando's* at the elbow in the road close to the mine entrance. For sit-down meals, the *Buffalo Ridge Spur* franchise is by the N1 off Sam Street; there's also a steakhouse at *Mudzwiri Lodge*, by the mine on the northern side of town, and a restaurant attached to the *Limpopo River Lodge*.

Beitbridge

On the South African side of the Limpopo there isn't much to **BEITBRIDGE** other than a tacky service station, a habitually long queue of trucks, some noisy minibus touts and the customs and immigration buildings (which include a duty-free shop). Two bridges cross the Limpopo (the river memorably described by Rudyard Kipling in *Just So Stories* as "great grey-green, greasy"), one for vehicles and one for pedestrians. The border is open from 5.30am to 10.30pm. For those arriving in South Africa, don't expect any great pomp and ceremony or even guidance. Be assured, though, that Messina is the direction to head.

Venda

To the west and north of Louis Trichardt lies the intriguing land of the **vhaVenda** people, a culturally and linguistically distinct African grouping known for their mystical legends, political independence and their arts and crafts. Venda was demarcated as a homeland under the apartheid system in the 1950s, and became one of three nationally independent homelands in South Africa in the late 1970s. Of all the homelands, Venda was one of the least compromised, keeping both its geographic and cultural integrity, and largely being left to mind its own business during the dark years of apartheid. Its boundaries have regained their former fuzziness, within the Northern Province, but the region has retained its strong, independent identity.

Venda history and culture

The people who today call themselves **vhaVenda** are descended from a number of ancient groupings who migrated from the Great Lakes area in east-central Africa in the eleventh and twelfth centuries. Their identity gelled when a group under Chief Dimbanyika arrived at Dzata (which means "peace" in Venda) in the northern

Soutpansberg, where a walled fort was later built. From here they consolidated their power in the region, fending off attack from a number of different African groupings (including the Voortrekkers, whom they harried from their settlement at Schoemansdal, just south of the Soutpansberg in 1867). Although the vhaVenda suffered a reverse at the hands of the Boers in 1898, the onset of the Anglo-Boer War prevented that victory being consolidated. The British had little interest in such a remote region, and were content to allow their administration to be run by the local chiefs, a system of self-government which, in one contrived form or another, lasted through the apartheid years until 1994.

The culture of the vhaVenda is a fascinating one, steeped in mysticism and vivid legend. One pervading theme is water – always an important concern in hot, seasonal climates, but in which Venda is unusually abundant. Lakes, rivers, waterfalls and lush forests all form sacred sites, while legends abound of *zwidutwane*, or water sprites, and snakes who live at the bottom of dark pools or lakes. You can still even find older people who hold a taboo against fish, partly because the animals live in water and partly because they believe that if you eat fish the crocodiles will go hungry and turn on other available food sources, such as humans.

Many vhaVenda ceremonies and rituals still hold great importance, with the most famous the python, or *domba*, dance performed by young female initiates. Naked but for jewellery and a small piece of cloth around their waist, the teenage girls form a long chain, swaying and shuffling as the snake winds around a fire to the sound of a beating drum – another sacred object in Venda – often for hours on end. Although it is well known, your chances of seeing it performed are limited – although dancing can always be arranged (at a price, and with notice). The genuine thing is most common during spring; Heritage Day around the end of August or the beginning of September is a good time for celebrations.

Thohoyandou

A fairly direct, if slightly chaotic, 70km west of Louis Trichardt following the southern edge of the Soutpansberg along the R524, the Venda capital, **THOHOYANDOU** (pronounced "toy-an-doh"), is an ugly, dirty sprawl of broken concrete and undisciplined building glamorized by a money-spinning casino. Situated among the last of the foothills at the western end of the Soutpansberg, it's not a place you'll want to spend time in if you can help it; and if you're heading for Kruger the R524 mercifully bypasses the town altogether.

The highlight of the capital, at least according to the tourist authorities, is the **Venda Sun hotel and casino** (☎0159/21011, central reservations ☎011/780 7800; ④), a clone of the gambling dens tacitly encouraged in the homelands by the apartheid government and lapped up by South Africans denied such illicit entertainment in their own country. It is set in the heart of the downtown area, surrounded immediately by trees, but not far beyond the road and tatty shopping mall. To get to it turn left off the R534 coming from Louis Trichardt at the Delta/Toyota service station and right at the third set of traffic lights. As a hotel, it has decent, if expensive, rooms and a range of facilities including a swimming pool.

The only alternatives to the *Venda Sun* in town are *Bougainvillea Lodge* (☎0159/82 4064; ②), just up the hill from the *Venda Sun*, a simple motel-like travellers' stop, and *Acacia Park* (book through *Venda Tourism* ☎0159/41577; ①–②), a gloomy, monkey- and insect-infested caravan and camping park just off the R524 on the far side of the large sports stadium. It has some basic and poorly maintained chalets, which, along with the campsite, are used a lot by contractors working on sites in town.

In the shopping centre next to the *Venda Sun* there are a number of **take-away food shops**, including a *Nando's* and *KFC*. There is a pricier **sit-down restaurant** in the

Venda Sun hotel. **Minibuses** for Louis Trichardt leave from the large, chaotic taxi rank in front of the shopping centre.

Information – and seeing Venda

The **Venda tourism office** (daily 8.30am–4.30pm; ☎0159/41577) is based in Ditike, a collection of small buildings in an enclosed *kraal*-type arrangement on the left as you come into Thohoyandou, not far before the first main junction where you turn to get to the *Venda Sun*. They organize a number of rather santitised tours in air-conditioned minibuses with official guides to the most famous Venda sights, and the majority of the very limited accommodation options. The **alternative** to these tours is to travel completely independently, but this way you will find no tourist-oriented infrastructure whatsoever, and a general lack of familiarity with visitors and what they might be looking for. It is a lot less dangerous to travel through Venda than many other places in South Africa, however, and of course the travelling can be wonderfully rough, raw and rewarding. But you have to be prepared for the fact that you will be very much on your own.

Lake Fundudzi, the Sacred Forest and the Mabudashango Trail

Along the northern side of the Soutpansberg, through a valley traced by the R523 road from the N1 to Thohoyandou, is the most appealing core of vhaVenda history and legend. This is where you'll find the lush forests, waterfalls and mountains which give Venda its mystical atmosphere.

From Thohoyando, climb out of town to the north and then west, eventually shucking off the suburbs to get amongst the elevated green scenery which lies ahead so enticingly. You'll pass the **Vondo Dam**, created in the early 1990s and surrounded by pine forests, then climb over the **Thate Vondo Pass**, over the summit of which a small shack marks the entrance to a network of forest roads that take you into the area containing the most important lake in Venda, **Lake Fundudzi**, and the **Sacred Forest**, an area of dense indigenous forest which contains the burial ground of Venda chiefs. You can look at both from afar, but to get any closer is a matter of deep cultural sensitivity: you have to gain permission, which, without local leads to the right people, is not easy to obtain. Another thing which contributes to the mystery of the place is that there isn't a readily available map showing you the network of roads around the forest, and some of the roads require 4WD. Information is available from the tourist office at Ditike, where you'll be persuaded to take up one of the official tours, which does at least have access to the right roads and contacts. However, although the guides are very knowledgeable and interesting, you do get the sense that the tours are a little inflexible.

ANIMAL MAGIC

Along with their spiritual relationship with water-inhabiting creatures, the vhaVenda have an interesting affinity with a number of **animals** of the forests and mountains. The relationship is, in many ways, a lot less aggressive and more humanized than that found in other African peoples. With lions, the vhaVenda recall the story of their great leader Makado, who harried the Boer commandos from the north. He was captured and thrown into a lion pit in Pretoria, but, rather like Daniel in the Old Testament, the lions chose not to eat him. Around the hot spring at Mphephu the legend runs that a leopard controls the hillside, and that it's always wise practice to keep him informed about who's in the area. And towards the eastern end of the Soutpansberg range there is a Lion's Head-shaped hill (there are nice views of it across Vondo Dam, on the Thate Vondo pass road) called Lwamondo. It is inhabited by baboons which are now protected because they once warned the vhaVenda of an imminent attack from their enemies.

One option well worth considering is the **Mabudashango Hiking Trail**, a four-day, 55-kilometre walk which takes you as close as any road to the main highlights of the area, including Lake Fundudzi and the Sacred Forest. The trail is big on views – undoubtedly a spectacular aspect of the area, as well as lush vegetation and a real sense of the water-fed wonder of the sacred land. At each of the camps there is a shelter with water and toilet facilities; for details, contact *Venda Tourism*.

Mphephu and Dzata

After crossing over the crest of the pass the R523 follows the **Nzhelele River** down a valley of scattered but mostly unbroken settlement. About halfway along is a poorly signposted turning to **Mphephu Resort** (book through *Venda Tourism* ☎0159/41577;

ARTS AND CRAFTS IN VENDA AND GAZANKULU

The Venda and Gazankulu regions have established a strong reputation in **arts and crafts**. The best known of these are clay pots distinctively marked with angular designs in graphite silver and ochre. Also growing in status are woodcarvings, ranging from abstract to practical; though, while the best of these can be imaginative and bold, you will see a lot which are unfinished and overpriced. You'll also come across tapestries, fabrics, basketwork and painting.

One thing which adds to the attraction of the art and crafts of these rural regions is that you can still find it being made in the villages, using traditional techniques and skills. Finding your way to these villages, however, can be quite an adventure, as they are widely scattered, the roads are poor, and directions can often be vague and confusing.

In **Gazankulu**, the main route is along the R578 between Elim and Giyani. Travelling from Elim crossroads, look out for a track leading up to the **Rivoni** workshop (opposite the turn to Waterval), where blind and other handicapped people make sisal mats, furniture, candles and coffins – a line that evidently does a roaring trade. There isn't a great deal to see, but the place is industrious and there is a small shop. Turning left at the brow of the next hill, then up a right-hand fork, is **Tsonga Textiles** (Mon–Fri 8am–4.30pm), where screen-printed fabrics are produced and turned into such things as tablecloths, bedspreads and clothes.

The R578 then goes down a hill, at the bottom of which is a turning to Mbhokota village. Going along this, turning left at the T-junction and left again along a narrow track just past a small homestead with a busy garden, you'll find a run-down-looking collection of buildings where **Twananani** textiles are made – attractive and quite funky hand-painted and batik garments with traditional African designs made by around twenty people.

At the next junction off the R578 to Riverplaats, then along a right-hand fork, the Shangaan woodcarver, **Jackson Thugwane**, an almost mystical figure who has had a number of pieces exhibited in major galleries around the country and in Europe, has a house and small workshop. If he isn't there you won't find much to see, but if he is be prepared for a few absorbing hours of philosophy, theology, art and the state of the modern world. If you take the left-hand fork after the Riverplaats sign, you will eventually come to a village called **Mashamba** where villagers make clay pots in the traditional way. This is, however, a trek deep into the rural areas of Gazankulu and the condition of the roads is fairly unreliable. For an update, contact the information office in Louis Trichardt.

In **Venda**, the villages are even more scattered and hard to find. There are a number of sites situated to the south of Thohoyandou, including the workshop of **Noria Mabasa**, whose clay and wood sculptures have become widely recognized around South Africa. Another place to look out for is **Mutale**, to the north of Thohoyandou, where traditional decorative drums are made. You can get advice at **Ditike tourist office**, from where *Venda Tourism* offer their air-conditioned minibus tours; another option is to contact **Annette Kennealy** (☎0159/32096), an artist who is very knowledgeable about art (rather than crafts) in the area.

②), a government-run resort situated on the flanks of the Soutpansberg by a hot spring. There are chalets here, as well as a rather unglamorous complex with a takeaway, TVs and a shop, but the pools can be pleasant if there aren't too many people around, and the setting is relaxed and away from the unpleasantness of Thohoyandou. There are in fact two springs – one within the resort and the other behind a reed screen just outside, which is used by locals – with a strict division of hours for men and women.

Not far west of Mphephu, on the northern side of the road, are the **Dzata ruins**, where the vhaVenda had their first stronghold. They're very interesting historically, but, as with the rest of the tourism infrastructure, not very visitor-friendly. If you find the gate locked, you may need to toot your horn to rouse the gateman.

Further afield

Along the R525 which runs across the Messina plains towards **Pafuri Gate**, the most northerly of the Kruger entrances, there are a series of holiday resorts, all possible stopovers on your way to Kruger but really not worth taking time out for on their own. The first is an *Aventura* resort at Tshipise (☎015539/624; ②–③), followed by two *Venda Tourism*-run resorts – *Nwanedi National Park*, which has rondavels (②) and a campsite, and *Sagole Spa*, which has similar facilities. The most interesting of these is the last, partially because it is the smallest and least developed, but also because of the presence of a famous Venda herbalist (called Tshikovha), some old fortresses nearby and the hot spring itself.

The other common reason to venture deeper into Venda is in search of the art and crafts for which the region has such a reputation (see box, p.581).

travel details

Trains

Beit Bridge to: Johannesburg (2 weekly; 13hr 15min); Louis Trichardt (2 weekly; 3hr 45min); Pietersburg (2 weekly; 6hr 40min).

Louis Trichardt to: Beit Bridge (2 weekly; 3hr 45min); Johannesburg (2 weekly; 9hr 10min); Pietersburg (2 weekly; 2hr 35min).

Pietersburg to: Beit Bridge (2 weekly; 6hr 40min); Johannesburg (2 weekly; 6hr); Louis Trichardt (2 weekly; 2hr 35min).

Buses

Beit Bridge to: Johannesburg (5 weekly; 9hr); Louis Trichardt (5 weekly; 2hr 45min); Pietersburg (5 weekly; 4hr 15min).

Louis Trichardt to: Beit Bridge (5 weekly; 2hr 45min); Johannesburg (5 weekly; 6hr 15min); Pietersburg (5 weekly; 1hr 30min).

Pietersburg to: Beit Bridge (5 weekly; 4hr 15min); Johannesburg (5 weekly; 4hr 45min); Louis Trichardt (5 weekly; 1hr 30min); Phalaborwa (6 weekly; 3hr 15min); Tzaneen (6 weekly; 1hr 45min).

Phalaborwa to: Johannesburg (6 weekly; 7hr 45min); Pietersburg (6 weekly; 3hr 15min); Tzaneen (6 weekly; 1hr 30min).

Tzaneen to: Johannesburg (6 weekly; 6hr 15min); Phalaborwa (6 weekly; 1hr 30min); Pietersburg (6 weekly; 1hr 45min).

Flights

Hoedspruit to: Johannesburg (1 daily; 1hr 15min).

Phalaborwa to: Johannesburg (3 daily; 1hr).

Pietersburg to: Johannesburg (4 daily; 1hr).

CHAPTER ELEVEN

LESOTHO

The most liberating aspect of the aptly named "mountain kingdom" of **Lesotho**, particularly if you have come from barbed-wire-mad South Africa, is its almost total absence of fences. This means you can wander at will, meeting as you do a people who are also some of the most hospitable of the region. The other thing you'll notice pretty quickly is that Lesotho is virtually treeless, with the exception of the invasive and water-hungry eucalyptus and the peach trees introduced by French missionaries a century ago. Indeed the country, once the grain basket of the region, is in deep ecological trouble, and acres of irreplaceable topsoil, loosened by decades of over-farming, are washed away down its rivers each year.

The **Lesotho Lowlands** form an east-facing crescent around the country, and are where you'll find all the nation's major towns, including the nondescript but busily practical capital of **Maseru,** and a host of smaller settlements that began life as tax collection centres for the British administration. The Lowlands have other delights – the weaving crafts of **Teya-Teyaneng,** the extraordinary caves at **Mateka,** and **Thaba Bosiu,** the mountain fortress of Lesotho's founder, king Moshoeshoe I. But the true splendours of the country lie in its ruggedly beautiful **Highlands,** which are dotted with excellent and inexpensive accommodation. There you can visit the engineering masterpiece of the **Katse dam,** ski at **Oxbow,** fish from rivers everywhere, and above all wander the countryside, dividing your time between immaculately crafted dry-stone-walled villages and their relaxed inhabitants, and the peaceful solitude of the mountains.

Although the tarred **road network** is good and getting better, many Sotho still travel by **pony.** You can do the same, from pony-trekking lodges all over the country; along with hiking it's unquestionably the best way to see Lesotho. Most of Lesotho's over four hundred **San rock art sites** and the many more **dinosaur footprints** can only be visited this way – although there are still plenty close by the roads which you can reach with ease if travelling by car.

Some history
Lesotho exists because of the determined efforts of one man, Moshoeshoe I (1786-1870), to secure land in the face of intense social upheaval and the insatiable land-

---

ACCOMMODATION PRICE CODES

All the **accommodation** listed in this chapter has been categorized into one of seven price bands, as set out below. The rates quoted, unless otherwise stated, represent the most expensive per-person rate for a double or single room outside the high season (Dec & Jan), except for ①, which also includes dormitory accommodation. These Lesotho price codes correspond to the South African price codes used in the rest of the book. For more accommodation details, see p.31. For currency details see p.588.

① M0–50	② M50–100	③ M100–150
④ M150–200	⑤ M200–250	⑥ M250–300
	⑦ Over M300	

hunger of others. Before the arrival of Moshoeshoe's ancestors around 900 AD, the San inhabited Lesotho's hills and mountains unchallenged. Today the San are gone, exterminated by the British led by one Colonel Bowker, who led the last of many missions against them in the highland region of Sehonkong in 1873. However, they have left their mark through rock paintings, glimpses of their tongue in the Sotho language, and traces of their features in some Sotho people.

The Sotho first settled the fertile plains that today form the Lesotho lowlands and the Free State, before going on to colonize the mountains. They farmed these plains relatively peacefully for centuries, but by Moshoeshoe's time bandit clans from elsewhere had already forced thousands of Sotho off their land. Moshoeshoe proved his own marauding skills in 1809, when he rustled so many cattle from another chief that he was judged to have "shaved his beard"; Moshoeshoe is the "praise name" he earned for that feat – pronounced "Moshwehshweh", the name is supposed to represent the sound of shaving. Moshoeshoe became a chief in 1820, based on top of a mountain near Butha-Buthe, where he became patron to many refugees in search of safety. However, after a particularly vicious attack on Butha-Buthe in 1824, Moshoeshoe decided it was no longer safe and trekked south with his followers in search of a better mountain. Moshoeshoe found one at Thaba Bosiu, which was subsequently attacked repeatedly but never taken. Moshoeshoe meanwhile expanded his kingdom by securing other clan chiefs as clients, at the same time earning a reputation for wisdom and generosity amongst ordinary Sotho that is almost mythical today.

Moshoeshoe had heard from travellers that missionaries brought peace, and so welcomed the arrival in 1833 of three from the Paris Evangelical Missionary Society (PEMS). Moshoeshoe established them in Morija, and took an active interest in their work, but never officially converted, despite their efforts. The missionaries established what is now the Lesotho Evangelical Church, second in size only to the Catholics in Lesotho, whose missionaries founded Roma in the 1860s (see p.599).

The kingdom was encroached by land-hungry whites from the 1840s, and the Orange Free State (OFS) government invaded in 1858, their soldiers destroying Morija and then launching a failed attack on Thaba Bosiu. They nonetheless captured plenty of farm land whose acquisition was sanctioned by a British treaty in 1860. In 1865, the OFS government cited Sotho cattle theft as the pretext for a new war, though few could deny Moshoeshoe's bitter assertion that "my great sin is that I possess a good and fertile country". The ensuing Seqiti War mainly involved the destruction of Sotho crops by Free State troops, an event which forced Moshoeshoe into a humiliating treaty in 1866 which signed over most of his remaining good land. Even this was not enough, and war resumed in 1867, halted only by the British taking over what was left of the kingdom as the protectorate of Basotholand in 1868. The Treaty of Aliwal North in 1869 restored Moshoeshoe's land east of the Caledon but left the rest with the Free State, where it has remained to this day.

Moshoeshoe died in 1870 and the British handed Basotholand to the Cape administration a year later, which began taxing its new subjects, establishing a series of hut tax collection points which have since grown into Lesotho's modest collection of small towns. In 1879, in a bid to tempt the OFS and Transvaal into federation, the Cape government decided to confiscate all Sotho firearms. The result was two years of raids and futile skirmishes, known as the Gun War, an expensive failure that brought down the Cape government and so outraged London that Britain resumed direct rule in 1884.

Along with Bechuanaland and Swaziland, Basotholand rejected incorporation into the union of South Africa in 1910, with King Letsie II instead helping found the South African Native National Congress (later the ANC) in 1912. During the following years, the monarchy and chiefs' position declined, partly because British reforms forced their uneasy conversion into a junior arm of the colonial civil service, but also because social changes at work in the region, like migration, urbanization and rising education levels, proved too much for chiefs and successive kings to adapt to. In 1960, when Moshoeshoe II was crowned king, independence politics were in full swing, spear-headed by Pan-Africanist Ntsa Mokhele's Basotho Congress Party (BCP), and rivalled by the more conservative Basotho National Party (BNP). The BCP easily won the 1960 elections, but the 1965 ones were narrowly won by the BNP, who duly led newly named Lesotho into independence on October 4, 1966. However, after losing in 1970, prime minister Leabua Jonathan annulled the result, declared a state of emergency, and carried on ruling until he was toppled in 1986 by Major General Metsing

Lekhanya. Lekhanya ordered the expulsion of the ANC from Lesotho and signed an agreement that year with South Africa for the Lesotho Highlands Water Project (see p.611).

In 1990, Lekhanya sent Moshoeshoe into exile and installed his son Letsie III as king, but only lasted himself until 1991, when he was ousted by Major General Phisona Ramaena, who understood better than Lekhanya the implications of the imminent democratic election in South Africa and the likely victory of the ANC. Ramaena allowed Moshoeshoe II to return home in 1992 and held elections in 1993, which Mokhele's BCP won convincingly, although the BNP have never accepted the result.

Letsie, who remained king despite the return of his father until 1995, dissolved the BCP government in August 1994 for alleged incompetence, but regional pressure soon forced the restoration of the government and constitution. The next king, Moshoeshoe II, died in a car crash in January 1996, and Letsie regained the throne. He has not tried anything unconstitutional this time, but the factionalized nature of Lesothoan politics continues unabated, so anything is possible in the future.

When to go

The Lesotho **winter** runs from May to July, when it often snows in the Highlands and sometimes in the Lowlands too, which is great for skiing and very picturesque. Although the days are usually crisp and warm, it does get extremely cold at night and ice can make driving hazardous in Highlands areas. **Spring**, between August and October, is a beautiful time, when the snow melts, new plants sprout up everywhere, and the fields are tilled again. November to January is **summer**, when Lesotho gets most of its rain, which is often torrential, turning dirt roads into mudslides. Still, when it isn't raining the weather is usually lovely and sunny. **Autumn** runs from February to April, and is one of the best times to visit the country, as it doesn't usually rain too much, it hasn't started to get really cold, and also there aren't many other tourists about. Whatever the time of year, Lesotho can be very cold at night, particularly in the Highlands, and prone to rapid weather changes, for which it is always wise to be prepared.

Getting there by road

There are **twelve border posts** from South Africa into Lesotho – from the Free State, KwaZulu-Natal and the Eastern Cape. All the **Free State** border crossings, and **Telle-Bridge** (daily 8am–10pm) in the Eastern Cape, cross over into the Lesotho Lowlands and

LESOTHO PUBLIC HOLIDAYS

January 1 - New Year's Day	May 1 - Workers' Day
March 11 - Moshoeshoe Day	July 17 - King's Birthday
April 4 - Heroes Day	October 4 - Independence Day
Good Friday	December 25 - Christmas Day
Easter Monday	December 26 - Boxing Day

PONY TREKKING

Ponies were introduced to Lesotho in the nineteenth century, with one of the first given as a present to king Moshoeshoe I by chief Moorosi in 1829. Moshoeshoe learnt to ride that year, and rapidly acquired further steeds, which he distributed to his family and followers. By the time of Moshoeshoe's death in 1870, ponies were widespread throughout the kingdom and the Sotho had become expert riders.

Lesotho's ponies are famously hardy, capable of slogging away for hours and negotiating slippery rock passes. The Sotho rarely groom their ponies much, so they usually look pretty dishevelled, but that doesn't affect their performance in the hills, where for many locals they are the only form of long-distance transport.

A number of lodges offer pony trekking, for which no previous experience at all is needed. However, only a few are well-organized, with guides, routes and places to stay worked out in advance. Among the best places are the *Basotho Pony Trekking Centre* (☎31 4165), the *Malealea Lodge* (☎051/447 3200) and the *Semonkong Lodge* (☎051/922 7330). You might also consider trying the *Trading Post* (☎34 0202) in Roma, the *Molumong Lodge* (☎033/702 1050) near Mokhotlong and the *Mount Maluti Hotel* (☎78 5224) in Mohale's Hoek.

Of the three most professional outfits, the *Basotho Pony Trekking Centre* is cheapest, at around M70 a day; pony-trekking at Malealea and Semonkong costs about M100 a day. One way to decide which place to go for is to choose first what kind of countryside you want to trek in. Semonkong, Mokhotlong and the area around the *Basotho Pony Trekking Centre* are all high up, above the sandstone and into the basalt (see box, p.602); most of the the rest are lower down, where conditions are usually less harsh for you, though harder on the ponies.

Wherever you go, make sure you bring a wide-brimmed sunhat, sun protection cream and waterproof gear, and, if you are staying somewhere overnight, a sleeping bag and mat, food, and something to cook it on. A luxury, but one you'll definitely appreciate, is some kind of balm to ease your aching limbs and buttocks, which will certainly be sore after a day's trekking, even if you are used to riding.

are much more accessible than the others, which enter via the Drakensberg. The latter include the famous **Sani Pass** (daily 8am–4pm), which you need a 4WD to ascend, although alternative transport is provided by local backpackers' lodges (see p.607). The **Ficksburg Bridge** and **Caledonspoort** crossings, which lead into Maputsoe and Butha-Buthe respectively, are both open 24 hours a day. Lesotho's capital Maseru is right on the border with South Africa, and the **Maseru Bridge** (daily 6am–10pm) border is the busiest in the country. The easiest way to reach it is east along the N8 from Bloemfontein.

The **drive** from Bloemfontein to Maseru is an easy 200km east along the R64. If you are driving from Durban, turn off towards Ficksburg at Bethlehem, and then either cross the border at Maputsoe and drive down through Lesotho, or continue on to Ladybrand and cross the border at Maseru. Driving from the Eastern Cape to Maseru is more fiddly, and if you want to stay on tarred roads for as long as possible remain in South Africa at least until Wepener, from where you can cross into Mafeteng, or continue through Hobhouse on the Ladybrand road, taking the right-hand fork to Maseru.

Getting there by plane

Moshoeshoe I airport, 18km south of Maseru, is Lesotho's only **international airport**. There are no regular flights into Lesotho from anywhere but Johannesburg, from where *Lesotho Airways* (Johannesburg ☎011/970 1046; Maseru ☎32 4507) runs a twice-daily flight that lasts just over an hour.

TIPS ON TRAVEL IN LESOTHO

- **Accommodation** This is reasonably priced in Lesotho; you can get a double room for about M70 a person in most parts of the country, and for M120 a person in one of the middle-range hotels in Maseru. Be aware that most outside Maseru take cash only.

- **Banks** These are found in all Lesotho's towns, but Maseru is the only place where it is easy to change money at them. Banks are open Monday to Friday 8.30am to 3pm, closing at 1pm on Thursdays, and on Saturday from 8.30am to 11am. Saturday is not a good day to do any banking, as the banks are invariably heaving with customers. Banks do not as a rule have ATMs, and any ATM you do find is unlikely to accept foreign cashcards. The larger hotels change money in Maseru and the Lowland towns, but for ludicrously bad exchange rates, making them very much a last resort.

- **Books** The glossy official tourist literature has useful phone numbers but is otherwise thin on facts, in which case you should turn to Marco Turco's *Visitor's Guide to Lesotho* (Southern); Russell Suchet, who runs the *Sani Lodge,* has self-published the *Backpackers' Guide to Lesotho*, which has plenty of useful information. Some South African backpackers' lodges have copies; otherwise contact him direct for a copy (☎033/702 1401). For a very good 1:250,000 topographical map of Lesotho, you need to pop into the *Basotho Hat* crafts shop on the main Kingsway Road in Maseru. However, you can only get the sort of detailed maps you need for serious hiking from the Department of Land, Surveys & Physical Planning (see opposite).

- **Camping** Freelance camping is possible all over rural Lesotho, provided you check with the local chief first; the virtual absence of fences in the country means you can roam, and pitch your tent almost anywhere. Though some lodges allow camping in their grounds, there is only one official campsite, near the *Pony Trekking Centre*; its hard surfaces make it good for caravans, but otherwise it's one of the least attractive camping spots for tents in the country.

- **Costs** These are lower than South Africa's. Buying food and eating out are slightly less expensive, and so is public transport. Pony trekking costs about M100 a day at most of the lodges (see p.587). Imported items like film are more expensive in Lesotho than South Africa, and only reliably available in Maseru.

- **Credit cards** Most major cards, such as *Visa, Mastercard* and *Amex*, are of limited use. Hotels and lodges geared to foreign visitors accept them, as do a few Maseru restaurants and the craft shops of Teya-Teyaneng. Otherwise you need cash for everything.

- **Currency** Lesotho's currency is the Maloti (M), divided into 100 lisenti, which is tied to the South African rand (R1 = M1). You can use rands in Lesotho, so you don't need to convert them beforehand, but you cannot use or exchange maloti anywhere outside Lesotho, so make sure you use them up or exchange them before leaving.

- **Dialling codes** To phone Lesotho from anywhere but South Africa, the country code is ☎266, followed by the number (there are no area codes); from South Africa, dial ☎09266. To phone abroad from Lesotho, dial ☎00, followed by the country and area codes and then the actual telephone number. To phone South Africa, first dial ☎0027, then the area code and phone number. To call collect, first call the operator, ☎100. Where area codes are indicated in the text, the number in question is a South African number, and you will need to prefix it with ☎0027 if calling from Lesotho.

- **Embassies** *Canada*, 202 Clemow Ave, Ottawa (☎613/236 9449); *South Africa*, 6th Floor, Momentum Centre, 343 Pretorius St, Pretoria (☎012/322 6090); *UK*, 7 Chesham Place, Belgravia, London SW1 (☎0171/373 8581); *USA*, 2511 Massachusetts Ave NW, Washington DC (☎202/797 5533).

- **Gay and lesbian** Same-sex relationships are not explicitly illegal in Lesotho, but they are not approved of either, so it is safer to avoid public displays of affection. There is a gay scene, but it is underground, so make use of South African gay contacts to find it.
- **Passports and visas** Visa requirements for the kingdom of Lesotho change fairly often, but at the time of writing most people do need visas, including citizens of Spain, USA, Canada, Australia and New Zealand. Other Commonwealth citizens, except those from India, Pakistan, Nigeria and Ghana, do not need visas, and nor do citizens of Germany, France, Switzerland, Italy or the Netherlands. You may find that border officials, particularly at smaller entry points, do not know the new rules, and will demand a visa from you even if you do not need one. There is not much you can do about this, but since visas are available on the spot, and are relatively inexpensive (M20/R20 single-entry, M40 multiple entry), you may as well pay up. If you have travelled through a yellow-fever zone, you will need an International Certificate of Vaccination against yellow fever. Visitors not requiring visas are usually given as much time in the country as they ask for, but, should you need an extension, contact the Department of Immigration and Passport Services, Kingsway, Maseru (☎31 7339).
- **Tour operators** The Lesotho Tourist Board (☎31 2896, fax 32 3638) can arrange tailor-made tours of the country. Visit them at their information office on the Kingsway in Maseru, next to the *Victoria Hotel*. Alternatively, the *Malealea Lodge* (☎ & fax 051/447 3200) offers some innovative options, often involving pony trekking or 4WDs.
- **Water** Safe to drink out of the tap. Whilst Lesotho's rivers and streams are bilharzia-free, drinking from them is inadvisable without purifying the water first if you are in any doubt about what might lie upstream (eg people washing clothes, dead livestock).

HIKING IN LESOTHO

As an almost entirely fenceless country, and hospitable to boot, Lesotho is a **hiker's paradise**. It really is possible to set off into the hills and hike for as long as you like, with no prospect of an angry farmer yelling at you to get off his land – quite a change from South Africa. If you're camping, it's important to ask permission, preferably from the chief, although it's normally fine just to pitch your tent if there's no one around. A cosier alternative, where its available, is to stay in a rondavel, for which which you will definitely need to ask permission, and to pay a small offering – M10–20.

Always prepare adequately before setting out, and bring supplies for at least a day more than you think the hike will take. Lesotho's weather is notoriously fickle, and you should bring a sunhat and sunblock, as well as warm clothing and waterproofs, whatever the season. Other basics include a torch, plenty of food (there aren't many stores in very rural areas, and those there are don't often have much stock), a water container, water purifying tablets, an all-weather cooker with fuel (don't count on finding firewood), a genuinely waterproof tent, a sleeping mat and a warm sleeping bag. Also invaluable is a decent map and a compass. The 1:250,000 map available from the Basotho Hat Building in Maseru marks most trails and topography, although the really detailed 1:50,000 maps of specific regions of Lesotho, available from the Department of Lands, Surveys and Physical Planning (☎32 2376), on Lerotholi Road, near the corner of Constitution Road in Maseru, are far better. Be warned that in the highest reaches of the Drakensberg there are very few villages, and you can walk for days without seeing anyone. Lovely as this is, it is also risky, so make sure someone knows where you have gone, and don't hike there on your own.

Lesotho Airways also flies four days a week to Qacha's Nek (domestic reservations ☎31 2453), and you can charter twenty-seater planes from the company to a number of other domestic destinations for M2760 per hour. Chartering smaller planes from *Air Maluti* (☎35 0314) is less expensive, and those from the *Mission Aviation Fellowship* (☎31 3640) are the cheapest of all, at M120–220 per hour.

Getting around by road

Lesotho has a good tarred **road network**, though you cannot avoid dirt roads when heading to more out-of-the-way places of interest. There is a continuous tarred road north from Maseru to Oxbow, and by 1998 this should extend as far as Mokhotlong. The road to Sani from Mokhotlong, and the Sani Pass itself, is untarred (and will probably always be so) and is best tackled with a 4WD. The road off the main northern route from Hlotse to the Katse dam is tarred and of very high quality, though it goes over some punishing gradients. On the central route, the tar extends as far as the Blue Mountain Pass, just beyond the *Pony Trekking Centre*, and then reverts to dirt and gravel of sometimes poor quality as far as Thaba Tseka. The southern route from Maseru is tarred as far as Mphaki, but is passable in an ordinary saloon car up to Qacha's Nek. The road to Sehlabathebe National Park is impassable without a 4WD, though buses somehow manage it.

If you have rented a car in South Africa, make sure the **insurance** covers you for travel in Lesotho. Some companies are reluctant to do this, because of the condition of many of the roads. **Fuel** costs roughly the same in Lesotho as it does in South Africa. The **speed limit** is 120kmh out of town, and 50kmh in urban areas.

Public transport covers Lesotho well. **Buses** are slower but safer than **minibus taxis**, but they are both very inexpensive. Timetables do not exist as such; the rule of thumb is to check the day before, and get to the bus station early if you have a long distance to travel, as long-distance transport usually leaves around 6am.

Hitching is much safer in Lesotho than in South Africa and is a good way to get around. Some drivers expect payment, so you should negotiate this before you've travelled too far.

MASERU AND THE CENTRAL DISTRICTS

The most convenient entry point from South Africa, and the country's most sophisticated urban centre by far, **Maseru** is a good place to start exploring Lesotho. Apart from a few elegant colonial sandstone buildings, there is not a great deal to see here. But it's the best place to do all the banking and stocking up you need for the journey east into the Highlands, particularly if you fancy one of the justifiably celebrated Sotho blankets see box, p.605), which are cheaper in Maseru than anywhere else. There are plenty of bracing excursions into the hills and plateaus that surround the city, including the one to Lesotho's most famous mountain Thaba Bosiu, the so-called "Mountain of the Night" where the founder of the nation, Moshoeshoe I, ruled for almost fifty years.

Roma, less than 40km from the capital along good roads, is the educational centre of the country, surrounded by beautiful sandstone hills and with an historic Catholic mission – the ascent from Roma deep into the Highlands to Semonkong, through several mountain passes, is one of the most striking in the country. **Semonkong** is famous for its mighty waterfalls, and you can visit another set, the **Kentane Falls**, by trekking westwards by pony from the delightful *Semonkong Lodge*.

Any car can manage the drive from Maseru along Lesotho's **central route** to the luxurious *Molimo Nthuse Lodge* and the *Basotho Pony Trekking Centre* nearby – about the most inexpensive place from which to hire ponies in the country. However, continuing further on over the epic **Central Mountain Range** requires a rugged vehicle that can handle the poor and rocky roads. Though the final destination of **Thaba Tseka** is unspectacular, the journey more than compensates, and from Thaba Tseka you can continue to Katse and its massive new dam (see p.611).

Maseru

Sprawling **MASERU** spills east from the Caledon River, which marks the border with South Africa, and is the nation's capital and only big town. Maseru's older buildings, as well as some stylish new ones, are built from well-crafted local sandstone, now recognized as the town's vernacular building material, though a number of ill-thought-out concrete box buildings diminish the effect, and unfortunately dominate the skyline. Most of the daytime action happens on or around the Kingsway, the road which runs through town getting more and more downmarket and lively as it heads east towards the cathedral.

Maseru is the best place in the country to do any **banking**, as the banks are the only ones in the country adept at handling foreign currency exchange, partly because of the number of aid workers who have been based here since the 1970s. The city's **post office** is the best in Lesotho too, and the new one under construction promises to be even better. If you need to stock up on **supplies**, you should do so in Maseru before heading off elsewhere, although Maseru does not have the craft selection of Teya-Teyaneng. You can get all the **maps** you should need of Lesotho from Maseru, which is also the only place where you can book for the Sehlabathebe National Park.

Public transport is chaotic and crazily unregulated, but does at least go everywhere in the country from Maseru, invariably for low sums of money. You are only a short drive from some beautiful walking country, although the true splendours of the country lie further east and into the Highlands.

Some history

Maseru, which gets its name from the local sandstone from which it was first built, was established by the British as their administrative centre in 1869. Britain had annexed Basotholand, as it was then known, a year earlier (see p.585) and needed somewhere close to the Sotho royal stronghold of Thaba Bosiu that was relatively accessible from the Cape Colony.

Britain put as little effort into developing Maseru as it did the rest of the country, no doubt expecting it to become just a minor South African town when Basotholand was incorporated into South Africa – which is what the British intended. It's grown swiftly over recent years, not so much because it is booming economically but because the poverty in Lesotho's rural areas has driven people to the city in search of a better life. Few have found it yet, and the city has a high unemployment rate.

Maseru has been the location for most of the turbulence of post-independence politics, including two successful coups and several more unsuccessful ones – and, most recently, shoot-outs between the army and police force over pay and other disputes. These have yet to be fully resolved, but this does not appear to trouble other Maseru residents unduly.

Arrival, getting around and information

Moshoeshoe I international **airport** is 18km southeast of Maseru off the Main Road South (A2); there are frequent, inexpensive minibus taxis and buses into town during the day and early evening (arrivals and departures ☎35 0777). Private taxis are available but cost considerably more (around M40). You can also rent *Avis* cars from the air-

National Stadium △

△ ❸,❼ & Lancer's Gap

Bus Station

Roman Catholic Cathedral

REPUBLIC OF SOUTH AFRICA

Caledon River

Seputana River

Houses of Parliament

Radio Lesotho

Department of Land, Surveys & Physical Planning

Old Resident Commissioner's House

Royal Palace

QE II Hospital

High Court

Kingsway Cinema

Basotho Hat Building

Central Prison

Ministry of Agriculture

American Embassy

Train Station

Lesotho Police Border Checkpoint Customs Post

Caledon River

SOUTH AFRICA

Caledon River

Moshoeshoe I International Airport

ACCOMMODATION
1 Anglican Centre
2 Lehali Hotel
3 Lakeside
4 Lancer's Inn
5 Lesotho Sun
6 Maseru Sun
7 Phomolong Youth Hostel
8 Victoria

500 m

0

MASERU

LEAVING MASERU

Public transport from Maseru to the rest of the country runs from the station off the Main Road North (A1); turn left into Pitso Road just after the cathedral traffic circle and you cannot fail to miss the huge sprawl in front of you. Rather than trying to work out the method in the madness, just ask around for where buses and minibuses to your destination currently run from. The two main roads out of Maseru are the Main Road North (A1) and the Main Road South (A2), both of which begin life at the cathedral traffic circle. There are a few fuel stations scattered along both for their first few kilometres.

---

port. If you intend to stay at either the *Lesotho Sun* or *Maseru Sun*, they will provide free transport to the hotels.

There is no **train** connection to Maseru; the nearest station is in Bloemfontein in the Free State. None of the big South African **bus** companies go to Maseru except *Transtate*, which runs from Johannesburg three times a week, from Bloemfontein daily, and from Durban once daily from Friday to Tuesday. Otherwise, there are always the daily **minibus taxis**, which travel from all three cities and a host of smaller places nearer Maseru. All of them stop at the border, which you must cross on your own. From there, you can easily find public transport into the centre of town.

Maseru is small enough for **walking around** to be no bother, though some accommodation is too far to reach easily on foot. Walking around after dark is risky. There are plenty of **minibus taxis** going up and down the Kingsway and off into semi-urban areas, with each journey costing M1.40. Otherwise, there are a few **taxi** companies you can try (see "Listings", p.596). **Driving** is straightforward in town, though often slow. Bear in mind that the Kingsway becomes a one-way street in the direction of the border from 7–9am each week-day morning.

Information

You'll find the **Lesotho tourist information office** (Mon–Fri 8am–5pm, Sat 8am–1pm; ☎31 2896, fax 323 638), at the western end of the town centre, on the main Kingsway road near the*Victoria Hotel*. Although underresourced, the staff are helpful and can give you a town map, flyers from the few resorts that consistently supply them, reasonably up-to-date information on hotel costs, and the odd glossy brochure. You can also buy the handy booklet, *Hill Walks in and Around Maseru*, by Gary and Veronica Taylor, for about M4. To book at the Sehlabathebe National Park, contact Sehlabathebe Reservations at the Ministry of Agriculture, on Raboshabane, off Moshoeshoe Road, PO Box 92, Maseru 100 (☎32 3600/32 2876).

To find out about most of the limited public entertainment Maseru has to offer, and for information about new services aimed at visitors, pick up a copy of the monthly *What's On in Maseru* from either the tourist office or the main hotels.

Accommodation

Maseru is the only place in the country where there's much choice of **accommodation**, offering everything from camping and grim dorms to luxury suites in plush hotels. The most central options, on or near the Kingsway, are also the most practical if you don't have your own transport.

Anglican Centre, corner of Assisi Rd and Lancer's Rd (☎32 2046). Large and austere travellers' centre very close to the Kingsway, though tricky to find, with spartan doubles equipped with elderly mattresses. Male and female guests are supposed to be housed in separate rooms, and there is a 7pm curfew, although a night watchman will normally let you in later. Ask for Mrs Mokoena if you want to stay. ①.

Khali Hotel, off Pioneer Rd (☎32 5800). Slightly dingy, but the rooms are spacious, with TVs that broadcast the South African movie channel M-Net. You can camp here too, and there are condoms on sale at reception, which come in handy for some of the permanent guests. There are private and public bars. The hotel is 1500m south of the Kingsway; turn left off Pioneer Rd after the bridge. The bus/minibus taxi towards the *New Europa* takes you pretty close. Camping ①, rooms ②.

Lakeside Hotel, off Main Rd North (☎31 3646). Big, ugly, brick building on the edge of an industrial estate, though the rooms are OK, with en-suite bathrooms, soft mattresses and TVs with M-Net. The restaurant does solid and inexpensive meals, but the hotel's main attraction is its occasional choral music shows and competitions. Turn right off Main Rd North towards Mafeteng at the marked junction and the hotel is 100m further on the left. ②.

Lancers Inn, Kingsway (☎31 2114, fax 31 0223). Central, pleasant, sandstone building that's one of the oldest in Maseru, offering good rondavels and chalets with modern en-suite bathrooms. Has a good beer garden and restaurant. ③.

Lesotho Sun, off Nightingale Rd (☎31 3111, fax 31 0104). Behind the QEII hospital, this is the smartest hotel in town, with comfortable if smallish rooms with TVs and all sorts of sports facilities, a pool, casino, cinema, and one of the best restaurants in town. Transport is provided to and from the airport. ⑥.

Maseru Sun, Orpen Rd (☎31 2434, fax 31 0158). Decent, though box-like, rooms, in soothing well-tended garden surroundings that are popular with locals in the evening. A decent restaurant, and the slot machines are a big draw too. ⑥.

Phomolong Youth Hostel, Lancers Gap Rd (☎33 2900). Some way out of town, offering battered dorms with ancient mattresses, but decent bedding. You can use the kitchen, but meals are only provided for groups. Doors close at 10pm. Take the Lancers Gap turn off Main Rd North and carry on about 2km, where it's on the right, barely signposted. ①.

Victoria Hotel, Kingsway (☎32 2002 or 31 2922, fax 31 0318). Prominent city landmark with reasonable rooms, a popular dining room and bar with terrace attached, from which you can watch Maseru go by beneath you. Opposite the Basotho Hat. ③.

The City

The best place to start an exploration of Maseru is from its most famous landmark, the aptly named and hat-shaped **Basotho Hat Building** on the Kingsway, which houses a reasonable crafts shop. Heading east along the Kingsway, you'll find more crafts, mostly woven grass Sotho hats being sold by vendors on the pavements outside the tourist office. There's a more upmarket selection in *Mohair Cottage*, a foyer boutique of the *Maseru Sun*, which you can find by continuing past the Basotho Hat Building down Orpen Road. See p.604 for more on Lesotho's craft industry.

Continuing up the Kingsway, you soon come to the old **Post Office**, and opposite it the new one, which should come into use some time in 1998. A little further up on the left, it's worth pausing to look at the old **Resident Commissioner's House**, now a government department, built in sandstone in 1891 and now restored, making it one of Maseru's finest buildings once again. The large Queen Elizabeth II Hospital is a short distance further up on the right, and a turn before it takes you up a hill to the *Lesotho Sun Hotel*. From here on the Kingsway is busier, its low-priced shops thronged by shoppers, and informal traders touting everything from Sotho fast food to cutlery made of galvanized iron. Wander into the **Tradorette Building Complex** on the left-hand side just past the PEP store, where the *Lesotho Blanket Co.* sells the best-priced Sotho blankets in Lesotho and *J's Music Bar* has the widest selection of Sotho and South African music cassettes in town.

The Kingsway comes to an end at the traffic circle by the impressively large, though architecturally unremarkable, **Roman Catholic Cathedral**, and splits into Main Road North and Main Road South, the two major roads out of town. You'll find the chaotic **bus station** up Pitso road, the first left turn you come to on Main Road North. The **national stadium** is 500m or so further up the road. The Lancers Gap turn is a short drive further on the right, which takes you to a particularly striking **mountain pass** only a few kilometres out of town (see, p.597).

Eating, drinking and nightlife

Maseru has a very good selection of **restaurants**, certainly more than anywhere else in Lesotho but also better than most South African towns of the same size. There are also plenty of inexpensive takeaways and snacks to be had, particularly around the bus station and on the Kingsway during the day. **Nightlife** is considerably more limited, as there's only one nightclub of note and two cinemas. However, the club's a good one, and there are plenty of hotel bars if you're just after a drink or two.

Restaurants

Auberge, Kingsway (☎31 2755). Opposite the *QEII Hospital*, this well-frequented place has about the most innovative menu in Maseru. It's not excessively pricey, has excellent service, and also serves draught beers.

Boccacio, corner of Orpen and Bowker roads (☎32 5853). Very popular spot near the Basotho Hat serving well-prepared, mostly Italian meals. Closed Mon.

China Palace, Kingsway (☎31 5488). Good-quality, moderately priced Chinese meals. With a balcony that looks onto the street, next to the *OK* supermarket.

Chinese Garden, Orpen Rd (no phone). Interesting, reasonably priced Chinese menu in a setting of faded opulence, but the food can take ages to appear on the table. Closed Sun.

Early Bird, off Kingsway. Inexpensive fry-ups, chicken and pies to eat in or take away, opposite the *OK* supermarket.

Lehaha Grill, *Lesotho Sun*, off Nightingale Rd (☎31 3111). An often busy restaurant serving a tasty but somewhat pricey range of continental dishes.

Maseru Sun, Orpen Rd. This place offers a choice of buffet or à la carte, with the buffet probably the better and certainly the healthier bet.

Penthouse, Kingsway. Right at the top of the *Victoria Hotel*, with a bird's-eye view of the town, this serves respectable Italian dishes, grills and seafood amidst great splurges of faded velvet decor. Closed Sat lunch and Sun.

Rendezvous, Kingsway (☎31 2114). Situated in the *Lancers Inn*, with an unadventurous menu but a good carvery, reasonably priced.

Victoria, Kingsway (☎31 2992). Standard and unexciting meaty fare, but a spacious restaurant, and usually busy in the evening. The service is excellent. Best visited when they serve curries on Mon and traditional Sotho dishes on Wed afternoons.

Bars and nightlife

Maseru's **bars** are almost all attached to hotels or restaurants, with those at the *Victoria* and *Lancers* being among the most cheerful. The bar of the *Auberge* is popular, particularly at lunchtime, and the *China Garden*'s rather poky bar attracts a dedicated following, perhaps for the frequently fine music blaring from its hi-fi. If you want to drink in more typically Sotho surroundings, you need to head out of the town centre a bit and make for any of the numerous informal bars scattered about the outskirts of town.

With the closure of the Studio 1 Club at the *Lancers*, Maseru's **nightclub** options have been halved, and now there's just the *Crossroads Club* (daily except Mon 9pm–late) under the *Victoria Hotel*. Fortunately, the club is well worth checking out, both for the music and to see Maseru's youth strutting their stuff until the wee hours of the morning.

Otherwise, you have a choice of two **cinemas**, with the one at the *Lesotho Sun* screening mostly action movies (☎31 3111 for details) and the *Kingsway Cinema* (☎32 5424) next to the *Victoria Hotel* offering a reasonable range of Hollywood releases, usually a few weeks after they've hit South Africa. Don't rely on the billboard outside announcing films and screening times, or the advert in *What's On in Maseru*. Check with the staff instead to see what's playing that day.

Listings

Airlines *Lesotho Airways* (☎32 4507/513); *Air Maluti* (☎35 0314); *Mission Aviation Fellowship* (☎31 3640).

Airport Moshoeshoe I International Airport (☎35 0777).

American Express, *Maseru Book Centre*, Kingsway (☎31 2554; ☎32 4760 after hours).

Banks Main branches of the *Lesotho Bank*, *Nedbank* and *Stanbic* are easy to find on the Kingsway.

Books The best of Maseru's small range of bookshops, called simply *The Book Centre*, is on Kingsway, just past the *Lesotho Bank*.

Canoeing Lesotho is not an ideal country for canoeing, as the rivers are only deep enough during the summer and there are not many stretches of white water. But on the Phutiatsana River the water flow is good so you don't have to do much paddling. The *Lesotho–Durham Anglican Link* run trips, and a few unhurried hours will end you up near Mazenod, from where staff from the *Link* will take you back to Maseru. Trips cost M50 for a half-day, and M100 for a full day. Contact Paul Middleton at the *Lesotho–Durham Anglican Link* (☎ & fax 31 2614).

Car Rental *Avis* (☎31 4325/35 0328); *Budget* (☎31 6344); *Executive Car Hire* (☎31 4460).

Emergencies Ambulance ☎121; Fire ☎122; Police ☎123.

Hospitals *Queen Elizabeth II Hospital*, Kingsway (☎31 2501); Maseru Private Hospital, Thetsane Rd (☎31 3260).

Libraries American Cultural Centre, LNDC shopping centre, Kingsway (☎31 2335); British Council, corner of Kingsway and Lerotholi Rd (☎31 2609).

Philatelic services Lesotho stamps are famous and highly prized. If you're a keen collector, contact the philatelic bureau of the post office. Or Andrea Grimmett (☎31 6981), a collector with many years experience, has a wider selection.

Post office The main one is on Kingsway, with a new one being built opposite (Mon–Fri 8am–4.30pm, Sat 8am–noon).

Radio You can get better BBC World Service radio reception here than anywhere else in Africa, on 90.2FM.

Taxis *Citycab* (☎32 3490); *Hoohlo Bereng* (☎32 4035); *Max Taxis* (☎32 5935); *Moonlight Taxis* (☎31 2695); *Silver Star* (☎31 1603).

Travel Agents *Afric-Go-Tours* (☎32 5367); *American Express* (☎31 2554); *Execu Travel* (☎32 5113).

Around Maseru

Although it makes doesn't make sense to spend much of your time in Lesotho in Maseru, if you can help it, you'll find a number of rewarding places to visit within only a short distance of the capital.

The Word, the Flesh and the Devil excursions

Just behind the *Lesotho Sun* hotel, there's an easily accessible climb to three peaks known locally as **the Word, the Flesh and the Devil**, which were a favoured hangout for snipers during the Gun War (see p.585). Walk between the fences separating the hotel and *Friebel Houses*, and straight up the hill past a succession of large boulders. After less than twenty minutes you'll reach the northernmost peak, the Word, where you'll find a survey beacon and excellent views of Maseru and the distant mountains. From there you can walk along the ridge to the other two peaks, the Flesh and then the Devil, though neither provide such good views.

Lancers Gap

Lancers Gap is an extraordinary ridge a short distance from town, with a great gap in the middle through which the road passes, so named because a Lancers regiment was allegedly ambushed and defeated there during the Gun War. In fact, the regiment was ambushed somewhere else, but it doesn't really matter, as this is still a great place to scramble around and look out both on Maseru and the mountains in the east. To get there, take the Main Road North from Maseru, and turn right at the Lancers Gap turn, which is at a major junction with traffic lights. The ridge is a few kilometres further along, up a very steep incline which you ascend along a good-quality hairpin bend road.

Qeme Plateau

The large T-shaped **Qeme Plateau**, which measures over 25 square kilometres, is only a few kilometres south of Maseru, near the South African border. It provides superb vistas into the Free State and east into Lesotho and is a good place for a day-trip from the capital. The usual way to get there is by going along the Main Road South as far as Mantsebo, turning right at the crossroads, then turning left after a *Frasers Store*. Leave your transport there, look out for a diagonal line climbing the plateau from left to right and make for this. You soon hit a footpath which takes you to the top. To climb to the top and back takes three or four hours.

Alternatively, take the Pioneer Road off the Kingsway out of Maseru, which reverts from tar to a good dirt road once outside the city limits, and follow it down to a junction a few kilometres further down, where the road deteriorates, so don't take this route if it has been raining recently. If you take the left-hand fork, you'll find yourself driving down the east side of Qeme, and will eventually find yourself at *Frasers Store*. The right-hand fork is much less travelled, and takes you through beautiful countryside along the western part of the plateau. Look out for a cleft in the plateau's ridge, and park at its foot at the village of Ha Mapholo. Leaving your car here is quite safe. Walk through the village and make for the cleft; you'll find that the first part of the climb is pretty obvious, but two-thirds of the way up you'll need either inspired guesswork or the help of one of the many herd boys who are usually clambering around here with their cows and goats. The climb takes about two hours there and back.

Once at the top, the boulders and grasslands make for an excellent stroll and picnic spot, albeit not much else. Make sure you've left yourself enough time to get back down before dark. From Ha Mapholo, you can either return the way you came or carry on a few kilometres, at which point the road improves, finally taking you to Main Road South just north of Morija.

Thaba Bosiu

THABA BOSIU is Lesotho's most important historical sight, a steep mountain with a large flat top about 20km east of Maseru that was the capital of the kingdom in the days of Moshoeshoe I. Although it has been declared a world heritage site by UNESCO, nothing has yet been done to develop it, and there's not that much to see once you reach the top. However, it is a place of great significance to the people of Lesotho, and the burial ground of the country's kings, and as such well worth a visit.

Moshoeshoe I trekked with his followers to Thaba Bosiu in 1824, in a bid to settle somewhere far from the warrior clans then terrorizing the flat plains to the north and west, and somewhere that would be extremely hard for anyone to capture. Thaba Bosiu, with its good grazing and seven or eight freshwater springs on top, fitted the bill, although it wasn't long before warrior clans, including Afrikaner ones, found their way here – although none were able to take the mountain, which has earned it, and Moshoeshoe, a good deal of mystique.

The name means "Mountain of the Night", perhaps because, as the legend has it, Moshoeshoe first arrived there at night. A more compelling reason, and the one most Sotho prefer, is that the mountain, which does not look particularly high or impressive by day, grows inexorably as night falls, becoming huge and unconquerable, before slipping back to more hill-like normality during the daytime.

There is a tourist information building (daily 8.30am–4pm), where you arrive, which will charge a small fee for information leaflets and an official guide to show you around. He takes you up the **Khubelu Pass** where the Afrikaner General Louw Wepener was killed trying to storm the mountain in 1865 (see below), past the rock where Sotho warriors used to watch out for approaching enemy forces and to the remains of Moshoeshoe's European house, built for him by army deserters living on the mountain top. From there, it is a short walk to the slight remains of Moshoeshoe's royal court and then to the royal graveyard. The tombs of Moshoeshoe I and most of the monarchs are marked with simple stone cairns, except the latest, of Moshoeshoe II, who was killed in a car crash in 1996, which is a more elaborate affair, adorned with plastic flow-

---

TAKING THABA BOSIU (BY STRATEGY)

Fresh from conquering much of the flat land east of the Caledon in 1828, the Ngwane were the first to attack **Thaba Bosiu**, but were badly beaten, after which they never troubled Moshoeshoe again. The mixed-race Kora people also harried Thaba Bosiu in 1831, often making away with and enslaving the villagers living beneath it, but always driven off the mountain proper by Moshoeshoe's fighters. The warrior, Mzilikhazi, of the Ndebele, who later conquered much of modern-day Zimbabwe, tried to take the mountain the same year, but his men were defeated by the mass of great boulders flung down from the top by the Sotho; Moshoeshoe is reputed to have sent the Ndebele a large number of fat oxen after their defeat, an unprecedented move for a victorious chief – as if to say that he understood that their attack had been inspired by hunger and that he wanted to help them out. At any rate, Mzilikhazi never came back that way.

There followed a twenty-year period of relative calm, during which time, when Moshoeshoe was on the mountain, he would receive visitors in a beautifully tailored dark-blue military uniform, complete with cloak, and offer them tea from a prized china tea service. He allowed the French missionary, Eugene Casalis, to establish a mission at the bottom of the mountain in 1837, and employed him as his secretary and interpreter. In 1852, a British punitive force led by the Cape governor, Sir George Cathcart, didn't even make it as far as the mountain, instead being attacked a short distance away by a well-armed mass of Moshoeshoe's troops, who forced their hasty withdrawal. Afrikaner forces fighting for the Orange Free State (OFS) made a brief attempt on Thaba Bosiu in 1858, but came back in a more determined manner, armed with heavy artillery, in 1865, and began steadily shelling the mountain, launching two simultaneous assaults a few days later. Eight men made it to the top, but were seriously wounded as soon as they did so, and speedily retreated back down. A week later, more Afrikaner troops and the OFS president turned up, and another assault was launched. General Wepener led his men right to the top of the Khubelu Pass, but he was shot at the top and mortally wounded. The Sotho then pressed a counter-attack, and the Afrikaner forces withdrew. They continued the siege for a month, though, during which time most of the livestock on Thaba Bosiu died of hunger and the Sotho became so short of bullets that they melted down the shells being fired at them to make home-made ones.

Although they won this battle, the Sotho lost the war, and Moshoeshoe signed a humiliating treaty in 1866 which surrendered most of Lesotho's farmland to the OFS. Four years later, the old king died and was buried on the top of Thaba Bosiu. Since then, every Sotho king has been buried there, including the latest to die, Moshoeshoe II, in 1996.

ers. If you look to the east of the mountain, you get a great view of Qiloane, a strange cone-shaped mountain with a large nodule on the top, which apparently was the inspiration for the distinctive Basotho Hat building.

Around the other side of the mountain is a kind of cave village where the royal household used to hide during attacks, but which were lived in and decorated with rock paintings by the San who lived there before them. A guide who usually hangs around the Khubelu Pass can take you to them, and include a visit to the traditional healer who is living in one of the caves at the moment. The caves are about a four-kilometre drive from the Khubelu Pass, followed by a short walk.

Practicalities

To **get to Thaba Bosiu by car**, take the Main Road North, turn off at the Lancers Gap junction, and continue until a T-junction about 5km further along. Turn left at the junction and Thaba Bosiu is about 3km further along on the right. You'll find a number of **minibus taxis** going from Maseru to here and back during the day, from the main Maseru bus station.

There is good **accommodation** next to the mountain at the *Mmelesi Lodge* (☎35 7215 or 35 7216, fax 31 2369; ②), which has a plush bar and pleasant restaurant serving moderately priced meat and fish dishes, and comfortable rondavels out the back with en-suite bathrooms.

Roma and Semonkong

Southeast of Maseru, the historic Catholic mission and university town of **Roma** is worth a stop, and the road from here to the town of **Semonkong** is an epic drive through the sandstone and stunning basalt peaks of the Thaba Pusoa range of the Lesotho Highlands, past a succession of remote and relaxed-looking villages filled with Lesotho's characteristic dry-stone-walled rondavels. On the way you'll pass the *Semonkong Lodge* – one of the best places to stay in the country, and only a short distance from the spectacular Semonkong (LeBihan) Falls, which crash down from nearly 200m to the Maletsunyane River below.

Roma

About 30km from Maseru along a good road, the mission town of **ROMA** has a beautiful location in strangely sculpted sandstone foothills and is home to the unlovely campus of the **University of Lesotho**, which began life as Pius XII College, run by the Roman Catholic Church and, between 1964 and 1971, was the university of all three of the former British southern African protectorates, now Lesotho, Botswana and Swaziland. You can buy phonecards and make use of their public phone boxes, which are rare in Lesotho, but there's not much to see on campus, except of course the cream of Lesotho's young elite in action. A kilometre or so further up the road from the university, lined with a succession of schools and colleges, is **Roma Mission**, most of which was built in 1862. Though grander, and intentionally so, than its evangelical counterpart in Morija (see p.612), the mission is still a little run-down these days, and there's not much reason to linger – although its extension to accommodate the grave of one Father Gerard is a classic of Catholic kitsch. Father Gerard was a founder member of the Mission and celebrated for restoring a young girl's sight through prayer, for which he has recently and posthumously been beatified (he died in 1940).

Practicalities

There are several **buses** and many more **minibus taxis** travelling each day between Maseru and Roma, which is one of the busiest public transport routes in the country.

The journey costs M5. Once you're here, the Mission will reluctantly put you up if you beg them, but the best **accommodation** is undoubtedly at the *Trading Post Guest House* (☎34 0202; ①) at the western end of Roma. Built in 1903 as a trading store by the Thorn family, this self-catering guesthouse has been lived in by them ever since. You can camp, stay in rondavels, or in the house itself. They've added a swimming pool and have one horse for pony trekking in the surrounding sandstone hills. To find the guesthouse, look out for a sign on the right of the main road as you enter Roma from the Maseru side, marked to the *Manonyane High School* and the *Trading Post*, and travel 100m up the dirt road. The accurately named *Roberto's Liquor Restaurant*, mainly used by students and opposite the university, is the only place to **eat** in Roma. The restaurant dishes up inexpensive, good-value food which you can wash down with a spectacular selection of alcoholic beverages that far surpasses anywhere in Maseru for choice. Right next door is the last place you can buy **fuel** before Semonkong.

Semonkong and around

The road from Roma to Semonkong is one of the most spectacular in Lesotho, with views galore as you climb higher and higher into the Highlands. Where the tarred road turns to gravel at Moitsupeli, look ahead towards the twin summits of the appropriately named **Thabana liMele** ("Breast Mountains"). The northern summit is climbable without special gear if you can find the cleft on its northern side. Just park at the next village of **Ha Dinzulu**, let people know where you are going, cross the Makhalaneng River and make your way up as far as you can. If you make it to the top, it's about seven hours there and back.

The road from Ha Dinzulu continues to climb until peaking at 2000m on Nkesi's Pass and then dropping down to the village of Ramabanta, where you cross the Makhalaneng River and then drive up to 3000m by Thaba Putsoa itself, before descending gently to the curiously straggled town of **SEMONKONG**. Only inhabited by the San until the 1880s, Semonkong began life after the Gun War as a refuge for displaced Sotho from the Lowlands. In town, you'll find a few basic stores, plenty of bars stocking a quite remarkable selection of beers and ciders, and even a post office and bank, though you should not rely on either for vital business. The roads in town are bad but not impassable, and it's worth going to the ubiquitous *Frasers Store* just to check out the Wild West style clientele, dressed mostly in blankets and gumboots, with their ponies hitched to a post at the entrance.

Practicalities

Semonkong is about a six-hour drive from Maseru if you don't stop long in Roma. The daily bus takes considerably longer. If you miss the bus, which usually leaves Maseru before 7am (enquire the day before for current times), you can always take public transport to Roma and then a minibus taxi from there, though these stop running by mid-afternoon. Alternatively, you can charter a flight to the airstrip in town from the Mission Aviation Fellowship for M600 (☎31 3640).

There is **accommodation** right next to the airstrip at the *Mountain Delight Lodge* (☎32 0454; ②), which offers pleasant rondavels, a quiet private bar and restaurant, and a jovial public one with kitchen attached, serving inexpensive takeaways of Sotho food. Far more soothing though, in a valley by the river on the outskirts of town, is the excellent *Semonkong Lodge* (☎051/92 2730; fax 051/92 3313; ①–②), where you can self-cater, *braaing* or making use of the well-equipped and spacious kitchen, or just tuck into the lodge's excellent home cooking. There's a great bar area with a pool table and a good selection of music (when the CD player is working) and friendly, laid-back management. You can camp, or stay in cosy dorms or doubles. Unusually for accommodation outside Maseru, the lodge takes *V isa*.

DONGAS AND SOIL EROSION IN LESOTHO

Travelling around in Lesotho's scarred and treeless landscape, it's hard to believe that the country was once the grain basket of the region. Yet, during the nineteenth century, the kingdom exported food to the neighbouring Orange Free State (OFS) and to Kimberley and the Rand to feed the thousands of diamond- and gold-mine workers. The problems began with the expropriation of the best land by the OFS in the 1860s, which forced the Sotho to start farming hilly areas that had previously only been used for winter grazing. This process continues to this day, and you will even see crops being grown at over 2000m in districts like Semonkong and Mokhotlong. Mountains are no substitute for fertile plains, however, and Lesotho has been a net importer of food since the 1920s.

The ecological effect of the sustained and unrelenting cultivation of the Lesotho mountains has been devastating. Already poor soil fertility has plummeted and, more seriously, huge quantities of topsoil are simply washed away with each summer rains, often ending up as silt in the rivers of the Eastern Cape. In many places, so much topsoil has gone that great ravines called **dongas** have opened up. These, though they often look green enough, in fact tend to be so close to the surface rock that they are useless for serious cultivation.

Efforts have been undeway to slow this process for some time, most noticeably through the neat terracing of fields set on hillsides, with layers of grass interspersed with the crops. However, the sad truth, which underpins the call by Lesotho's politicians for the Eastern Tree State to be returned to the kingdom, is that Lesotho cannot support its two million population.

The lodge will also arrange pony trekking for about M100 per person per day, with an extra M15 for each night you stay out in a village en route, and M30 per day for the guide.

Around Semonkong: Kentane and Semonkong falls

From Semonkong, it will take you a day's walk or pony trek west (see "Practicalities") over some pretty high mountains to the pristine 120-metre-high **Kentane Falls**. The Falls are inaccessible by any other means of transport, and the pony trek is reckoned to be one of the best in the country.

Rather easier to reach are the **Semonkong Falls**, a pretty 5-kilometre-walk from town through the maize fields and grazings that adorn the banks of the Maletsunyane River, though the path is slippery in parts. (It's possible to drive but you risk getting your car broken into if you go down to the bottom.) Also known as the LeBihan Falls, after the French missionary who was the first European to see them, the dramatic Semonkong ("smoking water") Falls drop nearly 200m down a sheer and scary cliff surrounded on all sides by natural vantage points, and into an exotic and swimmable pool. There's a path down to the bottom which takes three or four hours there and back, though it's well worth the journey, particularly if you fancy the swim, or if you want to camp. The water at the foot of the Falls usually freezes by June, but the waterfall keeps going all winter, spraying the surrounding rocks with ice and forming an impressive ice cage over the pool.

The road to Thaba Tseka

The small village of **NAZARETH** is just beyond the turn to Roma on the central A3 route, which runs over Lesotho's Central Mountain Range to the small district capital of Thaba Tseka, over 100km from Maseru. A few kilometres north of Nazareth are what were once some of the finest rock paintings in the country at **Ha Baroana**. The paintings are still impressive, with clearly discernible figures of animals, dancers and hunters, but they have been vandalized and washed away by child guides who throw water at them to make them clearer for tourists. To get to the paintings, either walk or drive along a difficult dirt road to Ha Matela and walk the last 4km from there, or drive up the next turn to the left, also along a bad road, which takes you straight to the site.

East from Nazareth along the tarred road, the countryside gradually changes from the cultivated Lowlands to the more sparsely populated mountains. A short distance beyond Nazareth is the **Tollgate Caravan and Camping Park** (☎37 0206; ①), the only official campsite in the country. Close by, the **Molimo Nthuse Lodge** (☎31 2922, fax 31 0318; ②) is more luxurious, perched by a stream at the foot of a hill, off the road at the point where the tar starts to peter out. With comfortable rooms, some with open fires, and a stylish rondavel-type dining room, this is a good place to stay, particularly if you are interested in trout fishing or hikes in the surrounding hills – though its moderately-priced meals are rather mediocre.

The lodge is also the perfect stopping off point if you are on your way to the **Basotho Pony Trekking Centre** (☎31 4165), a short distance further down the road (2hr by bus but less by car from Maseru). This is about the least expensive place to pony trek in Lesotho, with a two-day/one-night trek for example costing only M125 per person, plus M10 for overnight accommodation. As usual, you need to bring all your supplies with you. A shorter trek, and also suitable for hiking (2hr each way), is to the impressive Qiloane Falls on the Makhaleng River, due north of the *Lodge* and *Trekking Centre*.

The tarred road finally gives way to dirt and gravel at the epic **Blue Mountain Pass**, more than 2600m high, from where you will find commanding views of the surrounding mountains, though the views are even better if you climb the hills on either side of the pass. From there, the road descends first into the village of **LIKALANENG**, and then, after briefly rising once more, to the village of **MARAKABEI** on the banks of the Senqunyane River, where you can buy fuel. The lodge marked on the roadside approaches to the village is now closed.

You can buy fuel too at **MANTSONYANE**, about 20km further east, where there are also a few take-away restaurants serving Sotho dishes and some sparsely filled trading stores. This is as far as you can safely go with a car that doesn't have high clearance; if you still want to press on, there are buses going on to Thaba Tseka.

Thaba Tseka

The road into **THABA TSEKA** is a dramatic one, peaking in the heart of the Central Mountain Range at the Mokhoabong Pass (2880m) before descending to the town, which is over 2200m above sea level. Once here, though, you may wonder why you made the effort, as there is very little in this 1980s purpose-built administrative centre except buses to take you somewhere else. The only place to stay is the *Agricultural Training Centre* (☎90 0304; ①), a long prefabricated building with a kitchen that's often full during the week. There are no restaurants in town, though there are one or two

---

SANDSTONE AND BASALT

Lesotho is the only country in the world that lies entirely above an altitude of 1000m, and as such thoroughly deserves the name "the mountain kingdom". The Lesotho Lowlands would be Highlands anywhere else, and are made of **sandstone**. Right across the country, at about 1400m, the sandstone gives way to a dark grey rock called **basalt**, which was thrown up by volcanic eruptions several million years ago. Roughly marking the beginning of the Lesotho Highlands, basalt is a hard rock and resists erosion, unlike the sandstone, which has been carved by the wind over the millennia into an infinite variety of shapes that have rendered the hills the natural sculptures of the kingdom.

stores serving Sotho food to take away. There is no road south to Semonkong and the Sehlabathebe National Park, though there are hikeable trails if you have the time. There is a road to Sani Pass from Thaba Tseka, but it is so bad that you should ask how it is beforehand and only attempt it in a high-quality, 4WD vehicle, in which case it should be a spectacular ride.

The road to Katse is much better and, although you still shouldn't attempt it in an ordinary saloon car, there are a number of buses plying the route. From Katse there's a perfect tarred road to Hlotse in the north (see p.606). Otherwise, your only option is to go back the way you came, towards Maseru.

THE NORTHERN DISTRICTS

The route from Maseru to Sani Pass takes in the best of both Lesotho's Lowlands and Highlands, from the wind-carved sandstone hills on the way to **Teya-Teyaneng**, a hill town famed for its woven crafts, to the epic mountain passes of the "roof of Africa route" that runs from **Butha-Buthe** to Sani, and the new road from **Hlotse** across the Central Mountain Range to the Katse reservoir. There are plenty of fascinating out-of-the-way treats along the way, like the remarkable **cave houses** at Mateka, or the **dinosaur footprints** near the Tsikoane Mission, a short distance from Hlotse. You'll find plenty of good places to stay (though some take a little finding), particularly in the Highlands where a succession of well-located lodges make the perfect bases from which to hike the surrounding mountain countryside. A new attraction is the just-completed **Katse dam**, which collects water from Lesotho's south-flowing rivers, from where it is pumped north, thanks in part to the 185-metre-high dam. In an ordinary car, you can get as far as **Oxbow**, southern Africa's best skiing venue; though if you have the time, the driving skill and a good enough vehicle (such as a 4WD), you can go on to tackle the infamous **Sani Pass**, which provides the most dramatic entrance there is into South Africa, down the western reaches of the mighty Drakensberg.

Maseru to Hlotse

Sped through by most travellers on their way to the more spectacular regions of the Highlands, you'll find the lowland stretch between Maseru to Hlotse nonetheless has a number of attractions to offer, if you look for them. The caves at **Mateka** are architecturally the most fascinating in Lesotho and well worth a special trip, and the woven crafts in **Teya-Teyaneng** are of superb quality and design. The busy town of **Hlotse** has less of interest, but nearby is one of the largest collections of dinosaur footprints in the country.

There are **two good roads** from Maseru to Teya-Teyaneng (commonly known as Ty). The most commonly used is the **Main Road North**, which takes you efficiently through the scenic, sandstone mountain-studded Lowland journey. Only a few kilometres after leaving Maseru, you'll come to the hexagonal, red-roofed *Palace Hotel* (☎50 0700, fax 50 0010; ②), whose rooms have opulent beds and decent bathrooms, but balconies with no divisions between the rooms, which makes the rooms less secure than they should be. The hotel restaurant serves steaks, chops and fish for moderate prices. The *Galaxy Nightclub,* next door, opens on Fridays and Saturdays till late, and fills up when there's something special on. From the hotel, it's only an hour's drive to Ty, though it takes a little longer by bus.

A good alternative to the Main Road North, which takes you near the most fascinating caves in Lesotho, is the **Sefikeng Road**. To take this, you follow the Main Road North out of Maseru, and turn right after a short distance at the sign pointing to

Sefikeng; you soon find yourself on the Berea plateau, from where you can look down on the Lowlands to your left. At Sefikeng, turn left at the *Paradise General Dealer*, along a short patch of dirt track, and then onto the tar road towards Mateka.

Mateka

Getting to **MATEKA** by public transport or hitching is possible, but is an exercise in considerable patience. If you're driving, leave your car at Mateka, and enlist one of the many children usually hanging around to take you on the half-hour walk down the hill to the cave houses. The seven cave houses here have been sculpted out of mud under a huge rock overhang, and look more like igloos or West African mud architecture than anything you usually find in southern Africa. They are still being lived in, but their laid-back inhabitants don't mind you taking photographs, or simply goggling at what are the best-kept architectural secrets in the country.

Due to the tragic death of the chief and chief's son who were running it, the *Teng Lodge*, which is signposted from Mateka, is not really open, but if you make the tricky eight-kilometre journey here, across a seemingly impassable river (wade in first to check the depth, and take it at speed) and some dodgy stretches of dirt road, the new chief (who is the old chief's wife) will let you stay there for a donation only, and send someone round to give you hot water in the morning. You'll stay in a lovely rondavel looking out onto the Berea Mountains, but you'll need candles, food and cooking gear as the lodge has none of these. The chief can also provide a guide to take you to some remarkable, unvandalized San rock paintings about one hour's walk away, through gentle hills, maize fields and charmingly secluded villages.

Once you are back in Mateka, it is only a half-hour drive to Ty, and if you are travelling under your own steam, you'll find the occasional minibus taxi or private vehicle plying what is a good, tarred road, though you will probably have to wait a while.

Teya-Teyaneng and around

TEYA-TEYANENG, which means "place of shifting sands" after the sometimes treacherous sandy patches on the nearby river, straggles out over a hill; it has a compact centre but suburbs that meander several kilometres north and east. The main reason for coming here, apart from to pass through on your way to the northern Highlands, is that it is the **crafts capital of Lesotho**, specializing in all manner of weavings, from luxurious jerseys to elaborately designed wall-hangings.

There are three **weaving outlets** in town. *Setsoto Weaving* (Mon–Sun 8am–5pm), opposite the *Blue Mountain Inn* off a signposted road west of the Main Road, has a good selection, as well as crafts from elsewhere in the region, like Shona soapstone carvings from Zimbabwe and candles from Swaziland. Just before Ty's centre, off the Main Road from Maseru, turn left down a dirt track to another tarred road to find the small showroom of *Hatooa Mose Moasali* ("women must stand up and work hard") (Mon–Sun 8am–5pm). This women's collective sells particularly beautiful weaving, though they keep a fairly limited range in stock. Their catalogue displays some very special wall hangings, which you need to order from the women, as they take a week or two to make. A signposted turn to the right off the Main Road, just before Ty if you are coming from the south, takes you to the pleasant sandstone Anglican **St Anges Mission**, the home of *Helang Basali Handicrafts* (daily 8am–5pm). The showroom has an excellent selection of woven crafts, again including some very elaborate items, and in the workshop next door you can watch the craftswomen working on the wall hangings from great looms that stretch nearly to the ceiling.

CULTURE AS FASHION: THE BLANKET AND THE HAT

In a region of Africa where **traditional dress** has all but died out among ordinary people, Lesotho stands out as the exception. It's true that the **mokorotlo** (the Sotho traditional hat) is not quite as widespread these days, but you still occasionally see its distinctive cone and bobble in Lesotho, and in South Africa it is widely worn by Sotho migrant workers in the South Africa, where it is a convenient badge of ethnic distinction. Modelled on the shape of the Qiloane mountain near Thaba Bosiu, and made of woven straw, the *mokorotlo* has become the standard Sotho souvenir, sold in every craft shop, usually for M20 or less.

More prevalent than the *mokorotlo* is the Sotho **blanket**, still worn by men and women all over the country. At the time when king Moshoeshoe I was presented with a blanket by European traders in 1860, there were hardly any in his kingdom, with people wearing *karosses* made of animal hides instead. However,by 1872 traders were reporting insatiable demand for the blankets. Made from high-quality woven cloth, they were originally manufactured in Birmingham, England, and are today made in Port Elizabeth, South Africa. The ubiquitous *Frasers Stores*, which you find all over the country, first established themselves by selling blankets, and still stock them today, although the *Lesotho Blanket Company* in Maseru is the cheapest place to buy them. Good ones costs about M200, and if you do buy one don't forget to buy an outsized safety pin to tie the blanket with.

The blankets are essentially practical items; they keep the body at an even temperature except when it's really hot outside (although the Sotho wear them whatever the weather); they don't absorb much water, and they do not easily catch light, which is handy when you are dozing by an open fire. Blankets are also associated with fertility, which is why some carry the design of a maize cob, a Sotho symbol of fertility and prosperity. Young brides are supposed to wear a blanket around their hips until their first child is conceived, and boys wear different blankets before and after circumcision.

Most blankets have stripes on them that are supposed to lie horizontally when you wear the blanket. A curious feature of the design of some blankets is their retention of British imperial symbolism. One popular design features a large crown at its centre; another shows warplanes sporting British military markings. However, although they always were (and remain) foreign imports, and are the commodities on which many European trader fortunes have been built, the blankets remain quintessentially Sotho, and a source of national pride.

Practicalities

Ty's **bus and taxi ranks**, as well as plenty of **fuel stations**, are all on the side of the Main Road, alongside a number of undistinguished fast-food and take-away stores. There is plenty of **public transport** running from Ty to Maseru, and further north to Hlotse and Butha-Buthe, and you rarely have to wait long.

You'll find the **post office**, which is reasonably functional, off the Main Road to the left, on the only other major road in town. Follow this for a kilometre or so to reach the *Blue Mountain Inn* (☎50 0362; ②), the only **accommodation** in town. A spacious hotel with old-fashioned but comfortable cottages at the side to stay in, the *Blue Mountain* also has Ty's only **restaurant**, which serves tasty, inexpensive meals with quite a good wine selection to accompany them, and the town's only **nightclub**, which is busy and recommended on a Saturday night. Both the private and public bars are popular too, and though the swimming pool is empty and cracked the surrounding garden is a fine place in which to drink and relax.

Kolonyama

A village about 10km from Ty, across the Phutiatsana River and then up the hill, **KOLONYAMA** is home to *Beadazzled* (daily 9am–5pm), which sells an excellent selection of bead crafts for relatively expensive (but fair) prices. There are plenty of inexpensive items if you are on a tight budget, and some temptingly spectacular ones for M75 and upwards.

Maputsoe

A rough border town opposite the South African town of Ficksburg, **MAPUTSOE** is not a good place to stay long, if you can avoid it. Fortunately, the border is open 24 hours a day, and there is lots of public transport to Maseru and Hlotse and the north, so you shouldn't have to linger.

The town's main streets are filled with migrant workers commuting between Lesotho and South Africa, among whom are an uncomfortable number of hustlers who can spot strangers in town a mile off. Many seem to congregate at Maputsoe's only **accommodation**, the *Maputsoe Hotel* (☎43 0621;①), near the border, and usually filled with heavy drinkers and gamblers stuffing money into the slot machines. The hotel's plain but functional rooms are around the back, a short distance from the general commotion. The main street also has plenty of takeaways, of which the *Captain Dorego's* is probably the best of them. There's a 50kmh speed limit leaving town and plenty of police about, so take care if you are driving.

Hlotse (Leribe)

A dilapidated but pleasant little Lowland town named after the local river, **HLOTSE** was founded in 1876 by the Anglican missionary, Reverend John Widdicombe, and suffered repeated siege during the 1880 Gun War. Since then it has kept a low profile and, apart from a few shops and department stores, the only thing to see in town are the battered remains of a small military tower built by the British and now practically falling down.

There is, however, one good local attraction, a set of **dinosaur footprints** a few kilometres south of the town, left off the Main Road to Ty, at the turn-of-the-century **Tsikoane Mission**. You'll need to climb up the rock overhang above the church, preferably with the help of a guide, where you'll find over forty pretty clear imprints.

On the road **north of Hlotse** towards Butha-Buthe, you will see on your right the **Leribe plateau**, which gives the town its other name, and the **Leribe Mission**, founded in 1859 by François Coillard, at its foot. French and Sotho missionaries headed from here to modern-day Zambia in the 1870s, founding the Barotseland Mission there. The mission is only a short walk off the main road, though frankly there's not much to see there these days.

Practicalities

There is plenty of **public transport** in and out of Hlotse, and it stops just near the post office. For **something to eat**, you'll find Sotho restaurants dotted all over the town, where you can buy inexpensive *pap* and stew or chicken. Otherwise, there's the *Pelican Bar and Steakhouse* just off the main road, which serves inexpensive and sizable meat dishes, or the restaurant of the *Leribe Hotel* (☎40 0559; ②), which is the town's main **accommodation**. At the hotel, you have a choice of rondavels or terraced rooms overlooking a pleasant garden, which are all fine except those with numbers in the thirties, which are next to a large and noisy tank. The somewhat staid restaurant serves moderately priced meat and fish dishes and the occasional vegetarian pasta, and also, unusually for Lesotho, filter coffee. The only other place to stay in town is the *Agricultural College* (①) on the old road from Hlotse to Butha-Buthe, just before it meets the new road. There are basic dorms here and, though the college is not really geared to taking in outsiders, its staff will let you stay if you ask nicely.

Butha-Buthe to the Sani Pass

The road from **Butha-Buthe** is the most popular route into the Lesotho Highlands and travels through some of the highest and most dramatic mountain passes in the country. Though there's not much to do in Butha-Buthe except stock up for the continuing journey, the Butha-Buthe mountain just beyond, where Moshoeshoe I first ruled as chief before moving south (see p.585), rewards the steep climb up with some great views.

Butha-Buthe and around

Not far from the South African town of Fouriesburg (with the Caledonspoort border open 24 hours a day), and the last major town before the Highlands, **BUTHA-BUTHE** has a frontier feel. The main road is clustered with take-away restaurants and stores, and the pavements are filled with Highlanders here for their monthly shopping trip. The town was founded in 1884 because the local chief refused to go to Hlotse to pay taxes, necessitating a new tax centre nearer his residence. Butha-Buthe attracted traders from the outset, and is one of the few towns in Lesotho with much of an Indian community. There is a small crafts shop a short distance up the road to the border selling inexpensive Sotho hats, and run by the owners of the youth hostel (see "Practicalities").

The **Butha-Buthe** ("lie down") mountain, just north of town, is where Moshoeshoe I had his first stronghold before retreating to Thaba Bosiu in 1824 (see p.585). Though a stiff climb to the top, it is not really too difficult to ascend, which was one of the reasons the king felt obliged to move. Once at the top, you get tremendous views of the surrounding area. Not too far from here, 7km north of town on the Main Road, the **Sekubu caves** are 9km down a signposted dirt track. They're worth a look if you have the time; guides will point out some pretty good rock paintings but rather faint dinosaur footprints.

Practicalities

There is absolutely no shortage of **public transport** in Butha-Buthe, all of which congregates at the market in the centre of town. As well as buses and minibus taxis going to Maseru, Katse and Mokhotlong, you can also find buses going to Bloemfontein and Johannesburg.

The only **accommodation** in town is at the *Crocodile Inn* (☎46 0223; ②), just off the main road on the left as you come in from Hlotse. The hotel, which offers large rooms with thin walls but tolerable beds, has seen better days and fills up at weekends with dedicated drinkers who pursue their art in its various bars until well into the next morning. Food at the restaurant is inexpensive, but unimpressive and pretty slow in coming.

More pleasant, but much trickier to get to, is the self-catering *Ramakantane's Youth Hostel* (①), affiliated to the HI, 3.5km from town in the village of Ha Sechele. The hostel is pretty basic, with no electricity but gas instead for lighting and cooking; but the management is friendly and it's a good place to meet Sotho villagers and hike into the hills nearby. You can't drive there without a high-clearance vehicle, so the best thing is to walk. Turn by the *Guys n'Gals* store on the main road and it's about an hour's walk uphill from there. A further choice is the *Cidi Lodge & Supermarket* (☎46 0616; ①), 10km north of town, just by the Main Road. The rooms here are basic but perfectly adequate, there's a bar with a pool table and two restaurants, one serving Sotho food and the other, decorated exclusively with mirrors, serving steaks and chops. The lodge is the last place to get fuel before Oxbow.

The road to Mokhotlong: Oxbow and the Moteng Pass

The road from Butha-Buthe into the Highlands to Mokhotlong is amongst the most dramatic in Lesotho, passing through some particularly striking sandstone cliffs before finally climbing into the basalt. Some 25km into the basalt, up an increasingly winding route, you come to the unpretentious and quiet *Moteng Lodge* (②), set into the mountain, with rooms that are plain and ugly from the outside but reasonably cosy inside. Heaters are provided, which is just as well, as the lodge, like everywhere else in the Highlands, gets freezing in winter. The restaurant, which is rarely busy, serves inexpensive Sotho food, while the private bar's restaurant offers fry-ups and steaks.

A further 20km, over the **Moteng Pass** (2820m) and through stunning mountains and ravines, each one of which would make for perfect hiking, you come to the *New Oxbow Lodge* (☎051/92 2247, fax 051/92 6093; camping ①, doubles ③), whose rooms are comfortable and warm, and you can ski nearby (see below). There is also a cosy and well-stocked bar, and an efficient restaurant serving reasonably priced meals. You'll find good trout fishing on the Malimbamatso River which flows by the lodge, and wonderful hiking in any direction. There are plans to introduce ponies too, but check with the lodge first. It's also worth checking about the state of the roads if you are travelling in winter, as they are liable to ice over from April onwards. If you are driving on from the lodge, remember that this is the last place you can buy fuel before Mokhotlong.

Construction is under way on the road from the lodge to Mokhotlong, but it hasn't been finished yet, and for the moment the road is impassable without a good 4WD, though buses from Butha-Buthe somehow make the journey on a regular basis. There is a steady trickle of private traffic, too, most of which stops off at the Oxbow, where you can ask for a lift. Drivers of government vehicles, however, are usually reluctant to give you one. The road is supposed to be finished by 1998, at which point the drive to Mokhotlong will become no problem, so telephone any of the accommodation at Mokhotlong or Sani to find out the latest.

A short distance from the *Oxbow Lodge* you'll find the *Ski Lodge & Maluti Ski Club* (☎011/887 1319; ①) perched up a track on the left. Run by the *University of the Witwatersrand Ski Club*, you'll need to telephone beforehand and become a temporary member to snow or grass-ski, and to stay at the lodge. The good thing is that skiing is very inexpensive here – M15 a day on the grass, and M80 a day on the snow, including skis, use of the ski lifts and instruction; the bad thing is the drunken behaviour of some of the students, which makes staying at the *Oxbow Lodge* and just going to the club for the skiing an attractive alternative.

The road on to Mokhotlong is often called "the roof of Africa route", and it's easy to see why as you travel over a succession of ever higher passes, peaking at the **Tlaeeng Pass** (3270m), and passing through bleak, sparsely populated but entrancing mountain countryside. If you are adequately equipped, this district is tremendous hiking country, and you'll find the hardy locals who eke out a living here amongst the most hospitable in the country. About 40km from the Tlaeeng Pass, the descent to Mokhotlong begins, and most transport, private and public, stops first at the small village of **MAPHOLA-NENG**, with two well-stocked bars. From here it is only 30km as the crow flies to Mokhotlong, although the road's twists and turns ensure that the actual distance is nearer 50km.

Mokhotlong

Perched on the banks of the Mokhotlong River, **MOKHOTLONG**, whose name means "place of the bald ibis" (although they are rarely seen these days), began life as a police post in 1905. Slowly, the post evolved into a trading centre for the Highlanders of the region, but remained cut off from the rest of Lesotho for years, with radio contact only established with Maseru in 1947. An airstrip was constructed in 1948 and a rudimentary road link built in the 1950s, but Mokhotlong continued to get the bulk of its supplies by pony from Natal, via Sani, for a long time afterwards. Even today, it looks, feels, and *is* remote, with locals usually riding into town for a shop and a drink on ponies, resplendent in their blankets.

Not much happens in town, which is dominated by hurriedly built and decidedly plain breeze-block buildings that compare unfavourably with the immaculately constructed dry-stone-walled dwellings of the surrounding countryside. On Tuesdays things liven up a bit, when Mokhotlong has its livestock sales. Or you can pick up decent cassettes, or just listen to the music blasting out from the *Mamolibeli Music Shop* on the main road at the western edge of town near the *Senqu Hotel*. But otherwise you'll find little to buy except for fast foods from a few stores near the bus stops in the centre of town.

There's no public transport to Sani from Mokhotlong, but there are two daily buses that stop at Butha-Buthe, one leaving at around 6.30am and the other at 8.30am. There are plenty of buses and minibus taxis doing short distances, including the 15km or so to the *Molumong Lodge* (see below), often marked in the direction of "Ha Janteau".

Accommodation

There is a surprising amount of choice of **accommodation** in Mokhotlong: the *Senqu* is the best option in town, the *Farmers' Training Centre* the least expensive, although much the nicest place to stay in the area, for its location, facilities and relaxed atmosphere, is undoubtedly the *Molumong Lodge*, 15km south west of town on the dirt road to Thaba Tseka.

Farmers' Training Centre (☎92 0235). A friendly place, but with limited bedding, hot water only if they are running a course, and no kitchen. You can camp here. Situated at the far eastern end of town, past the hospital, with a bright-red roof. Quite a walk but you can get minibus taxis. ①.

Mokhotlong Hotel (☎92 0212). Reasonable though rather bare rooms with functional en-suite bathrooms looking out onto the mountains, and a public bar popular for its TV, but with hardly any chairs. The restaurant serves moderately priced, but unadventurous, meat-dominated meals. The hotel is at the end of the tarred section of the main road, just beyond the hospital, and unfortunately right next to a blood-stained informal abattoir. ②.

Molumong Lodge (☎033/702 1050). Set in a wonderful mountain location in the village of Ha Rafolatsane, and clearly marked "Molumong" on its red roof. Self-catering, with very cosy double rooms and a great lounge to relax in, the lodge offers inexpensive pony trekking, and is a good place from which to explore and hike. To get there, either take a bus or minibus taxi from Mokhotlong or, if you are driving, take the junction just before Mokhotlong to Sani Pass and then the first right. ①–②.

Senqu Hotel (☎92 0330). The smartest hotel in town, and the first you come to from the Butha-Buthe road, with comfortable rooms, strangely poky corridors, a TV in the public lounge, and tolerable food in its high-ceilinged, echoing restaurant. ②.

Sani and around

Branching off from the Mokhotlong road 5km before the town, the rough gravel and dirt road to **SANI** twists its way in spectacular fashion for nearly 60km along the Sehonkong River, peaking at the **Kotisephola Pass** (3240m) before dropping to 2895m at **Sani Top**. There are plenty of rewarding hikes to be made from Sani Top, including the twelve-kilometre one to **Thabana Ntlenyana** (3482m), the highest peak in the region, which is walkable in a day if you start early enough, and the tough but stunningly beautiful forty-kilometre **Top-of-the-Berg** walk to the Sehlabathebe National Park, which takes about four days.

Although the descent from Sani, down the infamous, hairpin-bend-filled Sani Pass is just about possible in an ordinary car, you'd be much better off with a 4WD, and there is no way you can ascend the pass from the South African side without one. During the winter, the pass is frequently blocked with snow, and rain often renders it very slippery during the summer, so ring the chalet or lodge (below) in advance to find out conditions.

The only **public transport** from Mokhotlong to Sani is the odd minibus taxi, but otherwise you'll need to hitch if you don't have your own vehicle, in which case you should make your way to the junction off the Mokhotlong Road as early as possible, or better still try to arrange a lift in Mokhotlong the day before. From the South African side, someone from the *Sani Lodge* (see below) meets the *Baz Bus* (☎021/439 2323) travelling from Cape Town to Johannesburg at Kokstad, on Tuesdays and Fridays, and can take you directly to the lodge. There's also a door-to-door service from Port St Johns every Thursday (☎033/702 1228), and one from Durban and Pietermaritzburg (contact Pauline Jones: ☎033/701 1017 at home, ☎701 1030 at work).

The **border** is open daily from 8am to 4pm, and there's **accommodation** on both sides. On the Lesotho side is the popular *Sani Top Chalet* (☎033/701 1466; camping and dorms ①, doubles ②), where you can self-cater or let them do the work. Try to book in advance, as it is often full, though you can camp in the chalet's grounds if it is. The chalet's setting is superb, with commanding views of the mountains, and you can hire ponies from there to explore with. Some way down the pass on the South African side is the excellent self-catering *Sani Lodge* (☎033/702 1401; ①–②), primarily aimed at backpackers and run by the knowledgeable Russell Suchet, which has good dorms and doubles, and loads of information on what you can do in the region.

Katse and the Lesotho Highlands Water Project

The **Lesotho Highlands Water Project** is southern Africa's most ambitious engineering feat for decades, and its centrepiece, the **Katse reservoir**, with its huge dam, stands in stark contrast to the rural simplicity that surrounds it. Much of the effort since the project began in 1986 has gone into the road from Hlotse to Katse, and it is now a remarkable journey that's almost worth doing for the drive alone. Once in Katse, you should also take a tour around the dam, whose sheer size and bulk linger in the mind long after the construction's vital statistics and the project's careful propaganda have faded.

The road to Katse

Once amongst the most inaccessible parts of the country, Katse's future has been changed forever by the Lesotho Highlands Water Project, not least by the transformation of its **road**, which used to be a rough track, into one of the best tarred routes in the country. The road begins at Hlotse, from where it is a speedy, unexciting run through the Lowlands to dreary **PITSENG**. Just north of Pitseng is a turn on the right to the *Outward Bound Centre* (☎40 0543), which runs week-long adventure activities for groups, including climbing, abseiling, hiking and kayaking. If really pushed for accommodation, you can probably arrange to stay in one of their very spartan dormitories (③ full board). Pitseng is an important centre for public transport, and is the place to catch a bus or minibus taxi to Katse, and to buy fuel, but apart from that there's absolutely no reason to hang around.

After Pitseng, the road starts a very steep ascent, hitting over 3000m at the **Mafika-Lisiu Pass** in under 30km, making it a punishing journey for most cars, most of which are lucky ever to make it out of second gear. Thanks to some remarkable engineering, the road twists and turns around the mountains, sometimes cutting through them, sometimes jutting out instead, leaving you suspended on the edge, a terrifyingly long way from the ground. There are plenty of places to stop and take in the view, though there have been reports recently of theft (in some cases armed) of tourists who have done just that, so keep a good look out if you stop, and your vehicle in view at all times.

After the Mafika-Lisiu Pass, you start descending to the small village of **HA-LEJONE**, at the northern end of the massive Katse reservoir. Though signposted as if it offers accommodation, the *Marmeso Lodge* is in fact just a good bar with a pool table and customers likely to offer you illicit diamonds, which you would do well not to buy. From Ha-Lejone, the road follows the reservoir, and just after the unmissable **Intake Tower**, which marks the point where the long tunnel carrying water to Gauteng begins, it crosses the water on the impressive new **Malibamatso Bridge**. From here, it climbs once more, reaching 2600m at the **Laitsoka Pass**, and then descending on the approach to Katse.

Katse and the dam

The town of **KATSE** is drab and boring, with uniform box-like houses arranged in an uninspired suburban manner. But the massive dam really is impressive, even if you

---

THE LESOTHO HIGHLANDS WATER PROJECT: THE STORY SO FAR

Lesotho's abundance of water but its shortage of cash, and Gauteng's monetary wealth but water poverty, are the stark facts that have led to the stunningly ambitious **Lesotho Highlands Water Project**. The essence of the project is to divert Lesotho's major rivers, and particularly the Senqu River (which South Africans know as the Orange River), into the Katse reservoir. From here, the water is pumped 45km north through specially constructed tunnels, via a hydroelectric power station near Hlotse, to South African rivers that carry it to the Vaal Dam, which supplies Gauteng. For this, South Africa pays Lesotho $55million a year.

The treaty that started the project was signed in 1986, when South Africa had a government fond of imposing draconian states of emergency on its people, and Lesotho had a military dictatorship; unsurprisingly, popular consultation never featured very strongly in the treaty. There wasn't much of an assessment of the environmental impact of the project either, which is worrying in view of recently reported "seismic activity" induced by the reservoir, though the engineers have been busy assuring everybody that things are OK. Villagers whose homes have been flooded, or who can no longer get from one side of the Katse valley to the other, are not convinced, but their voices will never count for much in a project that is supposed to double the water supply to the most industrialized, influential and populated part of Africa – Gauteng.

The initial treaty only committed the two parties to complete the first of four proposed phases of the project, after which there would be fresh negotiations and agreements, and it seems likely that when these happen both countries will have much more accountable governments than were in place in 1986. Phase 1a, which is now pretty much completed, consisted of the construction of the Katse reservoir and dam wall, the tunnels to South African rivers, and all the road infrastructure. Phase 1b will see the diversion of several rivers into the reservoir and a new dam, all of which is supposed to be completed by 2003. After that, the new negotiations begin, but if all goes according to the original plan, the Senqu will then be repeatedly diverted into the Katse reservoir, and the whole thing will be finished some time in the 2020s. Right now, however, the most impressive engineering feat is the dam wall itself, curved inwards for extra strength to such a degree that when you look down from the top you cannot see the rest of the wall, and experience the uneasy illusion of being suspended in space.

aren't usually interested in engineering. To find out more, make for the blue-roofed **visitor's centre**, just before the town and dam, where you can take in the smooth public relations video of the Lesotho Highlands Development Agency (LHDA), which runs the site. The centre can also provide someone to take you around the dam wall, which is 185m high and up to 60m thick and, if you are lucky, into some of its amazing network of tunnels.

The only **place to stay** in Katse is the *Katse Lodge* (☎91 0202; ②), with functional rooms offering wonderful views of the reservoir and its impressive birdlife, and a good restaurant serving a decent selection of inexpensive meals. Unfortunately, the lodge is small and primarily intended for LHDA workers, so the staff only confirm your reservation a maximum of 48 hours before your arrival, and there's always a good chance that the place will be completely full. If it is, your only other option is the *Agricultural Training Centre* (☎90 0304; ①), which is a long drive on a terrible road in Thaba Tseka (see p.602). At least there is a steady stream of private and public transport from Katse to Thaba Tseka, so you should be able to find something going there, though rarely after 2pm.

For **boat trips** on the dam, which can include a braai, picnic and drinks, contact Alec in Maseru (☎31 7153 office hours, ☎083/250 8167 after hours).

THE SOUTHERN DISTRICTS

The **Southern Districts** of Lesotho hold some of the country's most dramatic countryside, perfect for pony trekking, which you can do from a number of scenically sited lodges. There are a number of small towns, some based around missions founded by the British in the last century – **Malealea** is probably the most handsomely situated, **Morija** the most historic. Further south, you can see dinosaur footprints at **Mohale's Hoek** and, more accessibly, at **Moyeni**, before moving on east to **Qacha's Nek** and the isolated delights of the **Sehlabathebe National Park** beyond, Lesotho's only national park.

Morija to Malealea

The main road south from Maseru, past the airport and the Qeme Plateau (see p.597), soon takes you to historic **Morija**, with its small cluster of mid-nineteenth-century buildings and the only museum in the country. A further 45km away, along a dirt road that gets increasingly scenic as you near your destination, **Malealea** has a smoothly run and comfortable lodge amid wonderful countryside that's perfect for hiking and well-organized pony trekking in wind-carved sandstone hills.

Morija

Just 44km from Maseru, **MORIJA**, the first mission to be established in Lesotho back in 1833, is a pleasant little town at the foot of the Makhoarane Plateau which houses the country's only museum, and Lesotho's oldest building, church and printing press. Granted to three missionaries of the Paris Evangelical Missionary Society (PEMS), Eugene Casalis, Thomas Arbousset and Constant Gossellin, by King Moshoeshoe I, they gave the place the name Abraham bestowed on the mountain where he was reprieved from killing his son by God (it means "God will provide"). Both easy to get to from Maseru with your own and public transport, with buses and minibus taxis running throughout the day in both directions, Morija is also a good spot to pick up transport going further south to Mafeteng and Mohale's Hoek.

The large, red-brick **mission church**, with its impressive teak-beamed roof, is almost always open. Begun in 1847, this is the third church built on this site, using the labour of Pedi economic migrants on their way to the Cape Colony, though its tall steeple was only built in 1905. You cannot, unfortunately, get in to see the historic **printing works** nearby, which have produced Sotho literature since the 1860s and the country's oldest newspaper, *Leselinyana la Lesotho* ("Little Light of Lesotho"), which has been in almost continual publication since 1863.

Most of Morija was razed to the ground by Afrikaner troops in 1858, and almost the only building left standing was the **Maeder House**, built in 1843 and now Lesotho's oldest building. Today, this simple stone house contains a small crafts shop (Mon–Sat 8am–5pm, Sun 2–5pm), selling inexpensive Sotho hats, dolls, carvings, tapestries and batiks. Close by, the **Morija Museum & Archives** (Mon–Sat 8am–5pm, Sun 2–5pm; M4) is a stimulating combination of a geological and fossil exhibition, ethnographic material and historic items of Moshoeshoe and his contemporaries, and a useful commentary on Lesotho's history and modern-day political issues. The geological and fossil displays are presented somewhat drily, although the dinosaur exhibits are striking, but you should find something of interest amongst the ethnographic and historical items, including a succession of treaties broken by the British, Moshoeshoe's china tea set, and a *khau*, the beautiful V-shaped neck ornament awarded to brave Sotho soldiers. The archives have yet to be fully organized and catalogued, but you are allowed to dip into them under supervision and see what you can unearth among the jumble of nineteenth-century missionary tracts and records and some valuable Africana. The museum also produces a **booklet** called "A Guide to Morija", which tells you everything and more that you could possibly want to know about the town, including some pointers to nearby sites of interest. Browse through it in the museum's **tea shop** (Mon–Sat 9am–4.30pm, Sun 2–4.30pm), either outside or in its cool little rondavel.

The best of the **walking trails** marked out from Morija takes about an hour there and back, and leads to a dinosaur footprint on one side of a large rock, halfway up the **Makhoarane Plateau**. To get there, make first for the *Ha Matela Lodge* (see below), up the hill behind the museum, and from there make for the plateau, across a donga, following a succession of red arrows. Though a stiff climb to the rock, much of the path is sheltered by trees and the footprint itself is impressive, though rather faint.

The only **place to stay** in Morija is the self-catering *Ha Matela Lodge* (☎31 6555 or 36 0306; ②), set in a pleasant and secluded spot at the top of the town on the way to the Makhoarane Plateau, and offering a small number of comfortable doubles in a house with a lovely verandah festooned with grapes in the summer. The lodge can also arrange pony trekking for competitive rates.

Malealea

Further on, 85km from Maseru, there isn't much to **MALEALEA**, apart from the popular *Malealea Lodge* (☎ & fax 051/447 3200; e-mail: malealea@pixie.co.za; dorms and camping ①, doubles ②), which has a superb setting in the approaches to the Thaba Putsoa mountain range, and skilled, professional management, that make it one of the finest places to stay in Lesotho. The lodge was originally a trading store, established by the British adventurer Mervyn Bosworth-Smith in 1905, and it was he who wrote the justified inscription "Wayfarer! Pause and behold the Gates of Paradise" at the mountain pass that takes you into the final stretch of the journey to the lodge. There is indeed a magnificent view from there, and if you have your own transport you would do well to heed his advice and pause a moment to take it all in.

The current owners, Mick and Di Jones, have extended the trading store and turned its back into backpackers' dorms and a dining room (though you are also free to self-cater), and have built a series of sturdy rondavels, double rooms and a great little bar nearby. Central to the complex is an open fire, around which local school children gather on some evenings to perform songs and dances for the guests.

Many visitors come to Malealea to hike, and the lodge has mapped out a series of trails, but the main activity is **pony trekking**. The lodge does not own the ponies, but instead acts as an agent for local horsemen who get the bulk of the money. It costs about M100 a day to trek, with a small additional cost for staying in a village overnight. Together with the horsemen, the lodge has worked out a series of guided trips, from short one-hour tours and half-days to as many days as your bottom and your wallet can stand. An excellent two-day adventure is the journey to the **Ribaneng Falls**, which takes you down and over steep sandstone valleys and hills. Although you need to take cooking and sleeping gear with you, the lodge ensures that there is an empty, well-kept rondavel with a gas cylinder in every village you stay in. If you have the time for a four-day journey, your guide will take you all the way east to Semonkong (see p.600), over some particularly beautiful mountains, and through quiet, friendly villages. A good, less pricey alternative to the pony trekking, which is quite hard on the body if you are not used to it, is simply walking and using a pony as a pack animal. The pony can carry four people's packs, provided they are not excessively heavy.

To get to Malealea by public transport from Maseru, take a bus or minibus taxi to Motsekuoa if you can find one, or Morija if you cannot, from where you can easily get one to Motsekuoa. During the day, there is quite a bit of transport from there heading towards Matelilie and the only possible slow bit is after you are dropped off at the junction to Malealea, which is about 8km away. However, almost all the vehicles going that way are likely to give you a lift to the lodge. There is a bus that leaves Mafeteng each morning a little after 6am which goes direct to Malealea. It makes the return journey from Malealea to Mafeteng at 6am.

Mafeteng, Mohale's Hoek and Moyeni

Though there is not much to detain you between **Mafeteng** and **Moyeni**, there are still some good walks in the sandstone hills that surround, including some that lead to interesting sets of dinosaur footprints. You'll also find the best meal for miles around at the *Mohale's Hoek Hotel*, where you can also hire ponies to explore the beautiful and little-visited Mokhele mountain range east of the town of **Mohale's Hoek**. Mafeteng, Mohale's Hoek and Moyeni are all close to the South African border, with Mafeteng the most practical one to use for border crossings, with the most public transport.

Mafeteng and around

The bustling town of **MAFETENG**, 20km from the Van Rooyenshek border post (daily 7am–8pm), is the first you come to in Lesotho if crossing from Wepener in the Orange Free State. It means "the place of Lefeta's people", after the son of a French missionary Emile Rolland, who was the district's first magistrate and was nicknamed Lefeta, or "he who passes", by locals, who regarded him as virtually Sotho except for the fact that he "passed by" initiation school.

The only building of interest in Mafeteng is the **council office** on the main street, which is worth a quick look for the carved animal heads studding its front wall, and a nice statue of a handlebar-moustached Cape Mounted Rifles soldier in the front garden. There are two good nearby excursions, though you'll need your own transport to get to them. The **Luma Pan**, only 3km from town, attracts a good selection of birdlife; you can find it by heading for Wepener, and turning right down the first substantial dirt road you come to. About 20km east of Mafeteng, along a road that deteriorates past the village of Likhoele to the point that you are taking a risk in an ordinary saloon car, is the impressive **Thabana Morena Plateau**, which rises above a village of the same name, and rewards your steep climb with good views of the Free State plains to the west and the Thaba Putsoa mountains to the east.

Practicalities

As befits a border town, Mafeteng has a very busy **bus station** from where you can easily find transport north to Morija, Maseru and Malealea, and south to Mohale's Hoek, Moyeni and beyond. There are **plenty of places to eat** by the bus station and on the main street, the least frenetic of which is probably the *Italian Paradise*, up some steps on the corner of the main street and the bus station road, which in fact doesn't serve Italian food, but chops and steaks instead. Opposite, on the main road, you'll find *Le Joint*, which serves some meals during the day, but becomes transformed at night into a packed but friendly bar. For **accommodation**, there is the *Golden Hotel* (☎700566; ②), an anonymous-looking building offering slot machines, a sad swimming pool, adequate rooms and a small dining room serving meat dishes, that overlooks the street, to the right of the Main Road South from Maseru, just before you enter Mafeteng proper. Your other, rather better choice is the *Hotel Mafeteng* (☎70 0236; ②), which looks like a 1960s airport control tower, and has pleasant rooms and cottages set in a secluded garden with a good swimming pool. The hotel restaurant serves a limited range of moderately priced meat dishes. You'll find the hotel signposted off the Main Road South to Mohale's Hoek.

Mafeteng has a better **nightlife** selection at weekends than most Sotho towns. You can check out *Lenta's Garden Restaurant* near the bus station, which sometimes has music on Friday and Saturday nights, or the rather seedy, mirrored *Las Vegas* disco in the grounds of the *Hotel Mafeteng*, which blasts out soul and South African *kwaito* sounds until 4am on Friday and Saturday nights. Also good for a laugh is the cinema of the *Golden Hotel*, which screens action movies to an appreciative and vocal crowd on Friday evenings at 6pm.

Mohale's Hoek

MOHALE'S HOEK, a short distance from the little-used Makhaleen Bridge border post (daily 8am–4pm), is a rather bedraggled little town, but with one of the best hotels in the area and interesting sites nearby, including some well-preserved dinosaur footprints. Mohale was Moshoeshoe's younger brother, who was appointed by the king as part of his bid to wrest control of the district from chief Moorosi. There are still quite a few of Moorosi's Baphuthi clan here though, whose language is in some ways closer to Xhosa than Sotho.

If you desperately need to do some banking, you'll find the *Standard Chartered* and *Barclays* banks on the main street more efficient than most banks outside Maseru, although changing money and travellers' cheques can still take some time. Otherwise, there's nothing to see or do here, but you'll find an excellent walk to the **Mokhele Mountain**, about 10km east of town. Travel a short distance south on the main road to the little village of Mesitsaneng, and then head 7km east along a rough dirt track to the Maphutseng mission. Just before the mission, turn right down a smaller track, and you'll see a plateau to the right a short walk away, where you'll find some dinosaur footprints and an inscription marking their "discovery" in 1959.

Practicalities

You'll find it hard to work out the system at the busy **bus station** in the centre of Mohale's Hoek, so instead just ask where the bus for your destination is standing. **Minibus taxis** congregate outside the *Standard Chartered Bank*, and between them and the buses you should be able to find transport heading either north or south throughout the day.

BOG STANDARD: THE NEW PIT LATRINE

A new feature of the Lesotho landscape are great numbers of improved **pit latrines** with white chimneys, which are easy to build and hygienic, but hardly to be found in neighbouring South Africa. Their main improvement on the old pit latrines, still in use in the Republic, are that they keep flies that have come into contact with human feces away from humans and their food. Flies are the big problem with pit latrines, as they invariably head for the latrine pit; but with this design once they are in the pit they never get out again.

Typically, flies enter the latrine when someone opens the door, and then fly down through the latrine seat and hole and then into the pit itself. With the old design, they would then fly out the way they came in, but with this one they are attracted by the light at the top of the chimney. However, they cannot escape from it, because of the chimney gauze. As long as people remember to close the lavatory seat and keep the latrine door shut, thus keeping light out of the latrine, this is pretty foolproof, keeping the flies buzzing harmlessly in the pit and chimney rather than on people's food or babies' mouths, and so preventing a great deal of unnecessary dysentery.

The first **accommodation** you come to if entering Mohale's Hoek from the north is the recently established *Monateng Lodge* (☎78 5337; ②), but its rooms are not very good and the lodge has been poorly built – though the public bar is lively and friendly. Much better is the central *Mount Maluti Hotel* (☎78 5224; ②), owned by a white family who have lived in the area for years and can offer plenty of good advice about what to see and do there, as well as arranging inexpensive pony treks and guides. The rooms are comfortable, with TVs, and there's a tennis court and small garden; but the hotel's highlight is its restaurant, which offers first-class cuisine, even for vegetarians, at reasonable prices. As usual, there are also plenty of inexpensive **places to eat** on the main street.

Moyeni and around

MOYENI, which means "place of the wind" and is also known as Quthing, is a curious split-level town established by the British after the Gun War in 1884. The upper half has the police station, the main hotel, a large hospital and one or two pretty useless banks, while the lower half has most of the shops, fuel stations and is where you catch public transport. During the day, there are always plenty of buses and minibus taxis running north towards Maseru, far fewer running east towards Qacha's Nek, and one or two heading for the nearby Telle Bridge border post (daily 8am–10pm), from where you can pick up transport to Sterkspruit in the Eastern Cape.

The most easily accessible **dinosaur footprints** in Lesotho are very near the Moyeni's lower half. Just continue a short distance up the Main Road from the Moyeni turn and they are signposted next to the road on the left. Unlike other footprints in the country, these have been treated to a special visitors' centre. This has fallen into disrepair and offers little information, although a man still works there who motions you towards the variety of clearly discernible prints in the hope of a small tip.

Also worth a visit is the **Masitise Cave**, situated a few kilometres west of Moyeni to the right of the main road. Follow signs to the Masitise Primary and High schools, and at the high school ask for someone to show you the cave. It is a small and sadly very dilapidated brick house, whose dank rooms are filled with decaying stuffed animal heads, built underneath a rock overhang by the PEMS missionary,

A little further on are some much-vandalized and greatly faded **rock paintings**. If you have made it this far, have a brief look also at the pleasant mission **church**, which has a fine bell tower but no bell to go with it.

Accommodation

With the Catholic mission at Villa Moria the only budget **accommodation** option, there are two hotels in town. Neither is of particularly high standard, though the *Mountainside* just about wins on points for its more intimate and friendly atmosphere.

Mountainside Hotel (☎75 0257). Halfway between upper and lower Moyeni, this is a small hotel with mostly decent rooms (check the mattress before you accept a room), half of which look onto the street, while the others are more secluded and quieter. There's a pleasant and cosy private bar, a friendly public one and a good restaurant with a tasty fixed menu that normally has something for vegetarians. ②.

Orange River Hotel (☎75 0257). An ungainly building decorated 1970s-style in hessian and pine, with reasonable but very stuffy rooms, some of whose ceilings are in serious trouble. Curiously, you have to pay in advance. The tolerable restaurant looks out over upper Moyeni and has a good view of the surrounding countryside. ②.

Villa Moria Roman Catholic Mission (☎75 0364). Set in the grounds of the very grand two-towered church, the mission offers clean, inexpensive rooms with communal bathrooms. The complex is just west of Moyeni, to the right of the main road. ①.

Mount Moorosi, Qacha's Nek and the Sehlabathebe National Park

A far less used-route into the Highlands than the northern road from Butha-Buthe to Mokhotlong, the mountain road from **Mount Moorosi to Sehlabathebe** is ruggedly beautiful, with the added bonus of the mighty Senqu (Orange) River winding majestically alongside much of it. If the Katse dam builders have their way, the Senqu will in a few years be much reduced, but for now the chocolate-brown river is normally in full flood. The highlights along the route include **Thaba Moorosi**, the mountain where the outlawed chief Moorosi made his last stand against the British in 1879, the San caves at **Seforong**, and the remote, inaccessible, pristine national park of **Sehlabathebe** itself, the only national park in the country – perfect for fishing, bird-watching and kilometre-upon-kilometre of isolated hiking.

Mount Moorosi and around

Situated near the mighty Senqu (Orange) River, the small town of **MOUNT MOOROSI** is dominated by the *Mitchell's Trading Store* (☎051/673 1011; ①), which serves as the town's main store, garage, fuel station and sole source of **accommodation** available – very pleasant, and complete with open fire and kitchen. All public transport heading east and west stops in town, and it is quite easy to hitch from here too.

Mount Moorosi is named after chief Moorosi, who moved to the region in the 1850s, living in the cliffs around the town. He was an ally of the San and had several San wives, but made an enemy of the British in the 1870s when they captured his son and Moorosi promptly captured him back. British troops retaliated by attacking his stronghold in 1879, but he held out for eight months, until finally captured when the soldiers used scaling ladders on the steep cliffs, and then cut off and publicly displayed his severed head. **Thaba Moorosi**, where the main battle took place, is a kilometre or so further along the main road on the right, and you'll find if you climb it that some stone slabs still bear the inscriptions of the soldiers sent to get the chief. It is quite a tricky climb, though, so be sure to let someone in Mount Moorosi know where you are going.

Bethel Mission

An inexpensive minibus taxi ride will take you down to the ferry point on the Senqu River, with the crossing costing even less. Once on the other side, it is a four-kilometre walk to the **Bethel Mission** (①), which offers lovely self-catering dorms and doubles set in an innovative training centre for solar technology, permaculture and business skills. Short-term visitors are welcome, but if you would like to stay longer write to the mission at PO Box 53, Mount Moorosi 750, as far in advance as you can.

Mphaki and around

Shortly after rounding Thaba Moorosi, the main road leaves the Senqu River, and heads swiftly into the Highlands, peaking after only a few kilometres at the **Lebelonyane Pass** (2456m). The views are superb, but don't enjoy them too much if you are driving as there are no barriers to stop you plunging onto the slopes beneath. You soon come to the small village of **MPHAKI**, which has excellent accommodation at the *Farmers' Training Centre* (②), whose self-catering rondavels are far better equipped than most, as well as a pleasant guesthouse. Ask for Matemoho Mapeli Matsoso at the training centre gate. If you don't fancy self-catering, the *Motsekuoa Liquor Restaurant* opposite the Centre provides inexpensive and tasty Sotho **food** as well as a well-stocked bar.

The tarred road continues for another 10km out of Mphaki, where it reverts to decent gravel. You'll find some interesting **San caves** a short hike off the road a few kilometres further on at **Seforong**, just before Sekake, though they do not – unusually – have rock paintings.

Qacha's Nek

Past Sekake, the road rejoins the southern banks of the Senqu, but deteriorates significantly in quality, though you can still make it with care in an ordinary vehicle. You'll find it a beautiful, undulating drive, amongst the loveliest in Lesotho, though once you reach the approach to **QACHA'S NEK** you'll see depressingly familiar soil erosion and dongas.

Qacha's Nek, named after chief Moorosi's son Ncatya, was an area famed for its banditry when the British founded the town in 1888, in an attempt to forestall the kind of trouble they had experienced with chief Moorosi. Many of the "bandits" were in fact desperate San people, who had been hounded out of everywhere they used to live and now had nothing to survive on. This left the British unmoved, and they hunted them to extermination throughout the 1860s. Moorosi's Baphuthi people had started moving there in the 1850s, rapidly wiping out all the game, and turning the land over to grazing and cultivation instead. The area has unusually high rainfall, and the weather conditions favour conifers, including a few massive Canadian redwoods, giving Qacha's Nek an atmosphere completely different from most of virtually treeless Lesotho.

There's nothing much to see in town, except the elegant **St. Joseph's Church** at its eastern end, but the entire surrounding mountainous countryside is great for **hiking**. Qacha's Nek is also an important **border town** (daily 8am–4pm) and there is usually plenty of public transport heading west towards Moyeni, which leaves from the Shell garage in the centre of town. You can hear the minibus taxis a mile off, because they have cowbells tied to their fronts,. You'll also find transport just over the border heading for the Eastern Cape town of Matatiele, from where it is a simple matter to find buses and minibus taxis going on to Kokstad and beyond.

The best **accommodation** in town is the *Nthatuoa Hotel* (☎950260; ②–③), which is the first building you come to on the left as you enter Qacha's Nek. The hotel offers four types of room, each more luxurious than the last, starting with a decent though smallish double and ending with a large, fancy suite. All tariffs include a substantial breakfast from a restaurant that serves the finest **food** in town (unless you are vegetarian, in which case there is nothing for you). Just past the hotel, and opposite the *Farmers' Training Centre*, ask your way to the excellent *Narna's Guest House* (☎95 0374; ①), which is close by. Though the owners do not speak much English and water supply is often a problem (as it is elsewhere in town despite the high rainfall), this is a friendly place with a good kitchen where you can either do your own cooking or just provide the ingredients and let the owner cook them up, for a small extra charge. Turn left past the fuel station in town for the *Central Hotel* (☎95 0439; ②) which despite its name is over a kilometre further on, nestled away next to the PEP department store. A sandstone building and full of character, the hotel has only six rooms and is often full. Even if you are not staying, it's worth visiting it at weekends for live music. There are a small number of inexpensive **places to eat** in the centre of town, but for more substantial meals you should really make for one of the hotels.

Sehlabathebe National Park

The only national park in the country, **Sehlabathebe National Park** (free entrance) is remote and inaccessible, but predictably peaceful and beautiful. Set on the border with South Africa, in the eastern reaches of the Drakensberg, the park has a few game animals, and is better known for its birdlife, excellent trout fishing, waterfalls, and seemingly endless open spaces that make for perfect hiking. Once here, you probably won't want to leave in a hurry, so bear this in mind when you book. Having said that, the weather can be so foul as to make you want to move on straightaway, with mists and rain emerging out of nowhere even on the finest days.

Sehlabathebe is managed by the Ministry of Agriculture, and is the subject of on going land disputes that primarily concern grazing access. The current state of affairs is a rather messy compromise, and you are likely to see herd boys grazing livestock all over the park, much to the irritation of environmentalists.

Practicalities

To **get to the park** from the Lesotho side you definitely need a 4WD. Failing that, there is a daily bus from Qacha's Nek to the village outside the park, which takes four to five hours; or you can sometimes hitch a lift from the junction about 11km from Qacha's Nek, but you are then faced with the problem of walking up the very steep 17km from the park entrance to the park's office. The only other way into the park from the Lesotho side is to walk the forty-kilometre Top of the Berg hike from Sani Top (see p.609). From South Africa, the only way in is a day's walk along the dramatic path starting at Bushman's Nek, which is a few hours' drive from Underberg and Himeville in KwaZulu-Natal.

To be sure of **accommodation** in Sehlabathebe's well-equipped and inexpensive lodge (①), book in advance in Maseru through *Sehlabathebe Reservations*, Ministry of Agriculture, on Raboshabane Road, off Moshoeshoe Road, PO Box 92, Maseru 100 (☎32 3600 or 32 2876). The easiest way to do this is in person when you are in Maseru. During the week, however, the lodge is rarely full, and even if it is, you can always camp (①). Neither the Ministry of Agriculture, nor the tourist information office nor the park office itself have any maps of Sehlabathebe; if you want to do some serious hiking, go to the Department of Lands, Surveys and Physical Planning (☎322376), on Lerotholi Road, near the corner of Constitution Road, in Maseru, where you should be able to pick up some good, detailed maps of the area.

travel details

Buses

There is no such thing as a bus timetable in Lesotho, and the following information is intended just to give a rough idea of frequencies and journey times. Minibus taxis supplement bus services everywhere and ensure that you can always find some form of public transport on major routes, though the story is very different on minor routes off the tarred roads, where you can expect long waits. Because public transport is so erratic, it's usually a better idea to just make for the next town on and find something from there rather than getting a ticket all the way to your destination (unless there's only one a day); your bus will stop at the next town anyway, and wait for more passengers, and you might be able to get a minibus taxi in the meantime.

Butha-Buthe to: Hlotse (4 daily; 30min); Maputsoe (4 daily; 45min); Mokhotlong (2 daily; 7hr).

Hlotse to: Butha-Buthe (4 daily; 30min); Maputsoe (5 daily; 30min); Maseru (8 daily; 2hr).

Mafeteng to: Maseru (5 daily; 1hr 30min); Mohale's Hoek (5 daily; 45min).

Maputsoe to: Butha-Buthe (4 daily; 45min); Hlotse (5 daily; 30min); Maseru (8 daily; 2hr).

Maseru to: Hlotse (8 daily; 2hr); Mafeteng (5 daily; 1hr 30min); Maputsoe (8 daily; 2hr); Qacha's Nek (1 daily; 10hr); Roma (4 daily; 1hr); Semonkong (4 daily; 5hr); Teya-Teyaneng (8 daily; 45min).

Mohale's Hoek to: Mafeteng (5 daily; 45min); Moyeni (5 daily; 45min).

Mokhotlong to: Butha-Buthe (2 daily; 7hr).

Moyeni to: Mohale's Hoek (5 daily; 45min); Qacha's Nek (1 daily; 7hr).

Qacha's Nek to: Maseru (1 daily; 10hr); Moyeni (1 daily; 7hr).

Roma to: Maseru (4 daily; 1hr); Semonkong (4 daily; 4hr).

Semonkong to: Maseru (4 daily; 5hr); Roma (4 daily; 4hr).

Teya-Teyaneng to: Maputsoe (8 daily; 45min); Maseru (8 daily; 45min).

Flights

Maseru to: Johannesburg (2 daily; 1hr 10min); Qacha's Nek (1 Mon, Wed, Thurs, Fri; 40min).

CHAPTER TWELVE

SWAZILAND

ooking at a political map of South Africa, you could be forgiven for assuming that **Swaziland** was another bizarre product of South Africa's apartheid engineering. This small, landlocked kingdom, with a population of less than one million, lies in the spanner-like grip of Mpumalanga which surrounds it on three sides. But in fact, although South Africa's influence predominates, Swaziland was a British protectorate from 1906 until its full independence in 1968.

During the long years of apartheid, white South Africans regarded Swaziland as a decadent playground, where sinful opportunities (gambling, interracial sex and porn movies), forbidden by their Calvinist rulers, were freely available. This image is fading fast, and though Swaziland still feels a lot more commercialized than, say, Lesotho, its outstanding **scenery** makes it well worth a visit. The country spans a choice portion of the southern African highveld's descent into the eastern lowveld and is blessed with easily accessible areas of great natural beauty, including **five national parks**, some featuring big game. With a car and a bit of time, you can explore some of the less trampled reserves, make overnight stops in unspoilt, out-of-the-way settlements and, if you time your visit well, take in something of Swaziland's well-preserved **cultural traditions**.

Despite encroaching political dissent, Swaziland remains one of the world's few absolute monarchies, and **King Mswati III**, educated at Britain's elite Sherbourne college, regularly appears in the country's sacred ceremonies, bedecked in the leopard skins of his office, participating in a ritual dance or assessing the year's crop of eligible maidens as they dance before him. He might even choose to add a few to his collection of wives, carefully drawn from a wide selection of clans in order to knit the nation more closely together. If you can, plan to come to Swaziland for **Ncwala** (around the end of Dec or start of Jan) or **Umhlanga** (Aug or Sept); both ceremonies are as important to the Swazis as New Year is to the Chinese.

Laid-back **Mbabane**, the country's tiny capital city, makes a useful base from which to explore the attractive **eZulwini Valley**, home to the royal palace, and the **Mlilwane Wildlife Sanctuary**. With a car, you can venture further afield, heading into the highveld of the northwest, and up to the fantastically beautiful **Malolotja Nature Reserve**, with its fabulous hiking country, soaring valleys and cliffs.

If you are trying to get between northern KwaZulu-Natal and the Kruger National Park in South Africa, Swaziland offers a good, fully tarred **through route** via the Matsamo Border in the north and the Lavumisa and Mahamba borders in the south, passing by the Mkhaya Game Reserve and Big Bend. Approaching Kruger this way is a far more attractive option than skirting through the eastern parts of Mpumalanga.

Some history . . . and modern Swaziland

The history of Swaziland dates back to the **Ngwane** clan, who crossed the Lubombo mountains from present-day Mozambique in around 1750. Blocked from moving into southeast Swaziland by the Ndwandwe people, the Ngwane eventually settled at

Swaziland is **malarial**. For details on necessary precautions, see p.18.

Mhlosheni and then Zombodze in the southwest, where **King Ngwane**, after whom the clan is named, reigned precariously, under constant threat of Ndwandwe attack. His son, **Sobhuza I**, was forced to flee north from the Ndwandwe, but they in turn were defeated by the Zulu king Shaka in 1819. Sobhuza then established a new capital suitably far from Shaka in the eZulwini Valley, and made peace with the Ndwandwe by marrying the king's daughter.

Sobhuza's power grew as he brought more and more clans under his wing. His alliance with the newly arrived Afrikaners, forged out of mutual fear of the Zulu, was pursued by his son **Mswati** (after whom the Swazi people are named), who stretched his kingdom north to the Limpopo River and east to the Indian Ocean.

ACCOMMODATION PRICE CODES

All the accommodation listed in the Guide has been categorized into one of seven price bands, as set out below. The rates quoted, unless otherwise stated, represent the most expensive per-person rate for a double or single room outside high season (Dec & Jan), except for category ①, which are per-person rates for a dorm bed in backpacker accommodation, or a campsite. For more accommodation details, see p.31.

① R0–50	② R50–100	③ R100–150
④ R150–200	⑤ R200–250	⑥ R250–300
	⑦ Over R300	

Europeans arrived in greater numbers throughout the 1860s, after the discovery of gold in neighbouring Transvaal and at Piggs Peak and Forbes Reef in Swaziland. Mswati's son **Mbandzeni** granted large chunks of his territory in concessions to the new arrivals, emboldening Britain to ignore his claims to most of the rest, and by the time Swaziland became a protectorate of South Africa in 1894 there was precious little land left. After their victory in the Anglo-Boer War, Britain assumed control of the territory and retained it until 1968.

The British invested in their protectorate, establishing the enormous **sugar plantations** on the northeast, and an **iron-ore mine** at Ngwenya in the highveld (today, the country's major export is sugar). Meanwhile, the new king **Sobhuza II** concentrated on buying back his kingdom, and had acquired about half of it by the time independence came in 1968. The Swazi aristocracy managed the transition to independence skilfully, with its Imbokodvo party winning every parliamentary seat in the first elections. In 1973, a radical pan-Africanist party won three seats, prompting Sobhuza to **ban political parties** and declare a state of emergency which has been in place ever since. A parliament governs Swaziland today, but final authority rests with the king, who continues to name the prime minister and approve or veto important legislation.

After Sobhuza's death in 1982, a period of intrigue ensued, with the Queen Mother Dzeliwe assuming the regency until deposed by Prince Bhekimpi, who ruled until 1985, dissolving parliament and purging all the opposition he could. The current king, **Mswati III**, the son of another of Sobhuza's many wives, was recalled from an English public school to become king in 1986, and parliamentary elections were held in 1987. New opposition began to emerge, most notably the **People's United Democratic Movement** (PUDEMO), which has strong support amongst Swazi workers.

Maintenance of tradition and appeals to broad nationalism have been key components of Swazi royalty's strategy to retain power, but since the breakdown of apartheid in South Africa political tensions here have risen. Relations with the new South African regime are uneasy: the ANC remembers the expulsion of its activists during the 1980s and wants speedy political change. Although Mswati III appears to favour reform, so far none has happened. A poor turnout marked the "elections" of 1993. Currently, Swaziland is the only country in the region not practising multiparty democracy. It seems only a matter of time before it is coerced into doing so.

When to go

Summers are hot, particularly in the eastern lowveld. Winter is usually sunny, but nights can be very chilly in the western highveld around the Malolotja Nature Reserve and Piggs Peak. In summer, rainfall is usually limited to short, drenching storms that play havoc with the smaller untarred roads.

SWAZI PUBLIC HOLIDAYS

January 1	August/September (Umhlanga Dance
Good Friday	Day)
Easter Monday	September 6 ((Independence Day)
April 19 (King Mswati III's birthday)	December/January (Ncwala Day)
April 25 (National Flag Day)	December 25
July 22 (King Sobhuza II's birthday)	December 26

Getting there by road

Of the eleven border posts serving traffic from South Africa, the main ones are **Ngwenya/Oshoek** (7am–10pm), which is closest to Johannesburg and is the easiest route to Mbabane; **Jeppe's Reef/Matsamo** (8am–4pm) in the northwest, which is handy if you're coming in from Kruger Park; **Mananga** (8am–6pm) in the northeast; **Lavumisa/Golela** (7am–10pm), in the southeast, close to the KwaZulu-Natal coast; and **Mahamba** (7am–10pm), in the southwest, off the N2 from Piet Retief in the KwaZulu-Natal interior. The northern crossing via **Bulembu** (8am–4pm) to Piggs Peak is perhaps the most spectacular in the country, but the bad road makes this journey hard going in an ordinary car.

TIPS ON TRAVEL IN SWAZILAND

- **Accommodation** at the mid- and upper range is generally better value than in South Africa. Backpacker and budget places are scarce and thus not cheap.

- **Banks** are easily found in the major centres. Opening hours are Monday to Friday 8.30am to 2.30pm, with some branches open on Saturday from 8.30am to 11am. Most banks and hotels should be prepared to change travellers' cheques, but usually at poor rates of exchange. ATMs in Swaziland are only for Swazi bank account holders and do not accept international cards.

- **Camping** is possible near almost every tourist attraction and in all the national parks except for Mkhaya.

- **Currency** is the **lilangeni** – plural emalangeni (E) – which is tied to the South African rand (1 rand = 1 lilangeni). The rand is legal tender in Swaziland, so you won't have to change any money. Emalangeni are not convertible outside Swaziland. There is a shortage of change in Swaziland, so if you do change money ask for a good amount of low denomination notes.

- **Credit cards** such as *Visa*, *Mastercard* (*Access*) and *Amex* are widely accepted in hotels, restaurants and shops. The national parks are supposed to accept cards, but only Mkhaya can be relied upon to do so. If you're visiting any of the others, you'd be well-advised to carry cash.

- **Costs** are similar to those in South Africa, with food and fuel somewhat less expensive.

- **Dialling codes** The country code for Swaziland is **268**, to be followed by the destination number (there are no area codes). The code for **phoning out from Swaziland** is **00**, followed by the country and area codes and finally the destination number. To phone **South Africa**, dial **07**. To arrange a **collect call**, dial **94**. Country codes are the same as those dialled from South Africa (see p.45).

- **Driving** is the best way to see Swaziland; distances are small, all the main tourist sites are near good, tarred roads, and the major gravel roads are in decent condition. Most

Crossing the border is usually very straightforward: you simply have to show your passport and pay a token E5 road tax.

Transtate **buses** from Johannesburg enter Swaziland at the Ngwenya/Oshoek border, stopping at Ermelo en route to Mbabane, and at Mahamba, stopping at Nhlangano and Hlathikulu. The *Baz Bus* goes from Durban to Pretoria via Mbabane, entering Swaziland at the Mahamba border in the south and leaving via Ngwenya on Mondays, Wednesdays, Fridays and Saturdays.

Getting there by plane

Swaziland has one **international airport**, Matsapha (often referred to as "Manzini"), situated between Mbabane and Manzini. *Comair* operates five **flights** a week from Johannesburg, while *Royal Swazi Airways* flies one to three times a day, every day, to and from Johannesburg.

The national parks

Swaziland has five **national parks**, between them exemplifying the country's geographical diversity, and all offering good-value accommodation. The Swaziland National Trust Commission in Lobamba (Mon–Fri 8am–1pm & 2–3.45pm, Sat & Sun 10am–1pm & 2–3.45pm; ☎61178) manages **Malolotja Nature Reserve** in the northwest highveld and **Mlawula Nature Reserve** in the eastern lowveld. Royal Swazi Big Game Parks (Mon–Fri 8am–4pm; ☎44541, fax 40957, after hours and weekends ☎61591) in

---

dirt roads are passable with an ordinary vehicle in dry months. The authorities permit a blood-alcohol level in drivers which is double that permitted in South Africa, and enough to make you think twice about long drives at night. For Swazi car rental, see "Listings" for Mbabane (p.629).

• **Passports and visas** – see p.13.

• **Tour operators** *Umhlanga Tours* (☎62180, fax 46416) operates from the *Royal Swazi Sun* in the eZulwini Valley and runs tours to the Lobamba royal village, game parks, nature reserves and crafts centres around the country. Staff can also arrange horse-riding, hiking, caving, climbing and white-water rafting. *Eco-Africa Safaris*, PO Box 199, Piggs Peak (☎ & fax 71319), is based in the *Phopanyane Lodge* near Piggs Peak and operates walking, and 4WD tours of the surrounding area.

LANGUAGE

SISWATI GREETINGS AND RESPONSES

Hello (to one)	*Sawubona*	Goodbye	*Sala kahle*
Hello (to many)	*Sanibona*	(person leaving)	
How are you?	*Kunjani?*	Goodbye	*Hamba kahle*
I'm fine	*Kulungile*	(person remaining)	

BASICS

Yes	*Yebo* (also a casual greeting)	Today	*Lamuhla*
No	*Ha*	Tomorrow	*Kusasa*
Thank you	*Ngiyabonga*	Yesterday	*Itolo*

TRAVEL

Where is. . . ?	*Iphi I . . . ?*	How much?	*Malini?*
Where can we stay?	*Singahlala hephi?*	Where are you going?	*U ya phi?*

Mbabane's New Mall runs the **Hlane Royal National Park** in the lowveld, **Mlilwane Wildlife Sanctuary** near Mbabane, and the upmarket **Mkhaya Game Reserve** between Manzini and Big Bend.

MBABANE AND AROUND

Tucked in the jumble of granite peaks and valleys that make up the Dlangeni hills, Swaziland's administrative capital, **MBABANE** (pronounced "M-buh-barn"), is small, relaxed and unpretentious, with a population of only 60,000. Just over 20km from Swaziland's western borders with South Africa, the city roughly marks the point where the mountainous southern African highveld descends briefly into middleveld, before bottoming out further east as dry lowveld. This is a good base from which to start

MBABANE

ACCOMMODATION
1 Chillage Backpackers
2 City Inn
3 Hill Street Lodge
4 Tavern Inn
5 Thokoza Church Centre
6 Youth Centre

AN ALTERNATIVE ROUTE TO MBABANE

While most visitors – and *Transtate* buses from South Africa – approach Mbabane from the Oshoek/Ngwenya border, a good **alternative route** is from the **Nerston/Sandlane** border post, about 35km further south, and roughly 70km from the city. Although a longer route, this road passes through some outstanding scenery and will take you past some excellent places to stay on the way.

Once past Nerston, where there are some interesting San paintings (ask at the church for someone to show you the way), the road plunges deep into the beautiful and vast **Usutu Forest**, which covers over ten percent of Swaziland. After some steep climbs, you'll start a long descent to the factory town of **Bhunya**, whose hub is a belching pulp mill – reason enough not to linger. Press on for another 15km or so on the road to Mhlambanyatsi, taking care when crossing the single-lane bridge over the Lusutfu River. Just before Mhlambanyatsi is a fine **hotel**, *The Forester's Arms* (☎26084/74177; ②–③), set in a picturesque clearing. Cosy rooms with wonderful mountain views and hearty **meals** included in the tariff make this a good place to stop over, and if you're here on a Sunday so much the better: this is when people from all over the country pour in to feast on the hotel's superb buffet and roast – you'll need to **book** ahead to be sure of a table.

Back on the road, Mhlambanyatsi itself has a small shopping centre and some filling stations, but little else. Keep going: the road beyond it enters a beautiful, lush river valley, with traditional houses dotted all around. Once you have gone 2km past a dirt road turn-off to Malkerns, there is a sign pointing the way up to *Meikles Mount* (☎74110; ②). Follow the signpost: after a steep 6km (take care with the road if it's been raining), you'll be rewarded with sweeping views and some of the best **self-catering accommodation** in Swaziland. Comfortable cottages with reasonably equipped kitchens and open fires are available for rent and there is a farm shop selling a limited range of fresh food. This is prime **hiking** territory: a particularly spectacular hike takes you all the way to the Mlilwane Nature Reserve. Horse-riding can be arranged for E15 an hour, and there is good fishing in the river, particularly for bream and barbel. You have to **book** for at least two nights on weekends and during public holidays. From *Meikles Mount*, it is only another 20km to Mbabane.

exploring Swaziland: the **Mlilwane Wildlife Sanctuary** lies not far south, and the royal village of **Lobamba** makes an easy day's outing – vital if you're here when the Umhlanga or Ncwala ceremonies take place.

There's not much to do, but you should find the city a more agreeable one than hectic Manzini, especially if you need to change money, find a comfortable bed or plan your trip ahead. Certainly, if you're without your own transport, Mbabane is the best base from which to explore the rest of Swaziland.

Arrival and information

Matsapha airport (☎84444), 35km southeast of Mbabane, just north of Manzini, is Swaziland's only international airport. There's no public transport from here into Mbabane, so if you haven't arranged with your hotel for a pick-up be prepared to take a **taxi** or **rent a car** (see "Listings" for details). You cannot change money at the airport, so have some rands or emalangeni handy.

Transtate (☎011/28 3562) **buses** from South Africa terminate some way out of town at the intersection of Usutu and Manzini roads, from where you should call a taxi, as the distance into town isn't walkable. The main bus station is off the Western Distributor Road, near the Swazi Plaza mall, and from here you can take a bus to almost anywhere in Swaziland. **Minibus taxis** ply the Mbabane–Manzini route and rank on the west side of the bus station – this is also where you can rent a **private taxi** for local travel.

Mbabane's **tourist office**, Swazi Plaza (Mon–Fri 8am–4.45pm, Sat 9am–1pm; ☎42531) has a good supply of maps and brochures and a free *What's On?* guide – very handy for information on forthcoming events. The **Royal Swazi Big Game Parks Office** (☎44541) in the New Mall has a similar selection of leaflets and very helpful staff.

Central Mbabane empties out at night, and **muggings** are a risk for those wandering the streets alone. If you're going out after dark, arrange for a taxi to pick you up.

Accommodation

As with most of Swaziland, Mbabane is a bit short on budget **accommodation**, and what it does offer in the lower price range is in a seedy part of town. However, there is a good backpackers' lodge west of the centre and a handful of fairly decent **hotels** on and around Allister Miller Street. If you have trouble finding anywhere, staff at the tourist office (see above) should be able to help out.

Chillage Backpackers, corner of Nicholson Crescent and Gilson Rd (☎48312; email: lizzie@realnet.co.sz). Laid-back and friendly backpackers' lodge west of the city centre, offering inexpensive dorms and doubles and a variety of guided 4WD trips to remote parts of the country, as well as abseiling and a weekly trip to Maputo. ①–②.

City Inn, Allister Miller St (☎42406, fax 45855). City-centre hotel offering spacious, en-suite rooms, all with TV. Rooms near the bar can get noisy, so specify what you want. ②.

Hill St Lodge, Hill St (☎46342). Basic rooms with shared bath in a quiet suburb west of Allister Miller St. ②.

Tavern Inn, corner of Allister Miller and Gilfillian streets (☎42361, fax 45229). Tranquil, 1930s mock-Tudor hotel with swimming pool, en-suite rooms with TV and self-catering apartments. The best rooms are by the pool. A good restaurant and a popular pub are attached. ②.

Thokoza Church Centre, Mhlanhla St (☎46681). Church mission, some way east of the city centre, offering drab but cheap two- or three-bed rooms. There is a 10pm curfew unless you make prior arrangement. The area can be rough at night. ①.

Youth Centre, Isomi St (☎42176). Southeast of town in the Msundusa suburb, this evangelical centre offers cheap, basic rooms. Public transport to and fro is scarce, and it's quite a walk to the centre from here. ①.

The City

Mbabane's hilly **centre** is a pleasant jumble of office blocks, markets, plazas and shacks that you can very easily explore on foot – which is just as well, as driving here can be stressful without a sound grasp of the street layout. **Allister Miller Street** is the city's main thoroughfare, running south into the central business district (CBD), and lined in parts by colonial administrative buildings which are attractive to look at, but can only be entered on official business. The real hub of the city is **Swazi Market**, at the end of Allister Miller Street on the banks of the Mbabane River. Here you'll find neat rows of curio stalls with a colourful selection of handicrafts and, though prices aren't cheap, you can always haggle. Further into the market, fresh fruit and vegetable stalls make for a tempting browse (though prices here are fixed).

Several blocks west of the market and the CBD, and southwest of the Western Distributor Road, are Mbabane's two major shopping malls, the **Swazi Plaza** and the more upmarket **New Mall**, both brimming with department shops, banks and restaurants.

Eating, drinking and nightlife

You'll find the ubiquitous *Spur*, *Steers* and *Nando's* in Mbabane, but the town also has a smattering of very good **restaurants**, as well as some lively **bars** and **clubs**.

Restaurants

Continental Swazi Plaza (☎43276). Cheap and cheerful pizzas and grills, with some outdoor seating. Closed Sun.

Indingilizi Gallery & Restaurant, 112 Johnstone St (☎46213). Very pleasant place to come for lunch. The restaurant is in the gallery's back garden, and serves light, wholesome dishes at reasonable prices.

Kowloon Fast Food, New Mall (☎48637). Reliable Chinese takeaways.

La Casserole, Omni Centre, Allister Miller St (☎46426). Upmarket but good-value restaurant specializing in German dishes, and offering vegetarian selections.

Lourenco Marques Gilfillian St (☎43097). Expect to pay upwards of E80 at this excellent Portuguese restaurant. Mouthwatering king-sized prawns are a speciality, and you can buy their explosive *peri-peri* sauce.

Marco's Trattoria, Allister Miller St (☎43823). The best Italian restaurant in town, with a mid-priced to expensive menu.

Mediterranean, Allister Miller St (☎43212). Despite the name, this is an Indian restaurant serving up wonderful dishes in a dark, cavernous setting. It's located just opposite the *Cinelux*.

Bars, clubs and entertainment

Two of the city's liveliest **bars** are to be found at the *City Inn* and *Tavern Inn* hotels (see "Accommodation"). Mbabane also has two **nightclubs** worth checking out. The first, *Maxim's* on Johnstone Street (parallel to Allister Miller Street), has a good bar which at night transforms into an even better nightclub, and is especially popular on weekends. Some 8km north of town is the newer and hipper *Club Xstacy*, which you can reach by turning off Allister Miller Street at Golf Course Road, and following this until the Pine Valley turn-off, from where the club is signposted. Women travellers on their own are likely to encounter some harassment in bars and clubs, but the pestering probably won't be aggressive or persistent.

Mbabane has one **cinema**, the *Cinelux* (☎42818), near the junction of Gilfillian and Allister Miller streets. The generally mainstream programme is advertised in the daily papers and the city's free *What's On?* guide.

Listings

Airlines *Royal Swazi Airways*, Swazi Plaza (☎43301). *Scan Air Charter Ltd* (☎84474) is a private airline with light aircraft available for chartered flights. There is no *SAA* representative in Swaziland.

Banks Most banks are lined along Allister Miller St or in the Swazi Plaza. Branches include *Barclays*, *Standard Chartered* and *Stanbic*. Opening hours are Mon–Fri 8.30am–2.30pm, Sat 8.30–11.00am. The best time to bank is a weekday morning.

Bookshops *Websters*, 120 Johnstone St, has a good general selection, while *Africa South* in the Swazi Plaza offers an excellent range of books on Africa.

Car rental *Avis* (☎86226) and *Imperial/Hertz* (☎84393) are located at Matsapha Airport. Cheaper than both is *Affordable Car Hire* (☎49136) in the Swazi Plaza.

Embassies *Germany*, 3rd Floor, Dhlan'ubeka House (☎43174); *Mozambique*, Princess Drive (☎43700); *Netherlands*, Gilfillian St (☎45178); *South Africa*, New Mall (☎44651); *UK*, Allister Miller St (☎42581); *USA*, Warner St (☎46441).

Emergencies Fire ☎43333; Police ☎999 or 42221.

Hospitals *Mbabane Clinic Service* (private), St Michael St (☎42423); *Government Hospital* (public), Usutu Rd (☎42111).

Internet The *Internet Café* (email: box31@icafe.co.sz; website http://www.iafrica.sz.icafe), at the Omni Centre, near the cinema on Allister Miller St. This isn't a café, but it does offer access to the internet, and is Swaziland's only public internet facility so far.

Laundries *Swaziland Steam Laundry & Dry*, Allister Miller St, Swazi Plaza.

Library *Mbabane Library* (☎42633).

Pharmacy *Mbabane Pharmacy*, Allister Miller St; *Philani Pharmacy*, Swazi Plaza.

Post office The main post office is on Warner St, and there's a smaller one in the Swazi Plaza. Opening hours are Mon–Fri 8am–4pm, Sat 8–11am.

Tour operators *Umhlanga Tours*, Swazi Plaza (☎62180, fax 46416). See p.625 for details.

The eZulwini Valley and Lobamba

Southeast of Mbabane, the traffic-clogged MR3 runs for some 25km through the busy but scenic **eZulwini Valley** ("place of heaven"). Nestled in the valley are two of Swaziland's biggest tourist draws: the royal residences of **Lobamba** and **Ludzinzini**. Since the 1960s, a succession of casinos, strip joints, hotels and caravan parks have sprung up here, all catering for mainly South African tourists. Now that gambling is legal in South Africa, the numbers of pleasure-seekers has dropped and the business is no longer booming.

NCWALA AND UMHLANGA

The most sacred of Swaziland's ceremonies, with its timing determined by royal astrologers, **Ncwala** celebrates kingship, national unity and the first fruits of the new year. Around the time of the new moon in mid-December men journey east to the ancestral home of the Ngwane on the shores of the Indian Ocean to collect foam from the waves. While they are there, the Ncwala ceremony begins, with songs and rituals performed until the afternoon of the full moon, when the six days of the full Ncwala begin. Young Swazi men meet at **Lobamba** and are then sent away to gather branches of the *lusekwane* tree, from which they build a bower for the king. Warriors gather and sing songs that can only be sung at this time, while the king dances with them and eats the first fruits of the harvest. On the sixth day, objects representing the previous year are burnt on a massive bonfire, and prayers are offered to Swazi ancestors, asking them to put out the fire with rain. The ceremony ends amidst raucous singing, dancing and feasting. Visitors are allowed to attend most of Ncwala, but photography is prohibited during certain times, so be sure to ask first to avoid having your camera smashed.

The **Umhlanga** is a **fertility dance** which gets its name from the large reeds gathered by young women and brought to the residence of the Queen Mother to repair her *kraal*, usually in late August or early September. The sixth and seventh days are the most spectacular: this is when you can watch the young women, dressed in elaborate and carefully coded costumes, sing and dance before the king and Queen Mother at Lobamba, giving the king an opportunity to pick **a new wife**. The former king, Sobhuza II, invariably plucked a new mate from the bevy of young beauties, but Mswati III has proved more restrained – no one has been chosen by him in the last few years.

Seemingly interminable construction work along the MR3 can turn what should be a relaxed drive through marvellous scenery into a nerve-racking test of patience, past bottlenecks, diversions, and local transport that does its best to ignore both. Take it slowly, stopping off at one of the many good restaurants for something to eat, or staying overnight in an inn, and you'll soon start to appreciate the valley's charms. Behind the noise of the slot machines and karaoke soar beautiful mountains and, stretching along the left side of the MR3, the lush **Mlilwane Wildlife Sanctuary** offers welcome respite, as well as a wide variety of wildlife.

Malagwane Hill

Soon after leaving Mbabane, the valley road begins its giddy descent down **Malagwane Hill**. Almost immediately, there is a turn to the left for the elegant *Mountain Inn* (☎42781; ④), wonderfully located and a great **place to stay**. Nearby, the *Friar Tuck* **restaurant** is a bit dark, but serves up reliable buffet lunches and à la carte dinners. If the *Mountain Inn* is full, you could try the *Swazi Inn* (☎42235; ③), a short distance further on nearer the road, in a pleasant, colonial thatched building with comfortable rooms and a decent (if unimaginative) restaurant.

Back on the road, a drive down to the bottom of the valley will take you past a collection of **craft stalls** that are among the most expensive in Swaziland, and the *Mgenule* (☎61041; ③), which has fairly decent **self-catering** accommodation, offering rooms with kitchens but no cooking utensils. Next door, there's a pleasant and inexpensive tandoori **restaurant** with conveniently long opening hours.

Tea Road

Just beyond the *Mgenule* is a small turn-off with a sign pointing to the *Phangisa Gearbox & Brake Service*. Following this will take you to the **Tea Road** and onto a truly spectacular drive into the mountains, ending up roughly 8km from Manzini. Stay alert if you decide to get out of your car to take some photos, as there have been reports of gangs stealing from cars left unsecured on the roadside. Take care too if the weather is wet, as the road can get slippery. Safe if unremarkable **camping** and spartan rondavels are available at the *Timbali Caravan Park* (☎61156; ①–②), just past the Tea Road turn-off, and up another small turn-off on the main eZulwini road.

Next to the caravan park you'll find one of Swaziland's swankiest **restaurants**, the *Calabash* (☎61187), which serves an excellent range of seafood and specializes in German, Swiss and Austrian dishes. Further up the road, *Martin's Bar & Disco* becomes pleasantly raucous and drunken at weekends and if you're in the mood for partying will doubtless deliver a night to remember.

Back on the valley road

Continuing along the eZulwini Valley road, you'll soon come to *Cuddle Puddle* (6am–6pm; E5), a beautifully warm pool of mineral waters surrounded by tropical vegetation and perfect for a dip on cool days – or even when it's raining. Nearby, the *Swazi Spa Health & Beauty Studio* (☎61164) offers gym and sauna facilities, and aromatherapy treatments, should you need a little reviving. Immediately beyond this lie three *Sun* **hotels** offering their usual blend of comfort and anonymity. The *Royal Swazi* (☎61001; ⑦) is the smartest of the lot, with a fine swimming pool, a good selection of restaurants and plenty of upmarket bars, as well as a swanky casino and a tatty adult cinema. *Umhlanga Tours* (☎62180) have an office in the hotel lobby, and operate reasonably priced **tours** to more or less everywhere in the country. Best value of the *Sun* options is the *Lugogo* (☎61101; ⑥), blessed with a well-priced buffet that is particularly enticing

---

CHOOSING THE KING

Swazi monarchs are always men of the **Dlamini** family, and over the course of their reign tend to marry a number of women who are carefully selected from different clans in the name of national unity. In theory, the king marries women from increasingly important families as he goes along, which means that the son of the last wife is always a strong contender for the succession. In practice, however, other wives with older sons are also in with a chance, and this ensures turbulence and power-struggles every time the king dies. After his death, the royal council, or *liqoqo*, selects the new **Queen Mother**, who rules as regent until her son is old enough to take charge. She usually has to work hard to ensure her position against ambitious uncles. The main advantage of this awkward process is that by the time the new king is old enough to rule, he and his mother have generally garnered enough support for him to do so effectively.

---

at breakfast. Just beyond the filling station, past the *Sun* hotels, the *1st Horse* **restaurant** (☎61137; closed Sun) serves up very good Chinese meals and has a large bar.

Some 2km further along the valley road, a right turn past the unremarkable self-catering chalets of *Smoky Mountain Village* (☎61291; ③) will take you up a dirt road (follow the signs to *Mantenga Crafts*) to an interesting collection of **craft shops**. Some of Swaziland's finest crafts are on offer here, including a selection of outstanding tapestries, and if you have credit cards or ready cash you may find it hard not to splurge. Continue a short distance on this road for the beautifully located *Mantenga Lodge* (☎61049; ③), with cosy **chalets** nestled on the hill rise, a good bar and **restaurant**, and a sauna room with especially good views.

Back on the eZulwini strip, the *Happy Valley Motel* (☎61061; ③) has decent accommodation and the dubious pleasures of a go-go bar, cabaret, striptease and X–rated movies. Beery and leery South African men make up the bulk of the clientele, although occasionally a good band graces the *Why Not* go-go bar, attracting a wider audience. The complex also has a sports bar – lively during major sporting occasions – as well as a pizzeria and a steakhouse.

Mlilwane Wildlife Sanctuary

An good alternative to staying in the eZulwini Valley is to head straight for the **Mlilwane Wildllife Sanctuary** (open daily; entry fee), signposted on the Mbabane–Manzini road, and offering 24-hour access, a variety of accommodation and a pleasant, relaxed atmosphere. The name **Mlilwane** refers to the "little fire" that is caused on occasion by lightning strikes on the granite mountains. This is one of Swaziland's most popular reserves, so it's a good idea to book ahead if you intend to stay overnight (see "Practicalities").

Mlilwane's **wildlife** are herbivorous in the main, including white rhino, giraffe, zebra and bountiful numbers of antelope, but also the odd crocodile. Over 100km of road enable you to drive through the park to view game. Alternatively, guided walks and drives are available through the park office at the main rest camp. Best of the **walking trails** is the "Macobane Hill Trail", a gentle, three-hour hike through the mountains. There are also **mountain-bike tours** and **horseback trails**, both fairly relaxed ways of taking in the park's attractions. If you're feeling less energetic, you can pass the time watching **hippos** wallowing in the muddy hippo pool, right next to the *Hippo Haunt* restaurant, near the rest camp. The hippos are fed every day at 3pm.

The most spectacular part of the park, to the west, near *Meikles Mount* (see p.627), is currently inaccessible, but plans are afoot for the construction of a railway which will open this part up to visitors.

Practicalities

To get to **Mlilwane** during the day, head for the **main gate**, taking the turn-off on the eZulwini Valley road for *Mantenga Crafts*, and continuing straight ahead, instead of turning right. There is another, smaller turn-off, also signposted to *Mantenga*, a couple of kilometres further along the valley road. After dark, you have to use the **south gate**, reached by continuing towards Manzini and turning right at a small sign saying "Night Gate", just over 1km after Lobamba village. The sign is not illuminated and it's easy to miss: if you reach the turn-off to Malkerns, you have gone too far.

The park's **accommodation** facilities (all ①) include the main rest camp, where wooden huts all have en-suite bath and kitchen; *Beehive Village*, a collection of self-catering thatched huts and dormitory rooms; a beautifully-situated campsite and a **backpackers' lodge**, *Sondzela House*. **Bookings** should be made through *Big Game Parks* in Mbabane (☎44541, fax 40957, after hours and weekends 61591). The only place to eat is at the inexpensive *Hippo Haunt* **restaurant**, near the main rest camp – meals must be booked in advance at the park's office.

TED REILLY AND THE SWAZI NATURE CONSERVATION STORY

Swaziland owes the creation and survival of three of its major wildlife sanctuaries – Mlilwane, Mkhaya and Hlane – to **Ted Reilly**, who was born in Mlilwane in 1938, the son of a British Anglo-Boer War soldier who had stayed on. As Reilly was growing up, Swazi wildlife and their natural habitats were coming under serious threat from poachers and commercial farmers. In 1959, Reilly lobbied the colonial government to set aside land for parks but was defeated by farmers who wanted the land for commercial agriculture. Undeterred, he turned the Mlilwane estate into a park anyway, and set about cultivating a relationship with **King Sobhuza II**, who was having trouble himself with poachers at the royal estate in Hlane. After Swazi independence, Sobhuza became much more powerful, and Reilly's relationship with him lent weight to his nature conservation efforts.

Despite rickety finances, the **Mlilwane Wildlife Sanctuary** opened in 1963, and the restocking and reintroduction of species has continued ever since (today the reserve is ten times the size of the original sanctuary). Meanwhile, Sobhuza asked Reilly to help stamp out poaching at Hlane. Reilly's approach was to get tough, and the resulting shootouts earned him the praise of some, but the enmity of many. Matters came to a head in 1992, when, with the help of the South African Police Endangered Species Protection Unit, Reilly tracked down a poaching unit that had been operating in Mkhaya. In the ensuing gunfight, one poacher was killed and another paralysed. Criticism of Reilly's tactics intensified.

Reilly's dependence on royal connections has also generated controversy: critics claim it has prevented the development of a single parks board and a participatory, grass-roots involvement in conservation that is the key to long-term success. Some also assert that Reilly subordinates wildlife management principles to the needs of the tourist industry. Reilly's answer to his critics is simply to point to the three game parks his company runs. It's a hard argument to defeat. Without Reilly, the parks would not exist, and Swaziland and its visitors would be much the poorer for it.

The royal villages of Lobamba and Ludzinzini

Some 20km south of Mbabane, along the eZulwini Valley road, **LOBAMBA** was originally built in 1830 for King Sobhuza I, and is the royal *kraal* of Sobhuza II. The royal palace and outbuildings are not open to the public, but Lobamba is still worth visiting, not least for fascinating exhibitions of Swazi life in its **National Museum** (Mon–Fri 8am–1pm & 2–3.45pm, Sat & Sun 10am–1pm & 2–3.45pm; small entry fee). The displays here provide a helpful potted history of the country, with displays of cultural artefacts and wonderful old photographs of Swazi people and royalty. There are photos of Manzini and Mbabane when they were literally one-horse towns, of sweaty British administrators in full colonial regalia attending functions of the Swazi royal house, and much more. Outside the museum stands a life-size recreation of a traditional Swazi homestead. Remarkably, given their size, these huts are portable. Back in the museum, the National Trust Commission (☎61178) handles bookings for the Malolotja and Mlawula nature reserves (see p.637 and p.639).

Lobamba's **Somhlolo stadium** is the country's venue for major events and football matches, which are usually highly entertaining. For a few emalangeni on a Sunday afternoon, you can treat yourself to violence-free games of occasional great skill, with a good-humoured and vocal crowd. Consult the local press for details, or ask almost any male Swazi.

Opposite Lobamba, the village of **LUDZINZINI** is the royal *kraal* of the present king, Mswati III, and the Queen Mother. Unlike Lobamba, Ludzinzini cannot be visited or even photographed at all except during Ncwala (around New Year) and Umhlanga (around the end of August) – at these times, you'd be mad to miss the place (see p.630).

If you are on your way to Manzini, an alternative to taking the main road is to follow the **Lozitha road**, which heads north from Lobamba and is less used and far more attractive, despite the chronic overgrazing of the surrounding countryside.

Through the Malkerns Valley

Continuing on the main road to Manzini, a turn to the south roughly 5km beyond Lobamba (just after the fruit market) will take you to the scenic pineapple-growing **Malkerns Valley**. There's a wonderful **restaurant** here, *Malandela's* (☎83115; closed Mon), which serves hearty English cooking in a stylish setting with soothing views of the adjoining fields and the mountains in the distance. Next door, *Tishweshwe Crafts* (open daily) has an enticing collection of **local handicrafts**, while *Grass Roots* sells woven mats and baskets for very reasonable prices. A little further on, the village of **Malkerns** itself (which derives its name from a turn-of-the-century trader called Malcolm Kerns Stuart) holds few attractions, unless you have a particular interest in pineapple canning.

Continuing on the road past Malkerns takes you to Luyengo, and then either to **Bhunya** or **Mankayane**, but a sharp left at the T-junction in Malkerns will bring you back onto the Manzini road. Before you get there, several more **crafts shops** are lined along the road: *Swazi Candles* (daily 9am–1pm) sells a bewildering array of brightly patterned wax candles; *Inqaba Crafts* specializes in woodcarvings; and *Baobab Batik*, 2km further along, sells all manner of colourful batiks. The Mbabane–Manzini road lies 5km ahead. If your appetite for crafts is still not satisfied, take a right turn towards Manzini, then a left turn after 2km, and continue towards the **Bethany Mission**, a collection of crafts workshops recommended for their fine woven cotton rugs.

MANZINI

MANZINI is Swaziland's largest town and its commercial hub. Almost all the country's industrial and commercial sector is based in or around here, and the city is dominated by office blocks and malls which obscure the few attractive edifices. With a rising crime rate and an atmosphere far less relaxed than Mbabane, Manzini would be an eminently missable place were it not for its outstanding **market**, which operates every day except Sundays on the corner of Mhlakuvane and Mancishane streets.

Much of Manzini's market is given over to the practicalities of life, such as fresh fruit, household goods and traditional medicines, but there's an upper section which spills onto the steps below and is devoted to crafts and fabrics. The **crafts** selection is bigger, more varied and much better value than any other market in Swaziland, while the **fabrics**, which are Zimbabwean, Zairean, and Mozambican, cannot be easily obtained anywhere else in the country.

Just north of the market, on Ngwane Street, stands The Bhunu, one of Manzini's new shopping malls, and handy for shops and restaurants. The Hub, south of the market, on Mhlakuvane Street, is smarter and has a good supermarket and several restaurants and takeaways. Manzini's only other point of interest is its original **Catholic mission**, an elegant stone building (not open to casual visitors) opposite the new cathedral on Sandlane Street (parallel to Mhlakuvane Street).

Practicalities

Buses from all over the country and South Africa pull in at Manzini's busy main bus station at the end of Louw Street, just north of Ngwane Street. **Matsapha Airport** (☎84444) lies 8km west of the city centre; if you're arriving here, you'll need to take a **taxi** into central Manzini.

Manzini has a limited selection of **places to stay**. Near the bus station, on the corner of Meintjies and Mahleka streets, the *Mozambique* (☎52489, fax 52586; ②) offers tiny rooms with paper-thin walls, but has a friendly bar and an excellent **restaurant**. The *Prince Velebantfu* (☎52663; ②) on the Ngwane road, on the way back to Mbabane, is run-down but houses the good-value *Swazi Restaurant*, which serves meat and *phutu* (cooked maize meal). For more upmarket accommodation, head for the *New George*, at the other end of Ngwane Street on Sitkei Road (☎ & fax 52061; ④), which has en-suite rooms, a swimming pool, café and a fairly decent restaurant. The nearest **campsite**, *Paradise Caravan Park* (☎84935; ①), lies 9km west of the city.

Manzini's other good **places to eat** include *Gil Vicente*, in the Ilanga Centre on Martin Street (☎53874; closed Mon), which serves up tasty Portuguese dishes; the *Mongolian*, Villiers Street, where you'll find the best Chinese food in town; and the *Fontana de Trevi Pizzeria*, in The Hub, Mhlakuvane Street. If you're in the mood for some no-holds-barred Swazi partying, head west out of town past the airport to *Salt 'n' Pepper* **nightclub**, which gets particularly busy at weekends.

PIGGS PEAK AND THE NORTHWEST

The highveld of **Piggs Peak** and the **northwest** is unquestionably the most beautiful region of Swaziland, with rolling hills perfect for hiking, countless sparkling streams, a sprinkling of waterfalls and, to round things off, some wonderful accommodation where you can relax after appreciating it all.

Approaches to Piggs Peak

Most visitors to the northwest enter Swaziland from the north, after going through the Kruger National Park (see p.537), but Piggs Peak is only 64km north of Mbabane and easily reached from there, too. The most spectacular – and rugged – entrance into Swaziland is via the Bulembu road from Barberton in Mpumalanga (see p.532), which passes through Bulembu village on the way to Piggs Peak.

From Jeppe's Reef/Matsamo border

The **Jeppe's Reef/Matsamo border** is open from 8am until 4pm, and the road on the Swazi side is good all the way to Piggs Peak. Some 25km south of the border on this road is a good **place to stay**: the *Protea Piggs Peak Hotel & Casino* (☎71104; ⑨), set in thousands of acres of mountainous pine forest. Despite the monolithic appearance of the hotel from the outside, the rooms have fabulous views, there's an inviting swimming pool with a bar in the middle, and a good buffet **restaurant**. You can buy hand-spun mohair products in the hotel lobby as well as from their source nearby.

Travel another 3km to reach a sign to the right pointing you to the privately owned **Phopanyane Nature Reserve** (☎71319; ③–⑤), which is five long kilometres away from the road. The reserve is small, but carefully laid-out trails ensure that there is plenty to see, including the Phopanyane waterfall on the reserve's eastern side. The vegetation is subtropical and attracts hundreds of colourful **bird species**. Animals include mongooses, bushbabies, otters and numerous snakes, but all are hard to spot. This is one of the most beautiful **places to stay** in Swaziland, offering cottages (⑤) with private kitchens and gardens, and safari tents (③) next to the Phopanyane River, with a communal kitchen and washing facilities. If you can't afford to stay, it's still worth stopping here for a short hike in the reserve and a meal in its secluded, mid-priced **restaurant**. Alternatively, you can bring your own meat to *braai* while the safari tents are down. The pool, although chillingly cold, has one of the world's great locations, looking out onto endless mountains and surrounded by luxuriant vegetation. The reserve's owner, Rod de Vletter, also runs *Eco-Africa Safaris* (☎71319), and can take you or direct you to otherwise hard-to-find sites, including San rock paintings and the Gobolondo mountain range.

A few kilometres south of Phopanyane, 1km north of Piggs Peak, the turn-off to Kuthuleni marks the start of a beautifully scenic fifty-kilometre drive along a good dirt road to **Bhalekane**. There is not much in Bhalekane except a prison, but you can proceed from here to Tshaneni and the **northeast** (see p.638), or head south through fairly remote territory to Mafutseni and then Manzini.

From Bulembu

The road from Barberton in Mpumalanga to Piggs Peak via **Bulembu** is briefly tarred out of Barberton, but soon deteriorates as it passes through some of the most rugged country imaginable, with the road near the border, which is open from 8am until 4pm, in particularly poor shape. Looking up, you can see the Barberton–Havelock cableway, which carries asbestos from the nearby Havelock mine to South Africa. Once in Swaziland, the road soon passes through Bulembu, with Piggs Peak a further 20km away.

Piggs Peak

PIGGS PEAK, a small forestry town straggled along the main road, was named after a French prospector called William Pigg, who discovered gold nearby in 1884, where it was mined until the site was exhausted in 1954. Apart from the attractive surrounding countryside, there's nothing much to see here, but if you're heading to Malotja Nature Reserve this is a good place to stock up on supplies.

The town's **bus station** and **market** are near the Total garage at the northern end of town, where there is also a small shopping centre with a supermarket. There is a *Barclays Bank* in the centre of town, but it is unused to foreign transactions, so either summon your patience or hold out until Mbabane. For an **overnight stay**, the *Highland Inn* (☎71144; ③), in a pleasant colonial building on the southern edge of town, offers simple but comfortable rooms. Inside, the *Woodcutter's Den* **restaurant** serves up steaks and other fleshy fare at fairly reasonable prices. For a quick snack, *The Ranch*, in the town's shopping centre, dishes out fast food, while the *Phopani* **bar** nearby does plenty of trade, rocking until late on weekends.

On to Malolotja Nature Reserve

Driving south, you soon leave the pine plantations behind and pass into rolling highveld grassland, peppered with rural dwellings, with the stretch across the Nkomati River valley a particularly beautiful one. Alongside the road are curio stalls, often staffed by young children dressed in leaves to attract your attention.

After about 30km, just after Nkhaba, you'll reach the entrance to the Malolotja Nature Reserve, with the main road joining the Ngwenya–Mbabane road at Motshane 20km further on.

Malolotja Nature Reserve

Swaziland's least tourist-trampled park, the **Malolotja Nature Reserve** (daily: summer 6am–6pm; winter 6.30am–6pm; enquiries ☎ 24241, bookings ☎61151; small entry fee) offers awesome scenery and some of the finest hiking in southern Africa. This is a place to come for rugged, wild nature and a real sense of tranquillity, rather than for game-spotting. The mountains here, among the oldest in the world (3.6 billion years old), are covered in grassland and graced by a myriad of streams and waterfalls, including the 95-metre-high **Malolotja Falls**.

Nearly three hundred species of **bird** are to be found in Malolotja, with an impressive colony of the rare bald ibis just by the waterfalls. You'll have to look harder for **game**, although wildebeest, blesbok and impala are often visible, and there are leopards and two very retiring elephants lurking somewhere in the gaping tracts of mountain and valley. There is also the 43,000-year-old **Ngwenya Mine**, the oldest in the world, where miners once dug for specularite and haematite, which were then used as cosmetics and for religious rituals. You can visit the mine with a guide, who must be booked beforehand. Nearby, the **Forbes Reef Gold Mine** can be visited alone, but you'll have to take care on the slippery banks.

Malolotja's small network of roads pass some fine viewpoints and picnic sites, but to really savour this park's rugged wilderness – and see its waterfalls – you'll need to hike. A variety of **hiking trails** are laid out in the reserve, from easy half-day excursions to seven-day marathons, with accommodation available en route (see below).

Practicalities

Brochures and maps are available from the reserve's **offic**e, just inside the entrance gate. The office also issues permits for Hawane Dam Nature Reserve – useful if you're planning on heading there next. Hikers would do well to ask for the *Hiking and Backpacking Guide*, which gives helpful information on hiking in the reserve.

Accommodation should be booked in advance through the Malolotja Nature Reserve, PO Box 100, Lobamba (π61151, fax 61875). The main rest camp (①) has fifteen sites with *braai* areas but not much wind shelter, and hot water in a communal bath area. There is also an A-frame chalet (①) which sleeps up to six people, and five well-located log cabins (②), which can also house up to six people each. A small shop at the entrance sells basic provisions, but you would do better to stock up in Piggs Peak or Mbabane. Seventeen **campsites** are scattered around the reserve for those attempting longer hikes: you'll need to bring all your own equipment, including a cooker, as no fires are permitted.

If you're on a long hike during the summer, be prepared for blisteringly hot days. Temperatures drop dramatically in winter, when nights can be freezing.

Hawane Dam Nature Reserve

A few kilometres south of Malolotja, on the Mbabane road, lies the **Hawane Dam Nature Reserve** (π24241; Mon–Fri free, Sat & Sun E10), a small area around the northern end of the Hawane Dam, protecting part of the Black Umbuluzi River wetlands. Hawane's main attraction is its wealth of **birdlife**, and a very helpful trail for birdwatching has recently been laid out.

Hawane Park (π43084, or ask for π44477; chalets ③, rondavels ①) is a little further on, with a small, inexpensive restaurant and friendly bar, as well as chalets and rondavels which are slightly too close to the road for comfort, but still offer soothing eastern views of spacious grassy plains dotted with gentle hills. The **Hawane Stables** (π24109), signposted down a track on the other side of the road, have ponies (and guides if you want them) that enable you to meander the plains in style for around E40 an hour, as well as 4WD vehicles for budding men from Marlboro country. You'll need to book in advance for both.

THE NORTHEAST

Northeast Swaziland is dominated by sugar plantations which stretch far into the distance, shimmering from the constant water spray, wreaking havoc with the water table and leaving many locals without, but earning the country valuable foreign exchange. Three large tracts of bush – **Hlane**, **Mlawula** and **Mbuluzi** – have been preserved as wildlife and nature reserves, and these are the main attractions for visitors to this region. Mlawula takes in a small portion of the **Lubombo Mountains**, which run in a continuous line from north to south and form a natural boundary with Mozambique.

The most direct and obvious route to the reserves from Mbabane is to follow the tarred **Siteki** road for 100km. The **northern route** is a little over twice as long and is part gravel, but makes for a far more spectacular a journey. Travel north to **Piggs Peak** from Mbabane, and turn right at the **Bhalekane** turn-off, roughly 1km later.

Tshaneni

The gravel road from Piggs Peak passes through some fabulous scenery before eventually winding up at the sugar town of **TSHANENI**. There's one **hotel** here, the *Impala Arms* (**☎**31244; ②), run by a Gauteng couple who have turned it into a South African outpost, complete with posters of Springbok rugby players and cricketers. The rooms are plain but comfortable and there is a bar with pool table, filled with exuberant Swazi on weekends (Friday is striptease night). The owners plan a sports bar, casino and sauna, all of which will increase prices, so phone ahead to enquire about current rates. If you need supplies, Tshaneni's *Score* supermarket will come in handy, and there is a Caltex garage nearby for fuel.

The **Mananga border** is 5km north (open 8am–6pm), from where the road leads to Komatipoort (see p.536). Heading south, the next town you'll meet is bougainvillea-festooned **Mhlume** and 20km further on is a junction at Maphiveni, where a left turn takes you to the **Lomahasha border** post with Mozambique (open 7am–5pm), another 20km away, while a right turn followed almost immediately by a left takes you to **Mbuluzi Game Reserve** and **Mlawula Nature Reserve**.

Mbuluzi Game Reserve

Privately owned and little-known, **Mbuluzi** (**☎**38861; ④; entry fee) is about 1km from the road to Hlane, and straddles the road to Mlawula. The reserve is set in classic lowveld bush, which means that it is hot in the summer, and filled with thorn trees. Currently the park is being restocked with game, including hippo and giraffe, which you can view in your own vehicle – as long as it's 4WD. Vehicles can be rented (E100 per day), and so can guides (E100). The absence of predators in Mbuluzi's southern portion means that you can walk along a network of trails in this section.

Mbuluzi's **accommodation** is its finest feature: four large and comfortable lodges with verandahs overlook the Mlwawula stream, whose luxuriant vegetation attracts birds and animals which you can watch from their verandahs.

Mlawula Nature Reserve

The main attraction of the **Mlawula Nature Reserve** (open daily; entry fee) is the section of the **Lubombo Mountains** which runs along its eastern border and provides fantastic views of both Swaziland and the western fringes of Mozambique. Unique species of ironwood trees and cycads grow on the slopes, which can be easily hiked along a **trail** marked by a series of beacons, each of which can only be identified once you have reached the one before it (try not to find yourself searching for these at dusk). The trails wend their way around the river heading for caves, a waterfall and a **rhino pool**, and vary in length from two to eight hours. Overnight camping has not been permitted since the camping hut was burnt down, apparently by Mozambican border-hoppers.

The Mlawula stream and more substantial Mbuluzi River both flow through this reserve, passing through some spectacular valleys, and early Stone Age tools over one million years old have been found along their beds. **Antelope**, **zebra** and **wildebeest** congregate near the water, but so do **crocodiles**, so resist the temptation to swim. Enquire at the gate for feeding times at the **vulture restaurant**, where you can watch the critters feeding on recently deceased carcasses.

Practicalities

Buses from Manzini travel to the Mlawula Nature Reserve once a day very early in the morning. To get here by **car**, turn off the Hlane road roughly 1km south of the junction with the Tshaneni road, and continue past the Mbuluzi Reserve for a few kilometres until you see a sign pointing to the Mlawula Reserve on your right. You can pick up a daunting range of leaflets at the park gate, but no supplies, so stock up beforehand.

Accommodation should be booked through the National Trust Commission, National Museum, PO Box 100, Lobamba (☎61178, fax 61875). Facilities include a shaded campsite (①) in the Siphiso river valley and a tented camp (①) where you can also use your own tent. The camp has one of the finest open-air bathrooms in southern Africa, consisting of a donkey-boiler, firewood, water and galvanized-iron washtubs, with a stunning view that looks west over the reserve and beyond, making it perfectly positioned for sunset. More comfortably (but less beautifully), you can stay in a self-catering cottage nearby (③).

Simunye and Siteki

Seven kilometres south of the Mlawula turn-off on the Hlane road, the town of **SIMUN-YE** (which means "we are one") is a sugar company town, designed to house sugar estate workers near the cane fields. You'll find some handy shops and a bank in town and, close by, the *Simunye Country Club* (☎52646; ③), aimed primarily at the upper echelons of the sugar estate workforce, with a **restaurant**, sporting facilities and comfortable **rooms**.

Perched spectacularly on a hillside and once the gateway to a busy border post with Mozambique, **SITEKI**, just over 30km south of Mlawula Nature Reserve, is a fairly lively regional centre. Although the border has now been closed for some years, Siteki remains busy, with a **bus station** which operates frequent services to Manzini, a colourful **market**, and a number of lively restaurants along the main street. Next door to the *Siteki* hotel, off the main road on the way out of town, is the headquarters of *Litiko Letinyanga* (☎34512), a traditional healing organization, run by Dr Nhlavana Maseko, which seeks to improve the credibility of traditional healing with Western medical institutions. You may be able to arrange a session with a traditional healer, but you'll have to phone beforehand (ask for Betty).

There's only one **place to stay** – the *Siteki* (☎34126; ③), which is nice enough, though the rooms feel a bit spartan. Downstairs, the hotel **restaurant** serves steaks and other meat dishes, and there's a great bar attached, which is popular with locals and gets very lively at weekends.

At the beginning of the road ascending to the town, you'll pass through a foot-and-mouth disease control checkpoint; the guards only check you on the way out, to confiscate any meat products that you might have tucked away.

Hlane Royal National Park

Some 67km northeast of Manzini, **Hlane Royal National Park** (daily; ☎42680; small entry fee) is the largest of Swaziland's parks. Formerly a private royal hunting ground, the main attractions here are the thrilling abundance of big game, including **elephant**, **rhino**, **lion**, **leopard** and two young **cheetah**. Hlane is also one of the few parks in southern Africa where you can view elephants and rhino **on foot**, with an armed guide – an unforgettable experience. These two species are in the northern area of the park, which you can visit in your own vehicle, with or without a guide. Walking or driving with a guide will cost you a small sum per hour, and rhino-sighting is virtually guaranteed.

The southern enclosure contains the lion, cheetah and leopard; walking around here is out of the question, but you can go on a drive around. The enclosure's small size makes the trip feel a bit tame, although the cheetah and leopard are great to watch. Sadly, Hlane has no vehicles of its own, so no night drives are possible.

The rest of the park is home to antelope and warthog, and there is an extensive **trail network** through this area, which you can walk – though most choose to drive. The marabou storks still mentioned in some official tourist literature have now departed.

Practicalities

The **entrance** to Hlane is roughly 4km south of Simunye, off the Manzini–Lomahasha road. Fom Manzini, you should follow the Siteki road, and turn left at the sign to Lomahasha and Tshaneni. Buses running between Manzini and Simunye stop at the park gate.

Hlane has two **accommodation** options, both of which must be **booked** through Big Game Parks, PO Box 234, Mbabane (☎44541, fax 40957). The Ndlovu camp, near the road and the two game enclosures, offers self-catering rondavels (①) and camping spots (①), but no electricity. Paraffin lamps are provided, and cooking is on an open fire. Near the campsite there is a large watering hole where you can sit and watch animals coming to drink – it gets particularly busy at sunrise and sunset. The Bhubesi camp, with its three comfortable stone cottages (①) overlooking a dry river, is 18km from Ndlovu along a dirt track, and feels more remote, even though the cottages here have electricity.

THE SOUTH

Approaching Swaziland from one of its border crossings in the south is an excellent option if you're heading on to Kruger National Park. The scenery, particularly along the drive from **Mahamba** to Manzini through the **Grand Valley**, is really superb, and the road passes near most of the historical sites of the Swazi royal house. The south is also home to the **Mkhaya Nature Reserve**, Swaziland's most upmarket reserve and a sanctuary for the rare black rhino.

From Mahamba to Manzini

The **Mahamba border crossing** (open 7am–10pm) is the nearest to Piet Retief in South Africa. Mahamba means "the runaways", which refers to nineteenth-century pretenders to the royal throne who ran here twice to escape retribution. The nearest major town is **NHLANGANO**, only 16km from the border. Nhlangano (the name means "meeting place", in honour of the meeting of British and Swazi monarchs George V and Sobhuza II in 1947) is a good place to change money and to catch **buses** to Mbabane and Manzini.

The town also has a couple of decent **places to stay**: the lively *Phoenix* (☎78488; ②) on the main street offers en-suite rooms, while the upmarket *Nhlangano Sun* (☎78211; ⑤), designed to resemble a ski resort, lies off a signposted turn-off just north of town and looks out onto the Makhosini Valley. Rooms are plush, and the hotel's reasonably priced **restaurant** is worth stopping in if you're just passing through. The hotel also has a casino.

The **Makhosini Valley**, 8km from Nhlangano on the Mhlosheni road, is the site of the main **royal burial grounds**, which are guarded and tended by the Mduli clan, who prevent any disturbance to their eternal rest. This includes not cutting the grass, which means that the grounds now stand out as islands of forest in a sea of cultivated land. The Mduli people also grind the king's medicines and snuff, and have the interesting task of preventing any part of his body (including his faeces, semen, toe-clippings, etc) from being used for magical purposes.

A little further on is a turn on the right to **Zombodze**, King Ngwane I's first royal residence in modern-day Swaziland, which is badly signposted – follow signs for the Ngwane High School, which is very close by.

Travel on for another 28km north from Nhlangano on a good road to reach **HLATHIKHULU**, perched impressively high on a hill and providing cool relief after the murderous heat below. Ngwane's grandson **Sobhuza I** fled near here from the attacks of the mighty Ndwandwe king Zwide, to a place called kaPhungalegazi ("place of the smell of blood"), though nothing is now left of the *kraal* he erected here. Sadly for the town, the main road steams right by it, leaving it forlorn on a diversion to the right. Transtate **buses** stop at the *Assegai Inn* (☎76126; ②) on the main street, which offers en-suite **rooms** – all of which, mysteriously, face away from the views – and a good bar stocking *Hardys*, one of southern Africa's few decent ciders. Best of the town's **restaurants** is the friendly *Style* at the other end of town, which serves inexpensive curries and ice-cold drinks.

The Ngwane clan fought a murderous but inconclusive battle with the Zulu under King Dingane in the nearby **Lubuya Valley** in 1839. This quiet valley is barely populated and, though there's nothing to remind you of the battle that once raged here, it's a good place for a picnic and a stroll. To get to the valley from Hlathikhulu, take the first turning right after heading north towards Manzini, towards Lugoje Nek, and a left turn at the fork here brings you to the valley. The battle left Dingane's forces much reduced, making him an easy target for his brother Mpande the following year.

From Hlathikhulu, Manzini is 74km away, with the bulk of the drive passing along the **Grand Valley**, through which flows the sometimes mighty Mkhondvo River. The valley is hot, overgrazed and almost barren, but offers stunning hiking possibilities and stupendous views from a car.

From Lavumisa to Manzini

The **Lavumisa/Golela border** (open 7am–10pm) is the first border you'll encounter if you're travelling north from KwaZulu-Natal. The border is named after one of the wives of Sobhuza I, whose son Malambule tried to overthrow Sobhuza's successor, Mswati II. Golela, on the South African side, means "many animals", and indeed this area was once predominantly a hunting ground. Today, however, the animals have gone and there is little reason to linger. Instead, press on to **Big Bend**, crossing the Ingwavuma River just south of Nsoko, about 30km from the border, and follow the road through the **Lubombo Mountains**.

Big Bend

Just before entering Big Bend, you'll pass by the Riverside, a complex on the main road housing a functional **motel** (☎36012; ②), an outstanding lobster **restaurant** *Lubombo Lobster* (☎36308), a good Portuguese restaurant, a scruffy nightclub and, downstairs, *Emoya Handicrafts*, which has a small selection of good-value handicrafts. Next door is the *Bushlands Butchery*, where prices are so good that many South Africans drive here to stock up on meat.

BIG BEND itself, dominated by a huge sugar mill, is only worth visiting for its excellent **hotel**, the *Bend Inn* (☎36111; ①–②), at the far end of town. A grand old colonial establishment with superb views of the valley and well-positioned bars, the hotel is now run by an Indian family from Durban who have transformed the place from a sleepy enclave for white expatriates into a lively Swazi haunt. If looking for peace and quiet, don't come here on weekends, when major parties take place. The rooms are spartan but air-conditioned and perfectly comfortable, and the hotel **restaurant** serves tolerable curries and grills for around E25–40.

From Big Bend, there are **buses** travelling to Manzini and Mbabane, and north to Siteki (see p.640).

NGUNI CATTLE AND MKHAYA

The long-horned **Nguni cattle**, herded by the African clans when Europeans encountered them in the nineteenth century, were descendants of the early Iron Age herds. Although they are hardy, disease-resistant and well-adapted to their environment, white beef farmers regarded them as too puny and unproductive for their industry, and replaced them with imported stock. By the 1970s, pure strains of long-horned cattle had virtually disappeared from Swaziland, and **Ted Reilly** initially purchased Mkhaya to save them. The sharp increase in the price of cattle feed in the late 1970s made the long-horns increasingly attractive commercially, enabling Reilly to sell them as pure bred breeding stock, using the money to fund the game acquisition programme at Mkhaya. Today, the cattle graze alongside zebra, wildebeest and antelope, just as they always used to.

Mkhaya Nature Reserve

Roughly 30km north of Big Bend is **Mkhaya Nature Reserve**, situated along a turn-off from the brilliantly named village of **Phuzumoya** ("drink the wind") in classic lowveld scrubland, filled with acacia and thorn trees. A sanctuary for the rare **black rhino**, Mkhaya also accommodates **white rhino**, **elephant** and the near-extinct **roan antelope** and its other more numerous relatives, like nyala and eland. Rubbing shoulders with them are ample herds of **Nguni cattle** (see box above).

Visits to Mkhaya must be booked in advance (see below). You cannot tour Mkhaya in your own vehicle, but must arrange in advance to be met at the gate, from where there are two pick-ups daily (10am & 4pm). The drive ensures that you see all the big game – a task made easier by an enclosure system that restricts their movement – and a generous lunch is included in the price. For overnighters, morning and evening game drives are included in the accommodation price, as well as late-morning escorted walks which offer you the chance to get much closer to animals than you can in a car.

Practicalities

You'll need to **book** your visit to Mkhaya through Royal Swazi Big Game Parks, PO Box 234, Mbabane (☎44541, fax 40957). Visitor facilities are definitely a cut above the norm, but you should be prepared to fork out for the luxuries. There are three **accommodation** options, equipped with bedding and towels and located in the heart of the park, on the banks of the usually dry Ngwenyane River. Toilets and showers are shared at the

WHITE-WATER RAFTING

One of the most exhilarating things you can do in southern Swaziland is to **white-water raft** on the beautiful Lusutfu River, near the Mkhaya Nature Reserve. The route runs for 15km in summer (a bit less in winter), and crosses over rapids classed in grades two to four. Anyone can tackle these rapids once they have had a safety briefing.

The scenery along the route is stunning, but hard to appreciate once you hit the rapids, which leave you paddling like crazy and doing your best not to fall in the water. Most people do capsize, but careful supervision ensures that everyone lives to tell the tale. Trips usually depart from the Mkhaya Game Reserve and cost around E100 a person, including a picnic lunch and evening sundowners. A cheaper package is available from the *Sondzela* lodge at **Mlilwane** (see p.632), which includes transport to and from the river, and two nights' accommodation at Mkhaya, for E300 – contact Royal Swazi Big Game Parks (☎44541, fax 40957) to make bookings.

fully furnished *Standard Safari Tent* (④), but are en suite at the *Luxury Safari Tent* (⑤). Alternatively, you can opt for *Shallows Nest Cottage* (④), whose ingeniously designed bathroom is both private and completely open to the bush. Cooking is done on a huge campfire in the main part of the camp, and staff have been known to treat guests to an after-dinner concert.

travel details

Buses

Big Bend to: Manzini (13 daily; 1hr 30min); Siteki (2 daily; 1hr 30min).

Manzini to: Big Bend (13 daily; 1hr 30min); Hlatsi (2 daily; 1hr 30min); Lavumisa (2 daily; 5hr); Mbabane (27 daily; 45min); Nhlangano (12 daily; 3hr 15min); Siteki (15 daily; 1hr 30min).

Mbabane to: Manzini (27 daily; 45min); Nhlangano (4 daily; 4hr); Piggs Peak (10 daily; 1hr).

Nhlangano to: Manzini (12 daily; 3hr 15min); Mbabane (4 daily; 4hr).

Piggs Peak to: Mbabane (10 daily; 1hr).

Siteki to: Big Bend (2 daily; 1hr 30min); Manzini (15 daily; 1hr 30min).

Flights

Manzini to: Johannesburg (2–5 daily; 1hr).

SOUTH AFRICA: THE HISTORICAL FRAMEWORK

No account of South Africa seen from the tail end of the twentieth century can avoid talking about its most famous social invention, apartheid. While apartheid was never inevitable, its roots lie in its 350-year-old colonial history. The extreme legalized system of segregation and repression that was put in place in the second half of the twentieth century may not have been intended by the British authorities, but they nevertheless began the process in the nineteenth century with wars of conquest, laws to control the movement of labour and segregated reserves. South Africa's twentieth-century history has been about the rise to power of Afrikaner nationalism, its attempts to suppress African rights and the ultimate victory at the end of the century of multiracialism and democracy.

PREHISTORY

When our ancestors climbed down from the trees, it is quite likely they did it in South Africa – if a growing body of scientific evidence is to be believed. In 1924, the world's **oldest hominid remains** and the first-ever evidence of human-like creatures to be discovered in Africa were dug up in the Northern Cape and identified as a "fossilized monkey skull". After a stint as a hum-

ble paperweight, the fossil came to the attention of Professor Raymond Dart at the University of the Witwatersrand, who identified the earth-shaking find as an intermediate species between apes and humans, with a small brain but an upright posture. Still a little shaky on its feet, our ancestor trod the plains of eastern and southern Africa, perhaps three million years ago. Dart called it *Australopithecus africanus*: **Africa's southern ape**. After the emergence of *A. Africanus*, hominids spent the next couple of million years or so perfecting bipedal walking, tool-making, speech and got big-headed (a huge expansion in brain size took place) until they finally strode forth as *Homo sapiens*: the modern humans. Another first for South Africa was the unearthing of the oldest fossil evidence of *Homo sapiens* in a cave at the Klasies river mouth in the Eastern Cape, reckoned to be between 50,000 and 100,000 years old.

THE FIRST SOUTH AFRICANS

Rock art provides evidence of human culture in the subcontinent dating back nearly 30,000 years and represents South Africa's oldest and most enduring artistic tradition. The artists were hunter-gathers, sometimes called bushmen but more commonly **San**, a relatively modern term from the Nama language with roots in the concept of "inhabiting or dwelling" to reflect the fact these were South Africa's aboriginals. The most direct descendants of the late Stone Age, San people have clung up to the present to a tenuous survival in tiny pockets, mostly in Namibia and Botswana, making theirs the longest-spanning culture in the subcontinent. At one time they probably spread throughout sub-Saharan Africa, having pretty well perfected their **nomadic lifestyle**, which involved an enviable twenty-hour week spent by the men hunting and the women gathering. This left considerable time for artistic and religious pursuits. People lived in small, loosely connected bands comprising family units and were free to leave and join up with other groups. In this egalitarian society, the concept of private property had scant meaning because everything required for survival could be obtained from the environment.

About two thousand years ago, this changed when some groups in northern Botswana laid their hands on fat-tailed **sheep and cattle** from northern Africa, thus transforming themselves into **herding communities**. The introduction of livestock had a revolutionary effect on social organization and introduced the idea of ownership and accumulation. Animals became a symbol of both wealth and social status and those who were better at acquiring and holding onto their animals gradually became wealthier. Social divisions developed, political units became larger and centred around a chief, who had important powers, such as the allocation of pasturage.

These were the first South Africans encountered by Portuguese mariners, who landed along the Cape coast in the fifteenth century. Known as **Khoikhoi** (meaning "men of men"), they were not ethnically distinct from the San, as many anthropologists once believed, but simply represented a distinct social organization. According to current thinking it was possible for Khoi who lost their livestock to revert to being San and for San to lay their hands on animals to become Khoi, giving rise to the collective term "Khoisan". This dynamic view of history is significant because it throws out the nineteenth-century idea that race was an absolute determinant of history and culture – a concept that found great popularity among apartheid apologists.

FARMS AND CRAFTS

Around two thousand years ago tall, dark-skinned people who practised mixed farming – raising both crops and livestock – crossed the Limpopo River into South Africa. San paintings from some time in the intervening period depict small ochre people and larger black ones in a variety of hostile and harmonious relationships, indicating contact between the two groups. These **Bantu-speaking** farmers were the ancestors of South Africa's majority African population, who gradually drifted south, to occupy the entire eastern half of the subcontinent as far as the Eastern Cape, where they were first encountered by Europeans in the sixteenth century.

Today there are four main **Bantu language groups** in South Africa; **Nguni** (comprising Zulu, Swazi and Xhosa) and **Sotho** (Sotho and Tswana) being by far the largest. The other two are **Venda** and **Tsonga**. Apart from highly developed farming know-how and a far more sedentary life than the Khoisan, the early Bantu speakers were skilled craftworkers and knew about mining and smelting metals, including gold, copper and iron, which became an impor-

tant factor in the extensive network of **trade** that developed.

The picture painted by the British of them as bloodthirsty Africans engaged in endemic internecine conflicts probably said more about the white colonizers than the Bantu speakers. The nineteenth-century traveller Ludwig Alberti underlined this fact when he observed that the Xhosa of the Eastern Cape "cannot be regarded as a warlike people; a predominant inclination to pursue a quiet cattle-raising life is much more in evidence amongst them".

THE CAPE GOES DUTCH

In the fifteenth century, Portuguese mariners under the command of **Bartholomeu Dias** became the first Europeans to set foot in South Africa. Marking their progress, they left an unpleasant set of calling cards all along the coast – African men and women they had captured in West Africa and had cast ashore to trumpet the power and glory of Portugal to the locals. Little wonder that their first encounter with the Khoi along the Garden Route coast was not a happy one. It began with a group of Khoi stoning the Portuguese for taking water from a spring without asking permission and ended with one Khoi main lying dead with a crossbow bolt through his chest – a rather disappointing start for friendly relations.

It was another 170 years before any European settlement was established in South Africa. In 1652 a group of white employees of the **Dutch East India Company**, which was engaged in trade between the Netherlands and the East Indies, pulled into Table Bay to set up a refreshment station to revictual Company ships trading between Europe and the East. There was no thought at the time of setting up a colony; on the contrary, the Cape was a rather bum posting, given to the station commander **Jan van Riebeeck** because he had been caught with his hand in the till by the company bosses. Van Riebeeck dreamed up a number of schemes to isolate the Cape Peninsula from the rest of Africa, including a plan to build a canal that would cut it adrift. In the end he had to satisfy himself with planting a bitter **almond hedge** (still growing in Cape Town's Kirstenbosch Gardens) to keep the natives at bay, symbolically representing an ambivalence about being European in Africa, which still haunts most white South Africans.

Despite van Riebeeck's view that the **Khoi**, who were already living at the Cape, were "a savage set, living without conscience", from the start the Dutch were dependent on them to provide livestock, which were traded for trinkets. As the settlement developed, van Riebeeck needed more **labour** to keep the show going, and bemoaned the fact that he was unsuccessful in persuading the Khoi to discard the freedom of their herding life for the toil of ploughing furrows for him. Much to his annoyance, the bosses back in Holland had forbidden van Riebeeck from enslaving the locals, and refused his request for slaves from elsewhere in the company's empire.

This led to the inexorable process of **colonization** of the lands around the fort, when a number of Dutch men were released in 1657 from their contracts to farm as **free burghers** on land granted by the company. The idea was that they would have to sell their produce to the company at a fixed price, thereby overcoming the labour shortage. The only snag with this was the land didn't belong to the company in the first place and the move sparked the first of a series of **Khoikhoi–Dutch wars**. Although the first campaign ended in stalemate, the Khoikhoi were ultimately no match for the Dutch, who had the tactical mobility of horses and the superior killing power of firearms. Campaigns continued through the 1660s and 1670s and proved rather profitable for Dutch raiders, who on one outing in 1674 rounded up eight hundred Khoi cattle and four thousand sheep.

Meanwhile, in 1658, van Riebeeck had managed to successfully purloin a shipload of **slaves** from West Africa, whetting an insatiable appetite for this form of labour. The Dutch East India Company itself became the biggest slave owner at the Cape and continued importing slaves, mostly from the East Indies, at such a pace that by 1711 there were more slaves than burghers in the colony. By the end of the eighteenth century there were almost 15,000 slaves and just under 14,000 burghers at the Cape. With the help of this ready workforce, the embryonic Cape colony expanded outwards and trampled the Peninsula Khoikhoi, who by 1713 had lost everything. Most of their livestock (nearly 50,000 animals) and most of their land west of the Hottentots Holland Mountains had been gobbled up by the Dutch East India Company. Dispossession and diseases like smallpox, previously unknown in South Africa, decimated their numbers and shattered their social system. By the middle of the eighteenth century, those who remained had been reduced to a condition of miserable servitude to the colonists.

Impoverished whites living at the dog-end of colonial society also had few options, but these included the real possibility of dropping out of its grindingly class-conscious constraints. Many just packed up their wagons and rolled out into the interior, where they lived by the gun, either hunting game or taking cattle from the Khoi by force. Beyond the control of the Dutch East India Company, these nomadic **trekboers** began to assume a pastoral niche previously occupied by the Khoi. By the turn of the nineteenth century, trekboers had penetrated well into the Eastern Cape, pushing back the Khoi and San in the process. Not that the indigenous people gave up without a fight. As their lives became disrupted and living by traditional means became impossible, the Khoisan began to prey on the cattle and sheep of the trekboers. The trekboers responded ruthlessly by hunting down the San as vermin, killing the men and often taking women and children as slaves, bringing them to virtual extinction in South Africa.

After the **British occupation of the Cape** in 1795, the trekboer migration from the Cape accelerated. Britain was now undisputed as the world's dominant naval power. In the ferment that followed the French Revolution, it feared for the security of the Cape sea route to the East and therefore sent a few war sloops into Table Bay and informed the Dutch officials there that they were no longer in charge.

RISE OF THE ZULUS

While in the west white trekboers were migrating from the Cape colony, in the east equally significant movements were under way. Throughout the seventeenth and eighteenth century, descendants of the first **Bantu speakers** to penetrate into South Africa had been swelling their numbers and had expanded right across the eastern half of the country, where the rainfall was high enough for their mixed farming economy. By the turn of the nineteenth century the territory was brimming with people and cattle who were fast grazing it out, the limits of expansion having been reached. Exacerbating this was a sustained period of drought.

Nowhere was this more marked than in **KwaZulu-Natal**, where chiefdoms survived by subduing and absorbing their neighbours to gain control of pasturage, thus creating larger and more powerful groupings. By the early part of the nineteenth century two chiefdoms, the **Ndwandwe** and the **Mthethwa**, dominated the eastern section of South Africa around the Tugela River. During the late 1810s a major confrontation between them ended in the defeat of the Mthethwa.

Out of their ruins emerged the **Zulus**, who were to become one of the most powerful polities in southern Africa. Prior to the defeat of the Mthethwa, the Zulus had been a minor clan under their domination. Around 1816, **Shaka** assumed the chieftaincy of the Zulus, whose fighting tactics he quickly transformed, supplementing the Nguni's traditional long throwing spear with a short stabbing one suitable for close combat. The throwing spear rendered a warrior unarmed once he had thrown it and was relatively easily deflected by a cowhide shield, but with a **stabbing spear** he could keep on fighting indefinitely. Shaka also introduced the tactic known as the "horns of the bull" by which the enemy were outflanked by highly disciplined formations spreading out to engulf them by means of two wings. The manoeuvre was used to devastating effect against the British at the Battle of Isandlwana in 1879.

By 1820, the Zulus had incorporated the fragments of the Mthethwa and had defeated the Ndwandwe. By the middle of the decade they had formed a **centralized military state** with a 40,000-strong standing army. The nature of war in the east changed from the almost symbolic skirmishes that characterized Nguni raids up to the end of the eighteenth century to decisive battles in which massacres of women and children weren't unknown. Nevertheless, the real strength of the system lay in its ability to absorb the survivors, who became members of the expanding Zulu state. Throughout the 1820s Shaka sent out his armies to attack his neighbours and take their cattle. In 1828, in a palace coup, he was stabbed to death by a servant and his two half-brothers, one of whom, **Dingane**, succeeded him. Dingane continued with his brother's ruthless policies and tactics.

The rise of the Zulu state reverberated right across southern Africa and led to the creation of a series of **centralized Nguni states** as well as paving the way for Boer expansion into the interior. In a movement known as the **mfecane**, or forced migrations, huge areas of the country were laid waste and people across eastern South Africa were displaced, dispossessed and driven off their lands, either attempting to survive in small groups or banding together in larger political organizations to survive. To the north of the Zulu kingdom, another Nguni group with strong cultural and linguistic affinities with the Zulus came together under Sobhuza I and his son Mswati II, after whom their new state **Swaziland** took its name. A few hundred Zulus under the leadership of **Mzilikazi** had taken refuge in Northwest Province after rebelling against Shaka. By 1829 their numbers had swelled to around seventy thousand, but in 1838 they were routed by encroaching Voortrekkers, against whose firearms they proved no match. They relocated to southwestern Zimbabwe, where they re-established themselves as the **Matabele** kingdom. In the Drakensberg, on the west flank of KwaZulu-Natal, **Moshoeshoe**, another chief from humble origins, used diplomacy and cunning to build up his state from the ruins of the *mfecane*. By providing a haven to refugees, he was able to build up a substantial state from disparate Sotho groupings. Believing that "peace is like the rain which makes the grass grow", he kept no standing army, relying instead on opportunism and good-neighbourliness to survive.

THE GREAT TREK

Back in the Cape, many Afrikaners were becoming fed up with British rule. Their principal grievance was the way in which the colonial authorities were tampering with labour relations and destroying what they saw as a divine distinction between blacks and whites. In 1828 the **Cape Ordinance 50** gave Khoi residents and free blacks equality before the law, while the **abolition of slavery** in 1834 was the last straw. One Voortrekker wrote: "it's not so much their freedom that drove us to such lengths, as their being placed on an equal footing with Christians, contrary to the laws of God and the natural distinction of race".

In this spirit 15,000 Afrikaners (one out of every ten living in the colony) set out to leave the Cape and once and for all shake off the meddlesome British. When they arrrived in the eastern half of the country, they were delighted to find vast tracts of apparently unoccupied land. In fact, they were merely stumbling into the eye of the *mfecane* storm – areas that had been temporarily cleared either by war parties or by fearful people hiding out to escape detection. As they fanned out further they hit up against the Nguni states and a series of battles followed. By the middle of the nineteenth century, the Voortrekkers had consolidated control and established the two Boer states of the **South African Republic** (now Mpumalanga, Northwest and Northern provinces) and the **Orange Free State** (now Free State), both of whose independence was recognized by Britain in the 1850s.

Britain wasn't too concerned about the interior of South Africa. Apart from its strategic position, South Africa was a chaotic and undeveloped backwater at the butt-end of the Empire that was of scant interest back in London. At this time the United States, which was first settled by Britons a mere thirty years before the Dutch hit South Africa, had a population of over thirty million people of European extraction and 80,000km of railways compared with South Africa's 250,000 whites and 120km of railways. Things changed first in the 1860s, with the **discovery of diamonds** (the world's largest deposit) around modern-day Kimberley and even more significantly in the 1880s, with the **discovery of gold** at Witwatersrand (now Gauteng). Together these discoveries were the catalyst that transformed South Africa from an almost feudal farming society to an urbanized industrial one. In the process great wealth was made by capitalists like **Cecil John Rhodes**, traditional African society was crushed and the independence of the Boer republics ended.

Although the **Gauteng goldfields** were exceptionally well-endowed with ore, they were also particularly difficult to mine, requiring the sinking of deep shafts, which necessitated capitalist intervention. Exploiting the mines required costly equipment and cheap labour to operate it. Capital quickly flowed in from Western investors eager for big profits and even up until today the West has retained strong links with the South African mines. Gold transformed the South African Republic from a down-at-heel rural society into an industrial

nation that was the world's largest producer of gold.

Despite the benefits it brought, the discovery of gold was also one of the principal causes of the **Second Anglo-Boer War**. Gold-mining had shifted the economic centre of South Africa from the British-controlled Cape to a Boer republic, while at the same time Britain's European rival, Germany, was beginning to make political and economic inroads in the Boer republics. Britain feared losing its strategic Cape naval base, but perhaps even more important were questions of international finance and the substantial British investment in the mines. London was at the heart of world trade and was eager to see a flourishing gold-mining industry in South Africa, but the Boers seemed rather sluggish about modernizing their infrastructure to assist the exploitation of the mines.

In any case, a number of Britons had for some time seen the unification of South Africa as the key to securing **British interests** in the subcontinent. To this end, under a wafer-thin pretext, the Empire had declared war and subdued the last of the independent African kingdoms by means of the **Zulu War** of 1879. This had secured KwaZulu-Natal and meant that all the coastal territories of South Africa from Namibia round to Mozambique were under British control. All that remained was to bring the two Boer republics under the Union Jack.

THE ANGLO-BOER WAR

During the closing years of the nineteenth century Britain demanded that the South African Republic grant voting rights to British miners living in the country – a demand that, if met, would have meant the end of Boer political control over their own state. The Boers tuned down the request and war broke out in October 1899. The British command, which had been used to fighting colonial wars against enemies armed with spears, believed they were looking at a walkover; in the words of Lord Kitchener, "a teatime war" that would get the troops home in time to open their Christmas presents.

In fact the battle turned into the most expensive campaign since the Napoleonic Wars. During the **early phase** of the war the Boers took the imperial power by surprise and penetrated into British-controlled KwaZulu-Natal and the Northern Cape, inflicting a series of humiliating defeats. By June a reinforced British army was pushing the Boers back and once again the high command was talking about being home in time for their Christmas pudding. But the Boers fought on for another two years of protracted guerrilla war. **Lord Kitchener** responded ruthlessly with a scorched-earth policy that left the countryside a smouldering wasteland and thousands of women and children homeless. To house these thousands of dispossessed, the British invented the **concentration camp**, which took the lives of 26,370 Boer women and children. This episode wasn't quickly forgotten: for some Afrikaners it remains a major source of bitterness against the British today. Less widely publicized were the **African concentration camps** which took 14,000 lives. By 1902, the Boers were demoralized and split between those who couldn't face another winter of near starvation (the so-called "hands-uppers") and those who wanted to fight on ("the bitter-enders"). In May 1902 the Boer republics signed a treaty surrendering their independence in exchange for British promises of reconstruction. By the end of the so-called "teatime war", Britain had committed nearly half a million men to the field and lost 22,000 of them. Of the 88,000 Boers who fought, 7000 died in combat. With the two Boer republics and the two British colonies under imperial control, the way was clear for the federation of the **Union of South Africa** in 1910.

MIGRANT LABOUR AND THE BAMBATHA REBELLION

Between the conclusion of the Anglo-Boer War and the unification of South Africa, the mines suffered from a shortage of **unskilled labour**. Most Africans still lived by agriculture, either as tenant farmers on white farms or in reserves created by the colonial government. They had no need to desert their traditional farming way of life for a thankless existence in shantytowns far away from home. To counter this the government took measures to compel them to supply their labour. One method was the imposition of **taxes** that had to be paid in coin, thus forcing Africans from subsistence farming and into the cash economy, where they would have to earn a wage. Responding to one such tax, a group of Zulus protested in 1906 and refused to pay up. The authorities declared martial law and dealt mercilessly with the protestors, burning their huts and seizing all their possessions.

This provoked a full-blown rebellion led by Chief Bambatha, which was ruthlessly put down by the colonial authorities, with 4000 rebels dying in the process. This marked an end to armed resistance by Africans for over half a century. After the defeat of the **Bambatha Rebellion**, the numbers of African men from Zululand working in the Gauteng mines shot up by sixty percent. By 1909, eighty percent of adult males in the territory were absent from their homes and working as migrant labourers. **Migrant labour**, with its shattering effects on family life, became one of the foundations of South Africa's economic and social system, and was a basic cornerstone of apartheid.

KICK-STARTING AFRIKANERDOM

In a parallel development, large numbers of **Afrikaners** were forced to leave rural areas in the early part of the twentieth century. This was partly due to the aftermath of British scorched-earth tactics during the Anglo-Boer War, but also a result of overcrowding, drought and pestilence. Many Afrikaners joined the ranks of a swelling **poor white working class** that felt itself caught in a vice: victimized and despised on the one hand by the English-speaking capitalists who commanded the economy, and on the other under pressure from lower-paid Africans who were competing for their jobs.

In 1918 (the year Nelson Mandela was born) a group of Afrikaners formed the **Broederbond** ("the brotherhood"), a secret society to promote the interest of Afrikaners and to forge an Afrikaner republic in South Africa. It aimed to uplift impoverished members of the *volk* ("people") and to develop a sense of pride in their language, religion and culture. Ultimately the Broederbond was to dominate every aspect of the way the country was run for close on half a century.

During the 1930s, a number of young Afrikaner intellectuals travelled to Europe, where they were inspired by the jackbooted march of **fascism** in Portugal, Spain, Italy and Germany. This extreme manifestation of nationalism appeared to hold the key to realizing Afrikaner nationhood. It was around this time that Afrikaner intellectuals began using the term **apartheid** (pronounced "apart-hate", not "apart-hide").

Among the leading lights of apartheid who could be found kicking their heels in Germany in the 1930s were **Nico Diederichs**, who became Minister of Finance under the National Party government; **Hendrik Frensch Verwoerd**, apartheid's leading theorist and prime minister from 1958 to 1966; and **Piet Meyer**, controller of the state broadcasting service, who named his son Izan ("Nazi" spelled backwards – but he later claimed this was sheer coincidence). Meanwhile in 1939, the Broederbond kicked into action with a scheme that launched 10,000 Afrikaner businesses in the space of a decade. Some of these, such as Rembrandt Tobacco, Volkskas (the country's third largest bank), the Santam insurance company and Gencor (one of the five largest mining houses) are still among the leading players in South Africa's economy.

AFRICANS' CLAIMS

Despite having relied on African co-operation for their victory in the Anglo-Boer War and having hinted at enhanced rights for blacks after the war, the British excluded blacks from the cosy deal between Afrikaners and Britain that resulted in the unification of South Africa in 1910. It wasn't long in fact before the white Union government began eroding African rights. In response, a group of middle-class mission-educated Africans formed the **South African Native National Congress** (later to become the ANC) in 1912. The founders weren't interested in overthrowing the white government; they simply wanted recognition by white society. Middle-class blacks already enjoyed the vote in the Cape Province (now the Western, Northern and Eastern capes) on the basis of a **qualified franchise** according to education and property ownership, and the early African leaders wanted this to be extended to the rest of the country. Taking as their model the evolutionary growth of democracy in Britain, they hoped that this would eventually lead to universal suffrage.

In 1914, the leaders set off as a deputation for London, to protest against the **1913 Natives' Land Act**, which severely restricted property ownership by blacks. The trip was unsuccessful and the Land Act came into force and provided the legal foundation stone for the subsequent formalization of apartheid some 35 years later. The Act provided for the division of South Africa into distinct African and white areas, with blacks, despite constituting the overriding majority of the population, confined to less than ten percent of the land surface.

Through the early half of the twentieth century, the ANC remained a conservative organization unwilling to shift from a tactic of deputations to engage in active protest. This led to accusations that its leaders were "good boys tied to the apron strings of the white liberals". In response, a number of alternative mass organizations arose. Among the largest was the mighty **Industrial and Commercial Union**, an African trade union founded in 1919, which at its peak in 1928 had gathered an impressive 150,000 members. But in the 1930s it ran out of steam. The first political movement in the country not organized along ethnic lines was the **South African Communist Party**, which was founded in 1921 with a multiracial executive. While it never itself gained widespread membership, it became an important force inside the ANC.

Throughout the 1930s the ANC plodded on with speeches, petitions and pleas, which proved completely fruitless. They suffered a major setback in 1936 with the **termination of the African franchise** in the Cape Province. The ANC's response was to send a deputation to Prime Minister Hertzog to protest. Hertzog treated them abominably, not even offering them seats. "Well you've seen the newspapers," he told them dismissively. These events left the ANC crippled and hobbling impotently into the 1940s.

World War II split Afrikanerdom. There were those like Prime Minister **Jan Smuts** who stood firmly in favour of joining the war alongside Britain. But for others, like **John Vorster**, Britain was the old enemy, so they supported Germany, some signing up with the **Ossewa Brandwag** (the "Ox-Wagon Torch Commando"), which carried out sabotage against the government. After the war there were hopes of reform from Prime Minister Smuts, who at the time was playing a leading role in the formation of the **United Nations**. Smuts even had a part in penning the Preamble to the Charter on Human Rights, but while his work for abstract "human rights" earned him a statue next to Winston Churchill outside Britain's parliament, he was in no hurry to grant such rights to the majority of South Africans. Even conservative African leaders were losing patience: one, Councillor Paul Mosaka, complaining that "we have been asked to co-operate with a toy telephone. We have been speaking into an appartus which cannot transmit sound."

YOUNG TURKS AND STRIKING MINERS

In 1944 a young hothead called **Nelson Mandela** got together with his friends **Oliver Tambo** and **Walter Sisulu** under the leadership of **Anton Lembede** to form the **ANC Youth League**. Strict Africanists, they refused to work with any other organizations – such as the Indian Congress. The League's founding manifesto criticized the ANC leadership as a group who regarded themselves as "gentlemen with clean hands". Lembede's radical brand of politics was based on his idea that "Africa is the black man's country". He continued: "We have inhabited Africa, our motherland, from time immemorial. Africa belongs to us."

The 1945 annual conference of the ANC adopted a document called "**Africans' Claims in South Africa**", which reflected an emerging politicization resulting from the experiences of the war and especially the defeat of fascism. The document demanded **universal franchise** and an end to the **colour bar**, which reserved most skilled jobs for whites. The Youth League was influenced by the industrial militancy it had witnessed during the war. Despite a ban on industrial action, between 1942 and 1944 there were sixty strikes. In 1946 the African Mineworkers' Union launched one of the biggest strikes in the country's history in protest against falling living standards. Virtually the entire Gauteng gold-mining region came to a standstill as 100,000 workers downed tools. Smuts sent in police who forced the workers back down the shafts at gunpoint.

In 1947 the ANC Youth League was thrown into confusion when Lembede died suddenly. He was succeeded by **AP Mda**, and **Nelson Mandela** took his first step into public life when he was elected general secretary of the organization. At the same time, the Smuts government was under pressure for change. Meanwhile, **European decolonization** was beginning in earnest, with Britain withdrawing from India in the same year. This seemed to have implications for political rights for black South Africans. But more important still was demography, with the relentless **influx of Africans** into the urban

areas breaking the traditional stereotype of them as rural tribespeople.

For years, the white government had been hinting at easing up on segregation, and even Smuts himself, who was no soft liberal, had reckoned that it was untenable and would have to end at some point. His deputy **JH Hofmeyr** had thrown caution to the winds and committed himself to scrapping job reservation, which excluded blacks from skilled jobs. "I take my stand on the ultimate removal of the colour bar", he went on record as saying. Playing for time, the government appointed the **Fagan Commission** to look into the question of the Pass Laws, which controlled the movement of Africans and sought to keep them out of the white cities unless they had a job. The laws led to millions of black South Africans being condemned to a ghetto existence in the rural areas, where there were no jobs, poverty reigned and infant mortality was high.

When the Fagan Commission reported its findings its 1948, it concluded that "the trend to urbanization is irreversible and the Pass Laws should be eased". While some blacks may have felt heartened by this hint of reform, this was the last thing many whites wanted to hear. For Afrikaners, the threat seemed particularly acute, and raised all sorts of fears about losing their identity and being swamped by blacks. For **white workers** the threat of losing their jobs to lower-paid African workers was a real one, while **Afrikaner farmers** were alarmed by the idea of a labour shortage due to Africans leaving the rural areas for better prospects in the cities.

Against this background of black aspiration and white fears, the Smuts government called a **general election**. The opposition **National Party** campaigned on a *swart gevaar* or "black peril" ticket which played on white insecurity and fear. The Afrikaner nationalists promised to satisfy a range of conflicting interests. With an eye on the vote of Afrikaner workers and farmers, they promised to reverse the tide of Africans coming into the cites and send them all back to the reserves. For white business they made the conflicting promise to bring black workers into the cities as a cheap and plentiful supply of labour.

On Friday May 28, 1948, South Africa awoke to the unthinkable reality of a **National Party victory** at the (whites-only) polls. Party leader **DF Malan** was summoned to Pretoria by the governor-general to form a cabinet. On arriving by train at Pretoria station he told a group of ecstatic supporters: "For the first time, South Africa is our own. May God grant that it always remains our own. We Afrikaners are not a work of Man, but a creation of God. It is to us that millions of barbarous blacks look for guidance, justice and the Christian way of life."

Meanwhile, the ANC was riven by its own power struggle. Fed up with the ineffectiveness of the old guard, and faced with the rabid DF Malan, the Youth League staged a putsch, voted in their own leadership with Nelson Mandela on the executive and adopted the League's radical **Programme of Action**, with an arsenal of tactics that Mandela explained would include "the new weapons of boycott, strike, civil disobedience and non-cooperation".

THE 1950s: PEACEFUL PROTEST

During the 1950s, the National Party began putting in place a barrage of laws that would eventually constitute the structure of apartheid. Some early onslaughts on black civil rights included: the **Coloured Voters Act**, which stripped coloureds of the vote; the **Bantu Authorities Act**, which set up puppet authorities to govern Africans in the reserves; the **Population Registration Act**, which classified every South African at birth as "white, Native or coloured"; the **Group Areas Act**, which divided South Africa into ethnically distinct areas; and the **Suppression of Communism Act**, which made any anti-apartheid opposition (Communist or not) a criminal offence.

The ANC responded in 1952 with the **Defiance Campaign**, which kicked off with a letter to the government demanding the same civil rights for blacks that whites enjoyed. During the campaign, eight thousand volunteers deliberately broke the apartheid laws listed above and were jailed. The campaign rolled on through 1952 until the police provoked violence in October by firing on a prayer meeting in East London. A riot followed in which two white people were killed, thus appearing to discredit claims that the campaign was non-violent. The government used this as an excuse to swoop on the homes of the ANC leadership, resulting in the detention and then banning of over one hundred ANC organizers. **Bannings** were designed to restrict a person's movement and political activities. A banned person was prohibited from seeing more than one person at a time or talking to another banned person; prohibited from entering certain buildings; kept under surveillance; was required to report regularly to the police and could not be quoted or published.

The most far-reaching event of the decade was the **Congress of the People**, held near Johannesburg in 1955. At a mass meeting of nearly three thousand delegates, four organizations, representing Africans, coloureds, whites and Indians, formed a strategic partnership called the **Congress Alliance**. Explaining the historic significance of the meeting, ANC leader Chief **Albert Luthuli** commented that "for the first time in the history of our multiracial nation its people will meet as equals, irrespective of race, colour and creed to formulate a freedom charter for all the people of our country". The **Freedom Charter**, which was adopted at the Congress of the People, became the principal document defining ANC policy.

The government found the breadth of the movement and its principles of freedom and equality too much to stomach and they sent in the police to round up 156 opposition leaders who were charged with treason. Evidence at the **Treason Trial** was based on the Freedom Charter, which was described as a "blueprint for violent Communist revolution". Although all the defendants were acquitted, the four-year trial disrupted the ANC and splits began to emerge. From within the organization, a group of Africanists criticized the Freedom Charter because it promoted co-operation with white activists. At the 1958 ANC national conference they attempted to hijack the leadership, but when they failed they walked out and formed the **Pan Africanist Congress** under the lead-

THE FREEDOM CHARTER

- The people shall govern.
- All national groups shall have equal rights.
- The people shall share the nation's wealth.
- The land shall be shared by those who work it.
- All shall be equal before the law.
- All shall enjoy equal human rights.
- There shall be work and security for all.
- The doors of learning and culture shall be opened.
- There shall be houses, security and comfort.
- There shall be peace and friendship.

ership of the charismatic **Robert Mangaliso Sobukwe**. Upstaging the ANC, the PAC launched an anti-pass campaign ten days before a similar one planned by the ANC.

SHARPEVILLE

On March 21, 1960, Sobukwe and thousands of followers left home to present themselves without passes to police stations. Sobukwe gave strict instructions to keep the demonstrations peaceful and not to be provoked by anyone. Across Gauteng and the Western Cape there were demonstrations which in due course dispersed, but at **Sharpeville** police station, south of Johannesburg, the crowd refused to leave, despite being buzzed by low-flying Sabre jets. A scuffle broke out, the police panicked and opened fire, killing 69 and injuring nearly 200. Most were shot in the back.

In a rapid sequence of events, demonstrations swept the country on **March 27**, and ANC activist Oliver Tambo (later to become the ANC leader in exile until the release of Mandela) illegally left the country. The following day Africans staged a **total stay-away** from work and thousands followed Nelson Mandela and Albert Luthuli in a public pass-burning demonstration. The day after that the government declared a **state of emergency** and rounded up 22,000 people. One day later, the United Nations Security Council resolution called for the government to abandon apartheid, to which it reacted swiftly with bans on the ANC and PAC. It was now illegal to be a member of either organization. Among white South Africans there was near hysteria as the value of the rand slipped, shares slumped and some feared an imminent and bloody revolution.

Later that month, Prime Minister **Hendrik Verwoerd** was shot twice in the head by a half-crazed white farmer and many people hoped his death would provide a speedy retreat from apartheid. But Dr Verwoerd survived, with his prestige enhanced and his appetite for apartheid stronger than ever. More than anyone else Verwoerd made apartheid his own and formulated it into a coherent system based around the idea of **notionally independent bantustans**, in which Africans were to exercise their political rights away from the white areas. The underlying aim of the scheme was to divide Africans into distinct ethnic groups, thereby dis-

mantling the black majority into several separate "tribal" minorities, none of which on its own could outnumber whites.

After the banning of opposition in 1960, Dr Verwoerd pressed ahead with his cherished dream of an all-white **Afrikaner republic**, which he succeeded in achieving in March 1961 through a referendum. For his pains the Commonwealth Prime Ministers' Conference in London kicked the republic out of the British Commonwealth and Mandela called for a national convention "to determine a non-racial democratic constitution". Instead Verwoerd appointed one-time neo-nazi **John Vorster** to the post of Justice Minister. A trained lawyer, Vorster eagerly set about passing a succession of repressive laws that circumvented normal legal procedures and flouted all principles of natural justice.

Some in the ANC realized that the rules of the game had changed irrevocably. "The time comes in the life of any nation when there remain only two choices: submit or fight. That time has now come to South Africa. We shall not submit", Mandela told the world, before going underground as commander-in-chief of **UmkhontoWe Sizwe** ("Spear of the Nation", aka MK), a newly formed armed wing involving ANC and Communist Party leaders. The organization was dedicated to economic and symbolic acts of sabotage and was under strict orders not to kill or injure people. Mandela operated clandestinely for a year, travelling in disguise, leaving the country illegally and popping up unexpectedly at meetings – all of which earned him the nickname, the "Black Pimpernel". In August 1962 he was finally arrested, tried and imprisoned. He was let out again briefly in 1963 to defend himself against charges of treason at the **Rivonia Trial**. Mandela and nine other ANC leaders were all found guilty and handed life sentences.

APARTHEID: THE DARK DAYS

With the leadership of the liberation movement behind bars, the Rivonia Trial marked the beginning of the decade in which everything seemed to be going the white government's way. Resistance was stifled, the state grew more powerful and for white South Africans, businessmen and foreign investors life seemed perfect. The panic caused by the Sharpeville massacre soon became a dim memory and confidence returned. For black South Africans poverty deepened – a state of affairs enforced by apartheid legislation.

There was a minor setback in 1966 when Dr Verwoerd was stabbed to death (and failed to return from the dead this time) in parliament by a messenger who went off the rails after a tapeworm had ordered him to do it, as he told doctors. The breach was filled by **Balthazar John Vorster**, whose approach was more pragmatic than that of Verwoerd. Not averse to travelling to Africa to shake hands with tame black leaders like Hastings Banda of Malawi in the interests of détente, his approach to black South Africans was rather less chummy. His premiership was characterized by an increased use of the **police** as an instrument of repression, while bannings, detentions without trial, house arrests and deaths of political prisoners in detention became commonplace.

The ANC was impotent, and resistance by its armed wing MK was virtually nonexistent. This was partly because up to the mid-1970s South Africa was surrounded by sympathetic white regimes – in neighbouring Rhodesia and Mozambique – making it close to impossible to infiltrate combatants into the country. But as South Africa swung into the 1970s, the uneasy peace began to fray, prompted at first by **deteriorating black living standards**, which reawakened industrial action. **Trade unions** came to fill the vacuum left by the ANC and neither Vorster nor any of his National Party successors proved able to stem the escalation of strikes, despite all the repressive resources at their disposal.

However, it was the Soweto Revolt of June 16, 1976, that signalled the transfer of protest from the workplace to the townships, when black youths took to the streets in protest against the imposition of Afrikaans as a medium of instruction in their schools. The protest spread across the country after police opened fire and killed 13-year-old Hector Peterson during one march. By the following February, 575 people (nearly a quarter of them children) had been killed in the rolling series of revolts that followed.

Even in the face of naked violence, protest spread to all sections of the community. The government was forced to rely increasingly on armed police to impose order. Even this was unable to stop the mushrooming of new libera-

tion organizations, many of them part of the broadly based **Black Consciousness movement**. As the unrest rumbled on into 1977, the Vorster government responded by banning all the new black organizations and detaining their leadership. In September 1977, **Steve Biko** (one of the detained), became the 46th political prisoner to meet his end in jail at the hands of the security police. In place of the banned organizations, a fresh crop had sprung up by the end of the 1970s. The government never again successfully put the lid on opposition as it escalated through the 1980s. There were rent, bus and school **boycotts**, **strikes**, and **campaigns** against removals. By the end of the decade business was complaining that apartheid wasn't working any more, and even the government was starting to agree. The growth of the black population was outstripping that of whites; from a peak of 21 percent of the population in 1910, whites now made up only 16 percent. This proportion was set to fall to 10 percent by the end of the century. The sums just didn't add up.

TOTAL STRATEGY

It was becoming clear that Vorster's deployment of the police couldn't solve South Africa's problems, and in 1978 he was deposed by his defence minister **Pieter Willem Botha** in a palace coup. Under Vorster's premiership, Botha had turned the **South African Defence Force** into the most awesome military machine on the African continent and it became central to his strategy for maintaining white power. Botha realized that the days of old-style apartheid were over, and he adopted a two-handed strategy of reform accompanied by unprecedented repression. Believing there was a total onslaught on South Africa from both inside and outside the country, he devised his so-called **Total Strategy**.

In June 1980, MK, the ANC's armed wing, made an unscheduled reappearance when it successfully attacked the heavily guarded strategic oil refinery at **Sasolburg**, taking the government by surprise. The 1980s saw the growing use of sabotage against the apartheid state. During 1981 there were over ninety **MK armed actions** against police stations, railway lines, power plants, military bases and army recruiting offices. Attacks were often co-ordinated with protest campaigns: for example, buildings at the British Leyland plant were bombed when workers were on strike there. Botha began thinking about reforms and moved **Nelson Mandela** and other imprisoned ANC leaders from Robben Island to Pollsmoor Prison in mainland Cape Town.

At the same time, he poured ever-increasing numbers of troops into African townships to stop unrest, while using economic incentives to attempt to draw neighbouring countries into a "**constellation of Southern African states**" under South Africa's leadership. Between 1981 and 1983 the army was used to enforce compliance on every one of the country's neighbours. An undeclared war against **Angola** reduced a potentially oil-rich country to war-ravaged ruins, while a South African-sponsored conflict in **Mozambique** brought a poverty-stricken country to its knees. Nor was Botha averse to sending commando units across the borders into **Botswana**, **Zimbabwe**, **Swaziland** and **Lesotho** to attack and bomb South African refugees.

Botha hoped that by making a few reforms that tinkered with apartheid and by creating a black middle class as a buffer against the ANC, he could get the world off his back and stem internal unrest. In both he was wrong. Unrest continued unabated and he found himself having to rely increasingly on force. Detentions and executions of political activists increased (in contravention of the Geneva Convention) and heavy sentences were handed down in political trials. Used to maintaining control through the barrel of a gun, Botha was lost for any real political initiatives. Nevertheless, in 1983 he concocted what he believed was a master plan for a so-called **New Constitution** in which coloureds and Indians would be granted the vote. But before anyone got too excited he qualified this with the revelation that each group would be represented in separate chambers, which would have no executive power. Meanwhile, for Africans, apartheid would continue as usual.

Botha hoped for a tactical alliance between whites, coloureds and Indians in opposition to Africans. The scheme was a dismal failure that only served to alienate right-wingers, who saw it as selling out white privilege. As Botha was punting this ramshackle scheme, 15,000 anti-apartheid delegates met at Mitchell's Plain in Cape Town to form the **United Democratic Front** (UDF) at the biggest opposition gathering since the Congress of the People in 1955. Under a leadership that included ANC veterans, the UDF was a multiracial umbrella for 575 organizations. It endorsed the Freedom Charter and became a proxy for the ANC. Two years of strikes, protest and boycotts followed. But there were sinister stirrings when **Mangosuthu Buthelezi**, chief minister of the KwaZulu *bantustan* and leader of the Zulu nationalist **Inkatha** movement, told a rally of migrant workers in Soweto that "the UDF seems to be another force for disunity and cannot succeed without Inkatha. From now on Inkatha will adopt the attitude of an eye for an eye." Attacks by Inkatha members on UDF and ANC supporters became commonplace and have continued to the present. (Evidence in the 1990s pointed to support for Inkatha from elements in the apartheid security forces, including the supply of weapons.)

In the face of intensifying protest, the government looked for ways to respond, and between March and December it offered to **release Mandela** no fewer than five times, provided he agreed to banishment to the Transkei *bantustan*. Five times he refused and this cat-and-mouse game continued right through the 1980s as the pressure mounted and South Africa's townships became ungovernable. Towards the end of the decade the world watched as apartheid troops and police were shown regularly on TV beating up and shooting unarmed Africans. The **Commonwealth**, despite the concerted efforts of British Prime Minister Margaret Thatcher to stop them, condemned the apartheid government. The United States and Australia **severed air-links** and Congress defied President Reagan and passed the comprehensive Anti-Apartheid Act which promoted **disinvestment**. In 1985, the **Chase Manhattan Bank** announced that it would no longer be prepared to roll over its loan to South Africa. Over the next two years ninety US firms closed down their South African operations. An increasingly desperate Botha now modified his conditions for releasing Mandela, offering to "release Mandela if he renounces violence".

Mandela issued a moving reply, read by his daughter Zinzi to a crowd at Jabulani Stadium, in Soweto: "I am surprised by the conditions the government wants to impose on me. I am not a violent man. It was only when all other forms of resistance were no longer open to us that we turned to armed struggle. Let Botha show that he is different to Malan, Strijdom and Verwoerd [previous apartheid prime ministers]. Let him renounce violence. I cherish my own freedom dearly but I care even more for yours."

As events unfolded, a subtle shift became increasingly apparent: Botha was the prisoner and he desperately needed Mandela to release him. On the one hand **black resistance** wasn't abating, while on the other Botha was facing a white **right-wing backlash**. At every by-election the ultra right-wing Conservative Party had been eroding government majorities. In the **1987 general election** the government polled just 52 percent while, so far to the right that it had slid off the political spectrum, the **Afrikaner Weerstand Beweging** ("Afrikaner Resistance Movement", aka AWB) broke up National Party meetings and threatened civil war.

CRISIS

In 1986 Botha declared yet another **state of emergency** and unleashed a last-ditch storm of tyranny. There were **bannings** of people and meetings, and **shootings** by the police were carried out with impunity. There were **mass arrests**, **detentions**, **treason trials** and **torture**. Sinister hit squads were deployed to assassinate the UDF leadership. Alarmed by the spiral of violence that was engulfing the country, a group of South African businessmen, mostly Afrikaners, flew to Senegal in 1987 to meet an ANC delegation headed by **Thabo Mbeki** (now the deputy president). A joint statement pressed for unequivocal support for a negotiated settlement.

Weeks after the world celebrated **Mandela's seventieth birthday** in July 1988 with a huge bash at London's Wembley Stadium, Mandela was rushed off to Tygerberg Hospital, suffering from tuberculosis. Although he was better by October the government announced that he wouldn't be returning to Pollsmoor Prison. Instead he was moved to a warder's cottage at Victor Verster Prison in Paarl. Outside the prison walls, Botha's policies had hit the buffers and even the army top brass were pushing for change. They told Botha that there could be no decisive military victory over the anti-apartheid opposition and the undeclared war in Angola was bleeding the treasury dry.

At the beginning of 1989, Mandela wrote to Botha from Victor Verster Prison calling for negotiations. "I am disturbed by the spectre of a South Africa split into two hostile camps – blacks on one side, whites on the other," he wrote. An intransigent character, Botha found himself with little room to manoeuvre. He had brought South Africa to a state of unprecedented crisis, yet he refused to change direction. When he was weakened by a stroke, his party colleagues moved swiftly to oust him and replaced him with **Frederik Willem De Klerk**.

Drawn from the conservative wing of the National Party, from the start De Klerk made it clear he was totally opposed to majority rule. But he inherited a massive pile of problems that could no longer be ignored: the economy was in trouble and the cost of maintaining apartheid prohibitive; the illegal influx of Africans from the country to the city had become an unstoppable flood; blacks hadn't been taken in by Botha's constitutional reforms; and even South Africa's friends were beginning to lose patience. In September 1989, US President **George Bush** let De Klerk know that if there wasn't progress on releasing Mandela within six months, he would extend US sanctions against South Africa.

De Klerk made a strategic calculation that the ANC was organizationally weak, having little internal base and having lost all its external support as a result of the enforced closure of its bases in Angola and Zambia, as well as having lost aid from eastern Europe with the collapse of the Iron Curtain regimes. He gambled on his own party's five-decade track record in gerrymandering and on his own ability to outmanoeuvre the ANC. In February 1990, De Klerk announced the **unbanning** of the ANC, the PAC, the Communist Party and 33 other organizations, as well as the **release of Mandela**. On Sunday February 11, at around 4pm, Mandela stepped out of Victor Verster Prison and was driven to City Hall in Cape Town, from where he spoke publicly for the first time in three decades. He told his supporters that the factors which necessitated armed struggle still existed, but that he believed that "a climate conducive to a negotiated settlement will exist soon".

That May, Mandela and De Klerk signed an **agreement** in which the government agreed to repeal repressive laws and release political prisoners, while Mandela persuaded the ANC to suspend the armed struggle. As events moved slowly towards full-blown negotiations it became clear that De Klerk still clung to race-based notions for a settlement. "Majority rule is not suitable for South Africa", he said, "because it will lead to the domination of minorities."

NEGOTIATIONS

The **negotiating** process which took place between 1990 and 1994 was fragile, and at many points a descent into chaos looked likely. Obstacles included ongoing violence linked to a sinister "**Third Force**"– elements in the apartheid security forces who were working behind the scenes to destabilize the ANC; **threats of civil war** from heavily armed right-wingers and a low-key war of attrition in KwaZulu-Natal between Zulu nationalists and ANC supporters had already claimed three thousand lives between 1987 and 1990.

In August 1990 this violence burst into the Johannesburg townships when gunmen opened fire on black commuters on a train. In June 1992, forty people were hacked to death in a midnight attack on a squatter camp near Johannesburg. Eyewitnesses reported seeing police trucks ferrying alleged Inkatha supporters to the scene. When Mandela arrived at the scene a crowd of youths sang: "Mandela, you behave like a lamb while we are being slaughtered." This response was very much to the advantage of the National Party as it gave the impression of an impotent ANC unable to protect its supporters and with no power to stop the violence. Mandela responded by breaking off negotiations and launching a **campaign of mass action** to pressurize the government. On August 3 and 4, 1992, the ANC called the largest **strike** in South African history, when four million workers stayed away from work. Subsequently negotiations between the government and the ANC resumed and in October 1992 President De Klerk apologized (conditionally) for apartheid.

But in April 1993, it looked like the whole process was going to unravel with the **assassination of Chris Hani**, the most popular ANC leader after Mandela. Hani's slaying by a right-wing gunman touched deep fears among all South Africans. A descent into civil war loomed and for three consecutive nights the nation watched as Mandela appeared on prime-time television appealing for calm. This marked the decisive turning point as it became apparent that the ANC president was able to hold the country together, while De Klerk kept his head down. Pushing his stategic advantage, Mandela swiftly called for the immediate setting of an **election date**. On June 3, 1993, the poll was proposed for April 27, 1994 and Mandela was able to tell his followers that "the countdown to democracy has begun".

By December 1993, South Africa had its first multiracial administration in 350 years, when the **Transitional Executive Authority** was installed. But this did nothing to stop the violence, which continued to endanger the transition, while Chief Buthelezi and the white right-wing continued to threaten civil war unless KwaZulu-Natal was given autonomy and the Afrikaners a *volkstaat* ("homeland"). Bloodshed and mayhem continued in KwaZulu-Natal and it looked like the election was going to be disrupted. In February 1995, the negotiating parties held fresh discussions to accommodate Chief Buthelezi and the right-wingers. But concessions accepting the principle of self-determination failed to draw either into the elections.

In March 1995, a popular uprising against the government of the **Bophuthatswana** *bantustan* resonated across South Africa. The territory's army and police mutinied and, in an attempt to shore up his regime, Chief Mangope asked the white right wing to help. Hundreds of armed AWB neo-nazis converged on the capital, Mmabatho, and South Africa watched as they were routed by the *bantustan* army. Televison images of armed white neo-fascists being ingloriously defeated by Africans put paid to any ideas about white invincibility and laid to rest the threat of a right-wing rebellion.

In response, the fractionally less right-wing **Afrikaner Volksfront** ("Afrikaner Peoples' Front"), an alliance of whites who wanted their own self-governimg homeland, announced that it would take part in the election, thus leaving Buthelezi isolated. Yet Buthelezi still insisted on boycotting the poll and threatened to lead a KwaZulu-Natal secession from South Africa. His supporters were whipped up into a frenzy of violence that swept across the province. The transitional government declared a **state of emergency** in KwaZulu-Natal and swamped the province with troops. One week before the election was due, the mercurial Inkatha leader agreed to take part.

Despite a last attempt by right-wingers to disrupt the election by bombing Johannesburg International Airport, the **election on April 27, 1994** went off peacefully. Along with millions of his fellow citizens, Nelson Mandela, aged 76, was able to vote for the first time in his life in his country's elections. On May 2, President De Klerk conceded defeat after an ANC landslide, in which the party took 63 percent of the vote. The ANC was also dominant in all but two of the provinces, the National Party decisively taking the **Western Cape** and Buthelezi's Inkatha sweeping to a paper-thin majority in its **KwaZulu-Natal** heartland, with ten percent of the national vote.

But for the ANC, the struggle had just begun. From the National Party it inherited a country of 38 million people. Of these it was estimated that six million were unemployed, nine million were destitute, ten million had no access to running water and twenty million had no electricity. Among adult blacks, sixty percent were illiterate and fewer than fifty percent of black children under 14 went to school. The gap between black and white was still gaping, one indicator being infant mortality, which among Africans ran at eighty deaths per thousand compared with just seven among whites.

Since the 1994 election the ANC has been absorbed in tackling these myriad problems as well as in **nation-building** – attempting to forge the fractured shards left by apartheid into a unified whole. One of the toughest nuts is how to bring about resititution and redistribution, while leaving the economy sufficiently unshackled to create the levels of growth needed to provide jobs to an expanding population. Two weeks after his inauguration as the first democratically elected president in South Africa's history, Mandela gave details of the **Reconstruction and Development Plan** (RDP). The plan targeted as priorities health, housing and education and the promotion of economic growth. But in August Mandela's keynote address to outline the ANC government's progress during its first hundred days in office, was greeted by industrial action protesting at the slow pace of change. In November the **Restitution of Land Rights Act** passed through parliament, aimed to restore land taken from black South Africans under discriminatory legislation.

THE TRUTH AND RECONCILIATION COMMISSION

One of the most significant processes of the post-election period has been the sitting of the **Truth and Reconciliation Commission** (TRC), under the chairmanship of Nobel Peace laureate, Archbishop **Desmond Tutu**, with the task of uncovering the truth behind political crimes committed under apartheid. Among the deeply moving **testimonies** were thousands of individual stories by parents, siblings and friends of people who disappeared never to be seen again, while others gave gruesome accounts of torture, bombings and murders on an extensive scale. A pattern emerged of a widespread **dirty war** carried out on an organized basis against opponents of apartheid.

Further evidence of a systematic and brutal campaign came to light during the trial in September 1996 of former police colonel, **Eugene De Kock**, who was pleading in mitigation after being convicted on 89 charges of murder, gunrunning and fraud. De Kock told the court that he had taken part in the 1982 bombing of ANC offices in London and of a trade union in Johannesburg in 1987. He revealed that his activities were not the work of a rogue unit, but part of a well-coordinated campaign by the security forces, carried out with the full knowledge of the apartheid government, including presidents Botha and De Klerk. In fact, he maintained PW Botha had himself been engaged in planning a number of raids into neighbouring countries in which innocent civilians had been killed. His most sensational allegation was that the South African intelligence services had been responsible for the **assassination of Olof Palme**, the Swedish premier, in 1986, as part of its **Operation Long Reach** to wipe out opponents of apartheid.

De Kock subsequently applied to the Truth and Reconciliation Commission for amnesty, his thousand-page application arriving twenty minutes before the deadline on May 10, 1997. Among the hundreds of other last-minute applications was one from former defence force chief **Constand Viljoen**, and former National Party minister **Piet Koornhof**, who said he wished to make reparation for his part in administering the pass laws. There were also 370 applications from the ANC, including some from a number of the party's cabinet ministers. The party owned up to the torture of dissidents and spies and admitted that there had been sexual abuse of female trainees at its guerrilla camps.

Notably absent were applications from former presidents De Klerk or Botha, or from Chief Buthelezi. Botha had already told the commission that he refused to apologize for apartheid and attacked the ANC for its "fierce and unforgiving assault on the Afrikaner". Speaking on May 14, 1996, De Klerk told the commission that he had not been aware of any atrocities committed under apartheid, a statement Archbishop Tutu said he found difficult to believe given the avalanche of information made available to De Klerk when he was president.

THE NEW CONSTITUTION AND THE FUTURE

On a more positive note, the **New Constitution** was approved in May 1996 and provided for South Africa to remain a parliamentary democracy with an executive president. It was one of the most progressive constitutions in the world, and incorporated an extensive bill of rights. Its main points were the **outlawing of discrimination** on the grounds of race, gender, pregnancy, ethnic or social origin, sexual orientation, disability, religion, belief, culture or language; **protection of freedom** of religion, belief, movement, association, expression and artistic creativity; **prohibition of** slavery, servitude, forced labour, torture, detention without trial, violence or cruel punishment; **guarantee of the right to life**, banning capital punishment but permitting abortion; appointment of an **ombudsman** to defend individuals against maladministration.

At the February 1997 opening of parliament, President Mandela acknowledged three serious problems facing the government. Firstly there had been **inadequate progress** with the Reconstruction and Development Plan, which meant that poverty wasn't being tackled quickly enough. There was a danger that the very South Africans who had suffered most under apartheid were feeling left out of the new deal. The second point he raised was **corruption**, which remained rife in the civil service and was hampering the ability of the country's infrastructure to operate efficiently and was undermining economic capacity. In 1996 more than 3000 police officers had been investigated for criminal activities. But it was **crime** that Mandela identified as the top priority. Figures revealed than one person was being murdered every 29 minutes, there had been 1052 bank robberies in 1996 and over a million women were being raped each year. The impact of violent crime was still disproportionately felt by the black community, while fifteen percent of the country's disposable income was going on security measures. Mandela committed his government to taking action on the whole gamut of criminal activity including rape, car hijacking, weapons dealing and corruption.

For many people the big question is what happens when Mandela goes? Mandela himself has tried to defuse the impact of this by announcing that he won't be seeking re-election after 1999 and has indicated that he would like to be succeeded by his current deputy president, **Thabo Mbeki**. Charismatic as Mandela is, even now his role is increasingly becoming that of a (highly significant) figurehead holding the nation together. Much of the nuts-and-bolts running of the country has already passed on to Sussex University-educated Mbeki, a shrewd, suave and eloquent politician who displayed his considerable diplomatic skill while in exile after his father, ANC veteran Govan Mbeki, was imprisoned in the 1960s.

LITERATURE

Without apartheid, some critics have argued, there would not have been any South African literature. Apartheid has delivered ready-made plots and subject matter for gifted and mediocre artists alike. Stories of the white minority's psychological and political alienation versus the legitimate struggle of the oppressed majority, illegal and clandestine interracial relationships, possibilities of reconciliation, revenge or revolution, apartheid and its colonial precursors, have provided a truth stranger than many fictions. Produced by people with vastly different life experiences and subject to different political pressures, it is impossible to avoid distinctions between the literature of white and black South Africans.

During pre-colonial times there was a variety of oral literary forms, sometimes known as **orature**, in the southern African region. Orature was male-dominated, but women played a significant part in genres such as **praise poems**, equivalent to the heroic epic and folk tales. In contemporary South African orature there has been a further blurring of the boundaries of genre and gender. Women produce oral works at political gatherings, traditionally a male prerogative, while men and women participate in the *toyi-toyi*, a direct descendant of the war songs originally performed only by women to exhort men in battle and now most commonly associated with resistance and political rallies.

COLONIALISM AND TRANSITION

Published in 1883 under a male *nom de plume*, **Olive Schreiner**'s *The Story of an African Farm* is widely regarded as the first novel rooted in South Africa. It stands in marked contrast to the frontier tales of **Percy Fitzpatrick**'s *Jock of the Bushveld* (1907) and **Rider Haggard**, whose "Boy's own" tales of colonial penetration and subjugation such as *King Solomon's Mines* (1885) or *She* (1887) find their direct and indirect descendants in **Wilbur Smith**, literary doyen of airport departure halls, and the late **Sir Laurens Van der Post**, spiritual mentor to Prince Charles.

Christian mission education, the only early route to literacy for black South Africans,

favoured men. As a result, African women did not have the literary opportunities open to the playwright **HIE Dhlomo**; the writer **Thomas Mofolo**, whose historical novel *Chaka* (1925) originally appeared in Sesotho and was translated into English, French, Italian, German, Yoruba and Afrikaans; or the journalist, translator and novelist **Sol Plaatje**. A founder member of the ANC, Plaatje's best-known works are *Mhudi* (1930) and *Native Life in South Africa* (1916). The former is the story of an African society in transition as it deals with the implications of the Afrikaner Great Trek and the social upheaval caused by the Zulu military state's raids and conquests, while in *Native Life* Plaatje documented the disastrous effects on Africans of the 1913 Land Act. This law denied them access to the land of their birth after the Anglo-Boer War and formation of the Union of South Africa had effectively resolved economic and political differences between the white settler interests and British imperial power.

JIM-COMES-TO-JO'BURG

The discovery of minerals and the growing urbanization and industrialization of South African society had a detrimental effect on African and Afrikaner rural society alike. From the white perspective, removal from the land threatened the "natural order" of race relations for landless Afrikaners and Africans arrived in the city as "equals". While the perceived "threat" to white civilization was greatly exaggerated, it had four significant consequences for white writers at the time: it shifted literary attention away from rural concerns towards urban-based issues, it provided the context for fears of miscegenation, encouraged a re-examination of the image of Afrikaners, and opened up new forms of narration.

Movement towards the city fostered what Nadine Gordimer later termed the **"Jim-comes-to-Jo'burg" novel**, in which a naive young African man moves from a protected and stable rural environment to city life and a variety of urban experiences and temptations. **Peter Abrahams**' contribution was *Mine Boy* (1946), often regarded as South Africa's first proletarian novel, while for **Alan Paton** the true nature of African culture was to be found in a rural setting and the *status quo ante*. Much later **Mtutuzeli Matshoba**'s short story "Three Days in the Land of a Dying Illusion", from his collection *Call Me not a Man* (1979), would invert and parody the genre.

MISCEGENATION AND ARCHETYPES

Roy Campbell, subsequently associated with Iberian fascism, is the best-known poet of the interwar years. Like **Guy Butler** after him, he tended to equate Europe with history, development and rationalism and Africa with unchanging archetypes. During this period **Sarah Gertrude Millin**'s fiction, particularly *God's Stepchildren* (1924), provided the starkest articulation of differences between Europe and Africa and white anxiety about the consequences of **miscegenation**. The basis for Millin's views lay in the notion of "good" and "bad" blood, and in the fear that the (male) colonizer's possession and control of the colonial territories would simultaneously confirm his dominance and open him to control by the "heart of darkness". Millin of course did not even begin to contemplate "the horror" of miscegenation involving a black man and a white woman. With the repeal of the so-called "Immorality Act" in 1985 which forbade interracial sexual relations, miscegenation has lost its literary and political significance. **Stephen Gray**'s *Time of our Darkness* in 1988 may well be the last serious work on a subject tackled by **William Plomer** in *Turbott Wolfe* (1926), **Peter Abrahams** in *The Path to Thunder* (1948), **Alan Paton** in *Too Late the Phalarope* (1953), **Nadine Gordimer** in her short story "The Country Lovers" (1967) and **Athol Fugard** in *Statements After an Arrest Under the Immorality Act* (1974).

FROM DISPOSSESSION TO APARTHEID

The separation of **Afrikaners** from "their" land, and their participation in an industrializing economy largely controlled by English speakers, encouraged sentimental literary representations of Afrikaners. **Pauline Smith**'s work, such as *The Beadle* (1926) and her short story collection *The Little Karoo* (1925), inadvertently fostered the myth of the Boer as a landless, economically oppressed victim denied his language and culture. While **Herman Charles Bosman**'s short stories such as *Mafeking Road* (1947) and *A Cask of Jerepigo* (1964) also focus on rural Afrikaner

life, they display far more irony. Narrated by one Oom Schalk Lourens, who in Mark Twain-like fashion is never fully aware of the implications of the stories that he tells, Bosman's humorous tales of backveld ambition, betrayal and desire presage the concerns and doubts about writing and the control of history, truth and identity that would increasingly characterize what the novelist **JM Coetzee** has called "white writing" – writing that articulates the "concerns of people no longer European, not yet African".

Alan Paton's *Cry, the Beloved Country* appeared in 1948, the year in which the Nationalist government came to power, and has been filmed twice. Despite its reputation as an anti-apartheid novel, Paton's representation of the Zulu language as the discourse of a past, heroic age, and the book's support for racial segregation, perpetuate nostalgic, pastoral myths of the "noble Zulu" found in the works of Wilbur Smith, Rider Haggard and that most Victorian of socialists, Friedrich Engels.

THE DRUM GENERATION

It is to the link between emergent, predominantly male **black writing and journalism**, centred on the Johannesburg-based **Drum magazine**, that the 1950s belong. The publication was one of the few outlets for black creative writers such as **Can Themba**, Es'kia Mphahalele, Bloke Modisane and Todd Matshikiza, many of whom chose to write short stories or autobiographical novels. Favoured because of its flexibility and compatibility with their fast-paced and fractured life styles under oppressive conditions, the short story has remained a popular medium for black and white South African fiction. The so-called "**Drum generation**" articulated black urban experience and aspirations, often in an Americanized B-movie style in their journalism, fiction and drama such as *King Kong*, a musical based on the life of an actual boxer-gangster which helped to launch the careers of Thandi Klaasen, Dolly Rathebe and Miriam Makeba.

In general, there was little space for women's journalism and fiction at this time. Covering her pre-Botswana years in South Africa, **Bessie Head**'s posthumously published *The Cardinals* (1993) is a rare exploration of the problems faced by one of the few black women journalists during this period who made the transition to novel-writing.

While many of the *Drum* generation died relatively young and in exile, **Es'kia Mphahalele** has been a survivor. His *Down Second Avenue* (1959) is often viewed as the definitive text of an era characterised by black male autobiographies such as *Tell Freedom* (1954) by **Peter Abrahams**, **Bloke Modisane**'s *Blame me on History* (1963) and **Todd Matshikiza**'s *Chocolates for my Wife* (1961). Mphahalele's subsequent novels, *The Wanderers* (1971) and *Afrika my Music* (1984) recorded the fragmented experience of exile, that "soul-mutilating process" which has affected so many South Africans in the last sixty years.

Sophiatown, the last area in Johannesburg where Africans had freehold property rights, was the heartbeat of the *Drum* generation. Its nearest equivalent in Cape Town was District Six, a multiracial but predominantly coloured inner-city slum which provided the backdrop for the early work of two Cape Town writers, **Richard Rive** (*Buckingham Palace, District Six*) in 1986 and **Alex La Guma** (*A Walk in the Night*) in 1962, and Achmat Dangor's anthology *Waiting for Leila* (1981). Other coloured writers of note are the short-story writer and poet **James Matthews**, one of four contributors to the short-story anthology *Quartet* (1963) edited by Rive, and the three anthologies *Sirens, Knuckles, Boots* (1963), *Letters to Martha* (1968), and the poet **Dennis Brutus** who devoted considerable energy to ensuring South Africa's sporting isolation during the apartheid years, and **Arthur Nortje** in *Dead Roots* (1973). Like the short-story writer **Zoe Wicomb** in her collection of short stories, *You Can't Get Lost in Cape Town* (1987), Nortje was prepared to explore the more ordinary and less obviously political aspects of life in South Africa by focusing on inner worlds and on the issue of coloured identity as marginal to larger political and national questions.

Rive wrote several Cape Town-based novels such as *Emergency* (1964), the latter about the events surrounding the declaration of a state of emergency in 1960. Several other novelists have set works in this and subsequent periods of repression: **Jonty Driver**'s *Elegy for a Revolutionary* (1969), **Lewis Nkosi**'s *The Rhythm of Violence* (1964) and **Alex La Guma**'s *In the Fog of the Seasons' End* (1972) for the 1960s; **Sipho Sepamla**'s *A Ride on the Whirlwind* (1981), **Mongane Serote**'s *To Every*

Birth Its Blood (1981) and **Miriam Tlali**'s *Amandla* (1981) for the Soweto period; **Menan du Plessis**'s *A State of Fear* (1983), **Hein Grosskopf**'s *Artistic Graves* (1993) and **Mandla Langa**'s *A Rainbow on the Paper Sky* (1989).

PRISON WRITINGS

Novels of resistance are inevitably accompanied by prison writings, and South Africa is not short of these. Among many books on the subject, **Albie Sachs**' *Jail Diary* (1966) and **Ruth First**'s *117 Days* (1982) record their detentions without trial in the early 1960s, and **Indres Naidoo**'s *Island in Chains* (1982) deals with his ten years on Robben Island after being arrested and charged with sabotage. Most prisoners served out their sentences, but Tim Jenkin, Alex Moumbaris and Stephen Lee managed to escape from Pretoria Central Prison where most white political prisoners were kept. **Tim Jenkin**'s tale, *Escape from Pretoria* (1987) reads like a thriller, while in *The True Confessions of an Albino Terrorist* (1983) **Breyten Breytenbach** manages to combine political critique with grim humour. Not surprisingly, fictional accounts of prison such as **Alex La Guma**'s *The Stone Country* (1974) and **DM Zwelonke**'s *Robben Island* (1973) rely heavily on their authors' own experiences, but are complex narratives. In the realm of non-political prison writings, **Herman Charles Bosman**'s *Cold Stone Jug* (1971) provides an ironic and beautifully written foil to the seriousness of "correct" accounts.

South African writers are gripped by what Mphahalele has described as "the tyranny of place". All but one of **Alex La Guma**'s five novels are set in Cape Town, and they are linked by a steady evolution of political consciousness and organization. A journalist, writer and political activist from the 1960s until his death in Cuba during 1985, where he was the ANC's Chief Representative, his early works, *A Walk in the Night* (1962) and *And a Threefold Cord* (1964) explore individual acts of defiance against the state, while his later novels, *In the Fog of the Seasons' End* (1972) and *Time of the Butcherbird* (1979) display more complex narrative structures and deal with collective resistance.

WHITE LIBERAL WRITING

If la Guma's concerns have been with the disenfranchised and the dispossessed, **Nadine**

Gordimer's novels and short stories stand as dispassionate and coldly sensual chronicles of the interior voice of white liberal and radical opposition to apartheid. They represent an alternative to Paton's stress on individual responsibility as the key to political change. Over the years Gordimer has moved from confessional, though not necessarily autobiographical, narratives such as *The Lying Days* (1953), to bolder and more complex explorations of time and psychological make-up, such as *July's People* (1991).

While the former explores the growing political awareness of her typical main character, a white middle-class woman resident in Johannesburg's prosperous suburbs, the latter is set in a post-revolutionary South Africa in which Maureen Smales, wife and mother to a white middle-class family, has become heavily dependent on July, their former houseboy. The novel explores her search for political and personal liberation, part of which involves her efforts to confront and break with the emotionally fraught and contradictory personal and political dynamics so often associated with domestic service relationships in a colonial context.

Gordimer is not the only white writer to explore the dilemmas of privilege and conscience. She was initially part of the "Sestigers", an innovative group of Afrikaans writers prominent in the 1960s that included **Breyten Breytenbach** and **Andre Brink**, who has acquired the reputation of being the foremost white literary opponent of apartheid. Brink's works explore notions of truth, history and freedom in the colonial setting through books such as *An Instant in the Wind* (1976), which rewrites the traditional frontier-explorer novel; *A Chain of Voices* (1982); and *The Wall of the Plague* (1984). In this he has much in common with Booker Prize winner and literary critic **JM Coetzee**'s first novel, *Dusklands* (1974). This book establishes psychological and behavioural parallels between America's presence in Vietnam and the behaviour of one Jacobus Coetzee during his South African frontier experience in 1760. The majority of JM Coetzee's subsequent novels have used the perspective of a borderline psychotic narrator to explore the political and psychological damage caused by colonialism and apartheid. An intellectually brilliant postmodern critic of apartheid, Coetzee has always distanced himself and his works from the demands of publishing in order to function as a "weapon of struggle". Though by describing himself in *Dusklands*, even parodically, as "one of the 10,000 Coetzees . . . that Jacobus Coetzee begat", he invites parallels with the self-hatred and self-obsession of **Rian Malan**'s *My Traitor's Heart* (1990), which establishes its author in Calvinist style as the seventh-generation inheritor of the founding fathers' sins.

While white writing became increasingly introspective and its ventures into the interior shifted from geographical to psychological terrain, black writing faced an entirely different situation. Impeded by the exile of many artists, intimidated by trials and arrests, and censored by the state during a period of severe repression in the early 1960s, it was largely dormant until the late 1960s and early 1970s. This period saw the growth of the Black Consciousness Movement and the increasingly effective organization of black workers, followed by the Soweto riots and the independence of Angola and Mozambique.

BEYOND SOCIAL REALISM

The dawn of the 1970s saw both white and black writing beginning to look beyond the conventions of social realism, but for very different reasons. In the case of white writing, **interiority** was a response to the dilemmas imposed by a conscience that could not be ignored and privileges that could not be sacrificed. For black writers, **poetry**, and free verse in particular, became popular because it facilitated indirect forms of political expression. Among the names associated with this phase **Oswald Mtshali**, *Drum* survivor **Casey Motsisi**, **Mafika Gwala**, **Don Mattera**, **Njabulo Ndebele**, **Mongane Serote**, **Mandla Langa**, Gladys Thomas and James Matthews from Cape Town are the most prominent. In subsequent decades, many of these also wrote short stories and novels.

Oswald Mtshali was working as a motorbike courier when his path-breaking *Sounds of a Cowhide Drum* appeared in 1971. For Mtshali and many of his contemporaries, a cultural nationalism that rejected "white" standards and asserted a specifically "black" aesthetic and identity was the route to political nationalism. They sharply criticized the self-destructive nature of township violence, and used the perspectives and experiences of children to point out the injustices and inequalities of apartheid. Like many of their predecessors Ndebele, Serote and Langa were forced to leave the country, but **James Matthews** stayed, and *Cry Rage* (1972), co-written with **Gladys Thomas**, still remains a powerful statement of black consciousness and protest poetry. Along with **Gcina Mhlope** and **Jennifer Davids**, Thomas was able to modify the traditional role of black women (at best) as significant but secondary figures in the national liberation struggle, typified by the idea of the powerful black woman as mother figure.

The early 1970s also saw a resurgence of **drama**. There were escapist and exploitative musicals such as *Ipi Tombi*, nostalgic and utopian works such as **Credo Mutwa**'s *uNosilimela* and **Gibson Kente**'s *Too Late* and *Survival*, both with strong political messages. For international audiences, however, **Athol Fugard** remains the most prominent South African playwright. Fugard would be the last to claim full responsibility for several of his works, which were produced under workshop conditions with actors such as John Kani and Winston Ntshona contributing their views and experiences to *Sizwe Bansi is Dead*, a play about strategies to avoid pass law controls, and *The Island*, based on Sophocles' *Antigone*.

PEOPLE'S HISTORY

Launched in 1977, and capitalizing on the limited cultural and political space occasioned by the apartheid government's moves towards a policy of "repressive reform" in the post-Soweto period, **Staffrider magazine** was the most important literary development of the late 1970s. Taking its name and image from township slang for people (frequently black youth) who rode the overcrowded African sections of the racially segregated commuter trains by hanging onto the outside or sitting on the roofs, the magazine had two main objectives: to provide publishing opportunities for community-based organizations and young writers, graphic artists and photographers; and to oppose officially sanctioned state and establishment culture. Selections from the magazine between 1978 and 1988 appeared in *Ten Years of Staffrider* (1988). Initially based on a hands-off editorial policy, the magazine focused on "**people's history**", thus helping to retrieve hidden

aspects of South Africa's past for a wider audience. The *Staffrider* tradition continues. Recently, **Charles van Onselen**'s tome *The Seed is Mine* (1996), **Isabel Hofmeyer**'s *We Spend Our Years as a Tale That is Told* (1994) have been outstanding contributions to this genre.

The magazine also popularized a return to traditional conventions and forms of oratory such as **Nongenile Zenani**, and **Harold Scheub**'s *The World and the Word* (1992) and **Sandile Dikeni**'s *Guava Juice* (1992). Much of the latter's poetry was delivered at opposition mass rallies and trade union launches. By contrast, **Mongane Serote**'s *Third World Express* (1992), his first published work since his return from exile, retains links with with an oral tradition but is more introspective than Dikeni's poetry. More recently, praise poets performed at the inauguration of President Mandela and the opening of the country's first democratically elected parliament.

From the 1980s onwards, debates around the political relevance of poetry became even more intense than those dealing with prose. Some of the more politically committed poets included **Kelwyn Sole** (*Blood of Our Silence*; 1988) and **Jeremy Cronin**, whose anthology *Inside* (1983) asks readers "To learn how to speak/With the voices of the land" return to introspective themes of language and the poet's sense of place. Others, such as **Christopher van Wyk**'s *It is Time to Go Home* (1979) and **Achmat Dangor**'s *Bulldozer* (1983), retain a strident anger mixed with Cape Town's acerbic slang.

INTO THE 1990s

By the mid-1980s, international condemnation of apartheid and support for the liberation movement coincided with the growth of **feminist** theory and an expanding feminist publishing industry. These developments favoured the emergence of black South African women's autobiographies such as **Ellen Kuzwayo**'s *Call Me Woman* (1985) and **Emma Mashinini**'s *Strikes Have Followed me All my Life* (1989). This form had seen little development since the appearance of **Noni Jabavu**'s *Drawn in Colour* (1960) and *The Ochre People* (1963) in the early 1960s. The late 1980s was also a favourable period for the publication of **black women's poetry** in anthologies such as *Siren Songs* (1989) and *Breaking the Silence* (1990) or in individual collections such as **Sobhna Poona**'s *In Search of Rainbows* (1990).

As the 1990s took hold, however, the politicized approach that saw publishers, writers and readers going for the "struggular" had to acknowledge the less dramatic and more byzantine process of negotiations towards a relatively peaceful transfer of power, and the emergence of splits and disagreements in the cultural sphere between the ANC and some of its internal supporters. In this context, **Phyllis Ntantala**'s *A Life's Mosaic* (1992) acknowledged personal concerns, **Mamphela Ramphele**'s *A Life* (1995) criticized ways in which the liberation struggle had been male-dominated, and **Barbara Schreiner**'s *A Snake with Ice Water* (1992), a collection of interviews, stories and poems by women about their prison experiences from the 1960s onwards, confronted the shame and sense of incapacity to which many women in the liberation struggle had been subjected.

Good insights into the troubled psyche of the white South African male in a period of political transition include **Ivan Vladislavic**'s short-story collection *Missing Persons* (1989) and his novel *The Folly* (1993), **Etienne van Heerden**'s *Mad Dog and Other Stories* (1992) and *Casspirs and Camparis* (1993) – casspirs are armoured personnel carriers used by the police and army – and **Mark Behr**'s *The Smell of Apples* (1995), which attached significance to the death of Hendrik Verwoerd, architect of apartheid, during their fictionalized childhoods. Behr's subsequent disclosure that he was a police informer during his days as an anti-apartheid student activist doubtless adds interest to this confessional narrative.

POLITICAL AUTOBIOGRAPHY

The tradition of **political autobiography** is now well-established. *Let my People Go* (1962) by the late **Albert Luthuli**, former leader of the ANC, remains as compelling an explanation of the struggle for majority rule as **Nelson Mandela**'s *Long Walk to Freedom* (1994). Dramatic political change and the acquisition of freedom has seen many politicians and public figures come and go. Inevitably this has encouraged several to write stories of the life they would like us to believe they led or, in the case of those involved in clandestine work such as **Ronnie Kasrils** (*"Armed and Dangerous": My Undercover Struggle Against Apartheid*; 1993), **Joe Slovo** (*Unfinished Autobiography*; 1995) and **Natoo Babenia** (*Memoirs of a Saboteur: Reflections on my Political Activity in India and South Africa*; 1995), of the life they could not previously talk about in public. National secretary of the non-racial Federation of South African women in the 1950s, **Helen Joseph** was banned four times, jailed four times, on trial for four years and periodically unbanned. Her autobiography *Side by Side* appeared in 1986.

. . . AND BEYOND

South Africa's recently acquired political respectability has meant that writers of the formerly international polecat state can now, in Michael Ondaatje's phrase, become "international bastards" if they wish, as postmodernism and magical realism, sometimes in combination with autobiography, have become more popular and politically acceptable. **Ashraf Jamal** in *Love Themes for the Wilderness* (1996) has been quick to capitalize on the space available. Two recent novels by **Zakes Mda**, already recognized as a major playwright, *She Plays with the Darkness* (1995) and *Ways of Dying* (1995), can also be classified as magical realism. While the former may rely upon aspects of a traditional African culture with which many urbanized black South Africans have no contact, the latter explores some of the country's more bizarre forms of death from the perspective of a self-styled "professional mourner". Meanwhile Wilbur Smith, and now his wife too, continue to churn them out . . .

Roger Field

SOUTH AFRICAN WRITERS

There's no better way to get under the skin of South Africa than through its writing. And, while no four extracts can ever hope to convey South African literature's richness and diversity, the ones we've selected can be useful as a taster of some of the country's unplumbed literary depths. What the writers below have in common is that, although they are well-known in South Africa, none is internationally a big-name author. For a more comprehensive survey of the literary landscape, see p.663.

STEVE BIKO

Charismatic Black Consciousness activist **STEVE BIKO** *(1946–77) died after police torture. These words, extracted from an interview some months before his death, give insight into Biko's extraordinary commitment to political change. The extract is taken from "I Write What I Like", a collection of non-fiction writing from 1969 to 1972. In 1973 Biko was banned and could no longer travel, speak in public or write for publication.*

ON DEATH

You are either alive and proud or you are dead, and when you are dead, you can't care anyway. And your method of death can itself be a politicizing thing. So you die in the riots. For a hell of a lot of them, in fact, there's really nothing to lose – almost literally, given the kind of situations that they come from. So if you can overcome the personal fear for death, which is a highly irrational thing, you know, then you're on the way.

And in interrogation the same sort of thing applies. I was talking to this policeman, and I told him, "If you want us to make any progress, the best thing is for us to talk. Don't try any form of rough stuff, because it just won't work." And this is absolutely true also. For I just couldn't see what they could do to me which would make me all of a sudden soften to them. If they talk to me, well I'm bound to be affected by them as human beings. But the moment they adopt rough stuff, they are

imprinting in my mind that they are police. And I only understand one form of dealing with police, and that's to be as unhelpful as possible. So I button up. And I told them this: "It's up to you." We had a boxing match the first day I was arrested. Some guy tried to clout me with a club. I went into him like a bull. I think he was under instructions to take it so far and no further, and using open hands so that he doesn't leave any marks on the face. And of course he said exactly what you were saying just now: "I will kill you." He meant to intimidate. And my answer was: "How long is it going to take you?" Now of course they were observing my reaction. And they could see that I was completely unbothered. If they beat me up, it's to my advantage. I can use it. They just killed somebody in jail – a friend of mine – about ten days before I was arrested. Now it would have been bloody useful evidence for them to assault me. At least it would indicate what kind of possibilities were there, leading to this guy's death. So, I wanted them to go ahead and do what they could do, so that I could use it. I wasn't really afraid that their violence might lead me to make revelations I didn't want to make, because I had nothing to reveal on this particular issue. I was operating from a very good position, and they were in a very weak position. My attitude is, I'm not going to allow them to carry out their programme faithfully. If they want to beat me five times, they can only do so on condition that I allow them to beat me five times. If I react sharply, equally and oppositely, to the first clap, they are not going to be able to systematically count the next four claps, you see. It's a fight. So if they had meant to give me so much of a beating, and not more, my idea is to make them go beyond what they wanted to give me and to give back as much as I can give so that it becomes an uncontrollable thing. You see the one problem this guy had with me: he couldn't really fight with me because it meant he must hit back, like a man. But he was given instructions, you see, on how to hit, and now these instructions were no longer applying because it was a fight. So he had to withdraw and get more instructions. So I said to them, "Listen, if you guys want to do this your way, you have got to handcuff me and bind my feet together, so that I can't respond. If you allow me to respond, I'm certainly going to respond. And I'm afraid you may have to kill me in the process even if it's not your intention".

Reprinted by permission of Bowerdean Publishers.

HERMAN CHARLES BOSMAN

HERMAN CHARLES BOSMAN (1905–51), *one of South Africa's most widely read writers, is best known for his wry and amusing short stories about Afrikaner life in the Groot Marico district of the then Western Transvaal, where he spent six months as a schoolteacher in 1925.*

A BEKKERSDAL MARATHON

At Naudé, who had a wireless set, came into Jurie Steyn's voorkamer, where we were sitting waiting for the railway lorry from Bekkersdal, and gave us the latest news. He said that the newest thing in Europe was that young people there were going in for non-stop dancing. It was called marathon dancing, At Naudé told us, and those young people were trying to break the record for who could remain on their feet longest, dancing.

We listened for a while to what At Naudé had to say, and then we suddenly remembered a marathon event that had taken place in the little dorp of Bekkersdal – almost in our midst, you could say. What was more, there were quite a number of us sitting in Jurie Steyn's post office, who had actually taken part in that non-stop affair, and without knowing that we were breaking records, and without expecting any sort of a prize for it, either.

We discussed that affair at considerable length and from all angles, and we were still talking about it when the lorry came. And we agreed that it had been in several respects an unusual occurrence. We also agreed that it was questionable if we could have carried off things so successfully that day, if it had not been for Billy Robertse.

You see, our organist at Bekkersdal was Billy Robertse. He had once been a sailor and had come to the bushveld some years before, travelling on foot. His belongings, fastened in a red handkerchief, were slung over his shoulder on a stick. Billy Robertse was journeying in that fashion for the sake of his health. He suffered from an unfortunate complaint for which he had at

regular intervals to drink something out of a black bottle that he always carried handy in his jacket pocket.

Billy Robertse would even keep that bottle beside him in the organist's gallery in case of a sudden attack. And if the hymn the predikant gave out had many verses, you could be sure that about halfway through Billy Robertse would bring the bottle up to his mouth, leaning sideways towards what was in it. And he would put several extra twirls into the second part of the hymn.

When he first applied for the position of organist in the Bekkersdal church, Billy Robertse told the meeting of deacons that he had learnt to play the organ in a cathedral in northern Europe. Several deacons felt, then, that they could not favour his application. They said that the cathedral sounded too Papist, the way Billy Robertse described it, with a dome three hundred feet high and with marble apostles. But it was lucky for Billy Robertse that he was able to mention, at the following combined meeting of elders and deacons, that he had also played the piano in a South American dance hall, of which the manager was a Presbyterian. He asked the meeting to overlook his unfortunate past, saying that he had had a hard life, and anybody could make mistakes. In any case, he had never cared much for the Romish atmosphere of the cathedral, he said, and had been happier in the dance hall.

In the end, Billy Robertse got the appointment. But in his sermons for several Sundays after that the predikant, Dominee Welthagen, spoke very strongly against the evils of dance halls. He described those places of awful sin in such burning words that at least one young man went to see Billy Robertse, privately, with a view to taking lessons in playing the piano.

But Billy Robertse was a good musician. And he took a deep interest in his work. And he said that when he sat down on the organist's stool behind the pulpit, and his fingers were flying over the keyboards, and he was pulling out the stops, and his feet were pressing down the notes that sent the deep bass tones through the pipes – then he felt that he could play all day, he said.

I don't suppose he guessed that he would one day be put to the test, however.

It all happened through Dominee Welthagen one Sunday morning going into a trance in the pulpit. And we did not realise that he was in a trance. It was an illness that overtook him in a strange and sudden fashion.

At each service the predikant, after reading a passage from the Bible, would lean forward with his hand on the pulpit rail and give out the number of the hymn we had to sing. For years his manner of conducting the service had been exactly the same. He would say, for instance: "We will now sing Psalm 82, verses 1 to 4." Then he would allow his head to sink forward on to his chest and he would remain rigid, as though in prayer, until the last notes of the hymn died away in the church.

Now, on that particular morning, just after he had announced the number of the psalm, without mentioning what verses, Dominee Welthagen again took a firm grip on the pulpit rail and allowed his head to sink forward on to his breast. We did not realise that he had fallen into a trance of a peculiar character that kept his body standing upright while his mind was a blank. We learnt that only later.

In the meantime, while the organ was playing over the opening bars, we began to realise that Dominee Welthagen had not indicated how many verses we had to sing. But he would discover his mistake, we thought, after we had been singing for a few minutes.

All the same, one or two of the younger members of the congregation did titter, slightly, when they took up their hymn books. For Dominee Welthagen had given out Psalm 119. And everybody knows that Psalm 119 has 176 verses.

This was a church service that will never be forgotten in Bekkersdal. We sang the first verse and then the second and then the third. When we got to about the sixth verse and the minister still gave no sign that it would be the last, we assumed that he wished us to sing the first eight verses. For, if you open your hymn book, you'll see that Psalm 119 is divided into sets of eight verses, each ending with the word "Pouse".

We ended the last notes of verse eight with more than an ordinary number of turns and twirls, confident that at any moment Dominee Welthagen would raise his head and let us know that we could sing "Amen".

It was when the organ started up very slowly and solemnly with the music for verse nine that a real feeling of disquiet overcame the congregation. But, of course, we gave no sign of what went on in our minds. We held Dominee Welthagen in too much veneration.

Nevertheless, I would rather not say too much about our feelings, when verse followed verse and Pouse succeeded Pouse, and still Dominee Welthagen made no sign that we had sung long enough, or that there was anything unusual in what he was demanding of us.

After they had recovered from their first surprise, the members of the church council conducted themselves in a most exemplary manner. Elders and deacons tiptoed up and down the aisles, whispering words of reassurance to such members of the congregation, men as well as women, who gave signs of wanting to panic.

At one stage it looked as though we were going to have trouble from the organist. That was when Billy Robertse, at the end of the 34th verse, held up his black bottle and signalled quietly to the elders to indicate that his medicine was finished. At the end of the 35th verse he made signals of a less quiet character, and again at the end of the 36th verse. That was when Elder Landsman tiptoed out of the church and went round to the Konsistorie, where the Nagmaal wine was kept. When Elder Landsman came back into the church he had a long black bottle half-hidden under his manel. He took the bottle up to the organist's gallery, still walking on tiptoe.

At verse 61 there was almost a breakdown. That was when a message came from the back of the organ, where Koster Claassen and the assistant verger, whose task it was to turn the handle that kept the organ supplied with wind, were in a state near to exhaustion. So it was Deacon Cronje's turn to go tiptoeing out of the church. Deacon Cronje was head warder at the local gaol. When he came back it was with three burly Native convicts in striped jerseys, who also went through the church on tiptoe. They arrived just in time to take over the handle from Koster Claassen and the assistant verger.

At verse 98 the organist again started making signals about his medicine. Once more Elder Landsman went round to the Konsistorie. This time he was accompanied by another elder and a deacon, and they stayed away somewhat longer than the time when Elder Landsman had gone on his own. On their return the deacon bumped into a small hymn book table at the back of the church. Perhaps it was because the deacon was a fat, red-faced man, and not used to tiptoeing.

At verse 124 the organist signalled again, and the same three members of the church council filed out to the Konsistorie, the deacon walking in front this time.

It was about then that the pastor of the Full Gospel Apostolic Faith Church, about whom Dominee Welthagen had in the past used almost as strong language as about the Pope, came up to the front gate of the church to see what was afoot. He lived near our church and, having heard the same hymn tune being played over and over for about eight hours, he was a very amazed man. Then he saw the door of the Konsistorie open, and two elders and a deacon coming out, walking on tiptoe – they having apparently forgotten that they were not in church, then. When the pastor saw one of the elders hiding a black bottle under his manel, a look of understanding came over his features. The pastor walked off, shaking his head.

At verse 152 the organist signalled again. This time Elder Landsman and the other elder went out alone. The deacon stayed behind on the deacon's bench, apparently in deep thought. The organist signalled again, for the last time, at verse 169. So you can imagine how many visits the two elders made to the Konsistorie altogether.

The last verse came, and the last line of the last verse. This time it had to be "Amen". Nothing could stop it. I would rather not describe the state that the congregation was in. And by then the three Native convicts, red stripes and all, were, in the Bakhatla tongue, threatening mutiny. "Aa-m-e-e-n" came from what sounded like less than a score of voices, hoarse with singing.

The organ music ceased.

Maybe it was the sudden silence that at last brought Dominee Welthagen out of his long trance. He raised his head and looked slowly about him. His gaze travelled over his congregation and then looking at the windows, he saw that it was night. We understood right away what was going on in Dominee Welthagen's mind. He thought he had just come into the pulpit, and that this was the beginning of the evening service. We realised that, during all the

time we had been singing, the predikant had been in a state of unconsciousness.

Once again Dominee Welthagen took a firm grip of the pulpit rail. His head again started drooping forward on to his breast. But before he went into a trance for the second time, he gave out the hymn for the evening service. "We will," Dominee Welthagen announced, "sing Psalm 119."

ALEX LA GUMA

ALEX LA GUMA (1925–85) was the son of one of the leading figures in the black liberation movement. He was politically active against the apartheid government – among other things, helping with the Freedom Charter in 1956 – until he was put under house arrest in 1962. He and his wife fled the country in 1967 to the UK, then moved to Cuba where he was the ANC representative. His writing was banned by the white minority government.

This extract is from La Guma's first work, a collection of short stories set in Cape Town's District Six, before the area was razed to the ground and declared an area for whites only.

A WALK IN THE NIGHT

Up ahead the music shops were still going full blast, the blare of records all mixed up so you could not tell one tune from another. Shopkeepers, Jewish, Indian, and Greek, stood in the doorways along the arcade of stores on each side of the street, waiting to welcome last-minute customers; and the vegetable and fruit barrows were still out too, the hawkers in white coats yelling their wares and flapping their brown paper packets, bringing prices down now that the day was ending. Around the bus-stop a crowd pushed and jostled to clamber onto the trackless trams, struggling against the passengers fighting to alight. Along the pavements little knots of youths lounged in twos and threes or more, watching the crowds streaming by, jeering, smoking, joking against the noise, under the balconies, in doorways, around the plate-glass windows. A half-mile of sound and movement and signs, signs, signs: Coca-Cola, Sale Now On, Jewellers, The Modern Outfitters, If You Don't Eat Here We'll Both Starve, Grand Picnic to Paradise Valley Luxury Buses, Teas, Coffee, Smoke, Have You Tried Our Milk Shakes, Billiard Club, The Rockingham

Arms, Chine . . . nce In Korea, Your Recommendation Is Our Advert, Dress Salon.

Michael Adonis moved idly along the pavement through the stream of people unwinding like a spool up the street. A music shop was playing shrill and noisy, "Some of these days, you gonna miss me honey"; music from across the Atlantic, shipped in flat shellac discs to pound its jazz through the loudspeaker over the doorway.

He stopped outside the big plate window, looking in at the rows of guitars, banjoes, mandolins, the displayed gramophone parts, guitar picks, strings, electric irons, plugs, jews-harps, adaptors, celluloid dolls all the way from Japan, and the pictures of angels and Christ with a crown of thorns and drops of blood like lipstick marks on his pink forehead.

A fat man came out of the shop, his cheeks smooth and shiny with health, and said, "You like to buy something, sir?"

'"No man," Michael Adonis said and spun his cigarette-end into the street where a couple of snot-nosed boys in ragged shirts and homy feet scrambled for it, pushing each other as they struggled to claim a few puffs.

Somebody said, "Hoit, Mikey," and he turned and saw the wreck of a youth who had fallen in beside him.

"Hullo, Joe."

Joe was short and his face had an ageless quality about it under the grime, like something valuable forgotten in a junk shop. He had the soft brown eyes of a dog, and he smelled of a mixture of sweat, slept-in clothes and seaweed. His trousers had gone at the cuffs and knees, the rents held together with pins and pieces of string, and so stained and spotted that the original colour could not have been guessed at. Over the trousers he wore an ancient raincoat that reached almost to his ankles, the sleeves torn loose at the shoulders, the body hanging in ribbons, the front pinned together over his filthy vest. His shoes were worn beyond recognition.

Nobody knew where Joe came from, or anything about him. He just seemed to have happened, appearing in the District like a cockroach emerging through a floorboard. Most of the time he wandered around the harbour gathering fish discarded by fishermen and anglers, or along the beaches of the coast, picking limpets and mussels. He had a strange passion for things that came from the sea.

"How you, Joe?" Michael Adonis asked.

"Okay, Mikey."

"What you been doing today?"

"Just strolling around the docks. York Castle came in this afternoon."

"Ja?"

"You like mussels, Mikey? I'll bring you some."

"That's fine, Joe."

"I got a big starfish out on the beach yesterday. One big, big one. It was dead and stank."

"Well, it's a good job you didn't bring it into town. City Council would be on your neck."

"I hear they're going to make the beaches so only white people can go there," Joe said.

"Ja. Read it in the papers. Damn sonsabitches."

"It's going to get so's nobody can go nowhere."

"I reckon so," Michael Adonis said.

They were some way up the street now and outside the Queen Victoria. Michael Adonis said, "You like a drink, Joe?" although he knew that the boy did not drink.

"No thanks, Mikey."

"Well, so long."

"So long, man."

"You eat already?"

"Well . . . no . . . not yet," Joe said, smiling humbly and shyly, moving his broken shoes gently on the rough cracked paving.

"Okay, here's a bob. Get yourself something. Parcel of fish and some chips."

"Thanks, Mikey."

"Okay. So long, Joe."

"See you again."

"Don't forget the mussels," Michael Adonis said after him, knowing that Joe would forget anyway.

"I'll bring them," Joe said, smiling back and raising his hand in a salute. He seemed to sense the other young man's doubt of his memory, and added a little fiercely, "I won't forget. You'll see. I won't forget."

Then he went up the street, trailing his tattered raincoat behind him like a sword-slashed, bullet-ripped banner just rescued from a battle.

Michael Adonis turned towards the pub and saw the two policemen coming towards him. They came down the pavement in their flat caps, khaki shirts and pants, their gun harness shiny with polish, and the holstered pistols heavy at their waists. They had hard, frozen faces as if carved out of pink ice, and hard, dis-passsionate eyes, hard and bright as pieces of blue glass. They strolled slowly and determinedly side by side, without moving off their course, cutting a path through the stream on the pavement like destroyers at sea.

They came on and Michael Adonis turned aside to avoid them, but they had him penned in with a casual, easy, skillful flanking manoeuvre before he could escape.

"*Waar loop jy rond, jong?* Where are you walking around, man?" The voice was hard and flat as the snap of a steel spring, and the one who spoke had hard, thin, chapped lips and a faint blonde down above them. He had flat cheekbones, pink-white, and thick, red-gold eyebrows and pale lashes. His chin was long and cleft and there was a small pimple beginning to form on one side of it, making a reddish dot against the pale skin.

"Going home," Michael Adonis said, looking at the buckle of this policeman's belt. You learned from experience to gaze at some spot on their uniforms, the button of a pocket, or the bright smoothness of their Sam Browne belts, but never into their eyes, for that would be taken as an affront by them. It was only the very brave, or the very stupid, who dared look straight into the law's eyes, to challenge them or to question their authority.

The second policeman stuck his thumbs in his gun-belt and smiled distantly and faintly. It was more a slight movement of his lips, rather than a smile. The backs of his hands where they dropped over the leather of the belt were broad and white, and the outlines of the veins were pale blue under the skin, the skin covered with a field of tiny, slanting ginger-coloured hair. His fingers were thick and the knuckles big and creased and pink, the nails shiny and healthy and carefully kept.

This policeman asked in a heavy, brutal voice, "Where's your dagga?"

"I don't smoke it."

"Jong, turn out your pockets," the first one ordered. "Hurry up."

Michael Adonis began to empty his pockets slowly, without looking up at them and thinking, with each movement, You mucking boers, you mucking boers. Some people stopped and looked and hurried on as the policeman turned the cold blue light of their eyes upon them. Michael Adonis showed them his crumbled and partly used packet of cigarettes, the money he had left over from his pay, a soiled handkerchief and an old piece of chewing gum covered with the grey fuzz from his pocket.

"Where did you steal the money?"' The question was without humour, deadly serious, the voice topped with hardness like the surface of a file.

"Didn't steal it, baas (you *mucking boer)*".

"Well, muck off from the street. Don't let us find you standing around, you hear?"

"Yes (you *mucking boer).*"

"Yes, what? Who are you talking to, man?"

"Yes, baas (you *mucking bastard boer with your mucking gun and your mucking bloody red head).*"

They pushed past him, one of them brushing him aside with an elbow and strolled on. He put the stuff back into his pockets. And deep down inside him the feeling of rage, frustration and violence swelled like a boil, knotted with pain.

Reprinted by permission of Heinemann.

MTUTUZELI MATSHOBA

MTUTUZELI MATSHOBA is a black writer who is well known in South Africa. The extract below gives an idea of the conditions of life in the Transkei, the first artificially created home-land or bantustan, after it was notionally given "independence" in 1976. Kaiser Matanzima, the repressive first leader of the Transkei, imprisoned political opponents without trial and imposed emergency regulations which he renewed annually.

THREE DAYS IN THE LAND OF A DYING ILLUSION

"Heh, heh," he had chuckled at my ignorance of the present world. "You don't know that Transkei is independent?"

"Independent from what, of what?"

"Of South Africa," and his eyes had completed the sentence with "bloody fool!"

"That's news to me," I said as sincerely as I could.

"You must have been in jail. Were you not in prison when Transkey got independence? Or maybe you were mad, at Sterkfontein."

"Maybe. If that's what you want – your fellow blacks to be in prison. What's the red tape?"

"Give me your pass."

Fortunately, for once I had it for identification purposes. What with everybody looking for "terrorists"under every stone. I gave it to him and he pages through it before throwing it back at me.

"You're Xhosa, neh?"

I nodded.

"Then go and apply for Transkei citizenship at Counter Six. Next!"

I could not suppress my indignation anymore. "When you look at me you imagine I could make an ideal Transkei citizen? When you arrive home this evening you tell your mother to apply for it so that she can go and learn witchcraft if she is not a professional already." I turned and stomped for the door without waiting for his reaction.

So there I was, rolling into Qamata with my third denomination comrades. The discussion petered out to a noticeable hush as everybody was diverted from the articulate lady by the crossing of an invisible Iron Curtain.

The soil was red, ironically reminding me of Avalon and Doornkop cemeteries back home, the land parched and scarred with erosion. In the first fields that we passed the maize had grown hardly a metre high. The weeds, blackjack outstanding, outgrew it. A woman in dusty traditional attire with a baby strapped to her back and two boys in inherited clothes following her, was searching for stems that might have been overlooked at harvest time.

We passed two cows shaving the roadside of sun-scorched grass.

"*Kakade*, what's the use of buying cattle that end up short of grass?" remarked one of my travelling companions.

"*Imfuyo* [stock] is no longer an investment these days," added another.

I had thought the animals looked acceptable. Perhaps that was due to my inability to judge good beef. However you looked at it, some of the animals that we saw were scrawny and others well-nourished. Probably the latter belonged to people who could afford to buy hay.

The mountains rose high, solid, silent and motionless until they melted into blue-grey and hazy horizons, the only sight that appealed magnificently to my eyes. Below them there were picturesque villages of perfectly circular, thatched rondavels whitewashed for about a foot just below the edges of the thatch and around the windows and doors. This architecture dotted the elevated parts of the landscape on both sides of the road for endless acres.

"*Awu*," someone ventured, "*esikaDaliwonga! Ilizwe lembalela* [a land of drought]. That is why he has left it to pick out the richest parts of the land for himself elsewhere; to bulldoze the people out of land that they inherited from their fathers."

"*Ewe. Natbi uyokusixina ngaphaya.*" [Yes. He also crowds us into the parts that remain ours.]

I was confounded by those words because they came from simple people. Things being taken for granted as they generally are, who could have expected them to nurture any misgivings concerning their share of that wilderness? I say wilderness because that was the most suitable description of what was unfolding before my eyes compared with the white-owned Free State country I had seen the previous day. Proof of its being wasteland lay in the fact that they had surrendered to the inhuman migratory way of life rather than stay and try to eke out a living in their "homeland". It showed there was just no way to suck blood out of a stone. The illusion of freehold in a free land had long faded in the imagination of my cheated people. Independence, *uburu*, had come, avowedly to break the chains of blackness and drive away poverty. Instead it had brought an ominous fog of helplessness that hung over a land marred with eroded ravines which gave one a clear picture of what the earth might look like after an earthquake. From the silvery trickles that traced erratic courses on the sandy beds of some of the shallow dongas, I concluded that they had been rivulets many aeons ago.

The maize refused to grow higher than a foot without water and scientific agricultural methods. It would cost decades in time and billions of rands in the form of irrigation, fertilizer and technology before one would see any advance beyond cross-plantation on the slopes, which was the only scientific land treatment about which I could write home. Where would the billions come from? Obviously from "white South Africa" with her own sick economy.

If anybody out there had figured that he could temporarily depend on South Africa by sending people there as slaves, hoping that they would earn enough to be self-sufficient after some time, he had dreamt up a nightmare. Slaves don't earn anything; they live from hand to mouth. His country would forever remain both a labour reservoir and a vacuum to suck discarded human labour units out of the South African economy.

We passed a village with a dusty filling station or garage that might have been constructed from the home-made mudbricks of the rondavels. Even if I had a car and happened to have a breakdown near that place, I would never risk taking it there.

Reprinted by permission of Ravan Press in association with Rex Collings.

BOOKS

For a country with such a low proportion of its population reading regularly, South Africa generates a huge amount of literature, particularly about subjects the literate feel guilty about – namely, politics and history. Almost all the books listed below are in print, and those that are not, and which are published in either the UK or US, should be fairly easy to track down in second-hand bookshops. Those books only published in South Africa may prove hard to find outside South Africa itself. Where two publishers are given, the first is British, the second US.

HISTORY AND ANTHROPOLOGY

William Beinart, *20th Century South Africa* (OUP, UK). Useful and concise account of South African history this century, with an emphasis on economic history that manages to emphasize the essential without descending into tedium. His predictions for the future seem wobbly now, but there's nothing unusual about that.

Axel-Ivar Berglund, *Zulu Thought Patterns and Symbolism* (Hurst, UK). Sensitive and knowledgeable account of rural Zulu world views, related as they have been described to the author, with the minimum of interpretation from him tacked on. He does, however, set the scene well, and make thought-provoking connections between the various views expressed to him, whilst bending over backwards to avoid tedious judgementalism.

Philip Bonner, *Kings, Commoners and Concessionaries* (CUP, UK). The definitive history (so far) of nineteenth-century Swaziland, by a skilled historian with a gratifying grasp of the source material and mostly reliable judgement.

Its one weakness is a lack of oral historical research, though fortunately useful work has been done on this recently by the Swazi Oral History Project, based at the University there.

Emile Boonzaier, Candy Malherbe, Andy Smith and Penny Berens, *The Cape Herders, A History of the Khoikhoi of Southern Africa* (David Phillip, SA; Ohio University Press, US). Recently published and accessibly written account of the Khoikhoi people of southern Africa, successfully exploding the many prejudices and myths that surround them and exploring their way of life, their interaction with Europeans, and what remains of them today.

Jane Carruthers, *The Kruger National Park: A Social and Political History* (University of Natal, SA). Specialist history that deals with broad issues. By examining the scientific and ideological forces that gave rise to the Kruger National Park, this fascinating book asks important questions about our notions of nature and conservation.

Stephen Gill, *A Short History of Lesotho* (Morija, Lesotho). Thoughtful and well-informed account of Lesotho's history and the best single volume you'll find, written by the chief archivist at the Morija museum. Gill clearly loves Lesotho and has little sympathy for its many invaders but is a little over-generous in his account of Lesotho's missionaries.

Barbara Hutton, *Robben Island – Symbol of Resistance* (Sached Books UK; Mayibuye Books, SA) Fast, straightforward and illustrated account of Robben Island from prehistoric times to the present, with a good overview of prison conditions in the apartheid years.

Hilda Kuper, *The Swazi, A South African Kingdom* (Saunders College Publishing, US). A combination of anthropology and history, written in the 1960s, whose theoretical perspectives seem pretty dated now, though Kuper's observations still sound sharp. Her political insight was often astute too, though she was too fond of the Dlamini royal house to provide much of a critical perspective on them.

Ben Maclennan, *A Proper Degree of Terror – John Graham and the Cape's Eastern Frontier* (Ravan, SA). Riveting account of the early nineteenth century in the Eastern Cape history, written with the cracking narrative pace of a novel.

Candy Malherbe, *Men of Men* (Shuter and Shooter, SA). Brief, simple and highly readable primer on the earliest inhabitants of the Cape, the Khoikhoi, who were systematically dispossessed, but have nevertheless left their mark on modern South Africa.

Noel Mostert, *Frontiers – The Epic of South Africa's Creation and the Tragedy of the Xhosa People* (Pimlico, UK). Academically solid and brilliantly written history of the Xhosa of the Eastern Cape and their tragic fate in the frontier wars fought against the British.

Dougie Oakes (ed), *Illustrated History of South Africa* (Reader's Digest, SA). Physically weighty, but written in a delightfully light style, this illustated history is an essential volume on the shelves of anyone seriously interested in the democratic history of South Africa.

Thomas Pakenham, *The Boer War* (Abacus, UK). Definitive liberal history of the Anglo-Boer War that reads grippingly like a novel, managing to maintain a panoramic sweep of events while homing in on the quirks and foibles of the individual player.

Jeff Peires, *The Dead Will Arise* (Ravan, SA) and *The House of Phalo* (Ravan, SA). The leading historian of the Xhosa people tells in beautifully readable prose the stories of the Eastern Cape before the arrival of whites' as well as the impact of colonialism on their lives and society in these two books that rely on both written and oral sources.

Marjorie Shostak, *Nisa* (Earthscan, UK). A fascinating book – both bawdy and romantic – based on the life of a San woman in a hostile Kalahari environment.

Leonard Thompson, *A History of South Africa* (Yale UP, UK/US). Reliable and elegantly written, this is among the best introductions to it subject.

Laurens Van der Post, *The Lost World of the Kalahari* (Penguin, UK). The author's almost spiritual quest to find, and film, San people still existing as pure hunter-gatherers. T*he Heart of the Hunter* (Penguin, UK), is the sequel, although it can be read on its own, dwelling on the San he met and their mythology.

Various, edited by Shula Marks and Stanley Trepido *The Politics of Race, Class and Nationalism in 20th century South Africa* (Longman, UK). Seminal collection of Marxist and left-leaning analyses of South African

social and political trends this century, with an emphasis on the micro-study that stands in deliberate contrast to the sweeping liberal histories that have preceeded it.

AUTOBIOGRAPHY AND BIOGRAPHY

Breyten Breytenbach, *True Confessions of an Albino Terrorist* (Faber & Faber, UK). In vividly poetic language, the exiled Afrikaner poet tells the entertaining story of his return to South Africa in 1975 - to be arrested and jailed for seven years.

Sindiwe Magoma, *To my Children's Children* (David Phillip, SA). Fascinating autobiography – initially started so that her family would never forget their roots – that traces Magoma's life from the rural Transkei to the hard townships of Cape Town, and from political innocence to wisdom born of bitter experience.

Nelson Mandela, *Long Walk to Freedom* (Abacus, UK). Superb best-selling autobiography of the South African president, which is wonderfully evocative of his early years and intensely moving about his long years in prison. However, when it comes to his love life, the byzantine intricacies of ANC politics during its long years as an illegal organization and the story behind the negotiated settlement, Mandela is more diplomatic than candid. Mandela's generosity of spirit and tremendous understanding of the delicate balance between principle and tactics come out very strongly, and the book is without doubt essential reading for the new South Africa.

Emma Mashinini, *Strikes Have Followed me All my Life* (Women's Press, UK). Moving account of this diminuitive but unstoppable trade unionist, who defied both injustice in the labour market and the deep sexism of her colleagues during her tireless struggles from the 1950s to the 1980s.

William Plomer, *Cecil Rhodes* (David Phillip, SA). There are countless books on Rhodes, most of which feed the legend, although the distance of time has made some historians ready to regard him as a flawed colossus. This is a re-publication of one of the most critical accounts, written several decades ago, against the grain, by a South African poet-novelist, when colonialism was still regarded by many whites as a good thing. It pulls no punches in presenting Rhodes as an immature person driven by his weaknesses.

Albie Sachs, *The Soft Vengeance of a Freedom Fighter* (David Phillip, SA). The ANC veteran relates the story of how, in exile in Mozambique, he was almost killed by a South African security police bomb. The book vividly traces his recovery and the mental difficulties he went through, only to emerge with a new vision of the struggle.

TRAVEL AND GENERAL

Dan Jacobson, *The Electric Elephant* (Hamish Hamilton, UK). Jacobson, who left South Africa in the 1950s, returned in 1993 to travel from Kimberley in the Northern Cape to Victoria Falls, along the old "Great North Road" built by Rhodes, and since trodden by generations of missionaries, colonists and freebooters.

Dervla Murphy, *South from the Limpopo: Travels through South Africa* (UK/John Murray). Fascinating bike journey through the new South Africa with a writer who isn't afraid to explore the complexities and paradoxes of this country.

Visitor's Guide to Lesotho (Southern, SA). Exhaustive account of nearly every town and village on the main routes through Lesotho, accompanied by constant exhortations for readers to get out and meet the Sotho. Helpful in places, though rather indiscriminate.

Marco Turco, *Visitor's Guide to Swaziland* (Southern, SA). Turco travelled everywhere to write this book, including some really out-of-the-way places, though his account is marred by his tendency to recommend everything, no matter how dull it turns out to be when you get there.

FICTION

Mark Behr, *The Smell of Apples* (Abacus, UK). Best-selling novel about a small white boy growing up in a military family under apartheid in the 1970s, and painfully resonant for many.

Herman Charles Bosman, *Unto Dust* (Human & Rousseau, SA). Superb collection of short stories from South Africa's master of the genre, all set in the tiny Afrikaner farming district of Groot Marico in the 1930s, with the narrator Oom Schalk Lourens revealing with deliciously wry irony the passions and foibles of his community.

André Brink, *A Chain of Voices* (Minerva, UK). Superbly evocative tale of Cape eighteenth-century life, exploring the impact of slavery on one farming family, right up to its dramatic and murderous end.

J.M. Coetzee, *Age of Iron* (Penguin, UK/US). Voted by writers in a *Mail & Guardian* poll to be the finest South African novel of the last ten years, this depicts a white female classics professor dying from cancer during the political craziness of the 1980s. She is joined by a tramp who sets up home in the garden, and thus evolves a curious and fascinating relationship that transforms her.

Achnat Dangor, *The Z Town Trilogy* (Ravan, SA). One of the best Cape Town writers, Dangor sets this trilogy in a town much like it, during one of apartheid South Africa's many states of emergency, which have started to burrow in intricate ways into the psyches of his characters.

Modikwe Dikobe, *Marabi Dance* (Heinemann, UK). Short novel celebrating the bittersweet nature of black Johannesburg life in the 1930s, where the daily humiliations of life are tempered by the prospect of wild *marabi* parties when the weekends come.

Nadine Gordimer, *July's People* (Penguin, UK/US). Liberal white family is rescued by its gardener July from revolution, and taken to his home village for safety, where Gordimer teases out the power dynamics of this fraught situation with customary insight and eloquence.

Alex La Guma, *A Walk in the Night* (Heinemann, UK). Evocative collection of short stories set in District Six, the ethnically mixed quarter of Cape Town that was razed by the apartheid government, by this talented political activist/author.

Dan Jacobson, *The Trap*, and *a Dance in the Sun* (David Phillip, SA). Two taut novellas in one volume, written in the 1950s, skilfully portraying the developing tensions and nuances of the white-versus-black lives of the era.

Zakes Mda, *Ways of Dying* (OUP, UK). Winner of the 1997 M-Net Book Prize, this brilliant tale of a professional mourner is full of sly insights into the culture of black South Africa.

Thomas Mofolo, *Chaka* (Heinemann, UK). Thomas Mofolo was Lesotho's first great fiction writer, who wrote this epic tale in Sotho of the

Zulu king Shaka in 1909, here portrayed as a man fatally controlled by his strong passions. The original English translation gave the text a misleadingly biblical slant, which has been corrected in this newer translation by Daniel Kunene.

Isaac Mogotsi, *Alexandra Tales* (Ravan, SA). Delightful tales of family life in the run-down, lively homes of Johannesburg's Alexandra township, all with a clever and provocative twist in the tail.

Es'kia Mphahalele, *Down Second Avenue* (Faber & Faber, UK). Classic autobiographical novel set in the 1940s, where Mphahalele grew up in the impoverished township of Alexandra in a large extended family battling daily to survive the problems and injustices of the age.

Alan Paton, *Cry, the Beloved Country* (Penguin, UK). Classic novel by one of South Africa's great liberals, describing with tremendous lyricism the journey of a black pastor from rural Natal to Johannesburg, depicted as a veritable Sodom and Gomorrah, to rescue his missing son from its clutches.

Sol Plaatje, *Mhudi* (Heinemann, UK). The first English novel by a South African writer, *Mhudi* is the epic story, set in the 1830s, of a young Barolong woman who saves her future husband from the raids of the Ndebele, at a time when the Afrikaner Great Trek had just begun. Plaatje was also a political activist and was one of the founder members of the ANC.

Olive Schreiner, *Story of an African Farm* (Penguin, UK/US). The first-ever South African novel, Schreiner wrote this in 1883 under a male pseudonym. Though subject to the ideologies of the era, the book nonetheless explores with genuinely open vision as it tells the tale of two female cousins living on a remote Karoo farm whose young lives are disrupted by an Irish traveller.

Sipho Sepamala, *A Ride on the Whirlwind* (Heinemann, UK). Set in the terrifying times of 1976 in riot-swept Soweto, Sepamala's novel explores the psychology of resistance and defiance amongst the angry township youth.

Mongane Wally Serote, *To Every Birth Its Blood* (Heinemann, UK). Serote's only novel is a powerfully turbulent affair that traces the evolution of a township man from someone interested only in jazz, drinking and sex, to political consciousness through the humiliations he is subjected to by the forces of authority.

Martin Trump and Jean Marquard (eds) *A Century of South African Short Stories* (Ad Donker, SA). Respectable selection of South Africa's finest short stories, including contributions from *Drum* writer Can Themba, Charles Bosman and Nadine Gordimer.

Shaun de Waal (Ad Donker, SA). Brilliant collection of short stories by a promising young novelist about a country – and a people – in the throes of transformation.

POETRY

Lesego Rampolokeng, *Horns of Hondo* (Cosaw, SA). One of the most promising talents unleashed by the Congress of South African Writers (Cosaw). Rampolokeng speaks with a fiery township voice, his poetry flowing to dread rhythms of rap and dub.

Mongane Wally Serote, *Selected Poems* (Ad Donker, SA). The leading light amongst South Africa's many protest poets, with a work that ranges from early rage to incantations of freedom, leavened with humour and startling imagery.

Various, *The Heart in Exile*, edited by Leon de Kock and Ian Tromp (Penguin, UK/US/SA). Well-considered anthology of South African poems written between the time of Nelson Mandela's release in 1990 and the democratic elections of 1994. An interesting balance of forward-looking and reflective work from some of the country's most accomplished poets.

Various, *Return of the Amasi Bird*, edited by Tim Couzens and Essop Patel (Ravan, SA). Comprehensive collection of black South African poetry, which stretches right back to the early colonial era and extends to the cries of liberation and beyond.

ART AND PHOTOGRAPHY

Ian Berry, *Living Apart* (Phaidon, SA). Superbly evocative and moving photographs spanning from the 1950s to 1990s that chart a compelling vision of the politics of the nation, but at a micro level, with a decidedly small "p".

S. Francis and H. Dugmore, *Madam and Eve* (Penguin, SA). One of South Africa's leading cultural exports conveys the daily struggle between an African domestic worker and her white madam in the northern suburbs of Johannesburg in telling and witty cartoon strips that say more about post-apartheid society than countless academic tomes.

J.D. Lewis-Williams, *Discovering Southern African Rock Art* (David Phillip, SA) and *Images of Power: Understanding Bushman Rock Art* (David Phillip, SA). Short, concise books written by an expert in the field, full of drawings and photos, that concludes that most of the paintings depict images seen while in a state of shamanic trance and reflect a San world-view in which the spiritual and material world were both a part of everyday life.

Jurgen Schadeberg, *Sof'town: Images from the Black '50s* (Jurgen Schadeberg, UK). Classic black-and-white photographic studies of the "*Drum*" era of the swinging Johannesburg, where, if Schadeberg is to be believed, every black woman was a beauty and every black man a dude in a zoot suit.

Sue Williamson, *Resistance Art in South Africa* (David Phillip, SA) and *Art in South Africa: The Future Present* (David Phillip, SA). Taken together, these two volumes map the course of South African art from the early 1980s to the present day, with a thoughtful text, which is minimal enough to let the artists' works speak for themselves.

SPECIALIST GUIDEBOOKS

David Bristow, *Best Hikes in Southern Africa* (Struik, SA). Well-written and reliable guide that does your homework for you, selecting the best trails from a confusingly extensive lot.

David Bristow, *Drakensberg Walks: 120 Graded Hikes and Trails in the 'Berg* (Struik, SA). An indispensable paperback for anyone exploring the Drakensberg, with detailed route instructions and informative background about the natural history of the massif.

Shirley Brossey, *A Walking Guide for Table Mountain* (self-published, SA). Useful and inexpensive guide to trails around the Table Mountain, with handy hand-drawn maps and a down-to-earth text.

Judith Hopley, *On Foot in the Garden Route* (self-published, SA). Excellent little guide, that's perfect if you're planning on exploring the coasts and forest of the Garden Route on foot.

Jaynee Levy, *The Complete Guide to Walks & Trails in Southern Africa* (Struik, SA). Encyclopedic hiker's bible covering over 500 trails suitable for all abilities, with useful practical information about what to take and where to book. One to invest in if you're a keen trailist spending time in the country, but definitely not light reading to take for a walk.

Mike Lundy, *Best Walks in the Cape Peninsula* (Struik, SA). Handy, solidly researched guide to some of the Peninsula's many walks, and small enough to fit comfortably in a backpack while you are walking them.

Tony Pooley and Ian Player, *KwaZulu-Natal Wildlife Destinations* (Southern, SA). Comprehensive directory of every game and nature reserve in the province, with useful practical and background information.

Charles Stewart, *Rock and Surf Fishing* (Southern, SA). Uninspiringly written, but the author does appear to have tried his luck from nearly every available vantage point on the South African coast, and the book is a useful guide to what he has found out on the way.

BIRDS

Hugh Chittenden, *Top Birding Spots of Southern Africa* (Southern, SA). Essential companion guide for any keen bird-watcher, with information on spots, how to access them as well as a rundown on the common species and any specials to look out for.

Gordon Lindsay Maclean Roberts, *Birds of Southern Africa* (New Holland, UK). The definitive reference work on the subcontinent's entire avifauna population: if it's not in Roberts, it doesn't exist. Alas the weight of this tome makes it more of a tome to consult in a library than to take on your trip.

Ian Sinclair, *Southern African Birds – A Photographic Guide* (Collins, UK; Struik, SA). Pocket-sized volume full of photos to help you bird-spot your way around the country, with pretty minimal textual accompaniment rather short on interesting little facts about the birds in question.

MAMMALS

Richard D Estes *Safari Companion* (Russell Friedman Books, SA). A long-needed guide on how to understand African wildlife, with interesting and readable information on the behaviour and social structures of the major species.

Chris and Tilde Stuart *Field Guide to the Mammal of Southern Africa* (New Holland, UK). One of the best books on this subject providing excellent background and clear illustrations to help you recognize a species.

TREES AND PLANTS

L. McMahon and M. Fraser *A Fynbos Year* (David Phillip, SA). Exquisitely illustrated and well-written book about South Africa's unique floral kingdom.

Keith Coates Palgrave *Trees of Southern Africa* (Struik, SA). The authoritative book on the subject, but big and too heavy to carry around.

Eve Palmer *A Field Guide to the Trees of Southern Africa* (Collins, UK). Covers South Africa, Botswana and Namibia and is small and more practical to carry than Coates Palgrave.

WINE

John Platter *South African Wine Guide*. Annually updated pocket guide to South Africa's current output, with reviews and rating by one of the country's top wine writers.

James Seely *The Wines of South Africa* (Faber & Faber, UK). Recently produced, and almost as definitive as it claims, this book tackles South African wine region by region, estate by estate, complete with tasting notes and recommendations. Written by an author who once imported wine to the UK for *Harvey's*, but now does so for himself, its a useful and inexpensive reference guide.

MUSIC

In a region dominated musically by Zaire's mighty rhumba sound, South Africa is the exception, not just for the remarkable profusion of local styles, but because of the power and influence there of African-American music. Although Zairean musicians are starting to make inroads in Johannesburg, in most of South Africa American soul (or r&b, as many now call it), aided and abetted by hip-hop, seems to reign supreme, dominating both the airwaves and the music shops, and shaping black and coloured township cool. White people, as ever, have gone their own way, also looking outside the country for inspiration, but this time to the white British and American rock scene.

Nonetheless, despite countless predictions of its imminent demise, South African music lives on, reaching depths in the South African soul that imported music, no matter how cool, can never hope to touch. While Western fans could be forgiven for thinking that the *mbaqanga* or township jive, made famous by Paul Simon's *Graceland* album, and touring South African artists like the **Soul Brothers** and **Mahlathini** are at the music's cutting edge, in fact they are viewed in the country as distinctly old hat. Far and away the most popular music in the country is **gospel**. Also huge amongst township youth is **kwaito**, a curiously tinny South African variant of house that comes complete with its own dress codes and formation dancing styles. Meanwhile, thirty-somethings are more likely to top up their daily dose of American soul with **bubblegum**, the youth music of their day, essentially based on a mix of *mbaqanga* and disco, or the **reggae** of

singers like Lucky Dube. In the rural areas and in the hostels, **neo-traditional music** holds sway, with songs accompanied by the accordion, guitar and a thumping bassline, constantly reworking themes of marriage, dowries, betrayal and village gossip. City sophisticates, particularly in Cape Town, tend to go for **jazz**, either of the old school, performed largely by those who went into exile in the 1960s and returned in the 1990s like **Hugh Masekela** and **Abdullah Ibrahim**, or of the new school, which draws heavily on American West Coast fusion sounds. Young whites have plenty of **alternative rock bands** to choose from, like **Urban Creep** and Cape Town's **Truly Fully Hey Shoo Wow Band**, and there's always at least one to see on the weekend in any of South Africa's major cities.

GOSPEL

Choral harmony and melody are perhaps black South Africa's greatest musical gifts to the world, and nowhere are they better manifested than in its **churches**. In the mainstream denominations like Catholicism, Anglicanism and Methodism, a tradition of choral singing has evolved that has taken the style of European classical composers like Handel but loosened it up, added rhythm and some great dance routines. This type of choral singing is immensely popular, with regular competitions involving amazingly attired choirs – some of which are over one hundred strong. If you can't make it to a competition, you can watch the choirs every Sunday on television's SABC 1.

In the **Pentecostal** churches, the music is more American-influenced, with plenty of "Hallelujahs" and "Praise the Lord"s. Even so, the harmonies and melodies remain uniquely South African and intensely moving. Pentecostal gospel music is the style you are most likely to find on cassettes, where you should look out for groups like **Pure Gold**, the **Holy Spirits** and the incomparable **Rebecca Malope** (see box, p.684).

Also worth seeking out is **Zionist gospel**. The Zionist churches have more members than any other denomination in the country, who are required to donate ten percent of their income to the church, live an ultra-clean life and attend all the services and conventions, in distinctive long robes, often adorned with sashes. Their music is both inspirational and mournful, with a tonality all of its own, rendering it perfect for the moving night vigils that precede funerals, as well as for regular church services, held outside and often in parks, where you are welcome to watch as long as you do so respectfully. Zionist gospel cassettes are easily spotted, as their covers invariably feature the substantial performing choir in full robes, often with the preacher out in front in some suitably religious pose.

KWAITO

Kwaito, South Africa's newest music and dance craze, is the least accessible yet to an international audience reared on the good-time grooves of the 1970s *mbaqanga* and township jive. *Kwaito* is heavily influenced by house music, and its production is deliberately thin, tinnier than the happiest of happy house, and a far cry from the rich, multitextured sounds we are so used to in modern music. To make matters worse for outsiders, the musicianship is minimal and repetitive, and the vibe downbeat and pretty mean. A lot of South Africans feel the same way about *kwaito* too, and add to its sins an association with gangsters and an overexplicit sexuality. All this matters *nix* ("nothing") to its young township fans, to whom *kwaito* embodies the style and groove of the new South Africa to such an extent for some that many are now almost entirely weaned off American soul music.

Kwaito, like all modern dance music from hip-hop and ragga to drum'n'bass, is meaningless without a party crowd to dance to it, and when you see the music in this context it starts to make sense. Black South Africans have a predilection for formation dancing, preferably with plenty of deft footwork and synchronized about-turns, and *kwaito* is perfect for this, with its *tsotsi-taal* (ghetto slang) lyrics contributing the necessary contemporary vibe, complemented in the dance by the distinctive *kwaito* fashion of the crowd – currently long trousers that are too short for the men and skimpy miniskirts for the women.

Kwaito music is like bubblegum (see opposite) in that no tune or performer lasts very long. There are some major stars to look out for though, including **Arthur**, who performed the controversial 1996 hit *Don't Call me Kaffir*, **Joe Nina**, whose biggest tune was the hugely suc-

REBECCA MALOPE

Diminutive 29-year-old **REBECCA MALOPE** is unquestionably South Africa's biggest music star. These days, she only plays in stadia, with nearly every concert a sellout. Every album she releases goes gold or platinum, popular magazines can't get enough of her photos, views and story, and everyone seems to know the lyrics to all her songs. Well, nearly everyone that is, for Rebecca Malope is virtually unknown outside the black community.

Rebecca's musical formula rarely varies. Her songs are anthems that manage to sound as though they have been around for ever, and to which you can sing along, wave your arms in unison, do nifty little dance shuffles, or simply weep tears of ecstatic joy – all of which you will see fans doing at her concerts.

Rebecca employs marvellous backing singers, the best of whom is **Vuyo**, a handsome, pig tailed and deep-voiced man who is now forging a solo career of his own. Rebecca's competent, unobtrusive band includes keyboardist **Zako**, who also produces her and writes most of her songs. Despite an obvious humility and a willingness to promote other talents, Rebecca remains the undisputed star, with a tremendous, soaring and sometimes husky voice, dramatic gestures as she becomes possessed by the spiritual power her lyrics unleash, and a total commitment to her songs and the gospel message they convey.

The daughter of a Sotho father and Swazi mother, Rebecca was born in Nelspruit, Mpumalanga in 1969, and soon began singing in the local Assemblies of God church, where her grandfather was a pastor. Her initial recordings were mostly forgettable pop, but in Johannesburg she was spotted by producer Zako, and under his tutelage and because, she says, of letters from fans pleading that she sing God's songs, Rebecca returned to gospel in 1990, where she has since been amply rewarded. Denying that she is apolitical, Rebecca says she does sometimes sing at rallies, but will select songs that tell the politicians what she believes they need to hear.

Safely huge in South Africa, Rebecca is keen to make it internationally, but a European tour in 1997 made little impact, despite her producing some of her most intimate and powerful performances in years. She will no doubt try again, when audiences may be ready for the woman who in South Africa rests unchallenged as the reigning champion of the local music scene.

cessful "Ding Dong", **Abashante** and the **AboBabes**, who are two popular female *kwaito* outfits, though currently dwarfed by the current queens of the scene, **Boom Shaka**.

BUBBLEGUM

Bubblegum is *kwaito*'s predecessor, and established the formula of ultra-contemporary throwaway music that loses its flavour after only a couple of plays, which is how it got its name. Essentially a mix of township jive and disco, bubblegum was the vehicle for success of a number of artists who now like to think of themselves as more serious performers, perhaps as an explanation for their rapidly declining popularity. Such artists include **Sipho "Hotstix" Mabuse**, who had a massive hit with the tune *Jive Soweto* in the 1980s but has now branched out into jazz and more pan-African sounds; **Sello "Chicco" Twala**, who today makes his bucks producing *kwaito* and **Yvonne Chaka Chaka**. Yvonne showed more foresight than most bubblegum artists in the late 1980s by assiduously cultivating a following in the rest of Africa, so that although she is barely rated in South Africa any more she can still draw a huge crowd in the rest of the continent. Her biggest hit, which still stands up to scrutiny, is *Umqgombothi*, which is all about the delights of traditional beer. Yvonne's big rival was always **Brenda Fassie**, a genuine pop star with a flair for self-promotion whose monster hits include *Too Late for Mama* and, to commemorate the release of Nelson Mandela, to whom she is related, *Black President*. Recently, Brenda has been experimenting with *kwaito* sounds and has duetted with Zaire's Papa Wemba on her new album *Now is the Time*.

RAP AND REGGAE

While **rap and reggae** are very popular in South Africa, particularly in the coloured community, credible local performers are a bit thin on the ground. By far the best South African rap group are the **Prophets of Da City**, who hail from the coloured townships of Cape Town, and have a distinctly political slant to their lyrics. The unquestioned king of the local reggae scene, though he has been pretty quiet recently, is **Lucky Dube**. Originally a township jive singer, his switch to Peter Tosh-style roots reggae in the early 1990s was an inspired one, and his album *Prisoner* became the biggest-selling South African album of all time. An energetic, disciplined and talented live performer, Lucky Dube can also come up with a falsetto like Smokey Robinson's, which adds a distinctly new twist to his otherwise familiar roots sounds.

NEO-TRADITIONAL MUSIC

The best way to see South African **neo-traditional music**, unless you're lucky enough to find yourself at an event where it's being performed live, is on SABC TV Channel 1's *Ezodumo*, every Thursday night, which is compulsory viewing in the few rural homesteads and hostels that have a television. The programme is a great showcase for the bands, all dressed in vaguely traditional attire, and usually consisting of a male lead vocalist, female backing singers and a small rhythm section, which often includes a concertina player. As with *kwaito*, the instrumentation is really just a backdrop to the lyrics – usually shouted at great speed – and the dance routines, which reveal grace of movement in even the largest of backing singers.

The king of neo-traditional music is undoubtedly **Thomas Chauke**, who is an *Ezodumo* regular, and probably the best seller in any of the neo-traditional genres, making heavy use of a drum machine, an electric keyboard and some often intricate lead-guitar work to complement his endless vocals.

Sotho neo-traditional styles have shown the least development over the years, largely because of a particularly conservative music policy on Radio Sotho during the apartheid era. Nevertheless, the basslines are good, and while you can take or leave the concertinas the shouting is definitely first class. **Tau Oa Matshela** and **Tau Oa Linare** are groups to look out for.

You will rarely hear Xhosa or Tswana neo-traditional sounds, but **Zulu music** is everywhere, both in its instrumental and a cappella form, known to the Zulu as *iscathamiya* (see box, p.42). A unique guitar-picking style (*ukupika*) is central to the instrumental sound, though it's often overshadowed these days by a hammily played electric keyboard. Each song starts with the *izihlabo* (an instrumental flourish), followed by the main melody, which is interrupted by the lead singer's *ukubonga*, a fast-spoken declamation, usually in deep rural Zulu, that always used to be some kind of praise poem, but could just as well in modern songs be a denunciation of a woman's cooking or the jealousy of a rival. For particularly fine examples of the art, look out for the singer **Phuz'khemisi**, whose cassettes are everywhere, particularly in KwaZulu-Natal.

JAZZ

Ever since its main exponents went into self-imposed exile in the 1960s, **South African jazz** has been the music most associated with the struggle against apartheid. Musically, though, the sound of the exiles represented a departure from the indigenous *marabi* jazz of the 1950s (see below), and a move in the direction of the American avant-garde, as personified by Thelonious Monk, Sonny Rollins and John Coltrane. The two prime exponents of this new fusion were the **Jazz Epistles**, featuring Hugh Masekela, Jonas Gwangwa, Abdullah Ibrahim (then called Dollar Brand) and the great Kippie Moeketsi, and the **Blue Notes**, who included in their line-up Chris McGregor and Dudu Pukwana. Most of the Epistles left South Africa in 1960, and the Blue Notes left in 1964. During their exile, South African jazz musicians sought to reincorporate South African styles, and *mbaqanga* in particular, into their repertoire. Today, the exiled artists, including Miriam Makeba, are back home, at last receiving the recognition and respect they have long deserved. Some, like **Ibrahim** and **Winston**

"Mankunku" Ngozi, continue to perform fairly regularly and you should catch them if you get the chance. Others have moved closer to politics, with Masekela working as a top-level cultural bureaucrat in Pretoria, and Makeba an ANC Member of Parliament in Cape Town, which leaves them too little time for practising or for original composition and innovation.

Ironically, you'll have more opportunity to hear **marabi jazz** than the old new-wave, thanks to the dedicated gigging of the elderly but tireless **African Jazz Pioneers** and **Elite Swingsters**, often featuring Dorothy Rathebe on vocals. When it first emerged in the 1920s, *marabi* was the music of the black Johannesburg slums, played on pianos in *shebeens*. Always revolving around a simple three-chord structure, *marabi* developed in the 1930s, with guitars, banjos and concertinas added to the line-up. In the 1940s, American swing jazz hit South Africa and it was the fusion of swing and *marabi* that led to *marabi* jazz.

A new generation of jazz musicians has emerged in South Africa, keen to move beyond nostalgia, *marabi* and 1960s-style avant-garde, often drawing instead for inspiration on American West Coast fusion, but their problem is that, so far, few South Africans have shown much interest in their efforts. Virtuoso pianist **Bheki Mseleku** has elected to stay in London,

LADYSMITH BLACK MAMBAZO AND THE ISCATHAMIYA SOUND

The most famous of all South Africa's neo-traditional music is the great Zulu invention of **iscathamiya**, sometimes also called *mbube*, which is unaccompanied and distinctive choral singing made famous in the West by **Ladysmith Black Mambazo**. The style began in the migrants' hostels after World War I, with the first hit going to Solomon Linda and the Original Evening Birds, whose song *Mbube* sold 100,000 copies, and has been used many times since, most recently in the Disney movie *The Lion King*, where it has been worked into the song *The Lion Sleeps Tonight*.

Although it enjoyed pan-ethnic popularity in the 1940s and 1950s, in the 1960s *iscathamiya* reverted to its role as the defining sound of Zulu men's hostels. This was cleverly used by Radio Zulu to promote the apartheid concepts of rigid ethnic identity and ruralism, and the station encouraged and recorded songs that dwelt on Zulu-ness, and the need to leave the cities and

return to the rural areas. In 1973, Ladysmith Black Mambazo recorded their first album, *Amabutho*, which quickly sold 25,000 copies and have since recorded about forty others, all of which have gone gold. Following their collaboration with Paul Simon on *Graceland*, he produced their album *Shaka Zulu*, which sold 100,000 copies around the world, and took *iscathamiya* to the international stage.

Having flirted with the Inkhatha Freedom Party's Zulu nationalist politics in the late 1980s, today Ladysmith Black Mambazo prefer to dwell on religious matters, and keep their politics to calls for peace. Though non-Zulu speakers can appreciate the group's smooth dance steps, immaculate singing and vocal arrangements, the true glory of their music for the Zulu is the beauty of the lyrics, composed by Black Mambazo's gentle lead singer **Joe Shabalala**, who is surely one of South Africa's greatest living poets.

and the talented young bassist **Sipho Gumede**, despite the critical acclaim he has received, is struggling to find a decent audience at home. Nonetheless, you can almost always find modern South African jazz in either Johannesburg or Cape Town on virtually any weekend of the year, and sometimes midweek too – you just need to check the press for details.

POLITICAL MUSIC

With the collapse of apartheid and the accession to power of the ANC, the heyday of South African **political song**s has passed. With lyrics singing the praises of Umkhonto weSizwe (the armed wing of the ANC), or stating bluntly that "uMama uyajabula uma ngibulala iBhunu" ("My mother is happy when I kill a Boer"), the songs were performed during marches, demonstrations, rallies and most of all at the funerals of slain activists, usually accompanied by the *toyi-toyi*. This combination of a march and a dance is performed on the spot or on the move, with knees brought high, and is still widely used, but the old songs don't really fit any more, and you hear them less and less.

Mzwakhe Mbuli made his name in the 1980s as "the people's poet", performing his articulate and angry political poetry at countless rallies around the country. His house was fire-bombed by the authorities, and Mzwakhe himself was harassed and detained, but his poetry remained defiant, with titles like *Unbroken Spirit* and *Now is the Time*. In 1989, Mzwakhe correctly discerned the signs of the times, proclaiming in one poem that "the bull is dying at last, kicking at random", and in the following year, while celebrating Mandela's release, he urged prophetically: "When you vote and get elected, think of those who died."

Today, Mzwakhe is a more contented man, asking his many disillusioned compatriots that "if this is not the time for happiness, when is?", but at the same time using his poetry to urge an end to social ills like criminality and drug addiction. His performances are always energetic, thought-provoking and increasingly plain good fun, and it's definitely worth taking the opportunity to see him if he's playing while you are in the country.

BOEREMUSIEK

Boeremusiek is what is left of Afrikaans folk music, originating in Dutch and French folk music, but heavily influenced over the years by American country and hillbilly music, with the legendary **Jim Reeves** standing out as a major hero of the scene. These days, it's definitely easy listening, with the style's major current practitioner **Bles Bridges** known for throwing roses, Barry Manilow-style, to his adoring fans. However, the jazz-tinged concertina virtuosity of the veteran **Nico Carstens** can be interesting, particularly since his recent experimental fusions with *mbaqanga*, which he calls *Boereqanga*. **Koos Kombuis** champions a blend of rock and Afrikaans music, though the lyrics are the key thing here and just listening to the rather average instrumentation is not much compensation.

You can be sure of hearing traditional *Boeremusiek* at any Afrikaner dayout in the *dorps*.

WHITE ROCK

It is the eternal lament of **white rock** musicians in South Africa that noone in Europe or America will take them seriously, and that 95 percent of South Africans will never be interested in what they are up to. Still, in the 1980s at least they had plenty to say, with **James Phillips** and his Afrikaans alter ego **Bernoldus Nieman** dishing up deranged tunes that laughed at and kicked against white orthodoxy, seeking refuge instead in the tried and tested formula of sex, drugs and rock 'n' roll. Today, apartheid is over and Phillips is dead, but the alternative white scene still looks healthy, despite the continued absence of decent sales. **Urban Creep** are currently South Africa's most successful white rock band, and are trying their luck overseas after establishing a solid support base at home. **The Dynamics**, who found fame in the 1980s for their Madness-inspired grooves, have re-formed, and perform tirelessly all over Cape Town. Also from Cape Town are the **Truly Fully Hey Shoo Wow Band**, whose great name accurately lists five of white Cape Town's favourite expressions, and whose exciting live act sometimes includes the almost-legendary Duncan Dragon as a guest fire-eater. More interesting for their name than their raucous stage act are the **Springbok Nude Girls**, who have a big following all over the country. New bands spring up all the time in all the major cities, and even though most of their music is derivative and poorly executed every so often you hit upon a gem that makes stomaching all the dross worthwhile.

DISCOGRAPHY

BUBBLEGUM

Brenda Fassie, *Mama* (CCP, SA); Great late-1980s tunes from South Africa's very own Madonna. *Now is the Time* (CCP, SA) gives you the current Brenda sound, incorporating snatches of *kwaito* and soukous in the mix.

Sello "Chicco" Twala, *The Best Of...* (Teal, SA). A fair selection of Chicco's biggest bubblegum.

Yvonne Chaka Chaka, *The Best Of...* (Teal, SA). Contains pretty much all the Yvonne you need to hear, packed with her 1980s hits.

GOSPEL

Pure Magic, *Ikhoni'mfuyo* (CC, SA). Rebecca Malope's backing band, with lead vocals courtesy of her dashing sideman Vuyo Mokoena, and some powerful compositions.

Choirs of South Africa, *Choirs of South Africa* (Roi Music, SA). Stirring gospel anthems delivered by mass choirs with exuberance and power. All that's missing is the visual spectacle of their members dressed in flowing garments and swaying to the mighty sounds.

Izikhova Ezimnqini, *Khangel'Umsindisi* (Gallo, SA). A large Zionist choir, here singing some of the most famous hymns from the Church's extensive repertoire, with an almost weary yet utterly unshakable spirituality.

Pure Gold, *Igolide* (Gramma, SA). Not even the slightly cheesy instrumental backing can mar this powerful male choir's vocal delivery, as they sing gospel of the Old Apostolic Church in Zulu, Sotho and English.

Rebecca Malope, *Uzube'nami* (CCP, SA). Rebecca's main effort of 1996, and a stunning set of stirring anthems.

Rebecca Malope, *Shwele Baba* (CCP, SA). One of Rebecca's finest albums, with the title track a strong contender for her best-ever song and the rest of the cuts all pretty good too.

Amadodana Ase Wesile, *Nkosi Sihlangene* (Drum Rock, SA). Stirring anthems from this popular Methodist male choir, who wear blazers and red waistcoats, keep time by thumping a Bible, and can make huge congregations sway and sing as one.

JAZZ

Dollar Brand, *Voice of Africa*, *African Sun*, *Tetenya* and *Blues for a Hip King* (Kaz, UK). Virtually definitive four-album compilation of the best of Abdullah Ibrahim's (Dollar Brand) prodigious output, including the seminal *Mannenberg (Is Where It's Happening)*.

Sipho Gumede, *Down Freedom Avenue* (B&W, UK). Intruiging jazz-fusion from this accomplished bassist at the cutting edge of the new South African jazz sound.

Jazz Epistles, *Verse One* (Celluloid, France). Seminal recordings of this great South African jazz band, featuring Hugh Masekela, Kippie Moeketsi, Jonas Gwangwa and Dollar Brand.

Jazz Pioneers, *Sip 'n' Fly* (Flametree, UK). Well-paced old-style *marabi* jazz by the veterans of the art.

Miriam Makeba and the Skylarks, *Miriam Makeba and the Skylarks* (Teal, SA). Two-CD set of 32 great recordings of South Africa's queen of song, from the 1950s.

Hugh Masekela, *The Collection* (Connoisseur, UK). Good budget-price compilation of Masekela's 1960s and 1970s hits.

Philip Tabana and Malomobo, *Unh!* (Elektra Nonesuch), *Ke a Bereka* (Tusk, SA). The masterful guitarist with a sound and a style entirely his own does his individualistic take on Afro-jazz. The second release veers in a more traditional direction, but is still unmistakably Tabana.

KWAITO

Arthur, *Die Poppe Sal Dans* (CCP, SA). 1996 release of the man who came to fame with the controversial hit *Don't call me Kaffir*, this time stirring up a storm once more with *Voetsek* ("fuck off" in Afrikaans).

Various Artists, *Sounds of Africa Volumes 1 and 2* (BMG). Not much *kwaito* on Volume 1, but plenty on Volume 2, including *Istokvel*, *Shambala* by Dr. Victor, and M'Du's classic *Tsiki Tsiki*, making this a particularly good introduction to the genre.

Various Artists, *Street Bash Volume 1 and 2* (CC, SA). Excellent compilations of the latest in *kwaito* sounds, with further volumes sure to follow.

Woza Africa, *Istokvel* (Teal, SA). The title track is by far the best on the album, celebrating the money-saving schemes of the townships that enable everyone to have a party once in a while. As the chorus goes "clear the table, count the empties. . ."

MBAQANGA

Mahlathini and the Mahotella Queens, *Thokolize* (Earthworks, UK). Perfect introduction to the 1980s sound of this most stomping of *mbaqanga* outfits.

Soul Brothers, *Jive Soweto* (Earthworks, UK). Good compilation of all the Soul Brothers tunes that

matter, including their masterly title track that still goes down a storm in South Africa.

Various Artists, *Zulu Jive* (Earthworks, UK; Carthage, US). Good selection of early 1980s cuts, mostly from Zulul *mbaqanga* ace Joshua Sithole, as well as more traditional stompers from Aaron Mbambo and Shoba.

NEO-TRADITIONAL

Bayete, *Umkhaya-Lo* (Polygram, SA). Not strictly neo-traditional this, but rather a seminal fusion of South African sounds with laid-back soul and funk, blended by lead singer Jabu Khanyile's unique mixing talent and spiced with his beautifully soothing vocals.

Busi Mhlongo, *Babhemu* (Sterns, UK). Weirdly produced, but Zulu *sangoma* (traditional healer) Busi's hypnotic power shines through powerfully anyway.

Ladysmith Black Mambazo, *The Best of. . .* (Shanachie, US). Respectable introduction to a

group who have never put a musical foot wrong, and whose back catalogue is gratifyingly mostly available.

Various Artists, *The Heartbeat of Soweto* (Shanachie, US). Misleading title for this fine collection of Zulu, Shangaan and Tsonga traditional styles.

Various Artists, *Singing in an Open Space* (Rounder, US). Superb compilation of Zulu traditional styles by Gallo's guru Rob Allingham.

POLITICAL MUSIC

Mzwakhe Mbuli, *Resistance is Defence* (Earthworks, UK). Great sample of the militant lyri-

cism of the people's poet, including a moving ode to Mandela's release.

RAP AND REGGAE

Lucky Dube, *Prisoner* (Shanachie, US). South Africa's biggest-selling album ever, full of stirring Peter Tosh-style roots tunes.

Prophets of Da City, *Ghetto Code* (Polygram, SA). South Africa's rap supremos' most recent release,

full of tough but articulate rhymes and some seriously funky backing tracks to wash them down with, all in true Cape Flats style.

WHITE ROCK

James Phillips, *Made in SA* (Shifty/Tic Tic Bang, SA). A collection of the best of this seminal singer, songwriter and bandleader, who died in 1995, going back to late-1970s punk-style protest to 1980s rock and 1990s r&b tackling the complexities and nuances of South African society.

The Kerels, *Chrome Sweet Chrome* (Tic Tic Bang SA). A taste of grunge South African-style, with lyrics taking a wryly jaundiced view of the world, while the guitars thrash away in the background.

Tim Parr, *Still Standing* (Tic Tic Bang, SA). Celtic soul meets African rhythms on a celebratory, swinging album.

Pressure Cookies, *Swallow!* (Shifty/Tic Tic Bang, SA). All-grrrl group with sharply observed songs delivered in refreshingly bouncy manner.

Springbok Nude Girls, *Afterlife Satisfaction* (Sony, SA). One of South Africa's most popular white bands deliver an album mostly of derivative funk-rock, though some songs have bite.

COMPILATIONS

Various Artists, *From Marabi to Disco* (Gallo, SA). Quite simply the best South African music compilation around, with superb tracks and informative sleeve notes taking you from the 1930s to the 1980s.

Various Artists, *The Indestructible Beat of Soweto Volumes 1–4* (Earthworks, UK). Superb compilation, mainly featuring 1980s *mbaqanga*, along with a few more traditional samples. As the compiler Trevor Herman writes, "best heard loud and standing up".

LANGUAGE

South Africa has eleven official languages, all of which have equal status under the law. In practice, however, English dominates as the lingua franca, and if you're staying in the main cities and national parks you'll rarely, if ever, need to use any other language. However, in remote areas such as the Northern Cape and Northwest Province, Afrikaans is the dominant language among whites, while in regions such as the Eastern Cape, KwaZulu-Natal and the Northern Province, many blacks speak Xhosa, Zulu or TshiVenda, and you will need to master some basic phrases to make yourself understood. If you're heading anywhere off the beaten track, it's a good idea to memorize some local words and phrases, even if only to remain calm if someone whispers *dagga!* to you (it means "marijuana"), or to understand that *roomys* means "ice cream", and not "rooms".

South Africa's eleven official languages are **English**, Afrikaans, Ndebele, Xhosa, Zulu, siSwati, Tswana, Venda, Xitshinga, Southern Sotho and Northern Sotho (Pedi).

Afrikaans is widely spoken by coloureds and whites throughout the country, and in provinces such as Free State it is the language of the media. Ndebele, Xhosa, Zulu and siSwati are all closely related to each other. Also very similar are are Tswana and Southern and Northern Sotho. **Venda** is spoken in the Northern Province, and **Xitshinga** in the Northern Province and Mpumalanga. **Ndebele** is spoken in the Northern Province while **Xhosa** is used in the Eastern and Western Cape, and **siSwati** in Mpumalanga and Swaziland. **Tswana** is spoken primarily in the Northwest Province, and **Northern Sotho** in the Northern Province. **Southern Sotho** is spoken in the Free State, Lesotho and Gauteng. **Zulu**, the main language of KwaZulu-Natal, is also used in Gauteng.

In addition to these languages, there's enough English vocabulary unique to South Africa to fill a dictionary, the *Oxford Dictionary of South African English* in fact, which makes an interesting browse.

AFRIKAANS

Contrary to popular belief outside South Africa, most **Afrikaans** speakers are not white but **coloured**, and the language, far from dying out, is in fact spoken by more South Africans than any other language.

Broadly speaking, Afrikaans is a dialect of Dutch, which became modified on the Cape frontier through its encounter with French, German and English settlers, and is peppered with words and phrases from indigenous tongues as well as languages used by slaves. Despite this heritage, the language was used by Afrikaners from the late nineteenth century onwards as a key element in the construction of their racially exclusive ethnic identity. The attempt by the Apartheid government in 1976 to make Afrikaans the medium of instruction in black schools, which led to the Soweto uprising (see p.471), confirmed the hated status of the language for many urban blacks, which persists to this day.

ZULU AND XHOSA

Zulu is the most widely spoken black African language in South Africa. In common with Xhosa and Sotho, it contains a few clicks inherited from San languages, which can be mastered with practice. Zulu is closely related to **Xhosa**, **siSwati** and **Ndebele** and, as with other African languages (and unlike European languages), most of the changes to words happen at the beginning of them, rather than at the end. Don't confuse Zulu with Fanakalo, which is a pidgin Zulu mixed in with other languages and still sometimes spoken on the mines. It is not popular with most Zulu speakers, although white South Africans tend to believe it is.

AFRIKAANS WORDS AND PHRASES

BASICS AND GREETINGS

Yes	*Ja*	Good evening, miss	*Goeienaand, juffrou*
No	*Nee*	Good night	*Goeienag*
Please	*Asseblief*	What is your name?	*Wat is jou naam?*
Thank you	*Dankie*	Go away	*Weggaan*
Hello	*Hallo*	Do you speak English?	*Praat u Engels?*
How are you?	*Hoegaandit?*	I don't understand	*Ek kannie verstaan nie*
Fine, thank you	*Goed, dankie*	How much?	*Hoeveel?*
Good morning, madam	*Goeiemore, mevrou*	When?	*Wanneer?*
Good afternoon, sir	*Goeiemiddag, meneer*	Where?	*Waar?*

FINDING YOUR WAY

Where is . . . ?	*Waar is . . . ?*	Arrival	*Aankoms*	Right	*Regs*
Town (small)	*Dorp*	Departure	*Vertrek*	Rooms	*Kamers*
Airport	*Lughawe*	To	*Na*	Beach	*Strand*
Garage	*Petrol stasie*	From	*Van*	Hiking trail	*Wandelpad*
Station	*Stasie*	Ticket	*Kaartjie*		
Street	*Straat*	Left	*Links*		

DAYS OF THE WEEK

Monday	*Maandag*	Thursday	*Donderdag*	Sunday	*Sondag*
Tuesday	*Dinsdag*	Friday	*Vrydag*		
Wednesday	*Woensdag*	Saturday	*Saterdag*		

NUMBERS

1	*Een*	5	*Vyf*	9	*Nege*	40	*Veertig*	
2	*Twee*	6	*Ses*	10	*Tien*	50	*Vyftig*	
3	*Drie*	7	*Sewe*	20	*Twintig*	80	*Tagtig*	
4	*Vier*	8	*Agt*	30	*Dertig*	100	*Honderd*	

Greetings are an important part of Zulu, and you'll find that knowing a handful goes down very well. If you're driving around, it's worth investing in one of the Zulu language cassettes available in bookshops. These can be fun to play while you're travelling and can easily help you to master the greetings and basic phrases we've listed in the box overleaf.

Xhosa is similar to Zulu, but with far more words with clicks and a seemingly endless vocabulary. The Zulu vocabulary listed in our box would be understood by a Xhosa speaker, with a few differences which we've listed below.

For information on siSwati and **Sotho**, the languages spoken in **Swaziland** and **Lesotho** respectively, consult the relevant chapters in this guide. Siswati basics are very similar to Zulu basics; you can use all these phrases in Swaziland and be understood easily.

ZULU AND XHOSA PRONUNCIATION

o as in "ore", not "hope".

c a click, done with jaws slightly open, placing the tip of your tongue against the upper teeth, then pulling the tongue backwards.

ch like "k" only more pronounced – never as in "chew".

hl aspirated sound created by forcing air out from between the tongue and the sides of the teeth.

k like "g" as in gallant.

q the click most people can do. With jaws open, press the tongue against the roof of the mouth, then pull it sharply downwards.

x the sound you make to urge a horse on when riding. With jaws slightly open, press the tongue against the top teeth, then pull it to one side across the back of the teeth, making a kind of squelching sound.

ZULU WORDS AND PHRASES

BASICS AND GREETINGS

Yes	*Yebo*	Please	*Ngicela*
No	*Cha*	How are you?	*Unjani?*
Me	*Ngi*	How are you (plural)?	*Ninjani?*
You	*U*	I am fine	*Ngiyaphila*
You (plural)	*Ni*	We are fine	*Siyaphila*
Hello	*Sawubona*	We are hungry	*Kodwa silambile*
Hello (plural)	*Sanibonani*	Do you speak English?	*Uyasazi IsiNgisi na?*
Goodbye (if leaving)	*Sala kahle*	What is your name?	*Ungubani igama lakho?*
Goodbye (if staying)	*Hamba kahle*	My name is . . .	*Mgingu . . .*
Thank you	*Ngiyabonga*		

FINDING YOUR WAY

How much is this?	*Kubiza malini lokhu?*	How do I get to . . . ?	*Ngifika kanjani e . . . ?*
How much is the fare to . . . ?	*Yimalini ukuya . . . ?*	I understand	*Ngiyezwa*
Where is . . . ?	*Iphi i . . . ?*	I don't understand	*Angizwa*
		Ancestors/bless you	*Amadlozi*

XHOSA WORDS AND PHRASES		Thank you	*Enkosi*	Yes	*Ewe*
		Please	*Ndicela*	No	*Xha*
Hello	*Molo*	How are you?	*Usaphila?*	I don't understand	*Andiyeva*
Hello (plural)	*Molweni*	I am fine	*Ndiyaphila*	Ancestors	*Izinyanya*

INDEX

A

Accommodation 31
Accommodation price codes 32
Addo Elephant Park 269
Adelaide 284
Afrikaans, language 138, 691
Agatha 568
Aids information 57
Airlines
   in Australia and New Zealand 12
   in South Africa 28
   in the UK 4
   in the USA and Canada 10
Airport tax 57
Alexandria 272
Alice 304
Aliwal North 308
Amanzimtoti 366
Amatola Trail 305
Anglo-Boer War 651
Arniston 178
Augrabies Falls National Park
   238

B

B&Bs 34
Babanango 420
Backpackers' lodges 33
Baden-Powell, Robert 511
Baker, Sir Herbert 467
Ballito 371
Barberton 532–534
Barkly East 310
Barkly West 231
Basotho Cultural Village 438
Bathhurst 283
Battlefields 414–425
Beaufort West 162
Bedford 285
Beitbridge 578
Betty's Bay 170
Big Bend 642
Biko, Steve 302, 657, 669
Bilharzia 17
Bisho 303
Bizana 332
Bloemfontein 429–436

Bloemhof 516
Blood River Battlefield 416, 422
Blyde River Canyon 524
Blydepoort 527
Blythedale 373
Boesmanskloof Hiking Trail 165,
   166
Boknes 272
Bosman, Herman Charles 507,
   670
Botha, PW 186, 657–659
Buses 25
Bushman's Nek 387
Bushman's River Mouth 273
Butha-Buthe 607
Buthelezi, Mangosuthu 372, 658
Butterworth 318

C

Caledon 164
Calitzdrop 158
Calvinia 250
Camping 33
Cango Caves 157
Cape Aghulas 178
Cape Hangklip 169
CAPE TOWN 61–121
   Accommodation 68–78
   Adderley Street 79, 80
   Airport 64
   Arrival 64
   Bo-Kaap 84
   Buitenverwachting 94
   Bus services 66
   Cafés 111
   Cape Flats 107
   Cape of Good Hope Nature
      Reserve 104
   Car rental 68
   Castle of Good Hope 80
   Chapman's Peak Drive 99
   Cinema 116
   City 78–88
   City Hall 81
   City transport 65
   Clifton 98
   Company's Gardens 82
   Constantia 93
   District Six 81
   Fish Hoek 101
   Government Avenue 82
   Grand Parade 81
   Green Point 97
   Greenmarket Square 82
   Groot Constantia 93

   Historical Mile 100
   History 63
   Houses of Parliament 83
   Hout Bay 98
   Irma Stern Museum 89
   Kalk Bay 101
   Kirstenbosch National Botanical
      Gardens 92
   Klein Constantia 94
   Langa 108
   Listings 119
   Long Street 81
   Lower city centre 85
   Map, Cape Town and peninsula 62
   Map, city centre 69
   Map, southern suburbs 90–91
   Melkbosstrand 106
   Milnerton 106
   Mitchell's Plain 108
   Mowbray 89
   Muizenberg 99
   Nightlife and entertainment
      111–115
   Observatory 89
   Restaurants 109–111
   Rhodes Memorial 92
   Robben Island 86
   Rondebosch 92
   Rosebank 89
   Salt River 89
   Sandy Bay 98
   Scarborough 99
   Sea Point 97
   Shopping 118
   Simon's Town 102
   South African Museum and
      Planetarium 83
   South African National Gallery 83
   Southern suburbs 88
   Sports 116
   St James 101
   Table Bay 106
   Table Mountain 94–97
   Taxis 67
   Theatre 115
   Tourist information 65
   Townships 107
   Waterfront 86
   Woodstock 89
Cape Vidal 401
Car rental 29
Caravan parks 33
Cathedral Peak 391
Cattle killing, Xhosa 319
Cederberg Wilderness Area 215
Ceres 147
Champagne Castle 390
Charter's Creek 402

Chauke, Thomas 685
Children 58
Christiana 516
Cintsa 317
Citrusdal 216
Clanwilliam 217
Clarens 441
Clocolan 444
Coffee Bay 323
Colesberg 437
Cradock 285
Credit cards 22
Crime 52, 452
Cwebe Nature Reserve 322
Cycling 30

D

Darling 208
De Beers 225, 226
De Hoop Nature Reserve 179
De Kelders 176
De Klerk, FW 659–660
De Rust 159
De Vasselot 204
Diamond Fields 223, 232
Diamonds 512
Dias, Bartholomeu 183, 184, 272, 648
Diepwalle Forest 198
Disabilities 54
Diving 51, 266, 359, 408
Dolphin Coast 370–373
Domestic flights 28
Drakensberg 381–393
Drinking 43
Drugs 53
Dullstroom 519
Dundee 421
DURBAN 337–362
  Accommodation 344
  Airport 340
  Arrival and information 340
  Beachfront 352
  Berea 353
  Bus services 342
  Cato Manor 354
  City centre 346
  City transport 342
  Eating and drinking 354–357
  Ferries 343
  Grey Street and around 350
  History 339
  Listings 362
  Map, city centre and beachfront 348

  Map, Durban suburbs 338
  Nightlife and entertainment 357–359
  Outdoor activities 359
  Shopping 360
  Tours 343
  Victoria Embankment 351
  Warwick Triangle 351
Dutch East India Company 63, 102, 648
Dwesa Nature Reserve 322
Dyer Island 177

E

East London 296–301
Elim, Western Cape 178
Elim, Northern Province 576
Email services 44
Embassies, South African abroad 14
Emergencies 58
Eshowe 416
Exchange rates 21
eZulwini Valley 630–634

F

False Bay Park 403
Fanies Island 402
Farmstays 34
Ficksburg 444
Flight agents in the UK 5
Flower tactics 246
Food and drink 41–44
Fort Beaufort 307
Fort Hare 303
Fort Nottingham 381
Fouriesburg 443
Franschhoek 142–146

G

Gansbaai 177
Garden Castle 387
Garden Route 180–207
Garies 247
Gay and lesbian 56
Genadendal 167
George 185–187
Getting there from Australia and New Zealand 11
Getting there from Britain and Ireland 3
Getting there from the USA and Canada 8
Giant's Castle Game Reserve 388

Gingindlovu 416
Golden Gate Highlands National Park 440
Goniwe, Matthew 287
Goudveld State Forest 197
Goukamma Reserve 189
Graaff-Reinet 288–293
Grahamstown 277–282
Graskop 523
Great Fish River Reserve 284
Great Trek, The 650
Greater St Lucia Wetland Park 399
Greyton 165–167
Griquas, The 436
Groot Marico 506
Groot Winterhoek 210
Grootbos 176
Groutville 372
Guesthouses 34

H

Ha-Lejone 611
Haenertsburg 565
Haga-Haga 317
Hamburg 295
Harold Johnson Nature Reserve 373
Hawane Nature Reserve 638
Hazyview 535
Health 13
Helpmekaar 420
Hermanus 171–176
Hibiscus Coast 368
Hiking
  Barberton 534
  Blyderiverspoort 526
  Boesmanskloof Trail 165, 166
  Drakensberg 383
  Drakensberg Escarpment 440
  Garden Route 204
  General 50
  Giant's Cup Trail 386
  Kruger National Park 549
  Lesotho 589
  Letaba 569
  North Eastern Cape 313
  Wild Coast 316
Hillside 389
Himeville 386
Hitching 31
Hlane Royal National Park 640
Hlathikhulu 642
Hlotse 606

Hluhluwe-Umfolozi Park 396–399
Hluleka Nature Reserve 324
Hoedspruit 527
Hogsback 305
Hole in the Wall 323
Holidays, public 47
Hotels 31
Hunting 573

I
Idutywa 321
Ilam 280
Injasuti 390
Internal flights 27
Isandlwana 420
Itala Game Reserve 413

J
Jeffrey's Bay 270
JOHANNESBURG 449–481
  Accommodation 455–459
  Alexandra 468
  Arrival and information 452
  Baker, Sir Herbert 467
  Berea 464
  Bezuidenhout Park 464
  Braamfontein 462
  Bruma Lake 465
  Bus services 454
  CBD 461
  City transport 453
  Eating and drinking 472–475
  Entertainment, nightlife and
    culture 475–478
  Festivals 478
  Gold Reef City 469
  Hillbrow 463
  History 450
  Houghton 468
  Joubert Park 463
  Listings 479–481
  Local radio 476
  Map, central Johannesburg 460
  Map, Greater Johannesburg 449
  Map, Johannesburg
    accommodation 456
  Map, northern suburbs 466
  Melville 468
  Minibus taxis 454
  Newtown 462
  Observatory 464
  Parktown 465
  Randburg 468
  Rosebank 468
  Safety and crime 452
  Sandton 468
  Shopping 478
  Soweto 469–472
  Taxis 453
  Tours 455
  Yeoville 464
  Zoo Lake 467

K
Kakamas 237
**Kalahari-Gemsbok National
  Park** 239–242
Kamieskroon 248
Karoo National Park 163
Karoo Nature Reserve 292
Katberg 306
Kei Mouth 318
Keimoes 237
Kenton-on-Sea 273
Keurboomstrand 203
Kimberley 223–231
Kimberley's Big Hole 227
King William's Town 301
Kitchener, Lord 652
Klaserie 535
Kleinmond 170
Klerksdorp 514
Knysna 190–196
Kolonyama 605
Komatipoort 536
Kosi Bay 412
Krondraai 482
KRUGER NATIONAL PARK
  537–553
Kruger, Paul 450, 483, 488, 489
Kuruman 243
Kwambonambi 396

L
La Guma, Alex 672
La Mercy 371
Lady Grey 310
Ladybrand 445
Ladysmith 422
Ladysmith Black Mambazo 686
Laingsburg 162
Lake Fundudzi 580
Lambert's Bay 214
Lancers Gap 597
Langebaan 211
Leeu-Gamka 162
LESOTHO 583–620
  Getting around 590
  Hiking 589
  Map 584
  Pony-trekking 587
  Public holidays 586
  Tips on travel 588
Lesotho Highlands Water
  Project 611
Lesotho traditional dress 605
Letsitele 569
Lichtenburg 512
Lichtenburg Nature Reserve 513
Likalaneng 602
Lobamba 633
Long Tom Pass 520
Louis Trichardt 575
Lucky Dube 685
Ludzinzini 634
Lusikisiki 332
Lyndenburg 519

M
Mabibi 409
Mafeteng 614
Mafikeng 510
Magersfontein 233
Mail 44
Malan, DF 654
Malaria 18, 537, 558
Malealea 613
Malolotja Nature Reserve 637
Malope, Rebecca 684
Mandela, Nelson 81, 86, 327,
  380, 654, 658–662
Mandela, Winnie 470
Mantsonyane 602
Manyane Game Reserve 511
Manyeleti Game Reserve 551
Manzini 634–636
Mapholaneng 608
Maps 22
Maputsoe 606
Marais, Eugene 570
Marakabei 602
Marakele National Park 574
Margate 368
Maseru 591–596
Mateka 604
Matjiesfontein 161
Matshoba, Mtutuzeli 674
Mazeppa Bay 320
Mbabane 627–630
Mbuluzi Game Reserve 639
McGregor 150
Messina 577
Minibus taxis 26

Mkambati Nature Reserve 332
Mkhaya Nature Reserve 643
Mkuzi Game Reserve 403–406
Mlawula Nature Reserve 639
Mlilwane Wildlife Sanctuary 632
Mmabatho 508
Modjadji 568
Moffat, Robert 243
Mohale's Hoek 615
Mokhotlong 608
Money 21
Montagu 152–154
Morgan's Bay 317
Morija 612
Mossel Bay 182–185
Mount Frere 333
Mount Moorosi 617
Mountain Zebra National Park 288
Moyeni 616
Mphaki 618
Mtubabtuba 395

N

Naboomspruit 561
Namaqualand 245–256
National Parks 36
National Parks, accommodation 35
Nazareth 601
Ndumo Game Reserve 411
Nelspruit 530–532
Newspapers 46
Nhlangano 641
Nieu Bethesda 293
Nieuwoudtville 249
Nottingham Road 381
Nxaxo Mouth 320
Nylstroom 561

O

Okiep 252
Ondini 418
Opening hours 47
Oribi Gorge Nature Reserve 367
Oudtshoorn 154–157

P

Paarl 136–142
Palm Beach 369
Paternoster 213

Paton, Alan 378
Pella 253
Phalaborwa 528
Philippolis 436
Phinda Private Game Reserve 406
Photography 48
Phuthatijaba 439
Pietermaritzburg 374–380
Pietersburg 562–564
Piggs Peak 637
Pilanesberg Game Reserve 504–506
Pilgrim's Rest 522
Pitseng 610
Plettenberg Bay 198–203
Pofadder 253
Police 52
Pony-trekking, Lesotho 587, 614
Port Alfred 273–277
Port Edward 369
PORT ELIZABETH 261–269
  Accommodation 264
  Airport 261
  Arrival and information 261
  Beachfront 266
  City Hall and Central 265
  City transport 263
  Diving 266
  Eating, drinking and nightlife 267
  Listings 268
  Map, central Port Elizabeth 264
  Map, Port Elizabeth and suburbs 262
  Suburbs 267
  Tours 263
Port Nolloth 254
Port Shepstone 367
Port St Johns 328–331
Post 44
Potchefstroom 513
Potgietersrus 561
Prehistory 647
PRETORIA 482–495
  Accommodation 487
  Arcadia 490
  Around Pretoria 495
  Arrival and information 486
  Church Square 488
  City centre 488
  City transport 486
  Eating and drinking 492
  Hatfield 491
  History 483
  Listings 494
  Map 484

  National Zoological Gardens 489
  Nightlife and entertainment 493
  Paul Kruger's House 489
  Sammy Marks Square 488
  Sunnyside 491
  Union Buildings 490
  University 491
  Voortrekker Monument 492
Prince Albert 159
Private reserves 39, 551–553

Q

Qacha's Nek 618
Qeme Plateau 597
Qolora Mouth 319
Qora Mouth 320
Queenstown 308

R

Radio 47
Reilly, Ted 633, 643
Restaurants 43
Rhino Nature Reserve 482
Rhodes 310
Rhodes, Cecil John 226
Richards Bay 395
Richtersveld National Park 255
Riebeek West 209
Robben Island 86, 87
Robertson 150
Rocktail Bay 410
Roma 599
Rorke's Drift 420
Rosetta 381
Royal Natal National Park 392
Rustenburg 501
Rustler's Valley 443

S

Sabi Sand Game Reserve 551
Sabie 520–522
Safaris 38
Saldanha 212
Salem 283
San rock art 311, 381, 384, 647
Sani 609
Sani Pass 386
Schoemansdal 576
Scottburgh 366
Sedgefield 189
Sehlabathebe National Park 619
Self-catering 34
Semonkong 600
Sexual harassment 53

Shakaland 417
Shaka's Rock 371
Shamwari Game Reserve 270
Sharpeville Massacre 656
Simunye, KwaZulu-Natal 417
Simunye, Swaziland 640
Siteki 640
Skiing, Tiffendell 311
Smithfield 436
Smuts, Jan 209, 495, 653
Sobukwe, Robert 290
Sodwana Bay 407
Somerset East 285
Southbroom 369
Soweto 469–472
Spioenkop Battlefield 424
Spitskop Nature Reserve 236
Sports, participatory 50
Sports, spectator 49
Springbok 251
St Helena Bay 213
St Lucia 399
Stanger 372
Stellenbosch 128–132
Stellenbosch wine estates
  132–136
Sterkfontein 481
Stern, Irma 89
Storms River Mouth 206
Storms River Village 207
Strand 169
Suikersbosrand Nature Reserve
  481
Sun City 503
Surfing
  General 51
  Jeffrey's Bay 271
SWAZILAND 621–644
  Ceremonies 630
  Getting there 624
  Language 625
  Map 623
  National Parks 625
  Public holidays 625
  Tips on travel 624
Swellendam 168

T
Table Mountain 94–97
Tax (VAT) 58
Telephone codes, international
  45
Telephones 44

Television 46
Tembe Elephant Park 412
Teya-Teyaneng 604
Thaba Bosiu 597
Thaba Tseka 602
Thabazimbi 573
Thohoyanou 579
Timbavati Game Reserve 552
Time zones 58
Tipping 58
Tolkien, JRR 434
Tongaat 371
Tour operators
  in Australia and New Zealand 13
  in the UK 6
  in the USA 9
Tourist offices 23
Tours
  Battlefields 419
  Cape Flats 107
  Durban 343
  Johannesburg 455
  Kalahari from Upington 237
  Kimberley Mines 230
  Kruger National Park 542
  Soweto 470
Townships, Cape Town 107
Train services 27
Transkei 315
Travel insurance 19
Travellers cheques 22
Truth and Reconciliation
  Commission 287, 661
Tshaneni 639
Tsitsikamma National Park
  203–207
Tulbagh 148–150
Turtles 410
Tutu, Desmond 82, 661
Tzaneen 567

U
Ulundi 418
Umdloti 371
Umhlanga Rocks 370
Umkomaas 366
Umtamvuna Nature Reserve
  369
Umtata 324–328
Umtata River Mouth 324
Underberg 385
Upington 234–237
Uvongo 368

V
Vaalbos National Park 232
Vaalwater 570
Vacations 47
Valley of a Thousand Hills 363
Van der Post, Laurens 437
Vanrhynsdorp 247
Van der Stel, Simon 93, 102,
  128
Van Riebeeck, Jan 63, 648
Velddrif 213
Venda, arts and crafts 581
Victor Verster Prison 140
Victoria Bay 187
Visas 13
Vredenburg 213

W
Walker Bay 172–176
Warmbaths 559
Warner Beach 366
Watersports 50
Websites 22
West Coast National Park 210
Whale-watching
  Cape Town 100
  Hermanus 175
  Plettenberg Bay 200
White-water rafting, Swaziland
  643
Wild Coast 314–333
Wilderness 188
Wilderness National Park 188
Wildlife 40
Winelands 123–146
Wineries, Robertson Valley
  151
Wolmaransstad 515
Worcester 147

X
Xhosa language 690
Xhosa traditions 321

Y
Youth hostels 33

Z
Zeerust 508
Zinkwazi 373
Zulu crafts 361
Zululand, central 414–425

SODWANA SCHOOL OF DIVING

Sodwana's only PADI Dive Centre

Experience the magic of the Zululand Coast in Sodwana Bay South Africa's Premier Dive Site

We offer all the PADI courses from the beginners OPENWATER through to the professional DIVEMASTER plus the PADI Speciality courses.

We have a custom built 3m deep dive pool right next to our lecture room

- We offer you full time courses
- Openwater takes Four nights and five days
- Advanced takes two nights and three days
- The cost of your openwater course includes everything that you will need. No hidden extras
- Everything you need is in one place. Our school, our pool, our shop and not forgetting our beach
- Bring a friend and have a holiday
- Choice of Tent, Hut or Chalet Accommodation

Sodwana Bay Lodge, P Bag 317, Mbazwana 3974, South Africa.
Tel +27 35 571 0117   Tel/Fax +27 35 571 0055

PADI PADI DIVE CENTRE NO S - 3331

the perfect getaway vehicle

low-price holiday car rental.

rent a car from holiday autos and you'll give yourself real freedom to explore your holiday destination. with great-value, fully-inclusive rates in over 4,000 locations worldwide, wherever you're escaping to, we're there to make sure you get excellent prices and superb service.

what's more, you can book now with complete confidence. our £5 undercut* ensures that you are guaranteed the best value for money in holiday destinations right around the globe.

drive away with a great deal, call holiday autos now on **0990 300 400** and quote ref RG.

holiday autos miles ahead